TENDER
COMRADES

PATRICK McGILLIGAN AND PAUL BUHLE

TENDER COMRADES

A Backstory of the Hollywood Blacklist

PHOTOGRAPHS BY ALISON MORLEY AND
WILLIAM B. WINBURN

St. Martin's Griffin ❧ New York

Acknowledgments appear on page xi.

Library of Congress Cataloging-in-Publication Data

McGilligan, Patrick.
    Tender comrades : a backstory of the Hollywood blacklist / by Patrick McGilligan and Paul Buhle.
        p. cm.
    Includes bibliographical references and index.
    ISBN 0-312-20031-5
    1. Blacklisting of entertainers—United States. 2. Blacklisting of authors—United States. 3. Entertainers—United States—Interviews. 4. Authors—United States—Interviews. 5. Communism—United States. I. Buhle, Paul   II. Title.
  PN1590.B5M35 1997
  331.89'4—dc21   97-16178
                                                     CIP

First St. Martin's Griffin Edition: February 1999

10 9 8 7 6 5 4 3 2 1

To Faith Hubley,
my friend and inspiration,
and to the children of the blacklist
—P.M.

To the memory
of the blacklist victims
—P.B.

Contents

Acknowledgments

Portions of the John Berry, Jeff Corey, Jules Dassin, and Martin Ritt interviews were first published in *Film Comment*. The Faith Hubley interview was first published in *Film Quarterly* and then reprinted in the British Film Institute monograph *Women and Animation: A Compendium*.

The Alvah Bessie, Allen Boretz, John Bright, Karen Morley, Lionel Stander, and John Wexley interviews were originally conducted for a documentary called "Tender Comrades," which was filmed in 1983 but never completed. The authors wish to thank Ken Mate, the producer of that project, for permission to incorporate material from these interviews.

We are grateful to the UCLA Oral History Program for permission to excerpt from the interview with Alfred Lewis Levitt by Larry Ceplair.

The photographs of Norma Barzman, Alvah Bessie, Allen Boretz, John Bright, Jean Rouverol Butler, Jeff Corey, Jules Dassin, Edward Eliscu, Paul Jarrico, Robert Lees, Karen Morley, Martin Ritt, Joan LaCour Scott, Lionel Stander, and John Wexley were taken mainly in 1983, in conjuction with the documentary "Tender Comrades." The authors wish to thank photographer Alison Morley for allowing their use in this book.

The photographs of Walter Bernstein, Anne Froelick, Bernard Gordon, Faith Hubley, Marsha Hunt, Mickey Knox, Ring Lardner Jr., Alfred Lewis Levitt, Abraham Polonsky, Betsy Blair Reisz, Frank Tarloff, and John Weber were taken in 1996 and 1997 by photographer William B. Winburn expressly for this book.

The other photographs are used by courtesy of Eric Bercovici (Leonardo Bercovici), Hubert Niogret (John Berry), Mark Kegans (Millard Lampell), William Rapf (Maurice Rapf), John Sanford (Marguerite Roberts), Robert Boyle (Bess Taffel), Patrick McGilligan (Bernard Vorhaus), Anna Maria Levi Zimet (Julian Zimet).

William B. Winburn, who found himself between darkrooms, would like to thank Jim Galante, a New York City commercial photographer, for unlimited use of his darkroom for processing and printing the portraits in this book; and illustrators Gary Baseman and his wife, Mel, who graciously provided him with a place to stay in Los Angeles, as well as help navigating the unfamilar streets.

Special thanks to two researchers who supplied information for footnotes, Grace Wagner and Dorothy Szczepaniak.

Above all, appreciation and gratitude to our copy editor, Emily Garlin, who did her best to catch our mistakes, and to our editor, Calvert Morgan, Jr., for saying yes.

Introduction: Meet the People

By Patrick McGilligan and Paul Buhle

This book provides a unique opportunity to meet a representative group of the Hollywood figures named as subversives in the congressional hearings that took place from 1947 through the 1950s in Los Angeles, Washington, D.C., and New York City. Only a percentage of the people called before the House Un-American Activities Committee (HUAC)—only a percentage of those represented in this book—were actually given the thankless opportunity to appear in public and "defend themselves." All adopted the non-collaborative stance that set them apart from the "friendly witnesses." All were blacklisted.

Hundreds of people—famous and obscure—were cited in the public and private testimonies, their names added to the lists that suddenly proliferated in the hands of government and Hollywood power brokers. Only a small number were known outside professional circles, and most realized that their "naming" meant they might never work again in the film industry. They tried to think of evasive maneuvers; they fought their fate. But they knew that the only thing the Committee would accept was a public act of abasement and the submission of additional names—even though, as is now obvious, HUAC and the government already had all the names.

In the end, hardly anyone would fall through the cracks—the spies and informers were that thorough. If anything, the lists overcompensated, including non-Communist liberals and even some victims of mistaken identity. Hundreds forfeited their jobs; families foundered; lives were torn apart. The result was a dark watershed in America's cultural history and a stain on the national conscience.

The blacklistees had before them ten years, fifteen years—and more—of daily struggle to find work and find ways to cope. A surprising number vindicated themselves professionally, drawing on heretofore untested survival skills and racking up whole new résumés of achievements under pseudonyms. Those who could waited out the blacklist and clawed their way back to status, awards, and success. Others are still waiting.

In this book thirty-six blacklistees come in from the Cold War, many of them for the first time openly discussing the political beliefs that led to their victimization, as well as the time many of them spent in the Communist Party in 1930s and 1940s Hollywood. They are given the deserved opportunity, after five decades, to rebuke the "friendly testimony" of the left-wing turncoats and anti-Communist zealots who identified them to HUAC. Their group testimony provides a vital counterpoint to those lies and assertions.

One of the key charges of the HUAC grandstanders and their supporters was that Hollywood films were being tainted by Communist ideas. Yet the weeks of testimony turned up precious little evidence of this infiltration, beyond a handful of pro-Soviet wartime movies and a few absurd lines of script (the most notorious of which was written by Hollywood Ten scenarist Dalton Trumbo for Ginger Rogers in the 1943 film *Tender Comrade:** "Share and share alike—that's democracy!").

Yet the screen work that most of the blacklistees were doing *was* subtly humanist and progressive—a subtlety largely lost on HUAC. Here the blacklistees speak up not only for their politics but also for their impressive lives and accomplishments as screen artists. They tell their own life stories but also speak up for the larger body of the blacklisted generation—especially for the lesser-known or dearly departed, who were also named but are necessarily absent from this book.

Although the year 1947, when HUAC descended on the film industry, is widely regarded as the starting point of the blacklist, the real roots of that scoundrel time—in Lillian Hellman's apt phrase—can probably be found two decades earlier, in the Wall Street Crash of 1929, which ushered in the Depression that paralyzed America.

Not only did the stock-market collapse set the Depression in motion, it changed the complexion of the nation's still-young filmmaking population. Hollywood in 1929 had already embarked on a fresh stage of entertainment history, the era of the "talkies." Newcomers were streaming in from various occupations, but especially from those outposts that valued literacy. Now the influx speeded up, since Hollywood continued to make money and offer jobs in spite of the dire circumstances in the rest of the country. The early sound-era arrivals came from newspapers, vaudeville, Broadway, and the world of literature. An especially fertile crop was harvested from radio and the Yiddish theater.

Some of the more left-leaning newcomers had developed their political predilections from the cradle. The vast majority hailed from New York. They were Jewish, and a surprising number had Russian forebears, a fact to which few chronicles of the blacklist have paid sufficient attention. It is small wonder that so many of these show-business people would adopt a vigorously pro-Soviet attitude. Some paid little attention to their Jewish roots, or to the political emanations of the times, until—like the student protestors of the 1960s—they were educated by headlines or at the point of a policeman's truncheon. Some grew up fascinated by the aesthetic of foreign films, notably those of the realistic Soviet models of the 1920s, and were led to their politics partly by cultural sophistication. A few could boast of having actually visited

*Trumbo's title was not red propaganda. As Nora Sayre pointed out in *Running Time: Films of the Cold War*, "tender comrade" was Robert Louis Stevenson's term for his beloved wife.

the Soviet Union, where they observed the revolution firsthand and endorsed what they had seen.

The parents and grandparents of the Hollywood blacklistees were predominantly Socialist and radical idealists. But a small percentage came straight out of conservative Middle America and had longtime Republican ancestors. Those raised in Republican homes had this in common with the born leftists, however: They started out in life believing that America was the best, most promising country in the world. Most of the Hollywood Communists might have admitted feeling the same way, right up to the moment when they received their subpoenas.

Hollywood in the early 1930s was not immune to the spectacle of once-proud citizens picking through garbage and sleeping in doorways, desperate for a job or just for a bite to eat. The leftist community in the motion-picture industry had been scattered and disorganized before the hard times arrived. Now it was galvanized into action, as never before or since.

Hollywood would plead the case for President Franklin Delano Roosevelt's New Deal. Many the work of fated blacklistees, the best of the "social consciousness" films of the Depression era remain memorable documents of the American madness—the streetcorner apple Annies, dead end kids, wild boys of the road, and mayors of hell. Other films, neither topical nor issue-oriented, simply wore humanist values on their sleeves.

Off-camera, Hollywood was also nurturing its nascent social conscience. Aroused by the grim conditions of the times, film-industry figures threw themselves into controversial campaigns. They joined Upton Sinclair's quixotic EPIC (End Poverty in California) gubernatorial race of 1934 and proved a decisive factor in other elections. They wrote pamphlets, attended meetings, and collected money to uplift migrant workers and other downtrodden constituencies. They rallied around the banners of the unjustly arrested and imprisoned—Tom Mooney, the Scottsboro Boys, and, later on, the Sleepy Lagoon defendants and the Zoot Suiters. They established organizations to fight for courtroom justice, aid the cause of labor, and wage war against prejudice—although Jim Crow admittedly thrived in Hollywood as in the rest of the nation.

Those who were not politically transformed by domestic issues would find themselves radicalized by the international upheavals of the era, beginning with the rise of Hitler and Mussolini. The Sino-Japanese War of 1937, and finally the Spanish Civil War of 1936–1939, would raise Hollywood's political consciousness another notch. The drift was decidedly leftward, and these issues created a community of solidarity in the film industry.

Some of the Hollywood leftists were definitely not Communists of any sort; indeed, some took pride in counting themselves to the left of the Party. A small number of non-Communist liberals made the mistake of supporting the same political goals as Party members—or, later on, of speaking out in defense of the constitutional rights of the Hollywood Ten. Guilty by association, they would be blacklisted just as vigilantly as their Party-accredited contemporaries.

The majority of the Hollywood people represented in this book, however, and probably the majority of those who were blacklisted, *were* members of the American Communist Party, whether for a few weeks or for decades. The core group was in place even before the Spanish Civil War (among the original members of the Party's Hollywood section were also the founding members of the Screen Writers Guild). In their interviews, those who were Communists shed light on the first Marxist study groups, the early Party branches, and the organizing structure of the Hollywood section. They are forthcoming about their motivations for joining and their ideological and strategy differences with the leadership. They remember well the constant drudgework that membership entailed, which added to the noble feeling they had of sacrificing personal ambitions in favor of higher goals.

It would be no accident that all of the Hollywood Ten—the first ten people to be called to testify before HUAC in Washington, D.C., in October 1947— were one-time members of the Party. Nor was it an accident that seven of the Ten were scenarists well-known for their activism and their front-line positions in the Screen Writers Guild. Hollywood Communists vitally shaped the struggles to organize both the Screen Writers Guild and the Actors Guild, and Hollywood Communists were also crucially involved in the effort to democratize the craft unions, which existed under the iron-fisted control of corrupt bosses and organized crime. No events of the 1930s and 1940s were as bitter or divisive within the industry as the never-ending union battles.

Although the Hollywood section of the Party numbered at its peak only several hundred official members, it had an umbrella program with the kind of widespread appeal later enjoyed by Students for a Democratic Society (SDS) of the 1960s. Not only did the Hollywood section find surprising recruits and acceptance among the film elite, but its ideas and activities rippled outward, influencing many more liberals, who were always the bigger power bloc. So the "fellow travelers"—HUAC's label for those who traveled the same political paths as the Communists—were numerous.

Not everyone in Hollywood succumbed to liberalism or leftism, of course. The right wing, generally encompassing the ranks of producers and studio heads, was a cunning, well-entrenched faction. There were also vehement *anti*-FDR movies, and the Hollywood anti-Communists were as vocal and determined as their left-wing adversaries. There was constantly poison in the air, genuine resentment over the steps toward film-industry unionization. The rise of Fascism and anti-Semitism was a phenomenon that found many sympathizers in the film business, where Jews have always been prominent in the power structure. Personal and professional rivalries, as well as mere political disagreements, served to fuel the enmity of the opposing sides.

As the 1940s beckoned, there were warning signs of future trouble: The Hitler-Stalin Pact and the purge trials opened a few Party eyes. "We used to have a saying," one of the former Communists noted. "Whenever a train took a sharp turn, some would fall off." Fractious Party disputes stirred the waters of internecine dissension. Before the war, Party leaders criticized the anti-Semitic flavor of Budd Schulberg's roman à clef about Hollywood, *What Makes*

Sammy Run? After the war, Albert Maltz spoke up publicly for artistic license and was swatted down. Schulberg and Maltz were both well-respected, and what happened to them disturbed some Party members. Later these two episodes would also preoccupy the inquisitors of HUAC.

Indeed, the first embodiment of HUAC materialized in Hollywood back in 1940, drawn by the Los Angeles red squad, which was already notorious for instigating grand juries and spying on left-liberal screen personalities. A Washington committee, under the chairmanship of Texas congressman Martin Dies, captured sensationalistic headlines for a short time, but Hollywood managed to present a united front, and Dies beat a swift retreat. Within two years, America entered World War II, and Hollywood, left and right together, entered a period of temporary truce.

Studio heads, like employers all over the country, were determined to make a lot of money off the war. Desperate for labor peace, most of them were by now willing to accept the unions that the Hollywood left had been instrumental in establishing. The government's call for mobilization of all public energies drew volunteers from across the political spectrum in the film industry. Hitler was everyone's enemy—and Stalin, briefly, everyone's savior.

During the war, the Hollywood leftists contributed to some of the finest and most imaginative of the anti-Nazi films—though HUAC preferred to focus on the pro-Soviet ones. The Hollywood leftists also served as combat photographers, war correspondents, even OSS agents. In their interviews they tell of crafting the military documentaries and educational and instructional fare that helped bolster home-front morale. It is no accident that the leftist veterans were noticeably passed over in the first round-up of accused reds in 1947, since that particular career credit might have engendered public sympathy—and discredited the un-American image with which the Committee sought to brand them.

Meanwhile, during the war the Communist Party—and its Hollywood section—underwent a curious metamorphosis. Under the benign leadership of Earl Browder, the Party formally dissolved into the Communist Political Association, which unrealistically envisioned itself as sharing power in America's grand, postwar future. The Party in Hollywood grew bigger and acted more jingoistically than ever, relaxing its discipline and taking in record numbers of recruits—among them a number of those who turned the fastest when HUAC came calling a few years later.

As long as the war was on, Hollywood adversaries worked side by side. But it was an amity that wouldn't hold, and the FBI and the Hollywood right were making plans for a domestic counterattack even before Roosevelt's death and V-E Day. A series of hard-fought postwar jurisdictional strikes led by maverick craft-union leader Herbert Sorrell—a villain to the right and a hero to the left—put a flame to the fuse.

A newly-ignited HUAC returned to Hollywood in the spring of 1947, held closed sessions, and drew up its first lists. The Hollywood section of the Party had always been riddled with informers, whose secret depositions to the police and the Federal Bureau of Investigation (FBI) accumulated—as our subjects, readers of their own Freedom of Information Act files, can attest—into an accusatory mountain of sometimes fanciful and amusing information. The full extent of the infiltration and surveillance is unknown, since the informants are usually blacked-out in government documents, and many FOIA papers are still withheld. But the anti-red helpers included prominent moderates and liberals—among them one actor Ronald Reagan—as well as sham leftists.

As a result of the spring 1947 incursion, nineteen screen figures were summoned to the Committee's October hearings in the nation's capital, there to attract the press and publicity that HUAC desired. Eleven were called to the stand (they might have become known as the Hollywood Eleven, if German playwright Bertolt Brecht hadn't stumped the interrogators with his answers to their questions and then left the country the next day). A month later, in November, studio executives and producers convened a secret conclave on the growing controversy at the Waldorf Astoria Hotel in New York City. Their consensus to fire the Ten and to institute loyalty oaths and other measures effectively launched the industry-wide blacklist. Initially, the Hollywood Nineteen had attracted widespread support among celebrities and the public. Now support began to crumble away.

Workaday life and professional assignments for those under suspicion began to grind to a halt. Between 1947 and 1950, when the appeals of the Hollywood Ten were exhausted and the second round of hearings was scheduled, the fear and the reality spread among the hundreds upon hundreds of others with kindred beliefs or politics.

Most of the actual Hollywood Communists called before HUAC found that the best option was to say as little as possible about their political pasts. Some of them had left their Party days behind and had long since grown disillusioned by aspects of the Communist program or by the transgressions of the Soviet Union. Those who had already quit the Party, as well as those who still counted themselves loyal members, were confronted by HUAC with the dilemma not only of cooperating with a violation of their freedoms but of providing names of others. Ancient Jewish tradition proscribed the informer, an ethic that is still widely held in most societies. Informing, in the context of the blacklist, constituted a personal career move at the cost of damaged or destroyed lives. Whether or not to inform was, for those who refused, above all not a question of politics but a matter of ethics and morality.

The "cooperative witnesses" were not all paid agents. They had varied motives. Sometimes they testified out of plain fear and confusion, more often out of opportunism and the determination to keep their fancy houses and swimming pools.

The "named," ironically, had always thought of themselves as patriots; certainly they had never thought of themselves as spies, saboteurs, or social pariahs. Just the fact of their public excoriation made for a psychological wound from which some never recovered.

Many gladly dodged their subpoenas. Some elected to stay in Hollywood, where they tried to make the best of working "underground," operating through the good graces of those who offered to act as their "fronts." Others would find that they had little option but to search for employment outside the industry. Those who, rather romantically, traveled abroad and were able to construct new lives—often under false names—may have found a silver lining. A number of them did their most mature screen work outside U.S. borders, beyond Hollywood's box-office-minded grasp. In Mexico, England, France, Spain, and Greece, these blacklistees proved true communalists while acquitting themselves with fine films during the 1950s and 1960s. Although most would eventually return to the United States, Hollywood had lost them in their prime, and the torch of their creativity was never passed here.

The Hollywood and New York blacklistees acted as communalists too, chipping in on one another's scripts and pooling resources for loans to tide people over. For some, the beginning of oppression's end was signaled by the example of Dalton Trumbo, who led the way with his merrily defiant attitude. Trumbo wrote multitudinous scripts under various names, won an Oscar as "Robert Rich," and finally crashed through in 1960 with his name blazoned on the screen for *Exodus* and *Spartacus*. And, as these interviews make clear, Trumbo wasn't alone in finding holes in and making a mockery of the blacklist.

For some the blacklist ended thus—offers began coming in again, faces and names were restored to the screen. For others, though, the work never resumed. For one thing, too many had died young, the stress of blacklisting having added to the factors behind their premature deaths. For them, and for others who lived but suffered the worst, the blacklist never really ended. "It's not as if a bell rings one day," one of the blacklistees patiently noted in his interview, and someone announces, "It's over."

It would be pleasant to say that the survivors have met with late-in-life rewards. But the recent decisions by the Writers Guild to create a special pension fund for former blacklistees and restore a few credits, though laudable, are too little and come too late. And too many of the interviewees found themselves, after the blacklist was over, facing another blacklist—the age barrier against the older writer or actor and against script values now, sadly, considered old-fashioned.

One point about the "tender comrades" that is lost in most film histories is how varied and richly talented a group they were, and how varied and richly talented was their contribution to American film.

The films of the 1930s and 1940s that the Hollywood leftists were most proud of were not a transcription of the Communist Party platform, but stories suffused with feeling for people and their ordinary concerns. Political commitment was important in their approach to narrative conventions. They believed in the power of storytelling to illuminate social contradictions. They believed in the proper motivation of their characters and in conveying through the arc of the drama a pointed, significant moral.

Among them were realists who, it is true, wrote the hardest-hitting "social consciousness" films. Among them, it is true, were those who did their best to hold a mirror up to life, adding, with their politique, a keen sense of social context to films that offered sympathetic portraits of American underdogs. The realists turned into downright pessimists after World War II. Postwar film noir, in particular, was imbued with the awareness that crime was at its base about capitalism and capitalism about criminal greed. As the political skies darkened over their heads, some of the best films created by Hollywood leftists were conspicuous in their rejection of facile story solutions, just as their own biographies would become case studies in the thwarting of happy endings.

However, most of the Hollywood leftists were probably not hard-headed realists. Most were, in the words that one blacklistee used in describing herself, "optimists to the core." More than a few Party members were among the industry's highest-paid gag writers. (Laughter, flying in the face of puritanism, was a sublime form of subversion.) Besides the stark social dramas, the blacklistees also crafted award-winning love stories, short subjects, musicals, and westerns. They were instrumental behind the scenes, creating films not only for James Cagney and John Garfield but also for Roy Rogers and Gene Autry, Abbott and Costello and the Marx Brothers, Mae West and Katharine Hepburn, John Wayne, Walt Disney, and, yes, Ronald Reagan. The Hollywood left formed an integral cross-section of Hollywood's Golden Age, and this book, above all, constitutes a kind of last-look "Thousand and One Hollywood Nights."

The blacklist robbed them and us. America's iron curtain rang down on an era. Hollywood movies took a giant step backward; the humane traditions that the leftists had brought with them to Hollywood were jettisoned. The outrage over prejudice disappeared. Violence, which had always been part of film, would become ritualistic. The roles for actresses grew passive and cartoonish. The simple practice of constructing a logical narrative took a blow from which Hollywood is still recovering.

This book is not a straightforward introduction to the complicated history of the blacklist, although there is much in it, factually, that will require revision of previous blacklist histories. The film-reference volumes, too, will require new and improved entries, for there are revelations about credits, and behind-the-camera anecdotage galore, that shed light on legendary personalities and the studio machinery of a bygone era.

Instead, this is a group snapshot of the blacklisted generation, in their own words. They led remarkable lives, forged remarkable careers. Their example inspires, and their films remain their enduring legacy.

Patrick McGilligan and Paul Buhle
Milwaukee, Wisconsin, and Providence, Rhode Island
November 1997

I look back on two decades through which good friends stood together, moved forward a little, dreamed that the world could be better and tried to make it so, tasted the joy of small victories, wounded each other, made mistakes, suffered much injury, and stood silent in the chamber of liars.

—Dalton Trumbo, in a letter to Guy Endore, December 30, 1956

TENDER COMRADES

Norma Barzman
(and Ben Barzman)

NORMA BARZMAN, Los Angeles, California, 1983

INTERVIEW BY LARRY CEPLAIR

NORMA BARZMAN
(1920–   )

1946 *Never Say Goodbye.* Costory.
1947 *The Locket.* Uncredited contribution.
1952 *Young Man with Ideas.* Uncredited contribution.
       Fanciulle di lusso/Luxury Girls. Uncredited
          screenplay.

BEN BARZMAN
(1911–1989)

1940 *The Lady in Question.* Uncredited contribution.
1941 *Marry the Boss's Daughter.* Uncredited
          contribution.
1942 *True to Life.* Costory.
1943 *You're a Lucky Fellow, Mr. Smith.* Coscript.
       Swing Shift Maisie. Uncredited contribution.
1944 *Meet the People.* Costory.
1945 *Back to Bataan.* Coscript.
1946 *Never Say Goodbye.* Costory.

1947 *The Locket.* Uncredited contribution.
1948 *The Boy with Green Hair.* Coscript.
1949 *Give Us This Day/Salt to the Devil.* Script.
1952 *Young Man with Ideas.* Uncredited
          contribution.
       Imbarco a mezzanotte/Stranger on the Prowl.
          Uncredited contribution, also
          coproducer (as Noel Calef).
       Faithful City. Uncredited contribution.
1953 *C'est arrivé à Paris.* Uncredited contribution.
       Time Without Pity. Script.
1955 *Oasis.* Uncredited contribution.
1957 *Celui qui doit mourir/He Who Must Die.*
          Coscript.
1958 *Incognito.* Coscript.
       Méfiez-vous filletes. Uncredited contribution.
1959 *Blind Date/Chance Meeting.* Coscript.
1960 *Michael Strogoff.* Uncredited contribution.
1961 *El Cid.* Uncredited contribution.
       The Damned. Uncredited contribution.
1963 *The Ceremony.* Script.

1964 **The Fall of the Roman Empire.** Coscript.	1968 **Twenty-Four Hours of a Woman's Life.**
1966 **The Blue Max.** Coscript.	Uncredited contribution.
The Heroes of Telemark. Coscript.	**Z.** Uncredited contribution.
Judith. Uncredited contribution.	1972 **L'attentat/The Plot.** Coscript.
Der besuch/The Visit. Script.	1976 **La tête de Normande/Saint-Onge Normande.**
1967 **Triple Cross.** Uncredited contribution.	Coscript.
Justine. Uncredited contribution.	1990 **Korczak.** Uncredited contribution.

■

NORMA BARZMAN WAS born Norma Levor, in New York City, on September 15, 1920. Her parents, both of German-Jewish descent, were born in the United States. Norma's father, a successful importer, traveled to Europe regularly and particularly loved France. Just before the stock market crashed in 1929, he sold the business and their house in Westchester and embarked for a three-year stay in Europe with his wife and two daughters.

When the family returned in 1931, they spent a few years in Los Angeles, where Norma formed a close relationship with her mother's nephew, Henry Myers, a lyricist, screenwriter, and novelist. He encouraged Norma to pursue her dream of becoming a writer.

A few years later, the family returned to New York City, where Norma attended Julia Richman High School. She aspired to attend Wellesley College, and so, fearing that she already had two strikes against her—her Jewishness and her New York City education—she did not join any political groups. Despite an outstanding academic record, she did not get into Wellesley—the admissions office claimed it had lost all her records. She entered Radcliffe instead. At the end of her sophomore year, June 1939, she "ran away," sailing to Paris and getting a job on the *Paris Herald*. Her parents brought her back in September, just as World War II began.

One year later she married a mathematician, Claude Shannon (later known as the father of information theory), and accompanied him to Princeton, where he joined the Institute for Advanced Study. She went to work for the Economic Section of the League of Nations, then housed at the Institute. Her contact with the various Europeans there kept her aware of the worsening situation in Europe and the horrors of Fascism, but she still remained politically unconnected. Her father died in 1940. The following year Norma left her husband and traveled with her mother to Reno to get a divorce. They then went to Los Angeles to make a new life for themselves.

■

It was very foggy in our minds, what we would do in California. I knew I wanted to be a screenwriter and be near my cousin Henry [Myers];* that was

---

*Henry Myers (1893–1974), an early activist in the Screen Writers Guild, collaborated on *Meet the People* and other progressive musical revues. Named before HUAC by Gertrude Purcell, with whom he had written the screenplay of *Destry Rides Again*, he began writing historical novels, of which *The Utmost Island* was a best-seller.

clear. I would try to find a screenwriting school, if there was such a thing, and get a job on a newspaper. The very first night, Henry took me to a Russian movie, *Chapayev*. I had seen few Russian movies, so this was exciting to me. In addition, Henry introduced me to the progressive community of Hollywood, who regularly attended foreign-film showings. I met everyone who would later be named before HUAC. After the film we went to the Trocadero with Vera Caspary and her husband-to-be [producer I. G. Goldsmith], Bernard Vorhaus, and the Bob Rossens. They told me about the writers' school [run by the League of American Writers], and I enrolled in a screenwriting class taught by Gordon Kahn,* a script-reading class taught by Al Levitt, and a class on the American heritage taught by Jack [John Howard] Lawson.

Did you know the school was a Communist-front organization?

Shortly after I arrived, I came to understand that all the progressive people I liked and who were politically active were Communists. I ended up doing most of the things Party members were doing but not as a Party member—helping Yugoslav fishermen, lettuce pickers, the victims of the "zoot suit" violence. I probably never would have considered joining the Party, and might even have kept my distance, if I had come to Los Angeles prior to June 1941, because I could not have swallowed the Party line defending the Nazi-Soviet Pact. But by the time I arrived in September, the Soviet Union had been invaded; the Russians were fighting the Nazis and were our allies. Then it seemed normal to be working alongside Communists.

One of the things that attracted me to Communism was that Soviet women were allowed into all the professions. It appeared that the Soviet Union had a better attitude toward women than any other country, and it was strongly opposed to racism. I had also been profoundly influenced by the Depression, even though I was not one of the people who had suffered from it. My parents had invested in gilt-edged securities before we left for Europe, so when the stock market crashed, while we were in Europe, we only had to go to less-expensive restaurants. We did not feel the crunch.

But on our return to America, in 1931, I could see with my own eyes people selling apples on corners. A few years later, my high-school teachers, espe-

---

*Gordon Kahn (1902–1962) was one of the Hollywood Nineteen. A gifted journalist who covered the Lindbergh kidnapping and had a column in the *New York Mirror* before he went to Hollywood, he also wrote under his real name and various pseudonyms for the *Atlantic Monthly*, *Holiday*, *Reader's Digest*, *Esquire*, and *Playboy*. His published works include *Hollywood on Trial*, one of the first books about the blacklist, and, with artist Al Hirschfeld, *Manhattan Oases*, about New York speakeasies. Among his more than forty screenplays are *Ruthless*, *Her Kind of Man*, and *The Cowboy and the Señorita*. He also made uncredited contributions to *All Quiet on the Western Front* and *The African Queen*. His only novel, *A Long Way from Home*, set in Mexico during the Korean War and the McCarthy era, was written during the blacklist and published posthumously. His son, Tony Kahn, produced a documentary film about his father's life called *The Day the Cold War Came Home* and, later, a radio drama about the blacklist.

cially Mrs. Mandelbaum, my economics teacher, told us that capitalism was the cause of most evils: imperialism, war, the business cycle, economic depressions, and social injustice. Three books influenced me. *In Place of Splendor*, a book about the Spanish Civil War written by Constancia de la Mora, a wealthy aristocrat and a friend of the fierce Loyalist La Pasionaria [Dolores Ibarruri], showed that Franco's rebels were backed by Mussolini and Hitler. *Christ in Concrete*, a novel about the Depression written by Pietro Di Donato, and Dalton Trumbo's *Johnny Got His Gun*, linking capitalism and war, were the other two.

Were you worried that association with Communists and Communist causes might harm your career aspirations? After all, a red scare was in progress between the Nazi-Soviet Pact (August 1939) and the German invasion of Russia (June 1941).

I knew, of course, about the writers, directors, and actors who were anti-Communist, anti-Guild, and anti-union, who sided with the studio bosses. Henry Myers had to hide the fact that he was a Communist; otherwise he might have lost his screenwriting job. With those who weren't Communists or Party sympathizers, I kept my mouth shut.

What career path did you pursue when you arrived?

I wrote original stories for the screen and a very bad first novel [unpublished]. Then I got a job on the *Los Angeles Examiner*. I was hired only because the city editor, tired of training young male reporters who got drafted, was ready to take a chance on a woman reporter, even though he could not bear having her in his city room. He and the reporters made my life a holy hell. I was about to be fired when I stumbled on a great human-interest story, which won a prize as best feature of the year. William Randolph Hearst personally gave me a bonus and said he would be watching my career. Later, when the managing editor tried to fire me, because I was a "red," Hearst said, "I don't care what she is. She's a good reporter."

Meanwhile, I took my screenplays and original stories to the Party-run writers' clinic. George Sklar* headed it. He might have allowed me in because I was close to the Party. It was very helpful to me and was a wonderful example of how writers could work together. The atmosphere among Communist writers in Hollywood was like no other. People cared about each other, about ideas, about doing good things. It sounds Pollyannaish, but they enjoyed working collectively.

There are stories of John Howard Lawson being a discouraging presence at these clinics.

---

*George Sklar (1908–1988), best-known as a dynamic left-wing playwright of the 1930s (and especially for the interracial drama *Stevedore*, written for the Group Theatre), came to Hollywood with John Howard Lawson, hoping to sell an adaptation of their play *Merry Go Round*. Disappointed, he nevertheless returned in 1940, but he was never very successful as a screen-

My future husband, Ben Barzman, had such an experience. Ben had written a beautiful play called *The Factory*. Lawson, when he read the play, said, "Listen, Ben, this play is okay, but you don't want to be just another [Clifford] Odets, do you?" In other words, just another bourgeois writer. But my experience at the clinic was a good one. Albert Maltz, George Sklar, and the others did not look at scripts with Lawson's rigid point of view.

When, and under what circumstances, did you join the Communist Party?

Ben had been a Communist sympathizer since attending Reed College, which was pretty much divided between Communist and Trotskyist students during the 1930s. To put himself through Reed, Ben had been obliged to work for nine years "standing on my feet long hours" in a Portland cloak-and-suit factory. That, and the influence of an old-time Socialist father, make it easy to understand why Ben was left-oriented. His father, who played the trumpet in the czar's army, had deserted in 1905 and emigrated with his family to Canada. Ben was born in Toronto in 1911 and went to secondary school in Vancouver. Then the family moved to Portland.

But it was only when he came to Hollywood and was working with his brother, Sol,* on a musical revue, a West Coast version of *Pins and Needles* called *Labor Pains*, that he was approached by Party people. Henry Myers, Jay Gorney, and Eddie Eliscu [who together had written the successful left-wing revue *Meet the People*], Morty Offner, and the choreographer Jacobina Caro all offered to help Sol and Ben with *Labor Pains*. "Henry, Eddie, Jay, Morty, and Jacobina were terrific," Ben told me. "They gave selflessly, and I became convinced that Party people were better human beings. How could I think otherwise? They wanted nothing for themselves."

I met Ben a year after I arrived in Hollywood, Halloween 1942, at a cause party at the Bob Rossens'. He had already been in the Party for three years. Ben was irresistible, perched on a fuzzy white chair, cleaning his nails with his Phi Beta Kappa key, and telling stories in his inimitable manner. He was a great raconteur. We saw each other every day for three months, until January 25, 1943, when we were married by a defrocked rabbi who had been tarred and feathered and run out of Montgomery, Alabama, for defending the Scottsboro Boys and would eventually join the Communist Party and work for SovExport Film.† As a result, Ben and I always wondered, during our forty-seven years of marriage, whether we were really married.

In a very serious tone, just prior to the wedding, Ben told me, "I don't want

---

writer. His handful of credits includes *City Without Men*, *First Comes Courage*, and *The Bandit of Sherwood Forest*. Named by Martin Berkeley and others, blacklisted in 1951, Sklar concentrated in later years on writing plays and novels.

*Sol Barzman (1912–1990) collaborated with his brother Ben on two films before being drafted into the army. After serving in World War II, he returned to New York and began to write nonfiction, including *The First Ladies*.

†SovExport Film was the central Soviet agency for film import and export.

you to think you have to join the Party because of me." "I wouldn't join for
that reason," I replied. "I've wanted to for some time—you'll laugh—but I
didn't think I was worthy. I don't know enough, haven't had the experience.
I'm still so bourgeois." "You'll learn," he said, "you'll study. You're a lot more
dedicated than many members." In a way, I was. Some members paid their
dues, attended meetings in a perfunctory manner, did what was expected of
them, but didn't let it permeate their lives. They were few. Most were dedicated, gave their money, time, energy, the whole of themselves idealistically.
They really believed that Socialism would make the world better.

Describe Party life.

In the beginning, for me, it was classes and study groups and a great deal
of reading. [Friedrich] Engels's *The Origin of the Family, Private Property, and
the State* reinforced my feeling that the Party wanted to liberate women. With
the aid of my discussion group, I was able to make some sense of the labor
theory of value. We had lively discussions of subjects I was passionate about,
such as aesthetics. Ernst Fischer's theories were my bible. I believed then that
art needed to serve the revolution. After each meeting, magazines and pamphlets on a wide variety of subjects were made available to us.

I was busy all the time: a branch meeting every week and selling a certain
number of copies of the *People's World* [the West Coast equivalent of the
Daily Worker] and Earl Browder's *Victory and After*. We tried hard to recruit
minorities, sometimes artificially making friends with blacks and Latinos with
whom we had little in common. Some of us worked in the poor Jewish Boyle
Heights neighborhood, some in Watts. Recruiting was important. I didn't feel
sufficiently articulate about theory to invite someone else to join. So I deliberately looked for likely candidates who would be easy to convince—for example, one woman whose husband, a screenwriter was already in the Party.
She was a housewife and the mother of two. I convinced her that housewives
particularly should join the Party and agitate for women's equality. Her husband later named me. Party life was very social. After all, it was Hollywood.
Mostly we gave parties to raise money for causes.

The high point of the year was always the *New Masses* art auction. Communist and non-Communist artists, social realists—all donated canvases to
be auctioned for the benefit of the magazine. Sympathizers often gave paintings that had hung on their walls for years. It was fabulous, a chance to own
a Jack Levine, Moses or Raphael Soyer, Joseph Hirsch, Bob [Robert] Gwath-
mey, or, in my case, Milton Avery. The auction was a big social event organized by Jeannie Lees [wife of Robert Lees]. I helped with the big bash
afterward.

During the war, Party women agitated particularly actively for nursery
schools for working women.

So you were very gender-conscious then?

If you came out of Radcliffe when I did, you thought you could have it all: a good relationship with a man, children, and a career. My grandmother had founded a pin-cushion-and-comforter factory in Chicago in the 1860s. My mother, who regretted not having followed through on her ambition to be an actress, was proud of not being able to cook. My older sister was one of the first women to attend Columbia Law School.

At home, with Ben, who'd been brought up by a Russian-Jewish mother to expect to be waited on, my gender-consciousness teetered. Shortly after we married, Adrian Scott was thrown out of his house by his first wife [Dorothy Shipley]. He fell apart and came to live with us. I loved Adrian, enjoyed having him with us. But Ben and Adrian had a very close bond and, in their exchange of ideas, without being aware of it, relegated me to the scullery. I would make dinner, we would eat, I would clean up, and they would talk. I got quieter and quieter. The same thing happened at meetings. Those great, powerful personalities, like Herbert Biberman, would sound off, and I would feel like a little girl. They were all, Ben included, at least ten years older than I. I spoke less and less, had fits of hay fever and asthma.

Was Ben aware of what was happening?

By then I had a great career as a reporter, doing top stories and features, but Ben, who talked feminism at Party meetings and spent a weekend at a Party conference discussing "the woman question" and whether housewives should be paid a salary, complained regularly and bitterly about my hours at the newspaper.

While I was a reporter, in 1945, I got the idea for *Never Say Goodbye*. Ben asked if I wanted him to work with me on it. I said yes, because he had already sold three original stories for the screen. We worked on it at night and during weekends. I wrote it. He rewrote it. It was very much my story, with a big feminist point about young, divorced parents. The husband was a playboy, a man-about-town, who had not been a good husband or father. Their little girl decides, after he has moved out, to bring them back together. She sends a letter, with a photo of her mother, to a Marine overseas, thinking it will make her father jealous. The Marine turns up on furlough, stays with them, and is the ideal father and man-about-the-house, everything that the father isn't. The by-now jealous husband is forced to reform. The idea came from all the newspaper stories I had been doing about servicemen and their wives, most of whom were working mothers. The emphasis of the story was the woman, but the studio changed it when Errol Flynn was cast in the role of the husband.

We gave the story to Ben's agent, George Willner,* who immediately got

---

*George Willner (1905–1981) had many clients who were left-wing writers, including the Barzmans and Dalton Trumbo. After they were blacklisted, Willner helped clients to sell their work by means of "fronts" and pseudonyms. But when he was "named" before HUAC as a

an offer from Warner Brothers. The whole point of my working with Ben had been to get me off the newspaper and writing with him at the studio. "A big offer," George said, "only they don't want Norma on the screenplay. They've never heard of her. They want Ben to work with S. K. Lauren." I said, "You can't do that. It's my screenplay. I come with it." George then said that we would lose the sale. Ben said we couldn't afford to lose the sale. I said I was willing to work with Ben and Lauren. George said no; they just wanted Ben. I was dumb enough to give in. I never forgave myself, and I never forgave Ben. The whole episode made me sicker, with my hay fever and asthma. And even though Ben went to work at the studio, Warner Brothers did not award him screenplay credit, giving it instead to I. A. L. Diamond and James V. Kern [the director]. I was very upset when I saw the movie; it wasn't my story at all.

How was working with Ben? Was it a relationship between two equals?

Not until I eventually wrote a screenplay, "With this Ring," with Janet Stevenson, did I have a clue what a collaboration with two equals working together could be like.* Janet was ten years older than I, had gone to the Yale School of Drama, and had written a hit Broadway play with her husband [Philip], but those facts did not keep her from treating me as an equal. I'd gone to Janet with an idea of mine—about a woman, originally a teacher, who'd been turned by her husband into an unhappy, ineffectual clinging vine

---

Communist by another agent, Meta Reis Rosenberg, as well as by Harold Hecht, Isobel Lennart, and Martin Berkeley, Willner, a senior partner, was forced to sell his $750,000 interest in the Nat Goldstone Agency for $25,000. Having been a salesman before he entered show business as a talent representative, he took a job selling textiles. Then he was named again, by writer Melvin Levy. His name appeared on the front page of the Los Angeles newspapers, and he was dismissed from that job, too. He managed to support his family until the blacklist ended. Then he began working at the Marvin Josephson Agency, later becoming a top agent at the International Famous Artists Agency.

*Janet (1913–   ) and Philip Stevenson (1897–1965) have fallen through the cracks of most blacklist chronicles. They were playwrights who ended up in Hollywood when their play *Counter-Attack* was produced by Columbia as a motion picture in 1945. An adaptation of a Soviet play, it was about a soldier trapped in a small town held by the Nazis. Morris Carnovsky had played the lead on Broadway. In Hollywood, Paul Muni played the lead, Sidney Buchman was the producer, Larry Parks had a featured part, and former Group Theatre member Roman Bohnen played a supporting role. All this made *Counter-Attack* one of the special targets of HUAC.

Janet Stevenson also collaborated with her husband on other films, including *The Man from Cairo*. Philip Stevenson amassed screenwriting credits independent of his wife, including an Academy Award nomination for his coscreenplay of *The Story of G. I. Joe* (fellow G. I. Joe writer Guy Endore was blacklisted, and the third collaborator, Leopold Atlas, became a "friendly witness"). Once blacklisted, Philip Stevenson wrote novels and contributed to films under pseudonyms. Janet Stevenson concentrated on her work as an educator, historical novelist, and biographer, treating in her many books such varied themes as the lives of naturalist John James Audubon, opera contralto Marian Anderson, and pioneering feminists, the stories of the legal challenges to segregation and of the Montgomery bus boycott.

who kept the children out of his way and served fine dinners for his business associates to help him get ahead. On vacation, without the husband, who has stayed behind to conduct his business activities, she has an adventure with a soil conservationist. Alongside him, she teaches farmers and, as a result of working and being treated as an equal, she comes out of her shell. Milton Sperling of Warner Brothers read it, called us in, and suggested we situate the story at a ski resort in the mountains instead of an agricultural community. We foolishly said no. I so wanted to further my screenwriting career that I believe, if Janet had not been as strongly opposed, I would have given in. I would use this story again when I was on the blacklist and writing under-the-table television scripts for *Orient Express*.

Did the costory credit on Never Say Goodbye *help you get a screenwriting job?*

Everyone thought Ben wrote it. Not even the screenplay I wrote with Janet, which became known around town, helped. They might have hired me with Ben, but by that time Ben was working with someone else.

So it's mid-1946, and you are trying to get a screenwriting job.

Yes, and I am expecting a baby, suffering more from allergies, and realizing that my career might be babies. Then I did something really neurotic: I decided to have babies one after the other and get over the baby-having phase. After that I would have my career. I had Luli and Johnnie twelve months apart, tried to have another right away, which I lost, then became pregnant with Aaron. All that time, the *Examiner* was paying me maternity leave. I wanted to return, but Ben wouldn't agree. We had a housekeeper and a nurse, and my mother was around, so it wouldn't have been such a terrible thing to do. But he wouldn't let me. When I say he wouldn't let me, it sounds silly. I should have fought him, but he wooed me with a promise of collaborating on another story and a pledge that this time he would insist I go with him to the studio to write the screenplay.

So we wrote and sold another story, *The Locket*. It was a psychological thriller based on the déjà vu concept. Unlike the usual forty-page treatment, we always wrote near-screenplays of eighty pages. Hume Cronyn bought it but then sold it to RKO. They awarded Sheridan Gibney sole credit. We should have gone to the Screen Writers Guild for arbitration. I don't and I do not know why we didn't. It was 1948, we were raising money for the Hollywood Ten, everyone was feeling the effects of the subpoenas, some people were drifting away from the Party, and we were beginning to feel afraid.

What did you think of the film The Locket?

I'd been concerned about my own psychological state. I'd wanted to show how adult relationships between a man and a woman are frequently determined by events that happened many years before, during one's childhood. But the movie contained little of our story. Ben and I wrote another original story together, "Lost Memory," which didn't sell. I was frustrated. And the

Cold War was starting. So, in spite of having two babies, I took on part-time organizing work for the Party—the Committee for Soviet-American Friendship, headed by Pauline Townsend—who later named me.* We planned concerts and other benefits.

But I felt awful about my career. The hay fever worsened; so did the asthma. Also, and I was becoming very silent. The Party opposed psychoanalysis unless I went to a Dr. [Isadore] Zifferstein. I started to see him in July 1948, five days a week, and continued until we left the country, in February 1949. I resumed analysis in France in 1951.

Meanwhile, Ben and Al Levitt, who had just written *The Boy with Green Hair* for RKO, moved to MGM, with Dore Schary. They were in the middle of a script for Lana Turner when Eddie Dmytryk, who had been blacklisted in November 1947, came to Ben with the novel *Christ in Concrete* and asked Ben to write a screenplay that he could direct. Ben said, "Can't you see that I have a job? I'm in the middle of writing a screenplay for Dore, and I can't do anything else." "You owe it to me," Eddie replied. "You have to write the screenplay at night and on weekends."

Why did Ben "owe" Dmytryk?

They were very close. They had become buddies at RKO, when Eddie had directed Ben's *Back to Bataan* screenplay. The movie starred John Wayne, who went about making the most outrageous reactionary comments. So, to get even, Ben devised and wrote into the script agonizing stunts that Wayne, who worked without a double, would have to do.

Eddie also said to Ben, "You're still working. I'm paying for being a Communist, and you are not. I could take the screenplay to London and direct it there. It's a way of breaking the blacklist." I had loved the book, so I urged Ben to read it. He did, and he began writing a screenplay at night and on weekends.

Eddie took the script to England and gave it to [film magnate] J. Arthur Rank. He called Eddie in and said he liked it and wanted to produce it, but he had one question. "Uh-oh," Eddie thought. "He is going to ask, 'Are you now or have you ever been . . . ?'" Instead, Rank asked, "Mr. Dmytryk, do you believe in God?" Eddie thought for a moment and replied, "Well, if I didn't before, I do now." And they shook hands. The one condition of the

---

*Pauline Townsend was the wife of Leo Townsend, who also named the Barzmans. Leo Townsend's list of pre-HUAC screenwriting credits includes *It Started with Eve*, *Seven Sweethearts*, *Night and Day*, *Black Hand*, *Port of New York*, and many, many more after his testimony in 1951. He named thirty-seven people as Communists. Townsend told Victor Navasky, author of *Naming Names*, "I didn't name anyone who hadn't been named [before]." Investigating that assertion, Navasky established that Townsend was the first to name Joseph Losey and Losey's wife, Ben Bengal, Ben and Norma Barzman, Daniel James, Henry Myers, Mortimer Offner, Maurice Rapf, Bess Taffel, Phoebe Brand, Jay Gorney, and John Weber.

deal was that Ben come immediately to London to do rewrites and advise on the building of a lower East Side New York set.

Eddie telephoned us in the middle of the night, and we stayed up the rest of the night discussing the issue. Does Ben leave in the middle of a screenplay, does Norma leave in the middle of her analysis, do we leave Norma's sick mother, and do we travel with two babies and one in the tummy? We decided that it was important to break the blacklist, not only for Dmytryk but for the actor Sam Wanamaker, who had been blacklisted in New York and was now in England cast in the lead. So we sailed on the *Queen Mary* for what we thought would be a six-week stay. I left everything we owned in the bureau drawers and closets of our house on Sunset Plaza Drive.

Were you afraid that you and Ben might be subpoenaed?

Of course. Sooner or later it would happen. Maybe it was better for us to go abroad sooner rather than later. One hot day we'd been sitting on the front lawn when a convertible driven by a woman with blond hair turned around in our driveway. She told us that a sheriff's car was parked at the bottom of the hill and that the sheriff was taking down license numbers and asking people where they were going. He was asking about 1290, our address. "My name is Norma, too," she said, "and I am going to a party at Judy Garland's, up the hill." It was not until we were in Paris that we found out that the blond lady warning us was Marilyn Monroe. So to stymie the process servers we feared were coming, we swapped houses with Bernard Vorhaus. We were lucky—it was very hot, and their house had a swimming pool while ours did not. It would be good to get away, we thought, from this atmosphere of terrible fear.

Dore Schary felt Ben was being disloyal to him. He couldn't understand why Ben would want to leave a blossoming career. Joe Losey, who had directed *The Boy with Green Hair*, wanted Ben to do another picture with him.

What was your relationship with Losey in Hollywood?

Losey had been a New York stage director. He was terrified about doing his first picture, so frightened, in fact, that he tried too hard to get everything right. He even took a broom from a stagehand and started sweeping the set, which alienated the entire crew. But he was one of the few directors who respected every comma of the script. Whenever Joe wasn't sure what Ben meant, he would ask him for an interpretation and then really try to get it the way Ben had meant it. That went on for four movies, until the fifth, when they had all that trouble. But on *The Boy with Green Hair* Joe was grateful for Ben's presence on the set. We had been warned how difficult he could be, but we became close friends.

And how was London?

On arrival, we discovered the whole project was shaky. Dmytryk insisted Ben sign a paper stating that Ben had been paid for the script. Otherwise, Eddie said, the British crew would refuse to go on working. The film's producer later used that paper to deny Ben payment. All we ever received for the screenplay of *Salt to the Devil* [the title of the film based on the novel *Christ in Concrete*] were our tickets on the *Queen Mary* and hotel accommodations for the entire family.

Looking back, doesn't that seem foolish?

I think we would have done it no matter what. First, because of its subject matter—showing capitalism at its worst, the depths of the Depression, people starving, workers being pushed into betraying each other in order to get work. Secondly, because it was a superb project, and we knew it would make a beautiful film. In fact, it won prizes at the Karlovy Vary [now in the Czech Republic] and Venice film festivals. I will never forget how, when we traveled along with the film to the mines and factories of Czechoslovakia during the film festival there, thousands of people rose to their feet and bowed to Ben and me and cheered. The movie also became popular in Italy, and Ben became known and respected among Italian filmmakers.

Another result of the film was our friendship with Sam Wanamaker, who starred in it. Sam was a really great spirit. One of the first things he said when we met was that he had been walking all over London, especially Shakespeare's London, and that he intended to see that the Globe Theatre was rebuilt. He died in 1993, as his dream project was nearing completion.

Why didn't you return to the United States?

We thought that after six cold weeks in England, without even an egg (they were still rationing food), we ought to go to France for a vacation. In May, when the film was finished, we went to Cannes with our best friend, Adrian Scott—one of the Hollywood Ten—and his [second] wife, the actress Anne Shirley. They were staying in Europe until Adrian would have to return to the United States for sentencing on his contempt-of-Congress conviction. We heard things were getting worse in Hollywood, and we would never be able to get work if we returned. Adrian advised us to stay. He said he knew some producers in Paris who might give us work.

One morning Adrian turned up at our hotel in Cannes with his adopted son, Michael, who had been orphaned during the Blitz and was the model for *The Boy with Green Hair*. Adrian told us that Anne had left that morning, that she couldn't face his probable imprisonment and "life without Beverly Drive." It was the first time that we saw the domestic Cold War breaking up a family.

Shortly after that conversation, we moved to Paris. Ben figured we might have one last chance to do an original story for the Hollywood studios. Maybe, he said, Sammy Weisbord, our agent, would be able to sell it without our names on it. I came up with the idea, based on my sister Muriel's experiences cramming for both the New York and California bar examinations. Her boy-friend had left her, because she had no time for him. I said, "What if we told this story about someone losing her whole personal life while cramming for the bar?" I thought it would be great to have a woman lawyer as our main character, but Ben said no, we would never sell it with a woman; it should be a man. We called it "Young Man with Ideas" and used my father's first name, Sam, and my mother's maiden name, Levinson.

What were you paid for that story?

A lot. I forget how Weisbord did it, because he had to get us the money in such a way that it could not be traced. It was a great relief when the money finally arrived. Until then, my mother had been helping us.

Were there other Hollywood people in Paris when you arrived?

Only a few, temporarily on jobs. [Director] Lewis Milestone was there with his wife, and Ben started working on a project with him. Our new baby had whooping cough, the other two had chicken pox, and I had caught both diseases and was deathly ill. Our house was like a hospital. I told Ben to move out until we were healthy. When I got better, Ben and Milly [Milestone] were planning to go to Rome to see a producer, and I wanted to go. Ben said, "No. Milly wouldn't like that." I said I would not be in the way. Ben continued to say no.

He then felt he had to make it up to me. When an Israeli producer asked Ben to write a screenplay for a movie to be shot in Israel, Ben said to me, "You can come along and do the research." So in February 1950 we left my mother with the three children, a housekeeper, and two nurses. I stayed a month in Israel. Sam Wanamaker wanted to direct and star in the movie, but we had to use a Polish director [Joseph Leytes], a friend of the producer. We combed the country for an idea. I particularly wanted to visit the refugee children and orphans pouring into Israel from every country in Europe and North Africa. There was already in Israel a great deal of prejudice against Jews from the French-culture African countries—Algeria, Tunisia, Morocco. They were called "Franks" in the Israeli newspapers. I was curious to see if this prejudice was apparent among European Jewish children. I found a young American who had run a children's camp in the United States, come to Palestine to fight for an independent Jewish state and been assigned to run a school for orphaned kids from war-torn European countries. The building lacked water, and when water was trucked in, the trucks were frequently attacked and sometimes destroyed. The young American gave these isolated kids love, and by the time Israel became a state, he had restored their faith in people. This story became the basis for *Faithful City*, a good screenplay but a terrible picture. I did not get credit.

I returned to Paris without Ben. Bernie Vorhaus, who was cutting a film he'd shot in the South of France, called. We went to dinner. He had script problems on his next project. I started working with him. In the course of this work, I came up with an idea for a movie I had always wanted to do about a finishing school in Switzerland. My sister had attended a school like that in Lausanne. My parents had put me in the little girls' part of it. I lasted only two weeks; I cried so much my mother and father rescued me and took me with them on a fantastic trip to the Schwarzwald, Vienna, and Budapest. I used my sister's experiences in the finishing school and some of my memories of my freshman year at Radcliffe as the basis for the story. Bernie said he would move his wife—she was Welsh—and kids to England, and then we would form a company and do that movie.

Ben returned from Israel. Johnny Weber, a former William Morris agent, arrived with his wife and children, and money from progressive investors. Bernie returned with his wife and children, and money from his family. Ben and I invested the writing talent. We formed Riviera Films, with the idea of Bernie directing my script, but we ended up making two films, because we had a wealthy Italian-American in tow, a Texas oilman with ulcers who had been told by his doctor to find a less stressful occupation! He wanted to do a film at Forzano studios [Consorzio Produttori Cinematografici Tirrenia].

News arrived that Bernie had been named. Fearing that would kill the deal, he bought all the American newspapers within a radius of over a hundred miles, especially the *Rome Daily American,* which each day printed a special box listing those who had been named. I suggested Joe Losey for the Forzano film, *Stranger on the Prowl,* which Ben was writing. Weber said Losey would also be named. "Not right away," I said. "Let's get him out of America. He's going to be a great director."

With Ben's script, Losey got Paul Muni to agree to play the lead. Bernie rounded up a group of rising young stars, including Marina Vlady, to act in my movie, *Luxury Girls,* which was shot at Cinecittà. I, however, lost my passport and could not go to Italy for the filming. There probably would have been more work for me if I could have gone. Ben had been deprived of his American citizenship—he had been born in Canada—and couldn't travel either. Later on, he would receive a French passport for the stateless.

Were the names on the credits for Luxury Girls *real: Carlo Cavallero producer, Piero Museta director, and Ennio Flaiano screenplay?*

Cavallero was real. Museta was Bernie's assistant director. Flaiano, a fine writer, had translated my script into Italian. When I was named, by Leo Townsend [in September 1951], Flaiano's name replaced mine on the credits.

This was your screenplay; you worked on it by yourself?

I wrote the screenplay alone. Bernie consulted with me, as the director. It was about a very young girl who gets pregnant and wants an abortion. I thought it would be interesting to make her a wealthy girl with parents who will not allow an abortion. The other girls in the school support her position. After the girl attempts to kill herself, the parents give their consent. That was pretty hot stuff for 1951.

Did you like the finished product?

I saw the Italian version on television, in 1986, in my dying sister's hospital room in Rome. It was good, I thought, even after all those years. It was shown at the Edinburgh Festival about seven years ago.

Tell us about the Paris exile community.

By 1951 Jack [John] Berry, Tammy and Lee Gold,* and Julie Dassin had arrived. I had know them only slightly in Hollywood, but we became very close, a community. Lee Gold, who died a few years ago, was a fine man, a talented writer, and a dear friend. Tammy, who is still alive and splits her time between Beverly Hills and Paris, I still see. She is an example of a talented woman writer whose career was cut off by the blacklist. She has written two fine biographies and a good novel.

Could you be political?

Our French political life was limited to going to French ciné clubs, such as Ciné Action, that were Communist-oriented. Every time there was a *manifestation*—demonstration—we had to ask ourselves whether we could afford to participate. We had seen other foreigners bounced out of France within twenty-four hours for political activity of any kind. Socially we inhabited a Communist milieu. We saw the Joliot-Curies [Pierre and Irène Joliot-Curie], Jacques and Pierre Prévert, Yves Montand and Simone Signoret, Louis Daquin, and Vladimir Pozner.

Did you still consider yourself a loyal Communist?

Once we left American soil, we no longer considered ourselves, nor were we members of anything. We had no affiliations, but we continued to feel like Communists. Everywhere we went in Europe, people were always warm, welcoming. French intellectuals, whether Communist or not, treated us like heroes. As a result, we had a good feeling about ourselves, and since we were in a country where the Communist Party was a mass party, winning large blocs of votes, we felt part of the mainstream, not off in a corner. We had great friendships with our doctors, who were Communists, and who would not accept our money. They believed that by standing up to HUAC we had

---

*Lee Gold (1919–1985) and Tamara (or Tammy) Gold (a.k.a. Tamara Hovey) were writers who left Hollywood for France when their careers were imperiled by HUAC. Before the blacklist Lee's best-known credit was the script—written with Isobel Lennart—for Jules Dassin's film *The Affairs of Martha*. Tamara—the daughter of the famed screenwriter Sonya Levien—contributed to *Bagdad* and *That Midnight Kiss*. Residing principally in Paris for nearly forty years, the Golds wrote for many television programs and feature films, usually collaborating closely with the Barzmans and directors John Berry and Jules Dassin. Tamara Gold eventually turned to writing books. Her biographies of John Reed and George Sand were published under the name Tamara Hovey.

done something wonderful, and they wanted to do something equally wonderful for us in return.

The main problem of the American community was safety. We were frightened, didn't have any idea how long we would be tolerated in France without
passports or *cartes de séjour*. A lawyer told us that we might be thrown out at
any time, that we should make alternate plans. What could we do? Where
could we go? We queried Israel to see if that country would like a Dassin-
Berry-Barzman moviemaking kibbutz, but we were told by the cultural attaché
that Israel would lose a lot of support from American Jews if it sponsored such
a project. When we were not told to leave, we came to the conclusion that
a policy decision to give us a haven had been made in the upper echelons of
the French government. When necessary, we helped each other get papers.

Then the question was, how do we live financially? At the beginning Ben
was the only one getting jobs, writing French movies. Hannah Weinstein
arrived, made a television pilot that Jack directed, left for England, and began
to provide us with assignments for [the TV series] *Robin Hood*. Ben was making
much more money on the features he was writing than we—Jack Berry, me,
and Lee and Tammy Gold—were on our television scripts. With Lee I did a
one-hour pilot for *International Airport*, which aired in conjunction with another series. It starred Mai Zetterling and Herbert Lom. Most of our scripts
had either a progressive idea or at least something human about them. I
enjoyed writing the twenty-six-minute stories for *Orient Express*, another series. Jack and I rewrote his *He Ran All the Way*, putting it on a barge in the
Seine. Tammy and I wrote one based on the script I had written with Janet
Stevenson.

Were you and Ben, then, in reasonable financial shape?

Our group pooled all the money we made and divided it according to need.
But Ben felt put upon, because he was making most of the money. In the
spring of 1954 he decided we should leave Paris for the South of France. He
could not stand what he called the "herring barrel," herrings packed close
together in brine. We were sort of incestuous, sharing all our psychological
problems as well as security and financial ones. Everything went into the
pot—political, social, familial. So the Barzmans, to extract themselves from
the "barrel," began to live in a town above Nice, from April to August.

Ben wrote the first half of a novel, *Out of This World* (also called *Echo X*
and *Twinkle, Twinkle Little Star*), a science-fiction book that is now a collec-
tor's item. He had intended to write the entire novel while we were in the
Midi, but he began to get itchy for screenplays. He used to say, "Did the
telephone ring?" He meant, "Have they forgotten me as a screenwriter?" So
he took on a few German films with [actor] Curt Jurgens—*Michael Strogoff*—
and others.

*Ben and Jules Dassin formed an important collaboration around this time, didn't
they?*

Ben had helped him on *Rififi*, and then, when Dassin made another deal, it included Ben as screenwriter. That picture wasn't made. But one day, when Ben was laid up with a bad sore throat, Joe Bellfort, one of the executives of Fox-Europe, came bearing a thick book, Nikos Kazantzakis's *The Greek Passion*. He asked Ben to read it. We both read it, enthralled. Ben called Julie. We did not think it was a vehicle for Melina Mercouri, but Julie wanted to make a film in Greece starring her. Every morning Julie came to our house carrying the New Testament. He would dilate his nostrils and read Ben some passages in a very theatrical voice. After that he'd say to Ben, "Well, I've done my work for today. Now you do yours."

Julie shot Ben's screenplay, *He Who Must Die*, in Crete, but we could not go, because we still did not have our passports—this was in 1957. When we saw it at the Cannes Film Festival, Kazantzakis threw his arms around Ben and said, "Most authors of novels would be unhappy after seeing a film made from their books, but I can tell you that I am a very happy man. You, Ben, have extended my thought." The film received a special award at Cannes and prizes at other film festivals. Ben became well-known in France, and the French Ministry of Culture began to take notice of him and his work.

This movie led Henri Bérard, its producer, to say to Ben, "I think you could direct a picture, I think you should direct a picture, and I will let you do it. If, that is, Dassin agrees to back you up." Ben went to Julie and asked him to agree to provide whatever assistance Ben might need. Julie turned purple: "What makes you think you can direct?" Ben said, "You mean you won't help me?" And Julie replied, "Of course not. That is what I do, direct. That's me." And Ben said, while picking up a chair to hit Julie with, "After all I have done for you . . ." (the same words he used later with Joe Losey). Bérard came in and made peace. It was sort of forgotten, except that Ben never really forgave Julie. When I was in Athens recently, Julie filled my hotel room with flowers, took me to a fine restaurant, and presented me to the United States ambassador to Greece, who is helping Julie raise money for an art and archaeological museum named after Melina.

What was happening to your career?

I helped on the German films, including one about a woman obstetrician fighting for "painless childbirth," and wrote more scripts for the *Robin Hood* series. In one I was proud of, Eleanor of Aquitaine, a twelfth-century woman of great power and culture, goes around raising money for the ransom of her son, Richard I, the Lionhearted.

Suddenly Ben dispatched me to Paris to buy a house, and we moved back. We worked on a French film, with Yves Allégret, about young girls being sold into prostitution [*Méfiez-vous fillettes*]. Allégret, who did not know I was working with Ben, took Ben to a whorehouse to get the flavor of the place. Neither of us got credit.

Before discussing your new Paris life, let's deal with the relations between the Barz-mans and Joseph Losey. Let me quote from Losey's comments on the various movies on which he and Ben worked, and let you respond. In Michel Ciment's 1985 book Conversations with Losey, *Losey said about* Stranger on the Prowl, *"It was a very compassionate story that suffered from the fact that Barzman was still a Hol-lywood-oriented writer. It also suffered from the fact that Barzman and I were not able to work together on it at all because he was banned from Italy politically. [When it was shown in Paris] Barzman hated it. I didn't like it very much either."*

Stranger on the Prowl was a beautiful screenplay, before Joe got his hands on it, and one of the best scripts Ben had written. It was about a little boy and a criminal, outcasts who hide together and bond. We had not been around when Joe shot it, and we got the shock of our lives when we saw it in Paris. That magnificent screenplay had turned into something unbelievably corny. I don't know what happened to Joe. Yes, I do know. There was no one there to say, "Joe, don't do that." And Joe was having a terrible time with Paul Muni, who had cancer. There were many problems, so I cannot be too hard on Joe. But the problem was not with Ben's script. It was the direction.

Did Ben and Joe quarrel?

No. We did not tell Joe what we thought. We simply said we knew what he had had to contend with during the filming—including CIA types in Italy watching him and Bernie, and reporting to the U.S. State Department on the production of our two movies.

Why was Andrea Forzano credited with this script?

Ben had been named to HUAC. The Forzanos owned the studio where it was shot. I felt guilty about the whole mess. I had been the one responsible for bringing Joe to Europe.

Five years later, in 1956, Ben and Joe worked on Time Without Pity. *Losey told Michel Ciment, "Barzman and I turned the story on its head."*

It was based on an Emlyn Williams play, but the movie wasn't anything like the play. Ben saw in it the chance to do something against capital pun-ishment. It involved a father and son. The father, drunk all the time, could not get himself to England to save his son, charged with a murder he did not commit. That was the play. The film is really an exploration of . . . well, the audience knows immediately who has killed the girl. The murderer is a big industrialist, drunk with power, who has contempt for the girl, a maid, con-tempt for everybody, and is ready to see an innocent young man hanged for the crime. It was a fine film. It still is.

Did Losey work with Ben on the screenplay?

No. Ben wrote the screenplay in Paris, while Joe was in England. They had telephone conversations, and Joe came once to Paris for a conference. Joe shot what Ben wrote. Joe was still respectful of scripts, asking what Ben meant in various places, sometimes seeking Ben's advice on how to direct it. Joe was happy because the movie turned out so well.

Then, two years later, they collaborated on Blind Date/Chance Meeting. *Losey said that it was a rewrite of an Eric Ambler script that Barzman and Millard Lampell did in four weeks, with Lampell doing the love scenes and Barzman the rest.*

We received our American passports in July 1958, and in September we left for London. Harry Saltzman, the producer, paid for our trip. He wanted Ben to write *The Ceremony*, another movie against capital punishment.

So we were in London when Joe said that he needed a rewrite on this Eric Ambler script—in a hurry. Ben threw out most of the Ambler material and wrote a new first draft, but he was not working fast enough to suit Joe, who had a commitment with the Rank studios. Joe asked Ben whether Millard could help. Ben agreed and gave Millard the love scenes to rewrite. Then Ben put it all together.

Joe liked the script—no problems. We were still very close, although at one point, after the project was completed, Joe sent Ben a letter stating, "You do not care about me, you treat me very badly, you always act as if you are doing me a favor when you write a script for me, and I always feel humbled by you. I don't want to feel that way anymore." It was a terrible letter, which wound up with Joe saying, "Let's not be friends anymore." Right after we read the letter, Joe telephoned, saying we would receive a letter from him which we should not open or read. I told him that we had read it, but we understood why he had written it and did not hold it against him. One had to forgive his outbursts. He was so neurotic, and his mother and analyst had both just died.

And then came The Damned. *Losey told Michel Ciment, "I got Barzman to write a script, and he let me down very badly on it for reasons that were not entirely his fault, as he was at the time having trouble traveling for political reasons. Anyway, he didn't deliver a script that I thought I could do. I had to throw Barzman's script away and start over."*

First, Ben was having no trouble traveling. By this time he had a valid American passport. We were at our country house in Mougins, and Joe wanted to come there to visit us and work with Ben. Ben had already written a rough draft of the script, about children in England who had been exposed to radiation. While Joe was with us, Ben said that he was thinking about negotiating for another epic with Samuel Bronston and Anthony Mann. Ben had done *El Cid* and *The Fall of the Roman Empire* with them, and now they were talking about a life of Queen Isabella. They were all coming for lunch to discuss it. "Since they think I am working exclusively on that," Ben continued, "it would be best if they did not see you here, working with me on another screenplay." Joe blew up, shouting, "Are you ashamed of me?" Ben said, "No, but can't you see how awkward it might be for me? Couldn't you just get out of the way for the time of the luncheon?" Joe refused, so I called [film composer] Alex North, who lived in Grasse, and asked him to invite Joe to lunch in Cannes and keep him there for as long as possible. Joe accepted the invitation and went.

At five o'clock the phone rang. It was Joe, who said, "I am sick of getting drunk here in the Carlton bar. Are you coming for me, Norma?" Bronston and Mann had left, and I picked up Joe, who was in a roaring, drunken rage. He said, "Ben has sold out. He works with those guys so he can keep his swimming pool. He doesn't care about me anymore. He cares only about money and the good life, and I can't stand it. It is too shitty, and I won't work with him anymore." I tried to placate him, but he was very drunk and very angry. He stayed another few days, continued to work on the screenplay with Ben, and didn't say anything about his intention to get another screen-writer. I told Ben, however, that Joe had said he would never forget what Ben had done. Ben didn't think there was anything to worry about and continued working on the script.

Joe returned to England and hired another writer, without telling us. While Ben was doing rewrites, another screenplay was being written [by Evan Jones, who received sole screenplay credit]. That ended our friendship for a long time. He never explained or apologized. In sum, Joe did not dislike Ben's script for *The Damned* until Bronston and Mann arrived for lunch.

Did you continue to write?

I did less and less.

How were you and Ben getting along?

When we arrived in France, Ben had said, "I've been uprooted. Now every-thing is shit." And I said, "You have a lovely wife, lovely children, work, projects you probably never could have done in Hollywood, and lots of friends and exciting people all around you. We have the possibility of a wonderful life here." In fact, through our friend Vladimir Pozner, we would meet Picasso, Braque, Paul Éluard, and other progressive intellectuals at the Maison de la Pensée. But Ben was feeling culture shock, and I was not. After all, I had lived in France for three years as a child, I had returned for a few months prior to World War II. I could speak the language. For me, it was coming home. Ben may have resented that more than he showed.

His feelings were basic to our unhappiness. My unhappiness stemmed from bitterness about my career—hampered not only by the blacklist but by Ben's attitude toward my work—and from the loss of my passport and my inability to travel. In the years when I might have gotten work, I couldn't leave France. I resented being looked upon as a housewife. If it had not been for the "herring barrel," who were supportive of me as a writer, I might have lost all strength to continue working. Ben wanted me to take care of the babies and work on his projects. But what really got through to me was that he felt victimized and was constantly in a state of depression. Meanwhile, I was exhibiting symptoms again and went to a French analyst. I lost my symptoms but kept having more children.

At this time, Nikita Khrushchev delivered his speech revealing some of the evils Joseph Stalin had committed from the 1930s to the 1950s. How did you react?

I'm afraid we thought it was wonderful that the Soviet Union could admit to the dreadful things it had perpetrated, which we believed it had been pushed into by the worldwide conspiracy against it. Of course, we were shocked at the admissions Khrushchev made about the Stalin period, but Khrushchev's "telling the truth" seemed to us to indicate that the Soviet Union intended to live up to Communist ideals in the future, that it was going to begin afresh.

And the Soviet invasion of Hungary?

We had a hard time dealing with it, especially since our Communist doctor friends had published a letter in *Le monde* announcing their split with the French Communist Party. A large group of French intellectuals with whom we were friends did likewise. I don't remember why we remained so blind. Even when our friends the Mitelbergs—he was the great political cartoonist "Tim"—returned from Poland and told us about Communist Party anti-Semitism there, we rationalized that he was just looking for some excuse to leave his low-paying job at *L'humanité* and move to *L'express*. Yves Montand and Simone Signoret, standing in line with us to see Charlie Chaplin's *A King in New York*, after their return from the Soviet Union, told us how disappointed they had been. But we didn't listen. It took us until 1968 to admit the many things wrong with world Communism. The French Communist response, or lack of response, to the May 1968 revolution (*les événements*—the uprising of students, including our own children, and workers, defying the De Gaulle regime), plus the Soviet invasion of Czechoslovakia, their crushing of "the Prague Spring," dashed our hopes for Communism with a democratic face.

Let's pick up the Barzmans in 1957.

After I got my passport back in July 1958, we spent winters in London and summers in a country house in the South of France, in Mougins, which be-came by 1962 more and more our way of life. Eventually we decided to live down there and go to Paris for vacations. That decision isolated me; it con-tributed to my having more babies and trying farming instead of writing. I was always around when there was a problem with one of Ben's films, but mostly I was the lady of the manor, entertaining film people for Ben. I enjoyed it but now wonder how I could have stood it. Sophia Loren, who had become our good friend, pinched my cheek one day and called me "*la mamma,*" which drove me wild.

We had become close to Sophia and Carlo Ponti after Tony Mann had flown Ben to Rome to convince Sophia to do *El Cid*. She had refused to do it after reading the original script. Sophia had loved *Christ in Concrete* and told Tony that if Ben rewrote the script, she would do it. When Ben was ushered before Sophia, Carlo, and their friend, the screenwriter, Basilio Franchina, Sophia said to Ben, "My career is in your hands." "No, no," Ben replied. "I cannot promise anything. This is Friday. Tony starts to shoot Monday. I would have to write a completely new script directly for the cameras. I don't know if I can do that." She said, "Try." He promised to do his best. The next day they all flew to Madrid. Ben remembered that we had loved Gérard Philipe in Pierre Corneille's classic play *Le Cid,* so he called the French Embassy and received the ambassador's personal copy of the play. Ben followed it closely.

By the time I arrived, Sophia and Basilio and Ben were ensconced in apartments on three different floors of the Torre de Madrid, a new, swaying skyscraper. Ben worked at a frantic pace, Basilio consulted with him, and Sophia cooked her "light" meals of spaghetti and cannonball meatballs. A boy sat in the hall of Ben's apartment waiting for the pages. Ben typed, sometimes his secretary retyped, and when a few pages accumulated the boy took one set to Tony and another to Sophia. Basilio became an important figure in our lives, an uncle to our children, a very dear friend.

Charlton Heston, Sophia's costar, was sure that since Ben was "her writer," his role would suffer. So he would constantly call Ben and ask questions, such as, "When I spend the night in the barn with Sophia, what happens to my horse? My fans will want to know. It reflects on my image." So Ben wrote in a little business with a stableboy throwing a blanket over the horse and leading it away. There was a lot of tension between Heston and Sophia.

When I flew from London to Madrid, I was ordered to bring five kosher salamis for Phil Yordan, whose name appears on *El Cid* as the screenwriter. Ben's contract was not with Bronston, the producer and head of the studio, but with Yordan, who maintained a sort of stable of blacklisted writers. On arrival in Madrid, I immediately delivered the salamis to Yordan, who attacked one of them with his letter opener.

Now that a committee established by the Writers Guild is trying to ascertain correct credits for blacklisted writers, I asked Phil Yordan if he would be willing to write a letter stating that Ben should receive credit for the screenplay of *El Cid.* Yordan said yes, that all he had done was handle the business end and that he would be glad to sign a letter to that effect. I sent him such a letter. Time passed, and he did not return the signed letter. When I called to ask if he'd forgotten, he said no and that I should not expect him to sign such a letter. He'd remembered that in 1965, when Bronston had gone into bankruptcy, Ben had asked Yordan to honor the contract Ben had signed to write "Paris 1900" for Bronston, with Vittorio De Sica to direct. Ben, who had done a lot of work on the script, asked for a settlement and threatened to sue when Yordan refused. Phil, furious, agreed to pay Ben fifty thousand dollars, because he was in the middle of a big deal with Warner Brothers. "So don't ask me for a letter. Ben shouldn't receive credit on anything. He should be punished."

When did you start writing again?

I had to get a bad case of hepatitis, almost die. The doctor announced that he would hospitalize me unless everyone was kept away, that I mustn't think about the children or the house. I began to read, starting with Simone de Beauvoir and Jean-Paul Sartre. That stimulated me. I got an idea for a play about France's May 1968 *événements*. I wrote it with Ben. We had a lot of fun doing it. He was better with me than ever before. From then on, our collaboration was different. I guess he'd become convinced that I was talented, or maybe he was more secure about himself. Maybe I, too, was more experienced and surer of myself. As for the play, Simone Signoret said it was good but would not go in France, because it was "too American," and the French would never accept an American's view of their May 1968. American producers said it was "too French," and no one in America would know what we were talking about.

When and why did you decide to return to Paris to live?

In November 1973, our brilliant son, Paulo, dropped out of the *lycée*. We thought it would be wise to get him away from some bad influences. But we were actually glad to leave Mougins, which had changed after Picasso died, and return to Paris. The preceding year had not been satisfying professionally. Ben was beginning to feel too far away from the action. We'd had a succession of projects that in one way or another were disappointing. Ben had written a very full treatment for *The Blue Max*, a film about a German World War I flying ace, to be played by George Peppard. The director, John Guillermin, came down to Mougins to discuss the screenplay with Ben. Guillermin liked the treatment, but he complained that the hero was not very sympathetic, that something would have to be done. Ben replied that the German aviator was not a sympathetic character; he was a forerunner of a Nazi. "I tell you what," said Guillermin, all of a sudden very British. "You don't need to think so hard. It's easy to make him sympathetic. Just give him a little dog." "Just give him a little dog" became Ben's and my shorthand for a phony way of dealing with a story problem. And the result of that meeting, since some of Ben's contempt for Guillermin must have showed, was that he received only story credit.

The Blue Max was made under the supervision of Darryl Zanuck, then head of Twentieth Century–Fox, who adored Ben and had started working with him before the blacklist had officially ended. He'd given Ben a Fox-Europe French film, *Oasis*, which was unreleasable, even though it starred Michèle Morgan. "Do with it what you can," Zanuck told Ben. By overdubbing the actors with new dialogue and reediting, Ben found a way to make the story work. The picture was released, and Ben received a series of assignments from

Fox: an adaptation of Friedrich Dürrenmatt's play *The Visit*, starring Ingrid Bergman and Anthony Quinn; an adaptation of Lawrence Durrell's *Justine*; and so on.

But towards the end at Mougins, it was difficult to get a good project on its feet. Ben accepted an offer to help our Algerian director friend Lakhdar-Hamina on a film commemorating the Algerian struggle for independence. We were invited to Algeria. From that came *L'attentat* (called in English *The French Conspiracy*), directed by Yves Boisset. It told the story of the Moroccan leader Ben Barka, who was kidnapped and killed in Paris. Starring Michel Piccoli and Jacques Perrin, the film was credited with helping to topple the de Gaulle government.

Ben's work on *L'attentat* probably led Constantin Costa-Gavras and Jacques Perrin to send Ben the screenplay for *Z*. I had read the book and thought it was terrific. Ben and I read the screenplay and thought it was awful. Jacques, who was producing, and Costa came to Mougins. Ben told them what we thought was wrong with it. They asked his advice. Ben came up to the bedroom to ask me what he should tell them. I said that they should just go back to the book, which was wonderful. He told them that. They threw out their screenplay. Ben did an adaptation that followed the documentary nature of the book. Jorge Semprún rewrote and took a sole credit. Nevertheless, Ben helped them make a deal with the Algerians, permitting the movie to be shot there.

Ben suffered from a significant number of breaches of contract as well as credit deprivations.

European producers screwed screenwriters on pictures more than American producers because they could get away with it more easily. Ben had signed real contracts, drawn up by our lawyers, but unenforceable. And yet, when one of those producers approached Ben with a project so moving, so important, *Korczak*, we were both captured by it. We read massive amounts of documentation compiled by the Jews of the Warsaw Ghetto. In our discussions we saw emerging the story of a Polish-Jewish doctor who cared so much for the orphans he was tending and teaching that he chose to accompany them into the gas chamber rather than allow himself to be saved. We agreed to do it, partially because the producer, Artur Brauner, had a deal with Film-Polski, and we had faith that a studio in a Communist country could be trusted.

Ben wrote the screenplay, but just as we were about to leave for Warsaw, we received a telegram from Film-Polski telling us not to come, that the picture had been postponed. Brauner told us they were having political troubles. Ben had received only one-third of the agreed-on price. Then Alexander Ford, who had been signed to direct it, appeared in Paris, saying he was escaping from a pogrom in the Polish film industry. He was resented because he had been trained in the Soviet Union and he was Jewish. We helped him and his wife hide and then go to Israel. Last year, in Paris, I went to see a film entitled *Korczak*, directed by Andrzej Wajda, and my feeling is that what I saw on the screen was Ben's screenplay, with no credit assigned to Ben.

Did your return to Paris provide more work, as you had hoped?

Few really good projects came our way. We were reduced to taking one about the cider-drinking problem of the children of Normandy, a film we predicted would never be made. But with our children growing up and starting college, we needed more money. When I went south, to rent the Mougins house, I had dinner with our friend and neighbor Harold Robbins. That night, in the cold, damp guest room of another novelist friend's house, I couldn't sleep and got the idea for a Robbins-type book, with sex, drugs, and violence. The antihero was a writer like Robbins. My other novelist friend, Robert Littell, said it was very commercial, a possible best-seller, and since we needed the money, it should be gotten out as quickly as possible. He suggested I work with Ben to get it done faster. We had a good experience with it. We got an unbelievably enormous advance from Warner Books. But reviews in the United States were few, and the reviewers didn't understand, perhaps because of its computerized title *Rich Dreams*, that it was meant to be a satire. The French publisher, Presses de la Cité, titled it *Convoitise* [Envy]. It received excellent reviews in France and sold well.

Why did you decide, in 1976, to return to the United States?

While we were writing the novel, I realized I had gotten out of touch with America, even though we had made two trips back, in 1965 and 1969. Neither we nor the children had liked it. But to write in the English language for an American readership was a far cry from writing a screenplay in English that you knew would be translated into a foreign language.

There were other reasons for our leaving. Ben longed to go back, in spite of having come to terms with French culture. He'd even ceased to be bothered by his fractured French. But he still spoke nostalgically about his "roots." By now, too, we had a son and a daughter at UCLA, and Paulo was working for Jean Renoir in Beverly Hills as his literary secretary.

And, finally, on the vacant lot next to our lovely Auteuil house, the city of Paris had built a nursery school whose walls directly abutted ours, resting on our foundation. Our house was falling in, becoming uninhabitable, and I was spending all my time with architects, engineers, geologists, and lawyers. We sued and eventually won the case, receiving a huge sum from the city.

How was it, the return to Hollywood?

A shock—the community had disappeared. We found few old friends with whom we could share things. It was easier with those who had had some European experience. Many of those who had stayed behind, even those who had been able to work on the black market, appeared beaten down.

Nor was there a plethora of projects for Ben. The first was based on the book *Airlift to Wounded Knee*, written by the pilot of the rescue plane, but it worked out very badly.* The book's author [Bill Zimmerman] insisted on collaborating with Ben, and he wanted every decision to go his way, whether it was good for the script or not. They fought constantly, and the movie was never made.

Shortly after our return, Anthony Quinn approached Ben, saying he was dying to play Picasso and could probably get backing for such a movie. Ben did not think that a movie about Picasso could be done, but he said he would think about it. When I told Ben that I had read Françoise Gilot's book and other biographies that related all of Picasso's episodes with women, he became even more doubtful. But then I recalled for him Picasso's eightieth birthday party, which we had attended—a fantastic two-day affair. Picasso had not wanted a birthday party. He didn't like birthdays, because they reminded him of his age and how little time he had left to paint. We could deal with his struggle not to have a birthday party, I suggested, and in the course of it reveal much about his life and character. Tony liked the idea. Ben said it was mine, and that I would be working with him on it. Tony was very macho, both in his verbal language and in his body language, but he accepted my collaboration.

We wrote a long treatment, but the original producer died in the middle of making the deal, and Tony decided to take it to Broadway producers, to make it into a musical. We objected—it would take too long to come to fruition—and we almost succeeded, on several occasions, in selling the original treatment in France. Tony was angry with us for not agreeing to the musical.

Finally the William Morris Agency began getting us deals. We wrote several screenplays and earned a lot of money, but none of them were made into movies. There were projects about a money counterfeiter, newspaper ethics, and a Jewish boy raised by a Nazi couple, which Joe Losey was to direct. Ironically, I would have shared the credit on all of them. I was doing most of the writing by then, since Ben had suffered a massive heart attack in July 1979 that seriously weakened him and limited his activity during the last ten years of his life.

As Ben became more incapacitated, I did even more of the writing, plus taking care of him. When the assignments dwindled, our son Daniel got me thinking about returning to newspaper writing. The Los Angeles Herald Examiner hired me to write a column about aging. I wrote "The Best Years" for five years, for the Herald Examiner and then the Los Angeles Times.

In 1982 Costa-Gavras, perhaps out of guilt for denying Ben credit on Z, used his position as head of the Paris Cinémathèque to sponsor a retrospective

---

*Airlift to Wounded Knee was one of the first books about the occupation of Wounded Knee, South Dakota, in the winter and spring of 1973. Several hundred Indians, mostly members of the Oglala Sioux tribe, took over Wounded Knee, demanding a government investigation into the condition of American Indians.

of Ben's work. The films Ben had written were shown for a week; he was the first screenwriter so honored.

In 1985 we were invited to a film festival at Chateauvallon, near Toulon, to teach a screenwriting class. We were inspired by a pageant about the Renaissance written by Denis Guénoun. We got the festival's sponsor interested, he provided some financing, and Ben, Denis, and I wrote a screenplay. But the film proved too costly to make. While there, Jean-Luc Godard attacked Ben as one of the dinosaurs who never stopped believing in the well-constructed screenplay. Ben maintained that there was room for many different kinds of movies, some of which could be shot on the spur of the moment with a camera strapped to the shoulder and nonactors improvising their lines. For his part, he preferred a well-structured film.

I cite this incident because it's hard for Americans to understand why Ben was, for thirty years, in the forefront of French cinema. It all began with Pierre Rissient "discovering" Ben and Joe Losey. Now Pierre is production consultant for Ciby 2000, but back then he was a sixteen-year-old *lycéen* who managed to book *The Boy with Green Hair* into the Cinéma MacMahon. That provoked a long, bitter rivalry between the New Wave filmmakers of *Les cahiers du cinéma* and the MacMahoniens—the classic filmmakers—of *Positif*. Shortly before he died, Ben was awarded the Order of Arts and Letters by the French Ministry of Culture.

After Ben died, I returned to Cremona, where, years before, I'd researched a novel about [the famed violin-maker Giuseppe] Guarneri for my cousin, Henry Myers. That visit inspired my own novel, *The Violins of Cremona*, which I have just finished.

I know that you spent large chunks of time in London. Could you compare the Hollywood exile community there to the one in Paris?

There was terrific comradeship among the Paris colony. We all loved each other very much. The English colony was cutthroat. They did not have the language-culture problem to isolate them. Sometimes Hannah Weinstein wasn't speaking to Joe Losey, Losey wasn't speaking to the Stewarts [Donald Ogden Stewart and Ella Winter], and the Stewarts weren't speaking to the Vorhauses.

The English colony was also not as supportive. At one party there, I danced with Cy Endfield, who told me that the pickings were too slim in England and that he intended to go to Washington and "spill my guts."* He hoped

---

*Cy (Cyril) Endfield (1914–1983) was born in South Africa and educated at Yale and the New Theatre League School in New York. In Hollywood from 1941, he first made his mark writing and directing MGM shorts and Joe Palooka films for Monogram. His pre-blacklist films *The Argyle Secrets*, *The Underworld Story*, and *The Sound of Fury* are considered minor masterworks of suspense. After being named as a Communist, he fled to England, where he continued to write and direct films, sometimes under pseudonyms. The best-known of his British credits—

that act would get him a job directing a movie. I got him some television work with the BBC. But it didn't satisfy him, and he returned to the United States to stool. That would never have happened in Paris. He would have had financial support, encouragement, and people saying, "For God's sake, don't do that!" Among the Parisians there was no rivalry, whereas in London there was even social competition—between those who felt more "in" with the British and lorded it over those who did not. When Paul Robeson came to town, people vied with each for the privilege of giving the big party for him.

Looking back, what is your perspective on exile and blacklisting?

I've already told you—we were fortunate to leave America when we did. We found a whole new, exciting world out there, waiting for us. We left early, on our own terms, didn't have to worry about money, never had the hard times others did. The thing I most resented was that being away had deprived me of participating in the American women's movement. The French women's movement could not compare in scope or impact. And I feel that the blacklist can be only partially blamed for nipping my career in the bud. Much of my problem resulted from the position of women and from my not having fought adequately for my rights.

The truth is, thirty years of exile gave our lives a richness they would never have had. I don't mean just the fantastic opportunity of meeting famous men and women, or being exposed to other cultures, or the broadening experience of travel. The friendship, camaraderie, and stimulation we found with others of us who had thought as we did, and suffered for it, was strengthening. The blacklist in Europe tended to be less bitter, less beaten down. The blacklistees in Europe remained idealistic, even if their opinions changed. Sundays spent at Mike and Zelma Wilson's country house outside Paris, with the Jarricos, the Dassins, the Berrys, the Golds, had a positive effect on us and our children.

You can't talk about blacklisting without talking about the children. Yes, they had difficulties acclimatizing and, later, figuring out in which country and culture they felt most at home, but we exiles have a fine group of children, and in important ways they were not harmed by the Cold War red scare. They are, in fact, some of the best guides on how to avoid another such in the future.

Our seven children have turned out to be fine people. As for Ben and me, we weathered it all pretty well. Many families broke up. But Ben and I, despite our problems, very much enjoyed one another. We lived a sort of Hollywood screwball comedy. I am writing a novel about it now.

---

made for his own company, formed in collaboration with the actor Stanley Baker—were the rousing adventures *Zulu* and *Sands of the Kalahari*. Although the belief holds among many in the blacklisted community that Endfield made some under-the-table accommodation with HUAC early in the 1960s, the rumors have not been substantiated by any published accounts.

Leonardo Bercovici

PHOTO BY ERIC BERCOVICI

LEONARDO BERCOVICI, Los Angeles, California, 1988

INTERVIEW BY PAUL BUHLE

**LEONARDO BERCOVICI
(1908–1995)**

1938 *Racket Busters*. Coscript.
1947 *Moss Rose*. Uncredited contribution.
    The Bishop's Wife. Coscript.
    The Lost Moment. Script.
1948 *Kiss the Blood off My Hands*. Coscript.
    Portrait of Jennie. Adaptation.
1950 *Dark City*. Uncredited contribution.

1952 *Monsoon*. Coscript.
1954 *Maddalena*. Uncredited contribution.
    Casa Ricordi. Uncredited contribution.
1955 *L'ombra*. Uncredited contribution.
1956 *Carta a Sara*. Uncredited contribution.
1960 *Jovanka e l'altri/5 Branded Women*.
    Uncredited contribution.
    Under Ten Flags. Uncredited contribution.
1963 *Square of Violence*. Costory, script.
1970 *Story of a Woman*. Director, script.

■

A GRADUATE OF the Yale Drama School and a precocious playwright, young Leonardo Bercovici became a successful and versatile radio writer in the late 1930s and early 1940s. He could have stayed in Hollywood after a brief but fruitful sojourn there in 1937, coscripting *Racket Busters* with Robert Rossen. Instead he returned to New York and to top shows in radio. War called him to political commitments, including both documentary film work and pro-Soviet stage spectaculars, and then Hollywood beckoned again.

Starting in 1946, Bercovici quickly proved himself adept at several screen genres, from fantasy and light comedy to noir, often from a psychological angle. Two of his scripts, for *The Bishop's Wife* and *Portrait of Jennie*, became films now embraced as classics. Bercovici appeared headed for director or producer status until the Ten went to jail and he was named in the second round of HUAC hearings in the spring of 1951. He appeared before the committee on May 16, 1951, refusing to affirm or deny his Communist Party membership.

By 1952 Bercovici had fled Hollywood for Mexico and then Italy. There he remained active as a writer, working mostly uncredited and as a script-fixer for the next dozen years or so. It was not until the blacklist was over that Bercovici finally gained a few belated opportunities to direct films.

■

Tell me about your background.

I was born in New York City in 1908. We were very poor in my early years. My father must have come over to America in 1904 or 1905. He was a profoundly educated man, self-educated, a Romanian Jew. My mother and father quarreled in five languages! For a time my father worked in steel mills and as a salesman, selling various articles. During the First World War he became a Spanish translator for Texaco. After that he moved into being editor of the *Apparel Producer*. Later he became the labor editor of *Women's Wear Daily* and a reporter for the *New York World*.

We moved out of the city in 1920, and I grew up after that in a middle-class home in Morristown, New Jersey. I was part of the generation who knew we would go to college. My father wanted me to be a biochemist, so I could solve a few problems like tuberculosis, cancer, and immortality. [Laughs.] My mother's influence went in the direction of wanting me to be a different kind of success—a writer. They never pushed me, however. In high school, my best subject was mathematics. I went to NYU first and then to the Yale Drama School.

Your uncle was a writer, right?

Uncle Konrad Bercovici became quite famous writing Gypsy stories.* He claimed that he was a Romanian Gypsy and that his grandfather was a Gypsy bear-tamer. So I liked to call myself a Gypsy too. [Laughs.]

Was anyone in the family political?

Konrad was interested in politics. My father said he hated the whole subject, although he had been some sort of anarchist in Paris, en route to the United States. In theory, he was an anti-Communist, but the man he admired most of all was the Communist leader of the Fur and Leather Workers Union, Ben Gold, along with [the two leaders of the Congress of Industrial Organizations] John L. Lewis and Sidney Hillman. Lewis was for him a prophet and Sidney Hillman a gentleman, but Gold was incorruptible. Although for a time he served as the publicity director for the International Ladies Garment Workers Union, my father loathed David Dubinsky [the anti-Communist president of the union].

After my father left the ILGWU, he took on publicity for the Gold faction of the Furriers Union. I had already worked on the copy desk at *Women's Wear Daily*, so he got me the job, at twenty-two, of doing publicity for the gangster faction, as "Leonard Bennett."†

---

*A former reporter for the *New York World*, Konrad Bercovici wrote novels, Gypsy stories, and reform-minded nonfiction, including *Around the World in New York*, *The Story of the Gypsies*, *Iliana: Stories of a Wandering Race*, *On New Shores*, and *The Marriage Guest*. He was also a musician and composer who, in Hollywood off and on, was part of Charlie Chaplin's circle of friends. Bercovici made a disputed contribution to the script of Chaplin's *The Great Dictator*.

†The needle trades of the 1920s and 1930s, centered in New York City, were a hotbed of radicalized Jewish workers and labor activity, and also a hotbed of labor racketeering. Socialists, mostly of an older generation, had risen to the level of leadership in many unions and struggled to hold at bay the younger and more militant immigrants, often enlisting organized crime to muscle the rank and file. In the ILGWU, Communist rank-and-filers challenged the bureaucratic leaders. David Dubinsky, a major supporter of Franklin D. Roosevelt and the New Deal, was also a fanatical anti-Communist and soon afterward labor's leading collaborator with the new Central Intelligence Agency.

Dubinsky's chief rival in the needle trade, Sidney Hillman, was leader of the Amalgamated Clothing Workers, which represented menswear workers. A still more important New Deal figure (Roosevelt used to say, "Clear it with Sidney!"), Hillman was also a frequent ally of the Communists until his sudden death in 1945.

Ben Gold, president of the Communist-led Furriers Union, was considered one of the most heroic, least self-seeking leaders of the younger Jewish generation. He made his name in no small part by successfully fighting back the Lepke-Gurrah mob. Like Hillman, Gold played an important role in launching and sustaining the Congress of Industrial Organizations, which transformed American labor from a craft-based to an industrial-based movement and gave it a

How did you actually get into playwriting?

I had hated NYU, due to a clash on the subconscious level. What should I be: a writer like Uncle Konrad, or a biochemist, of all the possible things? My major was English; my professor was an authority on O. Henry and Keats. He was very elegant and also very tough. He wrote on a paper of mine, "It's a pleasure to read someone who thinks for himself."

I wrote a one-act play and sent it in to Yale and was accepted into the Yale Drama School. After I had been admitted to Yale, Heywood Broun wrote a column [in the *New York World*] about the superiority of the novel to the play. With all my eighteen or nineteen years, I wrote him a long letter about why drama was superior, and he published it, entire; it filled a full column. The next day he proceeded to rip me apart.

While at Yale I wrote a number of plays, including "Child of God," based on a novel by Roark Bradford, *Ol' Man Adam an' His Chillun*. I sent it to Bradford, and he advised me, "Take it to New York." Courtenay Lemon, a close friend of the playwright Marc Connelly's, was a founder and original reader for the Theatre Guild, so he read the play. But he never called me back. Someone from the Guild finally contacted me and asked, "Do you have the rights?" I called an agent, and she said, "I must tell you that last month Marc Connelly acquired the rights to everything Roark Bradford has written." When it was produced theatrically as *The Green Pastures*, it was ninety-nine percent from the novel and one percent from Connelly. And it opened to the best reviews of the century.

This was my first of several disappointments, some of them just bad luck. I had a few plays of mine done, and they created an enormous amount of interest in my work. In 1931, a group of us from Yale decided to produce a play, *Lost Boy*, in Provincetown. The author [T. C. Upham] was forty, much older than the rest of us, and he had inherited eight thousand dollars, so we took the play to New York and opened at the Mansfield Theater. We got wonderful notices from the *New York Herald Tribune* and other papers, which carried on a campaign for its success. It was about a poor boy who gets sent to reform school, and what happens to him there. Yet it coincided with no conscious political interest on my part.

Wasn't this also an early part for John Garfield?

It was John Garfield's first part. You knew he was star material right away. Certain actors have a glow about them. There he was.

Was the play commercially successful?

---

brief, radical phase from the mid-1930s to the late 1940s. The Communists themselves eased him out of union leadership during the McCarthy era.

It ran two or three weeks. But then the Mansfield Theater was sold, and the good notices in the *New Yorker* and elsewhere were no help. The new owners wanted too much of a cut.

How did you break into radio?

By then it was the middle of the Depression, and I was married [to his first wife, Frances Ellis Bercovici], with a child. I met a man named Bill Rapp [William Jourdan Rapp], who was the editor of *True Story* magazine as well as being a playwright. He did a play called *Harlem* that was fairly successful. I first started making money through him, writing little stories, twenty-thousand-word biographies of famous people. I was making a living in 1933 and 1934, but just barely.

In 1935 Bill Rapp and I sold a radio program, *Billy and Betty*, which was a big success. It was a good program, about kids in an American family. The plot was about a thirteen-year-old boy who was full of dreams and ambitions, and his sister, Betty. He organizes games and competitions, but she is always critical of him. What made the whole thing move was the accidental creation of the villain. In 1935, when the show had just begun, I took a house in Cos Cob, Connecticut, and someone lived near me with whom I had gone to college and who was a first-class pain in the ass. So I conceived this notion of a character just like him. I called the character Melvyn, the same as him.

He was superior and annoying, this Melvyn Castleberry. He ran as a dislikable character for seven years, played by a young fellow, Ted Reid. In 1955 I was in Rome at an event to which the American Embassy had invited bureau chiefs. A woman looked right at me, and she started to sing the theme song of *Billy and Betty*. It was Ted Reid's sister. This show had supported his whole family during the Depression!

By the time *Billy and Betty* was in its second or third year, I was writing it to serve the needs of friends: for abortions, for rent, and so forth. I had total creative control over the show.

Did it have any social orientation at all?

It had no social content except victory over Anglo-American snobbery. Billy was an all-American boy, and his sister was a doubter.

How did you get to Hollywood?

In 1936 or 1937, Bob [Robert] Rossen and I started writing a play. [Producer] Sidney Harmon knew Mervyn LeRoy, and LeRoy was coming to New York to look for writers. I had the flu, so LeRoy interviewed Rossen. LeRoy gave him a job. Rossen left immediately for California, and a few months later he said, "Come out here, we'll finish the play." I was tired of writing *Billy and Betty*, so I took the train out, arrived in the morning, and by late afternoon was being interviewed by LeRoy. He said to me, "Well, we've got the Dead End Kids under contract, and we're looking for something for them to do. Can you think of anything?" I answered, "There's a workshop at Columbia University [a leading center of social work study] where kids act out their traumas. One of these kids said an interesting thing: 'Who asked to be born?' " LeRoy picked up the phone and called Louella Parsons and said, "I've got a guy here with the goddamnedest story."

The next day, they were talking about a film to be called "Who Asked to Be Born?" by Mervyn LeRoy. I wrote a script with Bob, but nothing ever happened. Then I went to work for Warners and wrote an original screenplay with Rossen called *Racket Busters*, about [New York district attorney] Thomas Dewey, more or less. It was produced with Humphrey Bogart as the villain, one of his first good parts, and it was very successful. The night it opened at the end of 1938, I left to go back to New York.

I had just been given a radio offer by Bill Rapp and his partner, Charles Dexter Morris. I said, "I'll do it if I can direct." I was an incredibly shy young man of twenty-eight or twenty-nine, and I thought that directing would overcome my shyness. I was right: I desensitized myself. I directed *Central City*, an expanded-type *Our Town* which Procter & Gamble was willing to sponsor, a serious dramatic show. I used Van Heflin, when he was married to Eleanor Sher; I also used Arlene Francis and Sam Levene—the biggest New York theater actors, not radio actors. I called them in one by one and talked them into it.

That show was a big critical success. Soon I reached the point where I had five shows on the air simultaneously: *Billy and Betty*, *Betty and Bob*, *Helpmate*, *Central City*, and *Grapevine Rancho*, with Lionel Stander. *Central City* had the most social content but never had a high rating. It did best in Canada. When it closed, three or four hundred people protested in Vancouver. Procter & Gamble had stuck with it up to that point.

Why did Procter & Gamble back the show?

They respected it. During the war, I created the character of a minister who was very social-minded; he delivered messages about brotherhood and poverty, right out of the pages of the *Nation*. One of the most powerful men in radio advertising liked those speeches. But when I went to Chicago for a meeting once, he asked me, "Can't you take the show out of New York? New York is two-thirds Oriental." He meant that the production of the show was in the hands of Jews—non-whites. He himself was chairman of the Illinois Republican Party. I laughed.

In 1940, when Dewey ran for governor of New York, I got a call from his staff. The same executive had suggested that they call me. They wanted me to take over a major part of Dewey's speechwriting. I said, "Not for me." The big ad man called repeatedly, and I still said I wouldn't do it. He came to town and stopped over to see me and said, "I don't care what you think; this is just a job. Why should anyone care?"

Were you left-wing by this time?

At that point I wasn't very left, but the left did call on me occasionally. I was involved without being too involved. Twice I organized big Soviet-American friendship meetings. The main impresario of them both was Hannah Weinstein, but I wrote a great part of what the speakers would say.

Right out in the open—something that never came up with HUAC, which was very strange—we staged the famous 1942 "second front" meeting at Carnegie Hall.* We had Charlie Chaplin and all these other people on the dais. I wrote three-fourths of the speeches, including those given by [artist and writer] Rockwell Kent and [actor] Sam Jaffe. I was on the stage myself.

Just a short while later you joined the Communists.

In 1944, the American Communist Party dissolved into the Communist Political Association, and that's what I joined. I went to meetings in which a guy expounded on dialectical materialism. It was kind of oversimplistic, but what caught me was reading [Friedrich] Engels on my own. I fell into the English left tradition with Engels, who was an elegant and funny writer. I also read William Morris, the nineteenth-century left-wing poet and artist. Part of the tragedy of it for me was looking for someone with my interests in the Party. That was very rare. I found two. One was Dan James, a Latin scholar and a Marxist, later on a millionaire. He eventually became a famous and important author under the name "Danny Santiago."† My other friend, Waldo Salt, was also an intellectual in a real sense.‡

I know that you were notorious in Hollywood, later on, for having the effrontery to launch a dialogue between Marx and Freud.

---

*Chaplin was the keynote speaker at the October 14, 1942, mass meeting at Carnegie Hall, sponsored by the Artists' Front to Win the War, which was dominated by Communist Party members. The "second-front" campaign called for the U.S. to divert troops from the Pacific for an invasion of Europe, thereby forcing Hitler to back off from his relentless assault on the Soviet Union.

†A Yale graduate, Daniel James (1911–1988) studied writing under George Sklar at the New Theatre League School and appeared in a small role in a John Howard Lawson play. In Hollywood his pre-blacklist screenwriting credits include *Three Russian Girls*, although it is generally acknowledged that he also made an important but uncredited contribution to Charlie Chaplin's *The Great Dictator*. After being blacklisted, he and his wife, Lilith, worked for twenty years as volunteer social workers in Los Angeles, and he published many short stories in magazines. James edited and introduced *The Complete Bolivian Diary of Che Guevara* and wrote a biography of Che. In 1983 he scored spectacularly with *Famous All Over Town*, by "Danny Santiago," regarded as a key Chicano novel. His identity as the real author was not revealed until the book had received considerable acclaim.

‡One of the Hollywood Nineteen, Waldo Salt (1915–1987) went to work for MGM as a junior writer and scripted or collaborated on *The Shopworn Angel*, *Rachel and the Stranger*, *The Flame and the Arrow*, and the remake of *M* before being blacklisted. He worked pseudonymously in television during the 1950s and the early 1960s. His post-blacklist career was distinguished by Best Screenplay Oscars for *Midnight Cowboy* and *Coming Home*.

In 1946 or 1947, I tried to do something that was stimulating and important. I was a little ahead of the times. I wanted to create a kind of Marxist-Freudian group and to bring together certain screenwriters of the left and certain psychoanalysts in town. We had one meeting at my house. The people I remember coming were Dan, Waldo, Albert Maltz, and a couple of others. Up till then Freud was a bad name in the left, but without any explanation: criticism of him was just a slogan. I did all this before I went into analysis myself. But I had done a lot of reading about Freud.

Did the meeting work?

It didn't come off well. The analysts were some of the best in town, but each side was dogmatic, and I remember the first subject chosen to be discussed was F. Scott Fitzgerald's *Tender Is the Night*. The analysts were interesting, if kind of jargonesque. But Albert was very disruptive. Through an ignorant hostility or bias, he thought the book was just a pile of shit.

I don't think either side knew enough about the other. Dan and Waldo and I kind of bridged things for ourselves: we talked a common language, we could communicate and speculate, we had a sense of humor about Marx and Freud. Dan and Waldo—that was about the limit.

At that meeting there was a Hollywood analyst, Phil Cohen,* whom everybody went to; I didn't know him. The people who went to him were people like Richard Collins, as low as you can get.† Cohen later eased them into whatever they wanted to do in front of the Committee.

It sounds like you grew disaffected from the Party almost as quickly as you joined.

When I came to Hollywood in 1945, Waldo gave me a Party-written history of the U.S. in which they had excised any Marx and Engels, anything about the class struggle, and turned it all into a vulgar Americanization. But I did get involved, at first, and I accepted Earl Browder's ideas. I was in the Beverly Hills section with Dalton Trumbo, Ring Lardner Jr., and others. I then objected to the speed with which everybody turned around after Browder was repudiated. After that, I distanced myself rather quickly.

What precipitated some disillusionment for me was that in 1945 I got a job with the Office of War Information, working with Dick Collins, writing

---

*Philip Cohen, one of the most fascinating characters in the blacklist saga, came to Hollywood in 1942 after several years of psychology graduate school (but with no degree), setting himself up as a therapist. Because the Communist leaders thoroughly mistrusted psychoanalysis, yet the Popular Front milieu contained so many people eager for such services, Cohen became the left therapist of choice. By 1950 he was encouraging his patients to cooperate with HUAC. See Victor Navasky, *Naming Names*.

†Richard Collins was a scriptwriter and prominent Hollywood Communist of the 1940s whose many screen credits included collaboration with Paul Jarrico on *Thousands Cheer* and the story basis of *Little Giant*. Later he was one of the most prominent friendly witnesses to remain on the scene in film and television.

a film about the formation of the United Nations in San Francisco. When Collins vanished from the project, evidently because of the political risks involved, it hit me that the Party had taken in some terrible people.

You also ran into some conflicts with John Howard Lawson, Hollywood's section leader.

Jack Lawson was a man of real ability, a victim as well as a self-made victim. I wondered how he devoted himself to becoming a commissar; it was a pity. He was always very suspicious of me, but I was used to authoritarian characters like him, so it didn't bother me. He followed me up to San Francisco, when I was working on the UN film, and wrote his own script about the inevitability of the United States and the USSR marching into some kind of cooperative heaven. He tried to superimpose his ideas on what I was doing. Meanwhile, I found myself meeting daily with the Communist representatives from Eastern Europe, and they told me the exact opposite of what the Party here said.

All of these people were laughing at the American Communist position. Izzy [I. F.] Stone was up there; I knew him very well. So was one of the best columnists for the *Daily Worker*, Joseph Starobin.* I went to Joe, took the title page off both of the script versions, and said, "What do you think of them?" The next day Starobin showed me Jack's script and said, "This one's ridiculous."

After I came back here, there was a general meeting on Wilshire and Santa Monica, and I was asked to be a speaker. I planned to talk about what I thought was happening in San Francisco apropos of the UN. Jack called me and said, "Do you mind if I read your speech?" I said I'd bring it over. He read it and said, "I don't agree with any of this. I don't think you should give this speech. You're a dangerous man, because you write so well." "Jack," I said, "that's the speech I'm going to deliver." I predicted enormous strife and conflict instead of a honeymoon among nations. How Jack could have submitted . . .

Did the formal political discussions around the Party have any creative application?

None. None whatsoever. There should have been. When Ring [Lardner Jr.] and Hugo Butler were on the board of the Screen Writers Guild, I became chairman of one of the political groups of the writers' fraction. I felt there was an unhealthy degree of submission to the Los Angeles Communist leadership group. Everybody was just obeying orders, and I made a strong case about that. Dalton [Trumbo] listened and, without telling anybody, sat down

---

*Joseph Starobin, one of the most widely respected journalist-commentators for the *Daily Worker* in its most popular era (1935–1950), later wrote *American Communism in Crisis, 1943–1957*. I. F. Stone, a left-wing journalist who founded *I. F. Stone's Weekly* and published it from 1952 to 1971, became world-famous for his independent-minded commentary and his revelation of facts that the U.S. government attempted to keep secret. From 1971 until his death in 1989, his articles appeared in the *Nation* and other publications.

to write a thirty-page polemic about everything that I and others had said. He wanted it distributed to the various branches for discussion. But it fell into the hands of the Central Committee in Los Angeles. They decided that, while it was very interesting, the Party was not "sufficiently mature," as they put it, to discuss what was in this essay. The recommendation was that it "be burned." That's a quote.

Were you affected by the Maltz case?

The Maltz case affected me, but I never got along with Albert. We had known each other since 1932, and I never liked his novels. He used to ask me, "Did you read my book?" "Yes." "Did you like it?" "No." I remember the meeting on Beverly Glen, when Albert recanted his criticism of Party policies. I don't know what the hell he recanted for, and in fact I said to him later, "I don't know why you did what you did."

My friend Leopold Atlas was the scenarist of *The Story of G.I. Joe* and the only stool pigeon who broke my heart. He named three people, including me. When he described the Maltz meeting [in his testimony], he said the only person there who protested the decision was me. That wasn't true. That was Lee atoning for naming me.

In the end, Albert was such a stiff-necked character. I was teaching at the American Film Institute years later and we needed someone to teach with me. So I called Albert; I figured he would be a good teacher. What he was really good at was screenwriting. I guess he was surprised to hear from me. He said, "I can't. I'm not well, and I'm trying to finish a novel." He was happy that I called him. He died only a short time later.

Tell me how your film writing career developed.

My film career started because doing four or five shows on radio was hard work, and my partner, Bill Rapp, dropped dead at age forty-seven. The next day I got out of the business. That's when I went to work for the OWI [Office of War Information], and the first thing I did was a demobilization picture, *This Is Your America*, a very socially oriented four-reel picture. I wrote it on the basis of a very simple idea: when I was on my way to the draft board, it was raining, and I looked down, saw a quarter on the ground, then looked up and was almost hit by a car. From that incident I got an idea about the images that were on a penny and what they stood for. I went to Hollywood to finish the writing.

One day I was at Romanoff's, having lunch with Waldo Salt, when I spotted a man to whom I'd sent a play three or four years before with a vague hope of getting Irene Dunne to star in a film version of it. He was having lunch with a friend of mine, Donald Ogden Stewart. He came over and introduced himself: Charlie Feldman. Feldman was the most powerful agent in the business, also the most interesting and mysterious. He made me an offer: "Come over to my office at three and look at some stories; you can choose one of them to work on."

One was a novel called *The Bishop's Wife,* by Robert Nathan. It was a kind of serious novel about an angel who rebukes a bishop for not loving his wife. In my version the angel falls in love with the wife, which creates all kinds of disturbances. Also, it became a comedy. The next thing you know, everybody in town wanted my script. Everybody.

Feldman held off the bidding for a while, and then he finally gave it to Samuel Goldwyn for a quarter of a million dollars, which bought me a beautiful house. For the next fourteen months I did four scripts for him; all sold for about the same amount of money. I went up in price, and then Goldwyn called me in to make revisions on my script for *The Bishop's Wife,* and I did that little job, too. I also went to Dore Schary and did ten weeks on a script for sixty thousand dollars, and then to [David O.] Selznick to write *Portrait of Jennie.* Then I did an adaptation of Henry James's *The Aspern Papers,* which got produced as *The Lost Moment.*

I got credits on all these films. There wasn't anything social about them, but I was doing stories that I liked. I was riding very high. Maybe Ben Hecht got more money. But I was up to thirty-five hundred dollars per week. Finally I wound up with a contract with Hal Wallis to write, direct, and produce. At the end of seven years, my salary was going to go up to two million dollars per year.

I was just two weeks away from casting my first picture. I already had Claude Rains, and I was torn between Claudette Colbert and Bette Davis, when, *whoom!* That was it: the subpoena.

In fact, I saw it coming. I joined the group who took off for Mexico early to avoid their subpoenas. I was there, watching Rossen going through all of his agony and heart attacks, and it was so sad. I called my lawyer, who said, "I'll call Leonard Boudin." Boudin thought my prepared statement was fine. But he also said, "When it's over, at the end, you have to say, 'But I'm still a Marxist.' " [Laughs.]

So you testified?

So I did. I testified about myself only. A congressman said, "Well, this is something new." It later became a common thing to do, rather than refusing to testify at all. Martin Gang, one of the chief lawyers for friendly witnesses, said to me, "You should have gone to jail for what you did." I knew Gang. He had been my lawyer for a while, way back.*

---

*Martin Gang was one of the three key figures, along with Committee investigator William Wheeler and therapist Phil Cohen, in encouraging potential friendly witnesses to bow to pressure. A prominent Hollywood attorney, he had represented many Popular Front figures during the 1940s and even signed an amicus curiae brief for the Hollywood Ten in 1947. Ultimately he became the attorney of "friendlies" Lee J. Cobb, Sterling Hayden, Abe Burrows, Lloyd Bridges, Richard Collins, Sylvia Richards, Roland Kibbee, and Meta Reis Rosenberg, among others. Gang devised and carried out procedures by which the "friendlies" could clear themselves by implicating former comrades. He was known for extensively socializing with, as well as cooperating with, HUAC members. See Victor Navasky, *Naming Names.*

By the way, my Uncle Konrad had become a rabid anti-Communist. But during the blacklist, he was asked by the FBI about me, and he said, "Fuck you."

You went into exile?

From Mexico I went to Italy, like other people went to France or England. There was a whole group before me there; all of them left or got ejected from Italy after making a picture with Paul Muni [*Stranger on the Prowl*]. I came following that. One day I got a letter from the State Department and was told, "Go to the Embassy and turn in your passport."

I had among my friends the most eminent refugee from Mussolini. He had lived in America and returned to become the minister of transportation in the first postwar Italian government. He said, "They can't do that to you." He picked up the phone and called the prime minister: "I've got this American here; they've been persecuting him. . . ." Then he turned the phone toward me so I could hear the prime minister say, "Who do they think they are? They can't do that here. . . ." Between the two of them I was protected. In the next twelve years I worked on a lot of pictures. I wrote in English, and the scripts were translated.

What was your relationship with the younger generation of Italian filmmakers? Did you see them as a new school of film artists?

I don't think they had a school of filmmaking. I had no sense of them except as individual artists. One of my closest friends was [Roberto] Rossellini; in fact we lived a hundred yards from each other. I didn't know De Sica very well, but I thought he was the best of them. He had a certain fluid, poetic style that others might imitate but couldn't match.

I did make one film in that mode, *Maddalena*, which won prizes at film festivals in Edinburgh and Italy. But most of mine were pictures that were already going for someone else; I fixed them, rewrote them.

At one point I wrote a script based on Hawthorne's *The Marble Faun*, and the Rossellinis were going to do it as a family production, his wife, who was then Ingrid Bergman, playing one of the girls, and my then-wife [Swedish actress Marta Toren] playing the other. We gave it to an executive of United Artists in Rome, who was gung-ho to do it. However, United Artists in Paris killed the project because Congress had passed a resolution against Rossellini and Bergman, accusing them of moral turpitude.

Meanwhile, somehow or other, the script fell into the hands of Tyrone Power, who decided he would do the film with Bergman but without Rossellini directing. We had a number of meetings with Ingrid to make plans, until she told us that she was pregnant with Roberto's child. So that idea fell apart. Then Tyrone went back to the U.S. and asked me to write something else for him while waiting for *The Marble Faun* to happen.

So you came back to the United States?

By the time I arrived in New York, I had gotten a call from my lawyer in Hollywood, who said, "UA is nervous. Call Edward Bennett Williams in Washington." I made it clear to him that I didn't intend to do anything any different from before; I was not going to be a friendly witness. Williams said, "Excuse me for a half an hour. I'll find out what they've got on you." He came back and said, "They haven't got anything on you." Williams then wrote a letter to the committee saying, "He's a good American and there's no reason he shouldn't work."

I said to Tyrone, "Don't make a big thing of this." But he wanted to announce the project. Then, *wham!* I got a call from Thomas Pryor, later editor of *Variety* and then the film editor for the *New York Times*. The next day a big story broke in the *Times*, the following day in *Variety*, about a fellow who was going to break the blacklist. I had already signed the contract and finished the script for Universal. It was a good script and was supposed to be Power's next film—until one afternoon in Spain, where he was filming *Solomon and Sheba*, Power had a heart attack during a sword fight. They had told the doctors to go home for the day, to save money, and he died.

So I was the first to break the blacklist—but only for ten weeks. I got married that year [1959] to my third wife, Antonia [Madison], and the next thing I knew I was back in Italy, working for [producer Dino] De Laurentiis. I ended up staying in Europe another five years, again mostly rewriting and uncredited.

The picture I made that had the most social content was one I wrote, directed, and produced, *Square of Violence*. During the war, the Fascists in Italy had decided to kill massively in retaliation for any terrorist bombing. After one incident, they set a deadline of twenty-four hours for the guilty person to give himself up, and they ended up killing three hundred people. They picked up a lot of Jews, too.* You couldn't make this sort of film in Italy, but I had it all arranged in Yugoslavia, with Bibi Andersson, Broderick Crawford, and others. The story was about the doctor who actually bombed the Nazis and his moral crisis over turning himself in. It was all shot in English. Unfortunately, I was at the mercy of stupid people—they cut out the best scenes. Despite everything, it was still a very good picture.

---

*Partisans had killed thirty-three SS men on March 23, 1944, in Rome. On March 24 Nazi soldiers rounded up and killed three hundred and thirty-five men and boys in the Fosse Ardeatine caves outside Rome. Under the German standard, ten prisoners were to be killed for each German, but they added thirty-five more Jewish men from Roman prisons. The 335 were tied together and driven to the network of man-made caves along the Appian Way. Then, three at a time, they were forced to kneel down and were shot. At the end of the massacre the caves were sealed off. See Susan Zuccoletti, *The Italians and the Holocaust*; and Robert Katz, *Death in Rome*.

Was it distributed in the United States?

I sold it to Metro-Goldwyn-Mayer. It got wonderful notices at the Venice
Film Festival, and Metro was intending to release it in one theater at a time
in America. But they ended up not releasing it.

Eventually I came back to America again, and I didn't really break out of
blacklisting here until 1967, when I sold an original that I'd written in Italy
years earlier; I retyped it and sold it in twenty-four hours, and then I directed
it for Universal: *Story of a Woman*, with Bibi Andersson.

Do you feel that you ever managed to do anything in films of political value?

Doing pictures outside the Hollywood scene, like for the Office of War
Information, allowed for the kind of material that had political content. But
in entertainment motion pictures, political content is trivial. You are faced
with an inescapable problem: Pictures essentially reflect the personality and
the quality of the producer and of the studio that has them made. That's it.
No matter how hard you try, that's what comes off.

I'm not saying that it cannot be otherwise, but it isn't. Even so, there's a
huge difference between then and today. All you hear writers say today is,
"I'm doing it for the money." Earlier, in the thirties and forties, there was
anti-Fascism, which took the form of patriotism, acceptable anti-Fascism.

Wasn't there a chance to make strides, however briefly, after the war?

There may have been the beginnings of something, but the blacklist
changed the nature of social pictures. The studios got rid of eighty percent of
the best writers. I think there was a possibility for a new kind of filmmaking
when you think of things like Rossen's *All the King's Men*. But Rossen was
horribly split as a person. And even people like Jack Lawson would end up
writing mostly entertainment pictures. Sidney Buchman, too, wrote entertainment pictures. All the noble fellows of the left, what did they write? If
they were good, they got the better assignments. And the better assignments
were what? Big stars and a certain kind of story.

At one point I probably could have done something different with my
career, or rather I made a choice without knowing it was a choice. I could
have stayed on in Italy, for example, and made a picture every year in Yugoslavia. They made pictures like I wanted to make in Europe. In that environment you would have been more open to searching for social themes. But
I wanted to come back. Everybody succumbs to nostalgia, to the yearning to
be reaccepted into American society. No matter how much they deny it.
Everybody.

Walter Bernstein

WALTER BERNSTEIN, New York City, 1997

INTERVIEW BY PAUL BUHLE

WALTER BERNSTEIN
(1919–   )

1948 *Kiss the Blood off My Hands*. Coadaptation.
1959 *That Kind of Woman*. Script.
  The Wonderful Country. Uncredited
    contribution.
1960 *Heller in Pink Tights*. Coscript.
  A Breath of Scandal. Uncredited contribution.
1961 *Paris Blues*. Coscript.
1964 *Fail-Safe*. Script.

1965 *The Train*. Uncredited contribution.
1966 *The Money Trap*. Script.
1970 *The Molly Maguires*. Producer, script.
1976 *The Front*. Script.
1977 *Semi-Tough*. Script.
  Annie Hall. Actor.
1978 *The Betsy*. Coscript.
1979 *Yanks*. Coscript.
  An Almost Perfect Affair. Coscript.
  The Electric Horseman. Uncredited
    contribution.

1980 *Little Miss Marker*. Director, script.
1985 *The Legend of Billie Jean*. Coscript.
1988 *The House on Carroll Street*. Script.
1992 *Women and Men 2* ("Return to Kansas City"
 segment, telefilm). Director, adaptation.

1994 *Doomsday Gun* (telefilm). Coscript.
1997 *Miss Evers' Boys* (telefilm). Script.

■

WALTER BERNSTEIN MADE his way from a lower-middle-class Brooklyn Jewish background to late-1930s Dartmouth, where a boy's fascination with movies grew into an aspiration for a life's work. His budding skills meanwhile made him a natural for anti-Fascist intellectual tasks. Writing patriotic musicals for the Army and working as a foreign correspondent for the popular service weekly *Yank*, he never got movies out of his mind. But he came to Hollywood at a bad time for any left-winger, especially a young one—just as the Iron Curtain of anti-Communism was falling.

Bernstein considers himself lucky to have gotten in on the ground floor of network television, where indeed a handful of talented radicals and their friends quietly shaped some "quality" shows (as well as lively sitcoms) for a decade. The forgotten *Danger* series of half-hour dramas, the rightly exalted *You Are There* historical docudramas, the various live theater-anthology series, and *Colonel March of Scotland Yard*, starring Boris Karloff, all found him hard at work, usually hiding behind fronts or pseudonyms.

When the blacklist began to crack at the edges, Bernstein seized his chance to return to films. Within a decade or so, he had amassed an extraordinarily impressive dossier of credits in assorted genres, often the kinds of movies that were rarely made under the watchful glance of the studio guardians of old. These include the stunning anti-war drama *Fail-Safe*, the painstakingly accurate labor-organizing story *The Molly Maguires* (which Bernstein also produced), and *The Front*, a fictionalized blacklist document that found a large audience partly because it was also a comedy starring Woody Allen.

Bernstein was among the youngest of those on the Hollywood left, and, like his sometime collaborator and friend, director Martin Ritt, destined to carry their legacy of social consciousness forward. It is a burden Bernstein seems to carry lightly, as his creative work continues into the 1990s. His recently published memoir, *Inside Out*, focuses on the subject of his politics and the blacklist. We agreed to limit this interview to a discussion of the various degrees of blame and culpability assigned by blacklistees to key HUAC informers and friendly witnesses, some of whom Bernstein knew personally.

■

Do you have a general approach to understanding the motivations of the friendly witnesses, aside from the feeling that they all did it for their careers?

I think it's a mistake to try psychologizing. They are all different, and each has a distinct makeup. You could talk about Budd Schulberg's relationship with his autocratic father [Paramount executive B. P. Schulberg], for instance. Or about how [director] Robert Rossen, for egotistical reasons, was initially indignant not to be named as one of the Hollywood Ten. One's own reflections become highly personal, whether it's Rossen, whom I worked for, or Schulberg, whom I idolized, or [Elia] Kazan, whom I worked for, or [screenwriter Ben] Maddow, toward whom I had great fondness.

Let's talk first about someone you knew only marginally—choreographer Jerome Robbins. Some film and political scholars have sought to rationalize his willingness to testify against former friends by noting that he was afraid to be exposed as a homosexual.

I didn't really know Robbins; I met him only a couple of times, socially, in New York. But his testimony, if you read it, is relatively straightforward.* He went there to cooperate, he made the obligatory anti-Communist statements, and he got out of the spot he was in as best he could. To what extent he was fearful of being found out as a homosexual I don't know, although I think that probably would have been a factor. But Jerry had never been strongly identified with the left and has never been very political, either.

There were, of course, people who had never been in the Party, like Howard Koch, who were nevertheless very staunch in their refusal to cooperate.

It comes down to something I've said repeatedly: informing was not a matter of politics but a matter of morality. Jerry turned in some people so that he could get on with his life. He just went along. Later, Zero Mostel wondered if there would be any problem working with him in *Fiddler on the Roof* [which Mostel starred in and Robbins directed and choreographed], but there was no problem.

Jerry's testimony is easily the most conventional relative to that of Rossen, Kazan, and Schulberg. In Jerry's case, the Committee led him all the way. And he gave them what they wanted to hear.

What about Rossen?

I had worked for Rossen in the first job I had when I went to Hollywood, and I liked him. He asked me to write a screenplay from a Chekhov short story, "The Grasshopper." Then he switched me to working on an adaptation of Robert Penn Warren's novel *All the King's Men*. I didn't do very much work on the script; most of the time I was just listening to him. He had spent thirteen years as a writer in Hollywood for Warners, and he taught me a lot about movies as storytelling, about film drama the way he liked it: good, tough romanticism. He wanted me to help make his political ideas acceptable to studios. We would discuss some scene, and then he would go up and present

---

*Jerome Robbins's testimony, along with the testimony of Budd Schulberg, Edward Dmytryk, Elia Kazan, and others, can be found in Eric Bentley, *Thirty Years of Treason: Excerpts from Hearings Before the House Committee on Un-American Activities, 1938–1968.*

it to [Columbia studio head] Harry Cohn. When they were finished, the radicalism of the scene was usually deleted or toned down.

Rossen had wanted to be a prizefighter, and he constantly threw punches in the air, around me; I think I might have represented the Party's coercive authority over him, symbolically—although, to him, everyone was an opponent. But in his own mind, he was also a staunch Communist, very staunch.

Abe Polonsky related to me the feeling he had always had that Rossen was never to be trusted. Was that at all in your mind?

Yeah. I felt that there was something essentially corrupt about him on a personal level. In his talk about women or in his relationship to money, he gave you the impression that he was not a man of strong personal integrity.

This was no contradiction with his being a Communist hard-liner, someone who would as a matter of loyalty to the Party argue and vote against Albert Maltz's insistence on the individual's artistic freedom?*

There were various people who were known as hard-liners, people of entirely different moral fiber. Some had great integrity and honesty, people I would literally trust with my life. Others were slippery. There was even one member in New York—you could have called him a hard-liner in other respects—whom we expelled because of his dealings with women and money. Although he remained a Communist in his own mind, we felt that he didn't live up to the moral standards of what a Communist should be.

As to the discussions about Albert Maltz in particular, a lot of people, obviously including Maltz himself, went back and forth because of the pressure put on them. There was a certain fear about being cut off from the Party through disagreement with the Party's position. You had to toe the Party line in order to stay inside, or at least we thought so.

More than one person has said that Rossen was the kind of Hollywood Communist who pledged large amounts of money at public meetings, to impress other people, and then usually didn't pay.

---

*The Maltz controversy rocked Communist Party intellectuals in 1946, and none more than those in Hollywood. Maltz wrote a short essay, "What Shall We Ask of Writers?" in the February 12, 1946, issue of the *New Masses*, insisting that works of art be judged by their creative contributions rather than by their formal political positions. He singled out novelist James T. Farrell for praise, even though Farrell was a Trotskyist and thus strongly opposed to the Communist Party. American Communist leaders, shifting away from wartime amity with liberals, pressured intellectuals to respond harshly to this challenge. Denounced by rigid Communists in the *New Masses*, Maltz sought to defend himself privately, to his Hollywood comrades, at a meeting held in Morris Carnovsky's basement. Only a few Party members, including Abraham Polonsky, John Weber, and Arnold Manoff, rose to defend Maltz's position, and afterward Maltz himself recanted in "Moving Forward," published in the April 9, 1946, *New Masses*. Years later, several friendly witnesses pointed to this dispute as justification for their testimony. Ironically, some of them had been among the strongest attackers of Maltz and the most faithful to the Party line.

A couple of times I was asked to go collect back payments on Party dues. Rossen hadn't paid and sometimes he *still* didn't pay. You could tell that there was something slippery about him.

Would you have anticipated that he would crack?

No. As I say, I liked him personally, although after I worked for him, he was gratuitously not nice to me. He asked me to continue working for him after my contract was over. But Harold Hecht, who had just formed a production company with Burt Lancaster, offered me twice as much money. Hecht, who was also then a Communist and would become a friendly witness, put me together with Ben Maddow, who also taught me a lot about film writing. Together we wrote *Kiss the Blood off My Hands*, before it was rewritten [by Leonardo Bercovici].

Anyway, I had gone to Rossen and said, "I'd like to go on working with you, if you would match Hecht's offer." Rossen told me that he couldn't afford it, to go ahead and take the other job. I later heard from a couple of people that Rossen was knocking me, saying that I had quit on him and I'd been malingering anyway. I was more puzzled than hurt. I was just a lowly young writer, not a threat to him in any way. I wondered what need there was for him to do such a thing.

Then again, I just didn't know the Hollywood scene all that well. I went there for ten weeks in 1947 and ended up staying six months, but I never really learned the ins and outs.

Rereading Rossen's testimony recently, did you see anything new that might reveal something to you about his character?

The first time he testified, he only gave the Committee the Fifth Amendment and was excused. The second time he gave them a lot of junk, rationalizations about why he was testifying now.* I felt the same as I did while rereading Kazan's testimony: the two of them didn't believe anything that they were saying—unlike Budd Schulberg's testimony, which, upon rereading it, I found quite interesting.

Unlike those of Kazan and Schulberg, the films that Rossen made after he testified— especially The Hustler *and* Lilith—*didn't change fundamentally. They have no air of justifying a new political position. Particularly in their artistic striving, they continued to represent that peculiar mix of the thirties social film and European artiness which could also be detected in his earlier work.*

That's what Rossen wanted to do—that was his genre, what he was good at. He always used to talk to me about this play, "Corner Pocket," that he had written. It took place in a pool hall in New York. This eventually was

---

*Robert Rossen's testimony was published in *Communist Infiltration of the Hollywood Motion Picture Industry*, Hearings of the Committee on Un-American Activities, House of Representatives, June 25, 1951.

what he came back to in *The Hustler*—a reflection on his youth, where he came from.

Someone sympathetic to him once observed that his films were so deeply American that he couldn't possibly direct abroad, as Joseph Losey or Jules Dassin.

He was much more tied into the Hollywood system than Losey or Dassin. But Rossen could have worked somewhere, somehow.

Leonardo Bercovici, who was in Mexico with Rossen between Rossen's two testimonies, said that at the time Rossen was suffering, or at least thought he was suffering, from heart attacks.

That stress, the feeling that he was falling apart, that he was terribly scared, does help explain something about his becoming a friendly witness.

Let's turn to Budd Schulberg.

Rereading his testimony, I was fascinated by his account of going to the Soviet Union during the 1930s and not liking it there, because he is persuasive even if you don't wish to be persuaded. I could read it now and say, "Jesus, yes, that explains why someone could turn against the Communist Party." What's striking is the contrast between that kind of statement and the groveling by others before the Committee saying how honored they were to be there, how the Committee was doing a good job keeping American democracy safe, and so on. Whereas I didn't believe Kazan's and Rossen's changed positions for a moment, I could understand it in Budd.

But, of course, his main complaint was about What Makes Sammy Run? *being attacked within the Communist Party. Yet it appears that it was never a major issue on the Hollywood left like the Maltz case later. No one tried to stop him from publishing his novel, and compared to the day-to-day bullying of the studios, the pressure within the Party was pretty small potatoes anyway. Didn't he read his personal response and resentment back into history?*

Certainly. But having a *New Masses* reviewer first write a favorable review, and then change his mind to attack *What Makes Sammy Run?* in a second review, was a very disturbing experience. Here again, you're back into the realm of psychology, and you could make a convincing argument either way. You could say that something was done to him by the Party, and this is how he felt all those years, or you could say that he was rationalizing his testimony.

Apart from anything else, however, by giving friendly testimony you were collaborating with some very bad people doing some very bad things. These racists and anti-Semites running the congressional committees were the closest thing to Nazis holding positions of influence within the United States at the time. As far as I'm concerned, the buck stops there.

Still, I can sympathize because I liked Budd so much. He was such a hero to me in college. While I was still at school, Budd returned to the Dartmouth area to finish writing *What Makes Sammy Run?* He quickly became my friend and my mentor. That was part of a unique Dartmouth/Hollywood experience, because [producer] Walter Wanger, a Dartmouth alum, had donated film scripts to launch a college film library and sometimes sent various cameramen, editors, and technicians to lecture on their respective crafts. I went to all their lectures, and consequently I dreamed of going to Hollywood. Budd was already a Hollywood personality, also militantly left-wing. I aspired to have a life of politics and art, like his.

Visiting him after I graduated, bumming around in Hollywood, I found him married to this lovely woman [Virginia Ray] who had been courted by all the left-wing screenwriters.* He had won her. The two of them were the prince and princess of the young-left crowd of serious intellectuals and artists. More than ever, I wanted to be like him.

His screen credits before 1950 aren't particularly impressive.

But I don't know how much he wanted to be a screenwriter. He wanted to be a novelist. Rossen never wanted to be anything but a screenwriter and director. Budd was different.

That's evidence for the argument that he could have refused to testify and gone on to become a successful novelist anyway.

You could refuse to testify, and live, more or less well or badly. The actors and directors had more difficulty, the writers less difficulty.

Why did you say there was a shadow of Schulberg's father in his testimony?

That relationship is very key to Budd, apart from anything else. His father was a very tough bird, the head of Paramount in his twenties. One evening I met him at a friend's house, Lester Koenig's.† By this time, B. P. was being supported financially by his son. But while I was there he was giving advice to a starlet, and it was advice of the most immoral nature: "Dump the agent who got you where you are today," that sort of thing. I imagine that he was an awfully tough person to have as a father.

You said in Inside Out *that at the time you felt personally betrayed by Budd's testimony, even though, for example, he didn't name you.*

---

*Virginia Ray, nicknamed "Jigee," was considered one of the most glamorous women in Hollywood. Maurice Rapf introduced her to Budd Schulberg. Intelligent and well read, she served as hostess for Marxist study classes. She married Budd Schulberg on New Year's Eve 1936 but remained a center of glamorous mystery. She divorced Schulberg in 1944, married screenwriter Peter Viertel, gave "friendly" testimony on June 6, 1956, and died four years later in a fire, after a long period of alcoholism.

†Lester Koenig [1917–1977] worked closely with director William Wyler on *The Best Years of Our Lives, The Heiress,* and *Roman Holiday.* After the blacklist ruined his career in Hollywood, Koenig formed the Good Time Jazz and Contemporary music labels, recording many top jazz artists of the era, including Art Pepper, Ornette Coleman, and Benny Carter.

If I hadn't known him, I would still have scorned him and what he did. But because it was Budd, I was personally aggrieved. When I saw *On the Waterfront* later on, all I could see was a rationalization for his and Kazan's informing. Schulberg denies that this was the logic of the film; Kazan, in his autobiography [*A Life*, 1988], is very frank and pugnacious about it.

Let's go on to Kazan. Your relationship with him was very complicated.

At the time that he gave his testimony I was writing a play for him about a Jewish garment manufacturer who had been a gangster. I thought that Kazan was wonderful, terrifically charismatic, and on the same side as I was politically. We had been introduced by Marty Ritt.

As I said in *Inside Out*, Marty was Kazan's best friend within the theater. He had brought Marty into the Group Theatre, and Marty, although a born skeptic, virtually idolized him. When I met Kazan he was looking for a writer for a play he had in mind, with John Garfield playing the lead. Kazan, of course, was a mesmerizing actor himself. He had a seductive power that made him capable of getting performances from actors that actors didn't think they were capable of giving.

Before his testimony, did he you give any sign of a political shift?

On the contrary. He asked me if I could help him meet Blackie Myers, a Communist leader of the National Maritime Union.* I knew Blackie slightly, and we went down and met him and some of his merchant seamen friends in a bar one afternoon. We drank and talked about politics for a few hours.

This was part of the preparation for On the Waterfront?

Arthur Miller and Kazan had been talking about the subject. But Gadge [Kazan] actually did want to meet these guys. After we talked, as we were walking away, Gadge said to me how much he admired them, and how this was the side that he was on. That was his sincere view. Then he went and within a few weeks testified. Of course I immediately dropped the play.

No doubt there was big pressure on him from the William Morris Agency and also from his wife [Molly Day Thacher]. But I always felt that he made the choice between [Twentieth Century–Fox mogul] Spyros Skouras and Arthur Miller: that was deliberate. Even in his autobiography he still claims to be a Socialist of some kind.

I had no indication in my own relationship with him of the defensiveness that Kazan felt, the chip on the shoulder that he had toward the people he had worked with on the left, all the way back to the 1930s.

---

*Frederick ("Blackie") Myers, an important rank-and-file figure during the rise of the National Maritime Union in the 1930s, was for many years, until the McCarthy-era rightward shift of NMU president Joseph Curran, a key Communist in the union's leadership. See Bruce Nelson, *Workers on the Waterfront: Seamen, Longshoremen, and Unionism*.

How about from the testimony? Are the resentments more transparent now?

No, it's from the autobiography that you get that clear feeling. I never saw any of that at the time. He was really cock of the walk, the hottest director in theater and movies in America. He had directed *Death of a Salesman* and *A Streetcar Named Desire*, and he had won an Oscar for *Gentleman's Agreement*. To think that he had felt these old slights so deeply would have been inconceivable to me.

I feel in his case, working off the autobiography, that everything with him was personal, although I don't know exactly who he was getting even with. It all goes back to the Group Theatre, how he was treated there, how he imagined they felt about him, how he wasn't taken seriously. Even his nickname, "Gadge," describes the little guy who fixed things, not the great artist. Nevertheless, he played leads for them.

Marty Ritt told me an anecdote which sticks in my head. The two of them were standing around on a street corner looking at pretty girls, and Kazan said to Marty, "They wouldn't have anything to do with two funny-looking characters like us." That jibes with something that happened to me, watching him dress to go out on a date in New Orleans, while he was shooting *Panic in the Streets*. He was terribly nervous, even though for this girl it didn't matter at all how he was dressed. She was going out with a big director; that's all that mattered. I tried to kid him about it, and I realized you couldn't kid him. He was extremely insecure about himself in that regard.

Reading the autobiography, you gather that he had this feeling of estrangement, always. The fact that his wife was a Protestant with three names tells us something. He was insecure about his entrance into American proper society. Refusing to testify would amount to another instance of being cut off, or cutting himself off, making himself rejected, lumping himself willingly with the undesirables. Not to do that was of primary importance to him. Gadge was not in that sense a rebel at all, and had never been.

In his earlier milieus, it had not been particularly rebellious to be a Communist.

Not, at least, in the thirties or forties.

Adele Ritt, Marty Ritt's wife, told me that when Ritt heard that Kazan had testified, he was sure, at first, that it was a lie. He couldn't believe it.

Yes, I remember that. Marty had idolized him. When you read the testimony of Lionel Stander or Zero Mostel, for instance, what they say is marvelous. They were being themselves. But among Robbins, Kazan, Rossen, and Schulberg, only Schulberg represents anything of himself. By no accident, he's also the only one of the four who was a real writer, a novelist. He would have written his testimony carefully, as literature. Rossen came with a prepared statement, Kazan too, but Budd had a brief.

Let's talk last about Ben Maddow, who held out and was blacklisted until very late in the fifties when he chose to testify in executive session. What precisely he said to get cleared has never been made public. You were good friends with him. What was your impression of him, before and after?

Maddow I met when I first went out to Hollywood in 1947 through my agent, Harold Hecht, who had started a production company with his biggest client, Burt Lancaster. Ben and I worked on this movie I mentioned, *Kiss the Blood off My Hands.* Because of my inexperience, they wanted to pair me with someone who had been around. That was Ben Maddow, who had written a documentary, *Native Land,* under the name David Wolff, and who was also a talented poet. I learned a great deal about screenwriting from him, more than from Rossen. Ben had a much more visual sense than Rossen did.

I also admired Ben very much and we had a very good time. We did become friends. After I returned to New York, I saw him once in a while when he came east, and learned that he, too, had been blacklisted. After that, he had gotten work, especially from [writer-producer] Philip Yordan—Ben reputedly did all the writing for Yordan on the films that they did together.

In the late 1950s, I had gone to Los Angeles to try and help my friend Charles Russell, who was producing a television show. We were all still black-listed, but I heard from a friend that Ben was back working under his own name; in fact he was working at Fox. I couldn't believe that. I knew that nobody had been cleared unless they had named names. I called Fox and asked if Ben was there, and they said yes; actually, he was working for Kazan. We made a date for breakfast the next morning.

He immediately admitted that he had become a cooperative witness. I knew he had been working for Yordan, making a living. We all felt that the end of the blacklist was approaching, so why should he cross the line now? He said something I've never forgotten, that he was "tired of going into the screening room after the lights were out." He would be compelled to sneak into the private sessions where Yordan's films were shown, watch films that he had written, and then leave again before the lights went up. He said he couldn't take that anymore.

He told me that he had called up his agent at William Morris and demanded, as Ben put it, "Get me out of jail." The agent had arranged an executive-session meeting with Representative Donald Jackson. Ben named a number of people he had known. I asked how he could bring himself to do that to friends, and he said, "Well, I'm not friends with them anymore. We no longer have anything in common."

How about the reported claim that he said to you, by way of explanation, that everyone he named except Leo Hurwitz was already dead?

That was common among excuses, similar to, "Everyone I named was already named." Maddow and I parted very uncomfortably.*

---

*Ben Maddow reluctantly tells his side of the story as to why he eventually caved in to HUAC in Patrick McGilligan, *Backstory 2: Interviews with Screenwriters of the 1940s and 1950s.*

Do you assess him unkindly?

I was very fond of him, so I felt very sad; perhaps I should have felt more anger. I had always felt that Ben was a strange man in many ways. I was very surprised at what he did, although my friend Arnold Manoff* was not surprised at all, because he had always thought there had been something dark about Ben. But I feel uncomfortable assessing this or that degree of guilt because, once again, so much of that feeling, whether you admit it or not, is subjective. On the other hand, I can happily despise someone like Edward Dmytryk, for example.

You and several other blacklistees had a confrontation with him in Barcelona in 1988.

I was invited to the Barcelona Film Festival, where they were going to show *The Front* and where it had been arranged for a panel of blacklistees to discuss the blacklist. The panel were Jules Dassin, John Berry, myself and Rosaura Revueltas, the Mexican actress who had played the heroine in *Salt of the Earth*. Dmytryk was invited altogether separately to the festival because they were showing some of his movies. We made it very clear, individually and together, that we wanted nothing to do with Dmytryk, that we should not have to meet or deal with him in any way. They assured us on these points.

They showed *The Front*, and then we all went to a dais at this hall, and there sitting in the front row facing us was Dmytryk. Before the panel could start, Dmytryk grabbed the mike, giving his apologia for what he did, and actually attacking John Berry, for example, totally gratuitously. We were furious. I had to restrain Berry from going down and throttling him. Dassin got up with great dignity and said, "This is not why we came here." We all just got off the stage and left. It made a big splash in the papers the next day.

I always wondered: why did he do that? He must have known what our response would be. Evidently, he wanted to be recognized by his former comrades so badly that even being attacked (by us responding to *his* attacks) implied for him a possible recognition. I certainly recognized him. I'm proud to say that I called him "garbage" from the stage.

---

*Arnold Manoff (1915–1965) wrote a novel, *Telegram from Heaven*, later made into the musical *All You Need Is One Good Break*, which landed him in Hollywood following military service in World War II. There he wrote or contributed to *Man from Frisco, My Buddy, Dear Heart, Casbah, No Minor Vices* (a film directed by Lewis Milestone for which he earned a Writers Guild nomination), and *The Big Break*, before being blacklisted. Working with Abraham Polonsky and Walter Bernstein, Manoff helped devise most of the shows for the television series *You Are There*, under pseudonymous authorship. Unlike his partners, he suffered a series of setbacks in television and theater, and died before his career could transcend the blacklist. He was married to actress Lee Grant; their daughter, Dinah Manoff, is an actress often seen on television.

Is Dmytryk in the lowest category of informers for you? Or does Kazan rival him with his own qualifications? How do you assess the two of them, respectively, with regard to their ultimate contribution to film culture? Do either of them, for example, deserve any organization's Life Achievement Award?

First of all, Kazan was at times a brilliant director. Dmytryk was at best merely a competent director. In terms of their contribution to the culture of the country, I don't think there's any comparison. Kazan could direct on a level that Dmytryk couldn't approach.

I hate to quantify, although Dmytryk would definitely be among the lowest of the low for me. On the other hand, Dmytryk went to jail, which Kazan didn't, and didn't recant until afterward. I sympathize with him in the sense that at least he served time before he turned. One of the things that is different between them, however, is that Dmytryk has been vociferous over the years in defending himself, and he continues to attack the same people he attacked in his testimony, often gratuitously. Kazan has at least kept his mouth shut, except in his autobiography, where he remains defiant.

Recently there has been a controversy over whether either the Los Angeles Film Critics' Association or the American Film Institute should give Kazan their respective Life Achievement Awards. I don't think you can separate Kazan's work from what he did as a friendly witness. Such an award would only be given to him as a director, but it was as a director that he testified, hurting other directors, writers, and everyone who was blacklisted. Why give him such an award? It's one thing to say, on an individual basis, that fifty or so years have passed, and the wounds are old if not healed. But any official award given by an official film body would be given to someone who disgraced the profession.

It's important, too, what informing did to his work. Kazan in the 1950s directed a couple of arguably great films. But he also directed some junky ones. Then he began to write even more junky novels. As Marty Ritt once said to me, "He's writing the kind of novel that he would have once spurned as beneath himself to direct as a film." So informing compromised Kazan, and his cultural contribution lessened in the 1950s. It didn't make any difference in the case of Dmytryk.

John (Jack) Berry

JOHN BERRY, Lyons, France, 1995

INTERVIEW BY PATRICK McGILLIGAN

JOHN (JACK) BERRY
(1917–)

1946 *Miss Susie Slagle's.* Director.
  From This Day Forward. Director.
1947 *Cross My Heart.* Director.
1948 *Casbah.* Director.
1949 *Tension.* Uncredited script contribution,
      director.
  Caught. Uncredited directorial contribution.
1951 *The Hollywood Ten* (documentary). Director.
  He Ran All the Way. Director.
1953 *C'est arrivé à Paris.* Director (credited to
      Henri Lavoral).
1955 *Ça va barder.* Coscript, director.
  Je suis un sentimental. Coscript, director.

1956 *Don Juan/Pantaloons.* Coscript, director.
1958 *Tamango.* Coscript, director.
  Oh que mambo! Director.
1966 *Maya.* Director.
1969 *A tout casser/Breaking It Up.* Coscript,
      director.
1974 *Claudine.* Director.
1977 *Thieves.* Director.
1978 *The Bad News Bears Go to Japan.* Director.
1985 *Le voyage à Paimpol.* Coscript, director,
      producer.
1986 *Round Midnight.* Actor.
1988 *Il y a maldonné.* Coscript, director, producer.
1990 *A Captive in the Land.* Coscript, director.

■

JOHN BERRY'S REAL name is Jack Szold. Everybody calls him Jack. He has perhaps half a dozen other names—he forgets exactly how many, and what some of his names are—which he used with cunning to keep working during the darkest years of the blacklist.

His has been a career of peaks and valleys, weaving back and forth between theater and film, between, one is tempted to add, heights of artistic purity and expedient, wrongheaded jobs for hire. The credits cleave between New York and Los Angeles, stage and screen, then again, after HUAC rampaged through Hollywood, between the United States and France. To make matters more complicated, John Berry has served as actor, writer, director, producer—sometimes as all four. No wonder the reference books have a hard time charting him.

His show-business résumé starts in the early thirties, as apprentice, runner, stand-up comic, one-act player, and master of ceremonies in the Catskills. It continues with a stint as extra, apprentice, green man, and eventually assistant director for John Houseman and Orson Welles in the Mercury Theatre. The first, lost, or obscure items in his filmography are from this period: participation in a Frontier Films documentary, Welles's never-finished and never-released *Too Much Johnson*, and a 1943 remake of *Battleship Potemkin*.

Berry came out to Hollywood on a short-term contract at the end of 1943, happy for the temporary big bucks, skeptical about the lower art form of motion pictures. First at Paramount in its director-in-training program, he moved from studio to studio like a broken-field runner, directing increasingly prestigious projects while keeping up a heavy involvement with the Actors Lab Theatre. In 1951 he served as the uncredited director of a fascinating historical document, the 16-mm defense film made by the Hollywood Ten.

Berry's last American credit before the blacklist was a powerful *film noir* that has won a cult over the years, *He Ran All the Way,* John Garfield's final screen appearance before a heart attack killed the popular star. The movie was awaiting release in the summer of 1951 when FBI agents tried to serve a subpoena on Berry. He went out the window—literally. ("Out the Window" is the working title of his autobiography in progress.)

To escape the blacklist Berry went to Paris, where, although he has lived for long intervals in New York and London, he continues to reside, one of the last of the original group of HUAC refugees who settled in Paris. His family is there, and to an extent the highlights of his career have been abroad. Bertrand Tavernier, who featured Berry in a key role in *Round Midnight*, says that the expatriate's French films include several that are first-rate and highly personal, often concerning issues of friendship and betrayal. Tavernier adds that if Berry's films had been more widely seen, he would be acknowledged as one of the leading talents among the blacklisted generation.

Berry lives in an unfashionable Paris neighborhood. In the living room of his simple flat are a stack of sixties folk records and a small but prominent bust of Lenin.

■

All the film reference books say you were born in New York City.

They're all right.

Manhattan?

I was born in the Bronx, on Hoe Avenue, and then we did the classic thing that immigrant Jewish families did: our first move was from the Lower East Side to upper Manhattan; then the big move was back down to lower Manhattan. That was the trajectory of many of those families.

Were your parents born in America?

My real name is Jack Sold, or Szold. My mother was a Rumanian. My father, who for a long time claimed to be a Hungarian Gypsy, was Polish-born, from a small town outside of Minsk, in the Russian Empire. My father came from peasant stock. His story is magnificent in many ways. He was really the very prototype of the Jewish American immigrant who made good—with all that flair. When he was nine years old, he delivered fish for the Fulton Fish Market. When he was fifteen, he was a busboy, cleaning tables at Ratner's on Delancey Street. He was very clever in the restaurant business, obviously, because when he was nineteen years old, he became the manager of twelve to fifteen restaurants, a chain—the Busy Bee, I think, but I'm not sure. He'd ride the trolley car up and down Seventh or Eighth Avenue, visiting all the restaurants. That's when he met my mother, who lived on the Lower East Side, on Broome Street.

Did your father have any interest in the theater?

Never. My father ended up owning a very successful restaurant. He was extremely proud and loving of me, except after I decided to be an actor. He thought actors were bums. When I was first starting out, he would introduce me to his cronies as [sarcastically], "This is my son Jackie Szold; he wants to be an actor." Later on, when I started to get jobs he would say [proudly], "This is my son, John Berry; he's an actor."

He wanted me to be a lawyer or a boxer. A lawyer, because they say I was

terribly gifted with words as a child. A boxer, because I could make a million
dollars. He used to bring guys around to meet with me and teach me to box.
I did box—not professionally. I won a medal in one of those neighborhood
sporting clubs. I could have gone to the Golden Gloves, but I didn't because
I was fighting off my father's desires. Eventually I had to make a choice between being an actor and having a broken nose because, after all, I thought
I looked like Laurence Olivier, and I didn't want to hurt my chances of being
a great actor.

Who planted the seed in you that maybe you should become an actor? Your mother?

I really have no way of knowing that for sure. By the time my father was
thirty or thirty-one, he was the prosperous owner of a restaurant on Thirty-
eighth Street, right near the Thirty-eighth Street Playhouse. It was a modest,
medium-priced eating place with waiters—not a cafeteria. This was around
1924 or 1925.

My father organized a weekly crap game in the basement of the restaurant.
And I would go to stay with my father, so my mother would be free to go to
shul or the ladies' auxiliary. Of course, the gamblers didn't appreciate my
reaching out for the dice, so Pop arranged for somebody to take me to the
Thirty-eighth Street Playhouse, where very, very prestigious companies gave
matinees on Saturday. I remember seeing three plays: *Richard III*, in which
there was swordplay, blood, and shining armor; *The Pony Express*, which had
a horse and rider galloping across the stage, with sparks flying and the scenery
of the West on rollers (I remember the slogan "Nothing stops the U.S.
mail!"); and I think I remember a musical called *Maryland, My Maryland*, in
which Sherman's troops were marching through Georgia on their way to
Atlanta, while the chorus was singing "Maryland, my Maryland!" And I was
watching and weeping, at age five or six.

That was my father. My mother had me march in the May Day parade for
the Red Cross, sometime after the war, 1920 or 1921. I remember dressing
up as a doctor in a white suit with a little black bag, marching beside a
stretcher with a boy playing a wounded veteran. I remember also how pleased
she always was when I ran around the house with a colander on my head and
a wooden sword or rifle. It delighted her. My mother was a great storyteller
and a great entertainer, and when she realized I was interested in the theater
she really was happy.

My parents did take me to the Yiddish theater on Second Avenue—that
was my mother's influence on my father. I remember a play by I. J. [Israel
Joshua] Singer—not [Isaac] Bashevis—a tale of two cities, Warsaw and
Cracow. I remember *The Golem*, which was terribly impressive—the monster
with flames made with a fan and fluttering paper.

Did you go to movies as a family?

The only movies my father truly liked, that I know of, were those early
documentaries about Africa. Once, when my son, his grandson, who is a

director now, was seventeen, my father asked him, "What do you want to do when you grow up?" and my son answered, "I'd like to direct movies." My father said, "I hope you make better ones than the shit your father does." [Laughs.] My father didn't care much about movies.

Sometimes we did go to the movies—that was also my mother's influence. On Friday night, which is a Sabbath night, my mother would light the candles, hold the ceremony, and then we would go see Lillian Gish in *Broken Blossoms* or whatever was playing. It turned out my first picture in Hollywood was with Lillian Gish, and how extraordinary that was because I had adored her as a little boy.

How did your theatrical ambitions progress?

When I was done with high school, my mother got me a job at a summer resort where we used to go on holiday. I was hired as master of ceremonies, stand-up comic, dramatic actor, apprentice, and runner for five dollars a week, plus room and board. In the Catskills, of course, where else? The first play I did there was *The Valiant*, which was a one-act play, very, very popular in the twenties. The young man who was the dramatic director played the Valiant; I was the prison guard, who didn't have many lines. The *Valiant's* story was simple: A convicted murderer is about to be electrocuted; no one knows who he is or where he comes from. It is the night of his execution, and a young woman who thinks that she recognizes him, that he may be her brother, comes to see him. They have a long scene in which she keeps trying to evoke in him memories of the past. He keeps rebuffing her, but a very warm relationship springs up between them, because if he ever had a sister, he'd sure like her to be this one. She remembers that when they were children, her brother used to recite to her from *Julius Caesar*. The condemned man says he doesn't even know who Julius Caesar is. The brother used to recite the line of Caesar's that a coward dies many times before his death. She recites that line at the end of the play, then breaks down sobbing and runs out. Before he goes off to the electric chair her brother finishes the line: "But the valiant die only once."

I remember one of my jobs was to pull the curtains together. The first night of *The Valiant* I started to pull the curtains, which were supposed to come together in the middle. For reasons I was never able to discover, they wouldn't come together but kept rolling around the stage. We could never get the stage blocked off, so we had to do a blackout. That was my first contact with Shakespeare. [Laughs.]

The Catskills was where I worked for three years. I met a lot of the burlesque comics. Milton Berle was fifteen years old at that time, and he was already a big star in the Catskills, a legend and a myth. I worked the Kiamesha Ideal House, Lockers' Mansion, and others. I usually acted as the master of ceremonies. You have to understand that the master of ceremonies was also the social director of the smaller places. You had to keep people amused with jokes and games, see that the guests got to know each other, and romance and dance with some of the ladies. You had a little notebook in which you wrote down punch lines so that when you went for an interview, and the hotel owner would ask, "Have you got any material?" you'd say, "I certainly do," and open up your notebook and launch into punch lines.

The first night onstage was always a tryout. I remember one time, one place, nobody laughed. Not a smile. Nothing. I was sure that was it. I was out. When I got offstage, the owner said to me, "You have a certain amount of charm, and you can sure tell a story, but you don't understand something—you're talking to a Jewish audience that doesn't understand a word of what you're saying." I had to tell the jokes in Yiddish! Well, he liked me, so I stayed—maybe another two days.

Were your parents politically minded?

Not at all.

What about your father?

The only newspaper he read was the *New York Daily News* or the *Daily Mirror*. He would read it by just turning the pages, skimming the headlines. And he never read a book. Never! But my father was very bright and could comment on everything. He was very entertaining, a big sport, a volcano of incredible energy.

He was a Tammany Hall guy. He belonged to the Grand Street Boys. He helped break a strike. He was given an award for breaking the restaurant workers' industrial union strike in 1928 or 1929, and he broke it with goon violence and was awarded this plaque when one of the pickets slashed a strikebreaker's cheek with a razor, and my father, who had witnessed this, captured the poor bastard and beat the shit out of him. My father threw him into his restaurant and got the police to arrest him. This contradiction is enormous for me, you understand.

Did you have any reaction to it at the time?

Yes. My father was a hero, of course. He remained for me a hero but a confused man, politically. He was a petit bourgeois, with some fascinating ideas politically. At the height of the Depression, when I became politically minded and was always talking about the fact that we had to stop the starvation, get rid of overproduction, and stop throwing away food—which is what we're doing today, by the way—people in the restaurant would take offense. He'd say, "Wait a minute, listen to him, maybe he's got something there, because I tell you something, I know one thing, no man should be allowed to make more than a million dollars." That was a [Dr. Francis E.] Townsend idea.* After all," he'd say, "what would Rockefeller do with all his money if you sat him on the dock"—we lived on Dyckman Street—"if he sat

---

*The Townsend Plan, also known as the Old-Age Revolving Pension, was proposed in 1934 by physician Francis E. Townsend. One of several populist movements to address the social

there and he threw one dollar into the river all day long, he couldn't get rid of it all in his lifetime." This marvelous confusion.

Where did you get your politics?

Out of hunger, man. It grew very strongly for me. In 1934 my politics were to get rid of all the Bolsheviks and send them all back to Russia, where they came from. But at the same time I realized something had to be done about the fact that there were millions of people starving in the streets, no milk and no bread. I listened to all the speakers, including the speakers of the Communist Party, which was very popular in the neighborhood. But I also listened to the Father Coughlinites, who hated Communists, and other speakers all the time.

I was so terribly anti-Bolshevik at first that we formed a group of fifteen fellows or so to get rid of the bloody Reds. We met at my house because my family was doing pretty well because of my father's restaurant. We formed a political party that was surely fascist, having to do with being prepared to take on the Reds, arming ourselves, and all that bullshit. [Laughs.]

By 1936 you had the war in Spain. By that time I had been moved around a great deal, politically. I had become much more politically conscious and involved—from the time my father went dead broke because of the Depression and his own stupidity. I began to see what was going on in the world. I began to put feelers out.

Why did you join the Communist Party? Not everyone joined the CP.

They pretty much went one way or another, buddy.

Was there a moment when you turned into a radical? I remember Lionel Stander telling me that it happened for him, very specifically, when he was conked on the head by a policeman at a protest gathering.

I have no memory of that kind of experience. There was no specific incident. What happened to me was a very gradual process. I felt the injustice. I was very moved, for example, when I went to the river and saw the vets all living in those huts and hovels, people selling apples. And as I say, the Spanish Civil War was enormously important for me.

Did you connect your theater activities with politics? Did you have any association with the Group Theatre?

Not really. I wanted to be a part of the Group Theatre. I tried all the time. I knew them, and they knew me—or of me—because I was always around and because I was known as a talented young fellow, even though I hadn't done very much.

---

distress following the 1929 crash, it sought an old-age pension based on a general sales tax that its adherents believed would bring about generalized prosperity.

What was wonderful in those days, which is different now, is that there was a community, man. People used to congregate in front of Walgreen's drugstore every single day, and you'd meet all the other young actors and people trying to get jobs. A group of us—guys with free tickets for opening nights—called ourselves the "Bilious Boys." If we couldn't get free tickets, we'd walk in after the first act and stand in the back. We'd go to all the shows, then we'd meet afterward at the Lincoln Cafeteria and destroy whatever play, author, director, or actor we'd seen the night before. No matter what it was, it was totally unacceptable. Al [Alfred] Hayes was a part of that group; so was [director] Benno Schneider, the Lee Strasberg of his own period. Later on, I was in Benno's [acting] class. So was Gene Tierney, and also Gary Merrill, with whom I remained friends up until his death. Gary was a lovely guy with a style of his own.

Around this time Orson [Welles] announced a production of *Julius Caesar*. A modern-dress *Caesar*. I myself for a couple of years had been part of a minor Shakespeare company and otherwise had not done much, some Federal Theatre Project plays. Here we were, young actors basically without work, totally arrogant, and completely involved with ourselves, thinking, "Who the hell is Orson Welles? What nonsense it is to do a modern-dress *Caesar*!" We knew only that he was in the Federal Theatre, and we didn't know much about that. I had seen him in *Doctor Faustus*, and I couldn't figure out what this strange-looking, long-bearded kid was doing up there on the stage. It wasn't impressive at all to me. It was all black curtains, lights, smoke, bombs. No jokes. So what?

We were offended by the fact that this guy was going to do a modern-dress production. Together with another man, Lajos Egri, who wrote a very well-known book about playwriting, we decided we were going to do our own production of *Julius Caesar*. We were going to show what *Caesar* really should be. We were going to do togas and tunics.

But even while that was going on, I auditioned for the better job, the paying job—as Mark Antony—for Orson Welles. I did the Mark Antony funeral oration. And John Houseman said, "You're very, very passionate and talented. Your temperament is great. But your speech is impossible." It was very New Yawk. So John Houseman sent me to a lady—Laura Elliot, I believe—a great speech teacher of her time, and paid for the lessons.

Did you have any initial contact with Orson at that audition?

No. Although Orson was probably in the theater. So I was hired as an apprentice and extra for *Julius Caesar*. Eight dollars a week. After the play opened, I organized all the apprentices and extras and went to Houseman, because the NRA was in effect, and I said, "We want fifteen dollars a week." We threatened him with a strike. I betrayed him. He writes about it, somewhere. It was a big sweat for him at the time, but it was also amusing.

Some people have ambivalent feelings about Houseman.

What were the most fruitful periods of Welles's life, from my point of view? In the theater, certainly, with Houseman. That first movie, *Kane*—Houseman was there. They were a magnificent team. A magnificent team. It was really something to see. John at that time had a great and very wholesome effect on Welles. The thing is, they just couldn't work it out finally. Orson would probably reach out of his grave to pull me down if he heard this, but actually, when you look at Orson's whole career, it's just too bad he never found anybody else like Houseman.

Why, tell me why, under what circumstances and for what reason, would John Houseman be interested in giving John Berry speech lessons? Why? What was he expecting? What profit was in it for him? What would be achieved by this? He believed in talent, man. He wanted people to express themselves. If he thought there was something to get from you, he really tried to give you a shot. That spirit doesn't exist much anymore, man.

Do you think that's different from Orson?

I don't think Orson had time for that. Orson was Orson. Orson was a giant conceiver. Certain things that Orson felt were correct in terms of theater I did not. At the time I was not only arrogant, I was a nobody. I have come to understand how right Orson was about things, just recently. Orson always said, "If you want to see life, go down to Forty-second Street and Eighth Avenue. You'll see it. It's boring. We are in the theater. We are doing spectacle. If you are an actor, I want the audience to know that you are acting." I didn't subscribe to that. I wanted to involve them. I wanted there to be life on the stage.

You have changed your mind in retrospect?

I have changed my mind. Neither one is the total answer. It depends on what you're doing. Whatever works, man. Whatever does what it is supposed to.

How much interaction did you have with Orson?

A lot. And how. You understand, I was a tough street kid, and Orson was not at all. Very few in the Mercury were. Most of them were college kids with money and ambitions to become actors. Very few of them had my background. I was kind of fascinating to them. I remember, very early, Orson talking to me and trying to figure out what the hell made me tick and trying to catch on to me. He wanted to become one of "the boys."

Did you like him?

I loved him. Orson was incredibly important to me. He was one of the only romantics in the theater I ever knew. How many people put their own fucking money up to do a show? How many people save their own money to get their movies made? How many people live that way?

Orson was my spiritual father. Houseman was my savior. And Norman

Lloyd, whom I also met at the Mercury Theatre, was another incredible influence in my life. I loved Norman Lloyd, whom I consider to be the only
boy from Brooklyn who really is an English aristocrat. Norman really introduced me and forced me into areas of thinking about Stanislavsky. He had
an extraordinary quality as an actor. His performance as Cinna the poet in
Orson's *Julius Caesar* was hair-raising. Norman might have become, in other
circumstances, a Broadway star. Instead he went to Hollywood and played
that marvelous character part in *Saboteur*, then went his own way.

Did Orson have any politics?

Yes, he did. I would situate them as a wonderful, warm, human conception
of what life should be, and what we owe people, and what our responsibility
is toward our fellow man. Because of Orson, I got much more heavily engaged
in politics. Not because he tried to involve me, but because of his attitudes.
During the Spanish Civil War, for example, we had speakers come to the
theater and talk to audiences, trying to raise money. And I remember he
made an incredible speech before Actors Equity at the time of the civil war
in Spain in which he forewarned everybody about the future. He predicted
the coming world war with all its horrors. Orson was quite something.

All I know about him is that he never did achieve what, in my opinion,
he should have. I think Orson needed someone like Houseman, but Orson
could never trust anybody. You had to be prepared to take such an enormous
amount of guff and madness from him. I remember one day, at rehearsal, he
accused Houseman of trying to poison him. We were rehearsing for *Five Kings*
or *Heartbreak House* or *Shoemaker's Holiday*, and he asked for tea or something.
Houseman brought him his drink. All of a sudden Orson threw this big number—"Aaggh!"—accusing Houseman of poisoning his drink. Total nonsense.
Madness.

I'll tell you one of the things that happened to me with Orson. We were
rehearsing *Danton's Death*. It was two o'clock in the morning. I was now his
first assistant, very close to Orson. Not only was I his first assistant, I was the
green man. You know what the green man is? That means I was in charge of
plants—the prop man and set builder (Walter Ash was running the operation). Orson was onstage and he said to me, "I need some chalk." I said, "I
don't know where to get you chalk at two o'clock in the morning." He looked
at me with that wonderful, noble, aristocratic hauteur. He said, "Why? Must
you betray me too, booby?" I said, "I'll get you the chalk." I went down to
the men's room of the Mercury Theatre, got the fire ax, broke the wall, and
dug out some plaster and came back and said to him, "Here's the chalk." He
said, "Thank you."

At this time we were shooting a sixteen-millimeter film for a play we were
doing. We built sets on a vacant lot in Yonkers. We worked all night, so that
when Orson arrived in the morning to shoot, the sets would be up, because
he wanted the natural look of sunlight. We got the sets built, the limousines
with the cast started to arrive, it was maybe eight-thirty or nine A.M. Then

the wind came up and blew them down. Orson said, "What are we going to do?" I said, "We'll get them up, Orson." So I organized the crew, and we sat there and held the sets up, sitting in this vacant lot, one of us in the corner of each piece of the set, fighting the wind. Lunchtime—twelve, one o'clock. We'd been there all night. We'd been holding the sets up all morning. A caterer drove up and a long table was set up. Everybody was fed but the poor fuckers holding up the sets. Finally I said, "That's it, guys." We all stood up, and the sets fell down. Orson said, "What's going on, John?" I said, "We're going to eat, Orson, because we've been here all night." He had this enormously shocked and aggrieved look across his face. He said, "You haven't been fed? You must take my seat. Sit!" He got up. I said, "I don't want your seat. He said, "You must!" Of course, we all went back and continued to hold up the fucking sets. Orson did that all the time—operate, manipulate, function—but it was great fun and excitement for me.

That was Too Much Johnson, *your first film experience?*

Yes, a sixteen-millimeter picture, which we made to go with the William Gillette play, with Joe [Joseph] Cotten, Edgar Barrier, Arlene Francis. But there was another, even more obscure experience before that. I vaguely recall that Leo Hurwitz and Paul Strand did some kind of documentary picture in which my hands appeared. I think it was for Frontier Films and it was about union organizing. My hands were used as the hands of the FBI searching through files, which is ironic.

Too Much Johnson was for a play we were preparing for the second season of the Mercury, so that must have been 1939. It was twenty or thirty minutes of, I guess, chase—husbands and wives chasing each other. Aside from doing all those other things, I acted a part in it and was the assistant cutter. We tried the film and play out at a summer theater in, I think, Marblehead [Massachusetts]. It was not a film per se. It was chases that fit into the play and were interspersed with the play. The whole thing was a disaster, the film and the play. But Orson had a wonderful time making the film.

I know that I cut the picture, because I remember cutting it, and I remember that Orson was always fighting his hay fever, or asthma, or something. We cut it in the Waldorf-Astoria in a suite—Houseman, myself, and Welles. We smuggled the film and projector in. One time the film caught fire. What I remember, most remarkably, is me running with the projector in my hand, burning, trying to get out of the door and into the goddamn hallway, and Houseman racing for the door at the same time—so we had one of those comic who-gets-out-first moments; while Orson, with absolutely no concern whatsoever, was back inside, standing and looking at some piece of film in his hand, smoking his pipe.

We opened with *Danton's Death,* which was a disaster, and that was the end of *Too Much Johnson* and that was the end of the Mercury. Welles did the broadcast ["The War of the Worlds"] that year, and very shortly after the broadcast he went to Hollywood.

How long was it before you followed Orson to Hollywood?

I didn't follow Orson. Orson tried to get me to come. Some of the people who went with him paid their own way to go with him to Hollywood. But I had no interest in Hollywood whatsoever.

What happened was that in 1940 or 1941 Lionel [Stander] got a man by the name of Bernie Bernard to put the money up to finance a dramatization of [Richard Wright's novel] *Native Son*. Orson came back to Broadway and directed it, before the release of *Citizen Kane*. Then he went back to Hollywood, but since Orson thought I was talented and energetic, he charged me with keeping the production on its proper course, then let me take over the direction of it for the road, and then on Broadway, where I also played a leading part. I became terribly involved with *Native Son*. It was my first big part, and I was very happy. It was the beginning of my professional life on Broadway.

I can't help but notice that your first recorded film credit also comes around this time—in 1943—as an actor in a genuine obscurity called Seeds of Freedom.

Seeds of Freedom was a remake of Eisenstein's *Potemkin*, using *Potemkin* with a "frame." It's in flashback. It was directed by Hans Berger, a Czechoslovakian director as I remember. The "frame" was what was funny about it. The picture was made after the invasion by Hitler of the Soviet Union, and around the story were a group of Russian partisans fighting the Nazis. I played a young partisan, and Morris Carnovsky, unless I'm mistaken, played the older partisan fighter who tells the group the story of *Potemkin*. At the end of the picture the Germans attack us, and we attack them.

It was done in New York City, and other than that I have no memory of it, man. All I remember is the set, the director, Morris Carnovsky, and myself. I do remember that I saw the picture at the Stanley Theater at Thirty-eighth or Thirty-ninth Street and Seventh Avenue, and that I still conceived of myself as a young Laurence Olivier. When this kid from Brooklyn showed up on the screen, I slid under my chair.

How did you wind up in Hollywood, eventually?

Around this time, Jack Wildberg, who was a theater attorney and producer, did a play called *Cry Havoc*, about six nurses on Bataan, which later became a film [*So Proudly We Hail!*, 1943]. It had opened on Broadway and was a terrible disaster, so naturally he took it to Chicago. He asked me to come to Chicago and sit and talk about its problems. He wasn't paying me, as I remember, just buying me lunch and dinner and putting me up at the Pump Room in the Ambassador East. I went. I had nothing better to do. The Mercury was now gone. Orson was in Hollywood. And I preferred the theater, man.

Was your attitude that Orson had sold out?

I didn't make those kinds of judgments. I thought it was great that he went to Hollywood. I was quite honestly more concerned with where I was going. I was going somewhere in the theater. What happened was, [Elia] Kazan came from Hollywood to New York and stopped in Chicago. Jack Wildberg was a friend of [theatrical author, director, and producer] Cheryl Crawford's and part of the Group Theatre, so Kazan stopped by and saw a run-through of *Cry Havoc*. A young woman was directing it, and it wasn't very good. Jacqueline Susann was in the cast. Wildberg asked Kazan to help him out, and Kazan said—with his usual great charm—that he couldn't do it. Kazan said, "You don't need me. Get John to do it. He can do it." I knew Kazan—although he always claims he doesn't remember me—because I had worked for him as an actor in something he did for the war effort. Also, he was someone I really admired. He was one of ours—street tough, T-shirts and sweatshirts—one of the guys.

What happened was, I took over the directing, and in three days I managed to do amazing things with the play. Although it was still terrible, in four days I had restaged it and made it presentable. Because of that Jack Wildberg felt he owed me a favor and started introducing me around to Hollywood people. He introduced me to a man who was at Warner Brothers in New York, who invited me in and asked me, "Would you like to come to Hollywood?" I said, "To do what?" He said, "What do you want to do?" I said, "I want to be an actor, a writer, and a director." He said, "We don't need a genius." That ended Warner Brothers.

Then Wildberg got me another interview, this time with [Paramount executive] Buddy DeSylva, who was passing through New York. I met DeSylva at the Waldorf-Astoria. This interview, my big interview, lasted five minutes. I told him I wanted to be an actor, writer, and director. He was unfazed. "All right," he said. And he gave me a six-month contract.

I came out, I guess it was 1943 or 1944. I came out to Hollywood because it was two hundred and fifty bucks a week for a young actor for six months. I figured I'd put a hundred and twenty-five a week aside. If I could put that money aside I could hang out until I found a really good job as an actor. My feeling about film was somewhat less than complimentary. I was put on the set of Billy Wilder's picture [*Double Indemnity*]. My job was to sit around and learn, which I thought was amusing and interesting. I watched Billy Wilder and said to myself, "These Hollywood guys don't know how to move actors around." Because I was stupid and pretentious—what the hell did I know?—I thought anybody could do this.

You were wrong?

And how!

What was your interaction with Billy?

Billy was very kind and talked to me on occasion. His cutter, Doane Harrison, talked to me a lot about coverage and so forth; he was very helpful and came around later on when I was cutting my first picture. And a cameraman whose name was Johnny Seitz was great to me.

Were you consciously preparing to be a director?

I never prepared for being a director. I just directed. It's true I had gone to a lot of pictures. But the whole thing seemed to me obvious. You have to understand, I keep repeating, I didn't care about movies. I thought movies were really a very puerile form of entertaining people with no profundity. I was only interested in theater with a capital T. That was partly Orson's influence.

Meantime, Harold Clurman, the Group Theatre guy, was at the studio, and he was supposed to direct a picture called *Miss Susie Slagle's*, about a boardinghouse in Baltimore. John Houseman was producing it. I had met Harold at the studio. He was writing his book about the Group Theatre, *The Fervent Years*. I don't think Harold cared about movies. Anyway, his option was dropped, and John Houseman asked for me to step in and direct *Miss Susie Slagle's*. It was totally without sense. Houseman was always pushing my career somewhere. He was very, very important to me. He had a great feeling for my ability. He may have been right or wrong, but he had a feeling about me that was very, very good for me.

In today's world there are guys who would fall down, kiss your ass, or give you money to be able to direct a picture. At the time I thought to myself, "Well, that's all right. I guess I'll direct a picture." All because John had recommended me as director—and, of course, if John had said to me, "Go pick grapes," I'd be a migrant worker today.

How long had you been in Hollywood?

Four months. I'm not sure, I think I was 1946. Then I was asked to go meet Lillian Gish, who was starring in the picture. I met her in her dressing room and immediately she was so warm, so marvelous. She said to me, "Don't be nervous, because even though it's my fiftieth picture, I'm very nervous too."

I was asked to test the actors, at least that is what they told me. But I knew they were testing me, no question about it. By now all the arrogance had turned into total terror. [Cameraman] Ernest Laszlo did one of the tests. I had two cameramen—Laszlo for one scene and Johnny Seitz for another. Well, Johnny Seitz did a test for me that was better than anything I ever got in the movie, and for the movie I had Charles Lang, who was a helluva cameraman. But Johnny Seitz was absolutely sympathetic and wanted me to get the movie.

How was working with Lillian Gish?

Lillian was marvelous. She was in one of the test scenes. Naturally I was impressed because of who she was, but at the same time I had a great feeling for actors, and how you treated actors was one of my areas of expertise.

Could you give her direction, as a young kid?

Of course, I was able to give anybody direction as a young kid. It's much tougher now, you know. [Laughs]. You could always direct Lillian, but you should also listen to Lillian.

She was absolutely wonderful toward me. I made that picture with her in 1945 or '46. The blacklist came along, and I went away for twenty years. Then I found myself in a theater one night in New York, and sitting beside me was Lillian. I said, "I don't know if you remember me, Lillian, but my name is John Berry, and I directed you in . . ." "Oh, John," she said with this brilliant smile, "you were so talented. What happened to you?" [Laughs.]

You told her you had been blacklisted. What was her reaction?

I told her I had been in France for all those years. "Oh, that's why I haven't seen you for so long. I just couldn't understand where you had gone." She must have been fifty when she did *Miss Susie Slagle's*, and she was eighty when I did another thing with her, thirty years later, on television, a pilot called *Sparrows*. It was dreadful, but she was marvelous in it.

You bounced around the studios a lot in the 1940s. How did you go from Paramount to RKO?

Paramount loaned me to RKO to do a picture with Joan Fontaine. I believe that Joan Fontaine had been told about me by John Houseman, and she was making a movie, called *From This Day Forward*, for which Clifford Odets had written the script and that he was going to direct. Now, for reasons that I'm absolutely unacquainted with—either she didn't get along with him or she didn't like his script—Clifford didn't do the picture, and that's when they came to me. The picture's producer, a man named Bill Pereira, asked me to do the picture: New York story, New York kid; social content, socially engaged young fellow. Hugo Butler, who was also one of the writers on *Miss Susie Slagle's*, redid Clifford's script. I gave his script to Charlie Schnee, who was a buddy of mine, and we also worked on it. I like that picture very much.

Meanwhile, you stayed under contract at Paramount?

I stayed under contract at Paramount up until the time I finished *Casbah*. During that period of time I worked for RKO and Universal, as well as Paramount.

Why did you leave Paramount, eventually?

The studio dropped my option. I got into an enormous beef with Henry Ginsberg, who ran the studio at the time. Richard Maibaum had written a script called *O.S.S.* They gave it to me to read. I thought it was not very good. I spoke to Maibaum and told him what I thought he could do with it. I said, "If a guy becomes an O.S.S. operator during the war"—it wasn't terribly original, but this was my idea—"you have to start out with somebody who has all the qualities of a gentle human being and turn him into a killer; then at the end you have a guy who can't work it out in peacetime, because he has become a killer." I had some good ideas. It was set in France—what did I know from France? But I researched and found out that, for example, the fork goes in one place in France and a different place in America. Our main character wouldn't know that. I worked on the script with Maibaum, developing it. He thought I was the cat's pajamas.

So they put me on the picture. Then they told me they were going to cast Alan Ladd in the lead. I said, "Alan Ladd! If you cast Alan Ladd, we'll have a guy who is the very image of a killer at the beginning of the picture. It'll take away from the development of the story." Of course Alan Ladd was a big, big star. That didn't mean anything to me, you understand, a man of my integrity. [Laughs.] Richard and I went to one of Alan Ladd's pictures, and when I came out I said to Richard, "I think he's good for this stuff he's doing, but he can't play what I'm going to go for. He won't be able to pull it off." Richard said, "That's right!" I said, "Let's go tell the producers."

So we went to talk to the producers. I said, "He's not the right guy." They said, "Well, he's the guy we want." I said, "Well, maybe he's the guy you want, but he's not the guy I want, and if you want me to do it, you've got to go along with what I think. Richard himself says so." Richard said, "Now wait a minute, I didn't say that." So I walked out.

Afterward, Richard and I had lunch at Lucy's, and Richard said to me, "Please do the picture. They're talking to somebody else who has a contract at Warners, and they're perfectly happy that you won't do it. But I want you to do it because I know we'll make a good movie together." I said, "I won't make it with Alan Ladd." So I went to the top—I went to see Henry Ginsberg. He tried to be paternalistic with me, calling me "son"—I stopped that. I said, "You think I'm either nuts or talented. If you think I'm talented, let me do what I should do. If you think I'm nuts, let's break my contract." Well, you don't talk to the guy who runs a studio like that in that period. He said, "You won't work again until I put you to work," and Paramount laid me off. I had six months of doing nothing, then I did *Casbah* at Universal, for which Paramount picked up the money, then the studio just let the contract run out.

Frankly, I just wasn't very bright. But let's not kid ourselves—what are we talking about? We're talking about the manufacturing of a product—we were making nice, good-looking cars and hoping they drove well. Well, I was in another ball game. I came from the Mercury, I came from the theater, where we aspired to do art, and therefore, if I was going to make movies, the kinds of movies I wanted to make certainly wouldn't fit into the category of many of the movies that I did make, finally. Ironically.

Anyway, that's what happened at Paramount. In a place where people were career crazy, I wasn't at that time, and I'm still not. I don't think I became career crazy ever. It's been a flaw.

Where did you go after Paramount?

I went from Paramount . . . nowhere. I sat around for months until I got a one-picture deal at MGM: *Tension.* The producer was Bob Sisk. I think Allen

Rivkin wrote the script, which I thought was mediocre. I think I improved it a great deal. The funny thing is, since I was not the writer, I had to submit what I wrote to Allen. Being delicate, I didn't put down the characters' names. I put down, "he says," "she says," "the detective says," "the other guy says." Allen put in the people's names, and he got his credit.

For example, there's one scene in *Tension*, with [Richard] Basehart in a prison cell, which didn't exist in any version of the script, and it didn't exist in the budget. But I felt we had to have a crisis scene in which the character was in bitter trouble. I had a friend who had been Orson's business manager, Jack Moss, a fabulously knowledgeable moviemaker; he should have been a far more important figure than he was. He's the big, fat guy in *Journey into Fear*. He is the only man I have ever spoken to about movies who was always describing what was wrong with a script totally in movie terms. Everything was visual. Even psychological scenes were visual. I would say to him, "I don't know quite what to do with this moment in the story. . . ." He'd say, "Close shot. She's looking down. . . ."

He helped me on *Tension*, talking about scenes and rewriting. I wanted to make the murder suspicion much stronger than what had been suggested, and the only way I could think to do it was to put the character in a cell with the police questioning him. But there was no such provision in the sets, or budget. There was no such scene. I got up very early Monday morning, got the decorator, we went through the studio, and there was a subway station that had been built for something. The decorator said, "We could get some bars and . . ." I said, "That's the way we'll do it." We gave the actors the scene, we shot it, and Bob Sisk was furious. I got a phone call from Dore Schary: "If you ever do that again . . ." Another bad career move.

After that, I started doing plays again at the Actors Lab.* I did one play

---

*The Actors Laboratory Theatre, or Actors Lab, was formally announced in May 1941. According to Wendy Smith, writing in *Real Life Drama: The Group Theatre and America, 1931–1940*: "The Lab had its roots in both the Group Theatre and the Federal Theatre Project. It grew out of the Hollywood Theatre Alliance, formed by members of the Los Angeles section of the Federal Theatre Project after it closed down. At the time the [initial] Statement of Policy appeared the Lab's executive board included three former Group members: Virginia Framer, Joe [J. Edward] Bromberg, and Bud [Roman] Bohnen. They intended it to be a more realistic version of the Group; members were professional actors employed in films (the Lab didn't assume the Group's responsibility to provide a living for its members) who wanted to challenge themselves by exploring advanced acting problems in classes and public performances.

"The Lab flourished for nearly ten years, with its fingers in many different pies. It was active in war work, producing shows that were performed at Army camps, hospitals, and overseas bases under the auspices of the USO. After the war, it drew much of its income from a separate school called the Workshop, which offered classes for studio contract players and veterans taking advantage of the GI Bill's tuition appropriations. The professional members continued their studio work and appeared in the Lab theatre wing's full-scale commercial productions."

Red-baiters attacked the socially-conscious Lab once World War II was over, and state and federal un-American committees began to take their toll. The movie studios kept their contract

called *All You Need Is One Good Break*, directing and starring in it, which was of national interest because it was so timely. We had national coverage.* In the midst of that play Max Ophüls became ill, and I was asked to do *Caught*—from which they dropped me after three weeks when Max was recovered from his illness.

Is any of your work in the film?

I have never seen the film, nor did I really pursue the job. I was told that that was a scam between the agent and the studio. The studio had to give proof to the insurance company that they were making an effort to complete the picture. That was another case of not being career-crazy. Here was a picture with Bob [Robert] Ryan, James Mason, and Barbara Bel Geddes, whom I was very fond of, and I wouldn't give up the play that I was doing at the Actors Lab. I continued doing that play at night while I was shooting the movie during the day! [Laughs.] This may have ruffled some feathers.

Did you know Ophüls?

I didn't know Max. I got connected with *Caught* only because they were looking for someone to replace him temporarily.

Do you remember the scenes you filmed?

I vaguely remember Barbara Bel Geddes's character being taken to a hospital for some reason.

Around this time HUAC came to town and started their witchhunt of Communists and anybody vaguely pinko in Hollywood. You were leftist and you were certainly a director, but you would seem to be one of the least likely candidates to direct the Hollywood Ten defense film—or at the least, any one of the Ten could have done it himself. That short film is one of the most obscure items on your filmography. Who chose you? Were you something of a compromise choice?

Maybe it was Paul Jarrico. Maybe Eddie Dmytryk. Or the defense committee? Paul came to me first and asked if I would direct it, and I said no. I didn't want to stick my neck out. I said, "Are you out of your mind? You are asking me to do something that will put me in the shithouse. Let Eddie Dmytryk direct it, or Herbert Biberman, for chrissakes." Paul told me Eddie suggested me because he couldn't, on account of he was too busy trying to make a living. Eddie denies having anything to do with this, by the way; he says he

---

players away after the 1947 HUAC hearings; in 1948 the IRS revoked the Lab's tax-exempt status; in 1949 it was forced to drop its veterans-training program. Lab people were subpoenaed, attendance dropped, sources of revenue dried up, and the doors were closed forever in 1950.
*Written by Arnold Manoff and staged by John Berry and J. Edward Bromberg, both of whom also acted parts in the play, *All You Need Is One Good Break* was a tenement social drama that also had a brief run on Broadway in 1950.

would never have had me direct it because I wasn't a good enough director! What kind of bullshit is that to come up with? He's in the picture!

Anyway, I said no, but the defense committee came back to me and gave me that bullshit about my being a man of principle, so would I do it? So I became a man of principle. I said sure. And then Eddie Dmytryk kicked me in the balls later on. He's the guy who blew my name to HUAC. A typical hack. His pipe-smoking pose used to drive me up the wall.

Still, why would they opt for you? There were plenty of other leftist directors around town.

I knew most of the Ten. They were all terribly nervous and upset. I think the choice was made because they felt I would be able to calm them down and get them through it, getting something from them on camera without their being too stiff-assed.

It's in documentary format. Was it fully scripted?

Not in my memory. I just picked the shots and told them what to do.

Were there arguments at the time? Or were you completely in charge?

There were no problems. I really directed them. I don't remember much about it, except the horror of having all those wonderful people there, with whom I had warm relationships, and who were about to go to prison.

Tell me about your last movie before you yourself were blacklisted, and John Garfield's last before his death, He Ran All the Way. *I love the movie. What did Hugo Butler do on the script, as opposed to Dalton Trumbo?*

Hugo Butler, quite frankly, kept me from fucking up Dalton's script. Dalton did one script. Then Jack Moss went away with me, and we thought we'd fixed up Dalton's script. What we actually did was make some romantic piece of shit out of it, although we did find an ending that was quite extraordinary. When we came back, everybody was upset, so Hugo was put on the script. Hugo hated our script, said it was all bullshit. So he fixed our script by going back to Dalton's, although Hugo got the credit.

The big beef on the script was the ending. It wasn't Hugo's beef, it was Shelley Winters's. The one thing Hugo liked was our idea for the ending. What I didn't want was the ending of the book [the novel by Sam Ross], where she stabs him on the couch. I wanted an ending where a betrayal takes place . . . yet it's not a betrayal. I remember how Hugo wrote the end: They're coming down the stairs, and he's saying, "You love me? It's all garbage. Nobody loves anybody!" That's all Hugo's great dialogue. Shelley Winters refused to shoot that ending . . . coming down the stairs, saying those lines. She wanted to stab him on the couch upstairs, not shoot him downstairs. She said, "That's not the ending I agreed to do." [Laughs.] She complained that I was changing the whole meaning of the movie, that it ought to be the daughter's point of view. I remember telling her, "Shelley, it's not your movie, it's John's." She threatened to walk off. I said, "Go ahead, I'll get an extra and shoot the scene over the shoulder." She stayed.

While you were working on He Ran All the Way, *did you suspect you were about five minutes away from being blacklisted? Was Garfield worried about being black- listed? Was the filming affected by the atmosphere?*

No, we did not know. Absolutely not. We were combative. We had a feeling we would come off. We knew things were dangerous and all that, but so what? This was before the hysteria went wild.

Yet there's a feeling of doom about the film.

It's about doom. That's not coincidental. I wanted to do that story like that. And you must remember that Julie [Garfield] had had a heart attack, a slight heart attack, before the film.

Was he ill during the making of the picture?

Never.

You didn't have any inkling of his death?

Yeah, sure, but I didn't really think he was going to die. He died because he chose to die, in my opinion. You don't go out and booze and fuck and stay up all night, night after night, because you think everything is going to be okay in the long run. He was being driven toward a certain area that was pretty tough for him.

You mean informing?

I believe so. This is a guy I really cared for. We had a ball on that film. He and I would surely have had a very big and important relationship. We had a marvelous time working with each other on this one, and we were going to do *The Man with the Golden Arm* next.

He Ran All the Way is a helluva movie. That's one of the resentments of my life. What did I get out of that picture? Willie Wyler made a similar movie about the middle class called *The Desperate Hours* later on, and it became a big thing. *He Ran All the Way* has been ignored; the actor has been ignored— except by film buffs. I think Garfield is remarkable in that movie, so moving, so rich. He was as big a star as Bogart when he did that movie. Nobody knows about him anymore. They wiped him out.

Your best American film?

No question, up to that point, especially. When it comes to my American pictures, there is only that one and *Claudine* that have any real merit. Al- though I think *Tension* is all right.

Garfield was dead, and you weren't even in America, by the time He Ran All the Way *was released?*

I was gone. I'm not sure my name was even on the picture when it was first released.

Ben Barzman told me once that it was especially hurtful as a writer to have come to France in the middle of his life and have to pick up a second language, that no matter how good his credits with Joseph Losey were—and they were very good—to the end of his life he always felt he was lagging behind in his creative development, because of the blacklist.

Absolutely. How did all those fellows from Europe do it, who went into the Hollywood system in the 1930s and 1940s and succeeded so marvelously? Guys like Billy Wilder, et cetera. It's very individual. I find that I did things in France that I wouldn't have done anywhere else. At the same time it's fucking terrible to be without the total, familiar, and profound knowledge of your own culture and your own past.

Why did you choose Paris instead of, for example, London?

I didn't want to speak English, for one thing. And I always had wanted to come to France because I had seen many French pictures, and I thought French motion pictures, at that time, were really a leading example of film-making.

Had you ever been to France before?

No.

Did you speak any French?

Not a word.

Did your choice have anything to do with the other people who came here, the community of other blacklistees who were waiting for you here when you arrived?

No. I didn't know who was here. I didn't know some of the people. I just wanted to come here and work here.

Did you have a falsified passport?

I actually had a passport in my possession, because I was going to come through Paris back when I was directing *Casbah*, on my way to Algeria. Initially they were going to let me research the film in Algeria. That's a true story that is wonderful. The producer was a guy named Erik Charell, a movie and theatrical producer and director, who had produced an enormously successful operetta called *White Horse Tavern*. Right after the war sometime, it was going to be revived in Paris. He wanted to swindle a trip for the Paris revival. So he insisted it was absolutely necessary to research authentic North African music for *Casbah*. It was total nonsense. He kept saying to me, "Wait until you see Paris!"

But I never went. Nat Goldstone, another one of the producers on the picture, kept telling me I could go. But two days before I left, Goldstone said that if I went he would pull the plug on the picture. He said, "I don't want to be left here alone." Charell went. I didn't.

When you left America, was your point of embarkation New York City?

[Pause.] I'm not sure I should answer that.

Why not?

I'm just not sure.

Did you travel by air or boat?

Are you serious? If I had been on a boat, I'd still be out on the ocean.

Were there other blacklisted people on the plane with you?

Nah. There were only nuns, who were sure the plane was going down. They were praying, and believe me, so was I. Nuns, doing their beads. Seventeen hours in the air, man. I thought the plane was going into the sea, and I remember thinking . . . it's interesting, I remember thinking at the time, "If we go down, they'll never figure out why I didn't get the subpoena!" [Laughs.]

When you got to Paris, what did you find? Camaraderie? Panic? False confidence? Did everybody realize what had happened? Or did people think the situation was temporary?

When I walked through French customs, I had this enormous lift. I was out!—I thought. I was living a big adventure. The only person I knew for sure, and the person I knew best, was Georgette Knox, Mickey Knox's wife. Mickey was an actor and a buddy of mine from New York, and a very good friend of Burt Lancaster's. Georgette and Mickey had separated, and she was living somewhere in the vicinity of Paris. I took the bus into Les Invalides. I walked all day, finally I came to a hotel, I can't remember its name. I walked in and took a room. "How long are you going to stay?" they asked. I didn't know—a couple of hours. I didn't know where Georgette Knox was, exactly, I only knew she lived in a small town outside Paris. I told them the name of the town, and they said they'd try to find her for me.

Next afternoon, it was raining. About four o'clock somebody knocked on the door. It was Georgette. She fell down laughing. She told me I was staying in a hotel for hookers. "That's just where you would wind up. . . ." The lady of the hotel had sent a pneumatic message to the post office of the small town: "If you know Georgette Knox, there's an American in Paris who is looking for her." That is how she found her. Georgette immediately took me to the Deux Magots Café, where Sartre and all the French intellectuals went. Revolving doors turned, and in walked Vladimir Pozner, a Hollywood screenwriter and refugee I knew, in a trenchcoat. He opened his arms and said, "I've been waiting for you to arrive." He immediately took me to Ben Barzman, Bernie Vorhaus, and John Weber. Those were three of the key Americans.

It was pretty astonishing what was happening already. Ben Barzman, Bernie

Vorhaus, and John Weber had a company, and eventually they made two pictures. That's pretty goddamn extraordinary—a director, a writer, and an agent from Hollywood making two movies in France. How? How did they manage to do it? I sometimes wonder.

Was there a feeling of solidarity among the blacklisted community, and how long did it last?

There was a profound, extremely rewarding, and secure connection among those people, among all of us, and it was something absolutely marvelous in terms of human relations. We could count on each other. If you were broke or in trouble, you always had someone to call up. If your personal life was stressful and you needed someone to share your grief, you had somebody day and night, man.

How many people did the American blacklisted community number, in Paris, at its peak?

At its peak? There were the people I mentioned, Michael Wilson, Paul Jarrico, [musician] Mischa Altman, Lee and Tammy Gold, ten or twelve who were well-known, and many, many others on the periphery.

How long did that solidarity last?

Its most intense period was for about the first three years. After that, it went in and out of phase. We had to make our lives here. We didn't need each other that much anymore. We started searching in other areas.

At first, the adventure was mind-blowing. The war had been over for five years. The French resistance movement was still carrying on. The Communist Party got thirty percent of the vote. The country was being rebuilt. The enthusiasms were enormous. The struggle to do and be and rise was constant. All the political struggles in the world were of a highly energetic level. You'd go to a *manifestation* for the Rosenbergs with a great sense of being together. There was that kind of solidarity in every area, and illusions in every area also.

Norma Barzman told me a story about meeting Picasso at a reception and Picasso embracing her and saying, "Now you are one of us."

I know Vladimir [Pozner] brought Picasso and Chaplin together for a meeting, and probably some of the Americans were there. I wasn't.

What was the reaction to the Americans among the French film community, specifically?

From my point of view, I can only tell you the French were just absolutely cordial, gracious, welcoming, enthusiastic. It was very fashionable to greet the refugee Americans. Of course you couldn't just fall into work. You had to go out and meet producers. It's curious, that, because I never analyzed what the feeling was in Hollywood when it was the other way around, when all of the

French, German, and other guys, escaping the repression in their countries, came over to America. I think they were welcomed, but it must have been very difficult. The same was true for us: we were welcomed, but it was also tough. Believe me, you couldn't get a job!

For a long time I worked closely with a group of people—Julie [Jules] Dassin, Ben, Norma, Tammy and Lee Gold, a few others—who had an ability to get around and meet producers who wanted some kind of bargain setup. In the beginning we did television series, one after another. Barzman, Gold, and I wrote all kinds of television scripts between 1951 and 1953—*Mr. Potter, Foreign Agent*, something about Orly Airport, some American series, some English. We would do anything, well, almost anything. I remember we all tried to get Julie Dassin to do a *Captain Valiant* series set in the desert, with us, and I remember him saying, "In spite of the fact that I am desperate, I can't do that."

How long did it take you to learn French and feel at home?

I'm still doing it.

Let me ask you about some of the French films you made during the time of the blacklist that have never been widely distributed in the United States. They're all but unknown here. Your first was C'est arrivé à Paris.

That was an English-French picture with Henri Vidal, Michèle Morgan's husband. I got the job through Ben Barzman. My name isn't on it. I had to take a pseudonym, one of my pseudonyms—I can't keep them straight.

I remember Louella Parsons came on the set to do an interview one day, and I had to hide in the men's room. I told the assistant to keep working as though he were the director. I went upstairs—it was in the train station of the Gare de Lyon—to the restaurant, which has a balcony. I stood in the balcony and watched them set things up and shoot without my being there. Jacques, my assistant, would sneak up and ask me, "What else? Good, no good?" Then they would shoot the scene again. All the time Louella was down there doing interviews on the set.

Did you know her? Would she even recognize you?

Sure, I knew her, but even if she wouldn't recognize me, in my head she would. In my head, the entire U.S. was looking for me.

Did it turn out to be a good picture?

No.

How about Ça va barder?

That's a takeoff and commentary on an American *series noir*, an American private-eye story with a French sense of humor and a real wink at the audience. There are wonderful stunts in it. If you really wanted to compare it to something, you would say it was, in its way, a precursor of the James Bond pictures, though it took itself much less seriously than even they did. It had a complete complicity with the audience and made fun of all the movie clichés of that time.

How did you get that job?

That's a great story about how I got that job. Julie Dassin's agent, Claude Briac, got Julie a job doing *Rififi*. Another job came up, and Claude brought me to a man who was doing a picture called *The Street of Painted Lips*. It was a story by Maurice Dekobra, a very popular pulp writer of mysteries here. This one was about an Englishman who marries a French girl, who he thinks has been unfaithful to him. In order to punish her, he sells her to a brothel in Algeria, where for one year or so she manages to maintain her chastity, until a group of French sailors come and this French journalist stands them all off and saves her.

I was in terrible financial and work need. However, after reading that, I said, "I can't do this piece of shit." The group that I have been talking about told me I had to do this picture. The agent said to me, "Just sign to do the picture. Write it any way you want. Who gives a damn what's in the book?" So I went to meet the producer. I got fifty thousand francs to sign the deal—at the time, that's maybe a hundred dollars—and was told by the producer, "You get more when you give me the first version [of the script]." I said, "Maybe I could sweep out the office with a broom up my ass, too, for a hundred bucks!" We managed to work out a bigger deal—a hundred a week for six weeks. And I had been earning seventeen hundred a week when I left Hollywood!

So I signed. In six weeks I wrote a totally different story. I had told the producer, "What do you like about this story? You like the whorehouse. Well, I'll give you the whorehouse." My assistant read the new story in French to the producer and his wife on a hot Sunday night in August. I remember they lived in a rather rundown hotel with that kind of ostentatious, totally false, rich look of no consequence whatsoever. We started reading at eight-thirty P.M.; by ten o'clock he was asleep, but his wife was absolutely enchanted. He woke up about eleven-thirty or twelve, just as we were reaching the end, and he said, "Clara?" She said, "Shh!" When we got through reading it, she said to her husband, "He has an extraordinary point of view about France in this picture. We should do it." He said, "We'll do the picture if you can get Gérard Philipe for the lead."

The picture was about as far from Gérard Philipe as *Rambo*. I said, "Gérard Philipe would never do this!" The producer said, "Then I don't see how we can do the picture." My assistant happened to know a buddy of Eddie Constantine's, and he spoke up, "There's an American here named Eddie Constantine who just had a successful picture. He would be perfect." The producer said, "Well, if you can get Eddie, okay."

Did you know Eddie?

I didn't know Eddie at all. I gave my assistant the script to give to Eddie, and Eddie liked it. In fact he postponed another picture he was going to do in order to do it. Once I had Eddie, I said to the producer, "Since my story has nothing to do with that other story, why don't we change the title?" We did, and it became *Ça va barder.*

Was Eddie Constantine in France for political reasons?

Are you serious? He was over here because his wife was a ballet dancer who wanted to take lessons here, and he himself was a failed chorus boy from New York. Have you ever seen him in anything? He's not a great actor. But he comes off the screen, man. When Eddie Constantine was first mentioned, I looked at the two Lemmy Caution movies they had made before—the one with him, and the one without. When I ran the one with him, I realized right away he didn't know what he was doing, but man, he really did come off the screen. Why? I think it was his terror. The guy really came off.

Was the film a surprise success?

I knew it was going to be a terrific movie, even while shooting it, but it became one of the biggest moneymakers of that year in France, a big, big hit. It made Eddie Constantine the top moneymaking movie star of that period. Of course it was never shown in the U.S.

The next one, *Je suis un sentimental,* was another big success, critically big and a big hit at the box office. That's a terrific movie, too.

Eddie again?

And how!

Your circumstances must have changed.

I had gone from nowhere to become a big established figure. I bought a house, signed contracts, ran around, and was able to take care of the kids.

Je suis was another original story by myself and Lee Gold, a melodrama, with dialogue by a guy named Jacques [J. L.] Bost, who was a Frenchman but a very important element of this group. His brother was Pierre Bost, a very well-known screenwriter. It's a marvelous, funny, rich movie, very skillfully made, about friendship and ambition—and of course we know what wins under those circumstances. About an editor who is having an affair with a woman who's found dead, but he's not the killer. His reporter buddy has to save him. What happens is that the publisher's son is really the murderer. . . .

This was also a success?

A big fucking success. I owned some percentage of it. I think I made, like, nine thousand bucks on the whole movie.

You had a bad deal?

No shit.

Did you have a bad agent, or did you always make bad deals?

Both. I think they go together. My whole life! After that, I signed a contract for what seemed a very good deal, a two-picture deal with Cyclops, a motion-picture-producing outfit. The only condition was that *Don Juan* had to be the first picture, for which they had signed Fernandel. They were going to pay me a fair amount of money just to sit and pick my second picture from those things that they were going to suggest, and I could turn any one of them down, etc., over a period of three years. It was a marvelous setup on the surface, and I signed for it.

I should never have signed the contract. *Don Juan* could have been marvelous. Juan [Antonio] Bardem had written the original script with a guy named Maurice Clavel, both very well-known figures. It was a wonderful, intellectual, philosophical treatment. But I didn't completely like their script and I got the following idea, which may have been in the original script in some form. If I could get Fernandel and [Vittorio] De Sica—De Sica as Don Juan and Fernandel as Sganarelle—it would be such a coup. And then I could rewrite the script so that Don Juan has grown tired, tired of women and of having to prove himself a great lover all the time. So he says to Sganarelle, "You be Don Juan, and I'll be Sganarelle." It was a marvelous idea, especially with De Sica and Fernandel.

So I rewrote the script [as *Don Juan/Pantaloons*] and brought it to Fernandel, and Fernandel said he was absolutely enchanted with the idea. Then what happened? We couldn't get De Sica. We ended up getting a guy to play Don Juan by the name of Erno Crisa—fortyish, nice fellow, charming, half-assed star from Italy. And instead of my saying, "Forget it; I'm not making the movie with Erno Crisa—"

—as you did once upon a time in America with Alan Ladd—

Exactly. See what I mean? Instead of doing that on this one, having learned my lesson from Alan Ladd, I said okay. Well, the movie didn't fall flat, but it wasn't there. It couldn't work that way, not without De Sica.

I was stupid because I was not sufficiently desirous of . . . what? The opportunism creeps in and you find yourself becoming the image of a Hollywood director and not enough of the artist you pretend to be. Yet there are reasons for these things happening, so I don't have to beat my breast.

Did Don Juan *turn out to be a success at the box office, at least?*

No, it was not any kind of success. Now, we come to *Tamango*, which was the second movie for Cyclops, and which, ironically, was a bigger hit in America than in France. *Tamango* made a fortune for its producer [Sig Shore], who later made the Superfly pictures.

It's from a Prosper Mérimée short story about a slave ship, and as far as I know there aren't many pictures about the slave trade. It's a good movie, an adventure-type movie, with slaves fighting for freedom; very expensive, with an international cast that includes Dorothy Dandridge, Curt Jurgens, and Jean Servais. I wrote the script with Tammy and Lee, and Georges Neveux, a French playwright who did the dialogue. The picture has some wonderful stuff in it.

That was the first picture of yours to be shown in the United States since the blacklist?

And how! One of the fuckups, however, was that it took so long to get distributed in America. Go back to 1959, and your mind is gone if you think black pictures were being distributed. They weren't. It was distributed maybe three years after it was made, and it became an enormous hit. It showed under my name, because the blacklist was no longer in existence. It crossed the line, becoming one of the first black pictures, historically, to get distributed by the major chains.

I had concentrated on the American version because I wanted the picture to go in America. I shot the scenes twice—in French and English. The French was hysterical—a week went by between each line—and so was the English. Both versions have their problems. When I interviewed the actors, they spoke perfect English; when I got them on the set, suddenly it went out the window. I picked the best acting without regard to the language; then I dubbed it where it was needed.

Eventually it made money for you?

It made a headache for me.

Why?

The French intellectuals kicked the shit out of that movie. First of all, because it was from a Mérimée story, then because it was very expensive to make; because I was an upstart American pissant—yes, maybe talented—but they kicked the shit out of the picture. It was a big success in the U.S., but it didn't go at all here.

It hurt your French career?

It fucking near killed it. Of course, if you talk about that picture today, they have a different memory of it.

After *Tamango*, I had to prove I could make less-expensive pictures, so I made one called *Oh que mambo! Oh que mambo!* had an all-star French cast, was made on a limited budget, and at the time seemed a hysterically funny movie. A comedy about an overweight cashier obsessed with eating who works in a bank. He gets accused of a holdup in which the only thing that is actually stolen is a salami—I won't go into the details. It was a very well-done film. But it was badly distributed, and consequently I was finished in motion pictures in France.

Why did one failure like that wash you up?

I was partially responsible, because I moved away from France and moved back to New York and to London for several years. I said, "Fuck all this madness," and returned to the theater. I did five plays in London, two or three of which were marvelous experiences. I did a Sartre play, *The Condemned of Altona.* I directed and starred in *The Secret of the World,* a play by Ted Allan—a big success. In the States I did several plays, including Athol Fugard's *Blood Knot. Blood Knot* got terrific notices, and that brought me to the attention of the King brothers. And it was the King brothers who came up with an offer to do another picture, *Maya.*

Did you know the King brothers?

I knew them from years before, from my early days in Hollywood. They had wanted me to direct something back in the 1940s. However, one of the requisites for making a movie with them was that you had to put up with the older brother, whose name was Maurie. Frank was maybe tolerable, but Maurie! Maurie said things to me like, "John, what happens if the actor don't know his lines? What would you do?" I'd answer, "I'd talk to him." He'd say, "If he don't know his lines after you talk to him, what are you going to do?" I'd say, "I'd talk to him again, Maurie." He'd say, "Suppose he don't wanna learn his lines?" By now I'd be bored and say, "I'd hit him with a left hook and knock him on his ass." So Maurie would say, "Hey, what do you want to be, a director or a fighter?"

Why had your attitude about the King brothers changed? Was it anything like the Alan Ladd dilemma—and you no longer cared if the producers wanted to cast Alan Ladd?

Worse. It was changed because they were going to put my name back on the screen in America and from Hollywood.

Had you made trips to Hollywood, trying to get a job?

Yes. I made a trip there in 1961, I think. When people saw me coming near an office, they vanished. Very few people, even old friends, would see me. They were still so frightened.

So you never had one of those inner-office conversations where they ask you to sign a loyalty oath or something.

No, and I'm so glad. I'm afraid of what I would have done.

You never even got close to a film job in America?

Nothing. But I was on a pretty hot road as a theater guy in New York. I was doing some very interesting stuff. I was making enough money to live on. I was meeting people, reestablishing my life. I was doing some prestigious television—*East Side, West Side*. Meanwhile, it was great to be back in New York, and for a while I almost forgot about Hollywood. Maybe it was a mistake to go back to Hollywood.

Did the King brothers have any politics?

As long as you worked cheap, they couldn't care less about politics. So I agreed to do *Maya*, and I had a great time making it. I really did a picture that caught some of the quality of India, in spite of the fact that the King brothers gave me a script that was nothing but a travelogue. I got a great idea, which was to make it the story of an American kid who runs away from home and a Hindu boy whose father on his deathbed has told him if he will lead a sacred white elephant across India to this certain temple he will find a great treasure.

Did the King brothers interfere with the filming?

No, Frank King was marvelous about that. Here's an interesting anecdote. I picked a shot and went off the set and came back, and the camera had been set up somewhere else. So I said to the cameraman, "Gunther, why did you move the camera? This is not a good shot." He said, "I think it's a good shot." I said, "Well, I don't give a fuck if you think it's a good shot; here is the shot I want." Frank was there, so Gunther appealed to Frank. Frank said, "If he wants you to put the camera up your ass, put it up your ass. Let's not discuss it."

The King brothers were fine during the filming. Unfortunately, they cut the film afterward. I know I directed a far superior picture to what it is. If I had cut the movie, the movie would have worked. Because that is not where my real concentration was; the myth of the movie would have worked. The exoticism of India, the spiritual life, the horror, is enough to blow your mind. I know I captured some of that. I'm desperate to make another picture in India. I have a great story in mind, and if anybody reads this and wants to back me, I'll tell them what it is. *Maya* turned out all right, it even became a television series, but it was as prestigious as an empty sack.

Then it was back to France for A tout casser/Breaking It Up, *another Eddie Constantine picture.*

Right. I had come back to Paris to work on a script. While I was here I got a phone call from a guy who was in trouble on this picture starring Eddie Constantine, asking me if I would help. I said okay. I rewrote the script. It had Eddie Constantine and Johnny Hallyday in it, and it was a lark. But the experience turned out to be another pain in the ass. The producer took over the cutting and reduced a marvelous story that in allegorical terms predicted 1968, the student rebellion—to horseshit. I took my name off the picture.

So the film didn't reestablish you in France.

Not only did it not reestablish me, I got screwed out of my writing credit and my name was off it as director. I ended up filing a lawsuit. To be quite honest, I didn't win the suit. In the end everybody accepted a no-decision on it, and they paid me off. Later, much later, my name was put back on [as director]. In spite of all that, *A tout casser* was a very successful picture, although I don't think it was all that good. I don't like it at all.

But it wasn't your cut—

—and I had another big success without my name on the screen. The story of my life! Anyway, by that time my aim was the States, and all I wanted to do was plays. I went ahead and directed a play called *Boesman and Lena*, by Athol Fugard, that maybe was for me one of the most striking, completely achieved theatrical productions that I've ever done. Then I did a play called *Les Blancs*, on which I was asked to fill in. It had such bad press that by the time it opened it was already dead. Then I directed a musical called *Dr. Jazz*, which was a flop and maybe I shouldn't have done it, but I had a great time. And I directed *Othello* with James Earl Jones in California.

You got back into American pictures in a big way with Claudine. *How did you end up directing that one?*

I knew [producer] Hannah [Weinstein] from Paris. Back in the 1950s she had gotten divorced and moved to Paris and was starting a new life here with her three daughters. She asked me to read *Claudine* and give her my opinion, and I read it and told her I thought it was great. They tried to get a black director, but I guess they couldn't, so she ended up asking me if I would do it.

Did you feel at all defensive about not being black? I know Marty Ritt was always on his guard about Sounder.

It was not an issue for me, because they tried to get a black director and they couldn't. Anyway, there are things about life I don't know, but that is not one of them.

Did the picture turn out the way you wanted it to?

Pretty damn much. I think that picture is a warm, wonderful movie of a certain kind. I really like it.

Bertrand [Tavernier] says that what happened to you after Claudine *is a primary indication of your career wrongheadedness. You had this tremendous commercial and critical success. Anybody else would have capitalized on it, while instead you went on to direct* Thieves *and* The Bad News Bears Go to Japan.

True, somebody else would have capitalized on it, but I got into a whole series of weird fuckups after *Claudine*. I stood around doing nothing for several months. I had an agent who was just a flat-out liar who kept telling me about all these marvelous offers that never came through. Where I did make a mistake was doing *Thieves*, although I was offered other pictures—one of them was *Lipstick*—at the same time. I did *Thieves* out of loyalty to the guy who wrote it, Herb Gardner, because I had promised him I would do it. I was involved with that crowd, and I did like the premise. I always had problems with the script, and I could have made the movie work if everybody involved hadn't turned out to be such putzes. No question about it, I was an idiot. Stupid.

What about The Bad News Bears?

By then I needed a job, man. The script was better at the point I took the job than what it turned out to be. And we lost one of the kids we had cast, a very talented one who played an aggressive kid constantly in trouble with the Japanese. He was key to the project.

The Bad News Bears? That's an indication of some kind of interior horror story on my part. At those moments of choice, when you're down to the absolute certainty that you'll never get to do another picture again, ever, and you're wondering, "How will I live next week?" and someone says, "How about *The Bad News Bears?*—what do you do? You have to be very clear and very strong. I'm not clear and not strong about those things, that's all, and as I said to you in the beginning, in the long run I have not been career crazy.

Let me ask you quickly about just a few more titles, again, films of yours made in France that barely made it across the Atlantic: Le voyage à Paimpol *in 1985?*

That's a movie I made with the woman I was terribly in love with, and to whom I was married [Myriam Boyer]. I made it for her and because of her. It's about a young woman who's tired of being committed in every direction without any return. It's a pretty good love story, and it broke even. It was made by my production company, and if the romance between myself and my wife had continued, things might have blossomed into something wonderful. They just didn't.

Il y a Maldonné *is the next one, in 1987.*

A police story, about two teenagers, which has to do with informing and the question, do you give your friend over to save your own ass? It should have been done in the States. I shifted the locale to France and put my stepson [Clovis Corneallac] in the lead. It was the second picture we made, to keep the company going. I wrote and directed it, and it's got some really good stuff in it. It works. It was totally overlooked for distribution.

Tell me about your last movie to date, A Captive in the Land.

Yes, the one I filmed in the Soviet Union. Ex–Soviet Union. At Cannes in 1991 it got a standing ovation, but when it opened in New York, it played only a month. The producers have never done anything with the picture to attract an audience. I think *A Captive in the Land* is a very good movie. It's based on a James Aldridge book, which Lee Gold and I adapted.

You keep mentioning Tammy and Lee Gold. I don't think they are very well-known outside of blacklisted circles. Did they have Hollywood credits before the blacklist?

Lee worked on one of Julie Dassin's first pictures [*The Affairs of Martha*] in Hollywood. His wife, Tamara Hovey or Tammy Gold, is the daughter of a big Hollywood screenwriter, Sonya Levien. Lee and Tammy were always part of the group, and Lee was very important, very dear to me. He was very creative. I think he was a helluva writer. I think he never really achieved what he should have—lots of reasons, besides any of his own. He died about four or five years ago, before *A Captive in the Land* was finished. I miss him.

Are any members of that original group still residing in Paris?

[*Long pause.*] No.

Are any Hollywood people from the blacklist era still living here?

[Longer pause.] Let me think. No, I don't think so. I guess I'm the last one.

Is it true that one of the things you'd like to do is a My Dinner with André type of pseudodocumentary about Dalton Trumbo and the last time you met with him? Can you tell me a little bit about it?

I'll tell it to you in very quick terms. I made a trip to Hollywood in— what?—1976. I was there because of some movie job or a play, I can't remember, and I saw in the newspapers that Dalton had left *Papillon* and had been brought back to Hollywood and was being operated on. Now, Dalton was someone I went way back with and had a very warm, competitive, admiring, critical, completely different-world relationship with. He was a Colorado boy, a baker's apprentice, and I was a New York street kid. He was a Swiss Calvinist; I'm a hot-livered Jewish boy. He was movies personified but someone I really had a big admiration for. Trumbo enjoyed Hollywood. With all the bullshit, Trumbo enjoyed it—the living, the fighting, the winning.

My relationship to Dalton was similar in some ways to my relationship to Welles. He was another spiritual father. Dalton was someone to be with, man. There aren't a lot of people like that. You could really spend time with Doc— we called him Doc. There was heat, intellectual challenge, fun. We were very close, his other friends were [screenwriters] Michael Wilson, Hugo Butler, and Ian [McLellan] Hunter. We always got together when I was in Hollywood and when he was in Paris. When I found out he was on a very rough final trip, I called Cleo [his wife] and asked to see him. She said he was not seeing anybody. I said, "I know that. I just want you to say to him that I'm here and that I do want to see him, if he would find some pleasure in it." She told me to hold on, came back to the phone, and said, "He wants you to come at one o'clock tomorrow afternoon."

I showed up the next day at his extraordinary house, built on a hillside— Ives Avenue—where I had come frequently in the past. I walked in and went down the stairs, which were lined with all these photos of renowned people: his professional life, laid out before you. Cleo said he'd be right out. I stood in his marvelous garden, thinking how terrible it was that this poor bastard was going, and wondering how I would react when I saw him in a terrible, feeble condition.

The garden doors burst open and this guy in a black jumpsuit bustled out, bursting with energy, and he said to me, "How are you, you old shit?" His voice was raspy. He said, "You've got to excuse my voice—it's a little gone— and you've got to excuse my taking so many breaths because they took one of my fucking lungs away from me. But the painkillers are better than fucking marijuana, John! It's the best high you can be on, especially since I won't be around here very much longer." I said, "C'mon, Dalton, you'll live longer than I will." He looked me in the eyes and said, "I hope so, you sucker!" That was the opening.

We then spent from one o'clock to six—five hours—in his garden, in which we reexamined issues, the past, shared experiences between us. Dalton was an enormous absorber of good booze, and that was the one concession of my visit, that I would drink with him as we talked.

We talked about politics and the blacklist and the relationships. We talked about Mike Wilson, who was his close friend and mine; he was so close to Mike that he and Mike could collaborate by phone. Michael was an extremely gifted and serious screenwriter, while most of the guys who wrote screenplays in Hollywood were merely flying about. (Dalton said a funny thing about Mike. "The great thing about Mike," he said, "is that the pauses cost more than the conversation," which is true. If you ever said to Mike, "How are you?" he'd think about it before replying. He'd want to be entirely honest about the answer.)

We talked about the King brothers, who gave me my first picture after the blacklist. I thought the King brothers were vulgar shits. Dalton said to me, "Whatever they were, it was Frank King, whom I was fond of, who kept me alive and kept me working. He exploited me, but he was an interesting, funny man." We talked about scripts of mine that he had never responded to. One in particular bothered me. He admitted, "Maybe it was not quite proper of me not to read it."

We talked about society in general. He said the thing I didn't understand was that our society was a "money society." "You never really understood that," he said. "You have other naive horseshit ideas. If you're going to be here [in Hollywood], you have to be part of the money society."

He was writing his last book, and he said he only hoped that he would live until he finished it. He figured he had until August, which was why he wasn't seeing anybody. And would I like to hear part of it? Then he read me a chapter of the book, after which we stood up and took a leak in the garden. I remember him saying, "My father always said you were successful if you could piss in your own backyard."

He was noble, Doc was, writing in the bathtub, taking his pills, not seeing anybody. He said, "You know, I'm seventy-two, John, and I have no fear of dying. I have no belief in anything after. My life has been pretty goddamn good. I've done what I wanted, most of the time. I've achieved things. I've got a family I'm very grateful to have. Why should it go on forever?"

It was quite an afternoon. And as the sun was fading, the family gathered, including his son [Christopher], who had worked with me on the film I made for the King brothers; they gathered and watched us. We never came to a meeting of the minds, but that was of no importance because it was those differences that helped form our relationship.

Afterward, I thought about the experience and decided this would make a marvelous documentary. I told Dalton, "It would be important to have you on film so that a record will exist for others." He said, "Great idea. Half the money goes to me, because I've got to leave some money for Cleo." I said, "That's fine." He said, "I've got a great opening. The opening is the first picture I ever made, *A Man to Remember*, which begins with a funeral. Then you cut to my funeral, and we have the six doctors I paid a fortune to as pallbearers; otherwise I won't pay their bills."

I ran around Hollywood trying to get two cameras for me and Dalton. I couldn't raise fifteen thousand bucks. Maybe I didn't try hard enough, but there was a time limit, and in Hollywood they thought I was nuts. I came to France and talked to some more people, but no luck. Dalton died. It was a terrific loss.

Bertrand [Tavernier] and Pierre [Rissient] are after me to turn it into a script. I've written some of it. I still want to make that picture. Fucking A.

Alvah Bessie

ALVAH BESSIE, Los Angeles, California, 1983

INTERVIEW BY PATRICK McGILLIGAN
AND KEN MATE

ALVAH BESSIE
(1904–1985)

1943 *Northern Pursuit.* Coscript.
1944 *The Very Thought of You.* Coscript.
1945 *Hotel Berlin.* Coscript.
 Objective, Burma! Story.

1948 *Smart Woman.* Coscript.
1968 *España otra vez.* Actor, script.
1973 *Executive Action.* Uncredited contribution.
1985 *Hard Traveling.* Novel basis.

■

THE ONLY ONE of the Hollywood Ten to have served as a volunteer in the International Brigades in the Spanish Civil War (Ring Lardner Jr.'s brother James died there), Alvah Bessie probably had the least professional investment in Hollywood. A novelist and journalist, he joined the film industry late, in 1942, and worked as a scriptwriter for only five years before the blacklist hit. Nonetheless, he managed to compile some solid credits, including contributions to *Northern Pursuit, Objective, Burma!* (for which his original story was Oscar-nominated), and *Hotel Berlin*. His jailing in 1950 terminated his Hollywood career.

His books include *Men in Battle: A Story of Americans in Spain*, a memoir of his experiences as a member of the Abraham Lincoln Brigade; *Inquisition in Eden*, one of the best firsthand accounts of the blacklist; and the novels *Bread and a Stone*, about a decent man who commits murder (which his son Dan Bessie filmed as *Hard Traveling*), *The Un-Americans*, about a McCarthy-era perjury trial, *The Symbol*, about a haunted Hollywood sex symbol, and *One for My Baby*, covering his post-blacklist tenure as stage manager at San Francisco's the Hungry "i" nightclub.

■

Can you tell us a little bit about your class and family background?

I was born into a middle-class Jewish family in New York City in 1904, which was an awful long time ago. My father was an admirer of Cecil Rhodes, the great imperialist after whom he named me. My middle name is Cecil, which I've never used since I became aware of who Cecil Rhodes was and of his role in Africa. My father had been sent to law school in Ann Arbor, Michigan, but he never practiced law. He got a job with the American Tobacco Company tacking up signs—Bull Durham signs—on the walls of barns in Harlem, which was then mostly countryside in the 1880s and early 90s. Later he went into the soap business and sold soap. Later still, he invented a paper box, which made him quite well-to-do, a paper box covered with paraffin, in which they sold butter, lard, kidneys, liver, and tripe.

At any rate, this invention brought him lots of money until automatic packaging came in. He was a good, hard-ribbed Republican, completely sold on the free-enterprise system. He always wore a stiff collar and stiff shirts. He had some very strange ideas. He made my brother and me take ice-cold baths in the morning by running the bathtub full of ice-cold water. We had to get into the bath for five solid minutes. This was to harden us and to dim the passions of adolescent boys.

He wanted you to be a lawyer?

He wanted me to be a lawyer. I wanted to be a doctor. But I started writing when I was nine years old, and I kept right on writing.

When he died in 1921, I was seventeen. He had warned my mother, whom he had taught to play poker and to play the horse races, *not* to play poker or the horse races. He told her, "They will call you up from Wall Street, as soon as I die, telling you how sorry they are . . . and they will offer you tips on the market. Remember, now you will have two boys to bring up all alone. Hang up the phone." Well, within one day after he died they began calling, and she took all these tips on the market and promptly began to lose all the money that he had left her—which wasn't very much—with the exception of his life insurance. The reason he didn't have very much is that the week before he died he took a tip from a younger man who told him to take everything he had and put it into cotton futures. So he did. On Wednesday he had five hundred thousand dollars on paper, on Thursday he had seven hundred and fifty thousand on paper, and on Friday the bottom fell out of the cotton-futures markets. That night at three o'clock in the morning he woke us up and said, "I'm dying."

Why did you decide to become a writer?

As a boy I was mad about animals and natural history, because at a camp in Maine where I had been sent by my parents there was a marvelous counselor who was a Mohawk Indian. He used to take us out at night and build campfires and go off into the darkness and scare the hell out of us by pretending to be a mountain lion or owl. He got me interested in reading about natural history, and I first read the works of a guy who turned out to be one of these nature fakirs by the name of Ernest Thompson Seton, who made all of his animals human beings. He was probably my first literary hero.

Then I got interested in Jack London, and this was probably my first personal hero, both as a person and as a writer. When I was in public school, there were even Jack London Clubs, in which all members, boys and girls, pledged themselves not to go to any theater or circus where they had trained animal acts—which was an extremely difficult thing to do, because I loved trained animal acts. We pledged to get up and walk out and demand our money back and protest the use of trained animals, because Jack London said they were trained with methods of cruelty, not kindness. I read all of Jack London, and after that, when I got to college, people like Melville, Tolstoy, Dostoyevsky.

Already, by the age of nine, I had started to write. My first short story was called "The Wreck of the 999," which must have been an unconscious plagiarism from [the song] "Casey Jones." I'm afraid I've been a writer all my life, which is not a very safe occupation for anybody. I've done odd jobs as a writer of all kinds, including working on newspapers in New York and Paris and San Francisco. But I never made it big in any way; making money on one book out of nine or ten in a lifetime is not very impressive.

Radicalism is often a passion of youth. When were you radicalized?

In the early thirties. There was the Great Depression, I was living in Brooklyn, and I was out of work. I had married a lady who became the mother of my two sons, and she was working in a bookstore in Oyster Bay, while I was working in New York at various odd jobs. The odd jobs ran out, and we saw an advertisement in the paper, saying, "Wanted, a couple for a summer home in Vermont." So we went to Maplewood, New Jersey, I think it was, to meet a couple named Mr. and Mrs. Wilfred Falks. He was an architect, I believe. They had a summer home in Vermont and wanted a couple to take care of it for them; they were particularly delighted at the idea of a college-bred couple. They had a small child, and I was also engaged to teach the small child to swim.

This couple ferried us up there, including our furniture, and my wife became the cook and housekeeper while I became a gofer and sort of all-around handyman who was supposed to play chess with the visitors who came up over the weekend to drink bootleg whiskey. We were supposed to get our board and room and ten dollars a month, but they forgot to pay the ten dollars per month. At the end of the summer, the job was over, and we had to decide what to do. We couldn't stay in their house, but we could rent an empty house and live on a small piece of land in the same town for ten dollars a month, which was possible to do then.

That's what we did, and I put in a garden. I began corresponding with New York to get book reviews from the *Saturday Review of Literature*. I got a ride down to New York and called on the editor of *Scribner's*, who had bought one of my stories, a man by the name of Kyle Crichton.* Kyle Crichton was a major influence in my life because he encouraged me to write, got my stories published in *Scribner's*, and sent me books to review every single month. He would even send up packages of food because he knew what was going on in my life, and he would visit us in the summertime.

We had a very rough time in Vermont, but we did produce two children. We went there in 1931, and in 1935 I got a Guggenheim fellowship. I had been writing a novel, and I submitted this novel every year for three years in a further-advanced state of completion, and finally I got a contract for it. And when I got the contract they gave me a straight fellowship for two thousand

---

*Kyle Crichton was the most popular literary humorist on the left from the 1920s through the 1940s. Using the pen name Robert Forsythe, he was known for his columns in the *New Masses* and the *Daily Worker*, and for several collections, notably *Redder Than the Rose*. During the same period, writing as Kyle Crichton, he was an editor and columnist at *Scribner's Magazine*, *Collier's Weekly*, and other mainstream publications. After his political career, he published a book about the Marx Brothers and an autobiography, *Instant Recoil*.

dollars. I had met another guy who lived over in a different part of Vermont and who invited us to live on his property, so we went and lived there for peanuts. At the end of the fellowship I reapplied, naturally, and didn't get it again. I had met a man who was on the *Brooklyn Eagle*—he had a house in Vermont—who said, "Why don't you come down and help me on the *Brooklyn Eagle?*" This was the depths of the Depression, my fellowship was going to run out at the end of 1935, so I took a job as his assistant editor on two magazine sections of the *Brooklyn Eagle*. Then we moved from Vermont to Connecticut.

What was it about the experience in Vermont that radicalized you?

The Depression was one thing; Kyle Crichton was another. He sent me all kinds of Communist literature. He came up and argued with me. He sent me one of his books. He was probably the best satirist the left ever had. You can still find his books around, in second-hand bookstores.

At one point I went to work for some of the local farmers in order to get food. There was a farmer by the name of Richardson who had ten children and was way ahead of his time. He had put in a McCormick potato-digging machine and chemical fertilizer, which none of the other farmers used, and he got a tremendous crop of potatoes. I worked for him, taking it out in trade of potatoes—picking the potatoes and putting them in bags after the digger had dug them up. After several weeks, along came the A&P truck, and the A&P man said, "Mr. Richardson, you've got a great crop of potatoes. We'll give you twenty-two cents a bushel for them." He said, "What!? Why, I'd rather let them rot in the cellar than sell them for that. That won't even pay for my fertilizer, let alone my potato-digger." The man said, "Sorry, that's the price." So they did rot in his cellar until spring, when he began giving them away to anybody who wanted them. And the next summer he planted just enough potatoes for his family of ten children, his wife, and himself. What do you suppose happened? The A&P truck came along and offered him fifty cents a bushel. This struck me as very strange. I couldn't understand it. There were certainly not any more people demanding potatoes, nor any less, and certainly no scarcity of potatoes. What controlled the price of these darn things? I wrote my friend Crichton, and he said, "You don't read very well, do you? You must know by now that the so-called law of supply and demand applies only in certain instances. The market is rich. Didn't your capitalist father tell you that the man who is selling things to the public charges what the market will bear? If the market won't bear it, they'll lower the price. But these prices are artificial."

At any rate, I got convinced. I even got so convinced as to vote for [Communist Party candidates Earl] Browder and [James] Ford in the presidential campaign that year [1932] in Vermont. We were the only two people in that town who voted for them. People at the town meeting thought, "Who the hell are these people? There must be Communists here in town!"

Were you a Communist at that point?

No, we just voted for Browder and Ford. Anyhow, after Vermont, when I came down to work on the *Brooklyn Eagle*, I joined the Newspaper Guild. On the *Brooklyn Eagle* and in the Newspaper Guild was a marvelous police reporter named Nat Einhorn who began propagandizing me.* He suggested I should come to a Communist Party meeting and listen. The war in Spain had started. A very interesting situation arose, because I figured we ought to have in our magazine section an article about what the hell this war was all about. I was getting agitated about it from watching the newsreels and reading the articles and seeing the pictures of dead babies on the streets of Madrid. I went to the editor and said, "Don't you think we should have an article on this war?" He said sure. I said, "There's a girl by the name of Anita Brenner† who wrote an article for the *New York Times* a couple of weeks back, and maybe I could get her." He said, "Get her." So I got her, and she wrote the article, and two days later along came a gentleman named Father Edward Curran who had an organization in Brooklyn called the International Catholic Truth Society, with an article attacking her as a Communist. He brought the article to the editor and publisher of the paper, who was then Preston Goodfellow, and Goodfellow brought it to me and put it on my desk, saying, "Print this." When I read it, my eyes popped out and my hair stood up, what hair I had. It was the most incredible piece of crap you ever read in your life.

But I printed it, and then I went to Goodfellow and said, "Don't you think that Miss Brenner should have a chance to answer this man? After all, he has attacked her as a Communist. I happen to know she is not a Communist. I know her. I've met her many times. And I'm not an authority on Spain, but I could point out dozens of historical errors in this article." He said, "Yes, get her to write an answering article." So she did, and two days later in comes Father Edward Curran for a second time with an article four times as long as the first one. [Laughs.] And four times as ridiculous.

So I printed it, and again I went to Mr. Goodfellow and said, "I'd like to have Miss Brenner answer this one too." And he said, "All right, you can have Miss Brenner answer it, and that will be the end of the controversy. There will be nothing further published in the editorial pages or in the magazine section about this conflict, except in the news stories that will come from Spain." So that was it for Father Curran.

Father Curran had a whole group of young Catholic virgins going around

---

*Nat Einhorn was a founder and executive secretary of the Newspaper Guild's New York local and a leader of the Guild strike against the *Brooklyn Eagle* in 1938. In the 1960s he became a writer for the *Medical Tribune* and was noted for his articles on the role of African-Americans in medicine.

†Anita Brenner, well-known as a journalist from the 1930s through the 1950s, devoted most of her post-Spain years to Latin American reportage and translations from Spanish.

Brooklyn shaking cans for money for Franco. Really. And if you gave them money, they would give you a sealed envelope. I gave them a quarter in order to find out what was in the sealed envelope. There were a series of propaganda photos, horror pictures of atrocities allegedly caused by the Reds. I took them up to our photoengraving department and said, "What do you think of these pictures?" A guy looked at them for me and said, "Well, these are all foreign, made abroad." I said, "How do you know?" He said, "I can tell by the process that this is a German photoengraving job." I said, "German?!" He said yes and showed me some just like it. He showed me a picture of a naked woman lying on the grass, which was supposed to be a raped nun. He said, "There's one thing you might not have noticed—the sun is shining on this body from the right, but the shadow of the body is on the right. This whole photo was retouched in order to bring out the breasts and the hips and the thighs. But it is a very stupid retouching. If they had done the opposite side of the body, it would have been just as effective."

This was all part of the process of my joining the Communist Party. Then André Malraux came to New York, and I asked to go and interview him. Ralph Bates [a famed novelist of the 1930s who was one of the best-known British literati to fight in Spain] came to New York, and I went to interview him too. And then a guy came in from an organization called the Spanish Information Bureau, which was a propaganda organ of the Spanish Republican Government that was set up in New York City. He had found out I was sympathetic, and he asked me, "How would you like to come and work for me?" He offered to pay me more money than the *Brooklyn Eagle* did, too.

The *Brooklyn Eagle* strike also helped confirm the direction in which I was moving. Preston Goodfellow decided he would buy a Brooklyn paper called the *Brooklyn Times-Union*, which was a rival newspaper. But he also decided that he would not hire the staff of the *Brooklyn Times-Union*. Why should he? He had a staff. His idea was to put out both newspapers with the same staff. We called him in and told him, "If you intend to do this, we will go on strike, because we don't see any reason why we should put out two newspapers." He called a meeting in the city room and made a speech at which he cried, actually, real tears. He said, "If you boys and girls go out on strike, none of us will have a job, because I can't afford to hire these people from the *Brooklyn Times-Union*, so I will fold up this newspaper." Believe it or not, he said, "I thought this was one big happy family," a line from the movies. At any rate, we went out on strike, and he didn't go out of business. He took over the whole staff of the *Brooklyn Times-Union* and made more money than ever, and then sold both newspapers to somebody else.

By this time I had left the *Eagle* and gone to work for the Spanish Information Bureau, issuing releases and distributing photographs from Spain to all the newspapers and magazines, writing pamphlets and leaflets when Guernica was destroyed. After doing this for about six or seven months, I decided, "To hell with this. This is slumming. I want to get involved in this cause."

My marriage had broken up by this time, through circumstances having nothing whatsoever to do with politics. I was mad about flying and learning to fly; I was able to afford to take one lesson a week out of Floyd Bennett Field in Brooklyn. Out there I had met a famous test pilot by the name of Lee Gehlbach who had finished up the job for Jimmy Collins after Collins was killed.* Collins was the only famous test pilot who ever joined the Communist Party; he wrote a book called *Test Pilot*. Collins was testing the low-wing Grumman Fighter one day when the wings came off and he went into the ground with it. Gehlbach took the next one up and dived the wings off it also, but he came home, as he put it, "in his parachute."

Gehlbach came to my place for dinner one night and stayed for three weeks. He was a big drinker, when he wasn't testing flying planes. I'd go to work and come back home and he'd be lying on the couch. Finally one day my wife said, "I've fallen in love with this man." After a while he left, and I left too, to move into a hotel room. Gehlbach came to see me because I had talked to him about our writing a book together and in fact had gotten a contract from Modern Age Books. He said, "I think you should go back to your wife." I said, "Well, thanks." He said, "Look, women get very strange about men who fly airplanes. You've noticed that out at Floyd Bennett, haven't you? There are girls hanging around there who'll go to bed with any guy who can fly any kind of airplane." I said, "Yes, but that's not the kind of wife I have." He said, "No, but I am not in love with her, and I have told her so. I'm not seeing her anymore. I think you should go back. You have two kids." I said, "Thanks for the advice." But I didn't. Instead, I went to Spain. That was the end of that marriage.

You were a Communist by this point, right? Why did you join the Party?

Why? I was intellectually convinced that it was the right thing to do, and I thought—as any number of people thought—that this was the only organization that was actually fighting Fascism in the world, that was actually fighting unemployment, racial discrimination, national chauvinism. I believed it was, and I had evidence that it was, and God knows that during the Depression was the time when the Party reached its largest influence—it had close to one hundred thousand members, and many more than that with so-

---

*Jimmy Collins, "one of the most enigmatic aviators of his time," according to Richard P. Hallion in *Test Pilots: The Frontiersmen of Flight* was an Army Air Service classmate of Charles Lindbergh's who drifted into Communism and test-piloting. He also wrote as a reporter and developed a book, called *Test Pilot*, consisting largely of his columns. He died during publicized high-speed dive tests for the Grumman XF3 F-1 in March 1935. "The death of this popular and well-known airman shocked New Yorkers and became national news," wrote Hallion. Collins's autobiography, *I Am Dead*, was published posthumously and reviewed favorably by William Faulkner.

In May 1935 Grumman pilot Lee Gehlbach resumed trials on a later XF3 F-1 model and had to bail out during spin demonstrations. The third version of the new military aircraft finally passed spinning trials, and the F3F fighters were approved; they served the Navy fleet from 1937 to 1943.

called fellow travelers and sympathizers. It wasn't until later that it began to be obvious that the Party was not speaking the language of the American people. It took me almost twenty years to find this out. Now, this is pretty stupid of me, but though I was very deeply involved in the Party I never assumed any kind of leadership position beyond educational director of a group or being on a section committee. I had no qualities of leadership, not even in the war in Spain, although I got to be a sergeant adjutant, which is the rank that my grandfather held in the American Civil War. At any rate, I think joining the Party was the right thing to do at that time . . . for me.

Why did you make the decision to go to Spain?

I didn't go to Spain because the Communist Party told me to, although they were recruiting. I had almost made up my mind that I wanted to go even before they asked. In my particular group, some seven people signed up, and I was the only one who turned up to go. They had found other reasons to stay, or their families had dissuaded them. But I was a free agent at that point.

Why did Spain mean so much to you?

I wrote a whole damn book about it called *Men in Battle*, and I don't know how I could summarize things in a sentence except that I was very hot about the cause. I was very emotionally overwrought. I did not go under any illusion that this was an adventure of any kind. I had a very good idea what a war was about—although I'd never been in one, I had a very good idea—and I felt I would like to be involved in this war because it was probably the most important thing happening in the world at that time. There's even a book title that says it: *The Last Pure Cause*. It was a pure cause. It was easily recognized as such; a survey on the subject, taken by the League of American Writers, polled all the writers in the United States with any kind of name at all, and only one prominent writer declared she was on the side of Franco and Fascism . . . spelling it "fashism." She was Gertrude Atherton, an ancient lady who wrote romantic novels. Everybody was on the side of the Spanish Republic.

But you went to the lengths of actually heading off to fight.

I decided to fight, yes. I was thirty-three years old, and I wanted to be involved in something more important than my own reputation. All my life I had been, I suppose you would say, an egocentric person who was promoting himself as a writer and a personality. I didn't want to go as a writer, though I was advised by people like Kyle Crichton to get a job as a correspondent. I told him, "I don't want to write. I want to be involved in this fight." He said, "Good-bye. I'll weep for you." I said, "No you won't, because I'm one of these people who have charmed lives." I was determined to contribute what little I had as a soldier to the fight. I suppose you could say it was some kind of a death wish. Maybe there was such an impulse. I was unhappy. I had walked out of my marriage. And I could have repaired the marriage, because the night I left the lady said to me, "He is not in love with me. I am in love with him, but I will get over it. You have two children. You don't have to leave." But I had said no thank you and left.

What was your experience in the war like?

I refer you to the book I wrote. I can't easily describe it. It was an insane experience.

It was one of your proudest acts?

There are two things in my life that I'm particularly proud of. I'm proud of having been involved in the Spanish Civil War and making at least a respectable record for myself as a soldier. I didn't run away, although I was probably faster on my feet than most people. And I was ten years older than most of the guys there. I'm proud of that and of the fight that developed in Hollywood around HUAC.

How did you eventually get to Hollywood?

How did I get to Hollywood? I had always wanted to go to Hollywood to write movies, because I was fascinated by movies. Always have been. My friend Kyle Crichton knew an agent in Hollywood whom he personally engaged to get me there. He sent this guy all the short stories I had written for him, as well as my first novel [*Dwell in the Wilderness*]. And the excuse he got from Hollywood was, "This is a highbrow writer. We have no use for this kind of writer here." This was before I went to Spain.

Up to Spain I had been a respectable writer who regularly got into the best short-story collections of the year and could sell to any magazine that I sent things to. After I came back, I couldn't get a job on a newspaper, I couldn't get a job anywhere, I couldn't sell anything to a respectable magazine. It had to be a left-wing magazine. This made a complete switch in my life. It switched me right into the left-wing press. I had already switched myself by joining the Party, but being a Communist was not an issue in my career at first. It didn't become an issue until I came back from Spain, when the immediate identification as far as the media was concerned was that I was a red. After that, the agent in Hollywood began writing to my friend Kyle Crichton saying, "I can't get this guy a job now because he's a red writer."

Interestingly enough, on the boat back I had met this newspaperman with a press tag in his hat like they used to wear in the old days. He told me he was from the *New York World* and that his managing editor wanted to meet me. I said, "What does he want to meet me about?" He said, "He wants a series of articles about Spain." I said, "Great! I'm back in business." He said, "Tell you what you do. You write one article about how you guys got over the mountains over there . . . then give him a list of five or six more topics to choose from, because that's what he's looking for."

So I went to see the managing editor with the first article, and he sat reading it. He said, "It's great. Wonderful. But it's not exactly the kind of thing I'm looking for." I said, "Well, what are you looking for?" "Oh," he said. "You know. The romance, the drama—beautiful girls in their lace mantillas." I said, "In the first place, there was no romance and there was no glamour. I don't recommend the war to anybody for any reason whatsoever unless you have to fight, which we felt we did. And as far as lace mantillas are concerned, I never saw a girl in a lace mantilla. I never even saw a lace mantilla. They didn't display them in the shop windows of Barcelona at the time." He said, "I'm sorry. That's the kind of thing I would like." So I didn't get back into the newspaper business.

But I had met in Spain the editor of the *New Masses*, Joe North,* and I was able to get on the *New Masses*. They needed a drama critic. I told Joe, "I'm not a drama critic," and Joe said, "Well, you were in the New York theater for several years as an actor." I said, "I was in the New York theater for several years as a small-time actor, which is the reason I'm not in the theater anymore. It finally dawned on me that I would never be a great actor, and naturally I wouldn't want to be anything less than a great actor." He said, "Do you want to be anything less than a great writer?" I said, "This conflict I resolved a long time ago. I decided I would never write anything as great as *War and Peace*."

Lo and behold, along came World War II, and either all the writers in Hollywood were drafted or they joined the Army or they were serving in the motion-picture division of the military. Suddenly came an offer from Hollywood. In the winter of 1942, when I was in bed with the flu, the telephone rang and a voice said, "Is this Alvah Bessie?" I said yes. He said, "Well, I'm Jake Wilk of Warner Brothers. Do you want to come to Hollywood to write movies?" I said, "Don't give me any of that shit," and hung up. Well, it *was* Mr. Wilk [a longtime Warner Brothers executive], and he called back and said, "When can you come in and see me?" I said, "I'm sick in bed." He said, "When you're not sick, come in and see me." So when I got well I went in to see him. I asked, "What is wanted of me? I don't know anything about moving pictures, though I love them and have always wanted to work in them." He said, "Warner Brothers wants you for a contract." I said, "A contract?" "Yeah," he said, "they're offering you a hundred dollars a week." I said, "Why don't you speak to my agent?" By chance I had picked up an agent the night before who happened to be at a theater where I was reviewing a play for the *New Masses*. He said, "I don't want to talk to your agent. They want you, and you don't need an agent." I said, "I'm sorry, Mr. Wilk, but I would prefer that you talk to my agent." He said all right and got in touch with my agent.

So I went to have lunch with my agent and he said, "It just so happens

---

*Joseph North, well-known as a hardliner, was an editor of the *New Masses* in the 1930s and editor-in-chief for a time in the 1940s. He was the brother of Hollywood composer Alex North.

that Jack Warner is in New York right now, and I'll call him up." He called him up and got Mrs. Warner on the phone, and she said, "Why don't you come and talk with Jack? We'll be at the Stork Club tonight." He went and met Jack Warner there and said to him, "I don't understand your man Wilk offering my man Bessie only a hundred dollars a week. Bessie doesn't have to come to work for you for a hundred dollars a week. He has his own radio program. He has a best-selling novel coming out. He's going on a nationwide speaking tour. He has a home in the country. Why does he have to go to work for you for a hundred dollars a week?" Warner said, "Well, I don't know that I want him anyhow. I understand he's a red." So the agent, who, believe me, was not only one of the most reactionary men I've ever met in my life but practically a Fascist, a Southern Fascist at that, said, "Warner, you make me sick. Sick! Those goddamn reds are saving your fucking moving-picture business on the Stalingrad front tonight." And Warner said, "You're right! I'll give him three hundred dollars a week." That's how I got to Hollywood.

The last thing that was said to me by Mr. Wilk when he had me sign a contract for three hundred dollars a week was, "You don't belong to any organizations that you shouldn't belong to, do you?" I said, "What do you mean? I belong to the Newspaper Guild, and when I get to Hollywood I will join the Screen Writers Guild." He said to his secretary, "Put that down." The whole issue of politics never arose in Hollywood after that until the subpoenas came. It certainly never arose with any of the producing people or directors I was involved with. Except that I know Jerry Wald, the producer I went to work for, liked to hire people who he believed were reds. He told me why. He said, "Usually they are awfully bright, usually they are very good writers, and usually they know a lot more about people and what motivates people than the average guy does. That is why," he told me, "I wanted you to work on John Bright's play *Brooklyn, U.S.A.*"

First, tell us about meeting [Communist Party head] Earl Browder on the train coming out to Hollywood.

[Laughs.] That was funny. I had never met him, but naturally I had heard him speak many times at mass meetings. When I saw him in the dining car, I went over and introduced myself to him, since I'd been writing for the *New Masses* since 1939. He said, "I'm glad to meet you. I enjoy your reviews in the *New Masses*. So you're going to Hollywood . . . to set it on fire." I said, "I don't know whether I'll set it on fire. I don't know anything about the medium, but they've given me a job." In the course of the conversation I raised some questions with him. I was finding it very difficult to agree with certain ideas that he and the Party were putting out—that there could be such a thing as "progressive capitalism" and that it would be possible to have a peaceful transition from capitalism to Socialism in the United States. I said, "I can't envisage a situation whereby the capitalists of this country would say, 'Okay, boys, we can't run it anymore; you do it,' and quietly steal away." He said, "Can't you really, Alvah? Can't you really?" I said, "No, I can't . . . *really*." This was the only conversation I ever had with him. He was coming to Los Angeles to speak at a mass meeting along the same lines.

You had a similar conversation later on with John Howard Lawson.

I think it was, as a matter of fact, at the mass meeting where Browder spoke, at the Shrine Auditorium in downtown Los Angeles. I went with Jack Lawson because he had a car and I didn't, and riding back in the car with him I said, "I don't get this. I don't see a situation in which the boys who run this country just say, 'Okay, boys, we can't run it anymore, you do it.' I don't believe in that." And Jack said, "Don't you really, Alvah? Don't you really?"

Did you know John Howard Lawson from the time when you were knocking around in the theater in New York?

When I lived in the basement of a building on Patchin Place in the Village, Jack had an apartment upstairs. Also, I was an extra and a small-part player in one of his plays, called *Processional*, and rehearsed in another one of his plays, called *Loud Speaker*, which I never opened in because I was playing a butler, and they needed me to dance a tango with the young mistress of the house, and I couldn't tango. They hired a guy to teach me to do the tango, and it turned out he did it so much better than me that they hired him to play the butler; his name was Leonard Sillman, and he later became a big producer both on Broadway and in Hollywood.

I didn't know Lawson too well, but I impressed him and the director of *Processional*, even though I was only an extra. There is a scene in which the Jewish protagonist of the play gets caught by the Ku Klux Klan and is intimidated by them—the character was played by Philip Loeb, who incidentally was one of the suicides as a result of HUAC. The Theatre Guild director of this play, Philip Moeller, wanted the Klan to come onstage in some unusual way, and by accident I was in the front of the line. So I took a running leap in my costume and landed halfway across the stage, looking this way and that. Philip Moeller said, "That's great! How did you do that?" I said, "Eighteen years old. Genius." That didn't sit very well with him, but he said, "Keep it in, and all the rest of you, do the same." Nobody else could leap half as far. [Laughs.] They got all tangled up in their robes. My arrival invariably got a laugh from the audience, which was the whole idea, to make fun of the damn Klan.

Anyhow, I didn't really get to know Jack until I arrived in Hollywood many years later, because it was in the 1920s that I was in those plays. In fact, Jack was the very first person to take me to lunch when I arrived in Hollywood at Warner Brothers.

What kind of advice did he give you?

He said, as I recall distinctly, "You can do good work here, if you understand the limitations of this medium in this particular system." This is the exact opposite of what was told to me by the first man they teamed me with on the first script I worked on, the play by John Bright called *Brooklyn, U.S.A.*, which never got made. The first man was a writer whom I had practically discovered when I was on the *Brooklyn Eagle*, by the name of Daniel Fuchs—a very good writer. I had written the first big reviews he ever got, as a matter of fact. Lo and behold, when I arrived in Hollywood, Daniel Fuchs came into my office and introduced himself and said, "You and I are due up at Jerry Wald's office—the producer. I want to tell you this: Everything that you are given here will be shit. And you cannot make anything out of it except shit. That is all you can do with it. But," he said, "if you play your cards right, you can be on top of this heap in a year, making big money. Big money." I said, "Are you making big money?" He said, "Biggest money I ever made in my life." I said, "But you don't write well?" He said, "You can't write well. They won't let you write well." Well, he was right. He was right. It was enormously frustrating. But Jack Lawson was famous for being a real optimist, as far as the possibilities of doing good work in Hollywood were concerned.

When William Z. Foster* came out one time, there was a Party section meeting with him, and I remember something he said, which I thought was absolutely right on the nose. He said, "The best you guys and girls can do here in this industry is what I would call, in military terms, 'a holding action.' You can't really do very good work in this industry because they won't let you. But you can prevent them, if you know how to do it, from making really anti-black, anti-woman, anti-foreign-born, anti-foreign-country pictures. You can prevent them from making anti-human pictures, and that is a very worthy thing to be doing. You can also make straight entertainment in which no important issues are involved. This can be done very easily." I thought that was about as good a summation as I had ever heard of what the situation of Communist writers was vis-à-vis the motion picture industry.

Brooklyn, U.S.A., then, was, the first project you worked on.

I read the script on the train going to Hollywood and thought, "What the hell can I do with this? It's wonderful." So when I went up to the first story conference with Wald and Fuchs, and Wald asked, "What do you think of the script?" I said, "I think it's great." Fuchs kicked me in the ankle, and I looked at him. Wald said, "Yes, this play is great, but we want it brought up to date. There's a war on now, and we want you to bring in the fact that

---

*William Z. Foster, a regional leader of the Industrial Workers of the World and a founder of the rival Syndicalist League of North America, emerged into the spotlight as a leading organizer of the national steel strike in 1919. Two years later, Foster joined the Communist Party. An uncritical supporter of Stalin's policies, Foster remained a Communist leader for the rest of his life, temporarily eclipsed by his rival Earl Browder during the 1930s and during wartime, the Party's peak years of influence.

there's sabotage on the waterfront." When we left, Fuchs said to me, "Don't ever say a thing like that again. You were brought here to rewrite this thing. You don't tell a producer that a story he wants rewritten is great." I said, "Well, I think it's wonderful. I wouldn't know what to do with it." He said, "I'll show you how to handle it. No matter how good it is, you say, 'It stinks. I have a better way to do it.'"

Anyhow, we worked on it for a while; then Fuchs was transferred or something, and Wald put a young Italian American writer on the project by the name of Jo Pagano.

What psychological adjustments did you have to make to Hollywood?

I didn't have to make any psychological adjustments. I loved it. I loved the damn medium. I thought I could do something good there, even though Daniel Fuchs had told me I couldn't do any good. I was teamed with some guys who knew the operations pretty well, and I was fascinated by the whole technical end. The thing I discovered very rapidly, as every writer who goes there discovers, is that technically the craftsmen are marvelous. The people who do the sets, the people who do the costuming, even the research department—they come up with the most marvelous stuff.

For one picture I got onto, called *Northern Pursuit*, with Errol Flynn, they built a mine. Now this mine had several galleries, and went down fifty or sixty feet. It was a full-size mine with full-size beams—oaken beams that were weathered and wet and had moisture crawling down the walls and huge spiderwebs up in the corners with what looked like genuine spiders in them. I'm sure that if they had needed a spider in a scene they would have created one that could climb down. At any rate, I went through this set with the producer, and I said, "My God, what do we need this huge mine for?" He poked me in the ribs and said, "You know how much this costs?" I said, "No, how much does it cost?" He said, "It cost seventy thousand dollars to build this set." I said, "What are you going to do with it all? It's much too big. We have only one scene in here, in which Flynn drops from the rafters onto one of the Nazis." He said, "You'll write some more scenes." So I did.

Were you at all frustrated by the artificiality of stories?

Oh sure, sure. You got frustrated, and you got angry. I told you a lie when I said I didn't have to make any adjustments. Apparently, I did have to make some kind of accommodations. Within six months, I had developed pains in the belly. I couldn't eat, I couldn't sleep, I couldn't drink a bowl of soup without feeling full up to here. I went to a doctor, and every doctor he referred me to. One of the doctors laid me on a table and said, "Give me your hand." He put my hand on my stomach. I said, "My God, what's that?" He said, "That's your large intestine . . . that's your colon." I said, "It feels like a hard rubber hose." He said, "Yeah. You have a spastic colon. If you want to have ruptured ulcers pretty soon, just keep on the way you're going." I said, "What do you mean?" He said, "How do you like your job?" I said, "I love the job, but it's frustrating." He said, "You came here from a job paying you thirty dollars a week on the *New Masses* to a job paying you three hundred dollars a week. And what has happened recently? Have you gotten a screen credit yet?" I said no. He said, "You know, of course, that at the end of the first six months they will drop your option if you haven't got a screen credit." I said, "Yes, I've been told that." He said, "You're going to have to decide, unless you want to have hemorrhaging ulcers like your father, that you don't care whether you stay here at three hundred dollars a week or have to go back to the *New Masses* at thirty dollars a week. You're now on a layoff period because you're feeling ill, so take some time to decide." I said, "That's easier said than done, isn't it?" He said yes. So I returned after a week or two of layoff, and then I went back to my first conference with Jerry Wald.

Wald came up to me. He was always saying, "I've got a great idea . . . I've got the greatest idea . . . now listen to this! Blah, blah, blah." Usually I would argue with him. I would say, "No, that's stupid," fighting him on every god-damn stupid idea he came up with. This time he came forth with one of his ideas and asked, "What do you think of it?" I said, "I'll think about it." After I'd done this three times, he said, "What's the matter with you? When you first came here, you were hot as a pistol. You fought with me—I like that. Now you say, 'I'll think about it.' What is this with you?" I said, "I'll think about it." I've never had a spastic colon since then.

Is it true that there was a gradation between A writers and B writers in Hollywood, and that these distinctions also held true in the Party?

Yes, because the writers who earned five hundred dollars a week didn't associate with the two-hundred-dollars-a-week writers, and the one-thousand-dollars-a-week writers didn't associate with the five-hundred-dollars-a-week writers . . . to my knowledge. I know I didn't socialize with people like Dalton Trumbo and Ring Lardner Jr. I remember going to Dalton's house because we were both on the board of a magazine published in New York called *Mainstream*—first it was called *Masses and Mainstream*, then it became *Mainstream*, and after that it became *American Dialogue*. That was the first time I had occasion to meet him. And it wasn't until the subpoenas arrived that I met Ring, you know. I had more contact, for example, with Albert Maltz, who was making more than I did—he was making five hundred dollars, and I was making four hundred dollars—but I was more in his class. He came to Warners to work on a submarine picture, I remember, and we were very friendly. It wasn't until really after we were all out of jail that Dalton and I and the others became much closer friends.

Tell us about your role in the controversy behind closed doors involving Albert Maltz and the Hollywood section of the Party.

Albert wrote an article called "What Shall We Ask of Writers?" in which he objected to the strict criticism the Party made of writers for not following the line and promoting the interests of the Party in the way it felt the Party should be promoted. There was a meeting that was very hostile to Albert, and I myself attacked Albert.

I don't know how or why I ever objected to his article, because when I had been on the *New Masses* and was sent to review plays, on occasion they would send what I called a "Seeing Eye dog" with me to be sure that I felt the right thing about a play that they wanted certain things said about. One time I went to see Lillian Hellman's play *Watch on the Rhine*. I raised some criticisms of this play, but suddenly I found [writer] Ruth McKenney and her husband in the lobby asking me, "What do you think of the play?" When I started telling them what I thought of the play, they said, "Oh no, you're wrong about this and that . . . and so forth and whatnot . . ." One of my criticisms was that Lillian Hellman never identified the underground worker in her play. What was he? I said in my review that the man was obviously a Communist, because they were the kind of people working against Hitler in the particular period she was writing about. Why didn't she identify him as a Communist? I felt it was opportunistic of her. I felt it would have been accepted. They didn't object to that criticism, but they objected to others. I remember having a meeting with Joe North in which I argued, "I think we in the Party are the only people who can afford to tell the truth about anything, because we have a better understanding of what makes the world tick."

Yet you ended up attacking Albert.

I attacked Albert. I said, "We need more Party writers, and we need more writers who are more closely identified, not less closely identified, with the Party." Now, much later, I decided Albert was right and I was wrong—of course—and I told him so. He got treated very badly. But he also did something bad himself. This is the point at which he should have pulled out entirely, instead of criticizing himself and saying, "I was wrong."

It sounds as though it was a very brutal affair that broke everybody's spirit, even though the Party line was adhered to.

I don't know whether that's true. I don't remember anybody's spirit being broken. I remember feeling that he certainly was wrong at that time, and later I began thinking it over and thinking he was right. But we were trying to build a movement in a very difficult place, where it was almost impossible to build such a movement. It was very difficult to hold on to people even who were sympathetic. They were always finding reasons to move out. Whether the Party should promote and tolerate that kind of dissent became a disruptive issue. At least that's what was felt, and I at that time agreed with the criticism of Albert. I now do not agree with it at all. Albert was right and we were wrong, and if you want to go in for such a thing as poetic justice, this is one of the reasons why the Party has never made any headway in the United States since the Depression—because it does not know how to speak to the American people.

What the Party wanted of writers was that they should understand the forces which are operating in a society. Now, it is possible, obviously, to understand the forces operating in a society, without subscribing to Marxism-Leninism. And Balzac, as far as Lenin was concerned, was the proof of it, because Lenin pointed out that Balzac was a royalist, a convinced royalist—so much so that he even tried to make himself royalty by adding a 'de' to his name which he wasn't entitled to. Nevertheless, Lenin said he learned more about the French economy and society and the forces operating in that society from Balzac's fiction than he ever learned from all of the endless financial and agricultural reports that he subjected himself to in trying to understand the French system. If this is true, this means that Albert was right. One of the points Albert made is that there is no necessary connection between a writer and his politics. What he meant was: A writer shouldn't have to have a programmatic attitude toward any political system in order to understand the system in which he himself is operating.

Did conflicts and rivalries undermine the Party internally in Hollywood, before HUAC came to town?

I don't think so. It was a pretty cohesive organization. Mr. J. Parnell Thomas [chairman of HUAC] was correct in that there was a strong Party organization in Hollywood; there must have been two or three hundred people in the talent and crafts section alone, not counting the backlots and so forth. But they didn't stand up too well once the blacklist hit. People began avoiding each other, people began crossing the street when they saw you—people with whom you had associated for years.

The issue of Communism and the whole damn HUAC was a fraud from beginning to end. I was one of the people who at the first meeting of lawyers said, "Let's say, 'Yes, we are Communists,' and what business is it of yours?" The lawyers said, "Well, that isn't the point, Alvah. You can do that if you want. But then the next question will be, 'All right, what about so-and-so?'" That was the issue on which they chose to fight. We were choosing to fight on the issue of "What right do you have to ask questions which the Constitution and the Bill of Rights say are excluded?" The Committee would never answer this point. They said, "That's not the issue," and the courts held that that wasn't the issue, and the Supreme Court wouldn't hear the case, thereby upholding our conviction. The courts said the issue was "Were you subpoenaed, did you appear, did they ask certain questions, and did you refuse to answer them?" That was automatically contempt of Congress.

Your partner in jail was Herbert Biberman. Tell us about him.

[Laughs.] Well, I first knew Herbert Biberman in New York when we were both in the Theatre Guild play *Faust* by Mr. Goethe. His wife—I don't know whether he was married to [actress] Gale [Sondergaard] at the time or not—was the Queen of the Witches in the Walpurgisnacht scene, and I thought she was gorgeous. I knew I didn't stand a chance with her because she was attached to him. At any rate, I didn't like him in those days, on sight. He was always a pompous ass, and we used to say in Hollywood, "Herbert is a pain in the ass, but he is our pain in the ass."

But Herbert—as I said in my book [*Inquisition in Eden*]—would die in pieces for what he believed in. The man was enormously self-sacrificing. He went out on a limb. He did a great job of organizing the whole defense of the Ten, up until we all went to jail. Then I had the misfortune of being in the same jail with him. This experience began in Washington, when we left handcuffed to each other in the backseat of a car driven by a Texas marshal and a detective, all the way from Washington to Texarkana, Texas, where they deposited us on the way in two different prisons, one in Virginia and one in Nashville, Tennessee. We were sitting in the backseat, and Herbert, all the way from Washington to Texas [laughs] gave a lecture to the two gentlemen in the front seat about what our case was all about, what the American Civil War was all about, what the Russian Civil War was all about, and what the Russian Revolution, the American Revolution, and the French Revolution were all about. I was lying in the back just trying to go to sleep. Every once in a while the guys in the front seat would say, "Hey, Bessie, how you doin'?" and I'd open my eyes and say, "I'm alive," and try to go back to sleep.

Herbert always wore Édouard Pinaud's Lilac Végétal as an aftershave lotion. My father did, too. I therefore disliked the odor of it immensely. Anyway, we got to prison and we got booked in. At least fifty Mexican wetbacks were being booked in the same night. The place was always full of them, because they preferred to be arrested in the United States rather than live in Mexico, where they couldn't make a living for their families. We came up before a prisoner who was taking down information onto a typewriter and who asked us our name, address, age, religion. I said, "None." When Herbert came up, they asked him the question. He stood up straighter than he usually stood up—as straight as a soldier; he was in the National Guard in California—and said, "I am a Jew!" and sat down again. I thought, "Oh, Christ!" because I have never practiced the religion, my mother never practiced the religion, and my father never practiced the religion. The next day we both got Hebrew Bibles in our prison cells.

When we two got into quarantine, we had a lot of opportunity to talk. We had nothing else to do: you're not allowed to work when you're in quarantine, you sit in a different place in the dining room, and although you're allowed to go out for exercise, you exercise with other quarantined people. At one point, Herbert said to me, "You know, I think you behaved very badly on the way here from Washington." I said, "What do you mean?" He said, "You refused to talk to the two officers who were bringing us here." I said, "I refused to talk to them? Every time they asked me a question, I answered it." He said, "You'd lie in the backseat and when they'd ask, 'How are you, Bessie?' you'd say, 'I'm alive.' " I said, "Look, Herbert, in my opinion, on this trip I was in the hands of the enemy, and my only obligation was to be a gentleman and say 'Yes, sir,' 'No, sir,' and 'Thank you, sir.' When they asked me a question, I answered it." He said, "Well, you disgust me. You revolt me." I said, "In what way?" He said, "Look at you now. You're standing against the wall of the cell here, leaning against it. You don't even stand up straight." I said, "I never was in the National Guard, but I was in the war in Spain. We didn't stand up straight there either. We were the worst soldiers who existed from that standpoint. The Germans were very good at standing up straight. Anyhow, I'm very glad that I repel you, being in this situation."

Anyhow, Herbert and I didn't get along very well. We were both assigned to the same warehouse. He was made a worker; he was very big and strong and good at piling stuff onto the shelves and taking stuff down. I was made the clerk of the warehouse, with a typewriter, filling out endless bills of lading and receiving reports. They allowed me to use the typewriter for my own purposes, until it was confiscated by the chief guard and I had to go to the warden to get it back. I was writing a book of poems, bad poems. The men who ran this warehouse came to me one day when Herbert was sick and didn't come to work. They said, "Why aren't you like Mr. Biberman?" I said, "What do you mean?" They said, "He is the finest gentleman we have ever met in this institution. When he comes here in the morning, he says, 'Good morning, Mr. So-and-so.' And when he leaves in the afternoon, he says, 'Good afternoon, Mr. So-and-so.' " I said, "You want me to say that?" They said, "No, but why aren't you like him?" I said, "Because I'm not like him."

We had many contretemps. Once, when we were sitting outside in the yard, he said to me, "Alvah, I hate to say this, but the men in this institution hate you." I said, "They do? This is news to me." He said, "Alvah, they despise you. They loathe you." I said, "Don't be dramatic. What have I done? I am under the impression that I get along very well with everybody here." He said, "They complain to me. They say, 'What is the matter with your fellow fall guy? You ask him a question and he says, yeah, no, or uh-uh.' " I said, "Well, I'm a grouch. You know that. Why didn't you tell them I'm a grouch?" But I got so upset by this that I talked to a guy in the next cell to Herbert, who was a doctor. He was there for selling heroin, the most intelligent man in the prison at that time, except for us. [Laughs.] I told him this, and that it upset me. He said, "Alvah, the person the men hate is Herbert." I said, "Why?" He said, "He condescends to them. When we come back from the movies, he holds meetings out in the hall of the cellblock, asking, 'Well, fellas, how did you like the movie?' And if they don't like it, he explains to them why they should like it or why they are right to like it. He comes down a flight of steps to talk to people."

Anyhow, Herbert was a man of principle and a man of great courage, a man of enormous integrity and imagination, who worked day and night for months and for three years before we went to jail, organizing money and support and traveling all over the place making magnificent speeches. He was a great extemporaneous speaker.

I want to tell you one more story about Herbert. He and Edward Dmytryk were tried before a judge who took a much less important view of the case and who gave them six months and a five-hundred-dollar fine, instead of a year and a thousand. And he was let out at the end of five months for good behavior. We sat in the yard together on the day he was going to leave to take a bus into Dallas and fly home. He said to me, "Alvah, if there were any way I could do half of the rest of your sentence, I would like to do it, but I asked and I couldn't." I said, "Who did you ask?" He said, "The parole officer." I said, "Did you, really?" He said yes. I said, "Well, I thank you. I believe you would." So I ended up liking Herbert, basically. I think all of the Ten came to care a great deal about each other.

What were your physical circumstances when you got out of jail?

There were two of us who didn't have a dime when we went to jail, and that was Sam Ornitz and me. Sam hadn't been employed for years, and I had run out of whatever I had, so much so that I wasn't able to pay any of the expenses that many of the other guys were able to do. But there was a committee to support the two of us, which provided my wife and daughters with a stipend to live on and with the rent.

When did you quit the Party, and why?

After I got out of prison I went back into the Party. I couldn't get any job in Los Angeles of any kind, so I moved up to San Francisco. That was in 1951, and I remained in the Party most of the time that I worked for the ILWU [International Longshoremen's and Warehousemen's Union, led by Harry Bridges]. But gradually I began attending fewer and fewer meetings, and when they asked me what the hell was the matter with me that I didn't come to meetings, I said, "I think I'm ready to drop out of this organization." You don't really resign, you just drop out—or you take a large advertisement in the *New York Times* denouncing yourself, like Elia Kazan and all of the great spirits like that. I just dropped out. I think it must have been 1954 or 55. I didn't feel the organization was making any headway in our country.

We know that you worked backstage at the Hungry "i" for a while.

After the ILWU job folded up because they had to reduce the international staff, I went looking for work and ran into a guy named Lou Gottlieb, who was a bass player for a group then called the Gateway Singers.* I said, "Do you know anybody in the public-relations business in this town who would hire a character like me?" He said, "Come down to the club." So I went down and met [comedy monologist] Irwin Corey. Irwin Corey got me a job there, running the lights, which I'd never done in my life but I learned. And it would have been an ideal job for a writer, because you work from eight or nine o'clock at night until one or two in the morning, then sleep till noon and work in the afternoon—except it paid such a bad salary. I was there for

---

*The Gateway Singers were a Weavers-like folk group who achieved some prominence and also performed left-wing benefits. When the group petered out in the late 1950s, a more successful folk group, the Limelighters, was formed by some of the same musicians.

seven and a half years, and rose from eighty-five dollars a week to one hundred and five dollars. And I had alimony and child support to pay at that time.

It was a good place, and an inexpensive place for people to go who didn't have large sums of money. I got to know Lenny Bruce there. He asked me to read a couple of screenplays that he'd written and offered to pay me if I could make them better than they were. I accepted, and he gave me three screenplays. I thought they were fairly interesting, and I rewrote all three of them, but they never sold. He had an agent working on them down in Hollywood, but they weren't good enough to sell, really. But this guy was an unmitigated genius and a marvelous human being. I loved Lenny.

Why did you never return to Hollywood?

I never returned because there was no way of making a living there. I did return in various peculiar fashions. My oldest son, who has been making small pictures for years in Hollywood, got a job with a company called Wakeford-Orloff, Inc. They got very rich making television commercials and decided they'd like to go into feature films. Dan worked with them doing animation for their commercials, and when they took an option on a novel—a very good novel—he talked them into hiring me under my own name to write the screenplay. This was about 1961 or 1962. It never got made, which is a long story, but after some years Wakeford-Orloff got involved in making one of the last pictures Trumbo ever wrote, when he was very ill, called *Executive Action*. They needed a quick rewrite and brought me down to do a rewrite for a week.

Do you have any regrets about having gone to Hollywood in the first place?

No, no. As I said, I enjoyed working in the medium. I've always liked actors and theatrical people, and, with notable exceptions, I get along well with them. I probably am a ham actor myself. And I think Hollywood was a very important part of my education as a human being.

Allen Boretz

ALLEN BORETZ, Los Angeles, California, 1983

INTERVIEW BY PATRICK MCGILLIGAN AND KEN MATE

ALLEN BORETZ
(1900–1986)

1938 *Room Service.* Play basis.
Trouble for Two. Additional dialogue.
1942 *Step Lively.* Musical remake of *Room Service.*
It Ain't Hay. Coscript.
1944 *Bathing Beauty.* Coscript.
Up in Arms. Costory, coscript.

1945 *The Princess and the Pirate.* Coadaptation.
1947 *Copacabana.* Coscript.
It Had to Be You. Costory.
Where There's Life. Coscript.
1948 *My Girl Tisa.* Script.
Two Guys from Texas. Coscript.
1949 *The Girl from Jones Beach.* Story.
1961 *El Cid.* Uncredited contribution.

■

ALLEN BORETZ WAS one of the people in Hollywood who were labeled as Communists by screenwriter Martin Berkeley, who set a record among informers by coming up with 155 names in his House Un-American Activities Committee testimony.

Boretz was well-known on Broadway as the coauthor (with his friend John Murray) of the farce *Room Service*, which was a smash hit in 1937 and then permanently entered the repertoire of stage groups around the world, making him a wealthy man several times over. Boretz had little to do with the 1938 film version starring the Marx Brothers, which, he always insisted, bore scant resemblance to the play. However, one of his friends among what he called Hollywood's "Social Democratic" circle was Groucho Marx, with whom Boretz, who joined the film-industry branch of the Communist Party in the mid-1930s, had long-running political arguments.

In Hollywood, mostly at MGM and later at Twentieth Century–Fox, Boretz was the proverbial jokesmith and script doctor, content with the paycheck, the creative challenges, and the frivolous fun. He anonymously brightened many a dreary musical comedy with a risqué punch line or clever scene; indeed, on more than a few occasions, he deliberately left his name off the final draft, enjoying his private trump of the front office's power over credits. Apart from vehicles for the Marx Brothers and Abbott and Costello, Boretz also had the distinction—dubious, he'd hasten to add—of providing the screen story for a 1949 comedy, *The Girl from Jones Beach*, starring Ronald Reagan. It was Boretz's last formal screen credit before the blacklist.

Boretz sailed through life. About the only thing he seemed to take seriously was his political beliefs, although he could also be hilarious on that subject. Once blacklisted, he returned to work in the theater, and later joined the ever-shifting group of Hollywood refugees in Spain. A few weeks before his death, in 1986, he was on the phone from his hospital bed, calling friends with the nonstop patter and asides that had always made people hold their sides from laughter.

■

My name is Allen Boretz. I was born August 31, 1900. The first contact I had with Hollywood was in either 1934 or 1935. At that time I was rather a hot boy on Broadway. I had three plays sold, all of them scheduled for production.

One of them was *Room Service*, which has since become a classic; another was called *School Teacher*, which got wonderfully reviewed in Provincetown, Massachusetts, at the theater where Eugene O'Neill used to have his work shown; and the third was a play called *As the Twig*, which was under option, and the director of it was going to be a young fellow by the name of Garson Kanin.

At this time, Irving Thalberg, who was the majordomo under Louis B. Mayer at MGM, came to Broadway looking for writers. They were always looking for what they called "fresh writers," and they signed me along with four other people. One of them was a fellow called Dick [Richard] Maibaum, then there was Gladys Hurlbut, and the names of the other two don't come to me at this moment.* I got offered the highest salary of all because of my prestige on Broadway—five hundred dollars a week, which in 1934 was a lot of money. For instance, I could rent a duplex apartment on Malcolm Avenue in Westwood for only thirty-seven fifty per month, furnished, and I was able to buy a suit downtown for twenty-two dollars, and a pair of Regal shoes for six. I used to walk around in those days with a wad of money in my pocket, enough to choke a horse, because I didn't want to put it in banks. So that was the beginning of my Hollywood career.

Tell us about the beginning of your political career. How did you become radicalized?

I became radicalized because, after a youth of indifference as to who ruled the country or why, I fell in—through the fact that I played the violin—with a couple of violinists, and one of them was a man called Harvey Gardiner whose parents were dentists—both dentists and both Socialists. I used to go to visit Harvey frequently because we were very close friends; we played duets together. From him and his parents I first heard this kind of Socialist talk, and I began to ask questions about politics. I really began to think seriously about what was going on in this country.

Even as a child one of the things that people in my family called me was "the *meshugena filosof*," which, translated from Yiddish, means "the crazy philosopher." After I developed my sense of injustice, I would expound on it to the point of boredom. I began to hear, of course, about Hitler and the Jews and the changes in Europe, and I began to be fearful of what was going to happen in the world. But I made no move to do anything about my feelings, until one time I went down to Cuba with Max Liebman, who later on became the majordomo of *Your Show of Shows* for a number of years and really changed the face of television. We went to Cuba because we were writing a play together, and we needed some atmosphere.

While we were in Cuba, a German pocket battleship came into the harbor. I don't know if you remember what a pocket battleship was, but after the First

---

*The other two "fresh writers" were Emmett Lavery and Everett Freeman.

World War Germany was not allowed to build huge battleships. So with their ingenuity they built ships with great firepower but of smaller stature and smaller girth, and this was one of them. Anyway, this pocket battleship of Hitler's came into the harbor on a visit, to show the flag, as it were. Of course, Havana then was not the Havana of today. It was under Batista's regime; it was a Fascist country, a haven for gangsters and gamblers, and whores prominent all over the place. It was really the pleasure land for American tourists. But when the crew and the trainees came off this pocket battleship to march down the Prado, there were demonstrations by radicalized Cubans throwing garbage off the roofs; there were catcalls and various kinds of derogatory noises.

This troop of trainees—there must have been three or four hundred of them—were glorious men. They were bronzed. They wore white uniforms. They were tall and blond. They looked like gods coming out of Valhalla. Nobody could defeat people like this. They looked purposeful, dedicated to death. It was a phrase that came into my mind, that they were dedicated to death. They were terribly impressive.

At the same time I had a terrible hatred of what they were doing to the Jews. They marched down the Prado without turning to look at anything, paying no attention to the garbage or the catcalls, just going their course until they finally came to a café which had a girl band in it playing sentimental waltzes. And they sat themselves down in this cafe. Max and I had followed them, Max rather timidly, I must admit—but I was so engrossed with my feelings that I didn't realize I might be getting myself into a somewhat dangerous situation. Anyway, I went into this café and sat down right next to a group of these Nazi youngsters around the table—they couldn't have been more than nineteen years old—and I began to speak Yiddish loudly. [He shouts Yiddish phrases.] Well, Yiddish is almost like German. I'm sure they understood some of it. I watched them very carefully to see what effect I would have on them. They didn't move. Nothing. They didn't blink an eyelash, as though I didn't exist.

When I came back to America, I said to myself, "I've got to do something about these people, because they look invincible. The nation has to be aroused. People have to understand the danger we're in." I looked up a friend of mine in Hollywood, a press agent who was radically inclined, Manny Eisenberg. I told Manny I wanted to get involved. He said, "Come with me, because we are studying Marxism in a group. You want to learn about things? This is the place to go." So I went with him.

I want to emphasize that it was a Marxist study group. These were not yet Communists, if they ever did become Communists. One of the men stood in a corner and said very little. His name was Dashiell Hammett. There was Philip Loeb, an actor who had appeared in *Room Service*. There was a man called Harry Kurnitz, who later on became a mystery writer and a big shot at MGM, a great wit—so-called wit—in Hollywood. There was an agent,

George Willner. Jack [John Howard] Lawson was there. John Bright was there, and his partner, Bob Tasker. And Arthur Kober.*

I remember the difficulties that Kober was having losing his background. He and Manny and I used to leave the meetings together, and he'd be in the middle between Manny and myself as we were walking along, saying, "I can't get it through my head. I don't understand it. Now, tell me again, what is Marxism?" He would really try to understand it, but he had no heart for it, and he had no mind for it. He was just a man who was married to the middle class—a social climber.

This was my introduction to Marx. Later on, of course, when the crunch came and I had to shit or get off the pot—I say that advisedly—I decided that I had to join the Party. Because it made no sense just sitting around in rooms and listening to a lot of talk about Marxism and what it meant, what I call "the physics of economy." So I became a member of the Communist Party.

What is great about your life story is that, perhaps because you wrote comedy, you seemed to move freely and be accepted in all kinds of political circles. We know you were often a script doctor in Hollywood and sometimes, ironically, a script doctor for the most right-wing writers and producers.

At MGM I was assigned to help out many dying or sick scripts, some of which had been on the agenda for a great many years. I was being trained to be a producer by Larry [Lawrence] Weingarten, and one of the first people I was assigned to help out on a script, which was called "Remember When"†— it had been on the hot stove for many years and hadn't been licked yet—was Harry Ruskin. Harry Ruskin was a right-wing little man who had happened to write one song, which for some reason or other became popular, called "I May Be Wrong, But I Think You're Wonderful."‡ When I walked in to greet him he regarded me with great suspicion because I had never hidden the fact that I was a man who was rather radical, to say the least. He was worried about me because he thought I was going to take his bread and butter away from him. The first thing I said to him was, "Harry, I'm not here to get a credit. I don't want a credit. Too many people have worked on this script. Besides, that's not my function now. My function is to help you out of the

---

*Novelist and screenwriter Dashiell Hammett (along with three others) would be jailed in 1951 for refusing to reveal the names of contributors to a bail fund for eleven Communist Party leaders convicted under the Smith Act. He served five months. Richard Layman, *Shadow Man: The Life of Dashiell Hammett*, traces his political development, literary career, and personal life.

Stefan Kanfer, in *A Journal of the Plague Years*, tells how actor Philip Loeb was hounded to suicide in 1955.

Satirist, playwright, and screenwriter Arthur Kober was married to playwright and screenwriter Lillian Hellman from 1925 to 1932. Her thirty-year relationship with Dashiell Hammett began in 1931.

†Possibly this was the comedy made into a film as *Remember?* in 1939, about a married couple who suffer amnesia and fall in love all over again.

‡From the 1929 Broadway revue *John Murray Anderson's Almanac*.

woods with this thing. I assure you, and I'll even put it in writing for you if you want me to, I do not want any credit on this picture." Well, he had never heard a Hollywood writer talk like that to him before. So I became kind of friendly with him.

In that office there was a lot of right-wing talk swirling around like a conspiracy. I hate to use the word "conspiracy"; it really wasn't a conspiracy. It was an attitude, a kind of unspoken diktat that they would all follow the rules that had been handed down by a man called James K. McGuinness, who was the real guru of the right-wing movement in Hollywood. He was a brilliant man, a man who could sell anything. As a salesman he was better than Reagan. Anyway, one of his diktats was, "Do not glorify the common man." Anytime there was a situation concerning "the common man" in a picture of any kind in the studio, he, McGuinness, would personally see to it—if the writers were right-wingers like John Lee Mahin, Howard Emmett Rogers, or one of that group—that any glorification, any good word about the labor movement, would be cut out of the picture. I remember he came into the office one day when I was there and he said, "Well, I got that son-of-a-bitch laboring man out of that film. He'll get back in over my dead body."

I firmly believe that these were men who never stopped hating what had happened when the studios lost their right to designate the screenwriter credits. When that power was given to the Screen Writers Guild by the National Labor Relations Board, they never stopped brooding about it. They were always looking for some way to get back at the writers who had instigated that. And when we won the NLRB election [in 1938], those writers who had left to join the company union had to come back to a meeting of the Screen Writers Guild and justify why they should be accepted back into our Guild.* It was a fascinating scene to sit there and watch as these people beat their breasts in mea culpa. The only one who didn't falter or fall down was James K. McGuinness. He presented such a treatise on why he did it and how he

---

*James Kevin McGuinness, John Lee Mahin, and Howard Emmett Rogers were leaders of the Screen Playwrights, the rival organization of screen writers announced in 1936 to counter the growing radicalism of the newly founded Screen Writers Guild. The new group closely allied itself with producers and executives and condemned the idea of a "closed shop." MGM contract writer Mahin was elected the group's first president; the original board included Kubec Glasmon (John Bright's former partner), Frank Butler (father of future blacklistee Hugo Butler), and Sonya Levien (mother of future blacklistee Tammy Gold). In general, its members were the older, more established movie writers, many of whom were rewarded with lucrative supervisory positions at the studios. The Screen Playwrights fought a long, bitter war against the incipient Screen Writers Guild, until it lost a series of NLRB rulings and eventually was subsumed by the formally recognized Guild. But its founders and leading members came back to haunt Hollywood after World War II, with several of the former Screen Playwrights prominent among the rightists who cheered HUAC on, testifying before the Committee and then, behind the scenes throughout the blacklist era, enforcing the lists of unemployables. See Nancy Lynn Schwartz, *The Hollywood Writers' Wars*.

did it, and so forth and so on, that it seemed almost justified. I mean, you almost sympathized with the man's situation. He was that good a salesman, that brilliant in argument.

Do you think they harbored the ambition that someday the tables would be turned?

Oh, there's no question about that. That was openly said. I said to Don Hartman, who had joined the company union—I was working with him at the time—"How can you do this, Don?" He said, "Well, I have a house, mortgage payments, cars, a pool, children. I can't take the risk of not being able to make the payments when they come due." That was his only reason. He told me these other guys would never surrender. They were just grousing all the time about what had happened to them. He said he thought it was a mistake that we were so harsh with them; they should have been taken back without the mea-culpa meeting. They should have just been handed their membership cards and told things were forgotten.

What were all the mea culpas like?

You know. "What was I going to do, take my wife out in the streets and starve? I've never had a job before like this. I never thought I'd be in Hollywood in my whole life. Here I was, stuck with a mortgage. I was overcome by the glamour. . . ." Things of this type that justify the human weakness for being successful and not wanting to insult the powers that be.

We know you were also friendly and sociable with a group you dubbed the "Social Democrats," which included Groucho Marx. They were more than just liberals but far short of being Communists, right?

I would characterize the Social Democrats this way: they were soft on capitalism and hard on Socialism. But they had a hard-on for Social Democracy. They were people who wished good, but without bloodshed. They did not like the idea of riots, protesters, inflammatory pamphlets. They wanted a slow and easy process under the goodwill of the big boys, with the money given up a little bit here and there. We used to have terrible arguments about that, because I asked them to point out to me where, in the Bible or history, a ruling class gave up what it had in favor of another class. There was almost always turmoil, and it was so much better to realize that in advance.

But they accepted me in their group—mostly because of my wife of the time, who was a champion cardplayer, and who used to play with their wives. I played reluctantly because I am a terrible cardplayer and always lost. But they accepted me because of my wife and because they didn't have enough players without me.

One of the people in that group—among others like [Nat] Perrin and [Arthur] Sheekman and the Epstein boys [Julius J. and Philip G. Epstein], all nice guys, really nice, but to my mind very lackadaisical and spoiled people— was Groucho. Groucho used to spout the Social Democratic line. He and I always had a kind of bout going, and there were many times that I topped him. As Groucho talked, it came out in tremendous spasms of jokes, ninety-nine percent of which were absolutely no good. Once in a while he got off a gem. One day he was sitting quietly, and I walked over to him after observing him and said, "Groucho, tell me the truth. The real truth. What is it you really want?" There was a little pause, and he looked up at me with his lachrymose eyes and said, "I don't want anything to change." So I understood him for the first time. He really was a deep-dyed Social Democrat, no matter what else he had to say.

The Social Democrats didn't mind that you were a Communist?

I had a table at the Brown Derby, and I also had a table at Chasen's, a very front table. The reason I got the front table was because I had known Dave Chasen in vaudeville when he was a stooge for [comedian] Joe Cook, so I was favored. George the headwaiter was told to do everything that I wanted him to do. Anyway, this table was always full of the Social Democrats, who could afford to eat at Chasen's. On Thursday nights, when the maids were off in Hollywood, we used to gather there, the Perrins and the Sheekmans and others of that ilk. Around eight o'clock at night, I would get up, and they would know exactly where I was going. They'd say, "Oh, he's leaving for the party . . . the Communist Party meeting." [Laughs.]

They never thought anything of it.

No, they accepted me as a kind of eccentric. After all, I was coauthor of a classic play which had played all over the world and still is playing all over the world. They had to accept me as a kind of a nut. I remember one of them coming into my home one day and noticing a heavy volume of philosophy. "Oh? You just put it there so people can think you study philosophy, huh?" They thought I was a show-off kind of guy. Which I was.

Politically, they just couldn't accept things like the Hitler-Stalin Pact.

When Stalin and Hitler signed the Pact, I understood. I understood that it was a maneuver. Churchill once said he would make a pact with the devil in order to defeat Hitler, or anybody else who was threatening England. The West wanted nothing better than to have Hitler dismantle the Soviet Union and turn it into a capitalist paradise.

I did not go for the purge trials.* I was very sad about that. I would rather

---

*Growing internal opposition to Joseph Stalin's dictatorship in 1934 prompted him to secretly order the murder of Sergei M. Kirov, a member of the Politburo and the secretary of the Leningrad Communist Party, and to then claim that it had been committed by counterrevolutionary conspirators. The NKVD (the secret police) arrested hundreds, then thousands, of former and suspected oppositionists. Arrests of middle-level officials coincided with a new "cult of Stalin." Within the next three years, former leaders of the Bolshevik Party stunned the world by confessing to an improbable conspiracy against the state. Leon Trotsky was condemned to death in absentia (in 1940, living in Mexico, he was assassinated by Stalin's

that they had not taken place, and I was not impressed by the evidence given. I was against the doctors' trials, too.

During the period of Browderism, in the 1940s, when the Party opened itself up to virtually anybody who wanted to join by making its politics broadly acceptable, a lot of people joined who didn't know or really care what Marxism was. Do you think the Party, in a sense, created the seeds of its own destruction, by creating a class of potential informers?

I didn't like Browderism. I never understood it. We let in a lot of people who joined for nefarious reasons. Some of them later said before committees and in public statements that they joined the Party to get the liberated girls. I fully believe that some of them really did that. I think there was a lot of that kind of opportunism.

The aura of desperation in the American soul hadn't shown itself yet. As with the Jews in Germany, people were looking for some kind of rascal to kick out, somebody to belabor, somebody to hit, because people were having troubles of their own. None of us understood that. We didn't think we were traitors; we thought we were actually patriots. We thought nothing was too good for the American people, and that by turning the system from outright capitalism, which it hadn't been for a number of years anyway, into a gradual Socialism, finally we would get the perfected man—a man who had nothing to do with opportunism, with gathering money together or exploiting people. The great universal drama that we didn't understand is that man's only opponent is his own nature. It was a shame that we took in too many people who never shared those ideals.

Another funny thing about your life story is that just as HUAC was coming to Hollywood for the first time, you were busy writing a screen story expressly for our future president Ronald Reagan. Tell us a little about the genesis of The Girl from Jones Beach.

I got a call one day from a man named [Alex] Gottlieb, who was a producer; he said that he needed a story for three people over at Warner Brothers. One of the three was Ronald Reagan—I think that's a name familiar to people now—and the other two were Virginia Mayo and Eddie Bracken. He asked

---

agents). With this series of developments, Soviet totalitarianism had grown full-scale. See Roy Medvedev, *Let History Judge: The Origins and Consequences of Stalinism.*

The "doctors' plot," an anti-Semitic purge of the Jewish intelligentsia during Stalin's began when the NKVD announced the discovery of a "pro-Jewish conspiracy" and arrested leading officials of Jewish extraction, including nearly the entirety of the Jewish Anti-Fascist Committee, which had served the USSR so well during World War II. At the height of the purge, just before his death, Stalin accused doctors at Kremlin hospitals of murdering top officials. Because Jewish-American Communists steadfastly denied the existence of Soviet anti-Semitism at the time, they suffered terribly from the gradual, full revelation of the facts. For many it was the final step in disillusionment; for others it discredited only the Soviet system, not the ideals of Marxism.

me if I had anything ready. I said no, and he said, "Well, I need it on Monday." I said, "You'll have it on Monday, but the price will be a thousand dollars a page." So I sat down over the weekend, and by Monday morning I had nineteen pages. He read it, he approved it, and they gave me a check for nineteen thousand dollars.

Of course I didn't write the script itself because I was under contract to another studio, and actually the story ought to have belonged to that studio, because they were supposed to own everything I wrote. So it was a sub-rosa deal, and I had to relinquish the script, which was written by a man with three front names, I. A. L. Diamond, a Columbia College graduate, in the same class with Herman Wouk. I did get on the set several times just to see how things were going and what changes were made—what Izzy had done with my work—and there I brushed elbows with the future president, Mr. Reagan.

I had very few words to say to him. To me, as an actor, he was, pardon the expression, a shit-kicker. They used to say that about Gary Cooper—meaning, usually, an actor who was ill at ease in the acting profession. I'm not saying Reagan was ill at ease; I'm saying that maybe he was really not an actor. He was a salesman, never anything else but a salesman. I observed the man. He was sitting there one day changing lines in the script. He was very closely attentive to it, you know, scribbling out and writing in lines here and there. Then he'd look up and kind of smile. He had very shrewd eyes; I always thought so. But I also thought he was totally insincere—I didn't believe anything he said. To me, he was an actor, and I have always found actors kind of babyish and egotistical, people who are not too sure of themselves. That was my only experience with him.

It's funny; after he became president, when he was interviewed about his career as an actor, supposedly he said—I don't know if this is an accurate quote or not, but it's near enough—that he never could permit any line to stay in a script that he couldn't say sincerely. Because if he tried to say it sincerely but he couldn't really mean what he was saying, then it would come over on the screen as phony. And for this reason he kept changing a lot of lines, rewriting almost every script that he ever had by tinkering with the lines.

You wrote comedies almost exclusively. But comedy could be very subversive, too. Were you at all involved in one of the great debates among Party members in Hollywood—that is, whether significant content or social messages could be inserted into American films? Where did you stand?

My feeling about that was that content could be put in. I don't like to say "put in." Content could be made an integral part of the structure of a film, if it lived up to its dramatic purpose and was not inserted willy-nilly. Otherwise it would stand out like a sore thumb. Everything depended on what effect it was supposed to have. It could be too strong, but it could also be too subtle, in which case it was useless.

In comedy we did things all the time to beat the standard censorship. We got in obscene lines, or at least off-color lines. We got them in continually. Those of us who knew the jokes used to guffaw when the censors came by to watch the film, while they wondered what we were laughing at. A very trivial example is a line I can quote very easily, someone saying about another man, "Well, he's half-sweet and half-acid." The audience would laugh at a line like that, and the censor would wonder, "Why are they laughing?" because the censor was usually a humorless man who had no idea what jokes were or how writers could twist them to their use. Again, the jokes had to be integral and not stand out like raisins in rice. And, of course, they couldn't be too subtle either or else the audience would just pass over them and wouldn't know what was going on.

You were eventually named as a Communist by someone with whom you had been sort of friendly, the most prolific informer, Martin Berkeley—well, prolific at least in terms of naming names.* I understand you went way back with Berkeley. Can you tell us a little bit about him?

When I was the hot kid on Broadway, I had a number of toadies. Martin Berkeley was a man who was very handsome—rather weakly handsome, I would say—tall, blond, blue eyes, with a kind of Teutonic face. He had the same agent I did in New York, a man called Dr. [Edmond] Pauker, who was also the agent for Ferenc Molnár. Molnár, probably the greatest playwright of his day, was Hungarian, and so was Pauker, and it so happened that I first met Martin Berkeley in Pauker's office.

When he found out who I was, he hastily gathered up my plays and read them, and he became my toady. He followed me around wherever I went. He talked to me constantly, wanting to understand who I was, and what I was, and how I had come to write like that, because even though he was an actor, he had ambitions to write. He wasn't very successful as an actor anyway.

Now, he went out to Hollywood before I did, he married a girl, and they established a little house in the valley, and they also had a walnut farm. When I came out, he looked me up again, and he became my buddy. By now he had written a couple of plays, and he had me read them. I read them, I criticized them, I advised him not to get them put on. He insisted on it, and they were flops, and that hurt him a lot. My curious relationship with him went on for a great many years, although Berkeley was not among the people in my group who used to come to Communist meetings. He was in another group, although he later lied about that. I never saw him at a meeting. He was in a completely different fraction.

One year, when he was employed at Metro-Goldwyn-Mayer, they were having an economy drive and wanted to get rid of the lesser writers. And he

---

*Accounts vary slightly, but screenwriter Martin Berkeley was the informer who named by far the most people—reliably calculated at 155—as Hollywood subversives or Communists.

was one of the lesser writers. He came walking into my office with this piece of paper in his hand, crying. I said, "What's wrong, Martin?" He said, "They want to get rid of me." I said, "How do you know that?" He said, "They assigned me to write a Laurel and Hardy picture. They know I don't write comedy. I could never write a Laurel and Hardy picture. What am I going to do about it? I can't just walk in and say, 'I don't want to do this picture.' It will just give them an excuse to get rid of me." I said, "Have you talked to George Willner?" George, at the time, had become our Hollywood agent. He said, "Yes. George can't do anything about it." I said, "Well, Martin, I'll tell you what I'll do. I'll write the script for you." He said, "What do you mean?" I said, "I'll write the whole script. It'll take me maybe a week, ten days. I'll write the script for you, and then you can walk in and hand them a script. I want to treat those lousy bastards to a little medicine of their own. It'll be a lot of fun for me to do it." He said okay. So I did write the script, and he took it in to his producer, a guy called Bob Sisk.

Now, Bob Sisk knew me. He knew me from the Theatre Guild in New York. Bob said to Martin, "You didn't write this. This is not your style. You don't know how to write this way. Now, tell me the truth about this." Well, he finally pinned him. And Martin, who was starting his career of finking, gave him my name, not thinking that maybe I would get kicked off the lot for doing such a thing. Anyway, Bob sent for me. I went to see him, and he was very complimentary. He said, "I have never heard of a man doing a thing like this before. Why did you do it?" I couldn't tell him why I had done it—that Martin was a buddy, a Party member, a comrade. I couldn't do that. I said, "Well, I don't have too much feeling about Louis B., and I just wanted to have a little fun, see?"

This wasn't the first time I had done a thing like that with some fun attached to it, because I had little use for the number of writers who got screen credit on pictures. They used to say they needed a fresh mind, and they would stick another writer on a script, so that most of the scripts came out with three or four names on them. One time, for example, they sent me a writer by the name of Frank Waldman who'd just gotten out of Harvard, and they told me, "We want to get rid of him, so keep him around the office for a while and then after a few weeks call us up and tell us he's not doing anything. He's just somebody who has a connection to Louis B. We'll get rid of him that way." Well, I didn't like that way of doing things, either. So when it came time for me to submit the credits for the scripts of this particular picture, which was called *Bathing Beauty*, I put Frank Waldman's name on as the writer, and he had not written a single line. My producer, Jack Cummings, called me up. He said, "Who is this Waldman?" I said, "That's the fellow you sent down."

Anyway, Martin Berkeley began to gradually lose faith in himself. He began to fear that he would not get what he really wanted in life, which was to be a top writer in Hollywood. He had some talent but no great talent. He was no [Dalton] Trumbo, let us say. He was not even a . . . me, when you come to think of it. Later, when I was working at Twentieth Century–Fox and he was working there too, he cornered me in the hall one day. He said to me, "Are you still dedicated to that labor stuff?" I thought it was rather an odd thing for him to say. I said, "Well, certainly, of course I'm pro-labor. What do you think I am, anti-labor? No." He said, "You know, it's getting good and tiresome," and he kind of sheered away from me.

How did Martin Berkeley repay you for writing that script for him?

Martin Berkeley repaid me very nicely by naming me to the Committee as a Communist. I was in my apartment in Hollywood, working for Twentieth Century–Fox, and my daughter came running in. She said, "Oh, Daddy, I just heard your name on television!" She was so delighted—she was about seven years old. Her father was famous—he was on television, which was her goddess, or whatever. I said, "Oh, thank you, that's wonderful." Within a few minutes after that I got a call from a prominent attorney, Martin Gang, saying, "I can get you out of this. All you have to do is listen to me, and I can arrange it for you." I said, "No thank you, not if it has anything to do with naming anybody or taking an oath of any kind. Forget it. Not me."

What happened next?

Oh, the next day I went to work, at Twentieth Century–Fox. But before I did I went down and bought myself one of those black tin lunch pails, and I painted on it BOMB, in very big letters, as big as I could make them, very thick. I walked in the gate, and since the doormen, the gate-holders, knew me, they didn't stop me. They didn't even look at the lunch pail. Maybe I concealed it; I probably did. I walked up the main drag, and everybody started running away from me. This nut was coming with a package labeled BOMB! Maybe he's really got one. [Laughs.] Anyway, I'd been named, and they were off me anyway.

The only guy who came over to shake my hand was a prominent Hollywood director, Richard Brooks—God bless him. We used to talk baseball together, and that was our common bond. He shook my hand right out in front of everybody, and that was wonderful. Afterward, that night, I went to Chasen's, and nobody would talk to me. They ran away from me. We sat at the table, my wife and I, all alone. I'm surprised they even served me, but they did.

How long did you stay on at the studio?

That morning, right after the bomb episode, I went in to my producer, who was George Jessel, and he assailed me. He said, "What do you need that for? Who are you, anyway? What do you want to do in this world? You're crazy! I've got this picture going, and we're doing great with it. I've got to finish it. You're the one to finish it. You rescued it, and now I'm going to lose you? That's terrible! Sit down. Sit down, and don't move! Stay in that chair until I call you."

I said, "Wait—" He said, "Don't move!" He left. I stayed in that chair for three hours. He came back and said, "Don't open your mouth. Listen to what I have to say, okay?" I said okay. He said, "You're staying on. Lew Schreiber [a studio production executive] said you can stay on as long as I want you *if* you don't get any publicity. That's the one thing you have to promise. Now, the second thing is, we have to reduce your salary from seventeen fifty a week to seven fifty a week." Well, what could I do? I was without a future anyway; I couldn't get another job in Hollywood. So I stayed at Twentieth Century–Fox for over nine months, until one day a columnist had an item in the *Hollywood Reporter* saying, "What's Allen Boretz the red, named by Martin Berkeley, doing working for Twentieth Century–Fox?" Of course that was the end of it.

It's ironic. When the informers made their mea culpas, some of them sounded like the Screen Playwrights at the Screen Writers Guild meetings, trying to rationalize the money they needed to make.

Oh, yes. There was a guy called George Beck who was one of the guys I thought shouldn't have been taken into the Communist Party. He was a fey guy, the kind of guy who would come down to the tennis club and into the dressing room and say to the first guy he met—they were all mostly writers there—"I just signed a deal at RKO, and there's this story that's bothering me." By the time he got done talking to everybody, he would have a full story; everybody had contributed to it, you see. He got to be known as a guy who sold light comedies.

After the exposé by Berkeley, a couple of days after that, I was walking down Sunset Boulevard in Hollywood, and there was Beck standing in front of Schwab's drugstore. Right next to him in the alley where you park the cars was this brand-new red sports car, a roadster. I said, "What's the car?" He said, "I just bought it." I said, "What is it, George, the payoff?" Well, he turned all colors, turned around, and tried to walk through the window of Schwab's. Of course, I walked away from him. There were many others like that; you could harass them if you found them. They didn't belong in the Party and should not have been there in the first place.

You were on the blacklist for a number of years. What did you do?

I went back to my old trade of writing plays. I wrote a play that was called *The Hot Corner*, and I was up in Rockland County, New York, helping to raise money for the play, where I met a playwright by the name of John Patrick who had lots of money because *The Teahouse of the August Moon* was one of his hits. In fact, he had several hits in a row. Well, he did not invest in plays. He said he needed his money for himself, to live in Hollywood until he was a success there—he had just signed a five-picture contract. But he liked the play very, very much, he recommended it to others, and others did invest because of Patrick. We began to produce the play, gathering money and whatnot, and suddenly one day I got a call from Patrick. He said, "I've signed my deal with Metro, and the first picture I want to make is *The Hot Corner*. Now, how much money do you want for the play?"

Well, I thought it over to myself very quickly. I didn't want to tell him my troubles, and I thought the best thing for me to do was to put a price on it that he—or the studio—wouldn't pay. I said, "It'll cost you half a million dollars," which was a tremendous price for a play in those days. He didn't bat an eyelash. He said, "I'll get back to you." The next day I got a call from him. He said, "Listen, are you in any political trouble? Am I going to have any political trouble with you?" I said, "No, not that I know of. Why don't you find out from the studio whether I am in trouble or not?" The next day he called me up and said, "Would you be willing to sign an affidavit saying that you are not a member of the Communist Party?" I said, "Gladly. I am not a member of the Communist Party." As a matter of fact, I hadn't been since 1943, and this was in 1955, after I'd been blacklisted for several years. He said, "Well, then we're all set. Sol Siegel and I are flying into New York to complete the deal. We'll be talking to you in a day or two."

The next day, I got another call. He said, "It's not enough. The affidavit is not enough. You have to appear before the Committee and make a full confession of all your political involvements." So I said, "Just forget it." The strange part of the whole story is that my producer, who was Eleanor Saidenberg, had also been a member of the Party, and she was also urging me to get on the stand and spill my guts for the five hundred thousand dollars. I told her that even if it were nine hundred million, she couldn't get me to do it.

Did you have any moments of temptation or weakness?

I must say I spent a whole night thinking about it and trying, with my clever Jewish brain, to find a way out of this impasse. I felt like a rat running around in some kind of enclosure that had no exit, no entrance, nothing. As idealistic as I am, money has a great power. [Laughs.] And I was used to money. Finally I just had to give it up. That was difficult. But I'm glad I said forget it. I never lost anything by doing so.

Do you feel that if you had had less money, things might have been different for you?

Yes, yes. I have to admit to myself that if I had been like some of these boys who had to become waiters and carpenters and do things of that kind, I might have had some second thoughts. I have to admit to that human weakness. But I wasn't faced with that problem. I was always a good money-earner, I had many things I could do, and so "cooperating" passed out of my lexicon . . . if we can call it that.

You ended up living in Spain at the end of the 1950s and working on a few movies there. What was the expatriate community like?

The expatriate community worked frequently, with different names on the films. Ben Barzman was working on a film for Sophia Loren. Arnaud d'Usseau was there working on a film. I myself worked on a number of films, including *El Cid* for [producer] Samuel Bronston, who was the biggest crook in the world.

Wasn't it a contradiction for a former Communist political exile to be living in Spain and prospering under a Fascist dictatorship? Were you struck by the irony?

I was. People said to me, "What are you—you of all people—doing in a Fascist country?" I said, "Well, I don't believe that we should exile or blacklist ourselves. The Spanish people should see how other people live, and maybe they'll want a change. Maybe they will do something about their plight."

The fact is that Spain was a cleverly run country in 1960. Franco was the dictator, and you would think you were walking into a repressive land. I was very surprised to find that it wasn't repressive, or at least not obviously so. People were allowed to say anything they wanted to on the stage, because the prices were high, and the common people couldn't pay them. In films you had to adhere to certain strict rules, so films were censored. But it's true that it was the good life for us, because the bohemians of France had sort of drifted down into Madrid. I enjoyed that part of my life, and so did others who came around to join in it. There was no unhappiness. I personally felt no repression of any kind. Nobody bothered me in Spain.

John Bright

JOHN BRIGHT, Los Angeles, California, 1983

INTERVIEW BY PATRICK MCGILLIGAN
AND KEN MATE

JOHN BRIGHT
(1908–1989)

1931 *The Public Enemy*. Costory, coscript.
    Blonde Crazy. Costory, coscript.
    Smart Money. Costory, coscript.
1932 *Taxi*. Coscript.
    Union Depot. Uncredited contribution.
    The Crowd Roars. Coscript.
    Three on a Match. Costory.
    If I Had a Million. Coscript.
    Madison Square Garden. Uncredited
        contribution.
1933 *She Done Him Wrong*. Coscript.
1936 *The Accusing Finger*. Coscript.
    Girl of the Ozarks. Costory.
1937 *San Quentin*. Costory.
    John Meade's Woman. Coscript.

1938 *Frankie*. Coscript.
1939 *Back Door to Heaven*. Coscript.
1940 *Glamour for Sale*. Story, script.
1942 *Sherlock Holmes and the Voice of Terror*.
        Coscript.
    Broadway. Coscript.
1945 *We Accuse* (documentary). Commentary.
1948 *I Walk Alone*. Coadaptation.
    Close-Up. Coscript.
    Open Secret. Additional dialogue.
    Fighting Mad/A Palooka Named Joe. Script.
1949 *The Kid from Cleveland*. Costory, coscript.
1951 *The Brave Bulls*. Script.
1954 *La rebelión de los colgados/Rebellion of the
        Hanged*. Script (as Hal Croves).
1955 *Mexican Trio*. Script (as Hal Croves).
1971 *Johnny Got His Gun*. Production associate.

■

IN HOLLYWOOD SINCE 1929, John Bright was a founding father of the Screen Writers Guild as well as one of the original "secret four" members of the Hollywood section of the Communist Party. At the same time that he was building his early reputation as an uncompromising, hard-boiled writer, he participated in every left-wing cause that came along.

With his first partner, Kubec Glasmon, Bright cowrote five seminal James Cagney vehicles, among them the one that launched an entire school of gangster movies, *The Public Enemy*. Sans Glasmon (after being kicked out of Warner Brothers for slugging Darryl F. Zanuck) he collaborated on *She Done Him Wrong* for Mae West. His second writing partner was Robert Tasker, a fellow Communist and former convict who had written a novel, *Grim Haven*, and edited the penitentiary newspaper while at San Quentin.* For a time they specialized in prison stories and scripts.

Later still, during the blacklist, Bright emigrated to Mexico—joining the group of Hollywood refugees there which included the Trumbos and the Butlers—and became "Hal Croves." As Croves, he wrote black-market scripts, including (he credibly claimed) a film in collaboration with B. Traven. In the 1960s, when he returned to Hollywood, Bright became a story editor for Bill Cosby's production company and worked behind the scenes on the 1971 film of Dalton Trumbo's antiwar novel *Johnny Got His Gun*.

Bright was one of Hollywood's maverick leftists, always getting in trouble with his peers for his iconoclasm. Lionel Stander, who produced his play *Brooklyn U.S.A.* on Broadway, paid Bright a high compliment. "He was a sophisticate," said Stander, "a night-lifer like myself." A lifelong smoker, drinker, and bon vivant, Bright surprised people merely by staying alive as long as he did. He lived out his years in conditions of shocking poverty in a Hollywood apartment, his mind and tongue acerbic to the end. When he died in 1989, his ashes were scattered at sea.

■

---

*Robert Tasker (1898–1944) died in Mexico City, after a quarrel with his wife, the former Gladys Flores, granddaughter of Costa Rica's ex-president, in 1944. His death was reported as a suicide by poison. Bright always thought the suicide was inexplicable and mysterious. Later, Bright wrote a novel about his partner, *It's Cleaner on the Inside*, published in London in 1961.

My name is John Bright, and I was born New Year's Day 1908 in Baltimore, Maryland—a few years before Ronald Reagan was a blessed event in another part of the country.

How did you become radicalized?

I gravitated toward a political point of view because of my earliest contacts with the anarchist movement. Not the movement per se, but the Hobo College on West Madison Street in Chicago, where I moved when I was young. The teachers were Emma Goldman and Ben Reitman,* and [Big] Bill Haywood, who organized the IWW [Industrial Workers of the World, or Wobblies], was one of the lecturers. From Haywood I learned about the IWW, and I learned anarchist theory from Reitman and Goldman. The ideas of [anarchist theorist Peter] Kropotkin and Goldman had a strong effect on me then and still do.

Later, you went to New York for a time.

I went to New York to attend the New School for Social Research, and it was about that time that Sacco and Vanzetti were in the twilight of their lives. I was intensely concerned about that case, as millions of people in the world were, and I and the entire faculty and student body of the New School went up to Boston for a last-minute picketing plea to the powers that be. We—and the world—lost. Sacco and Vanzetti were murdered. And I was plunged into a terrible despair, a great disillusionment with my country, because these were the days of Coolidge and Harding and Hoover; there was great prosperity for some but no labor movement, no left wing, nothing but conservatism. So I moved in another, rather apolitical, direction.

I became a writer and a disciple, really, of H. L. Mencken. Well, Mencken was a Tory and a snob, but he was anti-establishment too, and that appealed to me. Mencken's democracy was a circus, amusing and not terribly important. That colored my thinking until the Great Depression.

When did you first come to Hollywood?

I landed here October 29, 1929, the day of the market crash. I had twenty-nine cents in my pocket. I was chasing a girl, and I wanted to write a book. I had no intention of going into motion pictures.

Was there much of a left-wing movement in Hollywood when you arrived?

No. When I arrived in Hollywood, there was no left-wing movement at all that I was aware of. It was a bland climate of largely not caring about anything

---

*Dr. Ben Reitman, bohemian and physician, sometime companion of Emma Goldman, had abandoned a wealthy family to become a hobo and later aided Goldman in Chicago in various campaigns through his political skills and his connections with the local establishment. He also joined her in birth-control agitation in New York City, offering descriptive pamphlets until he was arrested, which precipitated national publicity.

but making money and buttering up one's ego. That was the Hollywood I came to.

You were accompanied by a friend, your first writing partner, Kubec Glasmon. He was very different from you, right? To begin with, politically he was conservative.

He and I went back to Chicago. He did disapprove of my political activity. He didn't want any part of it. He wasn't a reactionary, though.

Glasmon was born in Poland, one of four children. His father—they came from a small town—was something very familiar in rural Poland and Russia, a pharmacist and veterinarian; he was not an M.D., but he was called "Doctor." He was the only Jew the Gentiles tipped their hats to. He had dignity. Well, there came rumors of a pogrom several hundred miles to the west. The village was in a panic, and everybody was preparing to leave for America. Very reluctantly, the father left his position of dignity to go to America. The mother was one of those Jewish mothers, ninety pounds wringing wet, with a tremendous drive for America, the land of opportunity; she was going to send her children through college to be somebodies. The father, a family man, just went along. America appalled him. He had no identity here. He was jostled on the elevator. He was miserable. So eventually he left his family and went back to Poland to die. The mother stayed and raised the kids. That's practically unparalleled in a Jewish family, but Glasmon's father was not a *nogoodnik*, simply a crushed man.

The mother raised her children with the idea that a Jew compromises, a Jew can't fight, a Jew has to be smarter than everybody. A Jewish bourgeois idea—climbing out of the ghetto. She scrubbed floors, took in laundry, and sent all four children through college before she died at the age of eighty-five or ninety. Glasmon, although in a sense the black sheep of the family—his brother was a well-known gynecologist, his sister graduated cum-laude from the University of Chicago, and his other sister married a wealthy garment manufacturer—studied dentistry, flunked out, went to pharmacy school, set up shop, and became a playboy.

I met him when I was working in his drugstore, jerking sodas, when I was sixteen. It was the corner drugstore, and I used to deliver booze for him. We became friends. After I wrote my Big Bill Thompson book [*Hizzoner Big Bill Thompson: An idyll of Chicago*, 1930] we had this insurance fire and he decided to throw in his lot with me and try writing. He had subsidized the writing of the Thompson book, and now we had plans to do a novel together. We talked over the material. It was going to be called "Beer and Blood." When we went to California, the night before the boat sailed through the Panama Canal, we stayed up all night talking about it—one of those big, portentous nights when our lives were going to be changed forever. I was twenty, and he was thirty; he was a mature man, and I was a kid. "Beer and Blood" turned out to be over three hundred single-spaced pages long. We couldn't interest anyone in publishing it as a novel, so we tried to sell it to Warner Brothers. Zanuck himself made the decision to buy it and helped us with the focus. We had too many different characters and stories, too much social scope, and starting from the first story conference he made the suggestion to concentrate on "the public enemy" and his friend.

Glasmon and I were a good team for a while. His contribution was substantive; mine was more style. He was semiliterate at best, but he knew a good deal creatively and contributed his share. Later, when I was older, I was no longer as much in awe of him. That made a big difference. Therein lay the seeds of our ultimate breakup. I had grown up, had ideas of my own, and was no longer his stooge.

How did you and Glasmon pick up the techniques of screenwriting, in order to write the first draft of the screenplay of The Public Enemy?

I very early on recognized the great importance of the film editor, the unsung hero of Hollywood. I thought so when I first went to work at Warners, on *Public Enemy*, and I think so now. A top-flight cutter is worth his weight in gold to a picture. I felt I could learn a lot from these guys, so I started hanging around the cutting room, asking questions.

They thought I was a front-office stooge, checking up on whether they were smoking or not. They didn't have fireproof film in those days, but they sneaked smokes while cutting pictures. At first they resented me, but I finally convinced the head of the cutting department, an old-timer by the name of Ed McCormick [editor of *Public Enemy*] that I was sincere. I was twenty-one or twenty-two and felt I had a lot to learn. When they saw my sincerity, they fell all over themselves to give me their wisdom. And believe me, they knew a lot. I would ask questions such as "Why did you cut from this shot to that one? There must be a reason." They'd explain why they were doing it that way. I learned a lot about screenwriting, about structure, from these guys.

I would also ask them their opinions of the various directors of our stable. I promised them, "You won't be quoted." They told me, "Well, you can have them all." I asked, "What are your criteria for a good director?" Months after we started at Warners, we were deep into *Blonde Crazy*, and I wanted to know about Roy Del Ruth. Del Ruth was personally a terrible person, a male chauvinist pig who would leave his mail all over his desk for his secretary to pick up. She hated him, and he was surly to everybody—secretaries, writers— except big shots. I asked them, "What about Del Ruth?" They said, "That shit. He plays it safe. He has no imagination." I said, "What do you mean, he plays it safe?" They said, "Just watch on the set, and you'll see what we mean. He sets up an establishing shot; he moves in and has a medium shot, an over-the-shoulder shot, a tight two-shot, etc., and then he throws the whole thing into cutting and we make the picture. He's always just protecting himself." That's what they thought of him.

Later, I was on the set watching Del Ruth and I couldn't help but laugh to myself: establishing shots, medium shots, over-the-shoulder shots, tight twos, protection, protection, protection, and then into the cutting room, the whole goddamned thing. Zanuck—he was an excellent cutter himself with script or film—and the cutters did the picture.

You and Glasmon wrote an amazing number of pictures together—eight, including one under the table—in the two or three years of your partnership, before you broke up.

We turned out for Warners, in one year, six pictures. That was 1931. *Public Enemy, Smart Money, Blonde Crazy, Taxi, The Crowd Roars,* and *Union Depot,* an original for Douglas Fairbanks Jr. and Joan Blondell. There was one more before my contract expired, *Three on a Match,* with Bette Davis.

Tell us a little about Public Enemy *and James Cagney.*

Recent articles indicate that Cagney speaks nicely of me and Glasmon; he has been very gracious—unlike most stars, he recognized the existence of writers. But he probably doesn't know how he happened to get his break. I know I never told him.

Warners had just acquired First National, which was a big, sick elephant. Zanuck was the head of Warner Brothers, Hal Wallis was the head of First National. Jack Warner was buying all kinds of properties for First National, but Zanuck had to dream up his own material. Hence *Public Enemy, Smart Money, Blonde Crazy,* and everything else. To his credit—he was a tin-pot Mussolini—Zanuck was also a very capable man. I respected him professionally.

He learned subsequently how to cast a picture, but it was his weakness earlier. In any event, First National had made a picture based on a best-selling novel by Helen Grace Carlisle called *Mothers Cry,* and in that picture a young actor from the New York stage, Eddie Woods, had played a stool pigeon and given a remarkable performance. Zanuck ran the picture for us and said, "That's the guy who's going to play Tom Powers." Glasmon and I, only a few weeks in the motion-picture business, were sick about it. As good as Eddie Woods was as a stool pigeon, he was no more Tom Powers—less—than I was. It was terrible casting. James Cagney was due to play Matt Doyle, the subsidiary part. We scarcely knew Zanuck, but we could see how imperious he was, and we didn't say anything to him, but to each other we said, "That's going to ruin the picture."

Cagney had come to the studio at one hundred dollars a week, with Blondell, from a stage play, *Penny Arcade,* a flop. Cagney wasn't mentioned in most of the reviews because he couldn't project on the stage as marvelously as he later projected to the camera. He was practically inaudible. Warners took him because he was cheap and he looked good. The studio didn't know what it had. He played in *Doorway to Hell,* and that brought him to Zanuck's attention; Cagney was always hanging around the hallways, hoping that his part [in *Public Enemy*] would get bigger. We were sick about the whole situation. This was our baby, and Cagney was perfect for the lead.

Had you seen him on the stage?

No, we saw it in him *personally.* We tried out a couple of scenes on him, and he read them for us. That launched our first experiment in studio politicking. Bill [William] Wellman was Zanuck's macho pal; he had just come back from a hunting trip with Zanuck in Canada. He had been fired from Paramount for goosing an extra girl and ruining a camera. He was a crazy but very talented guy. He was very sensitive for a tough, macho character. Wellman had an office across the hall from us, and we told him that we thought that the casting was wrong. Cagney should be playing the lead.

The man who was supposed to direct *Public Enemy* was Archie Mayo, who had directed *Doorway to Hell,* but Mayo wanted to get away from gangster pictures. He wanted very badly to do a women's picture, particularly a Constance Bennett picture. But Zanuck said, "You do what you're told, you toad." That's the way he treated his directors. We told Wellman that we felt he would be the perfect director for *Public Enemy.* He understood that kind of story. We tried out a few scenes on him. He said, "Jesus, I want this picture!" So he went in to see Zanuck and said he wanted the picture and got Mayo off the hook. Mayo was happy and did a Constance Bennett picture. And Wellman was happy because now he was scheduled to direct *Public Enemy.*

The stage was set to bring in Cagney, and we did—we brought him in and had him read the Tom Powers part for Wellman. We knew we didn't have the prestige to question Zanuck's casting, but Wellman did. Plus, he was Zanuck's pal. Then I was treated to my first example of executive hypocrisy. Zanuck called us in and said (with no mention of Wellman), "I've come to a big decision—that Jimmy Cagney should play the part. What do you think of that?" We said, "Jesus, what a terrific idea!" He said, "All right. I'm shoving the production ahead three weeks." He had us write down the Matt Doyle part and write up Tom Powers, so Cagney would get more to do and Woods would get less. Well, that made us completely happy. That's what happened.

Cagney and Zanuck and Wellman all claim that filming had already started.

They were just doing establishing shots. They had no intimate shots at all, maybe a few, but nothing important.

Were you on the set for the filming?

A good deal.

What was Cagney's approach as an actor?

He had a great distance, always, with everybody. I'll tell you the real story about how the grapefruit scene evolved, though. There have been so many conflicting stories about it that you should hear the real one. In the first place, the scene is in "Beer and Blood."

Isn't it an omelet in "Beer and Blood"?

It might be a cantaloupe. But the scene is there, and it was a grapefruit in the first script. Because it's a famous scene in the picture, everyone's taken credit for it. Zanuck took credit; Wellman took credit; but Harvey Thew's widow [Thew came aboard to help with the dialogue and continuity] recently wrote the *Los Angeles Times* and said that the scene was in the original script and not attributable to anyone else. It was in Glasmon and Bright's script.

Here's the lowdown. It was one of the last scenes shot in the picture. Like most of the pictures then, the story was being shot out of continuity. It was also the last scene involving Mae Clarke. It so happened that she had a very bad cold. She came to the studio anyway. The makeup covered her red, distressed nose. She took Jimmy Cagney aside and said, "I've got a terrible cold, and my nose is so sore. Would you please fake it?"

Well, Jimmy was a gentleman and a very gentle guy, and he said, "Of course, darling, I'll fake it." He went over to Dev Jennings, the cameraman, and said, "Mae's got a sore nose. Fix the angle so I can fake it." Jennings said, "Sure." Wellman overheard Cagney, and as they were setting up the scene—I was two feet away and heard the dialogue—Wellman said, "Jimmy, look, this is the best scene in the picture. This scene will be talked about for a century. Don't fuck it up. It's got to be real, and if it's real this scene will make you one of the biggest stars in the business. I understand you made an arrangement with that broad to fake it. True or not?" Jimmy said, "Yeah. She's got a sore nose." Wellman said, "Well, fuck her nose. You give it to her, really give it to her, and I'll take care of Jennings."

So Cagney paced up and down. He was in a dilemma—should he double-cross her or not? He finally decided that he had to do it. Wellman was right. So the look on Mae Clarke's face in the film was real. Not only did Jimmy give it to her, but he added something of his own—he twisted the grapefruit. That grapefruit juice was like a razor—it cut into her, giving her agony; her look was one of surprise and betrayal. The minute that the scene was done she jumped to her feet and belted Cagney and said, "You goddamned son of a bitch! You double-crossing Irish no-good!" And she turned to me and said, "You too! You goddamned writer!" Because she was married to a rich man she said, "I'll never work in this studio again in my life." Well, she didn't— not for a while anyway.

The thing of it was, it was a single take. So we sat up all night waiting for that film to come back from the lab, because if it was no good we were fucked. Fortunately, it turned out. One take.

You followed up Public Enemy *almost immediately with another Cagney picture—* Smart Money, *pairing Cagney and Edward G. Robinson.*

Yes, we were called in to do a picture for them. It was originally called "Larceny Lane," named after the "peacock alley" of the Congress Hotel, where the grifters and con men used to hang out. Then we took that title and put it on our *Blonde Crazy* story later. The exhibitors changed that title too, calling it *Blonde Crazy* over our protests.

That's when I also became friends with Robinson. He was a graduate of the Yiddish theater and a Method actor. Cagney was just a personality projecting himself onto the screen. Robinson was a trained stage actor from a long tradition, an unbroken tradition that went all the way back to Czarist Russia and Poland.

We wrote *Smart Money* when *Public Enemy* was being shot; Cagney was still on the make, and so Robinson was going to be the star because of *Little Caesar*. Robinson had to come in to the studio to hear the story, and I learned for the first time how to sell a story. Zanuck was a fabulous salesman of a story. Robinson was prepared to say no. He wondered who the hell Glasmon and Bright were. He had a veto clause in his contract. Zanuck said to us before he came in, "I'm going to pitch it, and if I get in trouble, I'll cue you. One of you guys jump in. If I go like this with my cigar [he gestures], that means I'm stuck, and you jump in."

Zanuck started in telling the story, and it was incredible. He acted out all the parts, including a crap game where he got down on his knees and talked to the dice. Robinson was being very negative, so Zanuck lifted his cigar. I was tongue-tied; I didn't know what to say. Neither did Glasmon. Zanuck got an inspiration. He said, "Eddie, in this scene, do you remember the shoes you wore in *Little Caesar*?" That was a joke around the studio. Robinson had the studio make shoes worth two hundred dollars, like Al Capone was supposed to have had, but they were never in the picture—the shoes were under the table in the scene! Zanuck said, "You designed those shoes. Now I want you to design the costume for this scene of the small-time gambler coming to the city for the first time." Robinson then sat up and said yes. Zanuck only got one-third of the way through the story before Robinson was dressing himself in a complete wardrobe. He told Zanuck, "I love it," shook Zanuck's hand, my hand, Glasmon's hand, and said, "I'll do the picture." My wife and I went to the Brown Derby that night, and he hollered at me from across the restaurant to come over. He told everybody, "Johnny and his partner have just written the goddamnedest story." But he never heard the last two-thirds of the story!

How did Blonde Crazy *come about?*

Same circumstances. Blondell had a small part in *Public Enemy*, and afterward they made a decision to team Blondell with Cagney. By this time, *Public Enemy* had come out and was a big hit. So we wrote *Blonde Crazy*, tailoring it for both of them.

Incidentally, Zanuck won a bet with [*Hollywood Reporter* publisher W. R.] Wilkerson about *Public Enemy*. Zanuck was typical in his enthusiasm; everything he did was always the best! "This is the greatest goddamn picture that's ever been made!" It was kind of contagious, too. He told Wilkerson that the press had been barred from the set of *Public Enemy* on account of the grapefruit scene (it was also a good publicity gimmick), but then he went overboard by saying, "This picture will break the record of *Little Caesar* at the Strand Theater." Wilkerson said, "What?" *Little Caesar* had broken all records at the Strand, which was the Warners house on Forty-second Street. Wilkerson said, "Want to bet?" He bet Zanuck five thousand dollars in advertising against five thousand dollars in cash that *Public Enemy* would not break *Little Caesar*'s record. And it did. The newspapers had photographs of the lines going all around the block to see *Public Enemy*. *Variety* had a big story about it with the headline "*Public Enemy* Breaks House Record." What Zanuck did to collect his bet was to take a double-truck ad in the *Hollywood Reporter*, with one page featuring Wilkerson's review, which was a pan, incidentally. Wilkerson's review was headlined "*Public Enemy* Disappointing." He had expected a picture with a big social sweep, and instead, with his stunted view, he got a story of only two guys, so he panned it. Zanuck made Wilkerson eat his words in his own publication. The other page had a photograph of the lines around the block and a cutting from *Variety* saying *Public Enemy* was breaking records. We all enjoyed that because we hated Wilkerson.

Were these early scripts shot pretty much as written?

Zanuck would never permit improvisation.

Were you and Glasmon on the set doing any rewriting?

Very little. What happened was Zanuck would look at the rushes and then bring us into the office and say, "That scene stinks. Let's do it over." Mostly we were on the set out of curiosity.

How did you get involved with Howard Hawks and The Crowd Roars?

Glasmon and I were sent to Indianapolis for the 500 to work with Hawks on dialogue. He was a very superior director, one of the best in the business, and a very good judge of writing. But I didn't like him personally. He was a real WASP. We all lived—not Hawks but the racing drivers and the crew—at the Hotel Claypool. We called it the Hotel Cesspool. It was full of whores and con men. A very interesting place. I loved it.

I got to know the racing drivers and was fascinated by the milieu. They were the most amazing people, like stuntmen. All they cared about was racing, booze, broads, and gambling; nothing else in the world existed for them. They had a twenty-four-hour-a-day crap game going, with whores all over the place, and constant music. Finally the management couldn't take it and kicked us out. So the whores invited us to another place, just outside the city limits, a big Victorian, Charles Addams type of house, the biggest whorehouse in Indiana. We all just moved in there and continued making all the noise we wanted to.

The script was all ready to shoot and we were all satisfied with it—Hawks, Zanuck, and Glasmon and I. Then something happened. I was in a crap game, and during a lull Billy Arnold, who a year before [1930] had won the 500, turned to Harry Hartz, who had almost won it two times before that, and said, "You heard about Joe? Pretty rough." I sensed something in their manner, so I took Arnold aside later and asked, "Who is Joe?" It seems there was a racing driver, a pal of theirs, who had had his wife or girl taken by his best friend after a lifelong friendship. He was in a rage, and they were racing against each other a few days after the incident. Arnold explained to me that on a brick track that's banked you get scared, but that's nothing compared to a flat dirt track, because you skid your turns, and that's really dangerous; it's awful easy to kill a guy. It's the perfect murder. So this guy killed his pal. The fire department came as fast as it could, but the guy burned up. The smoke was still rising from his burning body, as the guy who killed him went round and round the track, realizing he had done something impulsive and killed his best friend.

I said, "Fucking Jesus, that's so much better than anything that's in our movie." I forgot it was three o'clock in the morning, I was so excited. So I called Hawks—who was too much of a gentleman to live with these rowdies and who was the guest of a Duesenberg in a mansion up in the hills. Hawks said, "Goddamn it, you're drunk." I said, "Maybe I'm drunk on a great idea." He said, "Goddamn it, call me tomorrow."

I stayed up all night writing. The next morning I apologized for waking him up and told him the idea. His face was very impassive. He said, "Thanks a lot." Well, in the three weeks that I had been there I had taken out the girl at the Western Union desk two or three times; she was kind of a cutie. So I went to her later and said, "Did Mr. Hawks send a telegram to Burbank today?" She said, "Yes, how did you know?" I said, "I just know. Can I see it?" She said, "Oh, I'd get fired." But she added, "It's ten or fifteen pages." I said, "I'll take it to the toilet, and in fifteen minutes I'll bring it back. I won't say a thing about your having given it to me." She said, "Do you promise?" I said, "On my word."

I read the telegram, and it was what I had given Hawks, word for word. It was Hawks wiring Zanuck. "Have I got an idea! You should postpone the picture." We returned to Hollywood at once on the next plane. Zanuck called us in and said, "Have I got an idea!" He gave it to me—again, word for word. At least Hawks mentioned me; Zanuck didn't mention Hawks! By this time I was seasoned enough not to say, as I would have a year before, "You son of a bitch." I said, "That's a great idea."

Did you ever go back to Indianapolis?

We never went back. We incorporated some of the ideas—the lore, the racing jargon of the drivers.

After you left the production, Niven Busch came along and did some additional work on the script.

He did some dialogue at the last moment. He was a close friend of Hawks. He had done a couple of pictures for Hawks. He'd been around for a long time, he was a good writer, and we didn't have any protection in those days. Hawks just arbitrarily put his own name on the script, and Busch's too.

Up until Taxi *you were having phenomenal success at Warners.*

My troubles probably started when I went out on strike at the beginning of *Taxi*. I was getting two hundred and fifty dollars a week, and this was our fourth or fifth picture. All of our old-timer friends said, "This is the time to hit them for more money, when you're hot." I said, "Glasmon, let's get sick!" Glasmon didn't go along with it. But I got myself a raise to seven hundred and fifty dollars, and so Glasmon got a raise to seven hundred and fifty dollars too.

Zanuck was terribly imperious, and he couldn't be crossed. He had miscast Loretta Young as Cagney's wife in *Taxi*—a Brooklyn cabdriver's wife, which was just ridiculous. I wanted Joan Blondell. But Blondell had played with Cagney in two or three pictures. Zanuck wanted to split them up; he owed Young a couple of pictures, and he couldn't be talked out of it.

We were using as the basis an unproduced play of Kenyon Nicholson, who was the Pulitzer Prize–winning author of *The Barker* and a professor at Columbia University. Zanuck had a great feeling of inferiority before cultured people, you see, and Nicholson was a very cultured man. Nicholson was interested in what we were doing, even though we ended up using hardly any of his play, so I told him that Zanuck was planning to use Loretta Young but that Blondell was more plausible as a Brooklyn cabdriver's wife. He said, "Oh, that's terrible." I said, "I protested to Zanuck. Would you? He'll listen to you." He said sure.

A couple of days later, at seven in the morning, I got a call from Zanuck's secretary, asking me to report to the studio. I called Glasmon—we were inseparable professionally—and said, "I got a peculiar call. Did Zanuck call you?" Glasmon said no. I arrived at the studio, wondering. Zanuck wasn't there. The secretary looked very uncomfortable; he was a stooge, but pleasant. He wouldn't tell me what Zanuck wanted to see me about, but he said, "You're in trouble." I said, "Well, I'm not going to wait around here. I'm going to the commissary. I haven't even had breakfast. When he wants to see me, he can find me in the office." Later, after breakfast, I was just walking in the door of my office when Zanuck accosted me. "You fucking stool pigeon!" I was completely taken aback. He was in a rage. He said, "Going behind my back, criticizing my casting—" He hadn't argued with Nicholson, because he was in awe of Nicholson, but he got very vituperative with me, so I hit him. I tried to throw him out of the window.

That was the end of my Warners contract. I had about five months until the end of my first option; then I was fired. Glasmon was kept and put into the reading department.

The first half of Taxi *is very pro-union, very tough and exciting; the second half is a typical gangster story.*

Yeah, that's what Zanuck wanted. He had his insistences. I thought it was a very flawed picture, for that reason. After *Taxi* was made and reviewed, I was walking on the Warners lot and caught up with Zanuck, who happened to be looking at the review in the *Nation*. I had read the review. I was a little surprised to see the *Nation* in Zanuck's hands. He said, "I want to talk to you. Here's a review in a magazine I never heard of. Did you ever hear of it?" "Yes," I said, "I've heard of it." He said, "This review says *Taxi* has great social significance." I said, "Yes?" He said, "Did you intend that?" I said, "Yes." He said, "I'll be a son of a bitch. I thought it was all cops and robbers."

What happened after you left Warner Brothers? Were you out of work for a couple of years?

One day. Zanuck gave out a story to the press—*Variety* ignored it, but the *Reporter* printed it—that I would never work in the picture business again, that I was incompetent, and Glasmon was carrying me. No mention of the fact that I had hit him. He had a typewritten list of writers under his desk: A, B, and C. The A writers were the ones he liked, the B writers he would use if he couldn't get one of the A writers, and the C writers were the ones he wouldn't use under any circumstances. He gave this list out to all the agents. I was on the C list. Another guy on the C list was Rowland Brown, a husky guy who once put Zanuck in the hospital. I could have sued Zanuck, but I didn't. Neither Glasmon nor I ever worked for Zanuck again, however.

At any rate, everybody in town knew that I had slugged him. I had saved some money by doing a black-market script for Paramount—Glasmon and I together [*Madison Square Garden*, 1932]. We wrote that under the table, and it was touted for an Academy Award; to this day, one of the guys who got the credit for it, Allen Rivkin, is very shame-faced about it. He's still ashamed when he sees me. He went up and took the bow for the picture. Harry Joe Brown was the producer, and we got twenty-five thousand dollars.

I gambled in those days. I had an expensive automobile, too. I went through the phase that people do when they first go to Hollywood: a home, an expensive car and lifestyle. I was at a big gambling joint on the Strip, the Clover Club, that night, to lick my wounds. I had just been fired, although the contract had a little while to go. Let's say I had been given notice. I was at the bar, jam-packed with people, and I found myself jostled. I was in a kind of savage mood. I gave this guy a shove back and said, "What the hell is the matter with you?" The guy lifted up his fist and turned, and I saw who it was. It was Myron Selznick, and he was drunk. He was a very belligerent guy anyway, and also the best agent Hollywood ever had. I was signed with him, but I was just one name on the long list of Selznick and Joyce. I said, "Mr. Selznick, put your hand down. I'm a client of yours, for Christ's sake." He said, "You're an actor?" I looked like an actor in those days. I said, "No, I'm a writer." He said, "What's your name?" I said, "John Bright." He said, "You're the guy who slugged Zanuck!" I said, "Yes, and I got myself fired. I'm never going to work in the motion-picture business again." He said, "We'll see about that. You'll be at work soon enough. Just stand there."

He had been sitting with Sam Goldwyn and Barbara Stanwyck, and he went over to them and pointed to me, and they looked at me, and Selznick shouted, "Johnny, come over here." He introduced us. "Mr. Goldwyn, Miss Stanwyck, this is John Bright." He said, "Sit down, Johnny. What do you drink? Sam, this is the perfect man for the job. Take him, and you can have Stanwyck too." They had been arguing about her and her salary. I said, "What's the picture?" Selznick said, "The number-one best-seller: *Stella Dallas*." I said to Myron Selznick on the side, "It's not for me," and my agent said, "Shut up!" Goldwyn sensed something and said, "Have you read the book, Mr. Bright?" I said no, and he said, "I'll have my secretary send the book over, and then we'll talk." So I said, "Very well."

I left, and the next morning the book was delivered. It was a crock of shit! I could no more write that than I could fly to the moon. It was a real soap opera. I said to Selznick, "It will come across as a *New Yorker* satire if I write it. I don't know how to do it. I could intend to do it, but I couldn't pull it off." So I showed up at Goldwyn's office, and I told him, "You probably have a big hit on your hands, especially with Barbara Stanwyck, but I can't do it. It's not for me." He said, "Why?" I didn't tell him it was trash. I just said, "It's not my kind of thing." Goldwyn said, "It's true that your credits are pretty formidable, but they're all pictures for men." I let it go at that. So I turned down Goldwyn. *Stella Dallas* was a smash hit and would have sent me off in another direction, I suppose.

When I told Selznick what had happened, he said, "Are you crazy? I pulled for two thousand dollars a week for you." I said, "It hurt me to say no." He said, "At least you're honest." Then he said, "Can you write a picture for Mae West? Have you seen [the play] *Diamond Lil*? Have you ever done anything for Paramount? They haven't got a writer for the next Mae West picture." I said, "That I can do. It's not a gangster picture and not about men, but that I can do." He said, "The job's yours." I went to Paramount that afternoon and ended up helping to write *She Done Him Wrong*. It was from her play, and it suited me. Mae West was a female Cagney oozing sex instead of violence.

You worked with Cagney quite a bit and became his friend. Did he ever try to have any script input or offer suggestions about his character?

Any director who worked with Jimmy would say the same thing: He was one hundred percent pro. He took direction marvelously. He was less of a prima donna than any star, ever, in Hollywood. Any suggestion that he had for anything came out of his own personality. The difference between him and a creative actor like [Laurence] Olivier or [Paul] Muni or Eddie Robinson or Walter Huston is that Jimmy never went beyond the limits of his own personality in creating pieces of business and so on. He was always very tentative in saying to a director, "How about if I go like this?" It had to be in his character.

That suggests, from the roles he played, that he had hidden depths of bitterness, anger, violence.

Yes, indeed. But he was well-controlled, personally. For example, he didn't drink—maybe just one drink; he never got into any fights with anybody, unlike Bogart or Flynn. It was customary for stupid fans to be macho and to say, "Hey, tough guy!" and challenge actors to fight. That was the experience all actors with parts like that had when they were out among people. It happened a couple of times when I was on the street with Jimmy. Guys would lean out of the car and say, "If you're so tough . . ." Jimmy would just grin. He handled it like that and wouldn't pick up a challenge the way Bogart did.

Did you ever get glimpses of the hidden anger?

Only on the screen and a couple of times socially. I saw him really angry only once or twice. Once was when he was trying to get out of his contract with Warner Brothers. I was trying to needle him to do it. I helped get him out of that contract; I got him his lawyer. I helped [actress] Ann Sheridan get out of her contract, and Bob Rossen too. They were yellow-dog contracts. Warners was the worst studio in those days. They just chewed up people. They would sign people, give them a couple hundred a week with the promise of thousands of dollars down the road, then after a few pictures boot them.

Cagney had started late, unlike most stars; he was in his thirties at the time of *Public Enemy*. I played on that. I said, "They're trying to do it to you." He did six pictures in one year, he was at the top of the charts, and he was making twelve hundred and fifty dollars a week. For chrissakes! He was making the studio millions!

You and Sam Ornitz got him involved in a lot of the early issues and causes.

He'd been a poor boy. He was on the side of the downtrodden and losers. He told me he had two or three friends, kids he'd grown up with, in the penitentiary.

Did you take Cagney to visit Tom Mooney in jail?

No, but I was instrumental in arranging it.

Tell us about it.

Sam and I got him involved in the Mooney case.* I took him to San Francisco. This was in 1931 or 1932, right after Cagney had hit it big with two or three pictures. Cagney was very interested in meeting Theodore Dreiser, and particularly interested in meeting Lincoln Steffens, who was going

---

*Labor activists Tom Mooney and Warren Billings were sentenced to death for their alleged part in a fatal bombing in San Francisco in 1916. After several prosecution witnesses recanted, the sentences were commuted to life imprisonment in 1918. They were never granted a new trial, but in 1939 the governor of California pardoned them.

to be one of the principal speakers at this big rally at the Longshoremen's Amphitheater, with ten thousand people. Dreiser, Steffens, Cagney, Ornitz, and I had dinner at John's Rendezvous. We had drinks and were talking; Cagney and Ornitz were speaking in Yiddish, which amazed Dreiser and Steffens. We were almost late for the meeting.

Cagney, I, Ornitz, Dreiser, and Steffens sat up on the platform. But something happened that got Cagney and me both in trouble with Jack Warner. Pretty soon I had to take a leak. My bladder was full. There were twelve or fifteen people on the platform, so I turned to the man next to me, and I said, in a very conspiratorial way, "Do you know where there's a can around here?" At this moment, Hearst photographers came up from the pit and took a picture of Cagney, Ornitz, me, and the other speakers, and in the Los Angeles and San Francisco Hearst papers these people were identified. I was identified as a Hollywood screenwriter, and the man I was conspiratorially whispering to was William Schneiderman, the state secretary of the Communist Party. [Laughs.] This was on the front page of many papers.

Well, Cagney and I were both called in by Jack Warner, who raised hell about us being Communist dupes. All of which was grist for the mill for Cagney's wife, Bill, who was very reactionary. She was the one who moved him steadily to the right—six inches more as he got every ten-thousand-dollar raise. She hated me for that reason; she felt I was ruining his career by involving him in left-wing causes. In the beginning I was very friendly toward her, but as time went on she was poison in her attitude toward me and Sam Ornitz, and ultimately Lincoln Steffens.

Jimmy became very chummy with Steffens for a time. He rented a house in Carmel near him and was taken under the wing of Ella Winter, who was married to Steffens and then [after Steffens died] Donald Ogden Stewart.* I had a house in Carmel, and that's how I knew Steffens in the first place. Of course I knew Don Stewart and Ella very well, too. Ella and Steffens sort of adopted Cagney, and because Steffens was a much more important name than I was, I guess Bill had to put up with it. All the other people around Jimmy were reactionary too, not just his wife. He had a brother also named Bill, and he was a terrific reactionary. The Irish crowd in Hollywood were all reactionary. Pat O'Brien, practically Cagney's closest friend, was almost a Fascist, also

---

*Ella Winter (1898–1980) was a well-known journalist first married to muckraker Lincoln Steffens, with whom she traveled to the Soviet Union in the early 1930s. She translated or wrote several influential books about Russia, including *Red Virtue*, and edited her husband's speeches and correspondence, *Lincoln Steffens Speaking* and *The Letters of Lincoln Steffens*. After Steffens's death she married left-wing screenwriter Donald Ogden Stewart (1894–1980), who won an Oscar for his sparkling screen adaptation of Philip Barry's stage comedy *The Philadelphia Story*. When Stewart was blacklisted they moved to London, where they lived from 1951 until their deaths. Her memoir *And Not to Yield: An Autobiography*, published in 1963, touches on her Hollywood years and exile in England. Stewart's 1975 autobiography *By a Stroke of Luck!* likewise provides a window on Hollywood screenwriting, politics, and the blacklist.

anti-Semitic. Another member of that crowd was Leo McCarey, who was also very anti-Semitic.

One time, I remember, Jimmy was due at some meeting for the Scottsboro Boys, and his wife didn't want him to go. He hated to drive; I was the executive secretary of the Hollywood Scottsboro Committee, and I was going to pick him up—that's how I happened to be there. He told me, "I'm not going to go," and I said, "Jesus, they're advertising you." She came to the door and said, "He's decided not to go." That's when he flared up and said, "*You've* decided that I'm not going to go." He finally went.

Politics broke up a lot of partnerships in Hollywood. Most people focus on the period of the blacklist, when certain writers informed on their former partners. But early on, political differences had something to do with your breakup with Glasmon, at the peak of your success together as a team. Right?

I suppose so. Years after we had split up, he went into the Screen Playwrights, and at that time the Guild was down to a skeleton. We hired Thurman Arnold as our attorney. He was preparing a hearing before the NLRB, and he said, "We're liable to lose unless we can get a number of the Screen Playwrights back in the Guild." We had a rump meeting at [screenwriter] Phil [Philip] Dunne's. Everything was on a personal basis. We talked about those Screen Playwrights who were not shit-heels, like John Lee Mahin. Outside of that category, there were people who were borderline cases, and Glasmon was one. When his name was read out, someone said, "Who will talk to Glasmon?" Everyone was surprised when I said, "I'll talk to him."

It was a scandal in the town that we had broken up. In the columns they said, "Why break up a good thing?" Like the Beatles, on a small scale. So I went to see him. He and I were both working at MGM by then. [Studio bosses Eddie] Mannix and [Irving] Thalberg and Benny Thau were smart enough to put us on separate floors. The Guild people were on the second floor, and the Screen Playwrights were on the third floor. We'd meet in the commissary, but there was bad blood. We had all been friends. It was like a small town. When I went up to see Glasmon, it was the first time we had spoken in two or three years, except in passing. I didn't know that he'd had a heart attack that had scared him and eventually took him off. He also had a bad gallbladder. He died when he was young—forty. He was scared and reconsidering everything.

I laid it on the line. "Maybe I am going to be the last person to talk to you about the Guild," I said. "I'm awfully glad you came," he said. And all of a sudden, he started to cry. He went over and pulled the venetian blinds. "That sunlight," he said. "It's uncompromising. I've lived my whole life, thanks to my mother, in a fucking lie. I've compromised all along. For years I thought you were a damned fool because you never compromised. In many ways you were. You've paid a price and you'll pay more. But you're not ashamed of yourself when you shave in the morning, and I am, because I've devoted my whole life to compromise. That's what my mother did to me. What do I need to do to get back into the Guild?" I said, "We'll just reenter your name." He died not long after.

The Communist Party was active behind the scenes of many of these early causes. We know that you were among the first members in Hollywood. What attracted you to the Party?

It was the only organization in the country that cared and did something about what I believe is the great cancer in this country—racial prejudice. The Socialists didn't do anything about it, and certainly the Democrats and Republicans didn't do anything about it. But the Communist Party did. That attracted me originally, and I went all out.

How was the Party organized in Hollywood?

By 1934 I was pretty well established as a writer in Hollywood, and I was also looking for a political home. I had worked in the campaign of [author] Upton Sinclair, who was running for governor, but I was unfulfilled and unhappy. And then from left field—no pun intended—a man appeared on the horizon named Stanley Lawrence, with credentials from the general headquarters of the Communist Party in New York.* He told me and my partner who succeeded Glasmon, Bob Tasker, that the Party nationally had decided on the organization of a Hollywood studio section which would not be answerable to the state or the county but only to headquarters in New York. I, Tasker, and two other people became the first four members of the Hollywood studio section. Very soon after that, the section grew to something like a hundred members within a year and two to three hundred within two or three years. We established a direct linkage with New York, and "Commissar" V. J. Jerome, the cultural head of the Party, came out to advise us. John Howard Lawson assumed the position of the indigenous Hollywood person who was the head of the studio section.

After Upton Sinclair's defeat, the Party worked hard to elect a Democrat as the governor of California and was heavily involved in the Culbert Olson campaign in 1938. Didn't part of the quid pro quo involve freeing Tom Mooney?

The Republican Party had ruled California for two decades, and things were ripe for a change. The Party organized a committee—the Motion Picture Democratic Committee—and we plunged into politics in the very familiar Tammany sense. The way we did it was, at that time, absolutely electric in its effect upon the voting public. We had big motion-picture stars exposing themselves in a partisan way for the Democratic slate. We had teams: Melvyn Douglas, for example, worked with Philip Dunne. I was on a team with John Garfield, speaking at churches and YMCAs and so on. The Republicans

---

*Stanley Lawrence was one of the first teachers of Marxism in Hollywood, tutoring film people in the early 1930s.

couldn't match that. They had no stars. John Wayne hadn't yet found his horse. So we were extremely effective and elected an entire slate from top to bottom, though the man who was selected to run for governor, Culbert Olson, was a kind of tepid liberal lawyer. There were some of us who wanted Robert Kenny, who ran for attorney general on the same ticket; Kenny was actually a stronger candidate, because when the votes were finally counted, he ran way ahead of Olson on the ticket.* But labor was behind Olson, and the Party supported Olson in consonance with other liberal, progressive, and left-of-center forces. The Party went along with what they felt was the will of the people, and they were absolutely right.

But the Party, working through the CIO and the trade-union movement generally, made a deal with Olson that if he were elected he would pardon Tom Mooney and Warren Billings. He was elected, and he kept his promise. Mooney and Billings were pardoned.

What happened when Mooney was released? He was a personal hero of yours, and you had worked a long time to get him out of jail. He had a lot of popular support in Hollywood.

There's an irony connected with the Mooney pardon and his presence as a free man among us. Bob Tasker had been for five years in San Quentin and had gotten out after writing a fine book. He knew Mooney very well. When Bob became a screenwriter and ultimately my partner, we used to quarrel about Mooney. Mooney was a symbol to me, like Sacco and Vanzetti, or the Scottsboro Boys. Bob would say, "He's a son of a bitch, a fucking prima donna. He looks down his nose at all the other cons. He's a half-educated celebrity who has picked up a few Marxist phrases and looks upon himself as a real martyr. The cons hate him." They didn't hate Mooney because he was political. As a matter of fact, the politicals were aristocrats in Quentin, among the most popular men there; they were not finks but stand-up guys against authority. The two McNamaras [brothers John J. and James B. McNamara], who blew up the *Los Angeles Times* building, and [Matthew] Schmidt,—they were the most popular men in Quentin with the other cons.† So were the

---

*Later Robert Kenny became one of the lawyers for the Hollywood Ten.
†On October 1, 1910, two explosions ripped the *Los Angeles Times* building. The blasts and resulting fire caused twenty-one deaths. Two brothers active in the International Association of Bridge and Structural Iron Workers, the secretary-treasurer, John J. McNamara, and his young brother, James B. McNamara, were arrested the following April and indicted for murder. Treated as a cause célèbre by organized labor, which designated Labor Day 1911 "McNamara Day," they were defended by famed lawyer Clarence Darrow. On December 1, 1911, they confessed their guilt. James received a life sentence, John a sentence of fifteen years. Matthew Schmidt was a Los Angeles anarchist also convicted of murder for participation in the *Los Angeles Times* bombing. Los Angeles remained an open-shop town partly as a result of this labor defeat. The passions of the case helped prompt the Federal Commission on Industrial Relations in 1912, permitting more union activities among workers in the skilled trades.

lesser politicals. But Mooney took his publicity like a movie star. It went to his head.

Well, I didn't want to believe anything bad about Mooney. But the symbol was not a reflection of what I wanted it to be. We got him out—I say that advisedly. We ran the Democratic campaign in California on the condition that if we threw our support to Olson he would pardon Mooney. And he fulfilled his promise. We threw a big party in Hollywood for Mooney. All the liberals and radicals showed up, as well as the half-assed liberals and radicals, to meet a world-famous man. That was a real crowd-gatherer. Bob and I were his chauffeurs in various affairs that he went to in Hollywood, and everything that Bob had told me about Mooney was true. He was personally a prick. The way he behaved that day was just dreadful. He insulted everybody. When he met some movie stars, for example, who treated him as if he were a hero, he said, "Who are you? I don't go to movies. They're a crock of shit." I don't think that's sound politics, and it certainly was bad public relations. I wanted no part of him personally from then on. We couldn't get rid of him fast enough. All the borderline people said to us, "We told you so."

Bob and I made a secret report of this to the headquarters in New York and proposed that Tom Mooney be kept under wraps from here on out, and he was. He died just a short while later [in 1942].

Tell us about the importance of the Scottsboro Boys and why you—and so many other Party members in Hollywood—got so deeply involved in their case.*

The Scottsboro case was, like the Sacco-Vanzetti case before it, a real watershed for me, and it followed logically from a great-man aspect of my thinking that also carried back through my forebears. My great-great grandfather John Bright was the minority leader in Parliament, a great friend of Frederick Douglass, and the author of a measure boycotting southern cotton, which contributed greatly to the North winning the Civil War. My grandfather was a circuit-riding preacher and an Abolitionist, and was stoned to death in Covington, Kentucky, for preaching to a pro-slavery mob. And my father's house in Columbus, Ohio, was an underground depot for runaway slaves before the Civil War. So my concern with racial prejudice I came by honorably—by plasma, almost.

From the very first days of their arrest [in 1931] and subsequent trial in Alabama I was interested in the case and became active on behalf of the defendants, leading to my being one of the principal organizers of the Hollywood Scottsboro Committee to raise money for their defense.

---

*The Scottsboro Boys were nine young black men from a small town in Alabama who were accused of the rape of two white women on a freight train in early 1931. After nearly being lynched, all were tried and convicted, with only the youngest escaping a death sentence. The trumped-up charges—doctors testified that no rape had occurred—and prejudicial miscarriage of justice made the cause of the Scottsboro Boys a passionate one among liberals and

*Whom did you approach for money? What kind of support did the Scottsboro Boys
have among people in Hollywood in general?*

Hollywood people didn't read much of anything, except about the successes
and failures of films, but to the extent that they did read about political issues,
most of them took a kind of liberal stance about what they read. In my original
efforts on behalf of the Scottsboro Boys, there were some surprising people
who assumed, of course, that they were innocent and that, of course, it was
a frame-up—Bing Crosby, for example, who subsequently became a Republican and a great friend of our peerless leader [referring to then-President
Ronald Reagan]. Frank Tuttle, who was directing Bing in a musical, introduced me to Crosby, whom I hit up for money. He asked one simple question:
"Nine colored boys in the South accused of rape. They didn't do it. How
much money do you want?" And he wrote us a check for a thousand dollars.
He had worked with black people in the music business all his life and had
never shown any prejudice. That was the early thirties. Later on, he became
very, very reactionary.

*Didn't you have an experience similar to the Tom Mooney one, later on, when
some of the Scottsboro Boys were released from prison and came to Hollywood for
a fund-raising event?*

Well, the Scottsboro trials were many, and four of the defendants were
eventually released—two were sent East, and two were sent out to us. Out
here we arranged a party for these two boys and invited everyone who had
ever contributed money to the Committee. It was in one sense very sad and
a little bit of fiasco. From the literary standpoint, it touched me deeply, because here were these poor, burned-out kids, and they didn't know who the
hell were Madame Chiang Kai-shek, Anatole France, George Bernard Shaw,
and other famous people who sent them cables of support. They'd never heard
of these world celebrities, all they knew was that they were miserable. They
sat there with their knees together, as a white-jacketed black man served
them, dropping their forks and dropping their napkins. Who the hell had
napkins in an Alabama jail? You don't even have toilet paper! So they were
very unhappy, terribly self-conscious, and everybody was feeling for them.

All of a sudden, the whole thing got dramatic. A guy I had known in another
connection as a hustler, a con man, and a pimp—a black guy from Central Avenue in the Los Angeles ghetto—had gotten religion. He came to me very disturbed and told me that there two white chicks in rabbit coats waiting in the
Clark Hotel for the boys. He had overheard the boys saying, "I hope this gets
over with soon, because of our dates." I said, "Holy Christ! Does that mean
what I think it means?" My friend said, "Worse! Let's get down there fast."

First we had to do something about the Scottsboro Boys. So we did some-

radicals. The case prompted successive appeals and new trials in 1933, 1934, and 1936. The
last surviving member of the group was granted a full pardon by Alabama's governor in 1976.

thing that was cruel and realistic, but very important. We got them plastered by spiking their drinks, and they had bad stomachs anyway from Alabama. So we took them away. Then we went down to the Clark Hotel on Central Avenue, and in the lobby were the two broads in rabbit coats. Around them were cops—we knew them by their feet. We went through the lobby into the bar and out into the back alley, and then we saw the nature of the possible frame-up: The Hearst press car was waiting there with cameras and equipment, and three squad cars besides. If those boys had kept that date, their blood brothers in Scottsboro, Alabama, would never have gotten out, and the prejudiced part of the population would have said, "You see, all they cared about was sleeping with white girls!"

Was the problem partly that the Party had such an unrealistic and romantic view of African-Americans?

There was a kind of romanticism the Party had which bothered me, although it was like warts on your brother. I didn't disapprove of it so much as I felt it rendered the Party less effective, specifically in the area of race relations. That was my greatest concern. The Party and Party people individually were highly romantic about black people, and personally they treated them in a very special way. I think this damaged their effectiveness, because nobody likes to be treated specially in the way they were treated.

How many black people were there in the Hollywood section of the Party?

There were virtually no black people at all in the Hollywood studio section. Hollywood was, and to a great extent today is, Jim Crow. To the best of my knowledge there was briefly one black member of the Hollywood studio section, a black writer. Otherwise we were all middle-class people who with a few salient exceptions had no connection at all with black people.

The Party could not reach the black working class in Los Angeles for the very simple reason that at that time there was no black working class. That came later. There were two kinds of black people in Los Angeles, generally. One were the church people, largely middle-class, rather stuffy, very conventional, and Christian. On the other hand were the theatrical people, the pimps, the whores, the hustlers, and the lumpenproletariat, as Marx once called them so fancily.

The Party, being indiscriminate in its attitude toward blacks, made some howling errors. One time the Party planned a big clambake, a money-raising event, and they selected the Dunbar Hotel for it because it was large and it was very well-known. Duke Ellington and Count Basie and other entertainers stayed there, but it was mainly a hangout for con men, hookers, hustlers, and pimps. The middle-class black people never crossed the threshold of that hotel. That was a place of sin. And here the Communist Party was throwing a big bash. The whole thing was dramatized for me in a very sick sort of way when I overheard two hustlers standing outside the hotel saying, "Let's go in, man; you can knock yourself off some white chicks. Yeah, those reds loves us

niggers." The result politically was that the black middle class, the only potential for Communist Party activity and persuasion, stayed away in droves
from Communist Party affairs.

*On the one hand you were a stalwart on the Party's race-relations committees. On
the other hand you were constantly challenging and contesting the Party in this area.*

More than once, when I made a formal complaint through channels, as
they say, about race relations and the Party, I was called on the carpet and
threatened with expulsion because I was guilty of "defeatism" in what I
thought was a facing of some very real social facts. They said that I should
be removed from that kind of work because my attitudes were wrong, that I
was politically immature. I was instructed to turn to other kinds of Party
activity: the Screen Writers Guild, the Hollywood Anti-Nazi League, and
other such work. I don't know how much was accomplished by my formal
protests. There was no particular change in the attitude of the Party toward
the problems, and I was the patsy.

Was this your first dubiety regarding the Party?

I felt certain qualms early on, certain dissatisfactions beginning on a theoretical level, not a technical one. I went to a Party school, an educational
fortnight up in San Bernardino, and it was presided over with great unction
and importance by V. J. Jerome, who lectured at interminable length. He was
a defrocked rabbi and said everything twenty times in very much the same
way. He was lecturing one day on an aspect of inter-Party structure called,
euphemistically, "democratic centralism." I listened with a great deal of respect and attention, and then in the question-and-answer period I asked,
"Comrade Jerome, what if a Party decision is made that you cannot go along
with?" And he said, "When the Party makes a decision, it becomes your
opinion." Well, that smelled a little like brainwashing to me. I didn't like it
at all. But I swept it under the rug.

This was really the beginning of a process of dubiety. For example, jumping
around a bit in time, I felt that the Party emphasis on the war effort was false,
because it omitted a very important aspect of World War II, which was to
preserve the imperialist interests of the United States and Great Britain in
the middle of the war against Hitler's Fascism. They ignored the fact that
Churchill's program of "the soft underbelly of Europe," the Mediterranean
campaign, might have been nonsense from a military standpoint, but from a
geopolitical standpoint it made good sense—to Mr. Churchill. That kind of
thing was swept under the rug by the Party because this was a war against
Hitler and Fascism, and nothing else could even be mentioned.

On the domestic front, also, I was bothered. A. Philip Randolph, a great
black leader, felt that the time was right for a protest against discrimination
toward blacks in the armed forces, and he organized an enormous march on
Washington, to [President Franklin D.] Roosevelt's tremendous annoyance.
The Party sided with Roosevelt, and the march was put off, due to Party

influence in the high places of Randolph's organization. Also, I need scarcely say that the Japanese relocation centers, the concentration camps for Japanese, though an administration decision, were supported by the Party, to its later shame.

In fact your last Party meeting—before you entered the military—was once again taken up with your opposition to the blindness to racial discrimination during the war.

The last Party meeting that I attended before I went into the service had a special character and a special disappointment. All of us who went into the military were advised to get out of the Party, sever any connection with the Party, for obvious legal reasons. So I went to a meeting of the section committee as a kind of guest; it was a little bit of a farewell for me. There was one item on the agenda, only one. That was, "What did you do for the war effort last week?" They went around the room, and I became increasingly appalled. Well, "appalled" is too strong a word. I was unhappy because these dedicated men were talking no differently than Republicans and Democrats. They said, "My contribution to the war effort was selling seventy-five thousand dollars worth of war bonds." Well, why not? The Bank of America certainly approved of that. All the other contributions were similar.

Out of courtesy, they asked me what I had done this past week, my final week with the Party. I said that I had spoken at a meeting at a black church in protest against racial discrimination in the armed forces. This was something that the Party didn't talk about, because it was a war against Hitler, and we were not to show that we were a country of prejudices. So I had, in my final week in the Party, done what was officially a very un-Communist thing. In the ruckus of indignation that followed this confession of mine, I was asked why I had joined the Party in the first place if I wasn't willing to accept its discipline. I said I'd joined originally because the Communist Party was eager and willing to do the things that nobody else would do, the unpopular and courageous things. That was the Party I had joined. I said, "It seems to me that at this moment I might as well be in some goddamned country club, not sitting around with Communists."

What in general did you think of Browderism and the patriotic drift of the Party during World War II?

From a theoretical standpoint, I looked upon it as backsliding, as a betrayal, really, of revolutionary purposes. It was the result of the ascendancy of Earl Browder into the leadership. He was an amiable Kansan and a very nice and very well-intentioned man, but he was a reformist liberal who talked in Marxist phraseology. In sum, Browder added up to collaboration with the administration, not support of the administration on certain issues and criticism of the administration on other issues. That to me should have been the role of the Party, not all-out support of the war effort and the Roosevelt administration. The Party, of course, woke up to this disastrous situation, but only after

[Jacques] Duclos*, the head of the French Communist Party, had written a stinging criticism of Browder and Browderism. After that, Communists dutifully went in the other direction.

Did you rejoin the Party after the war?

I really intended to, despite the many misgivings I had, because it seemed the healthiest place to be, politically. Browder had been deposed, and the Party was back on track. And the Party was obviously willing to accept me back, despite a certain maverick quality in my track record. I was merely waiting for the tap.

Two Party men—one of whom later became an informer—came to see me and offered me a plum. I was offered the privilege of reviewing a very important book for a magazine of the League of American Writers. John Howard Lawson was the editor, and very much the editor, of that magazine. This book was Norman Mailer's *The Naked and the Dead*, which I had read and admired, and I was delighted to be able to discuss it in print. But the Party position, as evidenced in a previous review in the East, was that the novel distorted the American scene somewhat by omitting the existence and potential of the left. In my review I took note of that, and I stated an honest disagreement with the Party. My honest opinion was that it was a distinguished novel, that Norman Mailer's platoon represented a cross section of America across the spectrum, and that he was correct in his omission because there really wasn't a powerful left wing in America. To introduce a Communist into that platoon would have been a falsification, artistically and politically. I said this, and in the last paragraph I lamented the fact of the disarray on the left and said that there was a new wave coming, in effect, and that we weren't prepared for it. We were liable to get slaughtered. The review was published, omitting this last paragraph. When I complained, I was told that, having won the war, America was on the course of a widening and burgeoning progressivism, and we had nothing to fear from the right. That dampened my enthusiasm for rejoining the Party. That was, you might say, my final dubiety. I wish the Party had been correct.

In spite of everything you have said about FDR, we know that you and other Hollywood Communists were his sincere admirers. And it is hard to imagine the blacklist happening if he hadn't died when he did, passing the torch to Truman. You had occasion to meet Roosevelt once, during World War II. Can you describe the circumstances?

---

*An essay by French Communist theorist Jacques Duclos, entitled "On the Dissolution of the American Communist Party" and published in the April 1945 *Cahiers du Communisme*, bitterly criticized "the notorious revision of Marxism" by popular American Communist leader Earl Browder. Considered a message delivered indirectly by the French from Stalin himself, this document ended the de facto Communist alliance with American liberals so important in Hollywood, helping to usher in a period of isolation and repression.

I don't want to give the impression from my criticism of the Party's collaboration with the New Deal that I disapproved of the New Deal. I didn't. As a matter of fact, I did admire Franklin Roosevelt enormously, and I had the great pleasure of meeting him under circumstances that had to do with my role as a screenwriter.

I'd sold a play [*Brooklyn U.S.A.*] that had been on Broadway to Warner Brothers, and it was a play about corruption and gangsterism on the waterfront. The studio was worried that the administration might not approve of it, so I was sent to Washington to consult with Isador Lubin, who counseled Roosevelt on matters of labor. I got along fine with Lubin, and after getting the green light for the picture, I went with him on the way to lunch. As we were going past the Oval Office door, it opened, and out came FDR himself, pushed in a wheelchair by a Secret Service man. He saw Lubin and said, "Izzy, come here. I want to talk to you." Lubin excused himself from me and went over to Roosevelt; they whispered a few moments, and then Roosevelt looked over at me and gave me a come-hither signal. I was a little overwhelmed, a little self-conscious, but I advanced. He said, "So you're a Hollywood screenwriter and you work at Warner Brothers, a good Democratic studio! Glad to meet you, John!" He remembered from that whisper my first name. Then he said something to this effect: "Give my regards to Jack Warner and all the boys. You're doing a great job for the Party out there." The Party, of course, in this case meant the Democratic Party. So I took his hand again and he repeated my name. I walked away on the wings of morning. The electricity of that man's personality was unbelievable.

What was the first hint you had of the coming blacklist?

The first hint of any personal difficulty that I might get into because of my political activity came around 1940.* I didn't take it seriously at all. It was almost comic opera. I got a subpoena to go to the downtown offices of the congressional committee headed by Martin Dies, who was a sort of spiritual father of Joe McCarthy at a later date. I showed up there with my lawyer, Charles Katz, who subsequently was one of the attorneys for the Hollywood Ten, and when we walked into the outer office, on a long coffee table were a lot of scrapbooks showing all these lurid reports from the Hearst press and other papers of Martin Dies—Martin Dies speaking, yelling, defending America from the red menace. We looked at this with considerable clinical interest, and suddenly a horse-faced woman appeared, grabbed the scrapbooks out of our hands, and said, "You can't look at those! They're classified! They're top-

---

*A grand jury, convening in Los Angeles during the summer of 1940, instigated charges that Communist and Communist sympathizes had infiltrated the film industry. Texas congressman Martin Dies, head of a panel investigating subversive activities (predecessor of the House Un-American Activities Committee), convoked a secret hearing into the allegations. But the film industry united against his headline-hunting, and the "Hollywood reds" furor temporarily blew over.

secret!" Stuff that had appeared in the Hearst press all over the county classified? Top-secret?

Miss Horse Face took the scrapbooks and put them into a safe, and then shielded the safe with her body as she closed it and the classified documents were taken away from our subversive eyes. A few minutes later, we were invited into the inner office, and the two Dies Committee investigators were like a team of cops anywhere. One impaled me with his gaze, as though I were a criminal, and said very little. The other one gave out with a lot of snow and con—asked me about my movies, praised me, complimented me with goose grease, and then said, "Here, you're subpoenaed to go to Washington." I turned to Charley with my hand out like this and said, "Do I accept this?" Charley said, "No, you don't have to. Where is the first-class airplane ticket?" One investigator said, "We don't have that now." Charley said, "Then the serving of this subpoena is illegal. Johnny, let's go." We walked out. That was my first taste of what later became something very serious.

When HUAC started going strong in 1947, you also had a close encounter with Richard Nixon. You debated him publicly, in fact.

I'm an old adversary of Nixon. In one of many subversive organizations, we had a radio show and debates on the air, and we used to poll the public to choose the winner of the debate. The subject of one show was "Resolved: That the House Un-American Activities Committee Is Un-American." The affirmative was supposed to be taken by Bob Kenny, then California attorney general, with Richard Nixon, then in the House, on the other side. I worked with Kenny on the first fifteen minutes of his presentation. But Kenny liked to drink, and he'd get lost in a restaurant telling old sea stories. He didn't show up. Phil Dunne was the moderator, and I said, "He's not going to show up. I'll substitute for him, though I hate to do it." Phil said, "You'll have to clear it with Nixon."

So he went in and talked to Nixon, who said, "Who is this man? Just a writer? Okay, fine." He was a little nervous against Kenny, because Kenny was a really good debater. So I debated Nixon, and according to the returns on the switchboard I won two to one, partly due to the fact that the people who bothered to phone in were sympathetic. Nixon took it very bad; he was furious. He came over to me, and you'd think he would offer his hand. He looked at me very narrowly and said, "Do you have a card?" I pulled out my wallet and gave it to him. It had just my name on it. He said, "That's just your name. You must live somewhere." I said, "Are you going to invite me to lunch, Mr. Nixon?" But for the record, I wrote down my address and phone number.

I wonder if he made a personal note of it for later on, when HUAC was expanding their lists beyond the original nineteen.

[Laughs]. Of course, pretty soon there was a subpoena out for me, but I ducked it. I went down to Mexico. . . .

Jean Rouverol Butler (and Hugo Butler)

JEAN ROUVEROL BUTLER, Los Angeles, California, 1983

INTERVIEW BY PAUL BUHLE
AND DAVE WAGNER

JEAN ROUVEROL BUTLER
(1916–)

AS ACTRESS
1934 *It's a Gift*
1935 *Private Worlds*
     Bar-20 Rides Again
     Mississippi
1936 *Fatal Lady*
     The Leavenworth Case
1937 *The Road Back*
     Stage Door
1938 *The Law West of Tombstone*
     Annabel Takes a Tour
     Western Jamboree

AS SCREENWRITER
1950 *So Young, So Bad.* Costory, coscript.
1952 *The First Time.* Costory, coscript.
1953 *Autumn Leaves.* Story.

1959 *The Miracle.* Uncredited coscript.
1963 *A Face in the Rain.* Coscript.
1968 *The Legend of Lylah Clare.* Coscript.

HUGO BUTLER
(1914–1968)

1936 *Arsene Lupin Returns.* Uncredited contribution.
1937 *Big City.* Coscript.
1938 *The Adventures of Huckleberry Finn.* Script.
     A Christmas Carol. Script.
1939 *Society Lawyer.* Coscript.
     Young Tom Edison. Costory, coscript.
1940 *Wyoming.* Coscript.
     Blossoms in the Dust. Uncredited contribution.
     Edison, the Man. Costory.
1941 *Barnacle Bill.* Coscript.
     Free and Easy. Uncredited contribution.
     A Yank on the Burma Road. Costory, coscript.

1942 *Lassie Come Home.* Script.
    The Omaha Trail. Coscript.
1944 *Miss Susie Slagle's.* Coscript.
1945 *The Southerner.* Adaptation.
    From This Day Forward. Coscript.
1947 *Roughshod.* Coscript.
1949 *A Woman of Distinction.* Costory.
1950 *Eye Witness.* Costory, coscript.
    The Prowler/Cost of Living. Coscript.
1951 *The First Time.* Costory, coscript.
    The Highwayman. Uncredited contribution.
    The Big Night. Coscript.
    He Ran All the Way. Coscript.
1953 *The Adventures of Robinson Crusoe.* Coscript
    (as Philip Roll).

1954 *World for Ransom.* Coscript.
1955 *La escondida.* Coscript.
1956 *Torero!* (documentary). Coscript, codirector
    (as Hugo Mozo).
1958 *Los pequeños gigantes/How Tall Is a Giant?*
    Coscript, director.
    Cowboy. Uncredited contribution.
1961 *The Young One/La joven.* Coscript
    (as H. B. Addis).
    A Face in the Rain. Coadaptation.
1962 *Eva.* Coscript.
1963 *Sodom and Gomorrah.* Coscript.
1968 *The Legend of Lylah Clare.* Coscript.
1969 *Figures de arena/Sand Sculptures.* Story basis.
1972 *Running Scared.* Adaptation.

■

JEAN ROUVEROL BUTLER, the daughter of a successful playwright and early scenarist, first found her way into films as a teenage actress playing featured parts in such vintage films as *It's a Gift* and *Mississippi*—both W. C. Fields vehicles—and *Stage Door.* She met and married Hugo Butler, son of the veteran screenwriter Frank Butler. Butler *père* wrote Laurel and Hardy comedies and Bob Hope and Bing Crosby "road" pictures, and shared an Oscar for coscripting *Going My Way*; Hugo Butler specialized in family and literary fare at MGM (the classic films he scripted include *Huckleberry Finn*, *A Christmas Carol*, and *Lassie Come Home*) before evolving in his career toward a collaboration with Jean Renoir and increasingly adventurous material. Frank Butler, a frequent writer for director Leo McCarey, one of the leaders of Hollywood's noisy right-wing faction, was as profoundly conservative as his son and his son's wife were resolutely left-wing.

On the surface, during Hugo Butler's peak years of the 1940s, the Butlers seemed a typical Hollywood success story. Working closely with Hugo on many ideas for films, Jean Butler observed his methods and purposes. She also began selling magazine fiction. Then the blacklist arrived, forcing both Butlers out of the Hollywood mainstream.

The Butlers had been Communist Party members, and although their activism had waxed and waned, they remained faithful to the left. Hugo Butler was one of the first to go "underground" to dodge a HUAC subpoena, and the Butlers left Hollywood shortly after the Ten got out of jail, forming the advance guard of the Mexico City refugees. Living in Mexico and then in Italy, raising children and, later, coping with her husband's declining health, Jean Butler did occasional work as a screenwriter. The credits, sometimes in partnership with her husband, were pseudonymous for a time; after her husband's death in 1968, she wrote extensively for daytime television.

The Butler family tradition, three generations of Hollywood screenwrit-

ers, continues with Jean and Hugo's son Michael Butler, whose script credits
include *Brannigan*, *The Gauntlet*, and *Pale Rider*.

■

Let's talk about your family background a bit.

Women from Utah had voted for quite a while and my mother, Aurania
Ellerbeck, was a Republican feminist. She had been a change-of-life baby, the
youngest of twenty-two children, only eight of whom were born to her
mother. My grandfather was an apostate Mormon. After two years of trying
to figure out a name for her, someone noticed that a Cunard liner named the
Aurania had docked in San Pedro, and they all thought, "What a nice name!"
My mother went to Radcliffe to study playwriting, and while she was there
in 1912 and 1913, she marched in a famous suffragette parade. She also succeeded Alice Brady, playing Meg in *Little Women* [on Broadway and on the
road] at a time when no so-called "decent woman" went on the stage.

My father was a bank teller from a family of amateur stage performers. My
mother wanted children, so she married him. When I was three, she abandoned him, taking along myself and my brother, who was a year and a half
younger than me. The only thing she kept was his last name, but she dropped
the original spelling, "Rouveyrol," when a numerologist friend of hers told
her it was bad luck. Then she and her two sisters came out to California, and
I grew up in Los Angeles. My mother taught English for a while. That's when
she wrote a play, *Skidding*, upon which the Andy Hardy series was based.
Skidding outran everything in New York the year of its production, 1926,
except *Abie's Irish Rose*.

MGM wanted to buy the play. My mother's nephew was an attorney, and
he said, "Wait a minute." She had the sense to demand a contract for use of
the characters in film. Every year she would get a payment of five thousand
dollars for the rights. It was enough to live on comfortably, in various parts
of Los Angeles. Finally, she took us up to Palo Alto. When I was in the ninth
or tenth grade, she went under contract with Metro, and they put her to work
on gangster pictures. She even had to write an orgy for one of them! Her
best-known picture was *Dance, Fools, Dance*, with Joan Crawford and Clark
Gable in the cast.

How did your own career begin?

I graduated from Palo Alto High School in 1933, and I wanted to be an
actress. Instead of going straight through my senior year, I went to New York
to attend the American Academy of Dramatic Art. But my mother was not
feeling well and insisted that we both come back. I got accepted at Stanford,
and she did a play for me, *Growing Pains*, in Pasadena. From her experience
with *Skidding*, my mother had discovered the "amateur market," all the high
schools and small towns that needed to do family-type material with a few
characters and one set, and didn't want to pay much for it. In Pasadena, Anne

Shirley and several other former child actors who had reached the awkward age appeared with me in *Growing Pains*.

How did you find your way to the left?

There's nothing in my family background that moved me into the left. I was doing *Growing Pains* at the Pasadena Playhouse when Paramount signed me as an actress for the lead in *Eight Girls in a Boat*. But I was feeling not ready and terrified, so my mother took me out of that production. Instead I went to New York with *Growing Pains*, though it only had a very short run.

On the train back from New York, my mother was taking a constitutional, and she saw a young man hunched over a typewriter, typing something in the dramatic form. She introduced herself, he introduced himself as Maurice Rapf, and of course she knew the name of his father, Harry Rapf. She brought Maurice back to me almost like a mother cat with a mouse. She didn't know that he quite promptly invited me to my first Communist study group, on Christmas 1933. I think it was at the house of Tess Schlesinger that he asked me to be part of the group. He also introduced me to Budd Schulberg, I remember.

I had signed a film contract at Paramount with six months off and six months on. That arrangement gave me a chance to go to Stanford, and there I took something called "Introduction to Western Civilization." It was really a study of Socialism. At that point, I didn't even know what Socialism was. I found myself reading a little of [Socialist Party leader] Norman Thomas and [left-liberal economist] Stuart Chase; they were making awfully good sense. I got back after my first semester and rejoined the Marxist study group in Hollywood. I found myself reading all these political books that, except for a few, bored the hell out of me. *The Communist Manifesto* was a marvelous piece. Howard Selsam's *What Is Philosophy?* was a wonderful book. I can't remember anything else I really enjoyed.

My mother was convinced that the course at Stanford had corrupted me. She even told the Stanford regents that it had turned her daughter into a Socialist. Meanwhile, she told me that she would be very interested in belonging to a study group herself. She joined another study group, as a self-appointed double agent. This was funny: at one point she insisted that she was a capitalist, and a director's wife told her, "No, we're all workers." Meanwhile, the FBI interviewed her, and she cooperated with them, giving names and details.

As I got pretty involved in my career in my late teens, I was aware of a whole gang of young Hollywood types, some on the left and some who may or may not have been: Virginia Ray (who later married Schulberg), [actor] Maurice Murphy, Marian Edwards (she subsequently married Irwin Shaw), Marie Rinaldo, and a bunch of junior writers at Metro, including Fred Rinaldo, Bobby Lees, and Alvin Josephy Jr., who was not on the left but was a good Democrat. Some of these people became my friends.

I drifted away politically, because I knew that I wanted to be a writer and wanted to take the time to read serious fiction. Tolstoy, Dostoevsky, Romain

Rolland, and *The Magic Mountain* by Thomas Mann—that was my serious reading.

But your acting career also went on.

Yes, it got to where I was doing leads in little pictures and character parts in big pictures. In *It's a Gift* I'm W. C. Fields's daughter. I did ingenue leads in three westerns, with Gene Autry, William Boyd (that is, Hopalong Cassidy), and Harry Carey and Tim Holt. I was also in a little mystery called *The Leavenworth Case,* and I even played the screen's first schizophrenic, in *Private Worlds.* I also played in two *Crime Doesn't Pay* shorts, written by Bobby [Robert] Lees and Fred Rinaldo. Irving Pichel, later a director and one of the Hollywood Nineteen, was in one of them. It had to do with gangsterism in the dry-cleaning business, and I played the daughter of the owner.

By 1936 I was doing another play in New York, *So Proudly We Hail.* It lasted two weeks, the second of my two Broadway flops. Just before I came back to California, I wrote a scene for Maurice Murphy's screen test for MGM, and I acted in it with him. Meanwhile, a buddy named Waldo Salt, who had been on the crew of one my mother's plays in Palo Alto but who wanted to be a playwright, wanted to take me out so he could talk to my mother. By now Waldo was a junior writer under contract at Metro. Some friends said, "He's got a friend, the cutest boy, named Hugo Butler. You'd really like him." That wasn't on my mind. I only wanted to hear if there were any rumors about my screen test. Anyway, I called Waldo, who asked me to lunch at the Metro commissary.

Over lunch, he had his officemate along, a delightful Canadian wearing an argyle sweater and smelling faintly of aftershave. I said to him, "What are you working on, Mr. Butler?" He had been waiting for this. He answered, "I'm working on a screenplay from a property by Miss Aurania Rouverol." He meant one of the Andy Hardy films—although he never received a credit on that one.

Immediately I was entranced with Hugo. A few days later I was invited to a cocktail party up in the Hollywood Hills, and Hugo called to ask if he could take me, "to obviate your having to find your own way." I thought to myself, "Any man who uses the word 'obviate' in casual conversation is the man for me." His father was an old-time writer named Frank Butler who then or soon after helped form the Screen Playwrights and talked Hugo and Waldo into joining. It was the company union, created to forestall a real union. Subsequently it became a bitterly anti-Communist group. During this period I did more ingenue leads, including one in *The Road Back* (the sequel to *All Quiet on the Western Front*), and a character part in *Stage Door.* I then got a radio job as the wife of the youngest boy in *One Man's Family,** which was on once a week.

---

*One Man's Family, fashioned by Carleton Morse from John Galsworthy's *The Forsyte Saga,* ran from 1937 to 1959. From 1938 to 1951 Jean Butler played Betty, the wife of Jack, the young man in the family. See John Dunning, *Tune in Yesterday.*

I flirted Hugo away from another girl, we went together, and now came the spring of 1937. I was engaged to Hugo, and the Spanish Civil War was a big issue, as was the Japanese incursion into China. The left campaigned against selling scrap metal to Japan. The Abraham Lincoln Brigade was being formed and sent to Spain. We regularly canceled our subscription to the *Los Angeles Times*, which was a real right-wing rag.

Hugo was not a citizen yet, so he felt that he couldn't join anything. We had married, and in 1939 we had our first baby. She died of birth injuries. Simultaneously, the war broke out. By 1941, about eight months after I had started to work at Metro as a junior writer, we had our son, and then our oldest daughter in late 1942. We were pretty involved in family. In 1943 Waldo invited Hugo to join the Party. I thought of all that reading I didn't enjoy doing. A few nights later Hugo announced, "I gave Waldo the nod for us."

By now I was sublimating my acting career. Hugo was doing well as a writer. I was also pregnant and still going down to record *One Man's Family*. It was a full, rich life.

But I promptly found myself on subcommittees, collecting dues, picking up books, and so forth. Hugo was somewhat dismayed: he thought I was already spending too much time with the PTA and the YWCA board. Hugo was drafted in the spring of 1945, while I was still on *One Man's Family* and working on a novella.

Anyone going into the armed forces automatically got a leave from the Communist Party, and I took one, too. I found that a sort of relief. Our next baby was conceived on the parade ground of Fort Ord on a quiet day.

Not long after, I found out that I had sold my first story, for five thousand dollars, to *McCall's*. Hugo wasn't there for me to tell him. By now he'd become a corporal at Ord. He was elaborating the ideas of Earl Browder's *Victory and After** in the recreation-hall newspaper and making a big hit in the Army.

Let's stop here and catch up with some of Hugo's films. He did A Christmas Carol *and then* Huckleberry Finn. *He seems to have been the children's-classics specialist for MGM.*

Let me tell you about Hugo and adaptations: he understood that what you had to capture was the spirit, the quality, of each book. One exception was his rewrite of Waldo's script of *Huckleberry Finn*. The result was slapstick, mostly about "the Duke" and "the King," but nearly every time he wrote an adaptation, he strove to get the voice of the author as accurately as possible.

---

*Victory and After, by the secretary-general of the American Communist Political Association, Earl Browder, laid out a rosy scenario for the future: Russian-American cooperation would herald world peace and economic cooperation. Bitterly criticized by Communists themselves in 1946 (when the Communist Political Association renamed itself the Communist Party), *Victory and After* was seen retrospectively as an embrace of capitalism, and Browder was removed from office.

When he was writing *A Christmas Carol*, we were reading everything we could find about Dickens. And when he was writing *Huckleberry Finn*, he was immersing himself in Twain's *Life on the Mississippi*, and so forth.

In A Christmas Carol, the happiness of the Cratchit family is definitely a blue-collar moment, not just about the general human condition, as in the other versions. The other thing amazing about the film is that Scrooge is socially explained.

Hugo saw Scrooge as a lonely kid, someone nobody had ever loved. In the other film versions, it was all too damned cute. Hugo was still a junior writer at Metro (at the time); he was making either thirty-five dollars a week, which was his original salary, or seventy-five dollars, which was his promotion when his option was up. He wrote very efficiently and accurately.

Let me ask about the two Thomas Alva Edison biographies Young Tom Edison *and* Edison, the Man.

Hugo worked like a dog. He went back east for research. *Young Tom Edison*, starring Mickey Rooney, was partly rewritten by Bradbury Foote; the credit was shared. I think *Edison, the Man*, with Spencer Tracy, was more Hugo's own, and that got an Oscar nomination [for Best Original Story]. But they're both very nice pictures.

Lassie Come Home *was another one. Do you know why he was so good with this particular children's story?*

Hugo's memories of his own childhood, his boyhood, were very sharp. His family usually had a dog. *Lassie* he absolutely adored: he wrote it in something like two weeks, very early into our marriage, although it wasn't shot till a few years later. It's absolutely, totally faithful to the book. During the war a friend of ours met the novelist, Eric Knight, someplace in southern Africa. Fox had made of film of *This Above All* [another Knight novel], and Knight was kvetching about it, but he said, "On the other hand, the movie Hollywood made of *Lassie Come Home* was wonderful."

Was it clear right away that it was going to become a classic?

Nobody thought much about film "classics" those days. The only classics were Eisenstein, German expressionism, and *The Birth of a Nation*. We knew that we liked it very much.

There are so many wonderful things in that film.

It is important to remember that Hugo's parents were British, and he grew up in Canada. In U.S. culture, anything goes: you aren't boxed into your class, and you can go in any direction. In Britain there is this extraordinary social continuity or tradition that is represented strongly in *Lassie*.

Hugo had grown up among Brits and had a sharp sense of them. That was also the reason that he never could be a "friendly witness." No British or

Canadian schoolchild would ever rat on anyone, friend or foe. You just don't rat.

How about Barnacle Bill?

It was an interesting film. Marjorie Main was a strong, working-class woman, and Wallace Beery played a real proletarian. This was written at a time when Hugo was getting kind of restless at Metro. Out of every hundred pictures written each year, only twenty-five were made. Writers in those days were already thinking, "If only we could work independently, we could get out from under this terrible studio system." Anyway, when his contract renewal came up, they offered him some new projects and said, "These scripts will keep you out of the Army." He was so offended that he quit the studio, and that's when he was drafted almost immediately.

How about Miss Susie Slagle's?

It's from a novel [by Augusta Tucker]: Susie, who was played by Lillian Gish, runs a boardinghouse for medical students in turn-of-the-century New York. The film was directed by John Berry, one of his first. Hugo's was a fine adaptation, and it made a lovely, romantic picture. We saw a lot of the other scriptwriter, Anne Froelick, and her husband at that time. She was having a terrible time getting pregnant, and we had all these babies.

What can you tell me about Hugo's work with Jean Renoir on The Southerner?

The film was based on a book by George Sessions Perry, *Hold Autumn in Your Hand.* Hugo was the first writer on that script. He was absolutely captivated by Jean Renoir and by Renoir's lifestyle. Renoir lived about three blocks from us, and his whole house was all white, all plain, but here and there one of his father's pictures was hung. In the dining room there was a fireplace where they barbecued; the bread was laid out on a plank, and you just hacked off a piece. Hugo had never experienced French living, and he found all this absolutely fascinating.

Then he discovered that Renoir had another writer also working on the script. Under the Screen Writers Guild rules, that was strictly not allowed. Hugo was so offended, so hurt, because he had had such a crush on Renoir, that he walked away and took his name off the picture. Then he saw the completed picture's rough cut and realized that his contribution was substantial, so he asked for an adaptation credit, and Renoir gave it to him. Renoir could never understand why Hugo was so upset. He said, "That's the way I work." The second writer was, of course, William Faulkner.

The Southerner was "banned in Memphis," which turned out to be a way to get people into the theater to see the film. It's a fascinating, wonderful film. I have to tell you that the idiot character, the poor, wistful moron, was Faulkner's own contribution, a very good one.

Let's talk about one of my favorites, as a left-wing film buff: From This Day Forward, *adapted from Tom Bell's novel* All Brides Are Beautiful, *about working-class life in the Bronx during the Depression.*

I thought that it was a very nice picture. We didn't see these films with the same eyes as you do. But it was a little gem of a book. We were looking for material all through that time, and every time Hugo found something he really liked, it got made. He was in love with *All Brides Are Beautiful*.

I don't remember whether he was already writing seriously on it or had just begun. But we went to some premiere with the Lardners [Ring Lardner Jr. and Frances Chaney Lardner] and Ian [McLellan] Hunter and his wife, Alice Goldberg Hunter, who was a screen reader. Alice said, "With the war still on, you can't do this picture now; it's so pessimistic about the human condition." She meant: here we were in a holy war, in concert with the Soviet Union, and he ought not to write a picture about the Depression.

This depressed the living hell out of Hugo. He was awake all night trying to figure out how to get around the pessimism. That's why he wrote the film as a flashback from 1945, starting with an ex-GI in the unemployment office.

There's a lot in the film: working-class life, the struggles of a young artist, the miseries of the blue-collar housewife, the disappointed hopes of somehow getting out, like starting a chicken farm, and so on. But the scene which I have seen used in documentaries about the blacklist is the little boy asking a butcher if he can have a bone "for his dog," except that he hasn't got a dog, and the butcher knows it.

Hugo hated that scene. Someone else they brought in wrote that. I'm embarrassed when I see it used now in documentaries about the blacklist.

Nevertheless, From This Day Forward *is a unusual film, because it shows life on the factory floor and gives a radical, non-Hollywood view of life's disappointments.*

Being a radical was very good for Hugo as a writer because it gave him a point of view, an edge.

Now let's talk a little about the political scene, which was making Hugo's work, as well as yours, more and more precarious.

We had another baby, and that got Hugo out of the Army. It was time for him to go back to regular Party meetings, and he asked me, "Are you sure you want to go back? I'd never see you." It was okay with me not to go back; I wanted to continue reading the things that mattered to me. But I continued to work on the committees—I considered myself part of the ladies' auxiliary in HICCASP* and things like that, especially in the Henry Wallace campaign and the defense of the Hollywood Ten.

---

*HICCASP was the Hollywood branch of the Independent Citizens Committee of the Arts, Sciences, and Professions, a national group of liberals and radicals first drawn together to

You've been one of the few blacklistees to talk openly about the disparity between men and women on the left in Hollywood and the effect of the HUAC persecutions on personal relationships.

In the old days of the left-left, that is, of the Communist Party, the men were always working in a group in the Beverly Hills area, and the wives were sent out to the San Fernando Valley with the dentists' and doctors' wives. Within the studios, the most important writers were in the elite group, and the rest of us were in a hodgepodge with all the nonprofessionals, the script readers and so forth. I considered myself a professional entitled to be treated as a grown-up writer. But I was always out in the Valley with the other women.

I look back and realize that these men were just as chauvinist as anyone. They endowed themselves with a larger-than-life quality, so that we had to be keepers of the flame and feed into that elevation. They didn't think "the woman question" applied to them. Albert Maltz was extraordinary in this regard. The American left male articulated a very good position on women's rights. But he didn't live it in his own domestic relationships. There were very few exceptions. Nevertheless, when the men went to jail, the women were marvelous.

How did the blacklist creep up on you?

I remember being kind of puzzled by the outbreak of the Cold War. There had been a point during Stalingrad when Hugo's father had said, "If the Russians hold, I'm changing my nationality." But soon after the end of the war it all changed. I could see the political alliances unravel, but I couldn't understand why.

Dalton Trumbo had been secretly hustled up to San Francisco to write a speech for [producer] Walter Wanger in the early days of the United Nations. He met with Alger Hiss and other officials. It was only in retrospect that this acquired more interest; at the time it seemed perfectly normal.

Subsequently, during the hearings and the period of the Waldorf Conference,* there was a meeting at a little theater in Hollywood where Dore Schary [chief of production at RKO in 1947, he shortly moved over to MGM], Walter Wanger, and an MGM official addressed members of the Screen Writers Guild: "Just give us these ten [unfriendly witnesses] without protest and the hearings will end here,—no more persecution." After a discussion, the screenwriters agreed. Trumbo got up and, referring to Wanger, asked angrily, "How

---

support Franklin Roosevelt's reelection in 1944 and then reorganized to resist the rightward turn in the Democratic Party. The principal political organization backing Henry Wallace in 1946 and 1947, it merged into the Progressive Citizens of America (PCA). HICCASP served as the mobilization center for Hollywood's progressives across a spectrum of postwar issues.

*In November 1947 studio executives met in New York, at the Waldorf-Astoria Hotel, to discuss the HUAC hearings and decide the fate of the Hollywood Ten. The assembled moguls and producers announced the firing of the Ten and a new policy of political self-regulation that, in effect, ushered in an industry-wide blacklist.

dare this man say these things, when every political word that he ever uttered I put into his mouth?"

We were thoroughly involved in the defense of the Ten. Before the last denial by the Supreme Court, we were beginning to hear rumors about the McCarran Act. Congress was refurbishing some bill like the Alien and Sedition Acts, the right to intern "aliens and saboteurs."* We weren't feeling good about that, partly because we had not protested the internment of the Japanese. Back then we were so gung-ho about the war effort, we were shameless.

With all this going on, and reports of a subpoena out for him, Hugo was still productive.

He would meet with Joe Losey and others, secretly, in motels.

In the midst of all this, Hugo wrote A Woman of Distinction, *a funny little movie with Rosalind Russell as a college dean and Ray Milland as a visiting professor who provokes a scandal.*

It was written on the greylist, by Hugo and Ian [McLellan] Hunter.† They were both not working, both depressed, and they thrashed it out, just a film by two men desperate for money.

It's a reminder, though, that Hugo did write wonderful women's films, films about strong women.

I was a working mother, and my mother was a strong woman. He had known strong women. He was always impressed by the women writers at Metro, and his father had worked with Zoë Akins and others.

What was Hugo's contribution to The Prowler, *a Losey thriller that is rather dark and disturbing?*

Initially it was written by [Dalton] Trumbo. Hugo went on the project to cover for Trumbo, so there would be a writer on the set. He did make contributions. But it was really much more Trumbo than him.

---

*The McCarran Internal Security Act of 1950 established the Subversive Activities Control Board and made provision for the creation of holding areas (often referred to by the left as "concentration camps") for subversives in case of national crisis. The Alien and Sedition Acts had been passed by Congress in 1798 in anticipation of war with France. The Federalists claimed that support of the Republicans (then the liberal opposition party) by immigrants amounted to foreign influence and sedition. Lengthening the residency requirement for naturalized citizenship, making persons from enemy nations ineligible for citizenship, and authorizing the deportation of subversives, the Naturalization Act of 1798 set the pattern for later conservative measures. The Sedition Act prohibited assembly "with intent to oppose any measure . . . of the government" and likewise made it illegal to "print, utter, or publish" antigovernment views. Although the next president, Thomas Jefferson, suspended all enforcement, the statutes remained on the books for later use.

†The officially credited screenwriter is Charles Hoffman.

You've said that, ironically, just as the blacklist was beginning, Hugo was in the middle of a great transformation in his own writing.

Hugo had never thought of film writing as an art. But it was an intellectual challenge to him. And I can remember key moments in his life when he felt he had made a breakthrough toward new ways of telling stories. During this period Hugo had been hired to write the screenplay of *The Highwayman*, and when he had almost finished it, we went to see a preview of a picture written by Carl Foreman, *Champion*. The preview was miles out of town, and Hugo was absolutely blown away. As we were riding home, Hugo said, "You know, he's writing movies in a whole different way. He's jump-cutting in place of the dissolve, letting the audience fill in the obvious steps between point A and point C." When Hugo got back he called the producer and said, "I want to start the screenplay over from scratch, and I'll do it for free." This is one time he got into real trouble with the Guild—they said that he couldn't work without salary. But Hugo felt he had taken all that money on the wrong path. Subsequently, *The Highwayman* was made without Hugo's script, anyway. Henry Blankfort wrote the final version.*

From then on, that's the way Hugo wrote everything. Other writers were doing the same thing as Foreman, but much later I called Foreman, when he was sick, and I told him about the effect he had had on Hugo. He was very pleased. He told me, "I was flying by the seat of my pants. I didn't really know what the medium could do until *High Noon*."

All this as you were about to leave for Mexico.

Hugo knew that we would have to leave the country. He had grown up in Canada, and the climate there depressed him. Mexico was the obvious alternative.

We went up to see the Trumbos when Dalton got out of jail and spent a weekend with them. While we were there Cleo said, "There's a wonderful story published in *Harper's*."† I read it, and I almost died of excitement, it was so good. Hugo got Ingo Preminger to take an option on it, and Ingo gave it to Carl Foreman, who took it to Stanley Kramer, who said, "Yes, we'll do it as soon as Hugo is free." But when things got hot, Ingo notified us that what Kramer really wanted to do was to buy Hugo out for three thousand dollars. Would he sign a quit claim? Foreman rode over on his bicycle with a check for three thousand dollars. This became *The Wild One*. With that money Hugo went down to Baja and then to Mexico City.

Did Hugo make a contribution to the film?

---

*The script of *The Highwayman* is officially credited to Jan Jeffries. According to Jeff Blankfort, Henry Blankfort's son, Henry Blankfort supplied a rewrite of Hugo Butler's script, only to be dropped from the credits because of the blacklist.

†The story that became the basis for *The Wild One* was Frank Rooney's "Cyclists' Raid," which appeared in the January 1951 issue of *Harper's*.

No, Hugo simply spotted the property and took an option.

Meanwhile, you had your own script, your first to be produced, So Young, So Bad.

That was done with director Bernie [Bernard] Vorhaus. Every now and then, someone would come by the house with a project that Hugo was too busy to do. That's how I got most of my screen jobs. I was never really a scriptwriter in those days. This one happened because Bernie came to us with an idea for a film about a girls' reformatory, an idea he had got from a feature news story. He had talked to the author of the story, and we both did extensive research. Bernie and I visited a couple of reform schools including the Ventura Home for Girls, where there had recently been a scandal, with terrible things happening, like the girls' heads being shaved. We got all kinds of material and came back and wrote it. I don't think Hugo did anything. Bernie helped me structure the script.

I thought it became a very interesting film. Rita Moreno, Anne Francis, and Anne Jackson, all of them teenagers at the time, were in it, and, of course, Paul Henreid. The film was shot in upstate New York at a Jewish home for the aged and indigent blind.

And meanwhile you were also still writing fiction.

I was still trying to get acquainted with psychology, to learn more about how human beings functioned. Those problems, those relationships, made good drama. I had sold my first novella to *McCall's* for five thousand dollars while Hugo was still in the Army. John Weber helped me restructure the story.

By now Hugo and I had four children. I was pretty thoroughly immersed in being a mother, but I ended up writing and selling four novellas, and over the years I made about twenty thousand dollars writing fiction. Whenever Hugo had an idea he couldn't use, I'd take it up. One I remember: a day in the life of a five-year-old girl when her brand-new brother is being brought home, and what she goes through subconsciously, feeling displaced.

This was also the period when you shared your first cowriting credit with Hugo.

At the suggestion of producer Harold Hecht, Hugo and I wrote the story of a baby's first year and its effect on parents who were in no way prepared for the loss of control. It was the most apolitical story you could think of. The film was made as *The First Time*, with Barbara Hale, Robert Cummings, and Mona Barrie, directed by Frank Tashlin. It was playing in Mexico City on the day we arrived. In fact, three pictures that we had written were all playing then: *So Young, So Bad, The First Time,* and *The Big Night,* which Hugo had written for Joe Losey.

You and Hugo set right to work on various film projects in Mexico.

We got a lot of stuff written and made, both in Spanish and in English, in Mexico. George Pepper was already down there; he had gotten blacklisted first, as the head of HICCASP—the Hollywood Independent Citizens Committee for the Arts, Sciences, and Professions. Pepper became our producer, setting up a small production company with Hugo as writer.* That's the way George was able to package *The Adventures of Robinson Crusoe* with [director Luis] Buñuel. Hugo had the complete script ready before we went down to Mexico.

Hugo didn't think of himself as an artist with a capital A. But he was a terribly, terribly conscientious filmmaker who also loved literature. He tried to get the things that he read and loved onto the screen as nearly intact as possible.

Hugo had always felt that a big budget ruined a picture, because, as he said, "You've got to let an audience use its imagination." Later on, as he was beginning to get sick, he thought a lot about moral ambiguity in pictures. That, too, required the audience to participate in the project, to fill in the gaps in their own way rather than being presented with everything.

One of the things that made him a very interesting film writer is that he thought filmically. When I wrote my first screenplay, I had spent so many years acting on radio that I thought of everything in terms of the ear; I never really conceived of things visually. When I thought of scenes, I thought of what people said to each other—and pretty explicitly, "on the nose." I didn't discover subtext until I got into writing for the soaps. If only I had known about subtext when I first got into movies!

Had either of you made contact with Buñuel before?

Never. Buñuel was working in the United States, at the Museum of Modern Art, when he was attacked publicly by Salvador Dali and by the Catholic Church as a Communist. That was ridiculous: Buñuel was far too anarchistic ever to be a regulation Communist. But he had eventually gone to Mexico and had been working on films there since 1945. Meanwhile, Hugo, faced with Mexico's need for inexpensive production, knew that *Crusoe* was a very cheap property which could be shot in two languages at once. Pepper was getting investments from a group of blacklisted musicians for a feature-length picture. So he took the script to Buñuel and got a commitment; it was almost

---

*A violinist who developed arthritis in his fingers and thereafter threw himself into organizing the musicians' union and other political activity, George Pepper (1913–1969) was a leader of the Hollywood Democratic Committee in the 1944 elections and executive director of HICCASP in postwar Hollywood. Although a Communist, he was one of the great Popular Front organizers. "All who knew and worked beside Pepper attest to his intelligence, discipline, and uncanny knack for bringing together people of diverse partisan viewpoints," wrote Larry Ceplair and Steven Englund in *The Inquisition in Hollywood*. After being blacklisted and relocating in Mexico, Pepper served in an equally unifying role there, as agent, producer, and unwavering bastion of the community of Hollywood exiles.

set up before we got there. And that's how we met Buñuel. Hugo got interested in the avant-garde only after he began working with Buñuel.

Hugo and Buñuel worked together on the shooting script. But they had no actor to play Crusoe. By coincidence, we went with some friends in Mexico to see Orson Welles's production of *Macbeth*, because our friend Jeanette Nolan was playing Lady Macbeth. We were struck by the actor who played Macduff, Dan O'Herlihy. He looked good in a beard, and he became Crusoe.

Crusoe was received with a lot of admiration when it was finally shown in the United States, naturally without Hugo's name on it. Did you like the film?

Yes, it was a fascinating picture. But Buñuel always upset me; he was so idiosyncratic. He made Crusoe in the film a naturalist, because he was one himself. If he ever found a spider in the house he would scoop it up rather than kill it. He was full of these contradictions.

Meanwhile, you managed to work on another film, Autumn Leaves, on which you were given story credit, as Jean Rouverol, but not screenwriting credit. How did that happen?

It all started because [director] Bob [Robert] Aldrich was our buddy. He came down to Mexico to make *Vera Cruz*. Hugo had written for him what was called a "tits and sand" picture, *World for Ransom*, which was practically written over a weekend. Hugo stayed up for two nights and wrote it. Anyway, we helped find a house for him in Mexico. While he was working on *Vera Cruz*, Aldrich told Hugo that he was looking for a cheap property to make. Hugo said, "What about this?" and gave him the tear sheets from one of my stories in *McCall's*. Hugo was working on something else, so I started turning it into a screenplay, with Hugo quarterbacking me.

My story was based on one of Hugo's relatives, an aunt's husband, and was about an older woman who marries a younger man, a psychopathic liar. We had never met a psychopathic liar and had to do some research to understand such a person. We found out that it's usually someone who has no superego to begin with. I remember the secretary who typed the script crying and saying, "That's the story of my second husband!" Anyone who has a family member like that knows all about the condition.

Bob took it up to Hollywood, where [screenwriter] Jack Jevne represented us in story conferences. Jevne fronted for me but didn't really do any work. Two other writers worked on the script, too.* Bob kept in touch with us all the way through the production.

Were all the characters in the film yours?

---

*Lewis Meltzer and Robert Blees are formally credited, along with Jevne, for the *Autumn Leaves* screenplay.

They introduced another character, a landlady, someone for Joan Crawford to talk to. That was a substory I didn't write.

Most people think of it as a Joan Crawford vehicle.

That's how Bob [Aldrich] got to know her. Then, later, he got her for *Whatever Happened to Baby Jane?*

There is a lot of extraordinary material in the film—the psychological interpretation of a woman stuck typing for a living, frustrated and increasingly desperate as she sees her life go by. She is defined as lost, without a family or husband. She bravely attempts a marriage with a younger man, an uncertain and unstable character played by Cliff Robertson. One of the most impressive things takes place on the beach between them. She is very vulnerable. But when the ocean washes over them, their embrace in the ocean's spray signifies a release of sexuality. This scene looks like the original version of the famous beach scene in From Here to Eternity.

That was in my magazine story. My emphasis was, this woman in middle age is scared to death to reveal her body to this young man.

Autumn Leaves *starts like a women's film, but when she learns the truth about him, he starts telling lies, and the twist has a marvelous effect. The film is no longer a "weepie" but becomes more of a psychological thriller.*

Yes, she believes him until he picks up something to throw at her. In my version, there was only the threat of his being arrested for stealing something from the store where he worked, and she can't persuade him to take it back. I think it's much better the way Bob did it.

The film is a forerunner to the Hitchcock and other Psycho-style pictures of the 1960s, not only because of Robertson's character but because Crawford, too, is unstable; that is her main problem, rather than her socioeconomic status. Leonardo Bercovici told me that some left-wing writers had wanted to take a psychoanalytic viewpoint earlier, during the 1940s, but couldn't.

No, you couldn't. The Marxist position was violently anti-Freud. We didn't get around to forgiving psychologists until we got around to using them ourselves, and stood in great need.

Hugo did a number of small films in Mexico, mostly documentaries.

Hugo had always had an interest in documentaries. He figured out that you could make a film by utilizing news footage and staging only a few scenes. So Hugo invented the "docudrama" on his own. In many senses he was feeling his way.

He had become a real bullfight fan. He was present when an over-the-hill bullfighter staged the greatest bullfight of his life. Hugo described to me the audience carrying the fighter, Luis Procuna, all the way to his home, miles away, shouting, "*Torero! Torero!*" the whole way. My son happened to be coming home from a movie and passed this crowd, baffled by it.

Hugo made that bullfight the frame story of a documentary, *Torero!*, from Procuna getting ready for the bullfight onward. Hugo also codirected it with Carlos Velo [the left-wing documentarist who had worked on Buñuel and Dali's *Un chien Andalou*]. You can find *Torero!* in the archives of the Academy, because it won an Oscar nomination as a documentary, and it also won the Robert Flaherty Award for Hugo, at the 1955 Venice Biennale. Hugo used the name Hugo Mozo, which is "Hugo the Houseboy" in Spanish. Some of the Academy audience knew who it really was.

Was there any connection with Trumbo's film The Brave One, *in which the bull grows up a friend of the boy and eventually survives?*

Trumbo went to a different bullfight, with a bad kill. Dalton and Cleo left it with their faces white, horrified. So his experience went one way, Hugo's went another, from two bullfights just weeks apart.

I know Hugo made another well-known docudrama in Mexico.

This was also made under the name Hugo Mozo and was about the Mexican Little League team which won the world-championship game in Williamsport, Pennsylvania.* In English it was called *How Tall Is a Giant?*

So these were productive times, despite your exile.

Yes. I sold two more novellas to the slicks. Hugo and I both worked on a Mexican picture called *La escondida*. I've tried to do a memoir of the Mexico years, and I'm up to two hundred pages. I had to do so much thinking. You never know what you really know until you start to write it down, start having to analyze how you feel about a situation, how you got there, how you feel about it now, how much you are able to be articulate. For me, the richest, most wonderful years of our lives were in Mexico.

But you must have had some very difficult times, too.

The year our fifth child was born, all our possessions were in the national pawnshop. We let Trumbo pawn them because he swore that he had experience with pawnshops. Hugo had *Crusoe* coming out, and in late 1952 we were waiting for his first returns. We had exhausted all our savings. He had written certain people, including his father and my mother and several others, asking for five hundred dollars in exchange for one or two of his points in ownership of *Crusoe*. Hugo's mother collected all the checks and sent them.

Just then the successor to J. Parnell Thomas in the House Committee on Un-American Activities came down to Mexico and had a long conversation with the officials of the federal district. The mail didn't come and didn't come, and I was pregnant out to here. I asked the mailman about it, and he said,

---

*The team from Monterrey, Mexico, became the Little League champions in 1957 by defeating the La Mesa, California, team in the playoffs.

"The mail is censored." So I said, "I'll talk to the supervisor." I explained to the supervisor that we needed the money so badly—we had had to borrow from the cook that morning to buy groceries. The supervisor was appalled; he just saw me as a pregnant woman. I went home, went upstairs, and took a nap. Then I heard the whistle of the mailman. Hugo came upstairs and threw a whole handful of letters on the bed. He quipped, "Never underestimate the power of a woman." The mail included every check that had been delayed.

Hugo always felt he bore the financial brunt, even though one year I made more than he did. I worked on *The Miracle* with his father. Frank wanted Hugo, but Hugo didn't dare go up to Hollywood; some idiot relative of Frank's said that if Hugo went up, the relative would notify the U.S. marshal. Frank was very upset. He was in his late sixties or early seventies and was not too well. He had been given this assignment, and he needed help. He was almost weeping over the phone. Hugo suggested that I go up. In California Frank and I worked out a step outline; then, back in Mexico, I did the first draft of every scene and mailed it north, and Frank did the polish.

Did you like the project?

It was a pretty story: a nun breaks her vows, and everything bad happens to her. Our problem was getting the film off the Catholic Index, which proscribed "immoral" movies and could kill the box office. We made the character a novice instead of a full-fledged nun. She had made a personal promise to the virgin, and that was the real vow she broke.

Of course, I didn't get any screen credit. But we got ten thousand dollars for the whole job: two thousand five hundred of Frank's story money and ten percent, that is, seventy-five hundred dollars, of his screenplay money.

Let's talk about some of Hugo's other later films, like The Young One.

It was a Peter Matthiesson story that George Pepper found. He took an option on it and brought it to Hugo, who did the screenplay. They got Buñuel lined up immediately, so Buñuel had a lot of input on the screenplay. It was written when Hugo was already becoming more ill.

When I saw the film, I had the most terrible feeling. How could the man I married write that picture? It is such an amoral picture. Buñuel was a fascinating man, though. He lived with gusto. He also had a great wife who made great paella.

What about Sodom and Gomorrah?

Sodom and Gomorrah got us from Mexico to Italy. Hugo was getting very restless in Mexico. There were magazine stories about Italy with wonderful pictures of restaurant balconies overlooking green fields. Hugo got so excited that he wrote an original, set in Italy, called "Act of Love." It got optioned as a story several times, though it never got made.

Aldrich was the director of Sodom and Gomorrah.

Aldrich was in Italy with a script that he didn't want to use. Hugo went over and worked on the script, but he was unsatisfied with the result and also upset about how Bob planned to shoot it. In the end, Hugo didn't even want the credit, but he also didn't want to hurt Bob's feelings.

Aldrich had come down to Mexico when *The Young One* was being shot. He came to the studio and watched. I told him—I was just quoting Hugo—that Hugo found Buñuel very interesting, because he cut his pictures as he went along, saving money that way, and he shot almost everything in medium shot, very rarely using a close-up. Bob seemed either jealous of Hugo's interest in Buñuel or huffy about that means of telling a story. He said, "You can't get inside a character that way." Buñuel's view of people was dispassionate. Aldrich had his own extremely forthright way of telling a story, which was very strong, and right for him.

You said that at about that time, Hugo had begun to get ill.

In Italy Hugo really began to fall apart—even a little bit in Mexico, although I refused to admit that there was anything wrong. He began losing his temper in odd ways, and when we got to Italy, working with Aldrich, he really became a different guy. He actually conducted the first long affair he ever had in our twenty-five years and six kids. When I finally realized what was happening, I found the one English-speaking psychologist in Rome.

During this period Leonardo Bercovici and his wife sort of adopted us, as they did other Hollywood exiles in Rome. We adapted to living in Italy, but Hugo was getting worse physically.

How much work did he do on Eva, *directed by Joseph Losey?*

It was taken from a book by James Hadley Chase, better known for *No Orchids for Miss Blandish*. Hugo transplanted the setting from Hollywood to Venice after the Hakims [three Egyptian-born brothers who produced films from Paris] had brought the property to him, and it was Hugo who brought Joe Losey in. He hadn't worked with Losey since *The Big Night*.

Was there a reason?

We knew him as a friend, over the course of several marriages. But Hugo and Joe fell out, because Hugo wanted to do something with the script that Joe couldn't agree with, so Joe went to another writer [Evan Jones], although he kept much of Hugo's script. Joe also ended up marrying Hugo's secretary, Patricia Tolusso, who is now Losey's widow.

What did you and Hugo think of how the film turned out?

I ended up liking the film anyway. It was straight, Loseyesque, and cold. Joe didn't love himself much, and he didn't love mankind, either. He made some marvelous films, even if he was the most neurotic guy to work with. Hugo had little sympathy for self-indulgence. He was workmanlike himself.

How about Hugo's final major film, The Legend of Lylah Clare, *for which you share the script credit?*

Bob Aldrich had this TV teleplay that had been done with the same plot, a 1963 *DuPont Show of the Week.* Hugo had read a lot about vanished actresses, the myth or image of the star as opposed to the reality, and what happens when the legend is exposed as the "real" reality. Hugo did the major draft; then there was a hiatus of a year or so, and by that time Hugo was getting very ill. During rewrites, when he and Bob went over to England together, he was in the middle of a breakdown. I got a letter from Hugo, almost incomprehensible, really crazy. Bob had become so alarmed at his condition that he suggested I come over. I could see what was happening, and I was trying to shield Bob from the knowledge while doing Hugo's writing for him. The only writing I did myself was some rewriting on a few scenes, later on.

During this time, Hugo had been getting very interested—which scared the hell out of me—in existentialism, more and more interested in moral ambiguity. The mark of Buñuel was upon him—to be anti-Manichean, to reject absolutes. That was also in part a rejection of our illusions about Russia during the 1940s.

Had you engaged in much political activity after you left Hollywood?

Absolutely none, perforce, because we were on the run, and then, when we got to Mexico, if we had indulged in any political activity we could have been expelled without a trial. Everybody was scared to death, and we did everything we could not to be political.

So you came back to Los Angeles, with Hugo becoming increasingly ill.

We traveled through Italy in the summer of 1963, and we thought of moving there. We just couldn't bear to move our kids back to America: I hated the teenage culture in this country. We had loved Mexico and thought we might go down and try it for a little longer, so we rented another place down there. But finally we came back to L.A. at the end of 1964, when Hugo found a nice little house that we could afford. We thought he could get back into Hollywood pictures. Although he didn't get a credit for the work he did on *Four for Texas,* he did get his name on *Sodom and Gomorrah.* So he had this one credit, and now he was working openly for Aldrich. But his health was really failing.

Hugo died at fifty-three of a heart attack in January 1968. I got the results of the autopsy years later: it was arteriosclerotic brain disease, which causes large areas of brain death. It could have been stress-related, but Hugo had always had very high blood pressure.

Let's talk a little about your own later writing, mostly for television.

For about ten years I did soaps. I worked for more than a year, actually twenty months, on *Bright Promise*. That show was the creation of the Hursleys, Frank and Doris; they were known for a while as "Mr. and Mrs. Television." They created *General Hospital*.

I learned soap writing from them, and then I did six months on *The Search for Tomorrow* and four years on *The Guiding Light*, and then the whole team was taken over by Procter & Gamble to try and bring the ratings up for *As the World Turns*, so I worked another two and a half years on that program. However, by 1983 the soaps were going for the youth audience. I was then in my sixties, and I could hardly call myself a member of the youth audience. So I was let go, and my agent got me a contract for a book on soap scripting, called *Writing for the Soaps*. During Hugo's last year and in the first few years after his death I published six books, including one gothic novel. When *Writing for Soaps* went out of print, I got the rights back, updated it, and peddled it to Focal Press, the textbook division of Heinemann, with a new title, *Writing for Daytime Drama*.

The Marxist philosopher and sports historian C.L.R. James used to say that soap operas dealt with the contradictions in daily life. Did you ever think of it as anything but journeymen's work?

I deal with that in the book, in terms of its potential. Once in a while I got to write a scene that I adored. It seemed to me that sometimes you could really do a good job, mostly on human problems, very little else, and every once in a rare while the soaps would explore particular social problems. And, of course, they had fifty million viewers a week.

Were your soap scripts ever censored?

The entire story line is always done by the head writer, the week's progress is also his or hers, and the daily outline is done by the breakdown writer. I was given the breakdown to work from. I wrote some bloody good scripts within the limitations I was given. They used everything I wrote—once I learned about subtext. My team got a Writers Guild Award and an Emmy.

Can you give a philosophical view of film that you and Hugo shared?

It wasn't so much a matter of conscious philosophy. We never felt sufficiently in control of our lives or our own screen and TV work to make many choices. As far as we were both concerned, one did one's job as required— the best job possible under the circumstances. It was how we made a living.

Hugo was the real screenwriter of the family. I did a few screenplays, but I was more comfortable with prose. I thought that was where I belonged, mainly because I didn't visualize. Hugo visualized everything that he did. When he finally evolved a philosophy, it naturally had to do with film, and I guess he became a sort of existentialist. Down in Mexico we began to have these bigger questions in our minds. Marxist theory was all very well, but we were learning about many things that didn't fit. Hugo wasn't dogmatic about existentialism; he was an explorer, becoming more and more involved in moral ambiguity. Hugo considered himself very lucky to have done a picture by Renoir, three by Losey, and two by Buñuel. That was where he ultimately expressed his philosophy—through the films he wrote.

Jeff Corey

PHOTO © ALISON MORLEY

JEFF COREY, Malibu, California, 1988

INTERVIEW BY PATRICK McGILLIGAN

■

ACTOR JEFF COREY has delivered show-stopping performances as a heavy in potboilers for Republic, as Wild Bill Hickok in *Little Big Man*, and even, more recently, as Santa Claus on television's *Night Court*. Since the early 1940s—interrupted by twelve years during which the blacklist kept him off the screen—Corey has been a familiar and welcome presence in movies, with his rich vibrato, strapping physique, and unforgettable hawk-face.

Though unquestionably a patriot—he was a combat photographer of the kamikaze attempt on the aircraft carrier *Yorktown* in October 1945, which was deemed by naval citation "one of the great picture sequences of the war"—he refused to kowtow before the House Un-American Activities Committee. His brief, tight-lipped appearance was notable for its critique of the performance of an informer who had preceded him to the stand.

Thanks to the blacklist he was forced to become an acting teacher, and over time has become recognized as one of Hollywood's finest. Corey served as an acting mentor for James Coburn, Dean Stockwell, Jack Nicholson, many of the Roger Corman clique (including Corman himself), Harry Belafonte, Anthony Perkins, Dick Van Dyke, Donna Reed, Cyd Charisse,

Diahann Carroll, Rob Reiner, Penny Marshall, Candice Bergen, Ann-Margret, Richard Chamberlain, Ellen Burstyn, Cher, and Steven Spielberg. Corey estimates that he has taught roughly ten thousand students in the past forty years.

After the blacklist, Corey returned to acting with a vengeance, making appearances in *Mickey One, Seconds, In Cold Blood, Butch Cassidy and the Sundance Kid*, and *True Grit*, among other notable credits, while continuing to teach—not "screen acting" but his own blend of classical theory, Stanislavsky, hard work and practice, and playful devices.

■

You don't advertise; you don't publicize. Yet you're quite well-known among the acting community, not only as one of the best teachers but as an actor of distinction.

There's a category which is a solace to some actors: "actor's actor." People, particularly as you get older, pay homage to you when they work on a set with you. Even Peter O'Toole, when I did a day's work on *Creator*, bowed from the waist and said, "I am awed." I remember when I met Richard Burton on an adventure movie—I forget the name of it—and he reeled off all of these black-and-white films he had seen me in when he was a kid. It felt nice. I rather like that, though I don't require that kind of adulation.

Tell me about your own training as an actor. Did you begin in theater on the East Coast?

I started drama school the day Roosevelt closed the banks, in the very depths of the Depression. I remember getting out of the Fifty-seventh Street subway station and passing a branch bank that was closed. I had won a two-year scholarship in a national competition for the Feagin School of Dramatic Art.

While I went to the Feagin School, I also played in a Shakespearean repertory company at the old Jolson Theatre on Fifty-eighth Street and Seventh Avenue. So I had a very good start in traditional theater. It would be the equivalent of a painter starting in with academic training, learning to sketch, learning the color palette in a scientific way.

Were you initially schooled in the Stanislavsky Method?

No, no. I learned the Delsarte Chart. And I delight my students every now and then by doing the Delsarte Chart. It was a gesture chart proclaiming that there is an appropriate gesture for every emotional, physical, or mental condition. It was taught largely in this country and in Europe at the turn of the century. There's a charm to the Delsarte method, and a discipline, though it didn't hold up. It was pseudoscience.

But it was helpful?

It was helpful to know. I'm so glad I had that kind of training where you learned that if you had an expository passage you should look for the brass rail of the second balcony and be transported. Well, since then we've learned that expository passages are really a pain in the ass, and what you have to do is give them an *immediacy*.

I started Method classes at the Theatre Collective in about 1935. The Theatre Collective was a kind of left-wing theater, one of many that were springing up at the time, and I liked the way those people were acting. I was intrigued. Of course, they were barely audible, and—

Why were they barely audible?

They were searching for truth. [Laughs] But I always had energy and could be heard better than most. They liked me, and they were very encouraging. I liked the whole idea of Stanislavsky, and I really got very excited about the Method.

You were overwhelmed by this new style of acting?

By this new style of acting and by the fact that we did interesting plays. We trained with people like Lazar Galpern of the Habima, who did some body work with the people at the Theatre Collective—eurythmics, or stylistic movement, kind of an early version of Grotowski's kind of work—and we did some very stylistic plays in the Meyerhold-Okhlopkov tradition.

One play we did was Lope de Vega's Spanish Renaissance comedy *The Pastry Baker* at the Provincetown Playhouse. I remember Brett Warren, who had been am amateur prizefighter before he became a Method director, saying to me, "Kid, I want you to go to the Bronx Zoo and spend a morning watching a warthog." So I went! And I watched a warthog for three hours. I caught the voice of a warthog. It was supposed to be a warthog that had an acute case of dysentery—that was the nature of the farce. I remember a lovely young actress and graphic artist—her name was Tommy Bissell; she came from North Carolina, part of the Bissell carpet-sweeper family—making me a chamois cheek to wear, and I put rings in my nose for a porcine look. That was an exciting time in the theater.

What was the Method then, as opposed to how it has evolved?

There's been a consistency about the Method. Most people who talk about it don't know anything about it. I like to feel as though I've been a dose of salts; I try to proclaim that I really understand what the Stanislavsky system is essentially about.

Tell me.

Number one, Stanislavsky says that the flesh is accessible, that the actor in a performance must relate to the physical environment. His connection to faces, to people, to things, to an atmosphere, is much more important than trying to get the psychological truth. [Evgeny] Vakhtangov, who was Stanislavsky's greatest disciple and an innovator who locked horns with Stanislavsky later on, said that an inordinate search for psychological truth always leads to a psychological hernia. So all of this true feeling, really feeling the part, is such bullshit.

Stanislavsky's marvelous paradox was that the actor ought not to concern himself at all with the nature of the emotion of the scene. Don't think in terms of adjectives and adverbs. Think only in verbs. What's the problem? What must I do to get the scene resolved? What do I have to do right now? I don't think Stanislavsky knew Aristotle, but in his *Poetics* Aristotle, too, says that a character is neither good nor bad, except insofar as his deeds are judged. We say, "That is an unhappy man," because in his striving to do this and do that, the audience will judge that he's very unhappy. Rather than play unhappy, play frustration. All of this crap about real, real emotion is just bunk.

Harold Clurman very wisely called one of his books of essays *Lies Like Truth*. Stanislavsky talked about scenic truth, about make-believe. It's the truth of the stage. It's like the exchange in *Winnie the Pooh*: "Is that you, Rabbit?" "Let's say I'm not and see what happens." Acting is playful. It's make-believe.

You're saying that Stanislavsky was wiser than what is the popular conception of the Method nowadays.

He was wiser than the people who have misinterpreted the Method. I try to get actors to stop this goddamned feeling so much and to think about the part. What is the play about? What is the idea that is embodied in this play? If you understand that the story is only the illustration of a very cogent human theme, then you can play the part.

If I play that dangerous jerk in *True Grit*, Tom Chaney, well, I try to make a comment about how dangerous stupid people are. A community that just says, "Well, he's dumb, let him be," puts themselves in danger, because stupid people can destroy glorious people. That is how I played the part, and I'm glad I had a sense of what I should do. I was not trying to be high-toned and professorial. It comes easily to me as an actor to think: What's the meaning of this?

If the actor just plays a story without knowing the ideas resonating behind the story, it's going to become a rather mechanical performance. He will know his lines, and he will make interesting stage crosses.

To be "interested in the ideas resonating behind the story"—that is certainly part of the legacy of those who went through the theatrical ferment of the 1930s.

I had a wonderful enthusiasm about the Method in the 1930s. I also saw the Group Theatre's work, and they were thrilling. Their acting was unparalleled; there's never been anything like the Group Theatre in the United States, or anywhere in the world.

Why? It's hard for someone today to understand how people still talk about the Group Theatre performances.

Take [Clifford] Odets's *Paradise Lost*, which was not the greatest play. There was such a feeling of aliveness on stage. You weren't listening to lines. You were just observing people involved with a series of crises as it affected their interpersonal relationships. Things had to be done, coping with the most horrific confrontations. You cared, you got involved. I remember that Roman Bohnen's performance was absolutely poetic. He had embodied in that performance a kind of revelation of what a human being, every human being, has to undergo in the course of travails. I just didn't want to leave the theater.

What enabled the Group to reach that zenith?

Because they really had a program, and they also had a very gifted man, Harold Clurman, who knew how to work with a play and who understood actors. My friends Roman Bohnen, Art Smith, Joe [J. Edward] Bromberg, and Morris Carnovsky told me just countless wonderful stories about the joy of acting with Clurman, who was so respectful of what an actor is.

Saint Augustine said, "The artist is the man." And if you work with an actor, you have to start with this conclusion: No matter what the role is, if you can't personalize it and say, "I know about this condition every morning, noon, and night of my life, on a continuum," you can't play the part. Then you're making an editorial comment. You're saying, "I'm going to show you a good guy, I'm going to show you a bad guy." That's no good. You have to give the role, no matter what it is, a human dimensionality, so that when the audience sees you on film and on stage, they will say, "This man is part of a social environment and a psychological environment."

The Group Theatre was crazy about [James] Cagney, for example; as far as they were concerned, he was a Method actor. That is, he played in an organic way: a man in an environment trying to engage himself in working out some pertinent pattern.

Is part of the problem with the Method the way it has become fossilized?

Well, I don't regard it as a problem. Some people have understood the Method marvelously, understood it well and employed it well.

What's the proper way to employ it?

It ought not to be employed like a ritual. I'm a funny kind of Method teacher, because nobody in my class knows that I teach the Stanislavsky Method unless they get me in a corner and say, "What are we doing?" Stanislavsky's only one influence on my life, just as Bertolt Brecht is, just as Peter Brook is. I quote the American actor Joseph Jefferson, saying actors ought to be the head of their own academy. I quote Henri Matisse saying there are no rules outside of the artist. I say, "Find your own method."

It burns me up when people say somebody teaches so-and-so's method. That's offensive. Stanislavsky lived. He taught the Stanislavsky system. I'm old enough and respectful enough of my own life, and of my own personal history of acting and directing, that I teach my way. I say, "Take it or leave it." I'm not being defiant. You must respect your own way of operating. And an eclectic approach is an intelligent approach.

What was the progress of your career before you began to act in motion pictures?

I did Broadway. I toured in Leslie Howard's *Hamlet*. I toured with Clare Tree Major and his children's theater all over the United States. I acted in *The Life and Death of an American* for the Federal Theatre Project. I also did Chekhov's *The Marriage Proposal*, directed by a very talented director, Al Saxe, as part of a circus that played all over the parks of greater New York. I did it in clown makeup.

I didn't do radio until I came out to California. I had a running role in the *Philip Marlowe, Detective* series. I played Lieutenant Detective Ybarra. I did a lot of *Lux Radio Theater*, and oh, I loved that, just loved that. How exciting it was to know that everyone in the country was listening to you at that moment! Those marvelous actors I worked with: Ronald Colman, Charles Boyer, Bette Davis, Wallace Beery, Lionel and Ethel Barrymore, Cary Grant, Merle Oberon.

I came out here with my wife, just to visit California, in 1940. We came out in a Model A Ford. It cost us eighty-three dollars to make the eighteen-day journey across the country, including toll bridges and cigarettes. We got a room for three dollars and fifty cents a week on Kenmore near Barnsdall Park.

Then my New York friend Julie Dassin, who was a director-in-training at RKO, asked me if my wife and I could please stay at his house while he went on location. So we had a place to stay for a couple of weeks, and in a very naive way I walked Sunset Strip and went from agency to agency like you do in New York. Two out of the first three agents I saw wanted to handle me. I got an agent and began to work. We left our furniture in New York and continued to live out here.

Was that a difficult transition, moving from New York to California, and from theater to motion pictures?

No, no. I loved it. I was ready to give up the theater because things were so lousy in New York. Things had gotten just terrible on Broadway. I couldn't get work. I wanted a life. I loved my wife, and I wanted us to have a comfortable marriage. That was my priority. She wisely urged us to take a trip to California and take time to ponder any drastic decision. We sublet our New York apartment and made the carefully budgeted trip to California, and never returned to live in New York.

When you began acting in films, what kind of parts were you getting? How much work was there for you?

Oh, I was getting a good deal of work up until I went into the Navy for three years. I was in *The Devil and Daniel Webster*, *My Friend Flicka*, *Syncopation*. I worked a lot, and life was good. Many of my friends had come out to California, people in the Group Theatre, like Mike Gordon, Julie Dassin, and Howard Da Silva. We had a lot of friends out here. We had a house with a tennis court that we rented, and all the Group people used to come to play, including [Elia] Kazan, who was really a sorehead on the court. Many times I had him five to four, and then he beat me seven to five because he'd get so angry.

Were there differences you perceived, initially or developmentally, between acting for films and theater?

No. I don't believe there's such a thing as film acting. I think the important thing is to be a good actor. Of course, there is an awareness of knowing you're in a master shot or in a close-up, and I make those accommodations. I project myself in a particular way.

No, I was lucky because I was a pretty good actor as a kid. Even now when I see *The Devil and Daniel Webster*—I saw it at the RKO retrospective at the L.A. County Museum recently—I look at my performance and say, "Gee, I like that young man!" It's a nice feeling. I like looking at my old pictures. Even some guy who runs the PBS station in Arkansas sent me a clip of a Kay Kyser movie I did [*You'll Find Out*], and I liked me in it!

You spoke of a stage director as wonderful as Harold Clurman. Were there film directors who measured up as his equivalent, who were, in your opinion, stellar in their handling of actors?

Oh, you betcha! I like the old-timers like Vic Fleming and Henry Hathaway and Bill Wellman, for whom I worked a couple of times. Guys like Gordon Douglas, who was wonderful at action stuff and who had a wonderful feeling about characterization. God, they had such presence. In the best sense of the word they were ballsy. They were there. They were in charge. They were like the warrant officers on my ship during the war who had come up through the ranks. Vic Fleming had been a cameraman; Bill Wellman had been a flyer in the Lafayette Escadrille—marvelous guys!

Could they actually assist you with acting problems?

Oh, yeah. Henry Hathaway helped me many times. He used to give me line readings. I would say, "Henry, don't give me such good line readings. It's too intimidating, for Chrissakes! You read it so goddamned well." I would feel utterly intimidated.

Where did people like William Wellman and Henry Hathaway and Victor Fleming get their feeling for the truth of a performance?

Through experience, and they understood movies; they knew good acting from bad, and they knew what to tell you. Even a guy like [William] Dieterle, who was a martinet, though he would scream too much, he'd generate a lot of excitement on the set. Of course, I like some of the guys of the next generation too. Julie Dassin was always a joy to work with. I worked with Arthur Penn a couple of times later on, and I loved his intelligence and insight. And Johnny Frankenheimer and I always had interesting secrets going on.

Interesting secrets. You mean like the backstory of a characterization?

Oh, no. Like, he'd fire a gun in the middle of a scene just to get a reaction from me.

Is that a good idea?

Well, I like craziness of that sort. Of course it was in a creative, prankish, *Till Eulenspiegel* kind of context. Playfulness is important, yes.

During this early period in Hollywood, did you continue to study acting seriously?

In late 1940 we started the Actors Lab. We wanted to get some of the taste of theater that we kind of missed from our New York experience.

Who were some of the people behind the Actors Lab?

Jules Dassin and Roman Bohnen of the Group Theatre began to teach wonderful classes. A lot of the people from the Group Theatre—Ruth Nelson, Mary Virginia Farmer, Morris Carnovsky—were in Lab productions or were teaching for the Lab. Ultimately, people like Marty Ritt, Hume Cronyn, Jessica Tandy, Vinnie [Vincent] Price, and Karen Morley got involved. We had a very impressive array of people.

During the war we got a beautiful theater, a wonderful frame structure, and the Actors Lab began to do really interesting plays. *Life* magazine saw its production of *Volpone* and called it the best theater in America at the time. The Lab would have several productions going simultaneously. We did the first USO play! I remember *Declaration*, which was a "living newspaper" play about Jefferson that Danny [Daniel] Mann directed; and a series of Tennessee Williams's one-act plays, including *Portrait of a Madonna*, directed by Hume Cronyn, with Jessica Tandy. Through that she got to do the part of Blanche DuBois in *A Streetcar Named Desire* on Broadway.

The Lab was a very important theater at the time. Ultimately it was red-baited out of existence, and one of the charges put up by [California] State Senator Tenney was that the Lab did the plays of O'Casey, Chekhov, and Shaw. That was just a reflection of the idiocy of the times.

Was the Lab, in essence, a transplanted group of Easterners?

Yes.

What was the response of the motion-picture industry?

Oh, they loved it. They loved it. They sent students who were under contract to study at the Lab, including people like Marilyn Monroe. The Lab was the in place. It was really the hub of theater activity, and everyone used to come to see the Lab plays—Freddie [Fredric] March, Danny Kaye, the whole Hollywood community. For one thing, the Lab turned out to be a marvelous showcase, and gee, I remember some of the pictures at Universal at the time where half the cast seemed to be people who had worked at the Actors Lab.

Was there any sense in your lives, at this point, that what you were doing in film, the material, was in any way substandard to the kinds of things you had been doing and were trying to do in the theater? Was there any schizophrenia in the progressive community in the 1930s and 1940s—working in motion pictures for money on the one hand, and having pretensions toward being an artist on the other? Or was there more of an integration and the sense of having a career that was new and fun and challenging?

From time to time you did something silly—a gangster film at Republic that had very little merit, for example. On the other hand, after the war I did some *wonderful* gangster films, like Hemingway's *The Killers*, which was Burt Lancaster's first big movie, with Ava Gardner and Albert Dekker. I had a good role in that. Or *Brute Force*, about a prison breakout, the kind of film the French call *film noir*. I did *Canon City*, which was another prison breakout movie. So for a while my career was these successful gangster movies. I also did a series of cowboy movies like *Roughshod* and *Red Mountain*. After *Home of the Brave* and *Only the Valiant*, my career was zooming, and then along came the blacklist.

I really am not a lamebrain, and I know I'm an intellectual if forced to admit it, but I didn't go around feeling tortured or that I was selling my soul. I loved to act and I still love to act. Just recently, I did three films: *The Secret Ingredient*, for my friend Dan Tana, with Catherine Hicks, in Yugoslavia; I did a Charlie Bronson film where he's an investigative reporter—he doesn't kill anybody; and I did another film about what would happen if Christ came for the first time in 1990. (Of course, he'd be crucified.)

I'm not tasteless. I turn things down. But the thing that you describe, I saw very little evidence of it. I saw people who were frustrated because they didn't work enough or they didn't get good assignments, but in terms of contaminating the purity of one's aspirations, I didn't see too much of that. If I did, I would either laugh at such people or avoid them.

I don't like people like that. If you're an actor, you do what you're supposed to do. Shakespeare was a journeyman actor. He didn't realize his plays would be that great. The year that his own *Lear* was done, he played a minor role in somebody else's version of *Lear* done by his company. And he endured it. I don't like bellyachers.

The Tenney Committee, and later HUAC, may have been wrong, idiotic, to say that Chekhov and Shaw were festering at the Actors Lab, but they were right in the sense that the Actors Lab was the Barney's Beanery of its day, at least among the left-liberal community in Hollywood.

So what? We're nesters, and we like to nest with people we like.

When the blacklist came in, it pounced on the Group Theatre people, the Actors Lab people, and anyone with progressive political ties. Did the blacklist seem to come in quickly, or with ominous slowness?

Ominous slowness. I knew it was coming in 1947, actually at a time when my career was really in its ascendancy.

Did you have any feeling that it would spread so far and so deep?

I thought it would be worse. It was only twelve years for me. I thought it would be forever.

Why did you think it would be so bad? Because of the various schisms already existing in Hollywood?

Because we lived in this craven climate. Everyone knuckled under to this repulsive drunkard Joe McCarthy. It was a bad period. The "loyalty oaths" were instigated under the Truman administration, or at least, as far as I know, Truman went along with them.

Yes. Ring Lardner Jr. always makes a point of calling it the Truman era, not the McCarthy era.

Yeah. I don't think Truman was that great a president, though he was a very good senator; the Truman reports were wonderful during World War II.

But I admire my colleagues. Most of us were retired reds. We had left it, at least I had, years before. The only issue was, did you want to just give them their token names so you could continue your career, or not? I had no impulse to defend a political point of view that no longer interested me particularly. I always thought I was a good American, a patriotic American. I got three citations for World War II. The Committee was not interested in my making a statement about that. They just wanted two new names so they could hand out more subpoenas.

Faith Hubley tells me that it is her opinion that there was a foundation of payoffs under the whole blacklist, in the sense that if you gave them money in a brown paper bag, they would lay off the persecution; and that the payoffs underwrote corrupt unions, organized crime, and the future of the California Republican Party.

Lee J. Cobb, as I understand it, gave them twenty-five thousand dollars not to report his secret testimony, but then they double-crossed him, and people whom he had been seeing found out that he had mentioned them. I could've gotten out of it, too, by naming names. It was rough, you know. I had three kids to support. I'm very proud of the way we coped. I didn't go around bellyaching, just did what I had to do.

I felt a responsibility to keep the family intact. I was determined to give my children a good life, and I was able to go camping with them, for a month, a month and a half, every year for twelve years, all over the States and eastern and western Canada. In a sense they were wonderful times for us. I didn't have to worry about missing phone calls.

Friends were very generous. We'd not only get hand-me-downs, but sometimes I knew damn well that they bought the hand-me-downs. We converted the house from the loan we had to an FHA, based on the huge earnings I had made in prior years. I promised my wife I'd somehow or other come up with thirty-five dollars in cash every week for groceries, along with the staple costs of house payments, utilities, doctors, dentists, etc. Our doctor and dentist friends barely charged us for their generous services throughout the blacklist. We had a lot of pride. We weren't whiners.

But you didn't act in movies for twelve years. Did you do any plays?

I could've done a lot of plays, but I couldn't afford to do plays. I did one play at the Circle Theater that Mordecai Gorelik, the great stage designer, directed, a play that had been done at the Edinburgh Festival, about Irish construction workers. Then in 1959 I did *A View from the Bridge* at La Jolla with Marty [Martin] Balsam and Rita Moreno; I urged them to use Rita, and it was a landmark performance for her. Everyone saw that she was an extraordinary actress, not just a Latin bombshell. Stephen Joyce was in it, too, and my friend Bob Gist.

Bob Gist reminded me recently of the time my daughter Evie came backstage. She was sixteen years old, and she knew I had been a blacklisted actor. When she came backstage, we embraced, and Bob said all of the actors in the hallway went to their separate rooms to have a cry, because they knew it was a really singular moment when she saw her daddy do a play.

Why, at this time, during the 1950s, did you decide to teach acting?

I didn't choose to teach acting; it just kind of evolved through convoluted circumstances. At the time of the blacklist I didn't know what the hell I was going to do. I was working on construction and miscellaneous jobs, whatever I could. I was already teaching acting at the Stage Society, but I wasn't being paid for that.

What was the Stage Society?

The Stage Society was a very good group of people—Arthur Kennedy, Johnny [John] Ireland, Akim Tamiroff, Jack Laird, the playwright Richard Nash, Janice Rule—they had started an independent theater. Arthur Kennedy asked me if I could act in Eugene O'Neill's remarkable Strindbergian play *Ile*. I did it, and then they thought it would be a good idea to hold classes. [Russian actor] Michael Chekhov taught a class on Tuesday night, and I taught in tandem on Monday nights, with my own devices.

There was some kid in the first class who was not a very good actor, so the board of directors of the Stage Society voted to drop him. This poor kid, whom I had done work with at the Actors Lab years before, asked me if I would start an acting class. I said, "I really have no conscious wish to do anything like that." He said, "What if I start one for you?"

So, one night, about forty-five people—I'm not exaggerating—came to my house, and I heard them out. I asked them how they visualized such a class, because I had very limited experience as a teacher. And we started a class. Carol Burnett was in that first class—she was then a freshman at UCLA, as

I was, even though I was at least twenty years older than Carol. We started with a group of about twelve or thirteen, and it appeared to work. I thought it was just a temporary device at the time, till I was able to find a new occupation.

That would have been in 1951?

That was in 1951. I renovated a two-car garage we had at our house and expanded it, and that became my theater for seven years, until somebody in the neighborhood complained because it was a zoning violation. Then I began to rent places.

My theater became a very important place for people like Dean Stockwell, Bob [Robert] Towne, Richard Chamberlain, Robert Blake, Carole Eastman, and Jim [James] Coburn. Bobby [Robert] Blake and Jack Nicholson used to arrive early before class and inveigle me into a game of three-wall handball on our handball court. Bobby and Jack both came from working-class backgrounds in New Jersey; they used to come into our house, where the only available john was, and look through the French doors into our dining room. They were astonished. "That family sits and eats together!" It was outside of their experience.

Roger Corman came to class, to his credit, because he was tired of all these surly characters from New York with their damned Stanislavsky mystique, and he wanted to know what the hell the Method was. Being an engineer and a very practical man, he thought he'd come and work with me. We worked one-on-one, and he tried acting; then he came to class, and in the class he met these talented kids, and he put them to work. That was when Bob Towne and Carole began to write for him.

My class helped Bob and Carole Eastman as writers, I think. The discipline in the improvisations was to give them a lot of story and then have them not mention the story once while dealing with the implications of the story. Most improvisational work is just the repetition of a dull story. In an improvisation an actor should engage, say the subtext, and eschew the text. In a play you've got the text and you think the subtext. But to find out what subtext is, you ought to have the discipline of playing a situation and implying. It's much more economical and much more riveting, ultimately.

Sometimes the stuff Bob and Carole used to improvise sounded like Pinter or Chekhov. Whew! Boy! It came alive! Carole once told me that when she was having hangups about her writing, she would drive by the old place just to get a fix.

At any rate, word of mouth got around and kept the classes going. Other people taught with me from time to time. Leonard Nimoy taught for several years, and he taught very well. In general I would teach three hours in the morning, afternoon classes with children, and evening classes. I was also doing clinical work at UCLA in speech therapy.

I've never been listed in the phone book, and I never have advertised. I try to discourage people who call and just say they want to be actors, if they have no experience as actors and no frame of reference. I've told some people who sound pretty sincere about it, "Well, I'll tell you what. In the next three weeks, read fifteen plays—you choose which ones—and read one Shakespearean play; then call me up and tell me what you thought about the plays. Then I'll see you." One out of twenty calls back, and I'm respectful of their effort, even if they tell me, "I swear I didn't know what *Cymbeline* was all about."

What do you analyze or try to perceive about a new student when a prospect comes in for an interview? What do you look for in a striving actor?

Intelligence and that they seem like healthy people. I have no wish to uplift waifs, because that would be pretentious of me. This is no Pygmalion and Galatea thing. I like people to have energy and a sense of who they are. I want them to come eager. People very often ask if they can audit my classes, and I say I wouldn't ask anyone to audit except a dear old friend or colleague, and if they have any reservations about whether this is the class for them I'd rather they not come. They say, "How do we know?" I say, "That's just your problem." I'm not soliciting their trade.

Have you ever operated in reverse—seen someone in a small group presentation or met someone and—

No, I've never asked anyone to study with me. I couldn't in conscience do that. Acting is such a perilous occupation. When I start a new class, which is rarely, invariably I tell the new students that I am very respectful of how rough it is to make the tuition. I love their guts, and if I ever shortchange them, they can give me a swift kick in the ass and ask me for a refund.

I'm telling you this because it's easy for me to say: I care about people, and sometimes the work is just terrible. I have a kind of tenacity and sometimes I challenge my students. I tell them, when they became obdurate and resistant, "Look, I don't want to win a debate with you. If you persist in acting that way so you win this debate, you'll lose everything, because it's not going to help you as an actor. So please, lose this battle. Lose this battle."

Just yesterday I worked with a very beautiful actress, one-on-one, who is up for a series, and our first reading simply wasn't there. I asked myself, "How do I deal with this?" Then she told me what the producer had told her. They were looking for a person like "such-and-such a person" in that particular new series. So she had come in relinquishing her own persona and trying in a freaky way to be somebody else. I locked horns with her. I said, "No! What you are doing absolutely opaques you! There is no you! You are a very charming, almost irresistible woman. You are gifted, and you are obscuring it with this trying to be somebody else."

I remember that I recommended Ellen Burstyn for *Mickey One*, a film I did with Arthur Penn. They were very interested in Ellen. They spent a whole weekend talking to her; then she did a test. I couldn't believe the test! This girl who did lovely, inventive, astonishing stuff in class was terrible, and I had to ask her, "What the hell are you doing?" She was trying to be Grace

Kelly. Years later, when I went backstage to see Ellen in *Same Time, Next Year*, she said, "I have to thank you once again for persuading me I didn't have to be Grace Kelly."

Do you find that kind of feeling around the industry more epidemic nowadays, that people are not as free to be themselves?

Yeah. But it took forever to get kids to stop acting like James Dean, too, particularly when Jimmy was in my class. That was after you had finally gotten them to stop acting like Brando. Or, when I was a kid, we all wanted to be like Leslie Howard.

I had a wonderful conversation with Gary Cooper once. I screen-tested for *Bright Leaf*, starring Cooper, and he was in the screen test. Coop was apologetic. He saw how hard I was working to get the part. I was doing some pretty interesting work in the test that Michael Curtiz was directing. Coop said, "I've been away for the better part of a year, on safari with Hemingway. I just feel so stale." I said, "Oh, I really enjoyed working on the scene with you." He said, "I have only one or two tricks, at best. That isn't enough, is it?" I swear this is verbatim. Here I am, it's like Nina in *The Seagull* telling Trigorin, the establishment writer, "No, you're good . . . you're really good!"

I told Coop—I didn't call him Coop then; I didn't call him Coop until later, after we were in the picture *Bright Leaf*, together—I said, "There are a whole group of snobby New York actors—and I came from that group—who look down on what they call 'personality acting.' They say, 'Well, Gary Cooper is always himself.' But unconsciously, they're all imitating you! They're all trying to use Cooperisms. They're doing things that are derivative of your remarkable performance in *Mr. Deeds Goes to Town*." He said, "Really?" I said, "Yeah."

I told him I'd been working on a theory of my own, which I don't think is a unique one. I had heard people using the phrase "personality acting" pejoratively, and it was beginning to be my conclusion that the human being who is doing the acting is what the performance is principally about—that when Olivier is good as he is as Archie Rice in *The Entertainer*, we say, "God, what a remarkable man! Look what Olivier is doing with this part!" When Olivier does *Cat on a Hot Tin Roof*, we say, "Olivier is uninteresting, and his personality is diminished, is obscured, by this bloody acting." You see?

Here I was, telling Gary Cooper that he was fortunate being so beautiful and having the opportunity to work, work, work. There was a lot of good stuff in that guy, and he was *worth imitating*. For a while Coop and Pat [Patricia] Neal used to sit in on my classes.

I'm surprised. Coop used to sit in on your classes?

He wanted to be a better actor. He was interested in acting. He once told me how mortified he was that he had agreed to consider doing a Robert Sherwood play called *Abe Lincoln in Illinois*. When he read the script, he loved it, but he was frightened of it, so he didn't do the play; Raymond Massey did it. But Coop responded affirmatively to my first efforts in teaching. One of the very first classes I taught, he sat in on, and one day I asked him if he had any opinions about the scene that was being done. Oh, I shouldn't have done that! He just wanted to hide. He was not the kind of a man to be critical of an actor.

One of the legends about you is that even though you were blacklisted in the 1950s, as your reputation began to spread, all the studios began to send their people to you to study acting.

They did. Half of the people at Fox—for example, Rita Moreno, Sheree North, Virginia Leith, Diane Varsi, Al [David] Hedison, all under contract there. And some of the studio directors came to me, and we'd sketch out a strategy about what they really wanted to get out of the story they were going to film.

Can you give me an example of such a director?

I'd rather not.

How about a specific film where you did a lot of work?

When *Spartacus* was being prepared, [producer] Eddie [Edward] Lewis called me and said he wanted me on the set, except that the studio said they couldn't have me on the set. So I worked with Kirk [Douglas], and I went to some conferences about the story that took place at [Dalton] Trumbo's house, and I helped Kirk prepare for the role of Spartacus.

What would be the necessary preparation for Kirk at that point in his career? Wasn't he thoroughly ingrained as an actor?

Just to work on the part, and to get some notions. Actors sometimes came to me, I guess semisurreptitiously, to prepare for their roles. I didn't tell them ever not to listen to the director. I said, "You just come ready to collaborate." That's what happens: an actor comes prepared, the director is prepared, and you collaborate.

I'm wondering whether people in the studios—the neutral or even conservative people who may have been supportive of the blacklist—were coming to you, hat in hand, during the 1950s?

Oh, no, no, no. But I remember that [producer] Ross Hunter wanted me to work with John Gavin, who was doing some films for him, so John came and worked with me, and the studio paid for it. John felt compelled, because he'd heard about my political past, to say, "I must tell you, Jeff, that I respect you as a teacher, but man to man I don't approve of the stand you took before the Committee." I said, "I hear you John, but this is an open society. I didn't make the decision to do what I did lightly. I thought I did it with honor. I understand what you're saying, and there we are. It doesn't interfere with our work." Later on, in fact, he came to my class several times.

How did the blacklist end for you?

It actually ended in 1962, when [director] Joe [Joseph] Strick offered me a part in *The Balcony*. But in January 1960 I was offered a part in *The Untouchables* [on television], and I knew the newspapers would be calling. The *New York Times* called me, and Bob Thomas of UPI called me. I knew that if I made a statement I wouldn't work again, but I said to myself that I didn't want to work on this tenuous level. So I told them about the Committee's hanky-panky and about my personal history, about being asked to mention the names of people who had been mentioned before, and adding to the names, so I could work. And they printed those statements with pictures of me and articles laudatory of me, condemning the studios and the Committee. I didn't work again for two years, and my feeling was, "Well, fuck 'em. I can take it."

Then I worked for [producer] Ray Stark in London for two years, doing miscellaneous jobs. I worked with a lot of actors he had under contract, I read scripts, and on an expense account I saw plays in London for him. For a while I was working with Pat Boone, who was still under an arrangement with Ray Stark to do a picture at Fox. Fox was desolate then. No commissary; the place was just closed. They had to get a caterer to bring the food in.

There was a picture that Buzz Kulik was directing, a Rod Steiger story, and I was working on the part with Pat Boone. There was a part that would have been logical for me to get, and Pat said, "I'm going to talk to them about you playing the part." Pat came to my house one day saying, "We did it! We did it!" He had a meeting with—if I have the story straight—the legal department at Fox, and they knew that I had already done a film with Joe Strick. So Pat got me this part [in *The Yellow Canary*, 1963].

That's funny—Pat Boone helped break the blacklist for you.

Oh, Pat and I like each other.

What can you do with an actor like Pat Boone? I don't mean that pejoratively, but—

We had a lot of fun, and we did good work together. He'd come to my house. He loved the lunches my wife made, which seemed exotic to him. We never discussed politics. We used to talk about religion. I didn't put religion down, but I knew the Bible pretty well, and I tried to tell him that I had feelings about that wonderful carpenter from Nazareth—a pretty tough cookie, boy, a radical who wouldn't take crap from nobody, kind of a sorehead. I told him about the Italian film *The Passion According to St. Matthew*, and that Christ had a short fuse—none of this thy-will-be-done crap. We had some interesting discussions about religion. [Laughs.]

You say there was a part in the Pat Boone film that you were good for. How would you define a part that you would be good for?

Any part. I feel like Bottom in A *Midsummer Night's Dream*. I think an actor should feel he could play any part. I can play Pyramus, Thisbe, the lantern, the moon, the wall . . . I don't hesitate to tell an actress how she ought to play pregnant, even though she may have had three children. An actor needs that sort of assurance.

What appeals to you about a part?

Mostly, does the play make sense? Is it about something? And what would it be like to play this character? What kind of revelation is possible?

Does that hold true for film? You are talking about film interchangeably with play, right?

Oh, yeah. It may sound a little pretentious and artsy, but when [director] George Roy Hill offered me the part of the sheriff in *Butch Cassidy and the Sundance Kid*, it occurred to me—I didn't get self-conscious about it—that this sheriff had to say the truth, just as a Greek chorus has to say the truth. The sheriff couldn't indulge his own subjective feelings about these kids; he had to tell them their time was over—they didn't know it, but they were going to die. That was the function of the Greek chorus.

The thing that makes my art, the art of acting, a rich and lovely experience is that it all feels so good. You are so excited by what you know. I know something about this story; I know something about this human being. It's so exciting to have a chance to make it clear to the audience.

I would think you would advise an actor to know his or her range, but it sounds to me as though it's better advice for an actor to believe in an infinite range.

You're damn right. Otherwise, why be an actor? Michael Chekhov used to say to us, "If you're offered the part of Othello, you must say, 'Aha! At long last! The right role at the right time for the right actor!' It is irrelevant who else has played it. This is it." You must feel that way.

When I see an actor onscreen and I think, "That actor is limited," what am I really saying?

Well, you're saying that the actor has engaged a few safe and conventional devices which are kind of repetitious. That actor doesn't explore; he's giving you a kind of minuscule human being rather than the sort of crazy thing Charles Laughton gave you. Or Olivier in *Lear*. I didn't like Olivier's first three acts, but on the moor he was inspired. What an imagination!

If you're limited, it's like, I suppose, any human being who is overguarded and who opts in any social, real-life relationship to utilize only a very safe and circumscribed part of his nature; it just lacks excitement.

If it becomes too predictable, it's almost a shtick.

It's what Stanislavsky called "the despotism of acquired habits," if an actor doesn't explore a part. If you have a limited personality, you're going to bring limited stuff into the characterization. But if you have myriad qualities, you're going to be irresistible. People are going to be kind of astonished. They'll say, "God, that crazy actor, he can do anything!"

When you do scenes in your class, do you do scenes from classic film scripts as well as classic plays?

If it's a good film script, by all means, but I want my students to do the best material possible, and generally plays are more tried and true. I'm not being snobby about screenwriting. People have done wonderful scenes from *Midnight Cowboy* and stuff like that. But I'd rather do plays, although I rarely advise them what scenes to do. I say, "Surprise me."

Are there classical exercises that you employ?

No. Why should there be? Because if it makes sense, it should apply to Lope de Vega or Shakespeare or Chaucer. The other day—yesterday!—some kid came in with page fourteen of a very good translation of the *Illiad*: Achilles is telling Agamemnon what a fuckup he is. I don't like to just bracket: "Now we will do the classics."

Can you give me an example of the kinds of exercises you prefer?

I invented half of them, most of them. I might have the actors do five arbitrary physical tasks. One might be to kneel and cross yourself. The next one might be to look out the window and blow a kiss. The next one might be to take a cup of water and pour it on your head. The next one might be to do a tap dance. The next one might be to crawl under a table and pick up the table with your bent back and move the table around the room like a turtle.

The idea is the specificity of the physical task—doing it for its own sake, being very truthful. The idea is to really kneel and cross yourself, really get under a table and lift it up with your lower back. And while you are doing it, do "To be or not to be," or do the lyrics of a Gershwin song, or "Little Boy Blue," or a monologue from an Arthur Miller play. This would be to illustrate the importance of not complicating a role with all sorts of psychological gyrations; if I have a physical lie, it's going to beget a psychological lie. Most important, what is the body doing?

I'll do an exercise with people where I'll ask them, while they're improvising, "What does your body feel like doing? What does your hand feel like doing? What does your foot want to do?" And I will explain to them that the physical impulses we curb in the course of any experience are what subtext is about. You look at a woman and you get an impulse; you say, "God, I'd just love to stroke her hair." You talk in that situation about the things your body wants to do but doesn't do, and you find that this is a rich way to find out what subtext is about. It's a very physical thing, as well as an internally verbal thing.

What's the difference between someone who comes to you as a student and is terrific in class and winds up having a successful career—like Jack Nicholson—and someone who is terrific in classes and doesn't?

I used to think that everyone who is terrific would ultimately get a good career going. Every now and then I even went over to an actor who was kind of in despair, and I'd put my arm around him and say, "Don't worry. You're going to have a good career." I was working with Peter Fonda one-on-one at the time *Easy Rider* came out, and I was so impressed with what Jack did. That really surprised me.

Why?

Because I thought Jack had become a writer, principally, and I didn't hear much about him as an actor. Then this great opportunity came along, and he was just wonderful. I'd like to think a lot of his crazy ideas were stimulated by me. But I've never been able to say, in all honesty, "I taught this person everything they know." There are a couple of instances when people came to class, and I know I helped them a helluva lot; but it's an arrogant game to go around claiming that. If Jack says very warm things about his experience in class, I accept it, and that pleases me, but I would never go around suggesting that if it weren't for me, so-and-so never would've gotten where they are. That's crap.

I'm wondering whether the people we see who shine on the screen are necessarily the people you have seen shine in your acting class. Was Jack Nicholson shining in your class at one point?

I never kicked him out of class! He was a very agreeable kid. He claims that one day I said to him, "You need more poetry in your work," and he said, "There's a lot of poetry in my work, only you don't see it." That appeared in a *Time* magazine article. That's a good quip on Jack's part. I was never sure about Jack's way of talking so that you could always hear his larynx rattle. It turned out to be a very good kind of laid-back quality in Jack, and he's made good use of it. [Laughs.]

I don't give career advice. There's a guy who's an airline pilot who comes to class now; he has three kids to support, and he was thinking of giving up piloting and wanted to know if I thought he should spend more time pursuing an acting career. I said, "I don't want to give you this sort of advice." He said, "How good am I?" I said, "Don't you know?" I'm helping him, and it would be dishonest for me to keep him in class if I thought it was futile. But every now and then I have to approach someone in class and say, "I'm not making an indelible judgment about you and your capacities as an actor, but it's frustrating you, and it's frustrating me, and I think we need a little relief from each other."

Do you think actors need to be well-rounded or richly experienced individuals in life, the way those old-time directors were?

That's none of my business.

What I'm wondering is, does shallowness in a person translate into shallowness as an actor?

Well, in my class I will suggest to people that they listen to music, commit a poem to memory, go to museums and see art; we do work from postcards like that [gestures to art reproductions on the walls of the studio]. We do exercises where you begin to view a situation through that face or that face. Or it may be as a piece of antique furniture. Candy [Candice] Bergen used to come to class, and I remember that one day she worked on equating herself with a kind of New England rocking chair in order to improvise something about a character.

Do you think, in some sense, that all good acting must be progressively rooted, or rooted in some humanistic fashion? I remember talking about John Wayne with people of the blacklisted community and laughing at how difficult it was for some people on the left to rationalize a terrific performance by John Wayne or by a reactionary like Adolphe Menjou. I believe Jean-Luc Godard, in his film-critic days, had the same twinge when he wrote about Wayne's performance in The Searchers.

Menjou was so good. And Duke—now, I worked with him twice. We did *Wake of the Red Witch* together and twenty years later *True Grit*. He knew damn well I'd been blacklisted. He put his arm around me and said, "Jeff, it's been too fucking long." We began to talk; mostly we talked about movies and food. God, he loved desserts. He'd say, "You've got to promise me. Get some wheels tonight, and you go to Telluride and go to such-and-such restaurant, and you get that Bavarian cream pie. And you tell me tomorrow, look in my eyes and tell me, if you ever in your life tasted anything like that!" And the next morning he'd say, "Well, did you eat it? What did you think?"

One day he had occasion to tell me how much he liked a scene that I had done in *Wake of the Red Witch*. He said, "Remember? You came in and you said that"—he remembered the dialogue—"and then Paul Fix said such-and-such, and I did this and that, and then such-and-such . . . and then I socked you, remember?" Duke remembered the whole bloody thing. He was always so interested in acting.

As I recall, he really took over directing the scenes for that picture. Edward Ludwig was the director, nominally, but Duke was really directing it. He loved being on the set. On his few days off, he'd come on the set. So I don't shortchange him. Incidentally, he told Barbara Walters on a taped interview shortly before his death that the only picture he consistently liked seeing was *Wake of the Red Witch*.

But you were talking about how, in effect, an actor has to seek the truth of the human condition. If someone is blindsided by politics—

Well, Duke—and Wally Beery was another—was a remarkable primitive. In painting you get Bombois, Rousseau, Grandma Moses, and they have their validity. They're primitives. Gary Cooper was a primitive. Jack Nicholson never did a play, so Jack in a way is a primitive, except that he did study in my classes for a long time.

Charles Laughton was a combination of primitive and slick. Somebody once said Charlie was the greatest amateur actor in the world—"amateur" from the root word *amar*, "to love." I myself, when people say, "You're a real pro, Jeff," it doesn't mean anything to me. I thought Alfred Lunt's genius was the fact that he was the antithesis of slick. He had rough ends; he was like an unfinished Michelangelo sculpture. He was not polished one bit. He could play all sorts of elegant, patrician people, but you knew he came from Minnesota.

One of the reasons why John Wayne is so interesting on the screen is, I think, because of his particular odyssey in life. Coming from Iowa, having been a football player, being a certain combination of bold and yet anxious to please. When you see him on the screen, he is communicating a lot of that about himself. You don't get that with a lot of young actors and actresses today, who are born and raised in Malibu, with less life experience to offer, perhaps, once they have taken up the profession.

I don't know. Marty [Martin] Sheen is a good actor. His kids are doing well. They live around the corner. And Sean Penn has done some pretty good work. He's a Malibu kid. So it doesn't hold up, what you say.

Now, in the case of Duke Wayne, he was lucky. He grew up in a period of time when they could put him under contract. His size and looks kind of embodied people's idea of a projected American myth. Gary Cooper had that kind of mythic quality. Monty [Montgomery] Cliff had it—a kind of romantic, tortured young man. Jimmy Dean certainly had it.

But Duke's work was not always great. Some things he looked damned uncomfortable in. I liked him best in *Red River*, *The Long Voyage Home*, and *True Grit*. He was lucky to have that good career. He shouldn't have smoked so much. He'd still be alive. Actually, in a way there are probably more good actors around than in the 1940s.

I'm surprised to hear you say that.

There are so many places where they can train—in academia, in neighborhood playhouses, and in classes around town, not only mine. I'm pretty impressed with a lot of the performances. Even in sitcoms, sometimes. I love the stuff that goes on in *Night Court*. Jesus! John Larroquette would have been sensational in the 1940s!

Jules Dassin

JULES DASSIN, Los Angeles, California, 1983

INTERVIEW BY PATRICK McGILLIGAN

JULES DASSIN
(1911–   )

1941 *The Tell-Tale Heart* (short). Director.
1942 *Nazi Agent.* Director.
     The Affairs of Martha. Director.
     Reunion in France. Director.
1943 *Young Ideas.* Director.
1944 *The Canterville Ghost.* Director.
1946 *A Letter for Evie.* Director.
     Two Smart People. Director.
1947 *Brute Force.* Director.
1948 *The Naked City.* Director.
1949 *Thieves' Highway.* Director.
1950 *Night and the City.* Director.
1955 *Du Rififi chez les hommes/Rififi.* Actor
     (as Perlo Vita), coscript, director.
1957 *Celui qui doit mourir/He Who Must Die.*
     Coscript, director.

1958 *La legge/La loi/Where the Hot Wind Blows.*
     Coscript, director.
1960 *Never on Sunday.* Actor, script, director,
     producer.
1962 *Phaedra.* Actor, coscript, director, producer.
1964 *Topkapi.* Director, producer.
1966 *10:30 p.m. Summer.* Coscript, director,
     coproducer.
1967 *Survival 1967* (documentary). Director,
     coproducer, appearance.
1968 *Up Tight.* Coscript, director, producer.
1970 *La promesse de l'aube/Promise at Dawn.* Actor
     (as Perlo Vita), script, director,
     producer.
1974 *The Rehearsal* (semidocumentary). Script,
     director.
1978 *A Dream of Passion.* Script, director, producer.
1980 *Circle of Two.* Director.

■

DURING ONE OF those long, elaborate, almost-midnight dinners that are an Athenian ritual, a prominent book editor told me, "Jules Dassin is beloved here, yet there is a great hunger to know more about him. People admire his work, of course, but he does not give many interviews and keeps himself a man of mystery."

Dassin is also a man of some mystery in America, the land of his birth. Stubbornly reticent when it comes to talking about himself, the director does not enjoy reminiscing about his film career, especially the Hollywood half, and especially the period of time he spent making MGM contract programmers. He prefers discussing the slice-of-life dramas he made for producer Mark Hellinger and Twentieth Century–Fox studio chief Darryl Zanuck—*Brute Force*, *The Naked City*, *Thieves' Highway*, and *Night and the City*—which made better use of his talent and intellect. His reticence means that there are few Dassin interviews on record, and his point of view is largely missing from film books and histories.

Because he was blacklisted in the United States and forced to hopscotch around Europe for work, many Americans have not been able to judge the variety of his later oeuvre or see many of the mature films he made in Greece beginning in 1957. Written and directed by Dassin, these generally star Melina Mercouri, the political compatriot whom he married in 1966. The best known are *Never on Sunday* (for which, in 1960, Mercouri shared a Best Actress award at Cannes and was nominated for an Oscar) and *Topkapi* (1964). However, their work together also includes *He Who Must Die*, *Where the Hot Wind Blows*, *Phaedra*, *10:30 p.m. Summer*, the two anti-junta documentaries *Survival* and (virtually unreleased) *The Rehearsal*, *Promise at Dawn*, and *A Dream of Passion*. Dassin, usually functioning as writer, director, and producer, often tossed in an acting plum for himself, appearing under the pseudonym Perlo Vita. He started out in show business on the bright side of the footlights and has had a separate life on the stage—in the 1930s in New York's Yiddish theater as well as later in Europe. No wonder his wandering, bountiful career is difficult to pigeonhole.

I first met Dassin in Santa Monica more than ten years ago, finding him surprisingly reserved, overly modest, and pained by the idea of an interview. This was shortly after *Circle of Two*, a misfire that implausibly paired Richard Burton and Tatum O'Neal, closed the door on his screen career. His Greek wife had already stopped acting to become a widely revered Socialist figure, a member of parliament, and eventually a cabinet minister. Since her death in 1994, Dassin has quietly guided a foundation in Mercouri's honor with a "who's who" of board members that includes Julie Christie, Sean Connery, Ian McKellen, Paul Newman, and Joanne Woodward.

When I told Dassin I was preparing a book to coincide with the fiftieth anniversary of the House Un-American Activities Committee hearings of 1947, he asked, "Do people care about that subject anymore?" I assured him that people did, and he agreed to welcome me to Athens. One night there, Dassin patiently answered several hours of questions at his elegant home near Mount Lykavitos. Nearing eighty-six then, he had the look and vigor of a much younger man (younger in years than many of his peers in Hollywood, he was long ago dubbed "the kid"). I find it poignant that he has never taken Greek citizenship, and he told me that one of the places he has never gotten around to visiting—he still hopes to—is Odessa, whence his parents emigrated to the United States.

The interview started, therefore, with roots, political as well as cultural.

■

When were you radicalized?

I guess from the time I was about six. You know, you grow up in Harlem, where there's trouble getting fed and keeping families warm, and you live very close to Fifth Avenue, which is elegant. You fret, you get ideas, seeing a lot of poverty around you, and it's a very natural process. Then, as you grow older, you read things and you see deeper, and this went on into the 1930s, when there was a big movement in America. I was particularly influenced by the writers and playwrights of the time. There was a real revolutionary theater in the 1930s—interesting and strong—and radicalization was just an inevitable process.

I think it's hard for people nowadays to understand the connection between theater and politics in the 1930s, and the connection between theater and Hollywood. Today there seems no great love for theater among American film fans, less background and little appreciation for theater. I think this is hard for young people to realize—how theater led to humanism for people of your generation.

The fact is that theater is so neglected in America, and some of the great theater is unknown. Some of the great playwrights are not done. I go to London nowadays just to hear Shakespeare, just to hear it.

Theater for us at that time was so strong. It was much beyond its ambience. It reached out. There were evenings in the Group Theatre: *Awake and Sing*—how we laughed, and how we cried! *Waiting for Lefty*—how we cheered! Not only the Group Theatre and the theater I was in, but playwrights like Sidney Howard and Elmer Rice and Robert Sherwood. It was a very exciting time. Actually, the plays were not always as wonderful as we would have wanted them to be, but there was that spirit.

Also, to keep alive at that time, a lot of us were in the Federal Theatre, and that was such a magnificent promise for the cultural life of the country. When that was assassinated—demolished—there was anger and protest. That was one of the mutilations of America's cultural force, not only of theater but of painters, architects, journalists, poets, collectors of anthologies of folk songs. The Federal Theatre had been so rich that we were just devastated when it was undercut. All that, plus what was going on in Europe, and the trade-union movement, and so on, tends to radicalize you.

You started out directing in the Federal Theatre?

No. I became part of a workers' art theater, and I was there for six years. It was a marvelous theater called the Artef, a Yiddish theater full of talented people, people who worked at ordinary jobs during the day. I really had to learn Yiddish in order to become part of that theater. We were amateurs as a matter of fact, unpaid, but we lasted some five or six years. Do you know the name Benno Schneider?

Yes.

Well, Benno was our director, our teacher, and our god. We loved him. He was so gifted in that atmosphere; he had to live in that atmosphere, where he was totally unchallenged. He couldn't quite manage it elsewhere. But he was a brilliant man—inventive, funny. Only three of us went out to Holly-wood: Benno—he went as a coach; the actor David Opatoshu, who was a friend; and I.

Were you more director or actor?

Happily, I learned early that an actor I was not, and I made tiny steps toward directing. I directed small stuff at the Artef, and I also directed in summer camps. I didn't know it was called directing at the time; it was called "putting on a show." But it was a rich and wonderful experience.

Were people of your generation conflicted between theater or film?

When we all went to Hollywood—that was after my Yiddish theater and the Group Theatre collapsed—we went out there feeling that we were be-traying the theater. We were ashamed. We were idiots. Theater was our be-trayed love for a while, but that stopped.

How long did it take you to accept film?

I loved film before I went to Hollywood.

As art?

Absolutely. Especially foreign films. The first job I was ever offered at MGM—I never knew I'd be so thrilled—was a film with Conrad Veidt [*Nazi Agent*, 1941]. I remembered as a youth sitting in a theater in New York watching Conrad Veidt with awe [in German films]! This first job was a typical MGM masterpiece, with Nazis and anti-Nazis, and Conrad Veidt playing two parts—the good German and the bad Nazi. I remember when I was introduced to Veidt. I had this problem of always looking very young, much younger than I was, even when I was young. I was brought to the executive office, and in came Veidt—a tall, tall, beautiful guy with these gray eyes. They said, "This is your director." And he looked down at me, said *"Nein,"* turned, and left. [Laughs.] He was persuaded to try it for one day.

He was happy after one day?

I owed that happiness to a man named Harry Stradling. Harry was a great lighting cameraman—if somewhat inarticulate, nevertheless a brilliant artist. Fortunately, he knew Conrad Veidt. They had worked together in Europe. So there I was with Conrad Veidt, with Harry Stradling, and I knew nothing. And I had just that one day to prove I knew nothing.

So I start with a shot—an insert of a glass. Then three or four such shots. And one simple long shot of Veidt reading a book. This gets me to about eleven o'clock. Harry Stradling asks, "What's the next shot?" I just look at him dumbly. Veidt comes over. "And now, *Herr* Director . . . and now?" For answer I say, "Lunch." He looks at his watch, then at me with a mixture of pity and scorn. He repeats, "Lunch," and goes.

Harry Stradling puts a friendly hand on my shoulder. I'm determined not to cry. "Harry, I don't know what I'm doing. And this guy paralyzes me." Harry, gently: "Tell me what's the next scene." I tell him: "It's when he suddenly feels a presence. He looks up and there is his brother, the Nazi." Harry says, "Here's what you do. Lay down a long track. When Veidt realizes who it is, you rush into a big close-up."

Veidt comes back from lunch. He looks down at the long track with interest: "Ah?" I quote Harry word for word. Veidt says, "Ah," again—but this time it seems to mean, "Perhaps I underestimated you." We make the shot. Veidt is pleased. And I pass.

That project certainly sounds fascinating, politically.

It was so superficial. You know who wrote it? John Lee Mahin, and I never met him. I never met the guy who cut the film! I never knew you were supposed to. That's how ignorant I was, and the studio seemed pleased to keep me ignorant.

What about Veidt? He is supposed to have been such a great actor.

He was. But you wouldn't know it from his Hollywood films. And in most of them, again and again, the only part he was given to play was that bad Nazi.

Do you have any fondness for any of your MGM films?

[Laughs.] No.

Did they show any of them at your 1995 Museum of Modern Art retrospective in New York?

I forbade it.

According to the filmographies, you appear to have specialized, for part of the time, in comedy.

I specialized in shit. They were awful. They were silly—as was I. I didn't know what I was doing, and God forgive me, I didn't care.

From the perspective of today, anyone would think you were sitting on top of the world with an MGM contract as director.

It was just plain unhappiness and embarrassment. First of all, you knew what you didn't know, and you knew that what they asked you to do didn't provoke anything in you to want to know more. To stay in that kind of mire was awful.

People would think that at least it was a kind of education, being a contract director at MGM—learning where to point the camera, etc.

Maybe, but can you imagine, except for one or two films that I made, I never met the writer? You'd have a situation like this: Louis B. Mayer asks you into his office, shows you a script. "I am trusting you with my biggest star—Joan Crawford." You reach for the script and say, "I'd like to read it." He's angry that you want to read it first!

The Joan Crawford film [*Reunion in France*] was Joe Mankiewicz's dirty trick. Joe was supposed to do this film with Joan as a heroine of the French Resistance. Joe got out of it by saying, "I'll produce. Let the kid direct it." I remember trying for weeks and weeks to get a story conference with the executives and Joan, because the script made no sense. Finally we got a meeting, and the only thing discussed at that meeting was how, when Joan Crawford becomes impoverished by her generosity in giving everything to the Resistance, we could dress her the way her fans want her to be dressed. That was the whole point of the story conference, which took hours and hours.

Did it matter to Louis B. Mayer that you were a radical? Was he cognizant of that?

Yes, he was. He once laughed at me and called me a "pinko." And I was tolerated, as were a number of the tribe of which he famously said (was it he or Harry Cohn?), "These guys are Communists, but the only reason we keep them around is because they're talented." You must remember that they only cleaned house when they were threatened and intimidated by the House Un-American Activities Committee.

You had to leave MGM to make strides as a director?

Right. I think one of the evil men was L. B. Mayer. An evil man. He was a schemer. He was a man who if you crossed him, or offered a different opinion, he could hate you. I'm part of a famous Hollywood story with him that shows you the kind of a creature he was. I had made all these shit films, and I said, "I can't stand it. Let me out, let me out of this contract!" He said no. I said, "Well, I'm just going to stop." I went on a one-man strike. I took a little house on the beach and caught up on my reading for a year. He kept sending my paychecks to my agent. After a year I went nuts. He knew I'd finally call him and say I needed work. He said sure. When I walked into his office, seated there like a jury panel were most of the executive producers of MGM. Obviously he was going to show them how you treated a rebel.

He began a long monologue, addressing them more than me. "Son"—he always called you "son"—"I'm glad to have you back in the family." When they say he cried easily, he sure did. He cried; he slobbered. "But I want to tell you a story first. You know I love horses. Did you ever hear of a horse named Pater? Let me tell you his story. There was a sale of two-year-olds in the East, and I went back with my trainer. 'I want that horse,' I said, 'the one named Pater.' My trainer said he cost a lot of money and didn't have much pedigree. I said, 'I want that horse.' In spite of my trainer's objections, I bought that horse and brought him out here to California, and, as you know, he became a famous two-year-old—he just kept winning races. He would fly to the front. Nobody could catch him. And he was my favorite horse.

"Son . . ." He's not looking at me at all. He's playing all of this for his panel, parading up and down before them. And they're looking up at him with that admiring and adoring look which president's wives wear as they watch their husbands perform. "Son, I tell my trainer to enter him in the Kentucky Derby. 'Oh, no, L. B. He can't win there. Those are the great pedigree horses of the world.'

" 'Enter him,' I say. 'That costs a lot of money, L. B.' 'I don't care what it costs. Enter him.' We did. Before the Kentucky Derby, the season starts here in L.A. We enter him, now a three-year-old, in a few local races. The first race, like always, he flies out front. But suddenly he stops cold and drags in dead last. I didn't think it was important. He just wasn't ready. But then it happened twice. Three times. Four times. He flies out front—no other horse near him—and then again he quits. My trainer, the son of a bitch, he's smug. He says, 'I told you, L. B.' 'Now, you listen,' I tell him. 'I believe in that horse. He'll come back. Just take him out on the farm a little while. Let him relax.'

"Now, listen to this. One day my trainer comes rushing in: 'L. B., I just found out why Pater quits all the time. That horse has developed the biggest balls I've ever seen on any horse. And after a furlong or so, they bang so hard against him he has to stop.' "

Now L. B. pauses. He looks at his jury. He looks at me. "So, my son. I gelded him. And he's winning races again."

I get over my shock and I say quietly, "Not my balls, you son of a bitch."

And he yells, "Get out of here, you dirty red!" And that's how I got out of MGM.

While you were still at MGM you became involved with the Actors Laboratory Theatre, which later became a big magnet for reactionary political attacks, right? Jeff Corey told me that you were one of the best acting teachers he ever had.

If I remember well, I was one of the founding members of the Actors Lab. A group of us got together and decided to found a workshop and theater. I remember I had two classes—one for beginners and one for professionals. Some Hollywood actors were so bored and unhappy with what they were doing in films that they used to come to class just to work and carry on their study. [Charles] Laughton was in my class, Tony [Anthony] Quinn, Alex [Alexander] Granach—it was great, great fun. My God, we did very, very good work!

Was there a political quotient to the classes?

No. We were what we were—but it was theater, film, acting, and directing. I guess the Actors Lab had that liberal taint, but it had nothing to do with the work at all. We did wonderful plays: it's not well-known that *A Streetcar Named Desire* was first done in the Actors Lab as a one-act play called *Portrait of a Madonna*, with Jessica [Tandy] playing the lead role and Hume [Cronyn] directing it. And the roots of the Actors Studio were in the Actors Lab, because we had a lot of Group Theatre people with us—including Morris Carnovsky, Bud [Roman] Bohnen, Art Smith, and [J. Edward] Bromberg. I remember the only satisfaction I had in those shit jobs [at MGM] was being able to give work to Bud and Art and Bromberg and Howard Da Silva.

Did that at least make parts of those MGM films good?

No! We were embarrassed by them. We considered ourselves serious people. I'll never forget how I gave a job in this Joan Crawford picture to one of my dear friends. She was from the [famous theatrical] Adler family—a marvelous woman whose name was Lola Adler.* There was a moment when Lola, who [in the film] was a former employee of Joan Crawford's, had to weep for Joan. She came to me and said, "You're going to have to tell me why I'm

---

*Jacob P. Adler, who came to the United States from Russia, was a preeminent figure of the Yiddish theater and led his own acting company from the late 1890s to his retirement in 1920. Members of the Adler family were more prominent on the stage than in films. Adler's son, Luther Adler, also starred in the Yiddish theater, acted on Broadway and with the Group Theatre (with leading roles in Clifford Odets's plays *Awake and Sing!* and *Golden Boy*), and played memorable character parts in Hollywood. Stella Adler—Jacob Adler's daughter and Luther Adler's sister—also acted in the Yiddish theater, was a founding member of the Group Theatre (she played the dominating mother in *Awake and Sing!*), and performed in, as well as directing, many plays. Her film appearances were rare. She studied with Stanislavsky and later became a celebrated acting teacher, for many years operating the Stella Adler Conservatory of Acting in New York.

weeping for that lady!" I gave her the greatest director's answer: "Fuck you, Lola!" [Laughs.]

When did you start feeling better about what you were doing and begin to have an idea that you were doing worthwhile work? After MGM?

I had a very unhappy time when I was under that seven-year slave contract at MGM. I was so unhappy and miserable with what I was doing that until I got out of that contract I wanted to go back to New York forever. After I got away from MGM, a kind of education began. I think I was learning how to make a movie. I was beginning to feel a little better; the films were improving. Then the blacklist came along.

I began to get the idea on the second film I made for [Mark] Hellinger—*Naked City*. The first one, *Brute Force*, was again a really dumb picture. [Laughs.] I remember saying, "But all of these prisoners are such nice, sweet guys—they're all so lovely—what are they doing in jail?" And then Hellinger says we have to get women into the story. Oy! And yet *Brute Force* was a start. Hellinger let me grope my way, let me begin to learn.

Richard Brooks told me that Hellinger was an unusually generous man with salary and contract terms, and afterward paid him a percentage of the box-office success of Naked City.

My salary was modest. After the film he [Hellinger] gave me a present of one-half of one percent of his share—which for some reason I never got, and I don't believe through any fault of his.

Brooks said his checks kept arriving even after Hellinger's death.

He was generous with Richard. He was very fond of Richard.

But you prefer Zanuck.

When I was given my retrospective at the Museum of Modern Art, I began by saying, "Look, I'm old enough to say whatever I feel. I liked Darryl Zanuck." [Laughs.] We were strange friends. I used to say to him, "Darryl, your ambition is to be a nice guy. It's too bad you can't make it." *Thieves' Highway*, which I made for Zanuck, could have been good, but I think we shot it in something like twenty-four days. *Night and the City*, which I did later for Zanuck, was certainly my best film up to that time.

After HUAC was in full cry, I went to Darryl and said, "I know you don't like the blacklist. Do you want to break it?" He said, "Yes, I do." I said, "I want you to buy a book called *The Journey of Simon McKeever*, written by Albert Maltz."

"Albert fucking Maltz!"

"John Huston is ready to do the screenplay. Walter Huston is ready to play the leading role. It's the story of a guy who has arthritis and hitchhikes from San Francisco to Los Angeles to find a doctor and has adventures on the way."

He said, "All right, we'll do it. But tell nobody. *Tell nobody!*" I said, "Well, some people *have* to know." He said, "I'll take care of the studio. You take care of Maltz." I called Maltz and said, "Albert, I've got twenty-five thousand dollars for you, but you mustn't say a word," because Zanuck's plan was for me to take a skeleton crew and start in San Francisco—all childish Boy Scout tricks—and by the time we reached Los Angeles it would be too late to stop the film. I told this to Albert, but the next day there was a headline in the *Hollywood Reporter*: "Albert Maltz Declares the Blacklist Is Broken." [Laughs.] And that was the end. Zanuck was angry.

Angry with you?

No. He protected me as much as he could, but when all of New York descended—with [Spyros] Skouras swearing at me and saying, "I'm going to step on your neck!" and things like that—Darryl said, "The kid didn't quite tell me." I forgave him all that. He did something, the same night, I think it was. He came to my house, and coming to my house was like visiting the tenements, because I lived on the wrong side of town. He said, "Get out. Get out fast. Here's a book. You're going to London. Get a screenplay as fast as you can and start shooting the most expensive scenes. Then they might let you finish it." That was *Night and the City*.

I really respected the guy. He did something else that touched me so. We were getting very close to shooting time, when he called me and said, "You owe me one." I said, "Yes, I do." He said, "I want you to write in a part for Gene Tierney." I said, "She's a star. What do you mean 'write in' a part?" He said, "This girl has just had *un grand chagrin d'amour*"—a big deception in love—"and is suicidal. I know her. She'll go to work, and it'll save her." This from Zanuck, the guy who is known for being so . . . so tough, so heartless. We wrote in a part for her. Darryl sent me a one-word telegram: "Thanks." That was the unknown Zanuck.

Were you a Communist before you went to Hollywood?

That is a question Darryl Zanuck asked me once! [Laughs.] He said, "How the fuck did you become a Communist?" It happened immediately after the opening night of *Waiting for Lefty*. I was tremendously moved, but embarrassed that I was not a member of the Communist Party. It was a rather extraordinary evening, that opening night. It was one of the unforgettable moments of my life. It was so moving, so irresistible, and it made such a direct personal appeal that you said to yourself, "I must do something. I must behave like those guys, who are showing so much concern and love." That's what did it for me.

Was it a mistake for the Hollywood Communists to keep their membership secret, since it became the main grounds on which they were attacked? I know this was a debate within the Party itself.

I don't know. There were arguments on both sides. This became an issue when we were allied with the Russians. That was the only time it was really proposed.

The movement to present every American Communist as a villain, as a traitor, was very strong. I imagine that some of the Party minds said, "We have to protect our people." Whether it would have worked the other way, I don't know. If you look back on things, you know what happened to the IWW, what happened at Haymarket in 1886, what happened to Sacco and Vanzetti. It took a lot of courage to say, "That's what we are, that's what we believe in," in the face of mass opposition to an idea. I don't know. It's a tough question.

The Party tried very hard to present Communist or Socialist ideas as an advance in America's development that was in fact rooted in American traditions. Well, they failed in this. The American people couldn't buy it. The association with the Soviet Union was too powerful. They tried to present it as Americanism at its best, but even if it was a right tactic, a right idea, they just couldn't make it work.

I was at Peekskill,* and I remember people yelling at Paul Robeson—artist, singer, all-American football player. A lynch atmosphere was created, and it was astonishing to see good American citizens go berserk. The police, at best, were indulgent, and people were attacked. People cried out slogans like, "Paul Robeson—go back to Russia, you nigger!" As if he had been born there! It was savage. I was embarrassed for my country. There was violence, many were hurt, but what I remember mostly is the bestiality that was aroused in these normal American citizens.

That was a sad, stressful experience I will never forget. The strength of the propaganda against us was so overwhelming and so easily sold to the American people that we just didn't deal with it very well. Heavens, we tried. But we were challenging the whole structure of the American industrial giants. And, by God, they are giants; they defend themselves, and they defend themselves well.

I don't see that the ideas we tried to present were wrong. And the intentions were, as far as I'm concerned, always pure. Whether we needed Madison Avenue minds to say, "Look, this is the way you sell an idea, this is the way you make it more accessible," I don't know. I'm just trying to look back at the failure, because it did fail. To this day, the prejudices, the misconceptions,

---

*The "Peekskill riots" broke out on August 27, 1949, when Paul Robeson attempted to give a benefit concert for the Civil Rights Congress in Lakeland Acres, New York, a few miles north of Peekskill. Veterans and vigilantes assaulted a group of people who arrived early, and the concert was postponed. Following a mass protest meeting in Harlem, a concert was planned for September 4, and 20,000 people attended. As they returned from the event, concertgoers were assaulted by an organized mob that wrecked cars and buses. More than 140 people were injured.

are as strong as ever. "Socialism" and "Communism" are words that still shock most of the American people. Even today, when Socialist governments in Europe are common, most Americans still wince at the word, as if it's a monstrous philosophy. So it still applies.

Would you characterize the Hollywood Party members as the best and brightest of their generation?

They certainly were the best citizens. They really cared. They were the purest, the most idealistic of the lot. They were going to make a better world. That was the naive, idealistic dream they all had. Whether they were the best minds I don't know. Other good minds opposed them. But I think they were the best people. They were pure to the point of naiveté, and that amused me. I loved them for it, but they were naive.

The guy in Hollywood who made a very handsome living, who was allowed to make movies, who could buy a house and have a swimming pool or a second car, this guy who said, "No, this is not enough for me, it's not just my world," he was a truly concerned American, a good citizen. I saw the elite, the intellectuals, go hand out leaflets on picket lines and sell Communist newspapers.

When people think of the radical movement in Hollywood, they think of the writers usually, not the directors. What kind of a hotbed was the Screen Directors Guild?

I don't know which director is going to be angriest with me, but we were not a hotbed; we were not even a tepid bed. We were just nice, well-meaning people trying to be good citizens. There were many deep and passionate concerns, but hotbed? There was nothing like it. The only thing hot were the attacks on us when the hearings began.

People think of directing as being such a self-oriented profession. Was the Party able to make inroads recruiting directors, or were there just a handful of directors who were Party members?

A handful. I don't remember many Communist directors. I'd be hard put to name more than five.

Did some directors actually read Marx and Lenin?

When you first were accepted into the Communist Party, you went to a school. School? Guys giving lectures on Marxism and Communism. They were all frightfully dull, and we didn't get much education out of that. That was the extent of it. By your own initiative you might say, "I want to read more," and very often one did. But the formality was classes.

Was there a Directors Guild fraction?

As a matter of fact, I don't think it worked that way. I think it had to do, actually, with where you lived, where the zones were. I don't remember a Directors Guild fraction.

Why did so much of the political activity—and the HUAC attack—revolve around the writers?

It was very clear that the writer, basically, was the potential enemy. He was the guy behind most of the organizations, and behind the [Screen Writers] Guild. These were guys who wrote scripts, but they were never considered dangerous because of what they wrote on the screen. It was a ridiculous idea that they were writing Communist propaganda or subversive stuff. It was howlingly funny. It was not that at all, but that the organization of a guild demanding rights and better financial arrangements, with people asking for royalties, as in the theater—this was impossible for management to accept.

I remember that I was once on a negotiating committee, and I sat in Louis B. Mayer's office and attacked the ridiculousness of other people cutting the director's film, and Louis B. Mayer said, "Look, do you think we're going to hand over control to you? We have a hundred million dollars to fight you. Can you match that?" That was it. The demand of the writer to be considered the creator—and to earn a fair distribution of what a film earns—this is really what brought the industry down upon them.

Did you have forebodings in the mid-1940s, when American Communists in the Popular Front were working alongside Republicans on patriotic committees? Did you have the feeling that on the one hand the strategy of rooting yourself in American traditions wasn't going to work, and on the other hand that the forces aligned against you were sooner or later going to prove triumphant?

Of course, it's all in retrospect, but the world enemy was the Axis and Nazi alliance, and any united front was a necessity. What I think the Communists and the Socialists didn't understand is that all of those who joined such an alliance could say to themselves, "All right, we'll get to you later." The Cold War began even before the hot war was over. But it was a historical necessity to make a united front against this terrible menace that hung over the world. And there were Russians fighting on our side, and we were fighting on their side.

I remember one slogan, "Defend the Soviet Union." Now, to the average American mind, that meant defending something foreign. It was not "Defend the Socialist Idea" or "Defend a Fairer System," it was "Defend the Soviet Union." Now, the reasons for the slogan are obvious, because there was hope that that revolution was going to lead to a brighter and better world. But I think that slogan was very dangerous and armed the opposition: "Those crazy Russian Bolsheviks—what do you mean, 'defend' them"? It was a tough slogan to sell, impossible.

Did you speak out against things that you thought the Party was mistaken about?

Look, there were stupid things in the Party. I was on the verge of expulsion many times. I was right to complain after Dunkirk, when I asked the guys to stop using the slogan "It's a Phony War," and I said, "It's a real war!" I was threatened with expulsion. Another thing that got me very angry was when Albert Maltz wrote a piece, I think for *the New Masses*, in which he said, "Look, we are writers and artists. It's not our job to go out on the streets on Sunday and sell the *Daily Worker*. We have our own work to do." And he was attacked. I said he was right, and that was another time when I was about to be expelled. So there was a kind of rigidity and lack of imagination in the Party, and truly a lack of understanding of the amplitude and size of America—and of American opinions and platitudes. It was a mistake being contemptuous toward people like John Wayne and [James Kevin] McGuinness and all these people who had power and were, I guess, sincere. Even if he was naive and a red-baiter, it was a mistake to label John Wayne a Fascist, when he was really, on his own terms, an American patriot and nationalist.

I passed over the fact that he was in that Joan Crawford film you directed. So John Wayne wasn't quite a Fascist. Was he a great actor?

No. But he was a very, very professional actor—always on time, always knew his lines, always very civil. He worked very hard on the set—unlike other stars I could name.

When did you first learn you had been named by an informer?

Actually, I heard about it when I was in Europe. I'd been asked to go to Italy to do a film based on the Communist novel by Giovanni Guareschi about the mayor and the priest, *The Little World of Don Camillo*. I went to Rome to meet the gentleman who was the producer, Giuseppe Amato, and we didn't agree on things. I went to Cannes, where there was a film festival, and that's when I heard that I had been named as a Communist. Maybe I read it in the newspaper. I can't remember.

Was it unusual for a Hollywood director already to be overseas looking for projects?

I wasn't really looking. I had become a hero to the Europeans because of *Naked City*, which they thought was a very important film, so they courted me a lot. I liked the idea of making a film in Italy. Everyone was full of enthusiasm for the Italian cinema at this time after the war. So it was very appealing.

What did you do?

One of the things that drives me, personally, mad is that it has been written about me and others that we fled. My immediate reaction was to go back, which I did. I really wanted to be questioned. I had all the heroic answers ready. I was going to be a hero. I came back, and nobody bothered me. I waited to be served [with a subpoena], because I thought I had things to say. And before I was served I was asked to do a revue with Bette Davis.

Bette Davis was one of the few, maybe the only one, who said, "I'm not going to listen to this nonsense. I'll work with anybody I care to work with." I thought it was a silly and idiotic revue, and I never knew why Bette wanted to do it, but I agreed to do it on one condition. Instead of opening in Boston and Philadelphia before coming into New York, I wanted to tour to about ten American cities which we would agree upon, and I wanted my name in lights. I wanted to prove that there would never be any demonstration or any protest of any kind, even though the American Legion had promised to organize groups against the Hollywood Communists. And we did play in ten cities, and they did have my name in lights. Nothing ever happened.

When we first started to rehearse, someone came with a summons. It broke my heart, because it was a black guy, and this hurt me. I told him, "Oh, I can't come to Washington now, because we're in rehearsal, and this is a big responsibility." He said, "Well, you're going to be called eventually." I said, "What can I do?" I mentioned that we had a lot of out-of-town engagements. He kept turning up from town to town, so that by the time we got East he was already a buddy, warning me, "You're heading for big trouble." Then we finally set a New York opening, and I told him I would be able to be in Washington the following day. That is when I got a telegram, signed, I think, by Eisenhower—or at least representing Eisenhower—saying all hearings had been called off. That was the end of my subpoena.

Were there people who were particularly exemplary in their behavior before HUAC, as far as you were concerned—people like Lionel Stander, later on, who really snookered the Committee with his attitude?

[Laughs.] He and others were fine, but I was one of those who didn't like the whole situation of the lawyers taking over. I didn't like the Fifth Amendment position, but you had to respect the decisions made by people who had to face jail. Finally, it came down to the fact that if you did not put yourself in the position of betraying, you behaved well. There were no heroes or Saint Joans of Arc. There were guys troubled by lawyers' opinions, by wanting to hold on to jobs if they could, by family problems. If you tell a guy that he can't work, it's tough.

What were you going to say if you were called?

All the cliché things: What right did they have? What horrible people they were! That I had the right to be what I wanted to be.

That's pretty much what John Howard Lawson tried to say.

I was going to say it prettily. [Laughs.]

Why do you think people like Lee J. Cobb behaved so ignominiously?

I think they simply placed career before honor. It's that simple. The need to work is very strong. And particularly in the arts—it's your oxygen; it's your life. And their betrayal is a continuing pain because these are the guys I loved. Lee Cobb was one of my closest friends. I loved him. I loved Kazan. I loved Odets. And this still hurts.

Were Elia Kazan and Clifford Odets the biggest blows? And Lee J. Cobb?

Kazan was king of the theater, and we loved him. We were old friends. Kazan hurt a lot. Odets? Maybe the most, for what he represented. Lee Cobb was my personal big blow—we were very close.

When there were rumors that Lee Cobb was going to cooperate, I said, "Over my dead body." I just could not believe it. These rumors were persistent. People were calling me because they knew we had been very close. I was living in Europe by then. I had just gotten my passport back, and I went to New York to see Lee. Interestingly enough, I saw him at a party with a group of old friends. I got Lee aside and said, "Lee, there are rumors . . . ?" He said, "I just want to know one thing. Do you believe them?" I said, "Of course I don't believe them." And the night before was when he had done it all! That, I think, was the one that broke me the most. That was the toughest one.

Did you ever see him subsequently?

I turned my back on him.

Was it especially hurtful when the informers were other writers or directors, former Hollywood colleagues? What about somebody like Robert Rossen?

Parenthetically, I'll tell you a funny story. I didn't like Bob Rossen. I didn't think he was a nice man, and this I shared in common with Billy Wilder. We both did not like Bob Rossen. I remember once, in a little Paris restaurant we used to love, where I knew that if Billy was around I'd find him there, I was at a table, and Billy walked in. I got up to greet him, and he commanded silence. I asked, "Billy, what's wrong?" He said, "I've got terrible news." I said, "What is it?" He said, "Bob Rossen made a good picture." [Laughs.]

When I think of Bob, I think of his kids, who first had to be told he was doing the right thing. That's one of the things people don't talk about much, the problems we had with our children. Some had problems with wives, but a lot with children. You'd find things written on the walls of your house. Other kids would say terrible things. How did you explain what was happening, to your own kids? And Bob Rossen, before he went to Washington, had to explain to his kids that he was doing the right thing. Then, later on, when he went the second time, they had to know he was doing the wrong thing. And those kids had to live with what he did.*

Was there always a personal component in who caved in and who they named? When Kazan's autobiography came out, I spoke to the actress Phoebe Brand,† and

---

*Robert Rossen was one of the original Hollywood Nineteen. But the 1947 hearings were suspended before he was called to the stand, and he was able to continue directing films until the 1951 sessions. Appearing before HUAC in 1951, he denied present membership in the Communist Party, but refused other probing into his past political ties. Blacklisted, he caved in, and testified cooperatively in 1953, naming over fifty film colleagues.

†Married to actor Morris Carnovsky, Phoebe Brand was one of the original members of the

she was adamant in her assertion that where Kazan chose to tell the truth in his book, the truth was selective. She said she had never liked Kazan anyway. One of his dishonesties was naming enemies, but not friends, some of whom were also likely candidates.

You look for forgiveness, you try to understand, but I can't manage it with Kazan. What he did was diabolical. And what he did afterward was diabolical—to try and reach and offer work to blacklisted people. He tried to corrupt them by giving them work and by doing so making them accept him.

He for some reason, I don't mind telling you, has tried for many, many years to get me to just see him. I think you can appreciate that I just don't want to. Some years ago he came to Greece, and he wanted to make a film here. My wife was minister of culture at the time, and she told me this guy, Kazan, was coming to see her and wanted to make a film in Greece. I said, "Look, Melina, there are a lot of shits who have made films in Greece. He's a shit with talent." That was my attitude. A mutual friend, an entrepreneur here [in Athens], knocked at my door and came with an envelope and a letter. It was a copy of Kazan's script treatment, and my friend said, "He asks if you will read it and tell him what you think of it, for old times' sake." "I don't want to read it," I told my friend. "Tell him to get out of my life."

Melina offered him all the cooperation he would need, but he said he needed the Army and the Navy, in which case he had to send the script to the minister of defense, which was done. The minister of defense called me a few days later and said to me, "What are you trying to do, you s.o.b.? This is the most anti-Greek film!" It had to do with Greek and Turkish history, I never read it, so I don't know anything about it, really. The minister of defense said, "You want me to give him the Army and Navy for this film?" "No," I said. "I'm not asking for anything. I don't have anything to do with it." Well, they wouldn't give Kazan the Army and the Navy for his film. A month later I read some interviews that he gave to the American press in which he complained about how I blocked his picture. That's Kazan.

Did anybody name you for personal reasons?

No. As a matter of fact, one of the people who named me was the director Frank Tuttle. [Laughs.] The last time I saw Frank Tuttle—we were both represented by the William Morris Agency—I was standing outside the New York office, and there was a terrible downpour. Out comes Frank Tuttle: "What are you doing here? Hello!" He told me he was worried because he was supposed to appear before the Committee. Then, all of a sudden, he had

Group Theatre and has had a long and distinguished career on the American stage. Although Phoebe Brand's appearances in motion pictures were few, Carnovsky was a prominent character actor before the blacklist, and most of the Group Theatre spent time in Hollywood, appearing in small parts in films or Actors Laboratory Theatre plays. See Harold Clurman, *The Fervent Years*, and Wendy Smith, *Real Life Drama: The Group Theatre and America, 1931–1940*, for additional detail and background on Group Theatre personnel.

a terrible attack—he was a diabetic. There was no getting a taxi. I carried him on my back to a hotel in that rain. The next thing I knew, Frank Tuttle had named me. [Laughs.]

How did it evolve that you felt you had to leave the country for good?

When the subpoena didn't turn up, I was offered a job in France, directing a picture with Fernandel.

Did you speak French?

A few words.

What happened?

I had to have the script ready the day before yesterday. It had to go right away. So I said yes. I wrote a script in, like, ten minutes, got it ready, and went to France. I still had my passport. A few days before we started filming, a man called Roy Brewer, a Hollywood union official, got hold of the French producer and told him that if this film were made with me, it certainly would not be released in the States, nor would any film he ever made afterward be released in the States.

The producer had hired Zsa Zsa Gabor. He thought she was a great big star, because her face was on all the magazines at the time. I didn't care who was the star. It didn't matter. I just wanted to get the job. After Roy Brewer got to the producer, he then went to Zsa Zsa, threatened her, and frightened her to death, and I was taken off the film—just a few days before shooting.

You were given a lot of support in France?

Oh yes, the French were wonderful at that time. They were very angry about what happened to me. It was called "l'affaire Dassin." Many people in French film came to my hotel and said this was awful and asked what they could do. There was big solidarity. They immediately declared me a member of the French directors' union. The French were wonderful. But nevertheless . . .

Was the Directors Guild in America any help to you?

This is my personal bitterness, if there is any. The behavior of all the guilds during that time was disgraceful. It was only when the thunderclap came that the real lack of character in the guilds was revealed. They just stopped thinking as guilds and defending their members, and each member began to think about his or her own personal future. One has got to understand that there was an intellectual reign of terror, including the comportment of guilds. They sacrificed their identity and their interests and were just swept away by fright. They stopped functioning as guilds.

I remember writing a letter to the president of the Screen Directors Guild at the time, after I had finally ended up in Europe and had my job blocked by Roy Brewer. I wrote that letter really more as an exercise. I asked, "What is your role as a guild?" Of course, there was never any answer. But the Directors Guild, like all the other guilds, failed, was cowardly, rejected its own identity, its raison d'être: to protect its members. We can't be proud of it.

Then it became hard to get work?

[Sighs.] It was hard to get work. People were afraid to hire you. I also had this great problem traveling. Our passports had been revoked. I can tell you one wonderful story. When I was in Paris, I was offered a job—I don't remember what it was—by a producer whose name was Romain Pines. It was going to be a French-Italian coproduction, and now I didn't have a passport. The producer took me to the Quai d'Orsay. He went right to the top official, storming into one of the offices. The guy who received us said to the producer, "You fucking Communist, what the hell are you doing here?" The producer said to him, "You son-of-a-bitch Fascist, I came here to talk to you about something." They insulted each other like that for about fifteen minutes. It turned out that they had been in the Resistance together and had saved each other's lives. Finally, the guy asked, "What do you want?" My producer friend said, "I want you to give my friend travel papers."

"What kind? What is your citizenship?"

"U.S."

"The only passport we can give you is one which says you belong to no country, and I can't do that if you are an American."

They began insulting each other again. He finally gave me a *titre de voyage* and signed it with his eyes closed. "If you tell anybody I signed it, I'll . . ." That helped me travel. But there was always a block, always something that happened, including being asked to leave Italy by the authorities at the insistence of Clare Boothe Luce.

The U.S. government went after you, wherever you happened to be?

She was the ambassador to Italy, and I had been asked to cowrite a film with one of Italy's beloved writers, Vitaliano Brancati—a great, wonderful man—adapting one of the Italian classics, *Mastro Don Gesualdo*. That got noise in the news. Cops came to my hotel and asked me to get out of the country. I phoned Brancati, and he came over right away. He was on the editorial staff of one of the important northern newspapers and furious that the producers had been frightened. He made an appointment with the prime minister, whose name was [Mario] Scelba, and Brancati went to his office— he was accepted and respected everywhere—and showed him the front page of his newspaper if I were kicked out: "Italy a Hollywood Colony?" The controversy dragged on for quite some time, and finally the issue had to be decided by the guy whose government is now being accused of having been Mafia-riddled—[Giulio] Andreotti, the former prime minister, who was then foreign minister. He ruled that I could stay, but by this time the producers had stopped loving me. This is what happened with different variations for over five years.

Jack Berry says there was a positive side, in that all of you formed a close-knit community with one another, sharing good and bad times and camaraderie, in Paris.

It's true.

Did you all think that you were eventually—sooner or later—going to end up back in Hollywood, that the blacklist wouldn't last?

I can't speak for the others, but I didn't think it would last, and I would have been happy to come back. But then, I must say, I thought of being back in New York more than California, although I enjoyed California some of the time because there were very many nice, pleasurable social times with friends, even a lot of fun. Forget the junk you were working on—that you put behind you and enjoy what you can.

Did you have pretty good communication with people in America from Paris? Did you keep up with the hearings?

Of course. We would follow them and weep and suffer for every friend who succumbed. I'll never forget how, every time one of our champions was scheduled, we said, "Well, all right. He's going to tell them off." I remember one early morning, when I was walking on the Champs Élysées, the chairs were heaped before the street cafés, and a man whose name is Harry Kurnitz—

The playwright?

And screenwriter. He sat there weeping, early in the morning at a French street café. I asked him, "Harry, what is it?" Harry was not even a left guy. He was a middle guy but decent. He said, "Clifford." I said, "No! Clifford?" He said, "Clifford, the poet of the working class," and began to cry. We all did.

During the five years you spent in France, what kind of things were you doing to stay alive?

[Sighs.] I don't know. We didn't know. We lived on each other's money, which we didn't have. We played cards, but nobody had any money to lose, so we just redistributed the pot all over again. It's called exile magic.

What rescued you from that period?

Rififi. I was through in Italy. I got a call from a guy who said he had a picture for me. I got back to France, and there the situation too was that I had to do the script immediately, get it out overnight. First he gave me this book [*R.F.F. chez les hommes*] to read. It was a weekend, and I had to be in his office on Monday to say yes or no. I couldn't even read the book. It was all in an argot that even many people in France can't read. I got hold of a friend, who sacrificed his love life to read it to me that weekend. I had no idea of what to do with the book. I went to say no but heard myself say yes.

The producer said I was the only person who could make the book into a film. I asked why. He said, "The problem is that all the bad guys in this story are North African, and at this moment relations between France and Algeria are explosive. But you can make the bad guys American." I said, "Has it occurred to you to make them French?" He was stunned at first and then accepted.

That was your first directing job in five years?

Yes, after five years of unemployment.

After that, did the jobs flow?

In Europe, yes.

Tell me what happened at the Cannes Film Festival that year, 1955.

Rififi turned out okay, and it was sent to represent France at the festival. I won a prize for the best direction, and the Americans were very embarrassed when the French flag was put up, the flag of the country that had presented the film. So some guy from the American Embassy was assigned to come and visit and talk to me, and it looked as though he wanted to give me my passport back. That would have fixed things, but you know the manner in which they wanted to fix things, so it didn't happen.

Incidentally, the same thing happened with *Rififi* that happened with the Bette Davis show. *Rififi* made a lot of money in Europe, but people said the film couldn't be released in the States unless my name was taken off it, or I said mea culpa to do so. American companies came and offered me large sums of money. I resisted. Apropos, it's generally agreed that the first blacklist film that appeared [with the credit of a blacklisted person] was Dalton's *Spartacus*, but I think mine was before that. *Rififi* was shown in one theater, the Plaza in New York, and it got limited distribution in the rest of the country. No major distributor would touch it. Some little guy showed it around, but there was never a single protest or any representation that American public opinion wanted a blacklist. That was another of the great lies. It was just not true.

How is it that you ended up in Greece?

A few years earlier, a lady I knew in France had asked me if I wanted to make a film of the novel *Zorba the Greek*. We disagreed about who should play Zorba, so it never came to pass. (Later Michael Cacoyannis made it, and it was a huge success.) But after *Rififi* I read another book by [Nikos] Kazantzakis, called *The Greek Passion*, which I decided to film, and that's really how my connection with Greece began.

Did you have any background in Greece? Had you ever visited here?

No. I had met Melina in Cannes when I was preparing the film. She was there representing a film called *Stella*. I was there with *Rififi*. I told her I was preparing this project, and there was a part for her if she was interested. Again, this was no-passport time, but her father was a deputy [in the Greek Parliament], and he managed to help. So the first time I came to Greece was in the winter of 1955, and then I ended up filming in Crete, where Kazantzakis was adored, albeit ostracized by the Church. It took some doing. That was my first Greek experience.

Then, lo and behold, this film *Celui qui doit mourir [He Who Must Die]*, which I wrote together with Ben Barzman, again represented France at Cannes, the year after *Rififi*. Again the U.S. Embassy had to deal with the French press needling it, asking, "What are you going to do about these Americans?" Now, that was a time when the embassies used to give big receptions, and the French asked the Americans if they were going to invite these two blacklisted Americans, Ben and me. We were filled in by people who knew what was going on. The telephone calls that went from Cannes to Paris and back lasted all day long. It reached the hour of the reception, with the press calling to ask if we had been invited. Finally an invitation was slipped under my door. A few minutes later they called, asking, "Are you coming?"

"No, I can't come, because you haven't invited my collaborator, Ben Barzman."

Again, telephone calls, and finally another invitation. Ben and I were invited, and the receiving line was peopled with functionaries and Hollywood stars. That very morning people had ducked under tables to avoid being photographed with us—such was the fear. Now, as we proceeded down the receiving line, backs were nimbly turned, and Hollywood stars held up champagne glasses to cover their faces; the French press enjoyed this, and Ben and I had a great time.

Things like that happened all the time at Cannes. I remember once going up to the Palais, where they were projecting one of my films, and seeing Gene Kelly approach the entrance. I kind of ducked away so that he wouldn't be embarrassed by fleeing from me. He saw this. And I shall always appreciate him coming after me and saying, "What the hell are you doing? Are you avoiding me?" He took me by the arm and led me up the steps of the Palais. He was the only one I knew willing at that time to be photographed with me.

What stopped you, once you became entrenched and successful in Greece, from continuing to use other blacklisted friends as writers? Was it better if you wrote the scripts yourself? Why not, for example, continue to work with Ben Barzman?

Truth to tell, writing with Barzman was a matter of all of us being in the same boat, in the same place, sharing the work. And I liked him. Then I went off on my own, made a new life in Greece, and for better or worse, from then on, wrote all my screenplays.

Nobody else from the blacklist settled in Athens. Were you gradually isolated from your Hollywood friends?

Pretty much.

People didn't come through Athens as often as they came through Paris?

They did not.

Was that difficult for you?

I went to see people. My kids lived in Paris, and every time I went I would see friends in Paris. I would go to London for theater and see Joe [director Joseph Losey] and have good as well as bad times with Joe.

You didn't go to Los Angeles very much?

No.

You had to write and direct so many of your films so very quickly. After Hollywood, were there a number of films where you had a leisurely amount of time, or is it partly the nature of the business always to be in such a hurry?

I'll tell you the truth. This is a fault, I know, but I never understood the guy who needed six months or a year to write a script. If you work six, eight, ten hours a day, you can write a script in a matter of weeks. Sacha Guitry wrote plays in two days. I did write quickly. I wrote *Rififi* in six days, and *Never on Sunday* in ten days, but I would work at least ten hours a day.

Which of your European films are you most fond of, the ones you made after Hollywood?

I'm fond of pieces of this and pieces of that. I can't say I'm totally delighted with any one film I ever made, but there are parts of films I like. But whatever the result, I enjoyed the luxury of freedom. I did what I wanted to do. I would count and rue the mistakes later.

Which of your Greek films represent for you the highest degree of creative freedom?

If I had to choose one single film, it would be a film that was never released. It is called *The Rehearsal*. In November 1973 Greece was in the grip of a dictatorship. Greek students, in protest, occupied the Polytechnic University. In answer, the Greek colonels sent tanks. There were deaths and bloodshed. I decided to make a film about it, a documented reenactment of the occupation and the massacre. We made it in New York. It was a moving experience. The cast was a beautiful meld of excellent New York actors and Greek students, along with Arthur Miller, Lillian Hellman, Maximilian Schell, and Laurence Olivier—all of whom volunteered their time and talent. The film was finished in June. The junta fell one month later. If there was a possible distributor, he lost interest after the fall of the dictatorship.

How long was it after the blacklist before you tried to work in Hollywood again?

In 1968 we were in America seeking support for the restoration of democracy in Greece, but Melina was going to tour making speeches and didn't need me. Paramount asked me to make, of all things, a remake of *The Informer* with black actors. I said yes. It was a disastrous mistake. But it did give me a reason to care about working for an American company. I thought the whole situation of blacks in America was dreadful and that a film should be made. It was also a rather exciting time. It was the beginning of the black revolt and the Black Panthers.

I thought I had written a good script, but I kept saying to myself, "Who do you think you are to write a script about blacks?" So I asked [actress] Ruby Dee and a man named Julian Mayfield to write a second script with me. In retrospect, I think I prefer the first. Also, James Earl Jones was supposed to play in the film but at the last moment said no. Julian Mayfield, who was a schoolteacher, ended up playing his part. It all went haywire, but I loved Ruby Dee and all those who worked on the film.

That was Up Tight. *Did you film it in Hollywood?*

We began to film in Cleveland, but that was a year of terrible riots, and we were very much resented by the community, especially because we couldn't get black people for our crew. Very bad things happened in Cleveland. We began filming a little after the Martin Luther King Jr. assassination; as a matter of fact, I filmed the riots and protests surrounding his funeral. We went into this atmosphere resented and not trusted and attacked—sometimes physically attacked. Then Bobby Kennedy was killed, and the mayor warned us to get out of town saying he could not be responsible for our safety. So we actually had to finish the film in Los Angeles.

Did you get other feelers, now that the blacklist was long over?

The black film was such a disaster that nobody called, except for small stuff. It was kind of accepted that I had become an expatriate forever or was dead.

You didn't accept that you were an expatriate forever?

No.

Your last film to date, Circle of Two, *was made partly in Canada, but it didn't turn out very well, right? Was it an interesting-sounding job at the time? Why did you do it?*

Money. Money—and a rather sweet little outline. It all had to do with an oldish man, played by Richard Burton, being enchanted by a magical young creature. Well, when you cast the [role of the] magical creature with Tatum O'Neal, you're dead. [Laughs.]

Are you responsible for the casting?

It was my fault. I went along with it. The producers were under the impression that Tatum was a huge star. I remembered her from a child's performance and was dumb enough not to ask what had become of her. I signed to do the film, and then I went to California to meet her, at which point I said to the guys, "Don't make the movie!" But I was bound. Well, it was a disaster.

Was there something so dispiriting about the experience of the production that you vowed never again to direct a film?

I would say so. That was it. What happened also was that in order to do something to help this film, I cut it in such a way that she would be least objectionable. They got their hands on it and turned it around, and I sued and asked to have my name removed. All of that and more. [Laughs.] That experience was hopeless, and that was kind of it.

One wouldn't think you even needed money after twenty or twenty-five years of such success.

Think again. To my great delight, however, I found that you could earn a good living in the Greek theater. It's been a very happy stretch. I've done many plays here that I loved.

I know most of the blacklistees kept in touch with one another for the rest of their lives. Many stayed best friends. What held this particular group together?

This particular group was held together by what they considered a principled way of behavior. Many of them changed their political ideas, many became disillusioned, many were angry about the way things turned out—particularly about the Soviet Union, which they had set such great store by, had such hopes for, hopes that were frustrated, defeated, and betrayed. But what held and holds them together is that they behaved well. And they respect each other for it, whatever differences there may be among them.

Was the blacklist a blessing in disguise for some people, like you?

I wouldn't call the blacklist a blessing in disguise. I was lucky. I was out of work for only five years. I was able to change my life and make another life, but I was separated from my cultural background, and I had to improvise and pretend to understand other cultures as well. The bitterness is not personal for me, but certainly there was no blessing. The blacklist was a horrible, monstrous idea—attacking a man in his most vulnerable, vital need, and saying, "Well, you just bloody well won't work." The fact that I somehow circumvented some of the sorrows and evils of it personally does not change my mind about it, and I would never use the word "blessed."

Do you consider yourself an American?

An American, and a New Yorker. An easterner too—one of those dangerous, eastern-thinking people. I'll always be an American, and I miss America very much.

Why do you continue to live in Greece?

My children grew up in Europe. I have grandchildren now. When the Greek dictatorship fell, I couldn't say to my wife, "You've been exiled for seven years, but now we can't go back and live there." I couldn't do that; I knew what exile was. So I lived and worked in Greece, and in Greek theater and films. I had been offered citizenship in France. I have been offered citizenship in Greece. I always refused. I am American, and that I will stay.

How do you regard Hollywood today?

I'm greatly concerned about the kinds of films that are being made. I'm dismayed by the size of budgets for American films. I'm aghast at the idea that a film could cost a hundred million dollars and more. I think the blockbuster mentality is pernicious. I'm dumbfounded that serious film critics support with enthusiasm obscenely expensive comic-strip movies. But, of course, some excellent films are made. There is an enormous concentration of talent in Hollywood, and I believe in a better future.

Edward Eliscu

EDWARD ELISCU, Los Angeles, California, 1983

INTERVIEW BY PATRICK MCGILLIGAN AND DAVID ELISCU

EDWARD ELISCU
(1902–   )

1930 *Whoopee!* Lyricist.
  Follow Thru. Lyricist.
  Queen High. Lyricist.
  Great Day. Lyricist.
1931 *The Prodigal/The Southerner.* Lyricist.
1932 *Rockabye.* Lyricist.
  Bird of Paradise. Lyricist.
  The Half-Naked Truth. Lyricist.
1933 *Flying Down to Rio.* Lyricist.
  Diplomaniacs. Lyricist.
  Professional Sweetheart. Lyricist.
1934 *Stingaree.* Lyricist.
1935 *The Silk Hat Kid.* Coscript.
1936 *Paddy O'Day.* Lyricist, coscript.

High Tension. Coscript.
Little Miss Nobody. Coscript.
Every Saturday Night/The Jones Family.
  Coscript.
1939 *Little Tough Guys in Society.* Costory, coscript.
  His Exciting Night. Coscript.
  Charlie McCarthy, Detective. Coscript.
1941 *Sis Hopkins.* Coscript.
1943 *Something to Shout About.* Coscript.
  The Heat's On. Lyricist.
  The More the Merrier. Lyricist.
1944 *Hey, Rookie.* Coscript, coproducer.
  Meet the People. Uncredited contribution.
1945 *The Gay Señorita.* Script.
1947 *Out of the Blue.* Coscript.
1950 *Three Husbands.* Coscript.
1951 *Alice in Wonderland.* Coscript.

■

EDWARD ELISCU IS an offbeat French-Romanian name for an offbeat man in Filmtown, USA. An aficionado of the theater from childhood, he was not devoted to films as either art or commerce and, like so many others, did not enjoy the Hollywood career game. Hollywood in the thirties and the forties, for him, was a place of great political activism and idealism. The happy experiences clash with memories of evil enemies like the Screen Playwrights, the Motion Picture Alliance for the Preservation of American Ideals, and the House Un-American Activities Committee. Consequently, he expresses little nostalgia for the "golden age" of motion pictures.

The history of American show business in the twentieth century is reflected in the sweep and accomplishment of his life. In the 1920s he proved himself on Broadway as an actor, songwriter, playwright, and director. Brought to Hollywood first as a lyricist in 1930, he stayed only briefly. He returned in 1932 under a short-term directing contract offered by RKO producer David O. Selznick and engineered by director George Cukor, who was a high-school acquaintance and a friend of Eliscu's wife, artist Stella Bloch. After writing a song for Cukor's film Rockabye, Eliscu settled down to a career as a contract writer, making stops at most of the studios in town.

But he and his wife never really felt comfortable on the West Coast or in the film business. They made a point of leaving in 1934 to study theater in Japan and the Far East, and of spending intervals in New York or Connecticut. One of the Hollywood achievements in which Eliscu takes pride is a musical revue, Meet the People, which was a huge success in 1939, running for a year in Hollywood before moving to Broadway. The revue was a cooperative venture, with Jay Gorney writing the music and Henry Myers and Eliscu contributing lyrics, writing sketches, and editing material.

Myers was a frustrated opera composer, a fountain of wit and whimsical imagination, and a published novelist. Jay Gorney was a songwriter, famous for "Brother, Can You Spare a Dime?" Mortimer Offner, another Eliscu friend from high-school days (in Hollywood he coscripted Sylvia Scarlett and Alice Adams), directed the sketches. Danny Dare was the choreographer and overall director of the show. The Barzman brothers, Ben and Sol, contributed the revue's innovative opening as well as other material. All would suffer from the blacklist.

"Meet the People was an exhortation to Hollywood to come out of its cocoon and realize what was going on in the rest of the world," Nancy Lynn Schwartz wrote in The Hollywood Writers' Wars, "a variation on the theme of Hollywood's responsibility to produce works of mature content that reflected the times. Those who worked on it considered it the only successful collaborative creative experience of their lives.

"It began with a Sleeping Beauty, Hollywood, peacefully dreaming away, serenaded by lullabies, while war, strikes, and starvation go on around her. Finally a prince comes and stabs her with a large pin, which wakes her up, and he tells her to come on out and 'Meet the People.' Sleeping Beauty then watches the world, a very funny left-wing perception of it, unfold before her eyes."

In 1941 Eliscu, Gorney, and Myers created and coproduced a second politically-inspired musical, *They Can't Get You Down*. ("They" referred to "the power structure.") "It was faulty in some ways, but it was also hurt by opening the week of Pearl Harbor," remembered Eliscu. The show contained a hilarious bit of musical nostalgia for the formerly privileged, now exiled Middle European aristocrats who had emigrated to the United States, a song called "That Mittel-Europa of Mine."

"There was a dance between Hitler and Stalin that showed Hitler with a knife at Stalin's back," according to Nancy Lynn Schwartz's book, "and a knife in Stalin's hand at Hitler's back. But the waltzing dictators apparently upset the [Communist] Party so much that the number was dropped."

By the time *Meet the People* had traveled to Broadway and returned, transmogrified into a 1944 film starring Lucille Ball and Dick Powell, its original purpose was all but unrecognizable. That, in microcosm, was what happened to Eliscu in Hollywood. He was fortunate to have coscripted Lou Bunin's all-puppet version of *Alice in Wonderland* in France, just before HUAC invaded. When he returned to America, Eliscu found himself one of the many named by the loquacious Martin Berkeley, and his career in films was over. By then he was happy to leave Hollywood, but even back East, creating meaningful work was a struggle. After a successful year as a television dramatist, adapting several classic plays for that medium, he was blacklisted in New York as well.

Nowadays Eliscu doesn't watch old movies, while some of the best of the newer ones incorporate his classic songs on their soundtracks (brightening, among other films, Woody Allen's *Crimes and Misdemeanors* and *The Fabulous Baker Boys*). In 1987 he was awarded the Richard Rodgers ASCAP annual award "in recognition of his outstanding contributions to the American musical theater." Recently Eliscu has completed his memoirs, entitled "With or Without a Song," which he assures us will tell the whole story of his life and career better than any interview.

■

What are the roots of your love of show business?

I'm sorry if we're starting with the assumption that I have a great love for show business. I'd rather characterize my lifetime experience as someone deeply and incorrigibly attracted to the theater.

I had a triple ambition: to be an actor, a writer, and a director. My absolute devotion to the theater, including the serious part, began when I was very young. Remembering my mother, I would say that she should have been an actress. She had all the equipment and temperament to be one. She and I used to go to the theater together. Going further back into the roots of the family, there were some predecessors of mine in the best part of the theater. One of them was a star for Charles Frohman, one of the leading producers on Broadway. Her name was Fernanda Eliscu. Matter of fact, we were almost cast as mother and son at one time.

What were the origins of your political sentiments?

My mother was a fervent reader of a Socialist newspaper in the Yiddish language, the *Jewish Daily Forward* [*Forverts*]. Also, my oldest brother, Charlie, actually ran for alderman on the Socialist Party ticket. I don't even know how he got the nomination, because he was a rather flighty fellow. But he was a Socialist candidate.

I suppose I always had some kind of Socialistic attitude. I was deeply affected by reading, as a child, Jacob Riis on poverty in New York City.* When I read Riis—I was eleven at the time—I suddenly realized that it wasn't people's laziness or stupidity that made them poor. I remember writing a composition about Riis's book that I was then asked to read in an assembly. I ended my paper with something like, "Let us put our shoulder to the wheel; we must abolish poverty!"

These two interests of mine were combined, you might say, when I began onstage at the age of nine, reciting Lincoln's "Gettysburg Address" on July Fourth to an open-air theater audience, for which I was given two dollars and a box of candy. It's true that I did not understand fully the meaning of every word in the Address. But coordinating the abstract word with action and understanding came as I matured.

When I was still in my lower teens, my mother and I used to go together to Saturday matinees of vaudeville. I remember very distinctly responding to an anti-war sketch in which [actress Alla] Nazimova played. The country she lived in—which was not mentioned; it could have been any country—was at war, and she had a son who, she said, she would not give up so that he could fight and possibly be killed. Instead, at the climax, she pretended to kill herself right onstage. A shot rang out when Nazimova "killed herself." I

---

*Jacob Riis was a Danish-born American journalist and muckraker whose book *How the Other Half Lives* (1890), with its shocking photographs, spurred President Theodore Roosevelt to improve conditions for New York City's poor. Riis also founded a pioneering settlement house. His autobiography is *The Making of an American*.

remember a moment of great silence. Then, suddenly, there was a great cheer of approval from the audience. The orchestra blared out a popular song, "I Didn't Raise My Boy to Be a Soldier," and the curtain fell. A year later the popular songs changed to tunes like the patriotic "Over There" or lyrics that extolled the Red Cross nurses, like "There's a rose that grows in no man's land." Anybody who expressed an anti-war sentiment would be cut down. The whole country's attitude changed, including my own. I didn't have much of a political focus for a long time.

You got your real start onstage as a director with college shows.

As a junior at the City College of New York, I kept myself going financially by putting on amateur plays. The very first job I got was to direct the plays put on by the various YMHAs [Young Men's Hebrew Associations] all across the city. The senior class at CCNY found out about this and put me to work staging the senior play, *Bye Bye Beowolf*, written by Francis Faragoh,* with myself writing the lyrics. We even engaged the Morosco Theatre. But it was really a college show with plenty of laughter, some of it unintended. Though we sent a notice in advance to all the newspapers, only one columnist, Bide Dudley of the *New York World*, ran an announcement of our appearance on Broadway. He wrote, "The Senior Class of City College will present its own play, *Bye Bye Beowolf*, this Sunday evening at the Morosco for one consecutive performance."

Didn't you also work as a social director at summer camps?

In the 1920s summer vacations for young people from New York underwent a change. Camps were started that attracted young people for two weeks of tennis, camping, and prospects of marriage. The "social staff" was engaged to provide entertainment and round-the-clock laughter for the guests. This was a way in which many people, like Danny Kaye and Sid Caesar, got their start, then graduated into the professional theater. I was formally what they called a "social director" at Camp Copake, in upstate New York. My own job, along with dancing with the girls and being cheerful all the time, consisted of putting on shows, being the director and star of the theater all summer long—writing, acting in, and directing them.

Once a week we did original revues. Morty [Mortimer Offner] was soon made my assistant at camp. We hired him because he was very talented, very

---

*Budapest-born playwright and short-story writer Francis Faragoh (1898–1966) was prominent as one of the socially conscious New Playwrights in New York before he went to Hollywood, where he earned a sterling reputation in the 1930s and 1940s, working on such films as *Little Caesar*, *Frankenstein*, *Becky Sharp*, and *My Friend Flicka*. One of the key film-industry radicals, he helped organize the Screen Writers Guild and served as the first chairman of the Hollywood Writers Mobilization during World War II. Named before HUAC by Meta Reis Rosenberg, Edward Dmytryk, and Martin Berkeley, among others, Faragoh was forced to leave Hollywood, and his credit never again appeared on the screen.

funny, and very good-looking. Morty and I were able to influence the owners, who were not typical Catskills-type resort owners, that we were not typical college graduates. They approved financially, morally, and theatrically of all the things we wanted to do. I had the nerve—I just did it to please myself—to do the plays or material of Oscar Wilde, Noël Coward, Rodgers and Hart, the Gershwins, a whole variety of entertainment, and also serious plays, by [Eugene] O'Neill, for instance. I even had the nerve to try to play the lead in *The Emperor Jones.*

That's a black man's part.

Yes, and I got the kind of ridicule that I deserved.

This was not part of "the borscht circuit"?

The borscht circuit was a step below us. We were way up in Craryville. Incidentally, Sidney Buchman was at our camp. He was an outstanding personality, a man who looked like Byron, with a long, flowing Windsor tie. He had just been with the Ben Greet Players in [Britain and] Europe and now was working as a waiter. He responded willingly to an opportunity to go onstage for us in a play from the Harvard 1947 collection, portraying a Swedish sea captain—originally he came from Duluth, Minnesota. Sidney was an excellent actor.

How long did you work at the camp?

I did it for five summers. During this time I also taught school for one year. I should include the fact that I played hooky for two days as an extra in a Marion Davies picture, *The Belle of New York.* After the third summer at Copake, I went into the theater professionally, tramping up and down Broadway looking for a job.

You had some measure of success on Broadway as an actor.

Yes, I did. I appeared with Helen Hayes in *Quarantine,* a frothy comedy in which she showed her versatility as an actress. In my third or fourth part I played the young punk brother of Edward G. Robinson in *The Racket,* the role that sent Robinson flying to Hollywood as [a gangster modeled on Al] Capone in *Little Caesar.* This was an extraordinary ensemble of actors, including [future film director] John Cromwell.

I was often a stage manager, but I had the ambition to become a director. All the time I was also trying to become a playwright. It was a question of whether I should be a writer, an actor, or a director, of where I fitted in best.

I gather you were a songwriter from an early age. How did you get into songwriting?

I began by writing parodies for occasions like birthdays and school athletic contests and for rhymed sections of camp shows. Ira Gershwin suggested I should try lyrics as a professional.

Meanwhile, you were doing writing of some type all the time.

All the time. I was always writing, from imitation Ibsen and Shaw to imitation vaudeville. Leonard Sillman was sixteen years old when he came East from Detroit for a weekend at Copake, because his cousins were guests there. I put him into the Saturday-night revue, and he killed the people—he was so young, so confident, so brash. He made a big hit. His first professional job was in a Gershwin road show.

One day I was about to cross Fifty-seventh Street and Seventh Avenue when someone hit me so hard on the back that I almost fell over. It was Leonard Sillman, just back from the Gershwin road show. He asked me to put together a vaudeville act for him and a girl he introduced me to the next day. She looked like a squeaky doll—she had that kind of voice, with a funny face and a funnier name, Imogene Coca. It seems to me that the act I wrote for them opened and closed at the same time. I blamed myself. Leonard blamed the audience, saying, "It's too intelligent for them."

It all leads somewhere. After doing this with me, Sillman called me up one day, shouting into the telephone, "I've found the most wonderful collaborator for you—you'll be another Rodgers and Hart!" I said, "Wait a minute!" He said, "This is for your own good! His name is Eugene Berton. His brother Vic is Paul Whiteman's drummer." Gene had just came back from Berlin. Leonard had met him at one of Elsa Maxwell's parties. He said I must meet him at once. I said, "All right. Tell him to call me." Leonard said, "I did. I gave him your number. He sings in French and German. No, he comes from Chicago, speaks perfect English. Very cultured. You'll thank me."

Although we were hardly well-matched types, it was a productive collaboration, but it also cost me terrific anguish, because Gene would just fly off—disappear—now and then. One of the first things we wrote together was *The Dagger and the Rose*. There was already a wonderful play about Benvenuto Cellini by Edwin Justus Mayer. Horace Liveright, who was a producer and a publisher—a kind of intellectual but an absolutely crazy individual—got the idea of taking the score from a musical that Gene and I were working up about Lucrezia Borgia and incorporating our music into the Cellini play. I got Francis Faragoh to write the book, Gene did the music, and I did the lyrics. Then I suggested George Cukor as the director.

How did you know Cukor?

We went to De Witt Clinton High School at the same time. We weren't friends—I didn't really know him very well—but he was a good friend of Morty Offner. He and Morty's cousin Stella Bloch and Morty were a trio who cut school all the time to catch every opening bill at the Palace. They were devotees of who was best in the theater. Cukor at that time was just beginning his career as a director with a stock company in Rochester. He was determined to be connected with the theater. I think I went up to Rochester to talk with him about *The Dagger and the Rose*. This was 1923 or 1924.

So Cukor directed the play.

It was the kind of play referred to in the theater as one in which someone writes a letter with a feather. Its failure didn't stop Liveright from throwing a big opening-night party. I can still see him sitting on the regal steps of the hotel with four girls on one side and five girls on the other, like a monarch with his harem. The play closed after one week.

What happened next?

I had been recruited into what was then the Song Writers Protective Association—Billy Rose's title, as if we were gangsters. This was in the mid-1920s. Somebody who had been at one audition after another and loved the score of *The Dagger and the Rose* got us an appointment to meet Max Dreyfus, the head of Harms, the most influential musical publisher of the time. Dreyfus advised producers of shows on the choice or match of lyricists and composers. Gene was very excited and told me, "Did you know that Dreyfus is a very cultured man? He doesn't have a cheap piano—he has a Bechstein!" And he pointed it out to me the next day, in the office.

I think Gene was so nervous that he blew his audition, part of it resembling an impersonation of a woman performing the songs. It was a bad sign when we were ushered out the door shortly after, because we should have immediately followed the presentation of the music with a discussion of the songs, leading to the subject of a contract. When I got to my apartment, there was a call from Dreyfus's office. "Mr. Eliscu, Mr. Dreyfus wants to see you alone."

Then I knew what had happened. My heart sank. I said, "No, we're together on this." Gene shook his head sadly: "No, this is a crucial moment for you, a real opportunity." It had been more Gene's goal, and now he practically wept. The next day Dreyfus had loosened up, appearing a different man. He said to me, "I'll put you on a contract at fifty dollars per week against future royalties" in return for my writing lyrics for shows of which Harms was the music publisher. And right away he gave me a show! He teamed me up with Joe Meyer—author of the song "California, Here I Come!"—for *Lady Fingers*, a mild show with a book by the star, Eddie Buzzell, at the Vanderbilt Theatre.

The show was less than a hit. The theatrical gravediggers blamed Joe Meyer and me for having failed to come up with a real hit to send the audience out of the Vanderbilt humming or whistling an irresistible song. Rodgers and Hart reluctantly pulled one such number out from the bottom of the trunk: "I love you more than yesterday but less than tomorrow, less than tomorrow." That didn't send the audiences whistling or singing on their way out, either.

Harms called me in after weeks and weeks to work on a German hit song, translated as "I Kiss Your Little Hand, Madame," and I was asked to write an American version along the same lines. I turned the job down, saying, "No. Americans wouldn't like that." After that I didn't hear from Harms for a while, because I hadn't been very flexible and agreed to the literally translated title. Another lyricist had, and "I Kiss Your Little Hand, Madame" was a raging hit. I was going up and down the elevator with Gershwin and Kern less and less frequently.

Then a young agent I knew vaguely called me. He said, "Listen, are you shaved? I'm taking you to Vincent Youmans! What's happening is that Oscar Hammerstein is on the lyrics for three shows at once, and he can't handle all the work. He and Youmans need someone to replace him in a show called *Rainbow* that's supposed to open in six weeks. You're not still tied up with Harms, are you?" I said, "I haven't heard from them in a year."

Just stepping inside Youmans's anteroom, I couldn't help but notice the difference between his modern style and Dreyfus's stuffy oak—the difference between Bierstube and Bauhaus. I went in, and there was Oscar Hammerstein lying on a couch, very exhausted, and there was Youmans. The difference between Hammerstein and Youmans was that Hammerstein was a gentleman, very nice, and Youmans was not. Hammerstein asked me, "Can you play or sing something?" I said, "Well, I don't play the piano." Youmans looked as though he wished I would jump out the window, so he wouldn't have to throw me out. "You can sing a cappella, can't you?" Imagining that an unseen piano was accompanying me, I sang some songs from *Lady Fingers* and from *The Dagger and the Rose* which Hammerstein seemed to like very much. When it was all through, he said, "I think you can handle the job." Youmans said, "One thing we have to know—you're not tied up with Harms, are you?" I said, "I haven't heard from them in a year."

I plunged into the job, doing the whole score for *Rainbow*, one of the biggest shows on Broadway. Hammerstein had written it with Laurence Stallings, one of the writers of *What Price Glory?* I worked my head off getting the ensemble numbers together and was just about starting on the principal numbers when we began rehearsals in the theater. I was in the aisle talking to someone when a strange man approached me and asked, "Are you Edward Eliscu?" He handed me a summons from Harms, which said that I was hereby forbidden to work on any music which had the probability of being published. I was going to be thrown out! Now Youmans wanted to murder me, saying, "God damn it, I asked you about this!" I protested, "But I never got any statement from accounting, just my weekly drawing account."

I tried to get Dreyfus, but they told me he was not to be talked to. But his sidekick told me that according to my contract I owed Harms fifty-four dollars for the advances that had been paid to me. I said, "I'll make out a check." He said, "No, that's not the way it's handled. You are entitled to work for someone else only after you have earned the fifty-four dollars on Harms's songs. You have not done that. So you can't work for Youmans."

It took me a while until I got the idea. Of course. Dreyfus was using me as a cat's-paw. Youmans, instead of letting the man who had built his career step by step know that he wanted to go into business for himself, had just cut himself off from Dreyfus and set up his own publishing business. Harms was furious. Youmans had tried to take me and other lyric writers away. So there I was, absolutely and innocently in the middle. Can you imagine the misery? I was taken off *Rainbow* completely. The show wasn't a hit.

Dreyfus had his revenge, but being a paternalist who tried to substitute the reign of a strong patron for a business relationship, he suffered for that. On the other hand, Youmans aggravated the situation by not being frank and honest to a benefactor to whom he seemed an ungrateful son.

Two more years went by, and then Youmans sent for me again. Max Dreyfus came in with a show for Gloria Swanson, and Youmans had to get songs written for her fast. So I composed or collaborated on all the songs with lyrics in *Great Day*. "Great Day," "More Than You Know," and "Without a Song" were all from that show.

You were also working with Billy Rose by that time.

Youmans wanted every song that he had a part in to sell a million copies. He thought I was being too refined and that his music needed a touch of the popular-minded person. So he brought in Billy Rose, who had been responsible for "Barney Google," "Does the Spearmint Lose Its Flavor on the Bedpost Overnight?" and similar songs. But I must acknowledge that he was also a very ambitious and serious person, not only so far as writing songs was concerned but in the sincere effort to associate himself with the arts and some good causes, like the founding of Israel.

Ironically, *Great Day* was not a hit, but the songs were. After the show closed, maybe a couple of years later, Benny Goodman picked up the score and popularized it. And the songs from *Great Day* have been heard in numerous movies—quite a few even after I was blacklisted, I'm happy to say—including *The Helen Morgan Story, Funny Lady,* and, most recently, *The Fabulous Baker Boys,* and Woody Allen's *Crimes and Misdemeanors.*

You don't sound as though you liked Youmans very much.

He just had an attitude about me—that I was not a collaborator but just someone who was there to service his music. I almost walked out on the next one, *Flying Down to Rio.* But Morty advised me, "Stick with it. It's painful, but it's all riding on his music." It was a good thing, too. Youmans had a big reputation, and his music did carry the show.

Can you tell us how you got to Hollywood?

In the depths of the Depression, 1930. The same day that I decided I would have to go to an agent's office even if it meant becoming an actor again, I went outside and I saw a crowd gathered. Someone had just jumped out a window of the building. Anyway, I use that incident to point out that there was opportunity for neither an actor nor a lyric writer on Broadway at the time. I was sitting at the edge of my bed wondering what was going to happen to me professionally when the phone rang and a strange voice said, "Is this Edward Eliscu? This is Nacio Herb Brown."

Of course I knew who Nacio Herb Brown was. He was one of the important people in the new era of movie musicals. He had written "Pagan Love Song," songs for *The Broadway Melody,* and a dozen other hit songs. It turned out that he was staying at the Roosevelt Hotel, right there in Manhattan—I had assumed he was calling from Hollywood—and he said that he wondered if I would be interested in collaborating with him. I said yes—and then my only problem was how to get to the Roosevelt Hotel. I borrowed three dollars from Morty Offner, who lived around the corner, took a cab, and spoke to Brown. He was a different type of songwriter from the ones I had met.

I was used to Harms, the great publisher, where Gershwin, Kern, and all the other big writers of musical comedy were under contract. Brown was very different, a westerner with a waxed mustache, dressed differently from New Yorkers. At once he seemed very pleasant. He avoided discussing the theater, because that was not part of his background. He had been in real estate before going to Hollywood, but he had a good sense of melody. The very next day I was at his publishers, Feist, and was given a very extraordinary contract for Depression times: a guarantee of a year at four hundred dollars a week against royalties while in California and two hundred dollars a week if I returned to New York. Within a week I had the Feist contract in my hands, and shortly thereafter I was on the train to California.

My first picture was for Sam Goldwyn, which provided immediate and fast entree into Hollywood. Goldwyn told me, "Eliscu, I want you should know what kind of pictures I make. I make pictures that are not too high for the masses and not too low for the classes." This is not an apocryphal story; it's a bonafide Goldwynism.

What was your first picture?

The first one was *One Heavenly Night*, which starred Evelyn Laye, an actress who had just starred in Noël Coward's operetta *Bittersweet* on Broadway. Goldwyn had engaged two Pulitzer Prize winners, Louis Bromfield and Sidney Howard, to write this story of a flower girl at a Viennese ball. I believe it was at this point when I opened my eyes wide—that these people should be writing such a tawdry story!

That led to one more picture for Goldwyn, *Whoopee!*, starring Eddie Cantor, and we [Eliscu and Nacio Herb Brown] wrote one or two songs for it.

What happened after the Eddie Cantor picture?

The contract provided that I would get a set amount of money—a drawing account—against mythical royalties of four hundred dollars per week. The contract also provided that if I wanted to come back to New York from Hollywood, my salary would be cut in half. There were two reasons why I left, anyway, in the middle of the year, after seven months there. One, things had already changed. There seemed little possibility of selling any more of my songs. By now, Paramount, Universal, and particularly MGM either owned or were tied up with their own music companies. Feist had scant future prospects of placing any of its songs around town. Also, more important, by this time, Stella Bloch, with whom I had become acquainted in New York in the mid-twenties, had become the main influence in my life, and this was my opportunity to get married.

So you came back to New York.

It was important for me to develop myself financially and professionally in New York. When I returned to New York from Hollywood, I became very active in the theater again. [Dwight Deere] Wiman and [Tom] Weatherly engaged me to edit *The Third Little Show*, a revue, and to contribute sketches and lyrics. It starred Beatrice Lillie, a very distinguished cast of comedians, and others, like Edward Arnold, who became a well-known heavy in movies later. I also worked in various other revues with Billy Rose—for instance, *Sweet and Low*. John Murray Anderson, a distinguished director and producer, did a revue, *John Murray Anderson's Almanacs*, and I wrote the opening and other numbers. I also worked directly for J. J. Shubert doing lyrics for European imports. I could not complain personally when the Depression was so keen and bitter. I had work, and I was fortunate.

A year or more passed, and you returned to Hollywood.

It was another bad time in the theater. Suddenly I got a telegram from RKO saying that the studio would like to offer me a contract to direct films and would give me a hundred and fifty dollars a week. I was not the only one offered this opportunity. David Selznick, the number-one man at RKO, chose three more young, inexpensive proto-directors and engaged them to come out. George Cukor was behind the whole maneuver in my case, and I communicated with him, telling him I thought the salary was totally inadequate and unfair. I wanted more money. George advised me that it would be perfectly correct and justifiable to ask for more money, and so I did. A few days later RKO sent a telegram in which they agreed to raise the salary to fifty dollars more per week. Things being what they were, I accepted. Shortly after that, we were on our way to Hollywood.

How much of a chance did you get to become a director?

I coached the RKO stock company of young actors under contract. With the Depression building and the studio cutting expenses, I was kept on at RKO, but as a lyricist, not as a director.

Why did you ultimately gravitate to screenwriting rather than, for example, making your career, as some people did, only by selling songs for film musicals?

As I told you, from the time I was in public school I had always been writing. Francis Faragoh helped me to learn screenwriting. He said, "You just pretend your eyes are the camera." Having written for the theater, it was an easy transition.

Can you tell us something about Lou Breslow? Was he assigned to you as your first regular writing partner?

Through Allen Rivkin, a former newspaperman I knew who was now story editor at Western, Fox's less-important B-picture factory, I was assigned to collaborate as a screenwriter with Lou Breslow, mainly on pictures for Jane Withers, a pudgy rival of Shirley Temple. Breslow was a nice, salty character who had been a gagman and had been in the movie business all his life. I've forgotten which was the first feature we worked on—probably something for Jane Withers. They thought of Jane Withers as a natural assignment for us, because both of us were not hard-boiled people and we might be good on a picture about kids. We did more than one Jane Withers story. We took aboard Dore Schary as a third cowriter on *The Silk Hat Kid*.

Are you particularly proud of any one of those early films?

Every Saturday Night turned out to be the film I worked on that I liked best, the most enjoyable and gratifying. I wondered how the story could be worth the studio purchase price of fifteen thousand dollars. I went to see the stage production [by Katharine Cavanaugh] and found it a most enchanting American story about a family, without the fake clichés of romance or a chase. I had three and a half weeks to do it, all alone. Breslow and I were still good friends; by now we had done four or five films together. He said to me, "You'll never get by with this script. It doesn't even have a chase!" I said, "It's unnecessary." He responded, "I wish you luck."

The next thing I heard, Zanuck had screened this little picture, and it was going to become the first in a series about the same family. Zanuck canceled the booking of a bigger picture at the Carthay Circle—one of the major theaters—and substituted mine, and he ordered a new title to be put on the film, *The Jones Family*. It got very good notices for a practically unknown cast, and it did become a series, anticipating the Andy Hardy series. Although I wasn't given the proper solo screen credit, I was happy to do it. I'm proud of that film, partly because of the vanity of doing it all alone.

How did such a success affect your standing in Hollywood?

It was all very strange. The opposite happened. All of a sudden I began to be turned down for jobs! My agent, who was Sam Jaffe, told me, "I'm going to go talk to Sol Wurtzel." Jaffe, who was one of a kind, then walked into Wurtzel's office without being invited. He said to Wurtzel, "Either you double Eliscu's salary or I'm pulling him off the lot." Wurtzel was not a man to be talked to this way. He used some four-letter words and threw my agent out of his office.

Jaffe suspected something was afoot. He said he knew the producers' lawyers, whose offices were in an office building in downtown Los Angeles. We rode down to L.A. the next day, and he left me in a car in the parking garage underneath while he went upstairs. I almost was asphyxiated as I waited for two miserable hours.

My agent finally appeared, pale, excited-looking. He stepped into the car, closed the windows, and said, "I've just been through an ordeal. I'll tell you what it's all about, but if you repeat what I say I'll deny every single word." I said "What is it?" He said, "I just saw a sheet of paper with your name on it.

Do you want to know what they have on you?" I said, "Sure." He answered, "One, you were making speeches for the Screen Writers Guild; two, they know from your license plate that you go to foreign movies; third, they saw you buying a copy of the *Nation*." I said, "Thank you for telling me." But I thought to myself, "I'll find out what this all means."

Nothing happened for a while. I didn't get any raise at Fox, and worse, I was taken off contract. I couldn't seem to get a job anywhere else. It became apparent to my agent that not being wanted for screenwriting jobs was not an accident or coincidence but in some respects a pattern. I talked it over with Stella, my wife. Usually, when we had disappointments, we would go out to the beach or up to Arrowhead Lake to enjoy the quiet and pine trees. This time we said, "We're getting the hell out of this town."

We went to Will Wright's for a soda, a place where the walls were like peppermint. [Production designer] Hobe Irwin, a friend of Cukor's, happened to come in, and he asked us, "What are you up to?" We told him that we had decided to leave town. "Where are you going?" We said that we didn't know. He said, "Have you got anything against Connecticut?" We said, "We love it!" He said, "I've got a very nice house with one hundred and one acres, and you're welcome to it for as long as you want. I'll be here for months yet."

So we were in Newtown, Connecticut, the next week, and we've been here ever since. Hobe Irwin was a modest man but highly regarded among interior decorators. His house was far from being some little artistic shack; it bore the stamp of a man of exquisite taste. We felt that we were rid of Hollywood. I would be back in the theater, and Stella would be in the swim, with a much more appreciative audience for her work as an artist.

In two or three weeks, however, a telegram arrived from our Hollywood agent saying that all of a sudden he had a four-week job for me at Universal to do some work on a screenplay called "Talk of the Town."* This temptation made something very clear to me—a limited engagement was just what I wanted. That first blacklist, which the studios didn't acknowledge—whatever the reason was, I didn't work—was apparently cleared up. But after that, for me, Hollywood would always be a limited booking.

After a few weeks in Hollywood I came back East and started to work on a play about the flooding of Lake Candlewood. After a few more weeks, we discovered that Stella was pregnant. We decided that we would stay East until the baby was born. During this time I also wrote the Broadway operetta *Frederika*, originally produced in Germany with a [Franz] Léhar score, and here with Dennis King in the role of the young Goethe. It was hailed as "the first American socially conscious libretto." When one of those cold eastern winters started coming on, we thought, "California seems a more reasonable place to

---

*This project—not to be confused with the 1942 comedy *The Talk of the Town*, directed by George Stevens—was filmed under another title and does not appear among Eliscu's credits.

bring up David." So we invited David's nurse to accompany us to California, and once again we went Hollywood.

Wasn't it Cukor who sent for you again?

I called my Hollywood agent and asked him, "How did this restitution happen? How did I get kosher?" He said, "When you get back to Hollywood, be sure to let George Cukor know that you're back." I said, "All right." I called George, he asked about the baby and Stella, and I said, "I'd like to talk to you about my own situation." He said, "By all means. Come right over." He then disclosed that he had spoken to someone, a very important person, and that he was able to get me rehired at Universal.

Was that for Charlie McCarthy, Detective, *the one directed by Frank Tuttle?*

I don't recall the title; probably it was. The boss was a puffy pink man named [Milton H.] Feld, an ex-optometrist. I remember him, I think, from a studio Christmas party. I always tried to work at home, and Feld was telling a group why he let me. "I'll tell you a secret about Eliscu," he said, laughing. "He doesn't know, but we get twice as much work out of him by letting him think he's his own boss!"

Tuttle was a well-bred Yale graduate, the same vintage as Cole Porter. He was a diabetic or had some illness that brought on frightening seizures for which he carried the medicine. I never knew until recently that later on he named names.

How were your political views evolving? I know that when you wrote the lyrics for "Without a Song," one of the original lines you contributed was "A darky's born, he ain't no good, nohow, without a song." Later on, you made a point of having that changed to "A man is born, he ain't no good, nohow, without a song." Why did you begin to develop a social conscience?

On a certain day I did say, "This line should be changed," but my life led up to that point. Becoming a radical is not like getting a bee sting. It was something that developed quite apart from doing a workmanlike job in theater or movies. I responded to political urgencies. You must not overlook the effect of the thirties, the Depression, Spain, and the rise of Hitler, especially among writers who would like to have separated themselves and lived in a cloud world and didn't want to be involved in the real world.

The raging Depression politicized me. But the first real political meeting that I attended regularly in Hollywood was for the Spanish Refugee Committee, where a collection was made for children suffering because of the war in Spain. That really swung me over to a left attitude. For a long time I didn't know anything at all about the Communist Party, however. I joined the Hollywood Anti-Nazi League, and I was immediately put to work drawing up a petition denouncing anti-Semitism. It never entered my mind who exactly was pushing the League. I just thought of them as good, progressive people.

We know that some of your happiest moments in Hollywood, and some of your best political experiences, came not in films at all but on the stage, with a series of shows involving Henry Myers and Jay Gorney, two longtime collaborators of yours. How did Meet the People *come about?*

As Fascism and Hitler made themselves felt in Hollywood, I was able to use my training and experience to help write and stage material in evenings sponsored by the Screen Writers Guild and other organizations. There was one program, I remember, to discredit the Tenney Committee [the state of California's Un-American Activities Committee], but our first large-scale undertaking was a revue, *Sticks and Stones*. I wrote a neo–Walt Whitman opening, spoken by an impressive cast, including John Garfield and about thirty others. The staging of the show was undertaken by Garson Kanin and Herbert Biberman. The comedy was played by Bert Lahr and Jerry Colonna. The music was by Johnny Green and Jay Gorney, with lyrics by Ira Gershwin and me. The show was put on for two weekends.

That led to a move to establish a theater—the Hollywood Theatre Alliance—supported by Hollywood's leading liberals. A group of professionals led the move for a really important show. We rented a building with a stage. We encouraged other contributors who shared our anti-Fascist viewpoint. Supporters flocked in, mostly youngsters who had been trying in vain to break into the movies. Henry Myers and Jay Gorney put their sentiments to work. We made it a real cooperative undertaking to produce the first show for the Hollywood Theatre Alliance, which was given its name by Jerry Chodorov: *Meet the People*.*

At that time, movies did not deal with any real political subjects. Those who believed in serious theater belonged to the Hollywood Theatre Alliance. We did our script during a period of great agitation in late 1938 or early 1939, at a time when it was inevitable that people should use theater to express their feelings about Hitler's rise and their opposition to Fascism. In the course of working together, sometimes Henry and I did the lyrics collaboratively, sometimes he wrote separately or with Gorney, and sometimes so did I. The three of us got to be real coworkers and decided to band together as "MEG." We formed a cooperative trio that lasted for about fifteen years, on and off.

The opening scene of *Meet the People* showed Miss Hollywood asleep in her ivory tower, awakened by a young man who tries to get her to realize that all around her people are being slugged and dispossessed, cops are chasing robbers and robbers are chasing cops—a complete upheaval is going on in

---

*The Chodorov brothers—Jerome and Edward—were screenwriters and playwrights. Jerome Chodorov (1911–   ) was best-known for writing—with Joseph Fields—the Broadway hit *My Sister Eileen* and its musical version, *Wonderful Town*. Edward Chodorov (1904–1988) wrote several hard-hitting films for Warner Brothers in the early thirties—including *The Mayor of Hell*, starring James Cagney, and *The World Changes*, with Paul Muni—and then became a writer and producer at MGM, often of Broadway adaptations. When the blacklist arrived in Hollywood, both brothers resumed writing and producing plays in New York.

the world. Finally Miss Hollywood is awakened by the well-placed thrust of a pin, and she is exhorted to step out and meet the people. That's the song "Meet the People." The chorus is "Step out, meet the people, meet the common man, he's simply wonderful."

One of the best-known of the show's other tunes was "It's the Same Old South." It even became a hit record for Jimmy Rushing and later entered Count Basie's repertoire. All the songs and sketches had a political point. Nobody had ever seen this kind of material before in Hollywood. After we sold out in the small theater we had to reopen in a big theater. Then *Meet the People* went to New York, where it played for several months. There were actually several versions of *Meet the People*, including one that, in 1955, Jay presented alone at a supper club.

Is there anything to say about the film version of Meet the People, *which was turned into a romantic plot for a Dick Powell and Lucille Ball musical about workers putting on a show while building warships in Delaware?*

I never saw it.

Tell us something about Jay Gorney.

His father had brought him over from Europe as a child, and he had been raised in Michigan. He attended the schools in Detroit and the University of Michigan, where he led the band. He was a natural conductor. I first teamed up with Jay in the 1920s. We shook hands and joined forces, and I contributed to a revue Jay was working on, *Merry-Go-Round*. We wound up with two songs in it, one a campfire song, "Come Sing a Gypsy Song," and a second one, for Libby Holman and Leonard Sillman, called "Tomorrow You Go to the Dentist, But Tonight You Belong to Me."

Jay was not only a composer, he was an interpreter. He was very clever about adapting music to particular ideas. For example, in a number about Harry Truman wrangling with Congress, he would be sitting at the piano and singing, "My right hand doesn't know what my left hand is doing; they each play a different tune." And then he would punctuate a reference to Winston Churchill with a few bars of "Rule Brittannia." His songs were always very smooth with their references and, above all else, very humorous.

What about the background and talent of Henry Myers?

Henry Myers was a well-educated man who had written several books, including novels. He had studied to become a composer of operas in Europe. Early on, he served as press agent for a production of Gilbert and Sullivan's *Iolanthe* and went down in press-agent history. The ship for the production was designed by a scenic designer who had insisted upon a massive set of practically solid wood. It was a problem to transport it to the theater. To Henry's offbeat brain, this represented an unusual opportunity. He got permission to have the set transported across Broadway and through Times Square, and he arranged to have it "break down" right there. Thousands of

New Yorkers saw, that day, a ship break down in Times Square. The event was covered citywide by the press.

He, like Jay, had a wonderful gift for putting political issues and platforms to music. I remember when the question was whether Roosevelt should run for a fourth term, and Henry and Jay wrote a song well-known in our circle—although it never got any play outside these circumstances—called, "Mr. Roosevelt, Won't You Please Run Again?" Jay also put to music "The Bill of Rights," the rousing finale of Act One of *Meet the People*, with the full cast at the footlights ending "The Bill of Rights" with a spoken exhortation.

Later, when Jay was called to testify in front of HUAC, he was asked if he had ever written the music for a song about the Red Army. He said, "Yes, but I just wrote the music; General MacArthur wrote the words." And, asked about having been born in Russia and his arrival in America, he explained that his parents brought him here, that his father worked in Detroit, and that when his father applied to become a citizen, he first read the Bill of Rights to him. Here Jay faced the courtroom audience and bravely sang out, "Congress shall make no law . . ." and continued singing "The Bill of Rights" until the pounding of the gavel finally stopped him.

Hadn't your boyhood friend, Mortimer Offner, also become radicalized by now?

Morty was a person attractive to any number of people. He was charming and witty—he had all the social graces—and he was a most talented photographer and aspiring director as well. People were drawn to him, and he became a fine dialogue director for many shows and films. I don't know how he ever made it as a writer, since that really wasn't his forte.

During the Depression, anyone with any intelligence who was facing the economic situation would say, "This is bullshit." It was an honest kind of adjustment. For someone like Morty, it was damned unexpected, because there was absolutely no political past. His career had all been social and artistic up till then. In Hollywood, his associations, what he did and where he appeared, were definitely committed. I can remember him screaming about the capitalist system—alongside of Cukor's swimming pool!

We're in the late thirties now, and you're working on various films. What do you remember about Little Tough Guys in Society?

I'm laughing. I don't remember it at all, but I remember that it was terribly panned by some paper. I think that the plot had been used over and over again. I remember Morty working on it, but I don't remember myself, so I couldn't have made a notable contribution.

Do you have any memory of His Exciting Night?

Whose exciting night? It wasn't my exciting night! No, I don't remember anything about it.

What about Sis Hopkins, *a Judy Canova vehicle?*

It was a typical product of the Valley. If I recall correctly, I was assigned to do it with another writer. He said, "Why don't we have lunch together at my club?" and so he took me there. After lunch, he mentioned, "You know, we've never entertained a Jew under this roof. It's a strict rule of ours." I said, "You'd better write a new rule today—you've had your first Jew!"

What about Hey, Rookie? *You have coproducer as well as coscript credit.*

That's still a mystery to me. It started as a show we did for one of the Army camps, but when it became a movie, we had to sell the rights. I can't tell you more: I was never asked to serve on the picture itself. There was a brief possibility that those of us who had produced *Meet the People* would be engaged as a unit at Columbia. We almost went to work there, but it never panned out.

Can you talk a little about the musical Something to Shout About, *with Don Ameche and Hazel Scott?*

Most of all I remember the director, Gregory Ratoff. To understand to the least degree what Gregory Ratoff was really like, imagine this: Morty Offner hears a doorbell ringing very early in the morning at his house. He opens the door, and there stands Gregory Ratoff, without invitation. "I hear you do a wonderful imitation of me," he says. "Imitate me!" And Ratoff marches into the place. Morty does his imitation of Ratoff, and Ratoff says, "No, that isn't me," and proceeds to do an hour imitating himself.

The picture we worked on had a score by Cole Porter. I remember that one day Ratoff called me over to talk privately with him, which was unusual. Ordinarily he broadcast his news. He said, "You know that song by Cole Porter, 'You'd Be So Nice to Come Home To'? That's such a Russian song. I could sing it myself. Eddie, you write another song something like that, substitute it, and Cole will never know the difference!" I talked him out of it.

The story concerned a group of actors in a theatrical boardinghouse. We had been shooting a few days when Hazel Scott, a well-known, gifted black entertainer, came to Hollywood for a nightclub performance. "You know what" Ratoff said. "I'm going to put her in the picture." I thought that was a splendid idea. "How do you plan to use her?" I asked. "It's easy," Ratoff replied. "You know Harry, the boy who plays the janitor? She can play his girlfriend."

"Grisha," I protested, "Hazel Scott is a class act. Times have changed, especially since the war. She has to be treated in a more dignified way."

"I know. Of course," he replied, "we'll dress her in a beautiful bingham [*sic*] dress."

What about The Gay Señorita?

That was a picture Jay Gorney produced, and I think the star was Jinx Falkenburg, and that's all I remember.

Out of the Blue was a funny screwball comedy about life in Greenwich Village, starring George Brent, Carole Landis, Turhan Bey, Virginia Mayo, and Ann Dvorak, and directed by Leigh Jason. Wasn't it a collaboration between you and Vera Caspary?

The title was from a song that Max Steiner and I wrote. But please exonerate Vera. She never cooperated with anyone on a screenplay. She was very well-known as a wit, a bright woman, a good popular writer, but she shied away from writing movies. So by chance I ended up being assigned to adapt two of her stories.

The other one was Three Husbands, *a comedy with Eve Arden and Howard Da Silva.*

That wasn't really Vera's. The basic plot came from a much more successful film, *A Letter to Three Wives*, which set the standard for the humor of *Three Husbands*.

*You were also involved in one very remarkable non-Hollywood film—*Alice in Wonderland, *released in 1950 but actually made a few years earlier, in 1947, in France.*

It had a very interesting lineup of people. The main inspiration was a puppeteer, Lou Bunin, a very gifted man. Lou managed somehow to get an agreement with the postwar French government—at the time, very progressive—promoting a deal in which he would get the backing for a combination of live action and animation. He would train the French, who had no experience at animation, in return for which they would give him the run of a studio and supply the technicians.

Bunin engaged Henry Myers, Al Lewin, and me to do the screenplay. He tried to engage Hanns Eisler for the score, but somehow or other that didn't pan out. Sol Kaplan substituted for Eisler. Sol was also very capable; he had done the scores for several Hollywood pictures as well as for *The Banker's Daughter*, an Actors Lab production we had all worked on. Sol arrived in Paris, with his wife, Fran—a sister of actor Van Heflin—very pregnant and almost ready to be carted off to the American hospital. The baby was a boy, and his name is Jonathan; now he's a director in Hollywood.

Did Bunin make a point of hiring mainly blacklisted people?

In fact, there was no direct connection between the blacklist and the *Alice* project. This was still 1947, and Sol Kaplan, Henry Myers, and I were only on the way to being blacklisted. Al Lewin was never blacklisted, but, like the group of animators, he had worked with Disney. Several of those working on the animation had been on the picket lines at Disney, including [Eugene] Fleury, [Art] Babbitt, and others who had been discharged during the [1941] strike. They handled the animation and puppets.

What was it like making the film?

I can only tell you that it was a very, very difficult undertaking. The studio [in Nice] either had been bombed, or was just broken-down and unworkable. We were there for six months, and then we had to work in London as well as Paris. It was one thing after another—slow finances, broken-down equipment. Alice was to be played by an English girl who was prevented from coming to France because of British laws, so we had to substitute a nineteen-year-old who did not really look like the charming child that little Alice should be.

What did you think of the final film?

We had a good concept, but the combination of puppets, animation, and people under such circumstances only made things very disjointed. Walt Disney had first said he was going to do an *Alice in Wonderland* and then changed his mind. It was at this juncture that Bunin was able to make the arrangements and go ahead. Disney's version appeared later, in 1951. Inevitably, our *Alice* was submerged by Disney's production.

The two are like apples and oranges, really. Disney didn't have puppets; he had the best of animation for its time, and ours was not animation as we know it. Disney's was almost like a picture about childhood with Shirley Temple. The social and intellectual level of that film was very low. By contrast, we were very careful about introducing songs and about using the language of Lewis Carroll. We tried to integrate the kinds of lyrics and dialogue that would be consistent with the original novel.

The experience was enjoyable in many ways, however, including my first and only trip to Paris. Part of the contract was that we could bring our families over. I went there alone, with the other writers and some technicians, and later Stella brought the two boys, Peter and David, over to Paris. And our picture is still seen occasionally, usually around Christmas.

What were your relations with the Hollywood Ten?

I believe I knew all of them. I had had a close association with Jack [John Howard] Lawson, for instance, from the time when he was the principal playwright in the New Playwrights. That was the first time I ever met Jack. The New Playwrights—Lawson, [John] Dos Passos, Francis Faragoh, Mike Gold, and Em Jo Basshe—were a strange combination of various people who had started with a fifty-thousand-dollar gift from a banker, Otto Kahn. For a brief time I was their producing manager. After Jack, I may have known Lester Cole best. Later on, we befriended Lester's family when he was imprisoned in Connecticut, and they all moved here.

After the Ten went to jail, the blacklist was creeping closer to you personally.

The movie industry was getting it from the government. HUAC came on in a big way in 1947, but there was a lapse between the time when it all started and the time they got after nobodies. If you asked me, "How did it happen?" I could only say, "You would understand if you had lived through the whole thing." Some one hundred and fifty names appeared in the *Hollywood Reporter* on September 20, 1951. That son of a bitch Martin Berkeley had named me, along with the one hundred and forty-nine others. We were already in New York by that time.

Weren't you also named by Robert Rossen?

After all, we had practically lived next door; maybe he wanted to be neighborly and include me in good company. [Laughs.]

Why had you left Hollywood?

Why shouldn't I leave Hollywood? There was no reason to remain. We used to leave whenever we were fed up with the life there. If the work wasn't satisfactory, and it was all shut down for you, what were you going to stay for? To gripe and name people? We decided that we would clear out. When we left, we decided this time to put our furniture in storage and stay permanently in the East. I hoped to reestablish ties with the theater, which I tried a couple of times after being blacklisted.

But you were able to work in television for a while.

I wrote *The Late Christopher Bean*, in which Helen Hayes made her television debut, an adaptation of a play by Sidney Howard, taken from a French play, both of them very amusing. It was the first of a series on television, "The Pulitzer Prize Plays," for *The Schlitz Playhouse*. I did a few other good shows. But just when I thought that I was going to get a big contract for television, an assistant to a producer grabbed me and said, "Let's have coffee." We went downstairs, and he said that my name had appeared in *Red Channels*, although it had also appeared in other places. As I told [Victor] Navasky, and it's in his book [*Naming Names*], they wanted to fix it with me through the columnist George Sokolsky. I wasn't interested. Anyway, everything was off.*

You were never subpoenaed to appear before the Committee?

The FBI was at the door asking for me a couple of times. I'd go away for a while, they'd leave, and I'd be safe a little longer. But I couldn't hold out indefinitely, and one day they found me at home, and I got my subpoena. Imagine my surprise when they never called me to testify.

How did you suffer from the blacklist?

---

*Navasky wrote: " 'One day the boom fell,' recalls Eliscu. 'My agent said, "If you'd like, I can have you meet George Sokolsky. You're in trouble." I said I'd walk on two feet, not on four, and I gave up that agent. Then a story editor took me for a cup of coffee and said my producer subscribed to a checking service and they checked me out and got back two pages of entries.' Was Eliscu bitter? Not at all. 'I had been friendly with Dan O'Shea, the chief clearer at CBS—I had known him from my days at RKO. O'Shea was *really* friendly and sympathetic, and he thought it was an unjust situation, because I could have done the job well. I knew it was nothing personal.' "

I couldn't get back on television for ten years. It took that long to reenter, so it was television that directly blacklisted me, not Hollywood, where it was indirect. Finally I was able to continue, to a degree. I did the lyrics, for example, for *The Magic Nutcracker*, with Robert Goulet and Carol Lawrence. Sol Kaplan adapted the Tchaikovsky music to songs. But I never wrote another show in its entirety for television.

You ended up working quite a bit with Sol in musical theater, before and after the blacklist, didn't you?

Sol was a very attractive figure. He had started life in Philadelphia, where he was a musical prodigy who attended the Curtis Institute at the same time as Leonard Bernstein. The two had performed together. Then Sol came to New York and was very prominent in musical circles, until he finally got to Hollywood and wrote the music for films like *Tales of Manhattan*. After being frozen out of movies for years, he went back to television and wrote, eventually, for *Star Trek* and other shows.

In Hollywood, originally, Sol, Henry, and I had done a musical version of an old standard, *The Streets of New York*, which we called *The Poor of New York*, depicting the robber barons acting against the poor in New York during the Panic of 1857. It was produced by the Actors Lab. Howard Da Silva played the principal role, Morris Carnovsky played the rascal opposite him, and Lloyd Bridges was the handsome young man-about-town ruined by the Panic. Karen Morley was in it, too.

In New York, about 1950 or 1951, Sol and I settled in the same apartment house, Sol's family and ours, and we conceived of the idea of redoing *The Poor of New York* as a much more commercial production, in the score as well as the text. The two of us and Henry Myers rechristened it *The Banker's Daughter*. In New York the production was cramped into a church basement that called itself a theater. At that point, it was Sol and me working alone, because Henry had left us to go off on another venture of his own. You had to know Henry to understand how he got involved in these things. He was busy working on a novel to be called *The Winner of World War Three*, about the capture of the whole planet by cockroaches.

There was still another show, Time for a Change, *during the McCarthy era, produced at the Pythian Temple in New York. The political acuity and artistic accomplishment were remarkable, under the circumstances.*

The opening song really took off on the message "It's time for a change," which was the Republican slogan of 1952. In the show we did, the lyric was, "It's time for a change, it's time for a change, what's good for General Motors is just too bad for the voters."

Didn't you also collaborate with Sol on at least one industrial show?

Yes. In the 1950s Sol was working for MPO. The initials stood for three men who owned a studio and who mostly made commercials for television.

Sol wrote the music and conducted the musicians for the scores of the commercials and industrial films. Through him I landed at MPO, too. They had one of the largest clients in the industry, the Ford Motor Company. Every year Ford would do some kind of production film to inspire the salesmen and dealers to greater efforts. In 1962 Sol and I were assigned to do a live show for the salesmen and dealers. Also working with us on this was one of the most darling people, the former president of the Radio Writers Guild, Sam Moore, as funny and sweet a man as ever walked the earth. He was the principal man on the sketches.*

The name of the Ford show was *Got It Made*. The title song was sung to the tune of "Everything's Comin' up Roses," from the musical *Gypsy*: "Got it made, got it made, with the Sixty-two Fords on parade." Sol and I wrote a few original songs for the show, but it was my suggestion that we use a parody of an existing song. I felt it would sell the idea better, since the audience would already be familiar with the tune.

Ira Marvin was the producer and director from MPO. Ira, a childhood violin prodigy turned film-commercial producer, was the link to Lee Iacocca, whom I never saw. Originally we were going to do live shows in the largest theater or armory in each of several towns, but Ford came to their senses, so instead it was done as a motion picture with a vaudeville or revue format. Ira got Mickey Rooney and Harpo Marx to be in it. I was impressed by Harpo Marx's professionalism, but I found Mickey Rooney somewhat less disciplined, although very talented. We filmed it in Hollywood, at the tail end of the blacklist! I always found it ironic that three people who couldn't get a job in this town were being employed by an even bigger industry than the movies.

These jobs were few and far between, and they didn't always pay well. How did you manage to make a living, otherwise?

I was able to produce one show on Broadway, I had various deals under the table, and I wrote for magazines. I changed my style so that I could contribute poetry to magazines like the *Saturday Review of Literature*.

I was fortunate. I had a certain standing in ASCAP and in the theater, and I had received an income from song royalties all along. It was especially good by this time. In the thirties Benny Goodman had made the songs from *Great Day* popular. In 1952 we were lucky that the Republican Party chose "Great Day" as its banner song for Eisenhower. It was ironic, but think how ironic it was to do the MPO show in Hollywood, working for Ford, in the town where we were blacklisted!

I'm deeply grateful for not having suffered like most of the other blacklistees, because of the variety of sources of income and, more important, the

---

*Sam Moore (1904–1989) was a founder and president of the Radio Writers Guild. He wrote for many shows of radio's golden age, including *The Great Gildersleeve*. He was also coauthor of the book for the 1949 Broadway musical *Texas Li'l Darlin'*. He refused to answer questions when subpoenaed by HUAC in 1951 and was blacklisted.

influence of Stella and the continuity of socially motivated, if less intensive, activities.

What was important about the Hollywood left of the 1930s and 1940s, or important for people nowadays to understand, in retrospect?

There are two ways to answer. One is by saying how proud you are of the achievements. The other is by saying that you now realize how stupid some things were and how badly they would turn out for you. But at the time, you didn't exist alone. The most attractive thing politically about those times was that suddenly there were wonderful explanations, philosophical explanations, about world events and history, coming from people like Johnny Weber, who gave classes to people in Hollywood. But the force of prejudice against us was so strong that we didn't realize that sooner or later it would smash us.

When, in 1968, I was named as a nominee for the presidency of the Song-writers Guild of America, a letter to forty West Coast members went out, saying that I was too radical and should withdraw. Some friendly people here in the East said I should withdraw to avoid a split, et cetera. But, as much as they loved me, I know I made the right decision. Did I let them "smash me"? I said no. I paid no attention to the letter. I was elected and served for five years.

Would you now be prepared to answer whether or not you were ever a Communist?

I don't wish to answer that question. I can't say I haven't thought about it. But as I think about my past political associations, even now, I find myself being guarded. There is a kind of good-natured desire among various people to know my past aside from show business, a desire which I resist.

You still feel that there are oppressive forces that would smash you for revealing what you did long ago?

Yes, and if you think that they're not the same forces, you're not acknowledging them for what they are.

Anne Froelick
(Anne Froelick Taylor)

ANNE FROELICK, Los Angeles, California, 1997

INTERVIEW BY PAUL BUHLE
AND DAVE WAGNER

PHOTO © WILLIAM B. WINBURN

ANNE FROELICK
(1913–   )

1941 *Shining Victory.* Coscript.
1944 *The Master Race.* Coscript.
     Miss Susie Slagle's. Costory, coscript.
1947 *Easy Come, Easy Go.* Coscript.
1950 *Harriet Craig.* Coscript.

■

ANNE FROELICK (also known by her married name, Anne Froelick Taylor) is one of the strong-willed women who managed to make their mark in the mostly male-dominated world of screenwriting and the Hollywood left. The daughter of a former professional illustrator and, like her mother, a student at Smith College, she left home for Greenwich Village and the stage. From there she gravitated leftward culturally and politically, first as a model for avant-garde dress designer Elizabeth Hawes and then as a secretary at Orson Welles's Mercury Theatre. Howard Koch, on the cusp of a grand career writing films in Hollywood, helped make Froelick's transformation into a writer possible.

Froelick entered Hollywood just as the 1940s dawned. She collected only a handful of credits, though first-rate ones, before the blacklist ended her career.

■

When were you born?

I was born in December 1913 in Massachusetts. I grew up, actually, in Princeton, New Jersey. As a child, I don't remember my own father. When I was only three, my mother remarried. My stepfather, Louis D. Froelick, some years later adopted my sister, Peggy, and me. He was the founder and editor of *Asia* magazine.* He had gone out to Peking right after he graduated from Princeton, and there he got very involved with China.

So this was a prosperous Protestant family.

Yes, and I went to a wonderful school, Miss Fine's, in Princeton. It was difficult enough to have a last name different from my parents' and my half-brother's name. Nobody in Princeton came from a background of divorce in those days. After I was adopted by my stepfather and my name was changed to Froelick for school purposes, that was even more difficult. I also spent a year in France. Then, when I was fifteen, my mother and my stepfather separated. We moved back to my mother's hometown, Syracuse, New York, where she had a lot of friends.

---

*Asia, a leading organ of "the Old China Hands," was founded in 1899 and published by the American Association of China and the American Association of Japan. It was expanded from a newsletter to a slick magazine in 1917. Louis D. Froelick was a well-known editor and writer.

She must have been an independent spirit.

My mother was quite a character. Before she married my father, she had illustrated children's books. She did quite well at that. When we went back to Syracuse, she opened a dress shop for girls our age. She had my sister and me go to New York and pick out the clothes, mostly things we liked.

You left Syracuse to go to college.

First I went to boarding school, and there I was elected president of what would have been my senior class. But I already had enough credits to go on to college, and after I took the entrance exams and got a scholarship to Smith, my mother was eager to send me. I was only sixteen, and it might have been better if I had waited. But Smith is a great women's college. My mother went there, and I'd like to see my granddaughter go there.

How did you get along at Smith?

I loved it, and I still resent what my mother did. My scholarship was supposed to be based on my midterm marks. In my second year my marks went below what they should have been. I thought I had lost the scholarship. Later I got a letter saying that I could still continue, since I had improved my grades by the end of the year. But in the meantime my mother had just decided that she wasn't going to let me go back. She wanted my sister and me to take over her dress business. It wasn't a very hard job, but neither of us was remotely interested in it.

After a little while, I went to visit a friend in New Brunswick. On the spur of the moment, almost by accident, I decided to go to see my father in New York. He was very sympathetic about my relationship with my mother and asked if I wanted to come and live in Manhattan. He said he would give me a certain amount of money each month, very little but enough to help. I was nineteen and terribly glad to get away from home. I lived first down near the Village—at Fifty-nine Fifth Avenue—with three other girls, two from Syracuse and the other a Smith friend. We paid sixty-five dollars a month for our apartment, or sixteen twenty-five apiece! For the next seven years I lived all over the East Side, from Ninety-sixth and Madison to way over near the East River.

How did you get into show business?

I wanted to be an actress. I did get a few small parts in New York productions, and did some summer theater too. I even appeared in a Broadway show, if only a walk-on part. In the meantime, to support myself, I was working as a model. I used to do fashion shows at Lord and Taylor and other department stores. Then I got a job as a model for Elizabeth Hawes.* She was the best— the most fashionable—designer in the whole business.

---

*One of the few fashion designers deeply involved in progressive politics, Elizabeth Hawes attempted to revolutionize the fashion world thirty years ahead of her time. Trained for trad-

Did you know that Hawes was also a political radical?

Not at all. I was too naive, I guess. I didn't have any political opinions at that time. I often wonder about my father. He must have been quite conservative. Mother certainly didn't have any interest in politics.

But Hawes was awfully good to work for. She had three models. Each customer who came to see the clothes would be seated in a room with her own salesperson, who called for the dresses she might be interested in. If it was one of yours, you put it on and showed it; it wasn't like in a big American store, where you had to model all kinds of clothes for all customers all the time. I modeled, and I also kept her books.

That's how I found out that she had shown a collection in Paris the year before. There were copies of her invitations to all the leading French designers—and each of their refusals to attend. How dare an American presume to show them fashions?! I admired her for that.

You somehow went from Hawes's studio to the Mercury Theatre.

My father had suggested that I take a stenography course—typing and shorthand—which was a good idea. I wanted to act at the Mercury Theatre, so I took an office job with [producer] John Houseman until a part would come along. That's how I got to know Houseman and Orson Welles. I was Houseman's secretary until they hired Howard Koch to write, and then they assigned me to Howard.

What did you think about the creative atmosphere of the Mercury Theatre and of Welles's role in that operation?

Orson would come in at the end of the rehearsals, in order to add the finishing touches. Houseman always set everything up, got the script and the actors, and even staged the rehearsal, before Orson would take over. Years later, I would play bridge with the Housemans in Hollywood on Sundays, and I once asked him, "Why did you put up with that?" He had so much respect for Welles's talent that he never took any credit himself. Houseman could have done it by himself; Welles never could have. Anyone could see that. When Houseman left him, after *Citizen Kane*, Welles couldn't keep going in the same way, and he faltered.

What was it like working with Howard Koch?

---

itional couture in Paris in the 1920s, she wrote for the *New Yorker* as "Parisite" before returning to the U.S. in disgust with high fashion. Establishing her own business, she married director Joseph Losey in 1937 (they were divorced in 1944) and published a best-selling commentary, *Fashion Is Spinach*. Advocating unisex clothes, she was bitterly criticized, closed her shop in 1940, wrote for the left-wing newspaper *PM*, and then became a United Auto Workers organizer of women, until she was blacklisted in the late 1940s. Her 1967 retrospective at the Fashion Institute of Technology established her full stature as a design giant. See Bettina Burch, *Radical by Design: The Life and Style of Elizabeth Hawes*.

It was the beginning of my writing career, thanks to Howard. I started out as his secretary, but he soon began giving me dialogue to write, and some scenes, and he encouraged me to be creative. Then along came the famous broadcast of *The War of the Worlds*, based on H. G. Wells's novel. We transferred the setting to this country. I picked this place in New Jersey, some place near Princeton, for the imaginary spaceship to land. I worked on the script with Howard. I remember how they made us change the names of some things that people would recognize, and I resented that.

We wanted people to imagine a space invasion, if just for a little while. All we hoped was that we could get people a little excited. The commercial break was scheduled in the middle, and then there was a whole second act! I remember how we kept putting off the break, to keep the fun going a little longer. The night of the broadcast, Sunday evening, October 30, 1938, I listened to it and then I went to bed. The next day Howard went into a barbershop and had to ask what everybody was so excited about. We couldn't believe that people could get so hysterical and leave the city in droves and not even check by turning to another station.

So that was the start of your writing career. Did Howard bring you out with him to Hollywood?

I still had it in my mind to become an actress. I had only written for radio. But I had always had terrible stage fright, and when I began to figure out that I could get other people to stand in front of an audience and deliver my dialogue, I realized that was what I really wanted to do.

Howard wanted Warner Brothers to hire me as a writer in 1939, but Warners said that if I would start as his secretary, well, after six months they would promote me to a writer. It actually took them eighteen months. Howard was working on *The Letter*, for Bette Davis, who was under contract with Warners. In *The Letter* [based on a Somerset Maugham story] a British woman in Malaya kills her lover and disguises the truth from her husband. But it was really a psychological study of a woman, and a lot of my work was on the psychological themes.

William Wyler was the director. There were lots of rewrites from the original script, especially of Bette Davis's lines—and she had most of the dialogue. Howard asked me to start rewriting some of the scenes, especially the love scenes. The film was nominated for an Academy Award. But I thought to myself, "This is Howard's big start in Hollywood." I didn't mind that he got sole credit. And they gave me a contract as a writer.

Howard gave me my first credit, cocredit with him, on his next film, *Shining Victory*. This is a forgotten film. Howard doesn't even mention it in his autobiography, *As Time Goes By*. But the film was very important to me, and it was an interesting film in a way. *Shining Victory* was adapted from a Broadway play, by A. J. Cronin, about a doctor who is working on a serum injection that can cure mental disease. Hollywood did a lot of films then about the scientific approach to psychological problems. James Stephenson played the doctor. He falls in love with his assistant, played by Geraldine Fitzgerald, who doesn't know it. A hospital clerk [played by Barbara O'Neil] grows jealous and sets fire to their lab, and Fitzgerald risks her life to save the experiment.

It wasn't much of a plot. But Robert Lord was a sympathetic producer, and Irving Rapper was a good director. Howard structured the screenplay and gave me dialogue to write, especially the women's dialogue. And that was my big break.

You didn't find any more opportunities to work with Howard Koch?

After that, we were never at the same studio again. But we stayed friends, and I did one more very important thing for him, although I didn't know it at the time. He has a nice story about this in *As Time Goes By*. Howard's marriage had broken up, and he was assigned to work on *Mission to Moscow*, in 1943. He needed to go East to work on the screenplay and to consult with Joseph E. Davies, the U.S. ambassador to the Soviet Union, who had demanded that the film be made, on patriotic grounds. Howard planned to travel on the Santa Fe *Chief* and to work on the way, and he wanted me to go along with him as a secretary. But I had just gotten married, and I was about to start working on *Miss Susie Slagle's*. So, as he says in his book, he called me from the Mocambo, and I recommended a friend of mine, Anne Green, who had been a radio writer and had some experience as a secretary. He agreed, sight unseen. He even left behind his research materials, though she brought her own copy of Davies's book, *Mission to Moscow*. That's how the screenplay got drafted, on the train, with her drawing out his ideas. Later she did research in New York for some of the historical parts of the script.

Well, she was perfect for the job. She and Howard got married, and they stayed married the rest of their lives.

What was it like working at Paramount in those days? Weren't you one of the only women writers there?

It seems unbelievable that at the time I never thought of being the "only" woman writer or even a "woman writer." I was just "a writer." In the 1970s, when a women's committee was started by the Writers Guild, they brought out the issue of discrimination against women in the profession. But I never thought about it at the time. Living with my mother must have made me think that women could do anything.

Paramount was a good place to start. As Howard said in *As Time Goes By*, the studio was making a lot of films with social themes then, and left-wing writers were all around the lot. After that, I went to RKO.

You did The Master Race *there.*

My most political film. We had the idea in that film that Nazism wasn't finished. I was on the set doing rewrites, and that's how I got to know George

Coulouris, a great guy—he wasn't a Communist, but he was a good progressive—who played the villain. The movie was about a former Nazi officer who makes his way to a Belgian village which is just trying to rebuild after the war. He forces himself upon a middle-class family who have collaborated with the Nazis, and he takes advantage of people who have already been taken advantage of, like a woman who became pregnant by a German soldier and then had a little girl that she is afraid to show to her husband when he comes back from the war. *The Master Race* has lots of good drama in it. It was directed by Herbert Biberman, who also worked on the script. He was another good guy.

Then you went back to Paramount for Miss Susie Slagle's.

That's probably my favorite film. It was adapted from a novel [by Augusta Tucker] by myself and Hugo Butler, one of my favorite people and a wonderful writer. And it was directed by John Berry. He was such a young man; I think it must have been one of his first films. One of the costars was Lloyd Bridges, and we got to be great friends at the time.

Were you surprised that Bridges later became a "friendly witness" before HUAC?

Not just surprised—I was disgusted.

What did you like about the project?

It's about a rooming house in New York, at the turn of the century, where the landlady, played by Lillian Gish, presides over young men in training to become doctors. They have all sorts of troubles, and romances with nurses, and so forth. Veronica Lake wasn't much of an actress, but Sonny Tufts was delightful, a very funny guy to be around. We did a good job of creating the characters. It could have been just another doctors-and-nurses film, but these people came alive; they were real. The casting was obviously good, too.

You were still at Paramount to do Easy Come, Easy Go *in 1947.*

The best thing about that film was Sonny Tufts. Barry Fitzgerald played himself, more or less, as the Irish horse player who doesn't want his daughter to get married. I was out of the project by the time the film was made, and at least one person followed me on the script.*

Your last credit before the blacklist was Harriet Craig, *a remake of the 1936 film* Craig's Wife.

That was for Columbia. The original title of the film was "Lady of the House," a much better title. It was another psychological interpretation of womanhood, with Joan Crawford as the star.

---

*The *Easy Come, Easy Go* screenplay is credited to Anne Froelick, John McNulty, and Francis Edward Faragoh.

Many people would say that the film makes Harriet Craig seem manipulative, and that she might even be considered misogynous.

It depends on how you interpret her character. Harriet Craig has no choice, or she believes that she has no choice. Her father left her mother, and that's all she knows about the relationships of men and women. All that she has is her house and her husband; at least that's what she thinks. Other movies, like *Forever Amber*, written by Ring Lardner Jr., were going in the same direction—women acting as men had acted toward them.

After Harriet Craig, however, you were finished as a screenwriter.

Ironically, my career really had started to get going. Finally I had enough credits to get to the point where I thought I would be able to pick and choose what I wrote next. Then the blacklist started, and suddenly, even though I wasn't named for three more years, I didn't get offers.

For a while I thought I was such a minor person that I wasn't going to be mentioned to the House Un-American Activities Committee. Three years went by after the first hearing. Then, on the last day of the Committee's last visit to Hollywood, in March 1953, I was identified by some jerk* I hardly knew. I think that the Committee had my name much sooner, but that other friendly witnesses who knew me much better asked not to be the ones to name me if someone else did.

In your unpublished novel, "Fee Fi Foe Friend," your protagonist, Mollie, says that she joined the Party because the Communists were the only people who really tried to do something about fighting Fascism and organizing unions. Is that the way you felt?

That's correct. You couldn't see what happened during the Spanish Civil War any other way: it was the Communists against the Fascists. For a writer in Hollywood, the Communists in the Screen Writers Guild were the ones raising our professional standard, winning our rights in various ways. And they were way, way out in front of everyone else on Negro rights.

How active were you in the Party?

Not very active. I went to meetings and to a lot of events and activities. But I was also getting married about this time and trying hard to start a family. A lot of our activity in the Party was social. I saw a lot of Jean and Hugo Butler but also of Howard Koch [who was not a Party member] and his friends.

Did you ever wonder whether the negative stories about the Soviet Union and Stalin were true?

---

*Froelick was named by screenwriters Leopold Atlas, best known for his Oscar-nominated contribution to the script of *The Story of G.I. Joe*, and Sol Shor, who specialized in low-budget serials.

Not then, not seriously, especially not when the Soviet Union was winning the war against Germany. I see that a lot of books are being written now about how Lenin was supposed to have prepared the way for Stalin, but I don't believe them. We knew almost nothing about Trotsky and none of it good. But we admired Lenin. Even then, he was a lot more important to some of us than Stalin was. Lenin was the real revolutionary.

Did Party discussions help you with screenwriting?

Not at all. The theoretical discussions, or so-called theoretical discussions, sounded like harangues, and the books about theory were just terrible; they made me feel stupid. If only I could have read C. L. R. James then! But the Party made you feel that your favorite friends were all working together and that you were helping the world to be a better place in small ways.

How did you stop being active in the Party?

I don't know if I even thought about not going to meetings. During the blacklist the group just sort of dissolved. I suppose I stopped paying dues. A few years later we learned more about Stalin, and so forth.

People remember you especially as the person who knew the most saucy limericks in Hollywood. You quote one in your novel, about the New York Times *reporter Walter Duranty, because his popular book* I Write as I Please *was being read by everyone in those days. Here's the limerick: "Said a maid being laid in a shanty/'I fear you are going in slanty'/Said the man with a grin/As he wriggled it in/'I ride as I please; I'm Duranty.' " Was that one really your original?*

Yes, I wrote that one. But mostly I collected limericks, memorized them, and recited them at parties and events. Everybody enjoys getting a laugh, and I thought that they were terribly, terribly funny at the time. It wasn't that I enjoyed shocking people; you couldn't shock people in Hollywood. Maybe it was also that I was shy about making political statements, having intellectual arguments, so I liked to make people laugh instead.

The character Mollie, in your novel, also seems to have a grip on the lighter side of life, until the blacklist crashes in on her marriage. Did that happen to you?

That's right. My husband was a manufacturing planner at Lockheed. He joined the Party way after me, during the time when it was the Communist Political Association. Then when the hearings started, two years before I was named, guards came to his office one day and escorted him out of the plant. He loved his work, and it devastated him.

That was the source of our biggest conflict. We had one baby in 1946 and another in 1951, so we had a family going. But he was really bitter about what happened to him. I remember that I said, "You blame me for this happening," and he answered, "No, I don't blame you; I blame myself for being such a fool as to listen to you." Our marriage was in trouble.

In your novel Mollie responds to this crisis with self-medication—she hits the bottle.

That's just what I did. You could say that I fell into the bottle. All through the forties we drank—cocktails, at dinner, and sometimes a drink afterward. That was part of the socializing. When the blacklist hit I started drinking by myself and hiding my bottles, and my husband started hiding his bottles from me. It was terrible. Finally I went to Alcoholics Anonymous. I'm a recovering alcoholic.

But the blacklist didn't kill you, as it did others.

No, it didn't kill me. I survived. I even wrote a few plays that got produced and one funny novel that was published.* But I never made a living with my writing again.

---

*Her comic novel *Press on Regardless,* about a woman sports-car addict, was published under the name Anne F. Taylor, with Fern Mosk as her coauthor.

Bernard Gordon

BERNARD GORDON, Los Angeles, California, 1997

INTERVIEW BY PATRICK McGILLIGAN

BERNARD GORDON

(1918–   )

1952 *Flesh and Fury.* Script.
1953 *The Lawless Breed.* Script.
1954 *Crime Wave.* Coscript.
    The Law vs. Billy the Kid. Story, script (as John T. Williams).
1955 *The City Is Dark.* Coscript.
1956 *Earth vs. the Flying Saucers.* Coscript (as Raymond T. Marcus).
1957 *Hellcats of the Navy.* Coscript (as Raymond T. Marcus).

Chicago Confidential. Script (as Raymond T. Marcus).
Escape from San Quentin. Script (as Raymond T. Marcus).
The Zombies of Mora Tau. Script (as Raymond T. Marcus).
The Man Who Turned to Stone. Script (as Raymond T. Marcus).
1958 *The Case Against Brooklyn.* Script (as Raymond T. Marcus).
1960 *Studs Lonigan.* Uncredited contribution.
1961 *El Cid.* Uncredited contribution.
1963 *55 Days at Peking.* Coscript.

The Day of the Triffids. Script.
Cry of Battle. Script.
1964 *The Thin Red Line.* Script.
1965 *Battle of the Bulge.* Uncredited contribution.
1967 *Custer of the West.* Coscript.
1969 *Krakatoa, East of Java.* Coscript.

1971 *Captain Apache.* Producer.
A Town Called Bastard. Producer.
Bad Man's River. Producer.
1972 *Pancho Villa.* Producer.
Horror Express. Producer.
1984 *Surfacing.* Script.

■

BERNARD GORDON ARRIVED in Hollywood in 1940, following close on the heels of his lifelong friend from high-school days, Julian Zimet (aka Julian Halevy). He became a reader at Paramount, where he was active in the Screen Readers Guild, served as its president, and helped negotiate that organization's first contract with the film studios. He was marked as a unionist and a leftist by red-baiters in studio management long before he had any prominence as a writer. In fact, he was still at his desk in the story department at Paramount, in October 1947, when he read in the newspapers that he had been "named" as a Communist in the Washington, D.C., hearings. Gordon was fired in December, and he was subsequently listed by *Red Channels* and other ad hoc blacklisters.

Five years later, on April 14, 1952, he sat in the Los Angeles Federal Building chambers, scheduled to appear in public as a "Fifth Amendment witness," invoking his constitutional right to remain silent about his political beliefs. When local lawyers and doctors, caught up in the anti-red dragnet, put up an unexpectedly fierce fight before the Committee, the inquisitors ran out of time and never called some of the last Hollywood people who remained to be nailed. "More than forty years later, I suppose I am still under subpoena," said Gordon. "For I was never called and never testified." That "irritating limbo" in which he was never allowed to speak his piece about being named is just one of the ways Gordon has managed to slip through the cracks of film history.

In the five years between 1947 and 1952, Gordon worked as a freelance scenarist for producers whose wariness increased as the shadow of the blacklist grew and darkened. During this time he managed to write and have produced an unusual drama about a deaf-mute prizefighter, *Flesh and Fury*, and a solid western, *The Lawless Breed*, directed by Raoul Walsh.

After the 1952 subpoena, the blacklist descended and lean years followed. Gordon worked first as a salesman of vinyl-plastic items and then as a private investigator while he began to explore the possibilities of working under a pseudonym. Here again he proved his remarkable resourcefulness, first as John T. Williams, then more prolifically as Raymond T. Marcus (the name of a longtime friend who fronted for him). The hardscrabble ingenuity of those years can be detected in his wild range of uncredited films. Gordon wrote several crime dramas. He found himself unaccountably in demand as a science-fiction and fantasy expert on projects like *Earth vs. the Flying Saucers*, *The Zombies of Mora Tau*, and *The Man Who Turned to*

Stone. One of his most ironic credits was coscreenplay for *Hellcats of the Navy,* the only film to pair Ronald Reagan and Nancy Davis (Reagan) as its stars. In that instance Gordon took private satisfaction in having been hired to rewrite a friendly witness's weak script.

In 1959 he answered a fateful bailout call from an old friend, director Irving Lerner, to help with the postproduction fix-it of *Studs Lonigan.* After meeting the film's producer, Philip Yordan, Gordon moved to Europe to work for Yordan and alternated his career base between Paris, Madrid, and Hollywood for the next thirteen years. Yordan had affiliated with producer Samuel L. Bronston to work on his spectacle films. Gordon worked closely with Yordan on numerous Bronston productions and others, including *Day of the Triffids; 55 Days at Peking; The Thin Red Line; Battle of the Bulge; Custer of the West; Krakatoa, East of Java; Captain Apache; Pancho Villa;* and *Horror Express.* Some of these are considered triumphs of helter-skelter filmmaking; others, hampered by Yordan's very budget-conscious approach, are seen as downright turkeys. Let the fans and critics argue over which is which.

Yordan, one of Hollywood's bigger-than-life figures, has somewhat mystified his associates as well as film historians. Like the King brothers, who gave low-budget work to Dalton Trumbo and other blacklistees in the United States, Yordan employed American political émigrés in Europe. He collected them around him at bargain rates, using them, in shifting combinations, on films where he was usually credited as the screenwriter. Gordon has recently completed his fascinating memoir "Living in Interesting Times; or, How I Learned to Love the Blacklist," about his life and his career, including his long personal and professional relationship with Yordan.

"My title is ironic, obviously," said Gordon. "Mostly people think about the terrible personal effects, the ruined careers and lifetimes, even the deaths of people who were affected—all true enough and not to be slighted. Others think of the dark times in America during the McCarthy era, and the fear engendered not only in the entertainment industry but in the schools and universities, in the press and media. All true, too.

"But my own sense goes beyond even that. I feel that that black period laid the groundwork for much that has followed, the Nixon and Reagan regimes, which glorified the Cold War as a holy enterprise, which used the slogans of anti-Communism to construct a monstrous military machine that virtually bankrupted the country and placed the industrial-military complex in such a powerful position that even today, with the 'evil empire' gone, there seems to be no way to stop the expenditures for arms and the export of arms. Eisenhower warned of this in his farewell address.

"Beyond this, even, there is a sense that the convenient anti-Communism has become anti-government with respect to all social programs that came out of the FDR era. The rich and powerful, who grow more rich and powerful each day, used blacklisting and McCarthyism to dismantle everything liberal, to make liberalism a dirty word, so that today both parties vie to be more reactionary.

"The heritage of blacklisting and McCarthyism goes far beyond personal tragedies. The social consequences of realizing that even in America one must be afraid to dissent will be with us for a long time. The lesson for me is that the right to dissent is our most precious heritage. My fear is that that right has been lost. I hope that I'm wrong, that the wheel will turn again and we will remember a proud time when we were not afraid to speak out boldly."

■

Tell me about your first meeting with Philip Yordan and how much you knew about him beforehand.

I knew a lot about him from my good friend Irving Lerner. Irving had been working for Yordan for years, and he brought me in to help straighten out *Studs Lonigan* by writing the narration and helping to recut the film. I have a history of taking long, discursive novels and making scripts out of them. Yordan came over from Spain, and I met him in the projection room. He said, "Give me an example of one line you might write," and I had it ready.

What was your impression of him?

I had had so much told to me about what an operator he was that I didn't exactly encounter him cold. But my impression of him was that he was a tough, quiet man who knew exactly what he wanted and went right to the point and didn't waste any time, because he was always in a hurry, with more important things to do. When he said to me, typically, "How much money do you want to do the job?" I said, "Twenty-five hundred dollars." He said, "I don't have that." I happened to be in pretty good shape, because I had just sold a script I wrote with Julian [Zimet], and I had some money in the bank, so I said jokingly, "I'll lend it to you." Well, he liked that. He laughed and said, "Okay, we've got a deal." After that he asked, "Do you want to work in Spain?" I took it seriously enough to go out and buy a decent suit.

What was the feeling one had in his presence? Was he glamorous or magnetic? Certainly he had great success with women. In your book you describe each one of his wives, sequentially, as a more stunning beauty than the one before.

He was magnetic. Of course, you know he had a terrible problem with his eyes. He wore heavy glasses and squinted all the time. But he sold himself extremely well. It's the thing he did best, selling himself in terms of making deals and in terms of making relationships with movie stars. I'm not much of a judge of another man's magnetism, but he must have had it.

Let me put it another way—he must have charmed people. Was he charming?

He was not what I would call charming. Though he was a witty man and one who could turn memorable phrases (which made him a very good dialogue writer), he never tried to be funny in real-life situations. He did not try to gain approval by being entertaining. He was typically serious and authoritative without being overbearing. He was very straightforward, and I think that what women found in him—I can only assume—was not only a man who was rich and powerful but a man who knew his own mind, knew what he wanted, went straight for it, and could be relied upon. He had strength.

Why were you so ready and available to join him and his operations in Europe? What was it about your professional situation at the end of the 1950s that led you to take a job with him so readily?

My professional situation was that I was blacklisted. I couldn't get any work here in town, and I thought Europe was very glamorous. I had been over there on trips, but I hadn't been over there to work, and it seemed like an ideal situation for me to be able to go and live there and work and get paid. Also, Yordan always had so many projects going at the same time. It was an extremely attractive proposition to me.

You had functioned pretty prolifically during the 1950s, under a couple of pseudonyms. Were those kind of assignments getting harder to come by? Were the jobs drying up? Or was it just too much trouble to be constantly knocking on doors for work?

It was not the kind of situation where you could just knock on doors to get work. It had to come to you because of some prior contact. It was not satisfactory to have to work that way and to work for very small money.

Yordan's money was generous by comparison?

I knew from Irving, and from what had happened to Arnaud d'Usseau, who was already over there with him, that the living was good in Spain. I didn't know what the money was going to be, because we hadn't discussed that, although it turned out to be all right.

How was life in Spain?

Life there was deluxe—Hollywood in Madrid. Everything was on the house, that is, on [Samuel L.] Bronston, who was running up a humongous bill at the Hilton but seemed unconcerned. After I had been on the job only a few days, a man came around from the studio and handed me a bundle of two hundred dollars worth of Spanish pesetas—my weekly expense allowance. I really didn't need them for anything more than the *Paris Herald Tribune*. The fine dining room was at our disposal for three excellent meals a day, or as many more as we might like—all we did was add the tip and sign the check. It was summertime when we arrived, and they served meals in a great central garden-courtyard with a good musical combo. Even the harpist was pretty. I soon got the idea, though I never verified this, that Yordan was laying everything on as a Bronston expense even when he had people like me working strictly for a personal production of his own.

Yordan did very little writing during this period in Paris and Madrid, right? What was he like at a story conference? Was he useful, or was it your worry to sort all the snags out?

My problem was that I had not had any very significant history of accomplishment as a screenwriter. I didn't have any big credits, and here I was working with a man who was revered as an Academy Award winner [for *Broken Lance*, 1954] and who had all these great credits. I assumed he knew all the answers. For a long time I deferred to his opinions, and it was only rather late in the situation that I began to realize that I was right a good deal of the time and he was wrong. This was a revelation that came very slowly to me.

I had a conversation with Phil some years ago, after we were back here in Hollywood, when all of the work was over. I was driving him to the airport one day, and we were discussing *Circus World*. I said, "You know, you really blew that, because the way I had set it up originally was right, and what you and Bronston did with it turned it into a piece of junk." He said, "Yes, that's true. You were right." And I said, "I was also right about the end of *The Thin Red Line*. You blew that one, too. You were wrong about almost everything in those days." [Laughs.] He nodded and said, "Well, yes . . . yes." He didn't want to fight about it with me and he agreed that maybe I was right about those films. Looking back on it, I think I was.

It seems that he was very good on the big ideas—the concept of a film, or something that might bail out a scene.

He was a showman. He knew what would sell to the people who had to finance the pictures, what they were looking for in the way of show-biz ideas. He understood the business of moviemaking much, much better than I ever did, or ever will.

I remember what happened on *The Day of the Triffids*. Though Yordan blamed the producer [George Pitcher] and the director [Steve Sekely] for the problems, I believed the real trouble came from Yordan's unwillingness or inability to spend the money required to shoot the major action and special-effects sequences that had been planned for Spain. But he was also constrained by the need to spend most of the money in England to qualify for a government subsidy under the Eady Plan.* Whatever the reasons, when we were done there were only fifty-seven minutes of good film. Contractually, Yordan needed a feature-length film. Someone had to find or add close to

---

*The Eady Plan or Eady Levy, named after the civil servant who thought it up, was a tax on every cinema seat sold in Britain, which was paid back to the film that filled the seat, providing it was produced by British artists. The levy was paid very early in the film's distribution, so that the makers would start seeing some money long before the financing company had taken its share and begun paying off, if it ever did. The system, introduced in the 1950s, gradually became more elastic and therefore much abused, until it was scrapped.

thirty minutes. Apart from the cost of doing this, the other problem was that the cast—the principals and all other actors—were long gone. They could not be brought back without spending a fortune. It would be cheaper to scrap the whole film.

Yordan figured out in principle what had to be done: we would write and film another complete story that was related to the basic plot but independent of it, a story with different characters, therefore different and cheaper actors. What kind of story? I was stumped. The whole idea overwhelmed me. Not Yordan. A few days later, he came to me with his solution.

We could do a story of two people isolated in a lighthouse, just two characters who had somehow escaped the destruction of most of the rest of the world, and we could intercut their story with the one that was already shot. I liked it. I had to find two characters, put them in a lighthouse, figure out why they hadn't gone blind in the film like everyone else, make them interesting enough to watch for thirty minutes, and figure out how their affairs would intersect those of the original story. This seemed like a snap. I was relieved of my other chores, I set to work, and soon I had twenty-five or thirty pages I liked. I gave them to Yordan. He read them and rejected them. "Why?" I demanded angrily. "That's a good story." "It's too good," he retorted. "Your characters are too sophisticated; they have psychological problems. They don't fit in with the others in the rest of the picture." I thought he was dead wrong but shrugged and walked away from it.

Yordan had a British writer available. After all, the original novel was a British classic; the location of our lighthouse would be somewhere on the British coast and would have British characters and actors. Yordan asked Jon Manchip-White to write the new lighthouse sequence. Shortly, Jon came to my room with some script pages in hand. "I didn't think Yordan could write," he said. "What are you getting at?" I asked. "I just read a sequence he wrote, and it's really damned good," Jon said. I glanced at them and laughed. Of course, they were the pages of my lighthouse sequence. "Did he tell you he'd written them?" Jon nodded. I explained that they were my pages and that I had just received from him the most sincere compliment from one writer to another. I marched in to see Yordan and waved my pages at him. He shrugged, "What's the difference who wrote them?" Maybe that's the way he really felt. In any event, those were the pages that were shot, and many people have told me, since the film has become a cult favorite, that they like the lighthouse story best.

He was always looking for the truly big idea, the must-see picture. He had the notion, and he said to me again and again, that with television coming in, and people being able to sit at home and watch films for free, to get them out at night—paying for a babysitter, parking, and a big ticket price—there had to be a must-see aspect to a picture. That's what he kept looking for, especially in the Bronston days. That's why we came up with *55 Days at Peking*—because it was a big spectacle—and *The Fall of the Roman Empire*, as well as some of the others. He was always looking for "name" projects with a good deal of recognition that would attract big stars. He understood, better than I, that simple storytelling and personal scenes weren't the essence of commercial picture making. Big scenes with action and fireworks and trains racing through tunnels—that's what people paid to see, and that's what had to be included in a picture if you could afford it. If it could be done cheap. [Laughs.] Yordan spent only the money he needed to spend to get the job done.

Another obsession was to use his considerable collection of books and film properties, plus his prestige as a filmmaker, to create a new stock company with which brokers could sell millions of dollars worth of stock to (1) enrich Yordan and (2) provide capital for the production of films. As a man who was once trained as a lawyer, he had taught himself to be very good at the drudgery of preparing the kind of prospectus demanded by the Securities and Exchange Commission. He has done this repeatedly over the past ten or fifteen years. It never seems to work, but Yordan is convinced that there is gold in those hills and continues to sweat away at the effort.

Would his budget concerns constantly threaten any hopes you might have to script quality?

Constantly. An example: Writing the script, I described the initial action of the film *The Thin Red Line* after the soldiers came ashore on Guadalcanal. They were weary and frightened, having withstood the shelling of their ship in the harbor, and they were trooping raggedly toward combat positions in the interior. To give some visual reality to their condition and to help convey their misery, I had them slogging, falling, stumbling through a muddy patch of pathway. Yordan would have none of this. Impatiently, he explained to this neophyte that by writing these few words, the script told the production manager he'd have to prepare more than one set of uniforms for the actors. After they got filthy with mud, they'd have to have clean uniforms for subsequent scenes. What if the scene had to be shot more than once? How much time would be lost waiting for the laundry to return? How much extra would all that cost? Had I thought about that? Mud was out!

I protested that we were shooting a war film, that the reality of combat under the brutal conditions of the South Pacific was a crucial part of the whole, particularly for developing the character conflict around which I had devised the entire story. I appealed to the director, Andrew Marton, expecting support from him. But Marton would never side with me against Yordan. Marton, a successful second-unit director on major films, who had also filled in for Nick [Nicholas] Ray on *55 Days at Peking*, was eager to become a director in his own right. He was thrilled to have a film like *The Thin Red Line*, and Yordan had seduced him into believing that this was the beginning of a major career change. He refused to back me up on this or any other subsequent dispute. The mud was out.

I know that you tried, whenever possible, to inject philosophical or humanistic content into the scripts, or to contribute some idea that would make a film worthwhile for you personally. How was that possible, working with someone like Yordan?

Although I wanted commercial success and the money that went with that, I always felt an obligation to try and tell the truth in terms that I understood were true and in terms of what was happening in society—as long as it looked like it was going to be interesting on the screen, Yordan didn't care one way or another. When we did *Custer of the West*, I remember saying to Yordan, "Let's tell the truth about Custer and make him an antihero." I remember Yordan saying, "It's Jews like you who ruined the motion-picture business with this antihero shit." [Laughs.] It was also important for Julian [Zimet] and me to adopt a decent attitude about the Indians for *Custer of the West*, and we did. We set up the Indians as being in the right, and we showed that the American cavalry and politicians were destroying them, in violation of the treaties, and so on. When I saw *Dances with Wolves*, I thought to myself, "We did this twenty years ago."

He didn't care if those things were in the script as long as it didn't hurt the progression of the film. Another example: In a picture like *The Day of the Triffids*, I felt it was necessary to come up with some moral about the possible end of the world. *The Day of the Triffids* tells of a series of events that, first, blinds almost everyone on earth, and later, begins populating the earth with deadly three-legged plants (triffids) that roam about freely, attacking the helpless, sightless humans who remain alive. The story concerns the few people who, for logical reasons, have escaped being blinded and who must contend with the proliferating and unstoppable plants. For me, the problem of the book by John Wyndham was that the story meandered through many episodes and never came to a meaningful end.

Fortunately, I chanced on a story in a newspaper or in *Time* magazine about William Faulkner speaking to the Nobel Committee when he received their prize for literature. I paraphrase this poorly, but in essence he said that mankind will have a way of triumphing over all odds, that at the end, when the sun has grown cold and its very last rays are touching the peak of our highest mountain, even then, a human being will be standing there representing all mankind and mankind's triumph. I clipped this piece and pinned it to the wall as I wrote and typed away at the script. It gave me the clue I needed about how to finally end the story, on a positive note of humanity. I ended up saying that since life on earth arose from the sea, it would be that same broth of seawater that saves life as we know it. And with the help of a bit of seawater, man would eventually triumph even over the triffids.

It didn't seem to mean anything to Yordan. It gave the film a happy ending, so he was happy. The only time I had a really bad argument with Yordan was over the ending of *The Thin Red Line*. I thought I had a really good line to finish the picture. To end the story on a satisfyingly upbeat note, and to pay off the conflict between the sergeant (Jack Warden) and the soldier (Keir

Dullea), I had the sergeant mortally wounded in the final battle and the soldier comforting the dying man. True to his character, the sergeant scoffs at the imminent prospect of death—it's what he always expected, and he's a man who joined the Army, opted out of real life, and has been waiting for this moment. This is the root reason he's always felt contempt for men, like the soldier, who feared death, who believed living was all. Scornfully, the sergeant says, as the soldier is trying to comfort him, "What's the difference?" followed by the big question, "What do you want, anyway?" How does one answer the question "What do you want from life?" The soldier stands up and looks at the brilliant sky clear of battle smoke, an affirmation of the possible beauty of the world and of life. He drinks it all in and says, "I want everything." Fade-out. Many people who read my version of the scene found it moving and congratulated me on it. Phil's attitude, along with that of the toadying director [Andrew Marton], was, "The audience is cranking up the Fords." So, no dialogue. In the end, they shot Dullea fixing the sergeant's dog tag between his teeth. But my ending wasn't out because Yordan objected to the philosophy—it was out because he objected cinematically.

One of the things that mystify people about Yordan and his "factory of writers" in Paris and Madrid is that he chose to surround himself with so many blacklistees. Did he himself ever express any political beliefs or sentiments?

He never expressed any political sentiments. He never talked to me about the blacklist. I am sure that he knew I was blacklisted, of course, but there was never any discussion about it, and I don't think he had any interest in that topic, except that, in my opinion, it enabled him to find better people available cheaper.

The word "blacklist" never escaped his lips?

Never.

Was he sophisticated about, for example, Communism?

There was never any discussion of politics.

Did you share any common values?

I probably knew him better than anybody else who ever worked with him, because I worked with him for such a long time, and we developed a very close relationship which became social as well as professional. But you could never really tell about Yordan. He had a great ability to pose, to put on a "front" personality. On many occasions, for example, he expressed a strong sense of anti-Semitism—and, of course, he himself is a Jew—or made anti-Negro remarks. I sometimes felt he just enjoyed being provocative, yet I never knew for sure.

He grew up in a lower-middle-class Chicago Jewish neighborhood with all kinds of racial prejudices that he carried with him. I can remember a conversation with him when he complained about blacks eating in the good restaurants of Beverly Hills. I screamed at him about this, and he said, "It's nothing to get excited about. I don't care if they eat wherever they want to eat, just as long as they don't eat where I eat." I think he knew it was wrong to have racial prejudices, but he was part of the culture and the times. It's particularly ironic in his case, since much of his career stemmed from the success of *Anna Lucasta*, a play with an all-black cast.*

Someone told me a story, I think it was writer and producer Milton Sperling, about Yordan looking out of his window in Paris one day during the Algerian crisis and seeing a tank guarding the street. He said, "What is that tank for?" Sperling said, "The Algerian crisis." And Yordan supposedly said, "What Algerian crisis?"

That sounds very unlikely to me. I remember his reaction to the Algerian crisis when I was working for him. De Gaulle had gone on the radio and television, and warned the populace that there was a danger of terrorists flying in from Algeria. I didn't come to work that day, and he said, "Oh, any excuse not to come to work." That was his reaction.

He didn't read very much in the way of political or cultural material. He read a great deal but always for ideas for stories, and that seemed to be it. He could not have been totally naive about political issues. And yet he seemed to be totally indifferent to such matters.

I think it's hard for people to accept the paradox of good, committed, left-wing people going over to Europe and working for Yordan on his types of films without either being alienated from his kind of filmmaking or nurturing incredible resentments at the exploitation. As you say, he got the better people cheaper.

Most of the people who worked for him were seriously underpaid. I was not one of those. I was the only one who was well paid, so I did not have any reason to resent him on that score. I was getting better pay with him than I had gotten anywhere else. I started at about twelve hundred and fifty dollars a week and went up to about two thousand a week, which was damn good money in those days, especially in Europe. It was certainly good money for me, because I didn't have a history or record of high earnings.

As far as the others were concerned, yes, Arnaud [d'Usseau] resented him, Irving [Lerner] resented him, and so on. But they had no choice, and they were all people who enjoyed living in Europe, and this was their opportunity to do that. It was also a way of getting away from all of the mess in this

---

*Philip Yordan's play *Anna Lucasta* was first produced on Broadway with an all-black cast and ran from 1944 to 1945. The first movie version (1949), directed by Irving Rapper, had a Polish-American milieu and an all-white cast, including Paulette Goddard, Oscar Homolka, and Broderick Crawford. The screenplay was cocredited to Yordan (who also produced) and Arthur Laurents. The second movie version (1958), directed by Arnold Laven, reverted to an all-black cast, including Eartha Kitt, Frederick O'Neal, Rex Ingram, and Sammy Davis Jr. Yordan alone is credited for the screenplay of the second film, with Sidney Harmon listed as producer.

country and in Hollywood, so on the whole it was very much on the plus side, although people did feel exploited.

But people also liked him. He had a way of not putting himself above the writer and of being—not so much friendly as equal and decent and regular with people.

What was the camaraderie like among the blacklistees who worked for Yordan and who had come over from Hollywood? Was that always one of the pluses?

Yes. There was great camaraderie in Madrid and Paris. We felt very close and very happy to be together, and it wasn't just those of us who were working for Yordan but people like Mike [Michael] Wilson and Paul Jarrico and the Golds [Tammy and Lee]. We were all a community, and we socialized, we had meals together; it was a good feeling.

Did you keep up political involvements? What was your political drift?

We certainly weren't involved. We couldn't be, over there. We were foreigners who were, in a sense, free of political obligations, because we were living in a time and a place where we were out of the picture. We did have acquaintances who were left-wingers, and we knew all about the Algerian crisis, for example, and knew people who were engaged in it. We were concerned about what was going on politically. We hadn't divorced ourselves from political ideals or ideology, whatever you want to call it.

I know it gave one something of a cachet in Paris to be an American blacklistee. Was that also true in Spain?

No. People were very frightened of any left-wing connections in Spain. The Spanish police, pushed by the CIA, kept tabs on some of us, and we were aware of it.

You wrote in your book, however, that Spain had a very knowledgeable film-buff community, so some of you must have been well-known to them as Hollywood blacklistees.

I didn't have much contact with those people, so I don't know about that. The only one I knew well was Eugenio Martín, who directed *Horror Express*, *Bad Man's River*, and *Pancho Villa* for me, and he was very careful to stay away from all political discussions. I think he was frightened of Franco, and understandably so.

Can you give me close-ups of some of the lesser-known people who were important to Yordan, among his factory of writers or the circle of blacklistees living abroad?

Very important to Yordan were Ben Barzman and my old friend and collaborator, my almost-brother, Julian [Zimet], who frequently commuted from his home in Rome to Madrid and Paris and London to work on various scripts.

Besides them, tell me a little bit, for example, about Arnaud d'Usseau.

The blacklist destroyed his career. Arnaud was a man who had gone through a rough childhood, in the sense that his mother had been hospitalized for psychological reasons. He had really been raised after she died by a second mother who was an actress here in Hollywood, and by his father, who was an art director at Metro-Goldwyn-Mayer. From an early age he had lived in a real Hollywood atmosphere.

He had an early career as a B screenwriter at RKO, where he turned out quite a few inexpensive pictures in the thirties. Then he had become a successful playwright in New York with *Tomorrow the World, Deep Are the Roots*, and *Ladies of the Corridor*. The first two plays were with a collaborator, James Gow, who died at a very early age. On *Ladies of the Corridor* he collaborated with Dorothy Parker. That all took place in New York, and I didn't get acquainted with Arnaud until France and Spain.

He was a tall, handsome, beautifully set-up man, the kind of man who attracted women. He had a great deal of dignity and self-assurance, and a strict and straightforward morality, not in a narrow, sexual sense but in terms of what he felt was right and wrong about what was going on in the world. In later years, in fact, he had rather serious quarrels with a lot of his old ex-Communist friends, because he refused to accept all the demeaning of what had been going on in the Soviet Union and thought this was a cop-out. He continued to be very strong in his beliefs.

Was he a more talented writer than his very few credits with Yordan would indicate?

I wouldn't want to make a judgment about that. We worked together as friendly collaborators on quite a few things. It was a pleasure to me because he was a great playwright as far as I was concerned, and he thought I was a very good writer. We frequently disagreed about what we were writing on, but that's normal between collaborators. For some reason, though he started out with Yordan before me and could have become the person who took over in the sense that I did, he didn't. Whether that was a personality matter, or a matter of who was the better screenwriter or who pleased Yordan more, I don't know, I can't say, and I wouldn't want to say.

All I know is that one time, when I insisted on a raise from Yordan and told him that I did all of the work that was ever produced over there, he said, "Well, you're getting all the good assignments." Maybe that was true, but if I was getting all the good assignments, it was because Yordan thought I was able to do them, and Arnaud was therefore getting all the bad assignments, which never came to anything. Was that a matter of luck, or choice, or talent? I don't know how to answer that question.

How about editor and director Irving Lerner? When I interviewed Yordan once, the impression he gave me was, "I carried Irving Lerner." In other words, Lerner was a friend to whom Yordan gave work, but he was not a great talent. I get the opposite impression from reading your book: that Lerner was an immensely talented man but a good-souled personality who sometimes lacked the toughness that Yordan might admire.

Irving was not a forceful man. He was much too modest and decent to impose his will on anyone. But Irving was a wonderfully equipped man in almost every department of filmmaking. He knew film editing (which was his specialty), he knew sound, he knew lab work, he knew music (he was originally a musician). He was a really good technician, and more than a technician. He brought great value to everything that we worked on together. He did a couple of small pictures for Phil that were highly regarded in their day. Irving's talent was very considerable, and Yordan depended on him constantly to get him out of trouble when pictures had to be recut or scenes had to be dubbed, or whatever had to be done—Irving was on the spot. Yordan, unfortunately, treated him as a gofer. He exploited Irving very much and paid him very little.

I don't feel it was a matter of friendship between them, because when Irving died, and we had a memorial for him at my house, and all of his friends came, Yordan didn't come. Irving's wife has never forgiven him for that, and my wife, when she next met Yordan, chewed him out for not having come to Irving's memorial, when Irving had been his closest ally in filmmaking for many years.

What was Yordan's response?

Yordan's response was, "I don't come to funerals." My wife said, "Oh, you! You won't even come to mine." He said, "Oh, yes, I will." As a matter of fact, he did come up from San Diego for my wife's memorial.

You are rather hard on writer and producer Sidney Harmon in your book, depicting him as a kind of fifth wheel in the operation. He had script credits in the past, including an Oscar-nominated original story for The Talk of the Town *in 1942. I think he went way back, both with Irving Lerner and with Yordan. Did he have any political credentials? What function did he fulfill for Yordan?*

Whatever I know about this story I heard from Sidney, and it's not necessarily agreed to by Yordan. Sidney's account was that in the 1930s, when he was a young man of twenty, he was the coproducer of *Men in White*, a successful Broadway play, and working in a New York office he got hold of Yordan's first literary effort, which was a four-hundred-page script of *Anna Lucasta*. Sidney claimed that he gave that script to an old theatrical director, Harry Wagstaff Gribble, who was working with the American Negro Theatre in Harlem. Yordan had written it with a Polish background, and Gribble is the one who changed it to a black background, which is what made it so successful in most of its various theatrical and film forms. The play was performed and received very good notices in the New York press. This started a relationship between Harmon and Yordan which continued right through the next fifty years.

In my experience, Sidney was useful to Yordan principally because he knew people in Hollywood and could make approaches to actors, and Yordan thought he was very good at casting. It was not my experience that Sidney wrote anything at all; he seemed to me to be a hanger-on, one of a number of people Yordan kept around for comfort. Harmon was given producer credit on a couple of small, very low-budget films which Yordan made in Hollywood, but my favorite story about Harmon's credit is in the matter of *Battle of the Bulge*. They had run out of all the possible producer credits—producer, executive producer, associate producer, assistant producer—but having promised Sidney a production credit, Yordan gave him a whole card that said, "A Sidney Harmon." That's how it went out.

As to his politics, Sidney was left in his sympathies but not in his actions or in any organized way.

How about Lou Brandt? That's a name I wasn't familiar with until I read your book.

Lou was another left-winger who went back to the old days of the Yiddish theater in New York. He and his wife, Janet, had been active in small theater here in Los Angeles, and Lou was brought into the whole Bronston operation to be a production manager and to do whatever was necessary. They were socially friendly with Yordan, and Yordan hung on to them in the way he hung on to anyone he felt comfortable with.

Yordan was not at ease and confident in crowds. He liked one-to-one encounters, where he could be very persuasive. On one occasion, I felt he dragged me from Madrid to Rome, where there was to be a wrap party for *55 Days at Peking*, and naturally the attention would be focused on the stars and producers. He did not want to be left alone among strangers with egg on his face and no one to talk to. So I was there to be at his side, at least appearing to make conversation. He liked to be surrounded by people he knew and felt he could trust, and he would constantly bring the same people back to do whatever it was he was doing. Lou Brandt was one of them.

Were there many others? I get the impression of a dozen writers slaving away on different projects in his basement.

It was never a dozen in my experience, but it was probably half a dozen. We had somebody named Norman Borisoff, who was from Hollywood but living in Paris. I had known him when we were both readers, and I got him involved with Yordan. He was not blacklisted, but he was a left-winger. He was never a Party member; in fact he was a left-winger who was critical of the Party, and we used to have discussions about that which weren't always friendly. But by the time we were both working for Yordan there was no longer any real basis for contention.

There was a young man whose name was Dan Aubrey, a sort of would-be director. He wanted to be an apprentice and learn everything about filmmaking. Yordan kept him on the payroll at some kind of minimum, but he had his own family money anyway. Dan would take a shot at writing whatever came along. In Madrid, the key people stayed at the Hilton; the writers Yordan used there included Howard Berk and John Melson. In Paris, Yordan did have these rooms in the basement of his splendid home on Boulevard Suchet, once belonging to the Guggenheim family, and there he would have Arnaud d'Usseau, Norman Borisoff, Dan Aubrey, Lou Brandt, and other people. He would throw script ideas and problems at anybody who worked for him—Irving, too. His attitude was, "Who knows who will come up with something good?"

Kind of like, "Throw it at the wall and see if it sticks."

Yes. The writer I think was most important to him was in an earlier period, Ben Maddow.

Did you know Ben?

Yes.

Did Ben ever work for Yordan again after he gave his friendly testimony, or self-incriminating deposition, or whatever it was?

No, he didn't, because after Ben testified he got a fairly successful career going, writing without any blacklist problems, here in Hollywood.

Did you yourself ever encounter Ben again?

Yes, I ran into Ben a few times. Ben felt very guilty about what he had done. Ben was a very nice and decent man who had tried to hold out against the Committee for a long time and had suffered because of it, and he had had to work for Yordan for small money, although he was a very talented man, a poet and a writer of books. He finally knuckled under to the pressures. He was also very close to Irving, who never wanted to be censorious about Ben because they had been such good friends. I also felt Ben was a victim rather than an enemy. I never got close to him personally, but whenever I encountered him we were cordial.

Is that rare for you? Is there a small category of persons who did what Ben did, but whom you were able to forgive?

There were just a few cases like that, of people who broke very late in the game after trying to be strong. In those cases I felt one had to be forgiving.

It seems to me that one of the biggest resentments, among the blacklistees working for Yordan, would be that he put his name on scripts that they had written.

This was the blacklist.

Was it a constant issue with you, or not an issue because of the times?

It was not an issue because of the times. Things began to change around the time Ben Barzman came to work for Yordan on *El Cid*. The blacklist had tapered off in America because of what Trumbo had managed to do, writing so many pseudonymous scripts and then finally getting credit on *Spartacus* and *Exodus*. Finally Barzman got his name on *The Fall of the Roman Empire* with Basilio Franchina, who was also a strong left-winger and who was his Italian collaborator, thanks to the Italian movie star Sophia Loren, who at a certain point had balked at doing the film. After Barzman and Franchina got their names on *The Fall of the Roman Empire*, that was that.

When you finally asked Yordan for your first screen credit, after all those years of blacklisting, what was his reaction? I mean, what was his real reaction, behind the eyes?

That happened, of course, after Trumbo and Barzman, and after I had gotten credit on a small picture I had written, *Cry of Battle*, that was shot in the Philippines, which Yordan had nothing to do with. But he knew about *Cry of Battle*. When I asked for my credit on *55 Days at Peking*, he said, "Well, the problem is that Allied Artists made the deal with the idea that they would get a script from me. My name is important as part of the deal. I can't take my name off the film." Then he hesitated, and I said, "Look, there's no more blacklist. I wrote the damn script. I should have my name on it. Allied Artists isn't going to back out of the deal because of that." He said, "Well, go talk to Bronston, and if it's okay with him, it's okay with me—if you put your name on it with mine." That's the way it was done.

He seems to have done it, finally, rather good-naturedly, although it would seem to me that he was relinquishing a lot at that point—this great secret of his, that he wasn't really the writer of some of these Philip Yordan productions.

He did it ungrudgingly, yes. You have to remember that, by now, we had been working together for years and had a very, very strong personal relationship. But it's also true that he always pretended—or maybe he meant it—that the credit didn't make any difference to him. He had enough screen credits, and another screen credit didn't make any difference. He always said it was just a matter of practicality to him.

What happened when he himself finally had to sit down and write scenes for a script, together with you? You say it happened only once, and you report that incident in your book.

That's the one time I report. There was another occasion when we were struggling very hard to get going on *Krakatoa, East of Java*. Sidney Harmon was working with us. Yordan kept throwing out everything I was trying to do. When he came up with ideas of his own, I threw those out. We were throwing each other's ideas out.

Really sitting down seriously and trying to write together happened only once, on *Battle of the Bulge*. Bronston had collapsed financially, and Yordan had this new project going. I ended up rewriting half that script, although that is one instance where I made the mistake of eschewing any credit. Yordan and I sat in the hotel in Madrid, writing scene after scene together. That's when I had the interesting and amusing turnaround where basically he was writing for me. I refused to accept his notions of the scenes, again and again and again. We had one secretary, who was my secretary, and she typed both of our work. He'd offer me the scenes, and I would tell him why they were no good. I remember the look on his face when he finally brought me a scene to which I could say, "This is good! We can use this."

As I explain in my book, he was very troubled at that point. The whole Bronston operation had fallen apart, he didn't know what the future held, his marriage had gone down the drain, and his house here in Beverly Hills was under lease and he didn't even know where he was going to live next. He was under a lot of stress, and maybe that contributed to whatever problems he had in writing.

Do you think he was once a great writer who decided to channel his energies into business and promotion? Or is he one of Hollywood's greatest hoaxes as a writer, someone who never actually wrote?

Look, I can't answer that question, and I don't want to answer that question. I don't want to make a judgment. I consider him a friend. It's not possible for me to say what he did during his better days. When he was writing scripts for important directors and producers, I can't believe he was incapable of writing a good scene or a good script. He must have been. But I didn't see it. Maybe it's just that by the time I came around, things had so changed in terms of his priorities.

What is the Philip Yordan production you worked on, of them all, that you wish film buffs would never again mention to you—the worst of all your experiences?

I guess I'd have to say *Bad Man's River* with Lee Van Cleef. The script was terrible, and Yordan wouldn't let me cure it. He kept adding prologue after prologue after prologue, until it was ridiculous. Everything about the film was a mess.

Which is your favorite?

Horror Express—first of all, because it was my baby. Yordan left me alone, and I was a one-man operation. I made that picture from beginning to end, and I accomplished a great deal in terms of principal production that nobody thought was possible under the budget strictures we had. I had good performers. I had a director [Eugenio Martín] who trusted and liked me and went along with my ideas. And I had a chance to control the story: An archaeologist unearths a creature from outer space which has been trapped in an icy Siberian wasteland since a prehistoric period before even hominids existed. The creature is crated for shipment back to Europe on the Trans-Siberian Express. He revives. Having witnessed the development of the earth and of mankind, the creature intends to survive and return to his own galaxy. In order to do this, the creature must kill everybody he encounters. The scientists who are bringing him back on the Express finally realize that he is a terrible danger to humanity. They decided they have to kill him, and they do, but not before he makes a final, moving appeal to them, telling them that he represents something that is irreplaceable in terms of understanding the development of man. And it is true—the creature does represent something irreplaceable. I feel that *Horror Express* has some modest humanity. Some people like the film quite a bit and consider it a horror classic.

In other words, your favorite Philip Yordan production is the one he had the least to do with?

I didn't say that, and I wouldn't say that. You did.

Faith Hubley
(and John Hubley)

FAITH HUBLEY, New York City, 1997

INTERVIEW BY PATRICK MCGILLIGAN

PHOTO © WILLIAM B. WINBURN

FAITH HUBLEY
(1924–)

WITH JOHN HUBLEY AS CODIRECTOR
1956 *Adventures of an Asterisk*
1957 *Harlem Wednesday*
1958 *Tender Game*
1959 *Moonbird*
1960 *Children of the Sun*
1961 *Of Stars and Men*
1962 *The Hole*
1964 *The Hat*
1965 *Herb Alpert and the Tijuana Brass*
    Double Feature

1966 *Urbanissimo*
1967 *The Cruise*
    Windy Day
1968 *Zuckerkandl!*
1969 *Of Men and Demons*
1970 *Eggs*
1972 *Dig*
1973 *Cockaboody*
1974 *Voyage to Next*
1975 *People, People, People*
1976 *Everybody Rides the*
    Carousel
1977 *A Doonesbury Special*
    (television)

SOLO DIRECTOR
1975 *Women of the World*
1976 *Second Chance: Sea*
1977 *Whither Weather*
1978 *Step by Step*
1979 *Sky Dance*
1981 *The Big Bang and Other Creation Myths*
Enter Life
1983 *Starlore*
1984 *Hello*
1985 *The Cosmic Eye*
1987 *Time of the Angels*
1989 *Yes, We Can*
Who Am I?
1990 *Amazonia*
1991 *Upside Down*
1992 *Tall Time Tales*
1994 *Cloudland*
1996 *My Universe Inside Out*

JOHN HUBLEY
(1914–1977)

1937 *Snow White and the Seven Dwarfs.*
Collaboration.
1940 *Old Blackout Joe.* Collaboration.
The Dumbconscious Mind. Collaboration.
King Midas, Junior. Collaboration.
Pinocchio. Co–art direction.
Fantasia. "The Rite of Spring" sequence.
1942 *Bambi.* Co–art direction.
1943 *The Vitamin G-Man.* Collaboration.
Prof. Small and Mr. Tall. Collaboration.
He Can't Make It Stick. Collaboration.
1944 *Position Firing.* Collaboration.
Operation of the K-13 Gunsight. Collaboration.
Hell-Bent for Election. Uncredited contribution.
1945 *Tuesday in November.* Animation sequences.
1946 *Flat Hatting*
Brotherhood of Man. Coscript, design.
1947 *Human Growth.* Animation sequences.
1948 *The Magic Fluke*
Robin Hoodlum

1949 *Fuddy Duddy Buddy*
Ragtime Bear (first Mr. Magoo cartoon)
Punchy DeLeon
1950 *Trouble Indemnity*
Spellbound Hound
Barefaced Flatfoot
1951 *Sloppy Jalopy.* Producer.
M. Codesign.
Georgie and the Dragon. Coscript, design.
Grizzly Golfer. Producer.
1952 *The Four Poster.* Animation sequences.
Rooty Toot Toot
1953 *Heritage.* Script.
1956 *Adventures of an Asterisk*
1957 *Date with Dizzy*
1958 *Harlem Wednesday*
The Tender Game
1959 *Seven Lively Arts*
Moonbird
1960 *Children of the Sun*
1961 *Of Stars and Men*
1962 *The Hole*
Horses and Their Ancestors
Man and His Tools
1964 *The Hat*
1965 *Herb Alpert and the Tijuana Brass*
Double Feature
1966 *The Year of the Horse.* Animation sequences.
Urbanissimo
1967 *The Cruise*
Guilliver's Troubles.
1968 *Zuckerkandl!*
Windy Day
1969 *Of Men and Demons*
1970 *Eggs*
1971 *Uptight.* Titles.
1973 *Cockaboody*
Upkeep
1974 *Voyage to Next*
1975 *People, People, People*
1978 *Watership Down.* Uncredited contribution.
1985 *The Cosmic Eye*

■

FAITH AND JOHN Hubley broke away from Hollywood in the mid-1950s to form their own independent, small-scale studio in New York City, making animated films in an anti-Disney visual style that was closer in form and spirit to European surrealism and impressionism. They sponsored marvelous jazz and new-music sound tracks, and made (mostly short) films about adult and philosophical themes: the absurdity of war, the nuclear threat, environmental concerns, overpopulation, love, marriage, childhood development, spirituality, and feminism. Their highly original and straight-from-the-heart films have been feted worldwide—with three Oscars (out of seven nominations), film-festival citations from Jersualem to Zagreb, and museum anointings.

John Hubley was the senior artist, a noted background painter for Walt Disney on *Snow White and the Seven Dwarfs, Pinocchio, Fantasia, Dumbo,* and *Bambi.* He left the Disney factory after the bitter strike of 1941 and was among the founders of the alternative United Productions of America (UPA), source of Mr. Magoo and an alternative "flat" graphic style of animation featuring parody, serious subject matter, and abstract forms. A staunch unionist and cultural progressive, Hubley was production designer for the 1947 staging of Bertolt Brecht's *Galileo* and collaborated with director Joseph Losey on Losey's early films. The blacklist precipitated his move into animated commercials and into marriage and partnership with Faith Hubley.

Faith Hubley has her own history as a political activist and her own memories of Hollywood salad days. Her partnership with her husband lasted until his death in 1977. Since then, she has upheld the Hubley legacy and extended it with enchanting work on her own, including her 1986 feature *The Cosmic Eye,* in which three bebop visitors from outer space expostulate on the history and future of the human species. This interview was conducted mainly in New York City, with intermediate sessions in Madison, Wisconsin, where her daughter Georgia (on drums) and Georgia's husband, Ira Kaplan (lead guitarist and vocalist), were on the road with their alternative rock band Yo La Tengo.

■

Your official biography says that you were born in New York City and studied theater before coming to Hollywood.

I worked as a stage manager, and I studied with the New Theatre League at the New School. I studied the Stanislavsky Method for years—acting and directing—under Brett Warren and Lem Ward (in New York), and later with Lee J. Cobb, J. Edward Bromberg, Morris Carnovsky, and Phoebe Brand in Los Angeles. These were the old Group Theatre people—which brought me full circle, because seeing the Group Theatre, while I was still in high school, is how I became interested in theater.

While I was still a teenager, in New York City, I did some people's theater. We put on a play, for example, for the Transport Workers Union. It was a peace play, just before the Soviet Union was attacked [in 1941]. I took over the stage-managing. June 22 came, and we had to close because we could no longer be pacifist. We had to be more historically framed.

Were you studying art at all during this time?

This was when I was only sixteen to eighteen. I had always wanted to be a painter or a musician, but I had to earn a living first.

Did either of your parents paint or draw?

No. My father was a dentist, and my mother played the stock market, and, in fact, the reason I didn't go on to school was because they wanted me to be a dentist. I could have an education only if I would agree to become a dentist.

The reason you didn't go on to college, you mean?

I also didn't finish high school. That's why I started doing theater at fifteen. I'm a very loyal child, and I don't like to talk about my family, but I'll tell you a little bit, so you understand the context.

There was this hilarious pressure for me to become a dentist. For example, I had to pass "hygiene" in high school, but in order to pass you had to have a piece of paper signed by your parents saying your teeth had been cleaned. My father, who was a Russian-Polish immigrant Jew, was my dentist, and he wouldn't sign the piece of paper unless I agreed to become a dentist. So I left home and started doing theater at fifteen.

I got married to a radio announcer. He knew all about music and theater. That's how I got involved in the theater. Because I was a scholarship student, I had a lot of jobs to do, so I really learned how to put on a production. For example, I booked talent for the New Theatre League.

Who did you book them for?

Mostly unions and organizations. I met people like Marc Blitzstein and Earl Robinson, all the people of that time who were so wonderfully talented. I booked Woody Guthrie. Woody was always so vague—he was very grateful to have a sixteen-year-old girl who could tell him where to go and how much to charge. It was very exciting. I learned a lot from booking. I really got to talk to these people and to ask all sorts of questions about their work and that wonderful period of ferment in the theater.

How did your radical politics and lifestyle spring out of your upbringing?

Through my father—in a negative way. I had joined the American Student Union, as practically anybody with half a brain did, in high school. I was very anti-Fascist. My father had all of these tactics in order to get me to be a dentist, and at one point he came to the school and told school officials that I was a Communist and a prostitute, and I had a bad heart and I never brushed my teeth. It was part of his effort to turn me into a dentist.

I think my parents perceived me as their meal ticket. If only I would become a dentist, I could take over my father's practice and support them in their old age. So they kept turning me in to the FBI. Those kinds of experiences really had a lot to do with my becoming political, because I just had to survive.

As a teenager?

Yeah. We had a peace rally, when I was fourteen, I think. It was in York-ville, this Nazi neighborhood, with all these crazy German ladies and Nazis screaming, "They're dragging the flag on the ground!" The police were called and arrested us.

You make it sound as if you were very together, politically, for a teenager. Was it partly the era, partly New York City?

I was a very fortunate child. I had gone to one of the great public schools, in Hell's Kitchen, and had had wonderful teachers there, quite good teachers, who really taught us, when we were nine, ten, eleven years old, to think. We were told to read everything and anything we could. We could really weigh everything.

It was just a wonderful school. English was a minority language—mostly French, Italian, and Greek were spoken; there were Orientals and blacks; everybody was very poor. I remember that one student was a prostitute. Our teacher said, and I'll remember this until the day I die, "None of you make fun of her. None of you be cruel to her. She had no choice. Her father's an alcoholic; her mother's an alcoholic." I used to walk with her, I was proud to walk with her, and I guess my father saw me doing that and thought I was a prostitute because I was showing solidarity with her.

That's how we were raised at P.S. 17.

How did your marriage come about?

I decided I had to get married to obtain some legal rights, only I had never had a date in my whole life, and I had barely talked to boys. They had a musical quiz on the air at WNYC where if you knew all the answers or could identify the pieces of music you won a free concert ticket. My husband was the host of the show. Because I was shy, and because I had such a passion for music, I gave the answers to my girlfriend and she was picked out of the audience. He invited her to the ballet and later, when he found out it was me who knew the answers, he took me to the ballet.

If things were normal, we would never have gotten married. Marriage kept him out of the Army, and it kept me out of jail.

Obviously such a marriage couldn't work because we were too young. I left him and stayed with some friends in the New Theater movement until my father came to get me with the police. I came home from work one day and at the corner of Forty-sixth Street and Sixth Avenue there was my husband at one corner, and there were my father and two cops at the other. The cops said, "Either you go back to this man, or you go back to your father, or you go to jail." I couldn't figure out what I'd done wrong. I said, "What's my crime?"

Your crime was that you weren't old enough.

I was a little under seventeen.

What did you do?

I went back to my parents. My parents, at least, were a familiar torture, and it was just a matter of waiting it out until I was eighteen. I went to business school, earned money in an office, and worked in the theater at night. My father wanted me to get a divorce and take alimony. I was proud. I had a good brain and a good heart, thanks to P.S. 17, and I said, "I won't take alimony. It's immoral. I won't." So, when I was eighteen, I went to Reno for a divorce.

After you went to Reno and got your divorce, you kept going?

To Los Angeles. I wanted to be as far away from home as possible. The only people I knew there were Carl Lerner, who was working as a machinist, and his wife, Gerda.* This was 1943. I was so ashamed of this failed marriage that I just wanted to serve. My plan was to work in a defense plant till the war was over. I was going to go to school at night. I got a job at a place called Faith Plating. This is still on Santa Monica Boulevard, across the street from Goldwyn. I got fired for being too fast for them. "Slow down and don't be so serious," they said. I said, "There's a war against Fascism, and it is serious. I'm not going to slow down." They gave me three chances, and then they fired me. It was considered a disturbance on the assembly line. Without wishing to make trouble, I was a troublemaker.

So I decided to go into the movie business. One could do training films and learn a craft. I got a job as a waitress across the street from Columbia and applied for a job as a messenger. I waited and waited, and got hired.

It was during the war and the boys were all being drafted, so it was just a matter of time before one could get picked for something else and then could move up. It took about five minutes for any smart girl to figure out what jobs were available. The studio was wide open. You could learn budget and organization. They were training actors like Lloyd Bridges and Larry Parks, who were contract players, as young assistant directors.

Since they might need them as directors because of the war drain?

Possibly. It was a "progressive" studio—because of John Howard Lawson and Sidney Buchman, I guess. I picked Columbia because of Lawson. I knew his book *Theory and Technique of Playwrighting*, and I felt any studio that would hire him would have to be the best studio. There must be people there who could read and write and think. And Sidney Buchman was vice president, so, unlike any other studio, they took young people seriously.

Being a messenger at Columbia was like going to film school, because you could go anyplace, and you were sort of encouraged to ask questions and move up. For example, as a messenger you delivered the mail to the writers' room, so you could talk to all the writers. We kids knew almost as much about the studio as Harry Cohn.

---

*Carl Lerner (1912–1973) was a film editor and political activist who was nerver served with a HUAC subpoena but was blacklisted by his union, IATSE. His editing credits include *Requiem for a Heavyweight*, *Twelve Angry Men*, and *Klute*. He directed *Black Like Me*, with the script adaptation by his wife. Gerda Lerner is a novelist, a textbook author, and a preeminent feminist historian.

Did the studio live up to your expectations?

Yes. I would say I had a very good experience at Columbia, except that I wanted to be a music editor, and the only department, in editing, that would not consider women, oddly enough, was the music department. It was hard to get into the other editing departments, too, but it was possible.

Were you aware of being discriminated against as a female?

Oh, sure. You couldn't be a cameraman or a sound person.

How did they put it?

They just said, "You're a girl." [Laughs.]

Even the progressives?

They were a little more subtle, but same thing. [Editor] Dede Allen was my roommate and still is my dear friend. We both started out as messengers. Dede and I were trying to get hired in editing, and they would say, "No, you can't, because you're a girl." We'd say, "Well, why not?" They'd say, "Well, you're not strong enough." Then we would gain a lot of weight and show them we could lift heavy boxes, and then they would say, "We're not relaxed with you. You don't swear." Then we would practice saying "fuck" and "shit," walking through the studio saying "Fuck shit fuck shit," and then they would say, "That's no way for a girl to talk."

How did the Hollywood movement differ from the East Coast movement?

What I loved about the East Coast movement was that there was little separation between theory and practice. If you believed in people's theater, then you acted it out.

In New York we were very engaged in bringing culture to the people. One of the most exciting things was a project we cooked up with the cultural arm of the CIO where we convinced the Metropolitan Museum to do a history of labor for trade-union members, with parallel slides of what was going on in the history of painting.

In Hollywood there was a double standard. In Hollywood you made a lot of money, and then you helped the people. Even Jack Lawson wanted everyone to make a lot of money.

Was that dichotomy clear from the outset?

It was perfectly clear. I made a commitment to myself to work in the studios for four or five years and learn a craft, because I knew that it would take twice or three times as long to do that in New York at that time. I wanted to have a real strong hands-on background. I wanted to be never afraid of machines. I didn't want to be afraid of anybody. In a funny way I wanted to understand the economics, the budget and management, of the studios, so that I would never be seduced by Hollywood.

The people I really loved in Hollywood were the individuals. I loved Ben Hecht because I loved the movies he made, and I loved the fact that he was not two people; he was clearly one person. When I worked at Republic as a music cutter, because they hired women there, I was assigned to work on *Specter of the Rose*, which was directed by Hecht. I loved George Antheil, a brilliant composer who wrote all the scores for Hecht's movies. George let me cut stock music to make up the score for the film; then he took what I cut and wrote the score. My youngest daughter is named after George. Through him and his wife I met most of the refugees from the European community in Hollywood—Isherwood, Auden, Stravinsky, and so on.

How long did your progression up through the ranks at Columbia last?

A couple of years. I got real pissed when I found out I couldn't be a music cutter because I could read and write music, and most of their music cutters were musically illiterate. When I came to a dead end at Columbia, I went to Goldwyn, then to Republic and a couple of other studios; then I came back to Columbia.

When you went back to Columbia, did they allow you to cut music?

No. I was a script clerk, working script on westerns and the *Blondie* series and the Three Stooges. I seldom worked on anything I didn't really love.

You loved the Three Stooges?

I thought it was very important training—watching them improvise. And they weren't dumb. I tell you, that's something—to do continuity for the Three Stooges when nobody knew what they were going to do next, including them. They were fearless and funny, and they cracked me up.

During all this time in Hollywood, were you doing any painting?

Yes. I took a number of courses at the People's Education Center. I also took screenwriting from Edward Dmytryk, directing from Vincent Sherman, and a class with John Howard Lawson on the history of the American democratic tradition, based on the [Vernon L.] Parrington book [*Main Currents in American Thought*].

The screenwriting course was about the establishment of the status quo, the breaking of the status quo, and about how you resolve the breaking of the status quo on a higher level. [Laughs.] This went on for twelve weeks. *Quel* rip-off! But we took those courses in part because of the gossip. These were the guys working on the creative jobs at the studios, and it was a way for us to find out what was going on. And occasionally we learned something.

This is an example of how the movement was in California; I taught a class in Marxism! I taught a class in my living room to elderly people from the Fairfax neighborhood. I thought they were elderly; they were probably not as old as I am now. They would come and pay attention and listen and say, "Oh, yes, uh-huh . . ." This went on for about eight weeks, at the end of which they gave me a bottle of perfume—the only bottle of perfume anyone had ever bought me, up to that point. Their spokesperson said, "Darling, we didn't understand a word. We only speak Yiddish. But you're so nice. Every week you came, every week you talked to us . . ." [Laughs.]

My painting teacher (whose name I can't remember) looked at my work and told me I was a mixture of Persian miniatures and Milton Avery. I thought I had died and gone to heaven. I said, "Do you think I can paint?" She said, "Of course you can." She was wonderful. She persuaded me to take six months off out of the year, starting in 1945, and receive unemployment while free-lancing, and to use the rest of the time to paint and write and grow. That was my education. I was a young person, and I didn't need that much money. I was making a lot of money anyway, most of which I gave away, and not necessarily to the movement—to anybody who needed it.

Besides showing modern art, Clara Grossman's gallery also had a dandy film society [in Hollywood], the only film society which showed the classic films. The greats would come! Carl Lerner and Dede Allen and I took over Clara's film society, and we did a Russian series, a French series, and an American series. For the American series Irving Lerner was our mentor, so we found all the old documentaries of the 1930s, the independent films of Frontier Films. And we showed some Hollywood classics, like *Our Daily Bread*. We had eight hundred subscriptions.

How and where did you meet John?

I met John in Hollywood during this period, when he was in the Army. People used to say that we had the same smile and that we were apt to make the same jokes in different places. He was walking down Hollywood Boulevard one day, with Sy Wexler, who made educational films in Hollywood during and after the war.

There was Johnny, with his big teeth. I guess everybody has the same number of teeth, but his teeth seemed to jump out from his face. Then I saw his uniform, only it didn't look like a uniform; it was buttoned wrong, very creased. I walked up to Sy and said, "That's John Hubley, isn't it?" He said yes and we were introduced.

We became friends, and we were friends for a long, long time before we were married. We stayed in touch and were involved in projects together. For a while we were trying to do some documentary together, with Ben Maddow, called "The American Crime," I think. It was about lynching and civil rights, but we never made it. That was typical of Hollywood, even with the good folk. Endless dreams!

Were you beginning to think about animation?

I had seen Johnny's stuff at UPA, and I thought in my heart of hearts, while never articulating it, since I knew I was meant to be a painter and I loved the cinema, how lucky he was to be in this art form that was eclectic.

I thought, "Wouldn't it be wonderful to make something out of that art form, something more than meets the eye?"

Did you have a model for your thinking, at all?

No. But in our film society we showed the work of Georges Méliès, which I don't really like, but I like the idea of it because it is fantastical. I loved the avant-garde in France. I always loved surrealism and the experimental film-makers, because that is what we saw in Clara's gallery. There was a film we showed called *Ménilmontant* [1926]. I loved this film. I can't tell you why. It was a surreal film, a lot of action, full of canals and steps, by Dimitri Kirsanoff, a Russian émigré director. It was pretty close to a personal vision. [Laughs.] I just knew that someday I would direct films, and it didn't matter to me whether they were drawn or photographed. I still don't like that division. I just knew I was looking for a medium that would express what I was feeling inside. Don't we all? I knew it would be in film. It wouldn't be at the studios, because they were not set up for art, and I knew I'd have to be patient and work at it, and eventually it would happen.

At the time you met Johnny, he was gone from Disney, right?

Gone from Disney but not necessarily forever. I'm not a specialist on this, but I believe they were told they could come back after the strike, but they didn't want to afterward. By then they had finer things in their brains. At this time, Irving Lerner, who was a pal, had gotten this project to direct a sex-education film for junior-high-school kids. Eddie Albert was the producer, and UPA did the animation of the menstrual cycle.

Eddie Albert the actor? He was a progressive?

As you gather, I have a hard time putting people in boxes. After the war, Eddie Albert thought Hollywood was dreadful, and he wanted to spend the rest of his life trying to do something useful. He wanted to make educational films, so he got the money to do this film. Irving was to be the director.

It was a struggle to make that film. We were so broke at one point that I had to hand-code the whole film with a bottle of white ink. We worked like dogs on the boring live action. Johnny did the animation with UPA. He created this luminous body that looked like a Georgia O'Keeffe painting—it was beautiful.

It was a very successful film. It is the only documentary I know of that had to be remade because the clothing styles changed—so they reshot it fifteen years later. It was a historic film.

At the end of this period, in 1947, the House Un-American Activities Committee (HUAC) came to Hollywood, and I gather that you and Johnny were eventually both blacklisted.

Johnny was. I wasn't. His being blacklisted was just proof positive of how absurd the whole thing was.

How did Johnny find out that he was no longer employable?

I'll tell you what little I know. Johnny had to leave UPA, but I know he could have done a payoff at some point and continued to work for Columbia. Only he didn't. For one thing, it was too much money. A lot of people were offered [the chance to make] payoffs, and some could afford it, some couldn't, and some just said no. So Johnny was, as he put it, "on the lam."

What was your situation?

I was free-lancing. I had two goals: I wanted to edit one picture before I left California, and I got to edit Irving's picture. And I wanted to be a script clerk on one really expensive Hollywood movie with a lot of people and a lot of management. So through the union I got this job on a film called *Heaven Only Knows*, a two-million-dollar picture, which was at the time considered very expensive.

It was a western with special effects, Brian Donlevy, Robert Cummings, and a cast of thousands. When I finished with that job, it was time for me to do something else in life. I was still booking the next film series, which was the most important part of my life other than painting. But I hadn't clearly decided to leave Hollywood. I went back East for a vacation, and then I decided not to go back to Los Angeles because I just didn't feel like it. I was given to quixotic whims.

Did your decision have anything to do with the blacklist?

Maybe. New York was fun.

Had the blacklist started? Was this before the October, 1947 hearings?

It was on the cusp. I remember going down to Washington and helping friends in New York. I just wanted to work in New York. And mostly I wanted to go to Europe. I also wanted to work on a serious, heavy documentary, and I became Leo Hurwitz's assistant on *Strange Victory*. It's an interesting film, about how the war victory wasn't really a victory.

Did you finally go to Europe?

After I finished my work on *Strange Victory*, I went to Paris and then to this International Conference of Working Youth in Poland. The first thing that happened when we got to Poland was we all had to march through Warsaw; then we went to this church where, amid all these rococo angels, a priest gave his blessing to the international youth! [Laughs.] This conference was amazing. I will never forget it. It changed my life, grew me up.

At this conference we got to meet working youth from all over the whole wide world. We learned there was such a place as Vietnam! There were children who were working in the mines whom we could talk to about their working conditions.

Then I had made this promise to myself, way back in the messenger room of Columbia, that because I was a lucky girl who grew up in Hollywood, I owed the world something. I had pledged to work on a reconstruction brigade one day. And at the end of this conference, they asked, "Does anybody want to work on a railroad in Czechoslovakia?" and I raised my hand.

Really? For how long?

We dug trenches, and we laid railroad ties—for three weeks. I got a medal for bravery! [Laughs.]

Because the average age for girls on this international brigade might have been seventeen, I felt very maternal. We were working in a valley surrounded by huge hills. One day I saw this boulder coming down the mountain toward the trenches, and there was no stopping it and not enough time to jump out of the way. I saw this young girl who was going to get hit by the boulder, and I threw her aside and put my body between her and the boulder. I got hit, and I still have the scar. [She shows the scar.] After they cleaned up the blood we sang anthems; then they gave me flowers and awarded me a medal.

Then you came back to New York?

No, no, no. I went to Prague. Later when I was running out of money, I went to Rome, contracted meningitis and nearly died, spent four months in a clinic, and nearly lost my vision. Afterward I bopped around Italy with a friend of mine, wrote a screenplay about the Mafia with Basilio Franchina, whom I had met, went to a lot of movies, met a lot of people. I had the best time.

Was this the first writing you had done?

Yes. Because these near-death experiences made me feel as though life was not forever. Then I went to a Peace Congress in Paris and spent four months in Paris [at the Cinémathèque Française], as part of what I consider my home-made education, looking at movies and reading books.

My mother cabled me that I had a job waiting for me back in New York on a feature that was going to be shot. The director, Bernard Vorhaus, was blacklisted. So I came home and worked on Bernie's picture about delinquent girls, *So Young, So Bad*, with Anne Francis, Anne Wallach [Jackson], Rita Moreno, and Paul Henreid. I script-clerked it, in short order I became an assistant cutter, and before long I was editing a feature called *Go, Man, Go!* about the Harlem Globetrotters, directed by [cinematographer] Jimmy [James] Wong Howe.

Where was Johnny all this time?

In Hollywood. What he did as a solution to the blacklist was to set up a commercial company, Storyboard, and he started making a lot of money doing commercials. He had a front man, but he was making it big. The front was getting the business and signing the contracts. But everybody in town knew it was Johnny doing the commercials. They were good commercials, by the way—among other things, it was Johnny who brought jazz to commercials.

Ah, so he was the big jazz enthusiast.

Well, I was a jazz enthusiast too. Anyway, he had started to gain as much weight as he was making money.

Why?

Why do people overeat? Probably because he was unhappy. He was buying expensive clothes, and he looked like hell. Here was this really good-looking, wonderful-looking man—now he was fat and overdressed and drinking too much and miserable. I started writing him letters telling him he needed to get out and move to New York.

Then Johnny was hired by [lyricist] Yip [E. Y.] Harburg to do *Finian's Rainbow* as an animated feature. But Johnny was a fella who was famous for never being on budget, and certainly never being on schedule. So Yip, whom I knew from my youth in Hollywood, asked me if I would be Johnny's assistant in Los Angeles.

I said I had to think about it and asked if he had talked to Johnny. He said, "No, but everybody knows Johnny loves you and you love Johnny." I said, "That's different. That's friendship. You have to ask him." So Johnny was in New York doing something on *Finian's Rainbow*, and we met. He said he wasn't sure I should come to Los Angeles because we both knew that we had controlled our friendship for ten years, and after all, he was a married man with three kids. But we decided I would take the job, and so I went to Los Angeles again.

Then the picture blew up. All the preparations were done, the storyboarding was done, the score was recorded, the animation was in progress; we went out to lunch one day and came back, and there was a padlock on the door. That was it. The official word was the blacklist. They said it was because of Johnny. But I think it had something to do with some power struggle among the backers of *Finian's Rainbow*.

How far along was the film?

The sound track and all the dialogue were finished—it had Frank Sinatra singing "Necessity" and "Old Devil Moon" and Ella Fitzgerald and beautiful Louie [Louis] Armstrong, all kinds of great people, doing jazz versions of the songs. There are bootleg records of this track.

I am surprised someone like Frank Sinatra was willing to work with you, even though he must have known that Johnny was blacklisted.

Oh, Frank was always okay.

Lionel Stander once told me Sinatra was the only actor he knew who not only read
Marx but could comprehend it.

Frank was and still is partly wonderful. I know the things that he does for
people, and it's not all sentiment. He is trapped. He made a mistake with the
Mafia, and I don't think he had any choice after that. He was naive, and he
was captured by the Establishment.

But if we talk about politics in a profound way, I think Frank lived out his
politics. One can get shot for saying this, but Frank practices a lot that is
decent, and never mind who he endorses, politically, because he has no damn
choice. There isn't a jazz musician in need in this country who hasn't been
helped by him.

So . . . after Finian's Rainbow?

Then we went off to Europe on a trial marriage. We thought we should
travel together first. And we fought and fought and fought, but we did find
out that there is such a thing as a middle road, so we decided we were going
to get married. Johnny went off to get his divorce, which was hard, but he
did. This was 1955. Johnny opened up a New York office of Storyboard and
soon after sold the Los Angeles one.

That seems like quite a leap.

At the time it seemed simple. I didn't know all about doubt and uncer-
tainty; all I knew was that this was the luckiest moment in my life, and that
one could influence the outcome of one's life if one was clear about what one
wanted to do. When you're so in love, anything seems possible. I'm sure it
was different for Johnny—he's not here to tell his side of the story—and I
do know he was crushed by *Finian's Rainbow* exploding.

Everything seems a greater leap for him, greater than for you, since you had always
been more on the fringe.

I've got to stop talking about Johnny, because he isn't here to talk for
himself, and the anniversary of his death is coming up, and if I don't stop I'll
start to cry.

His grandfather was a painter from England, and everybody laughed at his
grandfather because he didn't make his money brewing beer like other members of the family. He was a beautiful spirit, an oddball, and he gave Johnny
his brushes and easels. Clearly, Johnny loved this man, and his love for him
was like a sustaining force.

Johnny never finished art school, because the Disney seducers came around
and offered him money and training. But he was always open. He always knew
there was more to life than Disney and being clever in Hollywood, and he
had a very profound feeling about art and literature and music. He always
thought there was something beyond, something around the corner, that he
was missing.

But wasn't it your influence, initially, that pulled him in such a radical direction?

It's broader than that. I think moving to New York was the big question. Moving out of the small industry town to where there is an intellectual and social life in the true sense of the word. I think, if you look at Johnny's evolution as a human being, his coming to New York, where he led a pretty isolated life as a pioneer in his chosen art form, allowed him to revive his goals. There was a pull. But for him to leave his whole past life and move to New York, where, in the beginning, he felt a lot like a country yokel, was very courageous.

Now, it was never total, he needed support and a lot of push, but I don't want to underestimate what he brought to it in the beginning, because from the beginning he was adventurous. He was a Renaissance person and always hungry.

How did you envision your partnership at the outset?

When Johnny and I got married, and we wrote our wedding vows, the agreement stated that we would make one short film a year and eat with our children. We would really try to have a family, meaning we would eat at home and share and be regular human beings, which is not the way people in Hollywood raise their families.

How did you finance your early avant-garde animation?

To begin with, Johnny had a commission on the way from the Guggenheim, to make *Adventures of an Asterisk*, a film about a child's vision. We had just had a new baby, and we tried hard to capture all that intensity in this film. The film turned out to be a visual experience about the vision of a little child, which is so pure and so wonderful, about how what is perceived by those eyes for the first time is tactile and felt, and about how that pure vision, as the child slowly grows in society, is made to follow certain rules.

For us, on a personal level, it was like starting over, because we were a new couple, newly partners, with this new baby.

It was a metaphor for your own careers.

Exactly. I've never enjoyed anything as much, and that enjoyment, that new release of energy, was sustained for five or ten years.

Were there other grants and commissions over the years?

Johnny and I never got a grant in our whole married life. Not one. *Moonbird*, for example, we financed ourselves, and it took about twenty-five years to pay off and only now is it making a little bit of money. There were some commissions, certainly; they would not be vast sums of money, not like in advertising, but it was money. And if UNICEF commissions one to make a film about how hunger affects the world's children, that's like performing your social obligation and getting paid for it.

I gather you have always done a little moonlighting.

In the beginning, I continued to work in live action for financial reasons, working on *Twelve Angry Men* and other movies, and also to give Johnny a little breathing space. Johnny kept up his commercial activity in New York, and I hated advertising, and I still do, with such a passion. I would've thrown those people out of my office.

Then along came Markie Maypo, which was different. [Laughs.] Are you old enough to remember Markie Maypo?

It rings a bell.

This was an amazing advertising phenomenon. Maypo was a cereal made by a little company in Vermont which was bought by a liquor company, Heublein, to offset their profits. The company wanted to do a commercial that was a non-commercial. So we did a commercial about this little boy wearing a cowboy hat who hates the cereal and goes "Yuck!" and his father has to force-feed him—"Here comes the airplane!" We named him Markie, after our son, who did the voice. It was a little one-minute documentary on feeding a child. And it took off, though it wasn't supposed to. It was supposed to not sell the product! We got paid a lot of money and were able to finance at least half of *Moonbird*. We lived from film to film like that for a very long time, until we began work on a feature [*Of Stars and Men*] on which we ended up owing an awful lot of money.

It seems to me that when you and John were working together, ironically, you had more of an upper hand when it came to actually choosing the subject matter, in the sense that, given his background as a more traditional and commercial animator, the films you began to work on seemed to spring more out of your sensibility. Privately, it seems, you were very—if not dominant, at least very assertive in terms of what you were doing together, and that's one of the things that kept John on track.

I think I have a natural ability to enthuse. It's genuine. I have to believe in what I'm doing, and when I have that enthusiasm, it's irresistible. So I think that's what happened, although, being flexible, we couldn't work around a theme until we found that part of the theme which Johnny felt good about, and that's what made the collaboration very strong.

Why were you, and are you, so opposed to a narrative form?

For my taste, I think the obligation of animation is to deal with material that live action can't, and to look for that form and content which is beyond an actor, which is beyond the adaptation of even a very fine book.

Was it easier to be abstract than to be linear, to go from A to B to C to D?

It was easier because a lot of it was free association. But if a film took us a year to make, six months of that time we spent working from the interior out.

How did your collaboration work, in terms of the initial writing?

It just evolved very naturally. We would discuss the structure; then we would each do a draft. The rule of the game was that if there was anything that either of us was violently opposed to, it was just out the window. You could fight for something you really loved a lot, but if the other person really hated it, you had to give it up. After a while, there would be something like three or four pieces of tape on a roll with John's name or my name, pieces that we had given up but really hadn't given up in our heart of hearts, hoping that when the whole thing was put together, maybe the other person would change his or her mind.

How much of what we see in the joint Hubley films are your own drawings?

Hard to say. Less than half. We would get the visual expression together, even if a lot of it was done in the privacy of our boudoir, then Johnny would usually do the amalgam. Especially in the films that deal with children or are about being a mother—I knew how certain things should look—but Johnny knew animation. Having had all the Stanislavsky training, I also had really strong feeling for how the characters should act, in some cases. Because it was not just drawing, it was character analysis, writing with the characters.

The story and the storyboard, how the picture looked, were joint. It was a two-people vision. Even though Johnny was a better artist and certainly had all this experience, I was like a primitive working with somebody who was very trained. There were great advantages.

There wasn't anything in the picture we didn't discuss together, but there was a conflict between the public and private image. The private image was fine. Working together was no problem; we could argue, yet have a healthy, strong collaboration. Whereas the public image was more Johnny. Johnny would do the public end, the handing out of the work to other people, till we got back to the editing at the end. That coincided with my training in live action because I had worked with a lot of directors.

The meeting with the animator, and the hand-out of the animation, is very crucial, because even though you have all the drawings, you need to communicate the timings, and the animator has to understand the spirit of the film. That is what the director explains. That was always private between Johnny and the animator, with the exception of Bill Littlejohn, because sometimes, especially on *Carousel*, I wanted to act out some of the characters.

I gather Johnny was always doctoring your scenes.

Yes, which made me feel very inferior. He was the senior artist, and he was ten years older. The turning point for me was *Carousel*, because I was sick by then and there were certain passages that I painted, really in my own hand, and which [for the first time] Johnny didn't change, or didn't doctor.

You were sometimes treated like a pupil. On the other hand, what a good school to be going to!

That's right. On balance, it was all okay. The big question was sharing the directing credit which happened for the first time on *Cockaboody* [in 1973]. It was the first time I ever got [an official] cocredit, a codirecting credit, which was very upsetting to him. It was difficult for Johnny to share as much as he had to. Later on, of course, Johnny began to change of his own accord.

Is there a way you can generalize for me the Hubley technique and approach, in animation, as opposed to the more traditional ways and means?

This is a good chance to say something that has to be said: Johnny was not an animator. Johnny was a designer-director. For years, we were scrupulous about saying, "No, we don't animate." An animator draws meticulously and makes this magic of things moving and turning and taking shape. Bill Littlejohn animates, or Shamus Culhane animates. We design and are filmmakers.

You should explain the difference to me.

There isn't a word for an animated filmmaker, but they're really two things. There's animation, the craft, and there's animation, making the whole film. In the Disney studios the craft people were the animators. Disney knew exactly what he was doing when he emphasized the craft separation so that nobody would have the filmmaking power; that's not only a political observation, it's an artistic one. People who did animation would start at Disney as little apprentices and spend fifteen years learning to do "in between," and if they lived long enough or were lucky enough to become animators, they would think they were at a pinnacle. Johnny, at Disney, was a background painter and a layout artist.

For the uninitiated, what is layout as opposed to background?

Layout is like staging a scene, designing how the scene is going to move, the action. But the layout person would probably have nothing to do with the sound, for example; he would just take the drawings from the storyboard artist and say, "How does this scene work?" It's like being a second-unit director. It's not conceptual.

So Walt Disney was really the filmmaker.

Absolutely. And he didn't allow other people to make films, and that's really what the strike [in mid-1941] was about, I think, about money and conditions and the control of the films.* To these young men Disney was

---

*A strike at the Disney studio, from May to August 1941, began after Walt Disney fired six animators, part of a group organizing the cartoonists toward affiliation with Herbert Sorrell's painters' union. Disney hated the nascent Screen Cartoonists Guild and refused to submit to collective bargaining with the Guild. A strike vote prompted Disney to launch an extended lockout. Mediators settled the bitter strike with the Screen Cartoonists Guild as bargaining agent, but the labor purges of the later 1940s sapped the Cartoonists Guild, and Disney em-

king, a god, and they had to kill the king in order to make artists of them-selves. It was amazing to me, because I remember how, after old Walt died, I couldn't believe my husband and [director of Famous Studios] Bill Tytla were sitting around watching television, talking about Disney with tears in their eyes. And I was thinking, "I thought this was the enemy!"

How would you generalize about the differences between the Disney style of ani-mation and the technology and the technique that you pioneered on a small scale?

The big change was that we figured out how to make films in a very small space. It's as simple as that—personal films that required half a dozen people.

From a technical point of view, since John didn't have to deal with the studio, he didn't have to use conventional ways, so we could do anything we wanted to do. Anything! We explored reticulation and paper as a medium, and it was the beginning of eliminating the hard cel and the hard line that I've always felt was ugly.

And cel animation is, was, inhibiting. One would have to have a certain kind of skill to do it as handmade mass production. I'm not a specialist in it; I just know I hate it—I hate the way it looks, and I don't like the feel of it. I hate the hard edge, and I don't see why anyone should learn to be tidy. I am a bit of a slob, and I like a free-flowing line and texture. That was our contribution, aside from content and the amazing changes in sound, using children, using jazz and wonderful composers, using improvisation—to lib-erate animation from itself, and to go to watercolors and to paint pastels. It was a big, big liberation and was resisted by the industry.

Your sources for films—from Harlow Shapley to Erik H. Erikson—are so, for want of a better word, esoteric. Is there any way you can generalize for me where you sought and derived your intellectual inspiration?

Remember, we had this ten-year friendship, followed by a very brief and intense courtship. The floodgates opened during the courtship, and we dis-covered that we both had always had this feeling about science. You know, for example, that Johnny always wanted to do the story of Galileo's life. He did the stage design for the Los Angeles production [directed by Bertolt Brecht and Joseph Losey] and helped block the scenes.

It was like being kids again, and we started asking each other what we really wanted to do in life. A lot of what we really wanted to do revolved around taking the ideas that were new, the emerging visions of the planet—which were being presented to the public in very technical jargon, almost in another language, a high-priest form—and breaking down the gulf between insiders and outsiders. It was a shared obsession. We wanted to be that bridge. I think we had very hungry minds.

---

ployees affiliated with IATSE. Some of Disney's most creative artists left him, as a consequence of the original strike. See Marc Eliot, *Walt Disney: Hollywood's Dark Prince.*

One of the things that strike me about your films is their relationship to jazz. They are very sensory, and you can let them wash over you and really enjoy them, and sometimes feel more than know something about what they are trying to tell you.

They're physical, almost like a good massage.

And, of course, some of them have such fabulous jazz soundtracks. I want to ask you about the jazz people, like Benny Carter and Dizzy Gillespie. When and where did you meet them? You've had such a long collaboration with both of them.

Benny I met independently of Johnny the first year I was in Hollywood. We were trying to raise money for an interracial hospital, and this classical pianist named Lucille asked me if I would go backstage with her to ask Benny Carter for some money. I said, "Of course!" Because, growing up in Hell's Kitchen, where there was a lot of jazz in the street, there was nothing more beautiful to me than a horn player.

When Johnny and I did our first film, *Adventures of an Asterisk*, there was no question that Benny would do the score. In fact, once he wrote a feature for us called "American Jazz," about the history of American jazz—a love story with two abstract characters. But we never made it, because we couldn't raise the money.

At one point, when we first got married and had these explosions of feelings, we did a film called *Date with Dizzy*, which is a live-action film, a satire on advertising. That was one of the first times we worked with Dizzy Gillespie. It had live action and some animation. We shot it in one day, and we had so much fun. An advertising agency paid for it. I'll never know why. It's an underground treasure, a record of Dizzy in 1957.

I gather you and Johnny were both profoundly influenced by the leading art of your generation, that is, by the surrealists and the modernists, the leading French painters.

Picasso, very strongly, for Johnny. For me, more Paul Klee and Miró. I was influenced by the side of them which is primitive and childlike and by how they allowed that to stay a part of their sophisticated vision. I like the directness and the passion of a child's vision.

You see, Johnny, in his heart of hearts, was a surrealist. John's humor and his interior were totally surreal. So once he perceived that life was getting short, that there wasn't much time left, the surrealism became dominant, or he wouldn't have survived. It was a joy for him to let go of "boy meets girl" and all of the rules of the game.

What was difficult, because there were difficulties, was in making a film like *Stars and Men* [in 1961], which I still think is a beautiful film, finishing it, and putting everything we had in the whole wide world into it, borrowing the money to finish it, having critical acclaim from Bosley Crowther of the *New York Times*, and then no distributor. Johnny would say, "I don't want to be an educator. I want to be seen."

Why did you feel the need to take the financial and creative risk of a feature?

Johnny always wanted to handle a longer length. And we wanted to do something that related to the marriage of science and art. Then we read this book by Harlow Shapley, *Of Stars and Men*, which was an overview of evolution. Dr. Shapley thought the next stage of evolution was psychic and that we had to start preparing for it. The first thing we had to do was stop destroying the planet and get rid of weapons; then we really had to work on new development, and he went through a kind of history of Western science to make that statement.

Of Stars and Men was a wonderful film. It played for all of a week in New York and then totally disappeared. We ended up owing all this money, which we eventually paid off, but it left Johnny with a sense of incompletion, because I think he really wanted it to succeed.

That haunted him. As time went by there were more debts, and there were more children. There was a middle period of work, including *Tijuana Brass*, which won the Academy Award, which is not our best work. It was commissioned by Herb Alpert and his partners, and they're lovely people. But the film represented, artistically, the compromise of those years.

Was Johnny giving voice to this compromise? Was it a struggle between you, behind the scenes, or was it inarticulate?

It was half and half. I know it was something we used to talk about. It coincided with a period when we had a policy not to do commercials, and we were doing a lot of stuff for the Children's Television Workshop—*The Electric Company* and *Sesame Street*—which was like a refined form of one-minute commercials, selling education to children. But it's not work from the heart, and I think, if you do a lot of it, it corrodes the eyes. There were some nice films during this period, like *Eggs*, but generally there was a lot of effort to launch features.

For example, we tried to do *Gulliver's Travels* with Ben Maddow. Johnny and Ben were best friends; probably Ben was Johnny's only close friend.

Yet this was after it became known that Ben Maddow had cooperated with HUAC. Wasn't that awkward or painful, considering that John himself had been blacklisted?

No, the painful part is what Ben did. I always find this discussion very interesting, because I don't believe in permanent guilt. There are some people I'll never talk to because I don't really like them. But I feel some people were victims—they were weak, and they became victims—and I believe they punish themselves enough, so I don't have to punish them.

When I worked on *Twelve Angry Men* as script clerk, I would be on the set with Lee J. Cobb. Now, I had been at Cobb's studio as a student, and we had a very deep relationship; I babysat for him and his wife, Helen, when he went into the Army, and I stayed with her. And on the set Lee would look at me and burst into tears and say, "How can you sit there looking at me? Who ever thought that I would be this disgusting person and you would be watching me?" So [director] Sidney Lumet and Henry Fonda would say, "Take that script and go hide!" There was no pleasure in that.

I didn't hate Lee. Later on, I went to see him backstage in New York when he was in *King Lear*, and I'm glad I did, because he died shortly thereafter. I told him he had given a wonderful performance, and he said, "You can't think I am wonderful. How can you? I am nothing. I am disgusting." I said, "Look, that was twenty years ago. . . ."

In Ben's case the blacklist probably came up, but I don't think we talked about it, and if we did start to talk about it, the subject was changed. Somehow, the idea of working together had come up, and at the time it seemed pleasurable.

Perhaps it is easier for you to forgive the excesses of the blacklist because you left Hollywood behind, and you have said to me that you were not really blacklisted, per se, whereas Johnny was.

And Johnny had a sense of loss about it. On the other hand, and I know this sounds totally irreverent, I think Johnny's life was made by the blacklist. I really believe that. It was very harmful to him, of course, but in a practical way it got him out of being a successful director in the studio system and into being an independent, and I don't think that would have happened otherwise.

What about Watership Down? *I know that sometime during the later stages of production John was relieved, in some fashion, as director. I am puzzled by the name Martin Rosen, someone I have never heard of as an animator, who is credited as director.*

He was our agent.

He's not an animator?

No. He asked us if we'd do *Watership Down* with himself as producer. I read the book, and I didn't like it and said I wouldn't do it. Johnny said he liked the book—I think he genuinely liked it—and this was his chance to do a picture and get paid very well. It was a bona fide offer, but it meant giving up his independence.

Martin came to see me. By this time I was a terminal cancer patient and I had all the freedom that you think you have when you're going to die soon. I said, with some rancor, "This doesn't interest me." He said, "Would Johnny do it without you?" and I said, "Ask him." It was a hard time for everybody; we had family discussions about it, and finally I said, "Johnny, you held out all these years; you've been a good pop, a good partner, and if you really feel this is what you want to do, you have a right to do it." He took the job and went to live in London. I ran the studio, and he would come back at intervals and stay for a week or two and help out.

Johnny was trying to live in both worlds, and I don't know, maybe it can be done, but he got sicker and sicker while he was commuting, and then he had a minor heart attack. I think *Watership Down* was ready to be mixed when I came over for a week of vacation and we went to Norway.

He was getting sick, and you had been diagnosed with terminal cancer.

Right. What a romantic couple! When that vacation was over, I flew to Venice, where we had spent many, many happy summers and where John was going to meet me and the two girls for one last weekend before going home, and he called up from London and told us he had been fired. For a person of Johnny's mentality, a kind of perfectionist, a golden boy, being fired was devastating.

What was the creative basis of the dispute?

It had nothing to do with creativity.

You told me that, previous to Watership Down, *there was a final period of working together which ended with an artistic flourish.*

It started with *Eggs*, when Johnny's spirit was returning, and for my taste it continued with *Voyage to Next*, the last short film we made together. By then I was sick, and there was the major work *Everybody Rides the Carousel* [in 1976]. It was commissioned by CBS during a period when they must have been under some pressure to do something decent for families and especially for children, and it is based on Erik Erikson's life cycle in *Childhood and Society*. It was just before *Watership Down*, it's seventy-two minutes long, and it's wonderful, though it wasn't a theatrical film, and it did have educational overtones.

I can remember when we finished it and we took it to Cape Cod, where Erik and Joan Erikson lived, for a showing at a lovely little theater. The last stage of the film is about the old age of wisdom, and we ended the film with the metaphor of a merry-go-round, this carousel, with the last horse going off into the fields to die. I had practiced learning death, or befriending death, and I remember sitting next to Johnny and starting to cry at the end because it was like I was saying good-bye to everybody. It was so ironic, in a way, that Johnny died, and I was supposed to die and didn't.

You and John had actually started work on The Cosmic Eye, *am I right?*

We had started a project with Carl Sagan, which I later turned into *The Cosmic Eye*. If we had gotten the money for "The Cosmic Concert," as we were calling it then, we would not have done *A Doonesbury Special*. *Doonesbury* was the backup if "The Cosmic Concert" didn't get financed. But if we had done "The Cosmic Concert," John was going to let me do one, maybe two, sequences of my own as part of what he called my "witch act"—because he didn't go along with all this mythology.

And spirituality and metaphysicality.

He thought it was interesting, and privately he would say to Bill Littlejohn, "She has something none of us know about, and we should let her go with it." So Johnny and I signed the contract for *Doonesbury*. We did the storyboard, Garry [Trudeau] wrote the script, we recorded the tracks, and then we took a vacation—after which Johnny went into the hospital for this so-called simple bypass and never came out. He hemmorrhaged and died on the table.

Can I ask you about your own illness? I understand you were diagnosed with terminal cancer many years ago.

In 1974 the first lumps were found. I was teaching the storyboard class with Johnny at Yale, preparing *Voyage to Next*. I'm not going to say cancer is fun; it isn't. But it has been an opportunity for growth. On occasion, I would have my sessions with students in the doctor's waiting room, which in a way was wonderful for them because, especially in the seventies, cancer wasn't talked about. The students would practice telling their storyboards to the other patients, so that in a sense they were practicing performing and getting other people's input. I could almost see the room change from a funeral parlor to a place with a real life force.

I had a mastectomy, and the initial assumption was that everything was going to be fine. Then, after the operation, my doctor said, "I think you should have radiation." Then, after I had radiation, I went in for a checkup and he said, "I don't like your lymph count. It's terrible. Take a deep breath, because I think you have to start preparing to die. I would give you, if I were being generous, a year, and if I weren't being generous, six months."

So for a while I was just living six months at a time. A lump was found in the remaining breast, and my doctor's partner told me he was going to book me a hospital room to have my other breast taken off. And I said no. I felt that it was just stress-connected, and that I was too mixed up about everything in life, and that what I really needed was a rest. So I rented a cabin in Maine and went away for a month in the summertime, leaving Johnny with the children. When I came back, the lump was gone. I changed my eating habits a lot, I had this very strong Italian chemotherapy program, and I kept growing more lumps, which I kept making go away, or they would turn out to be benign.

Up until Johnny's death I was still in and out of the hospital, with these lumps coming and going. The last time I was in the hospital was 1977. After that, I just went back every six months for checkups. After about ten years, they took me off the list of the doomed. I'm just now beginning to think I'll live. It's only in the last year that I have decided to plan for old age.

How did John's death and being diagnosed with terminal cancer influence what you began to do as a filmmaker, individually, without John?

There's something about accepting mortality that gives one courage. It certainly stood me up straight.

Finishing *Doonesbury* without John was honestly the hardest thing I've ever had to do in my whole life. I had to deliver one sequence at a time to NBC and go through censors and committees, and all the time suffering from cancer. They were trying to fire me because I was a mere woman. Garry was very, very supportive. It was just a horrendous period.

But, to be serious, I felt I had no choice. I could not afford to be unafraid. I could not threaten to commit suicide, because I was already dying. Every neurotic behavior pattern was just cut off.

How did facing death affect your subsequent choice of material?

I had always felt that every film had to make a statement, a serious statement, but now I felt I could waste no time. I felt very guilty about "The Cosmic Concert" after Johnny died, but I made the people take their money and go away. Yet I didn't want to give up the idea entirely, because I still wanted to do a long piece that was a continuation of *Of Stars and Men*, about how creatures from another planet must view us.

In time I finished *Whither Weather*, a film about the effects of weather on our planet. Then the Year of the Child inspired *Step by Step*, which dealt with the history of child abuse, the condition of the earth's children, and what their yet-to-be-gained rights are. After *The Big Bang and Other Creation Myths* and *Sky Dance*, I began to see how I could shape these elements into a feature film. I planned *Hello* as a short which would work as the climax, and in this roundabout fashion, after ten years, I completed *The Cosmic Eye*.

Has it been a problem, distributing as well as financing your films?

Most of the time. It has been up and down, down and up, up and down.

Would they ever be shown with Hollywood movies?

In the past, rarely. *Windy Day* played with *The Odd Couple*, I think. *Of Men and Demons* played with something, but I don't remember what. My film *Hello* played with [Bertrand] Tavernier's *Sunday in the Country* at the Paris Theater [in New York], and that was nice, although I received no fee. Since then, promises but no distribution.

Isn't that discouraging?

No, I swear I don't care.

Isn't that a paradox? To make movies that are about things which people should become aware of, or think about, or become concerned about, but the films do not reach them?

It's a paradox. But how much can you do? I know a lot of filmmakers, and Johnny used to be one of them, who would go to waste worrying about that paradox. You can't really lose your life's blood agonizing over the state of money or distribution. Either it will get better or it will get worse; it's out of our control. All we can do is do our best work.

But it sounds like it always got bad or worse—never really better.

But something would always come along. Nowadays I run into second-generation people who say, "You know, that film changed my whole life!" So maybe it was shown through churches or in schools or at a lot of Sunday schools; I really don't know. But the quality of the viewing was so serious that it could really touch a fellow human being. And the quality of an audience is much more important than the numbers.

That's not a very populist viewpoint.

Well, I'm not a very populist person.

That sounds elitist.

I don't think so. What I mean is, it's not the quality of the audience, it's the quality of the contact with the audience. If a film is shown in a quiet place where people can really see it once or twice, and think about it and talk about it, and contribute their personae to the film, if there are ten such people seeing the film, then to me that is worth more than twenty thousand in a big movie house. But I think all good ideas, and this applies to science, religion, philosophy, or politics, are shared first, intensely, and then it is exponential dissipation, or communication. I think that we're very misled by the electromagnetic force into thinking that we have to be on a screen simultaneously everywhere at once.

I believe my situation is changing, maybe because of the availability of the Disney home-video cassettes. In any case, maybe because I'm older and wiser, I don't lose energy agonizing over why there aren't more audiences in the United States. One has to have a personal adjustment and a social adjustment. My social adjustment is one of rage, and my personal adjustment is one that enables me to work.

For example, I've just begun work on a new short titled *Amazonia*, which presents two South American myths and a shaman's warning that we must save the vanishing rain forest. I will share the experience of developing the storyboard with my students at Yale this semester, who will in turn design their own visual pleas on behalf of the rain forest. If I stopped working to think about the problems of distribution or where I will find the rest of the budget of *Amazonia*, I would be paralyzed.

One of the things that I'm so grateful to Johnny about is that he was really brave and walked out on the mainstream. His insistence that the medium could handle—"handle" is the wrong word—that it could express much more has, I think, taken animation down a different road than the main one, in other directions. I am continuing down that road. It's a long way from growing up in Hollywood and what we thought then or what we perceived.

My choice as a working artist is not to play to the marketplace. It's not because I don't know how. I've chosen another path. As hard as my life is, and it is hard without Johnny, I wake up every morning, and I can't wait to get to work.

Marsha Hunt

MARSHA HUNT, Sherman Oaks, California, 1997

INTERVIEW BY GLENN LOVELL

■

ON CUE, MARSHA Hunt—who once earned the appellation "Hollywood's youngest character actress"—could be tough (as a nightclub singer in *Lost Angel*), flirtatious (as a wartime secretary in *A Letter for Evie*), stalwart (as a Polish teacher in *None Shall Escape*), bookish (as one of the quintet of unmarried sisters in *Pride and Prejudice*), spoiled and kooky (as a sympathetic socialite in *The Human Comedy*), or even vaguely sinister (the exotic "other woman" in *Smash-Up*). Given different circumstances, would she ever have become a full-fledged movie star? We'll never know.

Marsha Hunt was not among the Hollywood Nineteen or the Hollywood Ten. She was not even subpoenaed by the House Committee on Un-American Activities. Nothing so decisive or melodramatic was in store for this former fashion model and Paramount and MGM contract player. She ruffled feathers by simply being herself—articulate, involved, a passionate defender of minority rights, and, eventually, a Screen Actors Guild activist. Instead of being hauled before government inquisitors, Hunt, like others who protested from the wings, became the victim of innuendo and—most demoralizing—the Byzantine politics of her own union.

Following a stint as a Guild board member—during which she crossed swords with SAG founder and deep-dyed conservative Robert Montgomery—Hunt participated in the much-publicized October 1947 flight to Washington, D.C., with Humphrey Bogart, Lauren Bacall, John Huston, and other prominent members of the Committee for the First Amendment. The plan was to thumb their noses at HUAC and press home the point that the Hollywood community stood foursquare behind the Nineteen summoned by the tribunal. In Hunt's words, they flew to Washington "to reassure an alarmed public that movies were not, as charged, filled with subversive red propaganda."

It didn't work out that way. Immediately upon returning to Hollywood, Bogart, who had been called on the carpet by Warner Brothers, renounced the flight as "ill-advised." Hunt made no such public apology, and thus, though she had never so much as poked her head into a Party meeting, she became what Victor Navasky in *Naming Names* classified as "a guilty bystander."

In June 1950, on the heels of her return to Broadway starring in George Bernard Shaw's *The Devil's Disciple** and a newfound popularity as a guest on radio and television talk shows, Hunt's name appeared with 150 others in the pamphlet *Red Channels,* which targeted individuals in broadcasting. Listed under her name was an itemization of the leftist petitions she had signed, the anti-HUAC gatherings she had attended, and other political activities in which she had participated. Returning from a summer vacation in Europe—where, ironically, she had dined with Eleanor Roosevelt—Hunt found herself unemployable. Director Richard Fleischer, at producer Stanley Kramer's urging, cast Hunt as the French-Canadian mother in the film *The Happy Time.* He had no idea that, daily, she was being pressured by the studio to disavow political beliefs she had never held. "I knew that she had been connected in some way with that tragedy," Fleischer said, "but I didn't have much information about her. I just remember her as a stylish lady and a good actress."

In the years to follow—referred to by her as "the dark ages"—there were only a handful of parts. She played a mother in *Blue Denim* and *Bombers B-52.* Radio dramatist turned screenwriter Norman Corwin, who had cast Hunt in his radio program *Document A/777,* came through with a role in *No Place to Hide,* set in the Philippines. But after more than fifty plus films at Paramount and MGM, her career was all but ruined.

Offscreen, Hunt—whose energy and still-girlish demeanor belie her years—was better at playing a spirited survivor than an embittered victim. When the movie roles slowed to a trickle, she and her husband, novelist and screenwriter Robert Presnell Jr., persevered. Presnell kept writing (at one point he "fronted" without pay for the blacklisted Dalton Trumbo). Hunt toured in summer stock, did an occasional TV series (*My Three Sons, The Outer Limits*), designed the remodeling of their Sherman Oaks home, and embraced worthy causes (the United Nations, family planning, the homeless). Presnell, who had turned to TV writing and fiction, died in 1986. In 1993 Hunt published *The Way We Wore: Styles of the Nineteen-Thirties and Forties...and Our World Since Then.* An odd but irresistible amalgam of fashion layouts, production stills, and personal memoir, the book has become a valuable reference source for costume designers and social historians as well as movie buffs.

For years Hunt ignored queries about the blacklist. Now, however, after

---

*Earlier, in 1948, Hunt had starred on Broadway in *Joy to the World,* Allan Scott's comedy criticizing Hollywood's penchant for escapist entertainment, which was staged by Jules Dassin.

being featured compellingly in 1996 documentaries for both Turner Broadcasting and American Movie Classics, she is often sought out on the subject.
In AMC's Emmy-winning *Hollywood on Trial*, she provides the single most
poignant moment as she tells how over the years she has been scolded by
fans for "deserting the screen." "It was a shameful period, demanding conformity, stifling dissent," she now says. "Young people today don't believe
it happened. This being the fiftieth anniversary of the blacklist, I've been
asked to do some college lectures. I didn't want to talk about it before. I
wanted to get away from it, not look back. But now I think it's important
for young people to know, to understand the grip of hysteria, and paranoia,
that crippled our society, and to guard against it happening again."

   Hunt was interviewed in Sherman Oaks, California, where she has resided
since the days of riding stables, citrus groves, and dirt lanes "lined with huge
old trees that met overhead in a wonderful, leafy arch." Her converted
farmhouse, is pleasantly cluttered with books, memorabilia, sheet music,
pictures of four generations of Presnells ("no celebrities, just loved ones"—
including her late father-in-law, scenarist Robert Presnell Sr., who cowrote
the screen story for *Meet John Doe*), and the latest videocassette "screeners"
from the Academy. She was rehearsing lines for a staged production of *On
Golden Pond*, costarring William Windom and directed by her nephew Allan
Hunt, at the time of the interview.

■

Are you nervous about treading the boards again?

   I don't think I have the good sense to be nervous. I don't seem to get
nervous. I'm always so happy when I'm in a play. I get revved up, but I don't
think it's nervousness. I wasn't nervous on my first screen test when I was
seventeen. Maybe I mentioned that I don't have good sense. Even earthquakes
don't seem to panic me.

*After what you've been through, I can understand why it might take a lot to rattle
you.*

   The blacklist was an unhappy chapter in my life. When I did my book, *The
Way We Wore*, which is principally about the styles of the thirties and forties,
I decided also to depict the era and the public mood—including this terrible
blight on our society of anti-Communist fear. Now, having put it all down
on paper, I suppose I have pulled the cork out of the bottle, and I seem to be
approached again and again on this subject. Which is curious, because I was
never subpoenaed. I was never a Communist. I was never a figure of public
controversy. I just stopped working.

*Let's start at the beginning of your career. You were a teenager when you first came
to Hollywood, in the mid-1930s. You started out in programmers, like* Thunder
Trail *and* Hell Town, *starring with John Wayne.*

Four of the twelve films I did at Paramount were westerns. I wasn't thrilled about them. I kept saying, "Hey, I'm a New Yorker. I should be in easterns, not westerns." They said, "Well, Marsha, you're a tall girl. You'll look tall in the saddle against the skyline." So there it was. James Craig, who later on was in *The Human Comedy* and *Lost Angel* with me, played a second lead in *Thunder Trail*. He was just off the football field, big and handsome and likable. He grew into quite a competent leading man at Metro.

Soon you were appearing in MGM films with Greer Garson. One of your first A productions was Pride and Prejudice.

Pride and Prejudice was my first real shot at comedy. The bookworm sister, Mary Bennet, was such a delicious character for me to play—squinting through glasses, singing off-key, wearing sausage curls. I had the most fun. I dearly love comedy; I was never given anything close to it in my dozen films at Paramount. I played sweet young things, romantic leads, but pretty much empty-headed.

You're hilarious in the garden-party sequence, where Edmund Gwenn, as your father, tells you that one song is quite enough, thank you.

That's "Flow Gently, Sweet Afton." It was very hard to sing it off-key. Both my parents were musical.* I'm filled with music. I've written fifty songs. They had to coach me for weeks just so I could sing flat.

In fact, you appeared in three Greer Garson films— Pride and Prejudice, *Blossoms in the Dust,* and The Valley of Decision. *What was she like?*

I wish I could tell you. It was the same with Susan Hayward and Natalie Wood, whom I also worked with later on. Greer was entirely polite and civil. But there was no chatting, no chumminess on the set. She was pleasantly businesslike, letter-perfect with her lines—and then she retired to her dressing room. I don't mean to imply that she was queenly or in any way cold or unfriendly. It's just that you didn't get acquainted with her. Years later I ran across her socially, and it was delightful. I wish it had been like that on the set.

Clarence Brown directed you in The Human Comedy, *William Saroyan's slice of homefront Americana. It was a very prestigious production of its era.*

I played the spoiled rich girl. My character, Diana Steed, is wealthy and flighty. My favorite scene is the one where Butch Jenkins, the enchanting little towhead [playing the character Ulysses Macauley], befriends an older boy [played by Darryl Hickman] who's a little slow, and they visit the local library together and are awed by it. It's a wonderful scene. Overall, that film is pretty sentimental for the nineties. I don't know that it would hold today.

---

*Her mother was an operatic voice coach and accompanist.

But it was exactly right for the forties, the wartime years, when we needed that sense of all pulling together and holding tight to our values.

You were a Polish teacher in André de Toth's None Shall Escape, *with Alexander Knox as a Nazi on trial for war atrocities. It's a very good anti-Fascist film that really does stand up today. Was it any kind of turning point for you?*

It was a strong role in a significant film. I think it was the first film to show atrocities against Jews. We knew Hitler had to be defeated, that he wanted to take over the world, but there was a kind of self-consciousness in Hollywood about showing anti-Semitism. Most war movies were about fighting "the Japs." This film was different. It showed Nazi soldiers galloping into a Polish synagogue and using it as a stable. It showed Jews being rounded up and shoved into cattle cars and going off to who knows where. I think *None Shall Escape* was the first film to touch on that. The other thing that made it impressive was that it was a prophetic film made before World War II was over, yet it predicted the outcome. We shot it in 1943, and there was no assurance the Allies would beat the Axis. What it did was to prophesy the outcome and predict the Nuremberg [war-crimes] trials. The title *None Shall Escape* meant that none of these criminals against humanity should escape justice. Even the makeup of the international tribunal [in the film] was right: there are black judges, judges in turbans, Oriental judges. And the United Nations wasn't even in existence then.

None Shall Escape *was written by Hollywood Ten member Lester Cole. It reflected the Popular Front politics of the times, in that it was pro-Soviet—to the point where, in one scene, the American flag is shown flying proudly alongside the hammer and sickle. Did any of this come back to haunt you during the witch-hunt days?*

No, no one made reference to that film. I wasn't aware of any of the [pro-Soviet] lines until you mentioned them. Goodness, in those days we were allies. Oddly enough, it *was* written by Lester Cole, but I didn't know him when we were shooting the film. I just felt privileged to be in *None Shall Escape*. It had a social and historical importance.

It was also one of the first films in which you received star billing.

Top billing—not stardom, but it was a step in that direction, a challenging role. I got to play a young girl and then mature into the older years. Dramatically, it was a very good opportunity. But I had played "older" before. I played my first old lady when I was twenty-one. There was some aging involved in *Cheers for Miss Bishop*, made in 1941. Then, in 1946, I had the central role [as the program manager] in *Carnegie Hall* and got to play a character who ages from her teens to her late sixties. That was very challenging. All that's how I earned the proud title "Hollywood's youngest character actress." One day I counted up my parts, and I think I tallied just a few more romantic leads than supporting featured roles. It was almost evenly split in my career. And that was fine with me. I was not dreaming of stardom. I just wanted to be allowed to become the best actress I could, and mostly those opportunities came in featured roles rather than in lead roles.

All along I was sort of bucking the system: I didn't want any two roles to be alike.

Just before you made the flight to Washington with other members of the Committee for the First Amendment, you appeared in Smash-Up: The Story of a Woman.* *It's a sort of role-reversal version of* A Star Is Born. *Susan Hayward plays a dutiful wife who sacrifices her career and ends up losing everything to alcohol. You play Martha Gray, "girl Friday" assistant to singing idol Lee Bowman, Susan Hayward's husband.*

Smash-Up: The Story of a Woman. Ugh! It's frequently shown on TV. To me, it's the story of a weak, self-pitying woman who acquires a serious drinking problem because her husband isn't paying enough attention to her. The thinking is that he ought to understand what she's going through. Maybe I'm being a bit hard on the film, but I don't understand why it is so popular. My role is a red herring. I'm made to seem like the competition—"the other woman," whereas I only *wished* I were. I wore beautiful clothes in that one and got my hair pulled by Hayward. That's what all the fans want to know about: "Did it hurt when she pulled your hair?"

Can you describe yourself politically in the postwar years?

An innocent, almost a total innocent.

You weren't politically minded?

No, not at all. I gradually became involved, not as a partisan political advocate but as someone who cared about issues like fair housing, the civil-rights movement, equality for women, the danger of fallout from atomic tests—things I thought needed attention.

I know that you became involved in the Screen Actors Guild and were uniquely positioned within the leadership after World War II.

I guess it was in 1946 that I became a board member of SAG. Franchot Tone was going back east to do a play or something, and he asked me if I would fill out his term. I was so flattered, knowing nothing of organizations, never having joined anything. My father, you have to remember, was a very conservative Republican. I wasn't even sure about unions at first, because he hadn't thought too highly of them. And then, I didn't like having to join anything under duress. I did not join the Screen Actors Guild in the years at Paramount because I was already under contract. But once my contract ended [in 1938], then I was not able to get a job in films until and unless I joined SAG, which by that time had won closed-shop status.

---

*The screenplay was the last one for which John Howard Lawson received credit. He never returned to screenwriting under his own name after being jailed as one of the Hollywood Ten.

When I joined the board George Murphy was president, and then Ronald Reagan. I could have told you then that those fellows were destined for public office. They were such political animals. They had such a feel for politics, for the inner workings of organizations, for how to get things done.

How well did you know Reagan?

Slightly, socially. He was a dedicated liberal. Nice, nice fellow, but so political! And I certainly wasn't prepared for that arch-conservative about-face.

Any warnings from the studios or your agent about the potential damage to your career that joining the board might cause?

No, none at all. If it was frowned on, I didn't know it.

Boris Karloff was one very early SAG activist. I've heard stories about his having to park blocks away from Guild meetings to avoid surveillance.

In the formative years I think there was a good deal of surreptitiousness, because there was a professional price to pay for organizing a union. Once SAG came into being [in 1933], it was known as a "company union," by which is meant that the studio heads favored or tolerated a guild of actors, provided it didn't make waves that were too high.

The first month that I was on the board, I merely sat and listened, because I didn't know anything about boards of directors and seconding motions and tabling things. I didn't know about any of these procedures, much less the opposing camps that were developing.

But you evolved into quite an activist.

Gradually, I began to speak up. I remember Gene Kelly giving me a warning one day. He said, "Marsha, save your fire for when it matters. You are beginning to be heard. You're perfectly right about what you say; I agree with you. But don't waste your fire. Save it for a big issue, and then come on with your big guns. I know this board." And so he did. Most of them were extremely conservative. There were a few of us who were more liberal. And I was starting to be counted as one of the liberals. By this time I was married to Robert [Presnell Jr.], my writer husband, who was also known as a liberal.

Wasn't Anne Revere among the more outspoken members?

Yes, Anne was a really dedicated liberal. I was not. I just listened to things and thought, "Well, gee, that isn't quite right, is it?" Some of the expressed views just ran counter to my sense of fair play and evenhandedness.

One night, past president Robert Montgomery re-introduced a proposal from years earlier, which had lain dormant and might be worth reconsidering. It was to affiliate the three major guilds—directors, writers, and actors. It was felt that we could do better with the producers when union contracts expired if we had a united front. The concept intrigued the board. I either volunteered or was appointed to be on an exploratory committee. I think there were just three of us: [actor] Robert Montgomery [a founder of SAG and also a former president], someone else I can't remember, and me.

We met with our counterpart committees from the Screen Writers Guild and the Directors' Guild. They warmed to the prospect of tri-guild solidarity at contract-negotiation time with the producers, and it looked promising for the plan to materialize. But then Bob Montgomery tossed in a condition: all three guilds must officially disavow Communism and assert that all Communists would be barred from membership in their guilds. I was aghast. We'd had no such instructions from our SAG board; Bob set up that roadblock on his own.

Of course the others refused, finding political affiliation and philosophy none of their guild's business. And so the talks broke down.

Ever the spokesman, Bob gave a report of the breakdown at our next meeting, blaming the plan's failure on the negative and competitive attitudes of the others, and with no mention of his anti-Communist condition. Then it came to me that Robert Montgomery had introduced this whole concept, and steered it all the way, just to make certain it would fail! This was so convoluted, so sophisticated, a tactic, that I was staggered by it.

And you said as much?

After a few sleepless nights. I knew I couldn't tacitly go along with that distortion of the truth, and at the next meeting, with dry mouth and thumping heart, I told how my recollection of those talks differed from Bob's. In effect, I offered the board a choice of two versions, and clearly they chose to believe their venerated, trusted founder over this younger, inexperienced newcomer.

So you were shouted down?

No, worse. They heard me in silence and then turned to other business.

By the time I joined the board, the word "Communist" had begun to dominate activities and deliberations. I remember that there was a strike, at the Warners studio, of the set decorators' union, and the Screen Actors Guild had to decide about crossing or honoring its picket lines. But our discussion was less about whether or not its cause was just than about whether or not that union was infiltrated, if not dominated, by Reds.

Trying to get us back on track, I urged us to be concerned over the wages, hours, and working conditions of our fellow filmmakers, instead of over their political leanings and some possible Communists among them. As I spoke, I could see elbows nudging, glances exchanged, as if to say, "She must be *one!*"

That strike stirred up emotions. There was some violence, overturned cars and injuries, charges and counter-charges. Tension was high throughout Hollywood.

Everyone began taking sides.

There began to be camps of liberals and conservatives. Sam Wood—Samuel Grosvenor Wood, the director—was one of those who formed the Motion

Picture Alliance [for the Preservation of American Ideals], and he became its head. John Wayne and Ward Bond—a lot of very conservative members of the industry—became active in that organization. You know, I learned only recently, to my astonishment, that the hearings by the House Committee on Un-American Activities were requested by the Motion Picture Alliance! I had never heard that before. This hearing in Washington by a congressional committee on whether or not there was subversive Communist propaganda inserted into motion pictures was, in fact, inspired by a group of filmmaking people asking Congress to look into this matter. I guess their fear was quite sincere. But, oh, the suffering they brought about!

Edward Dmytryk makes the claim that his second appearance in front of HUAC, in April 1951, was specifically requested by Reagan, representing SAG.

These are inner workings I am not aware of. I do know that, because I contradicted Bob Montgomery on this matter of the three guilds coming together at contract time, as of then, I was "suspect." I must tell you that at one point we all had to sign non-Communist affidavits in order to serve on the Screen Actors Guild board. We were told it was now required of all U.S. union directors [serving on a board], to weed out that "dangerous element." I only later discovered that there was no such requirement, legally.

Do you trace your political activism to that first stand on the board?

I'm not sure I was an "activist"—that sounds so full-time! But once I became aware of things, I did speak up now and then. I thought the board should be concerned with our working conditions at the studios, rather than this tangent of anti-Communism, which just took over and absorbed all our time and our discussions.

You were so passionate about your craft. Why didn't you hold back, safeguard your career?

We didn't know the extent of the risk or the dimensions of the pall that would fall over motion pictures and broadcasting.

What happened when your term was up?

When my filling Franchot's term as a board member expired [in 1947] and a new slate came up, lo and behold, my name was not to be found. I was not proposed for the next board, even though I had a perfect attendance record and had served on three committees. One of the committees opposed Olivia de Havilland's suspension by Warner Brothers: was it slavery or not, prohibiting her to work anywhere else but taking her off salary until she behaved herself? Another committee was about minorities: trying to increase minority employment in movies and trying to get away from stereotypes, so that a man with an Italian accent wouldn't always have to play a cobbler in movies, a Japanese actor not always a gardener, a Filipino not always a houseboy. We visited the casting heads and producers' groups, lobbying them by saying,

"Let's see a dark-skinned or Oriental doctor without anything being made of the fact that he is a member of a different race. Let's see minorities represented in the higher professions, not just the menial kinds of jobs." These were issues that just struck me as fair. So I went to work on them and was happy to do it. I was discovering all kinds of things besides acting.

Did you ever feel that because of your public profile as an actress you were in any danger of becoming a political pawn?

No. Nobody ever cued me. Nobody was steering me in any direction. I think I'm probably too independent for that. I had no interest in Communism; I didn't inquire into it. I liked my country's system a lot and worked pretty hard for it, for patriotic things. No, I never felt like a pawn.

How did your friends and supporters in the Guild respond to your being dropped from the official ballot?

Some of the board members were so outraged by what had happened that they insisted I run on a petition for an independent slate. I can't remember whether I agreed to or not. I know I was terribly torn. I think I said, "Listen, if the board doesn't want me, I don't want to be a member. I don't feel like a combatant." The guilds and the industry were all being politicized very heavily in the postwar years.

My husband, Robert, having been a reporter [for *The Milwaukee Journal*] and a psychology major at Stanford, taught me how to read headlines and about the slanting of facts in the way a story is written or broadcast—in the choice of words. Some of what I was reading and hearing amounted to thought control, the steering of public emotions. This was all new to me—I had been a complete political innocent—but it was obvious that the anti-Communist fever that swept the land was manipulated and deliberate. And it was not a pretty sight.

You yourself never attended any kind of Party meeting?

Lord, no. No one ever asked me or Robert. There were, it turned out, several people we knew who were members of the Communist Party, but they never said so, except for one friend who was not in the arts.

Does that include screenwriter Richard Collins, who later was one of the most prolific of the people who "named names" and who later still objected to your casting on a television show?

I never met Richard Collins, but when he was in some executive post on *Bonanza*, a friend of mine worked with him. At one point, when I was recommended for a part, she was astonished to hear him say, "Don't bother bringing up Marsha Hunt to me. As long as I'm connected with this show, she will *never* work on it." He was so vehement and adamant about me, a stranger. I've since heard that he was someone who had been a Communist and repented, which was an enviable position. Perhaps it was better to have loved and lost, to be the repentant prodigal son. Once you saw the light, the error of your ways, you could beat your breast and vow eternally to get even.

Let's talk about the Committee for the First Amendment. How did the flight to Washington in October 1947 come about?

The flight was not masterminded by Communists. It was concocted by William Wyler and John Huston and Philip Dunne, who were having lunch at Lucy's, across from Paramount, one day and said to each other, 'We have to fight fire with fire, headlines with headlines! We've got to go to Washington with a star-studded brigade and get some headlines to fight these right-wing headlines that the Committee is getting.' " I'm kind of vague about all this, but I remember being invited to a small Sunday-afternoon gathering at Willie Wyler's house to plan and coordinate our actions.

What was the mood among the Hollywood celebrities who were on that flight?

We were revved up. We were doing something new to all of us and with a sense of mission. We went on a chartered plane. The whole industry had chipped in to pay for it. We stopped at two, maybe three, cities late at night— Kansas City and either Philadelphia or Pittsburgh. We were surrounded by throngs at the landing fields, huddled under umbrellas at one stop. Microphones were brought out, and we explained ourselves. It was heartening that there was that kind of attention at unscheduled stops, but we knew they were more interested in seeing the famous people than in the issue.

And once you were in Washington, at the hearings?

It was all so new to me. I had never been in a position of public controversy before. We were treated with skepticism and hostility, frequently by the Hearst press and some syndicated columnists. We were so misquoted. In my own case, I was quoted as saying things I would never say, at a function I never attended. This was almost libelous, and I wanted a retraction. But wiser heads said that we should let such things pass, that all of this would soon be yesterday's news and quickly forgotten.

Did you, as a group, do very much to make your presence known at the hearings?

No. The press did that for us—lots of pictures were taken. We sat there for two days. We were not given any role in the hearings at all. We were not there as anything but part of the audience. Later, back at the hotel, we held a press conference, which was well-attended.

The mood must have been quite different on the flight home.

Oh, there was a stark difference. The mood was to take whatever happened from then on with narrowed eyes. We went full of verve and dedication and outrage at what was taking place. We were going to try to explain and clarify things to a really confused public. On the flight back to Hollywood we were, I think, subdued and shaken by what we had witnessed and heard in the hearing room, by the ridicule and suspicion that the press afforded us. They thought we must be Communists, or sympathetic to Communism, or incredibly naive. We came home sadder, but I don't know if I'd say "wiser." We had certainly learned a good deal about pressure politics and distortion of our purpose.

The media were complicitous?

Yes, they were. We were belittled and made to look foolish. They took sides. There were some favorable editorials written; not all the press was hostile. A few columnists cheered us for having taken the trouble, for putting ourselves in a controversial spotlight and exposing the high-handed methods of the Committee. It was a divided press, but what we experienced mostly was damaging.

Were there tears or outbursts of anger on the plane?

No, no. We were more grown-up than that. I don't mean that we were in mourning over what had happened, but it was a sobering experience. We tried to handle it.

The leaders behind the scenes of the Committee for the First Amendment were Wyler, Huston, and Dunne. But Humphrey Bogart became one of the more public spokesmen on the flight. How well did you know Bogart?

I don't know that I'd ever met him before that flight. Betty—Lauren Bacall—and I had met as former models.

How did Bogart take what had happened?

He was angry—angry at the way we were treated and at what we had seen and heard in the hearing room. We all were. But we were also sorry that a few of the Nineteen had been so shrill and defiant in their demeanor. It hadn't helped their cause.

Later Bogart did an about-face. People say that he wasn't ready for that kind of controversy and therefore tried to distance himself.

What I heard—and none of this is firsthand knowledge—was simply that the brothers Warner called Bogart and Bacall into the front office and said, "Recant—or else!" These were booming careers the studio didn't want jeopardized, and so the Bogarts announced that the trip had been "ill-advised." Which was such a body blow to all the rest of us on that plane, because Bogie had been in the forefront; he had been as vehement, as angry, as any one of us—and also as prominent a box-office name. We were aghast at his turnaround.

Comic actor Danny Kaye is another one who was front and center in many of the press photos taken on the trip. What was his role?

Danny Kaye was the savior, our court jester. He danced up and down the aisle of the plane, making all kinds of fun and laughter. He really kind of saved the morale of the bunch. We all loved him for that.

Did you know any of the Hollywood Ten socially?

[Writer-producer] Adrian Scott was the only one I knew personally. And probably that's a big reason for our becoming a part of that protest movement. Robert and I knew and loved Adrian. He had married my dearest friend, Anne Shirley, a lovely actress. They did some of their courting at our house. We were very close to Adrian. He was the new boy wonder, "the new Thalberg." He had produced the first film on anti-Semitism, *Crossfire*, which was before *Gentlemen's Agreement*.

Years later, you were cast as Timothy Bottoms's mother in Dalton Trumbo's adaptation of his own antiwar novel, Johnny Got His Gun.

I had known Dalton very slightly. He knew we had gone to Washington to protest the treatment of the Hollywood Nineteen and had both signed the amicus curiae brief in hopes of reversing their convictions for contempt of Congress. Robert had fronted for Dalton during his blacklist years on at least one script, in order for Dalton to feed his family. Fronting was a very risky thing for any writer to do. I want to stress that Robert didn't take any money for it.

Years later, on the strength of seeing me in two short plays in Beverly Hills, Dalton called me and asked me to play the mother in *Johnny Got His Gun*. Such a long story, that movie. We had to shoot the death scene in the very room in downtown L.A. where Dalton's own father had died. No reason on earth for us to do it there, to drag the lights and cameras up those narrow stairs. But for Dalton it was such a subjective venture. He was so bound up in his own statement.

Let's go back to June 1950, and the publication of the so-called bible of the graylist, Red Channels.

Oh, gosh. Well, that ended my career. *Red Channels* came out in the summer of 1950, while—how's this for irony?—I was in Paris being invited to dinner by Eleanor Roosevelt. *Red Channels* was concerned entirely with the broadcast field. The film industry later had its own lists of victims. *Red Channels* included me because I had been offered my own TV talk show. I'd had beginner's luck on TV, being, as you can see, very voluble. I had been on a number of early talk shows with people like George S. Kaufman and Marc Connelly, bright, articulate folk. And I was currently quite successful on Broadway, having starred in *Joy to the World* with Alfred Drake [in 1948] and *The Devil's Disciple* with Maurice Evans in 1950. When *Disciple* closed, Robert and I and the Drakes went off to Europe together, and while we were there I was branded a "patriotically suspect citizen" in *Red Channels*.

When we returned from Paris, the offers had vanished, just mysteriously vanished. I called my agent and said, "I'm back, you know. How are things?" He said, "Haven't you heard?" Then he told me, and that was the first time I heard of *Red Channels*. They had listed several affiliations under my name—some I'd never heard about, complete lies. One, I think, had me attending a peace conference in Stockholm. I had never been to Stockholm, nor to a peace conference. The rest were innocent activities that *Red Channels* viewed with suspicion. One of these was the movement in the theater to stop a proposed bill in the city legislature to empower a "morality czar" of Broadway with the authority to close any production. The whole theatrical community rose up in protest over that issue, and it was duly reported in the press that I was part of it. The bill was defeated, of course, but that made me "suspect" in the eyes of *Red Channels*. *Red Channels*, I think, was what sealed my fate.

How bad was the news for you personally?

A few offers leaked through, but Stanley Kramer's *The Happy Time* was the only major film that was offered once the blacklist took hold. Before shooting began, I was in Seattle, on tour in a play, when my agent phoned me. He said the studio had received protests to my being cast in the film, and now they insisted that I sign a prepared statement or they would have to cancel my contract. In the statement I must swear to my non-Communism, past or present, and vow my fervent anti-communist efforts from then on. It was full of mea culpa and what an innocent dupe I had been of Communists who had secretly masterminded the Washington flight, which I now regretted with all my heart. I said, "But it's not true! The flight was conceived by Willie Wyler, John Huston, and Philip Dunne, none of them a Communist. I can't sign and swear to what I know to be a lie." And my agent said, "Well, then, they'll break your contract, and you won't be in that or any other film!" The irony: I had just returned from a radio broadcast, selling U.S. Savings Bonds as a public service for my country, only to hear by phone that I was supsected of being disloyal and perhaps even a traitor.

After some pacing, I asked myself, "Well, what *can* I swear to? What can I say that would be the truth?" Then I wrote out a statement expressing my pride and affection for my country's form of government, and saying that the flight to Washington had been a protest against the maligning of a good and patriotic film industry. I called my agent back and said, "Please get somebody to take down what I've just written." It was presented to Kramer's legal department, and they accepted it.

Even so, throughout the shooting of that film, I was constantly being summoned to the office of a man named George Glass—gosh, I'd nearly forgotten his name—who was an executive with Kramer. Glass would tell me that he had received more protest letters from the American Legion chapter in some far-flung part of the country—and a certain Catholic organization. They were protesting my presence in this film and threatening to boycott the film, to picket theaters wherever *The Happy Time* was going to be shown. Again and again I was urged to sign non-Communist pronouncements, affidavits, and things. Glass wanted me to take out a full-page ad in the trade papers, *Variety* and the *Hollywood Reporter*. These ads would swear to my hatred for—and unswerving opposition to—Communist doctrine.

I said to Mr. Glass, "I tell you what: If any of these shadowy groups wants to step forward and accuse me of some wrong, I will answer an accusation. But I'm not gratuitously going to take out a full-page ad, beat my breast, and shout, 'I'm not! I'm not! I never was!' Let somebody call me a Communist or charge me with subversive activities. Then I can answer. But I'm not gonna fight shadows." I held out.

You toughed it out.

Yes. The film had a gorgeous cast—Charles Boyer, Louis Jourdan, Bobby Driscoll, Kurt Kasznar, Linda Christian. I played Maman, a role I had originally turned down on Broadway. It was a nonmusical produced by Rodgers and Hammerstein. But I adored the film script, and the character was married to Charles Boyer. Who wouldn't enjoy that?

It must have seemed a sick joke, pretending to be part of this buoyant, idealized family.

It should have been a very happy time, and it was not. I loved the film and wanted it, of course, to be successful. And the fact that I—my presence in the film—might hurt the box office, and might make the film a source of ugly controversy, was a terrible weight to carry around while playing light comedy.

Did any of the other cast members ever broach the subject of the blacklist?

No, nobody knew my situation. I didn't confide in anybody. I can't forget George Glass telling me, "This is a time, Miss Hunt, for expediency, not integrity." And George Glass, I heard, had been a member of the Communist Party!* I guess they're the worst kind.

Like reformed smokers.

Yes, yes. Of course, the film came out and was never picketed anywhere. It went on to do very nicely. But after *The Happy Time* the offers stopped— or they were rescinded. You have to understand, I was never subpoenaed, not to Washington nor to Sacramento [where the state of California held similar hearings]. But clearly, they had researched my background and found me wanting, labeled me "subversive." I was articulate, an articulate liberal. And

---

*George Glass was a publicist who had become an executive in Stanley Kramer's company. According to Victor Navasky in *Naming Names*, Glass was a cooperative witness before HUAC. "Although Glass denied CP membership," wrote Navasky, "he told the Committee in January 1952 he had attended a half-dozen Party meetings and at the Committee's request named his fellow attenders." One of the people pressured to leave Stanley Kramer's company by Glass's testimony was Kramer's partner, high-profile screenwriter Carl Foreman.

people who thought independently had to be silenced, right along with anybody who had ever joined the Communist Party.

Though you were blacklisted—sorry, do you prefer "graylisted"?

These shadings are beyond me. I was denied work, and I know I must have been on the list that the studios and networks consulted before they hired anyone. If that's black or gray or charcoal it doesn't really matter—the result is still the same.

Okay—though you were blacklisted, you were still able to work a little.

Barely.

How did you make enough money to get by?

I don't think I could have survived without being married. Inexplicably, Robert was not blacklisted. I cannot tell you why. He was certainly more outspoken in his political pronouncements and outrage about what was going on, and enjoyed a good argument. He was without any kind of political discretion. And yet he kept working. Thank heaven. He was never a top-salary screenwriter, but he did work—and beautifully.

I, to keep functioning and also fill the larder, would do plays in stock. I did twenty or thirty different plays around the country during the 1950s and 1960s. That was not very rewarding financially, because you had to spend a week rehearsing and then one week playing. And you received a decent salary only for the week of performance, out of which you had to pay for your hotel, meals out, tips, taxi rides and all those things. It was a costly way to make a living. But I would bring home what I could.

Give me some idea of what the blacklist meant to you in terms of monetary loss. What had you been making as an actress at your peak?

I never was a moneymaker. I think the most money I ever was paid for a film was twenty thousand dollars. Now, of course, fifty years later, the cost and the standard of living are ten times that. Today that would be two hundred thousand.

What did you make playing in stock?

Probably one thousand dollars a show. That had to be spread over two weeks, because the rehearsal pay was almost a joke, it was so little.

I read somewhere that you were actually cast in Nicholas Ray's film Rebel Without a Cause and turned down the part.

I was cast to do it, yes. They wanted me for [James] Dean's mother. I had to withdraw. It was a scheduling conflict. I was already committed to do a play at the Carthay Circle Theatre [in Los Angeles], which had been a great old movie house. I did three plays there. This one was *The Anniversary Waltz*, with Howard Duff. Anyway, my view was that the part in *Rebel* was a terrible role. I was not looking forward to playing it. But the script [by Stewart Stern] was so impressive, it was clearly breaking new ground as subject matter. And although I felt the mother's part was stupid and contrived, I would have liked to be part of it. I had known Nick Ray socially, and I had already seen James Dean in a television show. I was so impressed by him. I thought it would be a fascinating project.

Warner Brothers and the producers [of the play] had even worked out a mutually agreed-upon arrangement not to use me on the film later than five p.m. every day or at all on matinee days. The studio had already done the publicity pictures with James Dean, Natalie Wood, Jim Backus, and me. I had done the first read-through with the cast. But when it came down to the crunch of other details, neither side would give in. My agent finally came to me and said, "I'm afraid you're going to have to make a choice." So I went with the play, because they were already selling tickets based on the announcement of the cast. I thought I was morally bound to the play.

Did you get to know Dean at all?

Dean was very busy being a rebel, showing his disdain for convention, picking his nose, scuffing the ground—generally being very individualistic. As we were being lined up for the [prop] family portraits, I mentioned the TV show I'd seen him in—[writer] S. Lee Pogostin's *Something for an Empty Briefcase*—and suddenly his eyes came into focus. He saw me for the first time. He got animated and intrigued. I told him I was fascinated with the way everyone moved [in that production]; they almost seemed choreographed. At that moment, we formed a kind of very brief bond. As we parted, he announced that I had "a gentle soul." That was my benediction from James Dean.

The mother really was a dreadful role. Ann Doran, who is an old friend, played her in the film. She was as good as the role would allow. The parents were cardboard figures who were meant to alienate the son with their lack of understanding—terrible, terrible. But it was an impressive film, as I knew it would be.

Key participants in the blacklist drama pop up behind the scenes throughout your career: Jules Dassin was your director for MGM's The Affairs of Martha, A Letter for Evie, *and then your first Broadway show,* Joy to the World. *Norman Corwin, well-known as a progressive, and Philip Dunne, one of the founders of the Committee for the First Amendment, gave you some of your few jobs during the 1950s. For Corwin, you appeared in* No Place to Hide. *Dunne was the writer as well as director of* Blue Denim, *in 1959. Coincidence or kindred spirits gravitating toward one another?*

Julie [Dassin], along with his wife and children, became a good friend. He was one reason I took the plunge and costarred on Broadway. I felt so safe in Dassin's hands—he was a superb comedy director. As for talking politics with him, I don't remember doing much of that. I knew that he was liberal in his viewpoint just from his remarks on this and that. But, to this day, I don't know if Julie had ever joined the Communist Party. It was none of my business. I never inquired into these things, and he never volunteered.

I suppose that later there was something of the kindred-spirits connection but not entirely. I will never know to what extent that was true. The people who employed me during the drought, the worst years, never said, and I never asked them if it was mercy employment out of sympathy for my plight. Those things just didn't get spoken aloud.

I have no answer, for instance, for why I was in *Bombers B-52*. This was in 1957, right in the midst of the dark ages. I didn't know anybody involved in the production. I had never worked at Warner Brothers before or since—I had worked at every major studio except Warners—when suddenly I was offered the role of Natalie Wood's mother, Karl Malden's wife. Maybe they just thought I was right for the part.

The Pentagon couldn't have produced a better promotional tool. Maybe your agent thought it was time for a right-wing, jingoistic film.

I have no idea how I was given that role. Normally my agents couldn't get me arrested. They were helpless in the face of that silent conspiracy to keep listed people off the screen.

How long were you blacklisted? When did the blacklist end for you?

Never really. Never fully. Well, I can't say the blacklist never ended, but what is true is that the momentum never was recaptured. I had such an ongoing, thriving career. What was it—fifty-some movies before the dark ages? Then, since 1950, I've made about eight.

You look twenty years younger than your real age; you're incredibly articulate; you have great energy and experience. I would think that as a character actress you'd be in great demand.

Thank you. I'm not. I can only tell you that my name doesn't come up. Of course, I'm still an actress. I don't think you ever stop having your bent for what you trained for and what you loved. You always relish the sheer joy of pretending you're someone else.

I think, for one thing, people casting and directing films today have never heard of me. They are very much a junior brigade; and they are making films for the young. I'm still a very active member of the Academy, serving on [the documentary-film nominating] committee. And I've been nominated for the Academy Board [of governors] three or four times. But I can't tell you I love motion pictures today. I think gimmicks are ruling the screen and not story, not character evolution or development, not relationships. I don't see many roles I wish I'd played.

Are you bitter about what transpired during the blacklist?

No point in it. Though I'm certainly entitled. They nipped a career that was just starting to flower. On the other hand, my life has gone into new directions that I have found deeply rewarding. The fact is that the blacklist opened up a lot of time for me in which I was able to make all sorts of marvelous discoveries. I was really closeted on a soundstage until then.

I've worked on committees for youth centers. I've done a whole lot of community work. I've emceed eight telethons [starting in 1954] for cerebral palsy, after the head of ABC, who was the father of a cerebral-palsy child, gathered a bunch of us in New York at "21" to talk about this condition, about which there was ignorance and superstition. In 1955 Robert and I girdled the globe, and I came back a different person. I became very involved in what the United Nations was doing. I spent time pounding its corridors, learning about health, nutrition, the basic needs of Third World countries. I was on the board of Planned Parenthood for ten years. I founded the Valley Mayors' Fund for the Homeless in 1983. And I'm still Sherman Oaks's honorary mayor.

You haven't stopped fighting the good fight on several fronts.

I don't suppose I'm able to stop. Besides that, after I was blacklisted it was too late to do anything but keep going; I was already unemployable, so I had nothing to lose. I remember how one night, as Robert and I were going to sleep, and we were commiserating about everything that was going wrong in that dark time, Robert said, "Cheer up—it gets worse." All you can do is laugh at a line like that. No, blessedly, I had enough joy and compensation in my personal life to make up for all the rest and keep everything in proportion.

Paul Jarrico

PAUL JARRICO, Los Angeles, California, 1983

INTERVIEW BY PATRICK McGILLIGAN

PAUL JARRICO
(1915–)

1937 *No Time to Marry.* Script.
1938 *I Am the Law.* Uncredited contribution.
The Little Adventuress. Costory.
1939 *Beauty for the Asking.* Coscript.
1941 *The Face Behind the Mask.* Coscript.
Man of the Timberland. Story.
Tom, Dick, and Harry. Story, script.
1943 *Thousands Cheer.* Costory, coscript.
Song of Russia. Coscript.
1946 *Little Giant.* Coscript.
1948 *The Search.* Additional dialogue.
1949 *Not Wanted/Streets of Sin.* Costory, coscript.
1950 *The White Tower.* Script.
1951 *The Las Vegas Story.* Uncredited coscript.
1952 *The Man Who Watched the Trains Go By/*
Paris Express. Uncredited script.

1953 *Salt of the Earth.* Producer.
1957 *The Girl Most Likely.* Uncredited remake of
Tom, Dick, and Harry.
1960 *Five Branded Women.* Uncredited coscript.
1963 *All Night Long.* Coscript (as Peter Achilles).
Call Me Bwana. Uncredited contribution.
1965 *Die pyramids des sonnengottes/Treasure of the*
Aztecs. Uncredited coscript.
1966 *Who Killed Johnny Ringo?* Script (as Peter
Achilles).
1968 *Le rouble à deux faces/The Day the Hot Line*
Got Hot. Script.
1976 *The Day That Shook the World/Assassination in*
Sarajevo. Script.
1977 *Bilitis.* Uncredited contribution.
1988 *Messenger of Death.* Script.
1992 *Stalin* (telefilm). Uncredited contribution.

■

SCREENWRITER PAUL JARRICO is a man of tireless radical zeal. He was, during the HUAC sessions, one of the most-named Hollywood Communists, his traducers led by his sometime writing partner Richard Collins, an eagerly friendly witness. A stalwart of the Hollywood section of the Party, Jarrico had doctrinal differences with John Howard Lawson, whom he succeeded as section chairman. In addition to fighting the blacklist in court, Jarrico was to produce the enduring *Salt of the Earth,* a militant strike film made against great odds during the McCarthy era. Created by the collective effort of blacklisted talent, *Salt of the Earth* remains a testament to the faith of these privileged Hollywood "comrades" in the grit of ordinary people.

Jarrico has long been a spokesman for others of his politically committed generation—a figurehead at events, a key person for journalists to interview, a campaigner in the Writers Guild to restore blacklisted credits, a speaker at funerals. Yet he rarely talks about himself in terms of his remarkable career. He was Oscar-nominated for his original screenplay for the Ginger Rogers comedy *Tom, Dick, and Harry,* and he also had a hand in the script of another Oscar-nominated film, *The Search.* He has solid credits spanning six decades—often, during the blacklist era of the 1950s and 1960s, under pseudonyms—and in his eighties remains actively involved with screen projects.

■

Tell me a little about your background.

I was born in Los Angeles in 1915, the only son of immigrant Jews from Russia. I grew up as Israel Shapiro, but in 1937, when I got my first job as a screenwriter, I changed my name to Paul Jarrico.

How did you decide to become a writer?

I'd been a writer of sorts from an early age. I was a high-school journalist, then a college journalist, and I began to write short stories in college, even began a novel.

Why did you turn to screenwriting?

It was unpremeditated, a matter of chance. I'd transferred for my senior year from UC-Berkeley to USC, and I also got married that year, and we were both about to graduate, when one of my professors recommended me for a junior writer's job at MGM. It paid thirty-five dollars a week, which was more in 1936 than a twenty-one-year-old newlywed could expect to make as a fledgling novelist. And, of course, I was excited about movies. Everybody was.

And that's how you started, as a junior writer?

No. I didn't get the job. But it took three suspenseful months for MGM to say no. And it was during those months that I got the bug. I put aside the novel I was trying to write and wrote an original story for the screen. A friend got it to Dore Schary, then a writer at Paramount—this was before his rise as a producer. Schary liked it and recommended me to Nat Perrin, a writer who was then producing B pictures at Columbia. It was now 1937. I was twenty-two. Perrin asked me if a hundred a week was okay. I gulped and said yes. "You'd take seventy-five, wouldn't you?" he teased. I gulped and said yes. "What the hell." He shrugged. "It's not my money."

Perrin assigned me to write a screenplay based on a *Saturday Evening Post* short story, called " 'Twas the Night Before Christmas," by Paul Gallico. I was installed in an office, and I phoned the story department and asked them to send me a script. "Which one?" they asked. "Any script," I said. They sent me several. That's how I learned the format. Perrin was supportive but hardly interfered at all as I wrote. When I finished my first draft, however, he blue-penciled a lot of my detailed camera directions. "The director doesn't follow them anyway," he explained.

The title was changed to *No Time to Marry*. In Gallico's story, a newspaper publisher remembers, belatedly, that he promised his kid a wagon pulled by a goat for Christmas. Though the stores are all closed by now, he sends his two star reporters (played by Richard Arlen and Mary Astor) and a photographer (Lionel Stander) to look for a goat. They have a lot of madcap adventures and are able to deliver the goat by dawn. My script went into production very quickly, as I recall, directed by an old hand named Harry Lachman. Though I was still at Columbia, having been rewarded with another assignment and a contract, I had very little contact with the director or with the shoot.

I should add here, I guess, that Lionel Stander sang the tune but not the words of "The International" as the trio ascended to the publisher's penthouse with the goat, mission accomplished. (The director had told them to ad-lib gaiety.) This, of course, has been cited and derided as a red plot to affect content. I met a Columbia vice president in charge of foreign sales, a few years after the release of the picture, and he asked me to tell him what was wrong with the picture. I was perplexed. "Wrong?" "It was banned in Brazil, banned in Argentina, banned in Venezuela, banned God knows where. I've run the picture a dozen times, trying to figure out why!"

Is it just my impression, or was Columbia a sort of hothouse for radicals? I am thinking of the presence on the lot of John Howard Lawson and Sidney Buchman. What kind of political activity went on at the studio?

I never thought of Columbia as a hothouse for radicals. It's true that Sidney Buchman wrote some films that are a credit to the left, like *Mr. Smith Goes to Washington*, and that as vice-president in charge of production he had some very real influence (though Harry Cohn still held the reins), but Columbia films, basically, were Capraesque rather than red. As for Lawson, he wrote *Blockade* for UA, *Earthbound* and *Four Sons* for Fox, *Action in the North Atlantic* for Warners, and *Smash-Up* for Universal. His only Columbia credits, I think, were *Sahara* in 1943, about the war in North Africa, and *Counter-Attack* in 1945, which was pro-Russian, but who wasn't? As for his [Lawson's] uncredited work on the screenplay of *The Jolson Story*, Buchman (with whom I spent some blacklistee time on the Côte d'Azur) used to deride his contribution.

As for what kind of organizing went on at Columbia, there was, of course, a continuing effort to strengthen the Screen Writers Guild, but that was going on at all the studios.

As long as we're on the subject of Sidney Buchman, what kind of a person was he? How much input and involvement did he have in Columbia production? Was it really his wife, Beatrice, as I have sometimes heard, who was the staunch leftist in that marriage?

Let me answer by saying that my second assignment at Columbia was to develop an approach to a movie inspired by [New York district attorney] Tom Dewey's fight against the mob. A small item on page one of the November 13, 1937, edition of the *Hollywood Reporter* said that Edward G. Robinson would star, Sidney Buchman would produce, and I'd been assigned to write the screenplay. Which wasn't true. I was feeding my notions to Jo Swerling, who wound up with a deserved sole screenplay credit on the film, called *I Am the Law*. Actually, I had no connection with Sidney Buchman at that point.

My pre-blacklist relations with Buchman were all tentative. I never worked for him or with him. I do remember his telling me once that he'd run *Tom, Dick, and Harry* twice, trying to understand its structure. I did get to know Beatrice well—a wonderful woman—and I have no doubt that she at least tried to strengthen his character. But Sidney and I were not in the same class—or class struggle. Not in Hollywood, anyway.

I was close to him for a while in "exile," and found him to be intelligent, talented, personable, but insufferably vain. He'd managed to transmute his paranoia into charm, but there was some dross left over. I really don't know about his political input at Columbia. Though I got my start there, the bulk of my experience during that era was at other studios.

What about Dalton Trumbo and Michael Wilson? You met them early on, didn't you? Can you give me a close-up of them, during these salad days?

I did meet Trumbo early in the game; it was at one of the first Writers Guild meetings I attended. He took me, after the meeting, to visit the huge bakery in which he had toiled, where ex–fellow workers greeted him with pleasure, and that first impression of exuberance and wit and scorn for pretension stayed with me over the years. I thought of him, and still do, as the Mark Twain of my generation. A truly remarkable man.

As for Mike Wilson, I got to know him several years later. He had taken up with my then-wife's sister Zelma, up at UC-Berkeley, and was headed for a literary career. Zelma thought he ought to talk to me about screenwriting. I preached the gospel of film as the art form that combines all the other arts, with the greatest possible potential for political influence. He was to emerge as one of the most esteemed screenwriters ever, and one of the most frustrated. He told an interviewer once that the only film he ever wrote in which his work was totally respected, shot as written, was *Salt of the Earth.*

Mike was an all-American boy, in fact, the boy most likely to succeed—handsome, athletic, ambitious, conscientious. He took his work and his politics seriously, though he had an antic sense of humor. He was my brother-in-law, my friend, my sometime collaborator. I'm convinced he would have had a happier life as a novelist.

Can I ask you, also, about Dore Schary? Did he have admirable qualities? How do you diagnose what happened to him later on, when he helped usher in the blacklist? I know that in some cases people feel sympathetic, or at least a sympathetic twinge, though still disliking their former friends who became turncoats. Is there any of that latent feeling in Schary's case?

I'd have developed ambivalent feelings toward Schary, I think, even if he hadn't played such a shabby role during the blacklist period. I was not the kind of radical who despised liberals. And Schary, I felt, was a sincere liberal, with genuine sympathy for the poor, for victims of discrimination, and so on. But he was also a classic opportunist, the kind who keeps telling himself, "If I make this compromise now, I'll be able to do much more for what I believe." And winds up on top, totally compromised. Do I still feel some sympathy for him? Yes.

When you got your first job in Hollywood, did you look up to certain people as screenwriters? Were there people who took you, a junior writer, in hand?

Well, that's a little hard to answer. Dudley Nichols was an exceptionally able writer whom I admired. Jo Swerling, whom I met at Columbia Pictures when I was really a neophyte—he had written *Man's Castle,* a lovely film, with Spencer Tracy and Loretta Young, about a relationship between a man and a woman living in a Hooverville—I admired a great deal. I admired Dore Schary a great deal. But no screenwriters took me in hand, although several older writers, and particularly Jo Swerling, were very nice to me. I was not considered a junior writer, incidentally, youngster though I was.

Did the writers at Columbia work closely with the directors?

Aside from Robert Riskin, without whom there was no Capra, the writers worked far more closely with the producers. This was true for me at all the studios, except for my relationships with Garson Kanin and Fred Zinnemann.

Did you have any contact with Harry Cohn?

I had no direct contact with Harry Cohn for some time, though his spirit was omnipresent at Columbia. When I was finally called into his Mussolini-type office (I don't recall why), he smiled and said, "I'll bet you thought I didn't exist." "I still don't think so," I managed to reply. Though there were many jokes about him, I rather liked him, and still, in retrospect, do. It was no golden age, but he was better at picking pictures than the computers that are doing it now.

Your father was a lawyer, I understand.

Yes, mostly for poor people, like the immigrants, Wobblies, and other radicals persecuted during the Palmer Raids—the Red Scare after the First World War. And he was a political activist, a Socialist, a Labor Zionist. I admired him a lot.

You grew up political?

You might say that. I can remember as a kid reading pamphlets proving that Tom Mooney was framed. I can remember, I was twelve I guess, when Sacco and Vanzetti were executed. What a solemn and tragic feeling there was at our dinner table!

Actually, then, you followed in your father's footsteps politically.

Well, he was certainly my role model—and still is. But by the time he died, at the end of 1933, I'd gone beyond his kind of Socialism.

You'd become a Communist.

I was getting there. I joined the YCL, the Young Communist League, at UCLA, as a sophomore. But for my junior year, 1934 to 1935, I transferred to Berkeley, and that's where I really got active.

Nineteen thirty-four. That was a big year for radicalism.

Was it ever! Harry Bridges, the longshoremen on strike, the whole city of San Francisco on strike, the Depression still going strong, Hitler on the rise. The students were more and more involved, especially at Berkeley. We had free-speech strikes, peace strikes, all kinds of demonstrations. It was a heady time for me.

How did that lead to your joining the Hollywood section of the Party?

As a matter of fact, it's connected with a meeting at the Los Angeles Philharmonic where André Malraux spoke to a large number of people about the cause of the Spanish Loyalists, because I ran into an old friend there who was an active Communist organizer. She asked me what I was doing nowadays, and I told her I had just gotten a job as a Hollywood screenwriter, and she said, "Are you in touch with people in the Party there?" and I said, "No, not yet." She said, "Would you like me to put you in touch with people there?" and I said, "I sure would."

Was there a social aspect to being in the Party, apart from the politics?

Oh, of course. That conversation at the Philharmonic led to my being invited to a luncheon at the Hillcrest Country Club where several young Communists looked me over. It was rather peculiar. My background wasn't really working-class, since my father was a lawyer; nevertheless, it felt rather strange to be sitting in this den of wealthy iniquity with two sons of film executives, and another screenwriter, asking me to join their club.

Why were there so many writers in the Party, as opposed to producers, directors, actresses, and actors?

That's an interesting question. Maybe it's because writers are smarter than other people. [Laughs.]

Looking back, was there an element of guilt involved in the reasons why some people joined the Party—because they were rich, or . . .

There's a Jarrico theory of guilt that will be found, someday, in textbooks of psychology, which is that most people who feel guilty are. Yes, there was a feeling that here we were, living middle-class lives, enjoying a higher standard of living than most people, being paid higher amounts of money for our work than most people got paid for their work, yet identifying ourselves with the oppressed and the poor. And there were people who said, "Well, if you're all that concerned with the poor, why don't you give your money away and become poor?" Yes, it was a question people discussed.

Maybe this guilt manifested itself later on in informing.

That's a connection I would not grant: that someone feels guilty about being better off than others and therefore becomes radicalized, and that somehow this is connected with that same person, later on, becoming an informer. No, I don't grant any connection there at all. I think people joined the Party primarily because they were against Fascism and against inequality and injustice, and if they were motivated by guilt, it was a minor motivation and not a major motivation.

Can you tell me about the differences between a branch meeting and a fraction meeting of the Party? And what was a fraction-plus?

Basically, as I recall, "fraction" was a term used for trade-union work. If the Communists of a union got together, even though they were in different branches, that was a fraction within that union. And a fraction-plus, a phrase that I'm not really familiar with, would mean, I guess, a meeting of Communists within a union to which non-Communists would be invited who might be expected to be sympathetic to the Communist point of view, as far as work within that union went.

What sorts of questions would you discuss at a meeting of a writers' branch of the Party in Hollywood?

A normal branch meeting would begin with an educational segment—one member of the branch would have prepared a talk on a certain subject—followed by a discussion of that subject by the entire branch. Then, probably, there would be a checkup of activities, just going around the room asking people to report on what they'd been doing, usually on the basis of assignments that they'd undertaken at earlier meetings: "How's that coming along? What's happening on that Guild committee? What's happening on that janitors' strike you were helping out with?"

How many people would be there? Where would the meeting take place? What was the atmosphere like?

It was relatively informal. There would ordinarily be about a dozen people at a normal branch meeting. It would take place at people's homes, a different home from week to week, or, more often, biweekly—every two weeks at a different home.

Was there pressure to stay active?

There was, but there was always a conflict, especially among writers, because writing is hard work, and a lot of people were reluctant to take the time off from their normal work of writing in order to engage in political activity. That was a constant conflict: "I haven't got time. I've got this assignment to do." "But, Christ, if you don't do this—if you don't talk to so-and-so in preparation for the next Guild meeting—it's not going to be done; you're the only one who knows him. You're the only guy who knows how to move him on this issue. You've got to do it." "All right, for Christ's sake, I'll do it!" More or less like that. It was not "Comrade, you are expected to do this. Report next week that you have done it!" It wasn't quite as stiff and autocratic as some people might suppose.

I'm fascinated by all the later testimony by HUAC "friendly witnesses" making reference to Party membership cards, which no one ever possessed or saw. Was there any sure way of people knowing who was in the Party and who wasn't? For example, people tell me that John Wexley was certainly in the Party—he was one of the most-named people in the hearings—but Wexley himself swore to me that he was not, and I tend to believe him. John Bright told me that Wexley was so tightfisted that he probably wouldn't have paid the Party dues. How could you ever know for sure?

If you attended branch meetings with people, you could assume that they were in the Party. There were some non-Party Bolsheviks, to adopt, I guess, a Russian phrase, who were close to the Party but for one reason or another were not in the Party, and I suppose if Wexley said he was not in the Party I have to believe him. And there were Communists who did not attend meetings, and who were given very special protection who were nevertheless Communists. But essentially, if you attended Communist functions with certain people over a period of time, you had every right to assume that they were Communists.

Can you give me an example of someone who was protected and did not attend Party meetings, someone who's dead, no longer alive, someone whom it wouldn't hurt, or someone who everyone knows was a Communist, then and now?

No, I can't. I speak very freely about myself as a Communist, and I speak very freely about John Howard Lawson, whose Communist affiliation was hardly a secret, but I'm still not prepared to talk about other people and whether they were Communists or not.

How about somebody like Paul Robeson? Is that a fair question?

Whether he was a member? I wouldn't know. He did educate me on the question of white chauvinism, and I considered it useful education.

Why Paul Robeson?

Because he was the man who knew more about it than anybody in the world. Paul Robeson was a man who had been under enormous attack because of his open admiration for the Soviet Union. He gave a concert in Peekskill where he and his audience were strong-armed by a Nazi-minded mob. He later came out to California, where he gave a concert, and I was one of the people—veterans of the Second World War—who formed an honor guard when he spoke and sang. He was a man I met under various circumstances a number of times, and I had occasion to discuss political questions with him, including basically the question of whether it was possible to root out the remnants of white chauvinism among people who realized that they lived in a society in which it was endemic.

I'm critical of the Party about many issues, and when I say I'm critical of the Party, I obviously mean to include myself. But there are a few issues on which the Party was right and on which the Party really fought all out, and one of those issues was the fight against white chauvinism. None of us who participated in those fights has anything to be ashamed of, ever. And a lot to be proud of. It's all very well to say you're against white chauvinism and you're against racism, but we grow up in a society poisoned by racism, and how do you get rid of that poison? How do you overcome it?

I can't quote him exactly, but I do recall the excitement of these discussions with Robeson, because he was a great man, and one felt it in his presence. And he was not all that judgmental. He hated racism, but he did understand that people reflect the values of the culture in which they're reared.

What was the role of women in the Party?

In theory, we believed totally, unequivocally, in the equality of women. But just as we never overcame our white chauvinism, we never overcame all of our male chauvinism, and the chairmanship of the branch tended to go to a man, and the organizational secretaryship tended to go to a woman. We had some of the best-run mass organizations in the country, and they were manned—if I may use the wrong word—by women. The women were so remarkable in their organizational skills that many of them went on to become successful organizers in bourgeois enterprises after the Party was no longer a force in Hollywood.

But to a certain extent women were excluded from leadership positions and from priority as a political issue.

I'm not saying they were excluded. But there weren't as many women in the leadership as their number and talent justified.

How did you see yourself as aligned within the Party in terms of the most important political questions that would arise inside of the Hollywood section?

Well, the Party line changed on a number of issues. Looking backward, for me the most significant division among the screenwriters, or among Hollywood Party members, was the question of whether the content of film could be basically affected by our work. There were those who felt that since the movie industry was owned and controlled by the ruling class, it was a part of the superstructure, and that its function was to defend the base—the economic base being a capitalist system—and that therefore we were kidding ourselves if we thought we could affect content at all. And there were those who felt that there was sufficient freedom in the film industry—enough choices possible—that one could affect content. Perhaps one couldn't make a revolutionary film, but one could certainly affect the attitude toward minorities, toward women, toward working people, or toward people in general—a humanist attitude as opposed to a Fascist, antihuman attitude. I was in this latter group, this second group, of those who thought that content could be affected. That put me, in Party terms, on the right; that is to say, I was a right-wing opportunist as compared to the left-wing sectarians. From my point of view, John Howard Lawson was a left sectarian and I was a true Marxist. From his point of view, I was a right-wing opportunist and he was a true Marxist.

Were these arguments with Lawson public or private? It seems in reading some of the literature that you became a sort of spokesmen for a minority faction when he was heading up the Party in Hollywood.

I don't want to say that I was the leader of the so-called opportunists. Certainly a substantial number of people shared my attitude.

Did you feel comfortable with Lawson's leadership?

Lawson was a friend of mine. You have to understand that the Party members were friendly toward each other. We could have disagreements, and sometimes very serious disagreements, without feeling personally betrayed or personally hostile, or without at least acting hostile. There were very, very serious discussions of the questions that I was talking about. The question of superstructure—base and superstructure—was one that was debated, analyzed, discussed; position papers were written on it, representing different points of view. This was not a minor scuffle. This was a basic political discussion that went on for years in one form or another.

Some of us didn't like Jack Lawson's leadership, particularly, but there wasn't much of a rebellion against him until he went to prison. When he came out of prison, he found that leadership had passed into other hands, and he wasn't particularly happy about it. He wanted his leadership back, and we wouldn't give it to him.

Most of the work of the Party had nothing to do with the issue of whether you could affect film content, right?

Obviously, the fight against Fascism was *the* priority from 1935 to 1939, and then again after the [Hitler-Stalin] Pact period was over, from 1941 to 1945. It was certainly the central priority. But there were always people who felt that the primary job of the Party in Hollywood was to organize and strengthen the trade unions. And there were many people who felt that the main job of a Communist in Hollywood was to help the struggle of people outside of Hollywood—to supply cultural materials, shows, skits, and speeches to people on strike, for instance.

Looking back historically, what did the Hitler-Stalin Pact mean to the Party's efforts to expand and to grow?

It was a disaster for the Party. Or rather, the Party decision to accept "What is good for the Soviet Union is good for us" as its basic orientation was a disaster. Clearly we lost whatever prestige we had built up in the course of the anti-Fascist fight, and in many countries Communists had to be the most self-sacrificial during the war in order to win back any kind of prestige at all for the Communist side. This was particularly true in France. God knows how many Communists lost their lives in the Resistance movement, in the effort to prove that they were patriotic Frenchmen and loyal anti-Fascists.

Do you doubt, historically, that the Pact was sensible?

I think the Pact made sense for the Soviet Union. The Pact was the Soviet Union double-crossing the double-crosser. It was a brilliant coup. It gained them some time, which they didn't use properly. Nevertheless, it achieved the aim of enabling the Soviet Union to deflect Hitler's onslaught or at least to postpone it. But the Communist Party here never regained, after the Hitler-Stalin Pact, the influence it had before. Even after the Soviet Union was invaded and the Party again switched back to an anti-Fascist position, the egg had been broken, the myth of Communist intelligence had been broken.

People like us had been the chief organizers in the Hollywood Anti-Nazi League, which had become an important organization. Then one day we found ourselves rising in meetings of the Hollywood Anti-Nazi League and saying, "I think we ought to change the name of the organization . . . and we ought to change the policy . . . after all, the war is imperialist on both sides." Certainly nobody who was a serious anti-Nazi would follow our leadership out of the anti-Nazi camp. That's what happened outside the Party. Within the Party, there were any number of people who just quit. I don't think the Party ever recovered nationally or in Hollywood, though I personally stayed with the Party through that and other disastrous twists and turns.

Later on, during World War II, wouldn't you say that the Party proved itself as patriotic as the DAR or the Republican Party?

It did indeed, but the suspicion that we had become patriotic on June 22, 1941, when the Soviet Union was invaded, was well-founded. And certainly it was easy enough to be patriotic when everybody else was. We didn't have any special vanguard position, except possibly the need to open a second front. Even that was looked upon with suspicion, again by people feeling we were looking out for the interests of the Soviet Union, not the United States. Now, I personally didn't find a contradiction between the interests of the Soviet Union and the interests of the United States. I thought the Soviet Union was a vanguard country fighting for a better future for the entire world, including the United States. That was an illusion, I dicovered. But the illusion didn't make me disloyal; it made me a fool. And that's what I wound up feeling like. Not that I'd been deceived, but that I'd deceived myself.

Let's get back on the career track. Where did you go after Columbia?

I really moved around a lot. After the three and a half months on *No Time to Marry* and the month or so on *I Am the Law* in 1937, I found myself borrowed from Columbia by Samuel Goldwyn to work on a script (never produced) called "The Duchess of Broadway." How this happened, why Goldwyn would have wanted a neophyte who'd just been put under contract at Columbia, I just can't imagine. Anyway, I was on "The Duchess" for six weeks or so, then back at Columbia to work on a Blondie story (unproduced) and "The Little Adventuress" (for a child actress named Edith Fellows), then back at Goldwyn for another month or so on "The Duchess." It was on the Goldwyn assignment that I got to know Garson Kanin, whom Goldwyn had employed as some sort of director trainee. Which led later to *Tom, Dick, and Harry.*

The contract at Columbia didn't last long, that seems evident, for I seem to have spent the period between the summer of 1938 and the summer of 1939 on a variety of assignments at other studios. I'm not sure of the order, but I remember a funny one at MGM on a script (unproduced) called "Frank Morgan for Senator." ("But no politics!" the producer warned.) There was also a short job at Universal on a treatment of "Probation Nurse" (unproduced); a screenplay of "Rip Van Winkle" at Monogram (which I've reacquired and am still trying to get produced, but that's another saga); an original screenplay at Universal called *Men of the Timberland*, which was rewritten, leaving me with a story credit. It dealt with the fight that Richard Arlen, Andy Devine, and some Dead End–type kids in the Civilian Conservation Corps put up against the timber barons. Premature environmentalism!

At any rate, I wound up at RKO at some point in 1939, working on the first stage—the original story—of *Tom, Dick, and Harry*, and on a rewrite of *Beauty for the Asking*. I was back at RKO for more work on *Tom, Dick, and Harry* at some point in 1940, but also worked at Republic again, on a story and screenplay called "All Night Program" (unproduced); sold a spec story called "That Was No Lady" (unproduced) to MGM; and went back to Columbia for a rewrite of the screenplay of *The Face Behind the Mask*. I don't think I even met the director, Robert Florey; I'm quite sure I didn't meet Peter Lorre, and although I have pretty full files on most of the things I worked on, I find nothing in my file on *The Face* but a step outline* and a favorable review in the *Hollywood Reporter* of April 24, 1941.

Then I went back to RKO for the final push on *Tom, Dick, and Harry* in 1941. Kanin kept me with him all through the shoot and even the editing— unprecedented. He had made few suggestions for changes in the script, but good ones, and he really wanted my input during the production. As I've said in other interviews, he really seemed to believe that the writer was to the director as the composer was to the conductor, or the architect to the builder. Which is why, presumably, he more or less gave up directing and became a writer.

When you were nominated for an Oscar, did your career get a jolt of electricity? Did your phone ring off the hook? Were you there for the awards ceremony that night, and how did you feel—being the David against the Goliath of Herman Mankiewicz and Orson Welles's Citizen Kane?

I'd been on the escalator from the beginning, and my salary had gone up a little with almost every assignment, but *Tom, Dick, and Harry* graduated me from B pictures to A pictures, and now my salary made a much bigger jump. Even before I got nominated for an Oscar. I was not there for the awards, and I was not surprised to be defeated by *Citizen Kane*. It deserved the Oscar.

I understand you thought Tom, Dick, and Harry *was a breakthrough in political content . . . at least at the time.*

Well, *Tom, Dick, and Harry* was a milestone picture for me—the first chance I got to write one for a big star, with a relatively large budget, and so on. I thought that I was writing an attack on the Cinderella myth and an attack on the success-story myth. And I did, I think, come up with some amusing observations on those questions. What I failed to realize until years

---

*A "step outline" is a brief, step-by-step presentation of scenes in the film.

later was that I'd reinforced, without meaning to, an even greater myth—the ultimate movie cliché—that love conquers all.

But I still think it's is possible to write films that say something. Take a film like *Network*, which attacks the television industry in the most profound way, even though it's in comedy terms. However, when I saw *Network*, I also prophesied, because I've grown more sophisticated since *Tom, Dick, and Harry*, that it would be bought for television, and it was.

I think [Herbert] Marcuse, who's difficult to understand in general, was fairly clear on one subject, which is the ability of the establishment to swallow the dissidents and to, in fact, profit from the dissidents. To turn the work of the dissidents, the anti-establishment people, into commodities. I think that happens. I'm jumping from one thing to another, but on that same theme, "Ballad for Americans," which Earl Robinson wrote, is a beautiful ballad about the cultural and ethnic diversity of America that extols the dignity of labor and says we are all Americans—there are a lot of important, good themes in that song. When I heard it played as the theme song of the Republican convention that nominated Wendell Willkie, I realized that we have to be very careful about defining progressive culture—that if it's too generalized it can be accepted by anybody or everybody, and that it can mean radical things to me but not necessarily to the other person.

What happened next in your career? How did you get roped into Thousands Cheer?

On the strength of *Tom, Dick, and Harry*, I got a job—with Richard Collins as my collaborator—developing an original screenplay called "Boy Wonder" for Universal. We designed it for Jimmy Stewart and Jean Arthur. The producer, Bruce Manning, had written some of Joe Pasternak's big successes at Universal, and Manning liked our work so much that he recommended us to Pasternak, who was, by that time, producing at Metro. Which is how we wound up writing *Thousands Cheer* at Metro, which is how we wound up writing *Song of Russia* at Metro, for both of those were Pasternak productions. To get back to "Boy Wonder," it languished on the shelf until it was rewritten for Abbott and Costello [as *Little Giant*]. Collins and I got original story credit and deserved no more.

I did not "get roped into" *Thousands Cheer*. The move from Universal to Metro was a step upward in both money and prestige, and though Pearl Harbor had not as yet been bombed, Russia had been invaded, the draft had shifted into high gear, and an entertainment about an individualistic draftee learning to adjust to the Army collective seemed like a good idea at the time.

What did you do during World War II, and how much was your choice influenced by the Party?

I'm a bit fuzzy on the chronology, but I think December 7 exploded while we were very close to completing the *Thousands Cheer* script. I began on December 8 to apply for a commission as a combat correspondent in various branches of the service, plus the OSS. There followed a series of turndowns.

The reason was obvious (and later confirmed): they knew all about my Party membership.

Then came Song of Russia, *right? A most unlikely MGM production.*

Hollywood was more than willing to do war films, but it took a lot of pressure by Roosevelt and the OWI [Office of War Information] to get the major studios to celebrate our alliance with Russia. So Metro bought a grim story called "Scorched Earth," and it was assigned to Pasternak, who produced musicals (mistake #1), and he asked Jarrico and Collins, who'd just done a successful musical for him, to do the screenplay, and at least one of them jumped at the chance. I knocked myself out to do it fast—the Battle of Stalingrad was raging—but Collins seemed to be dragging his feet. Gregory Ratoff was assigned to direct (mistake #2), Robert Taylor to star (mistake #3). When we finished the script, Collins said to me, shamefaced, "Look, I've done ten percent; you've done ninety percent. I don't deserve credit." I turned the offer down. "We were hired as a team," I said, "and we'll take credit as a team. But I don't think we ought to work together again."

How did you and Collins meet?

In the Party.

What was he like then as opposed to later?

He was a nice guy, and he became a shit.

Who did what in the collaboration?

I carried him—which was why, I guess, he knifed me. As I've said before, he wanted to stand on his own two knees.

What was Louis B. Mayer's attitude toward the project?

I wouldn't say he was enthusiastic about it, but he did do what the government asked him to do. And when he was told that I was a Communist, he said, "I know. I wouldn't keep him for a minute if he weren't such a good writer." That was his attitude before the Un-American Activities Committee said that he, Louis B. Mayer, had no right to employ a Communist.

There are funny stories about Louis B. Mayer's criticism of our script. He wanted us to take the word "community" out because it was too much like the word "Communism." The plot, if you recall, deals with an American orchestra conductor, played badly by Robert Taylor, who meets a Soviet pianist, played by Susan Peters, while he's on a tour of the Soviet Union. They fall in love, get married, and go off to visit her family, who work on a collective farm. Louis B. Mayer said it couldn't be a collective farm; it had to be a private farm. We said there was no such thing in the Soviet Union. He said, "Why can't it be just her father's farm? Why does it have to be a collective farm?" We finally reached a compromise. We wouldn't specify either collective or private. We'd just avoid the question. [Laughs.]

Why, when the film was done, did you ship out in the Merchant Marine?

It's complicated. Warner Brothers offered me a job to accompany an ice-breaker that was sailing to Murmansk as a gift of the Americans and to do a movie about it, and MGM refused to lend me to Warner's. I was furious, and I got in touch with some officers of the National Maritime Union I knew and arranged to ship out. I wanted to see the war, be part of it. I didn't feel like sitting around a studio.

What did that experience consist of for you?

It consisted of shipping out, being in North Africa and Italy in 1943, and seeing some action there. But I was a hitchhiker. As a volunteer, I could get off at any time the ship was back in the United States. And I did. It was a marvelous experience for me, and later in the war—at the tail end—I was drafted. I wasn't draftable earlier because I had a wife and a child. I was drafted into the Navy, but I didn't get overseas. By that time the war was just about over.

There was a period, after you got back from the Merchant Marine, when you did another stint at RKO, right?

I was borrowed from MGM by RKO, before my stint in the Navy, to do a screenplay based on a book called *I Am Thinking of My Darling*. William Dozier, then in charge of production at RKO, liked my script a lot. While I was in the Navy, my agent managed to free me from my MGM contract and to get me a dream contract as a writer-director at RKO. I was just getting started there after the war when Dozier was replaced by my old friend Dore Schary. As it happened, *Darling* was a fantasy, and Schary didn't like fantasies. That was the end of that project. The contract allowed me to turn down their proposals and them to turn down mine. A duel ensued. Omitting the blow-by-blow, it wound up in my writing the script for *The White Tower*. It was to be directed not by me, however, but by Eddie Dmytryk. Omitting details again, Dmytryk and I went mountain climbing, he got himself blacklisted, the project was shelved, and I was loaned out to a Swiss company to work on *The Search*. That all happened in 1946 and 1947. *The White Tower* wasn't shot until 1950, when I was long gone from RKO. Ted Tetzlaff, who directed, and Glenn Ford, who starred, respected my script, except for its heart, which was anti-war. They cut its heart out and failed to replace it with another heart, even an artificial one.

Tell me about The Search. *Were you around for the filming? How did you get along with Fred Zinnemann, the director?*

I reduced a 240-or-so-page script in German to a 120-or-so-page script in English and Americanized the hero (Montgomery Clift). Asked what kind of credit I wanted, I replied, "Subtractional dialogue." The quip cost me an Oscar; I got an additional dialogue credit, and the producer's son, an apprentice to the original writer, shared his Academy Award. I'd been given the job because Zinnemann asked for me, and we got along famously. His reactions to my work were always helpful, and he's gone out of his way, in interviews and in person, to praise my contributions. I was invited to stay for the shoot but declined in favor of a vacation with my family. Another mistake.

How involved were you with Not Wanted? *Did you work closely at all with Ida Lupino? Can you tell me anything about how she worked as a director?*

I wrote the first draft of the story and the screenplay of *Not Wanted* very quickly and barely met Ida Lupino. Saw it on tape recently. Embarrassing.

Then you were blacklisted. Briefly, I wonder if you could tell me the story of a movie you wrote for RKO that you didn't get credit for, The Las Vegas Story.

Well, *The Las Vegas Story* was not a script that I was particularly proud of, and I would not ordinarily have fought for credit on it. But I had just about completed that script at the time that I was subpoenaed by the Un-American Activities Committee, and Howard Hughes, who by that time owned RKO, reacted. First he ordered that the script be rewritten thoroughly so as to get rid of my credit, and they did make an effort to rewrite it thoroughly, but the picture was about to go into production, and they didn't have enough time to really take out the last bit of Jarrico poison. The Writers Guild, which then had control of credits, awarded me one of the credits. And Hughes declared that he would simply not have my name on the film, and if the Writers Guild didn't like it they could go on strike. So he not only violated his contract with me, which provided that I be given credit for my work, but he violated his collective-bargaining agreement with the Writers Guild, and several lawsuits ensued. I sued Hughes, Hughes countersued me, the Guild sued Hughes.

I lost my suit, and I lost it under the so-called morals clause. The judge decided that I had placed myself in public obloquy by refusing to cooperate with the Un-American Activities Committee—though we maintained that claiming your constitutional rights could not possibly be considered immoral. Nevertheless, the judge ruled against me, and the Guild got frightened. The lawyers for Hughes discovered that there was no enforcement clause in the collective agreement, and the Guild backed down. They not only gave up their campaign against Hughes, they surrendered their control over credits— not only in my case, in the case of that one film, but for the next fifteen or twenty years. That's why one saw such wild, ridiculous things as people winning Academy Awards whose names were not on the screen.

Anyway, the suit against Hughes got a lot of publicity, as did anything connected with Hughes. I was proud to have him as an enemy. A man's known by his enemies as well as his friends. [Laughs.]

I know that the story of Salt of the Earth *is a book in and of itself, but can you summarize the effort by a group of blacklistees to get into independent production*

*and the travail that you had to go through to get the film made and exhibited? Why
did you hire yourself as producer and not writer or director?*

The word "producer" covers a multitude of sinners, from independent mon-
archs like Goldwyn and Selznick to lowly deputies of studio heads who serve
as supervisors but have no real power. In theory, the producer is boss. He
hires and fires writers, directors, actors, staff, and crew; determines budgets
and schedules; runs the show. In practice, it doesn't work that way. He's the
coordinater of a number of major players.

What did I do in the case of *Salt of the Earth*? I joined Adrian Scott and
Herbert Biberman in forming a company determined to use the growing pool
of blacklisted talent to make films that said something. We had several scripts
in development when I persuaded my partners to put that story ahead of the
others. We agreed that Mike Wilson—an Academy Award winner before and
after the blacklist—would be the best possible writer for the job, and he agreed
to try it. Adrian would have been a more logical choice as producer, but he
wasn't well. In the event, Mike as writer, Herbert as director, and I as producer
were a triumvirate. No substantive decision was made unless two of us agreed
to it. So I was an unprecedented kind of producer.

I have said that *Salt of the Earth* was our chance to really say something in
film, because we had already been punished, we had already been blacklisted.
I used the phrase, "We wanted to commit a crime to fit the punishment."
The film dealt with a strike of Mexican Americans in which the women took
over the picket line. It was unequivocally prolabor, prominority, and pro-
women.

The effort to suppress the making of the film took dramatic forms. Our
leading lady [Rosaura Revueltas] who had come up from Mexico to play the
lead, was deported to Mexico before we had finished with her, on trumped-
up charges. There was vigilante action against us: attempts to burn down our
sets, gunfire directed against us, shots taken at a union organizer's car in the
middle of the night, our crews assaulted on the streets of the town in New
Mexico where we were shooting. Laboratories refused to process our film. I
had to trot around the country with cans of film under my arms, putting the
film through different labs under phony names. We had a lot of trouble, but
we did complete the film, despite the obstacles.

It won international prizes, but it was successfully blocked as far as any real
distribution—or even unreal distribution—went, in the United States. Now,
more than forty years after the film was made, the picture is finally beginning
to have a future in our own country. And I sometimes say that it's the only
picture I ever worked on that got better over the years instead of worse.

What types of projects did you have in mind if you had been able to continue?

We had several projects. We had a black writer named Mason Roberson
working on a script of a book we had acquired called *Scottsboro Boy*. Dalton
Trumbo was doing a script about a woman whose children are taken away

from her in a divorce case because she is accused of being a red. We were looking very hard for a film to star Paul Robeson, because we felt that he had been, historically, blacklisted and was certainly the most eminent blacklisted actor in America. But we lost our shirts on *Salt of the Earth* because of the boycott, and we were never able to realize these other projects.

I have gotten the feeling from some books that the Albert Maltz affair—that is, when Maltz was forced to recant his article in the New Masses *arguing in favor of creative freedom for the Communist writer—was another turning point for some people in the Party. But you have told me that it really wasn't. What were the issues involved there?*

The issue in the Albert Maltz affair was the definition of the cultural worker's responsibility to the political line of the Party—the nature of cultural work, really: whether an artistic piece of work that is positive in its human values is enough, or whether it's necessary for a work to be more sharply political and more definitely aligned to political needs. If the political need is, let us say, the war against Fascism, then your work, your cultural work, ought to be about the war against Fascism and not about how terrible poverty is in general, or about other issues that are not as central. This issue—this question of what is the relation between progress and culture, and the responsibility of the cultural worker who accepts political affiliation—is an old one. It goes back to Marx and Engels and has been continued up through the history of the First Communist International, the Second, the Third, and those to come.

In the Soviet Union, the Zhdanov line* was that the responsibility of the cultural worker is to serve the political line directly, not indirectly, not just by doing good work or even creating great works of art. That line became the dominant line in the Soviet Union and, by extension, in the American Party as well. Maltz was rebelling a little—not much, but a little—against the dogmatic assertions of the Zhdanov line, and he got slapped down hard. He was told that if he was a good Communist he would accept this line. And he did, which he later regretted.

But the point I am trying to make is that this was going on all over the world. Mao was saying the same thing to Ding Ling, saying she could not just write in general; she had to write what would help the Party directly, in the

---

*Andrei Zhdanov, considered a major theorist during Stalin's last years, intellectually justified and administratively guided the purges of intellectual and cultural figures in the post–World War II era. After a series of speeches in 1946 and 1947 denouncing "cosmopolitanism" and "worship of things foreign" (code words for Jews, among others), Zhdanov arranged expulsions from the Union of Writers. Not long afterward, arrests began, in the end destroying the Soviet Union's Yiddish literature and theater. So great did his influence grow that Stalin himself became jealous and "retired" the theorist-*apparatchik*, later blaming Zhdanov's early death on a "Jewish doctors' plot." Elsewhere in the world, "Zhdanovism" became synonymous with using logic-chopping on intellectuals to force them to toe the Party line carefully or face defamation.

current struggle. And Ding Ling accepted that—reluctantly—before she rebelled against it and got thrown into all kinds of terrible jails and exiled because of her rebellion.* The penalty for rebelling in the United States wasn't quite as tough.

The Party's relationship to things that writers wrote was somehow more strict when it came to non-movie writing than when it came to movie writing. Somehow one felt, or the Party felt, maybe correctly, that the individual writer was more responsible for a novel than for a movie, because the writer didn't have ultimate control of the movie, but he or she certainly had ultimate control of the novel. There were a couple of cases in which the attitude of the Party shifted, depending on the political situation, toward a work of art.

There was the famous case of Budd Schulberg's *What Makes Sammy Run?* Budd Schulberg is still groaning and bemoaning the fact that the Party mistreated him. The Party didn't mistreat him. Some members of the Party felt that if a Jewish hero, or antihero, was treated with the contempt that he deserved in Budd's book, he would feed anti-Semitism at the very time when the Hitler line was that Jews are like that—like Sammy. It was an ill-timed novel. Whether they were right or wrong, nobody said to Budd Schulberg, "You may not publish that novel." It was an opinion expressed by some people.

Similarly, Dalton Trumbo had written a marvelously graphic, compelling anti-war novel, *Johnny Got His Gun.* He had written that, I recall, before the Pact. It was considered maybe not too useful a book at a period when we were trying to mobilize collective security against Nazism. But when the Pact came along, and with it the slogan "The Yanks Are *Not* Coming," why, nothing was more perfect than Trumbo's anti-war novel. Except that when the line changed, and the Yanks *were* coming, then Trumbo's anti-war novel became an embarrassment again, although Trumbo was not forced to withdraw his novel.

You're saying, in part, that you feel that Albert Maltz was wronged more by this correct line-ism than, say, Budd Schulberg.

Oh, I do. I think Maltz was wronged because Maltz accepted Party discipline, and Schulberg just kicked about it—and kicked about it to the Un-American Activities Committee. What business is it of the Un-American Activities Committee? Part of Budd's being an informer was to talk about this terrible adventure he'd had of mind and thought control within the Party, which was a big exaggeration. It's true that my attitude toward Albert and my attitude toward Budd are quite different.

---

*Ding Ling, Red China's most famous writer and feminist, resisted Mao's doctrinaire view of "art as a weapon" and became a victim of the Cultural Revolution.

Why do you think so many people in Hollywood, and, in particular, Party members, were undergoing breakdowns and consulting psychiatrists after the World War II period?

I'm not sure there were more Party people going to psychiatrists and psychoanalysts than there were non-Party people, proportionately, but the Party did have a rule, as I recall, that no one who was in analysis could be in the Party. It was a security rule. So people going into therapy would either drop out or take a leave of absence.

Was there a kind of general anxiety or depression in people's psychologies at the time, related either to tensions within the Party or to politics after the war?

If there was, I don't recall it, because looking back at that period personally, I found it quite an exhilarating period and not at all a period of depression.

When the first HUAC subpoenas came down, was there initially a lot of popular support for the Hollywood Nineteen?

There was not only popular support, there was political support. The Committee for the First Amendment was formed, which consisted of a lot of important stars, including people like [Humphrey] Bogart and John Huston, celebrities of one sort or another, and sincere liberals who went to Washington at the time of the hearings to lend their support to the people who were called by the Committee. They went to lend their support to the thesis of those called, which was that the Committee on Un-American Activities did not have the right under the First Amendment to the Constitution to inquire into people's politics. Yes, there was all kinds of support—including newspaper editorials—which faded quite quickly not too long afterward.

Do you feel that you underestimated what was about to happen?

We underestimated the amount of fear and the quickness with which it spread. Once the producers got together at the Waldorf-Astoria and the leaders of the producers' association declared that they were going to blacklist the Ten—who by that time had refused to cooperate with the Committee and had been indicted for contempt of Congress—the liberal defenses collapsed, they just collapsed. Even though the target of the Committee, it seemed to me then and it still seems to me, was less a radical minority than the liberal center.

You underestimated the reactionary forces that were aligned against you.

We underestimated the direct connection between the Cold War abroad and repression at home. Looking back on it now, it seems very obvious. If you're going to call on people to give their lives in a fight against Communism internationally, you can certainly raise logically the question of why we should allow Communists or Communist sympathizers to express themselves domestically, here at home. I mean, there was a logic to the reactionary position, and we underestimated the strength of that logic.

How did you find out about your own imminent blacklisting? Who named you— and why, do you think?

I'd produced a fifteen-minute short about the Hollywood Ten on the eve of their imprisonment, made quickly and secretly by a small professional crew I recruited with promises of anonymity. Mine was the only name publicized at the time. I was pretty well-known as an activist anyway, and I didn't have to "find out about my imminent blacklisting"—I expected it. Who named me? I was named by thirteen (I think it was) informers, some of whom I don't think I ever met.

Most people were offered some sort of deal or cop-out. Were you?

No, and I'm afraid you're mistaken. Most people were not offered deals. Except for one or two people whose studio was rumored to have bribed somebody, there was no way to cop out. If you were named, either you named others or you were blacklisted.

Even if you were not a Communist?

Even if you were guilty by association, even if you were a liberal fingered as a radical by a malicious competitor, even if you'd joined the Party for a short or long period and then decided it was not for you. If you were named, whether falsely or not, you had two choices and only two. You could accept, or pretend to accept, the basic assumption of McCarthyism—that Communists were traitors—and plead that you were a dupe or a dope, and clear yourself by naming others. Or you could stand on the constitutional amendments that give you the right to speak out, the right to remain silent, and the right to believe any damn thing you want to believe. For those who were genuinely pissed off at the Party but reluctant to name others, the choice must've been difficult. For a person like me, a true-blue red, the choice was easy.

I know some of the informers really surprised—and hurt—people by their testimony. Which was the worst for you?

Richard Collins. We'd been friends, even after our collaboration ended, so the most painful betrayal was that of Collins.

Do you think high-handed tactics of the left in Hollywood undermined the left and contributed to the collapse, say, of the Popular Front leadership in Guild meetings, etc., and, later on, to the blacklist?

It's possible, though I'm not sure I know what you mean by "high-handed tactics." Mistakes? We made those, all right. And the Ten made mistakes.

Like what?

Like the pretense that they *were* answering the questions, which their law-yers had advised. But they were sure right in their fundamental claim, that they were defending the Constitution.

Any other mistakes?

Well, the liberals had been led to believe that though the Ten would not tell the Committee whether they were Communists, they would—those of them who were—identify themselves later. And they didn't. Which let the liberals off the hook, gave them a rationale for deserting the ship.

But it was a ship on which they were sailing too, not just the reds, so in deserting the ship they really allowed themselves to drown. They lost their own freedom. There were a lot more liberals than there were Communists, and they'd written some of the best films ever made—Nunnally Johnson's screenplay of *The Grapes of Wrath*, for instance. Well, after the Committee had its way, they couldn't write those scripts, even if they themselves were not blacklisted.

We have been talking about the tactics of the left wing. Can you characterize for me the types of tactics, and the efficacy, of the right wing?

The right wing in Hollywood, which had less of a following, I think, than the left wing did, was determined and well-organized, and showed a certain amount of revolutionary efficiency. [Laughs.] They did very well. They won the day.

After HUAC descended on Hollywood and wiped a lot of people off the map, professionally, many people either left town or quit the Party. Why did you stay?

I personally felt that I had things to do politically and that the fight was not over. Making *Salt of the Earth* was certainly part of the counterattack that we launched. And there were other things. We put out a newspaper called *Hollywood Review*, in which we tried to analyze what was happening to the content of films, and work remained to be done in certain organizations, non-Party organizations. The unions remained. There were plenty of things to do.

Is it true that you headed the Hollywood section in the mid-1950s?

I was the head of the Party in the sense that I presided over its liquidation—to use the Churchillian phrase. People were leaving the Party. Being chairman was not quite the prize that it had been in earlier years, though some people would never have considered it a prize. What was left of the Party we tried to hold together, but it was more or less a lost cause. When the Khrushchev report came along in 1956, even the slowest of us realized that the accusations against Stalin and Stalinism had been true—though we had denied they were true—and that we had been defending indefensible things. That, I would say, was the end of the Party.

Though not quite. Some of us participated in a movement to have the American Party declare its independence, so to speak, from the Soviet leadership. It was a movement that seemed for a little while to be succeeding. It was analogous to what was going on in Hungary in exactly the same year and for exactly the same reasons. But even after we won in a national Party convention—with resolutions to kick out the pro-Soviet leadership, and so on—they reasserted their authority and kicked us out, or kicked some of us out, and the rest of us resigned. That was early in 1958, and I didn't see any future for me in the Party. I no longer wanted to be part of a Party that considered itself "the holder of the franchise," to use the words of the leadership, the franchiser being the Soviet Union.

How did you quit?

Just quit. [Laughs.] Just said, "I'm getting out."

What were the worst mistakes of the Party in Hollywood?

The mistakes of the Party in Hollywood were probably the same as the mistakes of the Party everywhere in the United States. It was looking to the Soviet Union for leadership. But I think there was another mistake, which was probably special to Hollywood, and that was that our membership was covert. Secret. There are good historical reasons why Party members did not advertise their membership in the Party. But in Hollywood it was a disastrous course, because though we would have been one-tenth the size that we were [if we had been public], we would never have suffered the plague of informers that we did suffer. And we would have accomplished just as much, I think—or more.

Did you think at the time—do you think in retrospect—that a revolution in the United States was possible in your lifetime, if it hadn't been for the mistakes of the Party?

No. Nor were we leading a revolution. The Communist Party was not a revolutionary organization, not in the period when I was in it. It was a reformist organization, and for most of the years I was in it, it was the tail to the liberal-Democratic kite. The rise of Fascism had forced a basic shift of line, an attempt to build a Popular Front, a united anti-Fascist front, both domestically and internationally.

Around this time, when you left the Party, you also left the United States. Can you tell me why, and what that entailed?

One of the ironies of the blacklist was that they took our passports away. I'd been abroad a number of times before the blacklist, and I was pretty sure I could get work aboard, but it took a long, hard fight for the lawyers—notably Leonard Boudin—to get the Supreme Court to rule that the State Department did not have the right to withhold passports on political grounds. The moment that happened, which was in 1958, seven years after I got myself blacklisted, I took off. By that time I was getting enough black-market work to support myself. But I had built up such a head of steam that I just took off as soon as I could.

Where did you live, and what was the attitude toward you wherever you went?

Once I got to Europe in the fall of 1958, I lived in various places. Initially in Paris, then in London, the South of France, Switzerland, Paris again, Switzerland again, London again, and so on. I lived in a number of places, but Paris was the base to which I kept returning.

The attitude, obviously—or maybe it's not obvious—was very positive toward the blacklisted people who had gone to Europe. Generally we were made to feel welcome. And those who managed to get out of the country before their passports were lifted, but whose passports were lifted after they were abroad, got favorable treatment by the French government and even the British government. There was a general feeling that something unjust was going on in the States, and they were congratulating themselves that they were not part of the ridiculousness of McCarthyism.

Were you able to get work regularly, both on the black market, and openly?

I managed to support myself as a writer through the pre-blacklist, blacklist, and post-blacklist periods, fortunately. Not always to support myself well, but I managed to support myself. Yes, I got work. I got work at first under phony names, but in Europe at least the producers knew they were hiring me, and the reason for the pseudonyms was to help them get American distribution; my name might embarrass that effort.

*Ironically, your best-known film—*Tom, Dick, and Harry—*was remade during this time in the United States, as* The Girl Most Likely. *But your name didn't appear on the screen.*

The Guild awarded me a shared credit. It was impossible not to, since it was a remake of a picture on which I had a sole story and screenplay credit. They even nominated me for a Guild award for it. But the Guild made no demand I know of that the studio put my name on the screen.

After a while—finally, after seventeen years—in 1968, for the first time since the blacklist, I got credit under my own name on a film. It was no great shakes, but it was a milestone for me, and since then I've had my name on other films, and the blacklist is behind me.

Why did you ultimately return to Hollywood?

I was born and bred in L.A., I have lots of personal and professional connections in this area, I'd had enough of Europe, so I came home. From a job point of view, I should have done so years earlier.

I know you are one of the last of your generation who are still active in the marketplace. I can't help but notice that you worked on the telefilm of Stalin *a few years ago. Did that produce any qualms, or sense of irony . . . or feelings of poetic symmetry?*

I was hired to rewrite a script. I did so. I had no credit, because I'd not done enough, under Guild rules, to merit one. No, I felt no irony or nostalgia or poetry, or remembrance of illusions past.

I know there have always been divisions on the Hollywood left and, at times, friction among the blacklistees. But there has also been unusual solidarity through the years. What remains today?

There is still solidarity among the blacklistees—those who are still alive. The only period of division I can think of was after 1956, when a very few unreconstructed hardliners like Lester Cole accused everyone else of surrender. It's a dead issue now. The degree of solidarity? I'd say strong, then and now.

In thinking about your generation of leftists and Hollywood leftists, it seems to me to be to some extent a tragic story. Would you characterize it as a tragedy?

It was certainly tragic for some people. It was not tragic for me. I had thought of getting out of Hollywood and into independent production before I was blacklisted. I had, in fact, acquired the rights to a book called *Temptation*, by a Hungarian writer who used the name John Pen, which dealt with a youngster in Budapest between the wars and which had a radical theme. I'd gone to Hungary to try to set up a coproduction. The Hungarians had said yes, and I'd lined up some American funds before the Hungarians changed their minds. I mention it only to indicate that this was back in 1948, after the Ten but three years before I was blacklisted.

I would say that I personally found many positive aspects to being blacklisted. I don't recommend being blacklisted to others. But it really allowed me to have experiences that I would not otherwise have had. Apart from Paris and other cities, I had a chance to live in Czechoslovakia for some months in 1967, and for five months in 1968 during the entire period known as the Prague Spring, so I don't have to get my knowledge about Eastern Europe out of books. I really know what it's like to be there. I've had all kinds of fascinating experiences that I would not have had otherwise.

And my story isn't over yet. I mean, I'm not looking back over my life and saying, "It hasn't been a bad life," though, so far, it *hasn't* been a bad life. Because I still think I have a considerable future.

Mickey Knox

MICKEY KNOX, Los Angeles, California, 1997

INTERVIEW BY PATRICK MCGILLIGAN

PHOTO © WILLIAM B. WINBURN

■

MICKEY KNOX WAS set to be the next John Garfield. He had played good parts in fifteen pictures in three years. Then the House Un-American Activities Committee launched its witchhunt, and in 1951 he found himself unemployable as an actor.

During the years of exile, his ability to speak French and Italian helped him adapt. First, in Rome, he worked as a dialogue director for Jean Renoir. He proved so adept at it, and it was such an anonymous profession, that he was able to carry it off for several years in Hollywood at the height of McCarthyism. Dialogue directing took him to France, where he had the longest job in his life, on *The Longest Day*, working closely with Darryl F. Zanuck; then it was back to Italy.

For thirty-three years Knox lived in Rome, where his hospitality to important visitors and accidental tourists was such that in some circles he was dubbed "the mayor of Rome." His apartment on Via Gregoriana, where movie stars and literary figures mingled with scholars and diplomats, became "the closest thing to an international salon," in the words of Michael Mewshaw, who profiled Knox for *European Travel and Life*.

Knox continued to act in European and overseas Hollywood productions. But in Italy, and on the Continent at large, he became much in demand as a dialogue director, translator and adapter of foreign-language scripts, and dubbing expert. Probably his most famous credit is for writing the English-dialogue version of Sergio Leone's epic *Once upon a Time in the West*. Somewhere along the way, Knox also acted as the producer of one "spaghetti western" himself.

Not a bad life story, so far. All along the way Mickey Knox kept his tough veneer, his equanimity, and his impish sense of humor. It is only recently, thinking it over, says Knox with a laugh, that he has become bitter about the blacklist.

■

Where did the politics come from, for you?

My mother and father. My mother was a revolutionary in Russia, as a very young girl. Her mother, my grandmother, warned her, grabbed her, took her out of Russia, and brought her to America. My father is another question—he was a Marxist but very anti-Stalinist. My father and my mother were never married. They both came from Odessa. My mother got married to my step-father when I was five.

Where did your interest in show business come from?

I wanted to be an actor—I don't know why—from the age of thirteen. I was born in Coney Island and was raised there and in other parts of Brooklyn, where I first went to a Jewish school and learned to read and write Yiddish; my first play was in Yiddish. My stepfather was a house painter, a terrific guy who worked hard and supported us. But my mother was always very left-wing. My family moved to Washington, D.C., while I was in high school.

So you were really a "red-diaper baby"?

I was raised that way. When I became an adult, I knew what it was about and I believed in it. I really did.

You don't anymore?

I didn't say that. I believe in a society that is a government for the people but a government that is really for the people. I don't believe that corporate America is the last stop.

Did you study to be an actor?

I worked in the Civic Rep in high school, and I got a scholarship to Erwin Piscator's acting group. Piscator was a refugee from Germany, where he had been a famous theater impresario and during the 1920s directed remarkable productions. His group taught the valuable basics—dance, fencing, voice. "Your body is your instrument."

Then I went to Catholic University, in Washington, and Walter Kerr was my professor. He took the great excerpts from religious plays, wrote the speeches in between them, and called it *God's Stage*. I played I can't remember how many parts, and he directed. We toured the country in it.

I also did several seasons of stock, in which I played most of the leads as a young actor. Stock was an extraordinarily popular and successful enterprise all through New England, out in the Midwest, and down South. It was great for a young actor. You played at night, and you rehearsed during the day for next week. I did everything, from crazy, funny things, to serious plays, to melodrama. I once played a black Pullman porter in a melodrama! [Laughs.]

Before the war I also did my first Broadway play, *Jason*, written by Sam [Samson] Raphaelson. It's about a very austere critic—I guess he meant Brooks Atkinson of the *Times*—and a young, brash writer—based on Saroyan—who writes a play and crashes the critic's house and says, "You critics have to read the play first, so you know what the hell you're saying. Read my play and *then* come criticize it." I only played a small role, but I understudied the Saroyan part.

Then I toured the subway circuit with *Native Son*, which Jack Berry directed. I played the Communist lawyer. The subway circuit was exactly that: the Bronx, Brooklyn, New Jersey.

Then you went into the Army.

My first wife was an actress, a couple of years older than I (as was Georgette, my second wife). We met in New York, and she was the first girl I slept with on a steady basis. Before being shipped overseas I had a three-day pass, and we got married.

In the Army I had basic training as a medic (being nearsighted probably kept me out of the infantry). In England I was assigned to the Seventh General Dispensary in London. I was in a big production there of *The Eve of St. Mark*, by Maxwell Anderson. Later I got Army permission to put on a musical comedy. I wrote the book and directed it. We played at the huge Queen's Theatre, and it was always a full house, with the military of the various nations who came through London. The play was called *Three Joes in a Jam*.

Some months later I was transferred to the Signal Corps; that's where actors usually were assigned. Shortly after D-Day, my outfit was shipped to France, and my most exciting day during three and a half years in the Army was riding into Paris just after it was liberated. I got discharged in France (because I was getting married to Georgette) while in an artillery battalion.

You got divorced from your first wife, and you married Georgette, and she provided a fortunate connection for some people later on. Jack Berry tells me she was the only person he really knew in Paris when he first arrived there, fleeing the blacklist.

When I met Georgette she owned a bar in Paris, I was a GI, and it was heaven. I took all my friends there. I fell in love with her. I don't know about her—you never know about French girls. She'd close the bar, I'd have all my friends come in, and we had a party every night, drinking on her.

Is that where you learned to speak French, in Paris during World War II?

I learned it with her. Like all the French, she thought, "He must know French—it's the best language in the world." She would tell me stories about books and movies, talk and talk and talk—and a miracle happened. I woke up one day, and I was speaking in sentences. I was speaking French! I had absorbed it. Also, I evidently had the will; I wanted to learn it. I got a French grammar book and taught myself one irregular verb a day until I learned the grammar. To this day, I speak French quite well, and when I was blacklisted and couldn't get work anywhere, I first got work as a dialogue director because I knew French—and Italian.

Where did the Italian come in? How'd you learn Italian?

Georgette and I studied Italian after the war, because Italian [neorealist] pictures were just starting to come out—*Roma, città aperta* [Rome, Open City], et cetera. It's the only time I used the GI Bill. I got a private teacher from a school out here in Los Angeles. We both studied Italian, and I learned the basics, so when I went to Italy later on I had a language skill, which was pretty helpful. Knowing Italian and French saved my ass.

After the war, you came back.

After I got married, I came back to New York with my French bride. Very quickly after that I signed with Hal Wallis. He had a woman working for him who was terrific—Irene Lee. She was quite a dame. She had seen me in *Jason* and probably *Native Son*, and made a mental note of me. I was introduced to her, and she said, "I'd like you to meet Hal Wallis," and I said, "Great."

So, when he came to New York, I was introduced to him. It was a funny situation. I went up to his hotel. I was then wearing my Army trenchcoat, and he was then at the height of his success. He had produced *Casablanca*, after all. He said, "Why do you wear that coat?" I said, "Because it's the only one I have"—which was true. He said, "Oh!" and he signed me.

Had he seen you do any acting?

No, but she had. You know movies—they didn't give a shit if you could act!

You looked good.

He liked my look. I looked, oddly enough, very much like John Garfield, and for a long time everybody I met in movies—producers, directors—said I was "the new John Garfield." [Laughs.] Garfield was a big star then.

I pulled the first press release on you at the Academy of Motion Picture Arts and Sciences. It was dated January 1947. Since the first HUAC hearings were in October of that year, you must have had an all-too-brief buildup as a star before you were blacklisted.

I did fifteen pictures in three years.

What were your best parts?

Hal Wallis brought me out to be in *I Walk Alone*, and that was my first part. Then I played with [James] Cagney in *White Heat* and with [Clark] Gable in *Any Number Can Play*.

I had the lead in a very low-budget picture called *Western Pacific Agent*, and all of the reviews were put on a poster with a drawing of me climbing up a bridge. The reviews compared me to Cagney and Garfield. I played a *no-goodnik*. It was directed by a guy named Sam Newfield. You can't find it anywhere today. That was fun, because I had the lead.

There were two other parts I liked. One was in *Killer McCoy*; I played the lightweight champ. The other was the leader of the gang of kids in [the film version of the novel] *The Amboy Dukes*, or *City Across the River*, as they called it. I didn't see two pictures that I made, and I've forgotten how big my parts were: one was *Criminal Lawyer*, with Pat O'Brien, and the other was *Outside the Wall*, with Richard Basehart, for Universal.

When you worked on a set with Cagney, what did you see?

I saw a human being, not an actor, which is the key. He had energy. Without energy, you're not acting. I always thought Cagney was a great actor—I had probably seen all the pictures he ever made.

I was part of his gang in *White Heat*. I was one of those machine-gunned at the end, when he's up on top of the gas tank. A funny thing happened during the scene at the farm, when we're planning the robbery with Edmond O'Brien and Steve Cochran. In the scene, we were in the getaway car, and [Raoul] Walsh was directing, with one eye.

Was Walsh a good director?

He must have been, but he wasn't very articulate. According to him, he didn't even read the scenes before filming. He used to go over to the script girl and ask, "What the hell is this scene about?"

Somehow White Heat *turned out to be a great movie.*

Yes! It's a helluva good script, it's well-acted, and Walsh knew how to shoot a picture. Anyway, I'm in that old-fashioned car, with the other guys in back, and Cagney comes up to me, and he's supposed to say, "Don't forget. You go over the bridge and turn right . . ." He gives me the whole speech in very good Yiddish! And Walsh yells, "Cut! What the fuck are you doing? What is that language?" Cagney says, "He's Jewish." Walsh says, "We're shooting it in English." Cagney says, "Mickey understands me."

Cagney knew Yiddish. He was a *Shabbas bocher*, a "Saturday boy." All his childhood friends were Jewish kids. If you're a religious Jew, you can never turn a light on, strike a match, or do any work from sundown Friday to sundown Saturday. The gentile kid used to come and light the gas so they could cook.

Was he a personable guy?

He was very quiet and private. He was studying jujitsu. He was hard as a rock. Barbara Payton, whom I knew and who later made a film [*Kiss Tomorrow Goodbye*] with him, said to me that he had the hardest ass of any man she ever met. It was like granite. He was tough, really tough. We became friendly because I came from [the same type of neighborhood] where he had been brought up.

Had he turned right-wing by this time? What were his politics?

He was nothing. We had discussions. Get this: I had met him as a little kid. There was a place in New Jersey called Green Acres, a left-wing summer camp. He visited in the 1930s, when I was a little boy. He was very left-wing in the 1930s, to his credit. You had to be, if you had any brains in your head. The country was in such a disastrous state.

Here's what he told me when I knew him later. He said, "At a certain point I gave up reading newspapers, listening to the radio, and just removed myself from the world, really. I'm completely out of politics and everything that has to do with politics." I said, "Gee, that's a pity." He said, "No, it's not. That's the way I want to live. I don't want to read or hear about anything."

Can you compare your experiences with him and with Gable?

I played Gable's buddy and was by his side all through my part of the picture. The crew at MGM told me that when he was married to Carole Lombard, he was a totally different guy—funny, a practical joker, friendly to everybody. When she died, he made a hundred-and-eighty degree turn. He was nice, he was professional, but he was also solemn and quiet—no more practical jokes. He wasn't the Clark Gable that he'd been previously.

I kind of specialized in playing 'the buddy.' Humphrey Bogart's own company owned [the rights to Willard Motley's novel] *Knock on Any Door*. At one point, Hal Wallis was going to buy the book from Bogie for me and Wendell Corey; I had read the book and knew it would go over great. Then Hal called me in and said, "Bogie is hard-headed. He has decided he wants to solve the problems in the book and make the movie." But I got the part as John Derek's buddy. Then I also played John's brother in *Saturday's Hero*, based on a book written by Millard Lampell, who also got blacklisted later. John and I became good friends.

The funny thing about *Saturday's Hero* is how I was cast. The director was David Miller. I read with John Derek, and afterward David Miller and the line producer, who was Buddy Adler, were discussing it with all us—and Sidney Buchman, the executive producer—in the room. David said, "Okay, fine with me. What about you, Buddy?" Buddy said, "I don't know. Mickey's kind of too Jewish. They're supposed to be Polish kids." David was terrific about it. He turned to John Derek and said, "Are you Jewish?" John said, "Oh, no." David said, "Well, I can't tell who the hell is Jewish." Sidney Buchman said, "Okay, stop the crap. Mickey, you've got the part."

How about directors? In those fifteen pictures you made, did any of the directors take you by surprise with their talent and intelligence?

They took me by surprise by their *lack* of talent. All those big names—Mervyn LeRoy, for example, the so-called director of *Any Number Can Play*. Mervyn LeRoy was a big name at that time. He always smoked a long cigar. I was an actor who liked to ask questions. I found out you couldn't ask Mervyn LeRoy a question. I asked him a question about one scene and what I was supposed to do in it. He shoved the cigar in his mouth and [he imitates LeRoy growling unintelligibly] walked away. That is why he smoked cigars. That was Mervyn LeRoy.

Nick [Nicholas] Ray? When I found out I was going to be in *Knock on Any Door*, I thought, "Nick Ray! Great!" The first day on the set, I was so pleased when he put his arm around my shoulders and said, "I want to talk to you." He walked me all around the stage, *all around*, until we came back to where we had started, near the camera, and he never said a word. That was it.

That's very bizarre.

Very!

What was he trying to say?

To this day I don't know, and I got to know him very well. He was known in Hollywood for being a guy who, if your phone rang, and there was nobody at the other end, it was Nick Ray. To talk to him was torture, because he'd say, "Well . . . you know . . . uh, Mickey . . . uh, well . . ." Torture! Unbelievable. I was part of the Gene Kelly group. We used to have a lot of dinner parties together, and Nick would be there occasionally, and I began to find myself avoiding him.

Did any Hollywood director ever talk "character" with you?

No. The greatest director I ever worked with was Sergio Leone, and he didn't talk character with me either; I wasn't working with him as an actor. What Leone had, which only a few great directors, like John Ford, had, is that he saw the movie in his head before he ever did it. Plus he was a great storyteller. Leone was shallow as hell; he was bereft of profound ideas. But nobody topped him in the technique of making a movie.

Was there a better or worse studio, in your experience?

I worked at almost all the studios. Paramount, which was my home studio, was more *haimish*—friendly, nice dressing rooms, a homey atmosphere. Universal was run-down, shabby, except that they had a terrific western backlot. Columbia was like a factory—no grass, no nothing. MGM was just enormous, fifty soundstages, impersonal.

Meanwhile, you were doing other things to keep sharp as an actor. Did you hang out much at the Actors Laboratory Theatre?

I was at the Lab a lot. All my friends were there. We had acting classes there. Me and Tony Curtis, Janet Leigh, and Shelley Winters, a group of us, we got Morris Carnovsky to run a class. I also studied with a great, great actor and teacher called Michael Chekhov, who was different from Morris, less based on the Method.

Can you compare their approaches for me?

Morris was generally terrific as a teacher. We all had to do some Shakespeare in his class, and what he would do was have you sit down and think the scene, then get up and move and think the scene, then, while you're moving, just mumble the speech. Finally he'd say, "Now do it!" God, you just jumped out of your skin. You couldn't wait to do it. Morris's ideas were fantastic.

Michael Chekhov had an idea, which was enormously helpful to me as an actor, which he called "the psychological gesture," which is one physical quality that somehow embodies the character. He also had a very sharp and simple explanation about what almost every scene entails, which is convincing somebody—"bending them to your will," as he put it. What you do is get a mental image in your head of bending a steel bar—you really have got to concentrate to do it. You have to use all your effort to bend this steel bar. It creates a sense of directed energy that's extraordinary.

It worked against me, oddly enough, the first time I tried it. When I was called for an interview to read a scene at Warner Brothers, where I had worked, doing the picture with Jimmy Cagney, all I was told by the casting director was that the character was a gangster and that he was in this scene with somebody else. So I used that image of bending the bar. They didn't hire me. I said to the director, "I thought the scene was pretty good." The director said, "It was. It was *too* good. What you did was contrary to what the scene was. The man is a weakling." I explained what I was doing, "bending him to my will." He said, "People bend him to *their* will. He never bends anybody to his will. It just doesn't work. I'm sorry." You know directors—they don't think, "If he can do that, he can turn it around and do something else." [Laughs.]

Were you in any of the Lab plays?

No, the play I was in out here during that time was *Galileo*.

Brecht's Galileo?

The world premiere, starring Charles Laughton and with Joe [Joseph] Losey directing—but he wasn't directing, because Bertolt Brecht was there. What happened, actually, was that I replaced someone while they were in rehearsal. My agent called me and said, "We want you to read with Charles Laughton for the play." I said, "Great!" So I went up to his house and was met at the door by Elsa Lanchester [Laughton's wife]. She didn't say hello or anything to me; she thought I was just another one of the boys. She let me in and showed me into a room, a small study where there was a sort of love seat. He had me sit next to him to read for the part. I started reading it, and he put his hand on my knee. I said, "Mr. Laughton, do you mind if I sit across from you? I'd feel much more at ease that way, rather than looking sideways at you." He said, "No, that's fine, my boy." He understood that he made me nervous. But he turned out to be terrific; he cast me in that play, and we became friends.

I had a very difficult time with my part, because I was the Little Monk— a young monk who has a long scene with Galileo. He says to Galileo something like, "I can't accept your theory that the earth is just a grain of sand in the universe. Look at my parents. They're bent over from working all their lives in the fields. They believe that this is the center of the world, that this is God's planet." Here I was—I had been studying with Carnovsky and reading everything Stanislavsky ever had written, and I was doing the scene my way. Brecht came up to me and said, "No, no—don't do it that way. It's mathematical. Do you know what two and six is? Eight. It's mathematical, what you are saying. No emotion. You're telling him something that is like a mathematical theorem." It confused me. Later I understood.

Explain it to me.

His whole point was: it is better to be less emotional in a play and more intellectual. His plays were epic plays, and they dealt with—in his head, anyway—very important ideas and the philosophy of life. He said, "If you are emotional the audience will come out with *feelings*, but in the morning they won't remember anything about the play. My plays they never forget." Which is somewhat true. Also, they're beautifully written plays.

Were you ever in anything else that Losey directed?

No. As a matter of fact, we didn't get along too well. One day he put a note on a bulletin board—this was after Brecht had left the production— inviting *some* actors to meet with him and discuss what the play was really about. *Some* actors. And he left other actors off the list. He left me off. I resented that, and I told him so. I said, "How can you do that? How can you disrupt the cast? You want to meet with the cast? Meet with the cast." It got very unpleasant.

What was his explanation?

Nothing: "I am the director. I do what I want." I was about to say, "You're not the director, because Bertolt Brecht has been directing," but I didn't. I got upset, and Charlie Laughton was there. He took me aside, and he said, "Just leave it be."

How unusual was it that you were doing this major play and films at the same time?

It was unusual, because not that many actors were doing plays. There weren't that many plays like *Galileo*. Hal Wallis was delighted I was doing it, an important play with Charles Laughton.

He was open-minded about that?

Absolutely.

He didn't have that many people under personal contract at that time, did he?

No. He had Burt Lancaster, Wendell Corey, Kirk Douglas, me, and Lizabeth Scott. One day he said to me, "Mickey, you've been studying acting. Do you mind giving lessons to Lizabeth?" I shuddered inside. For once in my life I thought quickly, and I said, "You know, Mr. Wallis, she has a very special quality that's all her own. I think it might be a mistake to disperse it." He said, "Oh? I think you're right." Whew! [Laughs.] She was his mistress, too.

Eventually I asked, through my agent, to get out of my contract with Hal. He had brought me out for *I Walk Alone*, in which I played a baby-faced killer. The *New York Times* said, "A new baby-faced killer is born." Look it up. Then I was in another picture called *The Accused*, with Loretta Young, in which I played a truck driver. After that all he did was loan me out. He loaned me out for *Saturday's Hero* and *Knock on Any Door* and *Killer McCoy*.

L. B. Mayer wanted to sign me during *Killer McCoy*. A relative of his directed the picture—Roy Rowland—and L. B. had seen the rushes. The director came to me the next day at work and said, "Mickey, L. B. saw the rushes yesterday, and he said to me, 'Can we sign that boy?' " Mickey Rooney was the lead, and I was a guy training him to be a fighter. I was also the lightweight champ. I can understand what L. B. Mayer saw, because something happened in one scene between me and Mickey Rooney. My agent, who was then Herman Citron, said to L. B., "He's under contract to Hal Wallis," instead of saying, "Let's work it out." If I had signed with L. B. Mayer, I might have been put to work immediately; MGM made five hundred pictures a year, Hal Wallis made two or three. And I might not have been blacklisted. If you worked for MGM, you weren't necessarily blacklisted unless you were a writer. It all worked out badly.

I finally said to Hal, "All you do is loan me out. You pay me a small salary, and you're making money off me. You're not making pictures that you're putting me in. I'd like to try it on my own."

Was he offended by that?

Not at all. He really didn't make the kind of pictures I was in. He was funny that way. He signed people but didn't know how to use them. As a matter of fact, Hal Wallis never made a star. He had Kirk Douglas, whom he didn't like. He dropped Kirk Douglas, Kirk then made *Champion*, and that's when he became a movie star. Burt Lancaster would have been nothing if it had been up to Hal Wallis. You know who used Burt? Mark Hellinger, in *The Killers*. Then Hal started to use him. Up till then Burt was telling me every day, "I'm going back to New York. What am I doing out here?"

Hal Wallis had good writers, and at Warner Brothers he had all the Warner Brothers people. When he was on his own, as an independent producer, he never made a star. People like Kirk and Burt became stars in spite of Hal Wallis.

Did you like Wallis?

He treated me all right. He was a complicated guy. Very timid, cold. He had a very attractive young secretary. We started up an affair later on, during *The Rose Tattoo*. She told me that she was also his mistress. She said he had deep personal problems, sexual problems. All the time she was with him, she told me, he could never get an erection.

For a guy with such sexual problems, he seems to have had an endless number of mistresses.

It was the same way with Franchot Tone. I toured with Franchot in *Jason*. I had understudied the lead [on Broadway] originally, but then we toured all over with it, Franchot and I, with me playing the great part of the Saroyan character, the playwright.

Anyway, Franchot told me that he lost his potency when he married Joan Crawford. She made him impotent. Then, later on, he fell wildly in love with a woman I had an affair with—Barbara Payton, who starred in the picture I mentioned with Jimmy Cagney—a helluva girl, oh! He fell madly in love with her because she brought him back to life sexually. But she was also having an affair with Tom Neal. Franchot was not muscular, and he was drunk when he attacked Neal after he found out that Neal was fucking her. Tom Neal beat the shit out of Franchot Tone and put him in the hospital, nearly killed him. Neal was a monster. It's a funny story, because Barbara saved Neal's ass. Neal was going to be sued by Franchot and also put in jail. So Barbara went to see Franchot in the hospital and said, "Let's forget Tom Neal. You and I will get married. I love you. Let's put him out of our lives." That was the thing he wanted to hear. He said okay, and he married her. They went to New York on their honeymoon and had a big suite at the Warwick.

You make her sound like some kind of nymphomaniac.

She might have been. She really enjoyed sex. She kept me in bed once for three days and nights, even feeding me in bed. She wouldn't let me get out of bed. I had to crawl out on my hands and knees. She was terrific, though, because she was honest. She didn't want anything else from you. She just wanted companionship . . . or something.

Anyway, Franchot caught her on the phone with Tom Neal. He took her box of jewelry, and—he could have killed somebody with it—he threw it out of a window on the twenty-first floor. At which point she left him and went back to Tom Neal! Eventually, Tom Neal killed one of his wives, you know, after he and Barbara split up. Much later she committed suicide.

Did you know Burt Lancaster, growing up?

No, but Burt was my closest friend here.

Did Burt have any politics?

Left. When I first came out here, we were all very friendly, because Burt Lancaster and I saw each other almost every night, with my French wife and his wife. My first picture was with him, *I Walk Alone*. He was under contract to Hal Wallis, and so was I. Both of us were from New York. So we became like brothers. We were up until three or four in the morning discussing things. He had an extraordinarily inquisitive mind. He wasn't formally educated, but he read a lot, and he was very knowledgeable about a lot of things—classical music, for example.

I ask about his politics because his agent, Harold Hecht, was in the Party at one point.

I guess so—in the thirties. Anyway, Harold did end up being an agent, originally a literary agent. Sam Levene, who was in the only play Burt was in in New York, recommended Harold to Burt, and Harold became Burt's agent in New York. Then Hal Wallis signed him, and Burt came out here, and Harold too. Naturally, Harold was around most of the time when we were together. We were all very friendly.

Then, of course, when the shit hit the fan, Harold became one of the worst witnesses. On the stand he said, "Gentlemen, I think what you are doing is absolutely right and good for the country. Any help I can be, I'm glad to do. I'm opposed to all subversive elements. I'm yours to be used, et cetera." It was awful. Then he rattled off the names of everybody he knew from the WPA [Works Progress Administration] days. I just refused to see or speak to him anymore. At one of Burt's parties, Harold, with a big smile, came up to me when I came in and held his hand out. I walked right by him.

Twenty-five years went by before I saw Harold Hecht again, and now it was Italy, and I was working for Sergio Leone. We were starting to shoot *Once upon a Time in the West*. One day Sergio said to me, "Have lunch with me. Somebody's coming from New York, and you can translate for me." I said okay. So we went to the Cinecittà [studio] restaurant, and I asked who he was going to meet. He said something that sounded like "Harold Hecht." I said, "Harold Hecht!?" He said, "Yeah, he has the rights to two Dashiell Hammett books, and if I agree to direct them, they are going to be produced." At this point, Harold was a producer. I said, "Oh, really?" He said yes. In walked Harold. He changed color, from sort of gray to white, when he saw me. I did the translating, and finally Harold left. Sergio said, "What do you think?" I said, "Harold Hecht is a crook." Well, all you have to do is tell an Italian *that. That* they understand. So Sergio turned him down.

A few days later, I got a call from an agent I knew in New York, saying Harold Hecht had called him and asked him to tell me that if Sergio Leone agreed to do these movies, there would be twenty thousand dollars in cash in an envelope for me. I said, "Why did he say that?" The agent said, "He feels you might oppose the deal for personal reasons." I said, "Oh, no, I would *never* do anything like that." [Laughs.] That was my revenge on Harold Hecht.

Yet Burt—though a left-liberal—stuck with Harold throughout his career.

He stuck with Harold until Harold died. That's the way Burt was—loyal. Harold was his first agent, and really his first friend in Hollywood, and he stood by him. He didn't approve [of what he had done], but he was very broad-minded about it, I guess. Burt was very good politically, but he was never a dedicated leftist, as many people were.

When HUAC started up, I remember, Burt and I were in Tijuana together, going to the bullfights, and we ran into a writer who became a director, Richard Brooks, at a famous restaurant and bar there. Richard had written a novel about a revolt in America, then had completely turned around [politically].* I got to know him originally because he wrote *Any Number Can Play*, starring Clark Gable, and then L. B. Mayer said to him, "Go on the set and learn how to direct." That's where I had my first bad experience with Richard Brooks.

He was on the set every day learning how to direct. Mervyn LeRoy was the so-called director. Anyway, there was a scene in a gambling room where I played a dealer and a couple of robbers came in to rob the place. In the script Richard had my character reach for the guy who is holding the gun, played by Bill [William] Conrad, and try to yank the gun out of his hand. I said, "How do you do that? Here I am, three yards away, unarmed. How do I go after a guy pointing a gun at me?" Richard said, "Let's try it. Mervyn, do you mind if I see whether I can work this scene out?" Mervyn said, "Sure."

You know, actors rarely hurt each other, but Richard Brooks wasn't an actor. He was very strong, a former college football player. He said, "Try coming at me." The next thing I knew, he had grabbed me by the arm and swung me around and knocked me on the floor. I said, "Jesus Christ, Richard!" He apologized and asked to try again. It happened again! I said, "That's it, Mervyn. This is crazy." Richard apologized again and said, "Give me one more chance. I've got an idea!" That was one more chance too many, because he flung me against the side of a dice table. Luckily, I hit the table right under my nose—not on my nose or teeth—but I split my lip open and started bleeding like a stuck pig. Again he started apologizing. This time I said, "Fuck off!" My lip got swollen, and I had to miss the rest of that day. That was Richard Brooks.

Anyway, at this famous restaurant, we were sitting there—Richard, Burt, and I—and at that point, the amicus curiae [a legal petition on behalf of the Hollywood Ten] was circulating for signatures. Burt brought the subject up and said that he was going to sign it. Richard said, "Are you crazy? Are you really going to sign that? You're going to sign the amicus curiae and wreck your career for those guys, those Communists?" I said, "Richard, what's hap-

---

*Writer and director Richard Brooks wrote three novels. *The Boiling Point*, published in 1947, was a socially indignant novel about political tensions in a small southwestern town, focusing on a returned war hero.

pened to you? I read your book about the revolution that takes place in a town in America where strikers fight the Army." He said, "Times have changed." Richard went wild, trying to convince Burt not to sign the amicus curiae. But Burt eventually did sign it.

Your other great friend, whom you met during this period, was Norman Mailer.

To this day, Norman's my closest friend. A guy called [Sidney] Benson introduced me to him. Benson's mentioned in [Elia] Kazan's book [*A Life*]. Benson had several aliases. He was a Communist and a union organizer in the South who had gotten almost all his bones broken. I had met Benson at somebody's house, and one night he brought Norman over to my house in the Valley.

There was one good movie I was in, *City Across the River*, which Norman liked very much, so he was happy to meet me. We hit it off immediately. I had read his book [*The Naked and the Dead*]. Of course, I was doing a lot of reading then; when you're under contract, you have a lot of time. We hit it off, and we saw a lot of each other from that day on.

What was he doing in Hollywood?

He had come to campaign for [Henry] Wallace [1948 presidential candidate of the Progressive Party].

Was he flirting with the Communist Party at all?

No. Norman had nothing to do with the Party, but he had read Marx and was impressed as a student. As a matter of fact, we had a lot of talks about Marx, later on; he understood what Marx was about.

You and he have more than one connection. Eventually you became his brother-in-law.

I did, when I married Norman's [second] wife, Adele's sister [Joanne Morales]. I met Joanne through him and Adele. He and Adele were having a Thanksgiving dinner in Brooklyn, with Adele's family, and I came along as Norman's ally. There was this young, dramatically beautiful girl, only fifteen. Then I met her later, when I came back from Europe at the end of 1958 or the beginning of 1959, and she was babysitting for Norman and Adele. I went over there to visit, and she ended up making me hamburgers. When a beautiful woman makes you hamburgers, you're hooked. But Joanne was my third wife—that's jumping ahead.

Jumping further ahead, you had the distinction of appearing in two of the first movies Mailer directed, Wild '90 *and* Beyond the Law. *Norman has had an erratic career behind the camera. He strikes me as something of a frustrated filmmaker.*

Yes, I made those pictures with him! [Laughs.] It's funny how they happened. I was in his play *The Deer Park*, which played for months at the Theatre de Lys [in New York], and we used to get together, the actors and Norman, after hours and just have a terrific time. It was a very long play, and to relax after the show we used to meet in a bar, drink, and kid around. Norman said one night, "Jesus, we ought to do a movie." So we did, the three of us—Buzz Farbar was the third buddy who hung out with us. Norman got [documentary filmmaker D. A.] Pennebaker to shoot it. We got a loft, and Norman talked other people into dropping by. Norman said, "We're three gangsters who are going to the mattress," which means we were hiding out. That was it. No script—it was all improvisation with us talking like hoods. That was *Wild '90*. [Laughs.]

In the second one, *Beyond the Law*, we were three cops. George Plimpton played the mayor. That, too, was all improvised. There wasn't a word written down. And it's a pretty good movie.

How much did Norman actually direct?

He directed by being in it. He led the team, creating the drama, as an actor. There was a third one shortly after, an expensive picture called *Maidstone*, all shot on Long Island, that I wasn't in. During that one the famous incident occurred, a fight between [actor] Rip Torn and Norman. Of course, Norman later on directed a picture with a proper budget and a script he adapted from his book *Tough Guys Don't Dance*.

Back to HUAC. Did you ever attend a Communist Party meeting in Hollywood?

No. I was never a card-carrying member of the Party—and there were cards. I saw them; some friends of mine had them. I suppose that's the reason I was never called to testify and didn't have to give up my passport. When I came back from the war I attended one or two meetings of an entertainment branch. All we talked about was political theory, the civil-rights movement, unemployment, et cetera. It had nothing to do with subversion or overthrowing the American government, nothing like that.

Was there anybody in your New York group who later came out to Hollywood?

No, I was in a very small branch. Do you know that during our meetings, if you ever spoke about overthrowing the government, you were expelled? Out! Because the Communist Party was infiltrated by FBI agents, and they were agents-provocateurs. The guys who said, "Let's go there and bust heads" were always the FBI. All the extremists were FBI. I knew one for sure. I'm not going to mention names. A minor actor—a guy from New York. He caught me once and pushed me up against the wall and said, "You've gotta join the Party!" I didn't need him to tell me that. He was a very active guy in the Party.

How do you know he was also FBI?

I'm positive.

How much had being a fellow leftist helped you get jobs in Hollywood?

I had no connections. All the pictures I did during that first period were studio pictures. It was the casting people at Warner Brothers who cast me with Cagney in *White Heat*. The casting people at MGM didn't know my politics and never asked me. They were studio pictures; they weren't independents made by leftists like [producer] Bob Roberts or companies like Enterprise, who might have leaned toward me.

How much did being a leftist affect your acting, if at all? Did it inform your acting?

I guess so. Everything in your life informs your acting. Let me put it this way: A leftist has a certain view of life, which I think is more compassionate than the conservative view, and it obviously affects your acting, because that part of you is going to be dominant no matter what role you're playing. It makes you a more effective actor, I think. The actors who are strong Republicans, like Arnold Schwarzenneger or Charlton Heston or even Clint Eastwood—although he's grasped the techniques of movie acting very well—are cold actors.

What was the extent of your political activity in Hollywood?

I was active on behalf of the Hollywood Ten, once the hearings began. I went to one big meeting at the Coronet Theater where [John] Huston and [Humphrey] Bogart spoke. They were very vociferous in defense of people who were being hounded. They went to Washington, and evidently they met with the FBI, who told them to mind their own business—"You don't know what you're talking about—they're reds!"—and they both turned tail. They quietly slunk home. No wonder the liberals collapsed, because the two heads organizing the defense, Huston and Bogart, stepped aside, and everybody became afraid.

Did you know any of the Nineteen personally before they were subpoenaed?

The only one I knew was Larry Parks, the actor. I'd never worked with any of them. I went to meetings and gatherings and demonstrations where some of them were present.

What was the atmosphere like among the left-wing community in Hollywood as it got closer to the time when it became clear they were going to jail?

Among the people I was with, there was a lot of anger and concern.

Set the scene for me in terms of your own life.

Right around that time Georgette went down to Mexico and got a divorce. Actually, I was then living with Lois Andrews, who was not very political but leaned to the right.

Who was Lois Andrews?

Famous, famous. One of the most beautiful girls I've ever known. She was the child bride of George Jessel when she was fifteen. All the papers wrote about her. She had the lead in the last *George White's Scandals*. Tall, very beautiful, had a great body.

Then she came to Hollywood, under contract to Twentieth Century–Fox. She was very well-known in the movie business. When Georgette left, I had to get rid of the house in the Valley and find an apartment. Lois owned a big house on Doheny Drive and Beverly, just around the corner from Chasen's. She was a very clever woman. She knew a lot of rich people. She was also the mistress of a beer baron, and he lent her money, which she repaid, to buy real estate in Palm Springs and Los Angeles. As a result, she became quite wealthy and owned this whole building. I rented one of her apartments.

She took me under her wing immediately. [Laughs.] People kind of liked me just because they wanted to meet her. She gave great parties. They wanted to know this woman who was very famous and charming and entertaining and beautiful.

Were you worried about being targeted by HUAC yourself?

Not at first. I was not connected to the Communist Party [in Hollywood], but that didn't matter, as it turned out. When *Red Channels* and other lists came out, and things were getting hot for everybody, even people who had nothing to do with anything were fucked when the list-makers got the names all wrong, so by then I was thinking, "I guess it's going to happen to me too."

Did the job offers dry up?

Yes. It was very simple. I'd meet a young director; he'd come up to me— they all knew me; I had done all those pictures—and he'd say, "Listen, I've got a great part for you in this picture I'm doing." I'd say, "Great, call my agent," and never hear from him again.

Then I was told directly by Chester Erskine. Chester was a wonderful man. He had directed a famous play in New York starring Spencer Tracy, *The Last Mile*. Then he came to Hollywood and became an important director and producer. He produced *Androcles and the Lion* and *The Egg and I*—a big hit— and he had bought the rights to *Reader's Digest* for a television series. He had a beautiful home in Malibu where I used to visit. I was teaching him Italian.

Chester hired me as an actor for an episode of his *Reader's Digest* television series. Then he called me up and said he wanted to talk to me. He took me out of his office outside onto the street and said, "You're blacklisted." I said, "That's what I figured." He said, "I'm sorry. I can't use you anymore." He told the sponsor, which was Studebaker, that he had hired me, so he had to use me. They said, "Just this once, but that's it."

So they had finally found out you had been a Party member in New York?

No! The funny thing is, I was blacklisted because I had signed an ad in the *Hollywood Reporter*, along with three hundred other people, opposing the reelection of this California state senator named Jack Tenney. My name was on the ad. I don't even remember signing it. Mind you, I would have signed it, but I don't remember. There were a couple of other things like that which I didn't sign but that my name was on. I always suspected that this guy Benson I was telling you about just added my name, feeling I was sympathetic to the cause. Tenney was reelected and about eight months later he was given a three-year jail sentence for nepotism, because he had all his relatives on the payroll. He went to jail, and I was blacklisted.

After I talked to Chester, I went to the Screen Actors Guild, and I told my problem to the administrative head. He had a list of books like *Red Channels* behind his desk; he reached for one, went to the index, and looked me up. He said, "Did you sign the Tenney ad?" I said, "Well, I don't remember, but I probably would have, to be frank." He said, "Did you sign the amicus curiae?" I said yes. He said, "That's why you're blacklisted." There were a couple of other things, but the Tenney ad was what did it, I'm sure, because Tenney was a right-wing Republican.*

I asked this guy, "What can you do about it?" He said, "Were you a member of the Communist Party?" I said, "You know, I pay your salary. You have no right to ask me that. That is what this is all about. I don't think you have a right to ask me." He said, "Would you sign a loyalty oath?" I said, "If I can write it." He said, "Write it." I wrote, "I served my country during World War II, et cetera. As such, I am a loyal American, and so on." He said, "You're not saying whether or not you were a Communist." I said, "That's all I'm signing. Fuck you."

Eventually, years later, I got my FBI file. Somebody was certainly sending in a lot of reports about me, posting them from "safe" mailboxes in weird places like Cleveland. John Derek told me, years later when he was in Rome with Ursula [Andress], "You know, the FBI came to me and asked about you." I thought he was kidding. I said, "Oh, c'mon." But they did; it's in the files— all blacked out. He was cool; he didn't tell them anything—he didn't *know* anything.

Most of my FBI report is blacked out. But one thing is not blacked out. The very last page was the agent's review of the case. Let me read it to you: "No evidence has been developed reflecting Communist Party membership or activity. No further investigation is deemed warranted, and this case is closed." So I was blacklisted—but not for being a Communist!

Except that it's untrue. You were a Communist, right?

Not officially, but of course it's untrue. [Laughs.] Do you think the FBI knows what they're doing?

---

*For an account of Jack Tenney's career, during which he swerved from left to right and headed the California Un-American Activities Committee, see Nancy Lynn Schwartz, *The Hollywood Writers' Wars*.

So you were never subpoenaed and never had one of those weird face-to-face meet-ings with California Representative Donald Jackson where he offered people deals if they wanted to be cleared?

My feeling was that the only way to clear yourself was to name names, and I don't think I could ever do that.

Wait—I did meet Donald Jackson! I almost forgot. Remember I told you that Lois Andrews leaned to the right? One night, who was at one of her fucking parties but Donald Jackson! I tried all night to avoid him, but at one point I was in the bar of the house and I heard him say to some guys he was talking to, "Yeah, yeah, I did it. I wrecked John Garfield's career. I'm the one!" Garfield was a friend of mine. I had had a couple of dry martinis, and I came from Brooklyn, where we prided ourselves on being tough kids. So I jumped on him and knocked him down and started to strangle him.

Good for you!

I had my hands around his throat, and I was shouting, "I'm going to kill you, you cocksucker! I'm going to kill you!" Everybody pulled me off. He said to Lois, "Who the fuck is this maniac?" She said, "I think you'd better leave. I think he might kill you." And he left. That was my meeting with Jackson. [Laughs.] I always wondered if he remembered my name later on.

How long after your trip to the Screen Actors Guild and your close encounter with Jackson did you leave America?

It wasn't very long. A friend of mine, a director called Max Nosseck, a little German about five feet tall who spoke terrible English, invited me to Rome. He had had a couple of big hits. He directed *Dillinger*, with Larry [Lawrence] Tierney, and he directed *Black Beauty*.

Max went to Italy first, and he came back and said, "I have a deal to do *Othello* with Canada Lee," whom I knew.* I was supposed to be Iago. I said, "Great." I was delighted at the opportunity. He said, "I'll give Lois a part, of course." I said, "Great"—although I couldn't figure out which part she could play. So then we all went to Rome. Of course, I didn't know Italians yet; it was all bullshit. Max had found some poverty-stricken producer who, being Italian, put on a great show—nice car, well-dressed—and fooled him. The Italian thought Max was going to bring the money. Max thought he was going to put up the money. So nothing happened. There I was in Rome, and even-tually Lois went back and I stayed.

Why?

I loved Rome. It was beautiful. I had never been there before. I didn't know Italy. So I stayed, and I got my first job as a dialogue director.

---

*On the blacklisting and untimely death of the African-American actor Canada Lee, see Stefan Kanfer, *A Journal of the Plague Years*, 1973.

Wasn't it hard to split up with Lois?

They loved her in Rome. All the young princes were after her. She was something! But, c'mon, she was going to go back anyway—and I was black-listed.

Were you isolated when you first got to Rome? How did you hope to get work?

Everybody met at the Via Veneto. It was the great meeting-place. Americans got together automatically.

I ran into an American who was the dialogue director for Jean Renoir on *The Golden Coach*, and he knew I was an actor. He needed help, and he hired me. There were a bunch of kids who were hired to play in the troupe that toured with [Anna] Magnani in the picture. My assignment was to work with the kids, who had to speak English. Along the way I somehow endeared myself to Magnani. At a certain point, I remember, she was being pressed by this American dialogue director, who had a lot of hubris trying to tell her how to act the scene. I stood up and said, "Leave her alone. She's a great actress." I could see she was getting—not flustered but nervous. She didn't speak much English, so I said it to the guy, and I didn't even realize she could understand me. She told me later on, when I was hired for *The Rose Tattoo*, that she remembered what I had done that day and really appreciated it.

What was your interaction with Renoir?

Of course, I could speak French with him. He was an angel, and I loved him. So was his nephew Claude, who was the cameraman, a great cameraman. Renoir wore a hat all the time. Every time he said, "Action!" he'd take his hat off first and hold it close to him like this. [He demonstrates.] I asked him once, "Why do you do that?" He said, "Out of respect for the actors."

Was he always improvising, as people say?

He allowed the actors, especially Anna, a lot of freedom. The great thing about Renoir was, he knew exactly what he wanted. It wasn't like Mervyn LeRoy and some of these other Hollywood guys who were shooting postcards. They didn't have a clue what they wanted.

After lunch in Hollywood, I remember, the set would be cleared, and Mervyn LeRoy would have a chair put right in the middle of the stage, facing the set. The set would then be cleared by the assistant director. LeRoy would sit there, thinking about the next scene, right? I wondered about it, and one day I sneaked up on him. He was snoring, taking his nap every day because he had been up till four in the morning playing gin. He was a big gin player. That was a great Hollywood director.

Were there many other blacklistees in Rome at this point?

Ben Barzman was in and out. A friend of mine, Buddy Tyne, also a black-listed actor, was there. Luckily, Buddy had some good connections, and he ended up doing a lot of work in Europe, too, not as an actor but, like me, as a dialogue coach, mostly for Anatole Litvak. Buddy and I saw each other a lot in Rome, although he and his wife actually spent most of their time in Paris.

When The Golden Coach *ended, what did you do?*

Everything was very cheap in Rome. I had a few bucks saved up, so I stayed for about a year, but by then I was very close to being busted. So I had to go to Paris, looking for work.

Did you find any work in Paris?

None.

Who else did you know there?

Jack Berry was the guy I knew best.

Was he in any position to help you?

I helped *him*. He was trying to get a picture going. He had Evelyn Keyes ready, but she wasn't enough. He needed a French star to get the money from French producers. He wanted an actor called Henri Vidal, but at lunch he told me he couldn't afford Vidal because he was too expensive. I said, "No problem; he's a friend of mine." I called Vidal, and he said, "Come right over." Knowing Jack, he charmed him in ten minutes. Vidal said, "I'll make this picture. I don't care about the money." Later I said, "Jack, can I be your dialogue coach? You'll need somebody. Vidal doesn't speak English." He said, "Oh, I've already got somebody who's going to do that—a girl." Man! Jack!

At that point you'd been gone from the United States—

About a year and a half, and I came back. At that point I had no wife, no job. I went straight to New York first and stayed with Norman for a while. Then I enrolled at the Actors Studio.

From an outside perspective, it's curious to me that you would have had all this experience, yet you'd come back to America and choose to enroll in an acting class in New York.

I had to do something!

You had no offers?

That's the period during which I did some television. Oddly enough, I played the lead in *Golden Boy* on *The Campbell Playhouse* in New York, and another show I did was *And Then There Were None*, with Edward Everett Horton. These shows were all on CBS. Actually, CBS was one network that was lax about the blacklist. They resisted it until the end. NBC was kind of strong about it, and so was ABC.

Was the blacklist as palpable in New York?

For many, including me, it was palpable. I had one experience that I often think about. I had met Paddy Chayefsky in Paris when the war in Europe was over, but before the war with Japan was over. I believe he was writing some material for Armed Forces Radio. Shortly after I was brought to Los Angeles by Hal Wallis, I invited Paddy to come West and stay with Georgette and me at our small house in the Valley. At that point Paddy was unknown. I introduced him to Harold Hecht, who was then still a friend of mine. Harold told Paddy he needed a couple of screen credits before he could handle him.

Paddy eventually went back to New York and made a name for himself in TV. He wrote mainly for *Playhouse 90* when they presented live teleplays. Paddy wrote *Marty* and *The Bachelor Party*, among many others. I was in the cafeteria at the CBS building having coffee one day with Paddy, trying to get him to help me get a job on his show. He wasn't very encouraging.

Arnie [Arnold] Manoff, a blacklisted writer, came by, and I asked him to join us. All of a sudden Paddy stood up, took his cup of coffee, and said he was changing tables. I was stunned. I went to Paddy and asked him what the hell he was doing, and he said, "I can't be seen with a blacklisted writer." I said, "What about me? I'm blacklisted." Paddy brushed that off by, saying, "Oh, shit, you're only an actor." I don't think I ever spoke to Paddy again.

How long did you study at the Actors Studio?

Off and on during the 1950s. When I went to the Studio I was in Danny [Daniel] Mann's class first, and then Lee Strasberg's. Danny was the moderator, and he and Kazan and Bobby [Robert] Lewis were teaching, I think. Lee didn't start teaching until later.

Did you ever cross paths with Kazan?

Yes. I remember that when he was doing *Boomerang*, and I was looking for work, I went to see him. I said, "Gadge, I'm hungry"—meaning for work. He said to me, "You don't *look* hungry. What are you talking about?" To him I was a nobody. He was always a shit.

At one point, some years after I came back to America, I did a scene from *The Deer Park* at the Actors Studio because Norman asked me to; they were trying to raise money for the Studio. You know, *The Deer Park* is about the blacklist. Well, something happened that night. The place was full. Kazan was there, and a lot of people. Something happened which only if you were an actor would you understand—something magical. The scene just worked. I was playing L. B. Mayer, the guy who ran the studio, and I really got into the part. Norman's wife, Norris, was in the scene with me, playing a movie star under contract to my studio, and she was marvelous. Without her the scene might not have caught fire. We got such laughs, you can't believe. I love to do comedy, and I never did comedy in movies—always gangsters and killers. Kazan came up to me after the scene and looked at me as if he had never seen me before. "You know, Mickey," he said, "you ought to be in movies." I said, "Gadge, are you kidding?" He said, "No, I mean it." I said, "Okay, forget it," and I walked away. And he followed me, saying, "I'm not bullshitting. You should be in movies." Now, I don't know whether he knew I was blacklisted or forgot, or whether I was too small potatoes to even think about. But it was strange.

How did the approach of Lee Strasberg compare to those of Morris Carnovsky and Michael Chekhov?

I first had met Lee when I just got back from the Army and he was casting for Twentieth Century–Fox. I remember that he said, "I'd like to test you." All he did for Fox was sit in a little office and read the day's papers. I told him Hal Wallis was going to sign me, because I'd already met Hal. He said, "I'd like to test you anyway." I said okay, although I was already locked up. So he tested me, just to show Twentieth that he was working. It was just what they call a "personality test," where they ask you questions on camera— "What's your name? What do you like to do? Look this way, that way, and so forth."

Strasberg didn't teach; he analyzed. Sometimes he was brilliant. He never said much to me. He had his own acting class, which was private and had nothing to do with the Studio. At the Studio people came, rehearsed a scene, did it, and then were criticized—or analyzed—by the class first, then by Strasberg. He was very tough. He had his preferred students. He loved two or three. Strasberg loved stars.

Mainly I studied with Danny [Daniel] Mann, and then Danny went to Hollywood and was finished with teaching. Danny knew I had worked with Anna Magnani, and so he asked me to be dialogue director for *The Rose Tattoo*. He must have known I was blacklisted, but Danny was totally apolitical. It didn't mean anything to work as a dialogue director. I wouldn't get screen credit or anything. Hal Wallis immediately approved me.

So at the end of 1952 Norman and I drove across the country from New York to Hollywood. He said to me, "Can we go through Palm Springs? I'd like to see the place." We slowly drove through Palm Springs. That was right before he wrote *The Deer Park*, as a matter of fact. Later, when I read the book, I realized he had memorized the shrubbery and the architecture. Everything was inside his head.

Let me get this straight: you couldn't get hired as an actor, but you got hired as a dialogue director.

I couldn't get work as an actor. That was out. I didn't even have an agent then. But I worked in Hollywood as a dialogue director all through the blacklist period. Nobody gave a shit, because I wasn't acting. The blacklist listed actors. I was never listed as a dialogue director. I did *The Rose Tattoo* and then four or five other pictures with Tony [Anthony] Quinn, as the dialogue director, during the time I was living here.

And Hal Wallis, who brought you out to Hollywood as an actor in the first place, was the one who hired you as a dialogue director.

Well, Danny Mann hired me, but Hal Wallis produced *The Rose Tattoo*. Hal Wallis knew that the blacklist did not exist for anybody whose name or face wasn't seen on the screen.

Did you ever have a face-to-face with Wallis where the blacklist was brought up as a subject?

No. I saw him all during that movie, though. First we did some interiors here, and then we shot most of it in Key West.

What was his attitude toward you?

Very nice. Most of the Hollywood producers hated the blacklist. That's what people don't understand. The producers hated it. It deprived them of talent.

Did he ever say anything to you like, "This blacklist is a shame"?

I wasn't blacklisted with him.

It seems pretty brave of him to sponsor you.

Not really.

Pretty honorable of him, anyway.

Okay, I'll buy that. But it meant nothing. Let me tell you why—he didn't have to put my name on the screen. On the other hand, you're right. I don't want to put him down. I don't know what his politics were, but he hired me as a dialogue director, and I did *The Rose Tattoo*. I never mentioned the blacklist. He never mentioned it.

How did it happen that you and Anthony Quinn hit it off so well?

I met him the first night I went to Danny Mann's house. Magnani and the other cast members were there, and so was Tony. Tony and I liked each other instantly. We became very close friends, and he saw to it that I was hired on various pictures.

Why did he want you as his dialogue director?

He needed buddies. Tony liked me. We went out together, we went to Mexico together, we went to Las Vegas together. We went all over together.

What could you give him, in a one-on-one situation as an actor? You'd think that after so much time in the business he could almost sleepwalk through his roles.

Tony's a terrific actor, but he liked my ideas. You see that? [He holds up a trembling hand.] That's an actor—always. Even Marlon Brando is never sure. Tony, for whatever reasons, felt I had something to offer.

But when I'm hired on a picture as a dialogue director, I work with all the actors—all of them. Now, Tony and I had a personal relationship on the side. We would discuss the scenes, and things to take and give to a scene, and so forth. But normally, I was hired by the producers, and I had to work for my living, working with the other actors.

The dialogue director, especially in Europe, is always caught between the actors and the director. Did I side with the actors or the director? I was always with the actors, but I had to cover it up because I was working for the director, and especially in Italy, where the directors know very little about acting.

Were you able to make an okay living as a dialogue director?

Yeah.

Did any of the producers who hired you ever make any reference to your having been blacklisted?

Not once. Nobody knew it. Nobody ever checked me out. Remember, I was never credited. Nobody got credits then as they do now. Now there are a million credits. The credits are as long as the movie. Nobody got credits in those days except the top people.

Tony himself knew?

Sure he knew.

What was his attitude?

He knew about the blacklist. He liked to pretend he was left-wing. He had hung around the Actors Lab a lot, which put him on the graylist for a while. I'll tell you a story Tony told me. Tony says he was up for a picture with John Ford and Duke Wayne. The clearinghouse was Ward Bond. Ward Bond had an office to clear actors, and Tony was told he had to clear himself. Tony said okay, he would meet with Ward Bond. He told me, "I hated to do it, but I walked into Ward Bond's office and nobody was there. I called out 'Ward!' and a voice said, 'Hey, Tony, I'm in here. Come in.' There was Ward Bond on the throne taking a dump, and he said to Tony, 'Sit down there on the edge of the tub.' Ward said, 'Hey, Tony, are you a red?' Tony said, 'No, Ward. Jesus!' Ward said, 'Pink?' Tony said, 'No, Ward.' Ward said, 'You're sure?' Tony said, 'Sure.' Ward said, 'Okay, you're in the movie.' " That's how Ward Bond cleared Tony Quinn. Tony said he'd never been so embarrassed in his life.

Was there any kind of community of blacklisted people thriving under pseudonyms?

Yes, but I didn't know them—the guys in Mexico.

You had no contact with other blacklistees?

Again, mainly actors. Buddy Tyne was one; he was like me, working as a dialogue director. Lloyd Gough was another. But Lloyd was an open Communist, proselytizing all over the place. I did a picture with him [*Beyond the Wall*] once, and we had a lot of night shooting, and he used to sing, in a beautiful Irish tenor, accompanying himself on the concertina, all night long. The biggest laugh in *The Front*, for all of us, was the scene Lloyd is in, in the café, with two or three guys sitting around, where Woody Allen says to Lloyd, "Are you a sympathizer?" Lloyd Gough says, "Sympathizer? Shit! I'm a Party member!" Everybody who knew Lloyd fell over on the floor of the theater. He was always a Party member and never stopped telling people. [Laughs.]

Occasionally I ran into someone like Bob Rossen, but that's another story. Bob Rossen came up to me at a party and said, "Listen, I want to explain something to you." I said, "You don't have to explain anything." He said, "I have to. I did what I did because I have to work. I don't give a shit, I have to work. I did a terrible thing. I named my friends. But I have to work." I said, "You did what you had to do. That's fine. That's you." And I walked away.

How long did you stay in Hollywood?

About three years, although I went back and forth to New York a little.

Always as a dialogue director, never as an actor?

Not in Hollywood.

*What about these two films I come across in your filmography—*Singing in the Dark *and* Garden of Eden, *which I've never seen—that apparently you starred in, in the middle of the 1950s?*

Oh! [Laughs.] I would have completely forgotten all about those two if you hadn't mentioned them. They were done in New York. The director was Max Nosseck, my old friend who didn't give a shit about the blacklist.

Garden of Eden was a picture about a nudist colony, and I had the lead. Max was German, the producer, Walter Bibo, was German, and I think it was produced with German money. We shot it in Florida. I had a percentage because they gave me a minimum salary. Since it took place in a nudist colony, the picture went to court in one of the Southern states—not that there was anything sexual about it at all. The producer won in court and got good publicity, and so the picture was successful financially, but, of course, I never saw a penny.

The other one [*Singing in the Dark*] was with Lawrence Tierney and a famous cantor who was also a movie performer, Moishe Oysher. It was sort of a funny gangster movie with music. Max was not a great director, though he was a pretty good technician. He was a traffic cop, really, moving the actors and camera around. But he had taken a liking to me, and he didn't have to worry about the blacklist because the movies were too small, very low-cost B pictures.

That was it for acting?

Until Hal Wallis hired me to do *G.I. Blues* with Elvis Presley. That was my first one in a long time.

You got on the screen?

Sure.

What kind of part was it?

Elvis's buddy.

Good part?

All the way through the film.

Tell me about Elvis.

A lovely guy, extremely well-behaved. If a woman came on the set, he'd run over and offer her a chair. I asked, "Where'd you learn that?" He said, "My mother." I also asked him, "Where'd you learn to move like that when you sing?" He said, "All my friends growing up were black kids. I used to go to church with them, and that's how they moved when we sang."

Hal Wallis not only first brought you to Hollywood, he not only okayed hiring you as a dialogue director, but then he actually brought you back as an actor toward the end of the blacklist. I think you underrate him. He's the unsung hero of your story.

Now that I think about it, yes. Hal Wallis was a big wheel. He had an independent company at Paramount. He could do what he wanted, and he didn't give a shit about the blacklist. The producers had been forced into the blacklist by HUAC, *Red Channels*, and the like. But once a person like Hal Wallis chose to use a blacklisted actor, what could they do? Do you know that I keep getting residuals on the Presley film?

How'd you end up back in Europe?

I think what happened was, I was spending more and more time in New York, and at the Actors Studio, and then Sidney Lumet, whom I had known for years, hired me to be the dialogue director and to act in *A View from the Bridge*. It was a very tough job. *A View from the Bridge* had been bought by a French producer [Paul Graetz] and so we shot part of the picture in Brooklyn but then had to go to Paris to finish the interiors. I had to coach all the French actors who didn't speak English.

That's how I ended up in Paris in 1961. And then I got a job on *The Longest Day*—the longest job I ever had—with Darryl Zanuck. I ran into Gerd Oswald, who was supposed to direct all of the American sequences. He remembered me, although I didn't even realize I knew him: "Mickey, what are you doing in Paris?" "I'm looking for work." "Well, great, you've got it. I need you." So he hired me, but then he was fired and Zanuck took over the direction of the American parts of the film. I worked closely with Zanuck, although I worked with Bernhard Wicki, too, who did all the German parts.

That was a fascinating experience. Zanuck and I became very friendly. He would call the actors up to his office, John Wayne and Robert Ryan—a terrific guy—among them, and have me come in too. He would read them the scene. Badly. That was his direction to them. They'd all look at him like he was crazy. Finally he'd say to me, "Okay, Mickey, take the actors out and rehearse them." As we stepped outside, we'd be laughing. Me direct John Wayne and Robert Ryan and all the others? C'mon!

Did you work at all closely with John Wayne?

I got to know him very well. I kind of liked him. He had a sense of humor about himself. At one point we had an argument. He said about black people, "They're all monkeys." I said, "Duke, you're six foot five, and maybe you're gonna stomp all over me and kill me, but I still have to tell you you're a fucking idiot." He laughed and said, "Let's play chess." He loved to play chess during the breaks. Usually I let him win. [Laughs.] This time I beat him five games in a row. Then he really got mad. He did say those things, which were pretty bad, but it's hard to explain about him. He wasn't *really* a racist.

Could you teach him anything as an actor?

No, no. Duke was a good actor. In his early pictures he was callow; there was no worse actor. But he really learned the métier, just by doing it over and over. He was very professional—more than that. He told me this: When he became an actor, one of his early directors, Hawks or Walsh, told him it was very important for an actor who wants to be a star to have a walk: "Find yourself a walk." He did, a very distinctive walk. No, Duke knew what he was doing.

You watch him in his later pictures. He wasn't acting—he was always Duke Wayne—but he convinced you. Hey, acting is convincing people. I watch him over and over on television now, and he convinces me. That's acting.

Was he aware of your political history?

No.

Was Zanuck?

He didn't know. I was small potatoes. All those guys knew about were stars. It was the job of the casting people to know about people like me. The heads of the studios were just issuing orders: "No blacklisted actors." Why bring it up?

Zanuck himself didn't have any politics?

No, but he was one of the good guys. He hated the blacklist. It prevented him from hiring people he wanted to hire. Zanuck was absolutely apolitical, but, for example, he loved Kazan.

We were chatting together while having a coffee at the studio bar one day, and I brought up Kazan. I said, "You know, Kazan is going around telling everybody that people are lying about him, saying that he named names because he had a million-dollar contract with you." Zanuck said, "I thought the blacklist was absolutely wrong, but that's the way it was. The people in the East insisted that if I was going to use Kazan, he had to clear himself. We didn't have a million-dollar contract. What I did tell him, though, was that if he cleared himself, the studio was his. He could do any movie he wanted." I said, "That would probably add up to a million, wouldn't it?" He said, "Probably more."

Personally, I liked Zanuck a lot, although I had a very unhappy experience with him later.

What happened?

The picture [*The Longest Day*] was a hit, and Zanuck went back to running Fox. I had this idea to direct a picture on the Eady Plan. This was the Eady Plan: if there was a new director and an interesting project, the government of Great Britain would pay part of the cost. Philip Yordan, who lived in Paris, in a great apartment, said to me, "Why don't you find a property? I'll pay for it." I said, "Will you?" He said, "Sure." I found the property, one that Philip loved, a book called *Young Adam* by a writer called Alexander Trocchi. Trocchi was a terrible junkie; every time I saw him, I had to lend him money. But I got the money from Philip, who paid a thousand dollars for the option to the rights, and I started writing a screenplay.

Was Yordan going to produce? What did he get out of the deal?

Nothing. There were no strings. He bought it in my name. I had known Philip in Hollywood and got to know him better in Paris. We had dinners and lunches together. He loved to bullshit. It was amazing that he read the book [*Young Adam*], because he couldn't see very well. His eyes were bad, and he was going blind.

I knew about the writers he had in his basement. As a matter of fact, I went down there once, because I left my trunk there, and there were four cubicles with typewriters and paper. He was always writing five pictures at the same time. Everybody knew about Philip in Hollywood. But I'll tell you this: he treated me nice.

Had you ever written a screenplay up to that point?

No. So I sent the book to Zanuck in New York. Zanuck had a right-hand man, a Hungarian nicknamed Goulash—I can't remember his real name— who also introduced him to girls. Goulash went to London after *The Longest Day* with Elmo Williams, another person on whom Zanuck had come to rely a great deal. He was a very famous editor who had cut *High Noon*. He did a terrific job on *The Longest Day*, so Zanuck put him and Goulash in charge of the London office.

Unfortunately, Elmo Williams was also a prude. I found this out when we were all living in a hotel in Caen, in Normandy. I was there with Joanne.

We weren't married yet. He totally disapproved of me and her living in the same room, unmarried, because his kids were there.

Goulash called me first and said, "Mickey, we're doing the picture. Zanuck approved it. Hire a screenwriter." Zanuck had approved my directing it as an Eady Plan picture. A big mistake I made, but I didn't think about it. I should have said, "Hire the most expensive writer in London." All Zanuck knew was that I wanted to direct; he didn't know I was writing the script. I said, "No, no, no. I'm about two weeks from finishing the screenplay." Goulash said, "Send it to me." Too late—I fucked up. If they had hired a writer and spent money on the project, it probably would have gone ahead.

But, when my script got to Elmo Williams, he turned it down cold. I called him and asked why. He said, "Well, it's immoral." I said, "What do you mean?" He said, "Well, the woman is married to a big loudmouth on a barge, and he's impotent, and she makes love to a young man, and she doesn't pay for her sins." I said, "What do you mean she doesn't pay? Her husband is a big blowhard who can't make love to her." He said, "It doesn't matter. I don't like it." I said, "Okay. Can I come to London and talk to you?" He said, "Sure." At my own expense I went to London, but I couldn't shake him. I wrote Zanuck, and he wrote me back. I had the letter for years. It was a very nice letter. He said, "I rely a great deal on Elmo Williams. He runs my London office. I hate to go over his head. I can't help you. Try and convince him." But I couldn't, and Elmo Williams killed the project.

You moved from Paris to Rome in 1962. Why?

I loved Paris, and I would have preferred to live there. I had a big apartment. It was so cheap then. Paris is still my favorite city.

I was still not married, then. Joanne was a model, very well-known, on the covers of everything. It was embarrassing how much money she made. She was one of the most beautiful women in the world—half Peruvian, half Spanish. Perfect features. She was born in Brooklyn, and she'd come out on the runway with an attitude and get applause no matter what she wore. She had a "fuck-you" look, but very, very beautiful.

The French models who went to New York were beautifully treated by Americans, but the American models in Paris were treated like shit. And she hated Paris. Nobody was nice to her. I didn't care because I had absorbed the language, and I was working. After I finished the movie [*The Longest Day*], we went shopping for shoes one day, for Joanne. She tried a pair of shoes on and said, "They're too tight. Do you have a larger size?" The French saleslady said, in French, "Madame, it's not the shoes; it's your feet." She burst into tears and said, "That's it! We're leaving!" In three days I had packed up the car and gotten rid of the apartment. I had taken her to Italy before and knew she would love it there. Plus, I already had a job waiting in Rome.

To back up a little, when we were finishing *The Longest Day* I had run into Carl Foreman at the Hotel George V, where they made the only good martinis in Paris. He came running up to me: "Mickey, I've been looking for you! I'm directing my first picture, *The Victors*, and I need you, because I've never directed before. What are you doing?" I said, "I'm on *The Longest Day*." He said, "Well, you've got to get out of it." I said, "No, I've been on it for six months, and I only have two weeks left." He said, "You don't mind if Carl Foreman calls Darryl Zanuck and asks for Mickey Knox?" That's exactly what he said. I said, "No, Carl, I want to finish the picture." He called Zanuck anyway! But I went ahead and finished the picture, and Zanuck told me he appreciated that.

So we moved to Rome. The first scenes of the Foreman picture were going to be in Italy.

You had that job waiting for you?

Well—Carl! He wasn't a very nice guy. He used to say his problem in life was that since the day he was born his mother had insisted he was going to become the president of the United States one day. "I've been trying to be, ever since," he'd say to me.

Now get this: Carl needed me so desperately that I didn't start work on that picture until three months later. And this is what I heard from him. He wrote, "Columbia is getting very itchy about this picture. It's getting too expensive." I was getting the great sum of five hundred dollars per week. It wasn't bad in those days—like five thousand dollars today. He wrote, "They wanted me to cut you out, but I need you, for at least six weeks. I'm sorry I can't keep you on for the whole movie."

At that point, I felt like saying, "Fuck you!" I said to Joanne, "I'm going to turn it down." She said, "Well, it's money—plus going to London and so forth." And by now everybody I knew knew I was going to do the picture with Carl. I had told everybody, and I thought, "If I don't do it, it will be a black mark against me." So I had to do it, I felt.

It worked out, I guess. We went to London. Eli [Wallach], one of my oldest friends in the world, was in the picture, and I also got very friendly with George Hamilton, a lovely guy. But funny things happened with Carl.

I remember that Carl said to me before we started, "If you have any ideas for a scene, tell me before I shoot it, not later." You won't believe this: He was doing the first interior in London with that great actor Vince Edwards, who had played Ben Casey on TV, and an Italian so-called actress. They were playing a scene in which they had just met and were falling in love, a long dialogue scene. And it was going very badly—this Carl knew. I was standing there in back of him with the script. He turned around and saw me and asked, "Well, have you got any ideas, Mickey? That's why you were hired." I took him aside, because what I was going to say I didn't think he wanted anybody else to hear. I said, "As you can see, Carl, these people are not the greatest actors." He said, "I know that!" I said, "Well, it's too much dialogue for them. If you cut the dialogue down to the bare minimum, it might be somewhat more believable. They're having trouble with the dialogue." He said, "Fuck you!"—loud. Because he was the one who had written the script!

Everybody turned around. I said okay, I shut the script, and I quit the picture. I went back to the hotel, and I told Joanne, "That's it. I quit the movie." "Well," she said, "you're right." The calls started coming in from Carl's secretary, whom he later married, Eva. I wasn't answering the phone. Joanne was answering. Eva said, "I've got to talk to Mickey. It's very important." Joanne said, "He's not here." Eva said, "I must talk to him." Joanne said, "Try a little later." When she hung up, I said, "Fuck him." She called five or six times, and now she was desperate. "My job," she told Joanne, "hangs by a thread unless I can get Mickey on the phone." So I talked to her. She said, "Carl is having a special dinner party tonight for all the stars of the picture." All of a sudden, I was invited. I said, "Eva, you don't understand. I can't work with a guy who obviously doesn't respect me—and I don't respect him, frankly." She said, "You've got to be there. You know Carl. He's going to fire me otherwise. This is my assignment—to get you to the dinner tonight." I said, "Call me back in ten minutes." I talked it over with Joanne, and she said, "Look, I'm enjoying London. We have a nice hotel suite. Forget your pride and see what he says."

So I went to where everybody was meeting, at the bar of some big hotel where they had a restaurant with great prime rib. The whole time, I was standing there at one end of the bar, talking to someone, and Carl was at the other end. Finally dinner was going to be served, and everybody filed out of the bar to the dinner tables. Carl was waiting for me at the end of the bar— just him and me. He said, "Mickey, what happened to you today? You left." I said, "I left? 'Fuck you!?' What is that shit? Obviously, if you say that to me, you don't appreciate me or respect me. And I've got to tell you the truth, Carl. I don't respect you for saying, 'Fuck you!' to me." He said, "Aw, Mickey, what are you talking about? I say 'Fuck you' to my best friends. I tell Sidney Cohn*—that's my partner—'Fuck you' all the time." I said, "Carl, I can't

---

*Sidney Cohn, one of the many lawyers who represented accused Hollywood Communists, was known for his strategy of advising clients to take the "diminished Fifth" in front of HUAC, in which they confessed their own political pasts but refused to name other people's names. His clients included writer and director Robert Rossen, Leonardo Bercovici, and Carl Foreman. All were blacklisted anyway, although Rossen later reversed himself in revised testimony. Foreman, one of the more celebrated victims of HUAC—he had written *Champion*, *Home of the Brave*, *The Men*, and *High Noon* before the blacklist—represented a unique case.

Victor Navasky, in *Naming Names*, wrote that Cohn was different from most of the blacklistees' attorneys in that he maneuvered behind the scenes, seeking legal loopholes in the Committee's position. Although he was "constantly experimenting with new ways to circumvent the blacklist system," he claimed never to have represented any cooperative witness who exposed other people's names. At Cohn's urging, Foreman, "according to legend," in Navasky's words, went before an executive session of HUAC in 1956 and denounced himself but no one else. Then, reportedly, one of the Committee members received twenty-five thousand dollars under the table to "clear" Foreman. Foreman refused to show the transcript of his secret testimony to Navasky.

Some thought Cohn's legal maneuvering brilliant. To others, according to Navasky, "Sidney

work that way. If you want me to be there and be helpful, that's not the way to treat me." He said, "May I apologize?" Well, what are you going to do?

After *The Victors* we went to the States and got married, and then we came back and lived in Rome from 1962 on. I lived there for thirty-three years, until 1995. I loved Rome. Those years were beautiful. We had a sweet little apartment, and I was in love.

Why didn't you go back to the United States?

When I had done fifteen pictures in three years, everybody was asking for me. I was in great demand. I was an actor on the rise. I had a screen presence. Suddenly it all ended. And when I was blacklisted, I sort of felt that I had no more career as an actor in Hollywood.

At that point, if I had gone back . . . maybe it was the beginning of the end of the blacklist in the early sixties, but I didn't know that. I believed it was still in force for actors, and that there were no more roles for me in the United States. But thinking back over things in recent years, I've tried to decide for myself: What really happened to me? What was in my mind? I realized that I disliked this country deeply. I felt that any country that took a guy's livelihood away and could truncate a young career with such possibilities was not a good country.

Did you get much work as an actor in Italy?

Actor and usually dialogue director.

Between 1962 and now, how many films have you acted in, approximately?

I've lost track. I must have acted in seventy-five pictures altogether—acting and coaching. They weren't big parts, but I became the most efficient dialogue director in the world. It's not a big deal, but I have patience, and being a certain kind of actor gave me an ability to teach. I think it takes an actor who understands acting to be a good dialogue coach. And in Italy every picture has a dialogue coach. Also, it's shot either in Italian or without any soundtrack, and afterwards every picture is dubbed into English and Italian. So I did a lot of dubbing, too. We even had a dubbing organization, which I belonged to. I was one of the founding members.

What have been the best parts you played in Italian movies over the years?

I like the part I played in *The Tenth Victim*, which Elio Petri directed. I had a very good part as a television director. It was a futuristic picture, an international hit, starring [Marcello] Mastroianni. Another picture I liked because I had one of the leads was a little horror picture for kids, *Of Death and Love*, in which I played *"Lo Straniero"* [The Stranger], the sheriff of the town.

Cohn's tactics were unacceptable: to sell HUAC on the proposition that writers were naive types—moved to radicalism by the plight of Negroes and Jews—who didn't understand the realities of politics."

Did having been blacklisted give a person something of a cachet in Rome?

Yeah, because all the people I knew in Italy, all the people in the movie industry, in fact, up until the invasion of Hungary, were reds. All the directors were dedicated Communists. They were called "committed directors." I worked with Elio Petri, Francesco Rosi, Damiano Damiani, Mario Monicelli, [Michelangelo] Antonioni, [Bernardo] Bertolucci, and all those people.

But I was the dialogue director on the European sequences for many American pictures, too. I was on one picture that [Edward] Dmytryk ended up directing. I might have been acting in it too. He came up to me. I didn't know the man. I had never met him. But he said to me, "You know, I can tell from the way you're looking at me what you're thinking." I said, "What am I thinking?" He said, "That you hate my guts because of what I did." I said, "Well, that's peculiar, because I don't think I was looking at you that way, but you might have had a very good insight there." He turned around and walked away. [Laughs.]

What really got me on the map in Rome was not acting or even dialogue directing but doing about one hundred and fifty adaptations and translations of scripts from Italian into English. I built up a terrific reputation. That was my big living. My adaptations read like they were originally written in English. All the scripts I did, I tried to do my best. Again, it's no big deal, but that's why I was number one in Rome translating Italian scripts into English— because most of the films were done that way, and I gave them great attention. And when those scripts were sent to America to raise money or to get actors, the producers appreciated that fact that they were well-done.

That's how you met Sergio Leone, isn't it?

Actually, through dubbing. I met Sergio when he was making *The Good, the Bad, and the Ugly.* Eli Wallach's agent was a friend of mine, and he introduced me to Leone, who hired me to dub the picture into English. I wrote the lip-sync script and supervised the dubbing in New York. The toughest job I ever had, by the way. It took me six weeks—normally it takes two— just to get the script, because there was no soundtrack.

The obstacles were enormous. Sergio's prime need was to photograph it the best way he knew how, and screw the sound. He could always put it in later. Italian films don't care about sound. I kept saying to Eli, "What the hell did you say?" He couldn't remember. And the script was no help, really, because they were improvising a lot.

I had to read lips on the Movieola, over and over, in several languages. People were speaking Spanish, Italian, Chinese, German, whatever. Some people were just saying numbers instead of dialogue. Fellini was another one who always had people who were non-actors speaking numbers. It's a funny thing, but numbers are easy to dub. They're easier than German, for example. Spanish is easy because the lip movements are closer. French is very difficult, because the French mouth moves in a very peculiar way.

Then I did the dubbing with all the actors, except for Clint. Clint was the last one, and by that time Sergio, who was the tightest man in the world, felt he was going to save a few bucks by getting rid of me.

Did you know Clint?

I had run into him here and there in Rome, at movie theaters that showed pictures in English. I found him to be charming, sweet, and soft. By saying he was soft I don't mean to be pejorative. He was neither weak nor the kind of tough guy he eventually became in movies.

Of course, he was Leone's creation. Knowing Leone, I know exactly what happened when he took one look at Clint. He gave him that hat, low over the eyes, and that little cigar. As you recall, he always had Clint looking down at the audience over the brim of his hat and then slowly looking up into the camera, with an enormous close-up of his eyes. I don't by any means intend to put Clint down as a talent, but Sergio created the Clint Eastwood who later went on to such success in Hollywood in the Dirty Harry movies.

You are credited with writing the dialogue for Once upon a Time in the West.

I wrote all the dialogue in English. I had a deal with Sergio to have single-card credit. When we had a fight, he went back on his word and instead put me at the top of the list of all the technical credits.

Sergio was incredibly creative. He could describe exactly what he wanted, and then put down on film exactly what was in his head. But there was just plain ugliness in his character, actual as well as spiritual. He had no sense of gratitude. He was basically uncaring about people. He worked people to death, although with actors and especially leads he was always very careful. The stars loved him because of their long close-ups.

He was famously stingy, the stingiest man on the face of the earth. Although the salary was always a fixed sum, he skimped on the hotel and other living expenses. He never left tips. One day, while filming at an Indian-run motel in Utah, we had a big argument in a restaurant after having a meal when he refused to pay his share or leave a tip. The argument was stupid, but by then I was fed up with him, and he got his revenge—he screwed me on the credit.

Ironically, working with Leone is the one thing I am famous for. I was in Paris having dinner with a friend one time, later on, and at the next table I saw Joe Losey sitting with someone I didn't recognize. Now Joe acted friendly; now he was a big, important guy: "Mickey, how are you doing? Let me introduce you." Joe introduced me to Graham Greene. I said, "Wow, what a pleasure to meet you. I've read a great deal of your work." Graham Greene said to Joe, "I'm sorry. I didn't catch the name." Joe said, "Mickey Knox." Graham Greene said, "Oh, yes. You wrote the dialogue for *Once upon a Time in the West*, didn't you?" Graham Greene was a great movie fan, and he looked at *all* the credits.

You ended up producing one "spaghetti western," didn't you, Viva la muerte . . . tua! (*also known as* Don't Turn the Other Cheek)?

Westerns were very hot. Eli, who became a big star in Italy after *The Good, Bad, and the Ugly,* said he would do a picture with me. I got a book, a western *The Killer from Yuma,* by Lewis B. Pattern. I hooked up with a producer I knew called Salvatore Alibiso. Salvatore Alibiso had produced a lot of movies, including westerns with Franco Nero, whom I worked with a lot, but he never had his name on the screen. Only people in the business knew about him, as a big moneymaker. I told him that I had an option on this book. I told him I could get Eli Wallach and Franco Nero, and then all we needed was an actress—we ended up getting Lynn Redgrave. We put an agreement together. I was promised a fee plus ten percent of the picture, or what amounted to twenty percent of his end. I got a lawyer to draw up my contract. But it turned out to be a nightmare.

Why?

I had said to Alibiso, "Don't hire an Italian writer until you talk to me. I want to work with him. That's my forte." Unbeknownst to me, he hired two cheap, cheap writers to write this script, which he handed to me a short time before we had to shoot. I read it, and I was sick. I said, "Salvatore!" He said, "What's the difference? The picture's presold."

I had brought him Eli, who played a Mexican bandit, and that's all he cared about. Eli asked for a quarter of a million dollars for his salary. That's a hell of a lot of money. And he got it. After which, Alibiso knew Eli would do the picture no matter how bad the script was. I added some fun things where I could, but still the script was not good.

So we start making the picture in Spain. I was running the whole production. Salvatore stayed in Rome, except to bring me money in a paper bag for Lynn Redgrave. I had to take time out, regularly, to sit there and count it out with him, then again, later, with Lynn's husband—a nightmare, I tell you.

Could you make any kind of creative contribution under the circumstances?

No. I'll tell you why. That fucking Alibiso would not hire a very good director, a man named Sergio Corbucci who had directed a very good western, because Franco Nero hated him. Franco hated him because he had paid more attention to the other star. Franco said, "I'll never work with him again." I said, "But Franco, he's the best director." Franco said no.

So we had a nice guy as director, Duccio Tessari, who was out every night until four in the morning drinking with the bullfighters. In the morning he'd be dressed impeccably with a carnation. He wanted four cameras for every shot. Why did he want four cameras? He didn't know how to shoot a scene. If he set it up with four cameras, he couldn't miss. A very nice man, but it wasn't a good movie. It was a pity. It could have been much better.

Anyway, the picture came out, and I couldn't get my lawyer to look at the books for my end. Three years went by. Then, of course, the books were cooked, so I never saw a nickel from that experience anyway. After that, I said, "Fuck producing in Italy!"

You moved back to Los Angeles in 1995. Are you getting work here nowadays?

They're all kids running everything out here now, but a very peculiar thing has happened. All through the 1970s and 1980s I was making trips here once or two times a year to see my daughters, who lived here after I was divorced. I would immediately get parts in TV shows. I did *Hart to Hart, Quincy, Barney's Place, Perry Mason,* and lots of others. I was hired by one casting director, who said to me what everybody now says to me: "You're a new old face." Meaning I'm a new face, but at the same time I'm known to the industry. They cast me nowadays without even reading me.

You've had a pretty remarkable career. It strikes me that it wouldn't have turned out so remarkably if you hadn't been forced into unusual measures by the blacklist.

I did what I had to do. I had to live and make a living. I had to get along and still maintain my balance and my humor. I've become bitter only recently, thinking about it. [Laughs.]

AFTRA [the American Federation of Television and Radio Artists] had a meeting about the blacklist recently, held at this enormous auditorium in the valley. Marsha Hunt was among the other people on the podium. At a certain point in the program, she said to the very big crowd, "Will the people who were blacklisted please stand up?" And I stood up. There weren't very many of us. I'd never done that publicly before. And I've got to tell you something: I felt good. I really felt terrific.

Millard Lampell

MILLARD LAMPELL, Highland Village, Texas, 1997

INTERVIEW BY PAUL BUHLE

MILLARD LAMPELL
(1919–   )

1946 *A Walk in the Sun*. Lyricist, uncredited script
    contribution.
1951 *Saturday's Hero*. Story based on his novel,
    coscript.
1959 *Blind Date/Chance Meeting*. Coscript.
1962 *Escape from East Berlin*. Coscript.

1963 *Oro per i Cesari/Gold for the Caesars*.
    Script (uncredited).
1966 *The Idol*. Script.
1971 *Eagle in a Cage*. Script, producer.
    Hard Traveling (telefilm).
    Script based on his play.
1979 *Orphan Train* (telefilm). Script.
1982 *The Wall* (telefilm). Script based on his play.
1989 *Triumph of the Spirit*. Uncredited contribution.

■

BORN IN 1919, raised in a lower-middle-class home in Paterson, New Jersey, and educated as a football-scholarship student at the University of West Virginia, Millard Lampell made his way into left-liberal journalism and then became a key participant in the folk-song movement of the 1940s and 1950s. As an original member of the Almanac Singers, Lampell recorded several influential folk and topical albums and toured the country with Pete Seeger, Woody Guthrie, and Lee Hays, doing hundreds of agitational and fund-raising performances for labor and political audiences.

When Lampell and others weren't on the road, they were headquartered at Almanac House on West Tenth Street in New York's Greenwich Village, a three-story building which briefly became a residence and performing center that attracted socialites as well as Socialists. Before Lampell was drafted in 1943, he had written all or part of the lyrics to many songs, including Woody Guthrie's "Hard Travelin'." His famous cantata "The Lonesome Train"—with music by Earl Robinson—about the return of Abraham Lincoln's remains from Washington to Springfield, Illinois, after the president's assassination, was broadcast after Franklin D. Roosevelt died. It so impressed film director Lewis Milestone that he based part of his superb war drama *A Walk in the Sun* on lyrics that he assigned Lampell to write about the experiences of World War II GIs.

Lampell was also moonlighting as a radio writer. His radio dramas, originally produced by the Army Air Force, became an important vehicle for explaining the experience of war and the psychological difficulties of returning veterans.

As a novelist and screenwriter after the war, Lampell experienced initial disappointments in Hollywood and then a major critical success. Working with writer and producer Sidney Buchman, he turned his novel *The Hero* into *Saturday's Hero*, a compelling indictment of college athletics' professionalization by coaches, college administrators, and alumni associations. The raw exploitation of working-class boys' physical skills (unless and until they suffered debilitating injuries), the use of painkilling drugs, the hypocrisy of "amateur" athletics, were all exposed in this hard-hitting film. But Lampell's Hollywood career was foreshortened when HUAC and the other red-hunters started drawing up their lists of unemployables.

During the 1950s Lampell worked quietly in radio and television and scripted films abroad, before making his mark under his own name again, in television, during the 1960s and 1970s. Episodes of *East Side, West Side,* shows for *The Hallmark Hall of Fame,* a season of *Rich Man, Poor Man,* an acclaimed small-screen adaptation of his Depression-era play *Hard Traveling,* *The Adams Chronicles* on PBS, and the teleplay for *Orphan Train* (a three-hour historical drama based on Dorothea G. Petrie's novel about Manhattan slum kids traveling to new homes out West) earned Lampell an Emmy, several Peabodys, and one Writers Guild award. Today Lampell is working on his memoirs in novel form.

■

Did you start writing articles, short stories, and radio scripts before or after your time with the Almanac Singers?

I was a storyteller from an early age. I grew up in Paterson, New Jersey. My parents both worked all day, and I liked to make up stories for the other kids. But I had never thought of being a writer until I went to the University of West Virginia on a football scholarship, got injured playing football, and had my scholarship cut off by the college. Then I began ghosting master's theses for pay. The students did the research, and I wrote the papers.

Then I got interested in one particular subject—Fascist movements in America. My roommate was Ed Curry, a blond-haired, blue-eyed "Aryan," and together we ran around meeting people who ran Fascist groups. We presented ourselves to them as being interested in forming a Fascist student organization. From that experience I wrote an unsolicited article for the *New Republic,* "Is There a Fuehrer in the House?" The magazine published it, and pretty soon I was writing book reviews for them.

I didn't stick around for graduation. Instead, I hitchhiked to New York. By now I wanted to be a writer. I did a piece on coal-mining disasters for *Friday,* a short-lived left-wing version of *Life* magazine bankrolled by Sheldon Dick, who had inherited part of the A. B. Dick [tabulating machines] fortune. And I started to write short stories, not successfully.

Bruce Bliven, who was publisher of the *New Republic,* got me a temporary job as a spy for the Friends of Democracy, and they gave me an apartment with the rent paid. The Friends was a group supported by, and perhaps set up by, the Anti-Defamation League. It was headed by a progressive minister from Kansas, Reverend Leon Birkhead,* who had written a couple of the Halde-man-Julius Little Blue Books.† Birkhead had been Sinclair Lewis's adviser on

---

*A Unitarian minister in Kansas City, Birkhead founded the Friends of Democracy in 1937 after a trip to Germany. He came to New York in 1939 and thereafter was known mainly for his leadership of the Friends, his pamphlets and essays, and a semi-monthly anti-Fascist bulletin, *Democracy's Battle.*

†Mass-published pamphlet-sized paperback books, the "University in Print," from Girard, Kansas, the Little Blue Books offered hundreds of thousands of autodidacts world literature, as well as specially commissioned titles on politics, history, and philosophy, from the 1920s through the 1940s. Launched by Emanuel Haldeman-Julius, who had taken over the once-popular

Elmer Gantry. My job was to infiltrate the organization of a Fascist who traveled around New York City in a covered wagon calling himself "the anti-Jew
candidate for Congress." Another spy for the Friends was a guy who called
himself John Roy Carlson; he later wrote a popular exposé called *Undercover.*

So I was doing all kinds of writing before I hooked up with Pete and Woody
and Lee. I had read Lee's satirical stories in the *New Republic* about his father's
circuit-riding days, and he had read my articles there. I hadn't even played
an instrument as a kid, let alone thought of writing lyrics. But Lee and I took
an apartment together, and the group got going. Once the Almanacs became
well-known, we had a pretty busy road act. We considered ourselves organizers
who sang. We went across the country singing on picket lines, at meetings,
and for benefits. Everybody friendly to the liberals and the left, from Hollywood film types to CIO union members, just ate us up.

*During the early 1940s, like many subsequent blacklistees, you were a member of
the Communist Party, but rather briefly.*

Sure, I was in the Party, but under unusual circumstances. It was toward
the end of the Almanac days. If you had trouble sleeping, you could always
go to a Party meeting and fall asleep right away. We were never in one place
long enough to belong to anything like a regular branch. And the Party didn't
give us any ideological trouble.

The functionaries were obviously delighted to have us out there singing
peace songs, then anti-Fascist songs. Woody wrote a column now and then
for what he called "The Sabbath Employee" (otherwise known as the *Sunday
Worker*). We believed in what the Party was for generally, especially on the
home front, but when it came to international events, we didn't know that
much about them. I left the Party automatically when I was drafted, and I
never rejoined.

When did you first visit Hollywood?

We were on a cross-country tour, doing concerts and benefits, and Lee
stopped off in San Francisco. I went on to L.A. with Pete and Woody, where
we sang on picket lines and at fund-raising parties. That's where I met Lewis
Milestone, which was my beginning in films. I met all kinds of other people
at these Hollywood parties. The one who impressed me most was Bertolt
Brecht, although I'd never read any of his poems or seen his plays. I wasn't
yet very well-read.

Back in New York, early in 1942, Woody and I were working in the kitchen
at Almanac House. It was winter, and we had no heat except a kitchen stove;
that was the warm room. He was working on *Bound for Glory* [his autobiog-

---

Socialist newspaper the *Appeal to Reason* in 1919, the Blue Books included works by Charles
Dickens, William Shakespeare, W. E. B. Du Bois, Bertrand Russell, Guy de Maupassant, Clarence Darrow, Thomas Paine, James T. Farrell, and Margaret Sanger. Thousands of titles were
published, most for a dime or less, and distributed mainly by mail order.

raphy], and I was working on "The Lonesome Train". I finished it in my new apartment on Horatio Street. Earl Robinson read the first draft and wanted to set it to music, asking me to add a line here and there.*

What was your relationship with Robinson?

He would sort of check up on us Almanacs to make sure that we were following the Party line. In his wonderfully earnest Huck Finn—really, Tom Sawyer—kind of way, he would remind us of our political responsibilities. I always considered him an island of respectability. He had a wife, kids, and a brownstone in Brooklyn. Later on, he was playing "The Lonesome Train" around Los Angeles, and Milestone heard it. Milestone had the extremely original idea of starting his picture [*A Walk in the Sun*] with a song that would help develop the plot and characters. I did two things, not enough for a script credit but important to the film. I wrote three or four songs which come up intermittently in the film, with different melodies and lyrics. Earl Robinson wrote the music. The songs provide an advance look at the story line, including who is in the outfit and what they are going to do next. The narration spoken at the beginning by John Ireland was also written by me. But Robert Rossen wrote the screenplay alone.

Did you work much with Milestone?

No, I didn't. I did my work on the film from New York. Other than that one conversation in Hollywood, my connections with Milestone were all later on, during my work with the Committee for the First Amendment and my scripting of *Hollywood Strikes Back*. He came from a world, from the history of film, which even at that time in my life was still very remote and foreign to me.

---

*Earl Robinson (1910–1995), a crucial figure in the musical milieu of the left, composed the music for such enduring songs as "Joe Hill," "Abe Lincoln," and "The House I Live In," communicating his belief in revolutionary traditions in which all Americans could share. Born in Seattle, he attended the University of Washington, then in 1934 went to New York, where he joined the Workers Laboratory Theatre and the Composers Collective. He studied composition with Aaron Copland and Hanns Eisler, while writing his own music, including music for John Howard Lawson's play *Processional* and for the Federal Theatre Project production *Sing for Your Supper*. He composed cantatas based on the words of Carl Sandburg, Franklin D. Roosevelt and William O. Douglas. "The Lonesome Train" and "Ballad for Americans" (with words by John Latouche), which Paul Robeson performed on radio and recorded, were played widely during the war and afterward.

"The House I Live In" became a short film on tolerance in Hollywood, starring Frank Sinatra and written by Albert Maltz; it was awarded a special Oscar in 1945. But otherwise Robinson's scores for *A Walk in the Sun* and *The Man from Texas* did not establish him in the film industry. Blacklisted, he taught music and continued to compose, returning to films to contribute the theme to *Hurry Sundown* in 1966. Frequently Robinson was seen by labor and radical audiences, singing and accompanying himself on the piano, and even during his last years he retained his legendary charisma.

Obviously, you hadn't written for movies before. What had you thought of movies as a kid?

Most kids went to movies on Saturday, but I played football. The physical part of films attracted me. I wanted to be Fred Astaire, but so did everyone else.

You had done quite a bit of radio writing, however.

Really, I started just before going into the Army. A producer named Hi Brown, who did both the popular soaper *Joyce Jordan, Girl Intern* and the "squeaking-door" show, *The Inner Sanctum*, decided he wanted to contribute something for the war effort. By that time the Japanese had bombed Pearl Harbor, and Brown had a couple of patriotic radio shows on the air. One was called *Green Valley, USA*. It was about an American community during the war, and I wrote most of the episodes for that series.

I'm not sure how that all came about, but *Green Valley, USA* led to my writing for *The Prudential Family Hour*. Another producer, Howard Barnes, who had come to hear us at Almanac House, had the idea that I could write something about American folk heroes. By this time I had become self-educated by reading voraciously and knew a lot about folk heroes. Woody himself had invented "Jackhammer John," a modern industrial proletarian who was a twentieth-century folk hero. So I was well-acquainted with such notions and able to suggest a whole series of heroes for this program, each to be developed through a small dramatization of ten minutes or so.

This was Americana with a pinch of Jeffersonian left-wingism.

If you want to stretch it, the subjects were all workingmen—Mike Fink the riverboat driver, John Henry working on the railroad, Jim Bridger the backwoods pioneer, and so on. We didn't do any women. We hadn't developed our "Rosie the Riveter" consciousness yet. That was a little later, and *The Prudential Family Hour* wasn't about to include an anti-slavery figure like Sojourner Truth.

In the Army Air Force, you continued in radio.

When I was in the Army I went up to New York, because I knew people in the networks and wanted to sell them the idea for a series, *First in the Air*, which we launched in 1944, doing a new one every week. Colonel Howard Rusk had asked for such a program to prepare the GIs for coming home after the war, and to prepare their families for the men who in some cases had broken down and were now experiencing mental troubles.

One of the stories I proposed was "The Boy from Nebraska," about the only Japanese-American tailgunner, Ben Kuroki, who came from a potato farm in Nebraska and who flew fifty missions without ever getting a Purple Heart. The dramatic counterpoint was the treatment of the Japanese-Americans, the removal of them to internment camps. I also spoke up in another episode of that series for the Ninety-ninth Fighter Squadron, African-Americans in Italy.

As part of that series, the commanding general of the Army Air Force, Hap Arnold, proposed that we do a series of live broadcasts from Yale as an effort to bring together professional talent and keep various actors from getting scattered around the world prior to the making of *Winged Victory*. Moss Hart was writing *Winged Victory*, which was going to be an important morale-boosting show for the Air Force, but the work was going slowly. Suddenly, in 1945, therefore, I found myself at Yale in a special group, all in uniform, and I was directing as well as writing the shows. I always seemed to do things as though I had been doing them all my life. I remember we had an actor in our group with the wonderful name of Malden Sekulovich, which he later turned into Karl Malden. We also had Bill [William] Holden, Marty Ritt, and Chuck [Charlton] Heston. The *First in the Air* shows were later published as *The Long Way Home*.

Then I went to Italy for a short time, and suddenly I got orders to report back to the Waldorf-Astoria in New York. I had no idea why. There I was told it was because Mrs. Ogden Reid, publisher of the *New York Herald Tribune*, had taken up the case of Ben Kuroki. He was going to appear on this forum. This was a big deal; she was a big deal. Colonel Rusk had played the episodes that made up *The Long Way Home* for her, and she had personally called the secretary of war to find this writer who had written *The Boy from Nebraska*, so he could write a speech for Kuroki.

I got a lot of attention during my last twenty-one days in uniform, because I was also asked to appear on *Town Hall of the Air*, a national radio show, with the cartoonist Bill Mauldin and two generals, speaking on the topic "What the GI Wants." The generals were really bumbling. Bill and I couldn't lose; we were sergeants, ordinary soldiers, up against a couple of generals. The main issue we talked about was race policies and the constraints on the integration of the armed forces. I also talked about veterans' housing being stalled in Congress. I got over five hundred letters after that appearance. This also helped put me on the blacklist years later.

After you got out of the Army, you kept writing for radio.

After the war, I did radio shows for the United Nations as a hired gun, not as a regular employee. I went to the new state of Israel, which was still full of fighting, to write a radio play about Count Folke Bernadotte, called *Sometime Before Morning*.* Henry Fonda played Bernadotte. A fellow whom I had met in Chicago named Studs Terkel came to New York to play the taxi driver who became the driver for Bernadotte and was killed as well.

One other important thing on radio: by the time I got to Hollywood, in

---

*In a notorious and still controversial 1948 incident, Count Folke Bernadotte, a Swedish humanitarian and diplomat who had been sent by the United Nations on a peace mission to Jerusalem, was assassinated by members of a right-wing Jewish militia group, the Stern Gang.

1947, Norman Corwin, who had done his own series of dramas, had presented "The Lonesome Train" on the CBS network. That was a prestigious event, because Norman was considered the great radio director of the time.

Hollywood called?

By this time Warners had optioned *The Long Way Home*, but it wasn't long before Jack Warner decided that because the war had just ended, war movies were out. Earlier, during the war and at the high point of the Soviet-American alliance, the famous agent Charlie [Charles] Feldman had optioned "The Lonesome Train." It was to be part of a dramatization of four great world leaders: Abraham Lincoln, Sun Yat-sen, V. I. Lenin, and Winston Churchill. That was a crazy idea, and it didn't go anywhere, either.

Anyway, after *The Long Way Home* got stalled, it was pretty much up to me what I might propose next, and at first I had a ball trying to sort it out. I worked with Milton Sperling, a producer who had started out as [Darryl] Zanuck's secretary. Milton, who had been a Marine captain in the war, did something important for me. I hadn't seen that many movies, so for a month Milton had four run each day for me in the projection room.

It was a strange time to arrive in Hollywood.

It was August 1947, a few months after the Nineteen had been summoned to Washington, and just as the public defense was being prepared. It was a heady, marvelous time for me. All the celebrities were organizing to go with them to show support. The Committee for the First Amendment was developing an idea for a radio show. A few years earlier, during Roosevelt's last reelection campaign, in 1944, Norman Corwin and I had worked on a campaign radio show. It was run by [politican and public official] Chester Bowles out of Democratic headquarters. According to network rules political parties could buy time but weren't allowed to "dramatize" the political message. So we had decided to use real people, like a farmer from the Tennessee Valley or a Marine from Iwo Jima, and we even found a woman who had voted for Abraham Lincoln! She was a hundred years old. Of course, we wrote the speeches.

Anyway, now Norman said to me, "Let's do the same kind of show for the First Amendment." Humphrey Bogart or Judy Garland or someone else would start off their speeches by saying, "I'm an actor." This was *Hollywood Strikes Back*. Here I was, the new kid on the block, and the stars and directors were crawling up each other's backs to get on a show I was writing. Suddenly I met everybody in Hollywood—except Adolphe Menjou and John Wayne.

Did you know many of the people among the Hollywood left?

In Hollywood the people I knew best were Abe Polonsky and Albert Maltz. Alvah Bessie I found shrill, although I respected his having been a volunteer in Spain. John Howard Lawson and I were diametrically opposed about everything artistic, even the use of the English language. Abe was a great person-

ality, and Albert was very helpful when I was writing *The Hero*. I hadn't
written a novel before, and he was a true friend.

Some I knew from New York, where we used to play touch football every
Sunday in the fall, whoever was around. The group included Walter Bern-
stein, Irwin Shaw, and Marty Ritt. The only one who took it seriously was
Irwin—he used to come in football cleats and shoulder pads.

*You had only a brief spell as a Warner Brothers contract writer, and you didn't
really enjoy it, did you?*

I got bored with Warners, which assigned me to various projects, all of
them, it seems to me, called "South of St. Louis."* I worked on one project
for Jerry Wald, a movie for Joan Crawford to be titled "Miss O'Brien." She
had won an Academy Award for *Mildred Pierce*, and Wald thought any role
that she could do in a two-ninety-eight dress from the May Company would
get her another Oscar. I suggested, "Let's do one on a schoolteacher." I wrote
the story, but it was never made. You know how it usually happens in Hollywood.

To keep myself from getting bored out of my mind, I wrote a novel. I had
been a quarterback in high school, and I had played football on scholarship
at West Virginia until I suffered a shoulder separation, when a blocker missed
a tackler closing in on me. Then the school cut off my scholarship, and that's
the kind of thing I wrote about in my novel, which I called *The Hero*. I was
lucky; I got into writing, and the Alamanac Singers. But most of my friends
on the team were Poles or other Slavs from steel mills and coal-mining towns.
They had it worse if they lost their scholarships—they had nowhere to go.

When my contract ran out at Warners, I went back to New York, and my
novel was published. Then my agent called and said, "Columbia wants to buy
The Hero." Sidney Buchman asked me to write the screenplay. Sidney lived
on the Coast, but he also had a New York apartment, and he would travel
back and forth, so I knew him. He was a wonderful person, and, really, he
became my teacher about writing screenplays.

I wrote that screenplay in New York in 1950, and it was produced as *Saturday's Hero* that same year, very fast. They were already casting the picture
while I was still polishing the script.

Buchman is cocredited for the screenplay as well for producing it.

Under current Guild rules, he wouldn't have gotten credit. He wrote less
than twenty percent of the screenplay. But I didn't begrudge it to him. He
polished it up and saw it through as a film. More than anyone else, he taught
me that film was visual. Coming from my background, and with my interest
in literature and lyrics, I thought in terms of words. Sidney used to say, "I

---

*Milton Sperling is credited with producing a western with that title, released by Warners in
1948. Lampell claims no involvement.

want you to write the next three scenes with *no dialogue*." Even when dialogue was called for, it became a kind of marvelous exercise, showing what people were saying by what they did. And that, I learned, is the spine of film.

How much of a lefty was he?

He was a humanist. The heavy politics of the family were his wife, Bea's. Their marriage was chaotic, but he adored her. I remember about Sidney, though, that when we went out to the Coast, he really stood up to the studio. He had one knock-down-drag-out fight with the foul-mouthed head of the studio, Harry Cohn, and he really said to Cohn what everyone else wanted to say. The battle was over casting. We had wanted Jack Palance. Instead, we got John Derek, who was a contract player at Warners.

Saturday's Hero still stands up as a tough indictment of the way college athletes are treated. And John Derek was good in it, too.

Yes. Derek did a creditable job. He was a former paratrooper and had the physical ability.

Then I was "named," and I appeared before the Senate Judiciary Committee on April 2, 1952. My Hollywood days were finished for a while. I hadn't even seen the shadow hovering over me.

Who named you?

A guy whom I'd known—he didn't publicly appear—named Allen Sloane, who was already cooperating. He had been a friend of mine from high school in Paterson. Later he hung around Almanac House and then became a radio writer. In fact, I had helped him get jobs. He invented stuff for the Committee; he was a real Dostoevsky character. Of course, I was already listed in *Red Channels*, too. They did their research by looking up who had been reviewed in a friendly way in the *Daily Worker*, so they had me down from the Almanac days. One way or the other, I was out.

By the time I got my subpoena, I had already started to do a little television. Hume Cronyn offered me a job writing something he was working on, a thirteen-week series called *The Marriage*. I told Hume, "I'd like to write it, but NBC would never hire me." Nobody could believe such things would happen yet. Soon I appeared as an "unfriendly witness," and the executives at NBC decided, "We can't do this project with Lampell." I ended up working anonymously when another writer on the project—Ernie [Ernest] Kinoy, who later became president of the Screen Writers Guild—said that he would be my "front" while also writing for the show himself.

Hume was so wonderful to me. Guys like Howard Rushmore, who wrote a red-baiting column for the *New York World Telegram*, would be on the set, and Hume would be calling out my name: "Millard, could you come in here?" We were all learning in those early years how the blacklist worked.

How could you make a living if you were blacklisted in television also?

I did more work for the UN. The purge at the UN came a little later and didn't have any immediate effect on me, because I was a hired gun, not a regular employee. Then that ended, too. Finally I went into industrial documentaries. I would go to Paris and do some film like *Paris in the Eyes of Her Children*, sponsored by Air France. I also did two shows for IBM. These corporations didn't care about the blacklist.

How did you get involved with Joseph Losey on Chance Meeting, *a film noir about a painter framed for his girlfriend's murder?*

I was in London doing a documentary for Air France. I'd known Joe Losey from my Almanac days, when he used to come around to Almanac House in New York. I wrote the first draft while I was living in London. We handed it back and forth. I was reading Van Gogh's letters to Theo and used the spirit of them for one scene in the film. Joe was terribly nice to me. His drawback was his lack of humor, although he made some wonderful films. We did some rewriting later, but very little; once Ben and I were satisfied, Joe liked it.

You were blacklisted, so how did Chance Meeting *get distributed?*

Joe and Ben had left the country, of course, instead of being subpoenaed and testifying. But things were different in Europe. The picture was produced by Sydney Box and bought by Metro [MGM]. The head of distribution for Metro in London was not too aware of the blacklist. Why he would consider buying a picture by three blacklisted guys in 1959, I don't know. But Metro announced that they had big plans for *Chance Meeting*. They were going to bring a star over to the United States to publicize the film, and they even sent me a schedule of proposed television appearances. I would join them to promote the film, because I was coming back to New York.

Then the Catholic War Veterans got on the case and threatened to picket the theaters. I was told that a top MGM executive personally negotiated the fate of the film with Cardinal Spellman, telling him how much the studio had invested in the film. Spellman respected money—it was next to God. So Spellman decided, "You can release the picture, but you can't publicize it, and you can show it only as part of a double feature." So the film ended up being shown with a Clark Gable comedy, *It Happened in Naples*. That buried *Chance Meeting*.

Shortly afterward, though, you began to have more luck in the theater and on television.

First I had *The Wall*, a drama about the Warsaw Ghetto Uprising based on John Hersey's novel, produced at the Billy Rose Theatre in New York in 1960, with Morton Da Costa directing and the lead role played by George C. Scott. Another version was produced in 1964 at the Arena Stage in Washington, which was important to me at the time, and in 1982 it was again produced, this time by CBS as a three-hour television special which won a Peabody Award.

At any rate, in 1963, partly because of *The Wall*, David Susskind came to me to write for a somewhat controversial new television series, *East Side, West Side*. George Scott had suggested me, and Susskind was taking a gamble. But people were also getting ready to stand up.

Being able to write fast was useful on a television series. I had learned some valuable things during the blacklist. I had learned to work under vast pressure, because by the time the producer got to someone like me, he had already blown his writing budget, and what he wanted most of all was someone cheap who could deliver overnight.

Was that the case with Escape from East Berlin, *directed by Robert Siodmak, about a chauffeur who leads his girlfriend and family through a tunnel out of the Eastern Zone?*

Very much so. Other writers had done a first draft of the film, and Siodmak realized that it was unshootable. The producer got hold of me—I don't remember how—and I flew over to Berlin. That was a fascinating experience. Siodmak himself was a character, and it was wonderful to be in Berlin. I stayed at a house owned by my German publisher, Fischer Verlag, in Grünewald. Then this SS-looking man with a helmet would come roaring up late at night every night to pick up the pages for the next day—I was only a day ahead of the camera. As it turned out, we used part of the story from the other two writers [Gabrielle Upton and Peter Berneis], but I rewrote all the dialogue.

Was Siodmak at the end of his creativity by the time you worked with him?

I would say yes. The main thing about Robert Siodmak to me was that he was a wonderful tour guide to back-alley Berlin. He was very literate, like a personal epitome of the Berlin of the thirties, even more than Fritz Lang, whom I also knew. But Lang was ill by the time I got to know him, very much concerned with his aches and pains.

Are there any credits under the blacklist that I've missed?

Well, *Gold for the Caesars*, made in France in 1964 and directed by André de Toth. It was a bad Roman-slave story starring Jeffrey Hunter. I was asked by de Toth to write the script, and I did it all myself. I never saw the picture.

Back in the United States you got an Emmy in 1965 for Eagle in a Cage, *about Napoleon in exile on St. Helena. According to Victor Navasky's book* Naming Names, *you said to the awards-ceremony audience, "I think I ought to mention that I was blacklisted for ten years," after which you received a huge ovation. Did you plan to make such a direct and provocative statement?*

No. I didn't know what I was going to say. I didn't think I'd get the award, because of the blacklist. It probably worked the other way around—being blacklisted probably helped me get it.

I remember looking out at the audience and seeing at least three or four producers who had blacklisted me. They were all applauding. Then, a little later, the *New York Times* called and asked me to write about the blacklist. I wrote a piece for the Sunday entertainment section based on my testimony at the hearings, and they printed it without cutting a word. I guess it was the first article from the blacklistees' point of view published in a major paper.*

Next comes another theatrical release, The Idol, *which was treated badly by the reviewers.*

Probably rightfully so. That was Joseph E. Levine's project. We twisted Levine's arm to get Kim Stanley as the lead. The story line was about a student in London who has an affair with his friend's mother. We thought the mother would be a great role for Kim, who had just finished doing *Séance on a Wet Afternoon.* But she was much too heavy for the part. I went up to her house to convince her to go to a fat farm and take off forty pounds. She was a wonderful actress, and she acted thin that day! But she didn't like to fly, and by the time she arrived in London by boat not only had she *not* lost weight, she had gone back to drinking. It was a disaster.

So we ended up sitting in the Hotel Savoy frantically calling all over the world to see who was available. Finally we got Jennifer Jones. She simply did not fit the part. And it wasn't that good a script, anyway.

Your next film was an adaptation of your Emmy-winning TV show Eagle in a Cage.

Yes. After I had done it as a *Hallmark Hall of Fame* show, an executive from Westinghouse [film-production division], the same Howard Barnes from radio days, came to me and said, "We think it would make a good feature." They had a guy who was willing to put up half the money. So I set to work to convert my TV script, which meant really rewriting pretty much everything, because there's such a vast difference between what works on television and what works as a theatrical feature. At the last moment, the other financier fell through. Howard came to me and said, "All right, we'll finance it completely—if you'll produce it."

You had never produced anything before.

Yes, but it was another great experience of doing something new. Off I went to London, and we had a cast that included Sir John Gielgud, Sir Ralph Richardson, Billie Whitelaw, and Moses Gunn, who had been in my play

---

*Millard Lampell, "I Think I Ought to Mention That I Was Blacklisted," *New York Times*, August 3, 1966.

Hard Traveling. I wrote a part for Moses as a black general. There were actually black generals in Napoleon's army, from Haiti and elsewhere, although not with Napoleon on St. Helena.

I wrote the first draft when I was living in the Delaware Valley, in New Jersey, but then I went to Italy and finished the screenplay there, where we thought we were going to film it. The Italians really began to pile on the expenses, however, so we explored Yugoslavia, where a lot of movies were being made then, and finally we shot it there. Gielgud was wonderful, so was Richardson, so was Billie. Kenneth Haigh, who was a talented actor, just wasn't up to the part of Napoleon, however, and that hurt the film.

You seem to have had more luck over the long haul in television.

At a certain point I went to my talent agency and said, "Give me a television production that's in trouble." For example, I was asked to work on the second season of what had been a big hit, *Rich Man, Poor Man.* ABC wanted to continue with the show, and Irwin Shaw had tried without much success to do an outline for another year. When I went out to the Coast, I discovered there was nothing left of Shaw's book to do, so I had to create a whole new cast of characters. I used my wife's maiden name as the villain, which cheered my father-in-law immensely. And the second season was a big hit. So now it was easy for me to continue with television and get other important jobs.

One of my favorites was an adaptation of my own play *Hard Traveling.* I had contributed a couple of verses to Woody's song "Hard Travelin'," and later I turned this into a Depression play, a sort of *Candide*-like treatment of a sympathetic young man who travels across the country trying without much success to be a con man. It was also done at the Arena Stage, in Washington, like *The Wall.* The *New York Times* sent down a reviewer and gave it a rave, so PBS called and said they'd like me to do a television version, and I did.

Orphan Train was another one, a three-hour special that won me a Writers Guild Award. It stands up well, and an award that you get from other writers means a lot. I also did, for PBS, several episodes of *The Adams Chronicles.*

You have one last film credit, Triumph of the Spirit, *directed by Robert Young, about life and death in Auschwitz.*

Did I get a credit for that? Jesus! I was doing a screenplay for Orion, but it never got done, because Orion went into bankruptcy around that time. Mike Medavoy, Orion's head of production, had asked me if there was anything I'd like to write, and I came up with a project called "The Fever," about a young doctor who had to put in a year's service in the West Virginia hills. Anyway, Medavoy left, and after an executive has nurtured a project and then leaves, no one wants to do it anymore, because if it bombs, he takes the blame, but if it succeeds, the original boss gets the praise. So "The Fever" went on the shelf. But director Robert Young was working at Orion, and he and I had become friends.

Bob went off to Poland to make *Triumph of the Spirit*, and he realized, ten days before shooting, that the script was unshootable. I had warned him about that when he'd asked me to take a look at the script. So he called and asked, "Would you please see what you can do?" I went over for four weeks and probably got overpaid—no, that's not true, a writer can never be overpaid—for the little work I did.

Willem Dafoe played a Greek-Jewish boxer who is deported, with his family, to Auschwitz. Edward James Olmos was a magician, my attempt to lighten up the film by giving Olmos a character that I invented, like that of Joel Grey in *Cabaret*, who carried on satire under Fascism. But Bob and I had a disagreement about the picture. He wanted a ruthless, realistic depiction of Auschwitz. I said, "Bob, you're doing this as a commercial picture. You think that people are going to come to the movie from their comfortable houses, drive in their cars, and go home after the movie and feel as though they've just left Auschwitz? Are you kidding?"

This was a long time before *Schindler's List*. Steven Spielberg handled the subject shrewdly. The problem for us was the certainty of everyone dying and the relentlessness of day-to-day existence. In *Schindler's List* the mood is lifted by devoting large parts of the film to life in the factory or to Schindler himself. Bob went off on his own, improvising scenes, and the story began to get more and more grim. Although Bob is a very talented director, I couldn't believe it would work. After four weeks I just said, "Good-bye and good luck." It didn't work. Nobody wanted to go see an Auschwitz film.

Do you have any plans for future television work or films?

Strangely enough, a contract just arrived this morning. I had done a treatment years ago about [music producer] John Hammond and [jazz singer] Billie Holiday. Warner Brothers decided not to do it, but now they've just bought the treatment. I won't do the screenplay, though, because I don't want to do that kind of work anymore. I'm deeply into my memoir, and I've got two more books that I want to write.

Besides, with what's happened in the studios, it's a different world, and I don't want to do that dance anymore. I could no more go into a pitch session now than I could talk Swahili. Being a writer in Hollywood—and it has become more and more this way—is really humiliating. Since the latest round of executives took over, the guys from the business office are looking only for what makes big bucks here and abroad. If a bullet is a bullet is a bullet, you don't need dialogue. I'm too old for that kind of thinking. With a book, I'm totally my own master and make my own decisions. Right now, I teach a few university classes at night, and I write during the day. This is the time of life when, if there's anything you want to do, you had better do it.

Ring Lardner Jr.

RING LARDNER JR., New York City, 1997

INTERVIEW BY PATRICK McGILLIGAN

RING LARDNER JR.
(1915–   )

1937 *A Star Is Born.* Uncredited contribution.
   Nothing Sacred. Uncredited contribution.
1939 *Meet Dr. Christian.* Coscript.
1940 *The Courageous Dr. Christian.* Costory, co-script.
1941 *Arkansas Judge.* Coadaptation.
1942 *Woman of the Year.* Costory, coscript.
1943 *The Cross of Lorraine.* Coscript.

1944 *Marriage Is a Private Affair.*
   Uncredited contribution.
   Laura. Uncredited contribution.
   Tomorrow the World. Coscript.
1946 *Cloak and Dagger.* Coscript.
1947 *Forever Amber.* Coscript.
1949 *Britannia Mews/The Forbidden Street.* Script.
1950 *Swiss Tour/Four Days Leave.* Dialogue.
1951 *The Big Night.* Uncredited contribution.
1959 *Virgin Island.* Coscript (as Philip Rush).
1960 *A Breath of Scandal.* Uncredited contribution.

1963 *The Cardinal.* Uncredited contribution.
1965 *The Cincinnati Kid.* Coscript.
1970 *M*A*S*H.* Script.
1971 *La maison sous les arbres/The Deadly Trap.*
Uncredited contribution.

La mortadella/Lady Liberty. Coscript, 1972,
English-language version only.
1977 *The Greatest.* Script.

■

RING LARDNER JR. was among the nineteen Hollywood personalities subpoenaed to appear before the House Committee on Un-American Activities in Washington, D.C., in the fall of 1947. Along with nine others called
to testify—Alvah Bessie, Herbert Biberman, Lester Cole, Edward Dmytryk,
John Howard Lawson, Albert Maltz, Samuel Ornitz, Adrian Scott, and Dalton Trumbo—Lardner refused to answer, when asked, whether he was a
member of the Communist Party, and he was declared in contempt of
Congress. Bertolt Brecht, the eleventh, gave testimony that mystified the
Committee and shortly thereafter left the country. The ten became known
as the Hollywood Ten.

After their court appeals failed, Lardner served ten months of his one-
year sentence at the Federal Correctional Institution in Danbury, Connecticut. Released from prison, Lardner left Hollywood, finished *The Ecstasy of
Owen Muir,* a novel he had begun in prison, and found first a British and
later an American publisher for it.* Then he survived the blacklist largely by
writing, under pseudonyms, scripts for television shows that were shot in
England and sold to American networks.

Ring Lardner Jr. has a special status as the winner of Best Screenplay
Oscars before and after the blacklist. At the age of twenty-six he shared
with Michael Kanin the 1942 Academy Award for *Woman of the Year,* which
paired Spencer Tracy and Katharine Hepburn for the first time. In 1970,
with the blacklist over and his career recharged, he again won an Oscar, for
the screenplay of Robert Altman's *M*A*S*H.*

■

*How logical was the grouping of the Hollywood Nineteen? What did these people
have in common?*

From the week the subpoenas arrived, in September 1947, speculation began about how the recipients who came to be known as "the unfriendly
nineteen" were chosen. I felt then, and still feel now, that it was in part a
rather haphazard process. It is true the list included some of the best-known
Hollywood radicals: John Howard Lawson, Albert Maltz, Dalton Trumbo, and
Herbert Biberman. And there were another eight of us who were, along with
others equally eligible but not summoned, on the second echelon in terms of

---

*Prometheus Books is republishing Lardner's novel *The Ecstasy of Owen Muir* in its literary-
classics series in 1997. *The Lardners: My Family Remembered,* a family chronicle and an autobiography, was published in 1976.

publicized left-wing activities: Alvah Bessie, Lester Cole, Richard Collins, Gordon Kahn, Samuel Ornitz, Robert Rossen, Waldo Salt, and myself. Bertolt Brecht was a special case, as an expatriate who had just emerged from his wartime status as an enemy alien.

The remaining six were improbable choices. Howard Koch, Lewis Milestone, and Irving Pichel had each signed a petition or two that were deemed leftist, but there were dozens of other offenders on the same level of intellectual guilt. Koch might have drawn the Committee's attention as the writer of *Mission to Moscow* and Milestone as the director of *The North Star*, both of which were sympathetic portraits of life in the Soviet Union. And Milestone had the added liability of being both Jewish and Russian-born. But Pichel's closest connection to our recent ally and current enemy was that he had once played the part of Joseph Stalin before he gave up acting to concentrate on direction.

Adrian Scott and Edward Dmytryk had made themselves publicly known, not for their radical views but as the producer and director respectively of the movie *Crossfire*, which was a forceful attack on anti-Semitism. The fact that they were not only subpoenaed but among the ten actually called to the witness stand makes it all the more possible that it was their artistic rather than political malfeasance that had landed them in Washington. As for Larry Parks, he had been a little-known movie actor for five years before he drew a lot of attention with his portrayal of Al Jolson, the "Mammy" singer. The most likely reason for his inclusion was that some informer had named him as a member of the Communist Party—which he later admitted he had been—and the Committee members couldn't resist the chance to include a name actor in their roundup.

Most of you were in fact Communists, right? But some of you weren't.

It is true that most of the Nineteen were members of the Communist Party, as I was, so there must have been at least one informer in the ranks of the Party. Koch and Milestone were not members, and Brecht testified at the hearings that he had never joined the Party in Germany [or in the United States]. Pichel was the only one of the group besides Parks whom I had not known personally, in fact, had scarcely heard of, and it is almost certain that I would have known about him if he had ever been a Communist.

What were your personal relationships with those members of the Nineteen whom you knew best?

Trumbo, Cole, Collins, Salt, Lawson, Biberman, Rossen, Kahn, and Maltz had all been friends and comrades of mine over many years. Bessie, Ornitz, Scott, and Dmytryk I had also known but not as long or as closely.

Trumbo was my closest friend in the group. He was bright and funny and deeply concerned with what was going on in the world. He loved to talk, but unlike most people with that tendency, he was nearly always worth listening to. His writing was almost as facile as his speech, and he turned out an incredible quantity of material, especially during the blacklist, when his price per script was drastically cut.

Lawson was a hard man to get close to, but you had to admire his dedication to his role as political leader of the Hollywood section of the Communist Party. Intelligent and well read, he was also limited by the strictness of his adherence to Marxist doctrine.

I spent quite a lot of time with Albert Maltz over the years, but I never really felt at ease with him. He had considerable talent as a writer, but an overserious, slightly pompous manner diminished his charm for me.

Biberman was even more serious and more pompous than Maltz, but the very extremity of these qualities made him interesting and sometimes amusing to observe. He devoted almost all his time and effort to some form or other of political activity, and you had to admire him for it even if you felt some of his ideas were naive.

Lester Cole was a journeyman writer who seemed to recognize his limitations. We saw a lot of each other because of living close together some of the time and simultaneous service on the executive board of the Screen Writers Guild, but I never sought him out for companionship.

Gordon Kahn was the member of the group I had known the longest. When I went to work as reporter on the *New York Daily Mirror* in 1935 at the age of nineteen, Kahn was a veteran rewrite man there, and I often phoned stories in to him. Very small and distinguished by the monocle he wore, he had a devastating wit that made you enjoy his company. For some reason, he never accomplished very much in his screenwriting.

Waldo Salt was a prodigy who went to college and began creative writing at a very early age. He was smart and interesting, and a very talented screenwriter, and I always regretted not seeing more of him than I did. Luckily, I was able to make up for that in later years when we were neighbors in Connecticut.

Dick Collins was already a Communist when I joined in 1936. We saw each other frequently, both at Party meetings and socially, and I thought quite highly of him as a person, but somehow we never became close friends. I was completely surprised when a fellow inmate at the Federal Correctional Institution in Danbury, Connecticut, came to my cell and said they were talking about me on the radio, and I found it was Dick testifying as a cooperative witness and giving the Committee all the names he could think of.

The image Bob Rossen presented to the world was that of a plebeian with a lot of talent. He wrote some good movies, including the classic one about a lynching, *They Won't Forget*, which could conceivably have been a reason for southerners on the Committee to pick him out. He had just started a new career as a director when he was subpoenaed for the second time and decided to preserve that career at the expense of his former values. I was not as surprised as I had been by Collins.

Sam Ornitz was a novelist, known for his portrayals of New York City Jewish life, who had responded to a Hollywood offer in the early talking-picture days and remained there for the rest of his life, though his movie jobs were few even before the blacklist. He was something of a Marxist scholar and formed a team with another novelist, screenwriter Guy Endore, to address any group willing to listen to them on the subject.

Alvah Bessie had been a Communist and a writer for the *Daily Worker* in the East before he came west for a try at the movies. The most notable thing about his career was that he had joined the Abraham Lincoln Brigade early in the Spanish Civil War and then written one of the better books about that experience, *Men in Battle*. He was noted among the Hollywood Ten for his cynical pessimism, but almost every prediction of his about our future and the misdeeds of government agencies like the FBI turned out to be accurate or nearly so.

Adrian Scott and Edward Dmytryk were only casual acquaintances until the meetings of the Nineteen before the 1947 hearings and of the Ten during the nearly three years before we started serving our prison terms. Those meetings and some social contacts led me to form favorable impressions of both of them, Scott especially. Dmytryk's main drawback was that he always seemed to have special inside information about whatever was happening, and you never knew how substantial the basis for it was. After seven of us were confined to the District of Columbia Department of Correction (Lawson and Trumbo, whose trials were precedents for the rest of us, had already been sent to their permanent home-from-homes, and Ornitz, who was in bad health, was assigned to a prison hospital facility), I saw Eddie every day at our exercise period. The Korean War had broken out during the week between our perfunctory trials and our sentencing and confinement. All I knew about what was going on was what I read in the papers, but Eddie, as usual, had the inside dope. It was not the Communist North Koreans, he assured me, who had started the hostilities, but the South Koreans, with the blessing of our then secretary of state, John Foster Dulles, who had provoked the war.

It was perhaps a coincidence that Eddie and Herbert Biberman were sentenced by a different judge from the other six of us, but ours prescribed one year and theirs only six months. Alvah Bessie might have said, and probably did, that Eddie and his lawyer were already looking forward to his recantation, and that Herbert was included in the deal to make it look kosher. I know of no evidence one way or the other about that, but when I heard, also on the prison radio, about Eddie's statement on his release, after five months—he got thirty days off for good behavior—that the attack of the North Koreans on the South Koreans had so disillusioned him that he had renounced his Communist past and was now willing to cooperate with the Committee, I remembered one other observation of his: "You guys are all writers, and you can go on writing under pseudonyms, but I never had any craft except film editing and then direction. And I have no experience directing in the theater."

You mentioned that Milestone was Jewish. How much of a factor was that, in the Nineteen being chosen? Or the fact that none were U.S. military veterans?

I believe I was the first person to note that, in selecting the Nineteen, the Committee had not included any of the Party members or sympathizers who had served in the armed forces during the war. Since, in those immediate postwar years, such service, combat experience in particular, was an important distinction, I still think that this was probably a deliberate policy. Whether Jews were chosen over gentiles is more questionable, since the proportion of the former was not much greater among those selected than it was among the likely candidates for subpoenas.

Can you explain your legal strategy? It's very confusing to some people nowadays, who think, "Why didn't they just say they were Communists and be done with it?" Who was behind the strategy that prevailed, and why did it prevail? Did it have anything to do with personal and political prestige within the group?

When Dalton Trumbo and I figured subpoenas would soon be arriving, we considered all possible ways of dealing with the inevitable HUAC questions and came to the conclusion that the best course was to challenge the Committee's right to ask them. Invoking the Fifth Amendment at that time would have been putting ourselves in the position of saying, "It's a crime to be a Communist." Committee members could respond, "No, it's a perfectly legal party." Also, we would not be challenging HUAC's right to exist and to investigate areas protected by the First Amendment's right of free speech. If we said our political beliefs and affiliations were our own private affair (Alvah Bessie pointed out on the stand that Dwight Eisenhower was currently refusing to say whether he was a Republican or a Democrat), and that HUAC could not investigate where it was forbidden by the Constitution to legislate, then a victory for us in the courts could effectively demolish the Committee. And there were several Supreme Court decisions that seemed inclined toward those views, enough, at any rate, to make us think we had a chance of winning. When we lost by the Supreme Court's declining to hear our case, and the same court upheld the conviction of Communist Party leaders under the Smith Act, taking the Fifth became the only course for uncooperative witnesses: They would lose their jobs but stay out of prison.

When the Nineteen met as a group for the first time, there were some among us who said it was time to come out into the open and proudly admit to being Communists. But the lawyers who met with us told them they would immediately be asked to name names and had much less of a constitutional case on that score than they would if they remained quiet about themselves. Eventually, both lawyers and clients agreed that what Trumbo and I proposed was the best way of facing a bad situation and had the added possibility of a victory in the courts.

That was all we agreed on at that first meeting. At a subsequent one, however, the most prestigious of our attorneys, Robert W. Kenny, who had been attorney general of California and a Democratic candidate for governor, said, in effect, "Look, fellows, I don't think there's much chance of your being acquitted of contempt at the trial level, unless I have an argument that can appeal to plain American jurors who may very well sympathize with what you did but have to abide by legal instructions from a judge who tells them it isn't up to them to decide whether the law against contempt of Congress is a good thing or a bad thing; all they can decide is whether you have or have not committed contempt as that law defines it. So I need something that will give those sympathetic jurors some factual issue to enable them to vote in your favor. I want to be able to say that you were trying to answer the questions, but in your own way."

That seemed so valid a point and came from such a respected source that it affected how every one of us responded to HUAC questions. I don't think Kenny himself had any idea that the position he was suggesting would take the form it did in some of the testimony, notably that of Jack Lawson and Herbert Biberman, who was persuaded only at the last moment not to approach the witness stand singing "My Country, 'Tis of Thee."

Well, of course it turned out that Kenny's strategy didn't work in practice, and the various ways we all insisted we were trying to answer the questions, but in our own fashion, had an adverse effect on such supporters as the delegation from the Committee for the First Amendment, who came to Washington from Hollywood to observe the proceedings. They were, of course, unaware of Kenny's strategic purpose and felt we should have just declined to answer with firm dignity. Some of them, under pressure from their studios, used our evasions to withdraw their support; others, like John Huston, George Seaton, Philip Dunne, and Norman Corwin, continued to back us but were privately critical of what Dore Schary, the liberal executive in charge of production at RKO, called our "hysterical acting."

Did you have any idea that John Howard Lawson was going to behave in such a defiant fashion, starting off the proceedings on what some felt was a wrong footing?

I don't think any of us had any specific knowledge of what any of the others were going to say, beyond not answering the questions about the Screen Writers Guild and the Communist Party, and maintaining that we were trying to answer them in our own way. Jack Lawson was an exceptionally well-informed student of American constitutional history, and he used the opportunity to express his ideas on the subject. He regarded the Committee as an evil, undemocratic force, and when he was declared out of order he raised his voice to get that point across. I didn't realize at the time that he might be antagonizing members of the press and many liberals. In retrospect, however, I felt more was lost than gained by his particular style.

What were your personal feelings when you testified?

When the subpoenas were served in September, eleven of the recipients, including Brecht, were given specific dates for their appearance. I was one of the remaining eight who were told to wait until further notice of a date. We decided that despite this distinction the entire group should travel together and appear together at any meetings with the press or the public. A couple of wives, including mine, actress Frances Chaney, went along. We attended the hearings every day during the first week and the first three days of the second, on one of which a photograph of the two of us watching the proceedings was published prominently in a Washington newspaper. On Thursday of the second week we stayed in our hotel room listening to the radio coverage. Suddenly, the chairman, J. Parnell Thomas, called my name to take the stand. Bob Kenny explained that, not having a scheduled date, I had chosen not to attend that day. "He's been sitting there every day till now, right up in front," Thomas complained. Kenny simply promised to produce me on the following day. As a result, when the hearings were indefinitely suspended that Friday, October 30, I had taken the stand, and one of the scheduled witnesses (I believe it was Waldo Salt) gained a thirty-month respite from the blacklist.

I was not pleased with this turn of events. For one thing, I am not a particularly articulate person and do not seek opportunities to speak in public. I was worried about what kind of a presence I would make before the Committee. When I was suddenly called, I prepared a written statement, which I asked permission to read. Thomas said I could read it after my testimony, not before. When I was asked if I belonged to the Writers Guild and began to explain why that was an improper question, he broke in and said he would skip "to the sixty-four-dollar question." To that one I responded, "I could answer the question the way you want, Mr. Chairman, but I'd hate myself in the morning." That increased his rage, and he ordered me removed from the stand. I tried to remind him he had promised I could read my statement, but he just kept shouting for me to be taken away.

What was the group mood of the Ten after your experience at the hearings? Did you think you had won, or lost?

The only "unfriendly" witness to be called after me and Lester Cole that morning was Brecht. He had already explained to us that he was so anxious to return to Germany he could not face the long delay of a contempt proceeding. For that reason he told the Committee that he had never joined any Communist Party and then proceeded to an assured, dignified defense of his work and his associations. It was a high-level performance, and we admired him for it, and the fact that the Committee abruptly suspended the hearings that afternoon indicated that they were not too happy with the reaction they were getting.

For our part, we weren't too happy with our situation either. Although our lawyers had been assured by the head of the Motion Picture Producers Association, Eric Johnston, that they would never contemplate as wicked a thing as a blacklist, it took less than a month before they declared one for the ten of us and anyone else who took our sort of stand in the future. There was still the hope that we might win a case in the courts that would cripple HUAC for good, but there was an even stronger expectation that we would face prison terms. None of us regretted the position we had taken; under the circumstances, it was the only position you could take except complete surrender. But our individual view of what lay ahead ranged from Bessie, our outstanding pessimist, to Biberman, who led the optimistic camp.

What were the hopes for Henry Wallace's presidential campaign, and how did that cause figure into yours?

In the Henry Wallace campaign in 1948, there were, as usual, optimists and pessimists, and I tended generally to be on the pessimistic side. And John Howard Lawson, whom I had a great regard for, was on the optimistic side. It had a specific result in our case, because Lawson kept arguing that we should take advantage of every legal technicality to delay getting into the courts and being tried, so that the case wouldn't get up to the Supreme Court until after the presidential election. He argued that Wallace getting five to ten million votes would influence the country a great deal and would make for a more progressive atmosphere.

Actually, Wallace's showing was unimpressive, and the result of our delaying tactics was that instead of the case reaching the Supreme Court early in 1949, it was the fall of 1949, after the two most liberal justices on the Court—Wiley Rutledge and Frank Murphy—had died that summer, so that, whereas we needed to get four votes to be heard by the Court, we lost two of them and got only Black and Douglas. If we had been heard by the previous Court, it would have been very difficult for the Court not to uphold our position, because it was consistent with previous decisions. What the new Court did was to decide it wasn't an appropriate time to go into that matter. Jack's optimism may well have caused a setback.

After the October 1947 showdown in Washington, liberal support in Hollywood evaporated with astonishing swiftness. The only liberal supporters I ever hear mentioned were William Wyler, John Huston, Philip Dunne, and George Seaton. Were there many others? Why were liberals so impotent and disorganized in their response?

From those events in 1947 until the Supreme Court refused to hear our case in the late spring of 1950, we were never without some valuable support in Hollywood. First there were our comrades in or close to the Party, among them Zero Mostel, Jack Gilford, Howard Da Silva, Abraham Polonsky, Will Geer, John Randolph, John Garfield, Judy Holliday, Donald Ogden Stewart, Dorothy Parker, Lillian Hellman, and Dashiell Hammett. Then there were liberals who were against the Party and skeptical of the Soviet Union, but who continued a staunch defense of our rights: Frances Goodrich, Albert Hackett, Marsha Hunt, William Wyler, John Huston, George Seaton, Philip Dunne, Jane Wyatt, Gene Kelly, Groucho Marx, Frank Sinatra, and Danny Kaye, to name a few. There were people who hired members of the Ten anonymously, some of them out of conviction (Burgess Meredith and Franchot Tone engaged me to adapt a John Steinbeck story they wished to film, but I had to go to a bank to be handed the money by Tone in cash), some of them just because they could get us at greatly reduced rates, and some with a mixture of the two motives. Those of us most in demand, of whom Trumbo was outstanding, found some sort of work in the movie business, at home or abroad, during that period, and were thus enabled to support our families.

But with Cold War tensions mounting all the time, with Harry Truman's loyalty-oath program patterned after HUAC, with the advent of Senator Mc-Carthy on the scene, with the conviction of Communist Party leaders under the Smith Act, with the arrest and conviction of Julius and Ethel Rosenberg, the Hollywood we returned to from prison in 1951 was a much more hostile environment. The HUAC hearings were resumed, and each one of the scores of people named was added to the blacklist unless he proved his patriotism by naming others. No longer were there producers willing to hire proscribed writers out of sympathy or greed. Most disappointing of all was the way the talent guilds—writers, directors, and actors—refused to support their persecuted members. The Screen Writers Guild amended its rules about screen credit to permit the studios to omit the names of those on the blacklist. And the Motion Picture Academy decreed that none of us could be nominated for an Oscar.

I'm tempted to ask you if you got any support from Katharine Hepburn, since your career—your Oscar for cowriting Woman of the Year—*is closely associated with her name. You told me once that Hepburn, along with you and many others, worked for Wallace, and that she had a very powerful persona publicly, but that privately she was very insecure about politics; and that you were never quite able to read her politically.*

I remember one mass meeting in Hollywood, I think early in 1948, before Henry Wallace had declared himself as an independent candidate. He had already separated himself from the Truman cabinet and become the advocate of a sort of "one world" approach, opposed to Truman and Secretary [of State James F.] Byrnes's foreign policy. At this meeting Henry Wallace was the main speaker, and Katharine Hepburn was one of the other speakers. I was backstage, because I had some involvement in the meeting, and she seemed nervous just about speaking in public on politics, rather than nervous about endorsing Wallace—although, as I say, she was not really endorsing him, because this was prior to his election campaign.

But she went ahead and made a very good speech. She was actually quite a brave woman in many respects. I remember that when I was in prison in 1950 and it looked for a while as though we might be eligible for parole, we did mount a parole campaign and got people to write letters to the parole board. I wrote a letter from the prison to Kate and was agreeably surprised when she responded, sending a letter back to me in the prison with a copy of her letter to the board. Of course, she knew that her name would be noticed—letters to prison all got censored—so I thought it was a courageous thing for her to do. It happened that I didn't see her again until 1964, I think, when I went along with the producer Marty Ransohoff to try to persuade Spencer Tracy to play a part in a picture, *The Cincinnati Kid*, and saw Kate there at his house. I took the occasion to thank her for the letter she had written at the time, and she said, "Oh, I don't think I wrote such a letter. I don't remember anything of the kind." She dismissed it, wouldn't talk about it, and never did acknowledge it.

For which of the Ten did jail prove the greatest hardship, and why?

Since my incarceration, I have advised anyone contemplating criminal activity to commit only federal offenses, because federal penitentiaries and correctional institutions are much easier on the inmate than state or local facilities. The Federal Correctional Institution in Danbury, Connecticut, to which Lester Cole and I were sent, had a farm outside the prison walls where much of the food we were served was raised. The farm was worked by inmates classed as minimum security, among them Cole and J. Parnell Thomas, the HUAC chairman, who had meanwhile been convicted of misappropriating government funds. Passing Thomas in the chicken yard he took care of, Lester said, "Still handling the chicken shit, I see."

Our stay there was a little harder on Lester than on me simply because he was close to fifty and I was only thirty-five. But the fact is that a comparatively short sentence (ours were one year minus an assured sixty days for good behavior) is psychologically quite different from a longer one. With the latter, you have to reorient yourself to a whole new, more monotonous and confined way of life. But when it's a matter of only months, you just count the days till you return to normality.

For the older men, Ornitz and Lawson, the strain was greater. Ornitz spent his ten months in the federal prison hospital in Springfield, Missouri. I don't remember ever hearing from him on the subject during the few months before I moved away from California for good. Pure chance brought together in the same institution the two extremists in outlook, Bessie, with the standard one-year sentence, and Biberman, by a fluke, with six months—five in practice. Alvah confided to me later that he regarded Herbert's departure with great relief; with his own assurance that the world was headed toward self-destruction, he found it hard to listen to Herbert expressing his rosy outlook in the prison yard every day, and trying to convert the guards to progressive politics. The member of the Ten whose career suffered most from the whole experience of the blacklist and prison was Adrian Scott, whose success with *Crossfire* had changed him from a minor writer to a hot producer. He never regained that status.

Robert Lees

ROBERT LEES, Los Angeles, California, 1983

INTERVIEW BY PAUL BUHLE
AND DAVE WAGNER

ROBERT LEES
(1912–   )

1935–1940 (all coscript).
Robert Benchley Shorts:
How to Sleep. A Night at the Movies. How to Be a Detective. How to Start the Day. How to Train a Dog. An Evening at Home Alone. An Hour for Lunch.
Pete Smith Shorts:
Follow the Arrow. Pigskin Packers. Golf. Double Dives. Decathlon Champ.
Pete Smith Specials:
Chain Letter Dimes. How to Carve. Penny Wisdom. The Story of Dr. Carver. Weather Wise?
Crime Doesn't Pay:
Hit and Run Driver. The Perfect Set-Up.

Musicals (two reels):
It's in the Stars. Department Story.
Others:
Prophet Without Honor. The Flag Speaks.
1940 *Street of Memories.* Coscript.
1941 *The Invisible Woman.* Coscript.
Hold That Ghost. Coscript.
The Black Cat. Coscript.
Bachelor Daddy. Coscript.
Buck Privates. Coscript.
1942 *Juke Box Jenny.* Coscript.
1943 *Hit the Ice.* Coscript.
No Time for Love. Costory.
Crazy House. Coscript.
Substitution and Conversion (documentary).
1947 *The Wistful Widow of Wagon Gap.* Coscript.
Buck Privates Come Home. Coscript.

■

ROBERT LEES GREW up in a middle-class Jewish San Francisco neighborhood, the kind that seemed to make assimilation into American society comfortable and almost automatic. With this background, Lees had the confidence and some of the needed family connections to break into movies in the early 1930s, first as an extra, bit player, and chorus boy. Then, as a shorts writer, with his partner, Fred Rinaldo, Lees quickly achieved salary, status, and regular work. He also became a solid member of the Hollywood left.

Assigned to Abbott and Costello just as the stage and radio comics went into film, Lees and Rinaldo found their métier. Not that they didn't write other funny films—their scripts introduced Desi Arnaz, provided an early hit for the team of Dean Martin and Jerry Lewis, and gave Olsen and Johnson their best movie. But Abbott and Costello were headliners, and Lees, with his collaborator, provided the team with material for their most hilarious and successful vehicles.

Lees and Rinaldo knew how to visualize the subtext and build up the laughs. The climactic scene in The Wistful Widow of Wagon Gap, for instance, with Lou Costello in drag leading the women of the western town as they trash the saloons, operates brilliantly on several levels: the satire of the riot and shootout, the gender reversal of action, and the degree of femininity that the sexually ambivalent Lou achieves. The Lees-Rinaldo Abbott and Costello films were almost never as funny as they could have been, due to cuts and changes in the scripts. But many, many scenes still stand up wonderfully.

After the blacklist, Lees found his way into various corners of television. Today a voting member of the Academy living quietly in Los Angeles—his small house is cluttered with videotapes of modern-day films under consideration for awards—he looks back on his contributions with modest pride.

■

Let's begin by talking about your family background.

My family was middle-class, Jewish, successful. My father changed his name from Leszynsky to Lees. Many of my relatives turned out liberal, but most were very much Republicans, Jewish Republicans, until Roosevelt came in. Then some switched. My mother was very bright; her side was the Badts, German Jews, the ones most determined to get education. That side of the family was, however, quite conservative politically.

Our neighborhood in San Francisco was Presidio Avenue, right near the Presidio and very beautiful. Most of my friends were Jewish. I graduated from Lowell High School, which was preparatory for the university, and I went to the Concordia Club, which was also Jewish. My brother started golf at thirteen and became one of the club champions. Father used to show him off swinging a golf club in the living room for his friends.

So the fact is, my background was very much nonpolitical and liberal Reform Jewish. My father would blow the shofar at the temple. But religion was all a big game and fun. We weren't really strongly religious.

What did your father do for a living?

My father had gone through grammar school, left in the seventh grade, and become a self-made man. Until just before the Depression, my father had a chain of ready-to-wear jobbing houses from one end of the country to the other—Dallas, Chicago, New York, Seattle, Los Angeles. But he figured the Los Angeles office was the most viable and he should move there when all the others closed.

I started to go to the University of California [at Los Angeles]. I was there for about six months—not long enough to finish midterms. My father said, "What the hell are you doing there?" So I left college and went down to help out as a shipping clerk in the office. Meanwhile, my father had a connection with the Rapf family—which included Harry Rapf, a producer at MGM, and his son, Maurice Rapf, who was later blacklisted and was a very good friend of Budd Schulberg's, both of whom I got to know in the early thirties. Maurice's uncle, Joe Rapf, was also in the costume department at Metro—he had been my father's packer.

My father figured I could earn some money in the motion-picture business. So in 1931 I became a bit player, an extra, and a chorus boy at Metro-Goldwyn-Mayer. It was a very exciting experience.

My father and mother, meanwhile, decided to live out the Depression on a ranch in Nevada. It was run by Uncle Selby, my mother's brother, and my father had provided the capital for it when he still had the money. Now the ranch would be a haven for them.

My brother and I stayed in L.A., in an apartment. My share of the rent came from the studio, his from a job as a salesman in a downtown department store. I would have liked to have gone up to the ranch to live, but acting was more important to me. If the time came when extra work no longer paid off, I would keep enough for train fare and then join my parents.

What saved my neck was a chorus-boy job in *Dancing Lady*, Fred Astaire's first picture, with Joan Crawford—who couldn't dance a lick. I was also a bellboy in *Grand Hotel*, and I was in one scene as a boatman with Greta Garbo and Melvyn Douglas in *As You Desire Me*.

Somehow you became a dancer.

Not exactly. Some nice guys in the chorus tried to teach me the "time step," which I never could get right. They thought I'd never make the tryouts for *Dancing Lady*, because I was too short. I took care of this by rolling up toilet paper and stuffing it in the bottom of my shoes. Unfortunately for me, Sammy Lee, the dance director, ordered each of the guys he selected to do a time step. When it was my turn, a shoe flew high into the air and turned over, and the toilet paper came out like a serpentine roll and floated to the floor. Sammy Lee couldn't believe his eyes. After he was through laughing, he declared I couldn't dance and was even shorter than he was. But because of my determination, he said, he'd see if he could keep me around as some sort of assistant. I had a lot of adventures like that.

I finally was given the chance to do a screen test. I wrote the script myself. They thought my acting was lousy but the writing wasn't bad. I had done well as an actor at Lowell High School, but they were all character parts. When it came to playing myself, I was much too self-conscious. The writing, nevertheless, gave me an opportunity to become a member of the junior writers' department at MGM.

Your writing partner from the beginning was Fred Rinaldo. Tell us about Fred's background.

He was middle-class, Jewish, from New York. He went to Dartmouth, an English major, the same time as Budd Schulberg and Maurice Rapf. As you may know, after Maurice and Budd went to the Soviet Union they came back to Hollywood saying they had "seen the future, and it works." And here they were—with their heads shaved because they had caught lice—being treated kind of jokey in the press.

Fred Rinaldo came West, and Maurice said, "Why don't you look up my father [Harry Rapf]? They're doing a junior-writers program with kids from college [at MGM]. Maybe something will happen for you out there." And so Fred went into the junior-writers department.

The junior-writers department at Metro was a little fiefdom for a man who, I guess, had the job because they had wondered, "Where are all the new screenwriters going to come from when the older writers die?" This was what the junior-writers department was supposed to supply. This man was notorious for trying to see who he could lay among the young girls. He would try this line on them: "Which of these books do you think is literature—is it *Fanny Hill?*" Or some other erotic book that he would choose. One of these girls turned out to be the niece of an important producer. So the man in charge of the junior writers was fired.

Anyway, we never did get assignments to do really serious stuff. No producer would risk giving a kid earning thirty-five dollars a week—although it was good money in those days—a chance to write a script, when he could get any big-shot writer that he wanted. Thus the junior-writers department folded.

This is the moment when the two of you graduated into short subjects?

Yes. Fred and I got together, at Fred's suggestion. I knew about films, and he knew how to write and spell. He was an English major, and I had flunked the subject at UCLA. It looked like a good idea for a team. We heard that Pete Smith was going to do a short on chain letters, so Fred and I stayed up all night and wrote a script on chain letters, and then we went to Harry Rapf's office to see if he would be interested in our piece. Harry Rapf was in charge of the shorts department, among other things.

We had been there for two hours before Chic Sale showed up. Sale was an old-time comedian, and he asked, "What are you boys here for?" We said, "Chain Letter Dimes."* He said, "Well, I'm here for the same reason. What have you got?" We would never have gotten to see Harry Rapf on our own, but Sale read our script and said, "Hey, do you mind if I take this in to Rapf?" And we said, "Not at all." We heard them laughing through the door. Sale never did that short, but Pete Smith did, and we found ourselves in the shorts department. It was 1936.

What about your politics? Weren't you already part of a left-wing social crowd?

Not at first. As I said, I was far to the right. Fred Rinaldo, however, had learned a lot about politics at Dartmouth. Then, of course, Buddy and Maurice had gone to the Soviet Union, so I heard about that. There was a lot of political activity going on in Hollywood at this time. There was the organization of the Screen Writers Guild, the fight to raise money to save democracy in Spain, the activity against Hitler and Mussolini. All of us young people who grew up during the Depression remembered what *Variety* had said about the downturn in the stock market. "Wall Street Lays an Egg" was the headline. That told you something right there.

The girls I knew during my chorus days had all become politicized. Virginia Ray married Budd Schulberg. The girl I played opposite in my test, Ambur Dana, married Waldo Salt. Another girlfriend, Marian Edwards, married Irwin Shaw. Lefties all. Dalton Trumbo was also at Metro. We first met Dalton and all kinds of left-wing people who were around at this time.

Obviously, all this growing anti-Fascist activity was going on with the knowledge that if Hitler and Mussolini weren't stopped, World War II was on its way, and it was the Communists who were the leadership in all this. We were all swept up in this groundswell and damned anxious to be part of it.

The shorts department at MGM seems to have been a fascinating place to work.

Fred Rinaldo and I started off there with some Bob Benchleys and Pete Smiths and "Crime Doesn't Pay" and historical subjects. Metro used to have

---

*"Chain Letter Dimes" because the chain letters of the thirties asked for a dime from each recipient of the letter.

everyone under contract, and if personnel weren't working on a major picture, they did shorts. So we had some of the greatest productions. In fact, we even did a few musical shorts using guys who were really great lyricists. Fred and I won a couple of Academy Awards for the Pete Smith and Benchley short subjects.*

We also helped organize the shorts department for the Writers Guild, because there were some fifty-odd writers in the shorts department. Meanwhile, the Screen Playwrights—who were the big writers who didn't want to pay union dues—they liked to say, "We have agents; we don't need unions"— were also trying to get our vote. They would give us cigars and brandy and say, "Come join our club," which was actually a company union. But we got the shorts department for the Guild. Fred was more important to the Guild. He was more political. Once the Writers Guild made it, the actors and directors all followed.

You were going up in your career.

It was an exciting, wonderful period. We did about thirty-five shorts— some of the best Benchleys, like *How to Sleep* and *A Night at the Movies*, and Pete Smith's *Follow the Arrow* and *Pigskin Packers*. It was an education in screenwriting, visually figuring out what these guys could do on film.

We went to New York in 1938 because Bob Benchley said to Metro, "I'm going back to New York. My job is as a drama critic on the *New Yorker*. If you want films made, send the boys to New York." We did two Benchley shorts there, *An Evening at Home Alone* and *How to Start the Day.*

Fred and I were ensconced at the Algonquin Hotel. Across the street was the Royalton, where Benchley stayed, and these were the days of the Round Table. We were there for three months and were given carte blanche. The William Morris Agency gave us access to look at whatever acts we liked at Radio City Music Hall, like the bowler Andy Veripapas or the card shark Zingoni, both of whom we recommended for Pete Smith shorts.

You personally became further and further left?

When I married my girl, Jean Abel, in 1939, *Meet the People* was playing on Hollywood Boulevard, and Jean was given the job of doing the military map in the lobby. The map would have to be changed every other day, as Hitler took over more and more of Europe.

Finally, after some left-wing affair, a lot of friends were at my house. I was in the john when Paul Jarrico came through the door. He joined me, peeing in the bowl. And while we were at it, he said, "Have you ever thought of joining the Communist Party?" At this point my pee shut off entirely. I said, "What! What!" [Laughs.] I had always accepted a *Reader's Digest*, conserva-

---

*How to Sleep (1935) and *Penny Wisdom* (1937) won Oscars as Best Short Subjects.

tive, comic-book version of what was a "red," even though I was in the left wing. He said, "What's bothering you so much? Half the people outside in your living room are members of the Party, including your collaborator!"

That night Jean and I couldn't sleep. We had two big questions. The first was, "Should we?" And second, "What was wrong with us that they took this long to even ask?" To make a long story short, we joined.

Could you be very open about your politics?

Everybody knew what everyone else's politics were in those days, and nobody gave a shit. Jack Chertok, who was head of the shorts department, came to us one day and said jokingly, "The American Legion wants to do a short on flag etiquette, such as, 'Don't use it as a table cloth; don't use it as a diaper.' And you are just the boys to write it." We said, "Oh, Jesus." Then we started thinking. I thought of the title, *The Flag Speaks*, and we decided to make the flag itself the narrator.

We dramatized the struggle for women to vote, the fight for the Bill of Rights to protect freedom of speech, and the bigotry of the Ku Klux Klan. We laid it on. Then, to appease the Legion, once it was established what freedoms the flag stood for, we made it clear that the flag deserved all the respect that one could give, to honor it—thus, "etiquette."

We thought that the American Legion was never going to accept our script. But they did, and the film became used by the public-school system to educate kids. One day, decades later, my daughter came to me at a time when we were wondering when we were going to be called to appear before the Committee [HUAC] in Washington and said that she had seen *The Flag Speaks* at school. I said, "Don't tell anyone in school that your father wrote it." I could see her disappointment, but there was no way that I could explain why her father had suddenly become a pariah. I think that the children of the blacklistees suffered more than their parents. They were too young to understand what had caused this traumatic disruption of their lives.

Did you think of the Benchley shorts as being socially critical in any way?

Let me put it this way. I've given a lot of lectures about humor. Humor is essentially what are you afraid of—why are you whistling in the dark; why are you afraid of heights? You get Harold Lloyd, with the high and dizzy, or you get Benchley-type understatement. But humor is whatever bothers you—what you are dealing with is fear. One of the ideas oppressing everybody is the establishment. Who gets the biggest laughs slipping on a banana peel? The banker, the cop, the bully.

So a humorist invariably pits himself against the establishment for his jokes; that's where the laughs come from. What is it that is bothering you? Poor health, money troubles, racial prejudice? That's Jewish humor, too. If you don't laugh at it, whatever it is, you're in trouble. I used to have a phrase which is still worth repeating: if you can't whip them or join them, laugh at them. So I think humor has a real basis of social criticism. If you understand what is going on in the world, you can be funny.

I guess I was a comedy writer from the word go. I was the third and last child in my family. A lot of comics were raised at the bottom of the totem pole. Some were ugly or not popular.

I guess I'm leaping ahead to Abbott and Costello in asking you if this isn't a sort of tradition, from Chaplin to the Marx Brothers and the Three Stooges and so forth. Comedy often presents proletarian characters who come into the rich lady's house and accidentally put alum into her lemonade.

The idea is, you've got to have a straight man. And what is the best straight man to work your comedy off? It's the establishment.

If you look at Abbott and Costello, Bud Abbott, the straight man, is society's view of what is correct. Lou gets his laughs by doing it the crazy way, not the correct way; yet he succeeds. He does it, we used to say, by "the little x method." "The big X" is society, or the straight man, and the comic is "the little x." He's always the misfit, he's the one who's put-upon. If you really want to look at where comics come from, the answer is usually the village idiot or the people who mock God because they are so badly made in His image. What did the court jester do? He didn't wear the right clothes, he wore funny ones with bells, and he could mock the king because the king could not take on the jester; otherwise he would lose his dignity.

Sholom Aleichem used to say that when his muse would vanish, he would call upon "the little Jew" within him.

There you are—"the little Jew." So that's where the humor is. It has its political undertone whether or not you even know about it.

Paul Jarrico has said that what the writers learned from Marxism or historical materialism, and what they discussed in Party circles, really didn't help people in Hollywood at all as creative writers. But the sort of humanistic content helped in a much more general way. Would that be your opinion, too?

I'd add one thing more to that statement. Marxism did have something to say about structure. Because you were dealing with quantitative to qualitative change. The moment of truth is usually the second-act climax. A good example would be the character of Nora in Ibsen's *A Doll's House.* In the beginning she has the illusion (or thesis) that her husband is a paragon of virtue; then come various indications to the contrary (quantitative), finally causing a qualitative change in her attitude (disillusion, or antithesis). Now, what does she do about it? Should she stay with this man and live a life full of lies, or leave and slam the door? This is a coming-to-grips with reality, or a synthesis of what has transpired in acts one and two.

Marx, of course, was dealing with class conflict, but dramatic conflict, I believe, follows in much the same way, since conflict is the heart and soul of drama, from the disruption of the status quo of the protagonist to the resolution of that conflict at the story's conclusion: boy meets girl (thesis), boy loses girl (antithesis), boy gets girl (synthesis). Marxism, for me at least, has a lot to do with good story structure.

Including comedy writing?

Comedy is exactly the same thing as tragedy. The only difference is that it's stretched. It's either overblown like caricature—the big head on the little body—or it's English-style exaggeration or understatement—"Don't look now; a monster's following us." Like your reflection in a fun-house mirror, comedy logic is logic stretched out of shape.

Let's talk a little about your main comedic influences. Did you read the iconoclastic and anti-war humorist Thorne Smith?

He was great fun. And I read a lot of Benchley, too, before I came to Hollywood. Benchley was a hero of mine. And to think that I was actually writing for Benchley! Then, of course, I had some edifying experiences, like when I was still an extra and I worked with Buster Keaton. He was not a young man at this point. I remember one scene in which I was supposed to go down the aisle of a theater and sit next to a girl, his girl, in what was an empty seat next to her. The gag was, just as I was about to sit, he would sit down ahead of me, and then I would sit in his lap. In the rehearsals, I kept going faster and faster, but he would always beat me. Finally, he said, "Look, maybe you've been trying to slow up. Don't do that. You just get there as fast as you can. I'll get there faster." I never could beat that man.

He had great physical finesse.

Well, I know he played great baseball, too. We had a team at Metro, and Keaton would always be out there playing.

To get back to your personal history, we're chronologically in 1939.

In 1939 I became a member of the Communist Party, and I got married—not long before the Hitler-Stalin Pact. That was a terrible period, of course, because here we were, part of the Joint Anti-Fascist Refugee Committee and the Hollywood Anti-Nazi League, and all of a sudden we, the left in Hollywood, who had been joined with the liberals, found ourselves split on the Pact. We hated Hitler, but we were still for peace. Here were the liberals asking, "Where are you, the great anti-Fascists, now?" A terrible time.

There were people who left the Party. As they used to say, when the train took a sharp turn, some would fall off. I never fell off the train. Everything made sense to me at the time, up until Khrushchev [revealed Stalin's crimes in 1956]. I bought everything, because I thought the Party was the only alternative to capitalism and Fascism. Being children of the Depression, my friends and I found that the Party had the only people who made sense. You were dealing with people who were seasoned by *The Living Newspaper* of the Federal Theatre, *The Cradle Will Rock*, Orson Welles doing *Julius Caesar*, *Pins and Needles*.

Everybody decent, if they weren't in the Party, they were at least on the left. There was unity again during World War II, but it ended in Hollywood after the dropping of the atomic bomb and the start of the Cold War and the death of Roosevelt. When Roosevelt died, I remember, we played Earl Robinson's "The Lonesome Train" in our living room with a bunch of friends, all weeping. We sensed right then and there that this was the end.

It was a pretty brief period, after all.

Looking back, it's like Roosevelt was the aberration. America from 1917 on was anti-Soviet. I remember as a kid looking at the Hearst *San Francisco Examiner* and seeing a cartoon with a Jewish-looking fellow carrying a bomb behind his back. He was the Communist.

Meanwhile, it's 1940 and 1941, and your career continues upward.

We were doing very well, Fred and I. We were up to practically a thousand dollars a week each—not at first, of course, but that was a lot of money in those days, even for a top comedy-writing team.

We moved out of the shorts department into features. Jack Chertok wouldn't let us out until he got into features as well, because he knew that if we left he would not have as successful a shorts department. So at night we wrote a picture, on our own time, which we titled, "Tomorrow Never Comes." Metro got this from us without paying for it. Chertok gave it to Louis B. Mayer, and Mayer said it was not politically propitious. So it looked dead. This kind of thing happened in studios all the time.

Fred and I used to go to the gym across the way from our office; it was on the roof of one of the buildings. Lucien Hubbard, a producer, would also go to the gym. He was a polo-playing friend of Darryl Zanuck. We were boxing one day, and he ran into my glove with his solar plexus. I knocked him out. I was horrified, but Hubbard was the kind of guy who thought this was amazing and wonderfully daring. So he asked, "Have you boys written any features?" We showed him this script. He loved it.

Hubbard left Metro and went to Twentieth Century–Fox. Over there Zanuck told him, "You can do any picture that we have on our shelves." Hubbard said, "I want to do one that's at Metro." Twentieth Century–Fox bought it from Metro. We got nothing for it, of course. Zanuck told Hubbard, "If you want to do this with [Henry] Fonda, I'm going to produce it and you'll be an associate producer. If you want to do it as a B picture with an unknown cast, it's all yours." Hubbard decided to make it a B picture, and it went nowhere. That became *Street of Memories*, our first picture and our first feature credit.

Did it have any kind of political statement?

It did. The idea behind the story was to prove that even a successful businessman couldn't get a job, given a certain set of circumstances. If a man wasn't able to find a job, it didn't prove he was a bum. To do this we started out with an already successful hero who finds himself mugged and robbed of his identification. Then he comes to in a back alley, and he is unable to remember his past. He's shoved onto a freight car by well-meaning tramps and winds up in L.A. His experience there is typical of those on skid row. Finally, after he winds up in jail, people discover that he has suffered a concussion. And finally he and they realize his true identity. Although he recollects how powerless he was as an ordinary person, he can't remember the people who befriended him when he was a bum. It was kind of an urban *Grapes of Wrath*.

Then you and Fred went to Universal for a couple of films.

We went to Universal and worked on *Buck Privates*, for Abbott and Costello, and a few other comedies.

Let's talk about some of those non–Abbott and Costello films, like Bachelor Daddy *and* The Black Cat.

Bachelor Daddy had Edward Everett Horton in it. It took place in a bachelor establishment. Baby Sandy had been in a Bing Crosby picture when she was a year or so old and very cute, but by now she was three or four years old. The child was very unhappy on the set, a mixed-up kid who started to cry as soon as she got to the soundstage. The stand-in had to fill in some of the scenes. The story was of a kid dumped on a residence club of old bachelors. Later it became a familiar plot in films. I wanted to write a different story, about the father and mother of this actor kid exploiting her. I never got around to it.

The Black Cat wasn't a bad picture. It had Gale Sondergaard as one of its stars, playing a cat lover. It also had Hugh Herbert as an antique dealer. One of the best gags was Herbert boring holes in things to make them look old and wormy. Another was that he had an endless number of tools to fix things, but one tool was always breaking, and so he would have to get another tool to repair the first tool, and so on and on.

How about No Time for Love?

We found ourselves temporarily out of work as feature writers and decided we should write an original screenplay. Fred and I had this idea about a sandhog in a tunnel and a Margaret Bourke-White type who comes down into the tunnel to take some pictures. An accident happens—the sandhog falls off the scaffold, and she catches him. Somebody else takes the picture, and it hits all the papers. He is kidded by his fellow sandhogs, and of course the theme revolves around the reversed roles of the sexes.

We even did all the mimeographing ourselves to save money. We felt that the screenplay would spark some real competitive bidding from all the studios, since all of them had romantic duos. Paramount bought it for ten thousand dollars, because Warners came in too late with a much bigger bid. Worse, Paramount was interested only in the story idea and wanted to hand over the screenplay to Claude Binyon. Our contract called for us to make several weeks worth of revisions, at a raise in our basic salary. They actually had us redo the script as a treatment, then had us reduce it to an outline as a make-work gimmick, before saying good-bye. So our credit was reduced to "original story," whereas Warners would have been happy to do the film as we had originally written it. *No Time for Love* starred Fred McMurray and Claudette Colbert. But again we were very disappointed at the way things turned out.

What about The Invisible Woman? *It has all that wonderful* Topper-*style action, with hats and so forth floating through the air. And there are some great moments, just after Virginia Bruce becomes invisible, when she is tormenting the department-store boss for exploiting his workers. Then it drifts into somewhat familiar romantic-comedy territory.*

It should have been a better movie. I think it was a better movie in our script. The problem was, Virginia Bruce wasn't too good as an actress.

How about your one script for Ole Olsen and Chic Johnson?

That was *Crazy House,* a very good picture. The idea was that Olsen and Johnson had been blacklisted because they were such terrible characters. The picture opens with a big parade in front of a barricaded studio. The two are shot out of a cannon into the producer's office. The secretary hardly looks up before asking, "Who do you wish to see?" They say, "We're Olsen and Johnson." With that she screams, jumps into the typewriter desk, and pulls the lid down.

To do that, they dug a hole in the soundstage. The actress jumped into the desk through this hole, and a wire pulled the desk lid shut. But she hit her chin on the jump, and everybody thought she had been killed. Olsen and Johnson were horrified. She came out okay, however.

Back to the story: When the studio refuses to do a picture with such wild men, Olson and Johnson decide to make one on their own. They find what they think is a millionaire angel, only he's a lunatic with delusions of grandeur. They sign a star—the twin sister of the really talented one. Nonetheless, they get the film made and are ready for the preview, when raiders steal the last part of the film from the lab. Our hero [played by Patric Knowles] must get it back, but meanwhile Olson and Johnson have to stall the preview audience. In order to keep the people in their seats, they put on a show, for which we drew on the style of their Broadway show, *Hellzapoppin'.**

You reconciled vaudeville with film?

Yes. It was great fun, because we were actually pointing a finger at Universal, which had refused to let Olson and Johnson do their film (in the script, that is); then, at the end, it is Universal which buys the film from Olson and

---

*The 1941 Olsen and Johnson film used the title *Hellzapoppin'* and was based more directly on their hit burlesque revue.

Johnson when they auction it off to producers in the theater audience. The studio turned out to really have a sense of humor about being made fun of. We had one gag that has been used again and again since. We called Olsen and Johnson's company Miracle Pictures, with the slogan, "If it's a good film, it's a miracle."

Now let's talk about Abbott and Costello. Was either of them vaguely progressive, personally?

Like almost any big guys who earned lots of money, they would be Republicans.

But there was still an element in the Abbott and Costello films of, as usual, the establishment as the straight man.

No question. You couldn't avoid it, and, of course, that's where our thinking was.

Were you ever on the set with the production of their films?

Never. Our job was already over. So we usually had no relationship with the directors on the set at all.

Your first Abbott and Costello film, Buck Privates, was also their first feature. It made them possible as a Hollywood comedy team. But it is really mostly production numbers with a strong pro-Allies message. There isn't too much dialogue, but again you work into the film a lot of vaudeville, their style of vaudeville.

That's right.

Hold That Ghost is a much funnier film. It has Abbott and Costello as everyday guys who inherit a roadhouse where the money of a late mobster is supposed to be hidden. Along with the fake-ghost stuff there is a wonderful musical routine with Joan Davis. Isn't that the high point of the film?

Costello screwed up some scenes, or tried to screw them up, by objecting to her action and her lines. He was a fat little egotist. He couldn't stand the attention being drawn away from him, even if it made the movie funnier and better.

But you make room for lots of funny dialogue.

It was a good film. I must make it clear that despite Costello's offscreen personality, he comes across in films as sort of a lovable, chubby child who deserves the audience's sympathy. The audience needs to see him triumph over the opposition. The great thing about Costello was his total belief in the reality of the comic situation that he was in. On the screen, his fear in *Abbott and Costello Meet Frankenstein* was palpable enough for the audience to suspend disbelief, no matter how offbeat the situation. This is a must, in my opinion, for any successful actor, whether it be comedy or drama.

Abbott, for me, dramatizes a fundamental psychological component for

Costello. According to Freud, there are three parts to one's persona: there is the id (the pagan, uncivilized child), the ego (the adult), and the superego (the parent, society, etc). Abbott plays the adult as well as the stern parent to Costello's child. And, like a child, Costello often sees through Abbott's pretensions or tries to. It is this conflict that forms the basis for all their stand-up vaudeville routines and radio programs.

They never started out as visual comedians, the way Laurel and Hardy began their careers at Roach—Hardy, with his flapping tie, doing a slow burn while Laurel scratches his head and screws up his face, ready to cry. All the Laurel and Hardy gags, in fact, were visual ones. When Abbott and Costello wound up in films they preferred to resort to their own verbal stuff—great, of course—like "Who's on First?"

But their exquisite timing conformed to the laughter of a live audience. In films there is no such thing, which made them very uncomfortable as to what was funny. They worried about laying an egg, especially when they were presented with new material or purely visual routines. Costello would rather get a laugh from the crew than trust a scene to play in a movie theater.

Nevertheless, Costello turned out to be a superb physical comedian. He could do pratfalls and double takes with the best of them. His reaction to a scene was often funnier than the action itself. In *Hold That Ghost*, for instance, the roadhouse was formerly a gambling casino. Costello's bedroom looks normal enough, until Abbott picks up Costello's coat and hangs it on a hook before going to his room. The hook is a trick lever that causes the bed to roll over and become a craps table, the chandelier drops down and turns into a roulette wheel, and walls slide open to reveal banks of slot machines. All this time, Costello is gargling in the bathroom, getting ready for bed. The audience starts to laugh purely in anticipation of Costello's reaction when he sees the changed room. They aren't disappointed. Of course, Costello grabs his coat in panic and runs off to get Abbott. The released lever now returns the room to normal. Again there's laughter in anticipation of Costello's reaction to this new turn of affairs.

We used a somewhat similar routine in another film of theirs, when a tabletop is inadvertently placed on a single sawhorse so that it actually becomes a seesaw. A tablecloth covers up the mistake. The tipping table causes all kinds of trouble for Costello. A pile of silverware slides onto the ground before the table rights itself; Abbott accuses Costello of being sloppy. A bowl of salad placed on one end causes cakes to fly up into Costello's face, coating him with frosting, before a maid puts the salad bowl elsewhere; Abbott accuses Costello of sampling the dessert. Finally, a huge punch bowl, carried by the maître d', is plunked at the far end, turning the whole thing into a catapult. The cake sails over a hedge into a fancy garden party, like a bomb.

How about your third Abbott and Costello film, Hit the Ice? *Once again, there are so many production numbers that not much room remains for outright humor.*

Some of our dialogue, good dialogue, was changed by Abbott and Costello's third writer, John Grant, an old fogy who had worked with "the boys" in vaudeville. We had a good producer [Alex Gottlieb] and a good director [Charles Lamont]. Another director we worked with was Eddie Cline, once a Keystone Kop and an oldtime western director, who made a memorable crack when we were in an office conference. We said the scene would be easy to shoot. He shook his head and murmured, "Everything's always downhill and shady in the office"—but never on the set, he meant. [Laughs.] We quoted that line again and again.

After *Hit the Ice*, we went to Paramount to do a picture to be called "Ready, Willing, and 4-F." It was the idea of a comic going into the Army to join his straight man, who has been drafted, but the comic can't get in because he is deaf in one ear. We wrote this picture for [producer] Buddy DeSylva, and it turned out to be a really good script. Paramount tried to get Bob Hope; then they tried to get Eddie Bracken. At this point the war became too grim for comedy. So they put it on the shelf.

Fred and I were under contract to Paramount for fifty-two weeks a year, and they wouldn't let us go because we would be drafted. The studio was defined as a "war industry" and didn't want to lose any of its writers. By this time I was married and we had our first child, and that kept me out anyway. Fred and I went to Washington on a loan-out for nothing, to do training films with [director] David Miller, who had done a lot of our shorts. It wasn't until the Korean War that "Ready, Willing, and 4-F" was finally made into *Jumping Jacks*, Dean Martin and Jerry Lewis's sixth picture.

So you did a training film?

We did *Substitution and Conversion*, a six-reeler directed by David Miller, which played around the country as a public service, showing how factories could convert to war production and also save resources. We also did a lot of war-bonds shorts. If we had gotten into the Army, we would have been put to work under Hal Roach or somebody like that and probably would have ended up doing the same thing.

Then the war was over. We never got any film credits in the three years we were at Paramount, but they did loan us out to Universal to do some more Abbott and Costellos. In all, we did seven Abbott and Costellos. *Abbott and Costello Meet Frankenstein* is still the most popular. They were among the top box-office stars during the years we wrote for them.

One of my favorites from this period is Buck Privates Come Home, *because it exposes the resentments of enlisted men against officers, the kind of attitude that could hardly be expressed during the war. And it shows them as ordinary Joes having trouble making the adjustment back to civilian life.*

That's right. But the orphan girl, played by Beverly Simmons, was our big contribution here. She represented, to us, the victims of the war.

The late Jerry Garcia of the Grateful Dead is supposed to have said that Abbott and Costello Meet Frankenstein *was his favorite movie, and it is still shown widely in America on television every Halloween. Even the script has been published.*

Costello had to be talked into it, but of all the films we did for them, this one stayed closest to the way it was written. Its success has surprised me, though. We never took it that seriously.

Then there's your last Abbott and Costello credit, Comin' Round the Mountain.

We wrote it as "The Real McCoy," a much better title. We had a great routine in that picture. Abbott and Costello contact a witch in order to get Costello a love potion. She wants him to sign over his soul. In the process, she makes an effigy of Costello; he's smart enough to make one of her, and they have a duel of pin-sticking. Meanwhile, Abbott is the straight man who refuses to believe in witches. He keeps saying, "There's no such thing. I told you!" Finally, he looks at her broom, which has a windshield with wipers, like on a car. Now he *knows* she's a witch for sure.

Tell me about Holiday in Havana, *the film that launched Desi Arnaz.*

It was produced by Burt Kelly, who previously had done *The Invisible Woman* and *Hold That Ghost* at Universal. He was now a B producer at Columbia, and he knew things were going badly for us because of what was brewing in Washington with threats of investigations. He liked us and signed us to do this picture.

Arnaz was supposed to be a crazy Cuban who was very difficult to work with. We soon discovered that he was very bright and knew what was best for the film. We got on very well. The plot revolved around the annual event in Cuba of a battle between rhumba bands for a grand prize. I'm sure that if we hadn't been blacklisted, he would have been happy to hire us as writers for *I Love Lucy*. *C'est la guerre.*

Before things really got bad, you were the lefties in comedy-writing, along with Donald Ogden Stewart and some others.

We were the reds, all right. In fact, we picketed Universal for the Screen Writers Guild in 1945, although the Guild had already settled—but we didn't know it yet. The two of us were out there with signs by ourselves, and our producer had to come down to say, "Are you boys trying to close us down? The strike's over. Come back!"

This fellow happened to be none other than Robert Arthur, the executive secretary of the Motion Picture Alliance for the Preservation of American Ideals. But we were his best writers for Abbott and Costello. He used to have to go to the Screen Writers Guild and speak on one side of the fence, while Fred would speak on the other. The next day we would file in for a story conference with him. We thought he was a damn good producer, which he was. And we'd talk about our children and the Dodgers and everything but politics. But when he went before the Committee, he said he had to watch us very carefully to see that we didn't slip any subversive material into the Abbott and Costello scripts. How do you like that one?

What kind of political activities did you engage in during these years?

I was on the board of the People's Education Center, which was considerably more Marxist than the earlier League of American Writers school had been, and I taught screenwriting there. That was my main political job. I taught that you have to have a political consciousness. You can't be a writer without trying to understand people—people are your audience, and they are your source of humor. Writers actually *need* to be humanists. Writers can't help but be progressive, if they're people-oriented.

When Fred and I taught screenwriting at the League of American Writers school, maybe half my students were FBI agents, as I found out later. I hope they learned how to write! [Laughs.] Later I got raked over the coals by HUAC for teaching there. Anyway, several of the students did very well. One later became the president of the Screen Writers Guild.

So what happened when the blacklist hit?

We were in the middle of a show for Donald O'Connor and Jimmy Durante, a story about an old engineer on the steam engine and a new guy on the diesel. It was a good script that somehow or other was suddenly canceled. Then I got my subpoena. My Uncle Selby came down from Nevada to see the races, and we went together, all the time with this pink slip of paper in my pocket. I never told him what it was; I felt like I was dying.

Thinking back, I had very few problems with the Party at this point. There were factions, naturally, within Hollywood—people who loved [John Howard] Lawson or hated Lawson, loved [Samuel] Ornitz or hated Ornitz, loved [Lester] Cole or hated Cole. I loved them all. So at one point I found myself chairman of a group of one hundred and fifty members in the Hollywood branch. I was the only one everybody could talk to!

I have never considered myself really wise politically, though I got pretty learned after many years. Jean and I were the social end of it; we gave the fund-raising parties. I enjoyed the socializing, though I did a lot of political work, too. We had enough money to hire people to help take care of the kids while we devoted ourselves to doing something which we thought was going to change the world for the better.

You had one last collaboration with Fred Rinaldo.

Fred and I wrote a short comic film, *Speak Your Peace*, done under Party auspices right in the middle of the Korean situation, when we were not yet subpoenaed. It was a collection of sketches. It started with a guy in an aviation uniform singing, "I'm flying around in my B-29, looking for a place to land." He meets a Russian plane, flying from the other direction, whose pilot sings,

"Ha ha ha! Wait till you go back. You won't be able to find a place to land, either." Each of them has wiped out the other's country.

The last scene has a whole bunch of people in a park—that was Jack Lawson's backyard—all singing a song called "Speak Your Peace." [Hollywood columnist] Louella Parsons heard of it, because left-wing people in the labs were dubbing it. She said in her column that a terrible subversive picture was now being made. It played all around Europe, especially Eastern Europe, presumably distributed by the respective Communist parties. I have no idea whether a print of *Speak Your Peace* exists anywhere anymore.

And that was the end of your partnership with Fred.

Yes. The blacklist ended our seventeen years of collaboration. We realized that we'd have to find some other way to make a living outside of the industry. I was subpoened to appear before the House Committee on Un-American Activities [on April 11, 1951], in Washington, D.C. We were the first group to testify after the Hollywood Ten. In order to save legal expenses, Fred was advised to avoid a subpoena by leaving town. He hid out in his brother's mountain cabin. I visited him there to say good-bye before leaving on the train to join a group of other subpoenaed witnesses.

Our attorneys, Ben Margolis and Robert Kenny, decided that four days on the train together would give us time to prepare our defense. The First Amendment would be no protection now, and taking the Fifth Amendment, if not done properly, could be serious. If you were tricked into answering a question pertaining to a proscribed group on the attorney general's long list of subversive organizations, you were required under law to name all the other members you might know or find yourself in contempt of Congress and be jailed. For any of us to be an informer was, of course, unthinkable.

En route to Washington we did a great deal of rehearsing of our answers. For instance, if I were asked whether I knew Waldo Salt, I could safely say, "Of course. We came here on the train together." But then, if they asked whether I knew if Waldo was a member of such and such an organization, I'd have to plead the Fifth to avoid naming him and others.

Later, going over possible questions while trying to sleep, I "heard" them ask if I knew Fred Rinaldo. I was about to say, "Of course"—until I realized they might very well ask, "Do you know he is ducking our subpoena? Do you know his whereabouts?" I woke up in a sweat.

How did you finally handle the dilemma?

The lawyers said I'd have to take the Fifth the moment Fred's name came up. When I asked how in hell could I do that, all they could tell me was, "Play it by ear." Sure enough, when I came before the Committee, the first thing the prosecuting attorney wanted to know was the name of my collaborator! "You obviously know his name," I answered. "It's right up there beside mine on the screen credits." "Well, we don't see the pictures," he snapped. "Everybody in the business knows us as a team," I insisted. Then he said,

"Are you ashamed to tell us who your collaborator is, the man you have collaborated with for seventeen years!?" I answered, "Well, if you know we collaborated for seventeen years, you must surely be aware of his name, so why ask me?" This kind of thing kept going on and on, with the other Committee members joining in.

At one point I felt intimidated enough to declare that this harassment made me feel that I had to seek the protection of the Fifth Amendment, and so, without further ado, I did. Of course, there were more questions that made me look like a very dangerous agent of a foreign power. I would have liked to answer some of the questions, which were outright lies, but my only recourse was to stick with the protection of the Fifth. I was on the hot seat for over an hour and a half. When I came home, my testimony was all over the trade papers; they even reported I gave a "dapper Dan" performance. But it was the last hurrah. I didn't know of anything outside the film business that I could do to earn a living.

My father-in-law came up with what he thought was an answer. He was vacationing in Tucson, Arizona, getting over a serious operation. The Hotel Westerner, where he was staying, had a big dining room that they were willing to lease as a concession. His other son-in-law, a real sharpie who knew all the angles, was then operating a small restaurant in L.A. My father-in-law had never liked his other son-in-law's character, but he did like mine, in spite of my politics. I was honest, and I didn't name names, and since he was a former union man he was very sympathetic, especially when someone set fire to my lawn in the shape of a swastika. He figured that if I went in with the sharpie son-in-law, who was smart in business, perhaps I would learn how to make money, and perhaps my ethics would rub off on the other guy, and we'd both become examples for his grandchildren. The fact that the two of us hated each other's guts didn't matter.

So I sold my house and moved to Tucson, where we bought a place my wife figured we could sell at a later date for more than we'd paid for it, once she'd fixed it up. I became the maître d' of this restaurant. Before the year was out, my brother-in-law had moved back to L.A. He couldn't make enough out of the dining room alone, and the hotel wouldn't give up the bar. It took another six months before we got a buyer for our house. But the hotel kept me as the maître d' when they took back their dining room. Why? I'll never know, except that the help liked me and did their best to make me look good on the job.

Now, ironically, Jumping Jacks *comes out, with your credit on it.*

Yes, ten years after we wrote the film, now it was the Korean War, and Paramount decided it was perfect for Martin and Lewis. But because of the blacklist they wanted to take our names off it. They told another writer, Herbie [Herbert] Baker, to do a complete rewrite. Herbie was a friend of ours and told us the story a long time afterward. How in hell could he totally rewrite a story that they liked without destroying it? He couldn't and didn't.

Furthermore, the Guild still determined the credits, and the studios were bound by contract to honor their decision in such matters. All Paramount could do was take out a big ad in the trade papers explaining that, totally against their wishes, they were forced to allow our names to remain on the screenplay. So while I was playing maître d' in the dining room of the Hotel Westerner, *Jumping Jacks* was playing in a theater up the street, and so was an old Abbott and Costello film in its second run, both of them with our names in plain view. I think the situation was a lot funnier than the pictures. No one in the dining room made the connection.

So daily life went on in Tucson.

But it wasn't dull. The only political newspaper that I still subscribed to was the *National Guardian*.* It was national in its coverage, and to my great surprise I read an announcement that a documentary film about the Stockholm Peace Conference was to be shown in Tucson for the benefit of the Progressive Party at none other than the Hotel Westerner! And they gave the time and the room number. I told my wife to meet me after I closed the dining room and we'd take in this surprising event. We did. The audience was mostly from town—working-class, a few blacks, no guests from the hotel that I recognized. Though we were far from home, we had that feeling of déjà vu.

A week or so later, when I was trying to get cash out of the floor safe behind the front desk, I noticed a man appear above me wearing a hat. He told the receptionist—who almost stepped on my hand, as I fumbled with the combination—that he'd like to speak to Mr. Cohen, the hotel boss. I recognized him as the chief honcho of the local FBI, Shirley Temple's brother, Jack Temple. I did my best to stay down and keep out of sight.

Mr. Cohen came out of the door on my side of the counter, hardly noticing me crouched on the floor. The reason why the FBI was there—last week's Progressive Party meeting, of course. Cohen was an older man suffering from severe arthritis—the reason he'd decided to come to Tucson—and he was upset and nervous. Right off the bat, Cohen tried to explain that a hotel owner couldn't discriminate about renting space to political parties, even though, of course, he was shocked when he saw the types of people in attendance—blacks and all! But, he went on, the hotel had hosted a big brunch for the Democratic Party only a month previously, for a candidate in the presidential primaries, Averell Harriman—an affair, by the way, I had helped to set up; I got a warm handshake from Harriman, but no tip.

"I understand," Temple answered, "but this 'Progressive Party,' as these guys call themselves, is a bogus one to begin with." Cohen vowed he would

---

*The *National Guardian*, founded in the wake of the Henry Wallace presidential campaign of 1948, was the favorite weekly newspaper of the Popular Front left. "Progressive" but not Communist, it led the defense of "atom spies" Julius and Ethel Rosenberg and survived until 1991.

never give them space if they ever called again. Temple understood. What he was really after was the identity of the man responsible for renting the room to the group. He showed Cohen a picture. "That's the man," Cohen confirmed. Temple shrugged. "We can't do much about him, because he has a small business here." But Temple said he was very glad that Cohen wouldn't be making the same mistake again. So much for the FBI's "investigation" techniques—"intimidation" was far more like it.

Once safely back in the dining room, I heaved a sigh of relief, only to be told that Cohen wanted to see me immediately. No sooner did I enter his office than I was ordered to shut the door. Then, shaking an arthritic finger at me, he said, "Mistakes in the dining room you can make!" I didn't know what the hell he was talking about. "I knew you were up there with your wife," he went on. "My bellboy told me you were up there. Mistakes in the dining room you can make!"

Now I realized—Jesus H. Christ, he meant that if I did something like joining the Progressive Party, I would find myself out of a job. Here in Tucson I was going to be blacklisted all over again. I wanted to say, "Mr. Cohen, do you know who you are talking to? I just came back from Washington. I lost a job that makes a thousand dollars a week, and here you're paying me seventy-five! You know what you can do with your job!" But I kept my mouth shut.

All this was going on at the same time as *Salt of the Earth* was being shot by blacklistees in Silver City, New Mexico. Both Paul Jarrico, the producer, and Mike [Michael] Wilson, the writer, would make it a point to stop off in Tucson on their way through here and visit the dining room. As a rule, they'd hide behind a menu and ask for the maître d'; then, when I came out, they'd peer out with big grins on their faces. Naturally, I'd have them come back after dinner to say hello to Jean and have a drink.

When I told Mike about how guilty I felt for not telling old man Cohen off, he told me off. "How stupid can you be? You want to get yourself fired and lose another job? What we have to do is simply survive. You've already made your big speech in Washington. What are you going to gain by trying to argue with a frightened old man all alone in an office?" Believe me, I felt absolved by God. [Laughs.] And that was that.

Did blacklisting basically spell the end of your Party activity, too?

I believed that it would. I was out for a year and a half while in Arizona, and I didn't feel I would become a member again upon arriving back in L.A. Politically, things in the U.S. had gone from bad to worse, and the Party was now so weakened that there was little it could do to make things better. However, when I did get back to L.A., the House Committee was there, handing out subpoenas to appear at a hearing that would force more than just writers and other movie people to take the Fifth—doctors, lawyers, and teachers were all being targeted. Their opposition testimony was great, and it was recorded by various people all across L.A.—picked up from the radio and TV broadcasts of the hearings. Party members were assigned to that job.

Now I was assigned to take on the task of collating all these tapes and writing a continuity for this material, which would be recorded on a phonograph disc entitled, *Voices of Resistance*. It was pointed out that since this was a Party activity, it would be better if I did it under Party supervision. So I did come back as a member to do that job. The record turned out to be a very powerful document of the period and is still around in progressive archives. In fact, I'm using it for a project commemorating the fiftieth anniversary of the blacklist this year.

I stayed around another year or so, until I felt there was really no future in the Party. I wasn't happy asking people to do things I wasn't willing to do myself. It was an amicable parting of the ways.

So what did you do to make a living then?

I got through three more years of trying to make a living by using my family's connections in the garment business. My brother was a successful representative for a coat and suit house, and my first cousin in New York was a merchandise manager for Macy's. Between them, I got a variety of different dress and suit lines and traveled around Southern California, with my wife doing the modeling. We were told that we'd do much better if we went retail. With the last of the money we got from selling our Tucson house, we leased a store in Sherman Oaks and called it Country Casuals. It didn't do badly at first, and then the freeway came in, plus a big shopping mall, and we went downhill fast. It was then that I learned that the blacklist was showing some light at the end of the tunnel.

Writers were getting fronts or using pseudonyms to find work, with producers willing to look the other way. Unfortunately actors and directors, who had to appear on the set, couldn't change their faces.

I heard through the grapevine that the story editor on *Lassie*, Dick [Richard] Sanville, would be willing to accept material if the writer had a front whose name was in the clear. A good friend, Seymour Kern, was willing to let me use his name. We made a deal. He would turn over to me ninety percent of what was paid to him, just so he wouldn't get stuck with income tax. His ten percent would be the same as if he had acted as an agent. It was a good arrangement, even if I lost out on Social Security.

After a year of this "collaboration" my friend wanted out. He couldn't take being complimented by his family and friends for work he didn't do. I'd have to get another name. I talked to Dick Sanville, who suggested I use my wife's maiden name, Jean Abel. It sounded like a man, and I could also use her Social Security number.

This idea, which sounded so great, was quickly torpedoed by the front office. It seems a Rudy Abel was also being given screen credit as the show's unit manager—two Abels sounded like nepotism—and so "Seymour" had to find a new name. I chose J. (sometimes Jay) E. Selby—J. for my father-in-law, E. for my father Ed, and Selby for my uncle, the rancher.

At this point another story editor got hired just in time for a big story conference to be held in the office of the head honcho, Robert Maxwell. I'd never been in contact with him before. Dick Sanville, who was part of the group, made a mistake and called me Bob, someone else called me Seymour, somebody called me Jean, and the new editor called me by the latest name, Jay. Maxwell slapped his hand on the table and said, "For God's sake, what's been going on here?" He pointed to me and said, "You've been answering to four different names!" I went pale. I didn't know what to do. So I said, "Oh, well, all I wanted to do was be friendly." [Laughs.] And that seemed to take care of it.

So you kept doing television.

Right. More things opened up. The *Robin Hood* series with Richard Greene was being shot in England. The very progressive Hannah Weinstein was the producer who realized there was a gold mine of blacklisted writers waiting in the U.S. who would have no problem being hired for British productions since the blacklist didn't exist there. Ring Lardner Jr. headed one group writing the show in New York, and Adrian Scott did the same for L.A. I did four *Robin Hood* episodes, all with gag names on the credits, like Cecil B. Humphrey Smithe or Alfred Leslie Higginbottom.

A big break came when Richard Alan Simmons, a very good screenwriter who then lived across the street from me in the Valley, explained that he had been offered a job to write a special segment for *You Asked for It*, a popular TV program, about the transfer of the famous Hearst castle to the state of California as a public park. My friend didn't care to do it but felt I could land the job on his recommendation. He assured me that the blacklist wouldn't be a problem, because *You Asked for It* was always staff-written, and no screen credits would be involved.

So I appeared for a conference with the advertising agency in charge of the show—as Jay Selby. No questions were asked. They explained that Art Baker, the former host of the show, was to be replaced by a new, younger man. I got an idea, thinking about the old Benchley shorts, that a comic approach to the show would really be a departure. I suggested Wally Cox (then the star of *Mr. Peepers*) as the perfect personality. They were delighted enough with the idea (which they never carried out) to give me the assignment at four hundred dollars a week.

What turned out to be more unexpected was that I would be obliged to confer with William Randolph Hearst Jr. in his office at the *Los Angeles Examiner*. Not only was it the most reactionary paper in town, but it was the one where the film columnist Louella Parsons was champion of the blacklist. To my surprise, I found Hearst to be quite charming, and we hit it off in no time. Little did he know that in the back of my mind I was toying with doing the Hearst-castle show in the format of *Citizen Kane*.

I asked him about the indoor pool inlaid from end to end with imported tiles and purported to cost over one and a half million dollars. He said, "Oh, yes, and then we built the big outdoor pool." I asked, "Well, did you ever use the little one?" He said, "Oh, we hardly ever use that one anymore." He didn't seem to get the picture, even when I asked him to relate how they used a ladder to climb up over the immense fireplace to hang their Christmas stockings.

I was quite surprised when the head of their publicity department told me that Mr. Hearst had taken quite a shine to me. Then he asked, "What have you written previously that we can publicize?" I begged off just as fast as I could. "Wait until the piece is finished," I stalled.

I lasted a few more episodes of *You Asked for It* before they could no longer afford my salary. Years later, my namesake, Uncle Selby, went to Northern California for a visit and said he would love to see the Hearst castle. I called the *San Francisco Examiner*. They remembered the program, and after they got in touch with the parks department, my uncle was given the red-carpet treatment—no pun intended.

Now let me ask you about the politics of some of these television shows.

The early *Lassie* scripts that I wrote almost always had to demonstrate a lesson or provide a moral, like "sharing," for instance. Lassie finds a bone. What is the bone? It is a dinosaur bone, and it is needed to make the rest of the skeleton. So the idea is, Lassie finally realizes—well, through Timmy, though Lassie was a great intellectual dog, you know [laughs]—that the museum needs the bone, and she has to learn how to share. Another dog steals the bone, and Lassie has to get it back and turn it over. So, for the good of science . . .

Or "Share and share alike—that's democracy," at least for Lassie.

At least for Lassie. But every one of the *Lassies* had something to do with morality. I did one on Lassie's vanity in which the dog gets her picture taken as a prize for a magazine. They doll the dog up, hair in a bow and all the rest. When she comes back to the farm, she won't do anything to muss herself. She doesn't want to get dirty anymore. However, when the kid's ball falls into the pigpen and the kid gets cornered by a vicious boar, Lassie has to jump in to save him, and she gets filthy in the process.

Finally, the producers were saying, "You know, we've got to get a little bit more action"—almost violence.

They wanted the show to become more like Rin Tin Tin?

Because they were losing kids to other shows. So I did one with Lassie having amnesia. They said, "Amnesia? Can you do that for a dog?" I said, "Sure." [Laughs.] Someone is blasting stumps. Lassie covers Timmy, because the wood chips are starting to fly, and one of the pieces hits her on the head. Lassie doesn't remember her name. She can't remember her tricks. And if she ever leaves home, she's a lost dog, because she doesn't remember belonging anywhere. Sure enough, she does leave home, and she gets lost. So, until Lassie can get her memory back, there's a whole sequence of events about other people who pick her up and browbeat her and do terrible things. Finally, with her memory back, she returns home.

Now, a little later I was working on *Flipper*. I said, "Have you ever done amnesia?" They said, "What! Amnesia for a dolphin?" I said, "Sure." So I had them doing underwater explosions to construct a pier. Flipper swims too close, and the concussion gives her amnesia. From then on, of course, the plot develops similar situations. They bought it.

Still later I was working on a series called *Daktari*, about a vet who treats sick animals in Africa. He has a pet chimpanzee called Judy. However, I felt I couldn't plagiarize myself again, so I didn't suggest the amnesia angle. But would you believe that another writer sold them the same idea, which he must have stolen from seeing the other two shows?!

Didn't Flipper *have an inherent ecological edge?*

All these shows dealt with animals and with people who love animals and love pets. You couldn't say that what's good for people is not necessarily good for General Motors. But the idea of what's good for pets did have some decency in it. It was automatically built in—love for something; love conquers all. There was a great deal of good stuff in those shows for kids. Now it's all violence.

But you've got to understand that violence was also inherent in films from the time they made *The Great Train Robbery*. To digress a bit, motion pictures are motion pictures, action pictures. Violence has been built into film in the sense that an exploding car with flames is much more exciting than a bent fender. But you don't have to do that; we never did when I was writing films.

The Hays Office censors had a rule that you couldn't show a man being shot with both the shooter and his victim included in the same setup. You photographed the man firing the gun; then you showed his opponent being hit, separately. Now not only are the two together but you see the bullets strike the victim, the wounds spurting blood, black holes appearing on his forehead, and his brains splattering the wall behind him. Today scripts are written more for the computer graphics and so-called realism than for the development of the plot.

The producer used to be the belt in the production line. The producer would take the script from the writer and give it to the director. The producer would take the film from the director and give it to the cutting room. The producer kept the writers in their offices writing, the directors busy doing their directing. So everybody was working at what they were supposed to do—and the producer's job was to keep things running smoothly.

Now the creators themselves have far more control of the material than in the old days. A writer-producer or writer-director is able to ensure the integrity of his vision, which isn't diluted by the common denominator of everybody's input. Good or bad, at least it's a clear statement of what is envisioned. Certainly there is a depiction of themes that would never have been permitted by the old establishment and also a tendency to go overboard on sex and violence, in an attempt to increase the take at the box office but at the expense of reviving the threat of censorship.

But there is also a lot of good material in films today. I think there are a lot of good people today in Hollywood—and there always will be—because a good artist is of the people, he's by the people, and his material is for the people. If you get a script that does all those things, it's going to be progressive, and it's going to make a lot of money. That's the answer.

Alfred Lewis Levitt
(and Helen Slote Levitt)

ALFRED LEWIS LEVITT, Los Angeles, California, 1997

PHOTO © WILLIAM B. WINBURN

INTERVIEW BY LARRY CEPLAIR

ALFRED LEWIS LEVITT
(1916–   )

1948 *The Boy with Green Hair*. Script.
1950 *Mrs. Mike*. Coscript.
   Shakedown. Coscript.
1951 *My Outlaw Brother*. Adaptation.
   The Barefoot Mailman. Uncredited
      contribution.
1953 *Dream Wife*. Story, coscript.
1958 *The Two-Headed Spy*. Uncredited
      contribution.

1964 *The Misadventures of Merlin Jones*. Coscript
      (as Tom August).
1965 *The Monkey's Uncle*. Coscript
      (as Tom August).

HELEN SLOTE LEVITT
(1917–1993)

1964 *The Misadventures of Merlin Jones*. Coscript
      (as Helen August).
1965 *The Monkey's Uncle*. Coscript
      (as Helen August).

■

ALFRED LEWIS LEVITT and Helen Slote Levitt worked together in the Communist Party, the Screen Writers Guild, and various Popular Front organizations, and as cowriters of scripts for television and motion pictures.

While Al Levitt was rapidly moving up the ladder of screenwriting success in the 1940s, Helen Levitt virtually ran the Actors Laboratory Theatre in Pasadena. Named as Communists by Martin Berkeley in September 1951, Al and Helen appeared before the House Un-American Activities Committee and refused to answer its questions. Both were blacklisted.

While Al sought work on the black market, using fronts and pseudonyms, Helen coedited the remarkable if short-lived journal, the *Hollywood Review*, featuring some of the best Marxist and feminist criticism of film that had yet appeared. One of the blacklisted couples who did not emigrate, they also served as the nexus of support for those who stayed and those who returned.

In 1978 Al was able to rejoin the Writers Guild under his real name—he had been a member as Tom August since 1957; "Helen August," his regular collaborator, had joined in 1959. Al was elected to the Guild's board in 1981, and he and Helen served on several strike committees and in the group that worked out a formula to provide pension supplements for blacklisted writers. Helen also led a very successful workshop for African-American writers.

Their television and movie work varied with the opportunities. Al's best-known work remains *The Boy with Green Hair*, initiated by producer Adrian Scott, cowritten by Ben Barzman, and directed by Joseph Losey, all fellow blacklistees.

■

When did you decide to become a writer?

All my life I knew that I wanted to be a writer. I remember even writing poetry and stories as a child. When I got to high school I wrote for publications, and in college [at the New York University campus in the Bronx] I did a lot of writing, too.

I started writing about sports because then I got free tickets to everything. [Laughs.] I became sports editor of the college newspaper, the *Heights News*, and Helen and I went to all the games.

As a result, two things happened. I worked for a while for Joe Val, the sports editor of the [New York] World Telegram. Also, I was offered a job by Ned Irish, who ultimately owned Madison Square Garden. At the time he was a sports promoter; he introduced intersectional college basketball to the Garden. He liked my columns, and he wanted me to be his PR [public relations] guy.

My sports column in the Heights News was probably the most liberal in the country, because most of the people who were active in that field were hardly liberal. There were a lot of issues covered in those columns. I remember fighting a battle about a football player who had been injured in a game and had been paralyzed. The university just disowned him, as though they had no responsibility. I wrote columns about that, attacking the university.

Did you engage in any other political activities in college?

Bert Witt, a student leader and known radical, recruited me into a study group. We engaged in a lot of really ridiculous kinds of cloak-and-daggerish activities—Bert was an imaginative guy! [Laughs.] I don't even remember whether it was the Young Democrats or Young Republicans, but I was supposed to attend their meetings and report back to Bert. Bert was the leader of the [campus] ASU [American Student Union], and I was a member, of course.*

Were you in the Young Communist League?

That was in college, after my first year, 1932–1933, when the financial problems in the country became tremendous. I took a year off and worked for an uncle. It was really a great experience. Bert Witt did the same thing in the same year, so we went back and resumed our college work and graduated together. But I don't really remember a hell of a lot about the YCL. I just remember endless discussions of subjects that I didn't understand very well.

Did you read political works?

I read a lot of pamphlets, some of which were by Marx and Engels. I think I read Engels's Origin of the Family. [Marx's] Capital was pretty intimidating. [Earl] Browder impressed me tremendously. I mean that stylistically, he was way ahead of [William Z.] Foster, and all the things he said seemed right. I came into politics primarily both on a cultural level and as someone whose instincts were for the underdog.

All this time in college, meanwhile, your parents wanted you to become a doctor, because that's what all good Jewish firstborn sons did?

---

*Bert Witt was a prominent member of the American Student Union and the American Youth Congress. After the war he and other left-liberal supporters of Franklin Roosevelt formed the National Citizens Political Action Committee and Progressive Citizens of America to check the rightward drift of the Democratic Party.

I was a good student, and I was pushed by my family, who wanted me to go to medical school. I kept cutting all my science classes for my literature courses or my language courses. In fact, I got a job right after college because by that time Helen and I wanted to get married. Instead of going to med school I got a job in animated cartoons as a writer, with Terrytoons in New Rochelle.

How did that happen?

I had an uncle, Arthur Kalfus, who was a performer. I had great affection for him; he was really a marvelous guy who used the very imaginative pseudonym Arthur Kay. [Laughs.] He was in one Ed Wynn play [*Hooray for What!*, 1937]. I was still in college and writing funny sketches and pieces. The play happened to be in rehearsal, and he came to me. He said, "I think they're going to drop my big scene. Wynn doesn't feel it's funny enough, so I thought you could do something with it." So I worked on the scene, he turned it in to Wynn, and Wynn kept the scene in. That same uncle was doing voices for Terrytoons, and when he heard that they were looking to enlarge the staff with another writer, he immediately recommended me.

Then you helped Helen get a job there, too.

We couldn't get married on just what I was making. Helen was still in school, just finishing up. Paul Terry, who owned Terrytoons, was a very idiosyncratic man. He had a lot of pet theories. I wrote a letter to myself, purportedly coming from Helen, which she then put down in her handwriting, incorporating all his pet theories. I said to him, "Paul, I just got a letter from a woman I know. I think you might be interested." I handed it to him, he read it, and I waited for his reaction. He said, "This is really a bright woman! What does she do?" I answered, "She's just finishing school. I think she's considering a job on the *Philadelphia Inquirer*, but she doesn't want to leave New York." He asked me, "Do you think she's willing to work here?"

What did you do at Terrytoons, precisely?

I worked out story ideas for cartoons. I say "cartoon" in the sense of one-reel production. They accepted my way of working, which was on paper. And there wasn't the kind of competitiveness that I ran into later on at Merrie Melodies. The head writer who drew my stuff for me was a very funny old guy, John Foster. There was never any question about whose work was whose. He would put my name on the things he drew that were mine.

Did they have stock characters that you had to keep using?

No. Merrie Melodies and almost every other company had stock characters. We didn't, although I introduced a couple of characters that were repeated several times. I tended to work in characters that my uncle did the voices for.

Paul Terry was one of the pioneers of animated cartoons. [His character] Farmer Alfalfa went way back to the early days, long before [Walt] Disney.

He was also the most backward man I've met in my life. His company was the last one to go into sound. It was the last one to go into color. On a personal level, he was a very pleasant, sweet guy. In every other way he was really backward, as well as very reactionary politically. I remember that when Disney was working on *Snow White*, Paul Terry said, "It's too bad about Disney. He really has talent, but he's going to be wiped out. You cannot make a full-length feature in animation." With his usual clairvoyance!

You were fired for attempting to organize a union?

That's something Helen and I remember differently. She's more generous to Terry than I am. We tried to organize the Terrytoon employees secretly. We had spoken to some guys who had been organizing the Fleischer cartoon operation in New York. When they succeeded to some extent, [Dave and Max] Fleischer moved their whole studio to Florida.

When he heard about what we were doing, Paul Terry called all the employees together. He said, "I hear there has been some talk of a union among you. I just want you all to know that this company is really a hobby for me. I don't really need it anymore. And if it becomes unpleasant in any way, like becoming unionized, I'll just disband it and retire." That really shook a lot of people, because with Fleischer gone, this was the only studio left in the New York area. I guess he could have carried that threat through if he had felt like doing so, because he was very rich.

Helen feels that we were fired because there was retrenchment. My recollection is that all those who were fired in the retrenchment were people who had responded to our unionizing attempts.

Those ten months in New Rochelle were very intense. I liked our life there. I don't think we ever lived as well again. We were very political and involved in the community. We were active in a Communist Party unit, and we also were persuaded to join the temple. We organized current-events programs and cultural events. After all that, it was a shock to be fired. I remember that we couldn't even bring ourselves to tell our parents.

There was a period of a month or two when we were trying to get other things going and couldn't. I wrote to [Walt] Disney [Productions]. I wrote to Merrie Melodies. Disney sent me a cartoon comic problem to work on, but you had to do it in sketches, and I was a writer who didn't do my own drawing. I can't remember what I wrote to Merrie Melodies that got them to say, "You're hired," but I remember when that telegram came and the great excitement. We had never been out of New York, really. Now we were moving west.

I lasted at Merrie Melodies only about six weeks. It really was a fantastic introduction to all the clichés about Hollywood in all of its monstrous aspects. At that time, animated cartoons were not scripted, as they are now. They were storyboarded. The story department usually consisted of a group of sketch artists. I never was part of that. I would verbalize my ideas and put them down on paper, but someone else had to help with the drawings. When I first came out to Merrie Melodies, there was a guy who said, "I'll sketch your ideas as well as my own." My ideas would go up on a big board, along with those of other cartoonists.

Every Friday the studio manager would come through the department, and he'd look at the board and say, "Nice going, Joe. Very good, John. Terrific, Jack." When he said this to the guy who was drawing mine, I waited for the guy to explain that half of them were mine—at least half. He didn't. But after the studio manager left, I didn't say anything. The next week, the same thing happened. This time I said, "Don't you think I should explain which of those are mine?" He made me feel really crass for even suggesting anything. He said, "You know, we are all doing this together. This is a collaboration." I accepted that, feeling embarrassed for having been so gauche.

At the end of the sixth week, I was called in. The studio manager said, "Listen, we've given you six weeks. I have seen nothing of yours on the board." At that point, I just could not bring myself to say that this guy was taking credit for all of my work as well as his own, so I left. That was our introduction to Hollywood. [Laughs.]

Meanwhile, we knew no one out here. But when I was a kid there had been a counselor at the camp I went to, at Balfour Lake, back in Minerva, New York, named Mickey [Michael] Uris. I had heard that he married a counselor from the girls' camp there, an actress named Dorothy Tree.* On the May Day previous to our departure from New Rochelle, we had run into Mickey Uris's brother, George Uris, who was also a radical. When we told him we were leaving, he said, "Look Mickey up," and gave us his address and phone number. So we did.

They were your social entree to the Hollywood left?

Early on, through the Urises, we met a lot of really marvelous people. Dorothy [Tree] had a fairly good role in a picture called *Confessions of a Nazi Spy*, which was very well received by the left and made a splash. She invited us to the premiere, where we met [Donald Ogden] Stewart, Ella Winter, and the Endores [Guy and Harriet Endore].†

---

*Writer Michael Uris (1902–1967) seemed well launched on a successful Hollywood career, with script credits that included the musical *Happy Go Lucky*, the western *The Plainsman and the Lady*, and several Republic and Twentieth Century–Fox pictures. Uris was named by no less than nine "friendly" witnesses and saw his Hollywood career evaporate. Actress Dorothy Tree's biggest films, in a career that spanned the years 1938 to 1950, included *Having a Wonderful Time*, *Confessions of a Nazi Spy*, *Nazi Agent*, *Crime Doctor*, *Edge of Darkness*, *The Men*, *The Asphalt Jungle*, *Knute Rockne—All American*, and *Abe Lincoln in Illinois*. Tree (1906–1992), who never returned to films after being blacklisted, became a diction instructor and the author of several noteworthy books about speech and communication.

†Guy Endore (1900–1972), another central figure on the Hollywood left of the 1930s, worked as a scenarist on early horror classics (*The Devil Doll*), Astaire-Rogers musicals (*Carefree*), patriotic World War II films (*Song of Russia* and *The Story of G.I. Joe*, for which he was Oscar-nominated), and film noir (*Johnny Allegro* and *Tomorrow Is Another Day*). He served as editor

I remember the Urises also taking us to the beach quite often. That September of 1939 was very hot. There's a particular stretch of beach, named Sorrento [near San Diego], where all the liberals and leftists went. There I met Shepard Traube, a director from New York, who had been very successful in the theater, though he never made it big out here.* Guy Endore and his wife were often there, and Groucho Marx was another regular. I remember one time when we were all sitting in the sand, and Groucho walked to the edge of the water, turned around, spread out his arms, and said, "The Jews' last stand!"

Did you join the Hollywood section of the Party right away? Or did you begin to write screenplays?

Security was very important in Hollywood. We were sent to a Marxist study group, which was like being tested and checked. [Laughs.] Then we were assigned to a Party branch. This was during the period right after I was fired [from Merrie Melodies], when I had started writing screen treatments, my own originals, to try to sell. I got a lot of encouragement, but I never sold anything. Helen, meanwhile, went to work for the Motion Picture Democratic Committee.

Friends on the left introduced you to the idea of becoming a reader?

I found out that I could easily get outside reading assignments, which were a kind of preliminary to scriptwriting. If they liked what you did, you might be able to get a job. You made very small amounts of money and were paid by the piece. But I did get to know whoever was in charge of the reading department or story department at both RKO and Paramount. And then I got this steady job working as a reader for David O. Selznick.

Selznick's story editor was [producer] Val Lewton. He was the most remarkable man I've ever met in my life. He knew a lot of languages, including his native one, Russian. His English was impeccable. Anyway, he was very

---

of two early magazines of the Popular Front, *Clipper* and its successor, *Black and White*, and wrote the widely circulated Hollywood defense-committee pamphlets for the Scottsboro Boys and the Sleepy Lagoon defendants. He wrote many books, plays, articles, and polemical essays but is perhaps best-known for his novels, among them *The Werewolf of Paris* and *Babouk*. The films Endore contributed to, under various pseudonyms, during the blacklist period include *Captain Sindbad*.

*Shepard Traube (1907–1983) was the director of the 1940 Broadway hit *Angel Street*, which earned him an award as Best Director of the season from the New York Drama Critics circle. His career as a stage producer and director spanned forty years, and his stay in Hollywood, in the late 1930s and early 1940s, was fleeting but memorable. His story "Goose Step" provided the script basis in 1939 for the propagandistic *The Beasts of Berlin*, one of the first films about German underground opposition to Hitler, and among the handful of films he directed was *Street of Memories*, the first feature-length script by Robert Lees and Fred Rinaldo. Despite his long absence from the Hollywood scene, Traube was nevertheless named by Martin Berkeley and appeared before HUAC as an unfriendly witness.

nice to me. He said, "It's ridiculous for you to be a reader. I'm going to make you the assistant story editor. Same pay, but you can tell people you're an assistant story editor." Actually, all I was was a reader.

David O. Selznick at that time had some kind of project going that he referred to as the Lobero Theatre Project. The Lobero Theater was a legitimate theater in Santa Barbara. Playwrights submitted their plays, and he turned them over to me to read. One of the plays submitted was by a man named Martin Berkeley. It was terrible! Of course, his play was not among those selected. He found out that I was the reader, and I don't think he ever forgave me.*

Was being a reader good experience?

It really was an education. You learned to think objectively, because it wasn't your own work that you were judging. You saw a whole range of the kinds of mistakes that could be made in developing a story. You saw how one approach worked and another approach didn't. It was always easier to figure out why something didn't work than why another thing did.

Contrary to what some people used to say, and maybe still do, readers were not just trying to bury everything. Coming across something that was good made you feel like suddenly you had been handed dessert after a long meal. I remember reading either a full screenplay or a detailed treatment, a collaboration of Dalton Trumbo and Ring Lardner Jr. that was marvelous. I even remember the title, "The Fisherman of Boudrais." I was enthusiastic about that, but it didn't sell. On the other hand, another very detailed treatment that I read was written by Bess Taffel, Sol Barzman, and Ben Barzman, a three-way collaboration. I didn't know them then. I thought it was an absolutely marvelous idea and marvelously developed. That sold, and the movie was called *True to Life*.† The picture never lived up to what the script was, but I still think it was a great idea!

Bill [William] Dozier was the head of the story department, and the head of the reading department was Meta Reis Rosenberg.‡ Alice Hunter [wife of

---

*Martin Berkeley named Alfred Lewis Levitt as a Communist before the House Un-American Activities Committee on September 19, 1951.

†*True to Life*, directed in 1943 by George Marshall, starred Mary Martin, Franchot Tone, Dick Powell, and Victor Moore in a story about a radio writer who decides to live with a typical American family in order to get material for his soap opera. The detailed treatment by Barzman and Bess Taffel was turned over to the more experienced screenwriters Don Hartman and Harry Tugend, who altered it substantially.

‡Meta Reis Rosenberg worked her way up the professional ladder in Hollywood from secretary to script reader, agent, and producer. The name Reis came from her first marriage, to director Irving Reis, and Rosenberg from her subsequent marriage to agent George Rosenberg. She was long associated with the Berg-Allenberg Agency, which turned out during the HUAC hearings to harbor a hotbed of anti-Communist clients such as director Sam Wood, writer James Kevin McGuinness, actor Adolphe Menjou, and author Ayn Rand, who all gave incriminating and sometimes fanciful testimony. Meta Reis Rosenberg herself had been a Party supporter. When

Ian McLellan Hunter]—Alice Goldberg then—was also a reader there. Another of my fellow readers was Bernie [Bernard] Gordon. Dozier was a terrific guy to work for. He encouraged people. When I wrote something on my own, he tried to get a producer interested. He didn't succeed, but he tried. I was about to get my first movie assignment at Paramount when I got drafted. [Laughs.] This must have been 1942. I had been a reader for about two years.

How did you learn screenwriting?

I took a class that was given by the Hollywood branch of the League of American Writers, taught by [screenwriter and later president of the Screen Writers Guild] Mary McCall. The class consisted primarily of her telling anecdotes about her experiences. I remembered her anecdotal lectures when I started teaching—and knew better than to do that! [Laughs.]

The two guys who were most helpful to me were John Bright and [his writing partner] Bob Tasker. I wish I could be as patient as they were. I would write things, and they would read them carefully and discuss them in great detail. I got from them a sense of how to construct a screen story. They were both living on one of the cross streets near us. John was then married to Josefina Fierro, and Bob was also married to, or living with, a woman who was Mexican. Both were beautiful women, and both Bob and John were fluent in Spanish.*

Bob had been in prison for car theft or some other prosaic crime, and while in prison he had written a novel called *Grimhaven*. His own social conscience developed as a result of the response that the novel elicited from the public. Bob's background fit in with John's experiences in Chicago. They were two really very kind and generous men. They were also very handsome men. Tasker later died mysteriously in Mexico City.

By the time I got to know them, they had gotten in trouble at Paramount. Unintentionally, they wrote a story about an older man who was in love with a younger woman, and it was a story that, without their realizing it, called to mind the relationship of [producer] B. P. Schulberg and [actress] Sylvia Sidney. When they turned it in to Schulberg, he felt they were trying to parody him, and they were fired. They found it very difficult to get a job after that incident, and this was long before the blacklist.

For you, was Paramount a good experience?

---

the Committee subpoenaed her, she consulted writer Richard Collins on what to do; she had undergone therapy with Phil Cohen and was now represented by attorney Martin Gang. After clearing herself by denouncing her political past and naming names, Rosenberg went on to a highly successful career as an agent and a producer, mostly in television, where her partner was another informer, writer Roy Huggins.

*Josefina Fierro Bright was a principal figure in the Congress of Spanish-Speaking Peoples, the leading Popular Front organization to defend the rights of Mexican Americans. Later, divorced from John Bright, she was deported during the McCarthy era.

Yes, even though it was somewhat frustrating in terms of my career. I had some good writing experiences outside of Paramount during this period. I remember how an organization called the Hollywood Writers Mobilization held a big event at UCLA, and I got to write the speech for Henry Fonda, urging writers to write material that would bolster [wartime] morale.* I sat in the audience watching Henry Fonda deliver that speech, and it was an experience that I've never had before or since. He made that speech so much his own, without ever changing a comma. You had the feeling that here was a guy talking and saying things as they came to his mind, and it was tremendously effective. As a writer, I feel it's been downhill ever since. [Laughs.]

So in 1942 you were on the verge of getting started as a screenwriter—but you got drafted. What happened then?

John Garfield gave me a going-away party—Helen was working with him by then—and invited all my friends. Somehow, a crap game developed with Garfield and my friends, and he kept cleaning them out! It was really a funny incident, because I realized he was trying to lose, making outrageous bets. Finally, he had accumulated this big pile of money, and he just pushed it to the center and said, "I've got to take care of something else. You guys divide it up." And he left, so nobody would be embarrassed by losing. I was really touched by that.

Helen and I ghosted a number of things for Julie [Garfield]. I wrote an article under his name for *Theatre Arts* magazine. He was no great intellect, but I liked him. I think, on certain levels, he was really a kid spoiled by his success. But he certainly was kind to us.

Anyway, I was drafted. When I went into the Army, they sent me to the reception center in Monterey; from Monterey they sent me to Atlantic City, New Jersey, for my basic training; and from Atlantic City they sent me back to Culver City, to what was familiarly known as Fort Roach, where I stayed for the next year and a half. It was the Hal Roach studios, which were taken over by the government for the First Motion Picture Unit, called the FMPU.

There, every day for a year and a half, I would see Ronald Reagan, then pronounced "Ree-gan." He arrived on the post in a cavalry outfit, wearing jodhpurs and a campaign hat. Nobody could take him seriously; from then on, he was a laughingstock. I remember that one day he did something that I perceive in retrospect as being a departure from his being a liberal. There was a strike at one of the public utilities. He came in that morning in an absolute fury, and he said, "I'm a good union man and all that, but this is inconvenient." His choice of the word "inconvenient" stayed with me forever.

---

*The Hollywood Writers Mobilization, organized within a week of Pearl Harbor, drew on the talent of writers for victory-oriented goals and activities. Its first chairman was Francis Faragoh. The writers' organization later joined with UCLA to sponsor a widely-publicized Writers Congress, and members were instrumental in launching the *Hollywood Quarterly*, a journal of film study and analysis, the precursor of today's *Film Quarterly*.

Otherwise, my job at the FMPU was funny. On my Army record, as my last employment, it said, "Last employer: Paramount Pictures. Department: story." They didn't know that the story department was where the readers worked, and they assumed it was where the writers worked. So they sent me to write training films at Fort Roach, and I did. There was an interesting group of writers there at that time. There was Irving Wallace, Walter Doniger, Guy Trosper, Joel Malone, Mal [Malvin] Wald, myself, and several others. I think it was a really good experience for somebody aspiring to become a screenwriter. But I still was young then and foolish. I felt I really should be going overseas instead of living at home and driving to the post every morning.

When did you apply to go overseas?

It must have been the end of 1943. I didn't get chosen until sometime in 1944, and I was chosen by [actor] Van Heflin. He had a unit going overseas, and he had heard that I wanted to go. He said, "You want to come with me? This unit is mine." And I said yes. There was another part of the post where they trained people for combat camera units. Heflin and others were in that.

First I went over in the Hundred Sixty-second Camera Unit. We were attached to the Air Force. There were eight of us and two officers—two technicians in charge of the gun-sight-aiming-point cameras, which were referred to as GSAP cameras, attached to the planes. We were linked to the gun, so that whenever the firing button was pressed, these cameras would automatically operate. In addition, we were supposed to shoot whatever we could that we thought was important.

We were first stationed in England, and then we moved to France. Somewhere along the way, I was transferred to the Fourth Combat Camera Unit, and sent out in the field with ground troops to shoot footage showing the effect of air support on the ground action. When the war ended, they sent me back to my sixteen-millimeter unit. From there I was sent to Paris to do an American version of a film with [Henri] Cartier-Bresson. It was a film about the repatriation of prisoners of war and concentration-camp inmates. The French version was called *Le retour*, and the American version was called *Reunion*. The two versions were quite different, for a number of reasons.

That was really a marvelous part of my life in the war, because Cartier-Bresson was an incredible guy, one of the world-famous still photographers, who almost single-handedly elevated photography to an art form. The emotion of some of his footage was incredible. Also, Cartier-Bresson knew everybody. So through him I met such people as La Pasionaria [Dolores Ibarruri, a heroine of the Spanish Civil War] and many French cultural figures. All the time I was stationed at the Hotel d'Astor, eating in the hotel dining room, which had embassy rations and French chefs

How was the American version of Cartier-Bresson's film different?

It had a different quality. I finished my work on the American version in New York that winter but stayed only through the recording of the narration.

I left before I saw the whole film put together, although I ordered a sixteen-millimeter print for myself. After I got my print I received a letter from the guy who had done the editing on the film. He said that he was leaving government employ and asked me to lend him my print so that he could show people his editing. I ran into Irving Lerner, and Irving said, "Have you heard what's happened to your film?" He told me that the State Department—which had taken over the Office of War Information—had decided that the impact of the film was too strong. It had been translated into something like forty languages, but its message of peace carried too much impact, and now they were going to destroy all copies of it. I told him that this editor wanted a copy for his own professional purposes, and Irving said, "I wouldn't send it, if I were you." So I didn't. But I did use my sixteen-millimeter print to help get my first [postwar] jobs here in Hollywood.

How was Hollywood different after the war?

I don't have any recollection of it seeming different. I felt that I was different. I had been through a profound experience. Of course, Roosevelt had died. I was in Luxembourg the day the news of his death came, and I remember being awakened by a woman saying, *"Le President Roosevelt est mort."* I figured it was some kind of rumor. But when I got out in the field, GIs were weeping all over the place. It was a very moving occasion; no president in my lifetime has captured the imagination and had the inspirational quality that Roosevelt did. That was a big event politically.

In terms of real estate, there was a huge difference in postwar Hollywood. We had to scurry around to find a place to live. During my first attempt at getting work, Johnny Weber became my agent. He was a very political guy who had become an agent for [the] William Morris [Agency]. The first assignment I was able to get was to write a screenplay called "Double Crossroads," some kind of spy story. The producer, Jules Schermer, whom I knew from Fort Roach, wanted to hire me, but he was really uncertain. I had no feature-film credits, so he assigned someone to work with me as a collaborater. And the person he assigned was Ben Barzman. I had known Ben before, so the whole thing was very fortuitous.

This was at Columbia. We had a terrible time with the producer, but Ben and I got along. The picture was never made, and Ben went on to other projects. But I was able to get another assignment at RKO. My agent sold an idea I had to a producer named Ralph Steiner, who had never produced anything at the studio before. He had made documentaries in New York that won prizes.* Working with him at RKO in some capacity was Phil Brown,

---

*A significant figure in the history of American photography, the Dartmouth-educated Ralph Steiner (1899–1986) grew preoccupied in his work with documentary authenticity and everyday life. His photography influenced Walker Evans, among others. He was a prominent member of the New York Frontier Films group (which also included Paul Strand, Leo Hurwitz, Irving Lerner, and Ben Maddow) and later worked with Pare Lorentz and Willard Van Dyke on

one of the founders of the Actors Lab. I had a terrible time with Steiner; he and I did not see eye to eye on anything. What got me both of these jobs was my war film, *Reunion*. I gave it to my agent, he showed it to people, and that always got them interested in me.

My RKO idea was about a boy who is being brought up by an aunt who loves him but is very stern in the way she handles him. They live near the Columbia backlot. This kid finds an opening in the fence and wriggles through, and he wanders around looking at these marvelous sets. His imagination takes over. He starts to play roles in relation to each set. He solves, or he deals with, problems in his family through these scenes that he imagines.

One day, in the RKO commissary, I was sitting at a table alone. Adrian Scott, whom I knew, came over and joined me. He started asking questions about what I was doing. I told him about the story I was working on for Ralph Steiner, and he said, "Gee, that's a marvelous story, a terrific story." I said, "Yeah, but I can't get anywhere with this guy Steiner." And Adrian hired me for *The Boy with Green Hair* on the basis of that conversation. He said, "How would you feel about working with Ben Barzman?" I said, "Fine!" So we went to work on *The Boy with Green Hair*.

What was it like working with those two, Ben Barzman and Adrian Scott?

Ben was so good to work with. There was never any throwing of his weight around, although he had more experience than I did. He had credits.

Adrian was the greatest producer who ever lived. He spoiled me for anyone else. Adrian would challenge every scene, challenge every line in every speech, every word in every line, and he managed to do it in such a way that you couldn't wait to get back to the typewriter to try it again. He was absolutely marvelous, a lovely person, a gentle man who was also capable of being very tough if he had to be, but never for very long. I thought all producers were going to be like him! I found out that I was wrong.

Did you encounter any political problems with the studio?

We finished the script. Dore Schary was then head of production at RKO, and Dore liked it very much. He used to say—Adrian would get a call as we were waiting for our conference with him—"Okay, you can bring your Communist writers up now." Then we'd go to see him.

I remember that there was one big emotional scene, toward the end of the picture, where the kid's hair is being cut off by the barber. It's kind of a quiet scene: everybody looks at the kid, now shorn, and the kid gets up out of the chair. Pat O'Brien hands the barber his money, and the camera follows the

several path-breaking social documentaries, including *The Plow That Broke the Plains*, *The River*, and *The City*. Steiner worked off and on for MGM and RKO in the 1930s and 1940s, used primarily as a consultant. He never produced a feature film in Hollywood and was blacklisted.

kid without any sound until you hear the cash register ring. We wrote that in because the scene was so quiet.

We had this meeting with Schary. "Listen, guys," he said, "that's great, but you can't do it, because everybody will figure it out." We said, "Figure out what?" He said, "The cash-register bell is capitalism." This was so remote from anything in our minds—we just thought of it as a sound effect that would be an accent in a tense scene, but he was reading political meaning into it. If someone else had been writing that scene, I don't think that would have occurred to him. It stayed in, anyway. Sometimes the best things you write are unconscious.

But then Howard Hughes bought RKO.

Adrian had brought in Joe [Joseph Losey] to direct the film. Joe had never directed a feature before. When Howard Hughes bought RKO, Schary was out. Hughes took over, and he hated the script. Ben went off on another assignment. Meanwhile, Joe would get these notes from Hughes, and he would have to try to change each scene where Hughes felt the message was peace into a message of preparedness.

Then the Hollywood Ten [situation] happened, and Adrian was out. I remember when Adrian and Eddie [Edward] Dmytryk got their subpoenas. I was with Adrian when Eddie came into Adrian's office and said, "They can't prove anything on me." That was his total reaction at the time. I thought that the danger was just for big shots. [Laughs.] I never thought that it would filter down. At first, there was no thought that it was going to go beyond those people.

A man named Stephen Ames became the producer. Ames, because he was so conscious of his lack of qualifications, was a help to us. I stayed on. I wasn't being paid, but I was there every day with Joe on the set. At night we would take the memos that Hughes had sent that day and try to *seem* to do what Hughes wanted, without the effect he desired. And we did that pretty successfully, I guess, because Hughes ended up hating the film.

Did he know that you were doing the rewriting behind his back?

I'm sure he didn't.

How well did the cast understand the political message?

Pat O'Brien was a right-wing guy but very pleasant and genial to work with. He kept saying, "God, you guys must have read a lot of Sean O'Casey." I was surprised that he had read any Sean O'Casey! The kid, Dean Stockwell, was marvelous. I had some conversations with Dean, and he told me in his own way how he felt about playing the part. "I feel this picture is like being a Boy Scout," he said. "You're doing something really good."

Were you pleased with the final product?

We had to make some compromises in order to seem to do what Hughes wanted. What suffered was not the content but the aesthetics. Joe was very tense and nervous about a lot of the material. It was his first picture, and it was something to be tense about, with Hughes hovering around. When we wrote our screenplay, we detailed every bit of action for the actors. I think, in retrospect, that Joe resented that. He frequently made disparaging comments about the film. I remember that in the reviews he got credit for many touches we had written. They were, in some of the reviews, described as "director's touches." But that was my first experience on a film, and I learned to get used to that after a while. [Laughs.]

If it's a good collaboration, you don't remember who contributed what. Many years later, when I was teaching at [California State University] Northridge, we ran the film, and Ben came. Someone asked, about a particular line that worked very well, "Whose line was that?" Ben and I said almost simultaneously, "His." We each really thought it was.

You were finished at RKO, but you got other offers.

There was no possibility that I would be hired again at RKO. But when the movie was over, I did get offers. The next project that I worked on was at Universal, a picture called *Shakedown*, about a news photographer. Everybody was doing one-word titles. I did the script, and the guy who was going to direct it was a first-time director named Joe [Joseph] Pevney, an actor who had played in *Home of the Brave*. He was married to Mitzi Green, a former child star. Joe Pevney was a very talented actor; in fact he used to drive me crazy whenever we had conversations about the script, asking about the characters. Then, whenever he would suggest a new line of dialogue to me, he would act out the line that he was suggesting. [Laughs.] I could never tell whether he was performing or having a conversation with me about the script!

What was your next film?

I worked at Columbia on *The Barefoot Mailman*. That was originally a novel [by Theodore Pratt]. I worked directly with S. Sylvan Simon, the head of production there. He was an impossible man, and I left to work on *My Outlaw Brother*. Then they called me back to make changes on *The Barefoot Mailman*. When I heard what the changes were, I refused. So they hired someone else. Later there was a credit arbitration. [Producer] Bobby [Robert] Cohn called me and said, "I'm having trouble with this other guy. He's making a big stink about whose name goes first and says he feels you shouldn't have a credit at all." I said, "I've got a surprise for you, Bobby. Give the whole thing to him. I don't want my name on it." So that film was released without my name, even though they used some scenes of mine.*

Then I went back to work on *My Outlaw Brother*. That was really a weird

---

*The script for *The Barefoot Mailman* is officially credited to James Gunn and Francis Swann.

project. Ben [Benedict] Bogeaus was the producer. Elliott Nugent, a well-known Broadway veteran, was supposed to direct the film. He had been one of the authors of [the hit play] *The Male Animal*. I'd turn in pages, and my secretary would tell me, "Don't tell anybody I told you this, but all the pages that you turn in are being rewritten by the director." That's what he was doing; there was some kind of insanity about it. So I just finished the script inside of a week, did the whole job, ground it out. I hadn't wanted to take the assignment in the first place, but they had raised my weekly salary. Everything I did was changed by the director. Bogeaus was so grateful for my having done it so fast that he gave me additional-dialogue credit.

Pretty disappointing experiences. How were you feeling about being a screenwriter by now?

Really lousy. I was thinking of what else I could do to make a living. I was thinking about leaving the film industry entirely. But our agent, Sam Weisbord, Abe Lastfogel's right-hand guy, called me and said, "I want you and Ben to get together again and do something. I made a big sales pitch to somebody at Metro about *The Boy with Green Hair*, and they have a project that they want you and Ben to work on."

They had a book called *The Wild Country*, by Louis Bromfield, about a young kid and his relationship with his grandfather. There's something typically Hollywood about that logic. They thought, "These guys wrote one movie about a kid and his grandfather, so now they can write another one." [The producer] Carey Wilson was one of the really old-time producers. He had been a writer. He was always talking about Jean [Harlow] and Irving [Thalberg] and Norma [Shearer]. He had written the first *Mutiny on the Bounty*. Ben and I would sometimes have meetings with him that would go from ten to one; we'd break for lunch, come back at two, and resume—during which time we would get in maybe two minutes of our own ideas. All the rest of the time we were listening to him telling stories about the old days, reenacting scenes from *Mutiny on the Bounty*. He'd say, "Let's see, now. I'm Clark Gable, and you're the camera. The camera pulls back. Go ahead, pull back!" So I'd take a few steps back. It was surreal! It was also endless.

Was this 1950 yet?

No, 1949. After seven months of this, Ben left with his family; they went to Europe. He wasn't even blacklisted then. He left because Adrian Scott and Eddie Dmytryk were going to do *Christ in Concrete* in England, and Ben preferred to do that, so he went over to write the screenplay. I stayed for another three or four months of Carey Wilson, on a weekly salary.

But you went on to write Mrs. Mike?

The production manager on *The Boy with Green Hair* was a terrific guy named Ruby Rosenberg. He was also production manager on *Murder My Sweet*, which changed Dick Powell's career. Ruby dropped in to my office at

Metro one day and said, "There's a picture with Dick Powell that's starting up. They went into the first week of shooting without a finished script. They want a writer who will keep up with them as the shooting goes along." I said, "Forget it. I've just had eleven months on weekly salary, and I'm not going to put my head in that kind of a meat grinder." He said, "Just do me a favor and talk to the two producers. Tell them you don't want to do it." The two producers were Sam Bischoff and Ed Gross. Bischoff I had heard was a monster, and I said no even before I met him.

We were still living in this apartment on Riverside Drive in North Hollywood, and Dick Powell came to see me. He was a big star. I'd never met him. "Look," he said, "you really can write your own ticket. We're in terrible trouble. Every day that passes without shooting costs us an enormous amount of money. I know the salary you were getting. We're going to double that." I was tempted a little, but I said, "There is one condition: I never have to talk to Sam Bischoff." He hesitated for a moment and said, "Okay, I'll protect you."

They had stopped production. I had to write the rest of the film in sequence. I'd write a scene, my secretary would type it up with something like nine carbons, then I would take these copies down to the set and distribute them. I'd give them the material, and they would read it, and it was like waiting for the jury to reach a verdict. Finally they'd nod. They'd go out and shoot it. Then I'd go on to the next scene and be back just as the director said, "Cut!"

After several weeks of this, I got into a fight with Sam Bischoff, because Dick Powell had said, "Please, just meet with him once to take the pressure off me." I made that mistake. We immediately got into a yelling, screaming argument. I said, "I'll go up and clear out my desk." I moved off the lot. Then I read in the trade papers that production on *Mrs. Mike* had stopped again. About a week or ten days passed, and I got a call from Bischoff. He said, "I want you to come back." So my agent got me a raise, and I started right back in.

The leads in the film, Dick Powell and Evelyn Keyes, were marvelous to me. One of the temptations to go back was that they were heading out on location at Big Bear Lake. I demanded a house on the lake for me and my wife and my small son, and a babysitter every night. You can't bluff in that kind of situation. You have to be willing to walk away.

So we got this big house, right on the lake. Meanwhile, Dick Powell and June Allyson had a little room in a hotel, so our house was the only production office we had, and we had production meetings there every night. June Allyson and Evelyn Keyes and Dick Powell would come over to the house. Evelyn, June, and Helen would go bowling in the village, and Dick and I would work on the next day's shooting. Every time she came in, June Allyson would look around, and you could almost see the smoke coming out of her ears as she was thinking, "What's a writer doing with this house?"

While that script was painful and difficult, it was also a marvelous experience. We shot the film and finished it, and the film got good reviews. I think

I like it better than any other movie that I've written. After it was over, Dick asked me to a rewrite on another film that he planned to do. Powell was one of the great businessmen of this community, a multi-multi-millionaire even then, who did a lot of things that were money-wise. But he was very nice in all of his personal relationships.

Just then, the [court appeal of the Hollywood] Ten got going, and the amicus curiae brief was being circulated. Dick was an ardent Republican, but I decided to take a chance. I said, "Dick, I've got something I'd like you to sign." He said, "What is it?" I said, "You won't take my word for it and just sign?" He said, "Do you want me to?" I said, "You read it and then sign it." He read the thing, looked up at me and smiled, and said, "Give me your pen." And he signed it. He said, "I'll tell you something. If there were a gentleman in the White House, these guys wouldn't be in this trouble."

This was 1950 and you were about to write Dream Wife?

Yeah. Somebody had given me the idea, a guy who used to live up in the Hollywood Hills, near where the "Hollywood" sign is. He used to take walks, and there was a woman who used to walk her dog along with him. He got to know her, and they talked. She was trained to be an opera singer, and part of her training was to become fluent in Italian. She told this guy that when Howard Hughes was having an affair with an Italian actress who didn't speak any English, he hired this woman. She would be in the bedroom while these two people were screwing, and when the actress would say something Hughes would ask, "What did she say?" She'd have to translate into English, or from English to Italian if he wanted to say something to her. It was the most humiliating experience she had ever had, she said, but there was a lot of money involved.

That became the basis for an idea about a guy in the import-export business who has just returned from a trip in the Middle East. He is offended, upon his return, by American women's aggressiveness. He says to his partner, "You know, in a little village I know about, there's a woman who has been brought up to cater to a man's every whim. She would be perfect, a dream wife." He wants to send for her, but he can't speak her language. He fails to get a professor who is an expert in Middle Eastern languages, but the professor's daughter—it happens to be Deborah Kerr—can also speak the language, although she is opposed to this project in every way.

Dream Wife was really a marvelous vehicle for a lot of feminist values. Sidney Sheldon was the producer. I sold a treatment to MGM, and the studio guaranteed me twelve weeks' salary to do the screenplay. I finished the first draft somewhere around the eight-week period. Sidney read it and said he loved it. He sent it to Dore Schary. This was on a Thursday. Friday morning, when I came in, Sidney said, "Dore read the script and said, 'Don't change a word. I'm sending it to Cary Grant in the morning.' " "But," Sidney added, "it may take who knows how long for Grant to make up his mind or even to get around to reading it. Why don't you take some time off, take a little vacation? Look around for books or anything you like that you think will make a movie, and the studio will buy it for you. We're a team, and we're going to be making more pictures together." I said, "Great!"

I didn't hear anything for a long time. Finally I called and said, "How are we doing about Cary Grant?" He said, "Well, Grant feels that his part isn't big enough." I said, "You're kidding! The whole thing is about him. I mean, how could his part not be big enough?" He said, "Well, it isn't really a matter of size. He just feels that his part doesn't really motivate the story." I said, "Sidney, I don't know what the hell you're talking about, but I'll come in and make whatever changes we need to, because I owe the studio four weeks anyway." He said, "You know how they feel—that the first writer has written himself out, and they want to put another coin in the slot." I remember that phraseology. I was really thrown by it, but I was not suspicious yet.

By this time, the [second round of HUAC] hearings in Washington were over. When I finally got my subpoena, however, it was dated before that phone call from Sheldon! The studio apparently knew before I did. In the meantime, I had gone out to try and get other work. My agent was then Henry Lewis, who said that I was really hot and he was getting calls from everybody about me. He sent me to different meetings about different projects, and I kept running into strange roadblocks. Studio people professed to be anxious to see me, but when I got to their offices, there was something about their attitude that I wasn't able to identify. Then I had this really strange meeting with Jerry Wald, who ate his lunch during the whole meeting and talked on the phone without paying any attention to me in the least.

Our attorney had advised, "It would be good if someone would announce his subpoena, because then we could start to build rallies around the issue and begin to raise money for defense, as well as educate the public." So at one of the meetings of the people who had been subpoenaed, I said, "Look, I might as well announce it, because I know they know anyway. It's clear from the reception I'm getting at the studios that they know." I called the *Hollywood Reporter* and *Variety* to give them a statement. Both of them took the statement, but they never ran it in print. So I called both to place an ad. The *Reporter* wouldn't even accept the ad. Here it is, as it ran in *Variety*:

> Like most of you, I have been opposed to the Un-American Activities Committee for a long time. To change this attitude now that I have been officially challenged by the Committee's subpoena would be dishonest. To cooperate by sacrificing others' careers for one's own would be degrading. To repudiate past ideas and associations which dissent from the Committee's standards of orthodoxy, branding oneself a dupe, would be humiliating. The course of dishonesty, degradation, and humiliation feeds the Committee's insatiable hunger for publicity and aids in the ruin of the motion-picture industry. The Committee

has demonstrated that it thrives on submissiveness and hysteria. I am
with all who are for resistance and reason.

*You actually appeared before the Committee on September 18, 1951, and brought
a statement to read, which you were not allowed to read aloud at that time. So
would you read that into the record?*

Right.

> If you modify freedom of expression and conscience and association
> according to the current popularity of the words expressed and the
> beliefs held and the people associated with, you have destroyed those
> freedoms. They are destroyed not only for an unpopular minority but
> for everyone. For everyone must then consider his words and his be-
> liefs and his associations with caution, lest they be interpreted in an
> unpopular way.
>
> Every man has the right to be unpopular or even to be wrong in
> these areas without suffering the consequences of official censure,
> blacklisting, or jail. Most peace-loving people will find themselves
> unpopular with this Committee. A citizen may be held accountable
> only for his acts. This principle has been written into our Constitution
> and has been spelled out for this Committee often and eloquently.
> The Committee's continued intimidation of all people under the pre-
> text of attacking a few is its fundamental purpose.
>
> I do not, therefore, intend to enter my beliefs or my associations in
> a popularity contest in which the members of this Committee are the
> judges. I shall offer no cooperation to the evil purpose of these hear-
> ings, except that which the force of law compels. I shall resist the
> Committee in every way that the Constitution provides.

*Shortly after this, you wrote a similar speech for an actor who had been blacklisted,
whom you call Fred Smith.*

A number of meetings were held in various public auditoriums and some
in large homes, fund-raisers for legal expenses, primarily. Different writers
would be assigned to the blacklisted actors. I drew Fred and also Howard Da
Silva. Howard gave me a great compliment afterward. He said, "You write
words that fit my face." [Laughs.] The style in which I wrote speeches for him
was totally different from any way that I would ever talk, because Howard
was a florid man. It was really great to hear him say one of my speeches.

Fred was a young actor who, after the blacklist, became a furniture salesman. He never worked [as an actor] again, which is why I'm reluctant to use
his name. But here is part of the speech:

> For the past twelve years I have tried to become a good actor. I have
> studied and worked with little-theater groups, stock companies, and
> the Actors Lab here in Hollywood, and in a very small way in motion

pictures. In a personal sense, I feel that I have achieved some success. [But] I've won no awards. I've received no recognition from the public.

One Monday morning, I was served with a subpoena by the Un-American Activities Committee of the House of Representatives, and suddenly I found recognition thrust upon me. Before that Monday morning, very few movie producers knew my name. Since that Monday morning, every producer in Hollywood knows my name. I know that I was a little frightened at first, but I also was a little proud. I was proud and flattered at the company I was placed in.

But when I tried to trace back my activities through the years to find the things that had won me the right to this recognition, I became ashamed. I never spoke up boldly against injustice or evil. I never gave more than lip service to the struggle to win economic and civil rights for the American people. Except for signing a petition to outlaw the atom bomb, I never took any concrete action to help ensure a peaceful life for my child and all of our children.

Why me, Fred Smith, unknown? I did a lot of thinking about this. Almost hopefully, I wondered if maybe the part I had in *Union Station* was weightier than I had realized. But no, this wishful thinking lasted about ten seconds, and I faced the fact that I was still Fred Smith, unknown. If an Academy Award–winning actor is blacklisted or if a brilliant and successful screenwriter is blacklisted, it might not ring any warning bells in you who go about your anonymous jobs, unmolested as yet. But if the finger is pointed at Fred Smith, unknown, then all other unknowns had better watch out: the goal is conformity for the entire population. To those of you who turned to your neighbors when I was introduced and asked, "Who is he?" My answer is, "Who are you?"

Had you begun to plan your new life before you testified? Or was it only after your testimony that you had to begin to try and establish a new profession or a new way of making a living?

It was only afterward, and right away I had two more so-called opportunities to write scripts. Ed Gross had a movie for me. He said, "Would you be willing to write something under another name?" I said, "Yes," and he said, "I want to come see you. I have a project."

We lived on top of a hill. In those days, anybody who wanted to express their support would call, make a date, come up, and say hello, always arriving out of breath. I soon realized that they were parking their cars down at the bottom of the hill, because they didn't want their cars parked in front of our house. [Laughs.] Anyway, Ed Gross came in—out of breath—and said, "I've got a project in mind, and you would be perfect for it." He said, " 'The Larry Parks Story.' Here's the story: a guy's made some mistakes, he tries to go straight, and everybody kicks him in the ass. Who could write that better than you?" [Laughs.] I couldn't believe Gross had such an absolute lack of understanding that he really thought I was going to do that! He was kind of shocked when I told him I wouldn't.

Then there was a producer I had met because we were among the founders of the Oakwood School [a progressive secondary school in North Hollywood], and I was very active in the parents' group there. He called me and asked me to meet him somewhere, some remote place. He asked, first thing, "Are you willing to write something under a pseudonym?" I said "Absolutely." So we met, and he started to outline this picture. It was really a gung-ho, pro–Korean War story. I was listening, and I couldn't believe my ears; finally I stopped him. "Look," I said, "what the hell makes you think I'd be willing to write that? If I were willing to write that, I wouldn't be blacklisted!" He said, "What the hell's the fuss? Nobody's going to know. You're going to use a different name!" [Laughs.]

I had one more interesting encounter. Isobel Lennart asked me to meet her. She had gotten her subpoena while she and I were at Metro [MGM]. She was pregnant at the time, and she had gotten a doctor to excuse her from testifying. She thought she had beaten the rap, but she was being very careful. We met at this drive-in somewhere, and she said, "I'm doing very well. I want to put you on a weekly salary." I was really stunned by her gesture and very appreciative. But I did have some reservations about her, so I said, "Don't do it." She couldn't stay pregnant all the time. When they finally got around to her, she folded immediately. So I was fortunate to have kept my distance.*

Had there been any open discussion among the people subpoenaed in 1951 about the possibilities of writing under pseudonyms?

Unless you had reason to believe that somebody would be sympathetic to being a "front," you would usually try to get someone else, preferably an agent, to sound them out. If you went to another writer and said, "Look, I've got this idea which would make a good movie, and I'd be willing to do it under a pseudonym," and he said, "Well, let's hear the idea"—well, if he liked the idea himself and decided not to hire me, I could never go to court over the issue. That was one of the things that happened to everyone. We were taken advantage of a lot.

The blacklist provided temptations for certain people who would not or-dinarily ever have had them. There was another guy I knew from the Oak-wood School. Actually, we were in the Army together before I went overseas. He was a special-material writer. He used to write special material for acts in

---

*Isobel Lennart (1915–1971), an erstwhile Hollywood Communist, was among the most com-mercially successful women writers who became friendly witnesses. She wrote numerous screen-plays (earning two Oscar nominations), including *Anchors Aweigh, East Side, West Side, Love Me or Leave Me, Please Don't Eat the Daisies, The Sundowners, Two for the Seesaw,* and *Funny Girl,* from her own Broadway play. She died in an automobile accident at the peak of her career.

Las Vegas, for stand-up comics, and he also did some radio writing. He kept coming to me with projects that he wanted to write, but it was always his project, his name would be on it, and presumably I would be paid if it ever sold. But I hated every idea he offered. So I said to him, "Try to get a job where you get paid regularly. I'll write for you, and we'll split the money." He got a job writing for *The Colgate Comedy Hour*. I wrote some of the sketches, and he gave me half the money.

The more successful that show became, the more he resented me. He kept cutting my share lower and lower on the premise that "You sit in front of a typewriter all day, but I've got to go to these goddamned conferences. They ask me a question about the script, and I don't know what the hell the answer is. It's very tense work." He had me down to a third or a quarter of what he was getting. Finally, I said good-bye. I never saw him again, except on the picket line during every strike. [Laughs.]

You started doing some work as a photographer.

I had been interested in photography since my experiences with Cartier-Bresson. I started working with a professional photographer. He would take me with him on shoots, and I'd get a percentage, and then he began to turn some of the work over to me. For a time I stopped doing any writing at all. It was kind of funny, because we were doing high fashion. This guy had a great eye, and he understood fashion. I also had a good eye for photography, and boy, I really enjoyed that profession. Unfortunately, as I became more and more successful, the demands on me were greater, and I had to decide whether to make investments in more expensive equipment.

Then you got back into writing, this time television, almost by chance, while you were photographing a show in Las Vegas.

We had been very close friends with Jerry [Jerome L.] Davis and his wife. Jerry and I had occupied adjoining offices at Metro, and he was in my office most of the time with his story problems before I appeared before the Committee. Afterward, I never heard from him again. But later I learned that he and his wife had broken up, and that he had married [actress] Marilyn Maxwell.

I was in Las Vegas on a shoot, and she was doing a show there. The temptation to photograph her was irresistible. I worked my way through a crowd taking pictures, approaching her with a camera and flashbulb so that I faced her and Jerry's back was to me. I said, "Miss Maxwell?" She looked up and gave me the big starlet smile. He turned around, his jaw dropped, and I hit the flash button. I got this great picture of him with his mouth wide open. [Laughs.]

He said, "I want to see you in the morning." The next morning there was a knock on my hotel door, and he came in. He said, "I've got this assignment at Paramount, and here's the problem." He told me the story, and suddenly it was like no time had passed, like he was in my office at MGM again. One day, a short time later, he turned up at my [photography] studio and said, "Look, I've been thinking about it. Where could you find a better front than me, and where could I find a better behind than you?" So we started working under his name."

I was glad to have the money; I thought of it only in terms of money. I was never really able to get sufficiently ahead in photography. I had started too late in life. I told Jerry, "Take any assignment you can get." He then moved into the same little building, with an office above mine. We had extensions of each other's phones, and I rigged up a buzzer system. When he got a phone call and thought that I should be listening to it, he'd just buzz me, and I'd pick it up and listen in.

Because my name wasn't on any script that I wrote, I had a great sense of freedom. [Laughs.] I said to myself, "Who cares what kind of shit it is? Just do it, as long as it doesn't violate any real principles." Mostly we did sitcoms, and the worst you could say about them was that they were just silly and dumb.

How did you begin working under the name Tom August?

One day Jerry said to me, "Look, my psyche can't handle this situation with my name on your work. You've got to take a pseudonym, and we'll work as a team openly, but with you having a separate, different name." I asked, "Maybe we'll get caught that way?" He answered, "Nah, you're paranoid about that. Nobody gives a damn anymore."

He insisted, so I took the name Tom August. Actually, I'd taken the name Tom August before, when I had written the lyrics to the theme song for a CBS show called *Climax*. I knew André Previn, who was doing the music. I gave him the sheet with the typed lyrics. He put it on the piano, looked at it for thirty seconds, pulled out a little notebook with sheet-music paper, and wrote a melody. He handed it back to me and said, "That's the song." A day or so passed, after which I got a call from André, who said, "Metro won't release me to write for television, so you're going to have to 'front' for me." [Laughs.] So it was "Words and Music by Tom August." The arranger took what was a plaintive ballad and forced it into an up tempo, which he wouldn't have dared do if André's name had been on the song. But that song got me into ASCAP [the American Society of Composers, Authors, and Publishers] and actually made more money than anything André had ever written up to that time.

Did you share the money?

Of course. It was *his* music and they were *my* lyrics. So I already had the name Tom August. Then the first program Jerry and I got called in on was *Bachelor Father*. The producer was Everett Freeman, whom I had known at Metro. I felt that the risk was worth taking, because even though he was a conservative guy, I didn't think he would remember my name, although he might remember my face. That's exactly what happened. He said, "Oh, Tom, of course. I remember you from Metro." We worked on that show for quite a while.

Later on, you and Helen worked together on The Donna Reed Show?

The Donna Reed Show *was really good to us. Donna was terrific. I later learned that before the producer hired us, he went to Tony Owen, Donna's husband, and told him about me, getting his okay. Owen said, "But I don't want to know about it." That kind of thing happened a lot.*

We worked on that show for four years—doing other things, too—but in the meantime, that producer left. Tony Owen offered me the producership. I was afraid to take the chance, because it would put too much of a spotlight on me, and it might endanger him. So I said, "No, I don't feel comfortable doing that."

Jerry was made a producer at Warner Brothers, and that's partly why Helen and I started working together. I think we started in 1958, and we collaborated on other shows besides *Donna Reed*. Helen collaborating with me was really only a formalization of what we had always done, anyway. Anything I did I would always discuss with her, and she gave me input. She was terrified of meetings and conferences—not just in terms of the blacklist but those kinds of situations in general. I coached her about producers and how to handle them. A producer might have a problem with something that we wrote, and we'd pretend to argue about the possible solutions. Helen would say the right sentence, and the producer would say, "Of course, that's it!" But I didn't have to coach her very much. She handled herself very well immediately.

How was writing for television different from films?

Different and horrible. It's the worst job ever invented, from a writer's point of view. It grinds you down and has nothing to offer but money. Even with that, you have to work really fast to come out ahead. There are certain things we just would not do. We would not do any of the more violent shows or any of the other shows with crappy values. We tried to do some decent scripts, even though they didn't always come out as we would have liked.

Meanwhile, a lot of your close friends had left Hollywood. Weren't you feeling increasingly isolated here?

In a way. So far as I can remember, we were among the few blacklisted writers who never left the community. Helen was running a sort of USO for blacklisted people. Whenever they'd come to town, they'd call us, and we'd have some kind of a get-together. Helen and I were tempted to go abroad, but we felt we couldn't take the chance because of our daughter, who was ill during this time. We weren't remaining here solely as a matter of principle. [Laughs.] It just worked out that way.

Why did you leave The Donna Reed Show *ultimately?*

We had done something like thirty episodes for Donna. I guess I left because I was getting too much work on some of the other shows. Did I tell you about the [Dalton Trumbo] show I did for *Studio One*? After there was the big deal about [the Oscar-winning film] *The Brave One*, and people realized Trumbo had written it [as Robert Rich], he was beginning to get too many movie assignments. The head of CBS called him up and asked, "Would you do a comedy script for *Studio One* based on the Robert Rich masquerade?" Trumbo didn't think he'd have time to do it, so he recommended me.

I met with Bill Dozier, my old boss from when I was working at Paramount as a reader. I told him that I would be using the name Tom August. I gave him an approach to the story, and he liked it. "But," he said, "I'm a little worried. Nobody knows who Tom August is. Do you know someone who is not blacklisted and whose name we could put with yours as a collaborator? That would help." I said. "Yes, I know someone, Jerry Davis." He responded, "Terrific. He just wrote a show for us that was very successful." It was one that I had written which Jerry had put his name on! [Laughs.]

At this time Jerry actually had a job in Las Vegas working for Jerry Lewis. But he would come to Hollywood for the meetings every once in a while. *Studio One* was done like theater. You rehearsed it before a live audience; then it went on live. But CBS wouldn't let the series go on the air with this script. The guy could be blacklisted in the story but not for political reasons, so in the rewritten version he was blacklisted because he had slugged a producer! It was dumb. The director took me aside one day and confided to me, "I don't think you really know what you've written here. This isn't about a guy who slugs a producer; this is really about a guy who was blacklisted politically, and we're just using that plot as a blind. Now, I know a lot about the blacklist, because I know all those guys back East." In other words, he took me aside and explained the blacklist to me!

I was tempted to tell him. Ultimately I decided not to, because it would have compromised him.

When was the point at which you would say the blacklist was over and Tom August, or Al Levitt, was now an employable person?

It happened much later, at Twentieth Century–Fox. Helen and I were offered the story editorship of a show called *The Ghost and Mrs. Muir*. That meant going to the studio every day. Our daughter was then living at home, and Helen said, "There's no way I can do that; you have to take that job yourself. See if I can do a script from time to time." I asked the agent, "Who's the producer?" He said, "Stanley Rubin." I said, "You'd better tell him that Tom August is Al Levitt."

Stanley Rubin was a guy I'd known for a lot of years. He was, I think, briefly in the Party, and he had been a friendly witness. I figured I wouldn't have to make a decision. As soon as he was told who I was, I was sure Stan would say, "Thanks, but no thanks." Instead, he said he wanted to meet with me. So I figured, "What the hell. What do I have to lose?"

What year was this?

Around 1967. I went to see Stan, and he asked the question that always gets asked in this kind of situation: "Aren't you afraid someone will blow the whistle on you?" I said, "Nobody cares anymore." I figured I was not going to get the job, because if I were him, I wouldn't want Al Levitt there every day reminding him of what he had done. But he did hire me. I was hired as Tom August. And I've got to tell you, he was the best producer I've worked for since Adrian Scott. He created a really good atmosphere around the office in terms of the things necessary to get the work done.

The only time there was ever any mention of the secret between us was when he made a decision about something related to the show and afterward said, "God, I shouldn't have done that." It was a totally nonpolitical, purely aesthetic decision. He was annoyed with himself, however, and he kept saying, "I shouldn't have done that." I said, "There's no point in torturing yourself about it. You did it, and we'll be able to live with it." He answered, "God knows I've lived with enough guilt, so I guess you're right."

The first year *The Ghost and Mrs. Muir* was a good show, one of the few television shows that I didn't squirm at when I saw my work. While I was working on that show, I told my agent to try to market a screenplay under my own name. When the screenplay was sold, a trade-paper article said, "Tom August, story editor at Twentieth Century–Fox, sold a screenplay to Universal [Pictures] which he wrote under the name Alfred Lewis Levitt." Right after that, I worked for [director] Bob [Robert] Wise at Universal, and he knew my true identity. By that time I was back to using the name Levitt.

The Writers Guild magazine used to print a list every once in a while with the notice: "We have residuals for the following people. If you know them or any members of their family, please call the Guild and we'll send them their money." One day, when I was still Tom August, I saw "Alfred Lewis Levitt" on that list. I called the Guild and said, "I'd like you to send it to my attorney." I didn't want them to have my address; I didn't want them to link Alfred Levitt with me. They said, "You'll have to send us a letter authorizing us to send it to your attorney." I wrote the letter and gave them my attorney's name and address. When the package came, it contained an envelope, addressed to me, in care of Tom August. Inside there was a check made out to Alfred Lewis Levitt. On the check stub it said, "a.k.a. Tom August." I had gone through all this for nothing! [Laughs.]

Universal was apparently the first to know, because they were the first company to computerize. I always used my own Social Security number, because I had lost enough on the deals where I had used fronts and didn't receive any contribution to my pension plan or to Social Security. I didn't dream anybody would check my Social Security number. Mike Franklin, the executive director of the Writers Guild, then called my attorney and asked, "What do we do about the Tom August/Al Levitt situation?" I said, "Maybe it's time for me to go back to using Levitt, and I'll use August as a registered pen

name." So they changed my membership in the Guild from August back to
Levitt.

*Is it ever fair to say that the blacklist has ended for everyone? Do you feel that the
effects still hurt?*

It's frequently asked by people less knowledgeable than you, "When did
the blacklist end?" As though someone rang a bell and said, "Okay, now it's
over." Of course, it ended at different times for different people. But even
then it was never clear-cut. There were still people who were just as uncomfortable with blacklisted writers.

*I guess the natural culmination to the blacklist story would be the committee that
the Guild formed to supplement the pensions of blacklisted writers. Why don't you
explain how that got started and what it has accomplished.*

It was a by-product of another issue. The Guild had a pension plan which
placed the older writers at a great disadvantage. Most of those whose credits
were before 1948 got very small pensions. At every Guild meeting someone
got up and said, "It's outrageous," but pension plans are tightly controlled by
law.

The Guild decided to work out a formula to compensate writers disadvantaged by virtue of having been in the Guild longer: they would receive a
supplement out of the Guild treasury. They calculated it according to a very
specific formula that had to do with the years of work and number of credits.
When that happened, two people wrote letters to the Guild newsletter which
said, in essence, "What about the writers who are disadvantaged by virtue of
being blacklisted?" Those two writers were Lester Cole and Eddie [Edward]
Huebsch,* who wrote independently of each other. The Guild board decided
that blacklisting was a legitimate question.

The first step was to set up a committee, the Blacklisted Writers Screening
Committee. On that committee were Helen and myself, Frank Tarloff, and
several non-blacklisted writers, some young and some older. It would never
have happened without us, and others like us, who knew enough about that
experience to know that you could not simply transfer the criteria for older
writers to the blacklisted writers. It had to be much more subjective, and we
let some of the others take the lead. Some of these people were proposing
formulas richer than anything we would have dared to propose. We shut up!
[Laughs.]

---

*Described in *The Inquisition in Hollywood* as a key radical among those in the film industry
during the 1940s, writer Edward Huebsch (1914–1982) was a reader for Columbia in New
York during the 1930s. He arrived in Hollywood in 1945 and wrote or contributed to *Cigarette
Girl, Millie's Daughter, Sport of Kings, The Wreck of the Hesperus, Black Eagle, The Story of a
Horse*, and *Son of Dr. Jekyll*. Named and blacklisted in 1951, he found limited employment in
television but forged a relationship with director Robert Aldrich. He received a coscreenwriting
credit on *Twilight's Last Gleaming*, considered on of Aldrich's most political films.

Helen and I quickly learned to let others do most of the talking. What we did was to verify people having been blacklisted. Your book [Larry Ceplair and Steven Englund, *The Inquisition in Hollywood: Politics in the Film Community, 1930–1960*] was one of the official documents used. There were many interesting variations that came up. One guy came to us and said, "I was working all the time; suddenly I didn't get any work. I didn't know what the hell happened." Finally his agent told him, "You're on the blacklist for being a Communist." He told his agent, "That's impossible. I never was one." It turned out that the guy lived up in the Hills, he had converted his garage into an office, and he'd park his car on the street every day. What he didn't know was that his neighbor was a functionary of the Communist Party downtown, and that the FBI kept reporting that the writer's car was parked in front of his neighbor's house. We gave him a full blacklist supplement, because, indeed, he was a victim of the blacklist.

I think there were between twenty and thirty blacklistees who got special pensions. Of course, a number of blacklistees had already died. The supplemental pensions are an expense that keeps diminishing as the years go by, because there aren't any more people turning up for it. Recipients are dying.

Karen Morley

KAREN MORLEY, Los Angeles, California, 1983

INTERVIEW BY PATRICK MCGILLIGAN
AND KEN MATE

1946 *Unknown*
1947 *The Thirteenth Hour*
Framed

Six-Gun Serendade
Code of the Saddle.
1951 *M*

■

ACTRESS KAREN MORLEY didn't quite fit in at Metro-Goldwyn-Mayer in the early 1930s. Unconventional as a type, she fought the kittenish mold of the Hollywood ingenue, rejecting some parts that she found demeaning and seeking others with which she could better identify. Eventually, Morley behaved with unusual courage in breaking her studio contract in order to gain more freedom in her profession and then to go on the stage.

Before that happened, in the pre–World War II heyday of her career, Morley was sought-after by leading directors. She made her reputation in several well-remembered films, including Howard Hawks's *Scarface*, as the slinky mistress of crime boss Osgood Perkins; George Cukor's *Dinner at Eight*, as the understanding wife of Edmund Lowe, the doctor having an affair with Jean Harlow; *Arsene Lupin*, where she holds her own as the love interest of John Barrymore; John Ford's unlikely wrestling film, *Flesh*, as a duplicitous but sympathetic ex-con married to Wallace Beery; *The Littlest Rebel*, a charming Shirley Temple vehicle in which she plays one of the bemused adults; and *Pride and Prejudice*, as Greer Garson's friend, content with a loveless marriage. It attests to her intelligence in picking roles that the actress also appeared in several of the best-known "social awareness" dramas of the era, playing important roles in the New Deal fantasy *Gabriel Over the White House*, in King Vidor's *Our Daily Bread*, in Warner Brothers' coal-mining exposé *Black Fury*, and in the Spanish Civil War story *Last Train from Madrid*.

Off-camera, Morley was no less politically committed. Her first marriage, to a prominent director, Charles Vidor, a Hungarian-born Jew, led her into the anti-Fascist crusade and involvement in the cause of Spain. Later, in the South in the early 1940s, she joined a tobacco workers' organizing drive and then brought her unionist fervor back to Hollywood, becoming one of the few radicals in the Screen Actors Guild demanding action on longstanding wage and fairness issues. Her outspokenness during the final strike by the Conference of Studio Unions, an alliance of nine Hollywood craft unions, isolated her within the membership, and led to her being named as a Communist by several of the cooperative House Un-American Activities Committee witnesses.

One of her last screen appearances was in Joseph Losey's compelling remake of the early sound classic *M*, released in 1951. Her career was forfeited when she appeared before the Committee in 1952 and invoked the Fifth Amendment. In 1954 the former leading lady ran unsuccessfully for lieutenant-governor of New York State on the American Labor Party ticket.

Morley's second husband, the versatile character actor Lloyd Gough, was also named, and he also declined to give testimony. One of Gough's last parts had been a prominent one as the villain in Fritz Lang's western *Rancho Notorious*, filmed in 1951, shortly before his HUAC appearance. The producers couldn't cut him out of the plot, so his name was merely stricken from the end credits.

■

Writers and directors sometimes must cope with reactionary content in their scripts by exercising tricks of their craft, which is something that actors and actresses are not always able to do. What did you do when presented with characterizations that were either clichéd or degrading?

Well, I played lots of clichés. But about the only thing an actor can do, unfortunately, is to refuse a part—simply to turn it down—unless you are one of those people who have a great deal of influence in the studio. But ordinary actors under contract didn't have that kind of influence.

I remember one part I was offered, in *Viva Villa!*, which was made in 1933. It was presumably the story of the Mexican leader. According to the script I would play the daughter of a landowner when Villa was a peon, and I was supposed to whip him with a horsewhip. Later, when he was in a position of authority, he would give me a horsewhipping. I said, "It's disgusting. I won't do it." There was quite a little flap in the studio, with notes going back and forth saying that I was getting too big for my britches. But I didn't do it. I just refused. There isn't much more that an actor can do.

What did that role signify for you?

Well, it was symbolic, I think, with sadistic sexual overtones that I thought were ugly.

You were under a comfortable studio contract, yet you developed a reputation as someone who would not always do what you were told. How did you fit into the studio system?

I was terribly young—it seems to me now that twenty-one was very young—and I was headstrong. I didn't know how to handle difficult situations, except to refuse to play certain parts, which was not very smart. The studios at the time felt that they needed to guide their players, and they guided you to the extent that you felt that you were owned by your studio. The control of the bosses over actors was almost complete. What it amounted to was enormous interference in your personal life, especially if you were young and inexperienced.

Louis B. Mayer, for example, felt free to ask me if I was a lesbian; he told me I shouldn't marry the man I was going to marry—I should marry a man that he liked; and he told me that I shouldn't have a baby; and so on. The studio believed it could tell you to do just about anything that was good for the studio.

So, after I'd been at MGM a couple of years, I asked for my release, and eventually I got it. I don't think anybody else I knew of ever did that. I never signed a contract again, because I found that the intense pressures and the restrictions were just not for me.

You were married, early in the 1930s, to someone who had actually been a revolutionary. How did that influence your radicalization?

My first husband was [director] Charles Vidor, an Americanized Hungarian. He had fought for a couple of years, as a youth, in World War I. At the end of that time he had joined Bela Kun's forces and actually fought as a Communist revolutionary in Europe.* When that failed, he had to flee the country. He went first to Berlin and then came to this country. He was a true revolutionary at the time. In this country, however, he became a kind of fellow traveler who gave money to good causes. He didn't feel that this country was anywhere near ripe for revolution. I guess he was probably right.

It's impossible to remember what the thirties were like. There was this ghastly Depression, and there was this unbelievable horror going on in Europe. The effect of being married into a Jewish family during the 1930s, and of the growing terror against Jews in Europe, is what changed my whole attitude and my whole life. Although at first I didn't consider myself a radical, I became violently anti-Nazi, hysterically so, you might say. And when the tragedy of Spain came along, I think that really tipped the scales. After that I could be considered a radical.

You left Hollywood prior to World War II and went to North Carolina, where you helped to organize tobacco workers. Can you tell us about that experience?

After I was free from my MGM contract, I went to New York to make my way in the theater, which had been my first love. I did four flops, unfortunately, and I fell in love with a radical [Lloyd Gough]. When he went into the Army—the war broke out at that time—I followed, to visit him in North Carolina. That was where I really fell in love with the radical movement, in particular with the tobacco workers' union.†

---

*The revolutionary Hungarian government of Béla Kun (1919) attracted many intellectuals and artists, including philosopher, aesthetician, and literary historian György Lukács. It was replaced by the government of Miklós Horthy (1920–1944), one of the first Fascist regimes which, along with Mussolini's in Italy, helped set the stage for the rise of Hitler. Many Hungarian exiles in Hollywood rallied to the Popular Front left against Horthy and other Fascists.
†The United Cannery, Agricultural, Packing, and Allied Workers of America, uniting a diverse group of Mexican and Japanese field workers, southern black and white tenant farmers, and others, won its foremost victories during World War II, at the R. J. Reynolds Tobacco Company in Winston-Salem, North Carolina, at Campbell Soup in Chicago and Camden, New Jersey, and among workers in the cigar factories of the American Tobacco Company. Later changing its name to the Food, Tobacco, Agricultural, and Allied Workers, the union was one of the

People were organizing there under incredibly difficult circumstances. They were so brave, so clever, and so darling, and they were trying to organize black and white workers together, which was very difficult in the South. I had a lot of time on my hands, so I worked with them as a volunteer. I put on a radio program, I wrote articles, and I even drew cartoons for the union paper. We organized the Reynolds plant in North Carolina. I found the people absolutely wonderful, and that is when I truly fell in love with the left and wanted to be part of it. I came in the back door, you might say.

What happened, later on, to all those people you worked with and organized?

Don't ask. The union was destroyed in the McCarthy period, and people had a rough, rough time.

How did the repression of the Conference of Studio Unions strike in 1946 pave the way for the HUAC hearings?

I wasn't here for the first CSU strike [in 1945]. I was overseas with the USO. When I came back and returned to Hollywood, the CSU appeared to have won the strike, which had lasted the better part of a year. Then came the dream strike [in July 1946]. It lasted only three days. The CSU went out on a kind of general strike, the IATSE [International Alliance of Theatrical Stage Employees] respected the picket lines, and after three days there was a settlement, with a twenty-five percent increase in wages across the board. Now, this was thrilling, the kind of trade-union unity that people dream of. But the producers didn't dream of that, and, I believe, they went about making very, very sure that it never would happen again.

About this time, the actors were ready for their own contract negotiations. The Actors Guild had had a ten-year no-strike contract, and it was time for a new contract. Into this picture I came from the South and was happy to find a number of actors' committees getting ready with demands that they wanted incorporated in the new contract. The most important demand was payment for what were called 'reissues.' Movies were beginning to be rereleased back into theaters a second and third time, with the actors, of course, receiving no further payment. There were many other issues, such as a health and welfare plan, better working conditions, a higher minimum, and quite a number of issues like that.

In the rank-and-file committees we came up with ten major demands. When there was a mass meeting—the actors met once a year—our committee members got up one after another, presenting these proposals that they felt should be in the new contract. The excitement was unbelievable—people cheering and hollering and jumping up and down. We had assigned Larry Parks to make the summing-up speech. When he finished, he could have

---

most interracial to that date, with nonwhites (and women) in top leadership positions. It was expelled from the CIO in 1949 and all but destroyed in the McCarthy era, merging with the Distributive Workers Union and the United Office and Professional Workers Union.

been elected president [of the union] the next day. The members couldn't stop applauding. There was such gavel-banging from Robert Montgomery, but even he couldn't quiet them down. Montgomery and the other conservatives on the stage were absolutely aghast at what was going on, and I think they too made the determination that this was never going to happen again.

What were they worried about, ultimately—the craft unions merging with the talent unions?

This was very frightening to them, because the unions and guilds could very easily shut the studios down, if there was any real unity.

Do you think Larry Parks was singled out by HUAC later on because of his role in this campaign to present actors' grievances?

There is no question that this speech made Parks a prime target to be destroyed by the studios and HUAC.

Can you delineate the people who were politically to the right in the Actors Guild?

During the ten-year no-strike contract, there wasn't really much of a left or right. The Guild met publicly once a year, and we heard a report, but there wasn't much that could be done. People wanted conditions changed, but you couldn't get very much changed if you couldn't go on strike. It wasn't until the [third] CSU strike, at the end of the war [September 1946], that the Guild became polarized. Then it was Robert Montgomery and [George] Murphy and Leon Ames and Ward Bond—although he didn't do very much in the Guild, per se—on the right. On the progressive side were people like Anne Revere and Dorothy Tree and Julie [John] Garfield. There were other people with progressive ideas, but they didn't do an awful lot. There were never too many progressives, because you couldn't get elected to the board if you were a progressive. It was a very conservative board, the board appointed the nominating committee, and the nominating committee was very keen to nominate the same people all the time, so it was self-perpetuating.

The [first two] CSU strikes scared the conservative people in the Guild and frightened the producers, too, very much—because the producers had always known that the actors could shut the business down any day they wanted, any day. The actors never had any idea of their own strength.

What was the difference between the political complexion of the leadership of the IATSE and the CSU?

The IATSE was a very conservative union. It had a kind of smelly past. The CSU leadership varied a great deal. It was considered red, but it wasn't. There were all kinds of people represented in the CSU, and certainly the major leaders were friendly to the left, but they were not part of the left.

What was the response of the leadership of the Guild to the July 1946 CSU strike?

What happened, which was so clever and so sad, is that the producers gave the carpenters' union to the IATSE, which had never had the carpenters before. They knew very well that the carpenters could be persuaded to strike. Carpenters will strike very easily, because they can work somewhere else; they don't need studio work. The same was true of the painters. It was not true of the rest of the CSU—the screen editors, set designers, clerical workers, and so on—because they needed to work in the studios.

However, out the CSU went. The carpenters fell for it, the painters followed, so they dragged down the rest of the CSU with them; they fell for this stupid trap. The IATSE called it a jurisdictional dispute, but it immediately became a lockout of all the CSU unions. It's true that the strikers added some very important trade-union demands, but they also split the CSU from the IATSE. Who could believe at the time that the CSU would be destroyed? Nobody could believe it, and it took three years to do it, but the studios and the IATSE finally did succeed in destroying the CSU.*

A few of us had hoped that the CSU wouldn't strike, but once they had struck it was up to us to do our best to support them. This is what really split the Guild. It was so sad, because it split not on issues that concerned actors but on issues that concerned backlot workers.

When there developed this great interest in whether or not actors would cross the CSU picket lines, a huge, awful meeting happened. Outside the meeting, lined up, were thousands of workers in a silent vigil, and we had to go through their lines to attend our meeting. In that meeting, which was the most frighteningly rigged thing I've ever seen, there were huge guys walking up and down the aisles; you couldn't get to the mikes, and a maneuver was used to put an immediate vote of confidence on the floor and keep it there for two hours.

---

*To put it simply, the Conference of Studio Unions was left-wing in its orientation and had supported the activities of a number of Popular Front or Communist-led organizations throughout World War II. The CSU leaders hoped to organize and unite all non-IATSE locals in Hollywood. The issue that launched the third CSU strike, according to Larry Ceplair and Steven Englund, in their book *The Inquisition in Hollywood: Politics in the Film Community, 1930–1960*, was manufactured by Roy Brewer (international representative in Hollywood of the IATSE and a future ringleader of the blacklist) and the Producers' Labor Committee, "all of whom were spoiling for another go-round with the CSU."

Ceplair and Englund write: "Once again it was a question of jurisdiction, this time over set and prop building. Sets had always been erected by the carpenters (AFL) from material brought to them by grips (IATSE). Now, the IATSE claimed that 'set erecting' was different from 'set building,' and claimed jurisdiction over the former for a scab carpenters' local it had established during the 1945 CSU strike. The painters (CSU) refused to paint 'hot sets' (i.e., those 'erected' by IATSE people). The executives immediately locked all CSU personnel out of the studios."

The third strike would drag on for three years, according to Ceplair and Englund's account, resulting in the disappearance of the CSU, the purge of left-wing labor leaders, and "the end of the democratic labor movement in the picture business." Nancy Lynn Schwartz, *The Hollywood Writers' Wars*, also offers a detailed account of these labor struggles.

The atmosphere was really scary. Adolphe Menjou got up and said he was an authority on Communism, and this was a Communist strike if he'd ever seen one. Bob [Robert] Mitchum said he was going to hit that picket line with all of his one hundred and ninety pounds. [Frank] Sinatra said he'd have some friends to take him through the picket line, if necessary. It was just sickening. These were people they'd worked with all their lives, all their working lives, and they were standing outside waiting for our decision.

We were not interested in establishing whether there was confidence in the leadership; that was not the point. Anyway, finally the motion was moved, and yes, all right, they got a vote of confidence. Then, with great difficulty, I made the motion that we use our good offices to bring the strike to an end and until that time respect the picket line. This, of course, was ruled out of order—illegal. Why it was illegal I don't know, but that's the way it was; my motion was never voted on. So we went home, and the actors were just told that we would have to pass through the picket lines.

How did the strike end?

The strike simply petered out. The strikers either gradually went back to work or—most of them—were replaced by scab labor. About six thousand jobs were lost in that strike. What the strike really managed to do was make it clear who was who, because, you know, it wasn't very radical to be in favor of payment for reissues of movies; everybody was in favor of that. But this last CSU strike was used by the producers to make it perfectly clear who would cross picket lines and who wouldn't. The strike split all of the unions and all of the Guilds, the Writers Guild in particular. The people who didn't choose to cross the Writers Guild picket lines were particularly visible, and they and others became the targets when HUAC moved in for a nice list of probable names to investigate.

What was your initial response to the first wave of subpoenas, knowing that inevitably you would be subpoenaed and that you might have to go underground?

A number of people thought it would be important to see whether it was legal to dodge a subpoena, and so I said I'd be glad to find out. I went to the desert, to a tiny village, wore old clothes, just stayed out of sight, and used my brother-in-law's name. It was fun. It was also scary. I remember looking at the mountains and the desert, which are very dear to me, wanting to remember them very clearly if it turned out that I had to spend time in jail. But I found out that it's quite legal to dodge a subpoena.

As an actress whose face was well-known to the public and to prospective employers, were you able to find much work under the blacklist?

No. It was really murder to find work after being blacklisted, not just for me particularly but for all actors who were prominent, because their faces were well-known. I couldn't work anyplace where people might spot me. I couldn't even work as a saleslady in a fancy shop, for instance, which I might have done in New York. People in the theater like to say that it didn't have a blacklist, and technically it didn't. But I found that people went out the back door when I tried to look for work as an actress in the theater. So it was rough.

Benefit performances kept us alive. My husband played the concertina and sang his own satiric songs, and I did readings of poetry and bits in plays. I could work as an understudy, which I did, but not anywhere I could be seen. This kind of activity kept us going until my husband could get work in the theater. He worked as a standby and then finally got into a play. Alfred Lunt gave him a job. After that it became much easier, and a good thing, too. We managed, because he really supported me.

You also had a brief career as a public politician, when you ran for lieutenant-governor on a left-wing ticket in New York. Can you tell us a little bit about that?

Hard as it is to believe, I ran for lieutenant-governor of the state of New York on the American Labor Party ticket in 1954. We needed fifty thousand votes to stay on the ballot. We got around forty-eight thousand five hundred, because it was a terrible day, raining awfully. That was the end of the American Labor Party.* I ran on a totally feminist platform. I took care of women's issues for the Party at that time, which was lots of fun. I had a wonderful time. I like to think that I got more votes than a lot of people who are sitting in the Senate and House of Representatives from these little states with so few people in them.

What do you feel happened to film content—how women were treated in stories, and so on—in the 1950s, after all the progressives had been purged?

Movies just got worse. Movies have always been fairly violent, but in the old days writers tried to express human values. They tried, for example, to explain why a kid turned violent—he had been poor, his family was wretched, his boyhood was terrible. There was motivation other than just evil. The violence had to be motivated sensibly. This was a streak, I believe, of progressive thinking.

All that kind of treatment pretty much went by the board during the blacklist. Now violence became an art, a cult, and with it came the passive women. The beautiful, strong ladies went away, and the weak, beautifully

---

*The American Labor Party, founded in New York State in 1936 by a coalition of union leaders, Socialists, and Communists, enjoyed considerable success for a decade, repeatedly electing Representative Vito Marcantonio, the most left-wing figure in the U.S. Congress. The ALP also provided, through New York's open-primary system, hundreds of thousands of votes for President Franklin D. Roosevelt, Mayor Fiorella LaGuardia, and Representative Adam Clayton Powell. In 1944 an anti-Communist faction headed by David Dubinsky, president of the International Ladies Garment Workers Union, broke off to form the American Liberal Party. McCarthyism, along with the defeat and early death of Marcantonio, broke the ALP. It officially dissolved in 1956.

built women took their place, actresses chosen more for their figures than for their faces or for their characters. Then came "the ugly woman," "the cruel old woman," "the crazy old woman," "the despicable old woman." That saddened me, to see stars like Joan Crawford and Bette Davis playing such parts, which were really part of the "hate the ladies movement."

The passivity is what I found most distressing. Pretty soon there was not only passivity but cruelty toward women, and brutality and ugliness. Rape, or the threat of rape, which had in the old days hardly been ever more than faintly suggested, became part of almost every film. Now it's all over TV as well as the movies. Ladies had been treated better in the old days. There had been individual cases—the famous grapefruit scene that Jimmy Cagney did— but, on the whole, violence against women was very much frowned on. It was really out of the question. Only the worst heavy did it. Rape was only indicated in the most delicate terms.

What happened to themes of racial tolerance and justice?

One of the demands that our actors' committee had made was for the better treatment of minorities in movies and for parts that showed the true relation that minorities bear to American life. I needn't tell you that this was never adopted. The treatment of minorities simply disappeared, I would say, in movies in the 1950s. The issue simply wasn't treated at all. There were very few movies on the subject and few other than stereotyped parts.

Do you have any sympathy or feelings of forgiveness for informers?

Oh, that question of stool pigeons. During that period, it wasn't clear which way the country would go. There were strong Fascist elements on the march, and there was great fear as to what could happen. By the provisions of the McCarran Act, six concentration camps were set up; the money was allocated for them, and actually spent, about a quarter of a million dollars. And it was quite clear who would have been sent to them. It was in this atmosphere that people informed, and I believe that they didn't know whether they were only taking our jobs away or sending us off to something much, much worse. I think the informers realized the full extent of this, and that's why I personally don't forgive them, except maybe Sterling Hayden, who apologized publicly to everybody.*

You talked about the aesthetic effects and the jobs lost. How would you calculate the human toll on the people who were your friends?

I don't know how it could be measured. We know the spectacular cases— the deaths, suicides, divorces. The children suffered terribly. They felt that they had to sort of huddle together with the children of other progressive

---

*Actor Sterling Hayden was one of the people who named Karen Morley as a Communist in his March 21, 1951, testimony. In his 1963 autobiography, *Wanderer*, he denounced his opportunism bitterly, describing his appearance before HUAC as "a one-shot stoolie show."

families, because their classmates didn't understand what was going on or why their parents were being mistreated. They figured, of course, that their parents must have done something terrible. The stool pigeons' children did fine for a while. But I believe that our kids grew closer to their parents as they grew older and understood what happened, while a lot of stool pigeons' kids don't like their parents very much.

Abraham Polonsky

ABRAHAM POLONSKY, Los Angeles, California, 1997

PHOTO © WILLIAM B. WINBURN

INTERVIEW BY PAUL BUHLE
AND DAVE WAGNER

ABRAHAM POLONSKY
(1910–   )

1947 *Body and Soul.* Story, script.
     Golden Earrings. Coscript.
1948 *Force of Evil.* Coscript, director.
1951 *I Can Get It for You Wholesale.* Script.
1957 *Oedipus Rex.* Uncredited contribution.

1959 *Odds Against Tomorrow.*
     Uncredited contribution.
1968 *Madigan.* Coscript.
1969 *Tell Them Willie Boy Is Here.* Script, director.
1971 *Romance of a Horse Thief.* Director.
1979 *Avalanche Express.* Script.
1982 *Monsignor.* Coscript.
1991 *Guilty by Suspicion.* Uncredited contribution.

■

ABRAHAM LINCOLN POLONSKY, the son of a Jewish pharmacist, grew up in New York and graduated from City College and the Columbia Law School. He taught at City College and started writing for radio, scripting episodes of *The Goldbergs*, during the mid-1930s. By the end of the decade he was also writing for *Columbia Workshop Theatre* and Orson Welles's *Mercury Theatre of the Air*. As he continued working on plays and fiction, he visited Hollywood for the first time in 1937. But instead of immediately attempting a career there alongside so many other left-wing writers, he made a political choice. For two crucial years when the American labor movement was at the apex of both its influence and its collective idealism, he operated as educational director and newspaper editor of a regional CIO union north of New York City.

Right before world War II, Polinsky had a novel serialized in *Collier's* that attracted renewed attention from Hollywood. But military duty took precedence. After serving with the Office of Strategic Services, at times behind the lines in France, Polonsky returned to Hollywood at last, in 1945. After a disappointing start at Paramount, he became the leading scenarist for Enterprise, the best of the new, small production companies. With the hit boxing film *Body and Soul* under his belt, Polonsky then wrote and directed *Force of Evil*, considered by critics to be one of the best *films noirs* of the era, an intensely poetic, radically stylized work that nonetheless managed to observe the conventions of the crime genre. A script for *I Can Get It for You Wholesale*, produced while Polonsky was out of the country, rounded out his Hollywood life before the blacklist drove him out of the industry.

Polonsky had better luck than most of the blacklistees. In collaboration with Arnold Manoff and Walter Bernstein, he pseudonymously wrote the great majority of the scripts for one of television's "quality" shows, *You Are There*. In 1959 he wrote, without credit, a caper film for Harry Belafonte, *Odds Against Tomorrow*, the first of what was intended to become a series of projects with African-American stars and themes but which, like so many other blacklistees' projects of those days, failed to materialize. His "comeback" film, *Madigan*, directed by Don Siegel, is regarded as a classic cop drama, the model for Clint Eastwood's Dirty Harry series. *Tell Them Willie Boy Is Here* was one of the most unusual westerns of the late 1960s. *Romance of a Horse Thief*, which Polonsky took over as both scenarist and director in mid-production, offered a radical version of *Fiddler on the Roof*, the pre-Holocaust Eastern European Jewish saga as only an unbroken Marxist could tell it. Although they have their bright moments, his last two credits, *Avalanche Express* and *Monsignor*, were poorly received; in any event, both were impersonal jobs over which Polonsky exercised little control.

■

When and why did you join the Communist Party?

I joined the Party very late, after I got out of college, around 1935 or 1936, at the time of the Spanish Civil War. It was kind of funny, because I wasn't "joining" in the usual sense—I was already meeting with some of these people, mostly other instructors at City College, who were all members of the Anti-Fascist League. I myself taught English literature at City College from 1935 until the war started.

I came from a family of Socialists. Philosophically, I was always a materialist and a leftist. And I never felt alone. I came of age in a country that had come to a standstill, with fifty million people unemployed and the banks closed. I voted for FDR, and the New Deal was "left" enough for many of us.

What effect did your work in the Party in the thirties have on your development as a writer?

It didn't shape my artistic goals at all, because I had already taken a position of wanting to do socially significant art. The theoretical work of Marxism that everyone was talking about then I had already done. That kind of discussion with other Party members gave the political work around me some kind of intellectual basis. But we quarreled with the Party leadership, right from the beginning, on the various issues of writing. In our branch, anyway, at least among ourselves, we isolated the Philistines.

Let's go straight to Hollywood. When you arrived, you were already under contract.

Little, Brown published, as a book, a serial I wrote, *The Enemy Sea*. It was a potboiler which I wrote in three weeks. But it was a good story. I had been to sea, briefly, as an ordinary seaman when I left school, and I knew the subject. Paramount signed me to a deal which gave me fifteen or twenty thousand dollars on the rights and a job as a writer on staff. However, even before I received the contract, I went overseas to serve in the OSS [Office of Strategic Services].

When I got back, I took a military plane and went to see [producer] Bill [William] Dozier at Paramount. His secretary was Meta Reis. He kept me waiting, and I started calling him all kinds of names—to her. Either she told him what names I was calling him or he overheard me. In any case, when he finally called me in, he said, "You may have a contract, but you're not going to work here." I put a letter from [OSS director] Bill [William] Donovan on his desk, saying that the OSS was going to issue a story covering my new career in Hollywood, which it did. Dozier had no choice. My job was protected by a law that had been passed to preserve the jobs of GIs when they returned from the war. But behind my back Dozier said, "Fire that son of a bitch as soon as you get a chance."

How did you learn how to write screenplays?

I didn't have to learn how to write screenplays. I took one look at them and knew. That's not quite true. When I went to Paramount, I made sure I saw every movie they had in stock. On the other hand, I really didn't know how to direct. But I didn't come out to Hollywood looking to become a screenwriter or a director. I came here because I had a job waiting for me.

But you had a longstanding interest in movies.

I had an interest going back to childhood. In the Bronx, where I spent part of my boyhood, the Saturday movies influenced our daily play for the rest of the week. I grew up with movies.

But I started out in radio. The first time I visited Hollywood was in 1937, as a guest of Gertrude Berg, when I was writing for her radio show [*The Goldbergs*]. I was met by a *New Yorker* writer who asked me, "What the hell are you doing here? I'm trying to make enough money to get back to New York." He never could make enough money, because he drank it all up. He told me, "I'm going to show you how terrible everything is here." He took me on a set, and it was terrible—to him. He complained, "You see? This is what it's all about—chaos." But my reaction was, "This is wonderful!" All the small, marvelous details of film production I loved.

Your first film credit was at Paramount, with Golden Earrings, *a wartime romance with Ray Milland and Marlene Dietrich. Everyone remembers her line "I luff you, English."*

My script was about how the Gypsies became the first victims of the Holocaust. The studio cut all that out. They made it comic.

Then you moved to a much smaller, independent operation, Enterprise, where you got the assignment for Body and Soul. *Wasn't the story based originally on the life of the boxer Barney Ross?*

Arnold Manoff, who was also at Paramount, had been working on the Barney Ross story for six months. But Ross, a famous Jewish boxer, was a drug-user, and even though he was also a war hero, the studio eventually decided that they didn't want to make a movie about him.* Whatever Manoff wrote the studio wouldn't accept. So finally, one day, he was about to leave Paramount, and I happened to be visiting him in his office. He said to me, "Abe, I'm going back to New York. I can't stand this. They never make anything I

---

*Eventually the Barney Ross story was made as *Monkey on My Back*, directed by André de Toth, in 1957.

like." And then, "By the way, do you know John Garfield?" When I said, "Yeah," he said, "Let's go over and visit him at Enterprise."

Enterprise was two blocks away from Paramount, and while I was walking over I was also thinking of a boxing story for Garfield. And here comes the story that is *Body and Soul*. I got to Enterprise, and I told it to Garfield and his producer [Bob Roberts], and they loved it. Immediately they called a meeting of the heads of the studio and of production, and I told the story again. Now, since I'd had about an hour to think about it, I had a complete story.

I started to leave, and Charles Einfeld—he was second in command—said, "Where are you going, Polonsky?" I said, "I'm under contract to Paramount; don't you know that?" Einfeld said, "What should we do now that you've told us this story?" I said, "Get a writer; I'll make you a present of this story." And I left. I got to the gate at Paramount, and a guy stopped me and said, "They want you in the main office."

So you were loaned out from Paramount.

From then on, I was a two-thousand-dollar-a-week writer, even though I only got one thousand of it. Paramount got the rest. That was a lot of money. *Body and Soul* turned out to be a tremendous success. My script is the fundamental reason it turned out the way it did, although it was a wonderful job that James Wong Howe did. He had decided to use cameramen with experience at the battlefront, who had learned how to use hand-held cameras, in order to get some really unusual shots. That made *Body and Soul* kind of special for the time.

Enterprise didn't have that many hits.

Right. And no matter where you are working in Hollywood, there's nothing like having a hit. I went to see *Body and Soul* the first time it was being shown to the public at a preview. During the last part of the movie, the audience got up and started taking sides. People were arguing about Garfield's character, Charlie, when he faced the big decision of his life—"He should do this"; "No, he should do that"—as if the real thing were happening before their eyes. I never saw anything like that in a movie theater before. The head of the studio, Arthur Loew, turned to me and shouted, "It's a hit!" I said, "Maybe it's just a lot of noise." He said, "No, no, it's a hit!"

Robert Rossen was, of course, the director. How well did you know Rossen?

He was a good Warner Brothers writer; he made their kind of "social" pictures. He had that idea of himself.

His pictures frequently seem a mishmash of blue-collar melodrama and art film, as though he had always wanted to do both types of films and constantly mixed them up.

You have him down cold.

Was your script so tightly written that you were virtually codirecting?

No one codirects with Robert Rossen. You keep trying to prevent him from spoiling the picture, and writers hardly ever win those fights. We made Rossen promise that he wouldn't change a line of the screenplay, and then we found out he was handing out pages on the set, anyway. That was in his character.

I made sure he wouldn't change the picture in any substantial way. I was able to win a big fight about the ending because of my relationship to Garfield and [producer Bob] Roberts. Rossen wanted Garfield to go out and be killed, with his head stuffed into an ash barrel or something like that, which was just crazy. We shot both endings, his and mine.* When Rossen saw them both, he said mine was better.

People say that when Rossen, one of the original Hollywood Nineteen subpoenaed by Congress, didn't make the cut as one of the Ten, he was outraged. He thought that he was the great Hollywood Communist artist.

You wouldn't want to be on a desert island with Rossen, because if the two of you didn't have any food, he might want to have you for lunch tomorrow. The Communist Party was for years the best social club in Hollywood. You'd meet a lot of interesting people, there were parties, and it created a nice social atmosphere. He loved that. He was the kind of a guy who would go to public left-wing meetings and get up and say, "I donate a thousand dollars!" He never paid the money that he pledged. But he always got the applause. He was talented like Elia Kazan was talented, but like Kazan he also had a rotten character. In the end they both became stool pigeons. I figured all along that Rossen couldn't be trusted, but no one asked me.

Although Enterprise was not purely a left-wing operation, it relied heavily on various talented leftists, including you, Garfield, Rossen, Roberts, Manoff, Carl Foreman, and John Berry. Did that give you extra leverage to do projects your own way?

At Enterprise I was God, thanks to *Body and Soul*. I was the only one who had made that much money for them. Therefore, they thought that I could fix anything for them. For instance, one day Einfeld came to see me and said, "Ginger Rogers wants a picture made, and she says she'd like to talk to you." And Garfield insisted, "Go up and see her!" So I did. She wore a fur bikini outfit, and she took me down to her cellar and made me a black-and-white ice cream soda. She was very affable and nice. Since for those particular two seconds I was the most famous writer at Enterprise, she wanted me to write her picture. She had some book, and I took it and sketched out a possible

---

*In Polonsky's ending, the corrupt boxing promoter (played by Lloyd Gough) threatens Charlie Davis (John Garfield) after he wins a fight he earlier agreed to throw. "What makes you think you can get away with this?" he asks. Davis responds defiantly, "What are you gonna do, kill me? Everybody dies." In Rossen's ending, the promoter has Davis gunned down in an alley in revenge for not throwing the fight.

story line for her. But I didn't do any real work on it. I didn't want to work on a Ginger Rogers picture. I already knew that I wanted to direct my own picture.

It's surprising that she would pick you, given that she was well-known, along with her mother, for expressing conservative political views.

There's no vehemence against good writers working on a script. The vehemence comes before and after—before because "I can't get you," after because "You didn't do what I said."

How did Force of Evil *come about?*

Garfield said, "You want to direct? So direct!"—with him as the star, which would make it possible. "But," he said, "it has to be a 'melo' "—pronounced "meller," that is, a melodrama. We never called it a "melodrama"; we always said a "melo."

I knew a novel, *Tucker's People* by Ira Wolfert, which was about the numbers racket. I got Wolfert to come out here, and he stayed at Donald Ogden Stewart's house on the beach. There we broke the story down into what it needed to become a picture. I said to Wolfert, "I have to write the final screenplay, but you draft one and we'll see if there is something in it that we can use." Then I gave him coscript credit even though I didn't use anything in his screenplay except the lines from the book.

The book and the film show that it is an illusion to think that honest liberals and conservatives are going to clean up crime and make society better.

Here's a story Wolfert told me: He happened to be riding up in an elevator in the New York Supreme Court building with Governor Thomas Dewey, who had just arrested some big politicians and supposedly cleaned out the numbers racket. Dewey was getting ready to run for president in 1948 and boasting about his great victory over organized crime. Wolfert said to him, "If you promise in advance that you won't do anything about it, I can teach you something right now." Dewey accepted the offer. Then Wolfert asked Dewey, "How much would you like to bet on a number? This elevator operator right here will take your bet." The policy racket had simply moved the elevator operators to different locations. Nothing else had changed.

I'm the the the son of a pharmacist, *il dottore*, from a Sicilian neighborhood on the East Side where we lived after the Bronx. The Sicilians didn't teach me about organized crime; it was part of everyday neighborhood life. If your kid couldn't get a job, you went to Tammany, but you needed to have an old man with you. This old man was part of the organization. Thanks to him, you got a job pushing a cart someplace. It wasn't much, but you were working. According to this ethic, you had to take care of everybody. Meanwhile, the alderman made his visit to every store for a donation. Part of the money went to Tammany; part of it went to the organization.

Did you have any feeling that Body and Soul *had been compromised by Rossen, and that* Force of Evil *offered a second chance to reach the same blue-collar audience with a more sophisticated message?*

When you talk about the political problems of film production, it was not just Rossen, it was the whole system. You have to talk about what it means to be a radical working in a conventional medium, with certain kinds of aesthetic interests forced on you by the studio and certain kinds of aesthetic interests that you utilize out of the studio material. You also have to realize that we were in the film business not to change the world but to make films. To change the world we were involved in other kinds of things, like the labor struggle in Hollywood, against the studios and against the right-wing union, the IATSE [International Alliance of Theatrical Stage Employees].

You have described Force of Evil *as an avant-garde work. Is it avant-garde in the same sense as the postwar European movies?*

I mean avant-garde in the full sense of any modern art. And it is avant-garde. Garfield put up with all of that. He was marvelous. I did almost everything but cast the film. I was trying for one unified expression, and I got it! The film's moral standards are completely different from other films' standards—every act of love is also an act of betrayal.

In writing the script I was constantly thinking, "Am I pressing forward, getting a different view of everything?" I was afraid that once I was finished, they'd throw me out of town; they'd never let me make another movie. Of course, I didn't succeed completely, and I had all this trouble with the Hays Office trouble all the way through the picture. And they did throw me out of town, anyway, but for other reasons.

The film certainly breaks rules. Nothing is "right" in the standard Hollywood sense of making criminals pay for their actions. What problems did you have with the censors?

I was breaking every single rule that the censors had. We went full out, and it drove them crazy. They constantly said, "You can't do that." The biggest problem the censors had was that the Garfield character, the syndicate lawyer, doesn't want to improve humanity; he just wants revenge! I had to leave out the word "revenge," because according to the official rules you couldn't want "revenge"; you had to want "justice." I made it about as ambiguous as I could make it.

Did you have any difficulty directing actors for the first time?

Two of the principal actors, Tommy [Thomas] Gomez and one of the actresses, were gay; they both had their lovers on the set. Even so, Gomez and this actress couldn't act together. They hated each other. I asked a friend, "Are all homosexual actors that way?" No gay people that I knew were like that at all. He said, "No, these two just don't like each other." Then he explained a John Ford trick to me. You shoot one of them, and then you shoot the other. When you join them on film, it looks as though they're acting together in the same scene. As actors the two of them were marvelous—but alone, not together.

What kinds of discussions did you have with the cinematographer, George Barnes, about shooting the film?

We shot one day to see what the footage was going to look like, and I realized that for years George had been shooting all these female stars who were too old to be glamorous; they were fiftyish, and his job was to make them look thirty-seven. He was using a lot of diffusion and soft focus and stuff like that. He had started to shoot the same way for our picture. I said, "No, this is all wrong." He asked, "So what you do want?" Remember, he was famous, and I was new. I went out and got a book of Edward Hopper's Third Avenue paintings, and I brought it to him and said, "That's what I want." He said, "Why didn't you say so! Single-source lighting!" [Laughs]. And that made the picture look the way it does.

How involved were you with the score? The film's composer, David Raksin, was one more left-wing coworker who would later become a friendly witness.*

Before I made *Tell Them Willie Boy Is Here*, I didn't have the nerve to challenge the scoring. I knew that the music in *Force of Evil* was wrong, but I couldn't do anything about it. At the end of the story, the music soars, although the picture is going the other way. That is when I realized that musicians are stupid—like actors, sound men, everybody. Everybody but the director is stupid! [Laughs.] All Hollywood composers try to tell the story of the picture, as they understand it, through the music. But it's not always the director's idea of the story.

A few years later, at the time of the HUAC hearings, Raksin asked, "Would you mind if I used your name in my testimony? Everyone has already named you, anyway." I told him, "If you want to be a rat, you have to be a rat." He also offered me something as a consolation: "I can lend you money, you know." He wanted to bribe me, in a friendly way. I never forgot that.

Let's talk for a moment about one of the most famous scenes in the film, the so-called million-dollar-ruby scene. It takes place in the back of a taxi, where Garfield tempts his girlfriend—played by Beatrice Pearson—with an imaginary jewel. He expects her to reach out and take it, even though it represents a life of crime. It is

---

*David Raksin (1912–   )was famous at the time for writing the score for Chaplin's *Modern Times* and the hit mystery *Laura*. After he testified before HUAC in May 1952, when he named eleven Communist Party members, he scored *The Bad and the Beautiful* and *The Big Combo*, among many other films. In the ending of *Force of Evil*, Raksin's principal theme, titled "Regeneration," optimistically climbs a major scale even as the character played by Garfield, driven by grief, descends a series of staircases under the George Washington Bridge to find the body of his murdered brother.

a light, very seductive scene. Then, suddenly, it turns very dark. Garfield begins to contrast her willingness to be tempted for pure pleasure with his brother's refusal to join the numbers syndicate, to accept his share of the profits.

Let me just read these few lines of Garfield's as he stares out the cab window: "To go to great expense for something you want—that's natural. To reach out and take it—that's human, that's natural. But to get your pleasure from not taking, by cheating yourself deliberately, like my brother did today, from not getting, not taking—don't you see what a black thing that is for a man to do?"

This, to me, sounds a lot like William Blake when he said, with poetic hyperbole, that not to act on a wish is worse than killing a child. This logic is entirely contrary to what liberals—and Socialists and Communists—have always preached about revolutionary self-sacrifice.

That's right. It sounds like Blake, but it's really Polonsky. Garfield tries to win his brother over to being part of a bigger syndicate. He promises him, "I've come here to help you. I'll put you up in the clouds." Gomez won't listen to it and replies, "No, no, no." Gomez was great in that scene.

Incidentally, that was my whole attitude toward the Communist Party and its lack of understanding of what makes people tick. When I was a district educational director of the CIO, and we had to run a union election against the right-wing faction, we offered jobs in return for votes. After we won, the Party officials congratulated themselves, "We won because we're right, not because we could buy votes." I was brought up around the Tammany Hall machine, so I knew that wasn't true.

In the conclusion of Force of Evil, in a remarkable sequence of shots, Garfield walks all the way down from the George Washington Bridge, on a series of stone staircases, to the rocks along the Hudson River, to recover his brother's body. It's an incredibly effective montage, figuratively showing Garfield descending deeper into his own guilt, taking responsibility for the murder of his brother. Some people think this sequence is inspired by similar scenes in Battleship Potemkin. Is there any sense in which this was an homage to Eisenstein?

It's my homage to Polonsky, who knows his own streets—my city and my bridge and my steps, the most normal thing in the world for me to write about. Eisenstein would have enjoyed it, just as I enjoy Eisenstein.

The film doesn't present any hopeful alternatives. Unlike most other films, there isn't a single character to articulate the ideals of humanity.

That's right. The film is unrelenting, hard-boiled all the way through, and very well shot for that purpose by the cameraman. By 1948 lefties knew that social change was not going to happen so simply; the old straightforward plan of working-class triumph wouldn't work anymore. Of course, the Communist Party went on repeating the old words, like in a religion. Even when things didn't work out the way they had promised, they kept the words.

But something new was needed. It had to come. We needed to learn not from economics, which repeats the past, but from biology, from the biological innovations in nature which go in new directions and never repeat. Socialism had to be a biological invention, in that sense. Otherwise, everything, all history, became just the story of a bunch of crooks—as we've learned from all the defeats and disappointments since.

Let's move on to I Can Get It for You Wholesale, *for which you wrote a screen adaptation. The novel was a best-seller about the needle trades in New York, a satire about a Jewish labor organizer who takes union members out on strike and then cynically forms his own company and breaks the strike. The satire traded pretty fiercely in stereotypes. Zanuck is supposed to have said to you, "Fix this into a movie. The book's anti-Semitic."*

He didn't say it to me; he said it to [producer] Sol Siegel. The studio brought the author, Jerome Weidman, to Hollywood, and Zanuck asked him, "Can you change it?" Weidman said to Zanuck, "But I sold it to you!" Zanuck didn't give up: "Can you change it?" Weidman said, "Not me—but why not make the lead a woman?"

I was just about to leave for France when they called me in to do the script. I knew the book, of course, and I said, "Let's make it on the woman question," that is, on the issue of women's equality. So we made the lead a woman. She was played by Susan Hayward, a very fine actress who was perfect for the part.*

The Sam Jaffe character, the old tailor who runs the shop, doesn't appear in the novel at all. His appearance seems unmistakable as the film's conscience and the means by which you confront the anti-Semitism of the novel, through a zeyde, *or grandfather, figure who speaks with an obvious Yiddish accent. Where did he come from?*

Everything is meant to blunt the anti-Semitism of the novel. There's no anti-Semitism in the film. The Sam Jaffe character was my invention—the voice of experience. That character came from my own life. I had a grandmother like that; we all had grandmothers like that.

In fact, there's where I first learned to tell stories. I heard from my mother's mother all the stories that I would someday need. She used to get the stories out of the [Jewish Daily] Forward, stories that were translated into Yiddish to educate the Socialist readers.† Later on in life, I realized that I had learned

---

*I Can Get It for You Wholesale was later made into a Broadway musical starring Barbra Streisand and Elliott Gould. What made Polonsky's version memorable was its extraordinarily tough female protagonist, a character who was nonexistent in the book. To get rid of the problems with stereotypes in the original book, Polonsky changed the protagonist from a Jewish labor leader to an Irish-American dress designer. Even so, her more fiery speeches were rewritten at the studio's behest.

†The Jewish Daily Forward, the largest-circulation Yiddish-language newspaper in the world, was generally Socialist in its early decades but was also full of literary translations and original fiction. Later it became ferociously anti-Communist.

from her the stories of Tom Sawyer and Huck Finn, who happened, according to her version, to be Jewish boys on the Volga, with a Russian serf in the role of Jim, instead of gentiles on the Mississippi. I probably heard twenty percent of the *Arabian Nights* stories that way, and even two George Eliot novels. She read all this stuff, then told me all these stories in Yiddish. Incidentally, she wasn't the only one in the family to vote Socialist, so did my father. And my aunt, as I wrote in my novel *Zenia's Way*, actually went back to the Soviet Union after the Revolution.

Susan Hayward in the film is trying to fit into a man's world. There is a crucial scene with Dan Dailey in which he confronts her, insisting that she subordinate her career to his. Susan Hayward makes a speech that is considerably more feminist in your draft of the script than in the final film. Did you know the script was being changed, and did anybody consult you?

At the time, I had left Hollywood to write a novel. I was in the South of France when the film was shot, although I had some control through Michael Gordon, the director, who was blacklisted briefly before he turned "friendly" in front of the Committee. The ending in particular had to be suitable to Zanuck. Despite all of her resistance to Dailey's courting of her, which she sees as an attempt to push her out of the business, Hayward still has to go for Dailey in the end.

Wasn't there a vast canyon between theory and practice in the Communist Party in Hollywood?

Certainly, it was unsafe to jump across. But those who tried it were a rather large group, considering the small size of the Communist Party within the United States at large. Many of the Hollywood Communists had been attracted to the Communist Party because of the Russian Revolution earlier on—as a memory of childhood, so to speak—and the Depression, plus the Spanish Civil War, had made them feel that it was important to be a Communist. In that way, and in that way only, could people overcome what they felt was the major thrust of political action in the world, which was becoming Fascist.

Although progressive people in Hollywood became Communists for idealistic reasons, the working situation demanded a political and artistic synthesis that very often turned out to be elusive.

There's nothing unusual about that. Communists in New York and elsewhere often said that coming to Hollywood and writing films was a sellout. Why would anybody in his right mind write stupid pictures about ideas that he didn't really possess, when what he really and truly wanted to do was make a revolution and bring Socialism to the United States? Even many of the Hollywood writers who were Communists also thought it was a terrible or at least a questionable thing to be a Hollywood writer.

However, you can't possibly explain the Hollywood Communists away by saying, "They came to Hollywood for the money," although indeed they did. You can't possibly say that they came for the glamour, although some did, in fact. If they had come only for money and glamour, a lot more of them would have become stool pigeons—to hold their jobs, to continue making money and doing pictures. But only a small percentage of them became stool pigeons.

According to Marxist theory, no decent pictures could be made in Hollywood. In the meetings of the Hollywood clubs—a word we preferred to "cells"—one of the great discussions that used to go on all the time was: Should I be in Hollywood, and should I be writing movies? Or should I, say, do documentaries? Or should I try to make films apart from Hollywood that would in some way deal with the theoretical basis of why we are in fact in the Communist Party? This dilemma was not solved, and it couldn't be solved, because it was artificial and didn't exist. Filmmaking in the major studios is the prime way that film art exists. That doesn't mean that film, as an art form, doesn't exist apart from the studios. But when you want to get into making movies, and if you're fascinated with movies and care about movies, then there's only one thing to do: you try to make feature films for studios. It may not be the best solution to an artistic problem. It may end in the total defeat of every impulse that the writer, the director, and the actor has. But the fact of the matter is, that's the only choice, and that is why so many people who became Communists in Hollywood didn't rush to go elsewhere.

The left-wing writers took themselves the most seriously, fighting within the industry for content. They had the tendency to confuse aesthetics with content, which was normal. Meanwhile, the high-toned discussions of literary people about film made matters still more confused. Arguments in the high-class magazines were based on criticism of the other arts, distant from film. Film is a unique medium. There's something extraordinary about seeing someone on a screen, and if you don't understand that it's extraordinary, then you don't understand how films are made or the strange effect that film has on people—that is to say, film's "magic."

How well did the Hollywood left understand its efforts in theoretical terms, that is, in terms of Marxism?

The Party was a kind of social club here. A lot of people talking about Marxism were certainly not Marxists. They took the ideas seriously, but they didn't understand Marxism in any sophisticated way, and so there was a gap in all their lives and work. I'm not criticizing them; it's just a fact. Albert Maltz, in particular, was funny. He came to dinner years after the blacklist and said to me, "I didn't have to become a member of the CP. I could have done all the same things without being a member." I said, "Done what? You wouldn't have thought that way at all. Your talent resides in the fact that you embraced a political philosophy that you still don't understand." I wasn't trying to hurt his feelings. It's like the effect of religion on artists—you don't have to understand your religion in order to get the effect; you just believe. Albert joined, and he was a believer, but he was never really a Marxist.

Are you referring in part to the famous 1946 meeting, in Morris Carnovsky's basement, where only a handful of you in the Party supported Maltz's position of artistic freedom against the New Masses *editors? Party leaders had demanded the submission of artists.*

Right. When Albert wrote that article in the *New Masses*, and the fools in New York came down on him, Johnny Weber and Arnie Manoff and I decided to support him. We didn't know that he was about to go downtown to Party headquarters and make his peace with them and agree to take back his opinions.

That sort of typifies the limits of the Communist Party's creative contribution to screenwriting—from above.

The Party style of Marxism didn't have a chance here, or in New York either, among intellectuals. The leadership's behavior violated the whole intellectual life of Marxism, and the Party itself also did that constantly. Look how they ran their magazines and newspapers, with such a heavy hand. I had my fights with them.

What would happen when the Party's cultural commissar, V. J. Jerome, or one of the others came out from New York to lay down the line?

He would raise hell with about eleven people. We didn't give a shit. The cultural leadership obviously didn't know what they were talking about. We ignored them out here, and we did a lot of wonderful things despite them.

Maurice Rapf

MAURICE RAPF, Hanover, New Hampshire, 1986

INTERVIEW BY PATRICK McGILLIGAN

PHOTO BY WILLIAM RAPF

MAURICE RAPF
(1914–   )

1932 *Divorce in the Family.* Costory.
1936 *We Went to College.* Coscript.
1937 *They Gave Him a Gun.* Coscript.
1938 *The Bad Man of Brimstone.* Costory.
      Sharpshooters. Costory.
1939 *North of Shanghai.* Costory, coscript.
      Winter Carnival. Costory, coscript.

1940 *Dancing on a Dime.* Coscript.
      Jennie. Coscript.
1942 *Call of the Canyon.* Costory.
1946 *Song of the South.* Coscript.
1949 *So Dear to My Heart.* Coadaptation.
1950 *Cinderella.* Uncredited contribution.
      Adventures of Gallant Bess.
      Uncredited contribution.
1952 *The Detective.* Uncredited contribution.

■

MAURICE RAPF, LIKE his friend Budd Schulberg, grew up with a privileged backstage view of the motion-picture industry. He was raised a Hollywood prince. His father, Harry Rapf, was a prominent MGM producer, and his own golden road lay in the same direction. With Schulberg, who lived a block away, he went to public school and college, and spent a summer in Russia. They both chose to become writers and then joined the Communist Party, with Rapf working hard in the Screen Writers Guild struggle and becoming one of the people who helped set up the arbitration code still in use today. Eventually—after amassing solid screenwriting credits—both made separate, voluntary decisions to leave Hollywood.

Unlike Schulberg, Rapf stayed pro-Soviet and refused to act as a cooperative witness for the House Un-American Activities Committee; their opposing choices caused a thirteen-year rift in their friendship. Even today, Rapf declines to repent his Communist past and speaks up for the nobility of the cause.

The similarities and differences between his life story and Schulberg's are the subtext of this interview. But Rapf had a fascinating career in his own right, leapfrogging from studio to studio on mostly B projects, including John Wayne, Roy Rogers, and Gene Autry vehicles, and a legendary brush with F. Scott Fitzgerald on an ill-destined production called *Winter Carnival*. Curiously, Rapf wound up at Disney, the studio he liked best, working closely with Walt Disney, the boss he liked best. The animated films he helped write include *Song of the South, So Dear to My Heart,* and *Cinderella*.

Then, deciding to quit the Party and the movie business, Rapf headed east, where he dodged the blacklist and gradually found his way into animated industrial films as a writer and director, and, more gradually still, into academia. Today he is director emeritus and adjunct professor of film studies at Dartmouth College, his alma mater. His recently completed autobiography is called "Back Lot: Growing Up with the Movies."

■

Can you start by telling me a little bit about your father and the circumstances into which you were born in Hollywood?

Sure, but I was born in New York. My father was a vaudeville agent, actually, who also wrote acts. He had his office in the Palace Theater building, which was on Broadway and Forty-sixth Street, I think. We moved to California when I was seven years old, in 1921. It was on my birthday; that's why I remember it.

Before that, my father had led sort of a dual life. I really didn't know him too well in the vaudeville days, but I remember going with him, when I must have been four or five years old, to Brooklyn to see acts try out. It was very much like a movie preview. We would stand in the back, the act would be ten or fifteen minutes long, and there'd be a discussion of what the act could do to improve, to get more laughs, and so forth.

Then, about 1916, he started producing movies. He thought that was the coming thing. I have a number of full-page ads that he took out in the *Film Daily Yearbook* for his movies, so I know the titles of some of the films he made. Also, I was in a lot of them as a child actor. He always had children in the films, and I was free.

What was your biggest part?

[Laughs.] Well, he made a series of films with Wesley Barry, a young child actor, a freckle-faced kid. He made some in California and some in New York. I was in the ones in New York and not in California, because by that time I had started school and I wasn't free to be in movies. If you look at the coffee-table book that tells the Warner Brothers story, it will talk about Harry Rapf as being one of their first producers, and he was. When we went to California in 1921, it was for him to take up a job at Warner Brothers, where he continued to make the Wesley Barry pictures, and he also introduced the dog star Rin Tin Tin. Those were the most successful pictures Warner Brothers had at that particular time. I had three Rin Tin Tin puppies during that period, though none of them lived. In those days, they didn't have proper antibiotics to give to little dogs to prevent distemper; they were very high-bred—they all got distemper and died.

I remember one movie that my father made with Barry in which I played two parts. It was called *From Rags to Riches*. It was about a kid who is brought up on a farm; there were scenes in a country schoolhouse that I was in. Then his wealthy grandparents discover him and take him to some big city, and next he's in a fancy school. I'm in that school, too. Those scenes were shot in New York somewhere.

Did you have any youthful run-ins with Jack Warner and Darryl Zanuck?

I don't remember Darryl Zanuck in those days, but I certainly remember Jack Warner, because he was a neighbor of ours in Los Angeles, and my family and he and his wife and son went on picnics together and so forth. Jack Warner seemed to be pretty much of a clown who didn't care very much about movies, or about anything. The serious people in the Warners outfit were Harry and, at that time, another brother named Sam, who died in 1927. Jack was never the serious one in the Warner clan.

My father was sort of the fourth Warner Brother, but he could see that they weren't getting anywhere. The only successful pictures they made were his. He left there early in 1924, as I recall. I'm a little fuzzy about how he left. My recollection is that he left to go with [Louis B.] Mayer at MGM when the merger took place, and I was there the day the studio was launched, in April 1924. I don't remember my father working with Mayer down at the [William] Selig zoo studio, but apparently he did, because all the history books say he did.

One of the things that are not sufficiently appreciated about the Hollywood people of that era—and I think about many of the blacklisted people—is their familiarity with and fondness for vaudeville, for all areas of show business. That love of show business has gone out of movies, to some extent.

That's right. And my father had that love more than most, because he had gone into the vaudeville business early, in 1900. He grew up in Denver, and he used to stage minstrel shows and various kinds of entertainments there. But he always haunted the vaudeville theaters, because the vaudeville chains in those days were really like movies; they were where all the talent was, and they traveled around the country booked on a tour to all the key cities. Everybody knew everybody else on the bill. My father met Gus Edwards in Denver, and Edwards liked him; my father must have been about twenty years old. Edwards said, "Why don't you join the troupe?" He had an act called "School Days" in which he was the teacher. He had a very precocious bunch of kids, including Eddie Cantor, George Jessel, and Walter Winchell—all Jewish and talented: they could dance and sing and tell jokes. They were fresh kids. My father became the manager of that act about 1901, and traveled all around the country with it, sometimes with Edwards in the act, sometimes without Edwards. My mother was a secretary in Edwards's office in New York. That's how they met.

Edwards was also a songwriter; he wrote the song "School Days," which was the theme song of his act. He also wrote "In My Merry Oldsmobile" and other songs. My father remained loyal to those vaudevillians all his life. In fact, he brought back a lot of old vaudevillians in the first sound film he made. It was called *Hollywood Revue*. Jack Benny, who had been in vaudeville, was the emcee; he was too young to have been in the "School Days" act, but his vaudeville act consisted of telling jokes and standing alone onstage with his violin, which he would ultimately play very badly. That's exactly what he did in *Hollywood Revue*. My father brought out an army of old vaudevillians to be in that show, although what happened was that most of them got cut out. Gus Edwards is in it, however, doing a sentimental ballad called "Your Mother and Mine."

Our involvement with vaudeville persisted for many, many years. I remember that it was a standard procedure in my family to go down to see the acts at the Orpheum Theater, which was in downtown Los Angeles, out of bounds for most people in Hollywood; everything was in Hollywood or west of Hollywood, or later on, in the Valley. But because of the vaudeville connection, we went downtown—I won't say every week, because those acts were booked in for two weeks, but often. My father knew all the regular people, like Ted Lewis, Al Jolson, Herman Timberg, and, of course, Gus Edwards, who was still doing the "School Days" act in 1926. We always went to the Orpheum on a Sunday night, and my father went backstage to see all his old friends.

Did you have the same kind of "Hollywood prince" upbringing as Budd Schulberg, whose father was producer B. P. Schulberg?

Yeah. We lived a block apart, and we were very close friends from 1925 on. My studio was better than his for a playground because it was bigger, so on Saturdays we always went out to MGM and played on the backlot. It was a great childhood, ideal; you couldn't hope for anything better. We'd go to the prop department, and whatever was being shot at the time would provide all kinds of equipment. *Ben-Hur* was the first film we borrowed stuff from; that was wonderful—shields and helmets and breastplates. Then we'd go out on the backlot and act out *Ben-Hur*. Then came *The Big Parade*, with guns, bayonets, and helmets. Whatever it was, we'd just disappear for the whole day, playing in those sets. So the sets weren't imaginary for us; they were real. [Laughs.]

All of America's most famous people were your dinner guests?

Actually, who you socialized with was pretty well defined by the studio. That was another strange thing about that era that I don't think exists anymore. I can recall the early parties at my parents' house in the late 1920s. The studio would actually make home movies of sorts to run at the parties. They were very dirty and presumably funny. I was always excluded from watching those, because they were too sexy for me, but I'd go into the projection room and look through the glass. So I saw them anyway, and I never understood what was sexy about them.

I'm in one of them, and I have a print of it; [Irving] Thalberg and my father are also in it. It's headed "A Look into the Future," and it shows Thalberg and Rapf in the anteroom of their offices waiting for an interview with the boss. Well, I'm the boss. I'm about ten or eleven years old, I'm wearing a shirt, a bow tie, and a straw hat, and I'm smoking one of Thalberg's gold-tipped cigarettes. I go down the back stairs while they sit there waiting. I sign some kind of a paper for Mervyn LeRoy and get into a Rolls Royce, which is driven by Thalberg's chauffeur, an aging black man with white hair and a cane. I get into the back seat with Marie Prevost. That's the kind of stuff they used to do in their home movies.

How did your ambitions evolve before you went to college?

I wanted to be a writer all the time. I felt that movies could be a lot better if the writing was better, and I thought I could do that.

Was that due to your father's influence?

More or less. He always was griping about the scripts being lousy, and I read a lot of the scripts that he brought home. By the time I went to college, sound had come in, and actually he was grooming me to be a producer. No doubt about that; that's what he wanted. Nobody had any children at MGM at that time, so I was really in a very good spot to move up and be an assistant producer and then a producer. But that was beneath my creative dignity. [Laughs.] I wanted to be a writer.

How did it happen that you decided to attend Dartmouth?

I didn't go to Dartmouth originally. I went to Stanford. I transferred, and it was largely due to the presence in Hollywood of three people, one of whom I knew very well. That was [producer] Walter Wanger. Another was [screenwriter-producer] Gene Markey. The third was [producer] Arthur Hornblow Jr. There were only three college-educated producers in Hollywood, and they had all gone to Dartmouth.

You liked these people or were impressed by them?

Well, I knew about Dartmouth through them, that's all. Then my close friend Budd Schulberg went there. He and I got out of high school more or less at the same time; I got out in the winter, and he got out in the summer.

Beverly Hills High School?

No, L.A. High. We went to public school. We were both editors of the *Blue and White*, which was a daily newspaper published by the high school. The school was enormous, thirty-five hundred students, and was a very good high school. It was used all the time in movies set at colleges. It had a good football field and swimming pool, and it looked like a college. There was a series that RKO did called *The Collegians*, and that was the background they used.

I was barely seventeen, but I went to Stanford that fall of 1931.

Why Stanford?

It was the best school in California. One didn't ordinarily go east to school in those days. There were no airplanes, and it was too far. But Budd liked Dartmouth a lot, and I didn't like Stanford, so that was another reason I switched. I applied to three eastern schools, Harvard, Yale, and Dartmouth. I was accepted at all three, but I chose to go to Dartmouth.

Was it at Dartmouth that you were radicalized?

That's right. The trip to the Soviet Union had a lot to do with it, between my junior and senior year.

Was that a college-sponsored program?

No, it wasn't college-sponsored, but I found out about it in a college building. The activities building had on the wall a notice of a trip to the Soviet

Union for the summer of 1934, sponsored by the National Student League. I knew it was a Communist youth organization, but I didn't belong to it. My principal political drive before I went to the Soviet Union was peace. Peace was the big issue for students of my type in that particular period, and we had strange bedfellows, because it was after World War I, and people didn't want to see a repetition of that kind of war. We were not particularly aware of the growth of Fascism. We were aware of the Soviet Union, because that subject was taught in a number of courses we had. We were rather friendly toward the Soviet Union and recognized red-baiting even then as a reactionary tool, because it tended to inflame this country toward a war position. The congressmen and senators who were our heroes later turned out to be the biggest Fascists around, the America Firsters. I remember marching around the Dartmouth campus carrying a placard when the school was visited by a [Republican] senator from North Dakota named Gerald Nye. But he had a wonderful slogan, "Take the profits out of war." I supported that.

Then I made this trip to the Soviet Union in 1934. There were five or six of us who went from Dartmouth. This was before the days of foreign-exchange programs; it wasn't sponsored by the college at all. It was for an entire summer, three months, and for a very reasonable price, although I had a hard time convincing my parents to let me go. I couldn't afford it, even though it was only three hundred and fifty dollars, but I told them that Soviet theater was the most outstanding theater in the world; everybody was aware of the enormous achievements and experimentation that went on there, and the unorthodox approach of the Moscow Art Theatre, which was Stanislavsky's. On the basis of the fact that this group from the National Student League was going to be able to spend a week in Moscow at the end of the summer and then go to the theater—there was no theater in the summer, I couldn't lie about that, but in the fall we would have a week to go to the theater—I convinced my parents that I should go.

Did the five or six you mentioned include Ring Lardner Jr.?

No, Ring was a Princeton student. I met him in the Soviet Union. That was the first time I met him. He was a dissident, oddly enough. He published a wall newspaper, which in those days was standard in the Soviet Union, because they didn't have enough paper to print newspapers. We went to school in the Soviet Union. It was a real school, and that's where Ring published his wall newspaper. We had some very distinguished professors, although I didn't take the school part very seriously. We all lived in an ex-palace, and our classes were held there, too.

How many kids from the United States went to the Soviet Union that summer?

There must have been about fifty. It was called the Anglo-American Institute, so the courses were taught in English. It was not limited to American students; there were students from Canada and China as well, but they had to speak English.

When you say that Ring was a dissident, you mean that he actually put up a wall newspaper—

—attacking most of what we were saying, and attacking the leadership of the group, because we were led by Communists. I don't think any of us liked it very much, but we were forced to attend Marxist study groups and stuff like that. He came out with an open attack on all of us; he was the only one who sounded an opposition voice. So I knew him essentially as an anti-Soviet. [Laughs.]

Was Budd one of the Dartmouth group?

He was.

How did you start out—sympathetically?

I had a lot of arguments with people in the Soviet Union, but on the whole I was impressed. The thing that most impressed me and probably made me a Communist was that anti-Semitism was illegal in the Soviet Union, and that the Soviets were very anti-Fascist, which the United States was not.

I remember anti-Nazi posters, some of which I wanted to bring back with me, and some of which I did bring back—one in particular of a red fist up over a wall, and on the other side of the wall a guy in a storm trooper's uniform with a swastika around his arm. The caption under it was, "Keep Your Fascist Snout Out of Our Soviet Garden." I was impressed by that.

I also stopped off in Germany on the way back and got a chance to see what Hitler's Germany was like. This was 1934, very early. I was in Berlin for only five days. That was enough. I saw the Brownshirts marching down Unter den Linden. Anti-Semitism was really flagrant in Germany, but nobody in the United States was paying much attention to it.

Did you have any contact with the film industry in the Soviet Union?

Yes, quite a lot, because we were determined to do so. We ran into a guy who knew Budd Schulberg from Paramount; his name was Lars Moen. He was an American, or at least he had been in America a long time before they brought him over there to work in the movie industry. He got us into a lot of the studios. Don't forget, it was summer, and it's traditional to take vacations in summer, and nobody works. But they were shooting a movie at one big studio that we went to, where they had the so-called Cinema School. (I hate the word "cinema." I never use it. It should have been called a movie school—"movie" is a better word—but they called it a cinema school.) They were shooting the Gulliver story with puppets, so I saw that, and there was also a movie company not very far from our school that was shooting every day, and I went there very often, at least half a dozen times. It was an Armenian company. I eventually saw the movie they made. It was a costume movie about the early history of Armenia. They had a miserable little studio near our school. They had very limited equipment and miserable little sets.

What impressed me about that was that it was just like Hollywood. [Laughs.] Even though we were in the Soviet Union, it was the one place I went in the Soviet Union where democracy didn't seem to work. The director was giving orders; the assistant director was kissing his ass—it was just exactly like Hollywood.

When you came back from the Soviet Union you were a senior, right?

I was a senior at Dartmouth.

How did your political involvements and interests escalate?

My father was very upset by my letters from the Soviet Union. They were very positive and very strongly pro-Communist. He got very upset about that, in some respects. On the other hand, I was told by others that he was very defensive about me, too. When people would say, "Your son is turning into a goddamn red" he would say, "If he finds it a good place, it must be a good place." He defended me constantly, even though in a face-to-face discussion he would try to talk me out of Communism and say I could never have a career in movies if I was going to be a red.

Was he a Roosevelt supporter?

He voted for Roosevelt beginning in 1936, but he didn't in 1932. He was progressive in a certain way. He didn't want to confront me, so he turned me over to all of his friends and they lambasted me. It was one of the most interesting periods of my life, after I got back from the Soviet Union in September. First he met me in New York, and before I even went back to school I had to go to see Harry Warner about my pro-Soviet leanings. I really had to see the top brass of the movie industry to be dissuaded from my Communist point of view, and they were mean to me.

Mean? Harry Warner was?

Oh, terrible.

What kinds of things did they say to you?

I was going to destroy the movie industry, and not only that, but bring anti-Semitism down on the heads of all the movie people. I got the same treatment from Louis B. Mayer, whom I saw at Christmastime and who said to me, "It's people like you who cause anti-Semitism in the world."

Was it just you and Mayer alone in a room?

He and I. On the other hand, some of the younger people were a little more tolerant, like David Selznick and Irving Thalberg. They still attacked me, but they did it in a nicer way.

Your father set all this up?

Yes, so that he didn't have to do it. It just strengthened my convictions. I got more and more defensive. Apparently, a couple of books claim that I said something memorable to Mayer when he said that I should stop being a Communist because it was bad for the Jews. I supposedly said to him—because each year he would be announced as one of the highest-paid executives in the country—that I would be glad to stop being a Communist if he would stop being a capitalist. But I really never said it. I *thought* it. [Laughs.] I wish I had said it.

Did you like these people who were talking to you, or was it a little like being sent to the school principal?

Well, I liked Selznick. Selznick said something that I later acted on. Selznick pretended to me that he had been just like me when he was my age, which was bullshit, because I knew him when he was younger. His father gave him an allowance of a thousand dollars a week, and he drove around in a big car. He was very precocious and very different, but he certainly didn't have any radical point of view. He told me he read the *Nation*, the *New Republic*, and the *New Masses*, and he sounded off with that traditional line, "If you're not a radical when you're twenty, you're not worth a damn." But he did say one thing that was wise. He said to me, "I think you've got to choose between being a moviemaker and being a Communist." He didn't tell me how to choose; he just said that if you want to be a moviemaker, you can't be a Communist, and he was right. He was absolutely right about that— for the wrong reasons, probably. The reason I quit the Party ultimately was that I had no time to be a moviemaker. I was too busy being a radical. But I don't think he meant that.

Thalberg was also tolerant, and he also used the line about being a radical when he was young. But he didn't do most of the talking. I had lunch in his bungalow. At this time, late 1934, he had just returned after his heart attack, and Selznick was at the studio, theoretically to replace him. Thalberg originally had had an office adjoining my father's, and they made all the movies of the studio in the twenties right out of that little hub. Now he was making only five or six movies a year; he had his own unit, with his own dining room and bungalow and so forth. His assistant was a man who later became quite an impressive director, actually—a former college professor named Albert Lewin. He had Lewin there to confront me as an expert on Marxism. And Lewin was very tough. He was quoting stuff I didn't know anything about. I didn't know a goddamn thing about Marxism, to tell you the truth. I determined after that experience that I was going to learn something, because I couldn't answer Lewin's questions, which were very difficult. That's how Thalberg approached me.

After you got back from the Soviet Union, did you immediately get involved in a lot of political issues?

Not much. I wasn't an organization man then. When I got out of Dartmouth I went to New York. I wanted to get involved with moviemakers on the left. There were a lot of them, and I did get to meet them.

People like Leo Hurwitz and Paul Strand?

Exactly. That group, the Film and Photo League.* I wanted to work with them. Their headquarters were in Strand's apartment in the Village. I went to join them. But they didn't want me, and they couldn't pay me anything, because none of them were getting any money from the Film and Photo League. They had to make money elsewhere—like Ralph Steiner, who was my principal contact, because he had gone to Dartmouth; he was an advertising photographer who was making left-wing films on the side. They were making a movie at the time I met them, and I went with them while they were shooting it. It was called *Pie in the Sky*. Gadge [Elia] Kazan was in it, and his wife—Molly Day Thacher was her name, I think—was the director. Leo Hurwitz had something to do with it. I met the whole gang, and I thought they were on the right track, but I couldn't get in with them. Nobody tried to recruit me at all—for anything. I was just a hanger-on. They said they couldn't pay me, and I couldn't afford to work for nothing.

You were in no danger of starving, were you?

I starved anyway. My first job was with a theatrical producer, and I got fifteen dollars a week. The only meals I could afford were Nedick's hot dogs with orange drink. How the hell can you live on fifteen dollars a week and pay rent?

Were you booking acts, as your father had done?

I was an office boy in the office of a theatrical producer named Crosby Gaige. I didn't want to go to Hollywood, I didn't like the idea of Hollywood, but I found the New York theater to be more corrupt than Hollywood, to tell you the truth. I became totally disgusted with it. I had had great ideals about the New York theater and thought it represented art as opposed to commerce, which was California, and I found out that wasn't true. At least it wasn't true with the guy I worked for, who was producing plays that were absolutely impossible. I used to read all of his plays, and tell him, "Don't produce this one; it's a piece of shit," and he would do it anyway, because he made money whether the play was a piece of shit or wasn't. He had angels who put up the money. He didn't care. I decided I didn't like the theater at all. He wasn't making enough money with what he was doing anyway, it turned out, and

---

*Russell Campbell's book *Cinema Strikes Back: Radical Filmmaking in the United States, 1930–1942* charts the history and contribution of the Film and Photo League, Frontier Films, and other non-Hollywood filmmaking of the 1930s and 1940s

he finally asked me to stay on *without* the fifteen dollars a week, so I said good-bye. [Laughs.]

At about the same time my father was working on a project about a college reunion. He had come to my graduation and was very amused by the reunion that had taken place at the same time, the old-timers coming back to Dartmouth. He remembered a Warner Brothers film, directed by a friend of his named Archie Mayo, called *Convention City*, which was about a group of guys who leave home and go off to a convention and behave like children for a period of time. That's really what was happening at those college reunions. He wanted to make a movie about that, and I knew that he did. He wanted me to work on it, and by February or March 1936 I had no real job in New York, and he said, "Come on out. I'm stuck on this project. I'd like you to work on it." I did, because I had no other job, and I was going to be a junior writer at, I think, forty dollars a week.

I was assigned to work with Dick [Richard] Maibaum. This was Dick's first assignment at the studio. He'd had a play produced on Broadway, and in those days they thought that anybody who'd had a play produced could write dialogue, so all the studios hired these young writers who'd had plays on Broadway. There used to be four hundred plays a year produced on Broadway; today, I guess, there may be forty. In those days a play cost only twenty or thirty thousand dollars to produce, and if it lasted only two weeks it was okay. At any rate, I worked with Dick, we became good friends, and we turned out the script in six weeks. And it was shot. It was quite a good movie, actually.

That's We Went to College?

Yeah. It was about a college reunion. The original story had been written by Finley Peter Dunne Jr. [son of the famous humorist and brother of screenwriter Philip Dunne] and George Oppenheimer. It was promising. Apparently they were hired to do the screenplay and didn't make it, at least according to my father. But he liked what we did, our script was put into production, and it was the only film I worked on in Hollywood for eleven years on which I was ever allowed on the set as a writer. [Laughs.] And there was a reason for it—Maibaum and I were recent college graduates, and we could serve as technical advisers; otherwise we never would have been on the set.

Who was the director of that picture?

The director was a guy named Joseph Santley. He was the nominal director, and he got credit on the film, but there was one sequence shot by another director—that was sometimes done. The other director was Sam Wood, who was one of the most reactionary directors in Hollywood.

Was Maibaum the senior writer in the partnership, because he had a play that was produced on Broadway?

Yes, he was the senior writer, but we were both neophytes. We were very ambitious, and we must have written half a dozen original stories following

We Went to College. What happened was that after the film was previewed—it was a big success at its first preview—I was called in to the studio manager's office and offered a bonus. I'd received less than four hundred dollars for that script—six weeks' work. He was going to give me a five-hundred-dollar bonus, which was more than I had gotten for the script. I said, "I don't want it. I want a raise to seventy-five dollars a week." He wouldn't give it to me! [Laughs.] But he did give me the bonus. Dick was getting, I think, two hundred dollars a week.

We figured the only way we could crawl out from being writers of B pictures was to write an original for one of the stars. So we wrote a lot of originals.

Did any of them get made?

No.

Why is that?

I don't know. We weren't important enough. The producers don't know the difference between a good script and a bad script. We always gave them to my father first, but we were just a couple of kids, and he didn't go for them either. I didn't stay at MGM very long. After about six months during which we wrote the originals—all of which belonged to MGM, because we were on salary—my father bought an anti-war novel called *They Gave Him a Gun,* written by William Joyce Cowen, a man who was the husband of a writer he liked, whose name was Lenore Coffee. He had used Lenore Coffee on several movies; she was one of the successful female writers in Hollywood. Cowen had directed one film, and he wanted to direct this film.* When he sold the novel it was with the understanding that he would be allowed to direct it. The novel was a very short one, and it had a very simplistic but satisfactory notion. It was about a young kid who is drafted or enlists in World War I, becomes a sharpshooter and gets a medal for sharpshooting, comes back after the war, and can't get a job. He is given his old job as a grocery clerk but feels too important for that, and so he becomes a gangster. That was a familiar type of story, also done at Warner Brothers. In any case Dick and I were assigned to it, and we wrote a script; Cowen was kind of present, but he didn't do any writing—he was just making sure we adhered to the book.

Another writer was assigned to work with us. That was Cyril Hume. Cyril was a very experienced guy, much older than we were; he had been a contemporary of [F. Scott] Fitzgerald's at Princeton and had written one very, very successful, sexy novel in the twenties called *The Wife of the Centaur.* He was a very natty-looking fellow who wore a little bow tie, and he wouldn't eat in the studio commissary because they didn't serve booze. So every day at noon we left the lot and went to a saloon to eat and drink, and we wouldn't get back until about four o'clock. This project introduced me to alcoholism,

---

*W. S. Van Dyke ended up directing *They Gave Him a Gun.*

if nothing else. But Cyril was also very knowledgeable. Cyril, Dick, and I were a triad, which didn't make any sense, because you can't collaborate that way, but on the other hand, I learned a lot from working with Hume. We turned out the script, and I did get credit, with Maibaum and Hume.

At MGM, were there certain dos and don'ts for writers? Were writers urged, for example, to forgo camera movements and directions in their scripts?

I don't remember any of that. There were a lot of camera directions in our scripts—a lot. I've got the scripts, and I teach screenwriting nowadays, and I'm astounded at those scripts. They're very specific. I was very specific about camera instructions because I knew a lot about that. That was one of the things I thought I knew well; another was dialogue, which I thought I knew a lot about but really didn't. I did learn a lot from Hume about scene structure and dialogue and stuff like that.

At this point, you yourself were a member of the Communist Party?

Not when I first worked with Maibaum. My introduction to the Party in Hollywood was peculiar, very peculiar. I was in New York for almost eight months, and nobody ever asked me to join. All they would have had to do was ask me, and I would have joined; I was ready, but no one asked me. When I got to Hollywood, I arrived at the very time the Screen Writers Guild was going through its traumatic experience of trying to organize on a national basis. So the first week, working with Maibaum on *We Went to College*, I was approached by Lillian Hellman to join the Guild, and I did. I was honored. I was a punk, and here was an important writer asking me to join. I went to meetings with people like Dorothy Parker, Dashiell Hammett, Lillian Hellman, and Samson Raphaelson—these were my idols.

Did you know Lillian Hellman beforehand?

No. She was working to sign everybody up for the Guild. She could have asked me to join the local fire-fighters; I would have joined. It didn't make any difference to me—but I happened to be in favor of what they were doing, anyway.

During the course of going to all these meetings I met a lot of lefties, obviously. The next thing I knew, I was asked to join a group to study Marxism. I was very interested in that, because I'd had this terrible experience with Albert Lewin, who knew so much more than I did. I was told about a meeting, and I went to it. When I got there, I was amazed to see who was there, because it was a secret meeting; although it wasn't a Party meeting; it was a study group that met once a week. It was at the house of an MGM writer whom I knew—whom I won't name—and there were four or five other people there and somebody from downtown who was the instructor. I went to that study group for about four months, and then one day I was asked to join the Young Communist League.

You were amazed by who was there—why?

I didn't know they were lefties. They were all MGM people. It was really a cell at MGM, and they all knew my father. They worked for my father, as a matter of fact.

What was their interest and comprehension of Marx?

It was limited at the time. Remember, this was a study group, not a Communist Party group. We were given assignments to read things and report back. We were reading Marx and Lenin—not yet Stalin in those days—and it was tough going. I remember one of the people there. She was not in the movie industry at all but was a young writer from San Francisco who'd had tuberculosis and was recovering. I've seen her lately. She's very famous today. But I won't name her either.

You won't name anyone except yourself?

Only people who have named themselves.

Were there any people in that study group who subsequently named themselves?

No.

So it is a study group whose membership has remained secret—until now.

They're all dead, except for the one person I saw recently. She was about seventeen years old at the time, and she came to Dartmouth to lecture recently. It was partly a feminist gathering. I was probably the only man there. I went up to her afterward, introduced myself, and asked whether she remembered the study group. I mentioned the name of the woman at whose house the meetings were held. She cut me colder than hell. She didn't want to talk to me.

I mean this question as sensitively as possible: with so many people dead, and all of this having taken place so long ago, why do you have such a reluctance to name names?

I have never named anybody, and I never will—except those who have named themselves. I'm perfectly willing to talk about Ring, because Ring has written about himself, and I'm perfectly willing to talk about all the people who became informers, because they've already named themselves. And the others would probably have no objection. The dead ones certainly wouldn't object. But I don't want to talk about them as Communists. I did know a lot of people who were Communists—including some surprising ones. If you ask me who they were, I'm not going to tell you.

Can you tell me why you are so reluctant, in terms that will make it clear to people nowadays?

I feel it's up to any individual to describe his or her own situation in those particular years. I was approached a great many times in the 1950s by agents and investigators, and they knew everything about me; there was nothing they really had to ask me, except the dumb question which I could answer very simply: Have you ever been a card-carrying member of the Communist Party? The answer to that is no. Who would be so dumb?

Then they would go on from there, asking me about other people. I never denied that I had been a Communist. I don't deny it to this day. I just got back from an academic conference in Toledo, and I shocked everybody a little bit by starting out with the statement, "I've got to tell you that what I'm going to say is colored a little bit by the fact that I'm an unrepentant Communist." But I haven't been a member of the Party since 1946. I left the Party because I was bored and because eventually I agreed with David Selznick that I had to be either a movie writer or a Communist—I couldn't do both.

Is it also because in America, because of the way history is perceived and presented, even now such identification plays into the hands of reactionaries?

I think it does.

People are still tarred by a wide brush?

I think you run risks. For example, I've written a memoir, which I think is quite a fascinating book, and I can't get it published. I think one of the reasons I can't get it published is because I'm too frank. I tell exactly how the Party operated in Hollywood, which people don't like to hear. I had a big fight with a Trotskyite at the conference last weekend because I said, "If people like you hadn't deserted the Communist Party so completely, and attacked the Communist Party and relished so completely the demise of the Communist Party, the Communist Party might have survived." I feel that. I feel that very keenly, even though I don't argue about what happened in the Soviet Union, because I don't *know* what happened in the Soviet Union.

Getting back to this original study group that you joined—it was through this group that you were asked to join the Party?

But they wouldn't take me in the Party at first. I spent a year in the Young Communist League before I got into the Party.

Why wouldn't they take you in the Party?

I was too young.

You must have been twenty-one or twenty-two.

I was twenty-one.

What was the proper age?

I don't know. I don't know why they put me in the Young Communist League. I wasn't alone; there was another screenwriter in it. After a year of being in the Young Communist League, I complained that what I was doing there had nothing to do with my work. The Writers Guild was becoming reactivated. See, the Guild had collapsed after the initial organizing, and there was nothing for me to do in the Hollywood situation. I was too young to have any influence in some of the front organizations, like the Hollywood Anti-Nazi League and so forth. There were more mature people who made more money and could raise more money. So they assigned me to the Young Communist League, and that's where I stayed.

I worked on a newspaper which we published in the Young Communist League—I still have copies of it up in the attic. It was called the *Winner*. It was a very devious little paper. The idea was, it looked like *Variety* in that tabloid format, and on the cover of each issue was some athletic event. But inside it was pretty left. [Laughs.] The idea was to suck in young people with sports and then feed them a dose of politics when they got to the inside.

After a year, they did let me into the Party in Hollywood.

During this year you were still screenwriting?

I stayed at MGM through production on *They Gave Him a Gun*. Then Maibaum and I wrote the story for *Bad Man of Brimstone*. It was not our idea, actually. My father was active as a producer at that time, and there was a director there by the name of J. Walter Ruben. He had an idea for a Wallace Beery film, but he couldn't write, so Maibaum and I wrote his story. We didn't exactly stick to Ruben's idea. Then I said, "I can't hang around here; I'm getting out," and I left MGM. Maibaum isn't credited with the story; he could have taken credit, but I took it with J. Walter Ruben. Then Maibaum did the screenplay with [Cyril] Hume. He and Hume became a team and did several movies together.

What was the last straw for you?

I didn't want to go to work as part of a triad again. I didn't like that arrangement, because I was the low man on the totem pole, and it just didn't work for me. So I got a job somewhere else.

Wasn't that cheeky of you—quitting your father's studio?

I just felt I'd never get anywhere there, because I was a producer's son. I decided I had to prove I could do it on my own. I went to work, as I recall, in the B unit at Fox. One of the first things I did there was a picture called *Sharpshooters*, about a newsreel cameraman. I didn't do the screenplay. It was done by a guy named Jerome Cady. But I did do the story.

Did your father try to talk you out of leaving MGM?

Yes. He didn't think I should leave.

Tell me about Twentieth Century–Fox compared to MGM. What kind of environment was it for a writer?

It was pleasant for me, although I worked for a very tough guy named Sol Wurtzel. I got the job because he was a friend of my father's, it was really a nepotistic kind of job, even though Fox was a different studio from MGM. Wurtzel headed the B unit there. I didn't have anything to do with Zanuck until the latter part of my stay there. I worked only on B films, and I originally collaborated with another guy whose name was Lester Ziffren. This shows you how nepotism works—Ziffren was married to the daughter of Sol Wurtzel's brother, who was an agent. I worked with Lester for a while. He was an ex-newspaperman; he's still alive and a nice fellow. Then I worked with another nepotistic character named Jack Jungmeyer, whose father was a reporter on the *Hollywood Reporter* and who was married to the daughter of Charlie Skouras [brother of Spyros Skouras]. Jack didn't know anything about movies. I did; I knew quite a lot about movies, though I wasn't very skilled at writing.

At Fox, what was the working environment like, compared to MGM?

It was a better place. We had a lovely bungalow that once had belonged to Jesse Lasky. It was called the writers' building, and it was very comfortable and lush and away from the main administration building. The hotshot writers—many of them—worked in the main administration building, which is still there, just as you enter off Pico [Boulevard]. This Lasky bungalow consisted of about twenty offices. I worked there in the 1930s and then again in 1940, when I went back there and got moved up to Zanuck's unit to work with a guy named Milton Sperling, who was at that time married to Harry Warner's daughter. More nepotism.

Would you say writers were more valued at Fox?

I wouldn't say so, but they had more comfortable surroundings.

Did you have any more or less contact with directors?

None. Well, I had a little. I did a film there called *Jennie* for Wurtzel. Wurtzel had decided he wanted to do something a little better than what he had been doing. Ordinarily he did Mr. Moto and Charlie Chan pictures and other kinds of B pictures. He bought something from *Story* magazine—I don't remember who wrote it—called *Jennie*. It was an anti-Nazi story about a young girl in Pennsylvania who started an uprising against her martinet father, who was a German. I got to work on that story, with Harold Buchman. I met the director of the film, who was a man named David Burton, and I worked with him for a couple of weeks.

I later worked with Harold Buchman at Columbia too. I only did one film at Columbia, *North of Shanghai*. That had a funny beginning, because there I was working in what was known as a C unit, not a B unit. There was a lower category than a B. B films cost about one hundred and twenty-five thousand dollars. C pictures cost about sixty-five thousand. Columbia made C movies. A friend of mine was the head of the C unit. He too was nepotistically set up, because he was the son of the president of Columbia, who was not Harry

Cohn but [his brother] Jack Cohn. Jack Cohn's son Ralph Cohn was in charge of C pictures, and it was Ralph who gave me a job. Anyway, I went to work with Harold Buchman again. Ralph Cohn said, "We recently made a movie— *The Bitter Tea of General Yen*, with Nils Asther—which has a Chinese background. Before we tear down the sets, we want to use them for another movie. Go out and look at the sets and see what you can put together to use in a Chinese story, because that will make the production look very rich even though it's a sixty-five-thousand-dollar picture."

Sharpshooters at Fox was based on my original story about a newsreel photographer, and I used the same plot for *North of Shanghai*, more or less. This one was about a newsreel photographer who goes to China to cover the Chinese-Japanese war and meets a girl. I think Elissa Landi and James Craig were in the Columbia picture. They were sort of a Poverty Row leading lady and leading man. It was directed by a guy named D. Ross Lederman, who really made D movies. He was well-known as a maker of cheap movies and worked at Columbia for years.

Harold Buchman was Sidney Buchman's brother?

He was the younger brother of Sidney Buchman, who was a much more successful writer. Harold got blacklisted, too, and went to England and married a very rich woman, so he didn't have to do much work after that.

How did his talent compare to Sidney's?

He idolized his older brother. Sidney was more talented, but Harold was a competent writer, and I enjoyed working with him. I did two or three films with him.

You said Wurtzel was a tough boss but a good one.

He was very tough, and he had a murderous tic. I don't know if it's ever been written about. His tic was to grin at you. You'd be telling him a story, and he'd be grinning at you, and you'd think, "My God, he loves it," and he'd say, "That stinks!" Everyone knew about it except you, when you first went to work for him; it really was distracting as hell.

I was stuck with Wurtzel, but meanwhile some of my friends were working on the big pictures like *In Old Chicago*, which involved the Chicago fire. That was made to copy *San Francisco*, incidentally, which MGM had made about the San Francisco earthquake and fire. Zanuck said, "Aren't there any other cities that have had disasters?" and somebody said, "Yeah. Chicago had a big fire." A friend of mine named Richard Collins, who subsequently became an informer before the Committee, did the original story for *In Old Chicago*.

How long did you stay at Fox?

Over a year. I worked on a number of B films. Another one I did was a film called *Island in the Sky*, based on a story that Wurtzel bought. But they never used the story that we wrote; someone else rewrote it. I wasn't really a very good writer, so I was always being rewritten. I didn't like working in the B unit, but I never moved out of it during my first stay at Fox. I guess I got fired; maybe I quit. I don't know—but I moved on.

My next job was more satisfactory. I went over to Paramount. I had kind of a reputation as a writer of children's stories, or young people's stories, because I was young. I got a job over there working for William LeBaron, a totally different kind of producer. In the first place, he wasn't Jewish, which was unusual. He wanted to make a film using a lot of young people, and it was going to be a musical. By young people I don't mean children; they had to be in their early twenties. He wanted to discover new talent, and there were a lot of tests made to discover them. The story was about a bunch of unemployed actors who take over a moribund theater in New York and put on their own show. He had a script, and he didn't like it; I rewrote the script, and he liked it. They shot my script. It was called *Dancing on a Dime*.

But there is a funny story about that movie pertaining to the new talent. He went to Broadway, and he looked at dancers and whatnot, and one of the newcomers was a guy named Danny Kaye. I saw Danny Kaye's test with LeBaron, and LeBaron said, "No, we can't use him. He's too Jewish." [Laughs.] The next year Danny Kaye went to Goldwyn.

What was Paramount like?

I liked it. I was actually hired there to work on a Henry Aldrich movie, and I worked on that film, but I didn't get credit. Then I worked on *Dancing on a Dime*. Or maybe it was the other way around; I have no idea anymore.

What was good about Paramount?

Well, *Dancing on a Dime* was one of the few films I wrote that got shot as I wrote it. It was directed by the same guy who directed *We Went to College*, by the way—Joseph Santley. I thought the film, except for the rejection of Danny Kaye, turned out pretty well. It was a nice idea.

This brings us to Winter Carnival. *Let me ask you how you got hooked up with that legendary project.*

That's an interesting story, which I've written about at great length in my memoir. Here it is in brief: I got married in January 1939, and my wife, Louise [Seidel, an actress], and I had a small amount of money—four or five thousand dollars, which in those days seemed like a lot. So we decided that we would just spend the money and travel, and that when the money was gone we'd come back to Hollywood and go to work. We sold one car and drove away in another car, and we got as far as Hanover, New Hampshire, on our honeymoon trip. Our intention was then to go to Europe and stay in Europe until the money ran out.

But when we got to Hanover it was February, time for [Dartmouth's] winter carnival, and Schulberg was there with Walter Wanger and F. Scott Fitzgerald. They were working on the script of *Winter Carnival*. I was always a little bitter that Wanger hadn't hired me to work on the movie, but he hadn't. Schulberg had been on it for about a year and had been getting nowhere. Wanger was getting desperate, because there wasn't going to be another winter carnival until February 1940, and he knew he had to shoot some scenes this February. So he had hired Fitzgerald to work with Schulberg, maybe to goose Schulberg and get him off the ground—provided Fitzgerald was sober. The story that Schulberg tells about Fitzgerald [in his novel *The Disenchanted*]is accurate up to a point. Budd's father did come to the airplane to see them off in L.A., and he gave them two bottles of champagne. That kicked off Fitzgerald, who had been on the wagon but started to drink again. By the time they got to Hanover, Fitzgerald was pretty high, and, in short, he conked out. I met Fitzgerald there. I went to all the affairs with them because I was there on my honeymoon, but when Wanger blew his stack and fired Fitzgerald, he told Schulberg to hire me to work with him, and that's how I got on the movie. Schulberg doesn't remember that.

He doesn't?

I was on it for six weeks with him. The way in which it started is what he doesn't remember. He wrote in *The Disenchanted* that he got fired, too, and went to New York with Fitzgerald. He believes that now. But he didn't; he never got fired. He stayed right in Hanover, and Wanger said, "Call your friend Rapf and get him to work on the project." I didn't want to do it, because I was on my honeymoon and because I no longer had any desire to work on this movie, which by now was in serious trouble. Fitzgerald hadn't done a goddamn thing on the script, and they were really stymied.

Had you ever met Fitzgerald before?

No, I met him at the winter carnival for the first time. I went out with him to the outdoor evening, where he was fairly sober, and then after that he apparently went to some fraternity houses and drank all night. I was at the cocktail party where he came down the stairs and fell on his face. I saw that, too. Wanger had arranged a cocktail party to show off his prize author to the English department. The prize author came down the stairs right in the middle of the lobby of the Hanover Inn and—*clunk*—fell on his face. It was terrible.

Fitzgerald didn't write a single word of the screenplay?

I doubt it. I never saw a single word that he wrote. I inherited a little bit of an idea, but it seems to me that it was mostly Schulberg's. I got credit on that movie for both story and screenplay, and I shouldn't have. What happened was that Wanger fired me after six weeks. The script we finally wrote has everything in it that's in the final film. I have that script, and it's pretty terrible—just like the movie. I'd like to be able to say that Lester Cole, whom Wanger brought in afterward, ruined it, but he didn't. He did some extra work on it, made it a little more shootable, but it's the same script.

In any case, I got fired, and Schulberg, who had been on the production by this time for over a year, went to Wanger and said, "If he gets fired, I go." And Wanger used that old line that's always used by producers, "If you walk off this picture, you'll never work in Hollywood again!" Which is bullshit. [Laughs.] Schulberg should have walked off the project, but he didn't. He stayed on—which is some indication of his character—and Cole was brought in.

That was a strange circumstance, because Cole was a friend of both Schulberg's and mine, and since Cole later wrote a book, called *Hollywood Red*, in which he admitted he was a member of the Party, I can admit I knew he was a member of the Party. I couldn't attack Cole, so I left, and Cole and Budd worked on it for a few more weeks. [Lead actress] Ann Sheridan was coming on the first of April, and Wanger had to pay her whether he was shooting or not. I think I got fired in the beginning of March. He thought I was holding up the works, because I kept saying the script wasn't any good and we should rewrite it. He said I was being a perfectionist. He had to shoot; he had to get somebody in there who was really a craftsman and could put together something they could shoot. I was presumably buggering up the project by saying the script wasn't good enough. And it wasn't. I was right.

What was Lester Cole like at this time?

He was all right. Lester was always a very opinionated character and rather difficult sometimes because he had his own way of looking at things. He was very forceful. He had been an actor, you know, before he was a writer, and he knew how to present himself and his ideas. He was quite a skilled character and in the Party a very dominating character. I thought of him, at the time that he was brought in on this film, as sort of a hack writer, but Lester could turn out a shooting script; that's where the money was. Later on, Lester got into a relationship at Metro with [producer] Jack Cummings that apparently lifted him out of the professional situation he had been in, and he became a better writer.

Anyway, when the credits for *Winter Carnival* were issued by the producer, I didn't get a credit at all. I read the final script, and I was perfectly satisfied, because I thought the final script was terrible too, but my agent said, "That's ridiculous. It's your story, isn't it?" I said, "Yeah, it's my story all right, and it's got a lot of scenes in it that I wrote, but it's done so badly." He said, "Do you think you're entitled to credit?" I said, "Well, I'm probably entitled, but I don't think I should take credit." My agent insisted I should. He said, "It's an important picture. You've worked on nothing but B pictures. This is an A picture. It'll do you good. United Artists, Wanger, et cetera." I called up Schulberg when Cole was in his office and told Budd that my agent wanted me to protest the credits, and Cole didn't fight it, so I got credit. But I didn't have to take credit; I was nicely out of it. Unfortunately, it was very painful, because for six months after that picture came out, I couldn't get a job.

Why?

I'd go to a producer, and we'd be having a nice talk about what I was going to do with a certain project, and then as I'd be leaving and it looked as if it was all set, he'd say, "Didn't you work on *Winter Carnival*?" And I wouldn't get the job. [Laughs.]

It was a notoroius stinker.

Oh, it was listed by the *New York Times* as one of the ten worst films of the year. The result was, I was unemployed for six months. And because we ran out of money, my wife, Louise, went back to work for MGM as one of the inmates of a girls' school in a turkey called *Forty Little Mothers*, starring Eddie Cantor. It was her last work as a professional actress.

What kind of guy was Walter Wanger that he was unable to finesse this situation?

Wanger had no interest in making movies, to be honest about it. He just liked being a boss. He liked his position of prestige. But he really wasn't very good at making movies. He *acted* as if he was good, but I always felt it was a big chore for him to have to read a script. I got hired in Hanover, but when I first went to work for him I had to meet with him in New York. The understanding was that Schulberg and I could stay in Hanover and work on the script, and that sounded good—to get paid to stay in Hanover; plus, Walter doubled my salary, which was another reason I took the job.

First of all, he didn't abide by his promise to let us work in Hanover. He was in New York, staying at the Waldorf, and he said we had to come to New York because we had to confer with him. He was appearing on *Town Meeting of the Air*, which was a weekly program, very popular. It was to radio what PBS is to television today, a serious program, broadcast from Town Hall in New York every week, with distinguished people talking about major issues and answering questions from the audience. That's why Wanger was in New York. He loved that kind of thing. He liked to be a statesman. I don't think he was yet president of the Academy [of Motion Picture Arts and Sciences], but he was going to be very shortly, and he was a great spokesman for the industry. This particular *Town Meeting of the Air* was about world peace, or some damn thing; he was going to be on the program with Dorothy Thompson, who was a noted international correspondent, and he had someone writing his speech. That is what he was really interested in. He wasn't interested in *Winter Carnival*. After he did his chore and appeared on *Town Meeting of the Air*, he was going back to California.

He said, "You guys have got to come back to California with me." I said, "That wasn't the understanding. I'm not going back to California. I haven't even got a place to live out there. I am heading to Europe on my honeymoon." He said he'd buy me a railroad ticket back and forth and put me up at a hotel for the duration. I said, "What about my car?" He said, "We'll ship your car out there." He did do all of those things, and he did pay me the money for travel from and back to New York, but unfortunately, my wife became pregnant in the course of this time, so I never did get away to Europe. It was about sixteen years before I went abroad.

What about the picture you did next, Call of the Canyon?

I can't remember much about it, though I have a print of it, actually.

What studio was it?

Republic. I worked at almost every studio, to tell you the truth. My agent used to send me around from place to place, and I got jobs everywhere. I worked at Republic for quite a while. *Call of the Canyon* is a Gene Autry movie about a radio station in Las Vegas, as I recall. I collaborated a lot. Everybody felt that I was a kind of raw, undisciplined talent, so they would put me to work with old-timers. They put me with a woman named Olive Cooper on that project. They took me off it after I completed the story; I never worked on the script at all.

I was then assigned to a John Wayne picture, and they made the film, but I don't think it bore any resemblance to anything I wrote. It was called *King of the Barbary Coast.* I have a script upstairs that I wrote for it; it was a typical Wayne character, although it could just as easily have been Jimmy Cagney. It was a little bit of a take-off on *San Francisco,* with a gangster type who is a decent fellow. I stayed at Republic and did a Roy Rogers movie, but I don't remember what the hell the title was.

The Gene Autry movie was definitely my story, because I brought to it a personal experience, which is in *Call of the Canyon.* It's a modern-day western, which Autry sometimes did. He rides his horse occasionally in the film but also rides in a jeep and in cars. I had been in Las Vegas once—the old Las Vegas, not the modern Las Vegas; the old Las Vegas used to be a great frontier town, not like it is today—and I'll never forget one event. I was there on Labor Day, and there was a Labor Day parade. I saw all of the guys who worked in the casinos out on the street—pasty-faced guys, because they were always up all night, with eyeshades. They looked ridiculous in the sunshine, pushing baby carriages. It dawned on me that they were human beings. I had never thought of them as human beings. I thought that detail should be in a movie sometime, so it's in *Call of the Canyon.* [Laughs.] That's all I remember about that movie.

How was your involvement in the Party changing or accelerating in the late 1930s and early 1940s?

My main job in the Party was always the Screen Writers Guild. I was an active Guild member. The Guild was recognized after we won the NLRB election of 1937—we won on a studio basis, but not on an industry-wide basis—and I was supposed to help get a contract. But we couldn't get a contract from the producers right away; it took another three or four years for that to happen, as I recall.

The Guild leadership pushed me too far, I thought. My father thought so, too. They put me on the board and made me secretary of the Guild. The Party could control an election, you know. Otherwise, people like me and Harold Buchman and even Ring would never have been elected to the board of the Screen Writers Guild. We didn't deserve to be on the board.

How could the Party control the election?

Oh, by passing out a slate and urging people to vote for it. Not everybody voted, anyway. It was a concerted group who voted. I got elected secretary of the Guild on two occasions not because of the Communist vote but because of the vote the Communists *influenced*. A lot of people who were certainly not Communists had a lot of respect for me, because I ran the arbitration committee and set up the whole arbitration code that the Guild used.

You say the Party pushed you too hard. What do you mean?

Well, when we finally negotiated with the producers, I remember going to one meeting—this is recounted in Nancy Lynn Schwartz's book [*The Hollywood Writers' Wars*]—where I was on the negotiating committee, and I shouldn't have been on the negotiating committee with the producers. Those were all my father's buddies, and I had to get up and make the case for the Guild's credit proposal. In one instance, I said something about the producers violating the principle of the agreement, and Eddie Mannix sat up and said, "I'm not going to sit here and listen to that snot-nosed kid tell me that I violated an agreement." My father had predicted that this would be the case— the Party was using me as a front. And he was right, they were. I shouldn't have done that. I shouldn't have been on the negotiating committee. I wasn't a snot-nose, but I was a youngster, and I had known those guys since I was a child. You don't put that kind of person up in front of the negotiating committee.

They were using you for your name.

Yeah.

What were your other activities in the Party?

That was my primary activity. The only other activity I had was in the Democratic Party. I was on the Democratic County Committee at one time. I had been an organizer of the Westwood Democratic Committee. This was around 1940. It was an attempt to use FDR sympathizers for a lot of good causes. I was active in that, and finally I ran for office and got elected to the Democratic County Committee. I was on the ballot, in fact, although there was nobody opposing me.

Were you growing disillusioned with these assignments?

No.

Every time you moved to a different studio, you got assigned to a different group?

No, every time the Party changed its mind about how we should be organized. Once it would be on a neighborhood basis; once it would be on a studio basis; once it would be on a craft basis. It kept changing. The groups were never more than a dozen.

I stayed in the Party during the war, while I was trying to get into the service. The first thing I did, right after war was declared, was go to see Colonel [Irving] Briskin, whom I knew because he was a friend of my father's. He was vice-president of Columbia Pictures, and he had immediately taken an assignment as a colonel in the Signal Corps. I knew that he was hiring a lot of Hollywood people to go to Astoria, Long Island. I thought, "That's what I want to do." I went to see him, and he said, "What's your draft status?" I said, "Three-A," and he said, "Well, when you get to be One-A, come back to see me." But I never got to be One-A, so I never got into the Signal Corps.

I made some terrible mistakes during this period, because the Party was secret, you know, and yet everybody who talked to me—all the recruiters— they knew exactly what was going on in the Party, because they had so many informers. It was ridiculous to deny membership, but I did. It was one of the reasons why I wasn't accepted into the Navy. The first question the Navy recruiter asked me was, "Are you now a member of the Communist Party?" [Laughs.] I had gone down to enlist, and I was all set to go into a unit. I was only worried about my physical problems—my eyes, my nose, and things like that. But that wasn't what interested them at all. The guy started right out with that one question, and I lied. I shouldn't have. He knew! That's why he asked the question.

In the end, you didn't perform any military service?

No. I did work for various agencies, though. I worked for the Office of Inter-American Affairs on about four movies. You see, the Writers Guild had a service organization called the Hollywood Writers Mobilization. A lot of us signed up to do work, for no pay, for any branch of the service. I did several films with the Office of Inter-American Affairs; that was [Nelson] Rockefeller's group. The objective of those films was to keep South America pro-Ally instead of pro-Nazi. So we made films about subjects like "How to Purify Water" and whatnot. I worked on two films with a German émigré [novelist] named Lion Feuchtwanger, who spoke no English, so we really didn't confer about anything. He was a big name, and I was not a big name. He would write stuff in German, and it would be translated for me.

How did you end up at the Disney studio?

In fact, I started at Disney before the war ended. I was about to go into the Industrial Incentive Division of the Navy as an ensign. I had been recruited, and this was before that terrible interview I told you about, when I was asked, "Are you a member . . . ?" and I lied. I had about five or six weeks to wait until my commission came through. My agent said, "Do you want to work at Disney?" I said, "Oh, God, no. I don't want to go to an animation studio." He said, "Well, you've got five or six weeks, and they'll be glad to have you." The assignment was the Uncle Remus stories. I said, "He shouldn't make that into a movie, anyway, because it's going to be an Uncle Tom movie." He said, "Well, go and talk to Walt Disney anyway." So I went to see Disney, who had once worked for my father, and I told him, "You shouldn't make this movie."

Had you ever met Disney?

No. Disney said, "That's exactly why I want you to work on it—because I know that you don't think I should make the movie. You're against Uncle Tomism, and you're a radical. That's exactly the kind of point of view I want brought to this film."

Really? He said that?

He did say it. He always knew I was a radical.

How could he know?

He must have looked into my background before I went there to meet him. I had been named way before the big investigation.

In the State of California hearings?

No, in the *Hollywood Reporter*. There was a writer for the *Hollywood Reporter* named Jack Moffitt, and Jack Moffitt at one time wrote a piece saying that Ring Lardner Jr., Budd Schulberg, and Maurice Rapf controlled the Communist Party in Hollywood. To which Sam Goldwyn said, "If they're the ones who are running it, we've got nothing to worry about." [Laughs.] Moffitt is the guy who named me in 1947. He appeared before the House Un-American Activities Committee at their first hearing and named me—again.

Weren't you surprised, though, when Disney said these things to you?

Sure. But I had boned up on the project a bit. There was an author named B. A. Botkin who wrote a book called *A Treasury of American Folklore*, and he had a long chapter on Joel Chandler Harris, the author of the Uncle Remus stories, in which Botkin, a spokesman for American folklore who was also a progressive, said that the stories which Remus had told, and which Harris had, in a sense, simply transcribed, were really stories of slave revolt—the little guy outwitting the big guy. So I had a kind of rationale ready for working on this film. When I went to see Disney, and he said, "You're the person who is going to prevent it from being an Uncle Tom story," I accepted the job.

I went to work. After I had that experience with the Navy recruiter, I never got my commission, so I just stayed at Disney for two and a half years.

Song of the South took that long?

I wasn't just working on *Song of the South*. I didn't stay on *Song of the South* for very long. I was on that film for only six or seven weeks. I got into a fight with my collaborator, the guy who had written the original story, who was a southerner. The fight wasn't about the script at all. It was about the fact that my collaborator was pursuing a messenger girl on the lot and pretending to be me. I confronted him with that, and he wouldn't admit it, but I knew it was true because I had seen the girl, who had told me, "You're not the Maurice I know." So I went to the producer—not to Disney—and said, "I can't work with this guy anymore. One of us has to go." And I got fired. But Disney hired me back.

To work on what?

Cinderella.

How different was it to be writing animation?

I loved it. I thought Disney was the best producer I ever worked for.

Really?

The most imaginative, the most helpful, the most interested. He really cared about movies, which is more than you can say about a lot of guys I worked with.

What was Disney like in a story conference?

He was insatiable. He taught me something that I've carried with me to this day. He would say, "Well, I think it's damn good, but we've got to make it better." Anything that you think is good, you can make better; he taught me that, and I try to pass it on to students. It's one of the reasons he was a maddening guy to work for. He ended every conference by saying, "Well, I think we've really licked it now." Then he'd call you the next morning and say, "I've got a new idea." And he'd have one. Sometimes the ideas were good, sometimes they were terrible, but you could never satisfy him.

Was it always him, or was it sometimes his producers taking the creative lead?

It was him. He was the boss. A lot of the guys I worked with at Disney couldn't stand him because of that. He stuck his nose into everything. He would come around on weekends and snoop in their offices to see what they were doing and what their projects were like, before a story conference. He'd look at their storyboards on the wall. If you were working on a script—which was the case with *Cinderella*; I never did a storyboard, only a script—you could conceal what you were doing. But the difference between working at Disney and anyplace else was that if you were doing a storyboard you couldn't conceal it; it was up on the wall. And he'd come around on weekends to see exactly where you were and what you were doing—what the jokes were, and so on. A lot of guys didn't like that at all. I liked Disney and got along fine with him. He always knew I was a lefty, and I always wonder what would have happened if I had stayed there. Blacklisting me would have been embarrassing for him. He wouldn't have liked to fire me, but he would have fired me, of course. I left long before that had to happen.

How would you define Disney's politics?

He was very conservative, except in one particular—he was a very strong environmentalist. He once told me why he was conservative; I asked him. I said, "It doesn't make any sense for you to be as conservative as you are." He told me a story that I don't believe, but that he nevertheless told me in the presence of other people, explaining why he had become a conservative. He said it had to do with the fact that his father was a Socialist. They lived in Kansas City, Missouri, which was run by the Pendergast Democratic machine. There was an election coming up, and a bunch of Irish kids, sons of the ward heelers who worked for the Democratic machine, stopped him on the street and asked him, "How's your father going to vote in this election?" Disney said, "Well, he ain't going to vote for your candidates. He's going to vote for Eugene V. Debs." Or someone like that. Disney said that these kids then put hot tar on his balls. He said, "From then on, I was always a dyed-in-the-wool Republican." I don't believe that story, but he did tell it to me.

Was he at all a Fascist sympathizer or anti-Semite?

I never felt he was. He knew I was Jewish, too. But I don't think he was an anti-Semite. I think he was a decent enough guy who was very conservative, and it got worse as time went on and as he got richer. When I worked for him, the Disney studio was not very solid. They saved themselves during the war with war contracts, but he took all the money he made on *Snow White*—and he made a lot of money on *Snow White*—and poured it into this new studio, which was built to be converted into a hospital if he couldn't pay off the mortgage. It actually was converted during the war; a whole Army unit moved in and was quartered there for a period of time. Then, of course, the strike hurt him a lot, and that made him more reactionary because he felt the strike was Communist-inspired. He did believe that. His brother [Roy] must have convinced him, and he had a lawyer, Gunther Lessing, who was a leading anti-Communist "authority." So he was being fed all this stuff by his brother and his lawyer. On the other hand, he knew I was a red, and he liked me and other reds. It was a little like *Winter Carnival*, because the guy who succeeded me on *Song of the South* was a fellow lefty named Morton Grant.

Ironically, when the film was later attacked by the NAACP, I thought the attack was justified—I didn't like the film either. I had to go to a meeting in Hollywood, at the People's Education Center, which was a left-wing educational group. Speakers from the NAACP came, and I was supposed to defend *Song of the South*. But I couldn't do it. I had to agree with the attackers.

What remained of your writing contribution?

Oh, a lot. And my script was terrible. I've looked at it since. The script is just as racist as the film, although there is also a lot that is different.

How do you account for that? You weren't politically unsophisticated.

Disney didn't make it clear that the film wasn't about slavery and that it was set during Reconstruction. In my script I had the white family poverty-stricken, and that's a lot different from what you see on the screen. Their house in the film is immaculate, very white—it's a white mansion on a plantation. The women wear different dresses every time you look at them. I indicated in my script very clearly that they should be threadbare, because they lost the war. *Gone with the Wind* is pretty accurate in this regard. After the war, Tara is really run-down; Scarlett O'Hara builds it up by marrying the schlemiel with a business. This doesn't happen in *Song of the South.*

Also, the whole reason for the father leaving the kid in the first place is very different in the final script from mine. In mine he leaves because they haven't got enough money to pay the people who are working there; he goes to Atlanta to earn some money so he can pay the blacks who work on the farm. That's different.

Instantly Song of the South *became more notorious than* Winter Carnival. *It became your most embarrassing credit.*

It still is. [Laughs.] I keep getting attacked for that damn movie, and I constantly tell the story about going to see Disney and him saying to me, "I want you on it to prevent it from being anti-black." Disney and I talked about it all the time. There was always this great risk.

He told me another story that I don't necessarily believe, but maybe it was true. Of course, I was still working at Disney when the film came out and was attacked. He said the reason the film was being attacked was because of a leading black actor in Hollywood, an actor who had been in almost every movie in which there was a sympathetic black character. His name was Clarence Muse. He was in a lot of movies, and when they did the West Coast production of *Show Boat* he played the Paul Robeson part. Muse was the head of the local NAACP chapter. According to Disney, Muse had come to him and said he wanted to be Uncle Remus. Disney hadn't hired him. He went to New York and hired James Baskett, who had been on *The Amos 'n' Andy Show.* That's the reason the movie was being attacked, he said. I don't think it's true, but that's what he told people.

Somebody else who has researched the project told me that Muse was actually hired to be a technical expert on the film. If so, he failed in his job. [Laughs.] I stayed at Disney for another year after *Song of the South* was finished. Disney liked me, and he told me he wanted me to write a script on every property he had. I did them, one after another, except for *Alice in Wonderland.* I refused to work on that, because I didn't think it would make a movie. I still think I'm right.

But you didn't get a credit for Cinderella?

They really used my script on *Cinderella*, but I didn't get credit because of the blacklist. It came out after the blacklist, and the studio didn't want to give me credit.

What remains of your contribution?

A lot. I structured it to make her a rebel who fights for what she wants, as a result of which she is locked up in the tower and is never going to be able to try on the glass slipper when the guy comes around. That's what I contributed to the story—I made her a rebel. I also put the limitations on the fairy godmother, which they used. I thought I created the mice characters, but they insisted that I didn't. I thought that, although they are different characters in my script, what they did I invented.

The studio had to notify me when the credits were issued. There were twenty names on that movie, for the story, but not mine. I said, "This is ridiculous. Send me the script." And I read the script. It's different from mine, but those things I just mentioned are in it. There was a hearing; I didn't go to California for it. It was arbitrated by the Writers Guild in 1949 or 1950, when I was already blacklisted. The Guild decided that I had done twenty percent of the final film, but according to Guild rules you have to do twenty-five percent to get screenplay credit.

But that film wasn't credited by the Writers Guild, anyway. It was credited by the Screen Cartoonists Guild, so there are twenty names on it. This means that, if there are twenty names, nobody had to contribute more than five percent. Anyway, I didn't get credit, but I'm in the Writers Guild records as a contributor to the screenplay.

Disney didn't want to give you credit?

I don't know that it was Disney himself. I didn't correspond with Disney. I corresponded with his story editor.

Did you ever speak to Disney again, after leaving the studio?

No, because he was a different guy once television came in. Things changed a lot. I had no further contact with the studio. I never tried to go back there. But the experience helped me a lot in New York, later, because, having worked for Disney for two and a half years, I had gotten a reputation as an expert on animation. Which I wasn't. Although *Cinderella* was an animated film, and although there was a lot of animation in *Song of the South*.

Working in New York, in the 1950s, I found that animation was very popular, and I was able to do a lot of animation. I'm still invited to animation conferences. I was an animation *writer*, not an animator, although Disney was one of the only places I know of that took live-action movies seriously. They used to run movies at lunchtime for animators and directors to look at—

Chaplin movies, Buster Keaton movies, and so forth. That's where they got a lot of their comedy ideas.

Was the Disney studio the last place you worked in Hollywood before the blacklist?

Yes. What happened was that I quit the studio early in 1947 and found out that I had really burned my bridges by working there. My agent couldn't get me a job. People said, "Well, he's been working in animation for two years."

Why did you quit, ultimately?

Because Disney wouldn't give me a raise.

Personally, in a face-to-face meeting?

In a face-to-face meeting. He said to me that I was getting more money than anyone else at the studio, and that I couldn't get any more money as a writer. If I wanted to make more money, I had to become a producer. I regarded that as an insult. I didn't want to do that. All my friends in the industry, guys like [Paul] Jarrico and [Ring] Lardner [Jr.], were getting thousands of dollars a week, and I hadn't had a raise in two and a half years. I was still paid exactly what I was paid when I first went to work there.

Was Disney cheap?

To me it seemed cheap. I would have stayed for a hundred-dollar-a-week raise, but he wouldn't give it to me. He claimed that I got the highest salary at the studio among his creative people. Whether that was true or not, I don't know. But he wouldn't give me a raise unless I did something other than just write, and that's why I quit. I think it was a mistake. I shouldn't have quit. It would have been interesting to see what he would have done when the shit hit the fan later that year, because I couldn't get a job after I left Disney. I had no credits except *Song of the South*, and people considered that an animated film. *So Dear to My Heart*, which I also worked on, didn't come out until later.

Where were you when the blacklist came down?

I had left Hollywood. I heard that there was a subpoena out for me, sometime in September 1947. I hadn't had a job since I left Disney, which was in February or thereabouts. I'd gone four or five months without a job. Schulberg had been after me for a long time to get the hell out of Hollywood. So I decided this was as good a time as any to make the move. I went East in September. The 1947 hearings actually took place while I was in the East, looking for a place to move to.

What were you going to do, theoretically, once you left Hollywood?

Write a novel or short stories but not be dependent on the movie industry. Neither Schulberg nor I had a great deal of respect for the movie industry, because we were too close to it. It was a commercial business, in our view, and nothing more. The fact that once in a while a good movie or something special was made I never took seriously.

Let's go back a few months. When did you announce that you were quitting the Party?

I never announced it. I just stopped going to meetings.

When you stopped going to meetings, did people come and speak to you and try to coax you back into the routine?

No, nobody gave a damn about me. I don't remember, to tell you the truth, how it happened. I just remember that I stopped going. I think we were reorganized for the umpteenth time, and I probably had no place to go, anyway. So there was nobody to come after me. I was just a factotum in the party. I was a treasurer. I was a book distributor. I was active in the Guild. I did various chores. We all did.

Let me be sure I get this straight: You quit—but not out of any political disillusionment.

No, I had no political differences with the Party. I told you about the one piece of good advice I got when I came back from the Soviet Union: Selznick had said to me, "You've got to choose between being a moviemaker and being a Communist." In effect, what I chose to do, in 1947, was to be a moviemaker. I decided Selznick was right. It took too much time and energy to be in the Party. Although it's true that some people used the Party very strongly for their professional ends. There's no doubt about that—people hired Party people; they read each other's scripts and were helpful. But I never got any such help from the Party. I just decided I had to learn my craft as a writer.

It was at least six months before I left Hollywood that I stopped going to Party meetings. But I didn't stop my Guild activities. And I still considered myself a Communist. I even did when people came to see me in New York in 1951 to ask me that dumb question, "Are you now or have you ever been a card-carrying member of the Communist Party?" [Laughs.]

Let me ask you this question. It's always been my hunch that, as widespread and pervasive as the blacklist tried to be, some percentage of the people must have fallen through the cracks. True?

No, I don't think so.

Any percentage?

Very small. I think they got everybody. I don't know anybody who slipped between the cracks.

Not simply members of the Party but staunch left-wingers?

There were so many spies, and perhaps we should have known who were the informers in our groups. The informers knew precisely who was in the Party and who wasn't, but the Party people didn't know all the informers. The only meetings that were attended by non-Party people were fraction meetings, of the Writers Guild, for example, where there were non-Party people, and where you couldn't tell a Party person from a non-Party person. There'd be an informer there, and I would think he would later have named everybody.

Was there such a thing as an FBI agent or informer who actually became a screen-writer, eventually, with credits?

I don't remember any. [Laughs.] I think some of the screenwriters signed up with the FBI.

If you add up all the names of the people mentioned in various sessions and lists, you get up to several hundred. Was that the Party's strength at its height in Hollywood?

I'd say there were three hundred in the Party. I went to one meeting, about 1944, when obviously a lot of members weren't even there because they were in the service. It was during the period of the Communist Political Association, which was a fairly broad, open group. A lot of people came into membership under less scrupulous examination during that period than they would have had to undergo before. I remember going to one meeting, held in a hall, where there were about three hundred people, including a lot of people I didn't know were Communists. And I don't know for sure if they were. It was a big meeting.

It was rare to have a mass meeting like that.

Yes. Whenever I went downtown, I would meet with quite a few people, but not in Hollywood. The meetings were rather small. The writers' fraction was about the biggest group, as I recall, about twenty-five people. It was always a little surprising, actually, to find out who was in the writers' fraction, because you never really knew. They came from other groups. The writers' fraction crossed lines of individual cells.

So you went back East and found a place to live. Then what?

The hearings took place. I remember that I met another guy from the Party—whom I won't name—because we were staying at the same hotel. It was the Royalton, on Forty-fourth Street, across the street from the Algon-quin—it was like a cheap Algonquin. He was doing the same thing as I was, looking for a place to live before he brought his family east, because he was afraid he was going to be subpoenaed. I remember listening to the hearings with him while we were there.

I was going to Watertown, New York, and Redding, Connecticut, and all over, looking for a nice house, something interesting. Finally I found a place in New Jersey that was not far from Schulberg's, and then I went back to California for only two days. I picked up two of my children, and my wife and the baby came by airplane. I had found a place to live—a three-hundred-and-fifty-acre farm, later bought by [television anchorman] Chet Huntley and made into a beautiful place—but at the time it was very run-down, and it was hard to live. We didn't stay there very long. We moved to New Hampshire when summer came.

How did you go about getting work in the East?

I didn't get any.

For how long?

About three years.

None?

None.

What did you do for three years?

Well, we rented our California house when we left, for five hundred dollars a month, to [actress] Jeanne Crain's mother, and we lived off that rent for a while. I kept writing stories and they kept getting rejected. I also wrote two novels, and they were no good.

Then the next round of hearings began.

That's right.

One of the most prolific informers was your old friend Richard Collins. What was it about Collins that made him so well-liked before he turned tail and named everybody in front of the Committee?

I met Collins at Stanford, as a matter of fact. I don't know how he got started in Los Angeles—probably as a reader, because most of my friends started as readers. He was just a very engaging fellow. He was very erudite, too. I'll never forget his giving a lecture on "the history of art" once when we went off on a weekend jaunt. As time went on, he formed a collaboration with Paul Jarrico, and they worked on a lot of movies together and became quite successful. I always felt that Collins was riding a little bit on Jarrico's coattails, but at the same time Collins was a nice guy to be around. You could talk to him very easily, and I think that's one of the reasons everybody liked him. It was a great shock to find out that he was going to be an informer.

In fact, I was probably more shocked than anybody else, because he used to come to visit me when I lived in Norwich, Vermont, during the early blacklist period. Collins was thrown out of the industry, and his family lived in New York, and he returned to New York to go into business with his father. He had an idea for a business making patterns for ladies' dresses, but he needed money to get started. A lot of left-wing people who liked him, and who had money, invested in his business. He came to see me in Norwich, just before the second round of hearings, and I know that he wanted money, but I had absolutely no money. He stayed with me for four or five days, and I enjoyed being with him. I knew what he was going through. I knew it was very difficult. But two days after he left me, he appeared in Washington and named names.

You had no inkling?

None at all. It was really weird.

How do you diagnose what happened?

I don't know.

To this day?

His testimony raised a lot of complications, because it was not only unwarranted but false.* He named Budd Schulberg and was the first person to put Schulberg on the carpet. And Schulberg at that time had just completed his novel *The Disenchanted*, which had been accepted by the Book-of-the-Month Club for publication. I made a trip to New York shortly after Schulberg was named by Collins, and, as I say, his testimony created a big problem. I didn't know what the hell to do about it. I was really shocked by Collins's testimony, anyway.

He named you as well?

No, he didn't. No friend of mine ever named me. It was a very strange thing. Only the people I hated named me.

---

*In Victor Navasky's book *Naming Names*, Richard Collins explained how he—together with Meta Reis Rosenberg—decided who to name among their former friends and comrades and how this led to the inclusion of Budd Schulberg. "First we came up with a list of guys and ladies who were dead," Collins told Navasky, "and I said to Meta, 'I don't think that's going to work. That's a little soft; they're [the Committee] going to figure that one out.' So, between us, I suppose, or at least just to speak for myself, I must have known at least three hundred people from the Party. I had been in for ten years. I had been—what did they call it?—on the section committee, and in various branches, in fractions, and so forth, and so I really did know probably everybody. Maybe there were three or four people I didn't know.

"So we finally ended up with three categories. One was the ones who had died; the second was the ones who had been called [to testify], because we figured they were stuck already; and the third—and this was my mistake—were the ones who had left [the Party] a long time before. I had no idea that they would be bounced as hard as they were. I figured that having been out for ten years or nine years, like Schulberg, for instance, everybody would see that they *had* left. It was a tremendous mistake, because firstly the *New York Times* headlined Schulberg on the front page because he was a novelist of some importance, which is something that stupidly had never occurred to me. Then Martin Berkeley [whom he named], who had been out six or seven years, turned out to be the most voluble, I guess, of the witnesses."

I'm not sure that's so out of the ordinary. That's one of my theories about who was and who wasn't named, in some circumstances—that it had a lot to do with sub-textual or personal rivalries and enmities.

It's very odd, but Schulberg didn't name me, either, while I was named by guys like Martin Berkeley. He named hundreds of people. But the people who named me were not my friends. I didn't like them, anyway.

The point is, Schulberg never forgave me. I'm told—he never told me this, but I was told by his sister—that he was very bitter, because I didn't call him after Collins's testimony, to commiserate with him. However, I did meet with his mother in New York after Collins's testimony and commiserated with her about it. I said, "What is Budd going to do about it?" She didn't know. Shortly thereafter, I got a telephone call from a mutual friend of Schulberg's and mine—a guy who is now dead, so I can name him, also because he wasn't a Communist of any sort, just a friend of ours—named Paul Moss; I subsequently worked for him. Paul said, "I'm calling on behalf of BWS." That meant Budd Schulberg; I knew that. "He's going to testify tomorrow, and he wants you to know it. He also wants you to know he's going to do everything in his power to avoid implicating you"—and also somebody else he mentioned, who was a professor at Dartmouth. As far as I know, he did avoid implicating us; at least, in what I read of his testimony, he didn't include either me or the professor. But he didn't phone me himself.

I said to Moss, "Why isn't he calling me directly?" He said, "He thinks his phone was tapped." Maybe it was. This is what happened to Jarrico: He'd had a long talk with Collins, several nights before Collins testified, in which he tried to talk him out of informing. Later in the hearings the conversation was reported. So, conceivably, if Schulberg had called me, I would have said, "Oh, don't do it," and then he would have had to testify as to that. At any rate, he never called me, and we didn't talk again for thirteen years.

Are you saying—

Collins's implication of Schulberg is what prompted Schulberg to appear. Schulberg was never subpoenaed, you know.

It blew the door open.

Yeah. Schulberg was told by his father that he had to clear his name, or his book wouldn't be published by the Book-of-the-Month Club. It's not true, because the book was already accepted for publication but not announced. Budd did not have to appear, but he was talked into it and did it—just like Kazan.

Did you ever talk to Collins again?

Never. I've never had any contact with him.

Not after he left your home in Vermont and went to Washington to testify?

Right. He was here, and I have home movies of him here, and every time I look at those movies I get mad.

But you say you did speak to Schulberg again, after thirteen years.

I didn't know what to do about Schulberg. He had been my closest friend and had come to visit me maybe six or seven times between 1948 and 1951. Here in Hanover, when he visited, he would stay with me, and I would give a party, and all his friends would come. Well, that was over once he testified; people up here were kind of horrified by his testimony. It seemed very odd, when I moved to New York in 1951, that I would never run into him, but I never did. Others did, Lardner and so forth, from time to time, and didn't quite know how to behave. I didn't know what the hell I would do if I ever ran into him. I just didn't have any contact with him at all, although I saw his mother from time to time.

Was your contact with him thirteen years later accidental?

No, it was not accidental. It was very peculiar. It occurred this way: My youngest son and one of Schulberg's sons were both admitted to Dartmouth in 1964. I knew that, and I knew that he would probably bring his son to school just as I was bringing my son to school. There was a fair chance we were going to meet. So I called his mother, and I said, "I'm going to Hanover, and I imagine Budd's going to Hanover, too. We haven't seen each other in thirteen years, but tell Budd—I'm not going to call him—that if we run into each other we should act as if nothing has ever happened between us, because our problem is not our children's problem." Well, I arrived in Hanover and, believe it or not, the first person I saw was Budd Schulberg, standing on the corner right in the middle of town with his wife, actress Gerry [Geraldine] Brooks, and his son. We acted as if nothing had ever happened. We had dinner together that night and resumed our relationship without ever talking about the thirteen-year hiatus.

Is that still true? You have an ongoing relationship, and you still don't discuss the blacklist?

Yes. Well, we discussed it once. The one discussion we ever had about it arose because he wrote an autobiography, called *Moving Pictures: Memories of a Hollywood Prince*, which ends when he leaves for Dartmouth College. I read it, and I helped him a lot with that book. The original publisher was Abrams, but they weren't going to publish it unless Budd took it a few steps further. They wanted some stuff about the Communist Party, and they wanted him to conclude the book with the writing of *What Makes Sammy Run?* I told a representative of the publisher that Budd couldn't do that, because if he wrote about the next few years, he'd have to write about his joining the Communist Party, and he'd have to name names again. I told him that Budd had done that once and he'd better not do it again. Anyway, they backed out; they wouldn't publish the book without that material in it. Somebody else published it [Stein and Day, 1981].

He never put that material in?

Well, he promised this new publisher that he would write a sequel that took into account the period of time leading up to *What Makes Sammy Run?* We talked about that, and I told him he couldn't write that, and that if he did I certainly wasn't going to help him with it in any way, shape, or form. From here on in, he was on his own. I said, "How the hell are you going to write about the period at Dartmouth and the first couple of years in Hollywood without rehashing all of the material that you gave to the House Un-American Activities Committee, including names?" He said, "I don't know, but I'll figure out a way." He hasn't done the book yet, although he's still planning to do it. That's the only time we've discussed that situation.

That's amazing to me.

It is amazing, but we can't discuss it. We don't talk about our trip to the Soviet Union; we don't talk about our joining the Communist Party or any of that stuff.

Was there any interior logic to whom Budd named?

Lardner never forgave him for saying that he recruited Schulberg, because it was the other way around. [Laughs.] What really bothered me about the testimony were two things. One, I have no recollection whatsoever of his appearance before the Communist hierarchy in Hollywood to answer criticism of the book [*What Makes Sammy Run?*]. None. It does seem strange, since I was in Hollywood, that I wouldn't have been present if such a thing had taken place. However, I can't deny that it did, because he says that it did; he keeps saying it over and over—it's his main reason for leaving the Party. But I was never there.

I did read *What Makes Sammy Run?* in manuscript before it came out as a book, because his father and a few other people who had seen it felt that it was so anti-Semitic that it shouldn't be published. As I recall, he gave the book to a few people to read in Hollywood; he was at that time living in Vermont. He sent the book to F. Scott Fitzgerald, to me, to Lardner, and to a few other people. I got together with Fitzgerald to discuss Schulberg's book. Schulberg had said that if we all agreed it was anti-Semitic, then he wouldn't publish it. I didn't think it was. I was wrong, but I didn't think it was. Neither did Lardner. Neither did Fitzgerald. Fitzgerald was a little bitter about the book because he, at that time, was working on his own novel about Hollywood [*The Last Tycoon*], which he never completed, so he rather grudgingly liked the book but talked about its amateurish quality and so forth. As far as anti-Semitism is concerned, that is the only instance I remember when that book was submitted for discussion. But it wasn't discussion by the Party, because certainly Fitzgerald had nothing to do with the Party. It was simply given to friends of Schulberg's to read.

I thought the book was balanced. I recognized the character of Sammy—a composite of Norman Krasna and Jerry Wald. But there was also a character like my cousin who had accompanied us to the Soviet Union—he was the sympathetic Jewish voice who carried the story. The book did talk about Sammy's background on the Lower East Side; it was a little schmaltzy, actually, about the Jews in New York. So I didn't think it was anti-Semitic. But you know, what really happened with that book was that [Nazi propaganda minister Josef] Goebbels pirated it and published it in Germany as anti-Semitic literature. So it *was* anti-Semitic.

I didn't know that about Goebbels.

Well, I'm telling you. Five hundred thousand copies were published in Germany. Budd never got a nickel from them, but it was considered effective anti-Semitic propaganda by the Germans. So I was wrong; Fitzgerald and Lardner were wrong. The same thing happened to me, actually, with *Song of the South*, and I realized the effect of certain subjects on certain times. *Song of the South* got picketed by the NAACP, and they were quite right. On the other hand, that film can be run today, and it doesn't bother anybody, just as you can read *What Makes Sammy Run?* today and it doesn't bother anybody as a basis for anti-Semitism. In 1941 it was clearly useful anti-Semitism.

You said there were two things that bothered you about Schulberg's testimony. What was the other thing?

Only part of the testimony is in [Eric] Bentley's book [*Thirty Years of Treason*]. The Committee wasn't satisfied with Budd's testimony. They praised him for what he said about the Party's attack on his book and all that. But they said to him, "You were a leader of the group that was attacking the Committee, you gave parties at your house, and so forth"—which he did; he was in the forefront of the group that was fighting the Committee before he went and testified. They said, "What do you think of that? Don't you think you were wrong?" He didn't want to say he was wrong. In the testimony I read originally, he held out for about four pages and went all around the answer without giving the answer. What they wanted him to say was, "Yes, I was wrong, and I admire this Committee tremendously." He wouldn't say it, but he finally did. That's the second thing I objected to about his testimony. The rest of it may be valid. I don't know. He didn't lie, as far as I can see, and his excuse for the names he named was that they had already served jail sentences. And, of course, he named [Richard] Collins, because he wanted to get even with Collins. But that particular kowtowing to the Committee I object to. I know he never believed it. Because, basically, he's still a progressive guy, though he is very anti-Soviet.

This is why Schulberg and I began to split, a long time before he appeared before the Committee. He came under the influence of Arthur Koestler, to a large extent, and Koestler, who had also been a left-winger and a Socialist, was very anti-Soviet. Schulberg and I had exchanged a series of letters about the Korean War in which we were really in sharp disagreement about the nature of that war. And when Budd became part of the PEN organization, he lined up with all the anti-Soviets. Those people have some grounds for what they believe, but they're basically Trotskyites. [Laughs.] They hate the Communist Party, and they hate anybody who was associated with it. They think we should all get down on our knees and repent. I refuse to do it.

How about you and HUAC? Were you ever tempted to make any kind of accommodation?

Never. I was under subpoena all during the 1950s. But they never called me.

Were you being constantly stalked and confronted by investigators?

Yes, several times, once in particular. After moving to New York, I had been there only about a week, or not much more than that, when two guys appeared at the door and showed me badges and wanted to talk to me. I thought they had dropped my file somewhere, but they hadn't. It's just that when I was in New Hampshire I was of no use to them. But when I got to New York, I was interviewed by these two guys. Then I was subpoenaed. I was called almost immediately to appear at a hearing at [the federal courthouse in] Foley Square. I didn't appear, because the morning I was to appear I woke up with the mumps.

Was your interview with them a hostile one?

It was hostile, because I said to them, "I'll tell you anything you want to know about me, but I won't tell you anything about anybody else." But they really didn't want to know about me; they wanted to know about other people. So I didn't answer any of their questions, and they said they'd come back again. It was pretty harassing because they not only went after me, they went after my wife. They would stop her on the street and say, "Will you answer some questions?" She wouldn't do it, either.

The anecdote about why I didn't appear that time I was subpoenaed is really funny, because I was thirty-seven years old, and how the hell did I get the mumps at thirty-seven on the very day that I was supposed to appear before the House Un-American Activities Committee? I didn't have a doctor in New York, and my wife and I lived in a sublet apartment on West Eighty-sixth Street; she went downstairs and looked at the bulletin board to find a doctor, who then came to see me. He said, "You've got a problem. You've got the mumps." I said, "No, you've got a problem. I'm supposed to appear before the House Un-American Activities Committee in an hour, and you're going to have to call them and tell them I've got the mumps." He said, "Well, you've got the mumps." I said, "How long do you think I'm going to be sick?" He said, "How long do you think the hearings are going to last?" [Laughs.]

They didn't accept his word at all. They sent their own doctor. I really didn't have a bad case of the mumps, and by the time their doctor came I was fine. The hearings went on and on, and I was lying in bed pretending I had the mumps. Finally, the last week of the hearings—after three weeks of lying in bed—the doorbell rings one morning at nine o'clock. There's a young guy standing there in a Naval ensign's uniform with closely-cropped blond hair. If you ever saw the perfect Nordic, it was this kid—he was the doctor. Another guy was with him, the same type. This doctor looked at me, asked me to stick my tongue out, and poked around in my throat a little. He said, "Well, you've got the mumps, all right." I didn't have any mumps at all at this particular time. I said, "Well, how long to you think I'm going to be sick?" He said the same thing the first doctor had said. "How long do you think these hearings are going to last?" Extraordinary! [Laughs.]

These hearings ended a week later, after they had called about thirty people—almost everybody I knew in New York. That was in the fall of 1951, I think. Subsequently, I got subpoenaed again, for the Washington hearings. I was under subpoena for most of the 1950s, but I never got called. When I started working in sponsored films, it became a bit of a problem, since I was sent away a lot to different factories. I remember that once I was scheduled to be sent to Lancaster, Pennsylvania, to the Armstrong Cork Company, which makes linoleum, and it happened to occur during a time when I was under subpoena. I went to the producer of the film and explained that I had to let the House Un-American Activities Committee know where I was, that I might be called, and that I hoped it wouldn't be embarrassing for him. He said, "It won't. I'll say I never knew anything about it." That was the one thing the employers used to protect themselves. They would renounce you if you were called. It was understood. One guy, who was head of production for Screen Gems, wanted to hire me for a television job; this happened quite early in the 1950s. I said to him, "You know, I'm a blacklisted writer." He said, "You dumb son of a bitch! Don't you think I know that? Now I can't hire you!"

All this time, in the early 1950s, were you going in for interviews on television and radio scripts?

I was. I would go in to New York a lot when we lived in New Jersey and occasionally when we lived in New Hampshire. I kept trying to get jobs, but I was very honest, and I learned that I couldn't be honest. They'd say, "Why did you leave Hollywood?" Inevitably, somebody would ask that, and I would tell them the truth.

Weren't there friendly shows like Danger *and* You Are There *that you could apply to?*

For a long time I was tried to get a job at Dartmouth. I wanted to start a film program there, but it was premature, or else I was too left-wing—I don't know. When I realized that I couldn't get a job in Hanover, I moved to New

York, that was in 1951, and then I did find work after about six months. I did some television. I worked for Ring [Lardner Jr.] and Ian [McLellan] Hunter on some *Robin Hood* episodes. A lot of blacklisted people worked on those, at least everybody living in New York. There were several other series I worked on, always without any credit.

I did a movie, too, an uncredited movie. In England it's called *Father Brown*. The American title is *The Detective*—not the one with Frank Sinatra, but the one with Alec Guinness. It was made in England. This chap Paul Moss, who was a friend of Schulberg's and was the one who called me to tell me Schulberg was going to testify, wanted to break into the movie business. He had been a fight promoter, I think, and he was a very nice guy married to a very intelligent woman, Thelma Schnee, who was the sister of Charles Schnee, a movie writer and producer. She and her family had money and were willing to invest in projects for Paul to get into the movie business.

He got hold of the G. K. Chesterton stories about Father Brown and was going to make a movie. He wanted his wife to write the script, but she'd never written a script, so he hired me to work with her. I wrote a script with her, and they made the film. He went to England for the production; I stayed in New York. I thought I had a lifetime sinecure to beat the blacklist, because I was going to continue to work for him without credit. I was already working on a TV series for him. I had a full-time job with him. I didn't get very much money, but it didn't matter; it was enough. Then he had a heart attack and died right after that film was finished, and I lost my meal ticket. That was the only entertainment movie I worked on during the blacklist period without credit. His wife took solo credit.

I went back to Hanover in the summer of 1951, and I remember that this is when my life changed. I was out on the river with my children in a rowboat, fishing, when my wife came to the bank of the river and yelled, "There's somebody calling from New York about a job!" Well, I got back in as quick as I could and answered the phone, and it was a fellow from UPA, an animation studio that had just opened offices in New York. He had a project going and said, "I understand you write animation. Can you come to New York?" I said, "Sure, I'll be there tomorrow." So I went to New York, and I went to work for UPA, writing a sponsored film.

What's a sponsored film?

This one was for the Fragrance Foundation, and it was going to be about perfume. There were two jobs, actually. The other job was to start a series of educational but entertaining comedy shorts, with no sponsors, and I went to work on that, too. From then on, I was pretty busy.

Working exclusively for UPA?

No. I did two or three jobs for them; then I went to work for other people. Word got around that I was a guy who could write animation. It was then that I started to do storyboards also—that is, I worked with artists, and we did the storyboards together. It was all sponsored stuff. Ultimately, I began to direct these films, and they weren't all animation, either. Animation got priced out of the field, and by 1960 you couldn't do an animated sponsored film. They cost too much.

Just to be clear, a sponsored film is like an industrial film, right?

Right. I ended up doing about forty of them, writing and directing. I started directing in 1959, and from then on almost everything I wrote I directed.

Did you ever make a stab at working in Hollywood again?

No. I liked doing sponsored films. I liked it better than Hollywood.

Why?

Because I had more control. As a writer in Hollywood, I never got on the set, except on the first picture, whereas doing sponsored films, I did everything. I wrote them, I shot them, I cast them, I edited them, I put the music on them—I did everything.

Wasn't the subject matter sometimes dull or dispiriting?

Once in a while, but not often. I managed to make it interesting.

What year did you end up at Dartmouth?

About 1966. I started out as a visiting lecturer in film, coming once a year. I didn't quit working in New York for a long time, and I was still working up to 1980. That's when I did my last film, although that was an entertainment film for television—animation—called *Gnomes*, on CBS. It was about 1971 when Dartmouth decided they were going to have a film-studies program and asked me to head it.

You were always frank with them about your background?

Everybody knows I was once blacklisted, and everybody knows why.

I guess that's one of the virtues of so-called academic freedom.

It didn't exist in 1951, I can tell you that.

You said earlier that you're an unregenerate Communist.

Unrepentant is what I said. Because I never knew anybody in the Party—in all the years I was associated with it, which was a long, long time—who was seeking anything but humanistic goals. Certainly, there was never any attempt on the part of people I knew to overthrow the government of the United States. There were a few people I knew in the Party who thought there would be a revolution one of these days. In fact, I had one friend who always thought tomorrow was the day for the revolution. But it wasn't really going to happen, and certainly we weren't going to foment it if it did happen. We did believe in class struggle. I still believe in class struggle. The biggest problems I had with the Party were over the Nazi-Soviet Pact, because I was very pro-British. But, on the other hand, I believed that World War II started as an imperialist war—and I still do—and that it was intended to be a war against the Soviet Union but got turned around. I still believe that. I still think that the Cold War was responsible for more mischief in the postwar world than anything else, and I wasn't sorry to see the Cold War end.

I thought that the Party should cease to be an underground organization during the war itself. I fought very, very hard against the idea of maintaining secrecy about membership in Hollywood. I thought we should surface. When I went to that meeting at which there were three hundred people, I thought, "For Christ's sake, what the hell is the point of being a secret organization if you've got over three hundred people? Let's come out! It's the conspiratorial nature of the Party that scares everyone." I wasn't the only one who believed that, but we were squelched. That's one of the reasons I didn't want to stay in the Party, to tell you the truth. I really felt sick of leading a double life. I wanted so much to tell people about membership in the Party that it really used to drive me nuts. I wanted to be able to admit it.

As for all the revelations about the atrocities that took place in the Soviet Union—the so-called exposé of Stalin—by the time it began, I was no longer a member of the Party, anyway—and I don't believe half of it, either. I tend to be pro-Soviet—and I don't like what Yeltsin is doing—but I've come to recognize that human nature is the big stumbling block and that it's very difficult to get people to adhere to the noble principles that stand behind the Communist ideal. Call it Socialist if you want. It is the ideal of building a better world, a world that benefits more people than capitalism can. Unfortunately, human nature doesn't allow for that. When I was in the Soviet Union in the 1930s, I had all my arguments with the Young Communists about this. I said, "You can't change human nature." They said, "Yes we can." Well, I'm not so sure you can.

Betsy Blair Reisz

BETSY BLAIR REISZ, New York City, 1997

PHOTO © WILLIAM B. WINBURN

INTERVIEW BY PATRICK McGILLIGAN

■

ACTRESS BETSY BLAIR REISZ is proud to say that she was a sympathizer who asked to join the Hollywood section of the Communist Party. She was turned down, because she was then the wife of Gene Kelly and the Party leadership thought that her membership might endanger Kelly's stature as one of the film industry's most dedicated progressives. Kelly was on the planeload of celebrities who flew to Washington, D.C., in October 1947 to oppose the House Un-American Activities Committee hearings. Even afterward, when most of the liberal contingent of Hollywood caved in to the anti-Communist hysteria, Kelly stayed loyal to left-wing friends and beliefs. So did his wife, whose name, courtesy of *Red Channels*, was soon added to the blacklist.

Her life story is unique in many respects. Originally a dancer in a nightclub revue choreographed by Kelly, Betsy Blair played one lead on Broadway and then, in Hollywood, ever larger parts in movies, leading, in tangled fashion, to a starring role in *Marty*—which was almost denied to her because of her political associations. Critical acclaim, a Best Actress award at Cannes, and a Best Actress Oscar nomination in America meant nothing in Hollywood during the blacklist era. Apart from an undistinguished B western, the actress never got another offer from Hollywood in the 1950s or 1960s.

Betsy Blair moved to France in the mid-1950s, and then to England, where she has lived ever since with her second husband, director Karel Reisz. Her résumé would eventually include appearances in films directed by Michelangelo Antonioni, Juan Antonio Bardem, Tony Richardson, and Constantin Costa-Gavras. She was interviewed in London, where our conversation was interrupted by phone calls from grandchildren and arrangements for bridge with Antonia Fraser and Harold Pinter.

■

Why did you go to Hollywood?

I have to begin my story earlier. I grew up in Cliffside, New Jersey, right on the river, next to the George Washington Bridge. It was a completely normal small-town life. I went to dancing school, and I was good at dancing, so I entered an amateur show at the Fort Lee movie theater and won. I joined up with a kind of troupe of amateurs who toured around New Jersey. Although my mother was very enthusiastic about my dancing, she was also a schoolteacher, and I went to the school where she taught, so I had to be an extremely good student. I actually started school when I was four, because there was nobody to leave me home with; then I skipped a year, so I graduated from high school when I was fifteen. I always dreamed of a dancing career, but in fact I had a scholarship to Sarah Lawrence. When I went for the interview at Sarah Lawrence, they decided that emotionally and socially I was not mature enough for college. They suggested I go to junior college first for a year. My father wanted me to go to Katharine Gibbs and be a secretary. This was August 1939.

To make up my mind, I went to visit a girlfriend at her house on a lake, and when I came back to New York City on the train I met my mother at Pennsylvania Station. I happened to see a notice in the *Journal American* which announced a call for dancers that afternoon at two o'clock at the International Casino, on Broadway and Forty-fifth Street. I got off the train, saying to my mother, "I don't care what Daddy says! I'm going to this!" She sat me down, we talked about it, she counted her money, she took me to Macy's and bought me high heels, and she loaned me her lipstick. Then she took me up to Forty-fifth Street, and I got the job.

So there I was, dancing in a nightclub when I was fifteen. I was supposed to do it only until I went to college. I made thirty-five dollars a week, which was more than my two brothers, who had finished university. My father picked me up every night at two in the morning and drove me home to New Jersey. There I was, this little girl in the big, wide world.

The nightclub closed in three months. It was Mafia-run, and the owners disappeared with the money. But Billy Rose sent cards to all of us, because we were supposedly the youngest, prettiest chorus line in New York. I, at least, was the youngest. I went to the call at Billy Rose's Diamond Horsehoe, and Gene [Kelly] was the choreographer. I fell in love immediately. It took him maybe a little longer. But his best friend, Dick Dwenger—who later got killed in the war—was playing the piano, and Dick took pity on me, and they started letting me tag along after them like a kid sister. Gene was twenty-eight. I was sixteen by this time, January 1940.

Gene was extremely ambitious, artistic, learning everything like a demon. We went to museums, dance recitals, concerts, everything, all the time. Because I ended up not going to college, Gene is the one who gave me a sort of college education. I give him all the credit for that. He also gave Stanley Donen, who was a bright but uneducated southerner when he appeared on the scene, the same kind of education. Gene showed us things for the first time and took the time to explain everything to us. I guess he was a very paternalistic man. I can see that now, although I didn't see it then.

Eventually I was allowed to hang out with Gene and Dick and their friends in a bar called Louis Bergen's Theater Bar and Restaurant, which was on Forty-fifth Street between Eighth Avenue and Broadway. One thing I very quickly discovered was that everybody at the table, at least as far as I could tell, was some kind of very left-winger.

Except for Gene?

Gene was a strong sympathizer. Gene and Dick were, I would say now, Social Democrats, although Social Democrats don't really exist in America. But they were good left-wing people who believed in all the right things—trade unions, anti-racism. At one point, for instance, Gene took his father to Mexico on a summer holiday because he wanted to show his father the gold in the churches, which were surrounded by the poor people, and therefore prove to him that it wasn't a sin to have lost his faith in the Catholic Church.

Anyway, Lloyd Gough was one of this group, and he brought me pamphlets and things to read all the time. Gene used to say, "Leave her alone. She's just a kid." I'd say, "No, no! I want to learn!" Eventually I was invited to the Marxist classes at Lloyd's apartment twice a week from five to seven o'clock. I didn't have to be at the nightclub until eight. Now, this is 1940.

Lloyd was just providing the premises?

Yes, there was another man who taught. His name was Paul—that's all I ever knew. But, my goodness, he was very impressive, although we had the worst, most boring textbook in the world, *The History of the Communist Party in the Soviet Union.* One of the greatest things about the Marxist classes was the outside reading. *The History of the Communist Party in the Soviet Union* may have been very boring, but the outside reading was Upton Sinclair, John Dos Passos, [Ivan] Turgenev. The cultural side of the meetings was great, and I was always a voracious reader.

Did Gene go to those classes?

No.

Who else was in the group and later went to Hollywood?

Just Lloyd, I think, and Frances Chaney [who later married Ring Lardner Jr.].

So you went to these classes diligently for a while?

Very diligently.

How was your grasp of Marx?

Gene and Dick were more intellectual on the subject than I was, especially because I was very young. They were not Marxists, but they were able to have very specific arguments with the Marxists, arguing about things like: Since the legal system in Russia is under the Party, how can the legal system work? They could quote [Arthur] Koestler and George Orwell on the subject of Communism.

I remember one funny incident where a friend of Dick's challenged Lloyd about the purge trials in Moscow. Lloyd told him, "I went to bed for six weeks and read the whole transcript. The trials are completely legitimate." We knew he *had* gone to bed for six weeks and read the transcripts, so we believed him. Lloyd meant it, too—he believed what he had read.

Anyway, all this was going on as I was discovering everything in life. In a year and a half I went from a little Cliffside girl who knew nothing—to Lloyd's horror, I didn't even know about the Spanish Civil War—to being a dancer in the chorus of *Panama Hattie*, to meeting [William] Saroyan and playing the lead in his play *The Beautiful People* on Broadway, to Gene and I falling in love and getting married. Gene asked me to marry him, because he was going to Hollywood, and he sort of said, "I can't leave you at the mercy of New York, and I want you to be the mother of my children."

We got married in the Church on a side altar, although I wasn't even a Catholic, and I had to lie to the priest and say I would convert and bring up the children as Catholics. It was all done with Gene's collusion, and he thought it was hilarious. He told me we had to perform this farce, because it would kill his mother if we didn't get married in the Church.

We took two months driving out to California, went to Mexico first, and made a long side trip to San Francisco to see Saroyan, arriving in Hollywood on Pearl Harbor Day. I was intending all along to become a great actress, but I wasn't in any great hurry. I was now seventeen.

Gene was now twenty-nine?

Yes. He quickly became a movie star, and I was quickly pregnant (our daughter was born when I was eighteen). I had promised Lloyd that we wouldn't "go Hollywood," and for a long time I resisted getting a new car or a swimming pool, but we had a nice house. Many of our old friends from New York came to Hollywood—[Betty] Comden and [Adolph] Green; Lloyd, who came to live with Karen Morley—and we made many new friends. Life seemed great.

My political carryings-on about causes continued in Hollywood, always. I worked on all the committees. I worked for the Independent Progressive Party and the Henry Wallace campaign, for HICCASP [the Hollywood Independent Citizens Committee of the Arts, Sciences, and Professions], with Orson Welles on the Sleepy Lagoon case and the zoot-suit riots, for [Conference of Studio Unions leader] Herbert Sorrell during the strikes.* I was always on the very left side, and all the people I liked were on the very left side.

---

*According to *The Inquisition in Hollywood*, the Sleepy Lagoon case (August 1942) centered around the arrest of more than one hundred Mexican-American youths for the murder of a man named José Díaz. After a long trial, twelve were convicted of murder and five of assault. The Communist Party and numerous front groups helped establish the Sleepy Lagoon Defense Committee: "Sponsored by labor groups, professional guilds, ethnic organizations, educators, and film people—John Bright, Guy Endore, Dalton Trumbo, John Howard Lawson, Ring Lardner Jr., Orson Welles, Rita Hayworth, Dorothy Comingore, Canada Lee, and Joseph Cotten—

What kinds of things did you do?

When it was necessary, I went to downtown Los Angeles just to address envelopes and make phone calls for donations.

Because you were married to Gene, was your job sometimes to recruit celebrities or tap them for donations?

Yes, sometimes.

Who were the left-liberal celebrities whose support could be pretty much counted on in most instances?

The Garfields and the Contes—Nick [Richard] Conte and his wife, Ruth, especially. Nick was a working-class kid. So was John Garfield, although [his wife] Robbie Garfield was maybe the more astute one of them politically. Gene was practically a working-class kid too. None of them forgot where they came from.

When Gene first came out to Hollywood, he was under contract to David O. Selznick, who was always good for money. Orson, of course. Danny Kaye, John Houseman, Norman Panama, and Mel [Melvin] Frank. Bill [William] and Edie Goetz and Connie and Jerry Wald were also good givers, I seem to remember, and Dore Schary. Dore Schary gets a bad press nowadays because of the Waldorf Conference, but he was a great Social Democrat at the time. I think he was a great man.

Even though he later gave his imprimatur to the blacklist?

It must be very difficult when you're in a position of such power, when you think that you can make movies which mean something, and that becomes more important to you than anything else, so if you forfeited your position of power, what would you do? Go back to being a writer, or maybe become a

---

the Committee undertook a large-scale program to educate the Los Angeles population about the racism which existed in their midst and to gather support for a reversal of the conviction." The convictions were overturned on appeal.

Similar radio broadcasts, rallies, demonstrations, and benefit shows attended the cause of the zoot-suiters (June 1943). Scuffles between Mexican-Americans and white sailors were common in Venice and Ocean Park, in the racially charged atmosphere. A series of increasingly violent incidents began with eleven sailors claiming they had been attacked by a zoot-suit gang. Over one hundred sailors from the Chavez Ravine naval base drove in a caravan of cars and taxicabs to East Los Angeles and beat several Mexican-American youths in retaliation. They returned the next two nights, joined by Army and Marine personnel, their invasion climaxing on the night of June 7, when "an army of several thousand Anglos, including a number of civilians, raided the barrio and beat up every Mexican-American youth they could find while the police either looked the other way or arrested some pachucos," according to *The Inquisition in Hollywood.* "Hundreds of Mexican-Americans were injured; no whites were arrested." These events became known as the zoot-suit riots and crystallized the formation of hundreds of civic groups allied with the Hollywood left in trying to reverse the tide of racism and injustice.

small-time producer in Europe? I liked Dore and his wife very much. But it is hard for me to understand what he did.

Some people in Hollywood must have given money to left causes merely because it was fashionable.

I heard a story recently that illustrates something about Hollywood in those days. We gave Vanessa Redgrave's name to a friend, twenty-five years ago, who was organizing the fight against the Greek colonels. Vanessa told this person to ask David Hemmings for a donation. This man started to tell David Hemmings all about the cause, and he interrupted him, saying, "I don't want to hear all that. Whatever Vanessa gives, I'll match it." "So," our friend told us, "whenever Vanessa gave me five hundred pounds, I knew I had one thousand pounds." There was a lot of *that* in Hollywood.

You could, for instance, ask [Frank] Sinatra. He didn't *care* to know. He didn't want to talk about things. But he was a good Democrat in those days, and he was usually generous. If anybody was in trouble, he was very attentive and *very* generous.

Your political and social circle tended to emanate out of both your prior East Coast connections and also the MGM "contract family." Am I right?

Yes, we were transplanted New Yorkers, and Metro was the best place for musicals, and so we acted sort of snobbish about that, although we didn't think of it as snobbishness. Except for [composer] Saul Chaplin, who, I think, came from the time when Gene was in *Cover Girl* at Columbia—although Saul then went to Metro—we didn't socialize with people from the other studios. The people in musicals at Fox, for instance, were people we scoffed at—Betty Grable and Cesar Romero.

Describe a typical social evening at your house, and tell me who would be there, sitting around the table.

We had a table like this one. [Gestures.] This is a copy of that table. Only it was an antique, a round New England maple table with a lazy Susan. The Contes, because Ruthie was my best friend, were always there. Our close friends were the people who worked with Gene—Lois McClelland, Gene's secretary, who lived in the house with us for the first few years; Stanley Donen, who practically lived in the house; and Jeannie Coyne, who later married Stanley and then married Gene after I left. They were part of the household. Ted Reid, Nick [Nicholas] Ray, Saul and Ethel Chaplin (she's now married to Buddy Tyne), Adolph Green and Betty Comden whenever they were in L.A., Lennie Hayton and Lena Horne—oh, there would be ten or twelve people at dinner on a Saturday night, and after that it would be open house for twenty-five or thirty.

I don't know how to describe what it was like; other people can probably describe it better, and Saul Chaplin talks about it a bit in his book.* It was an extraordinarily warm and fun gathering that went on for years. Gene and I were insanely competitive charades players, and we were both very good at charades. We might play Ping-Pong and have drinks before supper; then came the charades, and then everybody would gather around the piano. Then, for two or three intense hours, we'd all sing like we were Ethel Merman, shouting and screaming and laughing. There was also an element of performance. Betty and Adolph would perform, and if Judy [Garland] was there she'd sing; Gene and Carol Haney would dance; Ted Reid did his brilliant character monologues.

Was there ever much of a political quotient to the evenings?

No, although sometimes there were petitions to sign.

Although most of them would fit into the "Social Democrats" category, it seems to me that the blacklist must have ruined this kind of fun for everybody, too.

I guess it probably did. It is true that some of our friends left town and that in general the parties changed around town. When I was in *Marty*, I used to get teased a lot about my producer, Harold Hecht, with people asking me what I was going to do about him, since he had named names before HUAC. I used to say, "I'm perfectly happy to work for him. I just won't have him in my house." And I never did.

Once you got to Hollywood, you never went to another Marxist study group or Communist meeting?

No. All of my theoretical discussions were at Schwab's or at the delicatessen across the street from the Actors Lab, where, believe me, with people like Arnie Manoff and Jack Berry screaming and yelling, we had big political discussions about everything.

Were you ever tempted to join the Party?

After the war I did ask to join the Party. This was in 1947 or 1948.

Who did you ask?

Lloyd Gough. He took me up on a drive in the Hollywood Hills to break the news to me that the Party had decided that it wasn't a good idea for me to become a member, because I was married to a very important man who wasn't a member of the Party and I could be just as useful outside.

Did he explain to you how that decision came about?

---

*Composer and arranger Saul Chaplin wrote *The Golden Age of Movie Musicals and Me*.

No. He just said, "The Party has decided." Whether that was the real reason, or whether they thought I was a sort of sentimental left-winger, I don't know.

Why did you try to join, so late in the game?

I thought all of the people I knew to be in the Party were wonderful. They all seemed to care about other people more than themselves. I was aware of my own fortunate life. I don't want to sound noble. I wasn't noble. But I wanted to give something back.

Were you hurt by the rejection?

I both was hurt and had a slight feeling of relief. It was when Gene came out of the Navy that he really decided all regimentation was bad. And I remember him saying to me one day, with affection, "You'd be the worst Communist in the world." Maybe he was right, and maybe I wouldn't be good at taking other people's orders.

Did Gene try to talk you out of becoming a Communist?

He never tried to stop me from doing anything. He was always very free with me.

Meanwhile, were you pursuing acting? Were you in any of the Actors Lab plays?

I studied acting at the Lab. My main teacher was George Shdanoff, who had run away from the Moscow Art Theatre with Michael Chekhov. But after about three months of teaching George realized that he didn't believe in teaching acting in a class situation, and he decided to teach privately. Patricia Neal and I left with him, and he became our coach.

I had decided I was not going to go the starlet route. I was very pretentious, coming from New York, you know—and I had only played one role on Broadway. Gene could have a contract with the studio, because he had a mission to fulfill—to bring dance to the workingman—but I was going to be a great actress with my own theater. I was probably quite obnoxious at the time, but because I was so young I don't think anybody minded.

You weren't trying all along to get a foothold in film work?

For the first few years, I was not even interested. I was in plays around town. Then George Cukor called up. We knew him socially, and I loved him. He said he and Garson Kanin, who with Ruth Gordon had written A *Double Life*, had a tiny part for me in the film. Would I do it for them? It would only take two days or three at most. By then—it was 1947—I was dying to be in the movies, but I didn't know how to reorganize everything I'd been saying all those years and how I'd been behaving. So I said, "Yes, of course, for you, George, I would." It was only a tiny part but very flashy. That was the first part; then I got other small and secondary parts. A fan in San Francisco once sent me a filmography he had compiled, listing nineteen movies that I had been in between 1947 and 1960, including the European ones. I had no idea I was in that many.

A Double Life was also important because that is where I met Paddy Chayefsky—on the set. Garson Kanin had read his first plays—unpublished, unproduced—and thought Paddy was talented. But Paddy was starving as a writer, so Garson got him a job as an extra. Paddy happened to be there on the days when I was working. We got into political arguments immediately, and I invited him home to dinner. He and Gene got on a treat because they were the same politically.

Were you at the initial mass meetings in support of the Hollywood Nineteen where people like John Huston and Humphrey Bogart spoke publicly? What was the atmosphere like at such events?

It's very hard to recreate those times. We thought that the mood in Hollywood was absolutely great, that Hollywood was with us, and that we would triumph. We didn't believe that America could go so wrong. One of the big things we all believed in was the right *not* to tell people whether we were members of the Party; we believed in the right to think whatever we wanted to think: That simple idea you learn in civics class when you're twelve years old. My mother was a very good Democrat, and that belief was very solid in me. I think it was solid in almost everybody.

Huston was a fantastic speaker. He was such a Hemingway-type character—a brilliant director, a wonderful writer, a charmer. Bogart I never believed, and it turned out I was right. I didn't know him and Betty [Lauren] Bacall well. I'd see them at parties, like at [Sylvia Fine and] Danny Kaye's house. I guess I never liked macho men. I remember that there was a French writer named Joseph Cassell who as a party trick would eat glass. He'd bite into a glass and crunch it down. Bogart, watching him one time at Danny Kaye's house, obviously couldn't stand it that this big, handsome Frenchman had bitten into a glass and was chewing it for everybody's benefit. So Bogart bit into a glass, and, of course, he cut his lip and bled all over his black tie and white shirt, while at the same time he kept wanting to fight with Joseph Cassell and had to be steered out into the garden by Gene and Danny. That was the kind of behavior that put me off.

When Bogart changed his mind about supporting the people who had been subpoenaed, he was forced to publicize his recantation. I saw a painful and wonderful program with his son recently, in which the son was asked, "Do you think your father changed his mind, or was it that he chickened out?" The son said, "I think he did understand more, so he did change his mind a bit, but also he chickened out."

Did you go to Washington, D.C., with the planeload of celebrities who were initially passionate in their support of the Hollywood Nineteen?

No, but Gene did. My daughter was a child then, and she remembers coming home from school to find me upstairs with the television set. I was glued to it, and then she was glued to it. Everybody I knew in Hollywood was glued to the television set.

Most books say that the liberals watched John Howard Lawson's forthright attack on the Committee and were horrified to discover that, indeed, they had a likely Communist in their midst; some of them had had no idea that these people were, or had once been, bona fide Communists. When they got back on the plane and returned to Hollywood, it became clear that the support had evaporated. They all chickened out.

Not Gene.

Gene didn't come back disheartened?

He came back disheartened by the tragedy that was happening, but he never would have said anything to disassociate himself from people or, like Bogart, said anything like "I am not a Communist." He never would have done anything like that. Gene's politics never really changed, and he stayed a supporter of people who were blacklisted. I know Gene helped Alvah Bessie and his family during the early years of HUAC, and gave money to people he really wasn't friends with for years during the blacklist.

Which of the Hollywood Ten did you know best?

Adrian Scott, I think.

Why him?

He was married to [actress] Anne Shirley—whom we knew—then. We were friends at dinner parties, and we were on the same committees. He was the most charming man. He was like the doctor in a small town, a really gentle American fellow. Therefore, if you met Adrian at a dinner party or a meeting, you'd naturally invite him to your house.

There was a period of time—three years, actually—between the first hearings and when the Ten finally went to jail. All along, did you still think you were going to win? Or did it dawn upon you by degrees that something terrible was happening?

By degrees. In fact, I went to a party in New York for Adrian the night before he went to jail. Even at that party, when he was going to jail the next morning, the idea was that HUAC wouldn't last. What was happening was seen as an aberration.

The mood was festive?

Yes—festive, wistful, brave. People said things like "This is right." "It's our revolutionary duty." "Every revolutionary goes to jail." And "We didn't expect it to happen in the U.S., but . . ." The mood was hopeful and still believing. We were people who believed. The truth is, we were idealists.

Of course, there *was* a Communist conspiracy in Hollywood. There was a conspiracy to get a black character into a movie or to express a liberal idea in a movie. It's a joke that it was a Communist conspiracy to overthrow the country. It was a conspiracy to do good work and establish the movie unions. People sneer at the "champagne Socialists." I never quite accepted that criticism, though I was sort of one, because I've never suffered much in my life. But it is false to think that you couldn't take those people seriously and that they were doing it for show. I never knew anybody who was doing it for show. Everybody I knew was doing it idealistically.

What was Adrian's mood the night before he went to jail?

He was such a well-spoken, polite, sweet man. I don't know where Anne Shirley was. I know they were still together, because I was in France when they separated later, and Norma Barzman and I had to take their belongings out of their suitcases and divide them up—he couldn't bear to do it himself. But she wasn't there that night. He was staying in somebody's flat downtown alone, and the next morning he was going to jail. I told him I couldn't bear the thought of him going off without some sort of good-bye. So I told him, "I'll come by in the morning."

I took a taxi from whatever hotel I was staying in, down to his apartment, Sunday morning, and on the way I said to the taxi driver, "I have a friend who is going to jail. What could I give him for a present that we could find now?" The taxi driver said, without hesitation, "An alarm clock. There is a drugstore open." So I bought Adrian an alarm clock, and when I came to the door, he was extremely nervous and didn't want to let me in, because he thought the FBI might be watching. I gave him the alarm clock, and off he went to jail.

When do you recall first becoming aware that the blacklist meant trouble for you, too?

Everybody was aware that there was trouble on the horizon, and then *Red Channels* was published, and my name was in it, along with all the "fellow travelers" and "pinkos." I happened to be in New York when it was published, and I came back from there with one of the first copies. There was a groundbreaking ceremony scheduled at the Actors Lab for the new building, and I spoke at the ceremony, along with Gale Sondergaard and Lloyd Gough. I spoke because I had the copy of *Red Channels*. Do I remember what I said? No. But you can imagine.

I remember now that I occasionally had help when I was giving a speech, from Adrian Scott or Michael Wilson. If I was having trouble with the wording, I'd talk to one of them, or if I didn't quite know what was the right thing to say. I also gave speeches for Gene sometimes, although Gene always wrote his own. One time he was supposed to speak at a reunion of the Abraham Lincoln Brigade, and he got laryngitis, so I went instead and read his speech. Years later, somebody found my file at CBS, and it said, "Spoke at the Abraham Lincoln Brigade." [Laughs.]

So you were in Red Channels.

Yes! I had been scheduled to be in this little movie at Metro, a B movie called *Kind Lady*, based on a famous English play, playing Maurice Evans's wife. After the groundbreaking ceremony at the Actors Lab, a reporter from the *Hollywood Citizen-News* called me up on a Saturday and said he had to see me on the morrow. I said no, I'd give him an interview anytime but not on a Sunday. He said, "No, it's not about an interview." And then he told me that the *Hollywood Reporter* on Monday was going to have a front-page editorial about the reds who took part in the Actors Lab ground-breaking ceremony—Lloyd Gough, Gale Sondergaard, and Betsy Blair. I said, "Thank you, but I don't really care." He said, "That's not all. On the back of the *Reporter* there will be a little item which reveals that you are being replaced in *Kind Lady* by a so far uncast English actress." So then I did care.

I called my agent at MCA, and I said, "I'm going to make a fuss. I'm not going to take this lying down. I have been coached for six weeks in the English accent by Gertrude Fogler at MGM, the costumes are all made, my portrait has been painted for a scene in the movie. I'm not going to accept it. There's no way they can fire me." He called me back later and said he had set up an appointment for me with L. B. Mayer on Tuesday.

On Monday it was all in the paper, and it was a little shocking. I got a bit frightened then. I wasn't at all frightened until I saw it published. By Tuesday I had collected myself, and I went in for a two o'clock meeting which turned out rather ridiculously, I can see now—actually, I could see it even then. L. B., whom I knew from all the parties at MGM, said all the corny stuff: "I had to speak to Spence and Kate, too. What's wrong with you people? This is the greatest country in the world." He was absolutely paternalistic: "I understand you're very talented, not some Betty Grable, and you have a husband who adores you, and a child. So what's wrong?" I kept trying to say something like, "Well, my mother always told me that in this country . . ." He interrupted me: "I knew you were the kind of girl who would talk to her mother!" I felt like giving up. It went on and on, with him expounding on marriage and life and pointing to photographs of him with the pope, with Roosevelt, with the king of England, until three o'clock came and the secretary came in to say, "Mr. Kelly is in the outer office."

Gene had been shooting, and when I didn't appear on his soundstage he thought he'd come up and see what was happening. L. B. said, "Oh, fine," and we went out to the outer office to greet Gene. L. B. put one arm around Gene and one arm around me, and he said, "Well, Gene, it's just as you said. She's a fine girl and as American as you and me." Walking down the corridor afterward, Gene said, "You must have given an Academy Award performance in there." Of course I had—me and my respectable white gloves.

L. B. Mayer had accepted all your explanations?

No, he accepted that I was going to go public and create a fight, so rather than have Gene tainted, he'd let me be in *Kind Lady*. That was it. I was in *Kind Lady*. Then I was definitely blacklisted.

Couldn't Gene help you out in some way?

Whatever kind of snippy kid I was, I didn't care. I told myself I didn't need the movies. I could be an actress on the stage, I might write a book, or I just might go to UCLA and become an archaeologist.

You didn't care?

Of course I cared, but I wasn't going to cry about it. Besides which, I was living on Rodeo Drive. Everyone I knew was fleeing or having trouble or was never going to work again. For instance, Alvin Hammer, who was Betty and Adolph's partner in the Revuers, with Judy Holliday, left and became a potter. We all know what happened to John Garfield. Canada Lee might have become as famous as Spike Lee. And Dorothy Comingore, the wonderful actress from *Citizen Kane*—she lost her career and her husband, since he gave names. Compared to such examples, I couldn't complain.

Did Gene take umbrage on your behalf?

I didn't put it on him. I was so busy refusing to be intimidated by the situation, because of what everybody else was going through, that I never asked him to do anything. I was in several plays during this period, including *Deep Are the Roots*, directed by Jack Berry before Jack himself disappeared out the window one day and went to France. I did try to write a novel. I didn't become an archaeologist. We also went to Europe for eighteen months during that period, in 1952. You didn't have to pay taxes if you stayed out of the country for eighteen months. We traveled on the Îsle de France and stayed at the Hotel Lancaster. I wasn't suffering too much.

It's ironic that Harold Hecht was the producer of Marty. *He had been a friendly witness in front of the Committee. Did working with him make your skin crawl?*

I knew him only slightly beforehand. I had seen him occasionally at left-wing parties in the old days.

You sound hesitant, maybe even slightly sympathetic.

Not to Harold, really, but I have sympathy for some people, like Larry Parks. Some people went through hell. I never actually thought about Harold Hecht going through hell, but now that we speak of it, it occurs to me that he was always so eager to please. I didn't study him, but my impression of him was this fellow who had been an agent, and therefore he was a fellow wanting to please already. And then he became Burt Lancaster's partner and a producer, and then he did this terrible thing, which for him was a terrible thing, too, and then he wanted to please people again, even more. He was so desperate to please, always, and maybe that was accentuated because of what he had done.

He resisted accepting your casting for a long time. How did you finally win the part?

I went through three auditions, and finally I read with Ernest Borgnine. [Writer] Paddy [Chayefsky] wanted me to be in it, and [director] Delbert [Mann] was very enthusiastic. The blacklist was never mentioned, although I hadn't worked in four and a half years.

Finally Harold Hecht said to me, "I'm sorry, Betsy, but anybody connected with me they look at very closely"—meaning, "It's *my* fault, but . . ."—"so you're going to have to write a letter." I said, "Harold, you know I can't write such a letter, but I'll try. I'll write something." What I wrote was hopeless: that I believed in American democracy and I loved my country, et cetera. I wrote like a twelve-year-old girl in civics class. Of course, it wasn't what they wanted, and it didn't pass.

Then I became really upset, because I did love that script. I really wanted to be in *Marty*. Besides which, it fit with all of my political ideas: it was about real people. So Gene, who was shooting *It's Always Fair Weather*, I think, went in to Dore Schary, who was the head of Metro at that time, and said, "Listen, Dore. Betsy says *Marty* is a great script, she's read for the director three times, she has all but got the part. You know her. You've played charades with her. You know she's not going to overthrow the country. You have to do something about her being blacklisted, or I'm going to stop shooting."

Dore telephoned the American Legion in Washington in front of Gene and said he would vouch for me. So I was in *Marty*, because someone had vouched for me, and it was the same thing as before—the blacklist was over, but only for one movie. I got an [Oscar] nomination, I won the [Best Actress] award at Cannes, I was hot for two hundred days, and I never got a single offer to do another Hollywood movie.

Did the politics of the blacklist help to break up your marriage to Gene?

Politics was the only thing we ever argued about, but Gene was always trying to explain things to me that I didn't agree with. Probably he was right, as things turned out. We probably had political arguments because that was the only area where I was slightly grown-up. But no, no, politics should have stopped us from breaking up, because Gene did help me. Our marriage broke up because I left Gene. I fell in love with a Frenchman and moved to Paris. Ironically, my love for Paris was owed partly to Gene, because we had never gone anyplace other than Europe for a holiday. That was very good of him. If Gene had wanted to go and lie on a beach somewhere, I would have gone, but instead we always went to Europe for culture.

What happened after Marty?

I played leads in European movies. Then I went back to California, in 1957, I guess. I went to see Lew Wasserman, then the head of MCA, which was still my agency. I told him I still hadn't had a single offer. "Maybe the Academy Award nomination is a jinx," I said. He said, "That's very strange, because I've heard your name many times from writers and directors here." Later he called me up and said, "You have to come in and talk to Captain Somebody." I forget his name—somebody in their office called captain from the time he was in the Army, an agent who was the person who cleared people. Captain Somebody said the same old things: "You have to write a letter, et cetera." I said, "I can't do that. I haven't done that all these years." So Lew Wasserman had a great idea. He would get me into a movie called *The Halliday Brand*, a little B western with Joseph Cotten, Viveca Lindfors, me, and Ward Bond. Lew said, "If you're in a movie with Ward Bond, they'll all *think* you're cleared." So I was in *The Halliday Brand*, I went back to France, and I never heard another word. It was the same as before with L. B. Mayer. I was never cleared. I never had another American offer, ever, during the 1950s *or* the 1960s.

Did Ward Bond wrinkle his nose at you?

No, Ward Bond was irritatingly perfect. He was so polite in the makeup room in the mornings. He knew his lines. He was on time. He was charming to everybody. I was furious.

Did he have any idea who you were and why you were in the movie?

They'd *won*. He didn't care.

The blacklist must have been ultimately a mixed blessing for you, at least in the sense that it must have had a deepening effect on your work as an actress. You got to do un-Hollywood things, like being in a Michelangelo Antonioni film. And you got to live and work in Europe.

It helped me certainly as a person and therefore probably as an actress. Any growth and development, any hardship or diversity, helps. In Europe, ironically, they thought I was big stuff, although I had only been in one Hollywood movie where I was the star. Steve Cochran and I were in the Antonioni film, ironically, because Antonioni thought our names would help at the box office. I don't have any regrets about my career, but it certainly wasn't much of a career. For all my ambitions when I was young, I think my life was always more important to me.

Martin Ritt

MARTIN RITT, Los Angeles, California, 1984

INTERVIEW BY PATRICK McGILLIGAN

MARTIN RITT
(1914–1990)

1944 *Winged Victory.* Actor.
1957 *Edge of the City.* Director.
 No Down Payment. Director.
1958 *The Long Hot Summer.* Director.
1959 *The Black Orchid.* Director.
 The Sound and the Fury. Director.
1960 *Jovanka e l'atril/Five Branded Women.*
 Director.
1961 *Paris Blues.* Director.
1962 *Hemingway's Adventures of a Young Man.*
 Director.
1963 *Hud.* Director, coproducer.
1964 *The Outrage.* Director, executive producer.
1965 *The Spy Who Came in from the Cold.*
 Director, producer.
1967 *Hombre.* Director, coproducer.
1968 *The Brotherhood.* Director,
 executive producer.

1970 *The Molly Maguires.* Director, coproducer.
 The Great White Hope. Director,
 coexecutive producer.
1972 *Sounder.* Director.
 Pete 'n' Tillie. Director.
1974 *Conrack.* Director, coproducer.
1975 *Der richter und sein henker/End of the Game.*
 Actor.
1976 *The Front.* Director, producer.
1978 *Casey's Shadow.* Director.
1979 *Norma Rae.* Director, coproducer.
1981 *Back Roads.* Director.
1983 *Cross Creek.* Director.
1985 *Murphy's Romance.* Director,
 coexecutive producer.
 The Slugger's Wife. Actor.
1987 *Nuts.* Director.
1990 *Stanley & Iris.* Director.

■

IN A CAREER spanning thirty years and more than twenty pictures, director Martin Ritt managed never to resort to multiple car crashes, dripping-blood close-ups, whiz trips through outer space, hollow patriotism, or teenage orgasms. This former actor made movies about subjects he believed in, about people he cared for deeply, about issues that ignited his passion.

In his life, as in his movies, Ritt proved himself a stand-up guy. He suffered but survived the blacklist of the 1950s, and throughout his life he devoted time and money to left-liberal causes. One of his funnier and more affecting films is *The Front*, yet it is deadly serious about the red scare, a subject that always cut deep with him.

Ritt started out as an actor on the fringe of the Group Theatre, where his friends and mentors included playwright Clifford Odets and director Elia Kazan; both later became friendly witnesses before the House Un-American Activities Committee. At seventeen, Ritt played a role in *Golden Boy* on Broadway. During World War II he was given leave from the Army Air Force to appear in the stage and screen versions of *Winged Victory*. He directed his first Broadway play in 1946. In the early fifties he directed and appeared on television in *Danger* and other shows. Then the McCarthy era forced him to make a living teaching at the Actors Studio, to the good fortune of such people as Paul Newman and Joanne Woodward, with whom he forged a long association.

Ritt came to film directing and Hollywood relatively late in life. *Hud* brought him recognition, but he was especially attentive to racial themes (from his first picture, *Edge of the City*, to *Hombre* and *Sounder*), labor issues (*The Molly Maguires, Norma Rae*), and literary material, ranging from Faulkner (*The Long Hot Summer, The Sound and the Fury*) to Hemingway (*Adventures of a Young Man*) to Marjorie Kinnan Rawlings (*Cross Creek*). Passionate conviction, goodwill, common sense and unusual sensitivity, an idiosyncratic narrative, discreet camerawork, and strong performances marked the best of his films.

He did not confuse ethics and politics any more than art and entertainment. In the late 1970s his name cropped up on a check forged by studio executive David Begelman, one link in the chain of events that became one of Hollywood's most celebrated scandals of recent years. When Mike Wallace called to invite Ritt to appear in a *60 Minutes* segment excoriating Begelman, the director demurred. "It [Begelman's crime] is of no importance," he told Wallace, "except as the aberration of a former agent." Alternatively, Ritt suggested that Wallace and *60 Minutes* do a critical segment on Judge Irving Kaufman, who had condemned the Rosenbergs to death. Wallace, said Ritt, "told me to get off his fucking back" and hung up.

Ritt was interviewed in his offices at Columbia, in Burbank, on the occasion of the release of his film *Murphy's Romance* in 1985.

■

How did growing up in the thirties affect your view of making movies?

Well, obviously it affected me a great deal. There was a great liberal surge in the country, emotionally and politically, and I was part of it. All the gifted people and all the excitement I knew around the theater were part of that sector of our intellectual thought. I was lucky enough to be working with an off-Broadway group, the Theatre of Action. I met Elia Kazan there. I was lucky enough to be around the Group Theatre, which was probably the single greatest group of theater intellectuals who ever existed together as a cohesive unit. When I look for material, I look in that area. That's where I feel most comfortable and now where I feel most needed, the times being so different today.

A liberal working in the mainstream is a very rare item today. Maybe a lot of liberals are working in the mainstream, but they don't make pictures about what they believe; they make other kinds of pictures. There's nothing wrong with that, but that's not my bag. I'm more of an activist about what I believe, which is the difference between a liberal and a left-liberal.

My generation was totally committed to humanism. Implicit in all of my films is a very strong and deep feeling for minorities, the disenfranchised, the dispossessed, be they blacks, Mexicans, Jews, or working people.

With widespread unemployment and labor inequity, racism, and threatening global war, why do we count so few socially conscious filmmakers?

It's very hard to understand the kind of historical time we're in. It's obviously a very conservative time—and not only here but all over the world. Filmmakers are not as affected or moved as I might be by certain dilemmas. I'm a complete reflection of the time I grew up in, as most people are.

I must say, to the everlasting credit of this country, that nobody has been shut up nowadays. People like me have been allowed to speak, whereas, in some other countries, I can well imagine that if I had the kinds of differences I have with the establishment, I might well be in jail. That kind of intrinsic strength which exists in our way of life is not in any way to be looked down upon—it's terrific. It makes it possible for good work to continue.

But it's tough to be a liberal, to try to make films about what you believe in. Because, starting with the corny old remark ascribed to Warners, Hollywood believes that if you want to send a message, try Western Union. People shy away—and those pictures have not been doing the greatest of business.

My present film [*Murphy's Romance*] is really a love story about a man [James Garner] who is kind of an idiosyncratic liberal and the lady [Sally Field] that he meets. Just in dealing with the human elements in the film, the film becomes, in my mind, a liberal film. Maybe I have a greater feeling about the broadness of what being a liberal means. It certainly doesn't mean only something that is direct politically, certainly not from a creative person, not from an artist.

I'm considered by many to be a very political fellow. But my films are hardly political, outside of two, maybe three—maybe *Norma Rae* would be included. I'm not interested in polemics, really. I'm not interested in making films that I feel are cardboard statements about what I want to say.

Why are most movies so valueless?

The whole psyche of the world is turned on to fast foods and comic books and teenage excitement and instant gratification. The country is conditioned to accept predigested food and prefabricated houses; the networks believe action-adventure is the best way to attract an audience. The studios partly believe that—along with horror films and teenage films. They are looking to make a size-twelve dress that the country will buy, and the only criterion they have is last year's hit, insufficiently realizing that a really good film is the individual impulse of some creative person.

I don't think most audiences have the patience to sit down to see a Satyajit Ray film. They want, "What's going on? What's happening!" Everything seems more hyped in this country because we're more developed and more organized.

It takes a superior artist to resist the dehumanization process, to resist the cops-and-robbers rut.

Absolutely. However, the good ones will finally find their way back to humanism, because there's nothing else. That's why the great directors are always dealing on some level with the human condition. It's the more difficult kind of film to make, which is another reason why the studios shy away from it. There's more room for failure. The films have to be better. You have to fit a film into a mold which commercial audiences are prepared to accept. Even if it's first-class, sometimes audiences won't quite accept it, and the film won't make the kind of money it should, and *that* will scare the studios. The other thing is so much more predictable.

The comic strip is the art form of this generation. Now the new generation is rejecting that for computers, listening to music, working at home, and isolating themselves, so the new corporate executives are having to find a different kind of drone to do their bidding.

Humanism is in eclipse, except in the very gifted of the young—because once you're gifted, it's going to appear in your work; it doesn't really matter what generation you are. When what is going on socially is a violation of our human instincts, the artist always emerges anyway, on a human level. If I had to entrust my life to anyone, I'd entrust it to artists before anyone else, before politicians. Artists are more related to the truth. They're less available to be bought. I believe that, I believe that deeply, and it has sustained me in times which looked very black to me.

Does a good movie have to be truthful?

I think so. A good one—not a successful one. I differentiate between the two, obviously. Yes, if it's really good, it has to have a true perception. It's naive to assume that any film is not political; they're all social at least. They're either selling escape or they're selling reality. Even the Disney films at one time were considered totally without message. That's childish. They certainly weren't without message. They were selling a different parcel of food, which the American public and the world public was prepared to buy.

According to that line of argument, there must be some good and truthful MTV videos.

I guess there are. The really, really good ones, yes—there will be some perception in them that makes the whole of MTV worthwhile even if it's only an extraordinary visual perception.

Does that hold true for video technology in general?

There's a whole new impulse in the industry that's very interesting, even if I don't totally like it.

What's the downside?

That it becomes an end in itself. That it becomes all style without substance. That it becomes so popular, so faddish, that that's what they come to expect from every film. Film can't possibly be as exciting as a three- or four-minute video. It's fast foods and comic books couched in more artistic terms.

Yet an occasional visual perception can be as truthful and as positive as a thematic message.

That's right. Because it's a perception by a creative person. That's where his talents lie; that's where his inclinations lie. The video artist is lucky because his work is in a form the marketplace is excited about.

The word "truthful" is kind of rabbinical. I don't want to sound that way, and I don't believe that way. I do like very few MTV videos. I don't remember a single one I really like. But I see things on MTV which I find very interesting and attractive from the point of view of form.

Why did it take you so long to come to Hollywood?

In the early fifties I don't think they were hiring anybody from TV, and the two plays I did in New York were sort of *succès d'estime* but not big, successful plays. Also, I was blacklisted, so in those years when some farsighted executive out here might have hired me at a cheap price, I was not hireable.

How did you find out you were blacklisted?

I was working at CBS, doing very well, when I got a call one day from Donald Davis (the son of the playwright Owen Davis), a very sweet man, a friend. I went up to see him on the fourteenth floor of old CBS on Fifty-fifth Street and Madison Avenue. He said, "I don't understand it, Marty, but you haven't been renewed." Well, of course, I understood what was going on; my antennae were out. I said, "This is it." He said, "Oh, Marty, not in this country." I said, "Okay, Donald, you'll see." I went home and I told my wife I was going to have to find some other way to make a living. Adele went out and got a job selling [ad] space for the New York telephone book.

I was hired, finally, to act in a show that Dan Petrie was directing, produced by a guy I had helped a lot in the earlier days of TV. Two days into the show I saw the executives come to Dan Petrie and start to chew his ear off. I said, "What's the problem, Dan?" He said, "They don't think you're right for the part." It was a thirty-five-year-old Italian truck driver. So I told Dan, who at this point was a kid just out of Chicago, what was happening, and he said, "What are you talking about?" Well, the show never appeared. They put on some old kinescope—and after that I didn't work for six years.

So I started to teach acting, professionally. And I really didn't work again until I was hired by Clifford Odets to be in *The Flowering Peach*, in which I played the small part of the oldest son. I went on to help him, because he needed time off to rewrite the play after we opened in Baltimore. I directed the play through the Boston opening.

Isn't it bizarre that Clifford Odets, who became an informer, would hire you as an actor?

The Clifford Odets thing is so bizarre that I really don't want to talk about it. Clifford and I had been close friends. We played in a weekly poker game that he often sat in on at CBS. Clifford came to the poker game after his session at the Committee—which was a very strange one, because he had screamed at the Committee and right after that started to give names. The poker game was an apolitical group if I ever knew one, and I didn't want to get involved in a conversation—but I hated what he did. He told us what had happened, and then he turned to me and said, "What's more, I have this play for you. There's a part in it for you. I'd like you to read it. Let's have dinner." It was bizarre as hell.

You became a movie director in 1957. That's relatively early in the history of the blacklist. Almost a fluke, wasn't it?

It was a fluke. Metro wanted me to make a picture, *Edge of the City*. They were in a proxy fight at that point. I was very cheap. I think I directed the picture for ten thousand dollars. The writer of it, a very good writer, Robert Alan Aurthur, was an old friend; he wanted me for the picture, so I got the job. But when Metro saw the picture, they hated it, in spite of the notices, which were terrific.

Fox offered me a job. I was broke, I was in debt, I hadn't worked from 1951 to 1957. I was happy to get a job in Hollywood. I came out here and immediately went into a long session of meetings with [Twentieth Century–Fox president Spyros] Skouras, who said I was being attacked for my politics and I would have to go before the Committee, and on and on. I said, "I'm not going to do any of that. I have nothing to hide, I've done nothing I'm ashamed of. I've worked here for three days; pay me for three days and I'll go home." He said, "Come to New York."

I went back to New York and went into nine or ten days of more meetings with Skouras, in which he waved the flag and told me what a great country this was. He had come here as a poor boy and he sold popcorn and became a multi-millionaire, et cetera, et cetera. I said, "All that is fine and well, and I don't bow to anybody in my feeling for my country, but I'm not going to do anything that I don't want to do, that I think is shameful." Suddenly, for no reason that I could discern, he said, "Okay, you're a good boy. You come to Hollywood and you make good pictures for Twentieth Century–Fox." That was it. I came back under contract, and it was clear sailing.

It's a historical irony that we now have a president [Reagan] *by way of Hollywood who insists that there never was a blacklist—just people in this country who did not warm to the notion that many artists and performers were American Communists. Of course, recently it was revealed that what some people suspected all along was true. Ronald Reagan was an informer for the FBI at the same time as he was supposedly testifying impartially before the Committee.*

I was called by CNN when that item broke [verifying that Reagan had been an informant for the FBI in the late forties and early fifties]. I was down at Del Mar and going to the races for the day. A camera crew interviewed me, and I said I was shocked to learn that he was an informant. He was then head of the union [the Screen Actors Guild]. The next day, [Ed] Meese came out with a statement that any red-blooded American would have done the same thing. My interview never ran. And the whole thing was quashed in one day—first you read that the president of the United States was an informant; two days later it is no longer in the papers.

It's part of the mentality that now says we won the Vietnam War. In other words, anything that Communists come off looking well for, in their behavior, is shuffled under the rug: "We don't want to know about it. We didn't do that. That's not true. That was the feeling of the American people." As you say, "That's what the president said."

The establishment will never admit to the blacklist because they would be liable. CBS, to this day, does not admit that there was a blacklist. I know why I was fired. They will not admit it, because they have no legal position—

they could very well be sued. There was a blacklist, unquestionably. It was imposed by the networks and the studios. It was unfair, it was unjust, and people suffered. In two cases, two of my friends were deeply cut up and died early in life because of the injustice of the blacklist.

It didn't make the people who were blacklisted any better than they had been before, artistically. Some of them were pretty good, some of them were not so good, some of them were bad, some of them were very good. That more or less remained. But the injustice was a terrible one. And a lot of people who might have developed never had that chance. The few of us who survived it are really among the most fortunate people in this country.

It seems a mystery to people today that so many capitulated, while so few others stood up to buck the tide.

A lot of people did stand up, certainly as many as capitulated. The country owes an everlasting debt to the people who stood up and were prepared to be counted at that point. Because without that body of people and without that body of thought, perhaps McCarthy would have been able to go a lot farther than he did. And perhaps any Fascist or neo-Fascist would be able to do a lot more than they've been able to do.

Philosophically, I don't think the country quite understands—nor do many writers and critics—the significant thing that happened when that small body of professors, doctors, teachers, musicians, actors, writers, directors, people from all kinds of professions, stood up to be counted against the grave injustice that was being done. It was a very significant point in American history to me. If those people had not acted as they did at that time, I would have had no chance to have any kind of career.

Does the bitterness toward informers still linger thirty years later?

There's a lot of bitterness, though personally I never had that kind of bitterness. I don't feel I have any personal scars, except for the close friendships and the people whom I love who have really been hurt. My wife, to this day, will not speak to certain people. I know several people who, if they saw certain people on the street, would spit in their faces.

You seem to have drawn strength from the experience.

Well, I felt they were wrong then, I know now they were wrong absolutely. I've been variously called a dupe or fool myself, for certain things that I did. I feel those people who've called me those names were wrong. I'm not and have not been a dupe. I knew what I was doing all my life. I made certain mistakes, obviously. I indulged myself in certain excesses. But I don't feel I have anything to be ashamed of. Everything I say or do now represents me.

I must say I don't know a single person who behaved, in my view, properly, and who has been any less of a human being for the rest of his life. And I know a lot of guys who behaved badly, and who have not really realized themselves as artists or human beings since that time.

How do you account for that?

They made a wrong move. They violated themselves. For an artist, it is the most dangerous thing in the world you can do. You can't deny who you are or what you are. If, suddenly, you find you're not popular because everything has swung the other way, you've got to have enough class to pick up the marbles and say, "That's who I am, that's what I am, that's what I am going to do, and if you don't like it, fuck you."

Does that hold true for Elia Kazan?

I'd rather not talk about Gadge. He was once my friend, my teacher. I've never been able to look Gadge in the eye, nor he me. Because he knows that I know.

What about his work?

I think his work suffered. I don't think he ever realized his great talent. I think his films before the testimony were better than afterward.

The blacklist was really a form of censorship, wasn't it?

That's right.

When you started directing movies, in the late fifties, films were bland, smug, repressed.

Oh, the fifties were probably the worst decade of the century.

Was there a permanent effect, or did the sixties bring it all back?

The sixties brought it back. But the eighties are in the same area as the fifties. Probably the nineties will bring it back again. The strength of the country is incalculable. It survives everything.

Could a blacklist happen again?

Sure, it's possible, but it's less likely because there was that core of people who did the right thing at that time. It has nothing to do with politics; that has to be understood. It has to do with morality. I have never in my life confused ethics and politics. I know some very ethical people with whom I have no agreement politically, and some very unethical people with whom I have all kinds of agreement politically.

You once told me that The Front *should never have been a comedy.*

We started to write a more serious film—the film was originally about Hecky, the Zero Mostel character. Halfway through, Walter [screenwriter Walter Bernstein] and I decided it was going to be maudlin and sentimental, so together we came up with the notion of "the front"—we remembered the story because it really happened—and decided that's what the film should be. And that's what the film became. I would like to make another picture that deals more seriously with that time and that subject. It might have a chance to be a better film.

Which of your films is closest to the way you'd want them to be?

I'd have to say the three pictures which were nominated for Academy Awards—Hud, Sounder, and Norma Rae. But I'd also have to include *The Molly Maguires, Conrack, The Front, The Spy Who Came in from the Cold,* and a little picture called *Casey's Shadow.* I've made about twenty odd films. Two or three of them I really don't like. Most of them I do like, in varying degrees.

Norman Jewison directed A Soldier's Story, *Robert Altman made* Streamers, *and now Steven Spielberg has directed* The Color Purple. *Very few white directors have shown an interest in racial subjects or themes. What are the problems in doing films like* Sounder *or* Conrack?

That you're not black, so that you're not as close to the material as you would like to be. There's no way anyone can understand what it is to be black unless you're black. Some of us make a pretty good facsimile thereof, and I hope I am one of those. But I'm very aware that blacks don't really get a shot.

I had a lot of arguments with some of my black friends about *Conrack,* a film that I really love. They felt I was doing a film about a white Jesus. They were into black studies and such, and I've been into integration for fifty of my seventy years. I said to them, "Make your own picture. Get off my back. This is what I believe in, and I'm not violating anything I believe in; if it's violating something you believe in, I can't deal with that." And they did not support the film.

Why do you persist in making movies about blacks?

That's what I have to make movies about. Because I cannot make movies about things I don't feel about deeply. I feel deeply about the dilemma of black people. I always have.

Certainly the blacks in this country have been disenfranchised for most of their lives. I'll never forget—I didn't intend to cast Cicely [Tyson] in *Sounder.* I had asked another actress to play the part, and she turned me down. When Cis came to me, I said, "Cis, you're a high-fashion model, a great beauty. I need a working-class, peasant woman." And she said, "Marty, there are no blacks in this country more than one generation removed from that experience." That sold me, because I realized the truth of what she said. I said, "Okay, you have the part."

She reminded me of what I was trying to say: that no amount of seeming sophistication or movement into another class—an upper-middle class or an intellectual class—would remove the genuine problem that has always existed. That every black really knew about all the time. That scar tissue is there and *deep.* I'm aware of it and very sympathetic toward it and feel that it is one of the most grievous errors we have made in this country.

I would like to make another picture about black people, but it would have to be a picture done at a price.

Would it have to be a comedy to satisfy Hollywood?

It would not *have* to be anything. Yet so many of them do seem to end up being in the South. I've found, singularly enough, that I'm very related to rural America. Why, I don't know. Certainly I was a big-city boy; I grew up in New York City, and I wasn't out of the city until I was forty years old. Why I have a feeling for rural America, I'm not sure. But I've learned to accept things about myself that I don't totally understand, particularly if they're good. I'm not putting any boundaries on it. I would just like to make a serious film about the contemporary black experience, be it in Mississippi, or Detroit, or anyplace.

Obviously one of your other great thematic concerns has been labor. Why?

Same reason. The dispossessed. I think working people in this country have gotten a raw deal.

Have I missed any of your other concerns?

I did one picture where Paul Newman played an Indian, *Hombre*—again, a disenfranchised group. God knows, if I could find a picture on that subject that was first-class, I would jump at the chance to do it. Because Indians don't even have the strength that the Negro population has. Because the Negro population, by virtue of their extraordinary gifts in show business and athletics, has dominated a lot of our culture in the last decades. The American Indian has really been neglected. That's a terrible tragedy.

What about feminism? Beginning with Norma Rae, *then* Cross Creek, *and now* Murphy's Romance, *you've made pictures that empower women.*

That's accidental, partly because women are suddenly bankable in Hollywood and acting as their own producers, partly because of my friendship with Sally Field. She's a terrific actress. I like her very much. And I like to work with people I like. I'm not much of a feminist, unfortunately. In fact, I've been called the opposite—by my wife—though we have a happy marriage of many years' standing.

Do you still have a predilection for Faulkner?

That really happened because of the Ravetches [screenwriters Irving Ravetch and Harriet Frank Jr.], because they are devoted to him. They think he is the greatest American writer, which he well may be.

The Long Hot Summer was a good, entertaining, commercial film. The other one, *The Sound and the Fury*, I didn't like. I made some mistakes on that. I shouldn't do Faulkner again. There's something in the language that's too rich. With great writers like that, it's very tough, because in a film you have to tell a story, and when the language becomes so much the star of the story, it's almost untranslatable.

Ironically, the one Faulkner film I have seen that I liked was *Intruder in the Dust*, directed by Clarence Brown and written by a man who turned out to be a friendly witness [Ben Maddow]. It was a much better film than either of mine.

What do you look for when you go about selecting story material?

I pick up something, I read it, and I'm affected. When I read that article about that woman in the *New York Times Magazine*, with her explaining to her two children how tough life was going to be because she was on the side of the union—out of which we made the film *Norma Rae*—I was very affected.

Do you feel inhibited because you don't write?

Somewhat. But every director writes, whether or not he really writes the written word. I've written two plays in my lifetime, and I've tried to write two or three screenplays. They're all serviceable. They're never really good. I've done seven films with the Ravetches. I know how good they are. I know the kind of talk they write, and I could never compete. I manage that talk sometimes in conversation but never when faced with the empty page. I feel that very often the performances in the films that I make illuminate the subject matter.

Why is it that you can achieve this, and another director can't?

It's partly having been an actor. I was trained as an actor at the Group Theatre, and I've taught acting at the Actors Studio and several other places. I love actors. I really love them. And as I see them begin to function, I can be very helpful. As an actor you look to complicate a part as much as you can. I think there's something very kindred between my training as an actor and the films I have made.

What's the value of complexity in a performance?

There is extraordinary value, because the mark of an artist, finally, is the complexity with which he deals with his subject. That facility, which some actors have to a very high degree, is of some importance, but it's not nearly as important as the ability to perceive things which make a character genuinely come to life.

How do you now categorize yourself politically, relative to Hollywood?

I would certainly think I am in the left of the Hollywood contingent, definitely. Also openly and admittedly. I'm not careful. I have not made a career out of being careful.

How do you categorize Hollywood politically, as compared to the rest of the nation?

Hollywood is probably more liberal than the rest of the country at this point—but not so it will hurt business.

Have you heard this joke? A guy walks into a bank and walks up to the girl behind the counter and says, "I want to make a fucking deposit." The girl says, "Whoa, wait a minute, sir." He says, "What do you mean, wait a minute? I want to make a fucking deposit." She says, "This is a bank, sir, you can't talk that way." He says, "I'll talk any way I want to, and I want to make a fucking deposit." She says, "Well, I'm going to have to call the bank manager." He says, "I don't give a shit who you call. Call him." She calls over the manager, who asks, "What's the problem?" "No problem," says the guy. "I want to make a fucking deposit, that's all." The manager says, "Wait a minute, this is a bank, sir." He says, "I don't give a shit what it is, I want to make a fucking deposit now. I just hit the lottery for two million dollars, and I want to make a fucking deposit." And the manager says, "And this cunt won't take your money?"

That's it—that's your short essay on capitalism.

What are the limitations for a progressive film artist in Hollywood? Altman ultimately became persona non grata here, while John Huston has to work outside the city limits. You are almost an anomaly.

Fundamentally, the studios don't want to make serious films. They just don't want to. They've come to the conclusion that they're not as good an investment as the other kinds of films. That will pass, too, as the horror films go by the wayside, as they have in the last year or so. Consequently, I think it's maybe a little easier to get a serious film on, but it's never been easy to get a serious film on. Never!

But in the heyday of the studios, the moguls put out four or five serious movies a year, either as a matter of ego, or for award purposes, or for their own personal aggrandizement.

And for the PR value.

Darryl Zanuck may have produced his share of fatuous musicals, but he also insisted on an occasional important picture.

Just think back. The five pictures that were nominated for Best Picture Oscars last year [1984] were all turned down by major studios—every single one of them. That has to tell you something about what the major studios are prepared to subsidize at this point. Any guy who is going to give them a picture that can't be channeled into some mold is going to make them nervous. They're nervous because business has fallen off. There were some mistakes made about the immediacy of cassettes. Cassettes are beginning to bury motion pictures in terms of economics.

It's even hard to criticize the studios, because it's just a business to them. They would like to make good pictures, but no picture is a good one to an exhibitor unless it makes money. By definition, that's a good picture—a film that makes money. Of course, we know that isn't true, and we've seen a lot of schlock in the last few years make bundles of money.

If I happen to find a picture I want to make that's too political for this gang, I'll find another way to make it. I may be able to sell them even a political picture by bringing it in at such a price that they can't resist it. No money up front. I'll get stars and I'll make the film. If I really found something—and I'm always looking—I'd find a way to get it on. For the films I've wanted to make I never charged the kind of money that I did for the others.

Can you even find stories where the writer pushes the limits of political acceptability?

It's very tough to find that kind of material. Most of it exists in the past. I haven't found anything on the level that I'm prepared to go to bat for. Now, this will probably bring me a rash of the worst goddamned scripts anyone could possibly read—crazy political scripts that are just godawful because it's all politics and they've forgotten everything else. They're cardboard. Agit-prop.

First and foremost, a movie has to be entertaining, because if it isn't entertaining, you're not going to affect anybody. Any film that is fundamentally cerebral will play to only a small segment of society, since the greater part of society is immediately inhibited. I feel I'm plain enough in my tastes that if I really like something, I will be able to get it across to most people. Because I feel I'm more or less like most people, maybe a little more sophisticated, a little fatter, a little more gullible, according to some of my critics, but I figure I'm pretty close to a lot of American joes.

Where are the great political screenwriters of today to help you solve the problem?

[Laughs.] I don't think there are a lot of them around, because they were developed at the same time that I was developed. Nowadays writers think, more or less, in terms of straight entertainment.

If you can't be political in Hollywood, at least you can be iconoclastic.

It's a safe philosophic form for political differences with the establishment. It's not political in the sense that it's against the establishment. It's artistic. Most true artists are iconoclastic.

Do you ever wonder whether you would have made more overtly political films if, as a result of the blacklist, you had been forced to work abroad?

Perhaps. I think making political films is a problem for leftist filmmakers all over the world. It's not really their time. They have to find some way to keep alive during this time, until the time comes back, and it will come back, because it always has.

Let's say you were invited to host a Martin Ritt weekend at some college and asked to show five great leftist films—great cinematically and as political statements. What would you show?

I know what I would show. I would show *The Battle of Algiers* first, and maybe second or third, because I love that film.

And if you had to add a few Hollywood films to your list?

I wouldn't be faring too well.

I've heard you express your admiration for John Ford's version of John Steinbeck's The Grapes of Wrath.

A great film. A great liberal film. I love the film. I love the director. The director is maybe the greatest director we've turned out.

And an interesting case—since Ford was a conservative artist, or at least a traditional man who created liberal, progressive films.

Because he was a great artist, and a great artist will always tell as much of the truth as he can. And it's my deep feeling that the greatest truth is in the liberal tradition.

It's unfortunate, and somehow indicative, that so many of the great directors of the forties and the promising directors of the fifties are no longer working steadily—Billy Wilder and Robert Wise, or even Don Siegel and Stanley Kramer. What happened to that generation?

Partly it's attrition. Partly it's the kinds of pictures that are being made. In some cases their work went bad, which I can't quite understand. I don't really know. I feel fortunate that I'm able to work.

Is it difficult for people of that generation to relate to the kids who run Hollywood today?

Do you want to hear a story? They swear it's true, but I can't believe it. It's too absurd. Fred Zinnemann "takes a meeting" with one of the young executives at Tri-Star. Introductions are made; there are handshakes across the table. The Tri-Star fellow turns to Zinnemann and says, "Well, Mr. Zinnemann, before we start, tell me a little bit about yourself. What have you done?" And Zinnemann looks at him and says, "You first."

It can't be true. It's too perfect!

Marguerite Roberts (and John Sanford)

MARGUERITE ROBERTS, Paris, France, 1962

INTERVIEW BY TINA DANIELL

MARGUERITE ROBERTS
(1905–1989)

1933 *Sailor's Luck.* Coscript.
    Jimmy and Sally. Coscript.
1934 *Peck's Bad Boy.* Coscript.
1935 *College Scandal.* Coscript.
    Men Without Names. Coscript.
    The Last Outpost. Coscript.
1936 *Hollywood Boulevard.* Script.
    Florida Special. Coscript.
    Rose Bowl. Script.
    Forgotten Faces. Coscript.
1937 *Turn Off the Moon.* Coscript.
    Wild Money. Uncredited contribution.
1938 *Meet the Girls.* Script.
1939 *They Shall Have Music.*
    Uncredited contribution.
1941 *Ziegfeld Girl.* Coscript.

Escape. Coscript.
Honky Tonk. Coscript.
1942 *Somewhere I'll Find You.* Script.
1944 *Dragon Seed.* Coscript.
1946 *Undercurrent.* Uncredited contribution.
1947 *The Sea of Grass.* Coscript.
    If Winter Comes. Coscript.
    Desire Me. Coscript.
1949 *The Bribe.* Script.
    Ambush. Script.
1951 *Soldiers Three.* Coscript.
1952 *Ivanhoe.* Uncredited contribution.
1953 *The Girl Who Had Everything.*
    Uncredited contribution.
1962 *The Main Attraction.* Uncredited contribution.
    Diamond Head. Script.
1963 *Rampage.* Coscript.
1965 *Love Has Many Faces.* Script.
1968 *5 Card Stud.* Script.

JOHN SANFORD
(1904–   )

■

"HER STANDING WITH the company was such that she was accorded privileges rarely enjoyed by other writers: each year, she received a six-week vacation with pay; her opinion was sought on casting and costume; she regularly attended the running of the "rushes"; she was sent out on location; and at executive story conferences, she often played the role of Scheherazade. Her salary, high to begin with, grew higher by stages, until she was one of the best-paid writers in the profession. With her earnings, she was enabled to provide for her parents, as she'd vowed to do, and she provided as well for your father and you. They were years of ease, of travel, foreign cars, racehorses, and bespoke clothes." Thus the career of Marguerite Roberts in the 1940s is described by her husband, novelist John Sanford, in his memoir of their life together, *Maggie: A Love Story*.

Marguerite Roberts had already forged one of Hollywood's quietly impressive careers when the blacklist interrupted her momentum. She had begun as an outer-office secretary, but soon took up screenwriting, first at Fox-Western and then at Paramount, proving fast, capable, and versatile in the early years of sound. At MGM, where she lodged for thirteen straight years, she was one of the dependable writers for the studio's most important stars, including Clark Gable, Robert Taylor, Lana Turner, Katharine Hepburn, and Robert Mitchum. She was credited with writing many first-class films and was the uncredited script doctor of as many more. She was a favorite of the studio executives, and when she was accused of Communist membership by HUAC informers, both Benny Thau and Eddie Mannix urged her to "cooperate" and escape the blacklist. She refused to name names, and the studio had to settle her contract, but she would be deprived of screen credit for her final MGM features.

For nine years Roberts did barely any writing, but in the early sixties, honorably restored to good standing, she came back with quality work, first for producer Jerry Bresler at Columbia, then under producer Hal Wallis, for whom she wrote several successful films. Born a midwesterner, and raised with horses and guns, she became a western specialist. Her return to form was capped by the adapted screenplay of *True Grit*, starring John Wayne as an over-the-hill sheriff. Thus Wayne, who was closely allied with the right wing in Hollywood in the fifties, won his only acting Oscar for a film written by a blacklistee and a woman.

John Sanford, who collaborated with Roberts on one MGM film—*Honky Tonk*, starring Clark Gable and Lana Turner—sat in on this interview, which took place in Santa Barbara in 1983. Marguerite Roberts died in 1989. After *Maggie: A Love Story*, which covers principally the blacklist years, Sanford wrote *We Have a Little Sister*, chronicling the early years of Marguerite Roberts's life up to the time Sanford met her in a Paramount elevator in 1936. Currently he's writing a third book that will focus on her later years and complete the story of her life.

In his nineties, Sanford, who has been hailed as one of America's unsung masters, continues to write. In 1997 the University of Illinois Press will publish his twenty-third book, *A Vision of the Americas*. "What the hell," he said. "If you're a writer, you write."

■

Were you born in Colorado?

ROBERTS: I was born in Nebraska, but I lived in Colorado. I came from Greeley to El Centro and from El Centro to Los Angeles. We were young, and we wanted to get away. I originally came to get work, with Mr. [Leonard] Roberts,* on the *Imperial Valley Press*, and he worked for a packing plant.

SANFORD: Then they split, and she came to Los Angeles.

When you came to L.A., were you still interested in doing work on a newspaper?

ROBERTS: I was always interested, but I couldn't get a job on a newspaper. So I got one with a contractor, and then a friend at Fox got me a job as a second secretary for [production chief Winfield] Sheehan. I was in the outer office, and I announced people and calls and sometimes took dictation from Sheehan. Big directors and actors and producers came through there. I worked for Sheehan for about a year; then he went to Europe. I was taken into the scenario department by Chandler Sprague, who employed me as his secretary. When he left and Al Lewis took over as scenario director, he took me on as a secretary. Lewis was a Broadway director; he and Max Gordon produced quite a few plays on Broadway. It was the transition period from silents to talkies, and when he left, I got a job in the reading department. There I met another reader, Charlotte Miller, and we concocted an original, which Fox bought—*Sailor's Luck*.

How long had you been at Fox by then?

ROBERTS: We wrote the screenplay in 1932. I had wanted to be a writer, and the reading department gave you good training. I was lucky. Raoul Walsh directed *Sailor's Luck*, and Jim [James] Dunn and Sally Eilers were in it. Crazily enough, it played the [Radio City] Music Hall—a silly little movie, but it was successful.

Charlotte and I were assigned to do another story for Dunn, and then they let Charlotte go and kept me. They paired me with another writer, Paul Perez, and we wrote *Jimmy and Sally* for Claire Trevor. I also did *Peck's Bad Boy*,

---

*Her first husband.

which was just something I did for my then brother-in-law, [director] Eddie Cline. It was for [producer] Sol Lesser. After that, I was out of work for nine months.

Did you have a contract at Fox?

ROBERTS: Not at that time. I got a hundred dollars a week when I was working.

What were the special demands made on writers in that period?

ROBERTS: There was no theory about anything. People were feeling their way. Al Lewis brought out from New York a great many writers and dialogue directors—who were useless and infuriated the real directors—and some reporters. The only women of note that he brought out were Maurine Watkins, who had written *Chicago*, and Sonya Levien, a most remarkable woman. Sonya was very well-known in New York and had been a friend of [journalist] John Reed's. She was sweet and kind and simple, and a damned good writer. She was also decent, and not many people in the picture business were. She became a big success and continued to write important films until her death.

You have one credit with her, right?

ROBERTS: *Ziegfeld Girl*. She wrote a script, and I rewrote it. I had known her since her early days at Fox. I used to see the people immediately when they got off the *Chief* [the train from New York]. I would meet them in Lewis's office. I met her, and Jean Arthur, who had a run in her stocking, and Spencer Tracy, and Leonard Spigelgass, who later wrote *A Majority of One*, and many directors and producers.

They were merely photographing plays in those days. No one knew what he was doing, although some of the old-time directors did. John Ford, or Frank Borzage, who did *Seventh Heaven*, they never needed a dialogue director.

How well did you know Raoul Walsh?

ROBERTS: I met him as a secretary, and I had a big crush on him. He was going to direct and play *The Cisco Kid*. He was a very handsome guy. He was driving through the desert one night, and a jackrabbit jumped up through the windshield, and he lost an eye. He wore a patch afterward. He was a rowdy guy, but marvelous. I don't know why he ever decided to direct *Sailor's Luck*. He did it in a wild and rowdy way.

He seems as though he would be hard to work with, as a man.

ROBERTS: I've always worked with men, and not for very many women. And for the same reason, I prefer Gable to Tracy, [Charlton] Heston to Robert Taylor. I liked stories about men, and I liked men; they amused me very much. For instance, Gable liked my stuff because he never took himself too seriously, never took sex too seriously. John and I wrote *Honky Tonk* for him, and he loved it. I did his next picture, too, *Somewhere I'll Find You*. In the middle of the shooting Carole Lombard was killed. Gable didn't make any pictures for a while; then he joined the Air Force.

SANFORD: The fact is, my wife has a certain manner. She gets along well with macho men. They told their men's stories, and she didn't blush or pull her skirts down. She just got along with them.

How did you end up at Paramount?

ROBERTS: I was out of work for nine months, and Al Lewis called up. He had become a producer at Paramount. He called me over to work with Maurine Watkins. I did work with her, but the project didn't get anywhere. He kept me on as a kind of inexpensive writer to develop ideas for him, and to do a script now and then. I stayed there . . . about three or four years. Just long enough to meet John.

SANFORD: She did a picture there called *Men Without Names.*

Was there any difference between working for Fox and Paramount?

ROBERTS: About the same. Writers were treated with disrespect.

SANFORD: Except that at Paramount the writing department was considered more important.

Did you feel that you were floundering?

ROBERTS: I don't think I ever floundered. I don't think my scripts were all successful, but they didn't take much out of me.

SANFORD: I think you wrote very easily and with confidence. And I've been watching you write pictures since 1936. Paramount brought me out in 1936, and we met in an elevator.

ROBERTS: I did more than a few before leaving Paramount: *Hollywood Boulevard, Florida Special, Turn Off the Moon, Wild Money,* and *Meet the Girls.* I was waiting to go to New York. I had written a play during one of my nine-month layoffs. We never got to Broadway with it. While I was waiting, I took a job at Fox and a small job at [Samuel] Goldwyn [Productions], working with Robert Riskin, something about Jascha Heifetz [*They Shall Have Music,* 1939]. After that I went to New York.

SANFORD: We're now in September or October 1938. Before she went, Jimmy Townsend of Myron Selznick's agency was after her. He got her the offer of a five-year contract at MGM. She said, against my advice, "I'm going to take it."

Why was Metro pursuing you?

ROBERTS: Earlier, I had done a script at MGM for [producer] Eddie Chodorov based on *The American Flaggs,* a novel by Kathleen Norris, and Dorothy Arzner was supposed to direct it, but nothing came of it. It was never made into a movie, but it got me my contract at Metro. They remembered that script.

What was the play you had written?

ROBERTS: It started out being called "Farewell Performance" but was put on in Boston as *West of Broadway*. It was about a couple like the Lunts [Alfred Lunt and Lynn Fontanne] moving to Wisconsin.

SANFORD: Unfortunately, the director of the play was hopeless. And Ruth Chatterton, the star, was a very arrogant lady.

ROBERTS: It was my first and last play. My MGM contract lasted for thirteen years without a break, with six weeks off every year, at a fantastic salary.

Did you enjoy MGM the most of all the studios?

ROBERTS: If you delivered for them, they treated you magnificently. They threw you right out the window if you didn't. [Louis B.] Mayer even gave one of my broodmares a free stud service from one of his crack stallions, Alibhai.

SANFORD: He used to invite both of us to his ranch for breakfast, and she would be asked to the [executive] lunchroom to meet important visitors like [U.S. diplomat] Ralph Bunche.

Sonya Levien and Isobel Lennart were also under contract at MGM, right? There were quite a few women screenwriters there.

ROBERTS: I knew both of them well. Lennart was very successful. She worked a great deal with [producer] Joe Pasternak. They made some very successful pictures. We used to talk. I really adored Sonya. I knew Helen Deutsch, and Gladys Lehman was a very decent woman. Dorothy Kingsley was very nice. But I never went to the commissary for lunch.

Were the women scriptwriters treated differently from the men?

ROBERTS: I have no beefs. Men have always been extremely kind and never tried to put me down.

Did you have any special booster in the front office?

ROBERTS: Benny Thau. He made the contracts at MGM. I didn't like Dore Schary. I got along with Mayer.

Let's talk about some of the individual credits. Did you get involved with Pearl Buck on The Good Earth?

ROBERTS: No. Jane Murfin wrote the script, and I rewrote it. We split the credits.

Your work on Undercurrent *went uncredited. How common was that?*

ROBERTS: That was another Hepburn picture. I rewrote it, but, no, I never did get credit. It was a favor to Pan [producer Pandro S. Berman]. I didn't ask for credit. I did work on something called *Desire Me*, which George Cukor had shot with Greer Garson and [Robert] Mitchum, but they couldn't release it. Cukor was a good director, but when he went bad, he went all over the place. Mervyn LeRoy and I redid the picture. It was one of those mystical things where a man goes to war and becomes friendly with another man, who is killed, and the other man goes back to the man's wife and sort of takes over. I never could figure out how the wife could mix them up that way. Then Mitchum comes back alive, and the men fight it out. It was kind of silly.

MGM is where you started to write westerns.

ROBERTS: I did one western for Eddie Cline, which I don't think was ever released.* But I also did *Ambush, The Sea of Grass,* and *Honky Tonk* at MGM.

You became a kind of western specialist.

ROBERTS: I like stories about men, stories about the West. I loved horses.

You rode when you were young?

ROBERTS: Soon as I could get on a horse, and I had a saddle horse for many years. My dad had been a sheriff, and we had lived in Wyoming and Colorado, so I knew quite a bit of the history of the West. I was drawn to it.

SANFORD: It wasn't always a matter of choice. If you were found to be able to write a western, they would say, "What about another one?" The western followed her around.

ROBERTS: I didn't say no.

Were you familiar with guns?

ROBERTS: My brother used to take me duck hunting, and there were always guns around the house. My first husband took me shooting out in the desert. My second husband—well, the less said the better. [Laughs.]

SANFORD: The Russian roulette in *Honky Tonk* was Maggie's concept, and it wasn't until later that we learned some people actually play it for real.

ROBERTS: I had a terrible guilt complex about that. We played it for comedy in *Honky Tonk*, but some people played it for real.

It's a wonderful scene.

SANFORD: When Gable walks away, there's a flash of light as he throws a bullet away. If you didn't see that, you missed the trick.

Did you have a feeling about the treatment of Indians in westerns?

ROBERTS: Yes. I had a big fight with [director] Sam Wood on *Ambush*. I had some marvelous stuff for the Indians to do. At one point the Indians waylaid the whites by digging in and, as the wagon train approached, rising out of the dirt. I also described the leader as a magnificent specimen. This was the story of a woman who had been kidnapped, and I wanted her not to

---

*Probably it wasn't released, and no western directed by Eddie Cline appears among Marguerite Roberts's official screen credits.

want to leave the Indians. She was in love with the chief. And of course Sam Wood went crazy! He was a very conservative man.

I remember that in The Sea of Grass *Spencer Tracy imagines settling on land taken from the Indians.*

ROBERTS: I'm not so proud of *The Sea of Grass*.

Tell me about The Sea of Grass.

ROBERTS: That was for Spencer Tracy, who was marvelous to work with, and [Katharine] Hepburn, who was so crazy about Tracy. I worked with Hepburn on another picture, *Dragon Seed*. She frankly wasn't one of my favorite people. I admire her, and think she's a very interesting person, but she's a snob.

It was a western with a definite woman's point of view.

ROBERTS: The Tracy character affected respect for the natural state of things, the undisturbed grass. He opposed the sodbusters, who wanted land. I had the Hepburn character note that his love for the natural state coincided with his becoming a millionaire off that very state. In other words, was his attachment mystical or opportunistic? [Director Elia] Kazan would have none of my viewpoint, only Tracy's.

SANFORD: I remember Maggie coming home at night, heartbroken, because she couldn't get her viewpoint into the script.

Sometimes the film does seem at cross-purposes.

ROBERTS: Thanks to Kazan. He didn't do any writing on the picture, but he was a chauvinist, and he wanted a woman to have his viewpoint. It was a point of honor with him.

SANFORD: The Tracy character was a man declaring nobility over something which was putting dough in his pocket.

ROBERTS: Kazan should have been called on it, and called hard. His politics were very liberal at the time—supposed to be liberal—but he was a chauvinist, and later a fink. That's what stopped him. It was a personal thing.

Were there pictures you wanted to work on, at MGM, but couldn't?

ROBERTS: *Madame Bovary*, but Pandro gave it to someone else. I wanted to do *The African Queen*, with Gable and Hepburn. I wanted to do *Zapata*, too. Both were snatched away from me.

Why Madame Bovary?

ROBERTS: I thought the novel was full of truth and social comment. The main character was a woman but a different kind of woman. At Metro, it was very difficult to write a woman, because the studio had the old-fashioned idea that there were two kinds of women—whores and angels. That was one thing that always turned me off. The women were clichés: "A lady wouldn't do this

... a whore doesn't do that. ..." They couldn't see past that. That was what drove me toward male characters. You could do anything with a man.

When you were writing a film for an MGM star, did you usually know who would be playing the lead role beforehand?

ROBERTS: We more or less wrote them for the stars. Gable was a marvel. Lana Turner was very easy to write for, too; she was limited, but certain things she could do very well. Robert Taylor was a stiff guy but a nice enough man, a reactionary who didn't like my politics—but he was all right. I had him in quite a few pictures: *Escape, Undercurrent, Ambush, Ivanhoe,* and *The Bribe.*

You wrote several films starring Robert Mitchum. Did you write them with him in mind?

ROBERTS: No. But I liked Mitchum. I think he was a very virile man, especially when he was young and good-looking. I remember when we were making *Undercurrent* and he came into Pandro's office because they were sending him around for interviews. He said they couldn't find any jackets to fit him; his shoulders were too broad. He was so proud of it, so childish. But I always liked him; I thought he was an interesting man.

Did you have preferences among the stable of MGM directors?

ROBERTS: I kind of liked Jack Conway, who did *Dragon Seed.* He did a good job on it, before he got sick in the middle of it.

Did you clash with Sam Wood?

ROBERTS: He was very nice to me. On location he took me to dinner every night. He was courteous. He was a hell of a good director and an intelligent man. But he just had a block. His daughter was [actress] K. T. Stevens, and I think he disowned her for being too liberal.

What about Robert Z. Leonard?

ROBERTS: A sweet man. He did *Ziegfeld Girl* and *The Bribe.* He did a good job on *Ziegfeld Girl* and made it a pretty interesting picture.

SANFORD: *The Bribe* was one of her last credits before the blacklist. She had her credit taken away from her on *Ivanhoe.*

I didn't know that.

ROBERTS: MGM settled my contract, and as part of the settlement they took my name off *Ivanhoe* and also *The Girl Who Had Everything,* with Elizabeth Taylor and Robert Taylor, and *Letter to the President,* with Shelley Winters.*

***Letter to the President,* apparently, was never released.

SANFORD: They took the credit for *Ivanhoe* and gave it to Noel Langley, an Englishman, but in the English release they credited her.

You had three uncompleted pictures and several years to go on your contract.

ROBERTS: But they gave me a marvelous settlement.

SANFORD: At all the conferences, the burden was, "We will pay all your expenses if you will give us some names." The answer was no every time.

Had you been named?

ROBERTS: By Martin Berkeley, who named about a hundred and fifty. The things that happened to people were terrible. We got along okay. They settled my contract, and not only settled it.

SANFORD: They could have said, "Go and sue." She worked for two months and finished her pictures. Many other people were told to get off the lot.

Did their attitude toward you change when you refused to name names?

ROBERTS: I think Benny Thau and Eddie Mannix kind of liked it. They were tough guys. They didn't like finks, although they were trying to get me to fink. We kept in touch with Benny for years.

Was it difficult to keep working after you knew you were scheduled to be released?

ROBERTS: I was just going through the motions. I finished up to the best of my ability.

So you went to England in 1952?

ROBERTS: We stayed for about four months.

Was it just a vacation?

ROBERTS: We just did not know what to do. We wanted to get away from Hollywood. It was a terrible thing for me, like having your father throw you out in the street. MGM was a very paternalistic studio. I was in a terrible condition. We went to England, and nothing turned up—we didn't try very hard to find anything—and then we came home. They picked our passports up the day we came home. We couldn't leave the country again for six years. I was blacklisted for over nine years.

When you returned from England, where did you go?

ROBERTS: We lived in Hollywood about six months more, and then we moved to Carmel for about a year. We've been here [in Santa Barbara] since 1955.

Did you ever think of working under a pseudonym?

ROBERTS: I never got any of that work. Nobody ever asked me.

What did you do professionally during the nine years of the blacklist?

ROBERTS: Almost nothing. I wrote a play and a screenplay, "Hotel de Dream," about the life of Stephen Crane and his mistress—a very interesting screenplay, but it was never sold. It got me some attention, and it got an option from James Woolf in England. He wanted it for Laurence Harvey. But it was long and expensive. I had castles and battles in it, and maybe it just didn't have what people thought would make a popular picture.

SANFORD: Woolf took an option on it in partnership with agent Nat Goldstone. It was that connection which finally enabled Goldstone to come to Maggie, saying he could place her either at Columbia or at MGM. She chose MGM for old times' sake, but he said it wasn't the same MGM she'd known, so she accepted the Columbia deal.

ROBERTS: I got a job through the good offices of Jerry Bresler. He was a producer. He signed me for *Diamond Head*, with Charlton Heston. It made money. It wasn't much of a picture, but it did all right. By 1960 the political climate was entirely different, although not at the major studios. Waldo Salt was working. Dalton Trumbo was working. I think Ring Lardner Jr. was working.

SANFORD: But Maggie was the first one to be employed by a major studio.

I thought that was Dalton Trumbo.

ROBERTS: Dalton worked for the King brothers and for [Otto] Preminger. *Exodus* was a Columbia release, but it wasn't *made* by Columbia. You could say it was the first release from a major studio.

But Diamond Head *wasn't released by Columbia until 1962, right?*

ROBERTS: In the intervening time I also did one script that I refused credit on, *The Main Attraction*. Jesus, that was terrible. I did a script for [producer] Ray Stark called *Rampage*, with [Robert] Mitchum, Jack Hawkins, and Elsa Martinelli. I split a credit; they rewrote it. And I did *Love Has Many Faces*, with Lana Turner, Stephanie Powers, and Cliff Robertson.

How did you hook up with Hal Wallis?

ROBERTS: I was at Columbia first with Jerry Bresler. He sent a script to Paramount, to Howard Koch, who sent the script to Hal Wallis. Wallis became interested in the script and in me. He took an option. He ended up not buying the script but called me in to work on something called *Glory Gulch*, based on a novel [by Ray Gaulden], if you want to call it a novel.

SANFORD: She took the script and put it up in the cupboard and wrote a whole new script.

ROBERTS: That was *5 Card Stud*. It was the first for Wallis; then I did *True Grit, Norwood, Red Sky at Morning,* and *Shootout*.

Can you compare him as a producer to someone like Pandro Berman, whom you worked with at MGM?

ROBERTS: Pandro was a kind of road-show producer, a good commercial producer. But Hal Wallis had class. Wallis was a hell of a good producer. He ran everything. He never went back on his word. And he could make decisions. I worked with him for four or five years and had more fun working on *True Grit* than any other film I ever did. Everything went right.

You worked pretty closely with Wallis?

ROBERTS: We could have story conferences over the phone. He was marvelous. We could talk to each other.

SANFORD: He wasn't a man who offered ideas. He'd say, "How do you want to do this scene?" Then she'd say, "This is how." And he'd say, "That's great. Let's do it."

ROBERTS: He wanted the writer to do the writing. He also wanted absolute control of the picture.

SANFORD: Anytime there isn't a person in charge, you're not going to have much of a picture. Wallis was a general.

ROBERTS: And he allowed no interference from the studio. Working with him was a fine experience. My only regret is that I didn't know him twenty years earlier, when I was younger and he was younger.

True Grit *certainly seems to be your most fully realized screenplay.*

ROBERTS: It was. I liked the director, [Henry] Hathaway, a tough guy but very good for that sort of picture. I thought Wayne was superb. I didn't like him at first, but I found that he was a nice guy.

SANFORD: He later said that *True Grit* was the best screenplay he'd ever read. And it was written by a woman and a blacklistee!

ROBERTS: He knew that I was a blacklistee, and when his friends found out that he was going to be in a movie written by me, great pressure was put upon him. He said, "This is a different day. I like this script, and I'm not being a censor." He was just great about it.

Screenwriter Philip Dunne told me a story once that made me think Wayne was not really a Ward Bond type of reactionary.

ROBERTS: No, he wasn't. He believed what he said—that we were a great nation with no flaws. He was a super-patriot.

Why do you think True Grit *turned out so well?*

ROBERTS: The chemistry was right. It was a marvelous little novel. The casting was very good. The direction was perfect. Nobody changed one word in the script, and the film came in just sixty feet over the estimated length. They only needed one preview.

SANFORD: Wayne had bid on the novel. He wanted to buy it himself. After Wallis bought it—I think he paid four hundred thousand dollars for the novel—he got a call from the agent of [author] Charles Portis, who wanted to work on the screenplay. Wallis said, "I have my writer."

ROBERTS: Portis was never a screenwriter. He tried a version of the script for Wallis, which had the ending. The ending was a good ending.

SANFORD: The ending was seven foolscap pages. People thought it was no good, but Maggie said, "There's a line in there we'll keep."

ROBERTS: But Wallis was in his English period, making those pictures that taught English people their history. In the middle of *Norwood* [the next production], which I thought was a good script, he went to England and turned the production over to Jack Haley Jr., and it didn't turn out.

SANFORD: I think we tried to see the picture six times.

ROBERTS: It could have been an amusing picture. Haley went for slapstick comedy and all kinds of crap. He turned a funny script into junk. It was really terrible.

I've never seen Red Sky at Morning.

ROBERTS: It was a nice picture. It didn't quite suit me. Wallis had a script and asked me to rewrite it. I thought it was kind of interesting. I liked the background of New Mexico. I liked the period. I liked the kids. I rewrote it, and [director James] Goldstone, I think, didn't do such a good job. And it was badly cast. Richard Thomas was nice, but I don't think the little girl [played by Catherine Burns] was very good. I don't think I've ever seen the whole picture.

SANFORD: Claire Bloom put me off. John Colicos—God!

ROBERTS: Wallis had him in everything.

That was your last picture.

ROBERTS: I got fed up. There was one more thing, for Reader's Digest Films, "Don't Launch Him . . . He's Mine." Helen Strauss was the producer—a literary agent, not a professional producer. I did the script, but nothing ever came of it. I wasn't offered any good theatrical pictures after 1971.

Why did you stop working with Wallis?

ROBERTS: He was at a kind of hiatus. He was mad at me, anyway. We had a little tiff over *Shootout*. He wanted me to rewrite it, and I didn't like his ideas. Anyhow, I was ready to stop.

SANFORD: She had been working since 1930. One day she came home and said, "What am I still hanging around for?"

Why do you think westerns stopped being so popular?

ROBERTS: They became passé. I don't know why. Now they have car chases and cars exploding instead of horses. The kids like it better. They like shooting, people being killed, car accidents. I think it's a new feeling for the same formula.

SANFORD: The western is a folktale about heroes. It's simple. This is a different world. We don't love the good as much as we used to, and there is no evil.

ROBERTS: There isn't much morality, and westerns are morality tales. I think the violence in westerns is different from today's violence—mowing people down, or the kinds of horror pictures they make.

SANFORD: The hero takes drugs or is drunk. That was once unthinkable.

Well, there is a tradition of hard-drinking western heroes.

ROBERTS: Rooster Cogburn was an awful drunk. There are good and bad guys in every picture, but morals have changed. I suppose that's the main reason for the departure of the western.

Was that part of the reason why you stopped working?

ROBERTS: I stopped working because I was tired and said to hell with it. I got so I didn't like to go down to Hollywood for interviews. I didn't feel at home there anymore. I couldn't get used to the changes.

Joan LaCour Scott (and Adrian Scott)

JOAN LACOUR SCOTT, Los Angeles, California, 1983

INTERVIEW BY PAUL BUHLE

JOAN LACOUR SCOTT
(1921–   )

1962 *The Magnificent Rebel.* Script
    (as Joanne Court).
1963 *Cairo.* Script (as Joanne Court).

ADRIAN SCOTT
(1911–1972)

1940 *Keeping Company.* Coscript.
1941 *We Go Fast.* Coscript.
    The Parson of Panamint. Coscript.
1943 *Mister Lucky.* Coscript.
1944 *Murder, My Sweet.* Producer.

    My Pal Wolf. Producer.
1945 *Cornered.* Producer.
1946 *Miss Susie Slagel's.* Costory basis.
    Deadline at Dawn. Producer.
1947 *Crossfire.* Producer.
1948 *The Boy with Green Hair.* Producer.
    So Well Remembered. Producer.
1950 *Gambling House.* Remake of *Mr. Lucky.*
1951 *Pardon My French.* Uncredited
    story contribution.
1960 *Conspiracy of Hearts.* Story basis
    (as Dale Pitt).
1964 *Night Must Fall.* Uncredited contribution.
1971 *The Great Man's Whiskers* (telefilm).
    Producer, story basis.

■

JOAN LaCOUR SCOTT'S LIFE in show business offers one of the fascinating and poignant untold stories of the blacklist. Raised by a former vaudevillian eager to get her daughter into movies, Scott survived a knockabout childhood and ended up at Hollywood High School with classmates destined to be famous. After a disastrous first marriage, she joined the Hollywood Independent Citizens Committee of the Arts, Sciences, and Professions (HICCASP), becoming one of the postwar younger generation who infused the dying Popular Front organizations with new energy. Very briefly a Communist Party member, she was subpoenaed for questioning about her role in helping to unionize television writers and was subsequently blacklisted under her maiden name. She married producer Adrian Scott after he was released from jail, becoming "Adrian's wife," the working title of her autobiography in progress.

With only minimum experience as a writer, she found her profession almost accidentally, fronting for her husband in television. She learned the trade rapidly. A productive stint working for Walt Disney might have led to more fruitful endeavors, if only her career had not been interrupted by the couple's relocation to England and then by Adrian Scott's tragic death.

■

Let's begin with your showbiz family.

My mother left home and school at thirteen to go onto the stage. She once told me that when she was on a vaudeville train and the school inspectors would come through looking for minors, she would dress up in high heels and makeup to look older. She traveled all over the country, including California, then came back East, where she was from.

We were born in New Jersey in 1921. My last name was LaCour, from my father. When my mother came to town in a vaudeville show, he saw her, and they got together. They were both nineteen and decided not to have children. But soon they had twins, myself and my sister, Jean.

My father moved out when we were two. Two years later my mother went back to vaudeville, just as it was winding down. My grandmother, her mother, took care of me for a little while. She had become a costumer on Broadway, with her own business. Her maid mostly took care of us, but it still got to be too much for her. Then someone had the idea of opening a boarding house for vaudeville kids whose parents were "on the road." My sister and I were the first residents. After about a year of that, my grandmother's father, who was in his seventies, needed someone to stay and help take care of him, in the little fishing village of West Barrington, Rhode Island. So my sister and I and my grandmother went there.

With my great-grandfather and me it was total love, the five years of my life in which I felt most happy and loved. Pretty soon, however, with vaudeville dying out because of the arrival of movies, my mother came to stay, "for a little while." My great-grandfather didn't like her one bit. She took a bath every day, she wore high heels and makeup, she stopped traffic walking through West Barrington. I never saw her when she wasn't flirting with anything male. Soon after my mother arrived, she decided to woo, and win, the manager of the local A&P store. A devout French-Canadian Catholic from a local family, he was absolutely thrilled by her. The Catholic Church issued her a papal bull forgiving her for having lived in sin and bearing two children out of wedlock. Imagine becoming a bastard overnight!

They came back from their honeymoon to a home in Riverside, Rhode Island, just across the bay from Providence. But she became totally bored, and acted out the pattern typical of all her four marriages. She showed more and more contempt for her new husband. To be absolutely fair, she was doing the best that she could with this new marriage, and once she had decided to do her best at something, she did work very hard at it.

She hit on the idea of putting us on the stage as a family singing group. She had never had a lesson in her life, but she taught my sister and me to sing harmony, and my stepfather, who sang in the church choir occasionally, also tried his best to fit in. Jean and I did sing on the radio in Rhode Island, and we even got into a studio in New York. But that day in the studio, when we were about to perform, my poor stepfather fainted dead away. He really caught it from my mother when we got back home.

With the death of vaudeville and the tightening grip of the depression, my mother was pretty defeated in her life plans. She decided that if we couldn't make it in the East at all, we might have more luck in California. She was sure that she could get us into movies, never realizing that we weren't the only cute twins in the U.S. and that a lot of other mothers who had twins were also dead set on getting their twins into pictures.

It was about 1933. By this time in the Depression, my grandmother was game to start over out West, and she and my grandfather were going to come along in a second car. My grandfather always had the brains of the family. His German-Jewish extraction made him the source of my one-eighth Jewishness. My grandfather had a reputation of being a killer cardplayer, and he firmly believed that we could make enough money to survive by playing cards as we went along from town to town. He and my stepfather were also going to sell guitars, with lessons, door to door. We were heading down South, and then across the country.

Whatever money we had went to buy bread and bologna, and we rigged up a "stove" by using an electric iron inverted over a chamber pot. I don't know how long it took my grandfather to find out that my stepfather just was not suited to be a door-to-door salesman. He would spend the day in the bar, or sitting in a park, sometimes crying. He was a lost soul. In Atlanta, Georgia, we ran out of money for a couple of days, and in the middle of the night my grandfather jumped from the hotel, three floors up. His note said the insurance money would get us the rest of the way to California. He died slowly, and we had to wait weeks for the coroner's jury to convene.

Finally we sold one car, all moved into the other, and started the trek from Georgia to Nebraska, where my grandmother's son lived with his family. In Lincoln we stayed with a retired professor who needed someone to cook and clean. My mother and grandmother saw to that themselves. As far as we two girls were concerned, we had a happy two months. Our first cousin was close to our age, and since my uncle managed two movie houses, the three of us went to the theater almost every day. It was freezing cold, but I remember us trudging through snowbanks, happily munching cranberry ice cream cones. At night we played anagrams with the old man. But I wasn't keeping up with my education. We had been enrolled in the Professional Children's School of New York, which mailed lessons to us at each of our stops. But my grandfather was the one who had always helped us, and after he died no one knew enough to help us with the difficult lessons.

Finally we got yet another old car and came down through Oklahoma and the desert to California, at first to San Diego. As it turned out, we had spent six months on the road, a lot of it waiting around in cheap hotels, and, when the car broke down—which it did frequently—stuck in hot roadside garages. From then on, I had the deep desire to stay in one place and have a normal life.

Finally you arrived in Hollywood.

Even when we finally landed in Hollywood in 1934—I was thirteen—my mother's wanderlust kept us on the move continually, from furnished apartment to furnished apartment. My poor sad-sack stepfather took to running away for a few days at a time. One of those times, my mother decided to move, and he came back to an empty apartment. We ended up renting a house near the MGM backlot, with hills and a river running nearby. All those incredible sets were our playground. As we had left Rhode Island, sound movies were just coming in strong. Now I was practically surrounded by them being made.

My sister and I graduated from Hollywood High three years later. Our classmates included Alexis Smith, my locker-mate, and Lana Turner, who was in my gym class. My mother and grandmother had set to work from the moment we got to California, and they were hard workers. For a while my mother was a singing waitress. Then the WPA Federal Theatre project came into being, with a headquarters in downtown L.A. My mother hooked up with a guy and his friend, and they resurrected two-a-day vaudeville shows in which my mother starred—singing, toe-dancing, you name it. In the summer of my graduation from Hollywood High, held in the Hollywood Bowl, my mother was still working for the WPA. My grandmother became a costumer in the same building where my mother was working on Federal Theatre projects. Jean and I worked after school, Jean as a salesgirl at Woolworth's and I as an usherette at a cut-rate movie house, required to wear a uniform that smelled of a lot of teenage girls before me. Thus, the family sort of limped along through the Great Depression.

Most vaudevillians had what could be called "liberal" ideas. They would never, ever, cross a picket line. When war production began I took a job, and I got married, in 1941, to a young man who was the same age as I, nineteen. My job was as a secretary in the "top-secret" department of RCA, where they were developing radar. My first husband, Bill O'Brien,* was drafted. We moved East for his training, and he became a second lieutenant.

The war was the best thing that ever happened to Bill O'Brien. He got to wear a uniform; he crossed the English Channel on a Liberty Ship, which was sunk by a Japanese midget sub; and later he could walk around with a Purple Heart—and a practiced limp. I settled in with another young second lieutenant's wife for about six months. I worked in a hospital in Salem, Massachusetts, and we lived at her mother's house in a poorer section of Boston, where it was "hot beds"—everyone working either the day shift or the night shift and taking turns sleeping in the two double beds. This working-class life in a war industry seemed to me quite noble, coming from my childhood. [Laughs.] Then I got a message from the Army that my husband was "missing in action." I'm not sure what I felt, but he had started drinking more and was becoming abusive toward me. I think I was disappointed when it turned out that he had only banged his knee when the midget sub sank his ship.

When he came back, he was transferred from Boston to New York Harbor, and so I moved there. He was assigned to the transportation corps and took longer and longer trips, in charge of prisoners, waste cargo, vital materiel, whatever. Personally, I was adrift, and I was getting pretty lonely. In this room I had rented, it was just me and the cockroaches.

Finally my husband came back. Though we hadn't been doing well before, now it was worse, because I had been on my own, growing up. He'd been away and seen the world and thought that I didn't understand anything. He was also getting drunk more often and becoming violent.

I left him and took a train back to California. By this time, my family had gotten a little house near Hollywood and Vine, from relocated Japanese, who had been forced to sell cheap. Those days, I would walk down Vine Street and see signs: "No Japs Allowed." It made me sick. I finally found the courage to divorce my husband—which wasn't easy in wartime—and tried to rebuild my life and my battered psyche.

You got involved in the upper reaches of the Hollywood left almost by accident.

---

*Bill O'Brien is a pseudonym.

I didn't seem to fit in anywhere. I heard about HICCASP and started off as a volunteer stuffing envelopes. All the women were older, in their forties, and Jewish. One day I told them that I was part Jewish, and they gave me such a look! There was no such thing as part Jewish, not for them. Then, suddenly, a secretarial job opened up there, in 1947, and I joined the staff.

George Pepper, the executive director of HICCASP and my boss, got his father to rent me a room. It was windowless, kitchenless, with the bed in the wall. There was such a scarcity of apartments in Los Angeles that I felt lucky. My place did have one window, which opened onto an air shaft, and I got quite a wide-ranging education about sex just by listening to my neighbors. I was still basically naive and afraid of relationships with men, after my five-year ordeal with Bill. But I was away from my family and no longer married to this madman, so I was happy.

Did you know what you were getting into?

Pretty much. HICCASP was a liberal-minded organization. In 1946 they were supporting candidates like Jimmy [James] Roosevelt and Henry Wallace and working to help "good" legislation get passed. George Pepper was married to Joy Pepper, who was beautiful and a dancer—she had been a ballerina. George was from a family of concert musicians. But he was splitting up with Joy, and I found myself getting attracted to him after only a little while. We started dating. Because I cared deeply about political and social issues, George encouraged me to join the Communist Party. The very words were a bit scary, but I wanted to try to do whatever I could to further "causes" I believed in. He put in an application for me, but at first I was turned down. I must have seemed like an outsider, too enthusiastic. Someone said, "You could be considered opportunistic." How could you work day and night for an organization, covered with mimeograph fluid and never getting enough rest and unable to afford a car to get to the office every day, and still be an opportunist? They finally accepted me—for a little while.

Assigned, as a fledgling Party member, to the Hollywood branch, I was in effect joining a very high-prestige, radical social club. We read books and talked about films being made. We talked about the problems of our country and the world. In the rest of Los Angeles and in the unions, from what I heard, ordinary Communists had much more difficult political lives—picketing assignments, circulating handouts, et cetera. Do I remember ever doing anything revolutionary? Hardly.

HICCASP became the Los Angeles branch of the Progressive Citizens of America, in time for Henry Wallace's Progressive Party campaign of the following year. My assignments now included handling some big people, like helping Katharine Hepburn and Henry Wallace to get around for events and helping them write their speeches. I remember especially working at a mass meeting where Wallace spoke. The FBI men who guarded him had guns, and they seemed very edgy. As I climbed the stairs to the platform to hand Wallace some flowers, I was literally tackled, and the bouquet of flowers torn apart. Apparently, they were checking for hidden bombs.

The Communists I met and worked with were mostly very successful writers and actors. I felt like a kid sometimes, because most of the Hollywood left was ten or fifteen years older than me. My first contact with Adrian Scott came when I was working as the stage manager of a mass meeting in support of the Hollywood Ten. One of my jobs was lining up the Hollywood Ten alphabetically. I remember that I took a dislike to [Edward] Dmytryk right away. He was an antsy-pantsy guy. If he'd had a couple more feet on him, he might have been more confident and a winning flirt. As it was, he was just this little man always trying to impress. He was very short, so he would always sit on a table in a group photo in order that he would appear as tall as the others. Anyway, at this meeting, when I was finally assured they were in alphabetical order, I noticed the last in line, Adrian, who seemed tired and tense, but still managed to be charming and considerate.

Raising money became another aspect of my job. Adrian was in my "silver book," the fund-raising book. He was always good for fifty or a hundred bucks, which was a lot then. I would also call Groucho Marx, which I'd rather be beaten up than do. Groucho would pretend that he was his own Japanese houseboy. He did make contributions, and he was even on the HICCASP board. But I was intimidated by him—unlike, for example, John Garfield, who was another person I used to chauffeur around. Garfield was a very nice person, kind of square and innocent, and still trying to deal with the death of his young son in the family swimming pool.

How long did you stay in the Communist Party?

Not long—about a total of six months. Feeling mixed up about men, life, and "my career," I went into therapy with a psychologist who became re-nowned for encouraging his Hollywood clients to inform.* Because of their bitter experiences with this man, the Party had made a ruling that it was either psychoanalysis or the Party. I said, "In that case, I'll take analysis." I had been in the Party for a total of about six weeks. I remember wondering if I had made the right decision when this psychologist said to me, "I want to talk about your sex life," as he got out the brandy and poured me a stiff shot to "relax me."

The once strong Popular Front of Hollywood was heading into near-terminal crisis.

People were jumping overboard out of the existing progressive organizations. The left didn't jump; that's how we "took over the organizations totally." [Laughs.] We were the only ones who stayed on the ship.

Even before HUAC came to Hollywood, it became clear that the wartime

---

*This was Phil Cohen.

alliance with the moderates and liberals was beginning to fall apart. Somebody hit on the idea of appointing a committee, representing the left, right, and middle, to meet day and night as long as was required to arrive at a "unity statement" to save HICCASP. I was assigned to be the recording secretary, which was quite an experience. Jimmy Roosevelt represented the centrists, along with Linus Pauling, who looked ninety even then. Dalton Trumbo and Jack Lawson represented the left. The so-called moderates were represented by Don Hartman and by Ronald Reagan. The radio writer True Boardman acted as the chairman.

I sat next to Reagan, who up until that time had seemed very liberal. But in a liberal-to-left organization he was more in the middle and drifting right. I remember that I didn't find him attractive or interesting in any way, and not intelligent, either. He didn't say one word in three days or nights. But after three days, son of a gun, the group did come up with a "unity statement," and nobody bolted from the room. I think Trumbo and Lawson were really brilliant—if you've been red-baited enough, you become pretty good at handling situations. The statement read something like, "We go on record as saying we are not Communists, we are not Prohibitionists, we are not Republicans"—they named every legitimate party—"but we support democratic rights." Well, everything went to hell anyway. People like Ronald Reagan had one foot out the door, and HICCASP disintegrated.

I had to get another job, and first I went to work for an awful PR guy, a shallow little man. Part of my job was to "dream up" PR stories for the firm's clients, and when I made up a gem about Tyrone Power and his girlfriend— she was our client—my boss was so delighted that he immediately called Hedda Hopper and got the lead story in her next day's column. I thought it was obvious that it was total fiction, but my dimwitted boss didn't realize that, and when I told him, he called Hopper back with apologies and fired me on the spot.

I made a few phone calls to guys like Bob [Robert] Kenny of Kenny and Cohn. Morris Cohn was another one of the lawyers representing the Ten. He was also a lawyer for the Screen Writers Guild. I went down for an interview, saw my first electric typewriter, assured everyone I could work it, and was hired to work for Cohn. It was 1949. I put up with a lot of what we would call sexual harassment on the job. It wouldn't have occurred to me to just get up and walk away, because I needed the job and I was getting a fabulous salary, plus I was learning a good profession, legal secretary. Time went by.

Now it was 1951, and Adrian came out of jail. He had been sentenced to a year but got off with nine months because of "good behavior." He went in three months after everyone else because he had to have colon surgery. He and Ring Lardner Jr. were determined to sue the studios on civil grounds: they had contracts but had been fired, notwithstanding. Morris Cohn was representing them, and I began to see Adrian again at the lawyer's office. I remember thinking how gorgeous these two guys were. Adrian was getting prematurely gray, but he was as handsome as could be. Ring was Ring, a pure golden American boy.

So we went to court, with Morris warning me that the judge was going to be very reactionary. It was like a courtroom movie in the old days when the lawyer would get up to make some point and the judge would say, "Sit down or I'll have the bailiff sit you down!" Later I would have recognized that as good screen dialogue. The judge would make statements from the bench like "I don't respect people like you jailbirds." The blue-ribbon jury of Pasadena was made up of elderly, upright citizens. To everyone's disbelief, they came in with a unanimous verdict for Ring and Adrian, whereupon the judge overturned the verdict. Ring settled, for a good price. Adrian made up his mind to fight the issue on principle, all the way to the Supreme Court, and he did, but meanwhile his money and his health ran out.

Anyway, Adrian, in my mind, was a rich and successful producer. Never mind that the man was half dead by now, physically and emotionally, and deep in debt after a year in a federal penitentiary and a broken marriage, and with a troubled adopted boy who had been dumped on him by his wife. One day he called the office, and I said, "You're calling about that brief Morris wanted you to read tonight." He answered, "Well, yes, I want to get that." I said, "Morris will be here any minute." Then he said, "But Miss LaCour, I'm really calling to see if you'd have dinner with me tonight." I went into shock.

We started dating and going to rallies together, and, of course, every head would turn, and you could hear the voices in the stands: "Adrian Scott! It's Adrian Scott!" They would be straining to look. I felt shy and self-conscious, but I also felt ten feet tall! I think I sort of sustained him during the first years out of jail, while he had no work, no prospects, and he helped me feel more confident and worthwhile as a person. But what helped him most was two years of intensive psychoanalysis with a skilled and wonderful doctor, Isadore Zifferstein, who died only recently. After three years or so, we were married, in 1955.

During this time, you also became executive secretary of the Television Writers of America, didn't you?

Yes, for two years, before Adrian and I were married. I got the job on the recommendation of Morris Cohn. We worked to win an NLRB election, and for a while it looked like the TWA had a bright future. Then the carefully orchestrated red-baiting by other guilds and unions mounted until the TWA was broken. At one point, I was sent to New York, along with the battle-hardened president, Dick [Richard] Powell, a wonderful human being, to organize the free-lance TV writers there and prepare for an NLRB election.*

---

*Not to be confused with actor, director, and producer Dick Powell, radio and screenwriter Richard Powell (1917–1996) was a successful radio writer who shifted to television, writing for *The Life of Riley*, *Topper*, and other series. His activism led him to serve as president of a

(Any meeting that we held was a little like *A Hundred Men and a Girl*, with Deanna Durbin—kind of bizarre, because I was always the only woman in the room; women writers were not yet working in television.) Then that creep Victor Riesel, the red-baiting columnist, attacked the union, identifying me as a red and claiming I was part of a conspiracy to get Communist propaganda into TV scripts. Half of the New York membership resigned after that column appeared.

When I went back to Hollywood and sat at the bargaining table, the networks' lawyer announced, "We will not sit in the room and negotiate with a known Communist." I just sat there, earnestly taking notes. The wonderful, warm, calm-but-strong NLRB official assigned to our election said quietly, "You *will* sit here, and you *will* negotiate with the legal bargaining agent for television writers." Later I suggested that I resign for the good of the union. Dick Powell said, "You're the lightning rod. If you quit, we're all dead." The big, successful comedy and drama writers in the TWA knew what had happened to the Ten, but they wanted to stick it out. There weren't even that many of us, but some of the struggle was wonderful, just the feeling of fighting back against McCarthyism.

Meanwhile, Morris Cohn called me and said, "We should get together." That was a code, meaning, "HUAC is looking for you with a subpoena. Get out of town if you can." After conferring with the union president, I went into hiding for two weeks, which I wouldn't wish on an escaped criminal. It was an awful feeling, moving from place to place. Finally, it was decided by the leaders of the union that I should testify, after all. Morris, who tried to get me ready, said "Of course, you'll deny that you've ever been a Communist." I said, "No, I can't, Morris." He was shocked. "You mean you have been in the Communist Party?" I answered, "A long time ago, and only for a short time. I'm not ashamed of it, but I won't admit it, because that would open the door for them to demand that I 'name names.' "

I was terrified as we were ushered into the hearing room, but Morris said it didn't show. The hearing became a fencing match: "Do you know so and so? What about Judy Raymond?* You knew her, didn't you?" She was the person who had named me. I knew her in passing, certainly not politically. Each time they mentioned someone, I'd respond in a quiet voice, "Has she"— or "he"—"been identified as a Communist?" The Committee members would look at each other and confer and say, "Yes," and then I would say, "Then I take the Fifth and First Amendments, and I won't answer that." They went

---

new writer's union, the Television Writers of America. Although not a Communist, he was sympathetic to the left and was blacklisted for his union leadership. He wrote under assumed names until the 1960s, when he was able to write openly for such shows as *Hogan's Heroes*. See "Interview with Richard Powell" in Paul Buhle, *From the Knights of Labor to the New World Order: Essays in Labor and Culture*.

*Judy Raymond, a former script girl married to producer Floyd Odlum, had become a HUAC informer.

down their list of names, and each time they got more irritated at my response. Finally one of the congressmen, Representative Clyde Dole, who was older than God, said, "I want a five-minute recess to talk to this young woman." He walked me down the hall, beseeching me to be "a good American, as nice a girl as I obviously was," to go back and say what he wanted to hear.

After more of the same, the Committee finally accepted that I wasn't going to answer their questions. Before the hearing, the reporters had wanted pictures—they actually asked me to pose crossing my legs and powdering my nose. I said, "Oh, come off it. We're not in a forties movie." After my session was over, I came out and all the photographers were waiting again; I felt marked with a scarlet "C." Naked. You never lose the feeling.

But, nevertheless, life went on in Hollywood for you and Adrian.

In 1956, soon after we were married, Adrian and I began to make payments on this little house in the Valley which we had mortgaged for nineteen thousand dollars. We lived there for five years, never making much of a living. I took temporary work as a typist. Adrian tried everything, right down to writing story lines for comic strips. Although he tried to find "underground" work as a writer, he couldn't quite grasp, or perhaps bear, doctoring someone else's scripts. At first, he didn't even know what a "treatment"* was and wouldn't write one. But that's the only way you got assignments, by writing a treatment first. He never got good at that, though he always wrote wonderful scripts.

Then Robin Hood *came to the rescue.*

Ring Lardner called Adrian from New York and said, "This woman in London [Hannah Weinstein] is producing the *Robin Hood* series. She's very simpatico and is reaching out to blacklisted people. You should get in on it." At first, on *Robin Hood*, it was difficult. Adrian was told he had to first write an "outline."† Then, when that was okayed, he could do the actual script. It was a struggle for him, a totally different way of working. Finally, he got the okay to go into "script." He wrote what I thought was a marvelous half-hour script. It went to England and Hannah said, "Get him to New York. He doesn't know how to write for television." It was different from movies. Styles were changing, and he'd been out of circulation for a while. He had trouble dealing with the form—the compression of things and the commercial breaks.

So he went to New York, very indignant. After three or four days of working with Ring Lardner and Ian [McLellan] Hunter and watching already filmed scripts, Adrian got the hang of it. He came back and made no further mistakes. I could see him gaining strength and confidence.

Meanwhile, he had to find a "front" for other shows. Now, some of the fronts were great and asked for nothing. Some of them, however, rooked you

---

*A "treatment" is a narrative summary of a television or film story line.

†An "outline" is a shorter, more concise version of the treatment, usually focusing on the progression of key scenes or characters.

completely, shamelessly. So, after thinking about it a while, it became obvious to Adrian that I should be his front—nobody would recognize *me*. It was a mistake in lots of ways. There were times when it almost severed our marriage. Then again, there were times when it also saved us. [Laughs.]

I started writing for television as Adrian's "front." Richard Sanville, a story editor at *Lassie*, started coming over and meeting with Adrian for hours, bringing along his own collie. Sometimes I'd sit in on the meetings, when they were trying to come up with a *Lassie* story. It was the fourth or fifth year of *Lassie*, and they were running out of plots. One night Dick and Adrian were sitting there bouncing ideas around, and I said, "What about 'Cry Wolf'? Have you done that?" And the story editor said, "Oh, my God, wonderful!"

Adrian said quickly, firmly, "She writes it." The problem was, I was blacklisted as Joan LaCour. If I went in as Joan Scott, somebody might have put it all together. There were people who might recognize either one of my names. We decided on a name which was a variation of my maiden name, just Anglicized. "LaCour" became "Court." I balanced it off with "Joanne" instead of just "Joan."

So I got the assignment, and it was the easiest thing I ever did. I couldn't understand what all the fuss was about. Dick Sanville said to Adrian, "My God, where have you been keeping her?" He changed only a few lines on the first script, and I thought, "What a piece of cake." Later it got harder. I found out why everyone said that *Lassie* was a tough show to write for.

There were funny things about writing for that show. You had to learn to think like a dog. We used to say, "Lassie is classy, not like Flipper." Sometimes the stories became ridiculous. In one episode, not one of mine, June Lockhart is in the woods caught in a bear trap, and she says to Lassie, "Go back to the house; get something to help me," but Lassie brings back a screwdriver. She says, "No, Lassie, the *wrench*," and sends Lassie back for the right tool! It was hard to write some of these scenes, as though Lassie could really understand what was going on. I always ended my scripts with this line: "If a dog could smile, Lassie would be smiling."

You were one of the few blacklistees who led a double life, fronting for your husband as well as using your pseudonym to write for your own career in television.

While I was writing for *Lassie*, Adrian was writing for *Meet McGraw, 77 Sunset Strip*, and *Surfside Six*, using his marvelous writing skills on these dumb shows under my pen name, Joanne Court. His specialty was this wonderfully old-fashioned studio tough-guy dialogue. I'd get a lot of attention from the male story editors and the producers who would come in "to meet the girl who writes like a man." I was still very young compared to the other writers; it was the season of fluffy petticoats, and I looked *very* young and, well, fluffy. So I would have to go in for the story conferences, me, this wisp of a girl. They would say, "God, you write like a man!" I'd smile graciously. I'd come home and tell Adrian the changes that they wanted to make, and he would be furious. He'd pace around the room, and I'd say, "Adrian, we have to change it." So he'd go off, fuming, and rewrite the thing.

One time I had a hundred-and-two fever. He was driving me to CBS, and as we arrived he handed me the script and said, "I finished the rewrites last night." I asked, "Is there anything new in it?" He said, "No, no." I walked in, and everyone was there, six production people, all men. They said, "Now, let's go over the entire script." I said, "Fine." I started turning pages. One of the production men said, "Let's look at such and such a page. I don't understand the motivation for this speech." I looked at the scene, and I realized I had never seen these pages, four or five of them. I hadn't a clue what Adrian had done in the rewrite. I was sitting there, and they were all looking at me and waiting. I said carefully, "Well, I see it as a matter of almost a subconscious issue. Our hero is questioning his own motivations, but he doesn't want to let on what he is really thinking." One of them said quickly, "Oh yes, Miss Court, that sounds fine."

There were good times as well as bad, but at one point we were really broke, because there wasn't that much work available. Dalton Trumbo had moved into one of his many mansions (we had been married there), a house at the top of a hill in Highland Park, looking down on the minions. I think it was Christmas. Dalton was working on something like eight scripts at once, on booze and uppers and downers, a man driven, writing under about four or five pen names to support his family and his penchant for high living. Adrian called him and asked, "Could you spare a couple of hundred dollars?" Dalton said, "Sure, when do you want it?" He sent his son, Chris, across town with the check, which was for the mortgage payment, and everything was temporarily fine. We called to thank Dalton, and he said, "Anytime!" In the meantime (he only later told us) he had four calls out to get the two hundred into the bank to cover the check. There was one time, later on, when he needed a hundred dollars, and we hurried to say, "Of course." And we had to scramble, ourselves, to get the money from another blacklisted friend and cover *our* check.

Anyway, I was slowly developing a TV writing career of my own, still using my pen name. I came up with a fresh idea about a woman pursued by a bounty hunter for *Have Gun Will Travel*, finished that script, and made it to more assignments. At the same time, I was getting into more and more ridiculous situations at the television studio, with male chauvinists wanting to pinch my behind and play games. I was disgusted half the time—it was hard work and, especially for a woman, there was not much respect. But enough money came in that we were able to pay off some of Adrian's debts, even to the psychiatrist who had saved him.

How did you end up working for Walt Disney?

The Disney studio sent out word that they were looking for a woman writer to do a story of Beethoven. Disney insisted on it being a woman, because women had "heart." Walt was such a strange man—all heart, you know, also an anti-Semite and a union-buster. One of the guys working there, in the writers building, was Fred Freiberger, a friend who was able to use his own name, who had no dark political past—or present. They all kept very quiet about their political ideas over there, anyway. Nobody felt really at ease. Disney was a frightening figure, a benevolent despot.

My agent first tried to send in this older European writer, a wonderful woman who could never have worked for Disney. She would have turned him over her knee and said, "That's junk. That's not true about Beethoven. I won't write that." I think that at the time I was practically the only other woman writer available. I was interviewed by virtually the whole production crew so that they could send word to Walt, who was in Europe, about whether they had found the right writer.

The first thing women are asked—not so much now—is, "What does your husband do?" I had talked to Adrian about that. He said, "They'll never ask." I insisted, "Of course they will!" So he said, "All right, tell them you're married to a lawyer." I said, "That'd be awfully easy to check. One of them might want to hire a lawyer." He said, "All right, then, I'm an English professor at some college." I said, "That's too easy to check." He said, "Well, if that's not good enough for you, come up with your own story."

Soon after I was hired, my producer, Jerry, took me out to lunch, and as we both looked up from the menu he said predictably, "Well, Joanne, what does your husband do?" [Laughs.] This was when the White Front discount appliance stores existed (much like today's Fedco), and all of us bought things like refrigerators and air-conditioners there; we couldn't bear to buy even an iron at full price. I said, "Do you know the White Front stores?" I was sorry to see I had piqued his interest. I was afraid he might be looking for a good buy, say, on a refrigerator. I said, "Well, my husband is a troubleshooter for White Front." He said, "Oh," and he started losing interest by the moment. So I said, "He goes down to the railroad cars when they come in, and he marks the things that are rejects, not good enough even for White Front. It's very responsible work." He said, "Well, maybe we should order lunch." I didn't want to be stopped. I wanted to get this guy bored for life. So I went on and on about my husband's important work. He said, "Well, yes . . . fine . . . right." In came the art director and he looked at the menu and then said, "What does your husband do?" The producer said, "Don't ask. I'll tell you about it later." Nobody ever asked again.

Then Disney came back from Europe. The whole project had started out with leftover footage with Mickey Mouse from *Fantasia*, the part with Beethoven's music. First Walt had wanted to make it into a half-hour program, and then he decided to go for an hour program. This was before I came onto the scene. So, by the time he returned, people were already researching and drawing and deciding on the music. I was in the writers' building working on concepts. Actually, I was thinking, "How the hell can I do this?" Nobody was telling me very much. I didn't even know whether we were going to have an animated Beethoven or maybe an animated duck or maybe the two of them talking to each other. All I knew was that the story was going to start when Beethoven was seventeen years old and then go up to his death—well, *almost* to his death, so the story could end on a high note.

We had our first conference with Disney. He anointed me with a pet name, "Little Bit," and told me to sit close to him over by his desk. He looked at me very intensely. I'm not very good at eye contact; I was looking everywhere but at him. [Laughs.] He said, "I understand you've got a very interesting approach to this material, Little Bit. Tell me about it." So I started reading from my notes, and when I got to the part where Beethoven starts to lose his hearing I looked up, and tears were streaming down Disney's cheeks. I looked around the room, and every one of those men were crying; I was the only dry-eyed person in the house. They cried like actors or trained seals. Disney wiped his eyes and held my gaze: "We're going to go for two hours on this show, Little Bit, and let's write it so we can put the two hours together later and release it as a feature film in Europe."

The next day, when we all trooped back to Disney's office, Disney announced that he was going to personally produce the Beethoven project. I didn't know enough to be afraid that I was going to have to work directly with him. It turned out to be a period of eight or nine months—three months of research for me, then writing the script, which had become by now two one-hour shows to be shown on consecutive Sunday evenings, known as "Disney's Television Specials." Following Disney's instructions, I wrote the two hours so that they could be knitted together as one and released theatrically in Europe.

At home, at night, Adrian would be my real "producer." I remember one day when my team—of art directors, composers, et cetera—went in for a story conference, and Walt didn't like an idea I proposed but didn't make it clear what he wanted. Adrian advised me, "Look, ask him what it is he wants exactly. It's not your place to sit there and guess." I said, "I don't think he'll like that." Adrian answered, "The hell with him. You're the writer, and you're going to have to stand up to this man somewhere along the way. You may as well start." His help not only was invaluable, it also kept my morale up. At the next meeting, sure enough, Walt asked, "What did you decide to do on that scene we talked about?" I said, "Well, I haven't done anything, because I wasn't clear on what you wanted in place of it." Suddenly, Walt threw the books, the scripts, everything, off his desk onto the floor, and my production crew was ushered out. Disney said, "I may see you after lunch. I may not." We trooped out into the hall, and the others all looked at me. I had betrayed the team, I had lowered the flag, we were all going to be fired. They said, "You can't talk to him like that."

I went back to the studio the next day, very nervous. The worst thing that could happen to tear into your gut was the loudspeaker going off, saying, "Joanne Court, Joanne Court, please join Mr. Disney in the conference room." And that's what occurred. Everybody else was already sitting there like silent, frightened little puppets. Walt stood up and said, "I want to apologize for losing my temper." My guys were stunned, in disbelief. After that, I could do no wrong, and we were all great buddies.

I was briefly the fair-haired girl at the Disney studio. They'd all whisper, "That's Joanne Court. She's working with Walt on the Beethoven special." Except one day I was on my way to the commissary to eat at the writers' table when Disney's chief assistant came running up and said, "I'm glad I caught you, Joanne. I am supposed to ask you what you are." I replied, "I don't know what you mean." He said "Well, are you Irish? Your name is Court." Ironically, with the name LaCour, I never got asked what I was—I was obviously French. Here I was with this meaningless name, Joanne Court, and no apparent history. So everyone around me waited breathlessly for my reply. I said, "Well, actually, I'm mostly French, Huguenot French"—everyone was happy about that—"and a little bit German, and French-Canadian and an eighth Jewish. I'm American hash." But Disney's assistant's face sank. I couldn't stop myself, although I knew it had been the wrong thing to say. We had a gloomy lunch. Disney would have to learn I was part Jewish—although being part Jewish wasn't as bad as being pro-union or both Jewish *and* pro-union. Of course, practically every writer on the lot was Jewish. Poor Disney thought that he'd finally found one of his own, with a name like Court.

Did Disney ever suspect you had an alternate identity?

Walt never called me at home, never sought me out in any way, never seemed even mildly curious about my personal life. But he liked my work and told me, when I turned in the "final draft," how very pleased he was with it. I remember that at some point in the script, Beethoven, during the shelling of Vienna, was losing his hearing and, lonely and frightened, was wandering around war-torn Vienna. I needed an emotional "beat." Adrian suggested the idea of Beethoven coming across a bedraggled white poodle and holding and protecting it. I thought it was saccharine, silly, but Adrian said, "Walt will love it." And he did!

Walt decided to shoot the film in Vienna, with the actual settings—the opera house, everything. They hired a full symphony orchestra there. Of course, I wasn't asked to go—writers never are (unless they are very "big"). My producer went ahead to find good locations, and Walt himself came about a week later. Walt took offense at something my producer said, and he was fired on the spot. Back at the Disney lot I saw the poor man once more. We had lunch, and I had to mop him up as he cried. All the Disney writers and producers had yachts they were paying installments on, college educations for their children, and, of course, homes. They were twenty-year "yes men" for Disney, and they knew they'd be there forever—unless they crossed that invisible line. My own theory was that if a young, pretty woman who was respectful of Disney crossed that line once—say, Tuesday morning at ten a.m.—it was okay. That he could accept.

Sometime after I finished the script, I got a call from my agent. Disney wanted me to come back and write a voice-over. I'd written this script in such a way that people didn't say, "Oh, here we are in Vienna in 1802, and this is a famous place for all aspiring young musicians." I had done it so you wouldn't need that kind of spelling-out. But Disney felt people needed to be hit over the head several times; otherwise they wouldn't get the point. He always had narration. I had even discussed it with him, saying at one point, "We won't have to have narration on this film, will we, Walt?" He planned to, anyway, and it was no insult to me. That was his finishing touch on the picture.

My agent set up a meeting on the day when they were watching the rough cut and the music. It was in an old-fashioned film-projection room, and I got a big hello. Walt hadn't seen me for a year, and there was all this wonderful display of friendship. Adrian had sat me down the night before and warned me, "You're going to hate the film. But then you'll grow to love it. Like a parent with a deformed child. They're going to have things in there that you didn't write, and they will have taken out your favorite scenes. Now, what are you going to say to Uncle Walt when the lights go up? He's going to ask how you like it." We agonized over what I should say while still being "honest" but not insulting to Disney.

Disney signaled to the projection room to roll the film. That marvelous music rolled over me. And then, with some of my best dialogue cut out and a great many scenes handled badly, my heart sank. I *did* hate it; it *was* awful. The lights came on, and Walt was behind me, patting my shoulder. I turned around to his face, and he said, "Well, Little Bit, what do you think of it?" With a straight face, I gave him Adrian's line, which was, "Walt, you've done it again!" [Laughs.] Disney was as pleased as punch.

The next day I was introduced to the actor who was scheduled to do the voice-over. As we went up to watch the Moviola, I felt I was sort of looking at Rosemary's baby—my monster. But each additional time I looked at the film, it seemed a little less awful. I began to think, "That's my baby." Soon all of us on the production team were toasting each other. We went up and down the halls and said things like: "Hey, that's not bad, is it?" "The music's great." "Yeah, I loved your dialogue there, Joanie." "You know, it's not a bad picture." It's a subtle studio process. Adrian had had it happen to him, and he knew it would happen to me, especially on my first movie.

I picked the spots where Walt wanted narrative. He wanted lines like, "A young man whose name will soon be known worldwide, and throughout all history, is arriving in Vienna." I remember writing something that was especially purple, and Adrian said, "I've never seen you write this badly! This is shit." I said, "Walt will like it." [Laughs.] Walt loved it.

It turned out that the actor couldn't be there, and I myself had to read the narration to Walt in the projection room when it was done. I said nervously, "Walt, I'm not an actress." He said, "You're not? I didn't know that." Except for my nationality and ethnic background, he had never asked *anything* about me. He told the technicians to start rolling the film as I began reading the narration. Afterward he said, "I love it. Don't change a word." I thought my narration weakened the film, but Disney was happy; that's what mattered.

He was so happy that he believed I was standing by to do another script for the Disney studio. But it was 1961, and we were already packing for London. As in old times, with husband, wife, and careers—and old times still prevailed—I had to give up my career.

Just before we left, Disney's assistant called me and said Walt was ready to have a conference on the new project. The next morning I met with Walt, and he said, "It's so good to see you again and to know we're going to work together again. I'm so happy." I replied, "Walt, I tried to make it clear to your assistant that I'm not available to do this script. I'd love to do it, but my husband has an offer of a job in England, and we're about to leave." He didn't ask, "Doing what?" Disney just fought for control. His face reddened, he took a deep breath, and finally he said, "Little Bit, I respect you. We'll work together again someday. I'm not going to let you go. I've got a studio in London. Don't worry. There's a property I want you to research when you get over there."

Several blacklistees who worked with Disney—Maurice Rapf, Al Levitt, and John Hubley among them—grudgingly liked or at least admired Walt, largely because of his creativity and his passion for his work. Did you feel the same?

The Disney studio did some shooting on its own backlot, which was ridiculously small. I remember one day watching them film *Davy Crockett* on some dusty little piece of road just behind the writers' building. The "Indians" were grouped together on horseback on a "knoll." The angle was so small that everyone not in the scene had to squeeze themselves up against the wall of the building to avoid being seen by the camera. Then I got paged to come to Disney's screening room. As I waited in the hallway, I heard a voice over my shoulder and felt an arm around me. "Hey, Little Bit, they're shooting that scene where the Indians attack the cowboys!" He was like a little kid. He loved his work.

You never worked with Disney again?

No, and Walt was terribly hurt. When we got to London, my agent cabled to say, "Disney wants you for such and such a project. Go to the BBC library and you will find . . ." The book he was interested in was in the public domain, from whence Disney got many of his projects. But turning it into a film never went very far, partly because the book was a piece of junk.

One more important thing happened before we left for England. We didn't have anyone to rent the house. It was a modest tract house, although by this time I'd bought us a pool with my Disney wages. One night the phone rang, and it was a rental agent who had called to say she had a great couple as the prospective tenants. The agent bounced over with a woman who looked like a starlet—all done up in mink—until she opened her mouth, when she sounded like a Brooklyn Dead End Kid. The woman said, "Oh, I know that my fiancé would love this place. Oh, it's so gawjus." [Laughs.] Adrian and I just sat there trying to keep straight faces. She added, "But we can only rent it for nine months. . . ." I thought of pregnancy, Adrian thought she had a role in some film, but we were glad to get any tenants at that point. She said, "I'll talk to my fiancé tonight and try to get him to come over tomorrow. He's not much for looking at places."

About an hour later the phone rang; it was her again. Adrian said, "I'm so glad you liked it and that you'll be coming by with your fiancé tomorrow. That would be just wonderful. And who is he? Oh, your fiancé is Mickey Cohen. . . ." Whereupon I just about slid down to the floor. We were storing our tax records and personal papers in the locked garage, but with Mickey moving in, the FBI or the IRS—or both—would have a dandy excuse to search our house.

Mickey Cohen [a notorious Los Angeles–area gangster] was especially in the news, because recently someone had been killed at his table in an Italian restaurant in the Valley, as his nineteen-year-old girlfriend sat next to him. A guy had walked up, pulled out a pistol, and shot the guy sitting on the other side of Mickey through the forehead. Mickey didn't bat an eye through the entire episode. He said to everybody "Now get up. Go out quietly. Go home. Dey'll come to arrest you soon. But dey'll want to talk to me first." He told me later that he ordered another bottle of champagne as the body was being taken out. [Laughs.]

It turned out that Mickey expected to be in jail for nine months on a pending charge, not the murder rap but something else. I thought we just couldn't rent to such people, but Adrian said, "Why not? We need a tenant, and I'm sure they'll pay the rent on time." The next day I heard a knock at the door, and there was Mickey, not much taller than I, with a bodyguard and the girl. He always had a bodyguard. I got Adrian, and we all introduced ourselves. Pretty soon, Mickey was saying to Adrian, "You're one of them guys? I don't believe it! We had the same lawyer! Geez, it's a small world!"

Anyway, then you went to London.

I was so happy there. I hated it in Los Angeles. I grew up there, and the memories are still unpleasant. I loved being six thousand miles away from my family. We had this wonderful life in London. We went to the theater and concerts and museums. We traveled all over Europe and went back and forth to New York and California a couple of times a year. We made wonderful new friends and had old friends among some of the Americans there who had fled the witch-hunts and were now bona fide residents of the U.K.

Adrian didn't really succeed, career-wise, in England.

No. The guy who hired Adrian, a college friend who was now head of MGM-London, had brought him over to be his top assistant in production. That was supposed to lead to producing MGM films under his own name.

But everything seemed to fall through. A film that was supposed to star Warren Beatty and have Joseph Losey as a director didn't happen. Adrian wasn't credited for films he did writing on, *Night Must Fall* among others.

I, meanwhile, was hired to work on an original script for a British production, *Cairo*, which borrowed heavily from *The Asphalt Jungle*, made in the U.S. many years before. It would be my first screenplay. Although I went in for story conferences with the studio head, again Adrian worked with me as my "producer at home," helping to make the script right. I ended up with a pretty good script. I thought the plot was a total giveaway, although, at the time it was released, the reviewers didn't seem to notice the resemblance to *The Asphalt Jungle*, so I ended up feeling a bit puffed-up. I hoped to parlay that into more writing, but there weren't that many jobs around, and the British industry had enough unemployed writers of their own.

Why did you come back to the U.S.?

Adrian got an offer from Universal studios in 1968, to return to Hollywood—all expenses paid—under a two-year contract as a producer. Albert Maltz sent Adrian a telegram that said, "Universal wants you. Don't say no." Jennings Lang, a former agent, now an executive of Universal, then made the trip to London to convince Adrian he should accept the offer. So we packed up. I wept all the way back on the plane. I couldn't hide my emotions, but I don't think Adrian wanted to notice. First I had given up my TV career to move to London, now, it seemed, I was giving up my happy life and was coming back to hell, and that's the way it came to pass.

At first, Adrian went off to the studio every day like a crazed teenager; he was so thrilled. I took to my bed for three months with Hong Kong flu and then a hideous migraine. They had me in ice packs. Adrian, who had been sick a lot of the time we were in London with one flu or another, now had to nurse me. He never even got a sniffle. Obviously psychological states are very important.

We bought a two-story house in Sherman Oaks. Adrian had a workroom and a whole library for himself downstairs. We caught up with old friends also just returning from havens in London, Paris, Mexico. But suddenly, the studio canceled Adrian's contract. They told him that either they would buy up his contract for the second year or he would have to come in to work and sit it out. Friends told us that Universal was cutting back in general, but I don't believe that was true.

Perhaps it was that Adrian was by now fifty-nine years old, which is the beginning of the "too old" list here in the industry. We talked about it quite solemnly and decided that he'd go crazy sitting in his Universal office for a year doing nothing. So when the studio offered seventy-five cents on the dollar as a settlement, we took it, But now it was a "new" old Adrian. He would go downstairs every day to his new study, sit there, and then come up at the end of the day. But he was unable to write. It didn't take me long to realize that he was severely depressed and I was losing him. He was totally withdrawing. He had been out in the cold more than twenty years. Why did they bring him back from London only to fire him?

In those days, a man didn't go into a women's beauty parlor to have his hair done any more than a woman would walk into a barbershop. Adrian had talked to a studio hairdresser, and I came home one night to find this man with his beautiful white hair dyed almost purple. I had to get out of the room, I couldn't bear to look at him. It didn't work, anyway. I could look at his scripts and see that the style of movies had changed. Adrian was a writer from another era, the thirties and forties. He still wrote marvelous dialogue, dialogue that nobody in real life actually spoke, of course. But I could see that Adrian wasn't writing modern film scripts. Now he had nowhere to go with his marvelous talent.

He did get one television film made, called *The Great Man's Whiskers*. Adrian had written it as a one-act play in his twenties, a fable about Lincoln visiting a little girl who had written him a letter. John Paxton did an adaptation.* Adrian's demeanor changed, and he seemed to enjoy making the two-hour TV movie, in which he had cast every blacklisted actor within reach. Dennis Weaver played Lincoln and created a warm and moving figure.

Adrian had gone in for a routine insurance physical, and they found a spot on his lung. They said, "It's TB or valley fever. It's not cancer." Nevertheless, they had to "go in" to "prove" it wasn't cancer. We toasted our seventeenth anniversary the night before Adrian's exploratory surgery. Albert Maltz, the next morning, came to be with me. He and Trumbo had feuded terribly— each felt he was "better for Adrian" and "a better friend of Adrian." Maltz was a very sober man and had this Christlike quality. But he was great to me, and I was glad to have him there. After the surgery, as Adrian was wheeled out of the operating room, the surgeon looked at me and said brusquely, "It's cancer." Albert again stayed with me, and he helped me deal with the traumatic news.

Looking back, I almost think Adrian willed himself to die. Life had gotten too painful. They didn't catch all the cancer, and Adrian died three months later. Six weeks after his death, the TV movie played and the credit read, "Produced by Adrian Scott." I felt my life was over. I didn't think I could go on without Adrian. It took two years of intensive therapy before I could even begin to function. I'm not sure how well I am doing that now.

To what extent were you able to resume your career in Hollywood?

I had been at the same studio as Adrian, Universal, working under my pen name, and there I wrote for *Marcus Welby* and again for *Lassie*. After Adrian

---

*John Paxton (1911–1985) was a former New York press agent and journalist turned screenwriter. His best-known films in the 1940s were collaborations with producer Adrian Scott: *Murder, My Sweet*, *Cornered*, *So Well Remembered*, and *Crossfire*. Although friendly to the left, he was not named or blacklisted. His later films include *The Wild One*, *The Cobweb*, *On the Beach*, and *Kotch*. *Crossfire* was nominated for a Best Screenplay Oscar.

died, a friend, Jean Butler, got me into the daytime soaps, and I worked for
a time on *The Guiding Light*. At sixty-five the "age blacklist" hit, just as it
had for Adrian. Now, if you're over forty, you can't even get an agent. The
entire industry seems to be run by twenty-five and twenty-six-year-olds—and
it shows!

You had some involvement in the 1991 blacklist film Guilty by Suspicion, *starring
Robert De Niro, didn't you?*

I had an interesting job, not writing but as "technical advisor" to the
company, and a walk-on acting part. Abraham Polonsky took his name off
the script after they mangled it. The rewritten script first shown to me was
credited to Irwin Winkler, who went on to be credited as the writer and
producer *and* director—not a good idea. De Niro and Annette Bening costarred in the film, which not even De Niro could save. I was hired to be on
the set and give the actresses—especially Annette Bening—"the feel of the
times." They used me in a small part. But after a couple of tries at a scene
with De Niro and Bening, I felt it wasn't going well, so I took myself out of
it. What remained for me was a brief bit as a schoolteacher. Mostly it was
fun, and I was treated well. After all this time in Hollywood, that's the only
time I've been in a movie. Ironic, isn't it?

Now I rarely see old friends. Many of the people we had known no longer
included me in their social plans after Adrian's death. Others have moved
away or died. It is a lonely, diminished life. There is no longer "the community
of the left." We are a dying breed.

But perhaps my autobiography, "Adrian's Wife," will keep those dark days
of the blacklist alive for another generation and show how many brave and
committed people tried to keep free speech, including the right to remain
silent, a reality.

Lionel Stander

LIONEL STANDER, Los Angeles, California, 1983

INTERVIEW BY PATRICK McGILLGAN
AND KEN MATE

LIONEL STANDER
(1908–1994)

1935 *The Scoundrel*
    Page Miss Glory
    The Gay Deception
    We're in the Money
    Hooray for Love
    I Live My Life
    If You Could Only Cook
1936 *Soak the Rich*
    The Milky Way
    Mr. Deeds Goes to Town
    Meet Nero Wolfe
    The Music Goes 'Round
    More Than a Secretary
    They Met in a Taxi
1937 *A Star Is Born*
    The League of Frightened Men

    The Last Gangster
1938 *Professor Beware*
    The Crowd Roars
    No Time to Marry
1939 *What a Life*
    The Ice Follies of 1939
1941 *The Bride Wore Crutches*
1943 *Hangmen Also Die*
    Guadalcanal Diary
    Tahiti Honey
1945 *The Big Show-Off*
1946 *The Kid from Brooklyn*
    Specter of the Rose
    A Boy, a Girl, and a Dog
    In Old Sacramento
    Gentleman Joe Palooka
1947 *Mad Wednesday/The Sin of Harold*
    Diddlebock
1948 *Call Northside 777*
    Unfaithfully Yours

■

TO GENERATIONS OF movie buffs, Lionel Stander occupies a permanent niche as one of Hollywood's immortals, unforgettable as an eccentric heavy in the comedies of Ben Hecht and Charles MacArthur, Frank Capra, Preston Sturges, and Harold Lloyd, usually lacing his portrayals with acid asides. His trademarks were a cigar, a gravelly voice, and a face etched from a totem pole.

Behind the career of one of the screen's premier character actors was a long résumé of left-wing involvement. Stander had been a prime mover in the struggle to organize the Screen Actors Guild, and in many anti-Fascist and civil-rights causes in Hollywood, since his arrival there in 1935. Twice he was blacklisted—first in the late 1930s, secretly, for taking on the corrupt unions and producers, and then during the McCarthy era for his cumulative "front" activities. After lecturing the Committee on the true meaning of un-Americanism, Stander vanished from the screen for fourteen years, the span of time between St. Benny the Dip in 1951 and The Loved One in 1965. He was able to do some work in the theater, to which he had always maintained a commitment, not merely as an actor but as a producer of serious drama.

For a time, this lifelong radical worked on Wall Street as a successful broker, an irony that certainly didn't escape him. Finally, Stander went to Europe, living in Rome for long spells and reviving his acting career abroad with memorable appearances in Roman Polanski's Cul-de-sac and several spaghetti westerns. A regular role as Max, the chauffeur, in the popular TV detective series Hart to Hart, from 1979 to 1984, provided the last laugh and the unlikely, triumphant capstone to his life story.

Stander died in 1994 at the age of eighty-six. Early in 1995 The Last Good Time, featuring his final performance, was released.

■

When were you first radicalized?

I was making a comedy short at Warner Brothers' Avenue M studios in Coney Island, and the studio usually supplied a car to take me home. But this day I had a date, and you could get home quicker by subway, so I took the subway. I lived in the Village and got off at Fourteenth Street and Union Square. As I walked through the park, I suddenly heard a loud noise and saw thousands of people running with signs and mounted policemen hitting people over the head. One cop went for me. I ducked and went up a side street, and next morning I read in the *New York Times* that this was a demonstration of the unemployed for unemployment insurance. I think it was 1931. The *Times* editorialized that the whole idea of unemployment insurance was Communistic and insane. And that started my radicalization.

What was Hollywood like, politically, in the 1930s?

To paraphrase Dickens, it was the best of times, and it was the worst of times—the best of times because you were young, and the worst of times because of the actions of Hitler and Mussolini, et cetera. Hollywood was the mecca for nearly every worthwhile intellectual of the 1930s from all over the world. You saw a lot of what was happening through the eyes of the German refugees—actors, writers, directors, technicians, and artists—who came here and through the activity of mass organizations like the Hollywood Anti-Nazi League, et cetera. The power of the left existed because it said all the things that everybody believed in and wanted to hear; it represented every person who believed in human decency, justice, and equality and was against racism and bigotry. And the Communist Party always took the frontal position.

It is very difficult to recreate the atmosphere, but I think that in general there were very few right-wingers and a minority of left-wingers in Hollywood. Everybody who was decent, however, was united on the necessity of doing something to prevent Hitler and Mussolini and Fascism from sweeping the world.

We know you were in the forefront of many of the early-1930s causes and issues. Were you active in the Salinas Valley lettuce strike?*

---

*A massive strike of lettuce workers in the Imperial Valley, beginning on January 1, 1930, ushered in a decade of farm workers' militancy. The Communist-led Agricultural Workers Industrial League took over the strike, integrating Filipinos among the predominantly Mexican unionists. Defeated through overwhelming force, farm workers struck again in 1934, now guided by the Communist-led Cannery and Agricultural Workers Industrial Union. The defeat of this strike, amid overwhelming repression, jailings, and deportations, signaled the end of the Communist Unionists' success in organizing farm workers and limited the success of farm workers' unionization until the 1960s.

I had friends who were. Lincoln Steffens was then married to Ella Winter; she later married Donald Ogden Stewart. Steffens lived up on the Monterey Peninsula, in Carmel. I went up there one weekend, and they introduced me to Jimmy [James] Cagney, who was also a guest of theirs, and John Steinbeck, who was helping the lettuce strikers raise money for their strike. I drove down in my car and met the strike leaders, saw conditions in the fields, spoke to a couple of strikers, and was aghast. They were striking for ridiculous wages, and their living conditions were like something you read about in some desolate spot in Asia, India, or Africa. I got excited about that cause and angry about it.

What were the issues in that case?

The issues were the issues that are always involved in a strike of farm workers. It was for union recognition and for certain hourly wages. I think they asked for forty cents an hour, or something ridiculously low. These issues are always the same in a labor struggle.

Were you able to organize people in Hollywood to support the lettuce strikers?

Yes. I went back to Hollywood and raised quite a bit of money from actors, sending it to Lincoln Steffens and Ella Winter for the strikers. At one point, the AFL [American Federation of Labor] had to decide whether or not to okay the strike. Kenneth Thompson, who was executive secretary of the Screen Actors Guild, was at a conference of the AFL in Sacramento, and he asked me to get some people to send a telegram and some money to help the strikers. I asked some friends of mine—Gary Cooper, Eddie Cantor, Eddie [Edward] Arnold, and a number of other people—and got anywhere from a hundred to a thousand dollars apiece. I cabled the money to Ken Thompson with a telegram.

Now, the press was covering the meeting, and when Ken Thompson read off my telegram, the first name he read was Gary Cooper—and the press dashed to the phone. The Hearst press was, of course, anti-AFL and anti-union, and they wanted to publicize the fact that the lettuce strike was really a Communist conspiracy organized by the Communist Party. Actually, it was an officially endorsed strike of the AFL, but the front page read, "Gary Cooper Gives Money to Reds." The reporters came to me the next day and asked me and everybody else who contributed, "Did you know when you gave that money that it wasn't going to the AFL—it was going to further the interests of a subversive organization?" Most of the actors said, "Gee, I didn't know that," and they would be quoted as such. But I'll always remember Herbert Marshall, who had given me five hundred dollars and put his name on the telegram. When they went to him and asked, "Why did you give money to the lettuce strike?" he said, "I loathe lettuce, and anything that keeps lettuce off the American table I'm for."

Weren't you also involved in the campaign to free Tom Mooney?

Yeah. I was a member of an organization that was asking for the release of Tom Mooney from jail, and I went up to San Francisco and met with [the militant leader of the longshoremen's union] Harry Bridges. Through a progressive sheriff or some such, we managed to get a visit with Tom Mooney, and I was very impressed with him. Of course, along with Sacco and Vanzetti, that was one of the cases that will live in infamy. A real act of repression that's almost unbelievable.

You were also one of the early organizers of the Screen Actors Guild. What were the conditions that were fundamental to its formation? Were you at the first secret meetings?

I joined the Guild before the Guild was recognized, when it was dangerous to be a Guild member, and when we had secret meetings. The attempt of the actors to unionize in the Screen Actors Guild was naturally met by the opposition of the producers, who were happy to have no union representing actors, because they knew that if the actors organized and we got recognized, we'd ask for a raise in wages and elevate the working conditions for actors— which we did. Eventually the Guild got affiliated with the AFL, and later on the AFL-CIO, and became a recognized trade union.

Before the Guild got power, there were no limits on an actor's working hours. You could work till midnight or two in the morning and be called for six o'clock the next morning. And the working conditions, particularly for extras and bit players, were terrible. We'd go on location and there'd be no water, coffee, or adequate toilet facilities.

Early on, the Guild became a struggle between left-wing and right-wing forces, with liberal forces caught in the middle. The right wing gained the upper hand in the Guild and kept it until very recently. Did you have any sense, from the outset, of these factions?

Oh, the Guild always had factions, but overall I'd say the Guild was liberal, just like Actors Equity was liberal. When the chips were down during the periods of repression, the Guild became right-wing. But actors are generally liberal. I'm proud to be an actor and among a group of professionals, or white-collar employees, who joined a union. Actors were involved early on in union struggles, and Actors Equity became affiliated with the AFL in 1919, even before journalists and other professionals became unionized.

But later on in the 1930s, the Guild did become highly divided, right? Was there any feeling early on that people like James Cagney, Robert Montgomery, Adolphe Menjou, and others would become your enemies at some later point?

Well, Cagney wasn't part of that right-wing movement; that came much later. During the 1930s, the early years of the Guild, when we were struggling for recognition, there was unity, and there wasn't much of a right-wing/left-wing split—not when we were fighting the producers. It was only during the McCarthy era, when the blacklist was really imposed and the Guild didn't take a stand against the blacklist, that the right wing took control of the Guild.

Writers could write their way out of a scene if the content was clichéd or derogatory or anti-humanist. What could actors do? What could you do?

Anybody who knows how pictures are made knows that it's completely ridiculous to think that any film in the thirties and forties voiced Communist propaganda. In fact, they might have been more interesting if they had. Of course, writers are historically liberal and pro-people, and if you equate being pro-people with being pro-Communist, then there were Communist films. But I never saw or heard of a Hollywood film that manifested the Party line.

Most of the films, like most of the films today, were dedicated to only one thing, and that was making money by purveying entertainment. Most of the films of the thirties and forties were apolitical, and the ones that were political were political only because they reflected the times—like Warner Brothers films, which took stories from headlines. And the really reactionary, anti-people films didn't come about until the McCarthy era, when producers tried to prove that they were anti-Communist by making out-and-out, blatantly anti-Communist propaganda films. People rejected them because they weren't entertaining.

How about the famous story of your singing "The International" in an elevator?

Oh, that again. [Laughs.] I was doing a mindless comedy [*No Time to Marry*], and I was in a scene waiting for an elevator, and the director told me to whistle something. As a gag, I whistled a couple of bars of "The International," thinking that surely they'd take it out. But they were so apolitical in Hollywood at the time that nobody recognized the tune, and they left it in the film.

Tell us about your involvement in Culbert Olson's 1938 campaign for governor of California.

Oh, that. Harry Bridges was and is one of my best friends. He came to me one day and said, "Look, the Democrats have a state senator who I think would be a great governor. I'd like you to meet him." I met him, and he was typecast for a governor—white-haired, distinguished-looking—and he was for all the right things. He was for the right of unions to have collective bargaining, he said he'd free Tom Mooney, et cetera, et cetera, right down the line. So I went back to Hollywood, and I helped organize the Hollywood Motion Picture Democratic Committee, and we ended up raising quite a bit of money for Olson. I went out campaigning for him, as did a number of other Hollywood people.

Now, Harry Bridges is smart. He said to Olson, "Look, the studios are anti-Democratic and anti-union, and Stander is sticking his neck out. If you win, you can take the political heat off him by appointing Stander to the boxing commission." Why the boxing commission? Because the prizefights were held at the American Legion Stadium, and the boxing commission was in charge. So the Legion was a really anti-radical group, and if I was made boxing commissioner, the heat would be off. This was the deal.

Well, Olson became governor, and nothing happened. So I called Bridges, and he got in touch with the governor's son, who was dispensing patronage. The governor's son said, "We'll take care of it." Much to my horror and amazement, a telegram came, appointing me to the Pest Control Commission of California at eighteen thousand dollars a year. I called up Harry and said, "This is impossible, a real double-cross." But I couldn't do anything about it. So I got my stand-in to be appointed to the Pest Control Commission. [Laughs.] That is politics in action.

Did Culbert Olson keep the rest of his promises?

No. He freed Tom Mooney, but like Jimmy Carter, when he got into office he rewarded all his enemies and punished all his friends.

The major struggle of the 1930s was opposition to Fascism and Hitler. At one point, you helped organize money to bring a boat full of refugee Jews into this country, eventually landing them in the Dominican Republic. Can you tell us that story?

That's when I became Jewish, realized I was a Jew. I think it was in 1938. The issue was getting German-Jewish refugees and political refugees out of Germany. I threw a party at my house, and the people who were there included Prince [Hubertus zu] Loewenstein from Germany—anti-Hitler, naturally; Otto Katz, who was the number-three man in the German Communist Party; and everyone in Hollywood you could think of, from Dorothy Parker and Robert Benchley to actors like Charlie [Charles] Butterworth and screen stars like Fredric March and his wife, Florence Eldridge. The speeches were so moving that, I remember, at that one party we raised over forty thousand dollars.

I realized that it wasn't enough to be Jewish; you had to be political. Though my family was Jewish, they weren't orthodox, and I'd had no religious training. But in 1938 I joined the group called, I think, the Committee of Thirty-seven, named for the signers of the Declaration of Independence. We had a double purpose. One was to use pressure on Germany to have Hitler stop the concentration camps and stop hurting Jews, by threatening to call off diplomatic relations with Germany and taking other political actions against Germany. Also, we wanted to save this boatload of twenty-four hundred Jews we'd managed to get out of Germany but who were on the high seas with no takers. England, naturally, wouldn't take them in, because it had a blockade of Palestine. France—even though a Jew, Léon Blum, was prime minister—wouldn't take them in. We went to the president of Mexico [Lázaro Cárdenas]—who had taken in a thousand Jews a year before, to the universal condemnation of the Mexican press and his opposition political party—and he wouldn't take them in. So I went to Washington for this double purpose—

to get the president to do something about taking action against Hitler because of his anti-Semitic activities and to get the United States to okay the boat to come in through a U.S. port.

Well, that's where I received my eye-opener. Harry Hopkins [the secretary of commerce] and Mrs. [Eleanor] Roosevelt were in my corner, but I was told by Mrs. Roosevelt that the president couldn't do anything because of the opposition he had within the Congress. So nothing was done. We had four hundred doctors among the twenty-four hundred people on the boat. I went to Morris Fishbein, a Jew, who was president of the American Medical Association—and guaranteed that the Jewish doctors wouldn't become public charges. Not only did he say that the AMA wouldn't approve their working in the United States, but a month later the AMA almost overwhelmingly passed a resolution that barred German physicians from working in the United States. They didn't say "German," they said "foreign medical graduates." I was stunned and aghast, and realized that nothing is simple, that just to simply fight for the Jews amounted to a highly involved international struggle.

Ironically enough, we finally got a port for these Jews through [President Rafael] Trujillo, the Fascist dictator of the Dominican Republic. He asked for five hundred dollars a head, but we had tapped out most of our backers. We couldn't raise enough for five hundred dollars a head; we raised a quarter of that amount. And he allowed that number of Jews to land in the Dominican Republic. We were in constant communication with the skipper of the boat and advised them to draw lots. But the Jews aboard decided to let the youngest of the twenty-four hundred land. This was tragic. Six hundred landed in the Dominican Republic, and Trujillo settled them in the worst part of the country, near the Haitian border. And the other eighteen hundred went back to Europe, to the concentration camps—they disappeared.

See, that's why nearly everybody today is guilty, because we weren't the only ones who knew about what Hitler was doing to the Jews. But nearly everybody kept quiet. You've got to pay tribute to the Communist Party and the left, which kept that issue alive—the fight against Hitler and against the extermination of Jews in Europe. How could anybody who believes in anything decent take an opposite, right-wing line to that? That's the power of the left that I'm talking about at the time—they represented what the majority of the decent people in America believed in.

You were often one of the people who volunteered to give fund-raising parties. Can you tell us a little bit about the parties at your house, and who might be there? Wasn't there a huge social aspect to the Hollywood left, in those days?

Well, I did give parties. I gave one party for Clifford Odets. I gave another party for André Malraux when he came [to Hollywood] during the Spanish Civil War. I gave a party for Ernest Hemingway when he came from Spain to show the film he'd made with Joris Ivens [*The Spanish Earth*, 1937]. When I gave parties, everybody would be there.

How about political meetings? Did you ever hold political meetings at your house?

Political meetings? Yes, but not in the sense of solidifying the Party line—political meetings about some specific issue, like aid to the Spanish Loyalists, or for China, or to get Jewish refugees out of Germany. That sort of thing.

Were these meetings sometimes very formal and dull?

No. I always found them exciting, because every intelligent person in Hollywood, concerned about things happening in the world was there. And history has proven these people right. Because there wouldn't have been a World War II if people had followed our thinking. We could have stopped Hitler and Mussolini before they had so much power.

Because of these and other activities, you were one of the first people to be blacklisted, years before anyone had ever heard of Senator Joseph McCarthy, right?

Originally, I was blacklisted—secretly, of course, because it's illegal to be blacklisted—because of my union activities during the strike of the confederation of motion-picture crafts led by Herb Sorrell [the Conference of Studio Unions]. The issue became whether or not the Guild would recognize the picket line. I got up at a union meeting at the American Legion Stadium, and I read the criminal records of George Browne and Willie Bioff, who were then the heads of the IATSE [International Alliance of Theatrical Stage Employees], the only union the producers recognized at that time. I said that we shouldn't have any truck with them and that we should support the strikers. At that time, Bioff and Browne—as the government brought out in their trial the following year—were [Al] Capone's henchmen in charge of payments to the mob by producers. And Johnny Roselli, who was a mobster working at Columbia as a producer—this I can't prove, it's from hearsay—got to Harry Cohn, and Cohn went before the Motion Picture Producers Association and said my contract was coming up and he wasn't going to renew it. He suggested that anybody who renewed me would be fined a hundred thousand dollars. That was the start of my blacklisting.

What year was that?

That was 1938 or 1939.

Later on, Herb Sorrell and his union offered the only alternative to the IATSE. Did you know him very well?

Yes. I liked him very much. He was head of the painters' union and head of the Conference of Studio Unions. He was a militant trade unionist, though I don't think he was a Party member. He was trying to get recognition for his union, but the other [small craft] unions, who were recognized by the employers' association, recognized only the gangster-controlled union, the IATSE. The opposition was so strong—the producers and the IATSE were against him—that I think it killed him.

At the height of these early struggles, Congressman Martin Dies came out to Hollywood and for the first time accused people of being Communists.

I forget what year the Dies Committee came out. I appeared voluntarily before Dies and swore under oath that I wasn't a Communist and never had been one.

Why did the Dies Committee invade Hollywood?

The motivation politically was that Dies and his group were opposed to Roosevelt and the New Deal, and they were using the Committee as a weapon against Roosevelt and his followers by trying to characterize anybody who supported him vehemently as being a red, being a Communist.

You were blacklisted, regardless?

No, that had nothing to do with my first blacklisting. My testimony supposedly cleared me, but it really didn't, because, as I say, this was a secret blacklist imposed by the Motion Picture Producers Association. I had been under contract to Columbia, and my contract just wasn't renewed. But I was able to work in films made by companies that weren't part of the MPPA, and for people like Preston Sturges or Harold Lloyd, who had so much individual clout and were friends of mine, and who asked, "Why can't we use him?" Well, of course, the studios couldn't explain why—they wouldn't give a reason—so my friends used me, anyway.

When the left wing was organizing and growing in Hollywood in the 1930s, what were the diehard right-wingers doing? Were they in the closet, talking to themselves?

Right-wingers, unfortunately, are never in the closet. They're all out night and day campaigning, making noise, joining moral majorities and moral rearmaments. They're actually an immoral minority, but they're always out there. The left should only be so active.

What were they up to in the 1930s, when the left was so predominant?

Taking pot shots at us, because it was very difficult for them to organize pro-Nazi, pro-Fascist organizations.

Can you give me an example of their tactics?

I'm not an expert on right-wing politics. I'm not an expert on any kind of politics. But they did it by saying that it was silly to join any political causes and that actors shouldn't be political. It's amazing to think that the right wing hit actors for being political, saying actors should only act, yet they, unfortunately, took a leaf out of our book and gave us an actor as president of the United States—a right-winger.

You told us that, in any case, very few Hollywood film stars were serious, committed leftists.

Well, the average star is so busy with being a star that he hasn't much time left over to be anything. It's tough enough to maintain yourself at the top of the heap. Politically, I don't think there was one star who was ideologically a Communist.

You told us that at one point you were friends with Frank Sinatra, who was one of the few who were able and willing to read Marx.

Well, Frank Sinatra was very intelligent, very intellectual, in fact, and he suffered from insomnia for many years. When you suffer from insomnia, you read a lot, and he read everything. He was very literate and very bright. He supported the left or at least was very liberal for many years. Now he's turned. But that happens to a lot of people when they get older. Why he turned politically is highly complicated.

What was your reaction when you first heard of the Hitler-Stalin Pact?

I was cool. I figured it was a temporary thing, which it was, and that the reason for the Pact was the inability of the democracies to line up with the Soviet Union against Hitler. It was a practical maneuver. I was never amazed or startled by the flip-flops of international diplomacy. Like everything in this life, international politics is highly complicated. I mean, who would think, after World War II, that today Japan and Germany would be the allies of the United States?

Did the Hitler-Stalin Pact separate the political lines in Hollywood?

Badly. A lot of people were all upset and left the mass organizations, the Hollywood Anti-Nazi League and others. But it wasn't a devastating effect. People like Melvyn Douglas and others talked to me about it. I took the long-term view that it was the destiny of the Soviet Union to be on the side of the United States against Hitler, and I was right. I've never subscribed to the anti–Soviet Union, anti-Communist hysteria. It isn't based in reality. When our president [Reagan], for instance, says the focus of all evil in the world is the Soviet Union, this on the face of it is ridiculous. The Mexicans had a revolution in 1910, before the Soviet Union existed. You'd have trouble in South and Central America and Africa whether the Soviet Union existed or not. The Jews and Arabs are at each other's throats. The Iranians and the Iraqis, the Greeks and the Turks—the Soviet Union has nothing to do with them. Actually, historically, the Soviet Union and the United States have never had much national conflict. The Russian Empire was the only colonial power that gave up its land to us without a fight. We fought France, we fought England, we fought Spain. Russia under the czar gave us Alaska for a couple of million dollars. The czar was quick to recognize the American Revolution. During our Civil War, the Russians supported the North. In World Wars I and II, we were on the same side.

When the purge trials were going on and became a source of right-wing propaganda as well as real concern to some people at the time, what was your attitude? What kind of knowledge did you have about what was going on?

Naturally, they received a lot of publicity in the press, et cetera. But I personally was not disturbed.

Why not?

As I said before, I'm cursed or blessed with a long-term, objective, historic view of things. I don't expect any government anywhere in the world to be perfect.

Did you feel at all betrayed by Stalin or by what Stalin appeared to be doing?

Oh, I don't believe in the perfection of government or humans. I think there is no Utopia, and no place is ideal, and I never had an idealistic view of Stalin. I respected him as the leader of the Soviet Union, but I always felt my problem was as an American, and that the government of the Soviet Union, like the government of any other country, was its own business. Where it conflicts with the things that I believe in, then I would oppose it.

Do you think some leftists, and particularly Hollywood members of the Party, had an idealistic view of Stalin that ultimately undercut their own organizing efforts?

I don't know. I've never given it much thought.

When we were leftists in the 1960s, some of us made the mistake of believing that we were going to see and make a revolution in our lifetimes. Did you have that view of yourselves in the 1930s—that you were actually going to experience and be involved in a revolution?

I wouldn't use the word "revolution." I felt, like most leftists in the thirties, that there would be a change for the better in the United States and that there was always room for improvement. I felt that capitalism, as it existed in the thirties, wouldn't continue in its present form. I didn't know we'd have a Reagan to try to turn the clock back. But this too failed, because it's impossible to be that reactionary. You cannot turn the clock back. It's impossible to cope with the problems of the 1980s with the philosophy of the 1920s. It's almost obscenely humorous. If I were an absurdist playwright, and I wrote a play with a president of the United States who, after being in office only three weeks, takes down a picture of Thomas Jefferson and puts up a picture of Calvin Coolidge as his role model, you'd roar with laughter. You'd say, "That's absurd!"

Did Hollywood leftists talk about any strategy for an American revolution in the 1930s?

No, I think Hollywood leftists were more concerned with the day-to-day struggles in their unions and in the mass organizations for the things that we believed in. There might have been a few ideologically sound members of the Party who were concerned with a future revolution, but I don't think that characterized the average leftist, of whom I was one.

Did you, or the average leftist, have a vision of how democracy and Socialism were going to coexist?

I must admit that I completely believed in [Communist Party leader Earl] Browder's principles of twentieth-century democracy, the extension of the Bill of Rights, the Constitution, and the Declaration of Independence—all the things that we hold sacred. If we lived up to those ideas, we'd have a wonderful country. That would be revolution. I never heard anyone advance the theory that we needed an immediate revolution, the violent overthrow of the government, and the establishment of the dictatorship of the proletariat. That I never heard.

Historically, this country is a revolutionary country. Even the most reactionary Republican will give lip service to our founding fathers, who were radicals and revolutionaries. The power of the left in the thirties and forties was based on this long-term populist tradition in the United States. This country recognizes dissent. Thomas Jefferson made statements that would have put him on the blacklist in the forties and fifties, like "The tree of liberty must be watered with the blood of a revolution every twenty years." Other founding fathers made statements like "It is our constitutional right to amend and change the government, and our revolutionary right to overthrow it." The tradition is here and always will be here, I hope. And the power of the left in the thirties and forties was that it was able to crystallize this into anti-Nazi, anti-Fascist action.

I'm not a great student of the Party, but I think the Party disbanded and became the Communist [Political] Association under Browder. Browder was a midwestern American, and he spoke a language that Americans understood. And it's no accident that under Browder the Party was more popular than it ever had been before or has been since.

You're saying Browder opened up the Party to its greatest extent, by making the umbrella bigger for people to come underneath?

Yeah, because there had been a feeling that the Party was dictated to by Moscow and that Europeans were in charge of it, et cetera, and the period when Browder was in charge, the so-called Browder era, was really very American.

Why did you never join the Party?

I've always been lefter than the left. Also, I'm very undisciplined. But I supported a number of the Party's positions. But not during the war, because I believed that the trade unionists should take advantage of the war to organize and cement and extend their power, whereas the Party had the line, "You've got to cooperate in the war against Hitler."

Did your not joining the Party have anything to do with your lifestyle and the way you preferred to live, as opposed to the way some Communists might want you to live?

No. I've always been cursed or blessed with a champagne style of living—Cuban cigars and French champagne.

Did people in the Party frown on your lifestyle?

Not that I know of.

Did people in the Party try to recruit you?

Yeah, but I had a very practical reason for not joining the Party. I'd sworn under oath that I was not and hadn't been a member to the Dies Committee. If I then joined and got a Party card, I could be subjected to legal action.

Was it part of the comedy of this whole period that so many people who were on the left believed that, in fact, you were a Party member, some of them believing that you went so far as to bluff your way through two congressional hearings on the issue?

No. I think the real Party members knew that I was sympathetic to the Party but that I wasn't actually a Party member because I didn't go to Party meetings.

Did you expect, throughout the 1940s, that this was a possibility, that you would be once again brought before a Dies-type committee?

Yes, and later on I pushed a resolution, which was unanimously accepted by the Actors Equity Association, condemning the Un-American Activities Committee. So I knew that if they ever moved into the theater, I'd be one of the first ones picked for it, and I was.

Do you think the blacklist was at all brought down on the left by its own mistakes? Or was it simply history bearing down on people?

I think that the left in the United States didn't make any grievous mistakes. I think that everything, as I say, is very complicated and complex. I think that the appearance of the blacklist was a result of the Cold War, and, again being historical, that it was like the Alien and Sedition Acts after the American Revolution. After World War I you had the Palmer Raids and another period of repression. After World War II you again had a period of repression. I think that the powers of repression were so powerful that they would split and weaken the left wing no matter how brilliant or clever, strategically, it was. There were things beyond their control which smashed the power of the left.

We understand you were one of the last people to hold a conversation with John Garfield in New York, before he was to appear before the Committee as a reluctant witness a second time.

It's very difficult to re-create the ghastly mood of that time among people in theater or film who were blacklisted or about to be blacklisted. Julie—I always called him Julie, because that was his real name, Julie [Julius] Garfinkle; he and I were very good friends—had been with the Group Theatre. There were a lot of left-wingers in the Group Theatre, and Julie had supported a number of left-wing organizations. They had called him before the Un-American Activities Committee, and he had appeared and made several statements. He didn't take the Fifth Amendment, on the advice of his attorney, and he was trying to not implicate anyone else, name any names, just talk about himself. He was never a member of the Communist Party, but he had been sympathetic. Now, the Committee wasn't satisfied with his testimony, he was told, and they were going to call him up again. He was very disturbed. I had a connection with the Committee, of all things, who told me what they were going to ask Garfield.

So I called up Julie on the phone and began to talk to him. I tried to explain on the phone, but he said, "Look, I can't talk about this on the phone." I said, "Come over to my apartment." He said, "No, I can't come to your apartment." I said, "Where do you want to meet?" He said, "Central Park." We set an appointment, he came out of his apartment, which faced Central Park, and we walked through the park. I told him what the line of the Committee was. They were going to try to entrap him into either a contempt or perjury citation. I gave him my advice, which was, "Take the Fifth Amendment. They have no right to inquire into your political thoughts or beliefs." He said, "But Lionel, if I do that, I'll be blacklisted in Hollywood and pictures." I said, "Look, you're a rich man"—and he was; he had about four hundred thousand dollars, which was a lot of money then. "What do you need it for?" I said. "Star on the stage, and this thing will blow over, because history is on your side. Just tell the Committee to drop dead, like I am going to do." He thought it over and didn't give me an answer. A week later he had his heart attack and died, and I think what contributed to his death was the stress and strain about appearing before the Committee.

Tell us about your own appearance before the Committee.

As I keep saying, nothing is simple. It was highly complicated. Two years before my appearance in 1953, someone had named me [as a member of the Communist Party]—a man by the name of Marc Lawrence. I consulted a New York lawyer and sued Marc Lawrence in the state courts of New York, and the judge ruled that if he repeated what he had said on the stand away from the stand, I had a viable suit. But he enjoyed congressional immunity on the stand. Evidently, Marc Lawrence had a lawyer, too, because as soon as he finished making his statements, he left for Europe. That was it for the lawsuit.

I got in touch with the Committee and demanded an immediate appearance to refute his statements about me. Two years later, when they were on a campaign to get people in the theater, they called me before the Committee. When they asked me what my motive was in appearing before them, I told them the truth. I had a hundred-and-fifty-thousand-dollar motive—I had a television contract that would give me a hundred and fifty thousand dollars if I could clear myself with the Committee. But it had taken them two years to call me. Only when it was to their political advantage to call me did they call me.

Set the scene for us. What happened?

There is a play [by Eric Bentley] called *Are You Now or Have You Ever Been?* in which I am a character, and the dialogue is my testimony word for word.* It's rather amusing.

Only one person knew what my line would be, and that was Harry Bridges, whom I accidentally happened to bump into in Washington on a Friday. I had done a lot of research on the Committee and on other people who had tried to defy the Committee being cited for contempt, et cetera. I decided that when I appeared before the Committee I would expose *them* as being the un-Americans. That's the line I took. When I began to testify, I immediately said I had knowledge of un-American activities through my research. I said, "Look, I have a list of synagogues that have been burned. I have a list of homes of blacks in the South and in the North that Ku Klux Klansmen have defaced. I want to give the Committee all of my research and knowledge of these un-American activities." They said, believe it or not, "We're not interested in that." I said, "Let's make a note of that—you're not interested in these un-American activities that I have knowledge of." Then I defied the Committee, using every constitutional amendment there was to keep them from shutting me up, and showed that they had been in business around seventeen years, with the purpose of recommending legislation to Congress, and yet they had never in all those years proposed a single piece of legislation. I attacked them as being part of a conspiracy to impose censorship on American theater and film, because as soon as you tell people who they can't and won't hire, you also tell them what they can and can't present. That was my line, and I got away with it.

Luckily for me, the press was in my corner, because a couple of days before, [Roy] Cohn and [David] Schine—the McCarthy boys—had accused Eisenhower of harboring Communists and the Army of being pro-Communist. Even the Hearst papers were in my corner. It was unbelievable that the press was completely on my side. I took Korea off the front page. The headline in the *New York Times* was, "Movie Star Lectures Committee," with a picture of me pointing my finger at them. Everybody told me I wouldn't get away with it, and more articulate, brighter, wittier people than I had tried to tangle with the Committee and had been cited for contempt or escorted out by the sergeant-at-arms. Why they let me do what I did I'll never know. I suppose I

---

*Stander's testimony, and that of many others, is in Eric Bentley, ed., *Thirty Years of Treason: Excerpts from Hearings Before the House Committee on Un-American Activities, 1938–1968.*

got away with it only because I have a very loud voice and I was louder than the Committee.

What was their response?

Anger. See, I inadvertently saved the careers of about twenty-six other people, because the Committee's program was as follows. They'd have a big name on Monday to get the press, and the next day they'd have ordinary people, then another big name on Wednesday. Every other day they'd have a big name because of the press. I appeared on only the third day of what were to have been weeks of hearings. The first day Artie Shaw had appeared and said he had been a dupe or a dope, and on the third day I appeared and said, "I wasn't a dupe or a dope, but, unlike a number of you congressmen, I'm proud of everything I ever said in public or private." When I finished my appearance, the Committee went into recess. Usually it was the witness who asked for a recess. The Committee went into recess and didn't resume those hearings. The next three weeks of hearings were canceled, and twenty-six other actors, writers, directors, and producers with subpoenas to appear never appeared; if they had appeared, it would have been tantamount to being blacklisted.

How long were you blacklisted? How long was it between pictures for you? Did they stalk and keep tabs on you?

Off and on I was blacklisted for twenty-four years. At one period during the fifties I was followed by the FBI around the clock—two men on eight-hour shifts, adding up to six men. God knows what it cost the government.

There's an amusing incident that occurred: I led a very actorish life. I'd stay up until about two or three every morning, usually at Sardi's or some other actors' retreat, and wake up at twelve or one and go out. Now, one day I had a TV show to do, and I had to be up at seven in the morning and out of the house by eight. Eight o'clock is when the FBI men changed their shifts. I'd never been up that early, and when I came downstairs and looked across the street, the car that usually had the two FBI men in it wasn't there. So I wrote a little note and tacked it onto my apartment door saying, "Don't worry. I'll be back at one o'clock and resume my usual dyadic routine." When I came back at one, the two men were there and invited me in for a drink at the neighborhood saloon. I sat down and had a drink with them, and they said, "Look, we've been following you for about three months, and we think you're a wonderful guy. We have a friend, an ex–FBI man who's a lawyer now, and we think he can straighten this out for you." [Laughs.] I said okay, met the lawyer, and hired him on a contingency basis. If he could get the FBI off my tail and straighten me out with the Committee, I'd pay him. After three weeks he came back to me and said, "It's impossible."

We understand that at one point the FBI tried to set you up, like Charlie Chaplin, using the Mann Act. Can you fill us in on that story?

Yeah. After I appeared before the Committee, I was in the revival of a musical comedy called *Pal Joey*. We went on the road, and I left it in Chicago—with a girl who I later married. We went back to New York to live, and we'd been living there about three months when one morning I went to a delicatessen to buy some food, and when I came back my girlfriend was gone. Her clothes were there—I'd left her in a negligee—but her coat was missing.

About two hours later she came back with the coat on over the negligee and told me the following story. Just after I left there came a knock at the door. She went to the door, thinking it was me, and opened it, and there were two men. They identified themselves as FBI men, showed her their cards, and asked her to please come down to the hotel manager's office, where they wanted to talk to her. She went down to the manager's office, and they asked her: "Whose idea was it to leave Chicago? What hotel did you stop at? Et cetera, et cetera." She told them we were going to get married, which was true, but that the mayor of New Rochelle, a friend of mine who was going to marry us, was away on a vacation, and we weren't going to get married until the following week, when he came back. They asked her all sorts of questions, like, "Did he perform cunnilingus on you?"—things like that—trying to find out if we had had sexual intercourse. Well, she lied, and they left her with the following bit of advice. "Look," they told her, "he's gone out with many, many girls. He's promised marriage to them all. He won't marry you. If he doesn't, and if you ever need a friend, call us—we're your friends at the FBI."

Well, I immediately brought my girlfriend over to the lawyer, and he saw immediately what they were after. They were trying to frame me on the Mann Act. I was going to marry the girl, anyway, so I thought I'd kill two birds with one stone. I married her, and the FBI's plan went down the drain.

How long was it between pictures for you?

I'd made fifty or sixty films before HUAC, including some for independent producers and TV, et cetera, even though I was blacklisted by the Motion Picture Producers Association. But finally, in 1953, after I appeared before the Committee, the blacklisting was complete. I couldn't work anywhere in films. I worked on the stage some, and I worked as a stockbroker—there was no blacklist on Wall Street, fortunately for me. But it seems that if my face or figure got on the screen, so delicate was the balance of the American socioeconomic and political scene at the time that I would throw the thing off the tightrope. But I could go to Wall Street and invest the savings of widows and orphans with impunity.

How did you live when you were on Wall Street?

Very well. First I worked in a brokerage house as a "customer's man." Then I got backing and set up my own shop as an over-the-counter broker.

You told us once that Wall Street was the only place outside of Hollywood where you could afford your preferred lifestyle.

That's true. See, when I got blacklisted, I had a problem. I was used to a minimum salary level of fifteen hundred dollars a week—that's in the thirties. I couldn't in all conscience ask a friend of mine to back me in a business, because the average business is lucky if it makes ten percent profit a year and pays off in ten years. So there was only one place where I could live and make enough money to support myself in the style I was accustomed to, and that was Wall Street. I became a stockbroker, and a successful one.

What do you think of Hollywood nowadays?

Hollywood is always interesting and exciting, because whether you like it or not, it's the cultural center of the Western world, still—although the Hollywood of today bears no relationship to the Hollywood of the thirties and forties, like everything else. Except that there are certain things that never change in a never-constant world, and one of them is the stupidity at the top. [Laughs.]

How do you regard the ironies and contradictions of your present success—playing a continuing character in a highly rated TV series—when you compare it to your political history?

Well, my politics have never had much to do with my career, except that my politics helped me get blacklisted. Today I enjoy the best job I ever had in my life. I'm in a television program that is always among the top twenty, that is shown in sixty-seven countries in the world, helping to lobotomize the entire world. [Laughs.]

How does that job square with your politics?

I was always realistic, and I never felt that being in motion pictures or television, which is a medium dedicated to the production of profits—and, quote, entertainment, unquote—was very political. Except that every picture or play has a message—but the message of the average play or television show is complete escapism. Ironically, when I look back at my career, and I try to think of a picture that I really believed in politically and socially, with a message that I could endorse, I'd have to say I was never in any such film. I never will be.

How do you characterize yourself politically today—differently from how you would have characterized yourself politically in the 1930s?

No, I'm the same schmuck I was when I was thirty, and I believe in the same things. I believe in liberty, equality, fraternity, justice, and real economic and political democracy. I believe in the right of dissidence. I believe in all the things I believed in then, even more firmly.

Bess Taffel

BESS TAFFEL, Malibu, California, 1953

INTERVIEW BY PATRICK MCGILLIGAN

BESS TAFFEL
(1915–   )

1943 *True to Life*. Costory.
1946 *Badman's Territory*. Additional sequences.
1947 *A Likely Story*. Script.
       Honeymoon. Uncredited contribution.
1951 *Elopement*. Script.

■

A CHILD ACTRESS in New York's Yiddish theater, Bess Taffel played roles in several productions of Maurice Schwartz's respected Yiddish Art Theatre and other professional groups. After graduating from college, she came to California in 1938 to pursue her combined master's degree in speech and literature at the University of Southern California. She taught English for a semester at Emmanuel Arts High School, but soon her involvement in the Hollywood Theater Alliance, at the time of its greatest popularity, swept her into contact with influential people in the film industry and on the Hollywood left. By leaps and bounds she became a contract writer whose handful of official screen credits do not accurately summarize a busy career of originals, rewrites, collaborations, canceled productions, and salvage jobs, mostly at Paramount, RKO, Columbia, and Twentieth Century–Fox.

Shortly after joining the Hollywood Theater Alliance, she also became a Communist. Although she had no reservations about telling HUAC all about her own motivations and activities, what they really wanted to know were the names of other people, whose lives and professions they could then seek to destroy. And so, when she was subpoenaed, she felt that she had no choice but to decline to cooperate with their interrogation. She appeared before the Committee on September 18, 1951, refusing to affirm or deny Party membership, and thereafter her big screen credits ceased. Her career was cut off as it was peaking. She is married to famed art director Robert Boyle, who worked long and closely with Alfred Hitchcock.

■

How did you get involved in motion pictures?

I had been in the Yiddish theater as a child, I acted in two plays at USC, and I always gravitated toward theater. I started working for the Hollywood Theater Alliance, helping out and going to meetings, and I ended up being executive secretary of the office. That's when I first started to meet a lot of people in the film industry, and most of my subsequent relationships radiated out from the Hollywood Theater Alliance.

You joined at the time the Alliance was producing Meet the People?

Yes. It was a wonderful musical. It became a big success and went to New York, although I don't think with the original cast. Through the Hollywood Theater Alliance I got to know the Barzmans—in particular, Ben and Sol.

Ben and his brother as a team were working on the skits for *Meet the People*, while at the same time they were trying to sell original script ideas to the studios. Ben was more of a scriptwriter; Sol, who was a talented lyricist, was essentially a songwriter.

Ben and I were friends. He had a sweet wit that rarely had a barb to it. We'd have dinner together and talk about the scripts he was working on. When he was stuck, we would brainstorm to come up with ideas. One day he said, "You've got to write. Let's collaborate." At first I was more flattered than anything else. All my life people had told me I should write: "Your letters are great! You should be a writer!" I thought it was nice that they liked my letters, but I never considered myself a writer. I thought writers were great storytellers like Robert Louis Stevenson or Charles Dickens. I never considered writing as a profession, and when I saw movies—of which I saw very few—I never gave any thought to the fact that they might be written by someone.

But Ben and Sol and I did begin to write originals together and afterward we tried to sell them. We didn't sell the first or second script we wrote, but I think we sold the third, to Paramount, for what was considered a pretty good sum in those days—twenty thousand dollars.

How did the first script you sold, True to Life, *develop as an idea?*

I don't know exactly how the idea started. It may have been that in the morning, when I woke up and opened my eyes, I always used to turn the radio on right away, and as I went along during the day I would listen to the soap operas. I used to laugh at them, but I also found myself becoming interested in what was going to happen next in the stories. They were absurd stories, but then I'm an easy reactor.

Our script was about two soap-opera writers whose plot ideas run dry. I used to think about the writers and wonder, "How can they keep this story going and going?" In our script the two writers have locked themselves up in a room and haven't shaved for days; they're stuck for ideas. One of them goes out and wanders down the street late at night and stumbles into an eating-place run by a woman; in the film it's Mary Martin, who ended up playing the part. She is a fey character who thinks he is down-and-out. He orders coffee and begins to notice her. He is taken with her speech and the way she phrases things—one of her lines was, when it was raining, "Hey, it's washday for the clouds!" He plays the down-and-out part to the hilt. She takes pity on him and decides to bring him home with her. He stays at her place, observing the wild goings-on, and then he writes about them for radio. The radio program—and the film—were titled *True to Life*.

Although the Barzmans and I worked together on it, it's hard to say who did what. I know we based some of the characters on my own family. One was a medical student, and my brother was a medical student who used to bring cadavers of animals home and store them in bags in the closet, from where they'd fall out at the weirdest times. He'd be working on these cadavers while eating an apple with one hand and poking around with a tool in the other. We put incidents like that in the script, although I don't know whether they stayed in, even in our own versions, before the studio took it over.

When Paramount bought True to Life, *was that your entree to a studio contract?*

No. Paramount did buy it, but Sam Goldwyn also called us to say, "Why were you in such a hurry to sell it? I was going to buy it. I was only up to page ninety, but I was liking it!" We used to write very full treatments, which was a habit I could not get out of all the time that I worked. People in Hollywood don't prefer treatments anymore. Now, writers pitch their stories and then go right into the screenplay. Back then, that's how you submitted something—with a detailed treatment. I always wrote the treatment, and my screenplays, too, as if the picture had already been made, with an enormous amount of description of what was going to happen up on the screen. It was a waste of time, I learned later, because directors rarely read the single-spaced paragraphs of description. They only scanned the dialogue.

In one case, I remember particularly, I sold a screenplay to Columbia about an acting couple like the Lunts who were very competitive with each other. In one scene, while rehearsing, they get into a small spat on the stage. Although there is no audience in the theater, the husband puts forth an argument, and then he doesn't like his reading, so he tries it again. The producer reading the script looked up and asked me, "What do you need this line a second time for?" I said, pointing, "Well, you didn't read that. It says, 'He doesn't like his reading.' " The producer said, "Oh, that's funny." [Laughs]

Anyway, Sam Goldwyn called and immediately hired the three of us. We joked with each other that probably he had grabbed us so that Paramount wouldn't get us. Goldwyn wanted to bring Danny Kaye in from Broadway to star in a film. This was during the war, and an idea called "Swing Shift" was presented to us, about women going into the aircraft industry. We were sent down to San Diego to do research, because there were many factories and working shifts there. Later we had a story conference with Goldwyn, and we told him a story that we had devised, and he said he loved it. He told us, "Put it all down on paper. I have to send it to Washington to get it okayed." Hollywood was a defense industry during the war, and it seemed everything needed to be approved in Washington.

Working for Sam Goldwyn, did you feel you had arrived professionally?

No. I was very nervous about the job. I was suddenly a writer, and I suddenly had a secretary and an office. I remember Ben just walking across the floor one day and, on the basis of that, saying, "This walk just cost Sam so much money!" I was making more money than I'd ever thought I'd make in my whole life, although we never saw all of the money from the script that the figure indicated, because Ben, in an earlier period of financial hardship, had given our agent part ownership in the script.

His agent was Nat Goldstone?

Yes. And by virtue of that, Nat Goldstone became my agent.

Goldstone represented many left-wing people in Hollywood. He was also notorious for handing out loans to people in need and then taking part ownership in their various projects.

I think Nat got the biggest amount of cash. I was a Janie-come-lately and had only a one-third interest, after what the agent took.

Did you find that Goldwyn was of any use to you as a writer?

He was of use in that he had a sure instinct. He wasn't the most articulate in expressing things, but if he didn't like something you'd better examine it very closely, because there was something there not to be liked. But we didn't have that much to do with Goldwyn. We had some story conferences with him, where he was king. His high-backed chair was like a throne, and he always had a glass of milk set out in front of him.

He was nice to us. We wrote a portion of "Swing Shift" without finishing it. Collier Young, who was then head of Goldwyn's writers, acted as our patron saint. Collie was lovely to us. We gave the story to Collie the night before we had a meeting scheduled with Goldwyn and then met him for breakfast. Collie told us, "It's great, exactly as advertised. The old man will love it." Well, the old man did not love it. He threw the script across the floor and said, "Where are all those wonderful people you told me about?" You must realize that nobody contradicted Goldwyn, because the first thing that usually came out of his mouth if you did was, "You're fired," although later he would probably hire you back. But I must say that Collie stood up for us. Collie told Goldwyn, "No, it's exactly the way they told it. The people are all there."

Goldwyn had changed his mind, and years later I found out why. I ran into my agent, Mary Baker, in London. She said, "You know, Sam would never have made a picture called 'Swing Shift.' He was so slow with everything he did that every studio in town would have beaten him to the punch." A film about a wartime swing shift was too topical an idea for Goldwyn.

What happened next?

We still thought the "Swing Shift" idea was pretty good. So when Goldwyn said he didn't want to produce the script, we asked, "Can we finish it, anyway? Don't pay us anything. If you end up liking it, you can pay us our back salary. If you don't like it, the script can revert to us, and we'll try to sell it."

But something else happened that was upsetting. There was a columnist for one of the trade papers whose name was Waxman, who I used to accompany to premieres and events. People assumed that we were a couple. Of course, I never told him about the script I was working on, because he and I never discussed my work. I had become a member of the Screen Writers

Guild, through the sale of the script, and I later learned that there was a rule in the Guild, evidently, that prohibited writing a script without getting paid.

The rule forbade active members to write on spec?

Right. Although I stress that I didn't know there was such a rule at the time. Then one day it appeared in Waxman's column that we were writing "Swing Shift" on spec for Goldwyn. Goldwyn was, naturally, furious, and there was a big stink. I was immediately suspect. All eyes turned to me, but I hadn't done it. I went to Waxman, and all he would tell me was that he couldn't reveal his source.

In any event, Goldwyn just canceled the whole agreement. We didn't break up with any kind of rancor, but I got the impression from Nat Goldstone that he thought I was sleeping with Ben, and that this was Ben's way of paying me off—getting me a screen credit. That happened a lot to women in Hollywood; it happened to me even when I was working alone. Later on, when I worked at RKO, I was friends with Clifford Odets, and the word came back that people suspected Clifford was writing my scripts for me!

Because you dated him?

I didn't date him! He was a friend of mine, and we never even discussed our scripts.

How did you proceed to get work on your own?

One of Nat Goldstone's partners was Harold Hecht, a very tricky guy who took me over and represented me for a while. But shortly thereafter, the Sam Jaffe Agency, in the person of Mary Baker, accepted me as a client, and Mary was very helpful. William Dozier at Paramount was the person who had bought *True to Life*, and now I was able to get an appointment with him. I knew Meta Reis, who was a rather important personage in the readers' department there, and we had become sort of friendly. Meta may have helped arrange the appointment.

Was Dozier happy to give you a job?

Not happy, although he did give me a job. They had a program called "junior writers," and I found myself one of the junior writers. That wasn't very exciting, but during lunchtime I got to sit at the table of the liveliest comedy writers ever gathered together at one time. They included the established writers for Bob Hope—Mel [Melvin] Frank and Norman Panama—and Abe Burrows, Arthur Phillips, and others. They were all writers taken from radio's top shows, and they were working on the *Road* pictures that Paramount made [with Bob Hope, Bing Crosby, and Dorothy Lamour] and other comedies for the studio. I used to look forward to lunch in the commissary.

There was another table in an enclosed room that we always passed by, where the top writers—[Frances] Goodrich and [Albert] Hackett, [Billy] Wilder and [Charles] Brackett, and others—were enthroned. In that room they were always busy playing word games for lots of money.

It sounds like Paramount was at least fun.

It was fine at Paramount. Lunch was pleasant, but otherwise some men would not work with me. Dozier told me there were actually men who refused to work with me, because they couldn't feel free to curse around a woman.

Were there ever very many women writers, wherever you worked?

No. Later on, when I started moving up the ladder, I worked at Fox, where there was only one other woman writer at the writers' table in the commissary. As a joke, the men would all rise as I came in. I kind of became their pet.

How did you get assigned projects at Paramount?

Dozier gave me scripts to work on that the studio's preferred writers couldn't do anything with. Then one day I was assigned to a producer whose name was Michael Kraike. He showed me a paragraph out of the *New York Times* that said the first people, and practically the only people, to resist the Nazis with force in Marseilles were the pimps, the whores, and the fences of the old quarter. He said, "See what you can do with this." So I wrote a screenplay which was very well-received.

One day I got a call from Kraike asking if I would have lunch with him, the head of the studio—I think it was Buddy DeSylva; I was there through a management change, and I can't remember who was the head at that time—and Katina Paxinou, the Greek actress who had just won an Oscar for *For Whom the Bell Tolls.* I went to lunch and met Katina, who said to me, "Oh, you're such a lovely girl to have written such a great script," adding, "When I heard that Paramount wrote a script called 'Marseilles,' I thought, 'Why am I not in it?'" The studio was delighted. She was an Oscar-winner, and I was going to rewrite the script to suit her.

Now, the heroine was supposed to be a young woman who is in love with a sailor. At the beginning of the film, she waits for the sailor, not knowing whether he has died or survived when the Resistance sank his fleet. She is the madame of the house, or maybe is one of the what we called "dancing girls"—whores. Kraike, who was a very cultured man, very interested in art, for example—he painted a little himself—talked at lunch with Paxinou about striving for something similar to [Maxim] Gorky's *Mother.* She said, "Oh, wonderful, wonderful!"

Afterward, I was heading back to my office, planning to rewrite in those terms for her, and she asked me, "Could I come with you?" I said sure. She said, "I'd just like to see your little writer's office." On the way across the lot she gripped my arm—I think I still have her finger marks there—and said, "If you make her a mother, I will absolutely not play her! I am an actress. If I want to be young, I can be young! If I want to be beautiful, I can be beautiful!" Then she left me—she never got to my office. She didn't want me to make her be Gorky's or anybody else's mother—absolutely not.

So I ended up making her not a mother but an older woman. I thought it would be more interesting, anyway, if the character were an older woman, in love with a younger man, who—in both the original version and the revised script—loses her sailor to another woman. I did make a final script out of it, and the studio was getting ready to produce the film. They even had the sets designed. Then the production was suddenly canceled. I asked why, and somebody told me that since Italy had surrendered and the war was nearing its close, by the time this picture was finished there would be no more call for war pictures. So they just canceled "Marseilles." I was very disappointed and tried to buy the script back. They wouldn't sell it. Other studios tried to buy it, but they asked too much money for it.

So I was put on a "notice title" for Dorothy Lamour called "Minnehaha on Park Avenue." It was about an Oklahoma Native American woman whose family struck gold but remained hillbillies. Well! And they also hired a very wry writer from the *New Yorker* as a screenwriter and put him in my custody. Part of my job was to guide him through this script. But the whole project wasn't my style, I hated the very idea, and I heard that the Army wanted writers to come to New York to write "rehabilitation pictures" for people coming back from the service and reintegrating into civilian life. So I voluntarily left Paramount and went to New York to write a couple of scripts for the Army.

At Astoria?

No. Our offices were in New York City. Ed North, who had been a writer out here, was our commanding officer. I was called an "expert consultant" and even got a merit citation for my work. I wrote "How to Read a Newspaper," "How to Look for a Job," titles like that. But I left before any of my scripts were actually shot, and I can't say I ever saw the films.

How long did you stay in New York, writing these rehabilitation pictures for the Army?

About a year, I would say. I really don't recall.

What happened when you returned to Hollywood?

I went to work for Columbia.

Why?

I had met Sidney Buchman earlier, maybe at [agent] George Willner's house—I knew George and his wife, Tiba. Sidney had become a vice-president in charge of production [at Columbia]. I had no big credits, so I was teamed with George Sklar, who was working on a story by John Huston called "Concertina." That was a really interesting episodic story of important periods in history, following a concertina as it came to America and changed hands. Huston had sold the story to the studio and bequeathed the actual script to us.

Sidney was the executive producer, although I actually never had a meeting with Sidney. Sidney was always overly busy. (We, in fact, formed on our floor what was called "the Waiting-for-Sidney Club," because so many people had scripts ready and were waiting for a conference with Sidney.) I can't even tell you what happened to "Concertina." After we finished the first draft—which is always overlong and not shootable in that form—it was held in abeyance. We were told that we'd be called back to work on it someday, but we never were, and the script was never produced.

Wherever you went, were you beginning to have perceived strengths? Did you yourself feel you had certain strengths?

I could write good dialogue, after all my years in the theater as an actress, speaking dialogue. I knew certain things intuitively that I think I learned through being an actress. I knew how to build a scene. I knew when a scene wasn't right. There are lots of books on how to build a scene and write a script, but I couldn't read them. I tried to, but I couldn't, because I didn't work that way. I didn't work according to rules. I wrote the way I felt and according to how something flowed. That's the way I always worked.

And after Columbia?

Then I went to RKO under contract. RKO soon discovered that I wrote usable stuff, and that contract lasted about four years. At the end of four years I had written in every mode imaginable—comedies, westerns, melodramas, even gangster movies.

Which of your scripts turned out best as films?

The ones that were never made. [Laughs.] None of them were really mine. If another writer didn't rewrite it, the director did something to it, or the actors rewrote their lines. Whenever I wrote comedy, for example, I was always very aware of the rhythm of the dialogue, but directors would come along and direct "according to their vision," and actors, who are always searching for the line, liked to put in the occasional pause or "well." I never used words like "well"! I know that some people think "well" is natural dialogue, but I don't believe that dramatic dialogue has to sound natural.

However, it sounds as though RKO was the first studio where you flourished.

I was kept busy all the time. But not everything got made there, either, which was endlessly disappointing. I remember one very good script that was on the cusp of being shot and was canceled for administrative reasons. It was a baseball-rehabilitation picture, a "rewriter" originally written by John Twist. Twist came to me later, after he read my version, and said he wanted to thank

me for the job I did: "You really improved my work." That was very good of
him to say. That was rare.

That script was ready to be made, and they were going to star Bill Williams,
who they were grooming as the new Van Johnson, along with his wife, Barbara
Hale, who later became Perry Mason's secretary on television. The production
was all ready to go. Then RKO made a deal with MGM. MGM wanted to
borrow Ingrid Bergman, in exchange for which RKO would take over a picture
that for some reason MGM had never followed through on making. The
MGM script was another rehabilitation picture. The studio decided they
didn't want to do two, and mine was canceled.

I worked hard on script after script. Another aborted project I worked on
was for [Alfred] Hitchcock. It was for Hitch's private company, which he had
formed with Cary Grant. They were going to do this script which, if memory
serves, might have been called "Weep No More." Hitch was shooting *Notorious* then, and I used to have conferences with him at a restaurant that
everybody from Paramount and RKO and another nearby studio converged
on, a wonderful place called Lucy's. It was very dark inside for trysts and
conferences, and outside there was a patio for tourists. Hitch had his regular
table inside.

What was a story conference with Hitchcock like?

The only time we talked about the story was when I thought I had developed the characters I was going to use and I was presenting them to him. He
listened and said, "That's all very interesting. What I want to hear from you
now is this: Let's say the movie has opened, is a big success, and is playing at
all the big theaters. And Mrs. Jones says to Mr. Jones, 'Are you playing cards
again tonight?' He says, 'Yes, I am.' She says, 'Then I think I'll go to see a
movie with Cary Grant.' When she comes home that night, he says—he's
lost a lot of money, and he doesn't want to be asked about it—'Did you see
the movie?' She says yes. He says, 'What was it about?' " And then Hitchcock
said to me, "What she tells *him* is what I want you to tell *me*."

You see, he wasn't *interested* in the characters' development. So I walked
back to my office on air thinking, "I've learned from the master himself!"
When I sat down to write, however, I realized that I had to develop the
characters before I could tell Hitchcock what Mrs. Jones said to Mr. Jones.
[Laughs.] On the other hand, there is something to what he said. I realized
the master storyteller was interested in the story above everything else, and
the characters would have to evolve out of the story.

Was Cary Grant in on these story sessions?

No. But I did talk to him about the script on a couple of occasions. I
remember that he said to me once, "Good script, but give him"—meaning
the character he was going to play—"some zzzzzz." "Pizazz," I think he meant.

This was about 1946. You had so few official credits up to this point, and none that would make me think of Hitchcock. How did you get chosen to work with him?

Well, I was under contract at RKO, and that was where he was going to shoot the film. But I became very highly thought of as a troubleshooter. Whenever a script was in trouble, I was yanked off whatever I was doing and put on that script. One picture I actually wrote under camera while I was still working with Hitchcock. I went out to locations and sat on a hill under a tree with a typewriter on a bridge table, and a secretary would hold the paper so the wind wouldn't blow it out of the typewriter. I'd write a scene and then hand it to the actors, and they'd film it. That was *Badman's Territory*. I was also called in to work on *Honeymoon*, which was the first adult film Shirley Temple made. I didn't get a credit. I had been called for only two weeks' work, and they asked Hitchcock if they could have me. So I went, and I stayed nine weeks, working closely around the clock with Colonel [William] Keighley—*very* Colonel—who was directing.

How did the Hitchcock project fizzle?

I heard that it fizzled because Hitch and Cary had a disagreement and broke up the company. Hitch swore he would never work with Cary again. Of course, he did. [Laughs.]

What was the disagreement about?

I heard that it had nothing to do with the script. For one thing, all I finished was a treatment. In any event, what little story there was came from material that Hitch had taken out of the studio library. But he could have taken anything out—it all revolved around Hitch's ideas. What he wanted to do was to have the climax of this particular film take place during a tobacco-auction scene. He always starts with an idea like that—like with *North by Northwest*, which my husband worked on as art director, where he wanted to do a chase on Mount Rushmore. I remember Hitch acting out the entire tobacco auction at Lucy's. [Laughs.] He had no story other than that a certain crime had been committed and that—but for one detail—it would have been a perfect crime.

In those days there was the Breen Office [the film industry's censor], and a writer couldn't let a crime be perfect. As a matter of fact, I wrote a script later on, called *A Likely Story*, which another writer had to change so the crime wasn't perfect. Ironically, there wasn't even a crime in my version; there was only the intention of a crime.

That story was also from the studio's stock material. It was about a man who is mistakenly told that he has six months to live. He meets a girl who is about to commit suicide because she is totally broke. He stops her from committing suicide, and because he knows that he has six months to live, he takes out an insurance policy and makes her the beneficiary. Of course, the diagnosis turns out to be a mistake. It was somebody else's diagnosis, and things don't happen that way in the movies.

Well, the Breen Office objected to having a happy ending! H. C. Potter was called in to direct the film, and I was called in to change the script, and Potter told me he would rather work with Waldo Salt, who had done a big picture, *Shopworn Angel*, with him. Waldo read my script and called me and said he didn't know what to do with it. He told me, "I will try not to ruin your script, but I can't turn Hank Potter down." Well, nothing would ultimately satisfy the Breen Office except to make the whole story a dream! [Laughs.] I got the solo credit, because Waldo very graciously deferred to me.

When did the politics start for you?

The politics began when I began to meet people through the Hollywood Theatre Alliance, people like Ben Barzman but especially people whose books I had read and whose work I'd studied—Albert Maltz and John Howard Lawson, for example.

The people I was most respectful of were the leftist people. I had a feeling they were wonderful people. They had everything going for them, but they still were trying to make conditions better for all people. They were leftists, but to me they seemed very patriotic. I admired them enormously and felt this was a good way to be.

So you became a member of the CP?

Yes. I was a member of the CP and very eager to be among them. They were the only ones who cared anything about Spain and other issues. I emphasize that the Communists were the most patriotic and that joining the CP was, I felt at the time, the most patriotic thing I'd ever done in my life.

The extent of my actual political activity was to work for the war effort and attend weekly meetings. However, on one occasion, Isobel Lennart was supposed to make a speech at the Writers Association, and at the last minute she couldn't appear. Paul Jarrico called me up and asked me whether I would appear. I thought I was saying no, but evidently I said yes. After I made that speech, my friends used to jokingly call me "Mother Taffel," after Mother Bloor.*

It was a speech about the treatment of women in screenplays, who were limited to subservient roles. I used some fairly strong language. The audience never expected anything like that from me, because they thought I was a mousy little creature.

I remember being very nervous. On the program were John Howard Law-

---

*Mother Bloor was Ella Reeve Bloor (1862–1951), a feminist, labor agitator, and Communist leader who looms large in the history of the American left. She figured prominently in early twentieth-century strikes and causes and in her lifetime was widely considered "the foremost American woman Communist."

son, [black actor] Rex Ingram, Eddie Eliscu, and myself. I had been called late. I wrote out the speech, I scribbled on it, I inserted and crossed out things, and I had no time to make a clean copy of it. I was invited to Albert Maltz's house for dinner, and then afterward it was intended that we'd all go to the meeting. I thought all the speakers were invited, but no, I was invited alone. Albert asked to read my speech, and I said no. He said, "Why?" I said, "Because what's there is what I'm going to say. I'm not going to change anything. You asked me to speak, and I'm going to." He tried, and I insisted. The real reason was that I didn't want him to read my sloppy writing on this piece of paper. [Laughs.]

Did your politics make any of the studios inhospitable to you?

RKO became inhospitable because the [third Conference of Studio Unions] strike took place while I worked there, and I had become the studio representative of the Writers Guild. The morning we heard the strike was on, I was on the phone to the Guild asking, "What do we do?" I was sympathetic—should we go to work? They said, "We're having a meeting on that. When you go past the picket lines, tell them the Writers Guild is meeting on the issue." I did, and therefore I was seen talking to the picketers—fraternizing with the enemy. That was something I was not allowed to get away with.

There was one producer who was particularly inhospitable to me. I remember around this time turning down a job at Universal, where I had been referred by RKO to rewrite a Deanna Durbin picture. Deanna Durbin was going to play a switchboard operator for the Supreme Court. The whole picture was about these members of the Supreme Court trying to find her a date. Robert Arthur was the producer, and after reading the script I told him what I thought: "Your Supreme Court is faceless. They're interchangeable. We never know who's who, and we never see them doing any Supreme Court work. It sort of diminishes the whole institution. Have a scene where they are at least talking about something else besides a date for Deanna Durbin." He said to me, "Do you believe that every picture must have a social message?" I said, "No, but I do believe that when we are dealing with Washington, which is our capital, that we should treat it with some respect." He repeated, "So you do think every film should have a message?" I said, "No, I don't, but I really don't think I'm your man. I think you ought to get somebody else."

What was his reaction?

He was very surprised that I would withdraw and sort of respectful of that.

You say that your activity on behalf of the Party was minimal. Some people tell me that they eventually quit the Party because membership put too many demands on their energies.

I'm not an organizational creature, and I was always busy with my scripts and my own life. However, I was very sincere in my belief in the policies and principles. There was a lot of reading involved, but I was used to a lot of reading. I eventually did become less active over time because of the demands of my career.

Your last major credit before the blacklist is Elopement, *a comedy. It's a funny idea on paper, but seems like a bit of a mishmash on the screen. What happened there?*

Writers all did the things we had to do. It was Zanuck's own idea, and it was an idea that top writers had worked on before me and couldn't get right. When they first tried to hire me, I turned the project down. They wanted to make a picture, something like *Father of the Bride*, called *Elopement*. I turned the job down because, as I told them, "I don't want to make a pale carbon of *Father of the Bride*." Any film about elopement couldn't be *Father of the Bride*, which we all knew was like a big Benchley short. I remember discussing it with my agent, who was then Bernie Fine, and saying, "Immediately, with an elopement, the audience will be forced to take sides. Immediately you're either for or against the parents, who want to stop the marriage, either for or against the kids, who want to elope. It's complicated. There are all sorts of issues the writer will have to take positions on. You can't have *Father of the Bride* with an elopement." Bernie said to me, "Okay, you want to turn it down? Turn it down in person and tell them exactly what you told me."

So I went to see the man who was head of the writers at Fox, and I told him what I thought. He said, "Will you *please* try to make something out of Zanuck's idea?" I said, "I don't think I can, and I won't know until I've tried and either failed or succeeded." He said, "Go. At least try." As sometimes happened, I did find a way to make something out of it. I had the two sets of parents, and the girl and the boy, switch positions. The parents, who don't know about the elopement plans, initially blame each other, and they go off to stop the girl and the boy in separate cars. But I devised a way whereby they all have to get into one car, and I allowed time for these parents to expose themselves to each other and to find out that they like each other. They are all decent people. Meantime, the girl and the boy are growing nervous. She, especially, gets cold feet as they get closer and closer to their destination, and then in tricky ways she maneuvers the conversation into an argument. The parents come together, and the kids break apart. The parents go home, and then the kids come home. And the parents end up urging them, "Elope!" It worked.

Except that it was originally written for William Powell, whom I had in mind the whole time as a small-town lawyer. His daughter is named Jack, because he is someone who really wanted a son. She doesn't want to follow in her father's footsteps and become a lawyer, which is what he wants. William Powell could do all the silly things the father had to do in the film. But Zanuck read my script and liked it, so he said, "Let's put Clifton Webb in it, instead." Webb was big box office then. William Powell was not. And then Zanuck started making changes. He said, "Instead of a lawyer, let's make him an industrial designer who wants his daughter to be an industrial designer."

Well, at first I was elated, because Zanuck liked it. In his office I improvised some ideas about what we could have Clifton Webb do, but then again, once I got back to my office, I said to myself, "This isn't a Clifton Webb character. Changing the casting stands the whole idea on its head. It makes it all a lie. The script was a small truth, and now it's a big lie."

So I wrote a note to Zanuck—seventeen pages. I was diplomatic enough not to say that Clifton Webb shouldn't play the part. I said he was a good enough actor to do *anything* but that we shouldn't change the script in the direction Zanuck had proposed because all the revisions would hurt what I believed he'd liked about the story in the first instance. I made the mistake of showing the memo first to my producer, a very nice man named Fred Kohlmar. His secretary read it in the outer office while I was waiting to see Freddie. She told me, "This is a great memo!" Then I showed it to Freddie, standing there while he was reading it. As he finished it, Freddie looked at me, and his secretary spoke first, "Isn't that brilliant?" Freddie said, "Yes, it's brilliant," and began to tear it up. "But I'd rather have a bad picture with Clifton Webb than a good picture with William Powell," he said. Because Clifton Webb was a rising star, and William Powell was not as big a box-office draw. And that's what it turned out to be—a bad picture.

How was Zanuck to work with? Some writers sing his praises as a story editor, and I've heard he behaved very graciously to some blacklisted people.

He was very nice up until the blacklist, though I didn't work that closely with him. I never spoke to him after that, because when the picture appeared I was already blacklisted. But my credit on billboards and advertising—you usually can't read the writing credits—this time, "written by" you could read, and my name was really big. And on the screen the letters were bigger than any I'd ever seen, before or since. I don't know who was responsible for that. I've often wondered.

It seems your career was just about to go into high gear at the point at which the second round of hearings began.

Yes.

How were you named?

I think by Leo Townsend. He named a lot of people.

Did you know him?

Yes.

Why do you think he named you?

I was just part of a long list. I hardly knew Townsend. Martin Berkeley named a lot of people, including me, too.

Did you know him?

I knew him like you know a lot of people in the industry.

How did you find out you were going to be named?

I was told before I was named that I was going to be named.

Who told you? How did they find out?

Nobody had to tell me. I kept looking at the papers, and every day there would be more names. It was obvious that I would be named. It was a terrible time.

It seems as though many of the informers named people that they felt hatred or some kind of professional rivalry toward. Sometimes friends named former friends, but more often, it seems to me, people who gave names went a long way around the barn to avoid mentioning the names of close friends.

I never felt animosity from anybody. I believe that the people who named me did it to protect themselves. But the Committee didn't really need names, including mine. They knew everything about me. They knew my politics, and they knew that these were all my friends.

Did people who cooperated disappoint you? Did you lose friendships? What about Meta Reis?

Meta was a great person. It was a shock to all of us that she cooperated. She told me before; we were very good friends. Then she called me after I appeared and said, "You know, I did what I felt was right, and you did what you felt was right. I've always liked you, and I still like you. You made your choice, and I made mine." I said, "I just didn't feel I had a choice."

I really didn't know how to behave with her. I knew the pressures that came with one of those subpoenas. I knew how terrible it was. You knew you had to pull down a lot of people. That was the only thing that would untie the knot. There was nothing I couldn't say about my politics, nothing I was afraid of saying—except other people's names.

Frank Tarloff

FRANK TARLOFF, Los Angeles, California, 1997

INTERVIEW BY PAUL BUHLE

FRANK TARLOFF
(1916–   )

1951 *Behave Yourself.* Coscript.
1960 *School for Scoundrels.* Coscript.
1964 *Father Goose.* Coscript.
   The Double Man. Story, coscript.
1966 *A Guide for the Married Man.* Script.
1968 *The Secret War of Harry Frigg.* Story, coscript.
1969 *Once You Kiss a Stranger.* Coscript.

■

IT WAS PARTLY because of the blacklist that writer Frank Tarloff spent most of his career in radio and television, though he managed to dabble, with distinction, in films.

Throughout the 1950s and 1960s he was one of the mainstay writers on a number of father-maybe-doesn't-always-know-best hit TV comedies: *Make Room for Daddy* (a.k.a. *The Danny Thomas Show*), *The Dick Van Dyke Show,* and *The Andy Griffith Show.* Some years later he would return to TV comedy, working for Norman Lear on *Maude* and the wildly popular satire *The Jeffersons.*

In motion pictures his only major credit before the McCarthy era was the 1951 black comedy. *Behave Yourself,* about a young married couple and their dog who get mixed up in a chain of murders. But his name returned to the screen in spectacular fashion when the screenplay that he and Peter Stone had written for the 1964 Cary Grant comedy *Father Goose* won an Academy Award. According to *Inside Oscar,* by Mason Wiley and Damien Bona, Tarloff met Stone—who had succeeded Tarloff in the writing of the script—for the first time at the podium, after presenter Deborah Kerr announced the winners. "Our thanks to Cary Grant, who keeps winning these things for other people," remarked Stone. "He just stole my speech," said Tarloff.

■

Tell me about your family background.

My parents came from a small town in Poland. When I was twelve we visited the town, and I met my grandparents, aunts, and uncles. We were all poor. My father had been in the needle trades until he became ill. He had no political inclinations, except maybe he and my mother were Polish nationalists. They were also Yiddish speakers and readers, and we got *Der Tag** at home. Though they were barely educated, they did learn English, and— to me this is a miracle—they were part of a generation whose children ended up a million miles from them as doctors, lawyers, and writers. The whole emphasis for me was education, and I was a very good student. But if I got

---

*Der Tag [The Day], a New York daily, was considered by some to be the "quality" Yiddish newspaper, equivalent to the *New York Times.*

less than an A in conduct, I would have been in trouble, for teachers were regarded as holy people.

My father ended up owning small candy stores. But that life *is* monstrous, six a.m. to two a.m., seven days a week, in a business always economically marginal—and we lived upstairs. By the time I was twelve, my parents had made just enough to visit Europe. Then my father died, and my mother and sister went to work. Soon we lived in Brighton Beach, and my sister worked at Woolworth's for twenty-five cents an hour. I went off to college at sixteen in 1932. After being a good student in high school, I then became a terrible student at Brooklyn College, probably the worst math major Brooklyn College ever turned out. I was just not interested in anything. I was too young.

Did you think of becoming a writer?

I graduated with D's in my major and some A's but in other subjects. I was also a C or C-minus English student. So I never thought of being a writer. With luck I could have become an accountant or teacher. I got a civil-service job in New York City, making seven hundred and forty dollars a year with my first salary. The economy was so depressed that when the examination for Grade One* was held, those who got the jobs were all college graduates. We did want those jobs, but the work was just rote filing and similar tasks.

Did your politics evolve in parallel with your ambitions?

From boyhood, my closest friend was David Shaw,† Irwin Shaw's brother. So I saw what happened with Irwin, who was ahead of me at Brooklyn College and far along in his career. I saw the way he was able to live. He was writing for radio, making three hundred and fifty dollars a week; he was a rich man. Whenever we wanted to go to a play, we had to buy our tickets three months in advance, for fifty-five cents each. Irwin would call up the night he wanted to go and not even ask the price.

David was a good painter. But after he visited Irwin in Hollywood and came back, he said to me "We're funnier than they are." So he suggested that we write a play together.

Meanwhile, in college and before, I was also friends with Lenny Leader and Leo Rifkin, who were both Communists. We had deep political discussions. While at Brooklyn College.‡ I was involved in the demonstrations led by the National Student League and even got arrested for picketing at Dean's Caf-

---

*Grade One was the entry-level category for civil-service workers.

†David Shaw became a successful playwright and occasional screenwriter. His credits include *Commandos Strike at Dawn*.

‡Brooklyn College, an epicenter of the student strike movement of 1933 to 1936, was especially volatile because of a college president who openly admired Benito Mussolini and a student body that included many, largely Jewish, radicals. The National Student League, established by young Communists, was one of the two major student organizations leading the strikes and other political activities. It merged with the Student League for Industrial Democracy in 1935.

eteria, although unlike some of my friends I was never a Young Communist League member. The people I got arrested with were experienced lefties. They all gave phony names like "Irving Place." I was the only one who gave my true name, and I had to go to trial, and every day after court I'd go back to the National Student League headquarters and help them make up political songs. As the Party's contact with the student movement, Leo Rifkin had access to "the ninth floor," the Communist national leadership. Lenny Leader later became editor of the newspaper of the furriers' union and finally ended up teaching journalism at USC.

One day Leo came and said that the Party had given him the assignment of raising money through the Old Liberals Club at Vassar and that they needed to put on some entertainment. He said, "Let's do a play through the Theatre Arts Committee with [actors] Chubby [Hiram] Sherman and Will Geer"—a left-wing cabaret. We were one of the first to do light song and comedy for the left-wing movement; we even predated *Pins and Needles*. Eventually we wrote a musical, "Academic Epidemic"—just the three of us, David, Leo, and myself. This was 1937 or 1938. We ended up with six of us mounting the show and a musician who wrote the music for the songs. It was a smash at Vassar, very politically oriented, with Leo giving us the Party line and holding us back on certain points. When we had the wrong positions on an issue, he would say, "We really can't do that." We did three weekends at the New School with full houses.

Then one day Leo said that a Broadway agent who had seen the show thought we could be the next [George S.] Kaufman and [Moss] Hart. We knew you could not go into a project with seven collaborators, so we had to unload three of our closest friends. It eventually became a source of humor, because we're still friends. Buddy Tyne was one—he was later blacklisted, too. But then we spent a year trying to revise the play for Broadway, and we never could. It was too wild and silly, and it never quite worked.

Irwin advised us to go see a famous Broadway agent, Audrey Wood. Just to get rid of us, she told us that a musical was hard to do and a straight comic play would be a better possibility. Naive as we were, we wrote one, and we sold it. Seven producers wanted it. Al Bloomingdale and Lionel Stander were interested, even the Marx Brothers. We did it ourselves, but the play, *They Should Have Stood in Bed*, lasted only two weeks [in 1942]. The play was funny but also too ridiculous. Out of that experience, however, we landed a job on radio doing *Bringing Up Father*. We lasted three months on that show, until we got knocked off the air for being anti-Irish. We were three Jewish kids doing Irish drinking jokes. The show was canceled.

How did you make it to Hollywood?

The war began, and David got drafted. I was deferred, and I came out here to seek my fortune on my own. I got very lucky. I was hired by MGM as a writer. I was already left-oriented, and there were enough people who quickly got to me. I joined the Party at MGM.

I remember that Lester Cole made a speech to my wife and myself, as a sort of recruitment procedure. It wasn't necessary. I found myself collecting Party dues from Dalton Trumbo and other famous writers. They were wonderful, and the only way that I could have gotten to know them was through the Party. Dalton was making five thousand dollars a week, but we were comrades. Likewise Paul Jarrico, Dick [Richard] Collins, who became an informer later, and quite a few others. I was welcome at "the red table" at MGM, where all the left-wing writers ate. Everybody knew who the left-wingers were. I must say I have never regretted, to this day, having joined the Party.

Then you got into radio. How did being a closet red affect your radio career?

Knowing all these people gave me confidence as a writer. To have been accepted by them was very flattering, a very heady experience. I had no experience at all writing for radio, but I developed the self-confidence to think that I might be able to do it. Also, in radio all the comedy was being done by about a hundred guys, and we all got to know each other. They were ninety-nine percent Jewish, almost all from the same background, all very, very good friends. It stayed that way, even during the blacklist.

Here's how it started. A woman named Aleen Leslie had a radio show called *A Date with Judy*, and she was looking for someone to help her. I began to write it while I was still working at MGM. I was probably the least important writer at MGM, except for the shorts writers, and I was making very little money, about a hundred and fifty dollars a week. I started doing the radio show for two hundred and fifty a week. That seemed a lot of money to me, and so I left MGM for radio.

When I started writing for radio, there were absolutely no set working conditions and no minimum payment, just whatever you could negotiate individually. Occasionally they gave you a commitment for an entire season. I also never got any credit for my work on *A Date with Judy*. The announcement on the air was always, "Written by Aleen Leslie." She had contracted to write the show, and she was always credited as the official writer. That was the condition for my getting an assignment. But she and the others I worked with were also very nice people, and later on, when I got involved with the blacklist, they let me continue to do the show.

It was so much simpler being a comedy writer for radio, then. Compared to now, when television shows have huge staffs of writers, eight or ten or more, on radio either there was a small team or you were on your own. I myself almost always worked alone. I found it quicker and easier, and that way I got all the money.

I had a close friend [actor and writer] Stanley Prager, another future blacklistee. He was very funny. I wanted him for company, and so I went to Aleen and said, "I want to have him working with me." They said sure, and there was another two hundred and fifty dollars available for him. So I realized for the first time that my two hundred and fifty was a low price. Eventually Stanley and I broke up as a team, and they gave me the whole five hundred.

They had been prepared to give it to me before, but I hadn't known enough to ask. Pretty soon I got up to six hundred dollars per show with them.

I could put in whatever hours I wanted, because I did my writing at home. I would meet with Aleen at the office of [former actress] Helen Mack, who had become a big radio producer and director. I would say, "I have a story idea, this is roughly what I want to do with it," and they would say, "Okay, go do it." Compared to later years on radio, it was all very intimate. And it was good training for other writing.

There's a line I tell new writers, a phrase in a famous poem which goes, "Many a village Milton dies unborn." There are so many people who have marvelous talents but who are never made aware of it. I'm no Milton, but I discovered that I had talent. A lot of the big staffs, especially in the later variety shows, had people who specialized as joke writers. What attracted me was not the jokes but the continuity. I liked the idea of telling a little story. I quickly developed a very good reputation in the family-comedy field. I became eminently hireable and eventually did all the big radio shows—*The Hardy Family*, *The Baby Snooks Show*, *A Date with Judy*, and *Meet Corliss Archer*.

A Date with Judy and *Meet Corliss Archer* were very similar. Each involved a husband, wife, a sixteen-year-old girl, and her younger brother. I did one script for *A Date with Judy* which they didn't want. When I began to write for *Meet Corliss Archer* I figured, "Well, I've got one ready." I just changed the names in the *A Date with Judy* script and gave it to them, and it was fine. A lot of the shows of that period were practically interchangeable.

What kind of control over the programs was exercised by the sponsors?

I was never in a position to know. I never got involved with either the sponsors or the network. All I knew was that I had to please the person who owned the show. I don't think we had any trouble unless there was something glaring.

Did you know Sam Moore, who was president of the Radio Writers Guild and then later was blacklisted?

I didn't know him very well, but I remember him as being a wonderful guy. He was the real organizer [of the radio writers], the first to get any kind of minimum conditions and pay for the writers.

How did the union get organized?

I must have been one of the early members, although other writers needed the protections much more badly than I did. Not only did the Radio Writers Guild establish better conditions, its members carried over their activity into television. We comedy writers quickly learned that we were the second-class citizens in television, and so we were the ones who also organized the Television Writers of America. It was still a small world.

Your only screen credit before the blacklist is Behave Yourself, *in 1951. What are your recollections of the film, and the director and cowriter, George Beck, who later cooperated with HUAC?*

Beck was the established writer, and I was the young kid who came aboard to help him. He did eventually become an informer. He just buckled, in order to continue working—which he didn't do anyway. He was a very dour man, very negative. I think he had reached a point in his career with this film where he needed help from somebody younger, someone not quite as jaded, perhaps. But he was very helpful to me. I got the job because of him. They were not hiring me, they were hiring him, and he said, "I want Tarloff, too."

Who rewrote whom?

I don't even remember how involved I was. I know the basic story idea was mine. Beck was always ready to quit; he was always throwing his hands up. The story was a mystery, and the mystery focused on a dog, somehow. We did only that one film together, and I never really established any position in the motion-picture industry.

Were you surprised at being named in testimony before HUAC or at the particular people who named you?

None of it was a surprise, although I still don't know why [cartoonist and writer] David Lang or Pauline Townsend picked on me in particular.* I knew them only very casually. I do have a story about David Lang. Years later, at the tennis club that I belonged to, a middle-aged woman who booked the courts told me about a man she was dating, a man who happened to be David Lang. I had a great dilemma. Getting a fellow was not going to be easy for her, so should I tell her what he had done? I wasn't sure what to do, but then I thought, "Fuck him. He doesn't deserve anything." Besides, she had a right to know something about his character. So I told her. What she did about it I don't know.

After being named, I went into television, but more from radio than film, really. And in television I worked all the time, as much as I wanted, except for right after I got blacklisted, and then I was out of it for only about six months. Then, through a friend, Artie Stander, and through Sheldon Leonard, producer and director of *The Danny Thomas Show*, I started to get steady work again. Sheldon had such confidence in me that after I satisfied him with

---

*Prolific scriptwriter David Lang was also prolific in the names he cited—including Frank Tarloff's—in his March 1953 HUAC testimony. Pauline Townsend, who also named Tarloff, was married to Leo Townsend, also a screenwriter with multiple credits, including collaborative work on *It Started with Eve, Seven Sweethearts,* and *Night and Day.* Leo Townsend testified without being subpoenaed, going out of his way to repudiate his Communist past and identify thirty-seven people as former comrades. He went on to a lucrative career that included *Beach Blanket Bingo* and *How to Stuff a Wild Bikini,* popular teen movies of the 1960s. His wife, Pauline, had no official screenwriting credits.

my first script, all I had to say was, "I have an idea" and he'd say, "Go write it." Most writers had to provide a full outline [of a script], but I was always able to avoid that. Television was a very good experience from the beginning.

On *The Dick Van Dyke Show*, I had only [writer and producer] Carl Reiner to deal with. As with Sheldon Leonard and *The Danny Thomas Show*, I never had to give Carl an outline. He did more rewriting of me, though, because he had written the first thirteen shows himself. In fact, I was the first outside writer on the show. When, after the first season, I read in the trades that *The Dick Van Dyke Show* was in trouble, I called Reiner and asked, "Do you want any help?" He said, "Oh, boy, do I want help!" I did three scripts, with the credit going to my "fronts." Later I also wrote on the black market for *The Andy Griffith Show*.

I had been able to make the connection with *The Dick Van Dyke Show* because my wife had been a singer at a place where Carl Reiner was top banana. Reiner continued to write many of the shows but was also happy to be a front, occasionally. Most of the other blacklisted guys were paying twenty-five percent to their fronts, but I was never charged anything by Reiner or anyone else.

How was television writing different from radio comedy?

In some ways it was harder and in some ways simpler. In the early days of television they wanted "movement," or something for the viewer to look at. You had to force yourself to write scenes in which the characters moved! On Joan Davis's show, *I Married Joan*, whatever we three writers put together, word would come back, "She wants more physical activity." We often had to go down to the set and do rewrites. Joan Davis was known as "the B company Lucille Ball."

The kind of stories that I would come up with generally, the kind which I preferred, were not physical comedy but broad. I much preferred stories with character development. Physical comedy was a departure for me.

Did most of the people you worked with on television know who you really were?

The producers and everyone important knew the real writer was me, eventually. With *The Danny Thomas Show*, I once asked Sheldon, "Does Danny know?" I would come to rehearsals, and it got so clumsy. Withholding tax was being taken and attributed to the front, and they would have to pass it along to me, somehow. Sheldon finally said, "This is terrible. We'll pick a name and establish it, and after one year you'll be right back with a big salary." My son's name was Eric Shepherd Tarloff, and I became Eric Shepherd. But I was told, "It's not a Jewish name. Get one like every other comedy writer's name." So I came up with David Adler instead.

I was in Schwab's one day, and two fellow comedy writers, not on the same shows as me, came in. One of them asked, "Who are you working with?" I said, "David Adler," and they both said, "He's great." The two other writers were Norman Lear, who was five to seven years younger than me, and Larry

Gelbart, who was still younger. Everyone on the shows knew who I really was, but everywhere else I still passed as David Adler. Not once did anyone say anything. People were very sympathetic. There were no informers among the people I knew in television. When I would go to rehearsals for *The Danny Thomas Show*, Danny would call to me, "Tarloff David!" and other names, mixing them up comically. He wasn't sympathetic politically, but he was friendly to my predicament.

Did you have many chances in television to emphasize a social message?

Working in comedy, being oriented commercially as I have been, I never, never aspired to be a fine writer who writes what he feels or to enlighten. My attitude has always been, "What will they buy?" In TV and radio, there was very little you could do anyway. Maybe there was a humanitarian attitude that pervaded my work in a very general sense, perhaps some iconoclasm. But you couldn't do much politically on television, and in movies you couldn't, either.

I've lectured on this to Lenny Leader's class on the blacklist, and one of the major points I make is that HUAC came to find subversive things in movies, but it was impossible. Radio and television had "standards and practices" departments, and motion-picture studios had story departments. You couldn't get away with things.

Well, in radio the shows I did tended to all be family-type comedies, where the general idea was that you could make a little fun of the father figure. But I could not say that that angle of humor was in any way related to my political orientation. It was in many ways the nature of that type of show, and I just went along with it. It would have violated the whole sense and feel of the show to do anything else.

Some of the television shows I wrote for also had fathers who served as patsies for the humor. You could go pretty far with Danny's character on *The Danny Thomas Show* before you had to pull back.

You had to go to England to get back into films.

I got back into film only by moving to London, specifically for that reason. In those days, if you were a television writer, you were a television writer. Many people thought that I moved to London to avoid the blacklist, but that's not quite true; it was only incidental. I was getting as much work here as I could handle.

I was visiting [producer] Betty Box and [director] Ralph Thomas [in London], and told them I'd love to write pictures. When Sheldon Leonard heard I might leave, he urged me not to and said, "I'll get you your own show and everything." But then, when I came over to England to look for work, all they said was, "We'll be in touch with you," and I went broke waiting for them to get in touch with me. I came back here, did some more television, and then went back to London again; by that time there was a possibility for me. Sheldon Leonard also arranged it so that I was able to continue to write for *The Danny Thomas Show* from England.

Betty Box and Ralph Thomas never did make a picture with me, but they brought me to a man named Hal A. Chester, a former Bowery Boy who had become a producer. Hallie had produced a number of the Joe Palooka pictures,* and he knew a lot of left-wing people. He himself was really a hustler. I met with Hallie in England, and I said, "I'm available." He had a script for *School for Scoundrels* which he couldn't get made. He hired me for a thousand pounds, roughly eighteen hundred dollars. After I did the rewrite, he was able to get the picture made, and I stayed on it through the whole production. But I never got a credit on the screen, because he said he wanted the film for the American market, and therefore, because of the blacklist he said he had to put his own name on it.

But at least I had gotten into the picture world. And *School for Scoundrels* has become a kind of a minor classic.

It's a very funny film. The gags in the film were all yours?

I rewrote the whole script, restructured it and so on.

Did you have to adjust yourself to British humor?

No. I had no problem with the Briticisms.

Were you happy with it politically?

Was I happy politically with any of my pictures? I never try to do anything with my political orientation. But I guess, in that sense, almost everything of mine was humanitarian, or at least for the underdog.

But School for Scoundrels *is such a patent satire of business morality.*

I wasn't thinking that way. I was just thinking about where the fun was in the material. It came out of a whole series of books [by Stephen Potter] on "one-upmanship," "gamesmanship," et cetera, all of them about how to win without actually cheating. The property was owned jointly by Carl Foreman and Hallie, but Hallie had the rights to make the movie. Eventually we tried to do a television series based on the film. Carl was very involved in that possibility, and I wrote a pilot which never sold. But it was through Hallie that I got the opportunity to do *Father Goose*.

How closely were you connected with Foreman?

When Carl came to England, he became legendary. I knew him from the old left, of course. We had offices in the same building in England, but I never worked with him directly.

---

*This series, based on a newspaper comic-strip character, served in the 1940s as a temporary home for half a dozen writers who were later blacklisted, including Henry Blankfort, Alvah Bessie, John Bright, Cy Endfield, Stanley Prager, Robert Richards, and Nedrick Young.

As for *Father Goose*, Hallie had bought a story called "A Place of Dragons" [by S. H. Barnett] and he brought it to me. He could get me to work on it very cheaply, because I just wanted to write pictures. My contract had an escalating clause based on the budget. I got something like sixteen thousand dollars to write the first draft. I was still writing *Danny Thomas Show* scripts from London, and that was supporting me while I was doing these several pictures for whatever I could squeeze out of Hallie.

I turned the project down at first, thinking of it as a poor man's *The African Queen*, about a bum with a classy lady and some romantic complications. *The African Queen* had some very prestigious people in it, however, and this was supposed to have been a small British picture. That's all Hallie was making at that time. Cy Endfield, who had written and directed some of the Joe Palooka pictures for Hallie earlier, was going to direct it.

How did things get changed around from the original story?

The original story did not even have the kids.* When I got the idea of bringing in the kids who need to be cared for, I thought to myself, "That's different," and I wrote it that way. The picture was still scheduled for a low budget. But Hallie was very smart, very shrewd; he could have been a major producer if he hadn't operated the way he did. Clearly, he recognized my script as a much better film than how it was planned, so he went to America, to meet with Universal. When he came back to London he said, "I think I have a deal."

And that was it. I was never further involved, although my name was permanently on the script. Later I got a call from Mel [Melvin] Frank, a director I knew, who said, "I hear you made Hallie rich." I said, "Well, I guess I made him fifty thousand dollars or so," and he said, "I heard it was a lot, lot more." So I got in touch with my lawyer, and it turned out as follows: Hallie was going to get five percent of the gross up to a million dollars. Plus, they bought a picture he had made in England for a hundred and seventy-five thousand dollars which they never released. So I ended up suing him.

When Hallie sold *Father Goose* to Universal, they wouldn't let him produce the picture. So he was out, and he was also very upset. But he was a man with no shame. I knew that he had cheated me, but after I got the Academy Award [for Best Original Story and Screenplay], I ran into him and he asked, "Why didn't you ever thank me for the Academy Award?"

Some of the film books say that you had a conflict with the other scenarist, Peter Stone, or that your approaches to the film clashed.

There was no conflict. I did the first draft. The draft Hallie sold was mine. Peter had just done a [Cary Grant] picture called *Charade*. It was very suc-

---

*The plot of *Father Goose* has Cary Grant as a bum on an island in the Pacific during World War II. He becomes a lookout for the Australian Navy and a guardian for a teacher, played by Leslie Caron, taking care of some schoolgirls fleeing the Japanese.

cessful, and he was the hot writer at Universal, so they gave *Father Goose* to him to rewrite. That was not an unusual thing to happen, especially when someone had just had a successful picture. But I still wish that they had given me a shot at it alone.

Tell me about The Secret War of Harry Frigg.

During the time of *Father Goose* I had sold Hallie an original script for a Paul Newman picture. He had bought a book, nonfiction, that dealt with a prisoner-of-war camp for general-level officers. At first I said, "I don't see any picture in this." But then I got the idea for this private who hates officers but has the job of helping several officers escape from prison, and that idea worked out. It was very much anti-authority. *The Secret War of Harry Frigg* was my original idea, my story, and my screenplay. But this script, too, eventually came into the hands of Peter Stone, because he was still the hot fellow at Universal, and he had just done *Father Goose*! I had sold my effort for very little money to Hallie, and once again he sold the script to Universal.

It certainly is a terrible title.

The title I hate. I don't know why Universal thought it was funny. I wanted something like "The Best-Kept Secret of the War."

"Frigg" means "fuck."

Of course—a silly title. I wrote the first script, and that was it. I had no further involvement.

What about you and Peter Stone this time?

I saw *Frigg*, and I thought my version was better, a more modern-type picture. They didn't reform him in my script. I wish they had done mine.

After Father Goose, *you did* The Double Man, *with Yul Brynner.*

This project is interesting mainly because of how it came about, again because of Hallie Chester being a very shrewd man. He heard about an unfinished picture with all the second-unit work already shot, including a lot of footage of skiing and mountains. We looked at the unfinished picture, and he said, "What I'd like is to find a way to use whatever footage there is and make a picture for very little money." That's a very hard thing to do.

At this point, there wasn't even a script. He just said to me, "Come up with a story where we never have to go outside again." My script was about the head of a CIA-type organization whom the other side has cloned in some way, after capturing the original one. That was the general idea. Alfred Hayes followed me on that script. By then I was suing the producer, and I was back in America by the time they filmed the rest of the picture. I never even got around to seeing *The Double Man*.

A Guide for the Married Man *was a tongue-in-cheek film about infidelity.*

When I was living in London, I was walking one day with a friend of mine, a guy who was married and had had several affairs. And he said to me, "Everything is easy about having an affair, but it's the little things that always trap you and drive you crazy. You have everything all set up, and then your kid gets sick. You always have to have a coin with you to get out of the house to make a phone call, or what will happen?" We laughed about his remarks, and then I thought, "What a good idea for a film—how to have an affair and not get caught."

I went to all the guys I knew who were having affairs and talked to them. Every one of the incidents in the film had really happened to someone.

According to the credits, the film is described as adapted from a novel of the same title, written by you.

They just said that for publicity. It was never a novel. I eventually had a book published here, based on the film, and went on tour all over the country talking about it.*

Originally, my lawyer—I didn't go through an agent—contacted [writer and director] Norman Panama, who had done a lot of films and television. He was a man I knew well enough. The script was sent to him to direct, and he wrote back a scathing attack on the subject—a shocking idea for a film! Two weeks after Panama wrote his attack, I sold the project. And who made the sale for me? Nunnally Johnson, a wonderful man. We had become friends after our sons became friends. I had given him the script to read, and he gave it to [producer] Frank McCarthy at Twentieth Century–Fox.

After Fox bought it, we had meetings on how to deal with the potential controversy. The studio was terrified. The censorship group in the studio wanted to head off any trouble. Everything was so clean back then.

This was Gene Kelly's first non-musical directorial credit.

When we sold the script I went to Frank McCarthy and said, "Who will direct the picture?" He said, "Frank Tashlin," who was a hack. It had to be done with style and class, or otherwise it would be sleazy. Walking down the hall in the studio, I looked at the directory and saw Gene Kelly's name. I walked back to McCarthy's office, and he said, "That's a great idea. We'll try it." Gene Kelly was in France. We sent him the script, and he said yes. I made him a director of non-dance features. I liked him. He was very easy to work with.

Kelly had been very active in the defense of the blacklistees, early on.

Most of his friends were on the left.

Were you on the set during the shooting of this one?

---

*A *Guide for the Married Man*, as told to Frank Tarloff, was published by Price, Stern, and Sloan in Los Angeles in 1967.

I was on that picture all the way through, every minute of it, right through to going to dailies, and even the publicity junket. I was very involved. Gene had said to me, "I don't need a writer standing over my shoulder, but let's try working together." Meanwhile, Gene told Frank McCarthy privately, "He won't last two weeks." He thought that he would have to get rid of me. But I had been around long enough to know the protocol. I asked, "When I have something to say, when should I do it?" Gene said, "When I've set up the shot." And that's what I did. When the actors came to me and said, "What about this line?" I always said, "Talk to Gene."

I got Walter Matthau the job on that film, also. They had first hired Jim Hutton, Tim Hutton's father, a big, tall, handsome guy who had been in *Where the Boys Are*. I said, "Frank, that's utterly wrong. It should be about a guy who is uncomfortable having an affair, someone like Walter Matthau." He said, "Write a letter to me." He took the letter I wrote to [Darryl] Zanuck, and so this became the first picture where Matthau got the girl. After that, Matthau got *Hello Dolly!* because Gene was directing it.

Were you satisfied with the outcome of the film?

It was not quite Academy Award material, but it earned more money than I had ever expected to see. And I was treated very, very well by Fox.

Now let's turn to the later phase of your television work, during the high-powered Norman Lear era of the sitcom. What did you do on these shows?

I worked on *Maude*, as a story editor, and also on *The Jeffersons*. There was a much more permissive atmosphere on television by now, and Norman Lear wanted a lot of anti-authoritarianism, especially on *Maude*. You could be pretty far out. On *The Jeffersons* you could have a go at bigotry, because Jefferson was as big a bigot as Archie [Bunker]. Norman was a great believer in rewriting. If he liked a script he would say, "It's a great script—to rewrite."

Were your later television scripts better for being done that way?

They were different but not necessarily better. Perhaps they were closer to what the producer had in mind. Norman really broke bounds in *All in the Family*, using the words "nigger" and "kike." Everything was fair game after that, almost whatever the writers wanted to say, however startling. It made people uncomfortable and hostile. Norman's shows hit much more on the head than anyone ever had before.

But not as dangerous as the English show that All in the Family *was based on.*

It was when I was still living in England that Norman bought the rights to *Till Death Do Us Part*, which was a wonderful show, really rough, much better than anything we did over here. There the father was one of the shits of the Western world; here he had to be lovable. But lots of people resented *All in the Family* because they were exposed to ridicule.

Television had a way of bringing the politics toward the center rather than pushing for a solution.

When a writer gets hired, he doesn't make the decisions; someone else is the censor. But *The Jeffersons* always had a black character you could root for—his wife, for instance. Then there were the mixed-marriage couple and the son. Some messages are almost sub rosa and very implicit—subconscious.

Bernard Vorhaus

BERNARD VORHAUS, London, England, 1997

INTERVIEW BY JOHN BAXTER

BERNARD VORHAUS
(1904–)

1925 *Steppin' Out.* Story.
1926 *Money Talks.* Coadaptation.
1928 *No Other Woman.* Coscript.
    Sunlight. Script, director.
1930 *Farewell to Love.* Associate producer.
1932 *Camera Cocktails, Nos. 1–6*
1933 *Money for Speed.* Story, director, producer.
    The Ghost Camera. Director.
    Crime on the Hill. Costory, coscript, director.
    On Thin Ice. Script, director, producer.
1934 *Blind Justice.* Director.
    The Broken Melody/Vagabond Violinist.
        Director.
    Night Club Queen. Director.
1935 *The Last Journey.* Director.
    Dark World. Director.
    Street Song. Costory, director.
    Ten Minute Alibi. Diretor.

1936 *Broken Blossoms.* Associate producer.
    Dusty Ermine. Director.
    Cotton Queen. Director.
1938 *King of the Newsboys.* Director,
        associate producer.
    Tenth Avenue Kid. Director.
1939 *Way Down South.* Director.
    Fisherman's Wharf. Director.
    Meet Doctor Christian. Director.
1940 *The Courageous Doctor Christian.* Director.
    Three Faces West. Director.
1941 *The Lady from Louisiana.* Director,
        associate producer.
    Angels with Broken Wings. Director.
    Hurricane Smith. Director.
    Mister District Attorney in the Carter Case.
        Uncredited directorial contribution.
1942 *The Affairs of Jimmy Valentine.* Director.
    Ice Capades Revue. Director.
1945 *Yalta and After* (documentary).
        Script, director.

1947 **Bury Me Dead.** Director.
   Winter Wonderland. Director.
1948 **The Spiritualist.** Director.
1950 **So Young, So Bad.** Costory, coscript, director.
1951 **Pardon My French.**
      Director, coproducer (uncredited).

1952 **Fanciulle di lusso/Luxury Girls.** Director,
      coproducer (uncredited).
   Imbarco a mezzanotte/Stranger on the Prowl.
      Coproducer (uncredited).

■

BERNARD VORHAUS BELONGS to a generation of filmmakers of whom most are long dead. His career began in Hollywood when D. W. Griffith was still making silent films, but the blacklist ended it before he could really test himself in middle age. Even so, the program pictures he made in Britain, and later in America for Republic and other low-budget studios, show a narrative drive and topical political flavor that suggest a considerable talent cut off at its peak. *King of the Newsboys*, for example, powerfully depicts New York City slum conditions and exploitation; *Fisherman's Wharf* has a beautifully sentimental perspective on the Italian-American working class; and *Way Down South*, before it turns cute and musical, opens a fascinating window on pre–Civil War slavery.

One word that sums up Vorhaus as a filmmaker and individual is "expeditious." He decided in the late twenties that Britain offered more chance of a career than Hollywood, and he moved to London. The British government's "quota" system, which forced American film companies to plow back part of their distribution profits into local productions—called "quota quickies"—gave him a chance to direct some tough, energetic films. He discovered actresses Ida Lupino and Margaret Rutherford, and plucked young editor David Lean from newsreels. Lean later said admiringly of Vorhaus, whom he acknowledged as an influence, "He really worked on a shoestring—highly inventive, with a real love of cinema, and as clever as a wagonload of monkeys."

Hollywood welcomed Vorhaus back at the end of the thirties, but he returned to Europe a decade later, after being named to the House Un-American Activities Committee as a Communist. Rather than battle the ragtag European film industry, like fellow political exiles John Berry, Jules Dassin, Cy Endfield, Joseph Losey, and so many others, he built a new career converting London's Victorian mansions to apartments. He was doing it still in his nineties, when he was interviewed.

■

According to the information I have, you were born on Christmas Day 1904 in New York City, and your father was a doctor.

Lawyer.

Which is, presumably, why you went into law.

It's why I avoided law. Father had wanted me to go into the firm, and we agreed that if I could get my degree at Harvard in three years instead of four, I could have a year to try to get into the film business.

You got interested in the film business while visiting Fort Lee, New Jersey, with your sister.

I caught the film bug very early, because my oldest sister, Amy, who was twelve years older than me, had sold some original stories to film companies, and she used to take me with her sometimes on the ferry across from New York City, where we lived, to New Jersey, where at that time most of the film studios were located, because Hollywood had not yet become the center of filmmaking. She would leave me on the floor to watch the filming while she huddled with the editor. I watched, fascinated. There was always music in those days to get the actors and the director in the right emotional spirit. The makeup was very extreme—thick yellow all over the actors' faces, with thick dark makeup on their eyes and lips. The acting was just as extreme. [Laughs.]

I usually managed to pick up a few bits of discarded film, which they left with amazing carelessness on the floor, considering it was so inflammable. In fact, there were some terrible fires in the laboratories at the time. I took some home, I had a projector that had been given to me as a birthday present, and I joined the film together and ran it, turning the handle.

This was a thirty-five-millimeter projector?

It was very simple and crude.

Did you actually go to see many early films?

Oh, I was very anxious to see films. My grandmother, who lived in West-chester County, which is a little way from Manhattan, used to take me to the local nickelodeon, and since it had hard wooden seats she would bring with her an inflatable cushion, a thermos bottle of coffee, and cookies, and we would watch the serials. But I was rather frustrated, because I'd always be left with the heroine tied to the railroad tracks while the train was approaching, or hanging over a cliff with the rope frayed, and then seldom would I get back to Westchester in time to see the sequel.

Given your later political activity, what was the political milieu of your childhood? Was your father a political person?

Father was very liberal. He was very enthusiastic about Woodrow Wilson in the First World War, about Wilson's promise to make the world safe for democracy, and about the founding of the League of Nations. Father had come to America as a poor immigrant at the age of seven, from a village in Austria, on the Polish border, near Cracow. He had worked his way through college and law school and developed quite an impressive legal practice. But

I had made this deal with him, and after I left Harvard I managed to meet Harry Cohn, who was the toughest of all the tough screen moguls.

How?

Through a salesman who had some connection with Harry Cohn and also with Father's business. When I met Harry on one of his trips to New York, he snarled at me, "What the hell makes you think you can write?" I replied, "Well, I've had a few short stories published." He said, "All right. Boy— Girl—Heavy. Got it?" I yelled back just as loudly, "Got it!"—although I hadn't gotten it at all, because I didn't know that "heavy" meant villain. He said, "Fire breaks out—Boy climbs up ladder—breaks through window—is shocked to find Girl in bedroom with Heavy. Now finish the story." Well, I was just as shocked as Boy was to find Girl with Heavy, but I ad-libbed something or other, and he said, "Okay, I'll take you on as a junior writer. But you'll have to pay your own way to Hollywood." That was how I started.

What was your impression of Cohn as a man?

He was a very tough character, absolutely ruthless, and he liked to embarrass people, but I never had any trouble with him. I wasn't at Columbia very long, in any case. One of the stories I wrote—which became the film *Steppin' Out**—helped Columbia break into bigger, first-run cinemas, and it got me my job at Metro [MGM] in 1925.

Nineteen-twenty-five was an *annus mirabilis* for Metro. *Ben Hur, The Big Parade,* and other tremendous films were made that year. For my twenty-first birthday, Mother came out to Hollywood—which, of course, was a five-day trip in those days—to see how her baby was doing in the wicked world of the film business. That evening, Metro was having a big banquet to celebrate their having become the number-one company. I couldn't get mother an invitation to go at the last minute, so I didn't want to go, but she insisted.

Anyway, Metro had all the stars—Greta Garbo, Norma Shearer, Jack [John] Gilbert, etcetera. I was very nervous and shy about meeting these world-famous characters. They had a big buffet with hors d'oeuvres and cocktails. This was the Prohibition era, so all the cognoscenti avoided the cocktails, and they all had their secret little whiskey flasks. I wasn't in the cognoscenti, so I downed one cocktail after another. They worked marvelously. I lost my unease. I was telling the funniest stories to Norma Shearer, while she was laughing like hell. But I never finished my stories. I never tasted that banquet. I passed out flat. Later that evening, Mother opened the door and a taxi driver carried this limp load of flesh over his shoulders, dumped it on the floor, and said, "Your son has had a little too much to drink." Poor Mother! Her worst fears were realized. [Laughs.]

---

*Steppin' Out, directed by Frank Strayer, based on the story "The Lure of Broadway," by Bernard Vorhaus.

I started by working as a junior writer to Carey Wilson, who was probably a very competent writer but a brilliant salesman and actor. He used to sail into Irving Thalberg's office and say, "Irving, have I got a story for you—with an opening that will kill you!" And then he would tell the opening, which did indeed kill Irving. He'd continue, "And you know how it ends? Now, this will really get you." Then he would tell an end that "got" him and would sell the story. The junior writer couldn't point out that this beginning, which "killed" Thalberg, and the end, which "got" him, had nothing to do with each other. You somehow had to write a story which connected these two absolutely incongruous elements.

Did you always connect them, or could you assume that Thalberg would forget their essential content?

I don't think I ever dared to ignore a beginning and end which Carey had sold. When I started writing—not as an amanuensis to Carey—I wrote, in partnership with Jessie Burns, a number of stories. We had a much less distinguished producer than Thalberg in Harry Rapf. How Harry got his job, I would think, was very largely because he was a brilliant pinochle player. I remember his telling us, "You writers don't appreciate what an important person the hero of this story is—he's at the pinochle of fame." Certainly some of the stories that are told about Goldwyn originated with Rapf. I remember the stories that went around when he made his first trip to Paris with a few friends. One of his lady friends said, "It's terrible, but I've been in Paris for several days, and I still haven't gone to the Louvre yet." And Harry said, "Me too. It must be the water here."

These early films at Metro were all silent, right?

Yes.

Then you decided to break off and make your own two-reelers as a director.

That's right. I had saved a bit of money, and I then put it into this two-reel silent film, *Sunlight*. It had ZaSu Pitts as the only professional actor. It got some critical notice, but just at this time the first talkie with Al Jolson was coming out in New York, so no producer was interested in releasing a two-reel silent film or engaging the director thereof. They were all rushing to New York to sign up stage talent. So I was pretty dejected, but I decided to give myself a two-week holiday in England with a bit of money I had left over, and the two weeks became seven years.

Before we go on to that, tell me a little bit about Sunlight. *Who were your influences in those days?*

I didn't know that I had any particular influences, I just wanted to make an effective character film with local Los Angeles atmosphere. So many of the films were ultra-glamorous.

So you arrived in England on holiday. Soon you found yourself working in the British film industry. How did that take place?

I don't remember exactly how, but I was offered a job as an associate producer with British Talking Pictures at Wembley Studios. Shortly afterward, the mother company, Tobis-Klangfilm in Germany, went bust. At that time, the two companies making sound-film equipment were RCA, which covered America, and Tobis-Klangfilm, which covered most of Europe. Anyway, Tobis-Klangfilm was in financial trouble and sold off its British company, so I was out of a job. But I managed, at next to nothing, to buy their library of films, because as the first talking-film outfit they had compiled a library of interviews with famous people, like George Bernard Shaw, as well as variety acts and news coverage of big fires or floods. I managed to edit some of this film and shoot bits silently myself, going out with a camera. I used some of the sound from the films over the footage, then sold it as "quota material" and got enough money together to direct and produce my own first feature film.

How could you edit together newsreel and variety acts? Did it purport to be a feature?

No. I sold a series of shorts called *Camera Cocktails* to Metro. Then there was a partly shot feature film that I managed to complete with a bit of silent material. It was all just stuff that I sold as "quota material" to get enough money together.

The "quota" operated how?

As you probably know, in the early thirties the government passed a law to encourage the British film industry. Distributors, along with their American or other foreign films, had to show a "quota" of British films. They normally paid a pound a foot when you delivered the material to them, and thereafter you had a percentage of the distribution, but seldom did you get anything by the time they deducted their expenses for distribution and prints.

Some producers just lined up actors statically and had them spout dialogue, because this was the quickest and cheapest way of getting footage. But there were some directors and technicians who really struggled against the odds to make good and interesting films.

So you went to Twickenham to make your first feature. There you must have run into the troublesome Harry Fowler Mear [often credited as H. Fowler Mear], whose story editing was infamous.

I always tried as diplomatically as I could to avoid letting Harry write a script, because he had masses of joke books—jokes about dentists, marriage jokes, motorcar jokes—and Harry's concept of a script was stringing "joiners" together over these jokes. I must say, to do him credit, he turned out the stuff at amazing speed.

Your first film was Money for Speed, *and then you made* The Ghost Camera *at Twickenham, with David Lean as your editor. Tell us something about that. Lean acknowledges you as a major influence in his career.*

I must say that David was very generous and complimentary in interviews, saying that I'd been a principal influence on his career. I had seen the cutting of British Movietone newsreels, and it was quite remarkable in its speed and imagination, entirely different from the staid Gaumont newsreels. I found out that a young man called David Lean was cutting it and persuaded Keith Ayling, who was the producer, to borrow him. It didn't worry me that David hadn't cut feature films before, because I had always done my own cutting and subsequently always did dictate exactly how I wanted scenes cut. What worried me was that David was staying on the floor of the soundstage all the time. I said, "Look, David, you've got to keep up with the shooting!" He said, "Don't worry. I'm working in the cutting room nights." And so he was. It was obvious that he was interested in becoming a director and wanted to watch everything that was happening on the floor.

There were a few firsts in *The Ghost Camera*. It was the first time that anyone had run a section of film before the main titles. It was the first time that, when there was a flashback—that is, when one of the main characters was talking about something that had happened previously—and you flashed back to it, instead of seeing the person in the scene—since the person wouldn't have seen himself—I shot from the "I" point of view of the person who was talking.

Ghost Camera is also the film in which Ida Lupino started her career.

This was her first picture. She was only fifteen years old.

I bet she was a dish even then.

Oh, she was lovely and very, very able. Of course, she came from a theatrical family. Lupino Lane was her uncle, and her mother was Connie Emerald, also an actress.

I notice that you often used unknowns and vaudeville people, like Stanley Holloway, Will Fyffe, and Jimmy Hanley—people who were not at all big stars. Was this a policy decision?

I didn't hesitate often to use people who hadn't been on the screen before. For instance, I saw Margaret Rutherford on the stage and gave her her first film part, in *Dusty Ermine*, because I saw what a remarkable personality she was. It didn't matter to me whether she could act or not—in point of fact, she was a very competent actress—but she was such a vivid personality, such fun, playing this ultra-respectable crook.

Tell me a little about The Last Journey. *People said you couldn't make a train film on a Twickenham schedule.*

I was very intrigued by the project, because, for one thing, it was a cross-section story—the stories of several different groups of characters, with cutting between them—and also, I liked the background of the railway. It was very difficult shooting the stuff on location. For instance, for one shot, where one train was to overtake another and almost crash, you had to start the trains two miles back from the camera for them to develop the right speed, and then they went way beyond the camera before they came to a stop. So it would take about two hours before you could make a second take, and I had to make God knows how many setups in a day.

When we finished the exteriors, I thought, "Now it will be a cinch to do the rest in the studio." But this was the first time the people at Twickenham had used back projection, in which the background, in this case the moving landscape as seen from a train, is projected onto a screen from behind it while the actors work in front of the screen, the set being in this case part of the train. Everything went wrong. The camera went out of sync with the projector, and the projector scratched the film, which was the only film we had. As we began falling behind schedule, I was increasingly worried about Julius Hagen's "editing." Hagen, who never read a script in his life, would edit a film in this fashion: for every day that the director was behind schedule, Hagen would rip out five pages from the middle of his script.

I went to see Hagen in his office, which was at the bar of the pub across the street from the studio, and said, "Mr. Hagen, please come and see what's happening." Reluctantly he came, he sat, and he watched. He got whiter and whiter. Finally, he went back to his "office," downed one double whiskey after another, and passed out. The next day he had a hangover, and by then the stuff was working properly, so we were able to finish the film without his editing. Thank goodness.

It seems to me that The Last Journey *sort of lives in the shadow of a number of other quite distinguished films of the same period. It's quite like* The Lady Vanishes, *something like* La bête humaine, *a little like* Twentieth Century. *Is this a case of parallel evolution, or were you picking up things from other movies? Were the Twickenham films seen as "the answer to . . ."?*

I certainly wasn't influenced by nor was I in any way copying any other film. In fact, a number of the things in my film were copied in the other railway films.

It was a brilliant idea to have the commanding and gentlemanly Godfrey Tearle as the hypnotist and psychologist who climbs onto the footplate with the crazy engineer and uses his skills to calm him down and to save the train.

Godfrey Tearle was a very strong personality, and it was a pleasure to use him—except that, as president of the Screen Actors Union, he was always terribly tough about making us finish right on the minute. What was usual at Twickenham was to work all hours without overtime. In fact, the two compensations were "free lunch for everybody" and a very friendly atmosphere. At Metro you had this enormous restaurant, with Louis B. Mayer at a long table in the center and everybody else, in decreasing importance, sitting further and further away from Louis B. Here it was very casual. Some of the actors whom I used—Merle Oberon, Ida Lupino, or John Mills—would sit down, and next to them might sit the property man or the man who swept the floor. A very nice, palsy-walsy atmosphere. And the food was pretty good.

Except that one film I made had an exterior street scene built in the studio, and there was a fish store which we were supposed to shoot the first day, but because of the illness of the actors it was deferred. From day to day this fish was under studio lights. Well, you can imagine! At the end of the filming of that scene, the menu that day was—you guessed it—fish and chips. I asked for an omelet. [Laughs.]

How did Dusty Ermine *come about?*

Twickenham bought a number of plays—bad plays, because they could buy them cheaply—and this one was about a family with connections in the House of Lords, hence the "ermine," and "dusty" because a black sheep in the family had become a counterfeiter. Well, I had already become enthusiastic about skiing—and incidentally, on one skiing trip got to know Leni Riefenstahl, who became a very distinguished maker of Fascist films. At the time she was a very beautiful girl and very impressive, always wanting to be center stage. A talk with Leni became very much listening to her.

You must have been in an interesting political and moral dilemma, faced with an attractive woman who represented everything that you by then were growing to loathe, I imagine.

You're so right. I was indeed. [Laughs.] But it was easy to make a distinction between the two things.

Let me just tell you that I wanted to introduce skiing into this film because I was stuck on it and thought it would lend some excitement. It was quite logical that a group of counterfeiters would locate in the Alps, where they could get their stuff across all these international borders—Germany, France, Italy, Switzerland. So I said to Mr. Hagen, "We can get wonderful box-office value by setting this in the Alps." He said, "Are you crazy? I wouldn't send a company out in England for a couple of weeks on exteriors!" I urged him, "But Mr. Hagen, it's such good box-office value." He insisted, "Nothing doing. It's too cold—the women will have to wear so many clothes that you won't be able to *see* anything." I gave up.

A few days later he called me into his office. He said, "Look, you've made some good films for me. You've made them fast, and they've made money. If you're so keen to go to the Alps, I'll let you." I said, "Oh, Mr. Hagen. This is wonderful. You won't regret it. I'll have a new script ready in two weeks." He said, "Oh no. You and the company leave this weekend." I protested,

"But Mr. Hagen, we have to write a whole new script." He said, "That's all right. I'll send Harry Fowler Mear with you." The last thing I wanted was Harry Fowler Mear!

Anyway, Arthur Macrae, who was one of the actors, was also quite a competent writer. Between us, overnight on the way to Kitzbühel [a ski resort in the Austrian Tyrol], we wrote a new outline and then over a few following nights finished a new screenplay. It was only much later that I found out the reason behind Hagen's generosity in sending us to the Alps. This was the time of a big boom in the British film industry. They were building the studios fast, but they couldn't build them fast enough to meet the demand. An international company with a very expensive cast had come to Hagen. The studio space they had wanted wasn't available, because the previous company was behind schedule. They said, "Mr. Hagen, give us your studio for two or three weeks, and we'll pay you double." Hagen said, "You'll pay me triple." They said, "I guess you've got us by the balls." He said, "That's right, and I'm squeezing." That is how we got to the Alps.

Dusty Ermine was followed by Cotton Queen, right? It's an interesting film.

Well, it was an interesting subject, but I didn't get a chance to write a proper script on it, really.

Again, it sort of seems to me to be like Hindle Wakes [a Stanley Houghton play and Victor Saville film, centered on Wakes Week, a traditional holiday for the people who worked in the cotton mills of the British Midlands], with the idea of the people from the mill going on holiday and enjoying themselves. As you say, you were not being influenced, but obviously these ideas were in the wind.

Yes, I always liked to have working people in a film, because the prevailing fashion was very much to use upper-class, suave characters.

By now it was the depths of the Depression. What was happening to your political development?

When I was shooting *Dusty Ermine* in the Alps, we were in Austria, on the German border, on a mountain called the Zugspitze. Over the horizon came a detachment of German troops, quite indifferent to the fact that they were invading Austrian territory, and with guns at the ready they demanded the names of the Austrian ski teachers whom I was using as actors. Well, these young men were among the group who had resisted the first German attempt to annex Austria [in 1934]. The Germans had in the process killed [Chancellor Engelbert] Dollfuss, the then head of state, but they were defeated. The ski teachers, knowing they were on the blacklist, instead of giving their names did the fastest jump turns I've ever seen and went racing down the mountain. The Germans shot after them but luckily did not hit anyone. But I did get a shallow wound on my face, which, more deeply, was the beginning of my deeper involvement in politics.

When you returned to America, did you become involved in political activity?

I became quite involved, as did my wife, Hetty, in the Spanish Civil War. Actually, it was an invasion, aimed at overthrowing the legitimate, democratically elected government of Spain, by [Francisco] Franco, using Moorish troops from North Africa and Spanish troops, and backed by the very wealthy people. The bulk of the people in Spain were very grateful for the moderate reforms which this new democratic government had given them. It was the first time they had universal education, good health programs, and so forth.

I went to a lot of meetings and signed petitions, trying to get the democratic governments of Europe and of America involved. They took a neutral attitude. They established a blockade of Spain, so neither side could get ammunition. In point of fact, this prevented the legitimate government of Spain from getting the munitions to defend itself, while Hitler and Mussolini were sending masses of stuff to Franco and German bombers were actually bombing Spanish towns and killing lots of civilians. We did everything we could to try to lean on governments, to stop this blockade, but I must say we didn't succeed, and even Roosevelt in America, because he was afraid of losing the big Catholic vote, would not do anything about it. As you know, a lot of people volunteered and joined the International Brigades.

Did you know some people who did?

I knew some of them, and some of them who were killed in the war.

People from the film business?

I can't remember any who were in the film business. There undoubtedly were some. But I must say I was very much influenced by a book by a Communist writer—I think it was R. Palme Dutt; the title was *Fascism and Social Revolution* [1934]—who pointed out that these democratic countries did nothing, really, to stop the flow of Fascism.

*You were a member of the Left Book Club, I suppose.**

Yes, I was.

Were you, like so many other people, impressed by John Strachey's The Coming Struggle for Power [1932]?

---

*In May 1936 local societies were formed across Great Britain to discuss books to be published by the Left Book Club, an imprint of the London publishing house Victor Gollancz, from manuscripts selected by a circle of prominent Marxists. A range of participants, from Labour Party members to Independent Labour Party members and Communists, used this forum to conduct Marxist education, and by 1938 one thousand local Left Book Clubs existed. This experiment was ended by the changing positions of the Communist Party. By that time, three million copies had been published, providing most of the left-wing literature read by the British until the postwar years. Among them were these books by R. Palme Dutt and John Strachey, which were also published in New York, as were many of the other Left Book Club titles.

Yes, I was.

I remember Donald Ogden Stewart saying that it virtually changed him into a Communist overnight. So you went back to the United States in 1937?

The British film industry went into a slump even bigger than the boom which had preceded it. Herbert Yates, owner of Republic, having seen a few of my films, offered me a job as producer and director. Going to Republic, I made the biggest mistake of my life. Instead of playing it safe and choosing for my first film a suspense story with comedy, which I was always able to do successfully—something in the Hitchcock manner—I became very intrigued by *King of the Newsboys*, a story of a boy and girl growing up in the Depression years that followed the Crash of 1929. The boy has big ideas of what he's going to achieve; the girl doesn't have much hope of his succeeding, and to get herself and her family out of their grinding, desperate poverty, she becomes the mistress of a quite attractive gangster. The boy, very bitterly, resolves to outdo him.

I had been impressed by the play, written by Louis Weitzenkorn, a former journalist, called *Five Star Final* [filmed in 1931], and another play which he wrote, called *Name Your Poison*. This latter was about a group of crooks who hook up with a beggar, insure his life heavily, and then try to murder him. Each time they try, it fails. They give him a lovely banquet and put ground glass in his meal, and he doesn't even get indigestion; instead, he's grateful to these warm, friendly people. Anyway, because it had black humor, they had trouble financing *Name Your Poison*. At last they got a woman who was going to put up the money. They had a party to celebrate. Louis sat drinking. This woman who was going to put up the money said, "Louis, why are you staring at me like that?" He said, "You remind me of my mother." She said, "Oh, you dear boy." He said, "And every time I think of that woman, I want to kick that bitch in the ass." So *Name Your Poison* was never produced.

I didn't know at the time that Louis was an alcoholic. After writing a few effective sequences, Louis caved in to alcohol, and it became absolutely impossible to do anything with him. We tried for a few weeks, but there was nothing doing. The studio was not prepared to wait any longer for me to start production, so I quickly wrote something myself, but it was not the kind of material that I was good at at all. The film was not successful, though it had some interesting sequences in it. Thereafter, instead of my being a producer and director, Republic insisted on my directing and having a lot of very poor producers and stories shoved on me.

Actually, the technicians at Republic were quite competent, especially the miniatures department, but the producers were very untalented. If I could have controlled the scripts I directed, I think I could have made some really good films there.

It's a remarkably abrasive choice for your first film, especially at Republic.

It was a very stupid thing for me to do. [Laughs.]

One might say it was noble. At least you had the courage of your convictions. So you found yourself on the grind, as it were.

After I'd been working at Republic, I was offered what seemed like a very interesting story, for an independent producer at RKO, Sol Lesser. Then he decided, instead, that he wanted to make something else for a child singer, Bobby Breen, he had under contract. Well, the first thing I said to Sol was that we ought to make this kid into a normal boy in the picture. Sol said, "Oh, I agree with you. Go ahead." I went and found Bobby Breen just slumped over his desk. I said, "Come on, Bobby. Let's go out and kick a football around." He said, "I can't today. I'm too depressed." I said, "What's the matter, Bobby?" He said, "I'm afraid I'm going to have a nervous breakdown." I said, "What's the matter?" He said, "Look at this." He showed me these sheets of paper and said, "The stock of my company has gone down ten percent. My popular rating has gone down twenty per cent." This was Bobby Breen. Actually, I was lucky to get as my writer Ian [McLellan] Hunter, for whom this was his first screen assignment. As I mentioned to you, I was always willing to trust my own judgment on new people, whether it was writing or acting.

Was he one of Sol Lesser's people?

No, he had nothing to do with Sol Lesser. I had read a few things that Ian wrote, but he hadn't yet done anything in films.* Subsequently he wrote many very fine films, including, after he was blacklisted, the William Wyler film with Audrey Hepburn, *Roman Holiday*. Thanks to Ian, we got a pretty good script. Then Sol Lesser, who was anxious to be an intellectual and a creator, at the last minute redictated the whole script—not adding anything new, because he wouldn't have been able to, but just mixing around all the words, sentences, and paragraphs, so that some of it didn't make sense. I didn't know what to do. I said, "Look, Mr. Lesser, you know the original was very, very good." He said, "Well, we'll have an impartial decision." So he called his staff together—the secretary, the telephone operator, even the cleaner, half a

---

*Ian McLellan Hunter (1916–1991) often wrote in collaboration with his friend Ring Lardner Jr. They worked together on the Dr. Christian movie series, *The Adventures of Robin Hood* for television, and the 1964 Broadway musical *Foxy*, an adaptation of Ben Jonson's *Volpone* set in the Yukon. Hunter won an Oscar for Best Story for *Roman Holiday* in 1953, and shared a nomination for Best Screenplay with John Dighton, before being blacklisted. His numerous pre-blacklist credits include *Second Chorus*, *Mr. District Attorney*, and *A Woman of Distinction*. Initially one of the group of blacklist émigrés who settled in Mexico, he shifted his career to New York City. After years of extensive television and film work under pseudonyms, he wrote *A Dream of Kings*, under his own name, in 1969. He taught screenwriting at New York University for twenty years. The East Coast branch of the Writers Guild of America recently established, in his honor, the Ian McLellan Hunter Memorial Award for Lifetime Achievement.

dozen employees. He said, "Now, I want you to give me your frank impression. This is Ian Hunter's script"—he read a bit of it—"and this is my script"— which they gave their acclaim, of course. This was *Fisherman's Wharf*.

Subsequently, I did *Way Down South*, also with Bobby Breen. I persuaded Lesser to use as a screenwriter Langston Hughes, who was quite a distinguished poet but also a writer of fiction and plays.

Hughes was assisted in the writing by the actor Clarence Muse.

Yes.

How did you do that, and why?

I thought that as black people they would get some feeling into this story, and to a degree it worked. But again, at the last minute, Sol redictated the whole thing.

Did you know Hughes?

No. I didn't know him personally, but I had read some of his writing.

You got him out to Hollywood?

Yes. The memory I have is of waiting to have a script conference with him and Clarence at a popular hotel in Hollywood, and when we went in they said, "We're sorry, but we can't let you eat here." They were not prepared to accept two black men. I was terribly embarrassed, but Langston Hughes said, "This is so unimportant compared to the other discriminations. Don't worry about it."

Here's a black, Communist, homosexual New York intellectual being brought to Hollywood to write a film for Bobby Breen. It's a leap of imagination, improbable, to say the least.

I think it would have been successful if it hadn't been for Lesser's rewrite.

Did Hughes bring something to it?

Frankly, not as much as I had hoped. It was a disappointment.

And Muse? Was his contribution much?

Very little. He was very much a keen operator, not a particularly talented actor or writer.

You were surrounded by so many interesting writers at Republic—Ring Lardner Jr., Francis Faragoh, Gordon Kahn, Ian McLellan Hunter, Samuel Ornitz, Guy Endore—and a preponderance of people on the left. How did that come about? Was that by chance or intentional?

As I've said to you, I was already quite involved in politics. Shortly after we arrived, my wife had gotten a nightly program going, on radio station KFWB, on the subject of the unfairness of the Spanish Civil War and the fact that this only mildly progressive democratic country was struggling for its life against these Fascist forces. I got a lot of writers to work on the program, many of whom were left-wing, more or less—John Huston, Ring Lardner, Donald Ogden Stewart—and some actors, some of whom were also politically inclined. Sometimes the actors didn't turn up, and my wife, Hetty, and I had to handle the program ourselves, but we kept it going for the rest of the Spanish Civil War.

I remember one script, which I think was written by John Huston, and we got an actress named Helen Mack, who was quite apolitical, to deliver the program. She did it so movingly, the staff were in tears by the end of the program. I said, "Great! Oh, Helen, that was absolutely wonderful. Thank you so much." She said, "Not at all, Bernie, but tell me, whose side are we on?"

Was there any concerted attempt to create a group of writers at Republic who were of like mind?

No. I suppose I was inclined to get writers who had a progressive point of view, but chiefly to get talented people who were not too expensive. [Laughs.]

Some of them, like Ring Lardner, were quite young at the time.

Oh, yes. I gave both Ring and Ian their first film jobs.

What was your impression of Lardner at that age?

Oh, he was brilliant, with delightful humor. To begin with, he had to develop his sense of story structure, but this was one thing I was used to doing myself and he very quickly became tremendously competent in structure and just delightful in his characterizations.

Were Herbert Yates and other Republic producers particularly aware of what was going on in the stories of these films you were working on?

Yates had no idea at all. He was anxious to make good films but did not participate at all in the production of films, except that he insisted that some of his girlfriends be featured in the films. This was not too disadvantageous with Vera Hruba Ralston, a Czechoslovakian ice-skater, because, though rather wooden, she was young and quite intelligent in responding to direction. But one of his girls, whom I had to use in *Lady from Louisiana*, was much too old to be an attractive, bubbly young girl. Yates was ultra-right in his politics, hating Roosevelt more wildly than anyone else I've ever known, but I don't know that he was much concerned with the politics of his employees. The executive producer, Sol Siegel, being Jewish, tended to be anti-Fascist.

Did Yates ever object to a script—for instance, in the case of a film like Three Faces West—*which had very strong political content?*

No.

It was extremely left-wing for its time, and there's John Wayne in the middle of it, which is puzzling.

Well, John Wayne I quite enjoyed. He was obviously a superstar, and although he responded very readily to any tone that you wanted in a scene, the personality of John Wayne always came through. This is really characteristic of any superstar, though with someone like [Laurence] Olivier, who was such a great actor, very often he was so absorbed in the character that the personality of Olivier himself disappeared within the characterization.

But Wayne is always Wayne—yes. It's such an interesting idea—the fugitive Nazi doctor hiding out in North Dakota and the sodbuster who becomes the moral hero. This was very unusual material. Who wrote it?

It was Sam Ornitz's original idea, but most of it was being written by Joseph Moncure March while we shot, which was a bloody nuisance.* The script had various elements that were never adequately integrated. One thing about it that disappointed me was the way in which we were forced to handle a key scene. In the script the doctor's daughter, played by Sigrid Gurie, was engaged to a German before she came to America, and she felt obliged to abide by this relationship, especially after the man, a former Resistance fighter, is forced to flee Hitler's Germany; when he arrives in America, he turns out actually to be a Fascist. Well, this was so black-and-white. I said to the producer, "First of all, we ought to have not an obvious Nazi but a very attractive character, although maybe a bit weak, whom we believe this girl would have been attracted to. Secondly, I think we ought to have a feeling of 'How would we stand up to the ultimate danger?' I mean, if you were in the Resistance, and you were captured, would you be able to stand up to torture well enough not to reveal any names of friends? The character should, first, greet the girl very charmingly—'Oh, you're even more beautiful than in my dreams'—and then, when the question of how he has been able to survive and succeed comes up, he should say, 'You have to move with the times. It's no good just resisting and being killed . . . ' And gradually it should be revealed that he has become a collaborator." I couldn't sell Sol Siegel on this idea, and instead it became this obvious black-and-white scene of a Nazi arriving.†

How were these films received at the time? Did they go out in normal release? Was there much of a reaction?

---

*The screen credits for *Three Faces West* are: original screenplay by F. Hugh Herbert, Joseph Moncure March, and Samuel Ornitz.

†The character in question (played by Roland Varno) is at first thought to be a heroic Resistance fighter who has sacrificed himself to get the doctor and his daughter out of Germany. When he shows up in the U.S., however, he is such an apologist for Germany that he is shown to be almost certainly a collaborator.

I think there were some pretty interesting reactions to *Three Faces West*: "a timely film," et cetera.

Did it give you any leverage to choose future subjects?

No, that was the problem at Republic.

All this time, were you an active Communist?

For a while I was very active with the Communists in the anti-Fascist work they were doing. I came very quickly to disagree with "democratic central- ism," which I think is a very undemocratic system. That is what governs the Communist Party and is what governed the Soviet Union. I think it's the sad cause of the terrible despotism and corruption of Stalinism, under which millions of their own people were murdered. Of course, in the first years, the leaders of the government were very idealistic and not at all seeking self- aggrandizement. When the Soviet Union signed a nonaggression pact with Germany, I think the Soviet Union was justified in doing so because it had tried for years to get a united front of the democratic countries against Hitler and hadn't succeeded, because they were hoping that Hitler and the Soviet Union would come to fight each other and either destroy each other or greatly weaken each other. It was only after the total inability to do this that the Soviet Union got time to build up its own defenses by signing this nonag- gression pact. But I was also very opposed to other Communist parties reduc- ing their anti-German activities. I must say it was a very confused period, because the government of Britain was very reactionary at the time, under [Prime Minister Neville] Chamberlain, and until Churchill came to power and established a strong anti-Nazi attitude and started building up the Army, you couldn't be sure what would happen in England, whether there would be a deal with Hitler.

Not that this is important, but I was chairman of the Hollywood Theatre Alliance, which put on a very successful revue called *Meet the People*. Then, definitely against my wishes, they put on a pacifist play, which I was overruled on and which, incidentally, lost all the money that they'd made on *Meet the People*. It wasn't long after that I went into the Air Force Motion Picture Unit and cut myself off from all political activity of any kind.

How long did you actually serve in the military?

From shortly after Pearl Harbor.

The Identification of the Zero [about identifying Japanese zero fighter planes] is one film most often attributed to you.

I was in the Air Force Motion Picture Unit, and I used Ronnie [Ronald] Reagan in that film. I got to know Ronnie very well. I think the reason he did not become a bigger star is that Warners did not give him good material. There was a shortage of petrol at the time, so we used to take turns going in each other's car to the post each morning, and we also often used to dine together at his house or mine. At the time he was very liberal politically, because this was the popular thing to be. He was anxious to attend left-wing functions, such as a weekly meeting at which Sam Ornitz and Guy Endore discussed current affairs and made amazingly accurate predictions, but I have heard since that he was supplying information to the FBI at the time.* He always had a line of jokes and enjoyed embarrassing women with dirty jokes. He could be very amusing company—a strange mixture.

I must say he had more knowledge of political history than any other actor I'd ever met. For instance, some crisis was arising, and I said, "Well, certainly Roosevelt will do the right thing," and Ronnie said, "You know, when Roosevelt was the assistant secretary of the Navy [during World War I], he called out the Marines to destroy a popular government which had been democratically voted into power in Latin America, because they had nationalized some land which the United Fruit company had previously owned and therefore cut the profits of United Fruit." Well, I looked it up, and sure enough, Ronnie was right. [Laughs.]

He was a very shrewd operator on a superficial level. At that time he was very alert and very bright. To me, the significant fact about him is that he was the first politician to be a professional actor, and therefore his television appearances were much more effective than most other politicians'. Hence, his success was largely an example of the power of television today.

I understand you also used Alan Ladd in one of your military films.

We had a lot of well-known actors come into the unit who were sometimes used for training films. I used Lee J. Cobb again and again for narration. Without rehearsal, he was instantly marvelous and gave wonderful performances. As to Alan Ladd, I said to Owen Crump, who was head of the unit, "I don't know how the public will react to Alan Ladd." He said, "Oh, they won't even recognize him. Don't worry." Well, we made this one training film, and as soon as Alan Ladd appeared on the screen the audience of servicemen yelled, "Oh, there's Laddie boy. He'll win the war for us." It was hopeless. [Laughs.]

But they'd accept Ronald Reagan.

Ronnie Reagan wasn't the same kind of figure as Alan Ladd.

It always amuses people like me that John Ford got to make a venereal-disease film. How were these assignments handed out?

Hold on. I made the venereal-disease film!

It's usually attributed to John Ford.

---

*Virtually decisive proof that Reagan was reporting covertly to police and government agencies can be found in Dan E. Moldea, *Dark Victory: Ronald Reagan, MCA, and the Mob.*

He may have made the one for the Army, but I made the one for the Air Force.* Let me tell you about it. The Medical Corps and the chaplains wanted to make the film, because with these young recruits away from home for the first time, venereal disease had become really epidemic. I managed to persuade them that there was no hope of successfully exhorting these young men to remain celibate, that if we wanted to make a useful film we had to show the dangers of getting venereal disease and how to take practical steps to avoid it. Well, the Medical Corps agreed at once and the chaplains reluctantly, and I made this film, which I felt was pretty good, about a young recruit who falls very much in love with this lovely, innocent girl and has intercourse without safeguards and discovers he has got venereal disease. The Medical Corps saw it and said, "Absolutely great! Just what we need." But I wanted to test it on a group of recruits. I got a group of men and ran it. They assured me they were very impressed. I took one of them outside and said, "Look, tell me, man to man, what you think of it." He said, "I was very impressed, Major. If I could make it with a girl like that, I wouldn't mind getting syphilis—*and* the clap! [Laughs.]

Did the film go out in that format?

Yes. It was quite effective.

How did the subjects get chosen?

Demands would come in from various organizations within the Air Force to have films made. At the beginning, we didn't have any experienced writers. In fact, I organized a course to teach screenwriting to some of these young men. Later we got very experienced and distinguished screenwriters, people like Jerry [Jerome] Chodorov and Norman Krasna. All we would get was an order to make a film about such-and-such, and then we had to create the script and do the film. In fact, I was really functioning more as a producer than as a director, though I did direct a number of films. We got demands from generals all over the Air Force to have films made, and a lot of them were quite useless demands. Owen Crump and I agreed that some of the projects were a waste of time. Some generals wanted us to make films to show the exploits of their particular unit—purely for their own fame and glory, having nothing to do with training or anything else. So I had to go around to these generals and talk to them. I remember telling them they were no doubt familiar with a new directive from Washington which would cause very severe penalties for anybody who wasted resources or money. [Laughs.] I usually persuaded them not to make the film.

Toward the end of the war I was transferred to the Signal Corps in New York to make a film about the Yalta and Potsdam Conferences, which I think

---

*Vorhaus did make one for the Air Force. John Ford's venereal-disease film, *Sex Hygiene* (1941), was made for the Army, with Darryl Zanuck producing.

was probably the most important film I ever made. John Huston had covered the previous Teheran Conference, but he had just photographed the important people coming and going—Churchill, Stalin, Roosevelt. I realized that this was a great historical opportunity to show and present the resolutions of the conferences, and the forces which had brought on the war. The Yalta Conference declared that Nazism was to be completely eliminated, but that Germany should be left with the means of production, so that the mistakes of the Versailles Treaty at the end of the First World War would not be repeated—Germany was left in such a terrible condition that it went bankrupt, and this made possible the rise of Hitler as a solution to unemployment and desperate conditions. This plan was met very enthusiastically by the State Department.

For my film I was able to draw on newsreel material from all over the world, not just American and British and Russian but even captured German material. It ended up running as long as a feature film, and one of the Broadway cinemas wanted to put it on. The head of the [Signal Corps'] Astoria studio was delighted, because he had visions of his own future career in films after the war. Then after Potsdam came the big swing—the Soviet Union, which had been our ally, was now our principal enemy. Churchill gave his Fulton, Missouri, speech about the Iron Curtain descending over Europe. Orders came from the State Department, "Burn the negative; burn all the copies." Actually, my wife and I decided that we would risk keeping one copy, and later, when I was shooting a film in France and was named for the first time, I returned to America only briefly to settle my affairs. Since I couldn't take this film with me when I went back to Europe, we buried it in the hills behind where we lived on Wetherly Drive above Sunset Strip. [Laughs.]

What was the film called?

I think it was just called *The Yalta and Potsdam Conferences*.

That was your military swan song. Then you returned to "civvy street." Did you find that it was a different Hollywood?

It was a quite different Hollywood, and a lot of young directors had emerged in the years that I had been away. I was determined not to go back to Republic and had quite a struggle.

You did Bury Me Dead *and* Winter Wonderland *for Eagle-Lion and then a wonderfully atmospheric movie,* The Spiritualist.

The Spiritualist was also Eagle-Lion. I managed to get Ian Hunter to rewrite the script in a week. He had only a week, day and night, and he really gave it some characterization and humor. I also had John Alton as cameraman.

I gave Alton his first job in America photographing a film [*The Courageous Dr. Christian*]. He showed me some material which he had shot in South America, and I was very impressed with the lighting. I said, "The only thing is, John, on our schedule you'll have to do it very fast." He said, "Trust me. I'll be as fast as you want." To my amazement and delight, he was faster and more talented than any other cameraman I'd ever worked with, partly because he used so little lighting. In fact, when he did his first film for Metro, which was a prize-winner, he used so little light that they secretly sent someone around after him with a light meter to check, because they didn't trust him. John was such a joy to work with because he had such interesting effects. He always knew exactly what lighting was appropriate. He used very few lights. He regarded shadow and darkness as just as important as light. So you never had a fully lit set; you had this mix of highlights and darkness.

That's certainly true of The Spiritualist. *It's immensely evocative, with gothic shadows. The wonderful house with Turhan Bey and the séances are superb.*

I remember one scene Alton photographed. I was shooting toward a stage—a theatrical stage, which was all we had built. I just put a few people on a rostrum in front of the camera with a rail as if they were in the first balcony. I said to John, "Gee, it's a shame I have no possibility of shooting reverses from the stage because we don't have a theater built." John said, "Don't worry about it. We'll shoot the empty studio. Just be sure there are no light-colored objects around." So we shot reverses from the stage into this empty studio and just had a few people sitting on the floor in a few places with just a teeny bit of light, plus a few exit signs which we had quickly made up in diminishing size to give an exaggerated perspective.

This is how Lang did Waterloo Bridge in Man Hunt—*a large globe, then a smaller and smaller globe. After you did* The Spiritualist, *you directed* So Young, So Bad *in New York.*

I had done some research and written with Jean Rouverol [Butler] a story about four teenage girls with a reform-school background. Paul Henreid was going to play the leading part, and several studios were interested in financing it but held off because this was the beginning of the McCarthy period. Already, although the film was not political in any sense, anything that didn't present America as in every way the best of all possible worlds was suspect, and this was critical of a state institution. Meanwhile we were offered financing by the Danziger brothers [kings of B films in the European and especially British cinema of the fifties] if we shot it in New York, so we did, under pretty difficult physical conditions.

Where in New York?

A lot of it is exterior and a little bit was filmed at the Astoria studio.

What were the difficulties?

For one thing, the sound was so badly recorded that we had to post-sync the whole thing. But the film was very successful.

You had quite a good cast.

Incidentally, the four girls had not been in films before. They all had subsequent careers.

*Rita Moreno, Anne Francis, and Anne Jackson did, but the fourth girl [Enid Pulver]
never developed a career. After* So Young, So Bad, *you went abroad for an Italian
film,* Fanciulle di lusso [Luxury Girls].

That's right. I was offered a joint production by Cinecittà, which is the
state Italian company.

*You were still abroad when Edward Dmytryk named you. He said he had met you
at Jack Berry's house.*

Dmytryk, who was the first person to have named me before the Committee, claimed that he had met me at a Communist Party meeting. In point of
fact, I had never met Dmytryk, and I was stationed in New York with the
Signal Corps at the time this meeting in Hollywood supposedly occurred. It
was only a year later that I met Dmytryk for the first time, and the occasion
was to raise the money for his defense and others of the Hollywood Ten.
[Laughs.]

What was your reaction to being named?

Well, I was obviously very depressed. I just loved filmmaking, and there
was no point in coming back to America to appear before the Committee,
because not only did you have to report everything about your own politics
but you had to name your friends. Otherwise, you were guilty of contempt of
Congress and were sent to prison.

*Since your naming followed the jailing of the Ten, it was very clear what the results
would be.*

Yes. In fact, I was shooting another film [Pardon My French] in France at
the time. It was a nightmare. The script had no story whatsoever, though it
had been written by Adrian Scott, who had scribbled something to raise
money for his trial. Roland Kibbee, a talented comedy writer, came up with
some intriguing ideas, and in the circumstances, with the principal cast already assembled, we decided to start shooting while he was writing. Unfortunately, after a few sequences he dried up almost completely. I think he was
somewhat dazzled by Merle Oberon and the high society with whom she
associated.*

Merle herself, though always a delightful actress and comedienne, was a
nervous wreck at the time. She could never be got on the set until lunchtime.

---

*Roland Kibbee later became a cooperative HUAC witness and named eighteen people during
his testimony.

I had to rehearse the first scene with her stand-in so the cameraman could light it, and then we could at least be ready to shoot when she arrived. In a scene where she was to kiss the cheeks of some child actors, she insisted that their faces must first be scrubbed with alcohol.

This was Pardon My French?

Yes. I went back to America only very briefly, to sell my house and settle a few things. During that time I arranged with a friend, Ben Barzman, to switch houses, so that if they came with a subpoena to my house, looking for me, they couldn't serve it on him, and he could phone me and say, "Look out, they're coming"—and vice versa.

Donald Ogden Stewart told me he had a sense that, sooner or later, he would be named as a Communist, and so he left for Europe before he could be subpoenaed. "I wasn't caught," he said. "I was caught up with." Did you share the feeling that being named was inevitable?

Yes. I knew that sooner or later it would happen, but hoped to finish this film abroad. When I did finish the film, the screen projectionists' union in America, which was an ultra-right-wing outfit, said they would blacklist all United Artists films if it was released. The contract was that Cinecittà got the European rights, and I got the American rights. So my life savings were gone.

You had actually invested your own money?

Yes.

I see. Oh, dear. Of course, they knew the film had been produced, so there was no question of releasing it under another name. You had a family at that time?

I had two very young children. I was offered a very attractive contract by another Italian distributor, Zumalino. I couldn't get my *permis de séjour* [resident's permit] renewed in Italy, so I went to France briefly, then came back to Italy on a month's holiday visa, which was perfectly legal. But within two days I was picked up by the police in Positano and taken to the nearest police station. I asked, "What am I charged with?" The police said, "We don't have to tell you that. You can talk to the American consul in Naples." The last thing I wanted was to go to the American Consulate, which was American territory, because this was the height of the red scare—the Rosenbergs were being tried, and Alger Hiss had gotten a long prison sentence for allegedly hiding some secrets inside a pumpkin for Soviet agents. And I had had all this top-secret material going through my hands while I was in the Air Force—the first use of radar for a blind landing, the inventions for a vertical takeoff, the first reversible propeller. They were all graded top-secret. Also, I'd been very friendly with the Soviet chargé d'affaires in Los Angeles. So the

one thing I wanted to avoid was going to the American consulate and being
sent back to America.

Well, they kept me in prison overnight, and then these two Italian policemen took me to the head of the police in Naples. He was very angry, because
this was a Saturday morning, and he had planned a weekend with his girlfriend on Capri, and here he had this American lousing it up for him. Fortunately, they had not yet sent my file, so he didn't know why I was being
held; he thought I was an American insisting on being taken to the American
Consulate. It suddenly occurred to me that my only hope lay in getting him
more angry. He said, "You Americans! You think you own this country." I
said, "We do!" He said, "Another word from you, and you won't see the
American consul! You'll go across the border to France." I said, "You wouldn't
dare." He said, "Wouldn't I! Alfonso, Luigi, send this American son of a
bitch to France." But this proved to be the end of my film career.

Still, you could work in France, couldn't you?

No, I couldn't even get a *permis de séjour* in France. I returned to England,
and my passport shortly expired. I couldn't get a new one. A solicitor who
was very experienced in civil-rights cases advised me to lie low. I was offered
a film to do which had a very mediocre script, and there was no point in
running a serious risk by making what could only be a poor film. I was desperate to make money for my family.

We managed to buy the end of a lease on this house [in London] for next
to nothing, because at the time everybody wanted to move from big houses
to little flats, where they could save money on central heating, servants, and
so forth. I made a deal with Eton College, which owned this and loads of
other properties in the area, to get a long lease if I would convert it into three
self-contained units, which I managed to do for less than a thousand pounds.
I engaged an architect, but then I realized that this could be a profitable
business, so at night I learned just enough architecture to know what I was
doing and subsequently converted a whole series of houses—in fact, a lot of
the houses on this street—into flats which I then sold. It was a very demanding business—looking out for properties, arranging the financing, supervising the building as well as drawing up some of the sketch plans, and
supervising the sale of flats. I felt fortunate to have an increasing income to
support my family, but, alas, I was out of films for good.

How about your political life? Did this continue?

We didn't really have a chance to do anything politically. During the
Vietnam War I became a British subject, because my son was classified 1-A
[according to the U.S. draft]. The only way to keep him from being drafted
into the Vietnam War, which I was very much against, was for him to become
a British subject. The only way I could do this quickly was for me to become
a British subject myself. Since then, I've been an active member of the Labour

Party, but nothing dramatic. For a period I was advised to avoid notice politically.

When you look back on that period now, is it with embarrassment, or nostalgia, or a sense of achievement—or perhaps a sense of something not achieved?

It's with a sense of deep regret that my film career was cut off, because I loved making films, and I think I had just reached the stage where I knew what I could and couldn't do and would have been able to make really good and successful films if allowed to continue. On the other hand, if I had it to do over again, I think I would be obliged to take the strong anti-Fascist stands that I did. Considering the people who lost their lives volunteering for the International Brigades in Spain, mine was a very modest sacrifice. I am so glad that I was able to go from being completely broke to developing a reasonable income to support my family, so I don't feel bitter about the past, though certainly I did regret no longer being able to do the thing which I most enjoyed.

John Weber

JOHN WEBER, New York City, 1997

INTERVIEW BY PAUL BUHLE

JOHN WEBER
(1910–   )

1952 *Fanciulle di lusso/Luxury Girls.*
        Coproducer (uncredited).
      Imbarco a mezzanotte/Stranger on the Prowl.
        Coproducer (uncredited).

■

JOHN WEBER'S MARXIST credentials gave him a unique vantage point in Hollywood. A professional organizer, labor activist, and regional political functionary for the Communist Party, Weber became a classroom savant for the film colony in 1938, remaining for a decade a key figure in the Hollywood section of the Party. After teaching political economy and American history to eager film-industry pupils, he made his way into the business, starting at the bottom rung as a reader and assistant story editor. He might have been on his way to screenwriting or producing, but instead he found a niche in the William Morris Agency. There, as the rare Marxist on the other side of the agent's desk, he stayed until the blacklist.

■

Let's begin with your childhood.

I was born in 1910 on East One Hundred and Twentieth Street, in Harlem, then a mixed Jewish and Italian neighborhood. My mother and father both came from the Ukraine. While they were both from religious families, they were not religious in the U.S. My mother called herself a "freethinker."

They were not touched very deeply by radicalism. My father was what they called an "operator," a person who used a sewing machine in a needle-trades shop in the days when they carried the machines on their backs from job to job. He was also a faithful union member who would never dream of crossing a picket line. He read the *Freiheit** faithfully, down to his last days, but he was never active in the trade-union movement. I don't think my mother would have allowed him to be active, because she was absolutely determined for the family to be upwardly mobile. She was an incredibly dedicated and vigorous head of the family.

We later lived in downtown Manhattan, on East Fifteenth Street, where my brother Morris went to Stuyvesant High School. I remember him taking me across Tompkins Square Park to the public library, where I polished off all the fairy tales in a matter of less than a year, when I was seven years old

---

*The *Freiheit* [Freedom] was a Yiddish daily paper (with one English page) published by Communists but read by a far larger number of people, mainly in New York City. Known for its high literary quality and cultured language, it remained an inestimable force within Jewish life through several generations of Yiddish speakers.

and a voracious reader. Unfortunately, I was also a quick study, too clever for my own good.

My mother didn't succeed with her first son, my oldest brother, Joe, because they were too new to the country and couldn't keep him out of the pool halls. He didn't do anything bad—he played musical instruments—but he never succeeded in work. My next brother, Abe, and my next, Morris, both became dentists. My mother would bring lunch to Abe in his first office, in a low-cost district, East New York [in Brooklyn], which, she was confident, would become built up. Through a relative we managed to save up enough to get a house in East New York, where we moved when I was about eight.

My mother taught us to be honest. It was only later in life that I learned that "honesty is the best policy" was not only a moral credo but also very practical, the best way to get ahead. She also told us that she was descended from a long line of rabbis, back to the Baal-Shem-Tov, a kind of medicine man who dealt in herbs and founded Hasidism. Despite the fact that she had no religious leanings, we would observe the holidays as a matter of Jewish custom. I remember a rabbi who would eat at our house during the fasting on Yom Kippur—he knew we wouldn't tell on him. We also had a boarder who gave me a chess set when I was eleven. I took to it at once and borrowed a book on chess from the public library. When I was in my seventies, my brother Abe chided me for never having taken that book back.

Was there anything else you read that predicted your future?

My bent was in the direction of journalism. At the age of fourteen I had a very romantic year, which consisted of being a coeditor of the school paper, the *Mirror*, at Franklin K. Lane Junior High School, on Halsey Street, in Brooklyn. We editors were the intellectuals of the school. That same year I became a copyboy at the *New York Morning World*, in the Pulitzer Building, on Park Row, for me a very glamorous place. The *World* had FPA's column, "The Conning Tower"; Heywood Broun's column, "It Seems to Me"; Alexander Woollcott's drama criticism; Harry Hansen's literary criticism; and, on the editorial page, Rollin Kirby's cartoons. Naturally, I was hoping that one day I'd be able to write. I always picture an unkempt Heywood Broun bending over and tying his shoelaces. I admired him for saying, years later, "Newspapers aren't *for* big business; they *are* big business."

One day the Polish man who was in charge of us sent me up to the thirteenth floor, supposedly to get a line of type. A linotype operator handed it to me. I didn't realize it was burning hot, and I dropped it. That was my initiation as a copyboy. But the whole period I was there remains unforgettable, one of the most romantic times in my life.

Meanwhile, in high school, I was already becoming a Marxist, and I delivered a speech in economics class debunking the law of supply and demand. As a result, I was flunked in that class, and it affected my attitude toward college. My family thought that a personable, clever fellow like me could certainly become a successful lawyer. I agreed that they might be right, but I had not the slightest interest in going in that direction. Instead, I developed a contempt for City College. I don't know why, but I would cut classes before and after gym and instead spend three hours working out. It was a form of pointless rebellion, and I dropped out after two years, much to the dismay of my family.

I joined the Communist Party at age eighteen, and I was considered quite a catch. For all these foreign-born and foreign-accented people who had difficulty among the general population, I seemed like a personable young fellow who "talks American." They were quick to put me on soapboxes, where I did well. I learned that it didn't matter how well-grounded you were, so long as you could talk convincingly. I soon found myself in the Party's national training school, where I was given all the world's essential wisdom in six months. I became a "professional revolutionist." We wore that badge quite seriously. They shipped me out to become a district functionary, a "leader and tribune of the people," and made me a proletarian snob.

Did you have any special reason to be sent to Hollywood?

I had been a trade-union director and an "orgsec" [organizational secretary] on the district level. I had organized textile workers, guided hunger marches, and led strikes. By 1938 I had become—how shall I put it—an "experienced leader." That meant someone who knew everything and could teach everything.

Hollywood was a very romantic but also a very different assignment. I had been living with my wife for nine years without "bourgeois" marriage ties, but when I was assigned there, we had to become respectable. We got married at City Hall, by one of the corrupt Tammany politicians, for two dollars and the price of a gardenia. Then we went out to Hollywood on the *El Capitán*.

Had you been a big movie-watcher before you got to Hollywood?

Everybody was. If it was raining and you had fifteen cents, you went to whatever movie was playing.

As a Communist, would you have known any of the famous left-wing film writers before you got to Hollywood?

Not at all. There were no famous writers—their fame was in Hollywood, not elsewhere. You might think of Donald Ogden Stewart or Sidney Buchman, but they would be known for pictures that were not especially left-wing but were very witty and popular.

What was the importance of Hollywood, as seen by Party leaders?

It was an important source of funds but more than that. They had the notion that they could influence the content of pictures. In Hollywood, at the time, the Party was developing on a big scale. They had decided to create something new, a Marxist school, so they needed people to teach Marxism-Leninism. Arthur Birnkrant was the only other instructor; later he became an assistant to Sidney Buchman.* We, the two teachers, were the heads of the Marxist school.

What was the intention of the school?

It was to develop the minds of the people who were the creative heart of Hollywood. Almost all of the people taking courses were writers, directors, producers, actors, and technicians—three hundred of them. They could take any course they wanted. The idea was to inculcate the ideas of the Party in these people so that they would make use of the ideas in pictures.

The students were mostly not Party members but people who were attracted by the anti-Fascist movement, because we were fighting Hitler. Spain, of course, was a glorious example of human courage and high aims. The general struggle was broad enough to bring people into the Party orbit. People in Hollywood wanted to understand society and social forces better.

Were the school and its classes "open" or "secret"?

The school did not even have an official name, and it met in people's homes rather than in a regular office or building, for one simple reason—we couldn't invite any publicity. The arrangement was obviously protective, but we made no fuss about it and tried to maintain a sense of normality.

How and what did you teach?

Political economy and U.S. history, although not quite in the way the Party had envisioned. Earl Browder had developed the spurious slogan—which I nevertheless respected at the time—"Communism is twentieth-century Americanism." I found myself at odds with the dogmatic element without rebelling against it. I did a few seditious things. For instance, I made use of Leo Huberman's *Man's Worldly Goods*, Vernon L. Parrington's *Main Currents in American Thought*, and a number of other such books, together with Marx's *Capital* and the usual classics.

The Party would have looked down on my choice of material as insufficiently scientific, but it was simply better for teaching Hollywood people. I developed my own approach, for instance, to the idea that the American Revolution was founded on property, rather than constantly resorting to high-flown phrases. You could not properly teach people anything unless you veered away from the dogmatism of the Party.

How do you think the school influenced a generation of Hollywood radicals?

I think it influenced people to be more confident that they could present progressive ideas, one way or another, in any phase of their work as writers,

---

*A former trade-union lawyer, Arthur Birnkrant (1906–1983) served as a story and production executive for Columbia Pictures under Sidney Buchman in the 1940s and early 1950s. He was involved behind the scenes as supervisor of *The Jolson Story* and *Saturday's Hero*. Blacklisted, he became a playwright, and several of his puppet plays were produced by Bill Baird.

actors, directors, even technicians. It freed up the creativeness of an awful lot of people—way beyond the ideas of "the "insertion school," whose tactic was inserting political lines into films.

In a broader sense, the Hollywood left and the cultural left at large succeeded in spite of our political failures. We were defeated and crushed, but we did help to get good pictures made, good plays produced, and good novels written. We influenced people to get organized in important social and political organizations. We influenced the course of the country, even during the time when we were in the course of being defeated.

That's an old story on the left. Eugene V. Debs, in the Socialist Party's heyday, exerted an influence which is still alive today, and so is the influence of the Industrial Workers of the World and even of the Knights of Labor. It's not only their exemplary effect but the influence that they had in molding people who then influenced their progeny. There must have been a million people who passed through the American left of the 1930s and 1940s. Millions more were influenced by it, and millions are still being influenced by it indirectly.

But did the school accomplish what the Party had in mind?

The Party leadership's notions of what could be done with Marxist ideas in film were quite limited as well as stupid. You must remember, the leadership of the Party did not consist of highly educated or even highly cultured people, only highly dedicated people. People like Donald Ogden Stewart or Ring Lardner Jr., for instance, were gifted in ways beyond the Party's understanding. For these reasons the Party leaders had no real cultural ideas, and the Party gave no leadership in a cultural sense.

The Party itself could not possibly flower in American culture without the benefit of creative writers and other artists who tied the verities of political economy to the living circumstances of the people in a thoughtful and human way. Hollywood was certainly a better place because the Communist Party was there. But the prime influence on the people in Hollywood came not from the Party proper but from the general cultural development of the left.

Were there well-known Hollywood stars or big names whom you met or heard about but whose Party memberships were kept secret from everybody else?

One could guess intelligently, but one couldn't know whether they were secretly Party members or not. Contact with them was always on a one-to-one basis. A substantial number did contribute financially, lend their names, or in some cases become active in organizations such as the Hollywood Anti-Nazi League, the Hollywood Independent Citizens Committee for the Arts, Sciences, and Professions (HICCASP), or the Committee for the First Amendment. One couldn't always guess, either. It came as quite a surprise, for example, that someone like Rita Hayworth found herself so hard pressed later on to explain away having lent her name to HICCASP, the Sleepy Lagoon Defense Committee, and the Hollywood Democratic Committee.

What happened to the school?

By 1940 the Party was pulling in its horns, because of the Smith Act.* They closed the school. They also decided to cut down on all full-time functionaries and said to us, "Go into the industry," which was just as impractical personally as a lot of their other political directives.

Tell me about your role as Party representative in Hollywood during the early years.

First of all, the Hollywood people were very much underground, even within the Party. The Hollywood section was a separate organization, with a direct connection with the national office—the Central Committee—and no relation whatsoever to the Los Angeles Party, because it was not considered secure. After all, producers, writers, and directors could all lose their jobs if their membership were known.

In Hollywood only the Party leaders of the section were formally considered above me. Actually, I was on the same status level as they. Jack [John Howard] Lawson was the leader; Herbert Biberman, Richard Collins, Lester Cole, and a few others were on the leadership committee. The personal representative of the Central Committee to Hollywood was the high-flown pedant V. J. Jerome, who was just ridiculous in my eyes. But he didn't come out often or stay very long.

You won't believe this. It was my task, for example, to memorize about one hundred and fifty names, addresses, and telephone numbers, and I did. You don't believe you can do a thing like that. I realized later that it was a piece of stupidity, because the FBI had the names, telephone numbers, and life histories of every single one of the three hundred people taking courses, including the two hundred and fifty Party members. I could have saved myself a lot of trouble by calling the FBI and asking for the phone numbers. [Laughs.]

What salary did the Party pay you?

During the ten years that I had been a functionary, I had been living on five dollars a week. I was paid a little more in Hollywood, not much more.

How did the Party shape, or at least relate to, the lives and daily work of the writers?

Remember, many of the writers had been organized by Communists, in various activities, before they joined the Party. They had already come to see an essential rightness about the cause of the Party, which many people rec-

---

*The Smith Act, adopted by Congress in 1940, made it illegal "to teach, advocate, or encourage the overthrow of the United States government." Although it was first used to imprison American followers of Leon Trotsky in Minnesota, it was later used for extensive prosecution of Communist leaders. The Communist Control Act of 1954 made mere party membership a violation of the law. A Supreme Court decision of 1961 struck down the Communist Control Act and key provisions of the Smith Act.

ognized but which was not well served by the leadership of the Party in the United States, or by the international leadership, either.

The best writers concluded, and I did too, that a person could be an honest, dedicated Communist only if he or she was at the same time a humanist, not a cold devotee of certain notions about social revolution. We concluded on our own that Marxism was not some hardline Bolshevik dedication, that revolutionary transformation was not for ideas but for people, a dedication to the future of humanity, raising the standard of ordinary people's living, making a better world in all respects. Marx never undertook to outline exactly how that could be accomplished, nor did Engels or Lenin. Nor did we. We only knew that we could be dedicated to that better world. That put us more in league with people who considered themselves not Communists but progressives, and that is the area in which we found we had to operate in Hollywood. I listened to what the New York leaders had to say—and ignored it.

Was this approach largely shared on the Hollywood left?

No. Like Hollywood generally, the Party in Hollywood consisted too much of people who were fundamentally careerist. The major impulse of almost everyone in Hollywood was careerist. Career meant everything. Hollywood people all kissed each other, but their true spirit was best exemplified by a full-page ad in the *Hollywood Reporter* celebrating the relationship of Charlie [Charles] Brackett and Billy Wilder, each one with a dagger hidden behind the other's back. That was the meaning of the kissing game—not among the people like the script readers and technicians; they didn't have the power to do bad things. But everyone aspired in Hollywood, of course.

I realized this only much later on, from the behavior of leading members of the Party, like Richard Collins, as friendly witnesses. I couldn't understand Dick Collins until I began to associate personal weakness with political cowardice. I use him as an example.

Did the Party, or the school, succeed in teaching the writers what you would regard as a solid version of Marxism?

The problem was that even leading Hollywood Party people had a poor grasp of Marxism—Jack Lawson, Lester Cole, almost all of them. Not that they were not good people. They meant well, they worked hard, they did the best they knew how, and they deserve credit for what they did. They were also, necessarily, deeply involved in their own careers as writers, in ways that would satisfy the needs of the motion-picture industry. But they were not deep thinkers or Marxists and could not apply Marxist ideas to American life the way they should have been applied. As Abe [Abraham] Polonsky once said, "I don't try to get Marxist ideas into pictures. I write the way I do because I am a Marxist."

Let's move on to your next phase in Hollywood, as a screen reader. You had made potentially valuable contacts.

I certainly had friends in high places. You didn't use that.

Some writers rose fast, in and through the Party.

For a writer, that's perfectly true. For a person without any skill in the picture business, how could anyone do anything for you? It didn't occur to me that anyone could. So I did what was the normal thing to do—started at the bottom. I decided to become a screen reader. I picked a novel, a difficult book to synopsize because it was zany, a sophisticated comedy—Elliot Paul's *The Mysterious Mickey Finn*. I worked up a twenty-five-page synopsis and submitted it. Sure enough, it landed me a job right away as an outside reader at RKO and Paramount. I wasn't strictly employed but given piecework, the overflow jobs. The studios had too much work for the inside readers.

How many inside screen readers were there?

Perhaps one hundred and fifty, something like that. Everyone used readers. The heads of the studios and people who worked with them never read anything. They wouldn't have known how to crack a book. Louis B. Mayer had a very talented reader whom he called his Scheherazade.* She would come in and tell him the stories. Even the educated studio heads were the same way. They were accustomed to saying, "You can always buy brains." And it was true, by the way. But if you did a good job as a reader, you could get promoted. Not long after I started doing piecework, I became an inside reader at Paramount. There were about a dozen of us at Paramount, each in our own office.

What did the work consist of?

You had to read a lot of crap and treat crap seriously, because the studios did—plays, novels, an awful lot of stuff. We had studio hours, and we were not highly exploited. Quite a few people, including many important writers, had been readers at one time or another. Being a reader was an education in thinking for the studio, because you had to write a synopsis—which could be as much as twenty-five pages—and then write a one-page summary and then write a one-paragraph summary. Depending on the literacy of your superiors, one or the other would be read. Many studio executives couldn't read more than a paragraph.

How long were you an inside reader?

Six months or so. Inside readers often went on to story editing, and that happened to me. I also finally made some money, but money didn't mean very much to us. We were not of the same mind as people who came to Hollywood to make money; we had come to do our duty. The same thing had

---

*Over the years, L. B. Mayer had more than one Scheherazade. Harriet Frank Jr. was one. See the interview with Irving Ravetch and Harriet Frank Jr. in Patrick McGilligan, *Backstory 3: Interviews with Screenwriters of the 1960s.*

carried over to my job as a reader. I could not see myself doing anything without doing it well.

You maintained your activities in the Party?

Unquestionably. As a matter of fact, the first thing I did was to organize a [readers'] union. I did what came naturally.

Had a readers' union ever been attempted before?

Never. Nobody had ever "thunk" of it. There were two reasons for a union, and only a certain kind of Communist would think of them at the same time. One was economic improvement and the other was to raise the professional standards. You would not get that combination if you asked the leaders of the Party, who would feel that raising professional standards was already a bourgeois deviation. This was part of what laid the Party low. Of course, the combination was attractive to the readers, so we could get somewhere. I worked closely with Alice Goldberg, who later became Alice Hunter [wife of screenwriter Ian McLellan Hunter], and with Bernie [Bernard] Gordon. They were fine people, and we managed to organize and to win better conditions. We called ourselves the Screen Story Analysts Guild.

How did you prevent yourself from being nailed as a troublemaker?

First we called small, quiet meetings, and only later bigger ones. But bear in mind, the IATSE [International Alliance of Theatrical Stage Employees] was virtually a company union. It did improve conditions for its members, but it was controlled by the studios. By and large, the studios were making such a hell of a lot of money, they could afford to improve conditions. I attribute our success not to our brilliance as organizers but to the fact that unionism was tolerated at the time. We could negotiate openly.

We were successful with the union. A very interesting thing happened, one of the greatest compliments that I've ever received in my life. I was kicked upstairs to assistant story editor at Paramount during the time when we were negotiating the contract. I was now part of the administration, on the other side of the desk. But the Screen Story Analysts Guild members insisted that I remain on the negotiating committee. I almost busted my buttons. I was so proud that they trusted me.

How much of a secret was it that you were a Communist?

It was not made known. We didn't allow it to be a hindrance, either.

Was it much different being a story editor?

Even among the story editors there were gross stupidities. D. A. Doran [the executive story editor at Paramount, later a producer] who loudly proclaimed that any good story could be told in one sentence, was once asked how he would do Hemingway's *For Whom the Bell Tolls*. He answered, "That's simple: the fellow is told to go out and blow up a bridge, and he does!"

Around this time I ran into another way of thinking, still more vulgar. One of my brothers wrote a screenplay about a flood in a mining district during the New Deal, and the various social issues involved. We were beginning to talk about the real prospects of selling it, with me as an intermediary, for somewhere in the neighborhood of twenty-five thousand dollars. The script was turned down. That changed my brother's life, and it had an effect on me, too. The head of the studio then was Buddy DeSylva, a real Tin Pan Alley ignoramus. Bill [William] Dozier, the executive story editor, told me Buddy had concluded, "Who's going to make love to a goil [girl] with coal dust between her legs?" That was the basis of the decision. Vulgarity was the order of the day. Four-letter words were the ones most commonly used in Hollywood, and "love" was not often among them.

You felt that you weren't going to rise up much higher in that kind of studio environment?

I suppose I was not the kind of person the executives would look to as a sycophant, and I was too high-minded to impress them as a future nabob. I think so, anyway. It didn't matter to me. I was getting seventy-five dollars a week; there was nothing wrong with that.

Anyway, I had to serve a year and a half in the Army. My first daughter was born the day I was discharged, and now we had to begin to think in terms of money. I went back to Paramount. But it so happened that Donald Hyde, who had been in charge of the literary department at the William Morris office and was ambitious to become a talent agent, came after me and offered me a job as the new head of the literary department.

My wife was very much opposed, at first, to my becoming an agent. Most agents were seducers, constantly going around trying to steal clients from each other by telling them they could do more. That was the most normal activity. They were thieves and liars. As Fred Allen once said, "An agent's heart is small enough to fit into a flea's navel and leave enough room for two aspirin and an acorn." Not all of them were bastards, but most of them were thoroughly corrupt people operating in a corrupt culture. The same with producers—that's why, when Sidney Buchman became an executive producer at Columbia, it was such an exceptional occurrence.

I told her that I could be different. There was no model for behaving differently, but I was going to become "the good agent." Besides, do you have any idea how two hundred and twenty-five dollars looked to someone who made seventy-five? It was too big an improvement to turn down, especially for someone who was vulnerable to being fired. It's important to make more money while you're vulnerable, especially if you're a Communist. A Communist worker always felt vulnerable, for a good reason—bosses didn't like Communists.

Were you and George Willner the only Communists working in the talent agencies, or was there a network of lefties?

There might have been others, but I never heard of any. We used to think favorably of Paul Kohner, but pretty soon after the start of the blacklist he was advising writers to straighten themselves out with [lawyer] Martin Gang. His attitude was, "What do you have to lose? You can't take integrity to the bank." Ingo Preminger was decent and fairly progressive, unlike his brother, Otto, who allowed himself to make some progressive films but was fundamentally a careerist. George Willner was a very active, progressive-minded fellow who wanted to do good things, and he did do a lot of good. But George was primarily a salesman—he had been a furniture salesman. He always carried around a thousand-dollar-bill and let you see it when he opened his wallet. He had to adapt himself to Nat Goldstone, and he made a lot of money for the Goldstone Agency.

How many people worked in the William Morris Agency?

Hundreds. The New York office of the Morris Agency was for publishing, and the Beverly Hills office had the literary department for motion pictures and theater. It wasn't the strong department in the agency there; they didn't have an expectation of making a lot of money, but they needed a literary department to support the rest of their work. I was the head of the literary department for five years, 1945 to 1950. Among the left-wing writers I represented were Ben Barzman, Bernard Gordon, Julian Zimet, Ring Lardner Jr, Al [Alfred Lewis] Levitt, Joseph Losey, Vladimir Pozner, Jean Rouverol Butler, Bernard Vorhaus, John Wexley, and Ned [Nedrick] Young. As corrupt and money-grubbing as the people in Hollywood were, they all had respect for the left-wing writers and what they produced. That was the golden age of Hollywood. I also represented Zoë Akins, Hume Cronyn, the Epstein brothers [Julius J. and Philip G. Epstein], Garson Kanin, Lewis Milestone, and Jo Pagano, among many others.

Did you represent any of the future friendly witnesses?

They shied away from me. They were thinking, in their own way, that it was better to be represented by someone who could not be tainted by a connection to the Party.

Did you have occasion to meet Hollywood producers or moguls who impressed you with their intelligence or good politics?

I got a fairly close-up look at them, from Dore Schary to Sam Goldwyn. I found some of them smart, some of them stupid, but all of them venal. And I am the tolerant sort!

How did you learn the legal rigmarole?

I was a quick study. If you are sufficiently clever rather than wise, you can accomplish a hell of a lot. For example, there were situations where contracts had to be written, and time was of the essence. It was dangerous to wait the usual month or so until the thirty-page contract got worked out with lawyers.

So I learned to write, in a three-page single-spaced contract, everything of consequence for the writer and the studio. And these held up, until the thirty-pager would come through. How did I manage to do that? I read a thirty-pager and decided that a lot of it was balderdash, in there simply for the livelihood of lawyers. It was not really important for the studio or valuable for the writer. My version was called a "letter of intent," but it functioned as a contract.

Could you make any contribution to specific films?

I developed the talent of putting the elements together, like a producer. The main job of an agent is the juxtaposition of creative forces. For instance, I convinced Arthur Kennedy to take a part in *All My Sons*. I persuaded him with the drama of the scene in which he stalks the father around the room. I also had to convince Lana Turner to take a role in *The Postman Always Rings Twice* by describing to her how she would look in a beach scene with John Garfield, with her tan, in a white bathing suit.

How did you learn that the blacklist was going to fall on you at the agency?

I learned from Meta Reis. She was at the Berg-Allenberg Agency then. We had worked together in the Paramount story department.

This is Meta Reis Rosenberg, who was a friendly witness and still later an executive producer of The Rockford Files?

At one point she was married to Irving Reis, a film director, but she got around socially. Anyway, Meta told me that Bert Allenberg, who was merging the Allenberg Agency with William Morris, was close to the FBI. Therefore I knew that my days were numbered. Shortly after that conversation, I was fired.

Did the Party have any advice, or any good advice, on how the Hollywood left should deal with the approaching repression?

The Party leadership had no legal advice to give, because they had no idea of what to do. The normal position would be to take the Fifth Amendment, but the Ten decided by themselves to take the First Amendment. They probably could have avoided jail if they'd taken the Fifth. But it wouldn't have helped them with their careers or avoided the blacklist's effect on Hollywood.

Abraham Polonsky says that you nevertheless continued to be a leader of the Party in Hollywood, after John Howard Lawson went to jail, at least until you left for Europe. Others have suggested that Paul Jarrico and Michael Wilson held the Party together.

I was a leader all the way through, as long as I was there. Michael Wilson was a fine guy and a wonderful writer, and likewise Paul Jarrico. But they were not in a position to operate in the Party the way I was, from the point of view of national experience, training, and political knowledge.

But it was being smashed, anyway. I made the political mistake of thinking that if I went to Europe to produce a picture and came back later, things would get better. Things got worse—not only from Joe McCarthy but from Roy Brewer [of the IATSE].

Meanwhile, I never had much respect for the political acumen of people like Jack Lawson.

You once called him an "honest sectarian."

I respected him as a person. He might have been wrong, but he was not a conniver like some others. He was wrong on principle, following the wrong notion. Nevertheless, when he had a chance to do good film work he did. *Blockade* was a hell of a picture, written at a time when it was difficult to write such things. To end a picture like *Blockade* with the ringing remark of Henry Fonda, "Where is the conscience of the world?"—there you have the ability of the writer to make a great statement without waving any flag. That's not a line you slip in; it's a line prepared for by the entire picture.

If not for the blacklist, would you have continued to have an increasing role in the Hollywood scene?

Well, the opportunity actually arose to be an independent producer. My brother was willing to invest some money. He had a burning desire to be involved in pictures himself, and he thought that if I could be successful, he could go into the business as a producer, too. So I got together with Bernard Vorhaus, a B director who had been in the Party in Hollywood, and we developed the idea of doing several films together.

Ben Barzman was by then in Paris, and he was a good writer, well-known in Hollywood. Joe Losey was also blacklisted; he agreed to direct and managed to get Joan Lorring, an accomplished actress. I persuaded Paul Muni, who needed work at the time, to do the picture for ten thousand dollars. I made a contract with him, based on the screenplay [called "Encounter"] that Barzman wrote, adapted from a story, "A Bottle of Milk." The scenario was cribbed partly from *Crime and Punishment*, partly from *The Bicycle Thief*, partly from who knows what else. But it had the makings of a movie. I had an ideal setup: a good script, great stars, a capable director. How could I miss?

We went first to Paris. We spent a long time in Paris, dealmaking, casting, preparing to find a means of producing a picture, and actually making preparations for the picture—working around the clock. I did have an aptitude for languages, and so I picked up enough French to get along and, what is more difficult, some of the technical movie language in French. It's possible by immersion. Language is communication, not grammar. I was able to get along well after ten months in Paris.

To get the necessary money we had to make a deal with an Italian producer, which we did. His claim to fame, besides owning a rickety studio [Consorcio Produttori Cinematografici Tirrenia], was that he once had written a libretto for Puccini, who had lived in the region. We didn't know that this producer had also been famous for his relations with Mussolini. Pretty soon he ran out of money, and we found a second producer, who, we later learned, used to be known as "the lemon-squeezer of Livorno." This producer had made his money by buying up tax collections farmed out from the state to private individuals. We didn't know that he also had been a big shot with Mussolini.

So I found myself in very good company. [Laughs.] We headed first to Pisa and then finally to Rome, where we finally finished shooting at Cinecittà. Now I adapted to Italian. I had very little money with which to work and great difficulty extracting money from the Italians—and I had to work up all kinds of legal documentation in Italian for various people. Day after day I was working with very little sleep. I also had to keep in touch with my family in New York, and [Paul] Muni was not the easiest person in the world to keep happy. His wife, Bella, was always on the set telling him what he had to think.

Vorhaus, meanwhile, was developing his own picture, *Luxury Girls*, using Norma Barzman to write the script. If it could make some money, that was terribly important for us, and I became coproducer of that film as well. We also tried to dub Italian pictures to make some money. We messed around with some actors and actually dubbed four pictures. In any case, the main picture we were interested in was still "Encounter."

We had a fine photographer from France [Henri Alekan] and a fine cutter from England [Thelma Connell]. But we had all kinds of production problems. I still remember when we finally managed to get hold of a circus group to perform—for one day. During that day we had to do all the photography of Muni being chased through the circus, with a very talented Italian child actor [Vittorio Manuenta]. Muni was temperamental, interfering with the direction. The damned light was beginning to fade, and Losey was worried about how everything would turn out. We also had big problems with the music for the film and the lab development [of the footage]—you have no idea how valuable the technical production is in Hollywood until you work with half-assed people and equipment.

Meanwhile, there was more trouble from back home.

Our names appeared in *Variety*. We were red-baited in print half a dozen times. We had to explain to the Italian Department of Culture that we were kosher. It didn't matter too much to them, but it was a problem, and there was nothing we could do about *Variety* and the effect at home.

The result was, we had a deal with United Artists. Vorhaus had made it for us. Arthur Krim [one of the top UA executives] personally came over when the film was made and was ready for distribution. But Krim said, "Roy Brewer told me that the projectionists won't show these pictures. 'How can you distribute that picture,' he said, 'when Barzman, Vorhaus, and Weber are all named as Communists?' So what can we do?"

The stratagem was to change all the credits and give them all out to the Italians. Meanwhile Losey wanted more money, and I became furious with him. When he was working on the picture, we had managed to pay him forty thousand dollars, while I was living on one hundred and twenty-five dollars a week.

When it finally came time to distribute the film, UA even had to change the title to the disgusting *Stranger on the Prowl.* Krim agreed with Brewer on a very limited distribution in the U.S., and we didn't get a nickel out of the deal, nothing on the basis of the quality of the film. It is most often seen on late-night television here. I had worked my way up from screen reader to literary agent to producer—and the blacklist.

That was the end of your career in movies.

We came back to the U.S. after we had been gone two and a half years. We had some problems renewing our passports but managed to renew them. We got back in December 1952. You can't produce pictures underground, and so my career as a producer was over, thanks to the blacklist. Like the majority of the blacklistees, I never worked in Hollywood again.

By this time, my brother had "a great invention" for bonding porcelain to precious metals in dental surgery. I found myself taking charge of people who had more technical knowledge than I did, so I had to bone up on all these fields. And I had to build up his company and manage the selling of the product. I operated this way for about seven years. He went bankrupt; the business went bankrupt. Then the people whom we had employed created their own little company, which they later sold for ten million dollars. We got nothing out of it. The dental profession gained a tremendous development, however, and it changed the course of dentistry. We had made it possible.

John Wexley

JOHN WEXLEY, Los Angeles, California, 1983

INTERVIEW BY PATRICK McGILLIGAN AND KEN MATE

JOHN WEXLEY
(1907–1985)

1932 *The Last Mile*. Based on his play.
1938 *The Amazing Dr. Clitterhouse*. Coscript.
    Angels with Dirty Faces. Coscript.
1939 *Confessions of a Nazi Spy*. Coscript.
    The Roaring Twenties.
        Uncredited contribution.

1940 *City for Conquest*. Script.
1941 *Footsteps in the Dark*. Coscript.
1943 *Hangmen Also Die*. Script.
    Heroic Stalingrad/The City That Stopped Hitler
      (documentary). Commentary.
    Song of Russia. Uncredited contribution.
1945 *Cornered*. Story and adaptation.
1947 *The Long Night*. Script.
1959 *The Last Mile*. Based on his play.

■

ONE OF THE socially conscious playwrights who stormed Broadway in the early 1930s, John Wexley wrote the grim prison drama *The Last Mile*—which catapulted Spencer Tracy to stardom on the New York stage and gave Clark Gable the same boost in the road company—and a stirring defense of the Scottsboro Boys, *They Shall Not Die*. Wexley always considered himself a playwright first, although he worked in Hollywood intermittently from 1930 on and gradually accumulated sterling credits.

After false starts at Universal, Paramount, RKO, MGM, Columbia, and Twentieth Century–Fox, he found his footing at Warner Brothers, writing the kind of tough, timely, and authentic screen stories that were known as the studio's forte. He teamed with director Anatole Litvak on several films, including the early anti-Nazi exposé *Confessions of a Nazi Spy*. Three times, on *Angels with Dirty Faces*, *The Roaring Twenties*, and *City for Conquest*, he lent his talents to superior vehicles for actor James Cagney. Later Wexley would leave Warner Brothers and retreat to his farm in Bucks County, Pennsylvania, only to be summoned back by director Fritz Lang to work with Bertolt Brecht on *Hangmen Also Die*, Brecht's only credited work on an American film. Later in the 1940s still, Wexley would contribute to two productions—the anti-Fascist *Cornered* and the pro-Soviet *Song of Russia*—destined to be targeted by the inquisitors of the House Un-American Activities Committee.

Named as a Communist numerous times by HUAC friendly witnesses, Wexley left Hollywood rather than kowtow to the Committee. He liked to say in private that the irony was that he never joined the Communist Party, because he didn't care for the dues-paying; people who knew him well said it might be true, since the writer was notorious among his acquaintances for his thriftiness. His screenwriting career was essentially over, but he turned things around and distinguished himself by writing, in 1955, a nonfiction investigation of the Rosenberg trial, *The Judgment of Julius and Ethel Rosenberg*, one of the first detailed rebuttals of the government case.

■

Tell us where you were born and when you first came to Hollywood as a writer.

I was born in Manhattan, on West 109th Street, not far from Central Park, and I first arrived in Hollywood as a writer on July 4, 1930.

What brought you to Hollywood?

When I was eighteen or nineteen, I was already an actor in the Neighborhood Playhouse, which was down on the Lower East Side of New York. Many people came out of the Neighborhood Playhouse, including James Cagney. I didn't know him then; I came later. I was in a serious play there, an English version of *The Dybbuk* [by the Yiddish writer S. Ansky], translated by a columnist for the *New York Times*. That was my first [Actors] Equity job. Subsequently, I was with Eva Le Gallienne on Broadway in a theater called the Civic Repertory Theatre. I don't remember if I was with her one or two years. She did two or three plays a week. I remember the Chekhov plays *The Three Sisters* and *The Seagull*, both excellent productions. That was at the Fourteenth Street Theatre, which later became the Theatre Union, with which Albert Maltz was connected.

I was very much involved in writing at the same time. I had been to the Washington Square Playhouse of New York University on a dramatic scholarship. I wrote one-acters and other plays. Several other people came from the Washington Square Playhouse, including Robert Rossen, Leonardo Bercovici, and Sidney Harmon, who became a producer. They were all in my group of good friends, and they were all at Warners when I first came out to Hollywood. Unfortunately, Bob Rossen didn't hold up.

During the period I was with Eva Le Galliene, Josephine Hutchinson left her [theater] group to play in pictures. I wanted to take off too and see the country. Mark Twain, Jack London—these were my heroes. I drove a Chevrolet from city to city, in 1926, all the way to the Coast. I had a beard and took little jobs, working for food and gasoline and a place to sleep. When I crossed the Mississippi, there wasn't a paved road until you got to San Diego. Two thousand miles of dirt roads—that's how it was until the mid-thirties.

I knew an actor in Hollywood; he was a friend of my uncle's.* He had played in the East and was under contract to Metro to do silent pictures. My uncle's friend took me to Metro, and I watched for a couple of hours the shooting of a picture with Norma Shearer. I got the idea that I would work as an extra, get a line or two and then some more, and maybe become a character actor. I was always playing older men. My uncle's friend wasn't very helpful; he seemed reluctant to take me to an agent. So I went to Torrance and worked in a steel mill and wrote a couple of stories about the experience. Then I picked up a friend and headed back East, passing through the South and picking up experiences; a lot of that helped in what I later wrote. When I got involved with the Scottsboro case, I took a lot of the setting from my travel adventures, or peregrinations.

So you wrote The Last Mile *after you had already been to Hollywood for the first time?*

---

*Wexley was the nephew of Maurice Schwartz, founder and star of the Yiddish Art Theatre.

I kept acting at the same time that I was writing. I was in a group called Actors' Authors Associates, rather distinguished people, including Walter Abel—later well-known in Hollywood as a character actor—and a number of others who also became well-known. This group did Gorky's famous play *The Lower Depths* with a new title, *At the Bottom*, performing on Broadway. It was a show for the cream of the theater people, who were crazy about it.

While we were in rehearsal, Herman Shumlin bought the rights to do *The Last Mile*, and in February 1930 it opened on Broadway with an unknown actor named Spencer Tracy and became a hit. I was still acting with the Associates and had to get an understudy. Between the opening of the show and coming out to Hollywood in July, I went to Europe—a boyhood dream. I went for a couple of months. That's how I met my wife, on the ship coming back. A cast of the dice, really. She took the boat in Bremerhaven, after coming from Vienna by train. I saw her up on the second or third deck, wearing a floppy hat. Also on the boat was Katharine Hepburn, who had just done a flop on Broadway.

There was a good deal of interest in the play. William Morris arranged a contract with Universal; my agent, Adrienne Morrison, the mother of the Bennett girls [Constance, Barbara, and Joan], who herself had been married to a distinguished actor [Richard Bennett], sold the play to the first company she had contact with. Old Carl Laemmle was formally in control of Universal, but Junior ran the studio. They were two or three years into talkies. The cameras were all shrouded with heavy coats. There was a need for dialogue, so they wanted playwrights. The gave me a contract for six months that extended seven years.

I arrived July Fourth. The agency would meet you at the Pasadena Station, so you wouldn't get mixed up with the hoi polloi downtown. Two young men, who later became important producers, met me.

Was there a big influx of playwrights at that time?

There were a few dozen. Some stayed. Those who were wise took a little money and went back East. I wasn't wise enough. I did go back but came again.

I was there at Universal six months. My agent got me a lot of money, five hundred and fifty dollars a week. In 1930 you could buy a fine car for that, and a bungalow cost only a thousand dollars in Hollywood. I wrote a number of treatments, met Willy [William] Wyler, who had done a couple of westerns, and met Paul Kohner, who was the studio's European man. Kohner and I became fast friends for half a century. Paul would become my agent between agents. Nothing of mine got made at Universal, but at least my play was still running, and it was quite usual and expected that scripts would be started and not finished.

When I got there, they had just done, with great success, Lewis Milestone's *All Quiet on the Western Front*. In the few days after my arrival, Milestone showed me the set, the no man's land and shattered French villages still on the backlot. I had seen the picture in New York, a powerful picture at the time, compared to others. Milestone and I became good friends, too, and almost did pictures together.

Universal had an idea—why not do the same picture with submarines? I started on a story called "U-Boat," with sinking Allied ships, the personal stories, and so on. But already things were happening in Germany in 1930, and *All Quiet on the Western Front* was banned there. Paul Kohner was the distributor, and people who wanted to see the film had to go to Holland or Belgium. That discouraged us, because we wanted to use the Kiel Canal as the location for "U-Boat." But the German military wouldn't okay an anti-war picture. Willy Wyler was going to direct, but I signed over the rights, and it was never made.

Another one I worked on involved Robert Wyler, Willy's brother, who was hoping to be a producer. He wanted to do a picture about steel mills. I took him out to Torrance, where I had worked—not as a steel roller but as a helper, unskilled labor on the open hearth. That was another story they didn't take to.

I remember talking to the story editor at Universal, and him telling me, "There are four kinds of love—the love between a man and a woman, the love between a mother and a child, the love of a man for his friend, and so on . . ." It was baloney. The fellow running Universal, Carl Laemmle Jr., was silly. He knew nothing and didn't dare to do anything. He came up to your waist—he was five foot one—so you could never stand in his office; you'd have to sit. Other executives really ran the place—rabbits.

I'll give you one example of their ineptitude. Willy Wyler and I went to see the West Coast production of *The Last Mile*. We went backstage to greet the young, unknown actor Clark Gable. We arranged a screen test. I threw Gable his lines. He wore his convict uniform, unshaven, and he was good in the part, better than Tracy, less self-conscious, more dynamic. After we made the test, he took us aside and asked very sweetly if we would shoot a little more film: "I brought my tuxedo and a razor." He was like an adolescent. In the studio, later on, they ran the test, and a couple of these executives were there in the projection room. One or both of them said, "He'll never do. His ears look like sails on ships." I said, "You can paste them back. He's a good actor." People laughed. His agent was pleading for a seven-year contract at two hundred and fifty dollars a week. I'll tell you, they passed up a gold mine. So Columbia gave Clark Gable a job playing a milkman, with a few lines. That was the beginning of his success story.

What was Wyler like at this time?

He had done a number of westerns, starting with two-reelers. He didn't get far with Universal, because he was a relative. His father was the first cousin of Carl Laemmle; Willy and his brother were born in the city of Mülhausen, in Alsace-Lorraine. They were very articulate in French and German. Willy had a lovely mother and father and another brother. Carl Laemmle brought them all over. I was at their home many times, and there was always a family feeling.

I also met [Albert] Einstein at Universal. He had come to California to see the Mount Palomar telescope. He was distantly related to Carl Laemmle. I could understand some German, and I was a kind of symbol for the studio, because I had a play running on Broadway. So I was invited to a table with him and ten others, including Mrs. Einstein. They asked me to show him the writers' bungalows. This was a proud moment in my life. He was like a tourist, taking it all in, quite impressed. He told me that when he and Mrs. Einstein had gotten married, they had agreed to leave all the big decisions in life to him and all the little decisions to her, and it was only now, after they had been married for quite some time, that he realized there were only little decisions. He said all this in German.

Where did you go after Universal?

By mutual agreement, I tried elsewhere. I went to Paramount. I jumped from five hundred and fifty dollars a week to eight hundred and fifty, a fortune. It was a three-month contract. What did I do? I didn't do anything that I can remember. They handed out stories. I wrote treatments. Everything petered out. I recall that I did talk a lot to W. R. Burnett, and worked next door from Don Marquis, who wrote *Archy and Mehitabel* and other lovely ditties.

Was it frustrating, not getting anything produced?

It was so common that it wasn't thought of very seriously. My play was still on. I was making thousands of dollars a week, not counting the studio salary. I was in the upper echelon, a playwright, not a writer, who is always somewhat of an alien in Hollywood. I went twice a week to films, to the sneak previews at the Bijou, to see what the common herd had to say about a film. Afterward, we'd all meet outside, see what the cards had to say, and then go to the Brown Derby.

What did you do all day long at the studio?

Write letters home, to the East. Paramount was where I met Sergei Eisenstein. The studio brought him to Hollywood. We used to eat together at the Brown Derby. He and the studio didn't get along, and they just kept him waiting for an assignment. Upton Sinclair got some money together and sent him down to Mexico. I met Sinclair about that time, too, and was invited to his house in Pasadena two or three times. I thought very highly of him. I admired him because of his famous books on Chicago and Boston. And when he ran for governor, I got embroiled in that campaign.

After Paramount?

A short stint at RKO, where I got another boost in pay. A certain producer wanted me to help him out on a script. That one was subsequently made. I didn't get credit. I didn't ask for it. The jobs went on like this from 1930 to

1931, but what I really wanted very much to do was to finish a play called
Steel, based on my experiences and research in the steel industry. So after
RKO I returned to New York and resumed writing plays. *Steel* was produced
in 1931. I stayed in New York a couple of years and then came back out in
1932, after having gotten married in Vienna. I had gotten an offer to work
at Metro. Now we were in the depths of the Depression.

That was an interesting and amusing time. I met the great L. B. [Mayer]
and his lieutenant Eddie Mannix, a big shot there, though I still didn't get
any credits, joining the ranks of Dorothy Parker, Sidney Kingsley, Elmer Rice,
and other prize-winners at various studios who at that time never managed
to finish a picture or get a credit.

Boris Ingster and another writer had been hired by Metro to work on a
picture called "Red Square." They had Clark Gable to play the engineer, and
in return for borrowing Frank Capra from Columbia, MGM promised to give
Gable to Columbia at some future date—that's how *It Happened One Night*
happened. Gable was playing an engineer who was going to help rebuild a
destroyed dam. There was a beautiful blonde, Jean Harlow, in the story. They
had a few drafts; now they needed a new one. I was one of the new writers.

The United States had not recognized the USSR at this time. The Soviet
Union was a riddle wrapped in an enigma and shrouded in mystery—that was
the attitude, vaguely hostile. Because of what? A different system called Communism. Every day in the Hearst press the cartoons had bewhiskered people,
always in a cellar, manufacturing bombs. This script had scenes where the
commissar, Wallace Beery, had a claw instead of a hand. I remember [Irving]
Thalberg's definition of propaganda. He asked me, "What do you think of
the script?" I said, "Here and there there's something. The rest is unabashed
propaganda." Thalberg said, "Propaganda is when the Bolsheviks write books
or make pictures. This is not propaganda." He added, "I went to Boys' High
in Brooklyn, and I learned right away that Socialism doesn't work. It's no
good. If you want to make money and get anywhere in Hollywood, get on
the bandwagon, John."

I worked on that project for a while with another writer, a really successful
one [Jules Furthman] who turned out a lot of MGM pictures. Then I was
taken off the project at the request of a MGM producer, [former actor] Ralph
Graves. Frank Capra later got disgusted with the film. He was mildly progressive and had too much good taste for that shit.*

Ralph Graves, who had given up acting, wanted me to do a picture about
boys leaving their homes and families and taking to the road, riding freights.
In the press you could read about them; there were tens of thousands. I was
interested in that subject. It was to be an original story. I did research. I went
to places where the kids went for help, like the Salvation Army. But as Ralph

---

*The movie was never made. It is titled "Soviet" in Joseph McBride's biography of Capra,
Frank Capra: The Catastrophe of Success, where its development—and cancellation—are con-
clusively chronicled.

and I became friendly—we went to the Hollywood Athletic Club together—he started saying, "You know why people are poor? They're fated to be poor. There will always be the rich and the poor; that's the nature of human beings. The rich make it because they have drive." That's the guy I was working for. An excellent cardplayer, though, and that's probably how he got his job. In social situations he sat with the executives, playing cards, beating them, winning large sums of money. Maybe twenty thousand dollars was lost at a table, so Mayer said, "Put him on the payroll." He never produced anything! He was being paid off by the stockholders. I didn't find out about this until much later.

How long did you stay at MGM?

Not very long. Early in 1933 two men came to power, Franklin Roosevelt and Adolf Hitler, and it affected all our lives. I got involved in the Scottsboro Boys case.

Why was it so important for you to get involved in the Scottsboro Boys case?

Well, it's a long story. It was almost a natural development after *The Last Mile*, which dealt with capital punishment—an uprising in a death house of condemned convicts. Here we had nine black kids, ages twelve, thirteen, and seventeen, also waiting to be executed. We had the theme of justice, which I'd always been sensitive about, combined with many experiences from my past—the Sacco-Vanzetti case, the Palmer Raids, J. Edgar Hoover, and so on.

I had lived and worked in the South for a year or two and was aware of the climate there. There were many lynchings every year, even at that time. A black person couldn't vote in the South—couldn't vote at all. They had all these tricks, like the poll tax. Black people couldn't go into a white restaurant, couldn't drink at a fountain which said, "For Whites Only." Black wages were minimal. People were treated just one degree above a slave condition, and slavery had supposedly ended with Reconstruction. I have always thought that racism is one of the most serious problems, if not the most serious, affecting this country. And, in a nutshell, that's what attracted me to the case. The case of the Scottsboro Boys was a clear injustice, and the Supreme Court of the United States recognized that five times by stopping the executions. I studied the court records and interviewed people. I went to see the lawyer who defended the boys and followed him to trials, observing his style. Oh, and I met the mothers of the boys, and the key witness, a young prostitute, who gave evidence that she had been instructed to lie. Ruby Bates was her name. She'd come North to raise funds for the defense.

I worked rapidly and for months wrote all night long. I felt I had to save these kids. I started to write the play *They Shall Not Die*. In February 1934 *They Shall Not Die* was read first by Harold Clurman. He wrote me a letter which I still have: "This is a strong subject, but it doesn't have any women in it, and I couldn't recommend it for production." I was immediately pleased when it was bought by the second person who read it, John Galsworthy, who recommended it to the Theatre Guild, the leading theatrical institution in the country.

So I started working within the Guild and their board of directors. They put Lee Simonson, their top set designer, on it, and Philip Moeller, their top director. If you look at the usual published play, you will see thirty or forty parts, but this one had ninety. Helen Wesley, a black actress, played an important role, and Claude Rains, Dean Jagger, Tommy [Tom] Ewell, and Ruth Gordon were also in the cast. It opened in February 1934 and had a fair run, considering that it was a terrible season for Broadway.

Why didn't you try to adapt it into a movie script? What was the attitude in Hollywood toward African-Americans?

There you had in films the Stepin Fetchit kind of character, or the mammy, or the Negro maid with a shrill voice who never knew what she was doing, like in *Gone with the Wind*. There were no blacks working in important positions in the industry, and the attitude toward blacks was a stereotype, the same as with any other minority. Jack Warner would say, "We don't want any nigger pictures." They didn't think much of the return at the box office from black clientele.

How long was it before you returned to Hollywood?

One of the Guild directors got a job with Harry Cohn as a movie producer, and an agent called me with a contract offer from Columbia. If you had a play running on Broadway, you got a lot of offers. Again I went out on a six-month option. This was 1934, and it was the year I got into Hollywood politics. I remember the terror that existed in California then. There was a general strike, Upton Sinclair was running for governor, and the Tom Mooney case was also stirring up people.

Was there a lot of political ferment on the lot?

Around Hollywood, not on the Columbia lot, though there were kindred souls, like Sidney Buchman—and then, through him, I met his younger brother, Harold—and Jack Lawson, whom I already knew from New York as a playwright. Franchot Tone was there, too. Robert Riskin was progressive, but very mild, and didn't make waves. Jack—I had no idea he had any Communist connections, but we talked about the world, about Hitler, about Roosevelt, about the recognition of the Soviet Union after seventeen years.

I was assigned to "Eight Bells," a ship story. I had a run-in with Harry Cohn. He was a pleasant gangster, but they don't wear masks in Hollywood, or I could tell if they had masks on. I could cotton to them. They did a lot of ship stories—almost once a year someone did a ship story. In this one there was a mutiny, only it wasn't called such. When I began to develop it, Cohn started worrying. He said, "Whoever heard of a mutiny? It's a revolution." I said, "It happens very often." His secretary brought in the *Encyclopedia Britannica*, but we couldn't find any mutiny listed; we found out later they didn't want the word "mutiny" in the *Encyclopedia Britannica*, either—not even [the actual] mutiny on the *Bounty*! So he said, "You see!" I lost that argument.

Tell us a little bit about the Upton Sinclair campaign and Hollywood's response.

I was working for Columbia, and the atmosphere in the state of California was very frenetic, almost, because of the big strike that had been won by the dock workers and the stevedores loading the ships in San Francisco. San Francisco was a very pro-union city. Northern California always was pro-union; Southern California had more of the "right-to-work" kind of philosophy—against unions—dating back to the bombing of the *Los Angeles Times* and the McNamara case [in 1911]. Clarence Darrow had been very much involved in that case.

In any event, the California corporations—particularly, in Southern California, the Motion Picture Producers Association—were terrified of a revolution, as they called it. They were intent on defeating Sinclair, this great danger, and reelecting Governor [Frank] Merriam, who was in office, a rigid Republican. Of course, Upton Sinclair's EPIC plan, which is famous, was very mild. The studios were afraid of income taxes, which didn't exist then in California. The acronym stood for End Poverty in California, but they looked upon it as out-and-out Socialism and conducted quite a campaign showing propaganda stuff in between the features in the theaters. They were tremendously opposed, almost hysterical.

In all the studios they had different methods of opposing EPIC, but at Columbia, in the central plaza, as you entered the studio, there—like a flagpole—was a huge thermometer thirty or forty feet high. And the red part, indicating the degrees of temperature, went higher as they got in what they called "contributions." It was really a tax hitting the employees. The studio got close to one hundred percent very quickly. People were asked to give a day's or week's salary, I forget which, and, of course, with the stars and directors and some writers this was a considerable sum, because an average writer might be getting five hundred or a thousand dollars a week.

Jack Lawson worked right next to me in an adjoining office. He was just then involved in forming the Screen Writers Guild. I had known him as a distinguished playwright back in New York City, where he had had a number of plays produced, including the famous one, *Processional*, put on by the Theatre Guild, and we had taken up our friendship again when I came out to Hollywood. *They Shall Not Die*, my Scottsboro play, was running on Broadway, and that gave me some kind of additional prestige which I might not have had otherwise.

Harry Cohn used to come out on the balcony of his office and look across the plaza, and frequently he would see us talking in Jack Lawson's office or mine. [Laughing.] And maybe another writer or two was there, because in one of the adjoining offices was Sidney Buchman, who was one of the top writers then. We were always talking about the Guild and political problems and the Depression and Sinclair. And Cohn would yell up, "Wexley! Lawson!

Get out of Buchman's office, because you're losing time." In other words, "Get back to writing; don't talk politics." He would scream this across the plaza.

One time he called me down to his office, and he said, "What's this I hear, that you don't want to give a contribution of a day's salary?" I said, "No. I'm against Merriam, and I'm for Sinclair." He said, "We can't have that. We have to have one hundred percent." I said, "Well, do whatever you like. Put one hundred percent on your thermometer." He said, "No, no. We have to do it honestly. We can't fake it, because we have a whole list of people and names and their contributions." This evolved into a number of such calls to the oval office, so to speak. He began to bargain with me as the days went on, to try to manipulate me by saying, "Well, Jack agreed to give if you would contribute." And I'd say, "You're probably telling him the same thing about me." He would laugh. Harry was a gangster, really, and when you caught him at it, he would mischievously grin.

It came down to this: I was getting about seven hundred and fifty dollars a week, so I ought to have been contributing a hundred and fifty. Cohn would say "Give me a hundred dollars." I said, "I won't give you a nickel," and I would laugh at the same time. He would say, "What are you, an anarchist?" I'd say, "No, not quite." "A Socialist?" He'd go on with these names. And then finally he ended up by saying, "Give me fifty and I'll kick in the rest quietly." I said, "No, I won't."

After three or four of these summonses to his office, he became angry and said, "Give me five dollars—a symbol!" I said, "No. That's the whole thing. I don't want to give you a symbol. I resent the whole situation. I resent that you're the boss and you call me down here." He said, "Well, I can't fire you, because you've still got seven weeks to go on your contract. But I'll tell you what I'm going to do. If you don't give me anything, you're not going to work anymore." I said, "Well, you'll have to pay me, anyway." He said, "I'll pay you, but you'll have to come here at nine o'clock every morning and stay till five, and I'm not going to give you any work—that's going to be your pun-ishment!"

Jack Lawson told me subsequently that he was calling him down and giv-ing him the same business. "Give me just a dollar." That was the end of Jack Lawson, because he was not under contract; he was on a week-to-week basis. He was fired. I lasted six weeks longer than him and would bring in books to read, magazines and newspapers, teasing Harry Cohn. From the balcony I would wave to him. Finally he relented and asked me to read something for my opinion. It was more like a book review than a script, some story he wanted to buy. But he let me go after my contract ended. He didn't rehire me.

Subsequently, months later, I met him at Palm Springs, at a hotel, around the swimming pool, and there he laughed about it. It was long after the election. Merriam, of course, won.

He never fired you?

He couldn't. Then I went to RKO on a four-week guarantee. I can't even remember what I was working on. I had previously bought a farm with some of the money I had gotten from *They Shall Not Die*. It had no electricity or running water, even. When I came to Hollywood, we just closed the doors, we didn't even have locks. After RKO I went back East and remained there and started to build a wing as big as the original house. We stayed for a couple of years, and then I was brought out in 1936 by Zanuck at Fox to work on a film about an American agent on a mission from the president, during some historic event, maybe the Spanish-American War. It was called *A Message to Garcia*, and I think it was made, but I worked there for only three weeks.*

Maybe it was Kenneth MacGowan who had asked for me. Kenneth was a friend of [Eugene] O'Neill's, and he knew Samuel French, my publisher; later he founded the film school at UCLA and did a lot with the Pasadena Playhouse. I remember asking Kenneth, "What the hell am I here for?" I hadn't met Zanuck, I didn't have a clear assignment, it was a hot summer, and I wondered what the hell I was doing there. He said, "Write a note to Zanuck." I did, but Zanuck didn't even answer. Then I got word from Kenneth that this was my last week. I sent a hot telegram to Zanuck, telling him what I thought of him, but I never got an answer. Years later I worked for him, though, and he paid me an awful lot of money.

This all sounds terribly frustrating.

It happened all the time, around me and to me. I really got started only the next time I came out, in 1937. We were able to go back to the farm with ten thousand dollars and sink it into the farm; you could do a lot with ten thousand in those days. I spent a whole year on the farm, writing. I had already written a play about China, produced in between those years, as *Running Dogs*, a special at the Theatre Union. In theater I could realize something, whether it was sold or produced or not. I was in control. I didn't have to knock on doors and sit outside producers' offices.

I was always just a visitor in Hollywood. You had to have a continuity there, and I never did. I felt it was a trap, anyway—the swimming pool, the tension, the envy, the hatred. That was Hollywood.

But in 1937 you made a decision to stick with motion pictures for a long while.

I went under contract. A seven-year contract. I had a hell of a time getting out of it.

You were a reluctant screenwriter.

---

*A Message to Garcia was indeed filmed in 1936, starring Wallace Beery and Barbara Stanwyck, and directed by George Marshall.

I guess so. It was a second love. When I got good at it, and self-confident, I began to like it better. That was at Warners. Warners had some real quality—message pictures and Bette Davis "women's pictures."

I began there with the same trouble, futzing around, and finally they gave me something with a budget, with a beginning and an end, and they invested some money in it. That was *The Amazing Doctor Clitterhouse*. It was a London play that had played briefly in New York, unsuccessfully, and they wanted me to do something with it. I made it into an American story, with Eddie [Edward G.] Robinson playing the doctor and [Humphrey] Bogart playing one of the heavies. It was very successful. And that's when I got together with Anatole Litvak, the director.

I worked on that at first alone. Robert Lord was the producer, a very nice guy. While I was working I became very friendly with Johnny [John] Huston, who couldn't seem to get himself established. Johnny wasn't trusted by the studios. He was a writer, a rebel, an iconoclast who hung around with lefties and the Guild. I loved him and his father, Walter, whom I knew very well as a stage actor. We would see each other at our homes. We'd see each other two or three times a week socially, play tennis, meet with the same people.

One day Bob Lord said, "We ought to do something for Johnny. Would you mind putting him with you on *Clitterhouse?*" I was about halfway through the script, but I said, "By all means." It was more fun that way, and I wasn't concerned with getting sole credit. So John and I started working together. That's his first major credit.

We divided the remaining scenes. We very rarely wrote at the same desk. We didn't quite know the ending as we worked. The play had an ending, but I invented a trial at the end of the film and a bewildered jury—was Clitterhouse sane or insane? People would leave the theater with that humorous question in their minds. Johnny would help with a scene, or the dialogue within a scene; then we'd get together and make it uniform.

What was he like as a writer?

Johnny was very verbal. But he wrote strange, jarring phrases, things the character never would say. I liked a lot of it, but it didn't belong. We were dealing with how gangsters would speak and also with a psychologist who joins the gang—he becomes enmeshed and lives a double life—and it never sounded like gangsters or a doctor; it sounded like Johnny Huston. It wasn't anything great one way or another, but we always had to go back and fix what he did. I had to be awfully discreet about it with Bob Lord. That lesson may have helped Johnny later; he didn't do that kind of writing when he did *The Maltese Falcon*. I may, in fact, have introduced him to Dash [Dashiell] Hammett. I was very friendly with Dash.

One thing I remember well. Johnny was going to direct. I always objected to the constant movement of the camera, which I attributed to the anxiety of a director who didn't have confidence in the material, so he always had to give the actors business to do. You see this constantly in films. I'd say, "Here's a great scene. Why the hell don't they nail the camera down? Let them talk. These are good actors." He'd say, "I'll do it someday," and he did it. He had a scene in *The Maltese Falcon* that ran thirteen minutes, and he didn't move the camera.

Did you write expressly for the Warners stars?

Usually. Sometimes I got involved in casting the other parts. I loved George Bancroft's performance in [the suspenseful 1929 film] *The Wolf of Wall Street* long before I was writing in Hollywood. I cast that part. It was not one out of the book. There was always at the studios the same fellow who played the fellow at the diner or the taxi driver—always the same actor, always the same. I asked, "Why not a fresh face?" They said, "For many reasons. One, this guy won't miss his lines." I said, "But everybody knows he's an actor." They lived in a world of films. Their ideas were taken from other films they had seen that week or the week before at Grauman's Chinese [Theatre].

People like Bogart and Robinson, did they involve themselves in the scripts?

Eddie was very trusting. On the radio, Eddie played the editor of a paper in *Big Town*, with Claire Trevor. They were getting five or six thousand dollars to do that show, every week, for a big prestige advertising agency. I did three of them while I was under contract to Warners, in 1938 or 1939. I still have the scripts. I'd get two thousand dollars apiece for them. It was moonlighting but on a technicality, because I could have written them late at night or on Sunday. Nobody ever argued about it, and Eddie was too important to argue.

What was it like at Warner Brothers?

It was an exciting time politically—the Spanish Civil War and so on. There was a lot of ferment in people's homes, sponsored by one organization or another. When people like Vittorio Mussolini, an important Italian Fascist,* were invited to Hollywood and escorted through the studios, we refused to let him on the set. When Julio Álvarez del Vayo, a Spanish government minister,† came to Hollywood to raise interest in and funds for the embattled Loyalists, we invited him to the writers' table. Bette Davis, Henry Fonda, Jimmy Cagney, and others were all for him.

But the studio executives, Jack Warner and Hal Wallis, were against anything progressive. Hal Wallis was a cold icicle, impenetrable, smart, and it

---

*Vittorio Mussolini, son of the Italian Fascist dictator, Benito Mussolini, had a position of great power in the Italian film industry. For an account of the Fascist period, see "Italy" in Ephraim Katz, *The Film Encyclopedia*; Vernon Jarratt, *The Italian Cinema*; and Pierre Leprohon, *The Italian Cinema*.

†Julio Álvarez del Vayo, a minister in the Spanish Loyalist government and later a member of the editorial board of the *Nation*, remained a prominent human-rights commentator for decades. His autobiography, *Give Me Combat*, recounts a life spent mostly on the left.

was very difficult to feel any sympathy or rapport with him. He oversaw. Jack Warner was a clown. The progressive tradition came from the producers. Zanuck had been at Warners and then left. Robert Lord and others kept up the tradition. Another one was Milton Sperling, a nice guy who was married to Harry Warner's daughter Betty.

So you didn't like Jack Warner?

No, I liked him. He was a vaudevillian. I had an argument with him about costs on *Clitterhouse*. I had a scene where the gang of thieves rob a building to get some minks, and Eddie goes with them. Bogart tries to kill Eddie, locks him in a cold-storage vault. Bogart thinks he's dead; fortunately, Eddie gets out. We wanted a surprise ending to the sequence. It's a decisive sequence, because next Eddie goes after Bogart. Because I was from New York, I knew that there are elevators that come up on every sidewalk. So in this scene the cops would be standing around, and the top cop would say something like "He must be hiding somewhere." The sidewalk opens up, and Eddie comes up in the elevator, debonair, right in the middle of the cops. Eddie says, "No one down there," lights a cigar, walks off. It would get a big laugh.

But I got a note from Jack Warner saying, "We don't have these elevators [on the lot]. We'd have to dig a hole and get a crank to bring him up. It would cost too much." We were already shooting. I called him up and said, "What kind of a peanut brain are you? Fourteen hundred dollars is all it would cost. I'll pay it myself." That changed his mind. I called Lord and said, "Deduct it from my salary." Lord said, "I'll pay half." Warner finally paid. But that was how he was.

Later, my experience with Warner during the CSU [Conference of Studio Unions] strike was funny. I met him that day after a lot of fighting took place—in a steam bath, by chance. He said, "I saw you on that goddamn picket line. Stop striking. Fuck off!" He was angry. I was just a yapping dog annoying him. He never knew what to make of me or of writers in general. Writers were dangerous characters to him—people who took blank pieces of paper and did something with them. It was a mysterious process to him.

You ended up working almost exclusively with Anatole Litvak at Warners for a while.

Four or five pictures, and we became very warm personally. He would tell me all about his problems with women. He had a place in or near Malibu, and we preferred to work at his place. Warners would say, "Why didn't you come into the studio today?" I'd say, "Oh, I was with Litvak." They'd say, "Swimming, eh?" We actually finished more scenes there and also worked into the night; we didn't watch the hours. But they'd say, "You have to come into the studio and check in." I'd say, "Why?" They'd say, "Because all the other writers will want to do the same." I'd say, "So fire me." I had to do what they said in the beginning, but then they relented after we got a couple of box-office successes.

It sounds like you were always fighting rear-guard actions against, if not the right wing, then the studio itself.

On *Confessions of a Nazi Spy* we had big problems with the German embassy and consulate and the German-American Bund. We had diplomatic relations with Germany, and therefore Germany was a friendly country, even though it was riding roughshod over Europe. Then Martin Dies, who started the House Un-American Activities Committee—it was called the Dies Committee then—moved in. He came to Warner Brothers to try to change *Confessions of a Nazi Spy* so that it would include anti-Communists as well as anti-Nazis. But the Communists had not done any espionage, so we couldn't include them—besides which, we were dealing with an actual case.

Did you actually see Martin Dies in Jack Warner's office?

Yes. I saw Dies going out of Warner's office as I went in through an anteroom. I told Warner, "I saw Dies going out of here. Are you knuckling under to that pipsqueak congressman from Texas?" He said, "Oh, I told him off. But if you could work in something about the pinkos." I said, "No, no, no." He said, "Well, you ask the director and producer and see what they say." They said no just as flatly as I did, and that satisfied him. In any case, the picture was very successful at the time.

You left Warner Brothers and went back East for a while; then you came back to Hollywood yet again. Tell us about working with Bertolt Brecht.

Let me tell you about the film we worked on. I was called by Fritz Lang, a European director who settled in Hollywood after Hitler took over—he did *M* and other famous pictures—and asked if I would like to come out to Hollywood and work on an original idea that he and Brecht had concocted. This was in 1942, just after Pearl Harbor. Bert Brecht—Bertolt Brecht, full name—was in this country as an enemy alien. He was a German. He had arrived from Asia, maybe Shanghai, having left Germany through Denmark and then traveled through the USSR and made the journey across Siberia and so on. He had come here in 1941. In any case, he had to be at his home in Santa Monica between dusk and dawn. He was politely interned. And that's where he had his entourage—his wife, his secretary, and his friends. Everybody had to come to him, because he couldn't go out nights.

What happened was that he and Fritz Lang had an original idea on one or two sheets of paper about the assassination of the famous "hangman" [Reinhard] Heydrich, the *gauleiter* of Czechoslovakia, whom Hitler had installed there. As you may know, Heydrich was assassinated about that time, in 1942. To Lang, I was kind of an expert politically. I had written *Confessions of a Nazi Spy*, and I had done another film dealing with Fascism [*Footsteps in the Dark*, 1940]. I could also speak German or at least understand it. That was helpful, because Brecht couldn't speak English.

How did you collaborate with Brecht, then?

Well, Brecht never worked on the screenplay. He only worked with Lang and myself in developing the original story. Mostly I went over to his house, and we'd play chess. Hanns Eisler, the famous composer, wrote the music for the film, and he would come by and play some tunes for the picture, and I would make up lyrics for the tunes, hoping they would be used by him, but very few were. Brecht loved to hear me read the screenplay scenes out loud, you know. When he'd hear that Lang had cut something out of the story, he would become furious. He'd call him names: "Lang has gone Hollywood; he is commercial," and so on, which was true. Lang cottoned to the producers. In any event, Brecht, like many of the German refugees, had disdain for American writers or directors, and whenever he wanted to dismiss somebody, he'd say, "They've gone Hollywood." But he cottoned to me because he could talk to me in German. And we played a fair game of chess together.

You told us he was a sort of megalomaniac.

This is a postmortem characterization of him. He was tremendously egocentric and loved to be the center of attention, and various composers and writers—Thomas Mann, Lion Feuchtwanger, Franz Werfel, and other greats of German literature—would come to his house to see him. He loved to be the center of this attention, like a monarch with his courtiers.

Sometimes I would take him to a barbershop during the daytime to get a haircut. He would get the haircut, and they would still be working on me, and then I'd see him go over to the mirror and take a comb and carefully comb his forelock forward to look like Julius Caesar or like Napoleon. It was unusual. And then he wore this tunic, very much like a Nehru jacket or a Chou En-lai jacket, which he had brought from China. This made him look a little bit military, maybe like a commissar. He liked that look.

He had this secretary [Ruth Berlau], who was a mistress, living in the same house with him and his wife, Helene Weigel, who had been a well-known actress. If I spoke nicely to this younger woman, who was much more attractive than his wife, I would get these icy stares from Helene Weigel, and then Brecht would have to try to sugar up the situation a little bit somehow. We never knew what kind of a ménage à trois it was or what was going on, how many bedrooms they had.

Eventually, he went after equal screenplay credit, right?

After the picture was done and the credits were awarded [by the producer], I was asked if I wanted to come in on the original story, and I said, "No, let the boys [Brecht and Lang] have that, and I'll just have the solo screenplay." Well, Brecht raised a fuss about it and told me, "I really don't want the screenplay credit, John, but my agent tells me it'll help me get work." I told him that the Screen Writers Guild was formed to prevent this type of situation, where producers put their nephews and cousins or whoever they could think of on the credits. We had set up the credit-arbitration panel, and it was really the most important function of the Guild, to protect the credits. I said, "You can't come in for a free ride." He said, "Well, in Germany, we did things this way." I said, "Well, we don't do things that way here." He went ahead, nevertheless, to present his case. There was a three-man panel, and they voted unanimously that he would have no screenplay credit, and they even bawled him out for bringing up the issue and wasting their time.

We made up and remained friendly, and later he appeared before the House Un-American Activities Committee, after the war. There the official record will read that they asked him, point-blank, "Did you write the screenplay on *Hangmen Also Die?*" and he said, "No, absolutely not." Then he left the country. Subsequently, I met him in Zurich, Switzerland, and we had a little bit to eat and drink, and we laughed about it.

You worked on another famous World War II film, or maybe we should say infamous. At what stage did you get involved with Song of Russia?

After [Paul] Jarrico and the informer Richard Collins. I was working with [Zoltan] Korda on the island of Malta, doing a documentary about the terrific fight they put up against the Italians. Joe Pasternak, a very nice guy, asked to borrow me to help with *Song of Russia.* I remember L. B. saying, "Each studio is asked to make some kind of contribution to the war. This is a very reluctant contribution."

I was trying to touch it up and was there as a mollifier or pacifier—a diplomat—toward Robert Taylor, who was a very strong reactionary. He hated anything that had to do with the Soviet Union, and they kept trying to tell him it was his contribution to the war effort. For some reason, he respected me and wouldn't talk to the other two writers. I had never met him before. But now I would go to his dressing room or have lunch with him, and he would say, "I hate this line," and I would say, "How would you like it changed?" Actually, I changed very little. But the act of changing seemed to satisfy him. That was part of my job—four weeks on the set keeping him happy. [Laughs.] One scene I remember trying to fix, and the studio said, "Take out the word 'community.' It sounds like 'Communism.' " So I changed it. Then, in the scene on the farm before the invasion, I used the word "collective." They said, "We don't want any collective." I said, "What will you settle for?" They said, "Community." [Laughs.]

Taylor was a conductor somehow finding himself in Russia as the war breaks out. There was a beautiful Russian girl, played by a contract player [Susan Peters], who in fleeing the scorched earth dares to get dirt on her face. I remember when Mayer saw the rushes. I was there with Joe Pasternak. Mayer screamed at me. "The heroine! In all the pictures we have ever made the heroines never have any dirt on their faces! I won't have my lead actress shown with dirt on her face, and by the way, her hair should be dressed properly!" I said, "Your heroine is running through bombs. How can she look like she just came from the hairdresser?" He took me outside and said, "Look,

I built this studio on this policy. So don't tell me what to do. You're only a writer." That was MGM. Edicts came down from on high.

Tell us about writing Cornered. *Edward Dmytryk cited his experience there as a negative example of Communist influence on films after he got out of prison, switched positions, and named names in front of the Committee. He said you were trying to persuade him to put more content into the film he was making and that you took him to a meeting at which he was criticized by two or three screenwriters who later turned out to be Communists.*

No, no. You have the story almost right. I was trying to prevent him from taking *out* the content. I had done a lot of research on the story in Washington. [Juan] Perón was then dictator of Argentina. Cordell Hull had written an official white paper about the guilt of Argentina—the criminal acts, the anti-U.S. acts. Argentina was harboring German U-boats which were sinking American ships and killing Merchant Marines by the hundreds. The U-boats were being fed information from Buenos Aires. I wanted to show the operations of the secret police, which Perón, a fan of Mussolini, had trained. Later Argentina became a haven for escaped Nazis, and they're still down there.

Dick Powell, in the story, is trying to find the collaborator who helped in the killing of his wife, who was in the Resistance in France. Dmytryk wanted to take out some of the scenes. He called them "propaganda"—subsequently, not then. I think it was Adrian Scott, the producer, later one of the Hollywood Ten, who was very embarrassed about the whole affair. He was working under great pressure and ashamed of what was going on, with Dmytryk trying to take the content out before shooting his picture. It was in the trades, so it was in public print, that Dmytryk had gone to Buenos Aires, preparatory to shooting the picture, to get the government's approval of the script. That's like going to Hitler to get approval of an anti-Hitler story. [Laughs.] Dmytryk said he went down there for background shots, but I believe he went down there for their approval.

I gave the script to [Albert] Maltz, a colleague who was politically minded and who would know what we were talking about. Adrian Scott was in on the meeting, and there may have been a third writer. But it had nothing to do with any Party approval or getting consent from Moscow. It was to say to Dmytryk, "This is a more exciting story than if you take out the juice, if you want to use that word, the substance of it. Otherwise, it'll just be a melodrama." And that's what he turned it into. Now little bits and pieces of my ideas remained; he couldn't take out everything. So it still became a fairly good picture.

Why do you think so many people in Hollywood joined the Communist Party?

Several I knew very well joined because it built up their own feeling of ego. They felt more in the swim. To give you an idea of the opportunist nature of it, let's talk about Bob Rossen, who certainly didn't gain any jobs or assignments from being in the Party. His wife, Susie, was a very decent person. She was the real "lefty," you know, and that may have spurred his joining a little bit, too. I remember that we were sitting at one of these big meetings at the Philharmonic, while Olivia de Havilland and others were addressing the audience and making a pitch for money to help the anti-Fascist refugees from Spain and so on. They called for pledges, and Rossen would say, "A thousand dollars." So the guy on the stage would say, "A thousand dollars from Robert Rossen!" When they came through the aisles, I would write a check and drop fifty bucks in. He'd say to me, "You're crazy. Why don't you say a hundred, five hundred, a thousand? You don't have to pay it. I never pay it." And it was true. He told that to the House Committee when he testified, because they asked about all these pledges and contributions and he said, "I never gave a cent, you know." [Laughs.]

Let's talk about the book you wrote about the Rosenbergs, after you were named in the hearings and left Hollywood. Can you tell us how the climate in Hollywood during the HUAC hearings led up to the Rosenbergs' predicament?

Well, we had the hearings from 1947 on. Their arrest was in 1950. It was the height of McCarthyism, although McCarthy himself wasn't so prominent until he waved that list around. People were running helter-skelter, trying to duck subpoenas. The climate of fear was tremendous. It was daily. The Communists had stolen the atomic bomb from America, in some way. They were *muzhiks;* they weren't capable of making their own bomb—they had to steal it from us. There were headlines in the papers every day: Larry Parks pleading with the Committee not to make him crawl through the mud, Parks giving names. Even a wonderful actor like Sterling Hayden was weakened at that point; later he wrote a memoir telling about his shame—he was one of those who really tried to undo the mischief. It was endless, the number of people who would become blacklisted.

It wasn't only actors and writers and directors. It was teachers all over America. There were union leaders kicked out of unions. At the aircraft plants near Hollywood they would call a guy a Commie and beat him up. In Texas they made the punishment the death penalty—you can look this up if you like—for members of the Party. There was a woman who had a child and divorced her husband; the husband put in a custody claim, and the judge gave him the child because the woman had been against the Korean War. And so on. This was the atmosphere. It was really lunatic, and approaching a police state.

The original Hollywood Ten took a stand against cooperation and informing. Do you think that in some way the subsequent waves of informers paved the way for something as dreadful as the execution of the Rosenbergs?

Yes. I think anybody who cooperated—that is the word they used—with the Committee extended its life and gave it reason for being. Had everyone refused to deal with the Committee, it wouldn't have lasted. It wouldn't have gotten the appropriations. But they had enough people who weakened and fell apart, for many reasons. Wanting to work was one; I saw a lot of that, first hand, with guys I'd gone to school with, like Bob Rossen. They had tasted power as directors and saw a lost world for themselves if they didn't work. Some had gone to England—like Edward Dmytryk—and bummed around and gotten little jobs. But when Dmytryk got out of jail—he was remarried, to a young woman [actress Jean Porter], and they had a baby—one of his motivations was to continue to work. It was not that he changed his principles. They made him what Whittaker Chambers, in his book, *Witness*, called "a running hound for a bone." They can do whatever they like with you, once you have informed. So they trotted him around to American Legion meetings and other places where he would talk about the evils of Communism, Socialism, and the fifth column. Some of the worst aspects of anti-Communist hooliganism came out during that period: "Fry the Rosenbergs! Sizzle them! Tear them down! Hang them up!"

Was the Rosenberg case the low point of the 1950s, from your perspective?

Let's call it the high point of the McCarthy era, in another sense. The government had moved from arrests and jailings and so forth into charges of conspiracy—actual charges of conspiracy—to commit espionage. They couldn't prove espionage; they had no evidence like that—it had to be hearsay. In a state court such hearsay would have been thrown out. But according to the archaic federal law, they could use hearsay testimony. The brother-in-law [David Greenglass]* could say, "My brother-in-law, Julius Rosenberg, told me this." Or, "I went with Julius in his automobile and . . ." But you didn't have to submit actual evidence. That is why the charge was conspiracy to commit espionage, which carried the death penalty.

The Rosenbergs were arrested, you see, within a week after the Korean War broke out, so it was a question of coupling the death penalty with our boys being killed in Korea. When [Judge] Irving Kaufman—who was later promoted to the Circuit Court—sentenced them, he used that argument. "You have been responsible," he said to the Rosenbergs at their sentencing, "for the deaths of fifty thousand soldiers in Korea." He placed the blame for their deaths on this involved thought process—the Russians had the atomic bomb; therefore they could be bold enough to help the Koreans make war.

The period between their trial and their executions took three good years, from 1950 to 1953. I was in Mexico City when the case started. The country was alert to this impending execution, the first in our history on such a charge. The whole case dealt with this fearful subject of having the secret of the atomic bomb stolen from us and given to—in quotes—"our enemy" to use against us. There were thousands, eventually hundreds of thousands and millions, all over this country and the world, who held meetings, in the Place

---

*Ethel Rosenberg's brother, David Greenglass, with his testimony corroborated by his wife, Ruth, was a principal prosecution witness in the "atom spy" trial of the Rosenbergs.

de la Concorde, in Trafalgar Square, in the Plaza de Mexico—all over the world. The pope at that time [Pius XII] sent special messages to the presidents, Truman and then later Eisenhower, not to execute them. The Chamber of Deputies in France voted almost unanimously, I think, pleading not to execute them. The Houses of Parliament in London sent appeals. Bertrand Russell, Albert Einstein, Harold C. Urey, a Nobel Prize winner—an avalanche of people all over the world got involved.

Did their supporters feel despair when they were executed?

I was at a mass meeting on the night of the executions, in Union Square, and there were ten to twenty thousand people packed into the street running from Union Square to Fifth Avenue. You couldn't move between people, the street was so packed. And when somebody came up on this truck with loudspeakers and said, "It's happened" there was a groan that went through that crowd, and it was frightening, chilling.

The Rosenbergs prompted a remarkable turn in your work. You changed from a playwright and screenwriter into an investigative reporter to look into the evidence of the case.

Generally, the American public was misinformed. I thought I'd retrace the steps of the principal witnesses, and chief among them was this weird character called Harry Gold. He was the one who was supposed to have been appointed by the Soviet consulate. An official at the Soviet consulate, his mentor, was the one who supposedly told him to go to Albuquerque and meet with this soldier, David Greenglass. Greenglass was the brother-in-law of Julius Rosenberg, who had been instructed to give secrets to an intermediary who would come to him. It was a very melodramatic setup.

I wanted to know if Harry Gold had really gone there. Harry Gold had sworn in his testimony in court that he had taken the Santa Fe *Chief* to Chicago, and from there he had gone on to New York to meet with the Soviet official to deliver the secrets. This was a key part of the case, because here he was, delivering the most important secrets in the world. Did he go there or not, as he said? He said he almost didn't make it. He said he had to meet the Soviet official at ten in the evening in a certain place on Long Island.

His entire story, to me, was very suspect. Since he was the strongest link in the chain of evidence, I thought if you could break that link, then you'd weaken the case. So I went to the station in Chicago, and I asked the stationmaster to give me a schedule of the trains coming and going in that particular year and date. He went through the safe there for me, and what impelled him a little bit to help me was that I was a writer who had worked in Hollywood. The first question he asked me was, "Did you ever meet Bette Davis?" I told him that I had, that she was at the studio the same time as me. Then, "Did you ever talk with her? Did you ever shake hands with her?" I said yes. He took my hand and said, "I want to shake your hand." [Laughs.]

He wanted contact with Bette Davis this way, through a surrogate. I also told him I'd written a picture for Hank [Henry] Fonda, *The Long Night.* That helped, too. Hank Fonda was a hero for this stationmaster.

Anyway, the schedule revealed that if you took the time of departure that Gold claimed to have made on this train to Chicago and compared it with the train that he had to meet there to go to New York, he never could have done it. They didn't jell, these times of departure and arrival. So I had him on this. Later, in a Senate investigation of this particular detail, they gave Harry Gold my book to study, and they questioned him directly about the discrepancy. He said, "Oh, that's right. I didn't continue by train" because he couldn't have made the connection. He said, "Wexley was right. I ran to the Chicago airport and got an immediate plane to go to Washington, arrived in Washington, ran to Union Station, took a train to New York from Washington, took a subway to Long Island" and so on. All of which was impossible. I later covered how that was concocted in a foreword to the updated version of my book.*

How did your experience in Hollywood help you in unraveling the Rosenberg story?

When I read the court record, I became more and more fascinated with the case and the evidence. I began to say to myself, "The story is full of holes, big holes and little holes. It doesn't jell." There were big holes, like the train schedule, which showed he could never have made this trip, and little holes, like the entire business with the Hotel Hilton card, which I later exposed as an outright forgery done retroactively by the prosecution or possibly by agents of the FBI. Studying the case, I was reminded of story conferences we'd have at different studios when we were kicking around a story. I always prided myself on not having these bloopers where a thing couldn't have taken place because it fell on the wrong day or whatever. So that probably led to my wanting to retrace the steps of the witnesses and write the book.

It was obvious that Harry Gold was trying to concoct a Hollywood-like spy atmosphere in his story. For example, he claimed that when he went to see this David Greenglass, the soldier, to get the secrets, he had to walk up a flight of very steep, dark stairs to this bedroom apartment in a lodging-house where Greenglass lived with his wife when he was off-duty from Los Alamos. Well, it was not a steep, dark flight of stairs. It was an open little staircase, a mild, gentle climb. So his story had the elements of a bad B picture, not even a good one. And there were so many holes in it that I hardly knew where to begin.

---

*The original edition of *The Judgment of Julius and Ethel Rosenberg,* by John Wexley, with a jacket designed by Rockwell Kent, was published in June 1955 by Cameron and Kahn in New York. The paperback edition, to which Wexley refers, included his updated foreword and was issued by Ballantine Books in 1977.

Whether we are talking about one of your plays, films, or books, what would you say is the common theme that runs through all of your work?

Thinking back on it—when you're doing it, you don't think of it that way—I see it wrapped up in the word "justice." Whatever I wrote, I was concerned with the theme of justice. That has always concerned me. It may have been a biblical influence. There were two words, you know, that were given to Abraham, "justice" and "kindness."

This found expression in *The Last Mile*, dealing with capital punishment and treating people like animals in a cage, and then *They Shall Not Die*, which was clearly a case of injustice. A good many of my films had that theme: *Confessions of a Nazi Spy; Hangmen Also Die*, which dealt with the Resistance and the underground movement against Heydrich, "the hangman"; *The Long Night*; and even *Angels with Dirty Faces*, with Cagney and Bogart, had something of that theme. And so on down to the Rosenberg case, where the lives of two young people, the parents of two children, were at stake. There, too, "justice" was the key word.

Julian Zimet
(aka Julian Halevy)

JULIAN ZIMET, Rome, Italy, 1985

BY JULIAN (HALEVY) ZIMET

JULIAN (HALEVY) ZIMET
(1919–   )

AS JULIAN ZIMET
1941 *The Devil Pays Off.* Coscript.
1942 *Sierra Sue.* Coscript.
1946 *Helldorado.* Story, coscript.
1947 *Saigon.* Story.
1948 *The Strawberry Roan.* Story.

AS NINA AND HERMAN SCHNEIDER
1956 *The Naked Dawn/Le bandit.* Coscript.

AS JULIAN HALEVY
1958 *The Case Against Brooklyn.* Coscript.
1964 *Psyche '59.* Script.
Circus World. Coscript.
The Young Lovers. Based on his novel.
1965 *Crack in the World.* Coscript.
1967 *Custer of the West.* Coscript.
1969 *A Place for Lovers.* Coscript.
1972 *Pancho Villa.* Script.
Horror Express. Coscript.
Bad Man's River. Uncredited contribution.

WRITER JULIAN ZIMET left Hollywood during the blacklist and adopted the nom de plume Julian Halevy to keep working on movies produced in Mexico, Europe, and America. Occasionally he used other "fronts," including, for the screenplay of *The Naked Dawn*—a 1956 noir western directed by Edgar G. Ulmer—the names of his sister and brother-in-law.

A friend since boyhood of Bernard Gordon, Zimet has taken many of the same paths in life. Enthralled by movies, he and Gordon belonged to the photography club at De Witt Clinton High School in the Bronx. Both attended City College, where they operated a film society and made sixteen-millimeter amateur films. After diverse apprenticeships—working on Willard Van Dyke and Ralph Steiner's documentary *The City*, filming a project for the International Ladies Garment Workers Union, serving as jacks-of-all-trades behind the camera on Yiddish and African-American films—both went to Hollywood.

Zimet came first, arriving for an interview in late 1939 and then returning for a job as a reader at Republic in January 1940. Republic was one of the lowest rungs on the Hollywood ladder and the last stop for agents trying to sell story material. "My job as a reader was to read books, plays, and original stories submitted by agents and to write summaries of them that were circulated, along with a critical comment, among producers and studio executives," said Zimet. "It took me a while to catch on to the studio's needs, which were for stories suitable for westerns and folksy comedies for country-music singers, pictures that never played in New York City. I had never seen films of that kind and didn't realize that they formed the bread-and-butter product of the studio."

Most readers were ambitious to become writers, and Zimet was no different. He managed to scrounge a credit or two—he is not the only blacklistee to list Gene Autry and Roy Rogers westerns on his résumé—and was soon joined by Bernard Gordon, who found his niche as a reader at Paramount.

Drafted by the Army at the onset of World War II, Zimet served in the Signal Corps and administered a program in filmmaking, using a how-to pamphlet he had written with Gordon in college for use in their film-society showings. Later, posted to Fort Astoria, he collected and edited footage on war operations in the Middle East, Lend-Lease aid to the Soviet Union, and the Allied landing at Anzio. He helped compile newsreels of the liberated concentration camps, the dropping of the first atomic bombs, and the Japanese surrender.

Back in Hollywood in January 1946, he found himself an assistant to a producer of Roy Rogers westerns, which were substituting for the Gene Autry series (Autry had left Republic). Zimet also joined the Communist Party. Among the reasons for this he cites the political lessons of the Great Depression, the lynchings and discrimination in America, the anti-Fascist struggle by the Communists in Germany, Italy, and Spain, and the sacrifice of millions of Soviet lives in the Allied cause during World War II. "I was not blind to the evils of Soviet rule," Zimet said. "Even as a student I had attended meetings of the 'Communist loyal opposition' that was opposing Stalinist dictatorship. Arthur Koestler's *Darkness at Noon*, a novel about the show trials in Russia before the war, made a strong impression on me, although it was not until many years later that Khrushchev's revelations opened my eyes to the full horrors of Stalin's regime. Nevertheless, in 1946, the Communist Party of the United States seemed the organization offering the only possibility for working for the ideals and causes in which I believed."

After writing one Roy Rogers western, he left Republic and free-lanced as a scenarist in the postwar years. Among his credits is the story for *Saigon*, a 1947 Paramount film starring Alan Ladd and Veronica Lake. After the initial HUAC hearings, in October 1947, Bernard Gordon was fired from his job at Paramount, and so the two friends became a writing team, working on various projects at different studios while making slow progress in the screenwriting profession.

The Cold War was building. When the Hollywood leadership of the Communist Party decided that members who were in analysis or therapy had to take a leave of absence, Zimet ceased direct association with the organization. One of his continued political activities was as chairman of the program committee of the Hollywood Independent Citizens Committee of the Arts, Sciences, and Professions, which attracted a wide constituency of professionals, university people, and intellectuals from other fields as well as film and media.

In this capacity Zimet initiated a series of readings of Broadway productions that had not reached Los Angeles. One was a play by Dalton Trumbo that was set in an undertaking establishment. Another program he administered was a series of film screenings held in a movie theater on Fairfax Avenue, including the first documentary about the German occupation of Czechoslovakia and the first uncensored footage of the concentration camps to reach Los Angeles, made shortly after the liberation of Poland. "These were movies that in their rendering of reality put Hollywood to shame," recalled Zimet. "They were startling eye-openers for our audiences, which included many people from the local movie industry."

By early 1950 it was clear that the Hollywood Ten, friends of long standing, were headed for jail. Other friends who had been Communist Party members were planning to go "underground." While they were working at Warner Brothers, Zimet and Gordon read a front-page story in the local

Hearst paper, the *Los Angeles Examiner*, claiming that the police had discovered a Communist plot to poison the city's water supply. Was this the long-anticipated government ruse to justify a crackdown? They both decided to leave America, although Gordon stayed in Mexico only briefly before returning to Hollywood to eke out a living, first working at "day jobs" and later writing films under pseudonyms.

Zimet left New York in September 1950 on a French passenger liner bound for Le Havre. For a year he moved around Europe, and then he headed for Mexico, where he lived from 1951 to 1958 among other political exiles. A brief attempt to crack the blacklist in Hollywood didn't succeed, and he wound up in back in Europe, working—often with Bernard Gordon—as part of producer and writer Philip Yordan's "film factory" and for other European filmmakers. Later he took a job traveling around Africa, Asia, and the Middle East for the Food and Agricultural Organization of the United Nations, writing and producing films and teaching young people how to make films and audiovisual teaching aids. For almost forty years he has lived in Rome with his wife, Anna-Maria, the sister of author Primo Levi.

Asked whether he would agree to be interviewed for this book, Zimet wrote that he was not at ease in the question-and-answer format, which "tends to shift the focus of the reader's mind from the person being interviewed to the person doing the questioning." Zimet decided, instead, to write an autobiographical letter, which after several months of correspondence grew to a couple of hundred pages. This excerpt describes the years he spent in Mexico and his brief, eventful return to Hollywood in 1958.

■

I arrived in Mexico City in a yellow Ford convertible on October 12, 1951, having driven from New York and made leisurely stops to visit friends in Washington, Nashville, and Louisiana. The anti-Communist crusade was gathering momentum in the United States, and I was anxious to avoid being summoned to appear before the House Un-American Activities Committee and risk going to prison, along with the Hollywood Ten. Of the Ten—who had already served prison sentences for "contempt of Congress," punishment for refusing to name the people with whom they had been associated in political activity—several had moved to Mexico, along with others escaping persecution for their political activities.

In those years and earlier, Mexico was a place of refuge for political exiles. Refugees from Franco, Hitler, and Stalin were welcomed, and many stayed on after it became possible for them to return to Europe. Trotsky had made his home in San Ángel, a suburb of Mexico City, and had directed a worldwide anti-Stalin campaign from there until his death at the hands of an assassin in 1940.

In the early fifties the refugees in Mexico were Americans. Schoolteachers, doctors, writers, journalists, businessmen, college professors, and government employees dismissed for political reasons, and Communist Party members and functionaries, were members of the community that I was about to join. Some of them were well-known, such as Frederick Vanderbilt Field, who went to prison in 1951 for refusing to reveal to a federal judge the names of contributors to a bail fund for eleven Communist leaders convicted under the Smith Act, and Martha Dodd, daughter of Ambassador William E. Dodd, Roosevelt's man in Berlin from 1933 through 1937.* The Hollywood contingent included Albert Maltz, Dalton Trumbo, Gordon Kahn, Hugo and Jean Butler, and John Bright, a group whose screenwriting credits covered many of the best and most important films that came out of Hollywood both before and after the blacklist.

I remember the date of my arrival, because it was a holiday, Día de la Raza, celebrating Columbus's "discovery" of the New World, and I was struck by the irony of the largely Indian population enjoying a fiesta commemorating an event that began their colonization and enslavement.

My car was loaded with luggage. I was planning to stay in Mexico for a long time—my stay lasted seven years—and I brought with me clothes, books, a typewriter, tennis rackets, and a few cooking utensils of a kind I would be unlikely to find in a "developing country." One box contained a collection of fifty records of African tribal music that I had been asked to bring from the Musée de l'Homme in Paris, an anthropological museum, for an American composer in Mexico, Conlon Nancarrow, a close friend of Bob Allen, a friend from my time in the Army who had invited me to stay with him and his family in Mexico.

Allen's inviting me to stay at his home was not without risk for him. He was a correspondent for the Associated Press, the worldwide news service, and that organization was subject to pressures from the State Department and, in Mexico City, from the American Embassy. Briefing me about the "do's and don'ts" I was advised to follow in the way I was to go about getting settled in Mexico City, Allen said that, as he would be publicly responsible for my behavior, it would be wise for me to avoid joining the tightly knit community of Hollywood reds. In other words, it would be a favor to my host if I didn't bring to the attention of the embassy the fact that he was housing someone who was part of the Hollywood "red network."

Although I was eager to see Gordon Kahn, a friend with whom I had collaborated on articles and pamphlets supporting the Hollywood Ten, and Albert Maltz, who had been a regular tennis partner of mine in Hollywood, I didn't look them up right away. Kahn lived in Cuernavaca, so not seeing

---

*Frederick Vanderbilt Field, an heir to two famous fortunes, was in the same prison as Dashiell Hammett, one of the other four defendants in the Smith Act case. Field later wrote *From Right to Left: An Autobiography*. Martha Dodd edited *Ambassador Dodd's Diary*. Her own book *Through Embassy Eyes* records the experiences in Nazi Germany that led to her involvement in the anti-Fascist movement, while *The Searching Light* traces her later political development.

him didn't present a problem. Maltz, however, lived in San Ángel, close to Bob Allen's house, and the possibility of meeting him on the street and having to explain why I hadn't looked him up was of some concern.

Maltz had a rigid personality; he held himself and others to a strict code of behavior. I imagined—correctly, as it turned out—that his experience of having been in a federal prison for almost a year had made him sensitive, ready to take offense to any behavior that might suggest a snub. Privately, I resolved to find a way to meet or call on Maltz and pay my respects at the first opportunity.

George and Mary Oppen were the closest of friends, and we had been writing to each other during the year in which I had been in Europe and they in Mexico City. George and Mary had long histories in the Party. George came from a wealthy family, and in the early thirties he had published a book of poetry with an introduction by Ezra Pound. It was a vocation he abandoned at the onset of the Depression when he stopped writing poetry and devoted himself to work in the Communist Party, where he soon became a full-time organizer. Drafted into the Army, he was sent to France, where he drove an army truck through the countryside that he and Mary had toured in a horse-drawn wagon in the early years of their marriage.

After the war George and Mary settled down in Southern California, where they planned to raise a family. They gave up full-time political work but continued to be members of a Party chapter in Redondo Beach that George headed. When the crackdown on Communists in 1950 was accompanied by prison sentences for Party functionaries [under the Smith Act], George and Mary fled to Mexico with their daughter, an act for which George was expelled from the Party for "desertion."

Disillusioned about Communism and bored with the kind of artisan work he had been doing, George began writing poetry again in 1957, his first efforts after the long hiatus. Eventually, back in America, he wrote and published several books of poetry, for one of which he was awarded a Pulitzer Prize.* George and Mary are both dead. Their history reveals much about the role of intellectuals in the Communist Party and reflects light on my own saga.

I got in touch with the Oppens, and we arranged a meeting. They were understanding about the need for caution. Their ten-year-old daughter was not, however, and declared her intention to resume our friendship and get-togethers immediately. A compromise was arrived at; I saw the Oppen family at outings in the countryside, where we were not likely to be observed.

The effort to avoid making my presence known to the embassy proved, in the long run, to be futile. A year or two after my arrival in Mexico, a Mexican lawyer handling my application to the Mexican authorities for resident status advised me to provide him with my American passport as proof of identity.

---

*George Oppen (1908–1984) won the Pulitzer Prize for poetry in 1968 for his collection *Of Being Numerous*.

If I couldn't get a passport, he said, even the receipt from the embassy showing that I had paid a passport-application fee would suffice. My passport having expired, I duly applied for a new one at the embassy, where, after some delays, I was informed by an official that favorable consideration of my request depended on cooperating with him.

"What sort of cooperating do you have in mind?" I asked.

The official presented me with a list of names that included everyone I knew in the Hollywood community in Mexico and a number of others, all of whom were American left-wing refugees. "Tell us what you know about these people," he said. "It'll be confidential. Nobody outside the embassy will know that you've been talking to us."

I declined the offer. My application for a passport was "referred to Washington," and I understood that I was not to expect a reply. On a later visit, again at the urging of my lawyer, who was handling my case with chessboard moves, I applied again and this time asked for a receipt for the three-dollar application fee. I had given the official ten dollars. The official, a short, heavyset individual with a marked limp (typecasting for the role of a heavy), took seven dollars from a drawer and handed them to me.

"What about a receipt for the three dollars I paid?" I asked, following the instructions I had been given by my lawyer.

The official sneered and shook his head. "I'm not going to give it to you!"

At this point I was on my own; the lawyer hadn't foreseen a blunt refusal. I raised my voice and, as if preparing a legal case, recited, "Repeat that, please! 'I refuse to give you a receipt for the three dollars you paid as an application fee.' "

It was a bluff. If the official had repeated his refusal, I was resigned to accepting it and departing. What else could I do?

However, the bluff worked. Perhaps the official suspected that my request meant that a legal basis for a court case was being established, one that he preferred not to be involved in. In any case, he sat down at the typewriter and wrote out a receipt for three dollars paid for a passport application. A half-page of comment followed, the substance of which was a declaration that this document was not proof of my being an American citizen and did not imply a request that courtesies granted American citizens be extended to me. This document was duly signed and stamped and handed to me with ill grace. I thanked the official and left triumphantly.

"It's what I needed," my lawyer said when I showed the document to him. Some days later it was returned to me bearing Mexican stamps and signatures. Along with it I received the official residence permit allowing me to extend my residence in Mexico indefinitely.

But all this was yet to happen. I cite it now to illustrate the punitive measures adopted by the State Department toward people like myself and to explain why Bob Allen had been justified in his advice to me to avoid drawing attention to myself. The actions of the embassy clerk were part of the harassment suffered by American expatriates of our political breed and contributed to an attitude of suspicion that greeted my first attempts to make contact with my Hollywood friends.

During the first weeks after my arrival in Mexico, I applied myself to study, reading books on the history of Mexico and improving the Spanish that I had learned in school fifteen years before and never practiced. In the latter task, I had considerable help from Bob Allen's three children, who spoke no other language and who took charge of me as a new member of the family.

I had enough money in the bank to carry me for a year or more, but I would eventually have to find some way of making a living, and my study was largely directed toward preparing myself for that task.

The first notion that occurred to me in that department was that of making an educational film for Mexican farmers on hybrid corn. The yield of maize on the tiny plots cultivated by the majority of farmers would be considerably increased if, instead of planting native varieties, farmers took advantage of a program developed by the Rockefeller Foundation for educating farmers to use improved hybrid seed and more advanced methods of growing corn.

I contacted the foundation and presented myself along with a script for a film and a plan for eventually showing the film in isolated communities by using mobile projectors and truck-mounted generators. The people at the foundation liked the idea and the script. They agreed to finance the project, providing approval could be obtained from the Ministry of Agriculture. They were leery of doing anything that might reflect on the inadequacies of that department's functioning.

For a brief period I imagined myself in an admirable role, teacher and missionary. Soon enough, the reality of Mexico disillusioned me about the possibility of accomplishing anything progressive within the framework of society as it was then. Through friends I was able to get to see the minister of agriculture and explain what I and the Rockefeller Foundation had in mind to do. The minister heard me out and said that he wasn't interested in the project. "I'm in my last year in this job," he said. "I've got other things to do."

I explained that all we were asking for was permission to put the name of his ministry on the opening titles of the film. He and the ministry would be getting a free ride. It was useless. The minister wasn't interested. He suggested that I return the following year, when a new minister of agriculture would have taken office.

Through Bob Allen I became acquainted with an Englishman, Clive Smith, who had been in Spain during the Civil War and had been a soldier in the Republican forces. A few months after my arrival in Mexico I moved into a house that I shared with Clive Smith and his five-year-old daughter. He and his wife had divorced, and the daughter spent part of each week with her father.

Smith worked as the commercial attaché of the Canadian Embassy, but he was also a stringer for several publications and for Reuters. I did odd tasks for

Smith, covering for him when he was on holiday, and eventually I took over one of his jobs, that of reporting for *Oil World*, a trade magazine for the oil industry. Reporting for *Oil World* led to my submitting an article to the American publication the *Nation*, about the Mexican oil industry, which had been nationalized in the thirties. After the article appeared, the magazine published a letter from the Mexican ambassador to the United States praising the article for its truthful reporting. Actually, the article had been commissioned by *Oil World* but not printed; it was the policy of the magazine not to publish articles reporting favorably on an industry that had been nationalized at the expense of the multinational corporations. I wrote that article and other pieces for the *Nation* under the pseudonym Julian Halevy. In recognition of the *Nation* piece, the press office at *Petróleos Mexicanos*, in accordance with the local custom of paying for "favors," offered me part-time work translating into English the speeches of the government minister heading the oil industry, a welcome addition to my inadequate income.

During a visit to Cuernavaca, a semitropical city a few hours' drive from Mexico City, I paid a night-time call on my old friend Gordon Kahn, a blacklisted Hollywood screenwriter who was living there. The visit was a disaster. Kahn had been aware of my presence in Mexico and didn't believe my explanation for not having gotten in touch with him sooner. He suspected me of having become an informer for the American Embassy and as much as ordered me out of his house.

Kahn left Mexico soon after—having been cheated of his money by some unscrupulous business partners, a common occurrence in Mexico—and returned to the United States, where he died soon after of a heart attack. His son described him in an interview long after as having been, at the end, an angry, bitter man.

Kahn's suspicion of me spread through the local Hollywood community. A few weeks after the encounter in Cuernavaca, I took advantage of an opportunity to call on Albert Maltz, my former tennis partner, accompanying a doctor acquaintance who had made a call at my home and remarked that he was going on to Maltz's home in San Ángel for a routine house call. When we arrived, and the doctor's car was met by Maltz, I greeted him and extended my hand. He refused to take it. I was not welcome. There was no opportunity for me to explain why I had deferred visiting him.

Maltz's hostility toward those former Communists who had collaborated with the investigating Committee was violent and persisted until his death. In Hollywood, years later, it became a subject of controversy between him and Dalton Trumbo, who—despite having, like Maltz, gone to prison—had softened his attitude toward informers and, in a few cases, expressed understanding of and sympathy for them. Maltz wrote a number of sharply critical letters to Trumbo, letters that came with such frequency and intensity that Cleo Trumbo, defending her husband, who was stricken with cancer, began refusing to accept delivery of them.

Maltz's ill-considered treatment of me and his part in spreading the rumor that I was an informer for the Embassy was hurtful and, for a long time, made it difficult for me to renew old friendships and make new ones. It was only after three or four years, during which time I had written and published a novel that was considered by the left establishment to be meritoriously progressive, that Maltz reconsidered his hasty and ill-founded judgment. At a party that we both attended, he sought me out and apologized stiffly for his mistake.

A word about the novel, which I began writing not long after my arrival in Mexico. The enterprise was motivated in an odd way. I had finished reading J. D. Salinger's *Catcher in the Rye*, which I appreciated for its sensitive, tender treatment of the youth who is the book's central character, and I felt disappointment at that character's having ended up in a sanitarium with a nervous breakdown. It was a "dusty answer" that Salinger was giving to young people who identified with the protagonist and narrator of the novel, and I had an urge to write an "upbeat" resolution of the serious problems that were crippling our young hero.

The novel I wrote, *The Young Lovers*, was an attempt to do that. The Korean War and the military draft were the cutting edge of the problems facing young men in the early fifties, and their impact on the lives of three male college students and a young woman, an artist whose stability is threatened by a background of traumatic family relationships, was what I wrote about. The love story between one of the college students and the artist gives meaning to the lives of the group, and when the young lover, an idealistic dreamer, is drafted, and the artist, now pregnant, is in danger of a crackup, she is adopted by the two young men who stay behind.

I sent a copy of the manuscript to my old friend Bernard Gordon in Hollywood—where he was eking out a living doing odd jobs—for his criticism. He received a notice from U.S. Customs that he was to pick up a package addressed to him. On his arriving at the Customs office, an agent riffled through the pages of the manuscript and whistled in awe. "There's a fucking-match in every chapter!" he remarked to a colleague. "We can't pass this!"

Bernie telephoned me to report that my manuscript had been confiscated. It would have to be read by a commission that would decide whether it was pornographic, in which case it would be denied entrance to the United States and destroyed.

Lacking the constructive criticism from Bernie that I had been hoping for, I applied for help to several people whose judgment I respected. These included Hugo and Jean Butler, George Oppen, and Charles Humboldt, the literary editor of *Masses and Mainstream*, a Marxist review, another American refugee from political persecution. A lot of time and effort was called for, and each of the persons to whom I had addressed my request was willing to give himself to the enterprise. Their volunteering reflected the community spirit prevailing in our "little band of brothers."

After reading the manuscript, the four critics met with each other and then with me. The manuscript was gone over page by page and commented on; criticism and suggestions were made, not all unanimously; opinions were debated. The process lasted almost a week, after which I set about rewriting the novel in line with the constructive criticism I had received.

When the rewrite was completed, I faced the problem of getting the manuscript to the United States, the first step toward bringing it to the attention of an agent. Again, sympathetic fellow exiles came to my aid. A New York motion-picture exhibitor, Arthur Mayer, the father of my Army buddy Peter Mayer, who lived in Mexico and did movie-production work there, heard of my predicament while visiting his son and volunteered to carry back to New York the five pounds of manuscript.*

Arthur Mayer had connections in the publishing industry, having written a book of film history himself, and he offered to read *The Young Lovers* with an eye to expediting its sale to a publisher. As it turned out, he liked what he read, and when he got back to New York, he submitted the manuscript to Simon and Schuster on my behalf.

When I arrived in New York a few weeks later to visit my family and follow the progress, if any, of *The Young Lovers*, I ran into a new obstacle. The chief editor at Simon and Schuster, Jack Goodman, agreed to publish the book, but not if I insisted on signing it with a pseudonym, as I had planned to do. He wanted the author's real name on the book.

Behind this complication was the frightening threat to the media of the House Un-American Activities Committee. Jack Goodman had been summoned before the Committee and accused of Communist leanings; with some difficulty and expense, he had succeeded in clearing himself. Informed by Arthur Mayer that I had been blacklisted in Hollywood, he wanted to avoid being accused of conspiring to provide a legitimate cover to a known red by publishing his work under a pseudonym.

I had hopes of a movie sale, a possibility certain to be eliminated if my real name were on the book, and I refused to accept Goodman's condition for publication, although I knew I would be taking a big risk of not finding another publisher. I gave the manuscript to a literary agent in New York whom I knew, told him what had happened at Simon and Schuster, and asked him to submit the book to another publisher.

A couple of days went by before I got a telephone call from Goodman at Simon and Schuster in which he said that he had decided to accept my conditions; the book would carry the pseudonym Julian Halevy. Naturally, I was thrilled at having the book accepted.

The agent, Lurton Blassingame, had the embarrassing task of retrieving the

---

*Former exhibitor and publicist Arthur L. Mayer (1886–1981) wrote an autobiography, *Merely Colossal*, as well as a noteworthy history of motion pictures, *The Movies*, with Richard Griffith. From 1961 on Mayer taught film at USC, Dartmouth, Columbia, and other universities.

manuscript from the publisher to whom he had submitted it and apologizing for what in those days was considered improper behavior. He invented the excuse that I had submitted the book personally, without his being aware of it, to Simon and Schuster. His discomfiture was compensated for by his being given the commission for representing the book at Simon and Schuster, although he hadn't negotiated that deal.

The Young Lovers appeared in 1955 and was well-received by the critics, some of whom compared it to *Catcher in the Rye*, thus confirming that my wish to influence a similar audience of young readers had been, to some extent, recognized. The book did well, for a first novel, and was eventually republished in paperback in four or five editions. It appeared in nine countries (including Japan!). I like to think that the wide circulation of the book contributed to the popular anti-draft movement that resulted in Selective Service being eliminated.

During the period that I was working on the novel, I took time off during a dry spell to write a film script that became a movie. Its authorship was attributed to my sister and her husband [Nina and Herman Schneider], writers in other fields, who "fronted" for me. Although the picture was made with a modest cast and budget and didn't attract attention in the United States, where Universal skimped on marketing and distribution costs, it attracted interest in Europe, where it was shown with the title *The Bandit*—my title on the script was "Tierra"; Universal changed that to *The Naked Dawn*—and became a cult movie, especially in France.

I have in my files a clipping from a French periodical, *Cahiers du cinéma*, of a review written by François Truffaut in which he praises the film, attributing genius to the director, Edgar G. Ulmer, and urging his readers to organize a protest at the offices of Universal because the company hadn't given the film adequate publicity. What struck Truffaut particularly was its treatment of the relationship between a woman and two men. It made him think that it would be possible to adapt for the screen a novel, *Jules et Jim*, that had appealed to him. At that time, Truffaut had not yet given up writing film criticism for directing. Not long after, he began making films. *Jules et Jim* was his third feature-length film. The rest, as they say, is history.

The clipping has another story attached to it. A few years ago I received a letter from Sally Belfrage, an Anglo-American writer and an old friend. Her father, Cedric Belfrage, was a British-born journalist who had been editor of a left-wing American weekly, the *National Guardian*. After taking the Fifth Amendment during a hearing of the House Un-American Activities Committee, he was jailed as a "dangerous alien," served several months in prison, and then left the United States and returned to Britain in order to avoid further imprisonment. Sally asked me if I had written *The Bandit*. In Paris, where she was living, she had been present at a social gathering during which some French moviemakers had talked about the film, which they regarded as a "classic," and had questioned the authorship attributed to Nina and Herman Schneider, writers with no record of having written films either before or after the appearance of *The Bandit*. Sally wrote that her guess about my having written it was based on her knowing that I had lived in Mexico, where the story of the film takes place, and that the authors credited on the titles were my sister and brother-in-law.

I wrote back to Sally, congratulating her on her detective work and enclosing the clipping from *Cahiers du cinéma*. Shortly afterward, I received a letter from a film scholar, introducing himself as a friend of Sally Belfrage and enclosing a list of questions about the history of my writing of the film. He invited me to come to Paris, where he would arrange a showing of the film at a film museum or institute at which French filmmakers could meet with me. I had to decline his invitation. The writer of the letter was Bertrand Tavernier, who became a leading movie director in France.

The history of that film began some years before Mexico, in Hollywood, where I showed Bernard Gordon a Maxim Gorky short story, "Chelkash," that had appealed to me as a possibility for development into a movie. The story was about a single encounter between an old thief and a young, impressionable boatman during a night in Odessa. Bernie agreed with me that the character relationship between the two could be adapted to another background, and we began developing the idea. A movie job came along, and we put the project aside. The congressional hearings and our leaving the United States kept us from continuing with the project.

Three or four years later, in Mexico, it occurred to me that the story lent itself to a Mexican background. The Russian thief became a disillusioned ex-revolutionary who survives as a rural bandit; the boatman became a peasant with a tiny farm who has dreams of getting rich. The bandit befriends the peasant, who is dazzled by the older man's money and his manner of throwing it around. He thinks he could put the bandit's money to better, more respectable use and considers betraying his mentor. The peasant's wife, embittered by domestic slavery, asks the bandit to take her with him when he leaves. The bandit, who sees in the young peasant his own youthful aspirations for owning and farming a plot of land, tries to convince the woman that she will be better off staying with her husband despite his faults. Then the old man discovers that the peasant, whom he has begun to think of as a son, had planned to murder him. Disillusioned and angry, he leaves, taking the wife with him.

What happens next? Get the film from a rental library and find out!

From Mexico I sent the script to Bernard Gordon in Hollywood, where he was working as a private investigator for lawyers on cases involving claims against insurance companies, though he maintained contact with people in the movie industry. Through underground channels he circulated the script, which was bought for five thousand dollars—"no questions asked" about the unknown authors—and produced by Universal. I didn't get to see the film until years later, when I returned to Hollywood. I was glad to see that the director, Edgar G. Ulmer, had followed the script faithfully. No changes at all had been made. I think this was a once-in-a-lifetime experience; like all Hollywood screenwriters, I'm accustomed to having my scripts rewritten and modified to the point of becoming unrecognizable.

This memoir has been about what it was like for a blacklisted writer to adapt to the blacklist and find ways of getting around it, but I don't want to leave this section about Mexico without indicating that life there was both more complicated, meaningful, and rewarding than it will appear to have been from this summary.

Between 1951 and 1957—my life from the ages of thirty-two to thirty-eight—working to earn a living was only a part of living in Mexico, a small part, at that. More important, it seems to me now, were other things: the friendships I made in the community of exiles—American, English, Spanish, German—with whom I shared ideals and beliefs tempered by persecution, and a bonding with Mexico and its people that stemmed from a deep attachment to a Mexican woman and her children that has lasted a lifetime. I think of Mexico and my years there as the middle of my life, formative and rich. It taught me to value feeling above all, and it determined the choices that brought me to Italy and led to my marriage to an Italian and to my settling here.

For that fallout from the blacklist, I'm eternally grateful.

I returned to Hollywood from Mexico in early 1958, drawn by assurances from my agent, Mary Baker, that she could get me a job; in her opinion, the blacklist was beginning to show cracks. An eight-year absence from the city found me, once again, unprepared for the changes that had taken place.

The old studio system, in which studio heads like Louis B. Mayer, Jack Warner, Darryl F. Zanuck, and Harry Cohn ran their fiefs like Chinese warlords, was giving way to a system in which independent producers, some of them with ties to major studios, had room to operate. An independent, like director and producer Otto Preminger, could buck the studios and their Motion Picture Association of America to make *The Man with the Golden Arm* and hit the jackpot with it.

Powerful new forces had appeared on the scene. Television and the music-recording business had taken over studios, office buildings, and real estate that had once belonged to film-production companies. A movie industry that had once turned out three or four hundred pictures each year was now producing far fewer, perhaps a tenth as many. Individual talents—actors, directors, personalities—functioning as free agents had boosted their share of the take, although the multi-million-dollar deals of today were still undreamed-of. Costs had risen. A picture budgeted at a hundred thousand dollars in 1950 cost a million dollars to make in 1958. The TV market and competition for the advertising dollar was determining the content of movies; if the subject wasn't suitable for a prime-time audience, it was unlikely to attract star talent and important financing. Glitzy, big-budget spectaculars like *Solomon and Sheba* and *Cleopatra*, appealing to a world market, were in vogue. Those two titles come to mind because I was involved, in a very minor way, in those projects.

There were new people running the movie business and a new spirit prevailing. Television had absorbed many of the artists and craftsmen displaced by the changes. They, and the new recruits, had different talents and different values from the ones that had been appreciated in my day. The censorship imposed by the McCarthy witch-hunts and the Cold War had entered the minds of the creative talents making pictures and television shows. It no longer needed the naysaying of the Breen Office censors or the watchdog committees of the American Legion and the Motion Picture Alliance for the Preservation of American Ideals to kill a project; the abortions occurred in the minds of the writers, directors, and producers.

I was a fish out of water. The friends on whom I had depended for an exchange of ideas, for stimulation and intellectual and emotional support, were gone from the scene. Some of them were still working underground in Hollywood and New York, but they kept a low profile; others were in Europe and Mexico, surviving as best they could. I missed terribly the community of friends I had left behind in Mexico, some of them movie people, the majority political refugees from different countries and different professions.

To recapture my feelings at the time, I have dug out of my files an article of mine from the *Nation*, a publication for which I wrote in Mexico and, later, in Italy. Published on June 7, 1958, and entitled "Disneyland and Las Vegas," it provoked some letters from readers either supporting my expression of "fear and loathing" at the meteoric expansion and success of those pilgrim-infested shrines or attacking me for various reasons, the main one being my "lack of fantasy." I wrote the article in Mexico, where I was taking a vacation from my screenwriting in Hollywood. It begins:

> This is written in Mexico, my home in recent years. I've just returned from a visit to the United States and am now once more enjoying the taste of unfrozen orange juice and fresh fish, conversations lasting four or five hours in which all sorts of cabbages and kings are discussed, meetings with friends where no one asks if I watched TV last night to see Mickey Rooney do *Oedipus Rex* on the Benign Cancer-Producing Cigarette Walpurgisnacht Spectacular. Now I feel myself once again reassured of my personal identity and critical faculties to the point where this article, which I have been vainly trying to write from within the revolving U.S. Barrel of Fun, comes to my typewriter as easily as a remembered dream being noted down for the psychiatrist.

On my arrival in Hollywood, I did, however, find a base of support in the person of my friend and collaborator Bernard Gordon, who, after years of hand-to-mouth survival at odd jobs such as selling plastics and investigating accident-insurance claims, had developed an undercover system for selling his writing services to a producer at Columbia's B-picture unit. Using a "front" identity, that of Ray Marcus, an old friend, and with the complicity of the producer, Charles Schnee, Gordon wrote several science-fiction films that were successful. Although I had great expectations of getting a job through Mary Baker and the Jaffe Agency, I needed stopgap employment while waiting for the agency to make good on their assurances, and Bernie offered to share his lifeline connection with me.

Bernie was hiding behind the identity of Ray Marcus, and, without the knowledge of the producer, I was concealed behind Bernie. It was a sort of double masquerade. Together we wrote a script for Columbia that became the film *The Case Against Brooklyn*. If memory serves me, it dealt with crime and courtroom shenanigans.

Before long, Mary Baker came through with a job possibility. An appointment was set for me to meet with Arthur Hornblow and King Vidor, producer and director of an as-yet-undefined film entitled *Solomon and Sheba*. I was to appear in the unblemished guise of a novelist, Julian Halevy, author of *The Young Lovers*.

The meeting was not without theatrical aspects. As no reference to my past was made by any of the parties involved, and as Hornblow and Vidor, both old-timers in the movie business, would in the normal course of events have questioned my ability to write for the screen, I assumed that they were aware of my history and screen credits and were avoiding the subject deliberately in order to pretend, if in the future it became necessary, that they had not knowingly engaged in trafficking with a blacklisted screenwriter. As it turned out, I was mistaken in this assumption.

The interview hinged on the question of whether I was equipped to deal with the subject matter of the film. "We've read your book," Hornblow said, "and we know you can write love scenes. But do you know anything about the Bible?" The reply I made was apt: "If I forget thee, oh Jerusalem, let my right hand forget its cunning!"

I got the job. My salary had been established by my agent. It was a thousand dollars a week. Working conditions were flexible. "Go home and write. Let us know when you have something to show," I was told.

I went home and briefed Bernie on these developments. If he wished to come in with me, we would continue working as a team, sharing the income. He agreed. On this deal, however, his identity would be hidden behind mine. With Columbia, in his role of Ray Marcus, he would be the "front"; on the Hornblow and Vidor project, in my role as Halevy, I would be the "front." Neither of us would answer to our own names.

Bernie and I immediately set to work trying to invent a story line. A day or two later, Mary Baker, who was not privy to my arrangement with Bernie, telephoned and asked, "Did those guys give you the wink?"

I was nonplussed. "The wink? What about?"

Mary spelled it out. "Did they let you know in some way that they're aware of who you really are?"

"No, Mary. They played it straight."

The tangled web of deception we had woven was proving to have knots in it. "I'm sorry, but I have to protect myself," Mary said. "You have to go in and tell these guys who you are." Her problem was clear. If in the future the project or, even worse, the film were to be threatened by a boycott such as those imposed on Chaplin films by vigilante organizations, Mary didn't want to be accused by Hornblow and Vidor of having caused the disaster by selling them a ringer.

The next day, I called Hornblow with the excuse of wanting to talk about the story line I had worked out, and I arranged to meet with him and Vidor. The presentation went well; they liked the story line that Bernie and I had developed. Now came the sticky part of the meeting. "By the way, there's something I think you ought to know about me," I said. "Halevy is a pseudonym. My real name is Zimet, and I believe I may be blacklisted. I was named as a red before the Un-American Activities Committee."

There was a moment's silence. Hornblow and Vidor exchanged glances. Then Hornblow fielded the ball easily. He dismissed the revelation with a smile and a wave: "I couldn't care less. We like your stuff. Go home and keep writing!"

The next day I was fired. Mary Baker called to give me the news. She said Hornblow had called her to say that the deal for my services was off. "I asked him why, although I knew what had happened," she said. " 'He's too expensive; we can't afford him,' he said. So I said, 'Make me an offer.' He didn't know how to handle that. He hemmed and hawed and finally came out with 'Mary, you understand!' " It seemed the blacklist was still operative. Mary's optimism about its having cracked was overoptimistic.

Further proof of the blacklist's effectiveness was forthcoming. Samuel Goldwyn Jr., who had bought the film rights to *The Young Lovers*, learned that I was in town and called me to ask if I would write the screenplay. This time I met the situation head-on and told him that my real name was Zimet, that I had been a screenwriter in the past, and that I was blacklisted.

"That makes no difference to me," he said. "I'd still like you to do the screenplay." Despite his good intentions, Goldwyn retracted the offer after having consulted his lawyers and his financial backers. He apologized at a meeting we had and explained, "The money men won't okay it."

Goldwyn then came up with an unexpected offer: "Since I can't hire you, tell me who you want to write it." This put me in an awkward and potentially embarrassing spot. The writer I had long had in mind was Isobel Lennart, an old friend and the gifted author of many MGM screenplays, among them *East Side West Side*, *Anchors Aweigh*, *Meet Me in Las Vegas*, and *Love Me or Leave Me*. She later wrote *Funny Girl* for the stage and adapted it for the screen. Isobel was one of the few friends to whom I had said good-bye before slipping out of the country in 1950, and we had embraced in tears at the parting.

Isobel had been called before the Committee and, breaking under pressure from her husband and the studio, had named names. Navasky quotes from an interview with her made before she died in a car crash in 1971: "I believe with all my heart that it was wrong to cooperate with this terrible committee in any way, and I believe that I was wrong. I believe I did a minimum of damage, but I still believe it was wrong. I had a much bigger reaction to it than I thought I would. It was shame and guilt and nothing else. I've never gotten over it. I've always felt like an inferior citizen because of this."*

There was an unwritten code among blacklisted writers prohibiting fraternization with people who had testified as "friendly witnesses" and "named names," and when Goldwyn responded favorably to my recommendation of Isobel and suggested that we go to see her together—he had the notion that perhaps I could work with Isobel and stay in the background—I had to explain that it wouldn't be possible for me to see her or even to talk to her. I couldn't trust myself not to take her in my arms and comfort her, because I knew how much she had suffered. A reconciliation of that sort, whatever my motives, would have meant a break with the clan of surviving blacklistees, and I couldn't afford that, not in 1958. I've always regretted that I never had a chance to tell her that my feeling for her was sympathy and understanding, not contempt.

Goldwyn accepted my explanation for declining to meet with Isobel or talk to her and decided to call her himself, which he did, inviting me to listen to the conversation on an extension phone. After ascertaining that Isobel had read *The Young Lovers* and liked it, he asked her if she would like to do the screenplay. Her reply, as nearly as I can remember, was, "I know the author, and he wouldn't want me to write it."

I had a strong impulse to speak up and tell her that it was I who had suggested her to take my place, but I said nothing. The consequence of its becoming known that I had, in a sense, "forgiven" her—although my appreciation of her sensitivity and understanding of young people did not, to my mind, imply a pardon for her having named names to the Committee—would have been a break between me and those friends whose working lives had been destroyed by the Committee. I didn't want that, and I could hardly go around explaining to people that I wasn't condoning Isobel's self-serving collaboration with the Committee. It raised the sort of thorny question in my mind that I have never been able to resolve. Was it right to support a boycott of pianist Walter Gieseking's concerts—he had pursued a successful career in Nazi Germany—while, at the same time, enjoying, at home, recordings of his superb Bach interpretations? Book and record burning, prohibition of music written by Jewish composers—all these were rightly condemned in their time.

---

*Navasky's source was a 1970 interview with Isobel Lennart, conducted by Robert Vaughn as part of the research for his Ph.D. dissertation, later published as *Only Victims*.

Is the practice more acceptable if the book and record banners—a nice distinction from "burners"—are on our side?

Of course, judgment is determined by the temper of the time. The wreckage of lives by the Committee and those who aided them was still on the scene in 1958. Ten years later, the agent George Willner, who had been blacklisted, called Isobel, much to her relief and joy, and said, "You know, so many years have gone by, and we love you and want to see you."

And then there's the comment W. H. Auden made in his poem on the death of William Butler Yeats: "Time will pardon Paul Claudel, pardon him for writing well."

The screenplay of *The Young Lovers* was written, but not by Isobel, and in 1964 the film was made, directed by Samuel Goldwyn Jr. himself and starring Peter Fonda. I heard it didn't turn out well. I never saw it.

I am trying to describe what it was like to come back to Hollywood after an absence of eight years and find almost everything changed, not for the better. A scene that sticks in my memory may shed light on my feelings at the time and on my beginning to feel that I didn't want to spend the rest of my life in that part of the world.

It was at a party to which I was taken by a new friend, a writer from New York who was in the social swim. The party was at the home of Bette Davis. She wasn't there, but her husband, Gary Merrill, was, and it was he who was throwing the party. Among the guests was Roger Corman. About twenty-five people were present, gossiping, drinking, and dancing to recorded music. The atmosphere was informal; many of the guests knew each other. I was new in town and a bachelor, and with the help of the friend who had brought me to the party, I circulated, meeting people. After being introduced to a young woman, an actress, and exchanging a few noncommittal remarks, I asked her to dance with me. She hesitated, eying me appraisingly, then said coolly, "No." I was taken aback by this rudeness. In the past I had been accustomed to turn-downs delivered with some effort at politeness: "Sorry, I'm tired," or "Give me a rain check." This was new.

Perhaps I remember the incident because of my reaction and the effect it had on the girl. She may have expected me to wince and disappear, instead of which I stood my ground, eyed her even more coldly and appraisingly than she had done me, and said, "It's a pity that in this town it's hard for a girl to be both pretty and well-mannered." This put-down left her with nothing to say, and I walked away. Later I heard that she asked around to find out who I was and where I came from.

At the same party I danced with an actress with whom I got along swimmingly, or so I thought. She was a sexy blonde who had been pointed out to me by Roger Corman with the phrase, "That's the mark!" He mentioned that she had played, in the movie *The Brothers Karamazov*, a bit part as one of the hoydens in a drunken orgy. She gave me her telephone number and said, "Call me!"

With visions of a Karamazov orgy in my mind, I did call her, and I suggested we have dinner together. Her reply was to the point: "What's in it for me?" On that occasion, I didn't know what to say. Mumbling some excuse, I ended the conversation and hung up.

It seemed that in the years I had been away it wasn't only the moviemaking that had become more market-oriented.

Further proof? When I did, finally, after a couple of months of searching for "Miss Right," begin building a "relationship," it lasted only a few weeks, until it became clear to my new girlfriend, who had quit her office job shortly after meeting me, that I wasn't going to bankroll her new, hoped-for career as a nightclub singer and recording artist. She departed like a thief in the night, leaving behind only a pair of lace-up, knee-length ice skates. Her disappointment was of brief duration. With the help of her analyst, who made it clear to her that in choosing a partner there had been some confusion in her thinking, she was able to focus on her true goal and locate a generous patron who, fortunately, was waiting in the wings.

After a suitable period of mourning, I telephoned to ask if I could send back the ice skates. "Don't bother," she said cheerfully. "Throw them out." I tried to find someone who would take the ice skates as a gift, but nobody was interested. Having newly arrived from Third World Mexico, I was constantly being reminded that I had come back to a consumer society booming on a system of big demand and big waste. I couldn't get used to the idea that finding someone to repair a typewriter was a major task.

On the work front, I started a new project. In a conversation with Bernard Gordon about my years in Mexico, I told him about a colorful period in Acapulco, in 1952, long before the tourist boom peaked. At the time that I spent most of a winter there, a community of drop-outs was flourishing, Americans mostly, drawn by the easy living and the availability of marijuana. A number of them lived on money from home, some of it tied to Army pensions and GI benefits; a few skimmed tips and gratuities from the tourist trade; others were useful to wealthy Mexicans who kept vacation homes in the hills overlooking the beautiful bay; yachts and fishing boats offered part-time jobs; nightclubs aiming for the tourist trade found American know-how useful. There were a hundred ways of getting by without having to take a nine-to-five job back in the States.

Drop-outs were not as familiar in the United States as they were to become, and when I told Bernie about the milieu and the young Americans, a few of whom were would-be writers and artists, he was intrigued and suggested that they offered a background and characters for a movie. I agreed, and we began work on a screenplay that we called "Beach Boys," a title that was not yet the household word defining a series of movies and TV shows and a genre of popular music that it was to become.

We worked on the screenplay for about six months and turned it over to Mary Baker in December 1958. The title page carried the names of the authors, neither of which were our real names. Bernie used the name of Ray Marcus, the friend who had loaned his name for Bernie's black-market work, and I, of course, was the novelist known as Julian Halevy.

Mary Baker was enthusiastic about the script. She told me later that when she first read it she said to her staff at the Jaffe Agency, "I'm going to sell this one for a lot of money." Her marketing strategy called for holding off submission until well after the Christmas and New Year holidays, when studio executives would have returned to work. That was about as much as we were told. Mary's plans for coping with the blacklist problem were unknown to us. However, it was clear that agency conferences were being held and an elaborate game plan devised.

Encouraged by the agency's activity on our behalf, I went back to Mexico for the holidays and, having decided to end my exile there (I had a passport now and looked forward to returning to Europe), I gave away the furniture and most of the things I had collected during my seven years in the country and shipped the rest back to the United States.

I stayed with the Oppens, who were living in the house near the university that I had vacated. This was when George was beginning to write poetry again; thirty years had elapsed since he had given up poetry to devote himself to political activity. The revelations of the horrible crimes of the Stalin era had finally and irrevocably disillusioned him about the Soviet Union and the possibility of bringing about the Socialist ideal to which he and Mary had devoted much of their lives. They were thinking of returning to the United States.

Hollywood exiles, including screenwriters Albert Maltz and Hugo and Jean Butler, were anxious to hear from me a first-hand report on what things were like in the movie business for blacklisted writers. Things were changing, I told them, and in fact, it was not long afterward that they returned to Hollywood to test the waters.

In mid-January I was back in Los Angeles, on deck for the action involved in the submission of "Beach Boys." Bernie and I weren't kept informed of what was happening; probably Mary Baker didn't want us interfering with her conduct of the campaign. Things were tricky enough without us underfoot. The Jaffe Agency had clients in every studio—writers, directors, producers. Many of these were given the script before the official submission to the story departments, and they acted to bring pressure on the studio heads and to report back to the agency on developments.

Bernie and I didn't know what was happening until it was all over. Things moved swiftly. The agency was trying to get competitive bidding between the studios; the studios were trying to avoid getting trapped in a bidding war. "Beach Boys" was a hot property. Every studio wanted it, but all of them, with one exception, didn't want to meet the writers or, much less, to employ them. The studios were prepared to buy the script, pretending that the real identity of the authors wasn't known to them.

There were bids from Warner Brothers, Paramount, MGM, and Columbia.

Mary Baker told me, after it was all over and the money was in the bank, that at MGM a top executive—I believe it was Benny Thau—had proposed the following: "Mary, we'll make an offer. Then you have the right to make one telephone call, here in my office, and say yes or no. That'll be it!"

"How much are you offering?" Mary asked.

"Sixty-one thousand."

Mary telephoned the agency office and relayed the offer. After a few moments of enigmatic conversation, she hung up and gave MGM her answer, "No."

Benny Thau wasn't convinced by the performance, because performance it was. A week later he called Mary and asked, "Mary, when I made you the offer for 'Beach Boys,' had the script already been sold?"

His suspicions were justified. Mary's spies at MGM had informed her of MGM's intention to make an offer and the amount that they were offering to pay. Using that knowledge, Mary had negotiated a better deal at Columbia with Harry Cohn: seventy-five thousand and, more important, a ten-week writing contract for the authors, Ray Marcus and Julian Halevy. The fact that we would be working at a studio, albeit under false names, meant that Columbia was willing to risk defying the blacklist. If attacked, Cohn could retreat to a claim that he wasn't aware of the real names of the authors.

Mary had pretended to consider the MGM offer for two good reasons. First, she didn't want to reveal the fact that her intelligence network had provided her with the details of MGM's proposal and that she had used the information to get a competitive offer from Columbia. Second, for Mary to have sold the script without giving MGM a chance to bid—which is what she actually did—would have been an affront leading to retaliatory punishment by the studio—which was what happened after she confessed.

"I was barred from the lot," Mary said with a smile. "It didn't bother me." MGM's edict was a symbolic gesture. The Agency represented several studio employees, and, of necessity, other representatives than Mary had access to their clients and to the studio.

It was a big moment for me and Bernie, one comparable to the moment when, after a long, expensive battle, we won the right to have our passports returned to us. In recognition of the agency's skillful dealings on our behalf, we sent Mary and her staff bouquets of roses. Then, in order not to risk having the deal explode in our faces, we deposited our checks and left town for a week, giving the checks time to clear before we showed our faces at Columbia.

I flew to New York and celebrated by taking my mother and other family members to a series of Broadway shows, "best seats in the house." At *My Fair Lady*, my mother, who had retrieved her ancient Persian lamb fur coat from mothballed storage for the occasion and exuded a strong smell of camphor—I think I saw Rex Harrison, immediately above our front-row seats, wrinkle his nose when he got close to the footlights—hummed the tunes along with the singers.

Came the moment, a week later, when Bernie and I walked through the front door at the Gower Street Columbia lot, braced for what proved to be instant recognition. A producer, Robert Cohn, for whom Bernie and I had worked as writers on a project called "The Millen Case" almost ten years before, hailed us. "Hi, fellers! What's your names?" It was proof that Bobby was in on the game and was giving us what Mary Baker had called "the wink."

Our producer at Columbia, Roger Edens, reported to us that on learning of the "Beach Boys" sale and the two-thousand-dollar-a-week salary that was being paid to the team of writers, his fellow producer Charlie Schnee had protested, "That guy [i.e., Bernie Gordon in his Raymond T. Marcus guise] used to work for me! I'll never be able to afford him again!" At which the person to whom he was complaining replied, with mock sympathy, "That's too bad, Charlie."

Edens had just moved to Columbia from MGM, where he had been an associate producer to Arthur Freed on a series of major musicals, the most recent of which had been *Funny Face*, with Audrey Hepburn and Fred Astaire. He was a client of the Jaffe Agency and probably had been shown the script privately, thus adding to the pressure on Columbia to make the deal on "Beach Boys." He gave us no hint of his being aware of our true identities, although he almost certainly had been briefed by Mary.

The studio perks—adjoining offices, private secretary, executive dining room—were nice to have once again. There would be no more quick lunches at the food stands in the Farmers' Market.

Now that the major obstacles had been cleared, we faced another hurdle—that of nursing our script through revisions for casting and locations without its suffering too many basic changes. Edens and we got along famously; the revisions he asked for were minor. We saw eye to eye on the characters and their development. This ideal working relationship came to an abrupt and unforeseen end when the studio boss, Harry Cohn, died suddenly of a heart attack.

New bosses took over the studio and decided to change "Beach Boys" into a vehicle for the studio's big star, Kim Novak. The role for which she had been intended was not as big as that of the male lead, a tough, handsome surfer, "king of the beach boys," a role that had appealed to male stars, including Kirk Douglas, who had personally offered thirty-five thousand dollars to buy the script for his own production company. Action scenes of the beach-boy way of life—the inspiration for our writing the story—were to be replaced by indoor, bedroom-type scenes for Novak, who wouldn't allow herself to be photographed in a bathing suit because her ankles were thick.

Edens was new at the studio and in no position to defend his project from the *hochpolitik* maneuverings of the new bosses. He sat silently through meetings with them during which Bernie and I vainly argued against the big changes required to suit a Kim Novak vehicle. Resigning ourselves to the prospect of our script being mutilated by other writers, we fought the good fight as long as we could—that is, until we finished our stint at the studio in May 1958.

• • •

The Jaffe Agency had made a deal for us to write a novelized version of the original script of "Beach Boys" for Bantam Books, with an advance of ten thousand dollars, and we decided to go to Acapulco, where we could enjoy tequila margaritas and the ocean breezes while writing the book.

I flew on ahead to Mexico City while Bernie drove the family car all the way from Los Angeles. His family was to follow and spend the summer with us in Acapulco. On this occasion, my return to Mexico City was that of a conquering hero. I was the first of the blacklisted writers in our community of exiles to venture back into enemy territory and come back alive and successful. For my friends, who were delighted at my success, it also meant that political changes for the better were taking place and that chances for their resuming their careers in Hollywood and elsewhere were improving.

The gang celebrated my return with a poker party like the ones we had held regularly during my years in Mexico City. The core members of the poker-playing group were Luis Lindau, a Jew who had escaped Nazi Germany before the war and had done very well in business in Mexico, although his education had been in art history; Conlon Nancarrow, a veteran of the Abraham Lincoln Brigade in the Spanish Civil War, who had retired to Mexico after the Republic's defeat and devoted himself to writing music (a few years ago he was awarded a big grant by the MacArthur Foundation, and concerts of his music, played on mechanical player pianos because it is too difficult for performance by pianists, were given in Carnegie Hall and other prestigious concert halls); and Sam and May Brooks, who were New Yorkers and had moved to Mexico City to escape persecution because of Sam's history of activity in the Communist Party (May survived her husband and continues to live and write in Mexico).

I was a good poker player, and over a period of years, during which our poker games were held almost every weekend, I won regularly the equivalent in pesos of fifty to a hundred dollars at each session. For the other regular players, I had long ago become the enemy to beat. On the occasion of this return match, I played my usual game and won again. This time the good-natured raillery and threats that had always been the group's reaction to my winning were lacking.

The following day I was invited to lunch by Luis Lindau. There was something he wanted to talk to me about, he said. At the good French restaurant to which Luis took me—he had cosmopolitan tastes; on one occasion he managed to produce candied violets, in Mexico something of a miracle—he brought up the subject on his mind. It was about the poker game the previous evening. "I'm sorry, Julian," he said. "But you'll have to choose between winning at poker and keeping your friends."

I talked about this ultimatum to the Oppens, with whom I was staying, and George gave me his point of view on the matter: "As long as you were a refugee like everybody else, it was okay for you to win. It was a game, a joke, all in the family. But then you left home to seek your fortune. You did what none of them was able to do. And when you came back, having made it, a kind of success, it was just too much, at least too much for them to accept your beating them at poker—on top of everything else!"

At the next poker game, shortly afterward, I lost. By the standards of our play, it was a hefty loss, about two hundred and fifty dollars. It was easy to do: I drew to inside straights and asked for two cards to fill out a flush; I bluffed obviously and unsuccessfully. No one but Luis caught on to what I was doing. As my losses mounted, the spirits of the other players rose. By the time the game ended at the usual witching hour, laughing and joking had taken over in a general euphoria.

By the next afternoon, the news had traveled. Friends, particularly those who were occasional players taking part in our regular games, were telephoned to be told gleefully, "We finally got Julian!"

The gang couldn't wait to organize another poker game. The "luck" of the other players held; again I lost, not as much as on the previous occasion but enough, about a hundred and fifty dollars, to make the party a success. The reversal in fortunes, for a second time, gave rise to general hilarity. Only Luis seemed not to be enjoying my discomfiture. He phoned me the next day. He was annoyed. "I told you not to win," he said. "But I didn't tell you to lose!"

This farce was interrupted by the arrival of Bernie Gordon in his big convertible Buick, which he had driven from Los Angeles. For him it was a happy return. Nine years before, he had fled Hollywood to avoid testifying before the Committee and come to Mexico City, together with his wife and infant daughter. It had been a miserable experience, largely because of amebic-dysentery infections that had afflicted them and threatened his daughter's life. His Mexico sojourn had been brief; it ended when I summoned him to London to work with me on a script about Martin Luther, a project that also didn't work out. Now he was riding high and looking forward to a working vacation in Acapulco. His plan was to rent a house there in which his family would enjoy a summer holiday.

Bernie and I drove to Acapulco, the resort from which all our good fortune stemmed, and set up shop, preparing for the arrival of Gordon's family. We were not prepared for what happened next: the arrival from Hollywood of the "Beach Boys" production unit—producer Roger Edens, cameraman James Wong Howe, and Charles Vidor, the director of a famous series of Rita Hayworth movies.

We were obliged to pick them up at the airport and take them to their rooms at one of the best hotels, the one with the terrace restaurant that overlooked the cliff from which local divers plunged down to the shallow sea below, always in time to catch an incoming wave to give them enough depth of water to survive. This was one of the scenes in our script. At dinner we got acquainted, and the next day we toured the area, showing the producer, director, and cameraman the various possible locations.

Edens seemed nervous about his relationship with Vidor, a crude and boastful man who was preoccupied with finding some good-looking girls to "get laid." After a few days Vidor lost interest in the splendid scenery and announced that he wanted to get back to Hollywood as soon as possible, and, what was more surprising, he wanted us to come with him. We were the perfect people to get started on the revisions, since we knew the territory, and after all, we were the ones who had written the original script.

With misgivings, we agreed to the job with the caveat that we wouldn't be able to return to Hollywood for approximately two weeks. It would take us at least that long to wrap up the loose ends of our lives in Mexico. First-class airfare and another ten-week contract cinched the deal, and our plans for a novel were set aside. We returned to Los Angeles and went back to work at Columbia on the script of "Beach Boys."

This time, Vidor was adamant in story conferences; it had to be a "Beach Boys" starring Kim Novak. We tried as hard as we could, but it was a long ten weeks of artificiality and frustration, after which we were let go with the vague promise of being reunited with the project at some later point. We weren't. "Beach Boys" was produced as a film several years later under a radically different title, and neither Bernie nor I ever claim it among our credits, for the very good reason that it was a lousy film without the slightest inkling of the fun and ideas that we had optimistically invested in it.

A more important event took place in the final weeks that we spent in Hollywood in 1958. The author and artist Rockwell Kent had taken the denial of his passport to the Supreme Court, which ruled that the State Department had no right to refuse passports to United States citizens on political grounds. Suddenly it was easy for me to travel again.

Now that our new identities had been publicly accepted, Bernard Gordon and I were free to market ourselves as screenwriters. The blacklist had not been officially broken, but we were semi-officially permitted to circumvent it. But despite the attraction of steady employment at the Hollywood studios, I had a strong urge to get away.

During the years that I had been away from the Hollywood scene, I had changed, and the industry had changed. Whatever there had been of truth and beauty and poetry in what people call "Hollywood's golden age," and I'm not saying there was very much, had been dissipated by the pressures of censorship and the logic of market forces. What is obvious today—that Hollywood movies are made for teenagers and audiences of the lowest common denominator around the world, committed to not offending official, corporate, or religious authority, and relying on spectacular, bizarre effects for their appeal—was in 1958 already the outline of the future.

Before the Cold War, there were honest, truthful, artistic films made—not many, but enough among the hundreds of films turned out to give people like myself the hope of being able to participate in some exciting, rewarding endeavor. But the scene had changed. The war, during which propaganda films were in demand; the Cold War; the anti-labor-union strategies of the big corporations that were taking over the industry from the adventurers who had built it; the advent of television; the development of a global market: all these forces were at work, taking the life out of movies and the joy out of making them.

Along with the movie industry, all of American society was changing. Advertising, consumerism, mass marketing and the disappearance of artisans and crafts, the rise of suburbia and the decay of the inner cities, pollution and smog, the deterioration of newspapers and periodicals, schlock goods on the newstands and in the bookstores and in the supermarkets: all these were turning the California I had discovered and found a sort of paradise into a far less attractive place in which to live. The change in society was reflected in changing relationships between people. It was not something one could put a finger on, and my feeling that something was missing in friendships and love affairs undoubtedly arose from changes in my own needs. But I had a strong sense of wanting to live in a world where things would be different.

Although the movie industry has been a constant, more or less, in my working life, I have spent long periods divorced from it, working at other things or not working at all. Not being subject to the pressures of movie writing, especially under the stressful conditions imposed by blacklisting, has spared me many of the health risks that, like silicosis for miners, go with the job of writing scripts: ulcers, heart conditions, alcoholism, lung cancer from smoking, galloping neuroses, matrimonial disaster, and other miseries attributed to tension and stress. Too, I have enjoyed doing other things: being a journalist, writing a novel, and, for many years, traveling around Africa, Asia, and the Middle East for the Food and Agriculture Organization of the United Nations, writing, producing films, and teaching young people how to make films and audiovisual teaching aids. The rewards of these activities, though not comparable in financial terms to the occasional windfall income from a movie sale or screenwriting job I've had, have been considerable.

That, plus the experience of living abroad, first in Mexico and then in Italy, away from the high pressures of Hollywood, have been enough to keep me here in Italy for nearly forty years, resisting the temptation to go back to the USA to work in television or movies, although that option has long since expired, along with the generation of industry people with whom I had contact during my Hollywood days.

Selected Bibliography

The history of the Hollywood blacklist is documented in numerous books. Three of the best, which we highly recommend, are Nancy Lynn Schwartz, *The Hollywood Writers' Wars* (New York: Knopf, 1982); Larry Ceplair and Steven Englund, *The Inquisition in Hollywood: Politics in the Film Community, 1930–1960* (Garden City, N.Y.: Anchor Press/Doubleday, 1980); and Victor S. Navasky, *Naming Names* (New York: Viking Press, 1980). The list below is devoted to nonfiction and first-person recollections offered, in various venues, by the blacklistees themselves.

MEMOIRS AND OTHER NONFICTION

Adler, Larry. *It Ain't Necessarily So*. New York: Grove Press, 1984.

Bentley, Eric, ed. *Thirty Years of Treason: Excerpts from Hearings Before the House Committee on Un-American Activities, 1938–1968*. New York: Viking Press, 1971. Includes the testimony of Bertolt Brecht, Hanns Eisler, Lillian Hellman, John Howard Lawson, Ring Lardner Jr., Zero Mostel, Earl Robinson, and Lionel Stander.

Bernstein, Walter. *Inside Out: A Memoir of the Blacklist*. New York: Knopf, 1996.

Bessie, Alvah. *Inquisition in Eden*. New York: Macmillan, 1965.

Brecht, Bertolt. *Journals, 1934–1955*. Edited by John Willett. New York: Routledge, 1993.

Carnovsky, Morris. *The Actor's Eye*. New York: Performing Arts Journal Publications, 1984.

Caspary, Vera. *The Secrets of Grown-Ups*. New York: McGraw-Hill, 1979.

Chaplin, Charles. *My Autobiography*. New York: Simon and Schuster, 1964.

Cole, Lester. *Hollywood Red*. Palo Alto: Ramparts Press, 1981.

Hellman, Lillian. *Three: An Unfinished Woman, Pentimento, and Scoundrel Time*. Boston: Little, Brown, 1979.

Hunt, Marsha. *The Way We Wore: Styles of the Nineteen-Thirties and Forties, and Our World Since Then*. Fallbrook, Calif.: Fallbrook Publishing, 1993. (Box 5103, Sherman Oaks, Ca., 91413.)

Ivens, Joris. *The Camera and I*. New York: International Publishers, 1969.

Kahn, Gordon. *Hollywood on Trial*. New York: Boni and Gaer, 1948.

Koch, Howard. *As Time Goes By: Memoirs of a Writer*. New York: Harcourt Brace Jovanovich, 1979.

Kraft, Hy. *On My Way to the Theater*. New York: Macmillan, 1971.

Lardner, Ring Jr., *The Lardners: My Family Remembered*. New York: Harper and Row, 1976.

Lawson, John Howard. *Film in the Battle of Ideas*. New York: Masses and Mainstream, 1953.

———. *Film: The Creative Process*. New York: Hill and Wang, 1967.

Mostel, Kate, and Gilford, Madeline, with Jack Gilford and Zero Mostel. *170 Years of Show Business*. New York: Random House, 1978.

Robeson, Paul, with Lloyd L. Brown. *Here I Stand*. New York: Othello Associates, 1958.

Sanford, John. *Maggie: A Love Story*. New York: Barricade Books, 1993.

———. *We Have a Little Sister*. Santa Barbara: Capra Press, 1996.

Stewart, Donald Ogden. *By a Stroke of Luck!* New York and London: Paddington Press, 1975.

Trumbo, Dalton. *Additional Dialogue: Letters of Dalton Trumbo, 1942–1962*. Edited by Helen Manfull.

———. *The Time of the Toad: A Study of Inquisition in America*. New York: Harper and Row, 1972.

Wexley, John. *The Judgment of Julius and Ethel Rosenberg*. New York: Cameron and Kahn, 1955.

Winter, Ella. *And Not to Yield: An Autobiography*. New York: Harcourt, Brace, and World, 1963.

INTERVIEWS AND REMINISCENCES

Ciment, Michel. *Conversations with Losey*. London and New York: Methuen, 1985.

Corliss, Richard. *The Hollywood Screenwriters*. New York: Avon Books, 1972. Includes Carl Foreman, Howard Koch, Ring Lardner Jr., Arthur Laurents, and Michael Wilson.

Cowley, Malcolm. *The Paris Review Interviews: Writers at Work*. New York: Viking Press, 1959. Includes Dorothy Parker.

Fariello, Griffin. *Red Scare: Memories of the American Inquisition*. New York: Norton, 1995. Includes Frances Chaney Lardner, Jeff Corey, Paul Jarrico, Howard Koch, Ring Lardner Jr., John Randolph, John Sanford, and Frank Tarloff.

Froug, William. *The Screenwriter Looks at the Screenwriter*. New York: Delta Books, 1972. Includes Ring Lardner Jr.

Georgakas, Dan, and Rubenstein, Lenny. *The Cineaste Interviews*. Chicago: Lake View Press, 1983. Includes John Howard Lawson.

Jackson, Bryer R. *Conversations with Lillian Hellman*. Jackson: University Press of Mississippi, 1986.

Kisseloff, Jeff. *The Box: An Oral History of Television, 1920–1961*. New York: Viking, 1995. Includes Walter Bernstein, Lee Grant, and Abraham Polonsky.

Leyda, Jan. *Voices of Film Experience, 1894 to the Present*. New York: Macmillan, 1977. Includes Jules Dassin, Carl Foreman, Howard Koch, John Howard Lawson, Joseph Losey, Lewis Milestone, Martin Ritt, and Dalton Trumbo.

McGilligan, Patrick. *Backstory: Interviews with Screenwriters of Hollywood's Golden Age*. Berkeley and Los Angeles: University of California Press, 1986. Includes Donald Ogden Stewart.

———. *Backstory 2: Interviews with Screenwriters of the 1940s and 1950s*. Berkeley and Los Angeles: University of California Press, 1991. Includes Arthur Laurents.

———. *Backstory 3: Interviews with Screenwriters of the 1960s*. Berkeley and Los Angeles: University of California Press, 1997. Includes Walter Bernstein and Ring Lardner Jr.

Milne, Tom. *Losey on Losey*. Garden City, N.Y.: Doubleday, 1968.

Peary, Danny. *Close-Ups: The Movie Star Book*. New York: Galahad Books, 1978. Includes contributions by Alvah Bessie, Jeff Corey, Marsha Hunt, and Howard Koch.

Plimpton, George. *The Paris Review Interviews: Writers at Work, 3rd Series*. New York: Viking Press, 1967. Includes Lillian Hellman.

Sarris, Andrew. *Interviews with Film Directors*. Indianapolis and Kansas City: Bobbs-Merrill, 1967. Includes Joseph Losey and Abraham Polonsky.

Server, Lee. *Screenwriter: Words Become Pictures*. Pittstown, N.J.: Main Street Press, 1987. Includes John Bright.

Sherman, Eric, and Rubin, Martin. *The Director's Event: Interviews with Five American Filmmakers*. New York: Atheneum, 1970. Includes Abraham Polonsky.

Sherman, Eric. *Directing the Film: Film Directors on Their Art.* Boston: Little, Brown, 1976. Includes Abraham Polonsky and Martin Ritt.

Shorris, Sylvia, and Bundy, Marion Abbott. *Talking Pictures.* New York: New Press, 1994. Includes John Bright and Lester Cole.

Siegel, Robert. *The NPR Interviews, 1994.* Boston: Houghton, Mifflin, 1994. Includes Walter Bernstein and Abraham Polonsky.

Tavernier, Bertrand. *Amis Américains.* Lyons: Institut Lumière/Actes Sud, 1993. Includes Sidney Buchman, John Berry, Herbert Biberman, Edward Chodorov, Carl Foreman, Joseph Losey, Abraham Polonsky, and Julian Halevy Zimet.

Witt, Herbert. *Brecht: As They Knew Him:* New York: International Publishers, 1974. Includes contributions by Hanns Eisler and Vladimir Pozner.

About the Contributors

JOHN BAXTER The Australian-born journalist, broadcaster, and biographer, has written twenty-six books, most of them on the cinema. They include *Hollywood in the Thirties, Science Fiction in the Cinema, The Gangster Film*, studies of John Ford and Josef von Sternberg, and biographies of Federico Fellini and Luis Buñuel. His biography of Steven Spielberg was published by HarperCollins in the U.S. in 1997. His latest book is *Stanley Kubrick*. He lives in Paris.

PAUL BUHLE is a visiting associate professor in Brown University's American Civilization Department. He founded the Oral History of the American Left archive at Tamiment Library, New York University, as well as the journals *Radical America* and *Cultural Correspondence*. He has written or edited more than twenty books dealing with the history of the American left, including, in 1997, *From the Knights of Labor to the New World Order: Essays on Labor and Culture*, and he has contributed frequently to the *Nation, New Politics*, the *Village Voice*, and *Tikkun*.

LARRY CEPLAIR teaches history at Santa Monica College. He is the co-author (with Steven Englund) of *The Inquisition in Hollywood: Politics in the Film Community, 1930–1960*, widely regarded as the definitive history of the Hollywood left. His most recent book is the biographical study *A Great Lady: A Life of the Screenwriter Sonya Levien*.

TINA DANIELL toiled for *Daily Variety* and the *Hollywood Reporter* in Hollywood. She interviewed Philip Dunne for *Backstory: Interviews with Screenwriters of Hollywood's Golden Age*, and Betty Comden and Adolph Green for *Backstory 2: Interviews with Screenwriters of the 1940s and 1950s*. Her science-fantasy novels for TSR include *Dark Heart, The Companions*, and *Maquesta Kar-Thon*, in the best-selling Dragonlance paperback line. She currently works in public relations in Milwaukee, Wisconsin.

GLENN LOVELL, a recent National Arts Journalism fellow, is an entertainment writer for the *San Jose Mercury News* and Knight-Ridder Newspapers. He has been published in the *Washington Post*, the *Los Angeles Times* (on Edward Dmytryk and the blacklist), and the *Columbia Journalism Review*. He teaches film part-time at San Jose State University.

KEN MATE graduated from the University of Wisconsin at the height of the Vietnam War, then joined SDS and plunged into anti-war organizing. Later, Mate migrated to California, where he edited the magazine *City Sports*. In 1983 he served as producer for the never-completed documentary "Tender Comrades," which consisted of filmed interviews with surviving blacklistees. Subsequently, he worked as an investigative reporter for KCBS-TV, eventually winning five Emmys and numerous other awards for undercover reporting on street gangs, workers'-compensation fraud, and medical malpractice. He resides in Los Angeles, where he is a private investigator, specializing in corporate investigations.

PATRICK MCGILLIGAN has written notable biographies of actors James Cagney and Jack Nicholson, and of directors Robert Altman, George Cukor, and, in 1997, Fritz Lang. In addition, he edits the continuing Backstory series of interviews with Hollywood screenwriters. He is currently completing a biography of actor-director Clint Eastwood to be published in 1998. His next book for St. Martin's Press will be a biography of Alfred Hitchcock, timed for 1999, the hundredth anniversary of the director's birth.

ALISON MORLEY is a photographer and former director of photography for *Mirabella, Esquire,* and the *Los Angeles Times Magazine.* A lecturer, photo critic, teacher, and curator, she has published her work in numerous national magazines. Her photographs of Hollywood personalities also appear in *Backstory: Interviews with Screenwriters of Hollywood's Golden Age* and *Backstory 2: Interviews with Screenwriters of the 1940s and 1950s.*

DAVE WAGNER is political editor of *The Arizona Republic* in Phoenix. He is working on a reference volume on films of the blacklist with *Tender Comrades* coauthor Paul Buhle.

WILLIAM B. WINBURN has been a professional photographer since 1979. His involvement in this project comes from a long-abiding love of film and is an extension of the portraits he contributed to the Backstory series. A native of Savannah, Georgia, he worked as a newspaper photographer in Athens, Georgia, before moving to New York City, where he gained experience in commercial and editorial photography. He currently works as a unit-still photographer for films and lives in Maplewood, New Jersey, with his wife and daughter.

Index